D1481272

BASIC ECONOMICS

LITTLE, BROWN SERIES IN ECONOMICS

Richard E. Caves, consulting editor

- **Caves and Jones**
  INTERNATIONAL ECONOMICS
- **Eckaus**
  BASIC ECONOMICS
- **Martin and Grossack**
  MANAGERIAL ECONOMICS
- **Sherman, H.**
  THE SOVIET ECONOMY
- **Sherman, R.**
  ECONOMICS OF INDUSTRY
- **Singer**
  PUBLIC MICROECONOMICS
- **Thompson**
  STATISTICS FOR DECISIONS

BASIC ECONOMICS

RICHARD S. ECKAUS
Professor of Economics
Massachusetts Institute of Technology

LITTLE, BROWN AND COMPANY BOSTON

Library of Congress Catalog Card No. 71-172253

THIRD PRINTING

Published simultaneously in Canada by Little, Brown & Company (Canada) Limited

PRINTED IN THE UNITED STATES OF AMERICA

Contents

SIX: GROWTH AND DEVELOPMENT

Preface

Rationale This is a book of basic economics. It emphasizes the explanation of economic analysis and the application of that analysis to understand the role of private markets and the functions of the public sector. Special attention is given to the areas in which public policy and private markets are closely intertwined.

Stress is placed on the spirit, the language, the methods, and the main results of economic analysis. But the book is not abstract. It discusses current economic issues, yet it is not just a description of economic institutions or a catalog of this year's ten most pressing economic questions. Institutions and issues are examined throughout in order to create the environment in which the economic analysis moves.

A major objective of the text is to bring the style and approach of the professional economist into the first course in economics. Professional economists proceed by constructing models. These are simple characterizations of reality which capture the most significant aspects of the problems being considered. The theoretical models in this text are set out explicitly. This does not mean that the book is mathematical or abstruse. There is no mathematics beyond the customary graphs and an occasional equation. But a little arithmetic can carry an explanation a long way, and professional economists often resort to numerical examples to illustrate basic concepts.

Being professional and explicit has important advantages. First, the theory becomes easier because it is more clearly defined. In addition, the student for whom this is the first and last course in economics is introduced to the professional economist's approach. As an intelligent layman, he will appreciate that approach when he reads newspaper and magazine articles on economic issues. The student who is going to go further in economics will find the next steps more natural if he is already familiar with the basic models. The instructor who wants to use some advanced techniques will find that relatively easy also, because the structure of the analysis is set out clearly.

The proper approach to economics has itself become a more controversial issue in recent years and the controversy has rightly entered the introductory course. Some of the issues are presented in articles included in *Contemporary Issues in Economics: Selected Readings,* edited by Prof. Robert W. Crandall and me. *Basic Economics* is not a book of conservative economics or of radical economics or even of middle-of-the-road economics. Its function is to provide understanding. It does not offer cut-and-dried solutions to current economic problems, because economic analysis, in itself, does not provide solutions. Answers and policies require value judgments. The analysis in the text has, I feel, been carried far enough to indicate where such judgments are necessary, but I have tried scrupulously to avoid showing my own. My radical colleagues may complain that I have not criticized the status quo of the United States economy. That is right. I have tried to describe the economy and explain how it operates. My conservative colleagues may complain that I have been too blunt in the analysis of the system's weaknesses. I hope I have never distorted the truth. Both may claim that there are distortions because of what has been left out, if not because of what has been included. I can only offer in extenuation the exigencies of space and time.

This is a relatively short book, achieving brevity by omitting some of the purely descriptive material customarily found in economics texts. Yet there is enough descriptive and factual material to enable the book to stand on its own. It can also be combined effectively with *Contemporary Issues in Economics: Selected Readings.* Or it can be used with other volumes of essays on current topics. Elimination of the redundancy that often appears in texts and supplementary materials helps keep the price of the package down.

A good deal of attention is paid to student motivation. As a long-time teacher of elementary economics, I have again and again met students who failed to grasp the main argument because they did not understand where it was going and just why they should try to understand it. Other students get hung up on a minor part of the main argument and have a hard time getting beyond that. So I have tried to be especially clear and to tie up the loose ends as neatly as possible. Where the loose ends still show, as sometimes they must in an introductory book, I have recognized that explicitly, rather than pretend they are not there.

Some topics have been included for their pedagogic value. "Who is interested in the gold points?" asked one of my editors. They are covered in Chapter 33 as a minor feature of a gold standard which no longer exists. My answer is that a little exercise with the gold points helps the student understand the essential ideas of the gold standard and of foreign exchange rates. It also comes in handy in a later discussion of some recent proposals for international exchange reform.

There are many paths to learning. Some students benefit most from reading and careful rereading. Some cannot push themselves to a meticulous review but will chew over specific questions. Others like to do problems. The *Study Guide* that Robert W. Crandall and I have written to accompany this text contains a variety of review materials. Learning is like other kinds of exercise: It is more difficult at the beginning. Economics is a new kind of stretching of the mind for many people. It is harder at the beginning than at the end. So no student should despair if the going seems hard at the outset. Nearly everyone has had the same experience.

The organization of the book is one I would personally follow in a two-semester course. But for good reasons other teachers will find other organizations more amenable. And departments and colleges will have different opinions of what will be most successful for their students. I have great respect for these differences, because I believe that success in teaching and learning depends on the personal commitments of the participants. Whatever increases personal commitment should be encouraged.

The book has, therefore, been written so that it can be used flexibly. Some alternative one-semester chapter sequences are presented in the pages that follow this Preface. What is essential is that the instructor and the student feel that the topics covered are interesting and important.

Acknowledgments

Finally I have the opportunity to extend my appreciation in print to what seems like a multitude of people who have helped me in writing this book. The M.I.T. Economics Department is a tremendously stimulating place. I am grateful to my colleagues for their many suggestions, both offhand and pointed, on large and small issues. Professors Morris Adelman, E. Cary Brown, Jagdish Bhagwati, Robert Crandall, Evsey Domar, Charles Kindleberger, Paul Rosenstein-Rodan, Jerome Rothenberg, and Lester Thurow gave advice on specific questions. Professors Robert Bishop and Robert Solow joined in my use of parts of the manuscript in the elementary course in economics here at M.I.T. and they made suggestions based on their experience. Professor Paul Samuelson's contribution to the M.I.T. environment goes beyond his great intellectual achievements and deserves a special acknowledgment.

As his student and as his colleague, I have accumulated many debts to him which a little competition cannot obscure.

The manuscript has gone through several drafts and benefited from the criticisms of many readers, most of whom are unknown to me. They have been generous enough to encourage me and critical enough to bring about substantial improvements in the text. The detailed comments and advice of Prof. Richard Caves of Harvard University were especially helpful. Parts of the book were read and tried out in their classes by Profs. Stephen Beggs, Francis McLaughin, and Richard Tresch at Boston College, and I have benefited from their reactions. Several generations of graduate student teaching assistants at M.I.T. have provided useful comments on the manuscript, and Jerome Siegel gave it a thorough critical review.

Mrs. Diane Hurley provided an essential assist in indexing and in bringing together and organizing much of the empirical material in the tables and charts, and Mary Catherine Huddleson and Catherine Evers gave some useful advice. Mrs. Karen Crowley, Mrs. Mary East, Mrs. Linda Price, and Miss Betsy Willson helped generously in typing the various drafts. My secretary, Mrs. Carol Bromwell, not only did much of the typing but made the project more pleasant with her own cheerful personality.

I would like to break two traditions in publishing. First, I want to indicate my appreciation for the friendly relationship with Little, Brown, which has made the project a pleasant and effective undertaking. Basil Dandison, David Giele, Donald Hammonds, and, formerly, Warren Stone are the individuals most responsible. Second, I want to acknowledge publicly those usually anonymous "editors and designers." The presentation has been quite markedly improved by the editing of Margaret Castagno, and its appearance on schedule owes much to her efforts. Nat LaMar managed the overall editorial direction and production with great skill and dispatch.

With all of this help, the responsibility for any errors remains my own.

Though only one member writes and has his name on the cover, a textbook is a family project. Susan has borne a share of the burden and has my gratitude. Risha's share and inspiration have been so great that she has my book's dedication.

Suggestions for one-semester courses

Many introductory economics courses are one-semester or two-quarter courses, often with an option to complete the introductory sequence in another semester or quarter. It would be presumptuous of me to suggest a single course outline for the variety of introductory courses that are given. I believe that the variety should proliferate, that the individual instructor and his students should be provided with high-quality learning tools which they can use in ways they find most satisfying. The alternatives listed below are, therefore, intended to show feasible sequences. They also indicate which chapters do reasonably well standing by themselves and which need the support of other chapters. Many modifications are possible. Some instructors will want to spend more time on either the macroeconomic or the microeconomic sections and will not attempt any of the international trade chapters. Others may want to supplement quite heavily with outside readings.

"Let many flowers bloom."

Suggestions for a course with a microeconomic emphasis

1 The issues of economics and their interdependence

2 Methods and pitfalls in economic analysis

3 The fundamental economic questions: In model economies and in reality

4 Private market solutions and the pricing process

20 Demand analysis: The theory and its qualifications

21 Business organization and motivation and the variety of market structures

22 Resource use and cost factors behind supply decisions

25 The economic consequences of monopoly and imperfect competition
26 Market structure and the requisites of public economic policy
27 The functional distribution of income and factor pricing
5 The role of public economics
6 Taxes and the public sector
7 Measurement of the economy
10 Private aggregate demand: Consumption and investment spending
11 National income as determined by aggregate demand: The First Macro Model
17 Economic fluctuations and price inflation
18 Policies for full employment and price stability
32 The balance of payments and its equilibrium
33 Foreign exchange rates and their determination
34 The theory of international trade and comparative advantage

Suggestions for a course with a macroeconomic emphasis

1 The issues of economics and their interdependence
3 The fundamental economic questions: In model economies and in reality
7 Measurement of the economy
10 Private aggregate demand: Consumption and investment spending
11 National income as determined by aggregate demand: The First Macro Model
12 The macroeconomic effects of fiscal policy and foreign trade: The Second and Third Macro Models
13 The functions of money and the demand for money
14 Private banking and the supply of money
15 Public policy and central bank control of the money supply
18 Policies for full employment and price stability
4 Private market solutions and the pricing process
5 The role of public economics
6 Taxes and the public sector
21 Business organization and motivation and the variety of market structures
26 Market structure and the requisites of public economic policy
27 The functional distribution of income and factor pricing
32 The balance of payments and its equilibrium
33 Foreign exchange rates and their determination
34 The theory of international trade and comparative advantage
36 Balance of payments and exchange rate policy and international finance

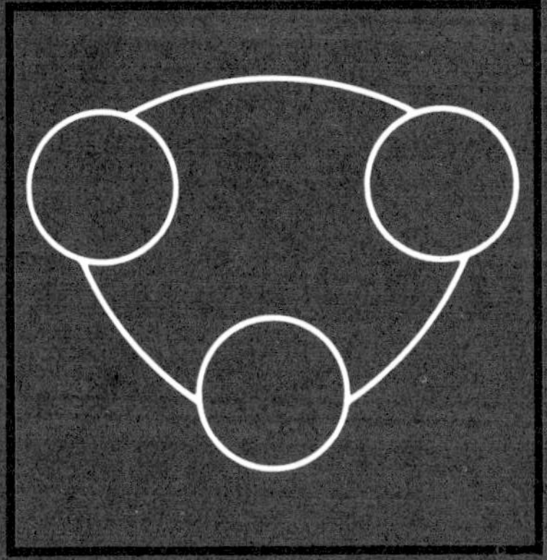

ONE

An overview of economics

Economics has sometimes seriously, sometimes jokingly, been defined as "what economists do." That is, of course, a cheat as a definition because it does not tell what it is that economists do. It does, however, suggest an essential feature of economics as a subject: To understand what economics is about, one must start working at it.

Learning economics is something like learning to swim. It cannot be done in ankle high water. One must get deep enough into the pool to stretch out and thrash about. On the other hand, there is no point in taking one's first plunge in the Colorado River rapids or a heavy surf.

Part I is the first plunge. It goes deep enough to provide a meaningful introduction to economics. It identifies the central economic questions and describes the general intellectual approach in economic analysis. This approach is then used to analyze the fundamental economic questions and the manner in which they are resolved. The economic mechanisms are described, and there is an introduction to price determination by supply and demand. The scope of public economics is defined, the functions of government are identified, and the way in which the government carries out its functions — via direct regulation, expenditure, and taxation — is analyzed. Part I concludes with a description of the way economists measure and judge the overall performance of the economy.

1

The issues of economics and their interdependence

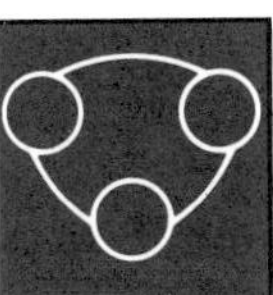

Economics is about goods and services: their choice, their production, and their use. It is relevant to politics, the humanities, and the fine arts. It intrudes into almost every aspect of human life, small as well as grand. It affects what people eat, their education, the length of their life and its style. It is involved in the great issues of the world. From arms control and atoms to urban blight and welfare, there is an economic accounting of every social problem and every proposed solution.

Everyone is aware of economic problems. The daily newspaper and the radio and television news programs take care of that for us. Understanding is something else — and more difficult to achieve than reading a newspaper or watching TV. An introductory book cannot explore all the fields of economics, nor can it resolve issues that have defied solution for many years. But it can help do two things:

1. Develop an appreciation of how the economic system as a whole operates, and
2. Develop methods of thinking that can be applied to a wide range of economic issues and can be used to judge the thoughts of others

In all economic systems, there are some areas in which private decisions prevail. These are given effect through markets. There are other areas in which public decisions dominate and are carried out by government institutions. In this sense all economies are "mixed," and there are no countries that are polar cases of pure *market economies* or pure *public economies.* Even in the most thoroughly centralized and government-controlled economy, the details of private consumption decisions are left to individuals.

And in the most thoroughly decentralized, private economy, the government provides many social services. The mix varies roughly from East to West, with a relatively greater role for public economics in the Eastern bloc of countries and a greater role for market economics in the West. Yet the term *mixed economy* is reserved for countries like the United States in which market economics has the predominant role. Since the mixed economy is the central focus of this book, understanding the workings of private markets will be a major objective. But since public economics has a direct and sometimes decisive effect on the availability of goods and services, as well as many indirect influences, it will be another focus of attention. The analysis of the interaction of market and public economics and the formulation of public economic policy is called *political economics.* It will be a continuing concern throughout.

The first step in analysis is to identify the major components or aspects of social issues.

Isolating the economic issues

Economics and politics are so closely related that their separation is almost always somewhat artificial. Nonetheless, we shall progress most rapidly, at least at the outset, by concentrating on each one separately.

Some problems do appear to be primarily political in nature, for instance, What is the best way to give effective representation to each group of citizens in a community? Some questions appear to be mainly sociological and cultural, such as, How can cities best be built and organized to achieve both the advantages of small communities and the stimulation of larger urban areas? Yet economics enters into all such questions, just as politics and sociology and culture affect such "strictly" economic questions as What is the proper rent for a landlord to charge for an apartment? The economic, political, cultural, and aesthetic components of social problems are not like building blocks, one resting on top of another in a pyramid or column. Rather they are the flesh, blood, and bones of society, intimately intermingled, mutually supporting, and at their boundaries virtually merging.

To begin, however, the economic aspects of society will be separated. This is done with full knowledge that it is always necessary to combine economics, politics, and sociology for a full appraisal of any social issue.

The big picture and the tough little problems

It is tempting to try to deal with economic questions at the level of "big think." Urban blight, for example, might be diagnosed as a disease caused by "prejudice, neglect, and exploitation." The prescribed cure could be a "a concerted effort backed by the good will of all parties." Yet, to understand the economic problems and, finally, to answer the policy question, What should be done? one must get down to the nitty-gritty details. Yes, there is urban blight. What will new residential housing or new factories contribute to its elimination? Does it make any difference what kind of housing it is, or who owns it, or who rents it, or who builds it, or who taxes it and how the taxes are used? Do the same questions apply to new factories too? How shall new construction be financed? What mortgage terms are feasible? Can private banks meet these terms? What is the effect of monetary policy on new construction? Will private property insurance be available at reasonable rates? The great problems of life are always composed of a myriad of little problems. These may seem technical and of little consequence, but they usually turn out to be the gut issues.

Practically everyone agrees on the great problems of mankind. Everyone is for "helping." Everyone wants the hungry millions of the world to be fed. Everyone wants the cities to be beautiful places to live. The real questions are, How can we help? How shall we go about feeding the hungry and making the city more humane? We will probably never vote on whether we are "for" or "against" urban blight, but we may well vote on specific urban renewal plans or on the officeholders who will promote them. Neighbors and even families have been known to divide in hot debate on such issues as where a new housing project will be located, whether a new school will be financed by taxes or by a bond issue, etc. When we reach out to grasp one of the great issues, we find it is a nettle, full of prickly little problems. And it is finally these sticky little problems that all the fighting is about.

These tough little problems start turning up whenever a great problem is investigated in any depth. We can see, almost with amazement at times, an intricate pattern of interdependence unfold. The costs of building new housing are high for many reasons. These include competition in the building industry or the lack of it, the requirements imposed by local government building codes, the cost of materials and the level of wages in the building trades, etc. Since construction costs are high relative to the income that can be earned by selling or renting houses to low-income families, only a small proportion of the new housing is constructed by private builders for poor people. In many instances, the blighted parts of urban areas were once rich neighborhoods. The relatively well-off families have moved away to luxury apartments or to the suburbs. They occupy housing which to some degree benefits from direct government subsidies in the form of insurance on mortgage loans and federal income tax deductions on local property taxes and on interest payments on loans. The commuters in and out of the city ride back and forth on government-subsidized trains and highways. The housing left behind in the city "trickles down" to lower-income families. Public housing projects constructed by government agencies and publicly subsidized private housing add to the supply of low-income housing. Why does it never seem to be enough? Why does inflation hit it so hard?

If we want to understand urban blight, we must look beyond the smoke and soot, the slumlord, and the unemployed worker. We must understand all the influences operating through private markets and public institutions — and not just in the city but also in its suburbs. Factors as disparate as the apprenticeship programs in building trade unions, the rationale of federal income tax deductions, and the financing of highways all have an effect. Separately, they do not appear to be *the* great problem of urban blight, but individually they have a perceptible impact, and collectively they *are* the problem.

To understand the great problems we must see them whole and we must see their parts, both the forest and the trees. If the issues seem monolithic, it is because we have not yet grasped their basic features. That requires hard work and a fresh view. The natural scientist and the physicist find nothing commonplace in the world and see a universe in a drop of water. So also the serious student of economic and social problems sees in each great issue a group of interdependent phenomena, each affecting the others and being affected by them.

Interdependence in economics

It is fashionable these days to refer to a problem like urban blight as a "systems" problem, one which has a number of interdependent aspects that must be considered as a whole. There is also a rural systems problem, an information systems problem, a transportation systems problem, a production systems problem, and so on. All these are aspects of the "economic systems" problem, which is the subject of this book. Our viewpoint here will be a comprehensive one. The object is to understand the functioning of the economic system as a whole. That means identifying the essential parts or aspects of the economic system, understanding the details of their operation and the role of both market and public influences, and finally putting the parts together and understanding the interrelationships.

The systems approach to economic phenomena has a number of important implications. First of all, the use of the word *system* suggests that there is some order or regularity in the phenomena and that economic events are not merely random and chaotic. It does not necessarily imply repetitive patterns or absolute laws, but it does imply continuity and orderliness. There are relationships, which, if we can discover them, will help us explain and predict the economic features and events of society. Second, interdependence means that the effects in one part of the system will tend to flow into other parts and be reinforced or offset as they are transmitted. For example, an economic policy intended to improve wages and working conditions will also have repercussions on employment and income.

Any systems analyst will tell you that the first steps in understanding a system are (1) to identify its functions or goals and (2) to understand the constraints or limits within which it must operate. The bigger and more complex the system, the bigger and more complex these tasks are. For urban systems alone, they would take a considerable amount of time and effort. We would find that the overall functions of providing habitations and places of production imply a number of subfunctions, and we would then begin to think of the other less obvious but essential functions of cities: serving as transportation and communication centers, providing the locations for schools, museums, and theaters, etc. With some effort, we could make a complete list of urban functions. There are also constraints. Some of these are technical, like the physical problems of designing buildings or transportation systems. But some constraints on urban areas have their source in political organization and, for example, the distribution of taxing powers among city, state, and federal governments.

Identifying the functions and constraints of the economic system as a whole is more difficult, not only because it is so much more comprehensive. We are more likely to be successful when dealing with urban systems alone, because we can contrast cities with rural areas and thereby gain some perspective. But one can hardly imagine not having an economic system. Like Archimedes, who said he could move the world with his levers if only he had a place to put them, we could understand economic systems more easily if only we could stand completely outside them and observe their operation. Since we cannot, we must consciously exert ourselves to become aware of what we normally accept as commonplace. Norbert Weiner, the great mathematician, wrote in his book *Cybernetics* that science has been most successful at the microscopic and astronomic levels. When we are dealing with units whose dimensions are so different from our own, our observations can be objective and will interfere very little with the functions of the units being studied. But in economics we deal with man and his organizations in just our own dimensions and that makes it difficult to be objective and to maintain perspective.

The goals of the economic system

On the other hand, there is a kind of obviousness to the question, What is the economic system supposed to do? The answer that it should contribute to human happiness is as good a start as any. But what does it take to make people happy? The economic values in life are only part, but an important part, of what is necessary.

Goods and services appear to rank high among the economic values that contribute to human satisfaction. There used to be speculation that there was an upper limit to human wants, that people would run out of desires for goods and services. That does not appear to happen, however. There is little evidence of economic satiation anywhere in the world.[1] Most people keep wanting "more and better." Moreover, success in acquiring and consuming goods and services seems to be addictive, although people get hooked to different degrees.[2]

This characteristic of individual and social behavior may be stimulated by large-scale advertising, though that is a historically recent and geographically concentrated phenomenon. Or it may be regarded as a basic "acquisitive instinct" and be endorsed or deplored, depending on one's values. But it cannot realistically be ignored. Some may even claim that it reflects an ideology which can be replaced by some other ideology. Even if that is so, no economic analysis of the world as it is can ignore the present force of the drive to acquire goods and services.

It is also important to recognize that people want more than material things from an economic system. They want the satisfaction and respect that go with employment. They want opportunities for advancement for themselves and their children. They want the economic system to provide for personal security and equity and national security and international responsibility. The exact content of these goals is not easy to define and any particular definition is likely to evoke controversy. But that does not mean that they are insignificant. Workers strike over "unfair" labor practices and people riot over inequality in opportunities. Though the goals are not always stated precisely, they are nonetheless the object of powerful drives.

Limitations on economic performance

While desires or wants may have no definite limit, there are limits to how far any economy can and will go in satisfying them. What determines those limits? First, there are several types of *constraints* or restrictions on economic activity. These determine the *potential* scope of operation of the economy, the maximum goals

[1] It is true that some small groups of people, mainly in the United States, have attempted to withdraw from the mainstream of the economy and society and reduce and simplify their consumption and production. But withdrawal is different from satiation, and in any case such communes are an isolated and numerically insignificant phenomenon.

[2] This is not intended pejoratively. People become addicted to all sorts of things, including Shakespearean sonnets and Rod McKuen poetry, Vivaldi concertos and rock records. The point is that most tastes require goods and/or services for their satisfaction and people seem to want to satisfy those tastes in greater and greater variety and volume.

which it can possibly achieve. Second, the *efficiency* of the economy will determine how successful it is in approaching its potential and where it will operate within its constraints. The concepts of constraints and economic efficiency are extremely important for understanding the operation of an economy and they appear again and again in economic analysis.

Constraints on the economy

There are three types of constraints on the potential operation of the economy. The first is technology. This constraint reflects the total of scientific knowledge and know-how that can be applied to production; it is the ultimate limit to the productivity of all resources and applies to any type of economic system. The limits of available technology are less restrictive today than ten years ago or even last year, because research and experience continually broaden our capabilities. But silk purses still cannot be made from sows' ears, nor iron transmuted into gold by alchemists. There are no magic fuel pellets, and the laws of thermodynamics guarantee that there can be no perpetual motion machines. There are rules of our physical environment which we know we cannot change. Undoubtedly, there are also new technologies yet to be discovered, which will relax the present technological contraints on the economy and expand its potential achievement.

Whatever the technology used, production requires resources. The limited availability of resources is the second type of constraint on the economic system. Even if we knew how to make silk purses out of sows' ears, the number of silk purses that could be made would be limited by the number of sows' ears available.

Land
Labor
Capital

Economists think in terms of a broad, three-way classification of productive resources: Land, Labor, and Capital. Land includes mineral deposits, water resources, and climatic characteristics, as well as fertile soil. Labor ranges from unskilled physical effort to the mental activity of the abstract scientist. Capital includes durable machinery, buildings, roads, and other construction, in fact, any lasting increase in productive capabilities which is created with labor and other resources.

These categories are not completely exclusive. Land, even fertile soil, is not useful until it is plowed and perhaps fenced and so has some attributes of capital. Likewise, a high waterfall is a beautiful and awe-inspiring sight but it cannot be used to produce electric power without a lot of construction work and electrical equipment. Some factors that contribute to productivity, such as enterprise and organization, do not fit neatly into the Land-Labor-Capital scheme. At this point, however, it is less important to set up a neat and comprehensive set of categories than to realize that the resources which can be used for production of goods and services at any one time or during any period of time are limited. Even in the richest economy there is just so much skilled and unskilled labor, improved land and mines and waterfalls and plant and equipment available. This constraint, in turn, sets an upper limit to what an economy can achieve with its technology.

The third constraint on an economy is a mixed bag of social customs and institutions that limit the ways in which resources and technology will be used. These include the reservation of certain areas for private market decision making and the reservation of other areas for public decision making. Social constraints are seldom absolutely fixed, but they are often slow to change. For example, the building code laws which enforce standards of safety and sanitation and use of materials are slowly changing social constraints. These codes become outdated by the development of new materials and technology. They are, therefore, somewhat arbitrary limits to what can be achieved in urban construction. Legal constraints may be imposed on a nationwide basis, such as the limitation on child labor. Some social constraints are imposed without laws. Union regulations, which are private agreements, define exactly what a carpenter or plumber can do. In most countries, it is unthinkable for women to work in certain occupations. There are also limits imposed internationally. For example, it is possible that controlled nuclear explosions could facilitate big earth-moving projects, such as a new Panama canal. But present nuclear testing treaties to which the United States and the U.S.S.R. have agreed in the hope of decreasing the threat of nuclear wars and reducing radioactive fallout make it difficult, if not impossible, to use such methods.

Technological, resource, and social constraints change over time. Scientific progress leads to technical improvements. The labor force grows. New mineral deposits are discovered, and old ones depleted. Capital accumulates through new investment, and wears out in use. Customs and laws change too — as, for example, the slow change in building codes and the gradual opening of union apprenticeship programs to black men. The continuing changes should not be misinterpreted as meaning that the constraints do not exist and that anything and everything is attainable. At any one time or in any period, the technological, resource, and social constraints impose limits on what an economy can achieve.

Economic efficiency

The success of an economy in coping with its constraints depends on the *efficiency* with which it can organize and put to use the resources available to it, including its labor. As a concept, efficiency has an intuitive appeal, but on close examination it turns out to be somewhat elusive. There are no simple measures of efficiency. It implies, first of all, the avoidance of waste. There are obvious ways of wasting resources which an economic system should shun. Forest fires are a waste. Whenever more inputs are used than are technically necessary for a particular output, that is a waste. When men and women want to work and do not have jobs — that is a waste.

Less obvious kinds of waste have their origin in the way an economy is organized. When, because of discrimination by race or sex, men and women work at jobs which do not best suit their talents, that is a waste. When businesses operate with some degree of monopoly power or when they otherwise control the markets in which they buy and sell, that also can lead to waste, as later chapters will demonstrate. It is common to think of governments as wasteful, buying "too many" paper clips or the "wrong kinds" of punch cards for the computing machines. Waste of this type is probably less important than the incentives to be wasteful that are sometimes embodied in tax and expenditure programs.

A good deal of this book is about what makes an economy efficient or inefficient. In fact, economists have often been accused of being preoccupied with efficiency, particularly with respect to the production of goods and services. It is difficult enough to judge the efficiency of an economy even in the narrow sphere of production. But judging economic performance in achieving other goals — equality of opportunity, security, etc. — is still more controversial, and economists' opinions are no better than anyone else's. Even so, though equality of opportunity, security, and progressiveness are complex and controversial criteria, the economy's performance in these areas cannot be disregarded.

One final point about constraints and efficiency: The distinction between a binding social constraint and an inefficiency often depends on the definition of words rather than on content. But the distinction may also differentiate between conditions which are more difficult to change and those which are less difficult. For example, agricultural price-support programs are a source of inefficiency, as we shall point out in Chapter 16. Are such programs a binding social constraint on farmers and consumers? They are only so long as the support laws are not changed. And such laws are changed from time to time.

It is natural to want to know the consequences of change of this type and to expect economics to help provide answers. So economic analysis is more than working out the implications of existing constraints; it can also be applied to the study of social change.

Scarcity and choice

The constraints of technology and resources in particular are the source of what is known as the *Law of Scarcity*. This should not be interpreted as it often is by its critics as if it were a law of *poverty*. The Law of Scarcity simply says that the technical and resource constraints, which determine the outer boundaries of what any economy is capable of producing, limit its production to less than people would like to have. Notice that the notion of unlimited wants has crept in again. "Happiness," it has been said, "is income divided by wants." If we would all agree to be happy on bread and water alone, there would be no scarcity. People being what they are, the limits of technology and resources are real constraints.

One implication of the Law of Scarcity whose significance can hardly be overestimated is the need to make choices—that is to say, the *inevitability* of making choices. "Enough of everything for everybody" cannot be achieved this side of the Garden of Eden. When all resources are being used and the constraints on production are binding, then, if more of any good is to be produced, there will have to be less of some other. A choice has to be made!

There was a brief period in the 1950s and before that in the 1920s when it became popular to think of the United States and a few other countries as "affluent societies." They were capable, it was said, of supplying high levels of consumer goods to all their citizens and of achieving all their other national and international goals at the same time. Presumably we have learned better. In fairness to the proponents of the affluent society idea, it must be admitted that they usually acknowledged that choices were necessary. Their preference was for fewer privately owned and enjoyed goods and more publicly owned and enjoyed goods.

It is so important to understand why choices among economic alternatives are inevitable and to appreciate how choices are made that we shall come back to the scarcity and choice issues again and again. In fact, the choice issues are put at the center of definitions of economics such as *Economics is the study of how scarce resources are allocated among various uses*. This first approach to a concise description of the subject will be elaborated below.

Our view of an economic system, then, is that it is an organized and orderly set of methods for making choices, subject to constraints, according to some criteria. This view can be given more meaning by being specific about the kinds of choices involved.

The fundamental questions of economics

There are many different kinds of goods and services that can be produced in various quantities. There are many different kinds of productive resources and production methods that can be used to produce the various goods and services. There are also many different ways of distributing the goods and services among individuals and families and other groups. Therefore, we have three fundamental sets of questions that an economic system must resolve: the *Output*, *Input*, and *Distribution* questions.

The Output questions: What goods shall be produced and what amount of each? The economic system must lead to decisions about the production of goods and services. (1) There is an enormous range of *consumer goods*. For the most part, in a mixed economy such as the United States such goods are purchased and used *privately*: food and clothing, cars and motorcycles, rock and folk records, etc. Some consumer goods and services, like fire protec-

Figure 1-1

CHANGING PATTERNS OF OUTPUT IN THE UNITED STATES BY MAJOR CATEGORIES

Durable goods Output has shown major fluctuations but rapid growth overall. The growth of Output of services has fluctuated less and has also been rapid. The Output of nondurable goods has grown somewhat less rapidly, and the growth of Output of buildings and structures has been even slower. These Output patterns reflect the manner in which choices are made. Any economic system must generate similar decisions.
(Source: U.S. Dept. of Commerce, Office of Business Economics.)

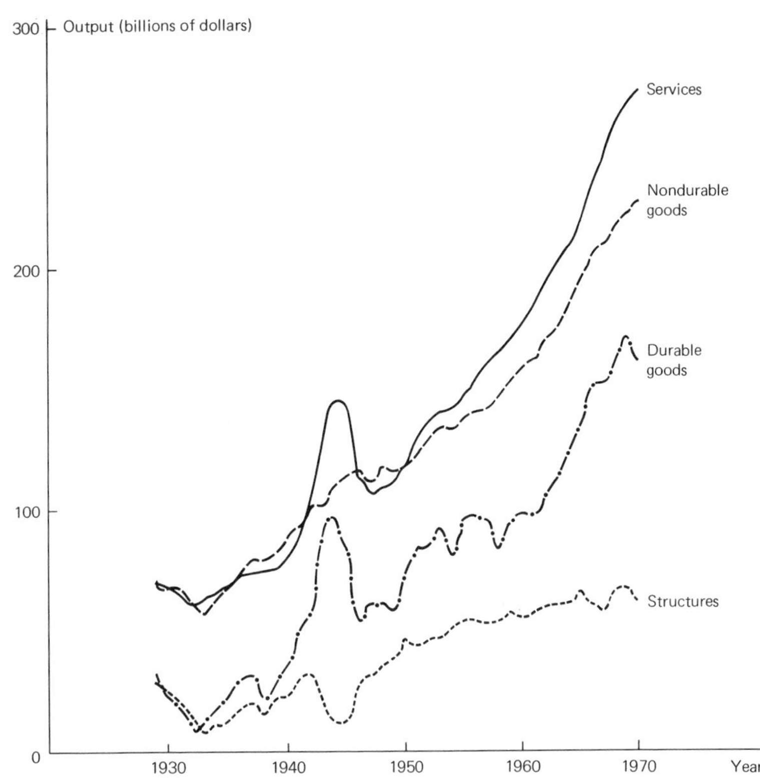

tion and mail delivery, are produced by government agencies and used by everyone. Government-produced goods which are to some extent consumed jointly, like weather forecasts and national defense, are called *public goods.* (2) There are many kinds of *capital goods.* These do not themselves yield immediate direct consumer satisfactions, but permit more production in the future: steel mills and bakery equipment, sewing machines and auto assembly lines. Most capital goods in the United States are *privately owned*. (3) There are also *publicly owned capital goods*, such as school buildings, post offices, and highways. These are created through government decisions.

One aspect of the resolution of the Output questions which deserves special emphasis is the time dimension. What weight should be given to future enjoyment of goods and services as compared with enjoyment now?

The Input questions: How shall each of the many goods be produced and how much of the various resources shall be used in production? The Input questions may sound like engineering problems which can be decided solely on technical grounds. But they are not. Physical science alone will not tell us whether new

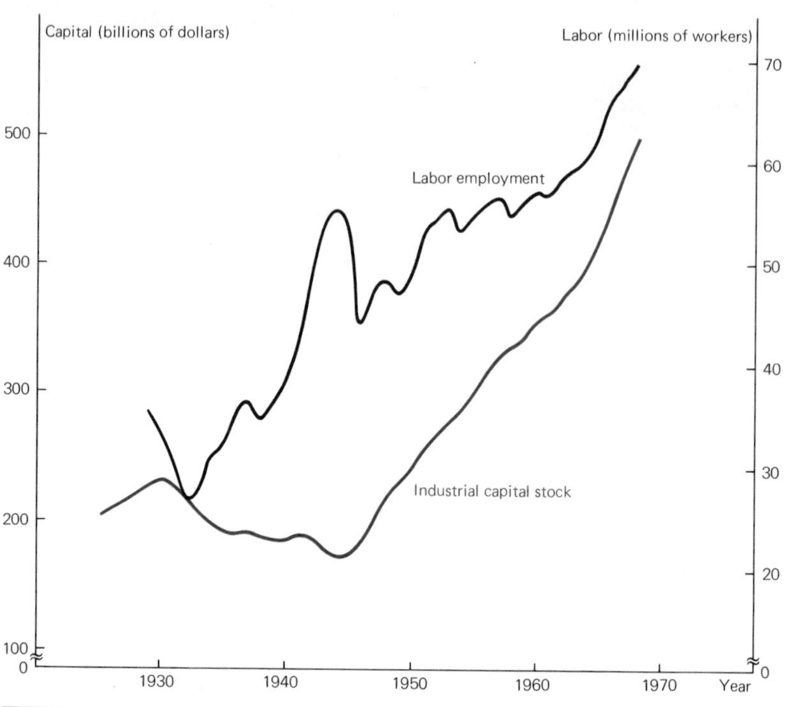

Figure 1-2

GROWTH OF LABOR AND INDUSTRIAL CAPITAL IN THE UNITED STATES (MILLIONS OF WORKERS)

Figure 1-2 traces the growth of aggregate capital and labor inputs. Notice that the capital stock has grown faster than labor since the 1940's. The capital aggregate includes many different types of productive plant and equipment. Likewise, the labor aggregate includes many types of skills and professional specializations. The resolution of the Input questions requires decisions about how these and other productive resources will be used. That, in turn, is closely related to the performance of the economy as a whole, whether or not there will be full employment, and whether there will be technological progressiveness — and what kind.

(Source: U.S. Dept. of Commerce, Office of Business Economics, and U.S. Dept. of Labor, Bureau of Labor Statistics.)

buildings should have steel, aluminum, or brick fronts. There are no scientific laws which in themselves determine whether nuclear power plants or coal or oil-fired power plants should be built to generate electric power. Physics and chemistry and electrical engineering contribute to the decisions, because they reveal the technical constraints that exist. Within these technical constraints, however, the final decisions on how resources will be combined depend largely on economics.

The Distribution questions: Who shall receive how much of the goods produced? The answers to the Distribution questions determine the allocation of the benefits of production. Who gets the new housing; who the old? Who eats hamburger; who has steak? Ultimately, these are questions about the distribution of income and wealth, because the goods go to the people who have the purchasing power. Some people have more; some have less. Is the distribution of income and wealth highly unequal or fairly equal? Is it becoming more unequal or less? Does the system permit or encourage economic mobility so that people have the opportunity to improve their life situation? How are these issues decided in the market sector? How does the public sector affect the final outcome? These are Distribution issues.

The Distribution questions have two aspects. One is the distribution of output as the return for the services of the various types of productive resources: Land, Labor, and Capital. This is called

Table 1-1

FUNCTIONAL DISTRIBUTION OF INCOME IN THE UNITED STATES

Income type	1960		1965		1970	
	Billions of dollars	*Percent*	*Billions of dollars*	*Percent*	*Billions of dollars*	*Percent*
Wages and salaries	294.2	71.0	393.8	69.8	599.8	74.9
Proprietorship and professional income (nonfarm)	34.2	8.2	42.4	7.5	51.4	6.4
Farm proprietors	12.0	2.9	14.8	2.6	16.2	2.0
Rents	15.8	3.8	19.0	3.4	22.7	2.8
Interest	8.4	2.0	18.2	3.2	33.5	4.2
Corporate profits	49.9	12.1	76.1	13.5	77.4	9.7
Total	414.5	100.0	564.3	100.0	801.0	100.0

the *functional* distribution of income because it focuses on the distribution of rewards according to the productive functions performed in the economy. This aspect of the Distribution questions is reflected in Table 1-1. That table shows the functional distribution of income in the United States in recent years. Income is divided among wages and salaries paid to labor of all kinds, interest, rent, corporate profits, and all the income received by owners of unincorporated businesses and independent professionals.

The other aspect of the Distribution questions is ordinarily the more familiar one. It is the division of output among individuals and families and is known as the *personal distribution* of income. Table 1-2 shows the personal distribution of income among households in the United States in 1969. The personal distribution of income depends on the returns to the different productive resources and on who owns them, as well as on the income received by different types of labor. It is also affected by taxes and by government payments to individuals, such as welfare and social security.

Interdependence of Output, Input, and Distribution questions

The three types of fundamental economic questions can be identified separately, but they are not resolved separately. They are interdependent. If the Output decision is to build brick apartments, that determines the physical Inputs. It also affects the Distribution question, since it means that bricklayers will have more employment than otherwise and more income and will be able to buy more consumer goods. If steel buildings are built, metal workers will be better off. If the Output decision is to rehabilitate existing buildings or build single-family housing, that is likely to mean more work and more income and more goods for carpenters. Yet the interdependence is not unidirectional. The Output decisions to build

Table 1-2

DISTRIBUTION OF INCOME IN THE UNITED STATES 1969

Household income	*Percentage of all individuals and families in this class*	*Percentage of all individuals and families in this and lower-income classes*
Under $2,000	10.0	10.0
$ 2,000–$ 4,000	12.4	22.4
$ 4,000–$ 6,000	11.7	34.1
$ 6,000–$ 8,000	13.2	47.3
$ 8,000–$10,000	12.9	60.2
$10,000–$12,000	11.3	71.5
$12,000–$15,000	11.8	83.3
$15,000–$25,000	13.4	96.7
$25,000–$50,000	2.8	99.5
Over $50,000	0.4	99.9*

*Total does not add to 100 percent because of rounding.
Source: U.S. Department of Commerce, Bureau of the Census.

or rehabilitate housing with brick, metal, or wood will depend, in part, on the cost of each method and, thus, on the wages received by bricklayers, metalworkers, and carpenters. In later chapters we shall investigate this many-sided interdependence.

With the more detailed specification of the fundamental economic questions, the definition of economics can be enlarged: *Economics is the study of choices in the market and public sectors which determine the composition of the Output of goods and services in the present and in the future, the use of scarce productive resources as Inputs, and the Distribution of the goods and services produced among individuals and social groups.*

Macroeconomics and microeconomics

The fundamental questions of economics are analyzed at various levels. When the questions are asked and answered for the economy as a whole — that is *macroeconomics*. Macroeconomics is, for example, concerned with the level of prosperity or degree of recession and the sources and effects of price inflation. *Microeconomics*, on the other hand, focuses on the operation of the economy at the level of the units making the basic choice decisions: the business firm, the consuming household, and the government. Macroeconomics makes its contribution by developing an overall view of the working of the economic system. The contribution of microeconomics is in exposing the detailed functioning of the economy and the interdependence of the details.

During the last thirty or forty years the relative emphasis in the economics profession has been on macroeconomics and the aggregate performance of the economy. But microeconomics has never been abandoned and in recent years has received a greater share of professional attention. This is partly because of growing concern about the detailed functioning of some aspects of the economy: pollution, traffic jams, crises in health care, and so on. Partly the swing in emphasis was the result of a feeling that the macroeconomic problems, if not solved, were at least well in hand. The experience of inflation and unemployment of the last several years has more or less disabused most people of that notion.

Both macro and microeconomic analysis are essential parts of economic understanding. Together they provide the necessary comprehensive and detailed view of the economy. But even more is required for economic understanding—an appreciation of the interrelations between macroeconomic and microeconomic phenomena.

It is clear that an immense number of details must be coordinated if an economy is to work well. The number of loaves of bread baked must be just about what consumers will buy. The same is true for men's suits and women's dresses, for kilowatt-hours of power-generating capacity and kilowatts of electricity used, for apartments available for rent and apartments demanded. The harmonious working out of all these matters is usually accepted as a commonplace event. Yet this meshing of a myriad details is really quite remarkable. Occasionally, when they do not mesh, the results are rather spectacular. Electricity blackouts which occur when circuits become overloaded are an example of failure to achieve consistency among the details. How is the necessary consistency achieved when the fundamental questions involve so many interrelationships?

Planned and unplanned economies: The role of the market and public sectors

If an individual has a big problem, he will probably make some informal or formal plan to deal with it. If a community has a problem, for example, improving its education system, it, too, will make a plan. The most characteristic human quality is sometimes said to be the ability to exercise foresight. It would therefore seem to be a plausible approach, in the face of the tremendous complexity of economic issues, to resolve the fundamental economic questions mainly by planned and centralized decision making. Some countries do try to run their economies this way. A central planning organization gives orders to the various producing units: Produce so much steel. Deliver it to just these plants. Use it to build so many buildings. Pay each type of worker so much in wages. Set up just so many stores to sell just these amounts of each good.

Consider, however, the tremendous task such a planning organization faces. There are thousands, even millions, of different goods and services and productive resources, many, many different technologies, and millions of people spread out across the country. There is so much detail that none of the planned economies attempt to take care of every last item from the center. All rely to some degree on individual initiative, but they differ greatly in how much individual decision making they encourage and allow. Resolving the fundamental economic questions by central planning is certainly one way of doing things. It has worked dramatically in some countries to modernize and industrialize the economies and to produce remarkable improvements in standards of living. It has also in some instances imposed unnecessary costs and great inefficiencies. Yet given the scope and complexity of the economic problems, it is no wonder that there are inefficiencies in planned economies. The wonder is that they work at all.

But what is the alternative? A system without a plan? No central organization to exercise foresight and decide the Output, Input, and Distribution questions and to give the necessary orders? In the United States and most other mixed economies, there is no overall planning and no central direction for the major part of the system. There is, to be sure, a large public sector which has great influence on private decisions. It does control some industries but usually does not attempt to manage details or even to set long-run economic goals. Rather public sector planning in mixed economies is generally used to create a favorable environment for the private sector. Most economic decisions are made privately as producers and consumers interact in markets.

How can a vast, complicated economic system like that in the United States function without some agency to coordinate all the separate private decisions? As with planned economies, it is no wonder that unplanned economies do not always work well. The marvel that we must ponder again and again is that they work at all. The methods by which planned economies operate are far from transparent. The operation of unplanned economies is even more difficult to grasp, because there is no formal framework.

For most people the understanding of an unplanned economy begins and ends with an assertion of the consistency of public and self-interest. Adam Smith summarized the argument excellently in 1776, the year of the American Revolution:

> Every individual is continually exerting himself to find out the most advantageous employment for whatever capital he can command. It is his own advantage, indeed, and not that of society, which he has in view. But the study of his own advantage, naturally, or rather necessarily leads him to prefer that employment which is most advantageous to the society. And he is in this led by an invisible hand to promote an end which was no part of his intention.

One of our major tasks is to understand the argument that leads to this conclusion, and its necessary qualifications.

There is an important implication of the argument so far which should be made explicit: *Planned, unplanned, and mixed economies all face the same types of Output, Input, and Distribution questions.* Both market and public economies are preoccupied with these questions. In all economies there must be mechanisms for making choices among alternatives. The facts of life – a scarcity of productive resources compared with an abundance of human wants – are the same for all. It should, therefore, not be surprising to find that some parts of the economic analysis developed for unplanned economies are also appropriate to planned economies.

Summary

Economics is concerned with the production and use of goods and services. There are economic aspects to nearly all the problems of society. To begin to understand the economic aspects, one must first separate them from other aspects of individual life and society. But one must always keep in mind the interdependence of all aspects of society. One of the most important distinctions is between market economics, on the one hand, which focuses on private decisions about goods and services which are effected through markets, and public economics, on the other hand, whose subject is public decisions mediated through government institutions. The economy itself should be viewed as a system, a whole composed of many interdependent parts in which market economics and public economics interact.

To understand a system, we start off by identifying its goals and the constraints within which it must operate. To satisfy its members, an economic system is expected to provide goods and services (for which there appears to no point of satiation) and to provide employment, security, equality of opportunity, equity, and progressiveness. It must operate within three types of constraints: (1) The limits of technical knowledge, (2) the limits of the productive resources available, and (3) the patterns of organization, behavior, and law imposed by social customs and mores. All these constraints can and do change over time, but at any one time they set limits on the operation of the economy.

The ability of an economy to satisfy the goals of its members within the limitations set by these constraints depends on its *efficiency*. Efficiency implies not only the absence of waste but also organizing and using the available resources effectively.

The existence of constraints on the economy, on the one hand, and unlimited human wants, on the other, is the source of the Law of Scarcity. Scarcity, in turn, creates the necessity of making choices among alternatives. The study of the manner in which choices are made is one of the central themes of economics. Three fundamental kinds of questions must be resolved by an economy: (1) Output questions: What goods will be produced and in what amounts? (2) Input questions: How will goods be produced and with what resources? (3) Distribution questions: Who gets how much of the goods produced?

Resolving the economic questions through planned public decisions is an obvious approach. It is difficult because of the magnitude and complexity of the detail. The operation of largely unplanned private markets to resolve economic issues is a less obvious approach and one which will be the focus of much of our attention.

Questions for discussion and review

1. The chapter asserts that economics pervades much of our daily life as well as the great social problems. As an exercise in gaining insight into this pervading influence of economics, describe its role in (*a*) the operation of the local school system, (*b*) the operation of a church, (*c*) the choice of a marriage partner.

2. What is the most nearly private economic decision about goods and services you can think of? What public economic elements enter into this decision?

3. When the nation faces a big problem like environmental pollution, why doesn't Congress just pass a law banning it? What are the tough little problems that make that impossible?

4. Are economic wants satiable? Do you think that people are manipulated to make them keep wanting "more and better"?

5. Give examples of how the three types of constraints operate to affect the welfare of older people in the society.

6. Discuss the following statement: *Economic efficiency is inconsistent with waste. Future generations will not condone our profligate use of resources and will mine our junk piles for minerals.*

7. Describe how the Law of Scarcity is perfectly compatible with the fact that the economy is in some obvious ways quite rich.

8. Describe, or give some examples of, the three fundamental economic questions.

Concepts for review

Market economics
Public economics
Systems analysis
Economic goals
Technological constraints
Resources constraints
Social constraints
Economic efficiency
Output, Input, and Distribution questions

2

Methods and pitfalls in economic analysis

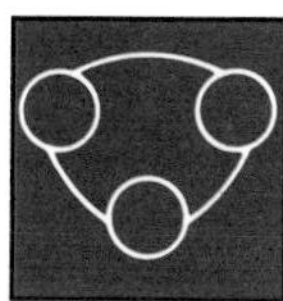

It is often assumed that common sense ought to be enough to untangle common problems. If we would just stop and mull over the issues, we should be able to get to the bottom of them. If that were true, it would be the way to resolve economic questions, for, as Chapter 1 argued, those questions are certainly common enough, that is to say, pressing and pervasive. Yet the conclusion can hardly be avoided that common sense, while no handicap to understanding, is not enough. The issues are too complex; their interrelationships are too intricate. Beginners can master chess principles but they cannot beat grand masters. Economics is more complicated than chess, and though most economic analysis has an intuitive plausibility, it takes more than ordinary common sense to really understand the moves.

To make progress in thinking about economics, one must be consciously scientific to avoid unwarranted generalizations either from individual experience or from special interest groups. Professor Paul Samuelson of M.I.T., who was awarded the Nobel prize in economics in 1970 "for the scientific work through which he has . . . actively contributed to raising the level of analysis in economic science," has spoken on this question.

> Anything and everything can be phrased so as to be plausible. Black is plausible; so is white; and so is grey. Until you have excluded some possibilities, or reduced their probability, you have accomplished nothing as a scientist.[1]

[1] Paul A. Samuelson, "What Economists Know," in Daniel Lerner (ed.), *The Human Meaning of the Social Sciences,* Meridian Books, Inc., New York, 1959, p. 185.

But how scientific can economics be? Are there "laws" or "rules" of economics which can be discovered? And if economics is a science, why hasn't it been used to make us all rich? Some first answers to these questions will be found in this chapter, but later chapters will return to them.

Economic statements: Tautological, objective, and normative

To lead to truth, economic analysis must obey the laws of logic. Conclusions must be valid implications of the premises. If we want to compute the value of output, we add up the separate components, using the logic of arithmetic; two and two must make four, not three or five or anything else. Statements which are logically valid simply because their words are defined to make them be so are *tautologies*. Tautologies can be deceptive when they are smuggled into an argument as more than the definitionally valid statements which they are. This is particularly dangerous to clear thinking in economics, which uses commonplace words, but with special definitions. When tautological statements that are valid for only certain definitions are treated as if they were valid for all the meanings of their words, they are seriously misleading.

Suppose, for example, that someone said, "In a capitalist economy there is private ownership of the means of production, and in a socialist economy there is public ownership." That statement does not convey any information about facts, though it may sound as if it did. It is simply a definition of capitalism and socialism. What if the speaker added, "Therefore, capitalism exploits workers." Is that a tautology, a statement of fact, or just one man's opinion?

Science begins with the distinction between opinion and fact, between objective and normative statements. *Objective*, or positive, economic statements are intended to describe facts, including the mode of operation of the economy. Such statements can be judged right or wrong only by testing them against facts. Either they agree or disagree, although in practice it is often not easy to determine which. But when we make judgments about positive statements, in principle, it is the facts which are decisive.

Normative statements, on the other hand, require or imply value judgments or preferences. That means that in the background there is some criterion or standard of behavior or performance to which the statement relates.

It is essential to recognize and respect the difference between objective and normative statements. Progress in the physical and natural sciences was possible only after the Renaissance pioneers declared their independence from tradition and authority as the arbiters of natural and physical law. Today no one would think of conducting a scientific argument in terms of how the sun and the planets or viruses and bacteria *ought* to behave.

Success in the social sciences depends on a clear separation of normative and objective statements. There is no more certain source of error than to confuse what really happens with what one would like to believe, good or bad, about the economy. Yet this confusion occurs again and again in the social sciences. It so easily intrudes into analysis that a special vigilance is required.

It is necessary to be meticulous because not all normative statements contain words like "should" or "ought" or "it is desirable and good," words that clearly indicate a value judgment. "Capitalism exploits workers" is a simple, declarative sentence which sounds like an objective statement of fact. But is it that, or a tautology, or a normative statement?[2] To decide what kind of statement such a sentence is, one should ask, Is it conceivably possible to find a fact that would disprove the statement? Or is it true by definition? If there are no facts that would contradict the statement, it must either reflect a value judgment or be a tautology. Suppose "exploitation" is defined as meaning that workers do not always receive the full sales price of the goods they produce. Then the statement, "Capitalism exploits workers," is a logically valid implication of a system of private ownership of the means of production, which follows some specific but widely prevailing market patterns. These result in workers not being paid the entire revenue from sales. In this sense, the sentence is also an objective statement that can potentially be disproved by reference to facts. But in this case the facts do not disprove; the statement is true; workers do not receive the full sales value of the goods they produce in capitalist economies.

The word "exploitation," however, is commonly intended to mean far more than the definition given above. When used in the statement, "Capitalism exploits workers," the meaning usually intended is something like, "Capitalism does not give workers the full amount they ought to receive." With this implication, the statement is a normative one, a statement of opinion. It cannot be refuted by facts because it is a judgment about how the value of output should be distributed. Nor does it imply any facts; a statement of opinion does not imply facts. Everyone is entitled to his own value judgments, of course. The point here is that it is essential to identify them for what they are.

The theoretical approach

The task of understanding the functioning of a mixed economy is truly a formidable one, and some way must be found to cut it down to a manageable size. Fortunately, there are plenty of hints and precedents which suggest how this can be done. The physical and natural sciences also have big and complicated systems to understand. They make their task manageable by simplifying or abstract-

[2] Tautologies can be normative statements ("By definition, whatever I like is good."), but not all tautologies are.

ing their problems and then explaining the abstraction. This is all that is meant by "theorizing." In the modern jargon of science, it is called *model building*.

A critical step in the theorizing or model-building process is finding the abstraction that does not do too much violence to reality. It retains the essential features of the problem, yet its simplifications reduce the number and complexity of the relationships involved. Thus, the scientist is able to gain insights that would otherwise be obscured. The abstraction of the problem should eliminate only those aspects which are not relevant for its explanation. The explanation must be logically correct. The theory will then yield objective statements describing reality or making predictions – statements that can be disproved if they are wrong.

In later chapters a number of economic models or theories will be proposed. At this point the objective is to understand in general how to formulate and test such models. There are three basic steps. First, the model must be described explicitly. This means that the concepts and terms used must be defined precisely. It also means that the conditions or assumptions under which the model is to be worked out must be stated clearly. Suppose, for example, a modern physical scientist were to describe the circumstances in which Galileo's experiment with falling bodies would work out exactly right. He might start by saying, "Assume there is a complete vacuum." Then he would have to define precisely what he meant by a complete vacuum. Likewise, if an economist wants to explain how an unplanned economy operates, he might start by saying, "Assume there is no government," and then go on to explain that this means that there are no taxes, no government expenditures, and no other means for government to control or influence the production and consumption of goods and services.

The second step in the process of constructing models or theories is to explain how the model operates. Any hypotheses about the behavior of the concepts employed must be specified. The logical implications of the assumptions and hypotheses are then worked out. The assumptions may go quite far in their characterizations, so that the logical chain of deduction may be relatively short, or vice versa. Scientists of all types, physical and social, prefer to make their assumptions as few and as simple as possible. That gives them what they call a "more fundamental" characterization for their models, since the implications they trace out can be applied to a far greater range of situations. If a physical scientist assumes the operation of the law of gravity on this planet, that tells him nothing about its operation on another planet. On the other hand, suppose he assumes only that there is something called mass with certain features and then derives the law of gravity from these assumptions. From this more fundamental abstraction, he can deduce implications about the operation of gravitational forces wherever the features of mass are found. Likewise the economists, explaining how competition works, may assume that there are many, relatively small business firms in the economy. Or this feature of an economy may itself be derived as an implication of more fundamental assumptions about the characteristics of technology and business organization.

The last step in the model-building process is testing. In many natural and physical sciences we would at this stage go off to a laboratory and flick the switch on the vacuum pump or do something else to simulate the abstract model we have created. We cannot do this in economics. Like some of the natural and physical sciences, meteorology and astronomy, for example, economics is for the most part an observational science. Controlled experiments are simply not possible in order to verify long-range weather forecasts or oscillations in radiations of certain stars thousands of light-years away. Nor is it possible for an economist to conduct a controlled experiment, for example, to find out the effect of an increase in property taxes on urban living. To do this, he would want to hold all the other features of the urban area constant with nothing changed except the property tax rate. This cannot be done. But like a meteorologist or astronomer, the economist can observe what is happening and look at past records and determine to what extent his observations are consistent with predictions made on the basis of his theory. Testing theories even in controlled experiments in a laboratory is not always easy. Testing theories outside the controlled environment of a laboratory, with many things changing at the same time, is an especially tricky business.

In the popular image, the theorist in economics and other sciences is someone who deals in finespun logical constructions that have little or no relation to reality. No doubt some of that posing and answering of abstract questions goes on in economics, as if the field were a branch of mathematics or pure logic. But the degree to which a theory corresponds to facts is always the final test.

A generalization is nothing but a theory or model of reality. It does not describe all the details of the subject, but it catches the essential features. If the object is to arrive at generalizations, there is really no substitute for theorizing and it cannot be avoided, however hard one tries.

Testing theories

One difficulty which often occurs to students and which is a real and continuing problem in economic analysis is: If economic theories always abstract from reality, and necessarily ignore some aspects of the real world, how can they avoid being contradicted by the facts thrown up by the real world? That is a fundamental and difficult question. Notice first of all that it does not ask, How can facts be used to *prove* a theory? Proof, that is, demonstration of the truth of a theory beyond every shadow of a doubt, is, strictly speaking, not possible in this world of imperfect knowledge. It is a good prediction that the sun will come up tomorrow, because it keeps doing so, and there is a theory that says it will, which has not yet been disproved. Nonetheless we can imagine cataclysmic happenings that might contradict the theory.

It would be more comfortable if all theories were either proved or disproved. Yet the world of science, especially the branch that includes economics, is not like that. Rather it is a world of theories which are held with different degrees of assurance and which gain in the sureness with which they are held according to the usefulness of the theories. That, in turn, depends on how well they explain and predict.

Notice that a theory is a conditional statement: *If* certain conditions hold, *then* certain results follow. To test the theory, one must try to reproduce the abstractions and conditions and look for the predicted results. Since it is not possible to make laboratory experiments which create the abstract conditions, the available facts must be examined carefully to see if the experiment has perhaps been performed in the course of the workings of the economy. It almost never has exactly, but often it has to some degree of approximation. Then one must try to decide whether the approximate results *disprove* the theory and thus force its abandonment.

The test for abandoning a theory is finally a pragmatic one: Is there another theory that explains and predicts better and which is, therefore, more useful? That does not mean that the test is an obvious one on which all men of good will can agree. There are heated debates, not just in economics but in the physical sciences as well, about when old theories should be abandoned and new ones adopted.

It is easy for people to accept the idea that a science such as economics is not a well-ordered system of logical theories and facts that prove them. It is not generally appreciated that the problems of economics as a science are the same in kind, though different in degree and detail, as those which arise in the "more scientific" fields of, say, physics and chemistry. And it is often not easy for people to accept the notion that, in spite of some theoretical and factual ambiguity, economics can be scientific and can make some highly reliable predictions on which to base policy.

To pursue this idea further, consider the example of steelmaking from the science of metallurgy. This has been called the age of steel. Steel is, perhaps, *the* essential material of modern life. It is made in big structures, called "furnaces," into which iron, coal, lime, and a few other ingredients are placed and "cooked," with the addition of some oxygen. Yet the metallurgical chemistry of what happens in that furnace is not fully understood. Moreover, every batch of ingredients that goes into the furnace is somewhat different and every batch of steel that comes out is somewhat different. Still the industry works in a reliable way to provide steel in huge tonnages. If the inputs or the furnace itself should change beyond the normal range of operations, the process will not work any more or, at least, not nearly so well.

In an analogous way in economics, when events fall within a "normal" pattern of behavior, we are pretty good at explaining and predicting them. We miss more often on "unusual" events. And in some ways — just as there are still mysteries in steel chemistry — we have not fully succeeded in bringing all the normal aspects of economic reality into the main body of our theories. But in steelmaking, the operations can be controlled to a much greater degree than in economics, and "normality" can be preserved. Economic life is not like that. We must take the unusual and the usual as they come and still try to explain and predict and make policy.

Identifying facts

It is not uncommon to hear some economic reasoning described as "good in theory but bad in practice." That suggests a distinction which is not legitimate. A theory that is bad in practice, that does not explain facts, is simply not a good theory.

To formulate theories and test them and predict with them, we must know just what the facts are. That in itself is no mean task. The facts seldom jump out at us. Discovering facts — in economics or in physics and chemistry — requires specialized skills. One runs into a whole series of problems.

There is, first, simply the problem of acquiring and assembling relevant information. For example, in a mixed economy with a large private sector, the behavior of private business firms is clearly of great importance. We know a good deal about that behavior, but there is still relatively little direct data on individual firms. Another example: Most of our information about markets comes from observing the results of their operation, but we have little detailed evidence on how firms make their decisions — decisions whose effects we observe in the markets.

Information is often intentionally concealed by business firms. The private nature of business operations makes this understandable, but it presents a major barrier to learning how businesses behave. Knowledge of such behavior would be useful, for instance, when economic policy makers set out to design a policy to stimulate technical progress. They would like to know, say, how various economic incentives would affect technological change. That would require information about the factors that determine the behavior of individuals and management in research and development laboratories in business firms, including consulting firms, in nonprofit organizations, and in colleges and universities. Yet the bias toward secrecy, particularly in business research laboratories, makes it hard to collect comprehensive data or even to find a representative sample.

Thus, the lack of direct evidence and the fact that economists must observe, rather than experiment, mean that we are often forced to rely on indirect evidence. We can seldom get inside business research laboratories to watch their decision-making processes in detail. But we can observe some of the results of their activity, for example, the patents they obtain. Unfortunately patents are not a good indicator of research effort. Some important developments are not patented at all, and the patents that are granted vary in their economic significance. That illustrates the disadvantages of indirect evidence.

Another difficulty in discovering the facts is due to the stochastic, or random, elements in many economic events and much of individual and business firm behavior. That does not mean that there are no patterns or regularities in economics. It means that the regularities are overlaid and somewhat concealed by randomness — in the same way that radio static can obscure a broadcast.

There is a lot of static in the behavior of individuals, but economics does not try to predict individual behavior. That is the province of individual psychology. Economics is concerned with the behavior of large groups of individuals and of business firms and of the markets in which they interact. There is a lot of static there, too. Fortunately there are ways of penetrating the "noise" of random elements to discover the regularities in the behavior of large groups. In part, the "law of large numbers" makes this possible.

Roughly speaking, this law states that as samples of observations get larger and larger, the sample averages become a better and better estimate of the average of the entire group. That is, in the behavior of large groups there is a canceling out of the extremely high and low observations. The larger the sample, the greater the chance that the canceling out will work better to make the average of any one sample close to the real average.

It is often possible to find exceptions to economic theories. Yet individual exceptions do not disprove theories that are meant to describe and explain the behavior of large groups. Nonetheless, such exceptions should be taken seriously. At some point, when they become significant enough, they "disprove" the theory.[3] At what point do exceptions become significant "enough"? The criterion is again a pragmatic one. When the exceptions become so important that the theory is less useful than another one, the first is abandoned. The use of statistical methods to test economic theories and describe economic processes is called *econometrics.* It is a flourishing field, and we shall have occasion to use its results.

Finally, facts should not be ignored simply because we are not certain that they fully depict the particular circumstances of a completely random and unbiased sample. Casual empiricism is stimulating though heady wine. We shall continually refer to interesting and insightful facts, but we shall be careful to avoid using them, as someone has aptly warned, "as a drunk uses lamp posts: more for support than illumination."

The use of the scientific method in economics is not fundamentally different from its application in other fields. But in economics, as in other fields, knowledge does not advance smoothly and steadily along a turnpike. There is usually intense interaction among the various stages of model building and testing. A fact will suggest an explanation which may not quite fit the fact. The origi-

[3] The aphorism, The exception proves the rule, is often quoted against using exceptions to disprove rules or theories. In the aphorism, however, "prove" is used in the sense of "test," as in "proving ground," and the aphorism, therefore, should be interpreted as, The exception *tests* the rule.

nal "fact" might turn out to be a rather special case, and a more general theory and more general tests will have to be tried. There may be a lot of fumbling insights and playing of hunches. Often it is only after the theory has been refined and tested conclusively that the road from assumptions to deductions to tests will be clearly laid out. That makes it possible for the student to grasp the ideas more easily. But the description is apt to be misleading if it suggests that some brilliant mind followed that straight and broad route from the beginning; usually the theorist, however brilliant his conclusion and however easy it may appear to us, spent many a day wandering around in the back roads.

Obstacles to understanding

Professional economists and other scientists find it hard to get on the scientific method turnpike of proposing and testing theories for the same reasons that new students find it hard. There are many obstacles to understanding. The entrance to the turnpike is a maze through which each person must pass himself. Since much of the maze is his own personal labyrinth, the student has to do most of the work to get through. Once we get out of the maze and onto the turnpike, economic theory helps us to move along quickly.

Semantics What creates the maze? Words do. We often use the same word for a lot of different purposes. Ordinary conversation does not require precise definitions, but careful thinking does. Semantics, the science of meanings, warns about the dangers of being misguided by the double or triple meanings which are given to words.

The word "capital," for example, carries a heavy burden of meanings. It is used to refer to money, corporate securities, physical plant and equipment, any durable productive resource, and, with "ism" added, to a particular way of organizing an economic system.

Words also generate emotions the way a ringing bell caused Dr. Pavlov's dogs to salivate. "Budget deficit" makes some people see red, and not just red ink. "High profits" are automatically "good" to some people and "bad" to others. "Unions" and "management" make some people choose sides immediately. "Exploit" carries so many emotional overtones that it is a danger to logical argument. The point is not that it is wrong to have emotions, even emotions about ideas. The point is that emotional reactions prevent real understanding when they are not recognized for what they are. In an objective discussion, emotions have to be put aside so that the issues themselves can be examined in a neutral fashion.

Folklore A related difficulty is that each of us is a walking encyclopedia of traditional economic folklore and mythology. We repeat the myths and maxims and hand them on from one generation to another.

This is a problem the physical and natural scientists do not have, at least not to the same degree as economists. In the physical and natural sciences, ignorance is more readily admitted. People do not pretend to know what the laws of thermodynamics "should" be. But nearly everyone has an opinion on whether or not the dollar should be devalued or whether taxes should go up or come down. This economic folklore is learned almost by osmosis and is reinforced by what we read in the daily newspaper. As examples:

> The dollar should have a sound backing.
>
> Savings are good.
>
> A healthy international trade position requires that we export more than we import.
>
> Prices go up when too much money chases too few goods.

Some folklore is true and useful, of course, but as long as it is just folklore we never know for sure. Is it true that "big business is bad for the consumer"? Or that "big business is progressive"? Only a careful analysis will reveal what truth these bits of economic folklore contain.

The intellectual baggage of economic folklore is an obstacle to real understanding. It introduces subconscious bias and mental blocks. The only remedy is to continually examine one's views and to try to sort out the mythology.

False analogy and other logical errors

Reasoning by analogy can be a powerful and suggestive way of working through a problem, but it is also a pervasive source of error in economics. It is dangerous, because it works only when the analogy is exact. For example, one of the most common arguments against deficits in the federal budget rests on the idea that the federal budget is analogous to the family budget. Families cannot live beyond their means and go into debt year after year without incurring bankruptcy, and, so goes the analogy, neither can governments. But is the analogy correct? Are families like governments? Do families have an indefinitely long lifetime? Do they borrow from themselves, as the government borrows from its own citizens when the debt is internal? Unless these and other similar questions are answered affirmatively the analogous reasoning does not hold. Government deficits may or may not be justified in particular circumstances, but the answer "yes" or "no" is not because a government is like a family.

One type of erroneous reasoning by analogy is so common that it has been given a name: the *fallacy of composition*. An explanation, perhaps quite valid, is formulated for the behavior of a single member of a larger group. That theory is then attributed to the group as a whole. But what is true for a part is not necessarily true for the whole. When one person stands up in the stadium, he can get a better view of the kickoff. When everyone stands up, no one can see any better and everyone might as well have remained seated. One person can take his money out of his bank without creating a ripple. If many people should try, the tidal wave would ruin the bank. One person out of work might, by his own efforts, be able to find a job. In times of high unemployment not everyone by his own efforts can obtain work.

If errors of logic and interpretation were easy to avoid, we would all be a lot smarter and a university could be, as Carlyle said, "a collection of books." Unfortunately, logic is not transparent and there are many pitfalls for the unwary user of common sense.

Another type of error often gets us into a logical whodunit. We confuse *association* with *causation.* For example, increases in advertising have been associated with increases in the national standard of living in the sense that both have occurred over the same periods. Did the former cause the latter? Some advertising men will tell you that it did, but it is hard to establish a tight logical argument and buttress it with facts.

A special form of the association-causation confusion is to presume that, because one event follows another in time, the first has caused the second. This is the *post hoc, ergo propter hoc* – after this, therefore because of this – fallacy. An event occurs; say, taxes go up. Another event occurs; say, prices go up. Did the first cause the second? Usually there is no obvious answer. Depending on the kind of tax, the way businessmen behave, and a number of other circumstances, some tax increases will sometimes lead to higher prices and sometimes not. The correct reasoning is certainly never as simple as *post hoc, ergo propter hoc.*

There is no substitute in economics for careful thinking and systematic reference to facts. This does not downgrade intuition. Intuition can sometimes indicate where we should look for answers to questions and, in a general way, how the answers might turn out. It cannot, however, demonstrate that our answers are correct. With issues as important as those which arise in economics, there are grave dangers in giving incorrect answers and making wrong predictions. These dangers justify the effort to be precise.

Summary

Because economic issues are complex and difficult, their analysis must be consciously rigorous and scientific.

Economic statements that are valid by definition are tautologies and convey no information about the manner in which the economy operates. Objective economic statements are intended to be descriptions of facts and of the manner of operation of the economy. In principle, objective statements can be refuted by facts. Normative statements are expressions of value judgments and, therefore, do not describe facts, but personal preferences. To avoid error in economic analysis, we must be able to distinguish these three types of statements.

The object of economics is to develop a general understanding.

Generalizations are nothing but theories. Theorizing or model building is, therefore, inevitable.

The building and using of theoretical models starts with the precise definition of the terms used and the explicit statement of all the assumptions that describe the model. Next, the implications of the assumptions and definitions are deduced. Finally, the implications of the model are tested against the facts.

To establish economic facts, one must assemble and interpret data. Direct economic information about the behavior of private individuals and firms is often difficult to acquire. As a result it is often necessary to rely on indirect evidence.

Interpreting economic data requires penetrating the screen of randomness that characterizes much of the economic behavior observed. Randomness does not imply unpredictability, at least for large groups, because the law of large numbers is usually valid.

There are many pitfalls to economic understanding, however. Semantic problems arise from imprecise and inconsistent definitions. A good deal of erroneous information is embodied in economic folklore. Logical errors arise in false analogies and in confusing association with causation. While self-consciously careful thinking may sometimes appear to be a roundabout approach, the importance of economic issues justifies the effort to be precise.

Questions for discussion and review

1. Do you think economics can be a science? Explain your answer.

2. Suppose you hear that "there is no business like show business." Is that a tautological, objective, or normative statement? What information does it convey?

3. *An economic system cannot be equitable and allow poverty to exist.* Is this statement tautological, objective, or normative?

4. Why does economic theorizing have such a bad reputation when the argument in the chapter makes it seem like a natural and obvious process?

5. Why is the law of large numbers important in economics?

6. What is argument by analogy? Can you give an example in economic reasoning other than the one given in the chapter?

7. Do you believe that there can be economic "laws"?

Concepts for review

Economic models
Tautological statements
Objective statements
Normative statements
Stochastic elements
Fallacy of composition
Post hoc, ergo propter hoc
Economic folklore

3

The fundamental economic questions: In model economies and in reality

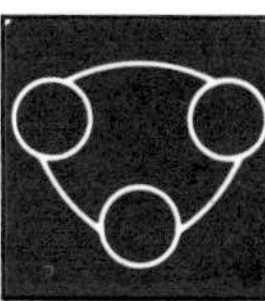

This chapter begins the analysis of the economic system at the microeconomic level of the basic producing and consuming units. The objective is a deep understanding of the character of the constraints on the economy, the fundamental economic questions, and their interdependence. This understanding will then be used to gain insight into some important current economic problems.

The constraints within which an economy must operate partially determine its ability to satisfy the goals of its members. These constraints are rooted in the economy's technology, the availability of resources, and the social customs and institutions of the society. While functioning within its constraints, any economy must somehow resolve the Output, Input, and Distribution questions described in Chapter 1. One of the most common mistakes made in thinking about economic matters is the failure to appreciate the interdependence which exists among these three questions. For example, public officials may make plans to do something about increasing the amount of urban housing. On the face of it, housing construction is an Output question because it has to do with *how much* of *what* goods are to be produced. But construction targets often are not met because the planners do not recognize the interdependence of this and other economic questions. There may not be enough skilled labor available, and the skills required are partly an aspect of the technology used in construction. These are Input issues; they are aspects of *how* the housing is to be built and *how much* of *what kind* of labor and other productive resources are to be used. Or the construction may be delayed by strikes over which union is going to get what part of the total work for its members. Or the work may be stopped by pickets demanding that more black workers be admitted into the construction unions. These Distribution questions are related to the Input questions. At stake is the allocation of *income earned* on the construction project, which will in turn determine *how much* housing, food, clothing, and the pleasures of life various individuals will enjoy.

The approach of the systems analysis of the basic economic questions is the strategy of science. We shall formulate abstract theories or models in which some essential characteristics of an economy are isolated. The models will then be analyzed. Finally, the results will be generalized. We shall strip the complex economic system to essentials by the simplifying assumptions used to decribe the models. The first steps are small ones, so small in fact that they hardly appear to represent any progress at all. In a sense they are steps backward, away from reality. But by stepping backward, we can get a running start which will move us along rapidly.

Three model economies will be studied in detail. The first model is an economy in which only two goods are produced with one type of productive resource. In the second model, there are two productive resources but only one type of output. In the third model, there are two goods produced and two types of inputs. Taken up successively, these models, by their extreme simplifications, will help us isolate and examine different aspects of real economies. They will also serve as a way of introducing some important concepts.

The First Model Economy

The First Model Economy is a simple world of production. We assume that there is only one productive resource. Call it Labor. All of it, as far as productivity is concerned, is identical. It is what economists call a *homogeneous factor of production*. So in this model we do not have to worry about some laborers being more skilled or faster or harder working than others. We will also assume, at first, that there is just so much of the Labor resource available. This can be thought of as restricting the analysis to a definite period in which there is no growth or decline in the amount of Labor. These assumptions define the resource constraints under which the economy must operate.

The First Model Economy is also a simple world of commodities. We reduce the great variety of production to manageable proportions by assuming that there are only two goods: Food and Clothing. Other things may be enjoyed, like fresh air and sunshine, but these are not scarce because they are freely available. Food and Clothing are scarce because the production of each requires inputs of the limited amount of available Labor.

We will suppose that the productivity of Labor, which is the output per unit of Labor, is constant. This is plausible, since all the

Labor is identical. The relations between inputs of Labor and the output of each of the commodities are, therefore:

Output of Food = (Labor used for food production)
× (Output of Food per unit of Labor)

Output of Clothing = (Labor used for clothing production)
× (Output of Clothing per unit of Labor)

Economists call these two relations *production functions*, because they relate the inputs used in production to the resulting output. They summarize the *technological constraints* on the economy. All the scientific and engineering information necessary to produce Food and Clothing is reflected in the productivity ratios of Labor in producing Food and Clothing.

The limited amount of labor available constitutes the *resource constraint*. When resources are used in Food production they are not available for producing Clothing. Therefore:

Labor used in producing Food + Labor used in producing Clothing = Total amount of Labor available

This constraint, itself, creates an interdependence between decisions about Food production and about Clothing production.

Finally we will assume that everyone owns his own Labor; it is not a resource which can be bought and sold. There is no peonage, serfdom, or slavery. Every man is his own master. But the Food and Clothing produced with Labor can be bought and sold. We can assume in this simple world that there is no need for a government, or if there is a government, it does not use any of the resources of the private economy. Alternatively we could assume that there was a government which used a fixed amount of the total Labor, and we would then concentrate on what was done with the rest. These assumptions define the *institutional constraints* under which the economy operates.

The assumptions defining the First Model Economy in themselves resolve some aspects of the fundamental economic questions. The others, as a result, become more clear.

The *Output* questions, which goods to produce and how much of them, boil down to how much Food and how much Clothing. The answer to those Output questions automatically determines the answer to the Input questions. The amount of Labor that will be used in the production of Food and of Clothing can be calculated quickly, since the productivity of Labor in each is constant. There is no problem of finding the best set of inputs in this model economy. There is only one resource and just one way of using it to produce each good. In this model there is no economic problem of finding the best way to produce the goods.

Likewise, the *Distribution* of the output among types of productive factors – the functional distribution – is no problem in this model. There is only one actor in this drama, only Labor. The personal distribution of income depends on how many man-hours of labor each worker provides. There are no capitalists and no owners and renters of land. Whatever is produced must go to somebody and there is only Labor, which owns its own services, so everything goes to it.

Production possibilities in the First Model Economy

We can work out fully and in detail all the alternative amounts of Food and Clothing that can be produced by the First Model Economy. This will provide a comprehensive overview of the options open to it. Suppose there are exactly 100 men available for work. The productivity of a man in producing Food is 10 bushels per day; the productivity of a man in producing Clothing is 5 standard pieces of apparel in a day.

Assume first that all the Labor is put to work producing Food. Then 1,000 bushels will be produced each day. Alternatively, if all the Labor were allocated to Clothing, the daily output would be 500 garments. These are possibilities *A* and Z, shown on the first and second lines of Table 3-1. These possibilities are also shown graphically in Figure 3-1 as points *A* and Z.

Intermediate points can be calculated just as readily. Suppose half the Labor were allocated to Food production and half to Clothing each day. Then 500 bushels of Food and 250 garments would be produced. This is possibility *M* in Table 3-1; it is shown as point *M* in Figure 3-1. Going from possibility *A* to possibility *M* means giving up 500 bushels of Food to get 250 garments. Similarly, going from possibility *M* to Z again means a trade off of 500 bushels of Food for 250 garments or 2 bushels of Food for 1 garment.

All the possible combinations of Food and Clothing that can be produced with the Labor available involve moving between possibilities *A* and Z in Figure 3-1, by shifting Labor from Food to Clothing production. One laborer moved out of Food production into Clothing production reduces Food output by 10 bushels and increases Clothing output by 5 garments. That is always the trade off: 10 bushels of Food for 5 garments or 2 bushels of Food for 1 garment. It is possible to think of shifting Labor, one worker at a time from Food to Clothing production and moving down a series of steps, which always go *down* by 2 bushels of Food, and *out* by 1 garment. This possibility is shown by the inset in Figure 3-1, which enlarges the region around point *M*. Since the trade off is constant,

Table 3-1

PRODUCTION POSSIBILITIES IN THE FIRST MODEL ECONOMY

	Labor in Food production	*Labor in Clothing production*	*Output of Food (bushels per day)*	*Output of Clothing (garments per day)*
A	100	0	1,000	0
Z	0	100	0	500
M	50	50	500	250
Q	40	40	400	200

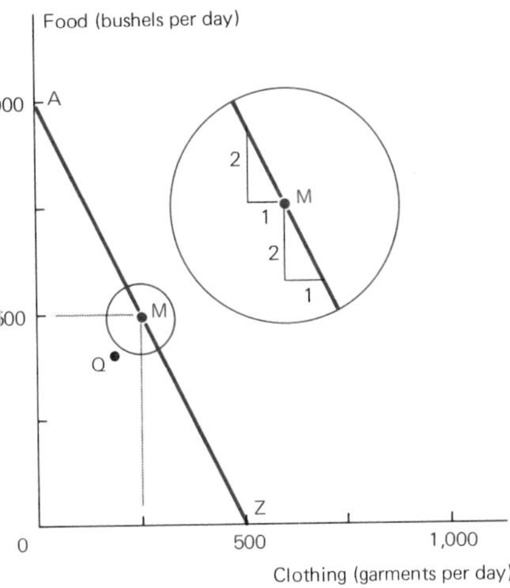

Figure 3-1

PRODUCTION POSSIBILITY LINE FOR THE FIRST MODEL ECONOMY

the line connecting *A*, *M*, and Z in Figure 3-1 and showing all possible Food and Clothing output combinations is a straight line.

In the First Model Economy, simple arithmetic can show us all the possible combinations of output of which it is capable. This is the economy's *production-possibility function*, or when it is plotted on a graph, the production-possibility line. The economy can move along its production-possibility line by shifting the productive resource, Labor, from one type of production to the other. In a sense, this shifting makes it possible to "transform" Food into Clothing and vice versa. That is why the production-possibility line is sometimes also called the *transformation function*.

To derive the production-possibility line, we always make use of all the Labor that is available. At each point on the line, resources are being fully utilized. So it is a relationship in which full employment is assumed. If the Labor available is not fully employed, less Food or Clothing or both will be produced. How much less? Any amount between the production-possibility line *AMZ* and the Food and Clothing axes. At point Q in Figure 3-1, for example, only 40 workers are employed in producing Food and 40 in producing Clothing; 20 are left unemployed. By leaving some of its productive resources idle or using them inefficiently, the First Model Economy can be inside its production-possibility line. On the other hand, the economy cannot possibly get "further out" than the frontier which the production-possibilitiy line represents.

The production-possibility line helps to demonstrate a number of important points. It shows the essential interdependence in the First Model Economy. The output decisions of Food and Clothing are interdependent, because the amount of Food produced depends on the amount of Clothing produced. Why? Because the Clothing decision will determine the use of Labor in that line and, therefore, the amount of Labor that will be left over and available to produce Food. In this way, the Input decisions, which determine the amount of Labor allocated to the production of each type of good, depend on the Output decisions.

The production-possibility line also clarifies the Law of Scarcity. Chapter 1 argued that scarcity is a pervasive and inescapable fact of life which imposes the necessity of making choices, since it is impossible always to have more of everything. That is true of an economy that is on its production-possibility function, with resources fully employed. But when resources are not fully employed, as at point Q, it *is* possible to have more of both Food and Clothing by using the unemployed Labor.

What is the source of scarcity when the economy is *on* its production-possibility line? The essential scarcity is one of productive resources. Scarcity is, therefore, not just a bourgeois, capitalist invention, but an inescapable fact of life in any system where the wants of the people push the economy out to the limits of its production possibilities. There are always limits on all the resources available at any time. It is that which imposes a scarcity of goods.

This simple economy has many commonsense analogies. A

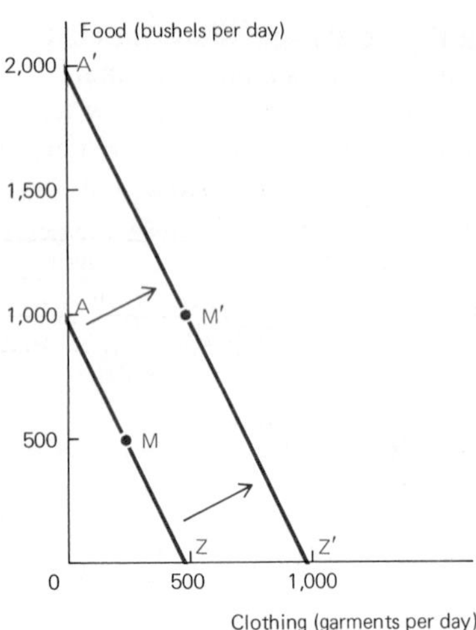

Figure 3-2

THE EFFECTS OF AN ADDITION TO THE LABOR FORCE IN THE FIRST MODEL ECONOMY

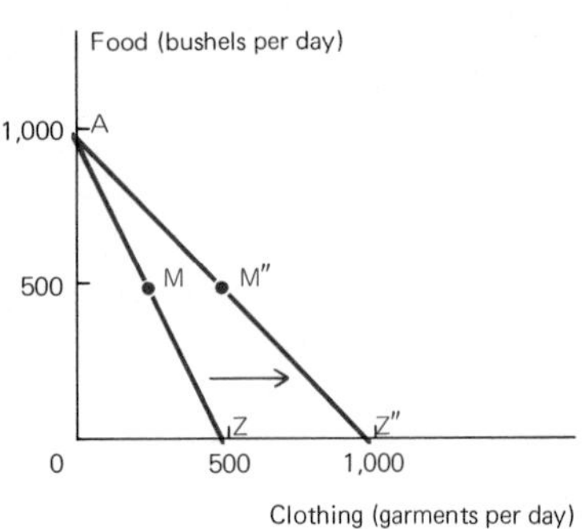

Figure 3-3

THE EFFECTS OF TECHNOLOGICAL IMPROVEMENT IN CLOTHING PRODUCTION

busy farmer knows that the more time he spends on his garden, the less time he will have for the field. The assembly-line manager with a fixed labor budget knows that the more labor he has assembling trucks, the less there will be for the passenger car line. The busy student knows that the more time he spends on economics, the less time he will have for other courses.

It is also possible to use the production-possibility concept to understand the sources of changes in the overall availability of goods. Suppose that there was population growth or immigration in the First Model Economy and the Labor supply grew to 200 workers. Then the entire transformation line would shift outward, as in Figure 3-2, from *AMZ to A′M′Z′*. Emigration, or a plague in which part of the labor force perished, would shift the production-possibility curve inward.

A technological change that increases the productivity of resources is similar to an increase in their availability, but the effects need not be the same in the production of both commodities. Suppose, for example, that a new sewing technique is discovered. As a result, Labor becomes more adept at making Clothing. The effect is an increase in Labor's productivity from 5 garments per man per day to 10 garments. If all the originally available Labor were put into Clothing production, it could now produce 1,000 garments. If just half the Labor were put to making Clothing, it could make 500 garments. But, of course, if all the Labor were concentrated in Food production, it could still produce only 1,000 bushels, the same as before. The new set of production possibilities is shown by line *AM″Z″* in Figure 3-3. The effect of the technological change in Clothing production is to swivel the transformation line outward from the Clothing axis. Therefore, it moves from the Food axis, except at *A*.[1] When there is complete specialization in Food production, an improvement in Clothing technology has no effect. But when some amount of *both* goods is produced, the effect of a technological change — even if it is confined to only one sector — is to increase the possibilities of production in *both* sectors. The technological change can be regarded as a particular way of saving resources in one type of production so that more can be used in the other type of production if that is desired.

Technological changes and increases in the supply of resources do not invalidate the concept of limited production possibilities when resources and technology are constant. When they shift, the production possibilities also shift.

An overview of the First Model Economy

If we think about how the First Model Economy could be operated as a planned system, that will help us to get a better overall view of it. Planning the First Model Economy would be relatively straightforward. After the planners determined the total Labor available,

[1] You should verify the positions of *A′M′Z′* and *AM″Z″* for yourself.

they could work out fully, as a matter of simple arithmetic, all the alternative combinations of Food and Clothing that could be produced. Then by administrative decision or by free consumer choice, the combination of Food and Clothing most desired could be chosen. Labor could then be allocated to produce exactly that combination. The relation between the Output and the Input questions is clear and direct. In a planned economy, however, the resolution of the question of personal Distribution of output would depend on the central authority's decision as to who should receive how much.

The assumption of only one resource and only two goods is a powerful simplifying device. We shall try it again — but in reverse — in the Second Model Economy.

The Second Model Economy

In the Second Model Economy only one good is produced, Food. But there are two productive resources that can be used to produce it, Labor and Land. The purpose of this abstraction is to highlight some of the characteristics of a real economy that are created by the availability of a variety of factors of production. So we simplify by reducing the number of goods produced to the absolute minimum. There is only so much Land and Labor available; this is the *resource constraint.* The available technological knowledge and production know-how constitute the *technological constraint.*

The *institutional constraints* specify the rules for hiring or buying Labor and Land. We shall assume that every man can be his own boss and buy or rent the Land on which he works, or he can work for wages on someone else's Land. As in the First Model Economy, there need be no government. Or if there is a government, we shall assume that it does not use any resources. Or we can give it a fixed amount of Land and Labor and concentrate on the use of the rest.

In the Second Model Economy the *Output* question appears in the starkest form possible. There is no problem of *which* good to produce. There is only Food. There is a question of *how much* Food will be produced. That is settled when we know the amounts of the two productive resources, Labor and Land, available and the technology used. The *Input* problem is somewhat more complex and more interesting than in the First Model Economy, because here there are two types of resources to be combined in production.

The most complicated economic problem in the Second Model Economy is Distribution. How is the output of the single product to be distributed between the two types of productive resources? This problem, which did not exist in the First Model Economy, emerges as soon as there is more than one kind of input in the production process. There is no engineering answer to the Distribution question. It is not even the sort of problem engineers analyze. Yet technology and resource availabilities are relevant.

Production and interdependence in the Second Model Economy

Just as in the First Model Economy, there is a relation between inputs of resources and outputs: a production function. It is a much more complicated relation, however, when there are two or more inputs. In particular, there are likely to be substitution possibilities between the inputs. That is, it will be *possible* to produce the same level of output with more than one combination of the resources. In the production of Food, there are many actual examples of substitution. Rice is produced in Japan with a lot of manpower in relation to the amount of land used. It is grown in the United States in Texas with a lot of land relative to the amount of labor used. Likewise, around the world, wheat, corn, and meat are produced with a wide range of variation in the proportions in which inputs are combined.

The production function is easier to conceive of than actually to measure, though there is a good deal of evidence on the characteristics of the production of different types of goods. These technological characteristics change over time as the result of research and innovation. At any given time, however, they impose a fundamental constraint on what an economy can produce and are an essential determinant of the basic economic questions.

In the Second Model Economy the amounts of Land and Labor available are specified. While it is possible to produce more or less output with the particular set of inputs available, there will be one specific technique which uses all the resources and produces the maximum output. Finding that technique will determine the level of Output and settle the Input question. It will also resolve the functional Distribution questions.

This last point is not an obvious one, and requires some elaboration. Suppose that there is a great deal of Land available and only a small amount of Labor. This was the situation in the American colonial era and along the Western frontier in the nineteenth century. Relatively speaking, it is the position of Texas as compared with Japan in the production of rice. In these circumstances, landowners will tend to receive a smaller share of the total output than if conditions were reversed. The relatively scarce productive resource does relatively better in terms of the return it can command. Where Labor is abundant and is crowding the land, labor incomes tend to be low and landlords receive relatively more. On the other hand, if Labor is scarce, or if technological changes make it possible to increase the productivity of Labor on the land, the resolution of the Distribution question will also change in favor of Labor.[2] The personal distribution question now depends on the ownership of Land as well as the amount of Labor of each worker.

[2] These results, though intuitively plausible, have yet to be demonstrated conclusively. That will be done for some special market conditions in Chap. 27.

The interdependence in the Second Model Economy is entirely on the production side, since there is only one type of output. Decisions about the use of, say, Labor in production cannot be made independently of decisions with respect to the use of Land. The way resources are combined to produce output makes the facts of technology an important source of economic interdependence.

Increasing and diminishing returns to a single resource

Though the precise characteristics of production functions will in reality vary from commodity to commodity, some qualitative features are quite general. The Second Model Economy can be used to demonstrate these.

Suppose that the arable Land available to the Second Model Economy is fixed in amount; no more can be brought into cultivation. Suppose further that the technology used in production remains unchanged. Population and the labor force grow, however, and output also, as more and more Labor is used on the Land. If we traced the history of output, what would it look like?

Figure 3-4 shows what is often regarded as a typical pattern. When population is sparse, output may well increase at a faster rate than the labor force. That is the stage from *O* to *A* on the output curve in Figure 3-4. In this phase there are *increasing*

Figure 3-4

OUTPUT FROM VARIABLE LABOR INPUTS WITH FIXED LAND INPUT

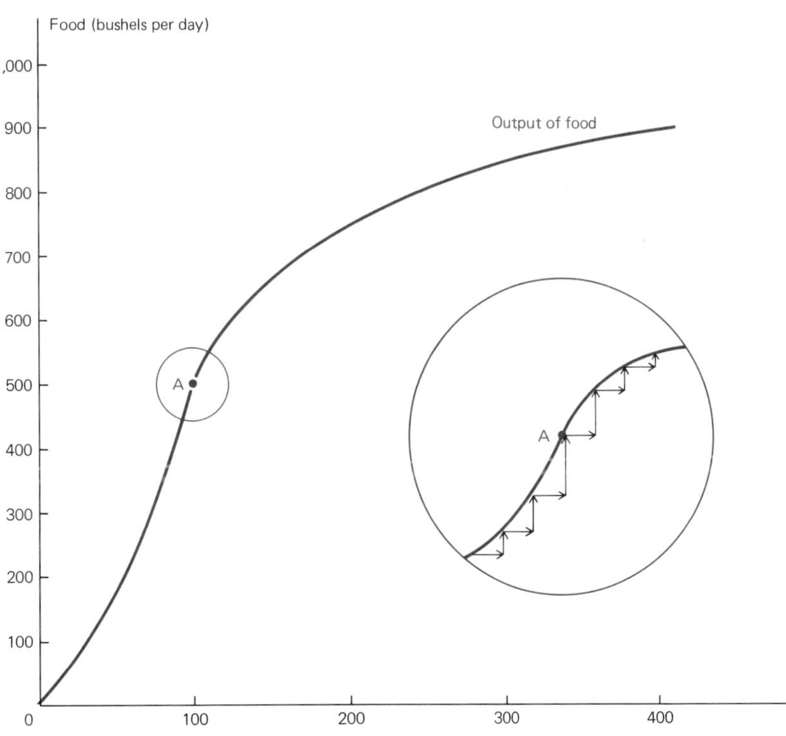

returns to the single factor, Labor. With the available Land fixed, the additions to output increase as additional workers are added. With more Labor available, workers can specialize in particular tasks and become more productive. If the labor force grows at 2 percent a year, output might increase by a larger percentage, say, 3, from *O* to *A*.

But this cannot go on indefinitely. As population becomes more dense, the opportunities for specialization are exhausted. Beyond *A*, *with the available Land fixed, the additions to output diminish with each additional worker.* This is the phase of *diminishing returns*, which occurs to the right of point *A* in Figure 3-4.

The inset in Figure 3-4 magnifies a part of the curve and shows the increments of output first increasing and then decreasing as additional Labor goes to work on the Land.

Law of Diminishing Returns

The numbers in Table 3-2 represent the output line around point *A* in Figure 3-4. Notice that the *additional* output of each *additional* worker falls after point *A*. This is sometimes called the Law of Diminishing Returns.

Diminishing returns, as defined, is not a logical proposition but a hypothesis about technology which is frequently observed in reality. As shown in Figure 3-4, diminishing returns need not prevail over all ranges of input, but the "law" has a way of finally working out. For this to happen, only one productive resource can be varied while all others are held constant *and* there are no changes in technology. Notice also in Figure 3-4 that output continues to rise even after diminishing returns set in. Diminishing returns is a remarkably general phenomenon. It turns up in agriculture and industry. Often it even describes the change in performance of students on examinations as they increase their study time.

Suppose, now, that the Land available to the Second Model Economy can also be increased, say, through a reclamation pro-

Table 3-2

OUTPUTS FROM VARIABLE LABOR INPUTS WITH FIXED LAND INPUT

	Number of workers (man-days)	*Total Food output per day (bushels)*	*Additional output produced when one more worker is added*
	98	589	
			5
	99	494	
			6
Point *A*	100	500	
			5
	101	505	
			4
	102	509	
			3
	103	514	

Figure 3-5

OUTPUTS WITH BOTH LABOR AND LAND INPUTS VARYING

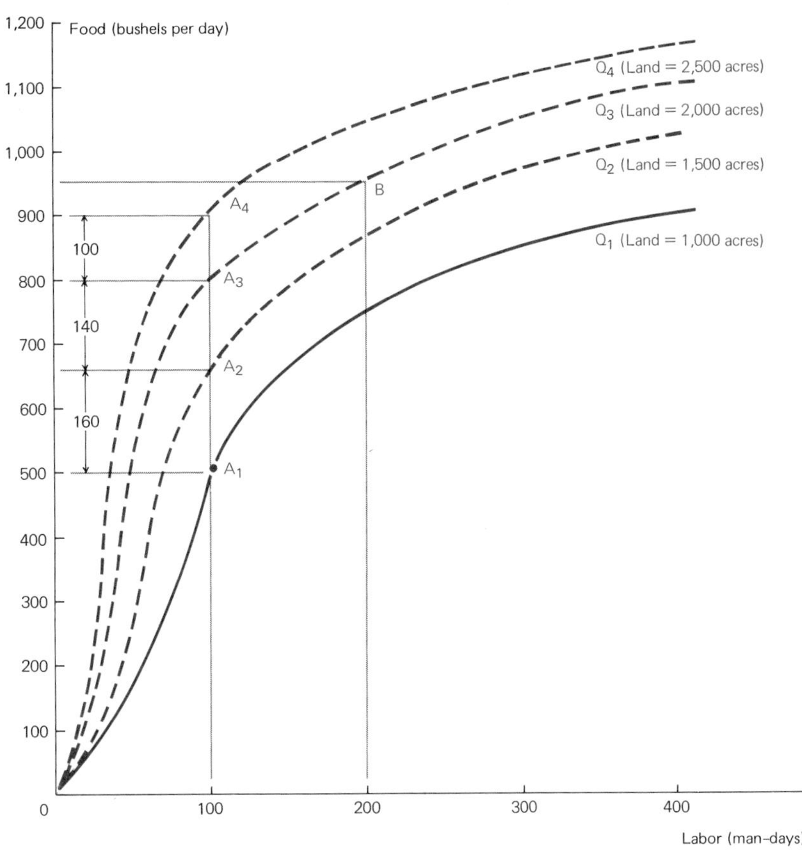

gram. Then, for each alternative amount of Land there will be an Output-Labor relation, as shown in Figure 3-5 by lines Q_1, Q_2, etc. In Figure 3-5 we can observe diminishing returns to Labor develop along each Output-Labor line. We can also see diminishing returns to Land work out across each Output-Labor line. With Labor constant at 100 workers, an additional 500 acres of Land increases output by 160 bushels per day, from A_1 to A_2. The next 500 acres, with Labor still at 100 workers, increases output by only 140 bushels daily, from A_2 *to* A_3; and with 500 more acres of Land and with Labor unchanged, output goes up by only 100 bushels daily, from A_3 *to* A_4.

Increasing and decreasing returns to the scale of use of both factors

Let us turn now to a somewhat different, but important, aspect of production relations. Up to now in our mental experiments with the Second Model Economy, we have held one of the inputs constant and varied the other. In reality, however, we frequently observe all inputs growing, and we would like to know what output behavior to expect when this happens.

Suppose we start at A_1 in Figure 3-5 and move to point B. We double *both* inputs, from 100 to 200 workers and from 1,000 to 2,000 acres of Land. Output goes from 500 to only 950 bushels per day and, thus, less than doubles. Here we have *decreasing returns to scale* of *both* productive resources. This is *not* the same as diminishing returns to the increase of *one* resource, while the other is held constant. Decreasing returns to scale is not an unusual technological characteristic, but neither is it a universal technological characteristic. In many lines of production there seem to be *constant returns to scale.* That is, when *all* inputs are doubled, output is also doubled. Or more generally: When all inputs are changed in the same proportion, output will change in that proportion also. Many manufacturing assembly processes seem to behave like this once they are at their most efficient size. One can also find examples of *increasing returns to scale*: A doubling of inputs will lead to more than a doubling of outputs. In general, in this case, output increases are larger than the proportionate increase in *all* inputs which causes output to grow.

A review of the Second Model Economy

Again we can obtain a summary view by asking how the Second Model Economy could be operated as a planned system. The Output problem boils down to the question, How much of the single product can be produced? That depends on the resolution of the Input problem, which is a matter of using the available amounts of the two types of resources in the most effective manner. Scarcity in this economy is again basically a matter of limited productive resources.

The most difficult issues in the Second Model Economy are the Distribution questions, because there are two types of productive resources. Functional distribution is a matter of the division of output between these two types of resources as returns for their productive contributions. As will be explained in greater detail in the following chapters, planners are aware that the division will have an effect on the efficiency with which resources are used. If, for example, nothing is allocated to Land, it will be used as if it were free and not scarce — when, in fact, its availability is limited. This suggests the relations between the Distribution issues and the Input questions.

Yet the system is not "locked in" or committed to a particular distribution of its output among individuals by its technology and resources. The personal distribution of income among individuals depends on many social and political as well as economic conditions. One person's income may be based entirely on his Labor. Another person may earn income only as a property owner; another may be both a worker and a landowner. All Land may be owned jointly and its share distributed equally. Land ownership may be private, and its income taxed away, all or in part, and redistributed. Depending on the planners' preferences, or the institutional constraints in a real economy, there are many possible answers to the personal income distribution question — whatever the functional distribution of income.

The Third Model Economy

In the Third Model Economy two commodities, Food and Clothing, are produced with two productive resources, Labor and Land. This system, though still quite simple, is sufficiently complex to provide a useful approach to analyzing many real problems as will be shown in the latter part of the chapter.

What kinds of complications in the basic economic questions can be expected in the Third Model Economy? Since this economy combines the features of the first two model economies, it has all the complexities inherent in *both* of them. Two goods can be produced, so there is a real Output question, as in the First Model Economy: How much of each of the two goods should be produced?

There are two productive resources, so there is an Input question: How much of each of the two resources should be used in the production of each good? With two resources there are possibilities of substituting one input for another in the production of each good — as there are in the Second Model Economy for one good. The resolution of the Input question depends in part on how the Output question is settled. If people insist on having a lot of Food and little Clothing, the amounts of the resources and the technologies used in the production of each good will be different from what they would be if people wanted a lot of Clothing and relatively little Food. The causal effects in the resolution of the fundamental questions are not one way, however. For example, the choices of the amounts of Food and Clothing to be produced will be influenced by the resources and technology available. If there is a great deal of Land relative to Labor and if growing Food is relatively easy, there will be a tendency to grow more Food than if Land were quite scarce.

The existence of two resources means that there is also a Distribution question involving the division of the Output, as there was in the Second Model Economy. This is again related to the manner in which the Input question is resolved — which is, itself, related to the resolution of the Output question.

In the Third Model Economy we have a truly interdependent system in which none of the basic economic questions is trivial. All the questions are present and must be accounted for.

Constraints in the Third Model Economy

The *technological constraints* in the Third Model Economy are embodied in the production function for *each* good. Production of each of the goods requires both types of resources. The output of Food depends on the amounts of Land *and* Labor used in producing

Food, and the output of Clothing depends on the amounts of Land *and* Labor used in producing it. Schematically:

Food production depends on	Land used in producing Food and Labor used in producing Food
Clothing production depends on	Land used in producing Clothing and Labor used in producing Clothing

There are diminishing returns in each line of production; if the amount of one input is held constant while constant increments of the other input are added to production, the additional increments of output will eventually get smaller and smaller.

The other aspect of the Law of Scarcity is the limited amounts of each of the two productive inputs which are available in any period of time. These constitute the *resource constraints*.

Land used in producing Food *plus* Land used in producing Clothing	= total Land available
Labor used in producing Food *plus* Labor used in producing Clothing	= total Labor available

The *institutional constraints* are embodied in the rules for buying and renting Land or hiring Labor. The system could be unplanned, or partially or completely planned. The basic economic questions remain the same in any case.

The production-possibility curve of the Third Model Economy

The production relationships and the availability of the two resources determine the production possibilities in this economy, as in the First Model Economy. In the first model, however, the calculation of the production-possibility line is a matter of arithmetic, because with only one resource, the input requirements per unit of output are constant. Even in the Second Model Economy, though there are two types of inputs, they can be used in only one type of production. In the Third Model Economy there are two inputs with substitution possibilities between them and two outputs in whose production they can be used. As a result, there are no simple arithmetic techniques that can be used to derive the production-possibility line for the Third Model Economy. Fortunately we really do not need to know precisely what that line is for our analysis, but we do need a general idea of what it is like. That can be worked out by relying on the experience gained in the First and Second Model Economies.

In the First Model Economy, the production-possibility curve was a straight line. It was derived by allocating all of the single Labor resource first to Food production and finding the maximum amount that could be produced. Then all of the single Labor resource was put into Clothing production, and its maximum was

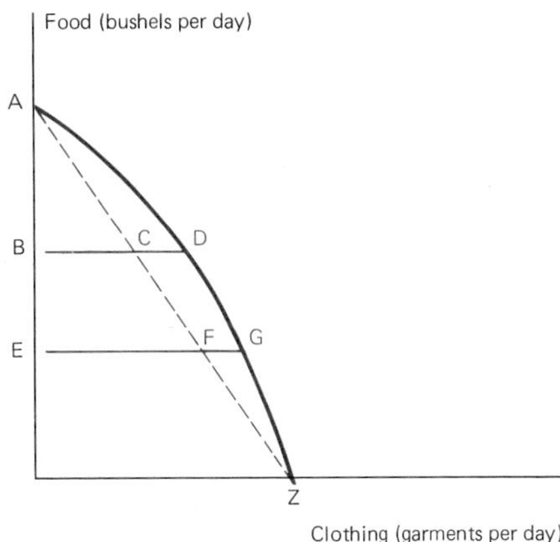

Figure 3-6

PRODUCTION-POSSIBILITY CURVE FOR THE THIRD MODEL ECONOMY

found. We then observed that the trade-off ratio between Food and Clothing was constant. Every additional unit of Food production required a certain, constant amount of the single resource. That meant giving up a precise, constant amount of Clothing. So the production-possibility or transformation function for Food and Clothing was a straight line. (This was verified by calculating an intermediate point which fell on the straight line joining the extreme positions.)

To determine the shape of the production-possibility curve in the Third Model Economy, we will adopt the same general approach. First, if all of *both* resources is allocated to the production of Food, there is some maximum amount that can be produced. That is point *A* in Figure 3-6. If all of both resources were put into Clothing production, some maximum of Clothing would be produced at point Z. Starting back at point *A*, if Food is to be transformed into Clothing by shifting resources from one type of production to the other, we should be able to do at least as well as in the case of the First Model Economy. We should be able to trade off Food and Clothing at a constant rate so that a straight line from *A* to Z would be a set of *feasible* combinations of Food and Clothing.

The production-possibility line is more than just a set of feasible production combinations, however. When the economy is on its production-possibility line, resources are being combined in the *most efficient* way possible. On the production-possibility line, for any specified amount of Food, the *maximum possible* amount of Clothing is produced. For any specified amount of Clothing, the *maximum possible* amount of Food is produced. So we have to ask if it is possible to do better then merely travel along the straight line between *A* and Z. "Doing better" means getting out beyond the straight line *AZ*; it means obtaining more Clothing than is indicated by the line *AZ* when any specified amount of Food is produced.

To do this, why not exploit the Labor-Land substitution possibilities? Why not take advantage of the fact that some combinations of resources are more productive than others in producing each commodity? The production of Food, for example, typically requires a lot more Land per worker than does the production of Clothing. That is no accident, but a result of the differences in the production functions of the two goods.

Suppose we stand at point *A*, producing all Food, and decide we want some Clothing. This is going to require that some resources be transferred from Food production. But let us be shrewd about it and take a relatively small amount of Land out of Food production and a relatively larger proportion of Labor. In that way the effect on Food production will be relatively small and we will get a comparatively large increase in Clothing production. In Figure 3-6, instead of moving along the straight dashed line *AZ*, we can move along the solid curved line. When Food production is cut

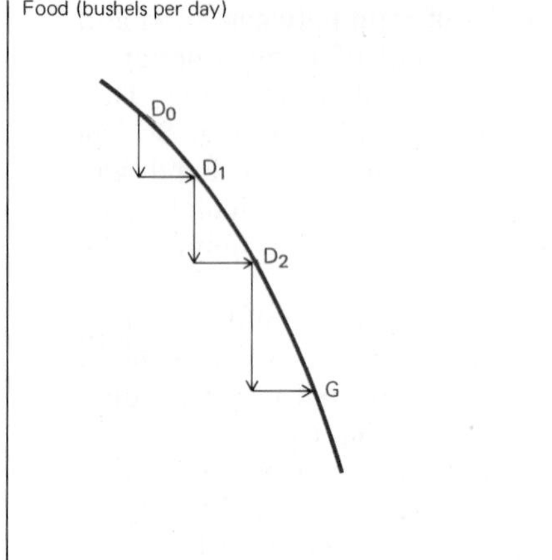

Figure 3-7

INCREASING OPPORTUNITY COSTS

Figure 3-8

TECHNICAL IMPROVEMENT IN FOOD PRODUCTION

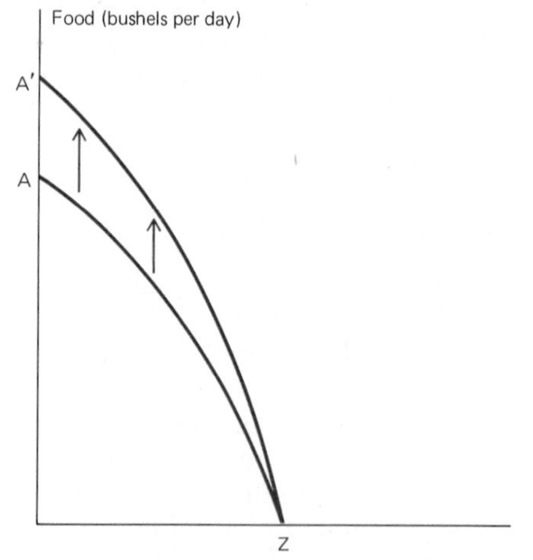

back to *B*, we will only get *BC* Clothing on the dashed line. But careful adjustment of the composition as well as the quantity of resources transferred to Clothing will enable us to produce *BD* Clothing. If we reduce Food production even more, to *E*, we should be able to get *EG* Clothing, rather than *EF*, which would only be on the straight line.

Try as we may, however, it will not be possible to continue to obtain such big increases in Clothing production as we move along the production-possibility curve by contracting Food production. The trade off of Food for Clothing will become more and more difficult, and more and more Food will have to be sacrificed to get the same increase in Clothing output. This phenomenon is so general it is also called a law: The Law of Increasing Opportunity Costs.

To understand this law, we must first be clear about what the "opportunity" part of it means. Producing more Clothing in the Third Model Economy requires that resources be transferred from Food production. So the real cost of producing Clothing is the Food that might be produced with the transferred resources—it is the opportunity of producing Food with those resources. Similarly the cost of using resources to produce Clothing is the opportunity of producing Food with those resources.

"*Increasing* opportunity costs" means that as more output of one good, say, Clothing is produced, the sacrificed opportunities for producing Food increase. Figure 3-7 blows up a part of the production-possibility curve of Figure 3-6. The horizontal arrows showing increases in Clothing output are placed so they show output increases which are always the same. But the vertical down arrows showing the necessary sacrifices in Food output get longer and longer, and the production-possibility curve will curve downward from D_0 to D_1 to D_2 to *G*. Overall this means that the production-possibility curve will bow outward.[3]

What technical facts lie behind the Law of Increasing Opportunity Costs? The production functions of these two goods are different and require inputs in different combinations to generate constant increases in output efficiently. This means that if the output of one good is reduced, the proportions of the resources released are likely to be different from the proportions used in the production of the other good. There will be some readjustment of the proportions of the inputs into both goods in order to get the maxi-

[3] It is possible that over certain ranges, particularly when relatively little of a good is produced, there will be economies of scale in its production. In this case the production-possibility curve may bend outward from *A* to *B* before bending back toward the axes, as shown in the accompanying figure. This could also happen in the *CZ* range.

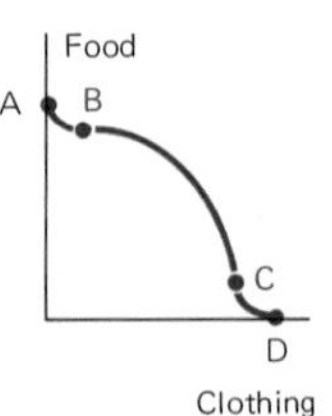

Figure 3-9
TECHNICAL IMPROVEMENT IN CLOTHING PRODUCTION

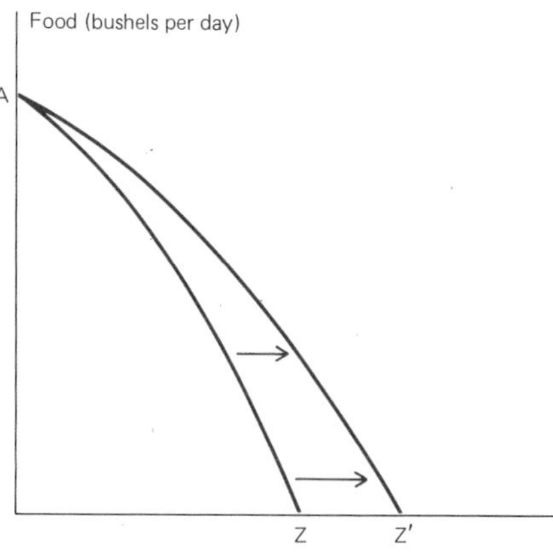

Figure 3-10
TECHNICAL IMPROVEMENT IN BOTH GOODS OR INCREASE IN RESOURCES

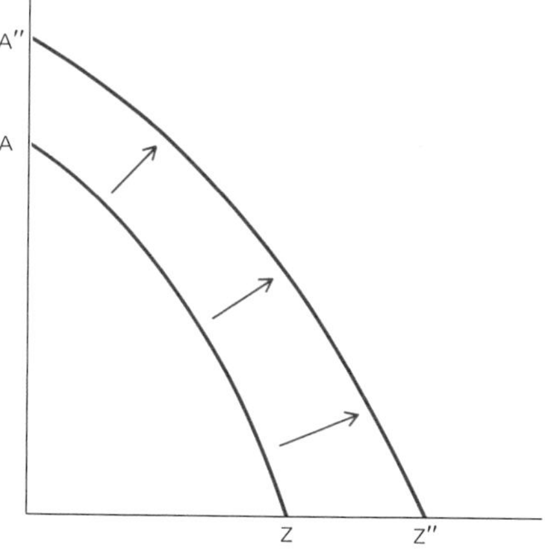

mum out of the resources, but the readjustment will not get back to the original efficiency of the resources. The sacrifices of one good necessary to obtain more of the other will increase.

In the First Model Economy we worked out carefully that the trade off between the production of Food and Clothing was constant. In the Third Model Economy, the trade off between Food and Clothing production depends on the particular combination of the two goods which is chosen. The trade off between Food and Clothing at D_0 in Figure 3-7 is different from at D_1, at D_2, and at G. The opportunity costs of Clothing in terms of Food *increase* from D_0 to G. Overall it becomes harder and harder to trade off production of Food to increase Clothing output.

In the Third Model Economy, as in the First Model Economy, the production-possibility curve provides a kind of menu or list of alternatives from which society can choose. Choices are necessary because of the Law of Scarcity, which the production-possibility curve embodies. If the economy were *inside* its production frontier as at point *C* or *F* in Figure 3-6, some resources would be unemployed. The economy could, therefore, increase its production of *both* Food and Clothing by putting all the available Labor and Land to work. When all resources are fully employed, the economy is *on* its production-possibility curve. In these circumstances, it is possible to obtain more of one of the goods *only by giving up* some of the other.

The representation of technological change in the Third Model Economy is analogous to its representation with the straight-line production-possibility line of the First Model Economy. In Figure 3-8, line *A′Z* shows the effects of technological change in producing Food only as the production-possibility line moves further out on the Food axis from *A* to *A′* but does not move from Z on the Clothing axis. In Figure 3-9, *AZ′* shows the effect of technological change only in producing Clothing. Line *A″Z″* in Figure 3-10 illustrates the effect of technical improvements in producing both goods, such as general improvement in the skills of Labor.

An increase in the available resources, say, by immigration of Labor into the Third Model Economy, would also push the production-possibility curve outward all along its length, as shown in Figure 3-10. We might expect the effect to be greater, however, for the commodity that tends to use relatively more Labor than Land — in this case, Clothing.

The fundamental questions in the Third Model Economy

We can return now to the fundamental economic questions and relate them to the production-possibility curve. The choice of a particular combination of goods from the menu provided by the production-possibility curve resolves the Output question. The choice, however, depends on the alternatives provided. We all know that our choice of dessert on a restaurant menu depends on how much we spend on the main dish. In the same way the Food and Clothing combinations to be chosen will depend on their opportunity costs or the trade offs between them.

To get on the production-possibility curve, we also had to resolve the Input question. The Input question of how much of each of the productive resources should be used to produce each commodity emerges as a full-blown economic as well as engineering issue. There is more than one way of using the resources available, and it is necessary to decide how they will be combined in the production of each good. The resources available for Food production and the choice of the best technique in producing Food depend on the resources and the technique used in Clothing production, and vice versa. A wide variety of techniques are available, and the particular ones used for each product depend on the output combination chosen from the production-possibility menu. Being on the transformation curve requires the most efficient possible methods for that combination of outputs. Other choices of technology will leave the system within rather than on the production frontier.

The Distribution questions, the division of the output between the factors and among individuals, are still somewhat behind the scenes, but closely related to resolution of the other issues. This may be seen most clearly at the extreme positions of production—either all Clothing or all Food. Labor will seem to be (and will be) relatively scarce as compared with Land when resources are concentrated on Clothing production, because Clothing tends to use less Land relatively than Food production. And in that case Labor will tend to get a relatively larger share of the product. The opposite is true at the other end of the production-possibility curve. At in-between points, also, resolution of the Distribution question will depend on the composition of Output.

Interdependence is a pervasive fact of life in the Third Model Economy. The choice of the amount of Food to be produced determines the amount of Clothing that can be produced. The two outputs together determine the inputs of Labor and Land and the particular technology used in the production of each good. The availability of the two resources and the character of technology determine the shape and position of the production-possibility curve. If there should be a change in the availability of either Land or Labor or in the technical conditions of production of one or both of the products, the production-possibility curve would shift. The choices of Food and Clothing in turn depend on the menu which the production-possibility curve makes available.

From two goods to many goods and back again

The model economies are useful abstractions because they each catch and isolate some critical features of reality. They make it possible to analyze those features and understand their significance more easily. Having completed a tour of those simplified economies

Figure 3-11

PUBLIC GOODS-PRIVATE GOODS PRODUCTION POSSIBILITIES

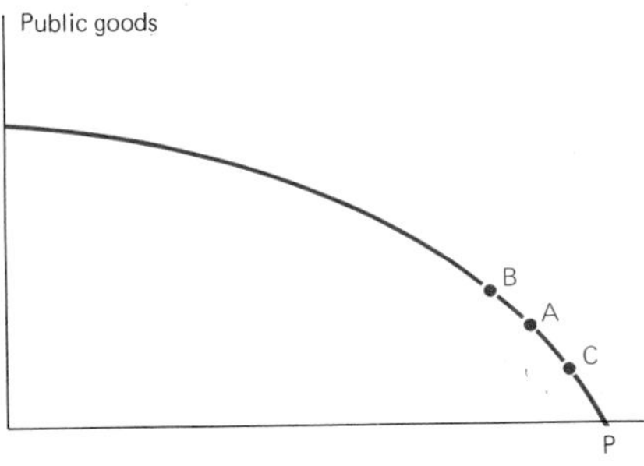

Why is A closer to the Private goods axis than to the Public goods axis for the United States? Would the representation be different for other countries?

we are ready to step into the world in all its complexity to see if we can understand it better.

Even in relatively poor countries not two goods but many different kinds of goods are produced: consumer goods, producers' goods, luxuries, necessities, new products, replacement products — the variety is staggering. And in every economy there are not two but many, many different kinds of inputs to production processes. Every type of land with a different fertility or climate, every different kind of machinery, every differently educated professional worker and skilled laborer is a separate input. Again the variety is overwhelming. In the face of this tremendous complexity, was it useful to spend time analyzing highly simplified models? The proof comes when we look at some of the economic issues that are currently being debated.

An important issue faced anew every year is the size of the federal, state, and local government budgets. These budgets provide funds for many different programs: education, welfare, parks, highway construction, military goods, space exploration, etc. These are programs for providing *public goods* from which everyone benefits to some degree. All require productive resources: engineers, skilled labor, plant and equipment, materials. The debate over the budget concentrates attention on the choice between *two* alternatives, public goods and private goods, and in this sense is like the Third Model Economy. *In times of full employment*, the problem can be posed as a debate over where the economy should be located on its production-possibility curve between public goods and private goods, *GP* in Figure 3-11. With the economy close to full utilization of its resources, it is not possible to squeeze out much more public goods production without pulling resources away from the production of *private goods*, such as new homes, automobiles, and dishwashers. If we are at *A* in Figure 3-11, do we want to move toward *B* or back toward *C*? We can also now see in Figure 3-12 why in a growing economy it is easier to resolve the debate about whether there should be more public goods or more private goods. Growth is represented in Figure 3-12 by a new production-possibility curve *G′P′*, outside the old one *GP*. When there is growth, through an increase in productive factors and/or technological improvements, it is possible to move from a point like *A* to a point like *A′*. Economic growth makes it possible to have more of everything, more private goods and more public goods.

Figure 3-12

GROWTH WHICH EXPANDS PRODUCTION POSSIBILITIES

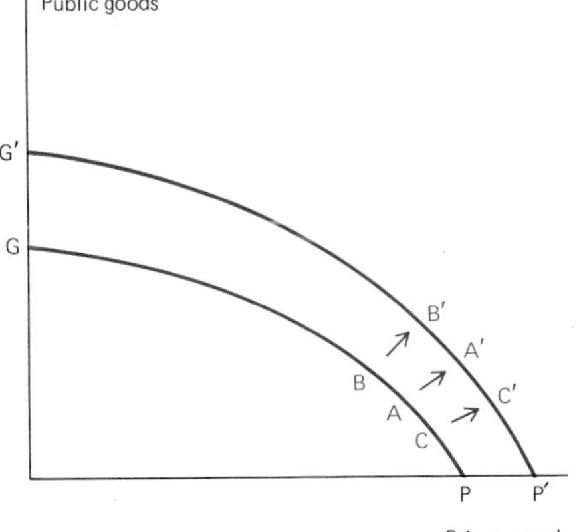

To turn to another application of the analysis we can clarify one of the sources of confusion about scarcity as a general economic condition. The confusion is caused by the failure to distinguish between conditions when labor and other resources are fully utilized and when they are not. Again the production-possibility curve can be used to demonstrate the significance of the distinction in the context of a classic example. Let us think of all goods, public and private, as either military or civilian. So we can again use a two-good production-possibility curve, as shown in Figure 3-13.

At the beginning of World War II the economy had not fully

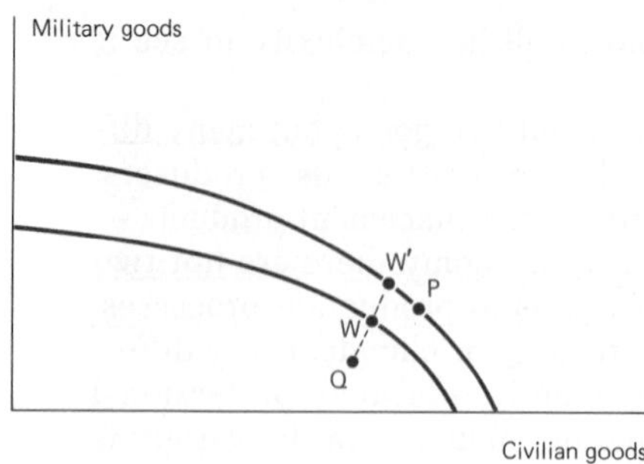

Figure 3-13
WORLD WAR II PRODUCTION CHANGES

recovered from the effects of the Great Depression of the 1930s. As a result, it was well inside its production-possibility curve, say, at point Q in Figure 3-13. As more and more resources were brought into production, the economy produced more of *both* military and civilian goods, apparently denying the Law of Scarcity. But the economy was moving from Q onto its production-possibility curve toward a point like *W*. That also led to overall economic growth. At the end of World War II, the economy was on a new production-possibility curve at point *W′*, further out in terms of both military and civilian goods than it could have been with full use of all its resources at the beginning of the war. Then, when the war ended, there was a sharp shift toward consumer goods, toward *P*.

This analysis can be extended to help explain the difference between the impact of World War II and of the Vietnam War. In 1965 when the rapid escalation of the Vietnam War began, there was relatively little slack in the economy. We were close to being on our production-possibility curve, at a point like *P* in Figure 3-14. The effect of the escalation was to increase the demand for and the output of military goods. Under the conditions of virtually full employment which prevailed then, that meant moving resources out of civilian goods production into military production in order to move to a position like *W*. That is a much more painful and difficult process than increasing output by the use of unemployed resources.

Figure 3-14
VIETNAM WAR PRODUCTION CHANGES

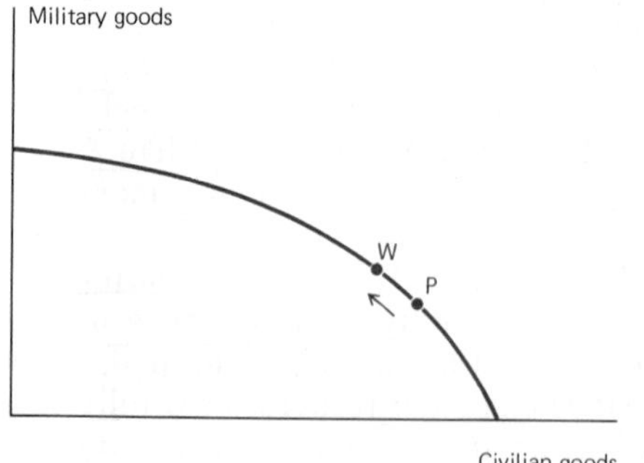

The analysis of the model economies also helps in understanding the indirect effects on the Input and Distribution issues of a change in Output decisions. The scarcity of resources for civilian goods production when military demands increase means that civilian technology changes somewhat. In the Korean War, for example, when steel became scarce, construction projects used more wood. During the Vietnam War, when copper was diverted from electric wiring to the production of bullet casings, the cost of electrical equipment went up. The Distribution of income and the goods that income buys also changes when the nation's resources are diverted to the production of more military goods.

A final example will demonstrate the generality of the model economy analysis. The most important issue that many of the poor countries of the world have posed for themselves is economic development. How can they improve the conditions of life of their people and become viable, independent modern nations? Development is a complex process requiring the successful interaction of many political, social, and even psychological features of society as well as economic resources. The analytical tools we have developed can begin to throw light on the process. Let us now divide all types of goods into two new categories: consumer goods and investment goods. Capital equipment created by investment is an important input into production. If development is to proceed, there must be more investment in new capital goods. That means that resources have to be diverted from consumer goods produc-

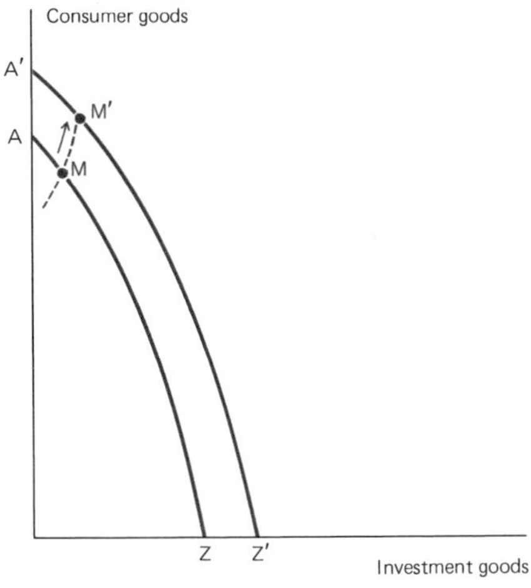

Figure 3-15

PRODUCTION POSSIBILITIES AND CHOICE IN DEVELOPMENT POLICY

tion to investment goods production. Figures 3-15 and 3-16 show the types of choices available and their consequences.

In Figure 3-15 some amount of investment goods is produced in the First Five Year Plan, at point *M* on the production-possibility curve *AZ*, but the concentration is on consumer goods. The new investment goods add to the available resources so that in the Second Five Year Plan more of both consumption and investment is possible on the new production-possibility curve *A′Z′*. The emphasis continues to be on consumption at point *M′*, since the policy makers feel that they cannot ask more sacrifices from the present poverty-stricken generation. By comparison, Figure 3-16 represents an alternative path to development. Here the policy makers decide to produce relatively less of consumer goods so that relatively more investment goods will be produced than originally, at point *N*. The accumulation of capital resources is, therefore, faster, and the production-possibility curve moves outward more rapidly to *A″Z″*. Consumption does not rise so quickly at first. More sacrifices are asked of the current generation, but the consumption potential for future generations is higher at *N′*.

Which path to development is better, *MM′* or *NN′*? The figures only pose the question. They do not answer it. They take the first essential step toward an answer, however, for choices cannot be made rationally unless the alternatives are clearly seen. (The analysis of development and growth problems will be pursued further in Chaps. 37 and 38.)

In this chapter, we have concentrated on the basic economic questions. We have seen that these questions must be confronted in every kind of economy. In Chapter 4, we will see how they are resolved by market mechanisms that work through the pricing process.

Figure 3-16

A MORE AUSTERE DEVELOPMENT POLICY

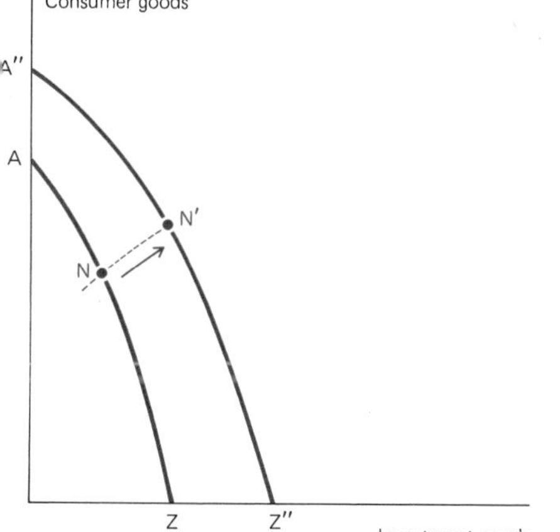

Summary

Three model economies were developed in this chapter to explain in depth the fundamental Output, Input, and Distribution questions and their interdependence.

The First Model Economy of two goods, Food and Clothing, and one productive resource, Labor, highlights the Output question of how much of each of the two goods will be produced. The relation of the Input question to the Output decision is straightforward in this model because there is just one productive resource with constant productivity. The output of each good is related to the Labor input by a constant labor productivity factor, and that relation is the production function for the goods. Because of the resource constraint, the more Food produced and the more Labor used in its production, the less Labor there will be available for Clothing production and the less Clothing which can be produced. The functional Distribution question of who gets the goods produced is simple in this model. The one resource receives all the Food and Clothing output. The personal Distribution of output depends on the amount of Labor each worker contributes.

In the Second Model Economy of one good, Food, and two types of resources, Land and Labor, the Output question is simply, How much Food can be produced? With two resources, the Input question is more complicated, as there are many alternative ways of producing Food. There may be substitution possibilities in the production function, which now relates Land and Labor inputs and Food output. The functional distribution of output is now the more difficult question of the division of the output between the two types of resources. It is related to the Input decision and depends on the relative scarcities of the resources and the way in which they can be used in production, as determined by the production function. The personal distribution of output is the division of the total output among individuals and depends on ownership of Land, as well as hours worked, taxes, and other social institutions.

In the Third Model Economy of two goods and two types of resources, nothing is simple. All the fundamental questions — Output, Input, and Distribution — involve choices among alternatives. In this economy, as in the others, all the questions are interdependent. Likewise, the causal influences do not run one way from Output to Input to Distribution, but back and forth among all the questions.

The production-possibility curve presents the menu of alternative combinations of outputs among which choices have to be made. When there is only one type of productive resource, the production-possibility curve is a straight line. When there are two (or more) types of productive resources, the production-possibility curve is bowed outward, and reflects the Law of Increasing Opportunity Costs. Economies can move along their production-possibility curves by shifting resources from producing one good to producing another. In the First Model Economy the trade-off ratio or opportunity cost of one good for another is constant. In the Third Model Economy the opportunity costs or trade-off ratios depend on the particular combination of outputs produced.

Behind the production-possibility curves are the technological facts of life, which are summarized in the production function for each good. When all inputs but one are fixed, and this one is varied, the Law of Diminishing Returns comes into play. This law says that, after some point, equal *additional* increments of the variable input will produce smaller and smaller amounts of *extra* output. Over some range of the variable input, however, there may be increasing returns to that input. When all inputs are increased proportionately and output grows more than proportionately, there are increasing returns to *scale*. If output grows in the same proportion, there are constant returns to scale. If the output growth is less than proportionate, there are decreasing returns to scale.

The production-possibility curve can be used to illustrate

many of the economic alternatives faced by an economy: the choice between public and private goods, between military and civilian goods, and between capital and consumption goods. Every Output choice implies also a decision about the Input and Distribution questions that face every economy, for all these issues are interdependent.

Questions for discussion and review

1. Discuss the following statement: *Economic scarcity is a capitalistic invention to scare the working class. In a world of mutual effort and sacrifice there would be unlimited abundance and no limits to the production possibilities.*

2. In the Third Model Economy the production-possibility curve was said to demonstrate the Law of Increasing Opportunity Costs. Are there opportunity costs in the First Model Economy? If so, are they increasing or decreasing?

3. Write down and contrast carefully the Law of Diminishing Returns, the meaning of decreasing returns to scale, and the Law of Increasing Opportunity Costs.

4. In recent years the introduction of new types of cotton picking machinery has had the effect of displacing labor in the Southern states. Describe the interaction of the Output, Input, and Distribution issues in these events.

5. Why does a bowed-out production-possibility curve illustrate the Law of Increasing Opportunity Costs?

6. Do you think it is easy for an economy to be on its production-possibility curve? How can you tell whether or not an economy is on its production-possibility curve? Would it be adequate proof if all resources were fully used?

7. Discuss the following statement: *There really is not a trade off between military goods and civilian goods, because the resources used in producing one kind of output cannot be used in producing the other.*

8. Why does technological change in the production of one good increase the production potential of many goods?

Concepts for review

Production-possibility curve
Law of Diminishing Returns
Law of Increasing Opportunity Costs
Decreasing and increasing returns to scale
Substitution possibilities
Functional and personal distribution of income
Production function
Output trade-off ratio

Appendix: Using the Second Model Economy to understand Malthus

Table 3-3

POPULATION GROWTH AT $2^{1}/_{2}$ PERCENT PER YEAR

Year	*Growth index*
0	100
1	102.5
2	105.06
3	107.69
4	110.38
5	113.14
6	115.97
7	118.87
8	121.84
9	124.89
10	128.01

The Second Model Economy will help us gain some insight into the problems of population growth. Suppose we let population grow in the Second Model Economy, but keep Land constant. With the tools we have developed, we can project the future of the Second Model Economy under these conditions. That future is a strict version of the dangers foreseen by the Reverend Thomas Robert Malthus in 1798 in his famous and lastingly influential *Essay on the Principle of Population.* According to Malthus, population has a tendency to grow geometrically at a constant percentage rate. A constant percentage rate means larger and larger annual increments. A constant 100 percent growth rate dramatizes this effect. It means that a labor force that starts at 100 first grows to 200, then to 400, then 800, 1,600, 3,200, 6,400, and so on. A $2^{1}/_{2}$ percent annual growth of population, which is not uncommon, generates the series shown in Table 3-3. At the end of ten years, a population growing at $2^{1}/_{2}$ percent per year will have increased by 28 percent. With this type of growth it would not be long, as history is recorded, before we would have to hang out the Standing Room Only sign.

Figure 3-17

THE MALTHUSIAN PREDICTION

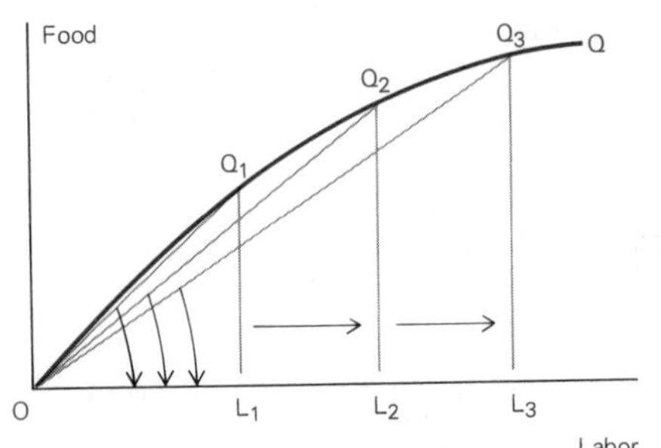

As population increases, the labor force also grows. But with a constant amount of Land, the Law of Diminishing Returns assures us that output will not increase as fast as the labor force. Malthus said that food production could increase only arithmetically — 100, 102.5, 105, 107.5, 110, etc. — so that by the tenth year it would be 125. But the larger and larger increments in population from a constant growth rate would lead, at best, to smaller percentage increases in food output. Or looking at it another way, the *extra* output produced by an extra worker would continually decline as the population growth went on. The result would certainly be a condition in which population growth was finally stopped by food shortage if the population growth tendency were not otherwise restrained. Because of this gloomy prediction of perpetual poverty, economics became known as the Dismal Science.

Figure 3-17 illustrates the Malthusian process. Population, and labor force, grows from L_1 to L_2 to L_3, etc. Output grows correspondingly from Q_1 to Q_2 to Q_3, etc. The average productivity of a worker in each instance is the *slope* of the line from O to Q_1, Q_2, *and* Q_3, and that slope continually falls.[4]

[4] The *slope* of a line is a measure of its slant or tilt. Numerically, it is the ratio of the height of the Q curve to the labor input which produces the output. The slope of OQ_1 *is* Q_1L_1/OL_1, for example. Since OL_1 is the labor input which produces Q_1L_1, the ratio Q_1L_1/OL_1 is the output per unit of labor.

Actually Malthus did not predict that man was fated to a life of bare minimum subsistence. He put diminishing returns and population growth together to establish a theory that would hold *if* population growth continued unchecked. But he and others have pointed out the existence of a number of checks on population growth. As income grows, there is a tendency for population growth rates to fall off. There is also a tendency for urban families to be smaller than rural families, so population growth rates tend to decline with urbanization. Education tends to lead to wider use of birth-control methods. (On the other hand, there have been periods of high birthrates in countries in which demographers thought that population growth had leveled off, notably in the United States and in most European countries in the 1950s.)

There is still another condition that must hold if the Malthusian theory is to work out: Technology must not change! If disease-resistant plants or better cultivation practices are discovered, the output curve will shift upward. The shift may not be uniform. The new technology may be more effective with one set of inputs than another. If technology continues to change, the output curve will continue to shift.

Technological change is a two-edged sword, however. For example, relatively inexpensive improvements in medical and public health practices are being introduced on a large scale in the poor countries of the world. They reduce infant mortality and increase human longevity, thereby decreasing the death rate. Birthrates, which are usually high in these countries, do not fall correspondingly, and as the gap between birth and death rates widens, the population growth rate increases.

While the Malthusian danger has been avoided in many countries, in others the race is still being run between income growth, on the one hand, and birth-control measures and population growth, on the other. It does not have to end as the Reverend Malthus predicted, but in much of today's world it is too close for comfort.

4

Private market solutions and the pricing process

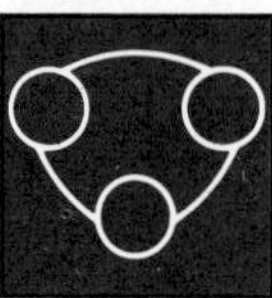

For anyone who has not been sick, cold, and hungry, it requires an effort of the imagination and, perhaps, the assistance of a great novelist to understand those feelings and to appreciate the comforts of health, warmth, and food. In the same way, it is difficult for anyone who has always lived in a reasonably well-functioning economy to understand just what it means for an economy to work badly or well. Most of us never give a second thought to the fact that more or less whenever we want, and without too much trouble, we can buy a loaf of bread or a pound of butter, an electric iron, or a hammer and nails. The goods are in the shops and we do not often have to stand in line.

Yet there is no magic in it. All the hurrying and scurrying about that seemed to characterize the model economies of Chapter 3 and which may have appeared a little strange and farfetched is the business of life. That traffic on the streets and those crowds on the buses and subways are not joyriding. On the whole, they are people going to work to produce goods and services and direct their distribution and people going to sell and buy the goods and services. Chapter 3 posed the fundamental economic problems and demonstrated their interdependence. The ways in which those problems are resolved is the subject matter of this entire book. Our objective in this chapter is to gain a bird's-eye view of the process. It will be valuable in itself and will also provide a guide to the more detailed analysis. Specifically in this chapter we shall concentrate on understanding the demand and supply interactions which determine prices – prices which in turn guide economic decision making through markets.

Types of economic systems: Centralized versus decentralized decision making

No two systems operate in exactly the same way in dealing with the fundamental Output, Input, and Distribution questions. Economies differ in the relative scope and importance of decentralized decision making through markets and of centralized government decision making. At one extreme is the philosophy of laissez faire which advocates that private enterprise and markets be completely free of government control. This philosophy, which was never really fully accepted anywhere, was widely expounded in the nineteenth century and the early part of this century. Since then the scope of both government enterprise and government regulation of private business has broadened nearly everywhere. In the Soviet Union, the countries of Eastern Europe, mainland China, and a few other places, all but a tiny proportion of productive activity is in the public sector, and centralized decision making predominates.[1] In between the extremes are the mixed economies in which some sectors are subject to considerable government control and others are guided primarily by private decision making.

In the mixed United States economy, government enterprise is confined to only a few areas of commerce and industry, though the influence of government extends more broadly through its taxing, spending, and regulatory powers. To understand the United States economy, we must, therefore, understand the operation of market economics, the manner in which the fundamental economic questions are resolved by private decision making. Recently there has also been a striking interest in decentralization of economic decision making in the Soviet Union and Eastern Europe as a possible way of increasing the efficiency of those systems. So an understanding of market processes will contribute to an appreciation of not only the United States economy, but of other economies as well.

Economies with central planning must be self-conscious about the fundamental economic problems. The unplanned economies are not self-conscious about these problems, and yet they are resolved with sufficient effectiveness to attract the attention of the planned economies.[2] How do economies work without planning?

[1] Yugoslavia is an exception in Eastern Europe. It has moved quite far toward reliance on market processes.

[2] This does not mean that the planned economies want to emulate all aspects of the unplanned economies or that the performance of the latter has not in some times and ways been disappointing. That makes it all the more interesting that policy makers in planned economies feel that there is something important to be learned from unplanned economies.

An overview: The Circular Flow of Economic Activity

A summary and overview of the structure of a mixed economy and its operation to allocate and combine resources and to produce and distribute goods is contained in Figure 4-1. This diagram is called the Circular Flow of Economic Activity. Unfortunately, we cannot show it as a motion picture in true-to-life color with a dialogue that really tells it like it is. Rather, it is a silent snapshot that puts most of the burden of interpretation on the viewer. Yet this one picture may be worth several thousand words, and will repay careful study. It shows the interdependence of the various parts of the economy and of the fundamental Output, Input, and Distribution questions. It also provides a graphic means of organizing much of the subsequent discussion of the manner in which these questions are resolved.

Figure 4-1

THE CIRCULAR FLOW OF ECONOMIC ACTIVITY

The Household Sector earns income from the services of the resources it owns which are used in the Business Sector and in the Public Sector. With this income it purchases goods and services produced in the Business Sector and pays taxes to the Public Sector. The Business Sector sells goods and services which it produces to both the Household and Public Sectors. It pays income to the productive resources it uses and pays taxes to the Public Sector. The Public Sector uses its tax collections to pay for the goods and services it buys from the Business and Household Sectors. It provides goods and services to the other sectors, makes welfare and other transfer payments to the Household Sector, and pays some direct subsidies to the Business Sector.

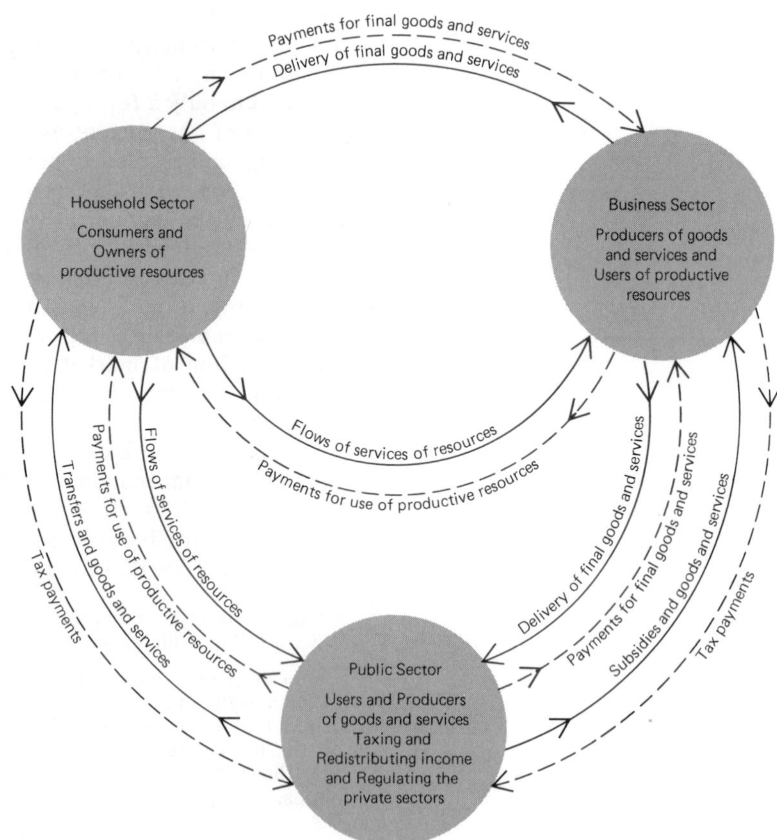

The three large circles represent the three sectors of the economy: the private consumer or household sector, the private business sector, and the public or government sector. The solid lines represent flows of goods and services among the sectors and the dashed lines represent flows of money payments. The red lines are transactions effected through markets and the black lines are those imposed or carried out by government. We shall take up the three sectors one at a time and trace their interrelations.

The household sector, the left-hand circle, is the buyer and user of consumer goods and services produced by business. For these goods and services the household sector must make payments to business. The household sector is also the ultimate supplier and owner, either directly or indirectly, of the productive resources used by business in the production of goods and services: labor, land, and capital plant and equipment. For supplying these resources, the household sector receives payments from business: wages, rent, interest, and profits. Businesses and individuals work for the government and rent buildings and equipment to it, and income is paid for these productive services. The government also makes some direct, transfer payments to the household sector — welfare payments, for example — for which no services are required. The government provides some services and, of course, levies taxes, and uses some of the tax revenue to make its payments to the household sector.

The right-hand circle represents the private business sector. Businesses are the hirers and users of productive resources to produce the goods and sevices demanded by consumers. They use the revenues from their sales to pay for the use of the productive resources and to make profits. The business sector also sells to the government sector, using resources owned by the household sector. The government sector pays the business sector for what it buys, using the tax revenue it collects from both the business sector and the household sector.

The bottom circle represents the government sector, paying for goods and services provided by the household sector and the business sector with taxes collected from both sectors. The government sector, in turn, supplies a variety of services itself, such as education and air traffic control. It also engages in a variety of regulatory activities that affect the terms on which transactions are made in the private sectors and between the private sectors and the government sector.

The fundamental economic questions are resolved in the interaction of the household, business, and government sectors. The household and business sectors constitute the private market part of the total economy, reflecting the fact that the flows of goods and services and payments between these two sectors pass through and are determined by markets. The "mediation" of the market for consumer goods and services means that the types and quantities of consumer goods purchased depend not only on the demands of consumers, but on the reactions of businesses to these demands. The mediation of the market for the services of productive resources means that the types and quantities of resources used depend not only on technology and business demands, but on the amounts of resources available to households. As the Circular Flow diagram shows, consumer expenditures are financed with income earned from labor and other productive resources. Therefore, the resolution of the Output questions reflects and is dependent upon the ways in which the Input questions, about the use of resources, and the Distribution questions, about the payments for resources, are resolved.

The public sector also affects these questions. The direct effects are through its demands for goods and services produced by the business sector and its demands for the use of resources owned by the household sector. The government payments for goods and resources are passed on via private markets into demands for consumer goods and productive resources by the household and business sectors, respectively. The tax levies and regulatory activities of the public sector directly and indirectly affect the composition of output, the use of inputs, and their payment. Again, we have a demonstration of extensive interdependence. But here there are new elements: the *role of markets* in directing the flow of goods and services and productive resources to government use and the *effect of government taxes and transfers* on the private sectors.

Market mediation and pricing

At the heart of the market mediation mechanism is the pricing process. The types and quantities of goods *consumed* depend on the prices of goods and incomes. The types and quantities of goods *produced* respond to the prices of goods and the costs of production. Costs of production depend on the amounts of the resources used in the production of various goods, the manner in which the resources are combined, and the prices of the resources. The prices of productive resources are the wage and salary rates and the rents and interest rates that labor and the owners of other resources receive. These, in turn, determine income.

Since all the fundamental economic questions in the private sectors are resolved by the pricing process, prices serve several functions and are themselves completely interdependent in these functions.

1. They serve to ration the produced goods and services among buyers.

2. They act as guideposts in the allocation of resources to the production of various goods and services.

3. They are the rates of payment of income to owners of productive resources.

Because prices play a central role in the operation of an unplanned economy, we must examine the price determination process carefully. The procedure will be to focus on how it works for some particular good or service. The analysis will again involve a simplification in that one market will be analyzed, separate and apart from all other markets. In the language of economics, this is called *partial equilibrium analysis.* It is an important type of analysis in itself, and it will prepare us to study the general interdependence of prices, markets, and the ways in which the fundamental Output, Input, and Distribution questions are resolved. We do not exhaust the subject of price determination in this chapter, but will return to it when we study particular types of pricing processes.

Markets and competition

The first step is to define carefully what economists mean by markets and market behavior. Most people think of markets as places, particular locations, where goods are bought and sold. The economist's definition is a reasonable extension of that: A market is composed of all buyers and sellers of the same good or service. The sellers may literally be located side by side in stalls or shops, with the buyers circulating among them. Or buyers and sellers may be spread out across the country or around the world and communicate by telephone and cable, as is the case for commodities like wheat and sugar.

We shall begin by assuming that the markets are competitive. (In Chap. 25 we shall investigate noncompetitive markets in some detail.) Actually we shall assume *perfect* competition, which is a strict version of competition and does not conform to the everyday usage of the term. It is a specific theoretical model. To economists, perfect competition means that no buyer or seller individually can affect the prices charged in the market. For this to be so, three conditions must be met: (1) The product being bought and sold must be completely standardized; (2) both buyers and sellers must be completely informed about the prices that prevail in the markets, and (3) the participants in the market must be small relative to the total volume of sales.

With many small sellers offering the goods — and all the goods alike — no seller can get a higher price than any other. And no seller need accept a lower price. Likewise with many small buyers, none will be able to exact special concessions from sellers. These rigorous conditions are not frequently met, and later we shall spend a good deal of time working out what happens when they are not met. For some markets, however, perfect competition is a reasonably accurate description. In wheat production there are many farmers who altogether produce about $1^1/_2$ billion bushels a year. But even a large farmer produces only about 100,000 bushels, which is about 7/1,000 of 1 percent of total production. For other markets, too, perfect competition is a reasonably good first approximation. There are roughly 400 textile firms producing cotton gray goods, which are standard types of fabric. In addition there are many foreign suppliers of cotton textiles who help maintain competitive conditions. Likewise there are many growers of corn and soybeans and many firms producing lumber. In a number of industries in which there is a "reasonable" amount of competition, perfect competition is not a bad working assumption.

It could hardly come as a surprise to anyone that we are going to analyze pricing in terms of Supply and Demand. The procedure will be to look at each concept separately and then put them together. We will start by studying the determination of price for a single, "typical" commodity purchased for consumption purposes.[3]

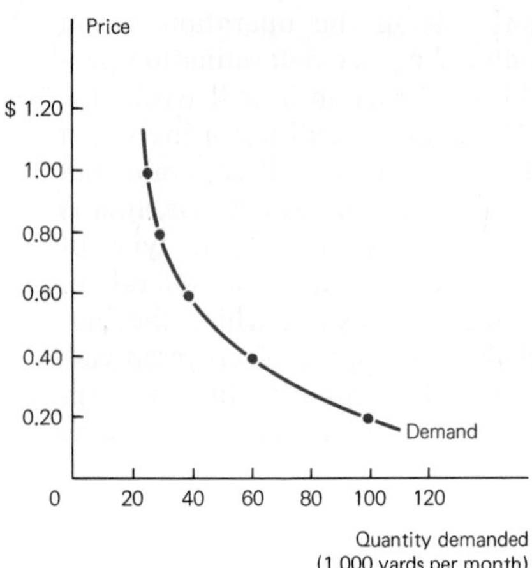

Figure 4-2

HYPOTHETICAL DEMAND CURVE FOR COTTON GRAY GOODS

Demand

Demand has a lot of different meanings, but in economics its meaning is rather precise. The demand for a commodity is the alternative amounts that people are willing to purchase at corresponding alternative prices during a particular period of time and in a particular "market area." There are several important aspects of this definition to note:

1. It is necessary to draw some boundaries around the quantities being considered. This is done by specifying (*a*) the time period, say, a day or a week or a month, and (*b*) the market area, say, the local supermarket or all the stores in the city or in the state. The market area is the geographic region within which the same physical commodity has the same price at the same moment. The demand in a market area is the sum of the individual demands of all potential buyers.

2. The next thing to notice about the definition is the test it imposes: There is no demand unless there is a willingness to purchase. Demand is not simply a *desire* to purchase, though goods will not be demanded unless they are desired. There must be the willingness to buy and the ability to pay for the goods.

3. Finally, demand is not a single quantity sold at a single price. It is a *relationship* between quantities and prices. It tells the alternative quantities that will be purchased — or the same thing, the quantities that will be sold — at alternative prices.

Table 4-1

HYPOTHETICAL DEMAND SCHEDULE FOR COTTON GRAY GOODS

	Price		*Quantity demanded (yards per month)*
If	$1.00	then	25,000
If	0.80	then	30,000
If	0.60	then	40,000
If	0.40	then	60,000
If	0.20	then	100,000

What is the nature of the demand relationship between quantities purchased and prices? Generally, it is like that shown in Table 4-1 and Figure 4-2, which present a hypothetical example. A greater quantity will be purchased at lower prices than at higher prices.

[3] The framework of the supply-demand analysis to be worked out can also be applied to the pricing of productive resources — with some necessary amendments.

This inverse price-quantity relationship is sometimes called the Law of Demand.[4]

Notice that the *demand schedule* in Table 4-1 is a set of "if-then" statements. Each line should be read: *If* the price is so much, *then* the quantity purchased will be so and so.

The prices and quantities presented in Table 4-1 are plotted in Figure 4-2 as the separate points. Figure 4-2 goes beyond the table, however, because the separate points are joined to make the demand line. That is intended to show how much will be purchased at all prices, including those intermediate to the prices quoted in Table 4-1. This is the *demand curve*, or *demand function*, as it is sometimes called. Remember that the demand curve slopes down and to the right when price is on the vertical axis and quantity is on the horizontal axis.

There is a good deal of factual evidence that downward-sloping demand is a typical pattern. Why should it be? Why does it seem plausible that—*everything else remaining unchanged*—more of a commodity will be bought as its price falls? First of all, because as the price of the commodity falls, there is a tendency to substitute it for other commodities. For example, when pork prices fall, pork is substituted for beef, and more pork is purchased. When chicken prices fall, chicken is substituted for both beef and pork, and more chicken is sold. If the price of electricity for home consumption should fall, its use would go up because it would be substituted for other types of heating fuels. These *substitution effects* are often quite explicit. A little casual observation at a department store "sale" will show a lot of it going on.

Figure 4-3

SHIFT IN DEMAND VERSUS CHANGE IN QUANTITY DEMANDED

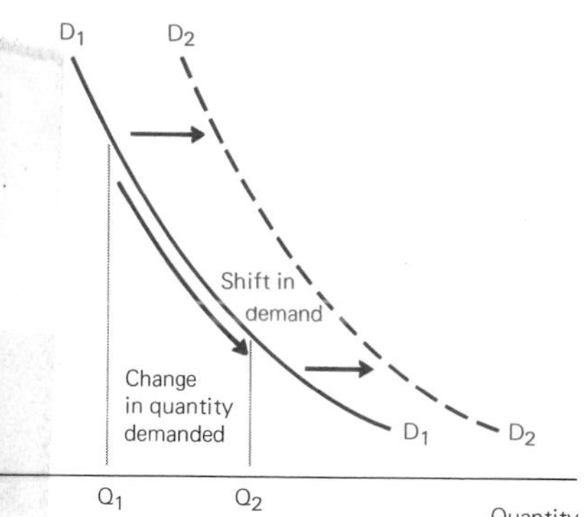

In addition to substitution effects, there are *income effects*, which strengthen the argument for the downward slope of the demand schedule. The electricity example is a good one. Suppose a homeowner already uses electricity for heating, and it costs him the not inconsiderable amount of $400 a year. If the price of electricity were to fall by, say, 25 percent, and he did not keep his house warmer, his heating bill would go down by $100. That is like an increase in his income. His wife, thinking correctly that the family is better off, buys a new electric freezer. They end up using even more electricity as a result of the reduction in the electricity rate.

The important distinction between a change in quantity demanded and a shift in the demand schedule is shown in Figure 4-3. The change in quantity demanded is a movement along a given demand schedule due to a price change (along D_1D_1). A shift in the demand schedule is a movement from one schedule to another (from $D_1\,D_1$ to $D_2\,D_2$).

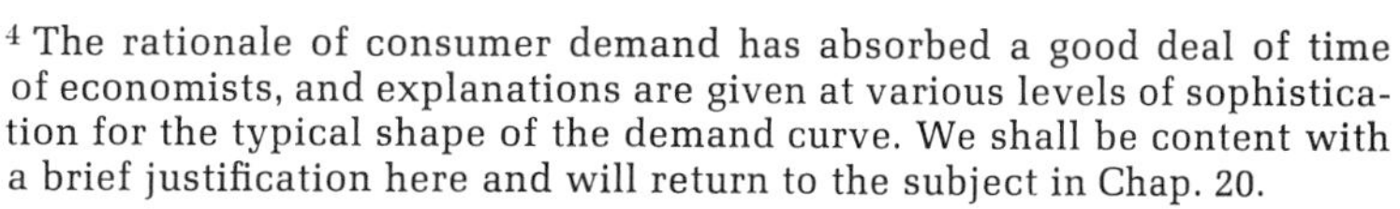
[4] The rationale of consumer demand has absorbed a good deal of time of economists, and explanations are given at various levels of sophistication for the typical shape of the demand curve. We shall be content with a brief justification here and will return to the subject in Chap. 20.

The determinants of demand and shifts in demand

It is natural to focus on the price-quantity relationship in demand, since we are interested in the role of prices in resolving the fundamental economic issues. The price-quantity relationship itself depends on a number of other things. What are the "other things" that are kept constant in the background of a demand schedule?

The tastes or preferences of consumers for the product and for other products. Economists do not have much to say about how preferences originate or why they change, though consumer preferences are fundamental economic influences. The advertising industry, with its substantial size and pervasive influence, is devoted to creating and changing tastes. It is not always easy to predict and measure the effects of advertising, but they can hardly be denied. On the other hand, it would be a mistake to believe that advertising is the most important influence on consumption trends. How much of the college life style is affected directly by advertising? Not an insignificant part, but not all by any means.

The prices of other commodities. We argued above that when the price of our typical commodity fell, *and all other prices were constant*, there would be substitution and income effects, which would lead to an increase in the quantity of the product demanded. Now, what happens if its price is constant and some other prices change? If the goods are *substitutes*, a rise in the price of one will shift the demand schedule for the other upward. Substitution effects are quite pervasive. For example, aluminum and copper wire can both be used in electricity transmission lines. Copper is a better conductor and is also stronger. But when the price of copper rises, substitution of aluminum wire for copper wire begins to take place. The quantity of copper demanded falls and the quantity of aluminum wire demanded increases.

A different type of relationship is observed when goods are *complementary* and are used together. Bacon and eggs, for example, are complements. If the price of bacon falls and more bacon is purchased, that will also result in an increase in the quantity of eggs purchased. A fall in the price of either eggs or bacon makes the combination cheaper and leads to an increase in the purchases of both.

Similarly, an increase in the price of copper wire will lead to an increase in the quantity of both aluminum and steel wire used

Figure 4-4

DEMAND SHIFT DUE TO INCREASED PREFERENCE

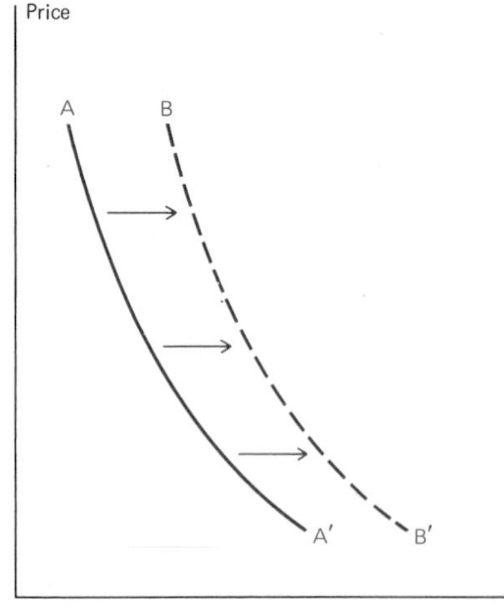

Figure 4-4 shows the effects of changes in tastes. *A heightened preference for the commodity shifts its price-quantity purchased relationship from AA′ to BB′, so that at each price more is bought. When beads become fashionable, the quantity purchased at each price increases. What would be the effect if the commodity went out of fashion?*

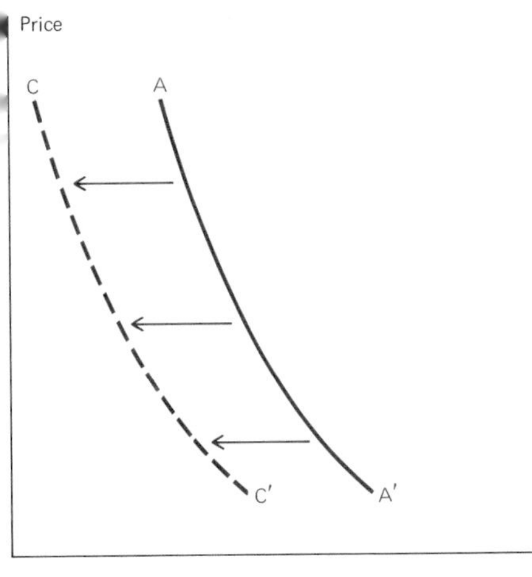

Figure 4-5 illustrates the effects of a change in the price of substitutes for the commodity, in this case a price reduction of such substitutes. The demand curve shifts from AA′ to CC′. At every price, less will be purchased. This illustrates, for example, how a reduction in the price of artificial fibers will affect the demand for clothes made of natural fibers. This could also represent an increase in the price of complementary products. How would the effects of an increase in the price of substitutes or a reduction in the price of complements be represented?

Figure 4-5

DEMAND SHIFT DUE TO REDUCTION IN PRICE OF SUBSTITUTES

for electricity transmission lines. Copper and aluminum wire are substitutes. Aluminum and steel wire are complements; owing to the relative weakness of aluminum wire, steel wire must be used with it as reinforcement in transmission lines.

The level and distribution of income. In general, there is a direct, or positive, relationship between changes in income and changes in the quantity demanded of any good. When income rises, people can buy more goods. This is just a manifestation of the apparent insatiability of wants, which we discussed in Chapter 1.

There are some goods for which this generalization does not hold. Purchases of *inferior goods* will fall as income rises, and with everything else constant. Because the individual can now indulge himself with more preferred items, he will reduce his consumption of less preferred ones. At a higher income he will buy more steak and less hamburger and more wine and less beer, if for him hamburger and beer are inferior goods.

Income distribution makes a difference also. Why, it is sometimes asked, is there a demand for luxuries when so many people go hungry? Remember, demand is not desire. Desire is effective only when backed with purchasing power. If income were distributed more equally, that would decrease the demand for Dior originals and increase the demand for food.

All of the determinants of demand affect consumer purchases. One of the most common mistakes people make in using the demand relationships is to confuse the effects of changes in one of these determinants with the effects of a change in the price of the commodity. Figures 4-4, 4-5, and 4-6 will help keep straight the effects of each type of change.

These diagrams show the *qualitative* effects of changes in tastes, other prices, income levels, and income distribution on the demand function. The precise *quantitative* effects of such changes

Figure 4-6

DEMAND SHIFT DUE TO INCREASE IN INCOME OR NUMBER OF BUYERS

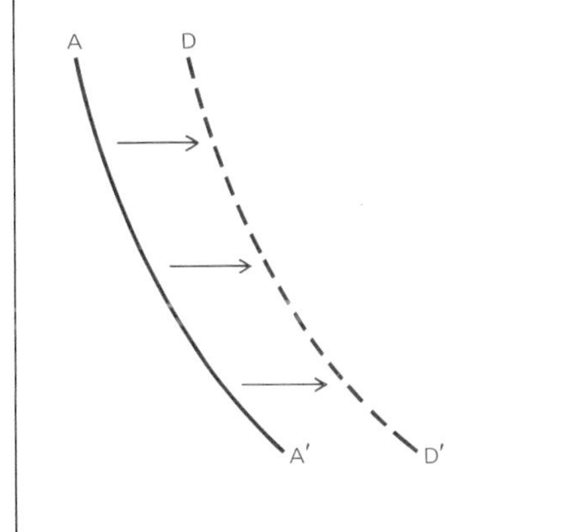

Figure 4-6 illustrates the effects of an increase in the number of persons in the market area and/or an increase in their incomes. The demand schedule shifts to the right. Would the effects be the same if the commodity were an inferior one?

can only be determined by a detailed study of the particular circumstances.[5]

Supply

The preceding analysis of demand gives us a broad hint of what economists mean by supply. The demand function is a schedule of alternative prices and the associated quantities that purchasers are willing to buy. The supply schedule or function for a particular commodity is also a series of if-then statements that indicate *the alternative amounts that will be offered for sale at alternative prices.* Plotted on a chart, it is the supply curve. Table 4-2 and Figure 4-7 show a hypothetical example of a total supply schedule.

Table 4-2

HYPOTHETICAL SUPPLY SCHEDULE FOR COTTON GRAY GOODS

	Price		*Quantity supplied (yards per month)*
If	$1.00	then	55,000
If	0.80	then	50,000
If	0.60	then	40,000
If	0.40	then	25,000
If	0.20	then	5,000

Are there any reasons why a typical supply schedule will look like that in Figure 4-7 or like anything else? In particular, why does it slope up to the right rather than down to the right like a demand curve? The upward slope means that, if the *quantity supplied* is to be increased, it is necessary to increase the price offered. Or to put it slightly differently, the amount offered for sale by producers will increase *only* if the price goes up.

Behind any particular supply curve lie: (1) the technical conditions of production, (2) the prices of the productive inputs used, and (3) the characteristics of competition in the market. These interact in complicated ways, and the full explanation of factors determining supply will have to wait until Part III. At this point, however, we will indicate the main outlines of the reasoning. For this purpose it is useful to recall the Second Model Economy of Chapter 3, because that was an analysis of the production of a single commodity. We observed there the operation of the Law of Diminishing Returns to additional inputs of one of the factors of production, with all the other resource inputs constant.

Figure 4-7

HYPOTHETICAL SUPPLY CURVE FOR COTTON GRAY GOODS

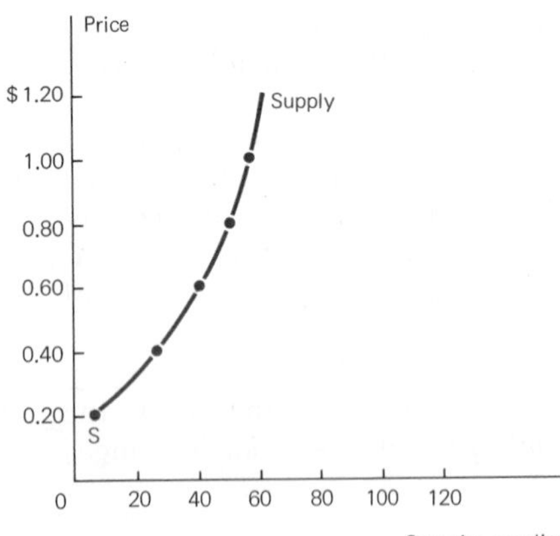

Costs will also rise or fall depending on whether the prices of the inputs used in production rise or fall. When, for example, labor's wages rise or the cost of fuel oil goes up, the costs of using specific quantities of those inputs will rise. As a consequence the offering price of the particular quantity of goods the resources help produce will rise.

[5] An example of a demand function estimated by an econometric study for the post-World War II period is the following, for all kitchen and other household appliances:

$$Q_t = 3.5249 - 0.1063\,P_t + 0.0222\,X_t$$

Q_t is per capita personal consumption expenditures on kitchen and other household appliances; P_t is the average price level of this category of goods; and X_t is total expenditure per capita. The prices and per capita expenditures are both measured relative to the prices that prevailed in 1954. H. S. Houthakker and Lester D. Taylor, *Consumer Demand in the United States*: 1929–1970, Harvard University Press, Cambridge, Mass., 1966, p. 82.

Diminishing returns means that as output expands, it requires progressively more and more of the resource that is varied to get an extra unit of output. In a real sense, extra units of output become more and more expensive in terms of the variable input. Because of this, costs will go up as productivity goes down, even if input prices are constant. The only way to have more and more offered for sale then is to raise the price offered so that it will cover the increases in cost.

Another way to increase the amount of a commodity available in a particular market area is to bring it in from more remote producing and warehousing sites. Transport costs are another reason why prices must go up in order to induce an increase in the amount offered for sale.

On the other hand, suppose there is enough time to raise output by increasing *all* the inputs, not just the easily variable ones. It is not necessarily true that costs per unit of input will go up. Costs may remain more or less constant or in some cases even go down. Thus, the shape and position of the supply curve depend in part on the time period that is considered.

Figure 4-8

A SHIFT IN SUPPLY VERSUS A CHANGE IN QUANTITY SUPPLIED

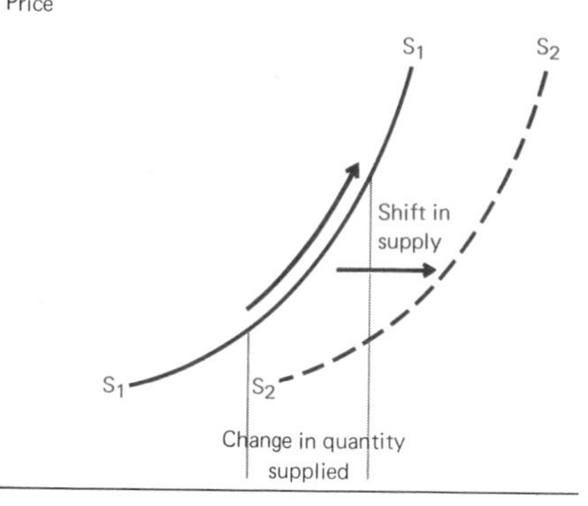

The prices at which goods are offered for sale depend also on how many producing firms there are and on how effectively they compete. The relationship between prices and sales shown in Table 4-2 and Figure 4-7 assumes that there are many intensely competitive firms. If there were only one seller, the relationship would be quite different. And there would be a still different relationship if there were only a few firms practicing a kind of live-and-let-live policy. All this means that the upward-sloping supply curve, while representative of many competitive situations, is not a universal truth from which there are never any deviations. We shall continue to work with it now, however, as a first approximation.

All the factors that determine the shape and position of the supply schedule are held constant for movements within the schedule or along the curve. If any of the background factors change, the supply schedule itself will shift. A shift in the supply schedule implies a movement of the entire supply curve. A change in quantity supplied is a shift along a specified supply schedule due to a change in price. These two different concepts are represented in Figure 4-8.

Price determination by supply and demand

The demand schedule is a set of if-then statements with respect to prices and the amounts that will be purchased. The supply schedule is a set of if-then statements about prices and the amounts that will be offered for sale. The *equilibrium price* is the price at which the *amount demanded* and the *amount supplied* are equal. It is the price which "clears" the market. At that price everything that producers are willing to offer will be taken off the market by purchasers. There will be no queuing up by consumers, for just the amount that is for sale at the equilibrium price will be purchased. Neither more nor less will be demanded. Likewise, at the equilibrium price, suppliers will not accumulate dusty, unsold stocks of goods. Prices are rationing devices, and *the equilibrium price rations exactly*: The quantity demanded exactly equals the quantity supplied!

The equilibrium price is of practical interest, however, only if there is a price-determining market mechanism which tends to move the price toward equilibrium. For that to happen, there must be competition in the market among buyers and among sellers. To see how it would work, turn to Table 4-3 and Figure 4-9, which reproduce both the demand and the supply functions for our typical commodity. It is clear that 60 cents is the equilibrium price, since at that price, the quantities supplied and demanded are equal at 40,000 yards per month. The eye is drawn naturally to the intersection of the two curves. But there is no law which says that the price *must* be there. What would happen if someday, for some reason, all or a few businessmen thought that the going price should be 40 cents? At 40 cents and at any price less than the equilibrium price, the amount demanded would exceed the quantity supplied. Many people willing to buy at 40 cents would find empty shelves when they came in to put down their money. Competition among unsatisfied potential buyers would bid prices up. Sellers facing unsatisfied customers would realize that they could have sold all their goods at somewhat higher prices. Thus, competition among consumers would tend to force the price up toward the equilibrium price.

Suppose now that sellers overreact. Say they raise the price to 80 cents and lay in stocks to support the sale of 50,000 yards of cloth per month – a rate of sales which they would be willing to maintain at that price. At 80 cents, however, buyers would be willing to purchase only 30,000 yards per month, as indicated by the demand curve in Figure 4-9. They could not care less if suppliers had more than that in their stores and warehouses ready to sell. The 80-cent price would limit the sales so that the quantity offered

Table 4-3

DEMAND AND SUPPLY OF COTTON GRAY GOODS

Price	*Quantity demanded (from Table 4-1)*	*Quantity supplied (from Table 4-2)*	*Difference between quantity supplied and demanded at the same price*
$1.00	25,000	55,000	30,000
0.80	30,000	50,000	20,000
0.60	40,000	40,000	0
0.50	60,000	25,000	–35,000
0.20	100,000	5,000	–95,000

Figure 4-9

PRICE DETERMINATION BY SUPPLY AND DEMAND

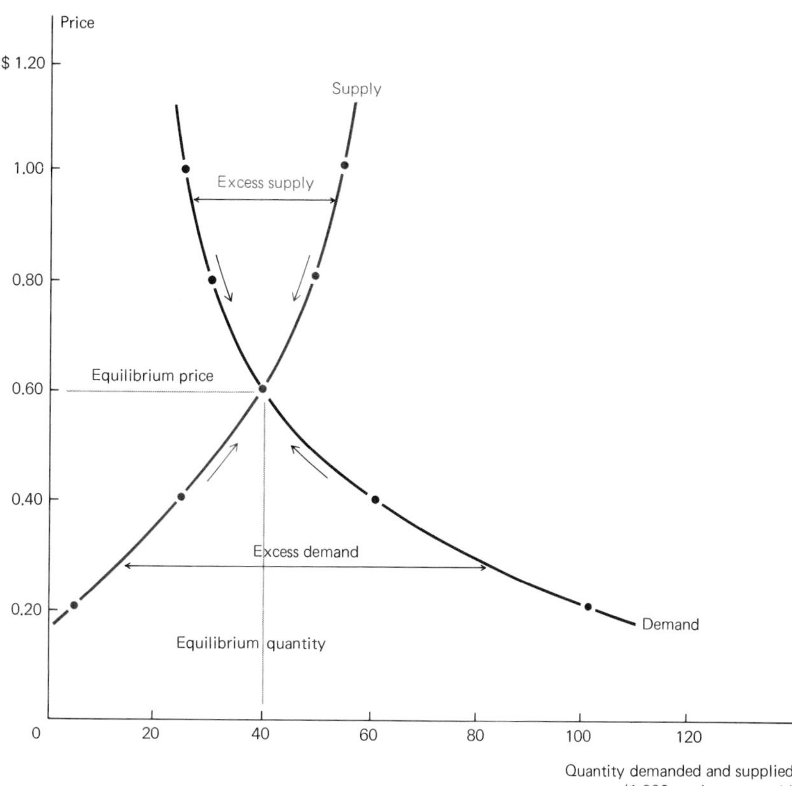

would be greater than the quantity demanded. Competition punishes as well as rewards. Suppliers cannot sell 50,000 yards at 80 cents. They must cut the price to increase sales, and if they are competitive, they will. The price will be bid down. At lower prices, sales will expand.

At prices *above* the equilibrium price there is an excess of quantity supplied over quantity demanded. At prices *below* the equilibrium there is an excess of quantity demanded over quantity supplied. The equilibrium quantity of purchases and sales clears the market at the equilibrium price.

The importance of the equilibrium price and quantity is not that they always and at every moment prevail. It is that they are the targets toward which the actual price and quantity tend to move. Realistically, one can expect a certain amount of random jiggling around even in the best of markets. Buyers change their minds, and sellers make bad guesses; no one is perfect, and competition works more smoothly at some times than it does at others.

Supply and demand analysis does not tell us what will happen at every moment in a market. If there is competition, however, markets will tend to clear at the equilibrium price, and that in itself is extremely important.

A qualification: How effective is the competition?

Competition among buyers and sellers is the mechanism that moves the market price and sales volume toward equilibrium at the intersection of the supply and demand curves. Without competition it is impossible to be really sure that the equilibrium is at that intersection. In fact, without competition, the whole notion of supply and demand relations becomes rather fuzzy. A monopolist may decide to ration his output among his customers by some means other than prices; since he has no competitors, there is nothing to force him to do otherwise. If there are only one or two buyers and sellers in a market, then the price and quantity decisions in that market will be to a large extent the result of bargaining processes, as they are in wage agreements between unions and management. There is no guarantee that the bargaining processes will lead to the same market-clearing result as perfect competition.

Strictly speaking, the supply and demand analysis developed here can be counted on to work only in the model of perfectly competitive markets. Few commodities and markets fit this model exactly. In many markets there are only a few buyers or sellers, or if there are many, some are quite large and influential relative to the others. Further, the commodities and services bought and sold may be somewhat different, and buyers may not be well informed about the differences. In some markets, personal services or special credit arrangements may keep competition from being perfect.

Nonetheless, the supply and demand analysis is a reasonably good approximation:

If there are a "reasonable" number of alternative buyers and sellers

If the effect on the market of the entry or withdrawal of a few of them is not "appreciable"

If buyers are "reasonably" well informed about quality differences

How can you know when the requirements are "reasonably" well satisfied? There are no blanket answers. In some markets, one dozen sellers may be more competitive than two dozen in other markets. It is necessary to look at each situation separately and come to a judgment about it. We shall return to these issues in Part III to provide some guidelines.

Applying supply and demand analysis

The purpose of this introduction to demand and supply analysis is not to try to develop the ability to predict a particular price in dollars and cents. Rather, the object is to get a general understanding of price-determining forces and of how prices lead to market adjustments. This means that in applying the analysis we shall focus on price changes and how and why they occur.

The equilibrium price will change if there is a shift in the demand schedule or in the supply schedule or in both. Therefore, to understand price and quantity changes, we need to know what shifts have occurred and why. Remember that in deriving the demand and supply schedules, we held a lot of things constant. Well, suppose that one of those things changes or that several of the underlying factors change simultaneously. The equilibrium price and quantity will also change as a result. Two kinds of knowledge are necessary to understand the direction and extent of the changes:

1. What *shifts* have occurred in either the demand or supply schedule or in both as a result of changes in their basic determinants?

2. How *responsive* are the quantities supplied and demanded to price changes?

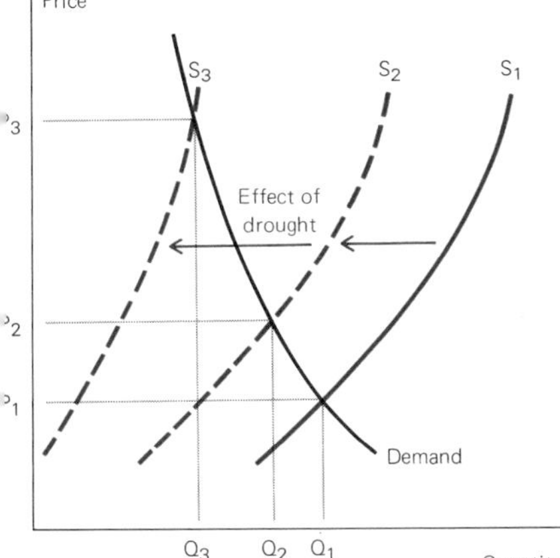

Figure 4-10

THE EFFECT OF SHIFTS IN SUPPLY

A full and deep discussion of supply and demand changes and their consequences will have to be postponed to Part III. But working through a few examples at this point will help to fix the fundamentals of the analysis.

Shifts in supply How would a drought in Brazil affect the price of coffee? Since Brazil is one of the world's leading coffee-growing areas, a drought there would certainly lower the available supplies. Still, Brazil has substantial stockpiles of coffee, and it is also grown in Colombia, Costa Rica, and other Central American countries, as well as in Kenya, Uganda, and other countries in East Africa. Suppose that the effect of the drought is described in Figure 4-10 by the shift from S_1 to S_2, which causes prices to rise from P_1 to P_2. If the drought continued for a second year, however, the supply shift would be larger, as the reserves in Brazilian warehouses began to run out. That would be shown by a shift from S_2 to S_3. As a result, the price effects would also be larger, and prices would rise from P_2 to P_3.

Shifts in demand

The tools of supply and demand analysis can be used to throw some light on the housing situation that is going to face the present college generation. This generation is part of the post-World War II "baby boom" which lasted until the late 1950s before peaking out. This generation is just approaching the years in which its rate of family formation will be the highest. Since men tend to marry at about twenty-three years of age and women at about twenty-one, the 1970s are going to be "marriage boom" years. Increases in the rate of family formation in turn mean increases in demand for housing. Figure 4-11 shows what that will mean for the price of housing, assuming that the supply of housing does not change. The housing price can be interpreted as the rental rates on apartments or as the prices of single-family houses. Either way, if the supply of housing does not shift up, the price of housing will rise.

Shifts in both demand and supply

To go on with the housing problem, the increase in demand which raises prices is also likely to raise profits in apartment building and in single-family dwelling construction. That will bring more contractors and capital into the housing field. Technological change is likely to continue to reduce the costs of housing construction. The effect of these changes is a rightward shift in the supply curve so that, at any particular price, more housing will be offered. What then will happen to the equilibrium price and quantity of housing in the 1970s?

The equilibrium quantities will certainly increase. But what happens to the price depends on the relative magnitudes of the shifts in the supply and demand schedules. Figure 4-11 illustrates the possibilities. The increase in demand, from D_1 to D_2 will push the equilibrium price from P_1 to P_2 and the equilibrium quantity from Q_1 to Q_2. If the supply schedule shifts from S_1 to S_2, the equilibrium price will be at P_3, an increase over the original price, but not as great as if there had been no supply curve shift. The equilibrium quantity will certainly be higher than before, at Q_3. But if the supply curve should shift enough, to S_3, not only will still more housing be used in equilibrium, but prices at P_4 will actually be lower than originally.

Figure 4-11

THE EFFECTS OF SHIFTS IN DEMAND AND SUPPLY

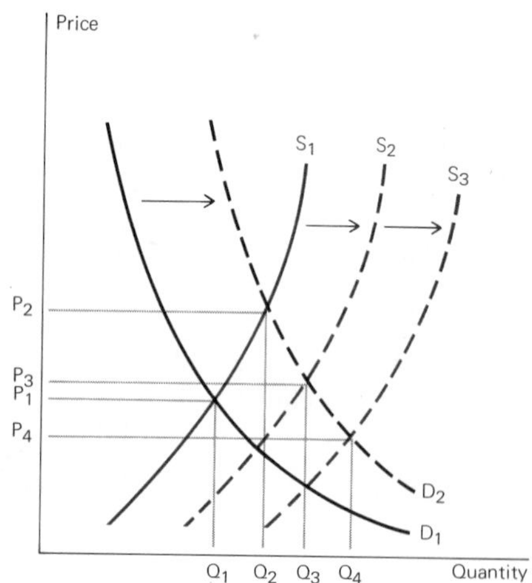

The world does not stand still for very long, and neither do demand and supply schedules. When *both* demand and supply curves shift, the final effect on equilibrium prices and quantities may be in doubt, depending on the relative directions and magnitudes of the shifts. Table 4-4 summarizes the possibilities.

In an economy with growing population and increasing per capita income, the demand schedules for most commodities are going to be continually shifting to the right. Does that mean that, inevitably, prices will keep rising? Clearly it depends on what happens to the supply schedules. Ocean- and lake-side properties, for example, are in fixed supply. Overall growth in income and, therefore, in demand will raise their prices. But that might be somewhat

Table 4-4

THE CONSEQUENCES OF SHIFTS IN DEMAND AND SUPPLY SCHEDULES

Shift in demand schedule	*Shift in supply schedule*	*Change in equilibrium price*	*Change in equilibrium quantity*
Increase	Increase	Up, down, or no change	Up
Increase	Decrease	Up	Up, down, or no change
Decrease	Decrease	Up, down, or no change	Down
Decrease	Increase	Down	Up, down, or no change

offset by technological changes in air transport which make the beaches of the Caribbean and of Latin America almost as cheaply accessible as those only a few hours' drive away by automobile.

Demand and supply analysis is a flexible and powerful tool with which to study the effects of the economic changes that continually occur. However, to say that demand and supply determine the price in a particular market seldom provides much understanding of what is happening. To gain that understanding, one must add to the demand and supply analysis factual information about what shifts have occurred and why.

Prices and the resolution of the fundamental economic questions

It is useful to take stock of what we have done in this chapter and compare it with what we started out to do. Chapter 3 posed the fundamental economic questions. In this chapter we were to explain how they are resolved. How did we get sidetracked from our grand objective of understanding how the economic system as a whole operates into a discussion of the prices of coffee and housing?

We started out by arguing that prices play a central role in an unplanned economy with decentralized decision making by consumers and business firms. Prices influence the amounts of goods that consumers purchase. They influence the amounts of inputs of productive resources that businesses purchase. They influence the quantities of goods that businesses offer for sale to consumers and other businesses. All this means that to understand the manner in which the fundamental Output, Input, and Distribution questions are resolved by market forces, one first must understand the price determination mechanism.

We made a start on that in this chapter by working out the demand and supply analysis under the special conditions of perfect competition. The requirements of the perfectly competitive model are so severe that they can seldom, if ever, be met in reality. Let us try to be clear then just why this unrealistic assumption was made. First, it was *not* because perfect competition is considered the most characteristic form of markets. By no means! Perfect competition is as idealized a condition as a perfect vacuum. The assumptions of competition can be violated in a variety of ways, and not just because of some grasping monopolist. *Nor* did we assume perfect competition because it is considered a utopia toward which we must all strive. As we shall see later, however, some important efficiency conditions are associated with perfect competition. The world of competition is a rigorous and even harsh environment. *Nor* does the assumption of perfect competition have any implications one way or another for the distribution of wealth and income among individuals, whether it is or ought to be equal or unequal. A competitive system for better or for worse reacts to the demands placed upon it and does not question the wisdom or justice of those demands.

We assume perfect competition in starting our work because it makes the economic analysis much, much easier than it otherwise would be. It is difficult enough as it is, and as we shall see, it becomes more complex as we make it more and more realistic. Our motivation, therefore, is that of positive economics, not normative economics. The theoretical model of perfect competition is, like all theory, an unreal world to some extent, but like all good theory it also catches some important facets of reality.

Now let us tie Chapter 3 and this chapter a bit closer together by analyzing what happens in an entire economic system when there is a change — as, for example, in the composition of goods demanded — and how prices mediate the process of adjustment. We have already put some effort into analyzing the effects of an increased marriage and family-formation rate on the demand for housing, so let us return to that example. All that we must do, really, is carry the implications of the analysis a little further. One general hint may help to remove a possible source of confusion. As already noted, the output of most goods is likely to grow in the future, so we should conduct the discussion in *relative* terms, having in mind the changes in demand for housing *as compared with demands for other goods*. Likewise, there may be a general price increase. Therefore, when we talk of an increase in the price of housing, we will really mean an increase *relative* to other prices.

A relative increase in demand for housing means that, overall, some consumers want the economy to be producing at a different place on its production-possibility curve. Comparatively more housing is desired and comparatively less of some other goods. But other consumers, older people and children, may not agree.

How will the difference be resolved? There is no central planning organization, political election, or meetinghouse discussion to resolve the difference. If the new families want more housing badly enough to direct their expenditures toward it, that will amount to a redirection of some part of total expenditures. There will be an increase in the demand for housing and a decrease, at least relatively, in the demand for other goods. Prices, that is, apartment rental rates and the prices of single-family houses, will rise relative to the prices of other goods and services. That will be the signal of the change that has occurred in demand, and it will induce other accommodating changes.

Real estate operators and housing developers will find that there are larger profits in housing than formerly. They will try to follow up the opportunity by providing more housing. In turn, that will mean that carpenters, painters, and electricians and cement, wood, paint, and wire will be employed to produce housing rather than, say, office buildings. And the builders will try to be efficient about it in order to make more profits.

The change in the composition of goods produced and in the use of labor and other resources means there is a change in the manner in which the Output and Input questions are resolved in the economy. There will be a corresponding change in the resolution of the Distribution question as well. The increased relative prices in the housing sector and the increase in incomes earned there will mean decreased relative incomes earned, say, in producing color TV consoles. The changes in income will be part of the process by which resources are pulled into the housing sector. The resolution of the Distribution question is thus related to the manner in which the Output and Input questions are resolved.

All these reallocations and changes in direction in the economy will occur without any overall plan or centralized decision making. It may, therefore, seem to be a rather chancy and unreliable way to run an economic system. But it works, not perfectly to be sure, but as was pointed out, well enough to attract the attention of centrally planned systems. What are the advantages of the market system? There are two: responsiveness to consumers and incentives to use resources efficiently.

That does not mean that everyone should be happy with the outcome. There is still room for many differences of opinion. Should private owners of land reap the benefits of increased land prices? Should construction unions be regulated to ensure that they do not discriminate against minority groups? Do the zoning codes generate desirable neighborhood environments? Do the building codes restrict technical change or promote safety? Is it possible to have the advantages of the market system and also regulate it to meet public standards of equity in income distribution, aesthetics in design, community in neighborhoods, and safety in construction? There are great debates over such topics. All we can say here is that we have learned enough about interdependence in the economy to know that every action—and regulation—has consequences beyond its immediate effects, and an informed debate must take these into account.

Summary

The fundamental Output, Input, and Distribution questions are resolved both through public decision making and through private decision making in markets. This chapter concentrates on market mechanisms which work through the pricing process.

The Circular Flow of Economic Activity provides an overall view of the interaction of the household sector, the business sector, and the government sector of the economy. The first two make up the private sector, and the third, government, the public sector. The household sector buys consumer goods from the business sector with income earned from the productive resources which are used by both business and government. The business sector uses resources to produce outputs purchased by both the household and government sectors and pays them with the revenues from its sales. The government sector taxes both the household and business sectors and uses the tax revenues to hire labor from the household sector and to buy from the business sector; in turn, it provides services to both. The fundamental economic questions in the private part of the economy are resolved in markets via prices. Market influences also affect and are affected by the public decision-making process.

Price determination is analyzed under the three conditions of perfect competition: (1) The commodity is standardized, (2) both buyers and sellers have complete information about prices, and (3) the buyers and sellers are so small and so numerous that the actions of any one have no effect on the market price. The assumption of perfect competition, though unrealistic, simplifies the analysis and still permits important insights.

The market or total demand schedule is a set of if-then statements. It tells how much will be purchased at different prices—with all other influences held constant. Typically, more will be purchased at a low price than at a high price, so that the market demand curve, when plotted with price on the vertical axis and quantity on the horizontal axis, is downward-sloping. This is called the Law of Demand. The "other influences" which are held constant for a demand schedule are (1) the tastes or preferences of consumers, (2) the prices of other commodities, (3) the level and distribution of income. If any of these factors should change, the entire demand schedule would shift.

The market or total supply schedule is also a set of if-then statements. It tells how much will be offered for sale at different prices. When plotted on the same axes as the demand schedule, the supply curve usually slopes up to the right. This reflects the higher costs of additional production and the higher prices needed to cover the higher costs.

The market equilibrium price is at the intersection of the demand and supply curves, where the amount demanded and the amount supplied are exactly equal. It is that price toward which competition of buyers and sellers tends to move the market price.

Changes in demand or supply are represented by shifts in the entire demand or supply schedule, and must be distinguished from changes in quantity demanded or supplied along a constant demand or supply schedule. The effects of shifts in demand and supply depend on the relative magnitude of the changes and the responsiveness of quantity changes in supply and demand to price changes.

The prices generated by supply and demand interaction are the guides in the private market sector of the economy to the resolution of the Output, Input, and Distribution questions.

Questions for discussion and review

1. Give several examples of the following types of interactions pictured in the Circular Flow of Economic Activity: (*a*) household-business interactions in resource markets, (*b*) business-government interactions in product markets, (*c*) business-household interactions in product markets.

2. It is often asserted that government has a pervasive influence on the economy. Does that influence extend beyond the collection of taxes and their use to buy goods and services?

3. Describe how the markets in which government buys and sells can affect the markets in which private households and businesses buy and sell.

4. What is the difference between the competition of the local drug stores and grocery stores in your area and perfect competition?

5. Prices have been rising generally in recent years, even in markets which approximate perfect competition. Quantities sold have also been rising. Does that mean that the demand curves are really upward-sloping, that the Law of Demand is not correct?

6. Discuss the following statement: *Advertising can persuade people to increase their consumption of a product even if its price goes up. That is a contradiction of the so-called Law of Demand.*

7. Using some simple demand curves to illustrate the changes, describe the effects of the following shifts which affect the quantities demanded of a particular commodity: an increase in the price of a complementary product, a redistribution of income away from the commodity's major consumers, a reduction in the price of the commodity, the appearance of competing products.

8. Define supply. Do you think that the quantity, say, of rental housing supplied in a particular market would increase if rents went up? Why or why not?

9. Suppose that in a more or less competitive market the quantities being offered for sale were less than the quantities that people were willing to buy. How would you describe this market, using supply and demand analysis, and what would you predict would happen?

Concepts for review

Centralized and decentralized decision making

The Circular Flow of Economic Activity

Market mediation

Perfect competition

Demand and supply

Changes in quantity demanded and changes in quantity supplied

Shifts in the demand schedule and shifts in the supply schedule

Equilibrium price and quantity

5 The role of public economics

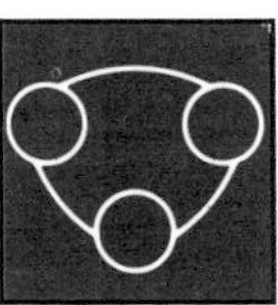

Public economics is about *the rationale, the methods, and the significance of the operations of the public or government sector of the economy*. To some people, discussing the role of government in the economy is like talking about sin: It should never be mentioned without being deplored. To others, like virtue, it is always to be praised. Still others believe that there are many things wrong with the present economic system but trust neither government nor private business and look for some new social arrangements. Whatever kind of system there is – whether it is primarily private, government, communal, cooperative, or any other – it must still somehow resolve the fundamental Output, Input, and Distribution questions.

The diagram of the Circular Flow of Economic Activity in Chapter 4 shows that in a mixed economy there are a variety of interactions between the public sector and the private household and business sectors. These include many market interactions in which the public sector buys and sells goods and services. The public sector's market operations, however, are seldom motivated by the same desires or carried out in the same manner as the activities of the private sectors. Moreover, in some of its economic activities, the buying and selling of goods and services are of little importance. The objective here is to get an overall perspective of public economics in the United States.

Two major problems arise in the discussion of public economics. One is the close relationship between politics and economics, and the other is the constant intrusion of value judgments, or normative economics, into the objective analysis of positive economics. When we try to understand why the government engages in particular kinds of economic activity, such as delivering mail or providing free public education, political explanations come quickly to mind. Sometimes those explanations are the best ones, though there may also be an economic rationale. Often the economic rationale is overwhelming. The concern here is economics and the economic rationale of government activities. We shall concentrate on that, without demeaning political influences in any way.

On the intrusion of normative economics, a word of warning is in order: There is hardly any other area of economics in which the intrusion of bias, folklore, prejudice, and ideological doctrine so impede understanding. Value-laden judgments come from the Left, the Right, and the Center. Therefore, one should be prepared to examine with skepticism not only the present discussion and the other fellow's statements, but also one's own opinions to see if they hold up under intensive scrutiny and new facts.

The intention in this chapter is to do positive economics. That will suggest different normative economic conclusions to different people. Everyone, including the author, has his own set of preferences about what governments can and should do. But the aim here is to avoid personal judgments. Opinions are easier to come by than understanding and the latter is the objective. Both reformers and standpatters should be interested in that.

Before we are through, we shall explore many of the sources of differences in opinion. When we have mastered a more complete set of analytic tools, we shall be ready to dig still more deeply into the issues. We can deal with the problems of government policy for economic stabilization, for example, only after we learn why and how stabilization is itself a problem. We can analyze government antitrust policy with greater confidence when we understand more fully the implications of competition.

The scope and growth of government

It is important, first, to appreciate in somewhat more detail just what we mean by the "economics of the public sector." The economic influences exercised by government take many forms. They are so pervasive that no single measure or perspective will adequately catch their range and impact. A survey of government expenditures is a good way to start, however. It will indicate the variety of government activities and provide one indication of their relative importance, and it will help keep the discussion relevant. Remember that several "layers" of government must be included in any tabulation: federal, state, county, municipal, and intergovernmental authorities. For convenience, we shall aggregate these into just two groups: (1) federal and (2) state and local.

Table 5-1 presents the total expenditures of the federal and all state and local governments and the major components for 1959 and 1969. One's first impression is that the amounts are astronomical. The federal budget is simply huge. No private business compares with it. The budgets of the fifty states and the thousands of local units add up to about 60 percent of the federal budget.

In 1969 military expenditures alone accounted for over 40 percent of all federal spending and about 27 percent of the budgets of all levels of government. The point is not that they are "too big" or "too small" but that they are large by comparison with other items in the budget.

Did you realize that education expenditures were so large comparatively? They are the largest single item in state and local spending and are not insignificant in the federal budget. Welfare and health expenditures are also a major item and growing rapidly. But some government activities that most people would concede to be important, for good or ill, involve relatively small amounts. The executive office of the President, which has a lot to do with national policy, had a budget of only $34 million in 1970, too small even to be distinguished in the gigantic amounts in Table 5-1. The Department of State had a budget of only $434 million, if economic assistance to less developed countries, which it administers, is omitted. The budget of the Department of Justice, which includes

Table 5-1

GOVERNMENT EXPENDITURES BY FUNCTION

	1959				*1969*			
	Federal		*State*		*Federal*		*State*	
	Billions of dollars	*Percent*	*Billions of dollars*	*Percent*	*Billions of dollars*	*Percent*	*Billions of dollars*	*Percent*
Total*	91.0	100.0	46.8	100.0	191.3	100.0	118.9	100.0
National defense	46.9	51.5	0.2	0.4	81.5	42.5	0.6	0.5
Space	0.3	0.3			4.0	2.1		
General government	8.5	9.4	5.3	11.3	18.7	9.8	13.9	11.7
International affairs	2.2	2.4			2.6	1.4		
Education	0.6	0.7	17.1	36.4	4.6	2.4	48.0	40.4
Health, labor, and welfare	17.6	19.4	13.1	27.8	52.0	27.2	33.7	28.4
Veterans benefits	5.6	6.2	0.1	0.2	8.4	4.4	0.1	0.1
Commerce, transport, and housing	4.9	5.4	9.4	20.0	9.8	5.1	18.6	15.6
Agriculture	3.0	3.3	0.5	1.1	7.0	3.7	1.2	1.0
Natural resources and recreation	1.4	1.5	1.3	2.8	2.8	1.5	2.9	2.4

*Detail may not add to totals because of rounding.
Source: U.S. Department of Commerce, Office of Business Economics.

support of the federal courts, the Federal Bureau of Investigation, and the Antitrust Division, was only $714 million in 1970.

In the last twenty years, perhaps the most remarkable changes have occurred in the health and welfare categories. The expansion of public welfare programs and the creation of Medicare, the health insurance program for elderly persons, has increased this budget sharply. Education expenditures have grown strikingly, and the space program has shown some big ups and small downs. The military budget, the largest single item in the federal budget, has shown major changes as a proportion of federal expenditures. In 1950 it was about one-third of the total. The proportion went up during the Korean War and after to almost two-thirds of the federal budget. The proportion fell in the early 1960s to about 40 percent, rose again to over 45 percent as a result of the Vietnam War escalation and has fallen again.

Figure 5-1 shows the growth in total federal and state-and-local expenditures over the last thirty years. A big jump in federal expenditures occurred in the early 1940s as a result of World War II. After that there was a decline in federal spending due to a sharp cutback in defense expenditures. In retrospect, the "big spending" of the 1930s, which generated so much controversy, is a barely noticeable increase in the rate of spending. In the 1930s, state and local expenditures were much larger than federal expenditures. That relationship changed permanently in the 1940s, and state and local expenditures now run at slightly less than two-thirds of federal spending.

The significance of the amounts in Table 5-1, even in the smaller categories of expenditure, can hardly be appreciated in isolation,

Figure 5-1

EXPENDITURES OF FEDERAL AND STATE AND LOCAL GOVERNMENTS

Federal government expenditures outran state and local government expenditures in the 1940s. But in the last decade, the rate of growth of expenditures has been higher for state and local governments than for the federal government. (Source: U.S. Department of Commerce, Office of Business Economics.)

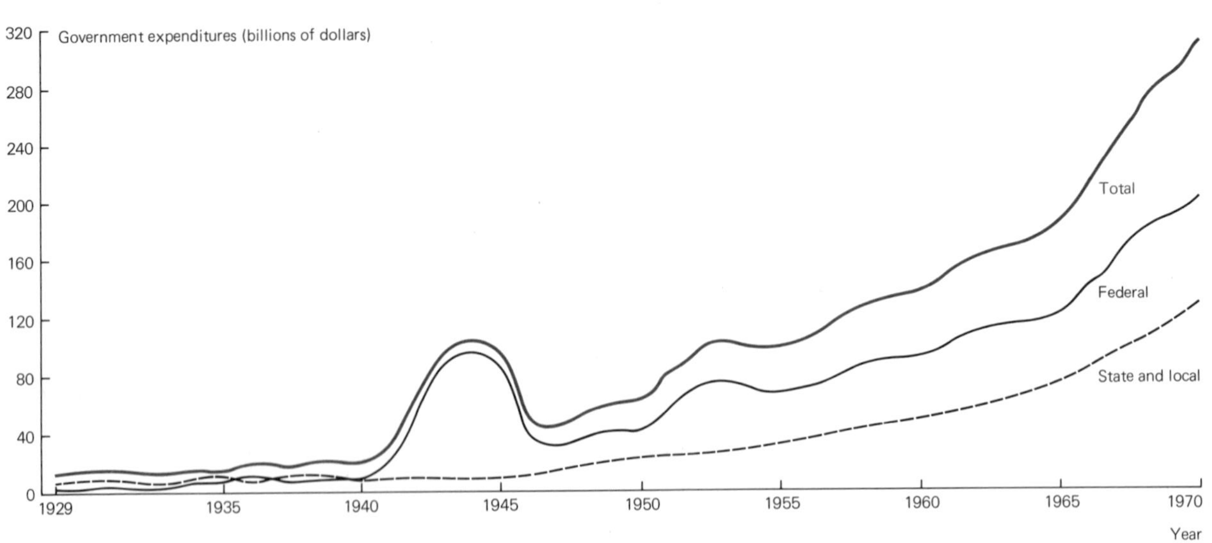

Table 5-2

PUBLIC EXPENDITURES AS PERCENTAGE OF GNP, 1961

Category	*West Germany*	*Sweden**	*United Kingdom*	*United States*
Education	1.9	2.5	4.5	3.7
Public health	3.9	0.8	3.4	1.3
Social security	12.2	5.6	6.4	5.0
Defense	3.5	4.3	6.7	5.0
Other current expenditure (including interest)	14.5	6.8	10.1	9.2
Investment	3.2	3.9	3.4	6.0
Total	39.2	23.9	34.5	30.2

*Includes central government only.

Source: Richard A. Musgrave, *Fiscal Systems,* Yale University Press, New Haven, Conn., 1969.

however. The United States economy as a whole is huge — the largest in the world in terms of its total production of goods and services — so we might also expect government expenditures to be large simply because of the size of the economy. But are government expenditures large relative to the country's total product? Table 5-2 addresses this question. It tabulates total government expenditures as a share of national production of goods and services for a number of countries. Some of these figures may be surprising. Notice that in West Germany, often regarded as a vigorously free enterprise economy, government expenditures are a higher proportion of the national product than in Sweden, which is usually regarded as more "socialist." The United States share is well below that of either West Germany or the United Kingdom.

Categorizing the economic functions of government

A close inspection of the categories of expenditure and income shown in Table 5-1 aids in understanding the economic functions of government. The descriptions more or less follow the tables of government organization: Military expenditures are made by the Department of Defense; education and welfare expenditures by the Department of Health, Education and Welfare, state and local education boards; and so on. That information is useful, but it is not conducive to the generalizations that would permit us to move to a higher level of understanding. For example, in underwriting medical care to the elderly and in undertaking space exploration, the public sector has assumed new functions or has expanded old ones. Why is that? Occasionally a government activity is reorganized to become, if not a private activity, something outside the normal range of government operations. This was done recently when the Post Office Department was turned into a public corporation. What is the rationale? And there is no doubt that governments have assumed a great variety of economic responsibilities around the world. Why? What accounts for the scope of public activities?

A general answer would be that the public sector, like the private household and business sectors, is involved in the resolution of the Output, Input, and Distribution questions. That is a true but uninformative statement. Governments vary a great deal in the economic functions they assume. In the Soviet Union the government takes full responsibility for the operation of the economy. One does not have to look for a special explanation for government housing construction: That, like all other production and distribution activity in the Soviet Union, with some minor exceptions, is simply part of the public sector. In the mixed economies of France, West Germany, and the United Kingdom, railroads, radio and television, and a number of other sectors are run by government.

On the other hand, in the largely decentralized, mixed economy of the United States, the actions of government are more circumscribed. Government influences on the resolution of the Cutput, Input, and Distribution questions are pervasive, but each type of government activity must have its own justification. Our next step is to analyze the functions of government in a mixed economy and the rationale for these functions. In the process a number of new concepts will be introduced. The analysis will also lead to a deeper understanding of how the private sectors of the economy operate.

The provision of public or social consumption goods and services

Many goods and services are not consumed and enjoyed on an individual basis but are used collectively. These are public goods. Because of their nature, they benefit more than one person — perhaps the entire nation. Of course, just as in the choice of private goods, people have different tastes and preferences in public goods, and one man's pleasure may be another man's pain.

Decisions about the availability of public goods are *essentially* political. While there are individual demands for such goods, they do not adequately reflect total, social demand.[1] Military expenditures are a good example of social consumption, in this case, national security. So is the international representation provided by the State Department. These examples also suggest the decision-making problems that arise in areas of social consumption. Unlike the choice of private goods, decisions about public goods and services are not left up to each individual. If the

[1] This point will be elaborated in Chap. 20.

community decides, by voting or some other political process, to have the public goods and allocates resources to their production, they will be available to everyone. There are people who believe that military expenditures for national defense include some "bads" as well as "goods." But as long as they are members of the nation, they cannot avoid the disadvantages – as they see it – and the advantages – as others see it – of all the military expenditures. If they want to change those expenditures, they must go about it through the political process.

Public highways and national parks are other examples of public goods, but they are used or not by each individual as he wishes, and their existence does not directly affect nonusers. Education is an example of a service that has both private and public consumption aspects. Individuals can benefit personally from publicly provided education which increases their earning power and income. Direct, but nonmarket, benefits occur when education makes better citizens or makes the neighbor's children better playmates for one's own.

The distinction between social consumption and socialized production should be kept clearly in mind. Socialized production, or socialism, means government ownership of the means of production. That may be good or bad, depending on your point of view, and we shall review its pros and cons in Chapter 6.

The maintenance of efficiency in the private market sector

It was pointed out in Chapter 4 that markets work well and are easiest to understand when there is competition. It is the competition of buyers and sellers, behind the supply and demand curves, which clears markets and ensures the efficient resolution of the fundamental economic questions. It was also pointed out in Chapter 4 that perfect competition is never fully realized in any market, though it is sometimes reasonably well approximated.

Noncompetitive markets can lead to a kind of economic inefficiency. They need not be so responsive to consumer demands or so effective in the use of resources and technology. In effect, when competition does not exist, the economy may not move out to its production-possibility curve.

One of the economic functions of government in a mixed economy is to maintain competition. The threats to competition have several sources. First, they may originate in fraud and deception practiced on buyers and sellers. Such practices can be described in an antiseptic way as impediments to the free and complete flow of knowledge which is necessary for the success of a competitive system. Another threat to competition is the existence of monopoly power. Monopoly in its pure form is an extreme condition in which there is only one seller of a product. But some degree of monopoly power may exist short of that extreme condition. Why do business firms seek some monopoly power? For businessmen, competition is a hard environment, with little opportunity for a quiet, secure life with lots of profits. It is understandable that businessmen would like to avoid the consequences of competition and that citizens should want their government to try to preserve competition.

One type of monopoly power that results from the lower costs associated with large-sized operations is sometimes called *natural*. Utility companies — electricity and telephone companies, for example — are sometimes regarded as natural monopolies. Under the conditions of natural monopoly, enforced competition would lead to inefficient rather than efficient use of resources. In such conditions government permits some degree of monopoly power or even, by exclusive licensing, creates it. Then government also assumes the responsibility for regulating it in the public interest.

The correction of market failures due to externalities

Private markets "fail" to achieve efficiency in the resolution of the Output, Input, and Distribution questions when there are important nonmarket economic relationships. This happens when there are *externalities* in production or consumption. These are familiar phenomena with an unfamiliar name. *Externalities are economic interactions among producers and consumers which do not involve purchases and sales of goods and services.* Pollution by private business and by private consumers is a prime example. Business firms that use the open sky, public rivers, and lakes to dispose of waste products are creating an *external diseconomy* to consumers and even other business firms by imposing a cost on them which is not charged in any market. Consumers impose diseconomies on other consumers when they pollute the air and water; these diseconomies are externalities also since they do not go through markets.

There are also *external economies*, positive benefits which are created by individual firms and which are not sold in markets. Say that a firm does research and finds that special kinds of lighting and combinations of optical and electronic equipment can be used to control a machine tool. The firm patents the idea. But then someone in another firm reads about it and adapts and patents an extension of the original concept to control a papermaking process; someone else adapts it to control a chemical reaction. The first firm has thus created benefits for other firms which did not bear any share of the original research costs.

When goods and services are produced and distributed and in the process external economies and diseconomies are created, market prices do not reflect the full costs and benefits to the producer or to the consumer. That means that *market prices, which must act as guides to the resolution of the fundamental economic questions, are simply unreliable indicators when there are externalities.* That, in turn, is the justification for government assuming the responsibility to have such externalities taken into account in production and consumption. It taxes and regulates polluters, for example, and sponsors a good deal of research.

Maintenance of high levels of employment and economic stability

Unfortunately the economy as a whole is subject to recurring bouts of unemployment and low-pressure economic activity. These are called *recessions* when they are mild and *depressions* when they are severe. Both mean lost production potential, wasted human and physical resources, and reduced individual and family incomes. For many years recurring periods of reduced economic activity were regarded as outside the scope of government policy. Now it is quite generally agreed that government has a responsibility to ameliorate the symptoms and treat the causes of recessions and depressions.

On occasion, the economy "overheats," with consequent inflationary pressures. These also impose hardships. People whose incomes lag behind price increases are hurt. People who have managed to save some money find that its purchasing power has fallen, unless they are lucky or shrewd enough to find a good inflation "hedge" – and not many people are. Elderly people living on fixed incomes from pensions and retirement funds suffer particularly during periods of inflation. So do welfare recipients when their payments do not keep up with rising prices. *The reduction of inflationary pressures and the maintenance of economic stability are now generally regarded as a major responsibility of the federal government.*

Achievement of greater economic equity

A competitive market economy tends to reward the owners of productive resources and labor according to the productivity of the resources. That creates incentives to use labor and other resources efficiently and helps determine the *functional* distribution of income. But there is no guarantee that it will lead to a distribution of *personal* income that everyone will agree is desirable, just, fair, or even tolerable. The distribution of the ownership of resources may be skewed because of the special ability and hard work of some individuals who have been able to accumulate wealth. But it may also reflect the accidental ownership of land found to contain oil, for example, and the ill-gotten gains of monopoly. Moreover, some individuals may work inefficiently or not be able to work at all, and yet be "deserving" by all standards except those of economic productivity.

Can people ever agree on what constitutes fairness and justice? Isn't it entirely a matter of personal values? Well, it is a matter of individual values, but it is not only that, for most agree on standards of equity. Two examples will demonstrate this. In effect the country has agreed that it is not equitable for elderly persons to be dependent on charity; the social security laws that have been passed and generally accepted provide the elderly with a regular income. The country has also agreed that it is not equitable for educational opportunities to be entirely dependent on the income of individual families. Access to tuition-free or low-cost education has, therefore, been provided at all levels in most states.[2]

Society does arrive at agreements on public policies to modify the effects of the operation of the private market sector and lead toward greater equity. These policies are among the most controversial but they are also among the most important in the interrelations of the public and private sectors.

The instruments of public economic policy

The private sectors of the economy are regulated and directed by the interactions of buyers and sellers in markets. How does the public sector interact with the private sectors? Here we will indicate the range and power of the instruments of public economic policy without going into detail about how they operate. That will be done at many points in the following chapters.

Direct regulation and control of the private sectors

There are many laws which say that the private household and business sectors must carry on their economic activities in certain ways. Regulation of the weight and length limits of trucks and safety requirements for automobiles, for example, are ways of determining the use of the public highways by businesses and individuals.

The rules of the competitive game have not been handed down on graven tablets. They need to be spelled out in detail, and this is one of the functions that government performs to help avoid market failures due to monopolistic tendencies. Moreover, government not only makes the rules, but through courts and regulatory commissions, *it acts as an umpire in enforcing the rules.*

Government also makes regulations to redress some of the market failures due to external diseconomies. Discharging smoke into the city skies and dumping polluting chemicals into lakes and rivers have been well within the rules of the game until recently. The rules are being changed, however, through new laws and regulations to control pollution.

Racial and religious discrimination, in addition to its inequities, leads to economic inefficiency. It is an inefficiency that the private market sector has been willing to live with and even perpet-

[2] There is a more important cost of education than tuition which is still borne privately. That is the "opportunity cost" of the income which could be earned from full-time employment by high school and college-age people if they were not in school. As long as this cost is borne entirely on a personal basis, there will continue to be a private, economic restriction on educational opportunity.

uate in some areas. Through direct regulation, which makes such discrimination illegal, government can not only reduce the economic inefficiency but also move the system toward greater equity.

Direct federal regulation and control of the monetary system and financial markets is intended to contribute to the overall stability and growth of the economic system. The wage-price freeze of 1971 is an example of the use of direct controls to try to moderate inflationary pressures. The nature and timing of the effects of such measures, as well as monetary, financial, and foreign trade regulations, are controversial. No doubt, however, they can have a great impact, for better or for worse.

Government production

All governments own some productive resources and hire and organize workers for production of both public and private goods and services. The production of some goods and services is even reserved exclusively to government. Military manpower is organized nationally, and there are no important private military forces. International representation is a service performed by the State Department. Educational services are, for the most part, produced by public employees in publicly owned facilities, though there are also important private educational facilities. Water, electric power, gas, and hospital services are sometimes provided by municipalities, but all of these are also produced privately. Police and fire protection are "produced" publicly, as is space research and exploration. The last example represents a remarkable expansion of the scope of government enterprise. Some people might argue, however, that it is not essentially different from the Lewis and Clark expedition commissioned by Thomas Jefferson in 1804 to explore the Louisiana Purchase area.

The Tennessee Valley Authority, a government corporation, has built a number of dams, power stations, and electric power distribution systems. When it was established in the 1930s, it was a new departure in federal policy and was both hailed and condemned as the beginning of a new era of government production. But, except for the space program, there have been no substantial extensions of government productive activity in the last thirty years. After World War II a number of government-owned plants were sold to private business. Government production of goods sold in competition with private enterprise has probably decreased in recent years. The federal, state, and local governments in the United States have never had any large-scale ownership of railroads, telephone systems, radio and television stations, airlines, steel mills, oil wells and refineries, or coal mines. Some people think the nation would benefit from more socialized production, and others would prefer still less.

One of the justifications for government ownership of the means of production is that, where there is public consumption, as in the use of public highways, for example, private enterprise will not respond adequately to community demands. Another pro argument is that, where the conditions of production and distribution lead to natural monopoly, say, in providing telephone services, government ownership will ensure the advantages of large-scale operation without the disadvantages of private monopoly. A supporting argument — one which has been heard more frequently in recent years — is that government-owned facilities can and will take into account the externalities, positive and negative, associated with production which are ignored by private enterprise. A case for government ownership is also made on the grounds that private ownership leads to a concentration of private political power and an inequitable distribution of income.

The arguments against government production also include the warning that concentration of economic power — in the hands of government corporations — is politically dangerous. Perhaps the most common criticism of government production, however, is that it is inherently inefficient: There is no competition or profit incentive to ensure that it is responsive to consumer demands and that it uses resources and technology most effectively.

There are grains of truth in all these pro and con arguments. How they balance is still largely a matter of personal judgment. There are the intangible political issues, such as the dangers of private or public concentrations of power, and the more tangible economic issue of efficiency. Not all the facts necessary for an objective judgment are available. Everyone must make up his own mind on this as well as other issues of public policy. The analysis to come will help.

Government expenditure on goods and services

The government budgets shown in Table 5-1 are for the most part listings of government expenditures on goods and services produced in the private sector. They are large amounts and have great influence on the resolution of the economy's fundamental economic questions.

Much of the discussion about government expenditure revolves around its role in stabilizing — or destabilizing — the economy and in helping to achieve high levels of output and employment for the system as a whole. But even when government expenditure is considered primarily as a means of exercising overall policy, there is no reason to neglect its detailed composition. A large share of government expenditure goes to provide public goods and services. Some of it is directed to improving situations that the market economy cannot successfully handle by itself. *The elements of public consumption and correction of market failure are often closely interwoven in government expenditures.* Government housing programs are a good example. There are externalities in housing which private enterprise cannot fully take into account. When an entire neighborhood deteriorates into a slum, the actions of single owners working entirely through markets cannot correct the situation. A landlord or homeowner does not reap the full consequences of improving his building or letting it run down. Some of the consequences are borne by his neighbors. Markets simply do not take account of interrelationships which are external to them, and this type of market failure is one reason for government housing programs.

Do good neighborhoods make good citizens? If so, this is just another way of saying that there are public consumption effects in housing, because the benefits of good citizenship are not confined to the individual. That provides still another reason for government housing programs.

Government expenditures on goods and services are also a means of achieving greater equity. This is the object of government distribution of purchased goods and services to improve the economic conditions of persons whom society regards as deserving but whose private incomes will not sustain adequate standards of living.

Government transfer expenditures

Parts of the federal, state, and local budgets are payments for which the government receives no corresponding return in goods or services. These payments are simply *transfers. Transfers reflect the general belief that income is not distributed by the private sector among individuals and families in a completely socially desirable way.* Social security payments, unemployment insurance, and other welfare payments fall into the transfer expenditure category.

In economic analysis, the distinction between transfer expenditures and expenditures for goods and services is very important. Goods and services purchased for public and private consumption draw directly on the total amount of resources and labor services available for production. Payments for them correspond to goods and services delivered. In this sense, these expenditures are *exhaustive*. On the other hand, transfer expenditures are *nonexhaustive*: They only shift from one group to another the ability to use the goods and services produced with the resources available.

Welfare activities, which are conducted mainly through transfer payments, are one of the most rapidly growing areas of government spending. Why is that? Are there more deserving poor, or does the nation have a more active social conscience? It is partly the latter. There is a wider acceptance of the idea that society has a responsibility to help everyone achieve a minimum standard of living. Also there has been a dramatic increase in what we regard as minimally acceptable. In addition there has been a greater participation in welfare programs by people who were always eligible but had not previously entered their claims. This also reflects the wider social acceptability of the programs.

We are learning, however, that simply transferring income is not enough to relieve poverty. Success depends also on the details of the programs. Some welfare programs contain "disincentive" features which discourage individual enterprise and even tend to disrupt family life rather than preserve it. This is the effect of the Aid to Dependent Children (ADC) programs that provide payments only to families without male heads. For a variety of causes—illness, lack of skills, and discrimination—some fathers cannot earn enough to make their family better off than ADC payments would make them. The law places these men in the predicament of being able to improve their family's economic position by abandoning them so that they will become eligible for ADC.

A rather new approach to the problem of achieving minimally acceptable standards of living for everyone has been supported by President Nixon and is now being tried on a small scale. This is the "income maintenance" or "family assistance" plan. Under this approach, government payments are made whether or not the family is headed by a working man. In addition, the payments are continued, at least partially, until the family income exceeds the level of the welfare payments. This type of plan helps create individual incentives to find employment and earn income.

Taxes

Government expenditures of all kinds are financed by taxes. But taxes are more than a means of providing the purchasing power that governments require to carry out their functions. Tax revenue also drains purchasing power from the private sector. This reduces the potential competition of the private sector for the goods and services demanded by the public sector.

But taxes are more than a means of finance. The power to tax, it has been said, involves the power to destroy. And it is also the power to perform many of the other functions of government.

Some taxes, for example, import duties on foreign-produced goods, can be used to regulate competition. Moreover, taxes can be used to change the prices of final and intermediate goods and services and productive resources. They can thus affect the resolution of the Output, Input, and Distribution questions.

Taxes can also be used to guide and control the private sectors of the economy. For example, the government can control pollution by direct regulation: Thou shalt not discharge black smoke into the air and sulfuric acid into the rivers, etc. Alternatively, the government can tax firms according to the amount of pollution they discharge. These "effluent taxes" transform an external *dis*economy to the system as a whole into an "internal" cost which must be borne by the polluting firms. The design of such taxes is still at an early stage, as is our knowledge of the effects of various kinds and amounts of pollution.

Depending on their composition and design, taxes bear with different weight on different groups in the population. One important implication is that the allocation of the burden of taxes and the availability of the social goods they finance can have significant effects on the distribution of real goods and services of all kinds.

Finally taxes are an important tool of fiscal policy to maintain high levels of employment and to stabilize the economy. A *reduction* in personal income taxes, for example, is like an *increase* in the purchasing power of consumers. It is, therefore, a stimulus to the purchases of goods by households, to their production by the private business sector, and to employment of labor to produce the goods.

Making government policy

We have identified the functions of the public sector and the instruments of public policy. But who decides how the instruments will be used to carry out these functions? Is there an "invisible hand" guiding the operations of the public sector to ensure an end "most advantageous to the society"?

The economist might try to duck these questions by saying, "All that is politics and not my line. I am just the technician, the cook who can tell how the ingredients of public economic policy can be mixed together to achieve the objectives which are set." But that is not really a satisfactory response. Public economic policy is not a recipe thought up in the political dining room and sent to the economists in the kitchen to be prepared. Nor is it chosen from an economic menu listing all the possible, feasible alternatives. There is constant interaction between the sometimes inconsistent and infeasible public economic objectives chosen by political methods and the economists' suggestions for policy and its design.

Essentially, the private sector responds to consumer demands, with each consumer having as much voting power as he has dollars to spend. This is called consumers' sovereignty on a *one-dollar–one-vote* basis.[3] In the public sector, decisions are made as the result of a political process. In a democracy, elected representatives make decisions about the precise content of public sector operations. On a *one-man–one-vote* basis it is a kind of "citizens' sovereignty."

At each level of government, the focus of much of public economic policy making in the United States is the budget-making process. No secrets are given away by the observation that budget making is to some extent a battlefield of people riding hobby-horses – people with axes to grind. But budget making is also the occasion for sincere people in and out of government to attempt to make wise policy.[4] Even if one does not agree with everything or

[3] We shall discuss in Chap. 20 the degree to which consumer demand is manipulated by business.

[4] It is sometimes thought that central planning is the key to the elimination of inconsistencies and the power of special interests. Yet comprehensive and rational central planning of consistent overall and detailed economic policy is an unachieved goal even in the centrally planned societies and is, perhaps, unachievable. At least no one knows how to do it now. Many experts believe that policy making in the planned economies is a muddling-through process, with some similarities to government budget making in the United States.

anything in Washington or the state capital or city hall, there can be little doubt that a lot of hard work is done in these places on ways to deal with current public problems and that a lot of interaction goes on among groups outside of government as well.

A method used more and more widely in government to improve the economic rationality of its decision making is called *benefit-cost analysis.* It is part of the Planning-Programming-Budgeting (PPB) approach. *PPB involves looking ahead to plan objectives, making specific programs to achieve them, and budgeting the cost of those programs.* Cost-benefit analysis helps policy makers choose among alternative ways of achieving the objectives.

When all the benefits of a project, fully included and properly valued, exceed the costs, again fully included and properly valued, the economic decision is positive: Go ahead with the project. If the benefits are less than the costs, the project is not worthwhile. In principle, this sounds and is straightforward, but, as always, there are difficulties in implementation. There are important advantages as well. The attempt to be inclusive means that all benefits and costs will be considered, not only the tangible ones that can be measured in money terms. It also means that an attempt will be made to include both external economies and diseconomies.

Some examples will illustrate the difficulties and advantages of the benefit-cost method. Suppose the federal government considers building a new dam. It is hard but not hopeless to try to capture and compare all the costs and benefits of such a project. Many of the costs can be assessed with some precision, because the inputs will have to be purchased from the private sector. Where there are important "inputs" that are not purchased or readily valued, say, a wildlife sanctuary that is going to be destroyed, cost estimation becomes quite difficult. Similarly, many benefits can be measured, but it is hard to be comprehensive and precise. We can compute the value of the electric power to be produced by the new dam. We can also make a rough estimate of the value of the property that will be protected from flood damage. When it comes to estimating the recreational benefits of the lake that will be created, however, we run into a number of intangibles whose value cannot be readily assessed.

Nonetheless, a benefit-cost analysis is helpful even if precise values cannot be placed on each benefit and cost component. The attempt to be inclusive and to measure all costs also helps to identify the particular segment of society that is going to bear the costs. Or if the costs are widely distributed but intangible, that is also recognized, even if not measured precisely. Likewise, the attempt to measure the benefits helps to identify the recipients of the benefits and tells us whether they are the same people who will bear the costs and deserve the benefits. Consider the issue of government sponsorship of a supersonic airplane. International passengers will save several hours in crossing the Atlantic. Will those passengers bear the full costs, and do they deserve the benefits?

The answer to the first part of the question indicates some of the objections to the SST. The costs of supersonic booms and the environmental change the SST might cause will be borne widely. Though these cannot be measured, they must be recognized. As to benefits, each person will have to judge for himself whether the international passengers are the deserving ones. Yet other benefits are claimed for the SST, such as international prestige and progress in United States aviation. Benefit-cost analysis helps give content to the question: Are those benefits worth what they cost?

Benefit-cost analysis is also applied in areas such as military spending, and there is a consequent improvement in the explicitness with which issues are posed. No one should think that the difficult issues are thereby resolved. Suppose the federal government considers undertaking a new missile system. The money costs are fairly readily identified and compared with, say, a new antiballistic missile system. What about the intangible costs in our international position? Such benefits as better "coverage" and increased security may be claimed for the new system. But are we sure of these benefits? Will the new system work? Again benefit-cost analysis helps bring the important issues out into the open.

The military-industrial and other complexes

Many people who fully recognize and accept the potentially constructive role of government nonetheless worry about the close relations between some parts of the public and private sectors. In his Farewell Address President Dwight Eisenhower in 1961 warned of the dangers of the "military-industrial complex." The space-industrial complex, the research-university complex, and other complexes have been identified more recently as areas of concern. But what is the worry? And is this economics, or is it entirely a matter of politics?

There is no doubt that the military budget is large, and so is the space budget. Moreover, the government sponsors most of the scientific research done in the country. But the United States is a big country, and when it undertakes to be prepared for military eventualities, it must operate on a large scale. Similarly, the moon is an expensive place to visit, and scientific research costs more than private business and nonprofit foundations are willing to pay.

Yet the worry is not simply a matter of size. Military, space, research, and many other areas of expenditure are distinguished by the dominance of the public sector. Compare the effect of government on, say, the purchase of carbon paper, typewriters, paper clips, and other office supplies. The public sector is a big buyer, in fact, the largest. But no one worries about the "office supply complex." The office supply sector must meet the criteria of responsiveness to private demands and efficiency in the use of resources which private markets impose. There is active competition among suppliers to sell products to both the public and private sectors. In both sectors the products must meet tests of performance which are more or less the same. All this contributes to an "arms-length" relationship between the producers and the government.

The markets for military goods and space equipment, and to a lesser extent research, are sometimes described as "enclaves" within the economy as a whole. Though inputs to these products are purchased broadly and mainly privately, the outputs are sold almost exclusively to the public sector. So the military goods market, the space equipment market, and to a somewhat lesser extent, the research market are enclaves on the output side, largely self-contained and separate from other producing sectors in the sale of their output. To be sure, government purchasing regulations impose certain tests of effectiveness. As was said about the Apollo spacecraft, "Every piece of equipment on board was produced by a low bidder." But it would be a mistake to believe that the bidding competition for government contracts is like market competition in private markets. The competition of the private marketplace is a much more fickle and difficult environment to predict and live in.

The problems of government-private industry relations cannot be resolved simply by enforcing competition. The goods and services involved are often public ones, and often there are important externalities and economies of scale in their production. In such circumstances, competitive markets would not work effectively either. The difficulties are fundamental, and there are no easy solutions.

Without active market competition, the possibility of collusion among buyers and sellers arises. This is one of the major fears underlying the worries about the military-industrial complex. Collusion is a source of economic inefficiency. Since the amounts of money involved are so large, a little inefficiency can go a long way. There are, of course, laws against collusion, but their enforcement is the responsibility of the public sector itself, which is one of the participants in the private industry-government complex. In such circumstances the performance of suppliers depends to a considerable extent on the personal honesty and good will of the men involved.

It does not impugn anyone's honesty to point out the difference between sectors in which personal elements play a large role and those in which impersonal markets call the tune. Competition is a "government of markets and not of men," to paraphrase the political aphorism. And like a government of laws instead of men, competition, as a government of markets, makes the system less dependent on personal virtue to be effective.

One of the dangers of collusion is simple economic inefficiency. But another danger is to be at least equally feared. The interest of private business is to make profits. The interest of government officials is to maintain national security and achieve other public goals. The danger of collusion is that these two types of goals are not kept separate.

Summary

Public economics is about the effects of government on the economic system. The federal, state, and local governments have great influence on the operation of the economy, partly because of the sheer size of their budgets. To appreciate the extent of government influence, one must also understand the economic functions performed by the public sector. These are : (1) provision of public goods and services which are, to some extent, used and enjoyed jointly; (2) maintenance of efficiency in the private market sector by preserving competition and regulating monopoly; (3) correction of situations in which markets fail to work well because of economic interactions which are external to the markets; (4) maintenance of high levels of employment for the economy as a whole and overall economic stability; (5) achievement of greater economic equity than is created by the private market sector alone.

These functions are complex, and their precise content is often controversial. There are difficulties in identifying the objective features in a situation and usually differences in value judgments about how the situation should be changed.

In carrying out its functions, the public sector uses five major types of economic instruments: (1) Direct regulation and control of the private sector is exercised, for example, through laws which regulate competition and noncompetitive practices, pollution, the monetary system, minimum wages, and participation in social insurance programs. (2) Government production includes such activities as education, fire and police protection, and also the big defense budget, space, and research sectors. (3) Government expenditure on goods and services provides the inputs used in its own production of goods and services and affects the availability of goods and services to individuals as well as the overall performance of the economy. (4) Transfer expenditures are mainly social security and welfare payments which affect the distribution of income and also the level at which the economy as a whole operates. (5) Taxes provide the public sector with purchasing power, help to regulate the private sector, redistribute income, and are also a major tool of policy to stabilize the economy.

Benefit-cost analysis is a method of public decision-making which involves the comparison and evaluation of all the costs and all the benefits associated with particular government projects. If benefits exceed costs, that justifies the project. While it is difficult to measure every cost and every benefit fully, the attempt to be comprehensive is itself an important virtue of the method.

Some of the differences between the operations of the public sector and the private sectors are illustrated in the debate over the dangers of the military-industrial and other complexes. The dominance of the government as the buyer in these sectors raises the danger of collusion without any independent party to monitor the transactions. By comparison, where there is competition, there are arms-length relationships which help guarantee the effectiveness of the markets.

Questions for discussion and review

1. Comment on the following debate:

A. *The government budget understates the role of the public sector because many important government activities require relatively small amounts of money.*

B. *The government budget overstates the role of the public sector because most government expenditures go back to the private sector to buy goods and services.*

2. Describe the difference between public goods and private goods and give examples. Can you think of any goods or services which combine public and private elements?

3. Do you believe that the incomes produced in the private sector should be redistributed in order to achieve greater equity in the system as a whole? Can you define what you think an equitable distribution of income would be: equality, guaranteed minimum incomes for all, minimum incomes guaranteed only for people over thirty, minimum incomes guaranteed only for people under thirty?

4. Is it true that the government can to some degree carry out all its functions by means of direct regulation and control?

5. Is there anything the government cannot do by means of taxation? Discuss your answer.

6. Describe the method of benefit-cost analysis and the problems in its application.

7. Do you think public policy can be made in a rational way or is it necessarily a matter of the compromise of conflicting interests?

8. Do you worry about the economic implications of the military-industrial complex? Why or why not?

Concepts for review

Public goods
Market failure
External economies and diseconomies
Income redistribution
Government regulation
Government production
Transfer expenditures
Government by markets

6 Taxes and the public sector

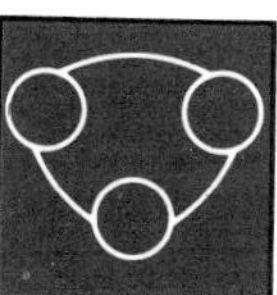

Taxes are a powerful instrument of public economic policy. They are used directly to carry out many of the functions of government. They are also used to transfer resources from the private sector to the public sector. Taxes are absolutely necessary, therefore, to support the other instruments of public policy that use or distribute goods and services.

Though taxes are an inescapable fact of life, that does not mean that one tax is as good as another as far as the total economy is concerned. *A tax is a burden on whoever ends up paying and will affect his economic behavior.* Different taxes place the burden differently on various groups or sectors. In transferring resources from the private to the public sector, taxes are likely to distort the way in which the private sector operates. Sometimes that distortion is desired; often it is not. We want to explore the issues involved in the location of the burdens of taxation and the distortions created by taxation. We can take them up in a more concrete way after surveying the tax system as it now stands.

A survey of federal, state, and local taxes

Table 6-1 shows the distribution of federal and state-and-local tax revenues. Note the sharp contrast between the two tax systems. The personal income tax is by far the most important single source of federal tax revenues. The corporate income tax generates about 42 percent as much revenue as the personal income tax. Social

Table 6-1

FEDERAL AND STATE-AND-LOCAL TAX REVENUES

	1959		1969	
	Billions of dollars	*Percent*	*Billions of dollars*	*Percent*
Federal				
Total*	89.7	100.0	200.6	100.0
Personal income taxes	38.4	42.8	92.3	46.0
Corporate income taxes	22.5	25.1	39.2	19.6
Social insurance taxes	14.8	16.5	46.5	23.2
Excise taxes	11.4	12.7	16.4	8.2
Estate and gift taxes	1.4	1.5	3.6	1.8
Customs duties	1.1	1.2	2.4	1.2
Miscellaneous	0.2	0.2	0.8	0.1
State and local				
Total*	46.0	100.0	118.3	100.0
Personal income taxes	2.1	4.6	10.0	8.5
Corporate income taxes	1.2	2.6	3.5	3.0
Social insurance taxes	2.7	5.9	7.1	6.0
Sales taxes	9.7	21.1	25.1	21.2
Estate and gift taxes	0.4	0.8	1.0	0.8
Property taxes	15.0	32.6	31.0	26.2
Miscellaneous taxes and fees	8.1	17.6	20.3	17.2
Federal grants	6.8	14.8	20.2	17.1

*Detail may not add to total because of rounding.

Source: U.S. Department of Commerce, Office of Business Economics.

insurance taxes (social security and unemployment insurance) yield slightly more than the corporate tax. Federal excise taxes, which include duties on foreign-produced goods and taxes on certain domestically produced goods, for example, gasoline, automobiles, whiskey, and cigarettes, generate a substantial amount of revenue also.

State and local finance depends most heavily on the property tax. Sales taxes are not far behind. But the personal income tax, the mainstay of the federal system, and the corporate income tax are much less important at the state level. Personal income tax revenues are the most rapidly growing part of the state and local

Figure 6-1

HYPOTHETICAL SUPPLY AND DEMAND SCHEDULES FOR WHISKEY (BEFORE TAX)

tax system, however, as hard-pressed state governments turn to it with increasing frequency.

Table 6-1 also shows state and local receipts from the federal government. These are grants which help support various types of programs, such as welfare, highway construction, and public housing. They now constitute about 19 percent of the revenue of state and local governments. Though originally tied to specific joint federal and state and local programs, the general revenue-sharing plans would grant federal money to be spent at the discretion of the state and local governments.

Tax incidence

It is natural to think that the burden of taxes falls on whoever actually pays out the money. Yet things are often not what they seem. We can demonstrate the possible difference between the taxpayer and the location of the burden of taxation (tax incidence) with the help of the supply and demand analysis of Chapter 4. Table 6-2 presents hypothetical supply and demand curves for some commodity, say, blended whiskey in a particular city. These are also represented in Figure 6-1. The equilibrium price is $4 and the equilibrium quantity is 100,000 quarts per week.

Suppose now that the city imposes a $2 tax on each quart of whiskey sold. The demand schedule does not change. With or without the tax, people are still willing to buy the same amounts at the same prices. The supply schedule changes, however, as shown in Table 6-3. Suppliers would still be willing to offer whiskey for sale in the amounts and at the prices shown by the supply schedule in Table 6-2 if they could legally do so. Now, however, the city government requires them to pay a $2 tax on each bottle sold. So suppliers must add $2 to the price at which they are willing to offer the old amounts. That creates a difference between the market price paid and the amount retained by the supplier, as shown in the first and last columns of Table 6-3.

Table 6-2

HYPOTHETICAL SUPPLY AND DEMAND SCHEDULES FOR WHISKEY BEFORE TAX

Price	*Demand (quarts/week)*	*Supply (quarts/week)*
$8	60,000	140,000
7	70,000	130,000
6	80,000	120,000
5	90,000	110,000
4	**100,000**	**100,000**
3	110,000	90,000
2	120,000	80,000

Table 6-3

HYPOTHETICAL SUPPLY AND DEMAND SCHEDULES FOR WHISKEY AFTER TAX

Market price	*Demand (quarts/week)*	*Supply (quarts/week)*	*Price retained by supplier*
$10	40,000	140,000	$8
9	50,000	130,000	7
8	60,000	120,000	6
7	70,000	110,000	5
6	80,000	100,000	4
5	**90,000**	**90,000**	**3**
4	100,000	80,000	2

The effect of the tax is to shift the supply curve upward by $2 for each quantity supplied. This shift is depicted in Figure 6-2 along with the demand curve. The new equilibrium price can be found at the intersection of the new supply and prevailing demand schedule at $5.

Figure 6-2

HYPOTHETICAL SUPPLY AND DEMAND SCHEDULES FOR WHISKEY (BEFORE AND AFTER TAX)

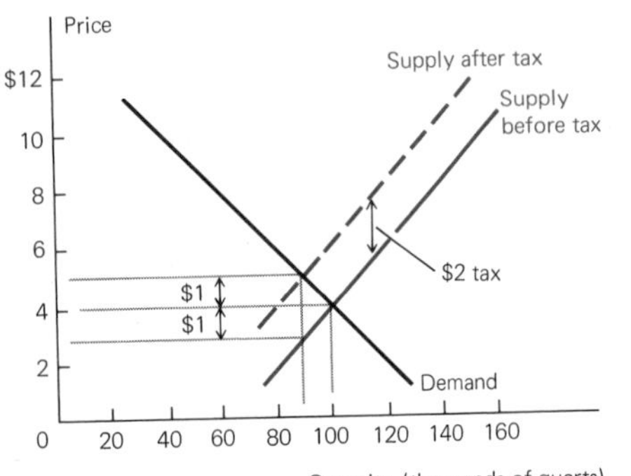

The new equilibrium price, however, is only $1 higher than the old price, and this is less than the amount of tax per bottle. That means that purchasers pay $1 more and suppliers receive $1 less per bottle. Buyers and sellers, therefore, share the burden of the tax between them. *The incidence of the excise tax is not only on the seller, who sends the tax collections to the city government, nor only on the buyer, but on both of them.*[1]

The example illustrates the point that the burden of some taxes can be *shifted* partly, if not entirely, from the person or business on which they are applied. The income tax is the clearest example of a tax that cannot be shifted: The burden falls on the individual who pays. The burden of excise taxes, such as the bottle tax on whiskey, and of sales taxes is less easy to determine, requiring an analysis of the characteristics of the individual markets. The incidence of a tax such as the corporate income tax is even more difficult to determine.

Recognition of the possible difference between the taxpayer and the actual incidence of the tax reemphasizes the point that taxes are not simply a withdrawal of purchasing power. They are a means of redistributing income. If the tax burden falls more heavily on the rich than on the poor, then the difference in their incomes will be less after taxes than before taxes.

Taxes which take a larger percentage of higher incomes than of lower incomes are progressive taxes. They shift a larger share of the burden of supporting government functions to upper-income groups. *Taxes which take the same percentage of income from all income groups are proportional. And taxes which take a larger*

[1] The equal distribution of the tax is a consequence of the particular hypothetical example and not a result that should be generalized.

share of the income of lower-income groups than of higher-income groups are regressive.

Tax distortions

Another implication of the example of Tables 6-3 and 6-4 is that the tax "distorts" the free choice of consumers. Instead of buying 100,000 bottles per week, as they did before the tax was applied, they now buy only 90,000 bottles per week. Likewise, the suppliers of whiskey are selling – and producing – fewer bottles per week. So production decisions are also distorted. These results may have been intentional. In the case of sumptuary, or regulatory, taxes, the tax is an expression of community desire to discourage a particular kind of consumption. Another example of the intentional distortion of private decisions by taxation is its use to internalize to business firms the external diseconomies of the pollution they create. This was mentioned in Chapter 5 as one type of remedy for the market's failure to take external diseconomies into account. *Often, the distorting effects of taxes on consumer and producer decisions are not intended*, but *are an unavoidable by-product.*

Excise taxes, such as the whiskey tax, can distort the decisions that both consumers and producers would make in untaxed markets. Other taxes – personal and corporate income taxes, for example – may also distort decisions about the use of resources. It is sometimes argued that personal income taxes reduce individual incentives to work because after-tax rewards are less than before-tax income. Conceivably the tax could make people work harder to get the same after-tax income. But that, too, would be a distortion. It has also been argued that the corporate income tax reduces corporate incentives to invest and produce to the extent it is not shifted to consumers. The degree to which distortion of free choice and decisions occurs depends on the particular characteristics of the market and on who bears the burden of the taxes. Tax incidence and distortions are two of the most complicated puzzles that economists have to deal with. We are far from complete success in untangling them. The analysis here demonstrates the potential significance of the issues, however, for the resolution of the Output, Input, and Distribution questions.

Tax principles

Federal, state, and local taxes often overlap, and the taxpayer seldom feels that his lot is a happy one. Is there any hope of finding a consistent application of tax principles in the multilayered United States tax system? Or can we agree on a set of principles on which the tax system should be based?

If we are to find such a set of principles, there is not much point in looking for them with economic analysis. Taxes are a means of transferring resources from private to public use and of redistributing income. They are also a means of influencing consumer and producer decisions directly. Ultimately, however, the questions of who is to bear the burden of the transfer, and to what extent, and whether private decisions should be changed are not economic questions. They are political in the broad sense of the term. Economic analysis can help determine the incidence of any tax, but it cannot say what that burden *should* be. Nonetheless it is useful to review some of the tax principles that have been proposed. In their most general form they command wide agreement. The disagreements turn up in the application of the principles.

Equity. Who would argue that taxes should not be equitable, that is, fair and just? But how many people will agree on what constitutes equity? Three formulas have been proposed to achieve tax equity.

1. The benefit principle says that taxes should be assessed according to the relative benefits received from government activities. This is a plausible rationale. Consider the commuter who pays tolls on an expressway. His benefits are immediate and clear. When his car gets stuck behind a truck, however, he becomes less certain that the tolls he pays represent his proportional benefits. In general it is difficult if not impossible to identify and allocate the benefits to individuals of government actions. This is particularly true if the benefits come from public goods provided for the community as a whole.

2. The sacrifice (or ability-to-pay) principle states that the sacrifices that taxes impose should be related to the taxpayer's ability to pay. Most frequently the application of this principle assumes that the well-to-do are able to bear heavier tax burdens than the less well-to-do. Therefore, to equalize the sacrifices of rich and poor, the tax should take a larger proportion of the income of the rich. That is, taxes should be progressive rather than regressive or even proportional. The sacrifice principle commands wide support, but its applications are always controversial. Comparisons of sacrifices are inherently a matter of personal judgment. That does not prevent the formation of a general consensus with respect to particular taxes, however.

3. The principle of equal treatment of equals (and unequal treatment of unequals) says people in essentially equal positions should be taxed equally and that people in unequal positions should be taxed unequally. The principle of equal treatment for equals is sometimes called "horizontal equity." It can be interpreted consistently with both the benefit and sacrifice principles by looking at both the ability-to-pay and benefit sides of taxation and government operation. Of course, the difficult problems of comparison and evaluation turn up again. Unequal treatment for unequals, or "vertical equity," also sounds like a reasonable guideline. In itself, however, the principle provides no indication of how slight or great the unequal treatment should be.

Neutrality. Taxes usually distort the consumption and production decisions of individuals and businesses. In some circumstances the distortions are intended, as with tobacco and alcohol taxes. *The principle of neutrality says that when the private sector of the economy is working "reasonably well" through markets, taxes should not distort production and consumption decisions.* It raises no barriers to the use of taxes, however, when markets are not working well, owing to market failures caused by either monopolistic elements or external effects.

Administrative efficacy. Several kinds of administrative criteria can be lumped together under this headline. *In principle, taxes should be simple and certain in concept and in collection.* They should be readily understood by the citizenry and easy to collect. They should also be adequate to provide the revenue that government requires.

Tax compromises

It is easier to enunciate principles than to enact them into law. There are always differences of opinion over the detailed applications of principles of equity. Powerful political and economic interests may oppose these principles because of self-interest. And implementation of the principles is always limited by essential inadequacies in available knowledge. In such circumstances, it is understandable that taxes and tax changes are highly controversial aspects of government economic policy. Nonetheless, tax laws are passed and changed and reformed from year to year. In the process, social compromises are arrived at which reflect the preferences and pressures of all voters to some extent, but not necessarily of any individual or group completely.

Social compromises are reflected in the entire structure of taxes. There are "users' taxes," such as the gasoline tax, which are justified on a benefit principle, though they are likely to be distorting. There are income taxes which place different relative burdens on different income groups, depending on their degree of progressivity or regressivity. The rationale of specific social compromises in the federal, state, and local tax systems will become more apparent as we survey in detail the structure of these systems.

The federal tax system

Table 6-1 shows the relative importance of each of the major generators of federal tax revenue. We shall take them up in this order.

The personal income tax

This mainstay of the federal tax system is also the major source of progressivity in the system. First of all the federal personal income tax has a progressive rate schedule, as shown in Table 6-4. The marginal tax rate, which is the proportion of each *additional* dollar

Table 6-4

MARGINAL TAX ON TAXABLE INCOME (AFTER DEDUCTIONS AND EXEMPTIONS) SINGLE PERSONS AND MARRIED PERSONS

Over	*But not over*	*Marginal tax rate %*
$ 1,000	$ 2,000	15
$ 2,000	$ 3,000	16
$ 3,000	$ 4,000	17
$ 4,000	$ 8,000	19
$ 8,000	$ 12,000	22
$ 12,000	$ 16,000	25
$ 16,000	$ 20,000	28
$ 20,000	$ 24,000	32
$ 24,000	$ 28,000	36
$ 28,000	$ 32,000	39
$ 32,000	$ 36,000	42
$ 36,000	$ 40,000	45
$ 40,000	$ 44,000	48
$ 44,000	$ 52,000	50
$ 52,000	$ 64,000	53
$ 64,000	$ 76,000	55
$ 76,000	$ 88,000	58
$ 88,000	$100,000	60
$100,000	$120,000	62
$120,000	$140,000	64
$140,000	$160,000	66
$160,000	$180,000	68
$180,000	$200,000	69
$200,000	—	70

of income which is taxed away, rises as income rises. This means that the average tax rate, the proportion of *total* income taken away by taxes, also rises with income.

The overall degree of progressivity or regressivity of the income tax is not determined solely by the rate schedule, however. It depends also on the various exemptions, allowances, and deductions built into the tax law. For example, a married couple with no children and with a combined taxable income under $2,300 will pay no income tax at all, whatever their age. If they are over sixty-five, they will pay no tax if their income is less than $2,900, and they can exclude the income they receive from social security benefits. Taxes paid to state and local governments and interest paid on loans can be deducted from the income which is taxed — a major advantage to people who own their homes and are paying off a mortgage. Medical expenses above a certain fraction of income can be deducted from income, as can certain charitable contributions, education expenses, and union dues; and gambling losses can be deducted from gambling winnings. Interest earned on state and municipal bonds is not taxed by the federal government, and losses on farm operations can be deducted from other income. These are all perfectly legal and aboveboard exemptions and deductions.

When does a deduction become a "loophole," and when does an exemption become an "unwarranted erosion of the tax base"? That again is a matter of personal opinion. We hear stories about people with high incomes who manage to pay little or no taxes by arranging to receive much of their income in forms which are exempt from taxation and by using various deductions against income. The evidence suggests that a very small proportion of income is able to escape taxation. Even so, from the standpoint of individual equity, this type of tax avoidance is not consistent with the intent of the tax law, as indicated by the progressive rate schedule. The income tax law of 1969 made some moderate progress in reducing the possibilities of tax avoidance and in imposing a minimum tax requirement on certain types of income that would otherwise not be taxed.

The corporate income tax

The tax on corporate profits starts at 22 percent and rises to a maximum marginal tax rate of 48 percent on profits above $25,000 per year. It is the second largest source of federal tax revenue and one of the most controversial of federal taxes. It is accused of being an instrument of double taxation, because the corporate profits which are taxed can be taxed again as personal income when they are paid out to individuals as dividends.

Debates over the incidence of the tax add to the controversy. One position claims that corporations shift the tax forward to their customers, so that it is like a sales tax. Another view argues that corporate stockholders bear the burden. On this ground, critics of the tax say that it discourages investment by corporations because it reduces the return to stockholders. Neither theoretical nor empirical studies have found definitive answers to these criticisms, and professional economists go at each other hammer and tongs over this question. Because the incidence of the corporate income tax is in doubt, its contribution to the overall progressiveness or regressiveness of the system is also in doubt. Part of the problem is that stockholders are not a homogeneous group. Although, in general, they have above-median incomes, some are retired persons living on relatively fixed incomes, and others have relatively low incomes – the "widows and orphans."

One important function of the corporate income tax is to help make the personal income tax work well. If there were no corporate income tax, stockholders could avoid taxes on corporate profits which accrued to them simply by not paying out the profits as dividends. The profits could then be reinvested or plowed back into the corporation to earn more profits and increase the wealth of stockholders without ever coming near the tax collector's books. The corporate income tax makes such complete tax avoidance impossible. Even so, when corporate profits are not paid out as dividends and, therefore, are not taxed as personal income, there is a potential tax advantage. Undistributed corporate profits are then taxed only once at the maximum 48 percent corporate tax rate. Thus, stockholders who are above the 48 percent personal income tax bracket benefit when undistributed corporate profits accrue to them without being paid out.

Payroll taxes Taxes earmarked for old-age retirement, insurance for survivors of deceased workers, disability insurance, hospital and medical insurance, and unemployment insurance are payroll taxes. Many people think of them as "premium" payments rather than taxes. This is partly because some of the programs are called "insurance" and partly because the amount of one's benefits depends on the payments one has made. Nonetheless, the payments are taxes; they are not voluntary, and in some instances when payments have not been adequate to cover claims, the government has used general tax revenues to cover them.

Social security taxes are a fixed percentage of wages and salaries up to a specified amount and are matched by employers. Self-employed persons also pay a fixed percentage of their income as social security taxes. The general consensus among economists who have studied the tax is that employees bear the burden of both their own and the employer's contributions. If it were not for the taxes, the employees' take-home wages would be higher. The social security tax rate was 1 percent on the employer and 1 percent on the employee on the first $3,000 of income when the law was passed in 1937. The rate and the maximum amount on which the tax must be paid have been raised since then and with particular frequency in recent years. In 1971 the tax was at the rate of 5.2 percent on employees on the first $7,800 of income.

Payroll taxes in themselves are regressive. They take a constant proportion of income up to a stipulated amount, and nothing above that level. So as incomes rise above the stipulated level, the tax proportion falls steadily. Moreover, the taxes are not paid at all on dividend or interest income.

The entire system of social security, Medicare, and unemployment payments is not so regressive as the payroll taxes themselves, however. The payments go mainly to people in lower-income levels, whereas the taxes used to finance the payments have a somewhat broader base.

Federal excise taxes There is no general federal sales tax, only specific taxes on certain goods and services. The most important in terms of revenue are liquor, tobacco, and gasoline taxes, but there are also taxes on telephone service, air travel, and fishing equipment, for example.

These taxes raise prices and reduce consumption, as was explained above in the discussion of the whiskey tax. Excise taxes are regarded as *sumptuary* taxes, when the items taxed, liquor and tobacco, for example, are regarded to some extent as morally or socially undesirable. The taxes probably do not actually succeed in curtailing consumption, however, because the amounts of these commodities demanded do not fall much as prices rise. As a result, the main burden falls on consumers.

The taxes are regressive when the items taxed make up a larger share of the budget of people with relatively low incomes than of people with higher incomes. They are also the type of tax that must obviously distort consumer choices.

Estate and gift taxes Taxes on the transferral of an estate at death and on the receipt of an inheritance are among the oldest types of taxes. Since one of the historical functions of government is to protect and supervise the transferral of property at death, governments have easily justified the taxation of that property. Since bequests are a source of ability to pay, death taxes have been justified on this ground. And, finally, though opinions differ considerably, one argument made for death taxes is that they have a leveling effect on the distribution of wealth and income. An argument against such taxes is that they reduce individual incentives to be enterprising and thrifty, because they reduce the proportion of an estate that can be passed on.

The federal death tax is a graduated tax on the size of the estate left by an individual. The federal gift tax is necessary to help make the estate tax effective. Otherwise, it would be too easy to avoid taxation by making outright gifts during one's lifetime. Neither tax has ever been a major source of revenue in the United States.

State and local taxes

As Table 6-1 shows, the state and local tax system is quite different from the federal system. The property tax is the most important revenue source for state and local governments, but it is not used at all on the federal level. Sales and excise taxes, which have only limited federal use, are the second most important generators of state and local revenue. Though state and local income taxes are expanding, they still contribute only a small share of total tax revenue at these levels.

The property tax The real property tax is levied as a fraction of the assessed value of real estate — land and buildings. This means that all such property must be inspected by the town assessor and given some value for tax purposes. Usually the tax assessment value is a good deal lower than the current market value. The discrepancy may be due to the use of an outmoded valuation procedure. Often it is due to the infrequency of assessment. Assessed values get out of date quickly when market prices change from year to year. People whose property values fall will apply for a revised assessment, but the others will keep quiet. With a small budget and a lot of property to inspect, the assessor does not make the rounds very often.

To set the property tax rate, the local government first computes how much total revenue is needed to maintain the streets, the schools, the police and fire departments, and so on. Then it makes an estimate of revenue from state or federal grants and from all tax sources other than property taxes. The difference between this estimate and the total needed has to be raised by the property tax. This amount is divided by the total assessed valuation to derive the property tax rate. There are no surprises in the process, however, because before the budget is finalized, the city fathers make an estimate of the taxes required to finance it and decide whether the tax rate is "reasonable" – one that will not precipitate an all-out taxpayers' revolt.

There are many potential and actual sources of inequity in the property tax and the way it is administered. Small properties tend to have a higher assessment relative to market value than larger properties. New buildings tend to be assessed at higher rates than older ones. The tax may not be related to either ability to pay or benefits received, especially in communities with diversified economies in which much of the wealth and income belongs to people who do not own real estate. All these factors make the property tax a regressive one, with the tax share it represents decreasing with higher incomes.

The personal property tax is used in some localities to supplement the real property tax and render it more equitable by bringing other types of property under taxation. Its impact is highly unequal, owing to the difficulty of finding and assessing personal property.

Sales taxes

Sales taxes are *general* taxes in that they apply one tax rate (usually between 2 percent and 4 percent) to the retail sale of a wide range of goods and services. Sometimes they are statewide; sometimes they are only citywide. Since the purchases to which they apply make up a larger proportion of low incomes than of high incomes, the tax itself is also a larger proportion of low incomes and is, therefore, regressive.

Some places have reduced or eliminated this regressivity by reducing the scope of the tax. Certain categories of goods, such as food and clothing, may be exempted altogether. Since these items form a larger proportion of low-income budgets than of upper-income budgets, this selectivity goes far toward reducing the regressiveness of the tax.

Interestingly enough, in spite of its regressivity, a sales tax is often more acceptable to the general public than is an income tax. This is probably due to the small amount paid on each purchase. By comparison, the income tax deduction from the paycheck looks big. It is a kind of myopia which prevents consumers from realizing that the sales tax is paid on many more occasions.

Other state and local taxes

Many states have personal income taxes. They resemble the federal tax, though the rates are often lower. Sometimes state income taxes give special exemptions or more favorable treatment to income earned within the state than to income earned outside the state. Often state and local income taxes are less progressive than the federal tax, and in any case, constitute a smaller fraction of tax revenues. So state and local income taxes do not offset the regressiveness of the rest of the tax structure at these levels.

There are also state corporate income taxes, gasoline and liquor taxes, state inheritance and gift taxes, and a bevy of license and permit fees, which yield a considerable amount of revenue. State death taxes are usually on the amounts inherited by individuals and are not only graduated but depend on the closeness of the relation between the decedent and the person receiving the inheritance.

Intergovernmental transfers

Intergovernmental transfers are of growing importance. The federal government grants funds to state and local governments for various projects, and the state governments make grants to local governments.

The federal government has used *conditional* grants, mainly to state governments, to encourage the state to undertake programs passed by Congress but requiring implementation at the state level. The states have been required to match the funds to some extent and meet other federal standards. The list of such programs is now a long one; it includes school lunch programs, water pollution control, hospital construction, vocational education, and unemployment insurance.

More recently the federal government has made *block* grants to both state and city governments. These do not require matching funds. They have been made for such purposes as urban renewal, public housing, and airport construction.

General *tax sharing* by the federal government has been proposed in recent years. The funds would not be confined to grants for particular programs, but could be used broadly in state government functions. *Essentially, tax sharing is a scheme to put some of the revenue-collecting power of the federal government at the service of state governments.* This is the major argument for the scheme, taking into account also the relative progressivity of the federal tax system. It is also argued that without federal aid local governments, perhaps even states, would go "bankrupt." Government bankruptcy would mean that bills would not be paid and government services would be cut back. The painful cure is raising taxes. The painless cure for the state would be to receive federal grants.

As one would guess, there are a variety of arguments against tax-sharing proposals. One claims that the states would not provide more and better government services, but only substitute federal funds for state-raised funds. As a result state and local government services would not be improved but only maintained with lower state and local tax rates than otherwise. Another argument says that if federal taxes generate surplus funds, federal tax rates should be reduced. If they were, money would not be available for general sharing.

In some cases, state governments also give grants to and share taxes with local governments. In part, such state aid is given because the state has taken over local revenue sources, the property tax, for example. It has also arisen because the state can more successfully impose certain taxes, such as those on personal incomes, than can local governments. In addition, state governments appreciate the fact that many services provided locally benefit the entire state.

An overview of the United States tax and transfer system: Who pays the taxes and who benefits

There are many kinds of taxes, many different levels of government collecting taxes, and many types of benefits provided directly and indirectly by all levels of government. Table 6-5 summarizes the best recent estimates of who pays and who benefits. The result may be a bit surprising.

Federal taxes as a percentage of income are regressive for income recipients under $2,000. A higher proportion of income is paid in taxes at that level than at higher levels. Above the $2,000 income level, the tax take tends to increase slightly as a proportion of income, though not rapidly until income reaches more than $15,000 per year.

State and local taxes decrease as a proportion of income over the full range of income and are, therefore, regressive overall. The share of taxes hardly changes in the middle-income range, that is, from $6,000 to $15,000, however.

Federal and state taxes together take a surprisingly large proportion of low incomes and, combined, they are regressive up to the $8,000 income level. Again, the percentage paid in taxes rises rapidly only above $15,000 per year.

However, transfer payments completely offset the regressiveness of the income tax system! Transfer payments to individuals rise as income falls. These consist of social security payments, welfare payments, unemployment compensation, and so on. If taxes and transfers are taken together, the *net* payments to government increase as a proportion of income as income rises. The tax and transfer system *as a whole* is progressive.

These conclusions raise important questions. Does it make sense to tax so much away from low-income groups and then pay transfers to the same groups? Are we sure that the transfer payments go to the same low-income people who pay the taxes? Do the high tax rates on poorer individuals work against their incentives? Is tax reduction on low-income groups an important

Table 6-5

TAXES AND TRANSFERS AS PERCENTAGE OF INCOME, 1965

Income classes	*Taxes*				
	Federal	*State and local*	*Total*	*Transfer Payments*	*Taxes less transfers*
Less than $2,000	19	25	44	126	—83*
$ 2,000–$ 4,000	16	11	27	11	16
$ 4,000–$ 6,000	17	10	27	5	21
$ 6,000–$ 8,000	17	9	26	3	23
$ 8,000–$10,000	18	9	27	2	25
$10,000–$15,000	19	9	27	2	25
$15,000 and over	32	7	38	1	37
Total	22	9	31	14	24

*The minus sign indicates that taxes were less than transfer payments to this income group.

Note: Between $4,000 and $6,000, the share of taxes in income does not change much in the case of either federal or state and local taxes. The share of transfer payments in income falls regularly as income rises.

Source: Economic Report of the President, 1969.

way of providing assistance to them? Does paying taxes help maintain an important feeling of civic responsibility? If you think so, then that is an argument for continuing to tax low-income groups. But is it an argument for a regressive tax system? Not at all.

We are not sure that the poor people who pay the high taxes are the ones who receive the transfer payments. Taxes do distort incentives, but it is hard to know by how much. Tax reduction for low-income groups was an important feature of the 1969 income tax law, but that law did not change the most regressive features of federal taxation: the payroll taxes.

Why do people disagree so violently about government economic policy?

Let us now step back for an overall view of the public sector and try to isolate the sources of the intense disagreements over the rationale of government economic policy and the instruments of that policy.

Hardly anyone these days would disagree about the need for government to perform the economic functions described in Chapter 5. And everyone knows that government must regulate, spend, transfer, and tax to carry out these functions. There is intense disagreement, however, on the precise content of public sector objectives and the exact form of its policy tools. While we cannot resolve these disagreements, we can sort out some of their sources and in the process help clarify government's role in the economy.

The disagreements stem from (1) differences in opinion over the successes and failures of private enterprise; (2) differences in evaluation of the effectiveness of government regulation, government enterprise, stabilization policy, and welfare policy; (3) differences in assessment of the incidence of taxes and willingness to bear tax burdens.

It is understandable that people should disagree about the successes and failures of private enterprise. Most of us look at the world from a snail's-eye view, and when we see other people who appear no more clever or more hardworking than ourselves doing much better than we, it is easy to blame the system. But apart from that natural tendency, there are real complaints that one could bring against private enterprise. There are monopolistic tendencies and inefficiencies, for example. Private enterprise may cut costs by using public spaces as a dumping ground. Inequalities in income or in opportunities for advancement may be regarded as inequities. There are many examples of consumer deception and of discriminating against consumers by charging different prices for the same product.

All these criticisms can be lodged against private capitalism. What would a defender of the system say? He might deny them all, but then, if pressed, say, "Nothing is perfect. One must take the bad with the good and strike a balance. Even Marx said there were many good things about capitalism."

All right, but what is there on the credit side to be balanced against the debits? Private enterprise is flexible in order to make profits. Through competition, it creates incentives for technical progressiveness and efficiency – for the same purpose. Further it tends to reward owners of resources and labor according to their economic productivity. It is responsive to the demands of consumers. Even when the exact requirements of competition are not met, profit-seeking firms still try to be efficient and responsive, it is argued, and may do so more effectively than they would if competition were enforced.

Now we can perceive more clearly the sources of differences in opinion. There are both desirable and undesirable features in the system, and we must always make up our minds with imperfect knowledge. Moreover, each person differs somewhat in his balancing of the goods and the bads. Some people are more willing than others to give up some efficiency and technical progressiveness for greater income equality, if that is necessary.

The differences in evaluation of government activities are just as profound. In the United States, as well as in countries with a substantially larger government sector, the complaints about government operations are strikingly similar to those made above about private enterprise. It has been argued that because of their monopoly – created by law – government managers of the postal system, for example, do not have to respond to incentives to meet consumer demands and be efficient in the use of resources. Government workers in politically protected jobs are often not rewarded for initiative and may not have to be assiduous. Government bureaucracies are bound up with red tape, and the rules often do not respond very readily to the changing complexities of modern life. Politicians and civil servants are not wise enough to stabilize the economy or to devise and administer welfare programs which do more good than harm. The inequity of tax and transfer programs reduces individual incentives.

But we also hear arguments in favor of government production and government control. It is claimed that government enterprise can avoid the inefficiency of monopoly and the inequality of income it generates, and that government planning can avoid the mistakes of myopic individual decision making. Government civil servants can be chosen for technical expertise and not salesmanship. Centralization can increase specialization and raise efficiency. Government economic policy can stabilize the economy and prevent depressions and inflations. Tax and transfer programs can stimulate individual incentives and redistribute income toward greater equity.

Again, we suffer from a lack of knowledge in evaluating the conflicting claims and criticisms. Moreover, even if we could agree on the effects of government versus private activities, we might well disagree again on the choice among goods and evils.

That does not mean that we must give up. The coming chapters will improve tremendously our understanding of the ways in which mixed economies work. Even so, gaps in knowledge will persist, as well as differences in personal preferences. That may be a little dismaying, but it also makes life more interesting, because there are still many unsettled issues and differences to argue about.

Summary

Taxes are the major means by which resources are transferred from private to government use. The incidence of a tax indicates the person who actually bears its burden on his income. The tax incidence may be different from the taxpayer if the payer is able to shift the burden of the tax to someone else. Taxes are progressive, proportional, or regressive, depending on whether they take a larger, constant, or smaller percentage of income, as incomes rise.

Since taxes change the prices of goods for sale in markets, taxes may change or distort the choices of consumers. They may also change the effective incomes earned by labor and other resources and thus distort producers' decisions about what to produce and how to produce it.

Tax principles set certain general standards. The standards must, however, be worked out in detail for each type of tax. Generally accepted principles include: (1) Equity: Everyone agrees that taxes should be fair and reasonable but there is disagreement about what that means. The benefit principle says taxes should be apportioned according to benefits received — but benefits are often hard to identify. The ability-to-pay, or sacrifice, principle says taxes should reflect individual ability to pay or ability to sacrifice income — but that is difficult to determine. Equal treatment of equals (and unequal treatment of unequals) is consistent with both these, but again hard to implement. (2) Neutrality: Taxes should distort individual decisions on consumption and production as little as possible as long as individual choices themselves lead to "desired" ends. (3) Administrative efficacy: Taxes should be understandable, easy to collect, and adequate to the needs of the government. Actual taxes reflect social compromises among these three principles.

The federal tax system is, on the whole, progressive, mainly because of the progressive income tax and the corporate profits tax, which are the major sources of federal revenue. Inheritance and gift taxes are progressive, but not important sources of revenue. Federal payroll taxes for social security and unemployment insurance are regressive.

The state and local tax system is, on the whole, regressive because of its major dependence on property and sales taxes, which tend to take larger proportions of lower than of higher incomes. State income taxes are growing, but still minor, revenue sources.

Transfers from the federal government are a major source of funds for state governments and a smaller but growing source for local governments. State governments also make grants to local governments. Intergovernmental transfers are usually tied to specific programs and require some corresponding funds or actions by the recipient. There is a movement for tax sharing by the federal government in which revenue transfers would be made to the states with no strings attached.

Taken altogether, the federal, state, and local tax systems are regressive over most ranges of income. Offsetting this are the transfer payments and other services provided to individuals by all levels of government. These are provided in greater proportion to low-income groups. If taxes, transfer payments, and other government services are considered as a whole, the system is progressive over all income ranges.

Disagreements about the role of government in the economy stem from (1) different diagnoses of the relative successes and failures of private enterprise; (2) different evaluations of the effectiveness of government action; (3) differences over how the burden of taxes should be and is distributed. These disagreements reflect both imperfect knowledge and a different balancing of the pros and cons as they are known.

Questions for discussion and review

1. Comment on the following statement, which is the kind commonly made whenever an increase in gasoline taxes is proposed: *The 2-cent per gallon increase in the gasoline tax will only result in greater hardship for the general public. The individual driver will have to pay the extra 2 cents out of his own pocket. Truckers will pass the extra 2 cents on to consumers. So this is not a tax on the gasoline industry but on consumers.*

2. Is it true that federal income taxes become confiscatory above a certain level? Does your answer imply that federal income taxes do not have effects on the work incentives of individuals? Explain.

3. Do you think there should be sumptuary taxes on whiskey, wine, cigarettes, fur coats, marijuana?

4. Is it always bad to use taxes to distort the production decisions that would be made by private enterprise? Explain.

5. Comment on the following statement: *Tax principles are so vague that they are no help at all in designing tax policy. They are like telling a child to be good when he goes out to play, when he really should be told how to deal with particular situations.*

6. Social security is generally regarded as an important step toward greater equity in income distribution. Yet the social security taxes are regressive. How can you reconcile these two views?

7. Suppose a sales tax is imposed which exempts food, clothing, and medicines. Is such a tax always more regressive than an income tax?

8. Why is the corporate income tax important as a way of making the personal income tax effective?

Concepts for review

Shifting and incidence
Tax distortions
Progressiveness
Regressiveness
Sumptuary taxes
Horizontal equity
Vertical equity
Ability-to-pay principle
Benefit principle

7 Measurement of the economy

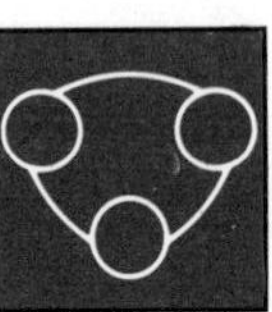

The issues involved in the overall performance of the economy are the subject matter of *macroeconomics*. This subject is concerned with the determinants of the total volume of output and income, agregate employment and unemployment, and general price movements. Macro issues are at the center of some of the great debates over tax policy, government expenditure, monetary and banking controls, and anti-inflationary measures. They are not remote issues. The unemployment statistics, for example, summarize not just numbers, but the unhappiness and frustration of individuals, women and men, who want to work and yet cannot find a job.

The macroeconomic problems of each year are different. The 1960s were touted, as the decade began, as the "super sixties" – a new era of growth and prosperity. But the decade started slowly. At first, the major economic problems were stagnation and high unemployment. In the mid-sixties, the New Economics, which we shall discuss in Chapter 10, made its popular reputation by the success of the tax and monetary policies it prescribed for those problems. After the Vietnam War began to have a major impact on the economy in 1966, the most pressing macroeconomic issues were inflation, on the one hand, and the conflicting claims of military expenditures and increasingly urgent domestic programs, on the other. A long congressional-presidential stalemate on tax policy put monetary policy at the center of the stage for several years, and there were two major "credit crunches." The 1970s started out with the unhappy combination of inflation and growing unemployment. The only safe prediction about the future is that it will bring new macroeconomic problems which will require new analyses.

Before we can take up macroeconomic analysis we must develop some new measures of economic performance. This first step is not such an absolute prerequisite in the area of microeconomics. The essential microeconomic concepts of prices, of productive resources, and of goods and services outputs are familiar parts of everyone's environment of ideas and experience. Macroeconomic analysis, however, moves away from the level of individual experience to an aggregate view. So aggregate concepts are required.

There is no point in pretending that measurement concepts are really exciting topics that will keep any conversation lively. Yet there is excitement in such questions as:

> Are we having or going to have a recession? Or are we heading for even greater inflation?
>
> Is the average standard of living rising or falling?
>
> Is the growth rate of the Soviet Union faster than that of the United States?
>
> Are we better off this year than last, or has price inflation taken away all the gains?
>
> Are the real gains in the availability of goods and services offset by a reduction in the quality of our environment?

To have a rational discussion about these questions, we must agree on what we mean by recession, inflation, and standard of living. How will we measure them? To compare growth rates, what will we measure?

The answers are not at all obvious; nor are they related to our everyday experiences. Our first task is to master these macroeconomic concepts. Then we shall turn to their use as measures of performance and will discuss their limitations as well. (The Appendix to this chapter discusses the macro accounts of the United States in detail and, for those who are not familiar with them, the principles of micro accounting.)

Macroeconomic accounts: General principles

A nation's macroeconomic accounts are a record of total output and income produced during a specific period. In the United States, the Department of Commerce makes more or less complete estimates of these accounts every three months and makes definitive estimates every year. Since national income and output accounts provide a comprehensive measure of a country's economic activity, they are the best single set of indicators of aggregate economic performance.

To get an overall initial view of macroeconomic concepts, look at the picture of the circular flow of income and output in a simple economy without a public sector, as shown in Figure 7-1. In this economy there are, on the one hand, only domestic consumers who

Figure 7-1

THE CIRCULAR FLOW OF ECONOMIC ACTIVITY IN A SIMPLE ECONOMY WITHOUT A PUBLIC SECTOR AND FOREIGN TRADE

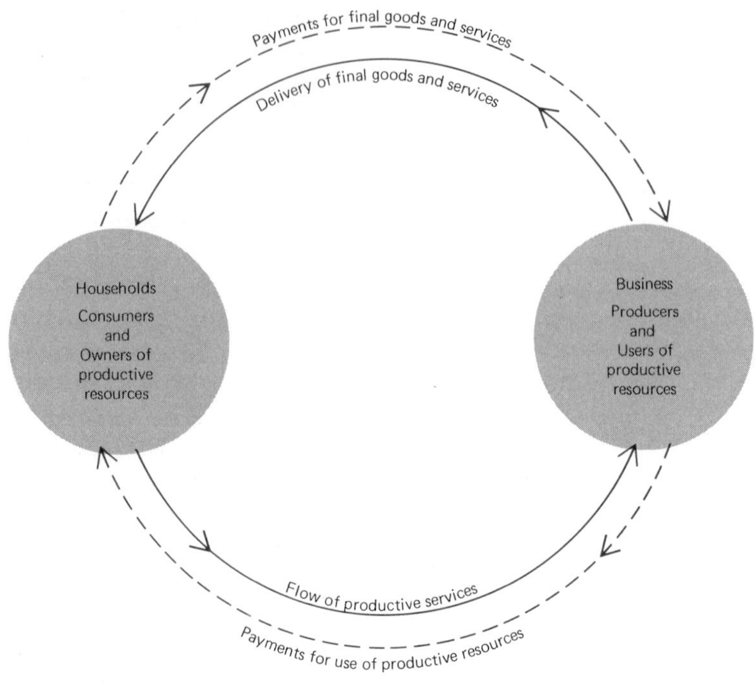

buy goods and services produced by domestic businesses. The consumers are workers and owners of land and other productive resources and they receive income payments from business for their labor and the use of their resources. On the other hand, there are the business firms which produce goods and services and sell them to consumers. They hire the labor and other resources from their owners and pay income for their use.[1]

The net national product (NNP) is the total value of final goods and services produced in the economy during each year. In the circular flow diagram of Figure 7-1, NNP is the sum total of the purchases of goods and services in the upper loop. It measures that hugely varied set of goods and services delivered by businesses to consumers: apples and oranges, bread and wine, refrigerators, television sets, and automobiles, banking and bartending, etc.

But how can we measure such a varied lot of things? Everyone knows we cannot add apples and oranges. But we can add their *values*. We get the value of apples by multiplying the quantity of apples produced by the price of apples. Then we add that to the

[1] The government sector, as well as the foreign trade sector, is left out of this simple model, and it is assumed that the only final products that businesses produce are consumer goods. We shall quickly relax these assumptions to make the accounts relevant to the real world.

value of oranges. We do this for all the goods and services the economy produces. The total is net national product.

In effect, to calculate the NNP, instead of adding up physical quantities of goods and services, we total up a *price-weighted* sum: (price of apples × quantity of apples) + (price of oranges × quantity of oranges) + (price of refrigerators × quantity of refrigerators) + etc. That is why the NNP is sometimes called "net national product at market prices." As we shall see in Chapter 23, competitive market prices have the special virtue of indicating the relative desirability of additional amounts of the various goods and services. Thus, if oranges cost 75 cents a dozen and apples 50 cents, it means that typically consumers act as if an extra orange were about 50 percent more desirable than an extra apple. The multiplication of quantities by market prices has the effect of giving each good a relative weight or importance which reflects the relative preferences for additional amounts of the good. Now we move on to the lower loop in the circular flow diagram.

The national income (NI) is the sum of all the income in all forms which is earned during the year. That seems clear enough, and it is, if we are careful to be comprehensive and yet not include things that should not be included.

First, the criteria of income should be kept in mind: Income arises from the performance of some kind of productive service—from individual labor, from natural resources, or from capital goods—and, in this definition, includes profits. Second the annual national income is the sum of *earnings*, including profits whether or not they are actually paid out. Social security *deductions* from paychecks, for example, are part of income, but are not paid out. So are undistributed corporate profits.

Suppose we insert a measuring instrument, like a water meter which measures the total flow volume, into the flow of income. The meter sums up the total of payments actually made. Is the sum of these payments the national income? Not quite. First, it will miss those earnings whose payment is delayed. Second, it will catch current payments of income that may have been actually earned a year or more ago. We need something like a geiger counter, which detects the existence of radioactivity and can measure it even though it is not visible. If we could put a radioactive tracer on all income, paid or not, our geiger counter could cumulate all those traces and provide the desired measure of national income.

The national income measures the *total annual flow* of productive services. There are many kinds of such services: skilled labor and unskilled labor, warehouse storage and factory space, the hours of operation of computer processing machines and milk-bottling machines. The services are not themselves commensurable, so we add up their values, which can be obtained by multiplying the amount of the service by the price of the service. The full name given to the national income concept is "national income at factor prices," because income is composed of payments to factors of production plus profits.

We have seen that the level of economic activity can be measured at two points in the circular flow: as net national product and as national income. Will we obtain different answers, depending on where we measure? It would be disturbing if it were so, but fortunately it is not. The final stage in establishing the foundations of macroeconomic accounting is to understand this equivalence: *The national product and the national income are identical.*

There can be no earned income without the production of goods and services. And there can be no production of goods and services that does not generate income. For every dollar of output there is a dollar of income, and there are no lost or unaccounted-for dollars of either.[2]

Most of the income generated in the course of production represents explicit costs paid for the services of productive factors: labor's wages, rents on land, and interest on loans. The income item that will adjust to make the value of output equal income is profits. Profits automatically take on whatever value they must take on to make NNP and NI the same. Suppose, for example, that a business operates for a year, produces a lot of final products, and pays out salaries and wages, rents, and interest, and then finds that it cannot sell the goods at prices that will cover costs. The income payments have been made, but the value of output cannot cover those payments. That seems to upset the identity of national income and net national product. We won't get rattled, however. We will just reduce profits by whatever amount is necessary to maintain the income-product identity. This helps explain why we have included profits in our national income accounts. Profits are the residual income item which adjusts as necessary to make the income and product measurements equal. It may be either a positive or a negative figure — a plus or minus.[3]

The equivalence of national income and net national product is in one sense a simple accounting identity. It is, in addition, an important insight into the structure of any economy. We shall rely

[2] This can be seen most quickly in the context of a simple system like one of the model economies of Chap. 3 in which only consumer goods are produced and there is no government. In the First Model Economy, with only one factor of production and one final product, it is clear that for every dollar of output there is a dollar of income. With two factors of production, as in the Second Model Economy, the income not received by one factor must go to the other factor, and the income of both factors must sum up to total income. That really does come out to be equal to the value of the final product, and will always be so.

[3] Profits are sometimes "justified" as a payment for entrepreneurship and enterprise. We shall take up the rationale of this position in Chap. 31. Here we are concerned only with the role profits play in national income accounting. This role is an exact carryover of the accounting procedure in the individual firm. Profits are the difference between the value of a particular output and all costs associated with that output.

on it again and again as we go on to deal with some of the important issues that arise in understanding the macroeconomic accounts of a real and complex economy.

Accounting for the national product

The details of macroeconomic accounting flow in a reasonably straightforward way from its general principles. Working through some of the most important details will help fix the principles in mind and will also uncover some interesting and not-so-obvious issues of macro accounting. We will start with issues involved in the measurement of the national product and then move to the income side.

National versus geographic production

The net *national* product of the United States, or the *national* income, is defined literally as the product or income of United States "nationals," i.e., citizens and other permanent residents. The income earned on investments in the United States by a Mid-Eastern oil sheikh is part of his country's national income, not that of the United States. Likewise, the earnings by United States companies and nationals abroad are measured as part of the United States national income. For example, the profits of United States oil companies in the Arabian peninsula are part of United States income. The *geographic* income, or product, on the other hand, is that earned within the boundaries of the nation, no matter who receives it, nationals or foreigners.

The distinction is not so very important for the United States, but it is important for countries with substantial foreign investments. These are mainly relatively small countries with large exports of things like oil or copper which are developed by big foreign corporations. In Chile, for example, prior to the recent law which fully nationalized the industry, most of the copper mined was produced by companies that were jointly owned, about fifty-fifty, by Chilean government agencies and private United States corporations. Therefore, half of the net profits these companies earned from copper production in Chile was considered – in both the Chilean and the United States national accounts – to be part of the United States net national product and national income.[4]

[4] This accounting procedure should not be interpreted as either an approval or disapproval of foreign investment. It simply reflects the fact that persons living abroad have a claim on the income and product created in Chile. It illustrates once again the dependence of accounting conventions on other types of institutions. When Chile nationalized the United States corporations' interests in its biggest copper mines, half of the profits which had accrued to their ownership moved from the United States national income accounts into the Chilean national income accounts.

Intermediate production versus output of final products

Suppose that for each producing unit we make a punch card that records the type and value of the unit's output of goods and services during the year. Then, at the end of the year, we run all the cards through a computer which sorts them, adds up the total value of each type of production, and computes the sum for all types of production. Will that be the net national product for the year? It *is* a kind of measure of national production, but it is not the most useful measure, because it contains a lot of *double counting.* A number of intermediate products, which are used up in the current production of other goods and services, would be counted twice, thrice, or even more often.

Suppose we instructed the computer to ring a bell every time it recognized on a punch card some output that it had previously added to the totals. We would have a lot of ringing!

The wool in the suit we bought in the store was recorded previously (1) as an output of the farm on which the sheep were raised, (2) as cloth produced in the textile mill, and (3) as a garment sewn in a clothing factory. Each of these stages is an *intermediate* one.

The value of output of each stage of production is shown in a hypothetical example in Table 7-1. If the computer were instructed to record only the "final product," it would skip over all the stages until the last one and record the value of the suit as sold in the store. If we included the output of each intermediate stage, the sum of column 2, we would be counting the same inputs several times.

Notice that the value of the final product at the store is the same as the total at the bottom of column 4 labeled "value added." Both are $50. *Value added at each stage of production is the difference between the value of goods sold and the value of the intermediate goods purchased.* The *sum* of the value added at each stage is equal to the value of the final product. So we could also

Table 7-1

VALUE OF OUTPUT AT EACH STAGE OF PRODUCTION

1 *Producing unit*	2 *Value of output at each stage*	3 *Cost of material input at each stage*	4 *Value added (column 2 minus column 3)*
Farm	$ 10	$ 0	$10
Textile mill	20	10	10
Clothing factory	40	20	20
Store	**50**	40	10
Total	$120	$70	**$50**

program our computer to sum up the value added at each stage of production and obtain the net national product in that way.

Suppose the clothing factory bought the textile mill and combined their accounts. We would lose some intermediate output in our total, though nothing essential would be changed in the economy. That is one reason why the total value of intermediate products plus final products (column 2) is an unreliable measure of economic activity. In the United States as a whole the gross value of expenditures on intermediate products is roughly equal to expenditures on final products. So the value of intermediate plus final products is twice the value of final ouput.

It is clear that the suit we buy in the store is a final product, but in general, how do we know a final product when we see one? Final products are goods and services that are not going to be resold, but are going to be enjoyed and used by the purchaser during the year. We shall identify their major categories when we turn to the detailed accounting.

Price deflation for real comparisons of net national product

We would like to use annual totals to measure overall changes in output and income from year to year. If we think a moment, however, we realize that it is not just physical quantities of the final products which change from year to year. Prices also change. The price weights in the national product are both a blessing and a curse. We cannot do without them, because we could otherwise not add up output values. But we cannot fix them absolutely either. In fact, we do not want to fix them because, as we have argued before, prices are the indicators of the relative desirability of goods. Prices must be free to vary in order to signal whatever changes are occurring.

Suppose there is a general inflation, and all prices increase. Or more rarely, there may be deflation, and all prices will decrease. Then our NNP yardstick will expand or contract, independently of changes in the real production of goods and services, as a result of overall price changes. Since we can easily confuse real changes in the production of goods and services with general price changes, the sophisticated NNP watcher always looks for the "deflated" estimate of annual NNP as well as the current-price NNP.

To obtain the deflated estimate, we must first measure the average price change from some "base year" – an arbitrary starting point from which to measure price changes. In most United States national income accounts, 1958 is used as the base year for price measurements. Suppose prices have gone up by, say, 40 percent since then. They are 140 percent of 1958 prices. Comparing the present net national product in current prices with the 1958 NNP measured in 1958 prices would overstate the true change in the output of goods and services. Part of the change would simply reflect a general change in prices. But if we *divide* present NNP in

Figure 7-2

NET NATIONAL PRODUCT MEASURED IN CURRENT AND CONSTANT PRICES (BILLIONS OF DOLLARS)

Note the effect of rapidly rising prices in the last half dozen years. NNP measured in current prices has risen rapidly, while NNP in constant prices has gone up more slowly, and even fell slightly in 1970. (Source: U.S. Department of Commerce, Office of Business Economics.)

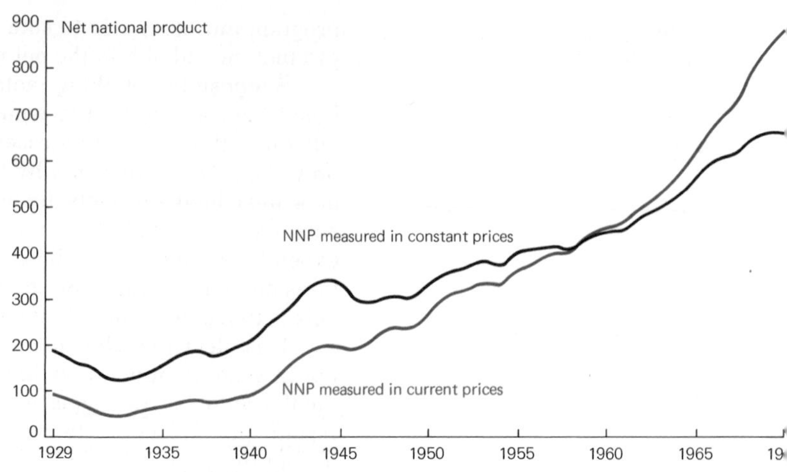

current prices by 1.40 (i.e., 140 percent), we can deflate current national product. This deflation procedure eliminates the effects of inflation in comparing current and 1958 NNPs or in any other year-to-year comparison.

Figure 7-2 shows the progress of the NNP of the United States in the last forty years as measured in the current prices of each year. That is often called "money NNP." Also shown is the NNP for each year after it has been deflated for price changes, using 1958 as the base year. This is usually referred to as "real NNP" or "constant-dollar NNP."

National production versus national expenditure on final goods and services

Net national product and national income refer to the final products produced by nationals and to the income earned in production. Total *expenditures* on final goods and services are often easier to measure and analyze than total *production*, and the two concepts are not necessarily the same. Expenditures are made not only for goods produced by nationals but also for imported goods produced by foreigners. For example, total wine purchases within the United States include those for French and Chilean as well as domestic wines. Electric turbogenerators installed in the United States are bought from English as well as United States producers. Similarly, part of our national production is exported to foreign buyers. In the total national product accounts, we want to measure only the expenditures on domestic production. On the other hand, we can include all expenditures — on both foreign and domestically produced goods and services — *if* we then subtract total expenditures on imports. To get the distinction, look at the following definitions.

$$NNP \equiv \text{total expenditures on nationally produced final products}$$

$$NNP \equiv (\text{total expenditures on nationally produced final products} + \text{total expenditures on imported goods}) - (\text{total expenditures on imported goods})$$

In the second definition, the expenditures on imports are first included as part of total expenditures and then are subtracted. It is clear that total net national product is left unchanged.[5]

When we take an expenditure approach to NNP, we run into several possible sources of error. One is the danger of omitting some types of final products for which there is no expenditure. A traditional example is the produce that farmers grow and consume themselves. In a specialized, highly market-oriented agricultural sector, such as our own, this is a relatively minor item. But if it were left out of the macroeconomic accounts of India, where a large part of the agricultural sector is still self-sufficient, it would be a major omission. A more important example in the United States is the output of *owner-occupied* housing. If a family rents a house, the rental payments are part of the national product. If the family owns the house, the building is still providing housing services, which should be included in the national product. And they are, by means of a special estimate of the rental value of owner-occupied housing.

Many nonmarketed services are left out of the national income accounts, more or less arbitrarily or because their value is difficult to estimate. The most important of these is, surely, the services of housewives. They do a lot of the nation's cleaning, sewing, cooking, baby-sitting, nursing, shopping, etc. When business firms and other individuals provide such services, their value goes into the national income accounts. When housewives provide the services, they are left unaccounted for. Is that a result of male chauvinism? Maybe so. But men perform some unaccounted-for services as well in "do-it-yourself" activities around the house. Since there are no dollar transactions involved, it is hard to estimate the value of all such services with any precision and that is the major reason for leaving them out.

The exclusion of capital gains (and losses)

When we shift from measuring production to measuring expenditure, we open up a second possible source of error. So let us recognize it here and then close that Pandora's box. *Expenditures and receipts are not part of NNP and NI unless they are for currently produced goods and services.*

Suppose that your friend sold the stamp collection he had been accumulating since he was ten years old. He came by and told

[5] The three lines indicate an identity or definition.

you that he figured it had cost him $500 and, since he sold it for $1,000, he had made $500 on it. Is that $500 part of the net national product for the year?

Somebody has spent $1,000 on the stamp collection, which is $500 more than your friend spent for it. But it does not meet the test of representing current production of goods and services. Those stamps are little pieces of paper whose prices have risen, on the one hand, because of a fixed supply and, on the other, because of increased demand as more and more people are collecting stamps.

Many types of expenditures do not involve current production. These include not only purchases of stamp collections, but purchases of many other types of property: real estate, stocks and bonds, and oil paintings. If prices have risen, the sellers sometimes make gains on the transactions. These are called *capital gains*. If sales are made at lower than original prices, there may be *capital losses*. Neither should be included in the net national product or national income.

The components of NNP

Macroeconomic accounts must be estimated from detailed, microeconomic data. For the estimation procedure and – as we shall see later – for analytical purposes, it is useful to categorize final products and expenditures on them according to use and purchaser. The following distinctions are helpful:

Consumption expenditures by consumers for their own use and enjoyment

Investment goods purchased by private business for the production of future goods and services

Government purchases of good and services of all kinds

Exports purchased to be sent abroad

Imports purchased from foreign producers

Consumption expenditures, C, include purchases of both durable and nondurable goods and a wide variety of services to be enjoyed now and in the future. Consumers purchase the goods and services for that purpose and not to realize a gain from their resale, though that occasionally happens.

Investment expenditures, I, are more complicated. These are purchases of *newly* produced capital goods – plant, machines, and equipment – which will be used for future production. These expenditures also include *additions* to the inventory stocks of goods in warehouses and factories which will be used for future production or will be sold in the future. These are all included in *investment goods*.

Should investment goods and services be considered part of the total of final production, or should they be considered intermediate goods? The fact that new capital goods and new inventories are produced means that the resources used in their production are not used to produce consumption goods for current use. In effect, current consumption is postponed in order to have greater productive potential in the future. It is true that one purpose of an economic system is to make people happy by providing them with goods and services *now*. But life goes on, and we will also value consumption goods in the future. Investment goods that contribute to future consumption are thus final products and are different from intermediate products, which are currently used up.

The total purchases of new capital goods and additions to inventories are called *gross investment*. Some of the total investment purchases are for replacement of worn-out capital goods, however, and some are for the creation of new productive capacity. The latter is called *net investment*. The difference between total or gross investment and net investment is *depreciation, D*. Net investment is always identically equal to gross investment minus depreciation. Depreciation is not income to anyone. It is an estimate of the amount of investment necessary to maintain the capital stock. (This is an important idea to which we return in a few paragraphs.)

Government expenditures on goods and services, *G*, include all expenditures by federal, state, and local governments. Government budgets encompass an enormous variety of items: They include the wages and salaries of government employees as well as large quantities of military equipment, postage meters, scratch pads, canned soup, etc. Most of the goods and services are purchased from private producers. Actual *production* by government agencies is a relatively minor item.

Government *transfer payments* must *not* be included in the national product totals. Transfer payments include social security payments, unemployment insurance, and welfare payments. The critical distinction is that they are not payments for current productive activity. Interest payments on government debt are also excluded from the national income and product accounts on the ground that they do not represent payments for current productive activity.

Exports, E, are likewise a mixed bag of goods; all types of things are purchased by foreign nationals for use abroad. The United States exports not only sophisticated machines and electronic equipment, but also a lot of agricultural commodities and industrial raw materials, such as wheat, coal, and lumber.

Imports, M, must be subtracted from the total of all these expenditures to obtain the NNP. Imports include many types of private consumption goods and services, as well as investment goods and government purchases of goods and services. They have already been included in the expenditure categories and must now be taken out in order to measure only national production.

Gross and net national product

The gross national product, GNP, is the sum of the production of all final goods and services, including all investment, whether for net new additions to plant and equipment and inventories or for goods that offset depreciation. It is

$$\text{GNP} \equiv C + I + G + E - M$$

The net national product, NNP, is obtained from GNP by subtracting an estimate of depreciation, D:

$$\text{NNP} \equiv \text{GNP} - D$$

While NNP is, in a sense, a more fundamental concept than GNP, it is much harder to measure accurately. The investment goods coming out of the factories are not labeled "new investment" and "to offset depreciation." To obtain the net investment figure, we first have to estimate depreciation and then subtract this rather chancy estimate from a much more accurate estimate of total production of investment goods and inventory accumulation. Remember that, in principle, depreciation is the amount by which the capital stock is used up or deteriorates; it is, therefore, the amount of investment that is necessary to maintain the capital stock. But who knows exactly how much a machine or a building is used up or deteriorates in a year? We can do better in estimating the amount by which inventories run down. All in all, the depreciation estimate is none too reliable. Because of this, GNP is the more commonly used estimate on the product side. In any case, GNP and NNP move along closely together. Table 7-2 presents the components of GNP for several recent years, including a special breakdown of investment expenditures.

A resume of the national product accounts

The national product concepts are not really very complicated, but there are some potential pitfalls. Remember the definition: NNP is the total annual expenditure on nationally produced final goods and services. Consider the following propositions:

> Not all expenditure is on current production.
>
> Not all current production is included in the net national product.
>
> Not all of the net national product is included in the total expenditure on final products.

If the paradoxes in these statements can be sorted out, some of the most troublesome aspects of the national product concepts will have been mastered.

The first distinction points out that there is a lot of buying and selling of things other than goods and services produced in the

Table 7-2

GROSS NATIONAL PRODUCT BY TYPE OF EXPENDITURE, 1968–1970 (BILLIONS OF DOLLARS)

	1968		*1969*		*1970**	
	Current dollars	*Percent*	*Current dollars*	*Percent*	*Current dollars*	*Percent*
Gross national product	865.0	100.0	931.4	100.0	976.8	100.0
Personal consumption expenditures	535.8	62.0	577.5	62.0	616.8	63.1
Gross private domestic investment	126.5	14.6	139.8	15.0	135.8	13.9
Fixed investment	118.9		131.4		132.2	
Nonresidential	88.7		99.3		102.6	
Residential	30.3		32.0		29.7	
Change in business inventories	7.6		8.5		3.6	
Net exports of goods and services	2.5	0.3	1.9	0.2	3.6	0.4
Exports	50.6		55.5		62.3	
Imports	48.1		53.6		58.7	
Government purchases of goods and services	200.2	23.1	212.2	22.8	220.5	22.6
Federal	99.5		101.3		99.7	
National defense	78.0		78.8		76.6	
Other	21.5		22.6		23.1	
State and local	100.7		110.8		120.8	

*Provisional.
Note: Subtotals may not add to totals because of rounding.
Source: U.S. Department of Commerce, Office of Business Economics.

current accounting period. These include real estate, used and secondhand items, and, perhaps, valuable antiques. In the process, capital gains or losses may be incurred by the seller, but these transactions do not go into the national product accounts.

The second statement refers to the distinction between intermediate products, which do not go into the net national product, and final products, which do.

The last apparent paradox is resolved by recognizing that there is some current production of final goods and services for which there is no corresponding expenditure. The services of owner-occupied housing, for example. The proposition might also remind us that some of the expenditure on final products is for imported goods, which we have to subtract in arriving at NNP.

The components of the national accounts on the income side

In actually preparing national accounts, we must modify the principle of the equality of NNP and NI slightly because of "indirect" taxes. These are taxes which are paid on goods and services when they are sold and which never get into any private business or individual pocket as income. They include state and local sales taxes and federal excise taxes, such as the tax on new cars. These taxes make the value of the sales of final goods and services higher than the total income earned in their production. In effect, the amount of the sales and excise taxes is included as part of the value of the goods, but not in income. To get NI from NNP, therefore, we must subtract indirect taxes, Ind.T.:

$$\text{NI} \equiv \text{NNP} - \text{Ind.T.}$$[6]

Since NNP $\equiv$ GNP $-$ Depreciation, we can define NI as:

$$\text{NI} \equiv \text{GNP} - \text{D} - \text{Ind.T.}$$

We pointed out in the discussion of the basic national income concept that NI is the sum of all types of income: wages and salaries, *w*, rent, *r*, interest, *i*, and profits, *p*. These distinctions are useful and important. Yet for proprietorships and partnerships, i.e., "self-owned" businesses, it is often difficult to distinguish these components. So we simply record all the income of such firms in one component: income of unincorporated enterprise. We abbreviate it as *iue*. Profits, *p*, are then just those of corporate enterprise earned from producing goods and services. Adding up all the income components, we get:

$$\text{NI} \equiv w + r + i + p + iue$$

Table 1-1 in Chapter 1 presents the national income as the sum of factor payments for some recent years.

Disposable and personal income

National income, which is the sum of all the incomes that are *earned* and accrue in production, whether or not they are paid, is the most fundamental income concept in the national accounts. But

[6] Strictly speaking, business transfer payments to be described below must also be subtracted.

it is not the most useful one for all purposes, because NI does not measure the annual flow of new purchasing power available for individuals to spend. There are two explanations for the disparity: Some of the earned income is not paid out and retained by individuals, and some of the regular payments that are made to individuals do not represent returns for productive services.

The *disposable income* concept, DI, measures the annual flow of new purchasing power available to individuals. We obtain it by (1) subtracting from NI that part which is not actually paid out for individual use, though it is earned, and (2) adding those regular payments to individuals which do not reflect current production of goods and services.

The earned income that is not paid out or retained for individual use consists mainly of various taxes: corporate profits taxes, social insurance payments, such as those for old age and unemployment insurance, and personal income taxes. Corporate profits that are "undistributed" or not paid out are also not available for individual spending. Other payroll deductions, such as payments on a pension fund, deductions to buy United States bonds, and health insurance deductions, are considered part of disposable income, which is available for spending. These deductions represent a voluntary decision on the part of income earners. Social security payments, on the other hand, are taxes and, therefore, involuntary deductions.

Undistributed corporate profits are part of the income accruing to individuals, and the individual stockholder may agree that all corporate profits should not be paid out, just as he might agree with the social security law. Since undistributed corporate profits can be withheld even without a stockholder's consent, however, there is again an involuntary element.

Personal income taxes are not available for spending by individuals. Ordinarily, they are deducted or withheld automatically. If they are not, they must be paid regularly in any case and are not available for spending.

On the other hand, some types of regular payments to individuals do not reflect current production of goods and services. These are called "unearned income." The most important are government transfer payments. For example, an elderly person receives a social security check or a poor family receives welfare assistance. Neither payment is for current productive services. Yet these transfers are an important part of the total flow of new purchasing power.

Business transfer payments are a minor unearned-income item. They include the voluntary gifts corporations make – for college scholarships, for example – and the involuntary losses businesses suffer when consumers default on business debt.

The last major item of unearned income is the interest paid by government on its debt and interest on loans to consumers. There is some controversy about whether these items ought or ought not to be considered earned income along with other interest payments.

The usual convention is that they should not be, though they are part of the annual flow of purchasing power.

In summary:

Disposable income ≡ national income
minus corporate profits taxes
minus undistributed corporate profits
minus personal income taxes
minus social insurance payments
plus government transfer payments
plus business transfer payments
plus government interest payments

Table 7-3

RELATION OF INCOME AND PRODUCT CONCEPTS (BILLIONS OF DOLLARS)

	1968	*1969*	*1970**
Gross national product	865.0	931.4	976.8
Less: Depreciation	74.0	78.9	84.3
Equals: Net national product	791.1	852.5	892.4
Less: Indirect business taxes and business transfer payments plus subsidies†	78.4	83.0	91.4
Equals: National income	712.7	769.5	801.0
Less: Corporate profits tax	40.6	42.7	37.9
Less: Undistributed corporate profits‡	21.6	18.5	14.3
Less: Social insurance payments	47.1	53.6	57.1
Plus: Government transfer payments	55.7	61.6	73.9
Plus: Business transfer payments	3.3	3.5	3.6
Plus: Government interest payments§	26.3	29.0	31.8
Equals: Personal income	688.7	748.9	801.0
Less: Personal income taxes	97.5	117.3	116.4
Equals: Disposable income	591.2	631.6	684.7
Less: Consumption expenditures	550.8	594.0	634.7
Equals: Personal saving	40.4	37.6	50.0

*Provisional.
†This also includes a small allowance for a statistical discrepancy and net returns on government enterprise.
‡Profits due to adjustment of inventory prices have been subtracted.
§This includes a small amount of interest paid by individuals on consumer loans.
Note: Government transfer payments to individuals are larger than social insurance payments to government. Transfer payments to individuals run between 9 percent and 10 percent of disposable income. Subtotals may not add to total amounts because of rounding.
Source: U.S. Department of Commerce, Office of Business Economics.

In the following chapters, when we begin to analyze the determinants of individual spending, we shall find DI a particularly useful concept.

Unfortunately, disposable income is hard to estimate as frequently as the macro account watcher would like, mainly because of the difficulty in finding out what current personal income taxes are. Reasonably good estimates can be made of all the other components of personal income on a monthly basis. So another income concept is defined: personal income, PI. It is simply DI plus personal income taxes:

PI ≡ DI plus personal income taxes

or

PI ≡ national income	minus	corporate profits taxes
	minus	undistributed corporate profits
	minus	social insurance payments
	plus	government transfer payments
	plus	business transfer payments
	plus	government interest payments

Table 7-3 relates personal income and disposable income to national income, net national product, and gross national product.

A resume of the accounts on the income side

We can summarize most of the issues involved in measuring the national income accurately by again posing three apparent paradoxes and relating them to the definition: NI is the sum of all income earned during the year.

Not all the money people receive is income.

Not all the income people earn is received.

Not all the income people receive is in the form of money.

The first statement makes the fundamental distinction between money and income. Money is the *means* of carrying out many kinds of transactions and serves other purposes as well. It can be used in paying income. It can also be used in purchasing property and stocks and bonds and in repaying loans and making gifts, none of which represent earned income.

The second statement distinguishes between income earned and income paid out and received. Undistributed corporate profits are earned but not received. Royalties earned by an author but not paid during the current year represent income earned but not received.

The last seeming paradox recognizes that some kinds of income are not paid in money. Suppose you get a job as a salesman and are allowed the full use of a car. The car is necessary for making your business calls during the day. But if you can also use it at night and on weekends, you will not have to buy a car of your own. The off-hours availability of the car makes the job more attractive. You may well be willing to accept somewhat lower commissions than another job without a car would pay. So the off-hours availability of the car is like income to you.

The uses of income

We shall later be interested in the ways income is used, so it is convenient to extend our definition making here. Part of individual income, that part which we have labeled *C*, is spent on consumption goods and services. The part that is left over is personal saving, *PS*. Notice that personal saving is not the number of dollars in savings banks, in time deposits, or in bonds; nor is it the amount that is added to any of these categories during a year. It is a residual: the amount that is not spent on consumer goods. Personal consumption and saving in recent years are shown on the last two lines of Table 7-3.

Suppose that we return for a moment to a simple model economy in which there is no government, and thus no transfer payments or taxes, or foreign sector, and suppose further that there is no depreciation and that corporations always pay out the full amount of their earnings. Then:

$$\text{NNP} \equiv \text{NI} \equiv \text{DI} \equiv C + S$$

In these circumstances:

$$\text{NNP} \equiv C + I$$

Then $C + S \equiv C + I$, or $S \equiv I$.

That is, when we do our yearly income accounting carefully, saving must always be equal to investment. Why must it be so? Because the concepts have been defined to make it so. Anybody can make up his own definitions, of course, and the burden is still here to demonstrate that the definitions are going to be useful.[7] But

[7] If we leave the simple model and put government and the foreign sector back into the picture and allow for undistributed business income, the essential definition does not change. Still $\text{NNP} \equiv C + I + G + E - M$, and $\text{NNP} \equiv \text{NI} - \text{Ind.T.}$ The last definition can be rewritten, using the earlier relationship between NI and DI, and $\text{DI} \equiv C + PS$.

$$C + I + G + E - M \equiv NNP \equiv C + PS + \text{corporate taxes} + \text{personal taxes} + \text{Ind.T.} + \text{undistributed corporate profits} - \text{transfers}$$

Collecting terms:

$I =$ (Ind.T. + corporate taxes + personal taxes $-$ G) + (undistributed corporate profits) + (PS) + $(M - E)$

Or $I =$ government saving + business saving + personal saving + foreign saving

with these so far plausible definitions, that is how it will come out.

Summary

In macroeconomic analysis, we need measurement concepts that can be used to describe the overall workings of the economy. The net national product, NNP, of the economy is the total value of final goods and services produced during the year. The national income, NI, is the sum of all the income which is earned during the year. NI includes profits as well. The profits item adjusts and takes on whatever value is necessary to make NNP equal NI. (In any real economy there are indirect taxes which are part of the selling price of output but which are paid directly to government and never become income to anyone. So $\text{NNP} - \text{Ind.T.} \equiv \text{NI}$.)

The net national product leaves out that income which is produced in the country but which accrues to nonresidents; it includes income earned abroad by United States residents, however. To eliminate double counting, NNP also leaves out production of intermediate goods. If NNP is computed by adding up all the expenditures on final products, including foreign-produced goods, then expenditures on imports must be subtracted. NNP and NI must exclude those transactions which do not involve production of goods and services. Thus, capital gains and losses realized on resales of goods are excluded.

Prices are involved in an essential way in the national product and income totals. Multiplying dissimilar goods and services by their prices makes it possible to add up total values of output and income. When the entire price level changes, however, the change in the value of NNP can be misleading, because it does not reflect a change in real output, but only a change in price level. It is customary, therefore, to compute a deflated value of NNP. That is calculated by dividing the money value of NNP measured in current prices by the percentage index of prices measured from the base year which is used as a reference point. The resulting real net national product reflects only the change in the actual production of final goods and services.

In preparing the NNP and NI accounts, economists attempt to be comprehensive by estimating important components for which there are no readily available market-determined values, such as the rental value of owner-occupied housing. On the other hand, many useful activities, such as housewives' services, are not accounted for.

The components of NNP are distinguished by their uses and purchasers. Consumption goods, C, are purchased by private indi-

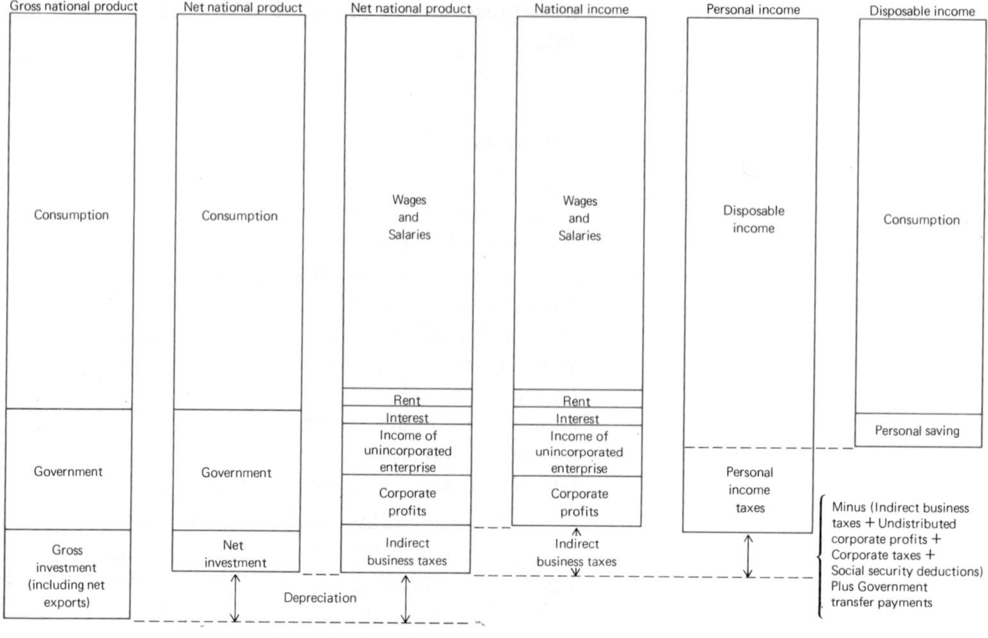

Figure 7-3

COMPONENTS AND RECONCILIATION OF INCOME AND PRODUCT CONCEPTS

viduals for their own use. Investment goods, I, are purchased by businesses as additions to inventory and as new capital plant and equipment to produce other goods and services. Government purchases of goods and services are included in G, and all exports in E. Imports, M, have to be subtracted from all expenditures. If all investment expenditures are included in I, then $C + I + G + E + M$ is the GNP, gross national product. When only net, new investment is added to the other components, the sum is NNP. Depreciation, D, is the difference between all investment expenditures on goods, called gross investment, and net investment. Depreciation is an estimate of the amount by which the capital stock has worn out or deteriorated.

National income, NI, is NNP minus indirect taxes, Ind.T. The national income is the sum of all types of earned income, including profits. Since it is difficult to disentangle the components of the income of unincorporated enterprise, it is added as a total, *iue*. Thus NI is the sum of wages, *w*, rents, *r*, interest, *i*, *iue*, and profits, *p*. Disposable income, DI, measures the purchasing power available to individuals for spending. Therefore, to get to DI, we must subtract from NI that income which is earned but not paid out and add in transfer payments which are not earned in return for productive services but do add to purchasing power.

The following definitions summarize the accounts:

$$\text{GNP} \equiv \text{NNP} + D$$

$$\text{NNP} \equiv \text{NI} + \text{Ind.T.}$$

$$NI \equiv w + r + i + iue + p$$

$$\begin{aligned} DI \equiv NI &- \text{corporate taxes} - \text{undistributed corporate profits} \\ &- \text{social security and other payroll taxes} \\ &- \text{personal income taxes} + \text{transfer payments} \end{aligned}$$

These definitions are shown graphically in Figure 7-3, at the top of page 140.

Questions for discussion and review

1. Explain the fundamental equivalence of national income and national product and the role of profits in maintaining that equivalence.

2. How is the NNP deflated for price changes when prices go down, say, by 10 percent?

3. If the receipt of capital gains makes someone better off, why aren't capital gains included in national income?

4. What is the difference between intermediate products and final products?

5. Can you think of any examples of income and output which are produced but not bought and sold other than those described in the chapter?

6. What would it mean if net investment were less than depreciation?

7. Why is disposable income a useful concept?

8. Demonstrate the definitional steps that result in the identity of measured saving and investment.

Concepts for review

Value added

Net national product at market prices

Real NNP in constant dollars

Disposable income

National income at factor prices

Net investment

Transfer payments

Personal saving

Appendix: Micro accounting and the official United States macro accounts

The logic of national income accounting is based on the logic of accounting at the microeconomic level of the firm and the individual household. While it is not necessary to learn micro accounting techniques to master the macroeconomic accounts, some familiarity with them can be helpful. Moreover, familiarity with accounting for the firm will help in later chapters, such as Chapters 14 and 15 where the operation of the banking system and the behavior of the firm are studied.

The balance sheet and the income, or profit and loss, statement are the two fundamental accounting tools. The balance sheet is understood best as a straightforward statement of the condition of a business firm *at a specific instant of time:*

Assets minus Liabilities = a residual called Net Worth

Assets are all the things the firm owns which have value. Typically, they include physical facilities of plant and equipment and inventories of materials and finished products. They may also include pieces of paper, stocks and bonds, or IOUs of individuals, which represent claims on corporations and/or persons. Liabilities are all the claims on the firm held by other businesses or persons or by government, except the claim of ownership of the firm itself. The value of the latter is reflected in Net Worth. That is simply what is left over after all the liabilities are subtracted from the value of all the assets.

The balance sheet equation is typically arranged in tabular form as shown in Table 7-4 in a hypothetical balance sheet.

Most of the items on the balance sheet are revealed by their names. But there is a certain amount of accounting jargon which one must learn to really be able to read a statement. The difference between current and fixed assets is that the firm expects to hold or turn over the former in a year or less and to own the latter for a longer period. A "sinking fund" is a group of assets, usually readily convertible into cash, which are set aside for a particular purpose. Depreciation is an estimate of the loss in value of the fixed plant and equipment since its original purchase. Estimates of deprecia-

Table 7-4

TYPICAL BALANCE SHEET OF A MANUFACTURING FIRM, DECEMBER 31, 1971

Assets			*Liabilities*		
Current			Current		
Cash		$ 20,000	Accounts		
Inventory		35,000	payable	$ 15,000	
Sinking fund		25,000	Tax reserve	5,000	
Fixed			Bank note	50,000	
Plant and equipment			Long term		
Original cost	750,000		Bonds	200,000	
			Total		270,000
Minus depreciation	300,000		*Net Worth*		
		450,000	Stock	200,000	
Intangible			Surplus	110,000	
Patents		50,000	Total		310,000
Total		$580,000	Total		$580,000

tion occupy a lot of the time and attention of accountants, who try to reduce the unavoidably arbitrary elements in its calculation. Intangible assets are things like patents or "goodwill" which are hard to sell and, therefore, hard to value. On the liability side, the "tax reserve" is a useful reminder that although a "reserve" may sound like an asset, when it turns up on a balance sheet it is a liability. Under net worth the value of the firm's stock which is outstanding is carried at some fixed, nominal figure. One should never make the mistake of thinking that it is calculated from the latest quotation on a stock market. Since the firm's outstanding stock is carried at a fixed figure and net worth is a residual which must be free to change, the item which does the changing is the surplus. That is a potentially misleading name too. Just think of it as the residual item on the balance sheet.

It is important to understand that the balance sheet is really just an equation and always must be. That will help make clear the rationale of "double-entry" bookkeeping. If you make just one change in an equation, it is no longer an equation. An offsetting change is necessary to maintain the equality. If any asset is changed up or down in any way, then something else must also change or the left-hand side will no longer balance the right-hand side. The something else may be a change in some other asset, or in the liabilities, or in net worth. If, for example, the firm spends $10,000 of its cash for a machine, it has $10,000 less in cash on the asset side but $10,000 more in machines. If it spends $10,000 paying off a tax bill or a bill for materials owed to another firm, it has $10,000 less in cash on the asset side, but also $10,000 less in liabilities. If the firm should just give $10,000 away, say, to charity, or as a distribution of dividends to its stockholders, then the residual item in net worth, the surplus, will have to fall by a corresponding amount.

The balance sheet is a description of the composition and net amount of wealth of a firm or an individual, or it may be constructed for the country as a whole. It reflects the condition existing at a certain moment, whatever the date on the balance sheet. It is a snapshot, not a history or a moving picture. Like a snapshot it is influenced by what has happened before and will indicate something of what is to come after. But it is no substitute for a history.

The income statement or profit and loss *is* a history of a special kind. It summarizes much of what has happened to a firm during a specific period of time. It too is understood best as an equation:

Revenues minus costs = a residual called profits (or losses if costs are greater than revenues)

The revenues are the amounts for which the firm sells its goods and services during the period. The total sales value is recorded whether or not the bills are actually paid in the period. Note that revenues are recorded, not actual production. Production may be more than sales and the firm will be accumulating inventories of its output. Or, if production is less than sales, the firm must be selling out of inventory.

The important trick in getting an income statement correct is to make sure that the costs which are charged against revenues are all those, but only those, associated with earning the revenues. The costs are all the charges, paid out or not, associated with producing the goods and services whose sales produced the recorded revenues. That may be different from all the payments made by the firm. Dividend payments to stockholders are not a cost, for example. Or, if the firm should buy a piece of land on which it plans to build in the future, that expenditure is not a cost of producing the goods and services whose sales are currently recorded. Other costs for which there have been no payments – unpaid bills, for example – should be included.

Again the income statement is typically arranged in a tabular form, as shown in Table 7-5. That should not, however, be allowed to obscure its essential character as an equation.

The names of the various rows are reasonably revealing. Note that the depreciation charges on the firm's plant and equipment each year are recorded as a cost of production. Even though the firm does not have to pay out any cash to meet these annual charges they are as surely a cost of doing business as any explicit expense.

The adding and subtracting of inventories is a device which ensures that only the costs of producing the goods sold are included. Suppose the closing inventory is greater than the beginning inventory. That means that some of the firm's recorded expenses during the period were to produce goods that have not been sold. That additional expense should not be charged against the revenues from the goods sold. Subtracting the amount of inventories accumulated over and above what the firm started with ensures that. If the firm's closing inventories happened to be less than its beginning inventories, then some sales were from its stock. They did not require any productive activity during the year. But the costs which had been incurred to produce them should be charged against revenues.

After the manipulation with inventories, the meaning of the other rows is fairly clear. Notice that interest on debt is a cost of operation and is subtracted to obtain before-tax earnings.

There are relations between an income statement and successive balance sheets. Depreciation charges for a particular period show up on an income statement as part of the accumulated depreciation charges on a balance sheet as of a particular date. Additions to (or subtractions from) surplus at the bottom of an income statement generate changes in the surplus item on successive balance sheets.

The income statement is the micro accounting relation which is most closely associated with the macroeconomic accounts. Those

Table 7-5

TYPICAL INCOME STATEMENT OF A MANUFACTURING FIRM (JAN. 1, 1971 THROUGH DEC. 31, 1971)

Net sales		$810,000
Less: Manufacturing cost of goods sold:		
Materials purchased during the period	$150,000	
Wages, salaries, and other labor costs	220,000	
Fuel and electricity and other miscellaneous expenses	40,000	
Depreciation charges	130,000	
Total manufacturing cost	60,000	
Add: Beginning inventory	25,000	
Subtract: Closing inventory at end of period	35,000	
Equals: Manufacturing cost of goods sold	530,000	530,000
Gross profit (or gross margin)		280,000
Less: Advertising costs	50,000	
Administrative expenses	80,000	
	130,000	130,000
Net operating profit		150,000
Less: State and local taxes (property, license fees)	20,000	
Interest charges	12,000	
	32,000	32,000
Net earnings before income taxes		118,000
Less: Corporate income taxes	59,000	
Net earnings after taxes		59,000
Less: Dividends on stocks		30,000
Additions to surplus		$ 29,000

macro accounts also reflect what has happened over a specific period. The macro accounts include measures of total output and income, which in theory and in fact are made up from the income statements of individual producing units.

Fine points in national income estimation

There are, fortunately, a group of dedicated people in the U.S. Department of Commerce who spend their lives improving the national income accounts. They receive considerable help not only from the Census Bureau, but also from other government agencies. We cannot explore all their problems, but a few issues are worth pursuing. We are concerned about fine points, not to nit-pick, but to strengthen our understanding. Some of the points are important, indeed, for they go directly to the heart of the evaluation of the system as a whole.

1. A classic question in national income accounting is to ask students to explain why, when a man marries his secretary, who nonetheless continues to do his secretarial work, the conventional measures of income and output should go down. The answer is that the conventional measures rather arbitrarily leave out certain types of nonmonetized income and output. As countries develop and societies become more specialized, household services and do-it-yourself activities decline in importance relative to those for which money payments are made. Home baking is being steadily replaced by commercial baking; home car washing is being replaced by mechanical car washing, and so on. As such activities move into the sphere of measured income and product creation, the national income figures go up, though people were washing their cars at home long before the car-wash machines were invented. These changes really do not make so much difference in the short-run measurement of ups and downs in the economy. They may well introduce substantial errors, however, in international comparisons of national income or in comparisons in the same country over long periods of time.

2. One of the great debates in national income estimation is over the treatment of government in the accounts. There are two objections to the conventional inclusion of government expenditures on goods and services. First, there is no appropriate market price at which to value many government services. The standard treatment is to value them at what it cost to supply them. But the justification for valuation given in the chapter was that market prices — not costs — reflect relative desirability. Is the cost of a stamp the correct valuation of the postal service? Should a year's grade school education be valued at its cost? Are these services worth more or less than they cost? Such questions cannot be answered unequivocally, and whether we agree or disagree with the standard procedure, we can only feel sympathy for the national income estimators in this dilemma.

The second objection to the conventional treatment of government in the accounts is that many government goods and services can be considered intermediate rather than final products. The fuel purchased by the federal government for its lighthouses is listed as a final product. But its warning services to private freighters is an input to a successful commercial voyage. This problem is not so difficult as the preceding one, however, and one can imagine a compromise that would be better than the present procedure.

3. We agreed that capital gains should not be included as part of an individual's income. What about capital gains that accrue to businesses when the prices of their inventories go up? To be consistent, we should also exclude those from the national income totals. In fact, there is an inventory-valuation adjustment made on corporate profits and the profits of unincorporated enterprise to eliminate capital gains there.

4. The rationale for using price weights to combine physical outputs in computing the national product is that, if the product markets are reasonably good, prices will indicate the relative desirability of goods and services. But what about those prices which do not indicate relative desirability, owing to government-imposed controls or some other kind of rationing procedure? In New York City, for example, there are rent controls on many apartments. Should these controlled rents be used to measure the value of housing services? Almost certainly they should not. But the adjustment process would be an exceedingly difficult one.

The number of rent-controlled apartments in New York City is not inconsiderable, but still it is small relative to the total amount of housing in the United States. That helps to justify our passing over the problem. But what should we do when nearly every significant price is a controlled one? What do the national income estimates mean then? That is a problem with which Western specialists in the economies of the Soviet Union and Eastern European countries have wrestled for many years. It becomes all the more critical when there are sharp changes in economic policy and important price "reforms."

5. To illustrate the variety of problems involved in consistent accounting, we will list a number of types of transactions and indicate briefly how they are handled in the income accounts.

Purchases of stocks and bonds: Not in income or product accounts

Commissions on purchases of stocks and bonds: In the income and product accounts

Interest on consumer debt: Not in national income but in disposable income

Interest on corporate bonds owned by foreigners: Not in income or product accounts

Interest on foreign bonds owned by United States citizens: In the income and product accounts

Illegal purchases and transactions: Not in income and product accounts

National income accounts of the United States

Aspects of the United States accounts have been presented to illustrate each of the concepts. Tables 7-6, 7-7, and 7-8 bring together some of the major accounts in a continuous series from 1929. These are measured not only in the current prices of each year but also in constant 1958 prices in order to provide comparisons in real terms. These comparative figures provide our most comprehensive picture of the nation's economic condition.

Table 7-6

GROSS NATIONAL PRODUCT OR EXPENDITURE, 1929–1970 (BILLIONS OF DOLLARS, CURRENT PRICES)

Year	Gross national product	Personal consumption	Gross private domestic investment	Net exports of goods and services	Government purchases of goods and services		
					Total	Federal	State and local
1929	103.1	77.2	16.2	1.1	8.5	1.3	7.2
1930	90.4	69.9	10.3	1.0	9.2	1.4	7.8
1931	75.8	60.5	5.6	0.5	9.2	1.5	7.7
1932	58.0	48.6	1.0	0.4	8.1	1.5	6.6
1933	55.6	45.8	1.4	0.4	8.0	2.0	6.0
1934	65.1	51.3	3.3	0.6	9.8	3.0	6.8
1935	72.2	55.7	6.4	0.1	10.0	2.9	7.1
1936	82.5	61.9	8.5	0.1	12.0	4.9	7.0
1937	90.4	66.5	11.8	0.3	11.9	4.7	7.2
1938	84.7	63.9	6.5	1.3	13.0	5.4	7.6
1939	90.5	66.8	9.3	1.1	13.3	5.1	8.2
1940	99.7	70.8	13.1	1.7	14.0	6.0	8.0
1941	124.5	80.6	17.9	1.3	24.8	16.9	7.9
1942	157.9	88.5	9.8	0.0	59.6	51.9	7.7
1943	191.6	99.3	5.7	−2.0	88.6	81.1	7.4
1944	210.1	108.3	7.1	−1.8	96.5	89.0	7.5
1945	211.9	119.7	10.6	−0.6	82.3	74.2	8.1
1946	208.5	143.4	30.6	7.5	27.0	17.2	9.8
1947	231.3	160.7	34.0	11.5	25.1	12.5	12.6
1948	257.6	173.6	46.0	6.4	31.6	16.5	15.0
1949	256.5	176.8	35.7	6.1	37.8	20.1	17.7
1950	284.8	191.0	54.1	1.8	37.9	18.4	19.5
1951	328.4	206.3	59.3	3.7	59.1	37.7	21.5
1952	345.5	216.7	51.9	2.2	74.7	51.8	22.9
1953	364.6	230.0	52.6	0.4	81.6	57.0	24.6
1954	364.8	236.5	51.7	1.8	74.8	47.4	27.4
1955	398.0	254.4	67.4	2.0	74.2	44.1	30.1
1956	419.2	266.7	70.0	4.0	78.6	45.6	33.0
1957	441.1	281.4	67.9	5.7	86.1	49.5	36.6
1958	447.3	290.1	60.9	2.2	94.2	53.6	40.6
1959	483.7	311.2	75.3	0.1	97.0	53.7	43.3
1960	503.7	325.2	74.8	4.0	99.6	53.5	46.1
1961	520.1	335.2	71.7	5.6	107.6	57.4	50.2
1962	560.3	355.1	83.0	5.1	117.1	63.4	53.7
1963	590.5	375.0	87.1	5.9	122.5	64.2	58.2
1964	632.4	401.2	94.0	8.5	128.7	65.2	63.5
1965	684.9	432.8	108.1	6.9	137.0	66.9	70.1
1966	749.9	466.3	121.4	5.3	156.8	77.8	79.0
1967	793.9	492.1	116.6	5.2	180.1	90.7	89.4
1968	865.0	535.8	126.5	2.5	200.2	99.5	100.7
1969	931.4	577.5	139.8	1.9	212.2	101.3	110.8
1970*	976.8	616.8	135.8	3.6	220.5	99.7	120.8

*Provisional.
Source: U.S. Department of Commerce, Office of Business Economics.

Table 7-7

GROSS NATIONAL PRODUCT OR EXPENDITURE, 1929–1970 (BILLIONS OF DOLLARS, 1958 PRICES)

Year	Gross national product	Personal consumption	Gross private domestic investment	Net exports of goods and services	Government purchases of goods and services: Total	Federal	State and local
1929	203.6	139.6	40.4	1.5	22.0	3.5	18.5
1930	183.5	130.4	27.4	1.4	24.3	4.0	20.2
1931	169.3	126.1	16.8	0.9	25.4	4.3	21.1
1932	144.2	114.8	4.7	0.6	24.2	4.6	19.6
1933	141.5	112.8	5.3	0.0	23.3	6.0	17.3
1934	154.3	118.1	9.4	0.3	26.6	8.0	18.6
1935	169.5	125.5	18.0	−1.0	27.0	7.9	19.2
1936	193.0	138.4	24.0	−1.2	31.8	12.2	19.6
1937	203.2	143.1	29.9	−0.7	30.8	11.5	19.4
1938	192.9	140.2	17.0	1.9	33.9	13.3	20.6
1939	209.4	148.2	24.7	1.3	35.2	12.5	22.7
1940	227.2	155.7	33.0	2.1	36.4	15.0	21.4
1941	263.7	165.4	41.6	0.4	56.3	36.2	20.1
1942	297.8	161.4	21.4	−2.1	117.1	98.9	18.3
1943	337.1	165.8	12.7	−5.9	164.4	147.8	16.6
1944	361.3	171.4	14.0	−5.8	181.7	165.4	16.3
1945	355.2	183.0	19.6	−3.8	156.4	139.7	16.7
1946	312.6	203.5	52.3	8.4	48.4	30.1	18.4
1947	309.9	206.3	51.5	12.3	39.9	19.1	20.8
1948	323.7	210.8	60.4	6.1	46.3	23.7	22.7
1949	324.1	216.5	48.0	6.4	53.3	27.6	25.7
1950	355.3	230.5	69.3	2.7	52.8	25.3	27.5
1951	383.4	232.8	70.0	5.3	75.4	47.4	27.9
1952	395.1	239.4	60.5	3.0	92.1	63.8	28.4
1953	412.8	250.8	61.2	1.1	99.8	70.0	29.7
1954	407.0	255.7	59.4	3.0	88.9	56.8	32.1
1955	438.0	274.2	75.4	3.2	85.2	50.7	34.4
1956	446.1	281.4	74.3	5.0	85.3	49.7	35.6
1957	452.5	288.2	68.8	6.2	89.3	51.7	37.6
1958	447.3	290.1	60.9	2.2	94.2	53.6	40.6
1959	475.9	307.3	73.6	0.3	94.7	52.5	42.2
1960	487.7	316.1	72.4	4.3	94.9	51.4	43.5
1961	497.2	322.5	69.0	5.1	100.5	54.6	45.9
1962	529.8	388.4	79.4	4.5	107.5	60.0	47.5
1963	551.0	353.3	82.5	5.6	109.6	59.5	50.1
1964	581.1	373.7	87.8	8.3	111.2	58.1	53.2
1965	617.8	397.7	99.2	6.2	114.7	57.9	56.8
1966	658.1	418.1	109.3	4.2	126.5	65.4	61.1
1967	675.2	430.1	101.2	3.6	140.2	74.7	65.5
1968	707.2	452.3	105.7	0.9	148.3	78.7	69.6
1969	727.1	467.7	111.3	0.2	147.8	75.7	72.1
1970*	724.3	477.2	103.0	2.3	141.8	67.7	74.1

*Provisional.
Source: U.S. Department of Commerce, Office of Business Economics.

Table 7-8

RELATION OF GROSS NATIONAL PRODUCT AND NATIONAL INCOME, 1929–1970 (BILLONS OF DOLLARS)

Year	Gross national product	Less: Capital consumption allowances	Equals: Net national product	Plus: Subsidies less current surplus of government enterprises	Less: Indirect business tax, business transfers, statistical discrepancy	Equals: National income
1929	103.1	7.9	95.2	—0.1	7.0	86.8
1930	90.4	8.0	82.4	—0.1	7.2	75.4
1931	75.8	7.9	68.0	0.0	6.9	59.7
1932	58.0	7.4	50.7	0.0	6.8	42.8
1933	55.6	7.0	48.6	0.0	7.1	40.3
1934	65.1	6.8	58.2	0.3	7.8	49.5
1935	72.2	6.9	65.4	0.4	8.2	57.2
1936	82.5	7.0	75.4	0.0	8.7	65.0
1937	90.4	7.2	83.3	0.1	9.2	73.6
1938	84.7	7.3	77.4	0.2	9.2	67.4
1939	90.5	7.3	83.2	0.5	9.4	72.6
1940	99.7	7.5	92.2	0.4	10.0	81.1
1941	124.5	8.2	116.3	0.1	11.3	104.2
1942	157.9	9.8	148.1	0.2	11.8	137.1
1943	191.6	10.2	181.3	0.2	12.7	170.3
1944	210.1	11.0	199.1	0.7	14.1	182.6
1945	211.9	11.3	200.7	0.8	15.5	181.5
1946	208.5	9.9	198.6	0.9	17.1	181.9
1947	231.3	12.2	219.1	—0.2	18.4	199.0
1948	257.6	14.5	243.1	—0.1	20.1	224.2
1949	256.5	16.6	239.9	—0.1	21.3	217.5
1950	284.8	18.3	266.4	0.2	23.3	241.1
1951	328.4	21.2	307.2	0.2	25.2	278.0
1952	345.5	23.2	322.3	—0.1	27.6	291.4
1953	364.6	25.7	338.9	—0.4	29.6	304.7
1954	364.8	28.2	336.6	—0.2	29.4	303.1
1955	398.0	31.5	366.5	—0.1	32.1	331.0
1956	419.2	34.1	385.2	0.8	34.9	350.8
1957	441.1	37.1	404.0	0.9	37.3	366.1
1958	447.3	38.9	408.4	0.9	38.5	367.8
1959	483.7	41.4	442.3	0.1	41.5	400.0
1960	503.7	43.4	460.3	0.2	45.2	414.5
1961	520.1	45.2	474.9	1.4	47.7	427.3
1962	560.3	50.0	510.4	1.4	51.5	457.7
1963	590.5	52.6	537.9	0.8	54.7	481.9
1964	632.4	56.1	576.3	1.3	58.4	518.1
1965	684.9	59.8	625.1	1.3	62.5	564.3
1966	749.9	63.9	685.9	2.3	65.7	620.6
1967	793.9	68.9	725.0	1.4	70.4	653.6
1968	865.0	74.0	791.1	0.7	78.1	712.7
1969	931.4	78.9	852.5	1.0	85.2	769.5
1970	976.8	84.3	892.4	1.7	92.0	801.0

Less:			Plus:									
Corporate profits and inventory valuation adjustment	Contributions for social insurance	Wage accruals less disbursements	Government transfer payments to persons	Net government & consumer interest payments	Dividends	Business transfer payments	Equals: Personal income	Less: Personal tax and nontax payments	Equals: Disposable personal income	Less: Personal outlays	Equals: Personal saving
10.5	0.2	0.0	0.9	2.5	5.8	0.6	85.9	2.6	83.8	79.1	4.2
7.0	0.3	0.0	1.0	1.8	5.5	0.5	77.0	2.5	74.5	71.1	3.4
2.0	0.3	0.0	2.1	1.8	4.1	0.6	65.9	1.9	64.0	61.4	2.6
—1.3	0.3	0.0	1.4	1.7	2.5	0.7	50.2	1.5	48.7	49.3	—0.6
—1.2	0.3	0.0	1.5	1.6	2.0	0.7	47.0	1.5	45.5	46.5	—0.9
1.7	0.3	0.0	1.6	1.7	2.6	0.6	54.0	1.6	52.4	52.0	0.4
3.4	0.3	0.0	1.8	1.7	2.8	0.6	60.4	1.9	58.5	56.4	2.1
5.6	0.6	0.0	2.9	1.7	4.5	0.6	68.6	2.3	66.3	62.7	3.6
6.8	1.8	0.0	1.9	1.9	4.7	0.6	74.1	2.9	71.2	67.4	3.8
4.9	2.0	0.0	2.4	1.9	3.2	0.4	68.3	2.9	65.5	64.8	0.7
6.3	2.1	0.0	2.5	1.9	3.8	0.5	72.8	2.4	70.3	67.7	2.6
9.8	2.3	0.0	2.7	2.1	4.0	0.4	78.3	2.6	75.7	71.8	3.8
15.2	2.8	0.0	2.6	2.2	4.4	0.5	96.0	3.3	92.7	81.7	11.0
20.3	3.5	0.0	2.6	2.2	4.3	0.5	122.9	6.0	116.9	89.3	27.6
24.4	4.5	0.2	2.5	2.6	4.4	0.5	151.3	17.8	133.5	100.1	33.4
23.8	5.2	—0.2	3.1	3.3	4.6	0.5	165.3	18.9	146.3	109.1	37.3
19.2	6.1	0.0	5.6	4.2	4.6	0.5	171.1	20.9	150.2	120.7	29.6
19.3	6.0	0.0	10.8	5.2	5.6	0.5	178.7	18.7	160.0	144.8	15.2
25.6	5.7	0.0	11.1	5.5	6.3	0.6	191.3	21.4	169.8	162.5	7.3
33.0	5.2	0.0	10.5	6.1	7.0	0.7	210.2	21.1	189.1	175.8	13.4
30.8	5.7	0.0	11.6	6.5	7.2	0.8	207.2	18.6	188.6	179.2	9.4
37.7	6.9	0.0	14.3	7.2	8.8	0.8	227.6	20.7	206.9	193.9	13.1
42.7	8.2	0.1	11.5	7.6	8.6	0.9	255.6	29.0	226.6	209.3	17.3
39.9	8.7	0.0	12.0	8.1	8.6	1.0	272.5	34.1	238.3	220.2	18.1
39.6	8.8	—0.1	12.8	9.0	8.9	1.2	288.2	35.6	252.6	234.3	18.3
38.0	9.8	0.0	14.9	9.5	9.3	1.1	290.1	32.7	257.4	241.0	16.4
46.9	11.1	0.0	16.1	10.1	10.5	1.2	310.9	35.5	275.3	259.5	15.8
46.1	12.6	0.0	17.1	11.2	11.3	1.4	333.0	39.8	293.2	272.6	20.6
45.6	14.5	0.0	19.9	12.0	11.7	1.5	351.1	42.6	308.5	287.8	20.7
41.1	14.8	0.0	24.1	12.1	11.6	1.6	361.2	42.3	318.8	296.6	22.3
51.7	17.6	0.0	24.9	13.6	12.6	1.7	383.5	46.2	337.3	318.3	19.1
49.9	20.7	0.0	26.6	15.1	13.4	1.9	401.0	50.9	350.0	333.0	17.0
50.3	21.4	0.0	30.4	15.0	13.8	2.0	416.8	52.4	364.4	343.3	21.2
55.7	24.0	0.0	31.2	16.1	15.2	2.1	442.6	57.4	385.3	363.7	21.6
58.9	26.9	0.0	33.0	17.6	16.5	2.3	465.5	60.9	404.6	384.7	19.9
66.3	27.9	0.0	34.2	19.1	17.8	2.5	497.5	59.4	438.1	411.9	26.2
76.1	29.6	0.0	37.2	20.5	19.8	2.7	538.9	65.7	473.2	444.8	28.4
82.4	38.0	0.0	41.1	22.2	20.8	3.0	587.2	75.4	511.9	479.3	32.5
78.7	42.4	0.0	48.7	23.6	21.4	3.1	629.3	83.0	546.3	506.0	40.4
85.4	47.1	0.0	55.7	26.3	23.3	3.3	688.7	97.5	591.2	550.8	40.4
85.8	53.6	0.0	61.6	29.0	24.7	3.5	748.9	117.3	631.6	593.9	37.6
77.4	57.1	0.0	73.9	31.8	25.2	3.6	801.0	116.4	684.7	634.7	50.0

Source: U.S. Department of Commerce, Office of Business Economics.

8

The dimensions of economic well-being and economic activity

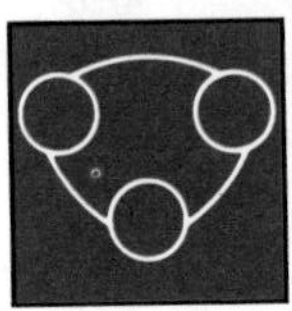

The grand numbers of macroeconomics are not merely impersonal accounting summations. They reflect the real work, enjoyment of consumption, and planning of individuals, families, and social institutions. It is easy to forget these microeconomic implications. One should try not to let that happen, however, in using the macro concepts.

In this chapter the macroeconomic aggregates will be used to gain an overall perspective of the functioning of the economy and to identify the essential issues in some of the current social debates. The Appendix discusses input-output accounting.

Eliminating a simple misconception about technological progress

Technological "progress" is now seen as a mixed blessing which creates as well as resolves problems. Careful macroeconomic accounting can help in evaluating the "mix." For example, it is not uncommon to read the following type of evaluation:

> Rapid technical change can bring to people the benefits of higher consumption and new products. It can eliminate many of the old scourges of mankind and improve his health. But because it also increases the productivity of labor and management, it reduces the need for workers of all types. Machines can be built to program their own production and repair their own

breakdowns. Man is becoming obsolete. There soon will not be enough income created to buy the tremendous output of which the machines are capable. We face a bleak future of a great production potential that cannot be enjoyed.

This reasoning is based on a simple, common, and profound error, which macro accounting can eliminate. *Macro accounting tells us that, fundamentally, every dollar of output produced is a dollar of income.* Measured output and measured income can never be different. Many problems must be solved as we adjust to technical change, but there can be no problem of an insufficiency of *income* of the type described.

Yet the quotation strikes a chord. The concepts of macro accounting can eliminate the simple error, but there are unarticulated worries in the quotation which accounting alone cannot resolve. Though measured output and income are always equal, can we be sure that even with new technology the output and income measured will provide jobs and general prosperity? Will the potentially higher incomes associated with new technology be realized? These deeper problems cannot be resolved by accounting, however good, but will require the macro analysis to be developed in the next chapters.

Gross national product or gross national pollution

"GNP – gross national pollution": The phrase reflects one of the more recent of our public worries, the general degradation of the ecological environment. The macroeconomic concepts developed in Chapter 7 help in identifying some aspects of the pollution problem.

"Gross national pollution" suggests that increasing pollution is associated with an increasing gross national product. It may even imply that, because of environmental pollution, the conventional gross national product overestimates the true benefits of economic activity.

These implications are undoubtedly true. *Increasing economic activity has resulted in more pollution.* Chapter 5 points out that public pollution is the result of the shifting of various private costs of waste disposal to the general public. This happens, for example, when sulfuric acid wastes are dumped into public rivers by factories and refineries. There are also pollution costs associated with private consumption, e.g., the exhaust fumes of automobile joyriding.

Pollution is a "bad" not a "good," a cost which is not accounted for privately. We noted in Chapter 7 that certain goods and services provide real satisfaction, but do not get into the national income and product accounts because they are not traded on markets. Similarly, pollution does not get into the national income and product accounts because it escapes market transactions. If we were comprehensive in our social accounting, we would include its effects.[1]

When the ecological environment is regarded as an inheritance that should be preserved, pollution is properly regarded as a cost that degrades the environment. The gross national product, which is gross of depreciation of produced physical capital, is also gross in that it includes depreciation of the environment by pollution. The net national product after depreciation provides a better estimate of the benefits of economic activity, and we should, in our present national mood, subtract depreciation costs due to pollution as well.[2] Pollution costs are difficult to estimate, however, just as are depreciation costs.

National income and product as indicators of economic welfare

Table 8-1

GROSS NATIONAL PRODUCT PER CAPITA, 1968 (IN U.S. DOLLARS)

Country	*GNP per capita*
1. United States	$4,379
2. Kuwait*	3,463
3. Sweden	3,315
4. Canada	2,997
5. France	2,537
6. West Germany	2,206
7. United Kingdom	1,861
8. Israel	1,459
9. Italy	1,418
10. Japan	1,404
11. Venezuela	944
12. Argentina	739
13. Chile	569
14. Mexico	566
15. Portugal	529
16. Brazil†	329
17. Philippines	301
18. Jordan	262
19. Ghana	238
20. United Arab Republic†	188
21. Bolivia	170
22. Indonesia	96
23. India	80
24. Malawi	58

*1966 data.
†1967 data.
Source: United Nations Statistical Yearbook.

Sometimes implicitly but often explicitly the national income and product accounts are used as a basis for judgments about economic welfare. Americans were said to be about twice as well off on the average in 1970 as in 1948 because the United States gross national product *per capita*, the GNP divided by the population, had doubled since 1948. United States residents are said to be roughly twice as well off as those of the Soviet Union because our per capita gross national product is about twice as high. Is this a valid use of the accounts, and are these valid comparisons?

While not entirely appropriate, no other comparison is better. The best single indicator of how well off an individual is, and the one we use most frequently, is his income. *The best available aggregate measure is gross national product per capita.* This is certainly the most comprehensive measure of how well an economy is doing on the average for its members. Table 8-1 shows the per capita gross national products for a number of countries, ranging

[1] Pollution is an example of an external diseconomy, a concept introduced in Chap. 5. It is external to market transactions, because its direct effects are not transmitted through market prices and deliveries of goods and services. It is a *dis*economy because it reduces economic welfare.

[2] This provides a good example of the "one man's food is another man's poison" adage. We now regard the natural environment as something whose deterioration is a cost which should be subtracted from GNP to get at the true benefits of economic activity. Our high estimate of the costs is associated with our relatively high incomes and wealth, however. For the poor countries of the world, where certain kinds of pollution are often more severe than in the United States, it has been said, for example, by Adam al-Jafri of Malaysia that "some of us would rather see smoke coming out of a factory and men employed than no factory at all. It is, after all, a matter of priority."

from the high United States figure to Malawi, the country with the lowest estimated average.

There are several difficulties associated with such comparisons. First of all, the composition of national products varies drastically from country to country. United States residents use a lot of durable consumer goods compared with citizens of other countries; they eat a lot of meat compared with everyone else, except the Argentines. Italians, on the average, have fewer automobiles and eat more wheat products than United States citizens. Indians are mostly vegetarians, and so on. This means that, in making international comparisons, we are faced with the old problem of comparing apples and oranges. Now the apples and oranges stand for the distinctly different market baskets that the national products of the countries represent. And we do not have a single consistent set

Table 8-2

COMPOSITION OF THE GROSS NATIONAL PRODUCT IN SELECTED COUNTRIES AS PERCENTAGE OF GNP (1968)

Country	*Private consumption*	*Government*	*Investment*	*Exports*	*Imports*
1. United States	61	21	18	5	5
2. Kuwait*	27	15	19	66	26
3. Sweden	55	22	24	23	23
4. Canada	61	15	24	24	24
5. France	61	13	27	14	14
6. West Germany	56	16	25	23	19
7. United Kingdom	63	18	19	20	21
8. Israel	66	30	21	27	43
9. Italy	64	14	20	18	16
10. Japan	52	8	39	10	9
11. Venezuela	63	14	25	28	30
12. Argentina†	68	12	19	10	9
13. Chile	74	12	17	15	17
14. Mexico†	79	6	18	9	10
15. Portugal	71	13	19	24	27
16. Brazil	75	11	15	6	7
17. Philippines	76	9	21	16	22
18. Jordan†	78	23	17	13	31
19. Ghana	72	18	11	18	18
20. United Arab Republic†	68	23	14	12	16
21. Bolivia†	79	10	14	24	27
22. Indonesia	91	6	9	12	17
23. Malawi	85	17	16	23	41
24. India‡	72	15	15		2§

*1966 data.
†1967 data.
‡GDP used from International Bank for Reconstruction and Development.
§Net import of goods and services including net factor payments abroad.

Note: Percentages may not add to 100 because of rounding.
Source: United Nations Statistical Yearbook.

Table 8-3

CONSUMPTION PER CAPITA IN 1967 (U.S. DOLLARS)

Country	*Consumption per capita*
1. United States	$2,470
2. Sweden	1,720
3. Canada	1,710
4. Kuwait*	1,515
5. France	1,390
6. United Kingdom	1,255
7. West Germany	1,175
8. Israel	990
9. Italy	870
10. Japan	650
11. Venezuela	565
12. Argentina	467
13. Chile	450
14. Mexico	417
15. Portugal	338
16. Brazil	250
17. Philippines	216
18. Jordan	211
19. Ghana	184
20. Bolivia	151
21. United Arab Republic	126
22. Indonesia	83
23. India	64
24. Malawi	60

*1966 data.
Source: United Nations Statistical Yearbook.

of prices that can be used to value and compare the different national products. Each country has its own set of prices, and none are identical. Consequently, we get somewhat different results, depending on whose prices we use to make the comparison.

It is even worse than that, however. Look at the composition of the national products of a few countries, such as shown in Table 8-2. Notice that the *share* of consumption in the total tends to be higher in low-income countries and lower in high-income countries. Absolute levels of consumption, however, are closely related to levels of income.

Perhaps we should focus on consumption per head in order to make comparisons among countries? Isn't that what determines the economic quality of life of individuals? Do the amounts that governments and businesses spend contribute anything to human happiness? Well, remember that business investment consists of the production of real goods – new capital goods – which will be used for future production. *So current investment represents a potential increase in the availability of consumption goods in the future, and that is certainly worth something now.* As for government purchases of goods and services, they are a mixed bag of controversial and noncontroversial items. Schools and hospitals get general approval. Highways are beginning to be controversial because they are associated with automobile congestion and air pollution. Military expenditures, which are the largest single part of most national government budgets, are even more controversial. Yet it is hard to say that the income of a man working on a civilian truck should be included in the national income and that the income of a man working on a military truck should not be.[3]

For purposes of comparison, Table 8-3 presents the consumption per head in the same countries listed in Table 8-1. Notice that the relative positions of the countries change somewhat, but there is no major shift.

The personal distribution of the national income

The country whose per capita national income has been highest in recent years is Kuwait on the Persian Gulf. Its GNP per capita is second only to the United States. These somewhat surprising facts are also somewhat disturbing if one wants to draw implications about relative economic welfare from the comparisons of national income or GNP per head. The Kuwaiti national product consists almost entirely of royalties on oil pumped out of the gigantic pool on which the country sits. The unsettling element arises because those oil royalties accrue almost exclusively to the Sheikh of

[3] The problems of comparisons among countries are also found in comparisons of different years in the same country, because the composition of output and prices change over time.

Table 8-4

DISTRIBUTION OF INCOME IN THE UNITED STATES, 1968

1 Income class	2 Distribution of families by income level (percent)	3 Cumulative percentage, total of all families	4 Share of income by class (percentage distribution)	5 Cumulative percentage, total of all income
Under $ 1,000	1.8	1.8	*	*
$ 1,000–$ 1,999	3.4	5.2	1	1
$ 2,000–$ 2,999	5.1	10.3	2	3
$ 3,000–$ 3,999	6.1	16.4	2	5
$ 4,000–$ 4,999	6.0	22.4	3	8
$ 5,000–$ 5,999	6.9	29.3	4	12
$ 6,000–$ 7,499	7.6	36.9	8	20
$ 7,500–$ 9,999	23.4	60.3	16	36
$10,000–$14,999	25.0	85.3	31	67
$15,000 and over	14.7	100.0	33	100.0

*Less than 0.5 percent.
Source: U.S. Bureau of the Census, *Current Population Reports,* Series p-60.

Kuwait. He is generous with their use, and Kuwait now has many new schools and hospitals, fresh water from ocean desalting plants, and so on. But the income is nearly all the Sheikh's and the averaging process is clearly misleading about the income and standard of living of most of the Kuwaiti people.

But what is most obviously true of Kuwait is less obviously but equally true of all other countries. *Averaging is always to some extent misleading, and to avoid being misled it is necessary to go behind the averages and look at the personal distribution of income among individuals and families.*

Table 8-4 shows the distribution of income in the United States. Columns 2 and 4 show the percentage of families in each income class and the percentage of total income received by each family in the class. Columns 3 and 5 record the cumulative totals, adding from the lowest income class, of the percentage of income received and of the percentage of families included in each income category and lower ones. The facts are no secret, but they come as something of a surprise to many people. There are a lot of people at the bottom, and life is hard there. There are relatively few at the top, and they live quite well.

One way to see the effects of inequality is to plot the data of Table 8-4. This is done in Figure 8-1 by preparing a graph in which *percentages* run from 0 to 100 on both the horizontal and vertical axes. On the horizontal axis we plot the percentage of families, and

Figure 8-1

LORENZ CURVE FOR THE UNITED STATES, 1968: INEQUALITY OF PERSONAL INCOME DISTRIBUTION

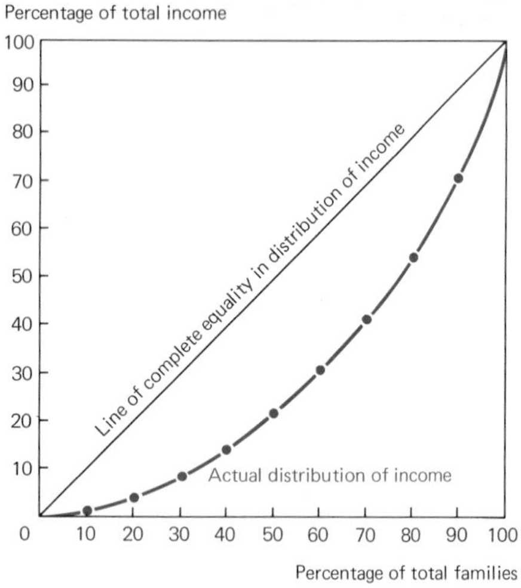

Figure 8-2

DISTRIBUTION OF INCOME IN THE UNITED STATES: 1935, 1945, AND 1968

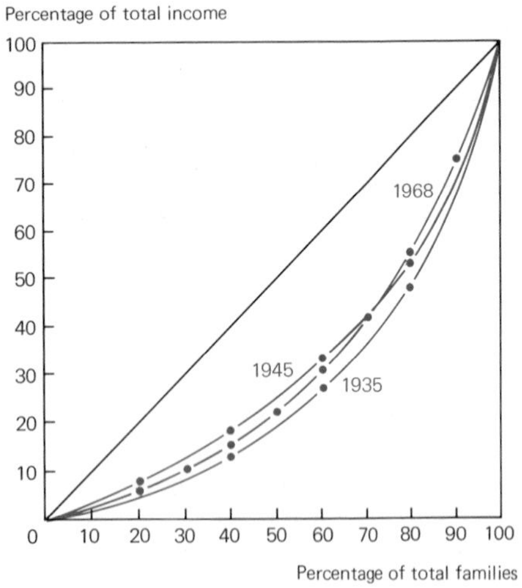

on the vertical axis we plot the percentage of income they receive. If 10 percent of the families received 10 percent of the income, and 20 percent received 20 percent of the income, and so on, there would be complete equality. The line representing such complete equality is the straight diagonal from the lower left corner to the upper right. *The actual data, plotted from Table 8-4, lie along the line bowed away from the diagonal. This line is called a Lorenz curve.* The general shape of the Lorenz curve for each country is more or less the same, although its exact position changes somewhat from country to country. In the United States, the distribution of income after taxes and transfer payments is more equal than the before tax and transfer payment income distribution because, as pointed out in Chapter 6, the tax and transfer payment system, taken all together, is progressive. There is some evidence that the distribution of wealth in the United States is more unequal than the distribution of income.

Whether any particular degree of income inequality is "good" or "bad" depends on one's own principles and appreciation of the consequences. The fact is that income inequality has not been increasing in the United States to any substantial extent. This is shown in Figure 8-2 which presents the Lorenz curves for the distribution of income in the United States for 1935, 1945, and 1968. There has been a clear reduction in income inequality since 1935. From 1945 to 1968 the changes have been slightly in the direction of a greater share for the upper-income groups. The greater inequality of the income distribution in the United States in 1935 as compared with more recent years is indicated by the fact that the 1935 Lorenz curve is further way from the 45-degree line than the other two curves. The 1968 curve crosses the 1945 curve in the mid-range, indicating some slight redistribution of income.

Income distribution in itself does not tell the full story about quality of life in each group. In the United States, the amount necessary to support a family of three at a level that most people would find minimally acceptable was estimated to be $3,026 in early 1970. About 10 percent of the population fell below this and the other somewhat arbitrary "poverty lines" for all families in 1970. The American dream of spacious and comfortable housing, bright and adequate clothing, and a generous table is clearly not within the reach of all Americans. Yet the number of people below the poverty line has fallen except during the most recent recession years. So the problems of poverty remain a major challenge. And when we analyze the determinants of the overall performance

---

Source, Fig. 8-1: U.S. Department of Labor, Bureau of Labor Statistics.

Sources, Fig. 8-2: 1935: Selma Goldsmith, George Jaszi, Hyman Kaitz, and Maurice Leibenberg, "Size Distribution of Income since the Mid-Thirties," Review of Economics and Statistics, *February, 1954. 1945:* U.S. Department of Commerce, *Office of Business Economics. 1968: U.S. Department of Labor, Bureau of Labor Statistics.*

of the economy, we must not forget its significance for all the individuals who make up the total.

The national accounts as indicators of the level of economic activity and of fluctuations

What do people mean by prosperity and depression, good times and bad times? Essentially they are talking about the changes in production and income that the national accounts measure. Figure 8-3 presents a long view of the economic history of the United States in this century. The potential GNP is an estimate of the amount which could have been produced with reasonably full employment of labor and capacity. When the actual GNP is less than the potential, resources are idle, and output which could have been produced is being lost. When the actual is greater than the potential, the economy is pushing up to its maximum production capabilities, and that, in turn, is a source of inflationary pressures. Clearly, we have had a lot of ups and downs. Some have been associated with wars. Some have not. The cataclysm of the Great Depression of the 1930s stands out as a giant down.[4] The prolonged prosperity of the 1960s stands out as a uniquely sustained up.

[4] Novels are better than economic histories in giving the flavor of a time. John Dos Passos' *U.S.A.*, Houghton Mifflin Company, Boston, 1963, is a good slice of the 1920s and 1930s, and the descriptive journalism of the same years in Frederick Lewis Allen, *Only Yesterday*, Harper & Row, New York, 1957, is excellent.

Figure 8-3

GROSS NATIONAL PRODUCT AND ITS MAJOR COMPONENTS (BILLIONS OF DOLLARS, 1958 PRICES)

(Sources: *John W. Kendrick,* Productivity Trends in the United States, *National Bureau of Economic Research, New York, 1961; Dept. of Commerce, Office of Business Economics; Ray C. Fair,* "Aggregate Price Changes and Price Expectations," Federal Reserve Bank of St. Louis Review, *Nov., 1970.*)

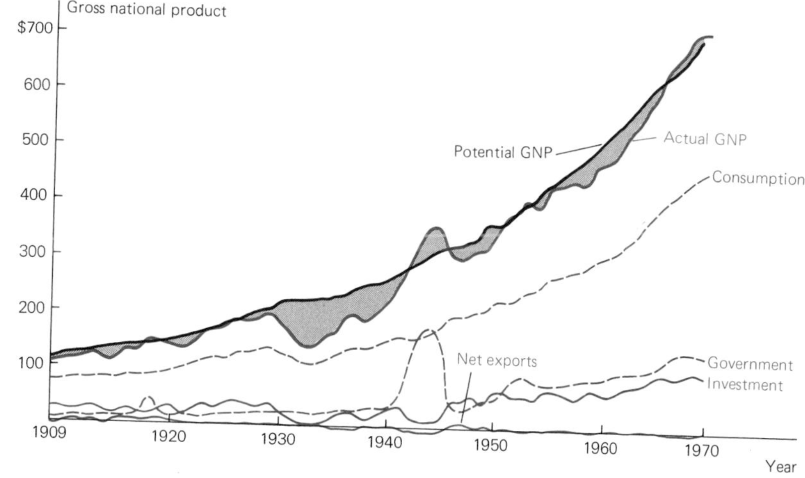

The pattern of the last ten years is of particular interest, partly because it indicates how the experience of the moment can shape the long-run view. The early 1960s were years of relatively high unemployment and stagnant economic performance. There was a general tendency to accept these as more or less permanent features of the economy and to expect them, as well as the relative "affluence" of the United States, to continue. Then in the middle 1960s a new design of economic policy led to much higher growth rates and levels of employment. Prices were almost stable, and the prosperity led to a general euphoria about the ability of the experts to design policy for both growth and stability. The late sixties dispelled that euphoria. The economy went through a roller-coaster ride of inflation, followed by higher unemployment, an economic slowdown in 1970, a retarded recovery, and continued inflation in 1971. *The inclination of the mid-sixties to downgrade the problems of economic fluctuations has been succeeded by a new realization of the difficulties of achieving economic growth while avoiding excessive ups and downs.* Those ups and downs were studied in the past under the now somewhat old-fashioned name of business cycles. It is more modern to call them "economic fluctuations." Under any name they still require careful attention.

Identifying economic fluctuations

Actually, "business cycle" is a somewhat misleading name for the ups and downs in overall economic activity. It is misleading because it suggests a degree of regularity in the pattern and timing of fluctuations that has not really existed. Though all economic fluctuations have certain common characteristics, each fluctuation has its own individuality. With this warning in mind, we will also talk about "cycles."

Eliminating seasonal variations. The problem is to identify different kinds of fluctuations. It is not so easy as may first appear. We are on the lookout for changes in the general level of economic activity. But the level of activity in some parts of the economy is always changing independently of overall changes. When housing construction and employment decline in October, does that mean we are in for a general decline in economic activity? When retail sales boom in December, does that mark the beginning of a general increase in economic activity? Not necessarily in either case.

Agricultural output is the most obvious type of seasonal production, but there are others as well. Beginning in October, and continuing through the winter months, housing construction and employment in the building trades always decline, because the increasingly cold and stormy weather makes outdoor work more difficult. Retail sales always boom in December, owing to the Christmas buying spree. Automobile production always declines in late summer as manufacturers change over to the new models. If we want to know whether such changes reflect a broader movement, it is necessary to ask, Is the change in output, employment, sales — or whatever — greater or smaller than normally occurs about this time of year? To answer that, we have to figure out what "normal" seasonal patterns are. Then we can compare the normal seasonal movement with the actual change and see which is larger.

After we make seasonal adjustments to the output and income estimates of each sector of the economy, we can add up these adjusted incomes and outputs and obtain seasonally adjusted estimates for GNP, national income, disposable income, and their components.

Correcting for trend. With seasonal variations eliminated, we see that the output of some sectors of the economy never seems to decline. Year-to-year production just grows and grows. Electric power output ordinarily behaves that way, for example. In these sectors there may still be important fluctuations, however, in the *rate of growth*. When the rate of growth of a rapidly growing industry declines, the direct and indirect effects can be quite profound. To try to identify these fluctuations, we can estimate the *long-term trends* in output, and then compare actual production with the estimated trend and find out which is larger or smaller.

The sophisticated economic data watcher looks for changes in rates of growth or decline. Often a reduction in the *rate of increase* of output, for example, is followed by an absolute fall. Or a reduction in the rate of decline may be followed by an end of a decline. There are many possible patterns, and if the data watcher falls into the habit of looking for only one kind, he can be disastrously misled. A trend is a trend only so long as movement in one direction continues. There is never any guarantee that a pattern will continue, nor is there any clear and unequivocal warning to mark the end of a trend and the beginning of a cycle.

The phases of economic fluctuations. The problems of identifying long trends in economic activity present in dramatic form the statistical difficulties economists encounter in measuring and interpreting fluctuations. There are thousands of things going on in the economy at the same time: wheels within wheels and partially connected wheels, all with different amounts of inertia. There is overall growth, which is the result of growth in particular sectors being transmitted as demands on other sectors. There are always some declining sectors whose decline tends to slow down the overall economy. *A cycle is a cumulation of many separate forces that act together through various linkages to speed up or slow down the economy as a whole.* If a cycle can be appreciated in that way, then it will be easier to see why cycles vary so much in length and intensity and in the industries and regions they most affect.

Having emphasized the differences in economic fluctuations, we must balance the picture and describe the similarities. The patterns are generally similar. A relatively long *expansion* phase is capped by a *peak* or *boom* period, which sometimes just peters out, but has in the past sometimes ended in a *panic* or *crisis* in the banking or financial system. A *recession* is set off, often shorter but

Figure 8-4

A SCHEMATIC VIEW OF BUSINESS CYCLES

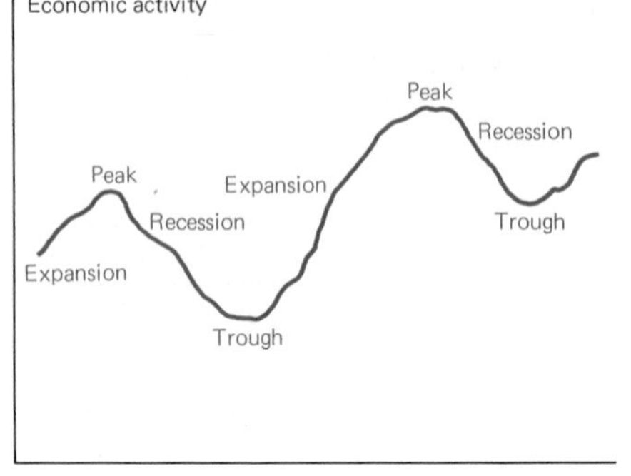

sometimes longer than the preceding expansion. Output, income, and employment fall cumulatively as the slowdown in one sector is communicated to the other. At some point, the downturn begins to slow, and the economy "bottoms out" into a *trough* through which it may move quickly or slowly before it moves again into the recovery and expansion period.

Figure 8-4 presents a schematic diagram of business cycle phases. It runs over two hypothetical cycles to show a few of the possibilities. Sometimes the peaking has been relatively sharp, as in the first cycle; sometimes there is a relatively slow roll-over into a recession. The recession phase, from peak to trough, is usually shorter than the recovery phase, from trough to peak. The bottoming-out process may be short and sharp or gradual and slow.

The duration of business cycles. Cycles vary so greatly in magnitude and timing and in the impact they have in different sectors that it is no easy matter to say exactly when one begins and ends. Economists used to think that it was possible to identify three or four different characteristic cycles to which they attached the following labels:

Not really applicable anymore

1. A "major" cycle of about 7 to 11 years
2. A "minor" cycle of about $2^1/_2$ to 4 years
3. A "construction" cycle of 15 to 20 years
4. A "long" cycle of 50 to 60 years

These labels are now regarded as inadequate. The actual ups and downs in the economy are a combination of coincident and contrasting movements in the various sectors. Sometimes the movements cumulate, and sometimes they offset each other. Rather than trying to identify repeating cycle patterns, economists now tend to emphasize their diversity.

There has not been a "classical" cycle in the United States since the late 1950s, and even the fluctuations of the fifties were rather abbreviated in form. That does not mean that the economy has been sailing along on an even keel. We are, it seems, always trying to avoid a recession or an inflation, looking for ways to speed up or slow down the economy.

Aggregate growth in the economy

Table 8-5 shows the development of the United States in broad outline in terms of the growth rates of a few major components of the economy decade by decade, over several recent decades. The table contrasts the disheartening experience of the 1930s with the more rapid growth of the 1940s. World War II set off that rapid expansion which continued after the war. The 1950s slowed down again, though still the average annual growth rate of GNP was more than twice that of the 1930s. The 1960s started slowly, but overall they represented quite a respectable performance.

Table 8-5

AVERAGE ANNUAL PERCENTAGE RATES OF GROWTH FOR THE UNITED STATES ECONOMY

Years	*GNP*	*Personal consumption expenditures*	*Gross private domestic investment*	*Government purchases of goods and services*
1930–1939	1.3	1.3	−1.0	3.8
1940–1949	3.6	3.4	3.8	3.9
1950–1959	3.0	2.9	0.6	6.0
1960–1969	4.1	4.0	4.4	4.5

Source: U.S. Department of Commerce, Office of Business Economics.

Employment and output

Figure 8-5(*a*) shows the amount of unemployment in the United States as a percentage of the total labor force since the beginning of the century. Note the marked decrease in the amplitude of the fluctuations in recent years. Note, too, the low average level of unemployment in the 1960s as compared with the 1950s.

Not even in the years of most intensive economic activity and

Figure 8-5

UNEMPLOYMENT AND PRODUCTIVITY

Figure 8-5(a) *will help you appreciate what the Great Depression of the 1930s meant to the older generation. In 1933 one out of every four people in the labor force was unemployed. Not until 1941 did the unemployment rate fall below 10 percent. In recent years the highest unemployment rate was in 1958. In late 1970 and in 1971, however, it went above 6 percent. The growth in productivity shown in Figure 8-5*(b) *has been so strong that a careful inspection is required to sort out the periods of more and less rapid change. (Source: U.S. Department of Labor, Bureau of Labor Statistics.)*

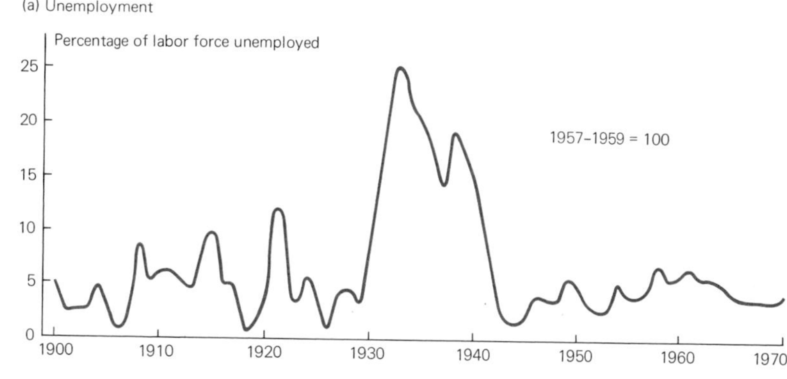

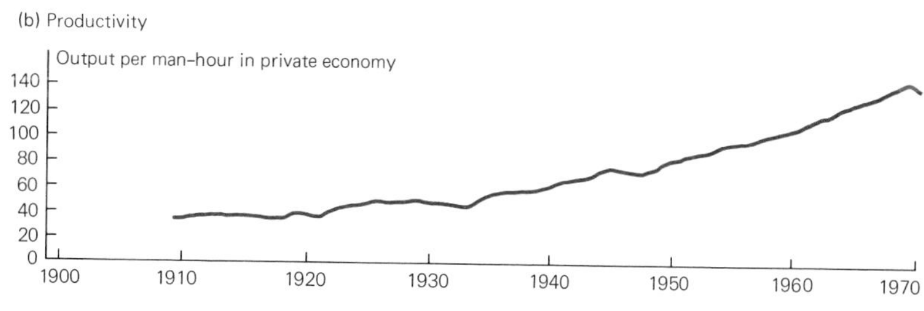

greatest prosperity has the unemployment rate fallen to absolute zero. This is due to a core of "frictional unemployment" which we always have with us. The frictional unemployed are the people who are reported as without work and looking for jobs even when there are jobs available. There is and always should be some turnover of labor in a dynamic economy. Workers move around in search of better opportunities, and manufacturers adjust their production processes to new techniques and market situations. It takes time, however, for workers to find new jobs that they like and into which they fit, though the jobs may exist.

Figure 8-5 (*b*) illustrates the behavior of another important economic ratio: output per worker, or productivity over time. There is a tendency for productivity to decline or not grow so fast when the unemployment rate goes down and to increase as the unemployment rate goes up. This may seem perverse, but there are several straightforward explanations. When business firms lay off workers, they try to keep their best ones as long as possible. When they hire workers, they tend to look for the ones with the greatest skills. That goes far in explaining why productivity tends to rise before employment recovers. It also helps explain why unskilled workers find it difficult to learn skills on the job when unemployment is high. In addition, when output falls, firms shut down the less efficient equipment first. That tends to maintain productivity. Other organizational and production-scheduling effects work the same way.

Frictional unemployment and declining productivity are barriers to zero unemployment. The closer the economy comes to zero unemployment, the more rigid these barriers become and the more difficult it is to reduce unemployment further. That is why economists and others speak of "full employment" even when a good deal of unemployment exists. For a long time in the 1950s it was conventional to regard an unemployment rate of 4 percent as full employment. The convention has changed with experience. In the late 1960s the unemployment rate stayed below 4 percent for several years, and some economists began to think that 3.5 percent was an achievable full employment rate. For our purposes, *fixing an exact percentage which represents the limit to higher employment is less important than knowing that there are limiting factors.* There is no absolute limit, but a yielding one. It becomes more resistant, however, as the level of unemployment falls. Therefore, when you think of full employment, make the mental qualification that it is not really zero unemployment.

The incidence of unemployment varies among different groups, as indicated in Table 8-6. It is always higher among unmarried men than among married men, for example. This indicates perhaps that the former are more willing to spend time searching around for jobs they like. Unmarried men also tend to be younger members of the labor force, and their higher unemployment rates indicate the relatively greater difficulty that the less experienced have in finding jobs.

Table 8-6

SELECTED UNEMPLOYMENT RATES, JANUARY, 1971

Marital status, age, and color	*Unemployment rates (percent)*		
	Male	*Female*	*Total*
Total, 16 years and over	6.4	6.8	6.5
White, 16 to 20 years	12.7	10.7	11.9
White, 20 to 64 years	5.0	5.7	5.3
Married	4.0	5.7	4.6
Unmarried	9.9	5.6	7.6
Black, 16 to 20 years	23.4	23.1	23.3
Black, 20 to 64 years	9.1	8.0	8.6
Married	6.1	6.9	6.4
Unmarried	16.3	9.2	12.5

Source: U.S. Department of Labor, Bureau of Labor Statistics.

Blacks, male and female, have higher unemployment rates than whites, both in periods of prosperity and recession. Typically their unemployment rates rise more rapidly as a recession comes on, though in the 1969–1970 recession, this general pattern did not entirely hold. There is no doubt that the high unemployment rates of black workers are due to past and present discrimination. Discrimination has been a barrier to the acquisition of skills and experience, and it continues to place black workers at a disadvantage in the competition for jobs. The highest unemployment rates in the labor force are among black teen-agers. In addition to discrimination, they are subject to the factors that affect the employment opportunities of younger workers generally.

The patterns of unemployment over time and among groups are of critical importance in evaluating the performance of an economy. Unemployment means low or no income, and its greater impact on lower-income groups makes its social effect all the greater. Unemployment also means individual self-doubt and frustration and social unrest. Every recession leaves a permanent mark. To understand the generation over fifty, for example, remember they came to maturity during the Great Depression of the 1930s. To understand the worries of young blacks and young engineers now, one should be aware that their unemployment rates went up sharply in the recession of 1969–1970.

Regional and sectoral changes in the economy

Macroeconomic accounting makes it possible to appreciate the significance of aggregate changes in the economy. We do not, however, want to lose sight of the detailed components of those

Table 8-7

PER CAPITA PERSONAL INCOME BY STATES AND REGIONS

State and region	*1949*	*Average growth rate, 1949–1959*	*1959*	*Average growth rate, 1959–1969*	*1969*
United States	$1,384	4.6%	$2,161	5.5%	$3,687
New England	1,425	4.9	2,338	5.7	4,076
Maine	1,174	4.3	1,780	5.5	3,054
New Hampshire	1,259	5.2	2,084	5.2	3,471
Vermont	1,073	5.0	1,739	6.4	3,247
Massachusetts	1,470	4.9	2,373	5.8	4,156
Rhode Island	1,437	4.1	2,154	6.0	3,858
Connecticut	1,660	5.0	2,695	5.5	4,595
Mideast	1,618	4.4	2,494	5.2	4,158
New York	1,749	4.3	2,661	5.3	4,442
New Jersey	1,663	4.8	2,634	4.9	4,241
Pennsylvania	1,401	4.6	2,196	5.2	3,659
Delaware	1,854	3.9	2,712	4.2	4,107
Maryland	1,456	4.6	2,269	6.0	4,073
District of Columbia	2,107	3.3	2,929	4.9	4,722
Great Lakes	1,517	4.4	2,322	5.4	3,928
Michigan	1,520	3.6	2,251	5.9	3,994
Ohio	1,474	4.4	2,276	5.1	3,738
Indiana	1,361	4.6	2,119	5.7	3,687
Illinois	1,685	4.3	2,581	5.2	4,285
Wisconsin	1,366	4.7	2,152	5.4	3,632
Plains	1,298	4.4	1,990	5.8	3,497
Minnesota	1,310	4.4	2,020	6.1	3,635
Iowa	1,316	4.0	1,949	6.2	3,549
Missouri	1,338	4.6	2,101	5.1	3,458
North Dakota	1,129	3.1	1,537	7.0	3,012
South Dakota	1,092	3.0	1,469	7.2	3,027
Nebraska	1,303	4.3	1,976	6.2	3,609
Kansas	1,287	4.9	2,075	5.3	3,488

changes. The various parts of the economy do not grow at the same rate, nor do they move up and down in the same way during overall fluctuations. But how shall we identify the "parts" of the economy? What are the most useful ways of dividing the aggregates?

Regional divisions provide one answer. Table 8-7 lists the regions and the states, their per capita income levels and average annual growth rates since 1949. The table will repay careful study. Notice, for example, that *the regions and states with the highest per capita incomes are not always the ones in which per capita income has been rising most rapidly*. The Southeast and the Plains states have relatively low per capita incomes and relatively high average growth rates. The same is not true of all the Rocky Moun-

Table 8-7 (continued)

State and region	1949	Average growth rate, 1949–1959	1959	Average growth rate, 1959–1969	1969
Southeast	953	5.2	1,585	6.4	2,916
Virginia	1,108	4.8	1,770	6.5	3,307
West Virginia	1,033	4.4	1,584	5.1	2,603
Kentucky	933	5.2	1,552	6.3	2,847
Tennessee	927	5.1	1,532	6.2	2,808
North Carolina	940	4.8	1,510	6.7	2,888
South Carolina	859	4.5	1,334	6.9	2,607
Georgia	947	5.4	1,609	6.6	3,071
Florida	1,191	5.0	1,936	6.2	3,525
Alabama	815	6.0	1,465	5.8	2,582
Mississippi	691	5.7	1,203	6.3	2,218
Louisiana	1,085	4.4	1,666	5.2	2,781
Arkansas	799	5.6	1,377	6.1	2,488
Southwest	1,256	4.2	1,899	5.4	3,216
Oklahoma	1,169	4.4	1,805	5.4	3,047
Texas	1,291	4.0	1,913	5.5	3,259
New Mexico	1,116	5.6	1,917	4.3	2,897
Arizona	1,269	4.4	1,949	5.6	3,372
Rocky Mountain	1,360	4.3	2,064	4.7	3,294
Montana	1,385	3.8	2,010	4.5	3,130
Idaho	1,249	4.1	1,872	4.7	2,953
Wyoming	1,606	3.4	2,234	4.2	3,353
Colorado	1,405	4.6	2,196	5.1	3,604
Utah	1,244	4.5	1,926	4.5	2,997
Far West	1,689	4.3	2,567	5.0	4,176
Washington	1,569	4.0	2,318	5.2	3,848
Oregon	1,573	3.4	2,191	5.0	3,573
Nevada	1,822	4.3	2,767	4.9	4,458
California	1,730	4.4	2,651	4.9	4,290
Alaska			2,509	5.9	4,460
Hawaii	1,354	4.8	2,156	6.2	3,928

Source: U.S. Department of Commerce, Office of Business Economics.

tain states, however. The relation between low-income levels and higher growth rates means that the regional differences in income are slowly being reduced.[5]

What accounts for the differences among the regions? Some of the reasons for long-run growth differences are obvious and do not require a course in economics: overall regional differences in natural resources and capital equipment and in the education and skills of the labor force. But those answers do not really get to the

[5] A more detailed regional breakdown would show a few "pockets of poverty," such as Appalachia, in which per capita incomes have been almost stagnant. These depressed areas present special problems of understanding and economic policy.

bottom of the question. The natural resources of the Northeast are more limited than those of the South. Yet per capita income in the Northeast is higher, and while it has grown more slowly in recent years, it must have grown more rapidly in the distant past. Questions such as this are easy to ask but difficult to answer. The analysis to come will help, but more regional economic analysis and history are necessary than can be offered here.

The regional economies also behave differently during short-term fluctuations. Some regions appear to contract pneumonia when the overall economy gets a little head cold. And some regions do not even sniffle. But these characteristic responses vary from time to time.

Further study would in fact show that much of the regional movement in income and output can be explained by regional specialization. The relative severity of the 1969–1970 recession in the Great Lakes region can be traced in large part to the concentration there of the automobile industry and its major suppliers. The Northeast has relatively little commercial agriculture now and relatively more manufacturing and service output. The Mountain states have a great deal of agriculture, forestry, and mining, and a substantial amount of manufacturing. Patterns change, however. The South, which was largely agricultural for many years, has become more and more a manufacturing area as well.

Summary

Macroeconomic accounting can be used to dispel misconceptions and to measure major features of the economy. It demonstrates clearly that technological change can never make measured output greater than measured income. While that is true, it still does not answer the question, Will the measured output and income be at high or low levels?

Conventional macro accounting leaves out some important types of productive activity, such as housewives' services. It also leaves out some deleterious effects of economic activity, such as pollution. Because of these unaccounted-for items, the macro accounts tend to be somewhat inaccurate measures of the net benefits of economic activity.

The macro accounts provide the best available though still imperfect indicators of relative economic welfare. One of the major difficulties is that their use as such indicators requires comparisons among the quite different collections of goods and services that make up the various national products. In addition, the averages conceal important facts about the distribution of income, which is often considered a major determinant of economic welfare. The distribution of income is far from equal in the United States, though there is no evidence that it is becoming more unequal.

The national income and product accounts provide our most

comprehensive measures of the level of economic activity and changes in that level. To identify economic fluctuations, we must remove the effects of annual seasonal changes in output, which may be due to the weather, to holidays, or to regularly scheduled production changes. We must also remove the effects of strong growth trends in some producing sectors so as to see clearly the fluctuations in relative rates of growth.

Although economic fluctuations do not repeat themselves with the regularity in timing and pattern that the term business cycles implies, the ups and downs do have some common features. Typically the economy moves through phases of expansion, peak, recession, trough, and expansion again. While economic policy in the sixties was successful in sustaining a long period of expansion, that did not mean the end of economic fluctuations, as the most recent recession has indicated. The expansion of the sixties did show, however, that the United States economy could grow relatively rapidly, with low levels of unemployment and fairly stable prices. This experience was contrary to the expectations of slow growth which had developed as a result of the relatively stagnant years of the late 1950s. But the late sixties and early seventies brought recession *and* inflation.

Zero unemployment cannot ever be achieved because it becomes more and more difficult to reduce unemployment as full employment is approached. That is why economists speak of full employment even when 3 percent or 4 percent of the labor force is unemployed. Uemployment hits various groups differently. Typically, unemployment rates are higher among young, unmarried men than among older, married men. Unemployment rates are relatively high among black workers, both male and female, reflecting the effects of discrimination.

The various geographic regions and producing sectors of the economy grow at somewhat different rates and respond differently to overall fluctuations. In general, the regions with the lowest per capita incomes have grown most rapidly in recent years, indicating a tendency for equalization of incomes among regions. Generally, also, economic fluctuations tend to be less severe in regions with fast long-term growth rates.

One of the most striking aspects of sectoral growth in recent years has been the strong and continuous uptrend in the output of services. Production in the investment goods sectors has been much more variable than production in the consumption goods sectors.

Questions for discussion and review

1. If factories became fully automated so that literally no workers were required to operate them, would income earned still be equal to output produced?

2. Besides pollution, are there any other "bads" whose costs should be deducted from GNP to obtain a more accurate estimate of NNP?

3. What are the strengths and weaknesses of comparisons of national income per capita as a measure of relative economic welfare?

4. Why is the distribution of disposable income less unequal than the distribution of earned income?

5. Would you consider a slowdown in economic activity a recession if national income did not fall? If disposable income did not fall? If the overall unemployment rate did not rise?

6. Do you think economic fluctuations in your region are more severe than in the country as a whole, or less severe? How could you find out for sure?

7. What about the growth rate in your region, is it faster or slower than the national average? How could you find out about this? What accounts for any difference that might exist?

Concepts for review

Personal distribution of income
Lorenz curve
Poverty line
Business cycle
Seasonal variations
Growth trend
Phases of economic fluctuations
Full employment
Sectoral variability in output

Appendix: Input-output accounting

Suppose we take the consumption, investment, and other final product totals and disaggregate them by producing sector. That would tell us how much each industry contributes to the totals. The results of such a disaggregation are shown in Table 8-8. In effect, we have simply stretched out the national product accounts for 1958 to indicate the sectoral detail.

Now let us stretch out the accounting system in another dimension. We shall record the deliveries of output by each sector not only to their final uses as consumption, investment, etc. We shall also record the intermediate deliveries of outputs of goods and services *by* each sector *to* every other producing sector. That is shown in Table 8-9, reading across each industry *row*. For example, the Materials sector delivered $8,069 million worth of output to Metalworking and $8,843 million worth to Construction. It also produced $3,994 million worth of final goods. The very first entry in the row indicates that there were $8,565 million worth of deliveries from one firm to another within the Materials sector. As

Table 8-8

DELIVERIES OF FINAL PRODUCTS BY EACH PRODUCING SECTOR, 1958 (MILLIONS OF DOLLARS, 1947 PRICES)

Industrial sector	*Total final demand =consumption + investment + government + exports − imports*
1. Materials	$ 3,994
2. Metalworking	19,269
3. Construction	39,348
4. Transportation and utilities	22,625
5. Services	137,571
6. Mining	−653
7. Agriculture	8,327
8. All other	82,996
Total	$ 313,475

Source: Anne P. Carter, *Structural Change in the American Economy,* Harvard University Press, Cambridge, Mass., 1970.

another sectoral example, the Agriculture sector delivered only $7 million worth of output to the Metalworking sector, and there were $18,091 million worth of deliveries from one firm to another within Agriculture.

If the total *intermediate* deliveries of *output* by one sector to all other sectors are added to the total production of *final* products by the sector, we obtain a measure of the total output of the sector. This is called *gross domestic output.* It includes not only the final products of the industry but all the intermediate flows which are carefully taken out in national income accounting.

Now, instead of reading across a row, let us look down a particular column of Table 8-9, for example, the Metalworking sector. Reading down, we see the intermediate *inputs* that every other industry has delivered to Metalworking. The Materials industry delivered $8,069 million of output to Metalworking. Within Metalworking, $6,996 million of inputs was delivered from one firm to another. Construction delivered $5 million of inputs, and so on.

Each column in Table 8-9 provides information on the *inputs* that the particular sector received from every other sector. Each row shows the distribution of output of each producing sector. So the table is, naturally enough, called an *input-output* table.

The next to the last entry in each row records the national income earned or value added in the sector. That is the sum of wages and salaries, rents, interests, corporate profits, and the income of unincorporated enterprise in the sector. The sum of the value added in each sector is the national income. If indirect taxes and depreciation were added to it, that, in turn, would be equal to the gross national product. This would lead us back to the sum of the final products produced by each sector.

As an expanded kind of macro accounting, the input-output approach reveals a great deal about the structure of an economy and the importance of each sector in producing intermediate as well as final products. It provides a remarkable picture of the interdependent flows of goods and payments within an economy. That is the major benefit of input-output accounting here. In more advanced work it is shown that input-output analysis can be used for making detailed forecasts of the effects of changes in the structure of final demand.[6]

Table 8-9

UNITED STATES INPUT-OUTPUT TABLE FOR 1958 (MILLIONS OF DOLLARS, 1947 PRICES)

Sector	1 *Materials*	2 *Metalworking*	3 *Construction*	4 *Transportation and utilities*	5 *Services*	6 *Mining*	7 *Agriculture*	8 *All other*	*Final demand*	*Gross domestic output*
1. Materials	8,565	8,069	8,843	3,045	1,124	276	230	3,464	3,994	37,608
2. Metalworking	1,505	6,996	6,895	3,530	3,383	365	219	2,946	19,269	45,100
3. Construction	98	39	5	429	5,694	7	376	327	39,348	46,322
4. Transportation and utilities	999	1,048	120	9,143	4,460	228	210	2,226	22,625	41,059
5. Services	4,373	4,488	8,325	2,729	29,671	1,733	5,757	14,756	137,571	209,404
6. Mining	2,150	36	640	1,234	165	821	90	6,717	—653	11,199
7. Agriculture	506	7	180		2,352		18,091	26,529	8,327	55,992
8. All other	5,315	1,895	2,993	1,071	13,941	434	6,096	46,338	82,996	161,080
Value added	14,097	22,522	18,320	19,877	148,614	7,344	24,923	57,777		313,475
Total inputs	37,608	45,100	46,322	41,059	209,404	11,199	55,992	161,080	313,475	921,240

Source: Anne P. Carter, *Structural Change in the American Economy,* Harvard University Press, Cambridge, Mass., 1970.

[6] Although the history of this type of accounting reaches back to the mid-eighteenth century French Physiocrats, its development and widespread current use is due to the ingenuity and enthusiasm of Prof. Wassily Leontief of Harvard University.

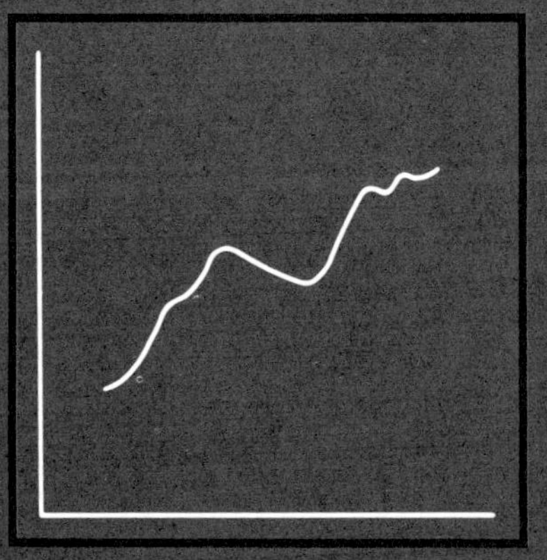

TWO

The determinants of the macroeconomic performance of the economy

The next ten chapters are devoted to the analysis of the determinants of the macroeconomic performance of the economy. The analysis owes a great deal to John Maynard Keynes, the great English economist who shook up the economics profession in the 1930s with his difficult and provocative book, The General Theory of Employment, Interest and Money. In this sense the New Economics to be presented here is Keynesian. But that is like describing a college student as someone who graduated from grade school. It is not untrue, but it does not tell us all that is relevant.

Macroeconomic theory has gone far beyond Keynes' book. It now stands as an approach on which there is wide consensus. That does not mean that all economists agree on all issues. There are wide differences in emphasis. Depending on one's goals and the interpretations of the facts, macroeconomic theory can be used to defend or attack a tax increase or tax cut, budget surpluses or budget deficits, and Democratic or Republican economics. The New Economics is a powerful set of tools which provides important insights into the great issues of prosperity, recession, unemployment, and inflation.

The world was in the grip of the Great Depression when Keynes' book appeared in 1936. Yet the economic theory of that time, what is now called "classical economics," had little to say about the causes and cures of such an economic crisis. Classical economic theory still echoes in the halls of power and forms part of the mythology of economics of the common man. Chapter 9, therefore, is devoted to understanding its strengths and fatal weaknesses.

Modern economics cannot accept the theory that the market economy is inherently self-stabilizing at full employment. Chapters 10, 11, and 12 explain the basic determinants of the aggregate performance of the economy in terms of the effective demand for output.

Monetary influences are brought into the analysis in Chapters 13 through 16. Basic monetary concepts are clarified first. Then the monetary system is explained, and its relations to aggregate economic performance are traced.

The effective demand and monetary analyses are brought together and the problems of economic fluctuations and public policies to deal with them are tackled in Chapters 17 and 18.

9

Does the market economy guarantee full employment?

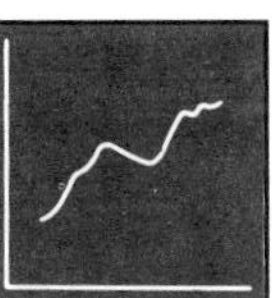

Until the mid-1930s the answer given by nearly all of the economics profession to the question posed in the chapter title was, Yes, except for minor fluctuations or major disruptions caused by outside forces such as wars or natural catastrophes. The answer given now, as a result of the analysis of the New Economics, is No. Our objective in this chapter is to understand the rationale of "classical economics" that lay behind the earlier Yes, and why it was wrong. The New Economics, which we take up in Chapter 10, tells us what does determine the level of output and income.

The motivation of this chapter is not just an antiquarian interest in what some old boys thought and wrote on the subject of macroeconomics. Those old boys were pretty smart, and we can profit from their insights as well as their mistakes. Although their mistakes were fatal for an understanding of the short-term behavior of the economy, their analysis contained a basic understanding of the determinants of what the long-run performance of the economy *could* be.

Potential versus actual GNP

The black line in Figure 9-1 shows the levels of GNP actually achieved since 1954. Its downward and upward bends show the slowdowns and speedups in overall economic activity. The red line is an estimate of the *potential GNP* of the economy in each year. Potential GNP is the volume of goods and services the econ-

Figure 9-1

COMPARISON OF POTENTIAL AND ACTUAL GNP

(Source: *Ray C. Fair, "Aggregate Price Changes and Price Expectations,"* Federal Reserve Bank of St. Louis Review, *November, 1970.*)

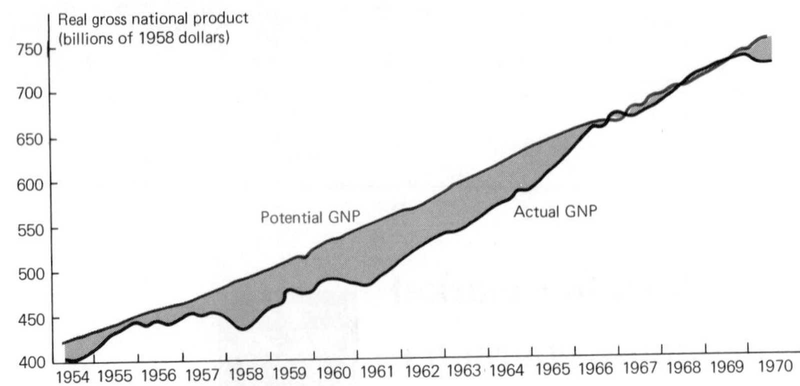

omy could produce if there were more or less full employment of labor and full use of other productive resources.[1] During most of the 1950s there was a substantial gap between actual and potential GNP, as shown by the shaded area under the potential GNP line. During these years prices rose relatively slowly, as can be seen in Figure 9-2. In the middle sixties the *actual-potential* gap began to close, and a few years later prices began to rise more rapidly. By the late sixties unemployment had fallen below 4 percent. Actual GNP rose above potential GNP at a 4 percent unemployment rate in much of 1968 and 1969 and prices started to go up at a comparatively fast rate.

Corresponding to such overall changes in national income and product, there are many detailed changes in particular regions and sectors of the economy. These reach down to the levels at which we all live. For example: Why were student loans hard to get last year? Because of general inflation and the monetary policy that was used to control it. Why did unemployment of young men and women under twenty rise from 1969 to 1970? When overall unemployment rises, the burden falls soonest and most heavily on young workers. Why did new construction of public housing slow down in 1969 and 1970? Again because of the macroeconomic policy used to offset inflationary forces.

The facts presented in Figures 9-1 and 9-2 indicate a real contrast between the late 1960s and the early 1960s. In 1967 and 1968 the United States economy was pushing against the ceiling on national output imposed by nearly full employment of labor and of productive capacity. These overall limits on the *supply* of goods

[1] Remember, full employment of labor allows for some unemployment. In Fig. 9-1 the unemployment rate implicit in the estimate of potential GNP is 4 percent.

Figure 9-2

AN INDEX OF PRICES OF PRIVATE OUTPUT

(*Source:* *Ray C. Fair, "Aggregate Price Changes and Price Expectations,"* Federal Reserve Bank of St. Louis Review, *November, 1970.*)

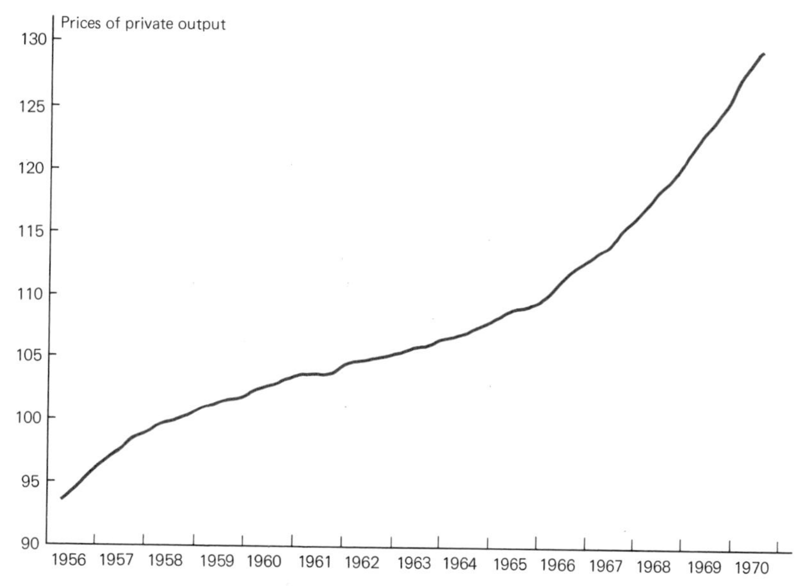

and services were the *binding constraints* on the aggregate performance of the system in those years. That certainly was not the situation in the 1950s and early 1960s when the economy was far below its full capacity and full employment ceiling. That ceiling was not the constraint. What were the determinants of output and income then? And what forces kept the system buoyant and bumping along the full employment ceiling in the late 1960s? In answering these questions, the New Economics stresses the *aggregate demand for output as determining the level of national income and output*.

A striking fact worth considering is that as long as classical economic theory held sway, economists generally ignored unemployment, even substantial unemployment persisting over several years. More importantly, the problems of economic fluctuations, in the aggregate and at the individual level, were not seen to be issues of public economic policy which required some positive government action. The classical theory, which was dominant throughout the nineteenth century and the first third of this century, still has a considerable following, often among people who do not realize that their views are classical. When people say that economic fluctuations do not create problems of public economic policy, they are implicitly asserting that a market economy is in itself capable of maintaining high levels of employment and income.

What is the attraction of this theory? What has given it such appeal and lasting power? In an oversimplified form, it has become part of our economic folklore. It is embodied in the old saying, Anyone who really wants to work can always find a job. Or as one of our leading poets put it:[2]

> No man is born into the world whose work
> Is not born with him; there is always work
> And tools to work withal; for those who will.

Our object is not to defend the theory or to destroy it, but to understand its rationale, its limitations, and its truths. In this way we shall also understand the new macroeconomics better.

The classical theory of income and employment

It is easy to see that in an economy of self-employed and self-sufficient workers there would be no unemployment. The economy would be poor or rich depending on the resources available and how efficiently they were used, but everyone would work as much or as little as he liked.[3]

In a modern economy of employers and employees, however, people are hired only if there is a demand for their output. Yet classical economic theory claimed that there were automatic mechanisms which would always operate even in this type of economy to create a level of aggregate demand sufficient to maintain full employment. The central argument in this theory was set forth by the French economist J. B. Say (1767–1832) and is known as Say's Law, or, more extensively, as Say's Law of Conservation of Purchasing Power. It is often summarized in the statement, Supply creates its own demand. On one level this can mean that every act of production creates an amount of income equal to the value of output. That is simply the income-product identity of national income accounting. It is as true at low as at high levels of income and employment. But to the classical economist, Say's Law had a more far-reaching meaning. It was that *there would always be sufficient aggregate purchasing power generated to demand all the output that could be produced at full employment*.

This argument will become clearer if we master several new concepts. The first is *aggregate supply*: the sum of all final goods and services that will be produced in an economy at alternative levels of NNP. That is not just NNP under a different name. NNP is the total production of final goods and services as measured at the end of a year. It is what economists call an "ex post" concept because it describes something after it has happened. Aggregate supply, however, is a forward-looking, or "ex ante," concept and is

[2] James Russell Lowell, *A Glance behind the Curtain* (1843).

[3] The model economies of Chap. 3 are composed of self-sufficient workers. The output of those economies depends on the real resources available to them, including the hours of work devoted to production.

Figure 9-3

AGGREGATE SUPPLY

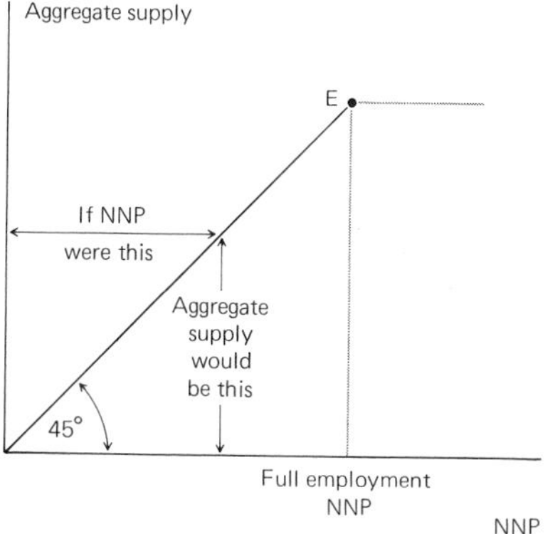

concerned with what is expected to happen or what is planned. Aggregate supply is the total amount of final goods and services that will be offered for sale at each level of the net national product. The amount that will be offered for sale at each level of NNP is the amount that can be sold.

In Figure 9-3 aggregate supply is the line from the origin; it has a slope of 45 degrees, because a line with that slope is equidistant from the axes. So the perpendicular distance to the line from the NNP axis is equal to the horizontal distance from the aggregate supply axis. The amount offered for sale at each level of NNP will be equal to the NNP. The line stops going up and turns horizontal at the full employment level of NNP. It is impossible to offer for sale more than can be produced.

This may seem to be a roundabout and unnecessarily complicated way of saying that producers will sell whatever they can sell. The roundabout approach has one great virtue, however. It emphasizes the important fact that production decisions and purchasing decisions are made by different groups of people for different reasons. There is no reason why, ex ante, that is, looking forward, the decisions of the two groups have to be the same. Unless there is some mechanism or process to make the decisions of purchasers and producers *come to be* the same, the economy will never be *in equilibrium.* If markets are out of equilibrium they will not even be approximately clearing in an orderly manner. Unsold goods will pile up in inventories; underproduced goods will be cleaned off sellers' shelves. In the latter situation, purchasers will be frustrated because they will not be able to buy the goods they want. Producers will have underproduced. In the former situation, producers will be frustrated because they will not be able to sell what they have produced. This is not the way the economy behaves. Although economic conditions change from year to year, or even from month to month, and inventories are built up and run down, the extreme conditions of *dis*equilibrium do not always prevail.

A tendency to move to equilibrium is a feature of classical theory, as it must be of any theory that accurately describes the way the economy works. The classical economic argument was stronger than that, however, as Say's Law indicates. The classical theory asserted that there were processes in the economy which would move it to equilibrium with full employment and full use of productive capacity. According to the classical economists, aggregate demand for NNP would always tend to be at the full employment level, at point *E* in Figure 9-3.

It is instructive to follow the reasoning of the classical economists. We can do this more easily in a simple model than if we try to deal with all the complications of reality. So let us define our First Macro Model as an economy (1) with no government spending or taxation and (2) no foreign trade purchases or sales. We shall also assume that there is no depreciation. Though these are extremely simplifying assumptions, we shall lose nothing of the essence of classical economic theory if we work it through in this context.

It is always useful to get the national income accounting straight for an economy. In our First Macro Model, since there is no depreciation, the gross national product, GNP, and net national product, NNP, are the same. That is, GNP $\equiv$ NNP. Since it has no government sector and no foreign trade, there are only two types of expenditures, consumption, C, and investment, I. So NNP $\equiv C + I$. There are no taxes and transfer payments, so NNP $\equiv$ NI $\equiv$ Disposable income, DI. Disposable income is either consumed or saved, S; thus DI $\equiv C + S$. Therefore, NNP $\equiv C + I \equiv$ DI $\equiv C + S$.[4]

Now suppose the economy of the First Macro Model happens to be at full employment with full use of capacity. The income generated at full employment will accrue to individual workers, to owners of land and capital, and to profit receivers. These people will spend their income on consumption goods – but not all of it! Some part will be saved. That part is a *leakage* from the circular flow of income. As shown in Figure 9-4, the saving leakage makes total consumption expenditures less than total income and, therefore, less than the total expenditures necessary to buy all the goods produced. That may appear to make the total demand for final goods and services always less than the total supply. But, fortunately, even in this simple model there is another source of purchasing power for another part of the final product. That is the expenditure on new investment goods purchased by business to create productive capacity. Investment expenditure adds to the aggregate demand for goods and services and is an *injection* into the stream of purchasing power.

Now we come to a critical question: Is there any reason to suppose that there is a mechanism or process which will make the expenditure on investment goods just enough to offset the saving by income recipients – no more and no less? The classical advocates of Say's Law asserted that the answer was Yes, but they were not always absolutely clear on the logic. Some of them told stories about savers looking for real investment opportunities and employing whatever of their income was left over after consumption expenditures to buy investment goods. In some classical arguments there was the notion that banks collected the current saving of individuals and channeled it into the purchase of new investment goods. In general, that is not what savers do or what bankers do either.

The more sophisticated classical theorists argued that there is a supply and demand adjustment process that makes the quantity of investment goods demanded equal to the quantity of saving

[4] Remember these are definitions. That is why the three-line identity sign is used rather than the equals sign. They are also ex post concepts; that is, they are measured after the events they summarize. But they also tell us in advance what kinds of spending to look for.

Figure 9-4
THE FLOW OF AGGREGATE DEMAND

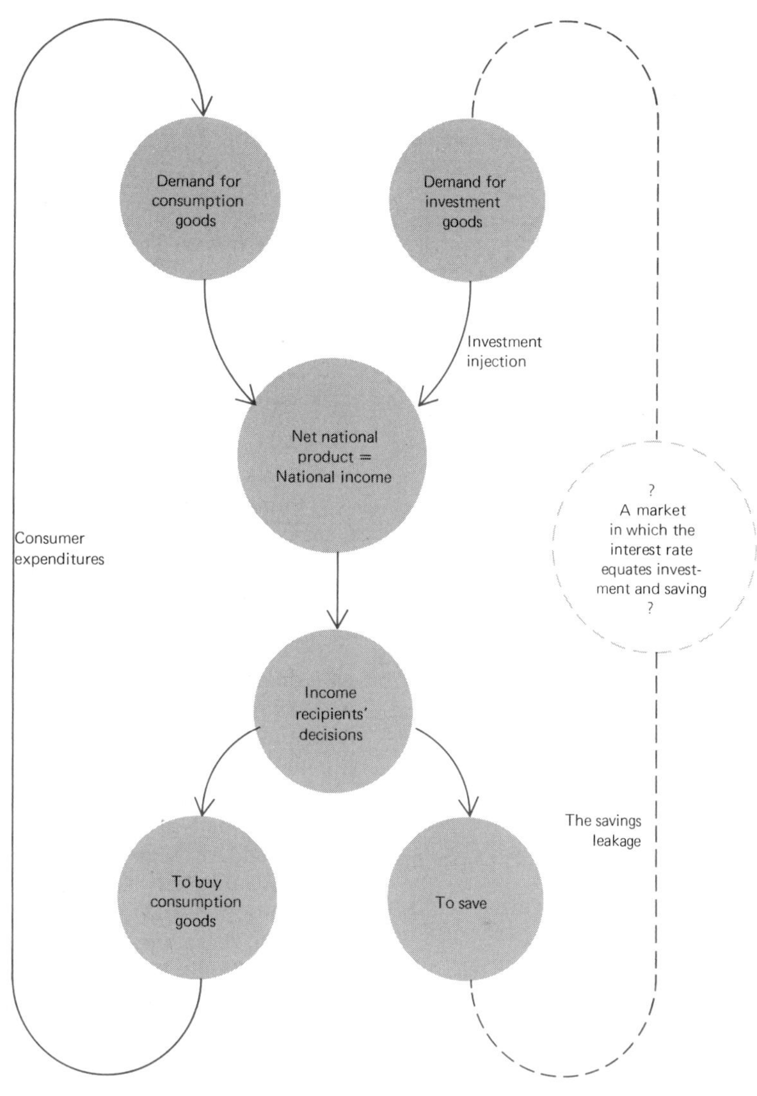

supplied. Adjustments in the interest rate are assumed to work in much the same way that price movements equate the amounts supplied and demanded in goods markets.

This theory is represented in Figure 9-5. The quantity of real resources demanded for investment is assumed to increase as the interest rate falls. At lower interest rates more investment would be profitable and, therefore, according to the theory, more would be undertaken. The amount of saving supplied is assumed to increase with the interest rate because higher rates make saving

Figure 9-5

THE CLASSICAL THEORY OF EQUALIZATION OF SAVING AND INVESTMENT BY THE INTEREST RATE

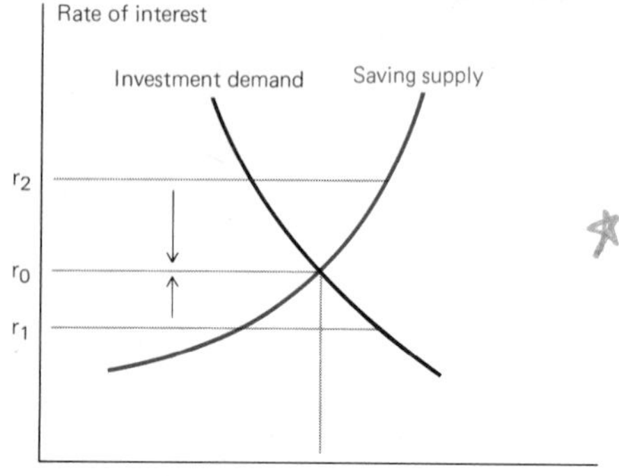

more attractive. The equilibrium rate of interest is at r_0, at the intersection of the investment demand and the saving supply curves. At interest rates above the equilibrium rate, r_0, saving would be greater than investment. Competition of savers and investors would force the interest rate from, say, r_1 to r_0, and push saving and investment into equality. Below r_0, say, at r_2, forces would work to push the interest rate upward[5] and equalize saving and investment. This process guaranteed, it was claimed, that the savings leakage would always be exactly offset by the investment injection and that the flow of purchasing power would be maintained.

But would purchasing power be maintained at just that level which would fully utilize the labor force and capacity of the economy? Another, but related, argument relying on competition and price flexibility in labor markets was put forward to resolve this question.

Suppose there *were* some unemployment. According to the classical economists, wages would fall as the result of competition among workers for jobs. That would (1) reduce production costs, (2) increase profits, (3) stimulate production, and (4) create more jobs. So workers would again be hired up to full employment.

This process is illustrated by Figure 9-6. There is some aggregate demand for labor, as illustrated by the curve *D*, and an aggregate supply of labor, exemplified by the curve *S*. If there were unemployment, the amount of labor supplied would be greater than the amount demanded, as at wage rate w_1. But labor market competition would bring wages down and make the amount of labor supplied at the equilibrium rate, w_0, equal to the amount demanded. At wage rates below the equilibrium rate, labor market forces would push the wage rate up and again bring the amount of labor supplied and demanded into equality. Likewise, if capacity were idle, there would be a similar competition which would lower costs and finally lead to the full use of the capital stock.

Figure 9-6

CLASSICAL LABOR DEMAND AND SUPPLY INTERACTION

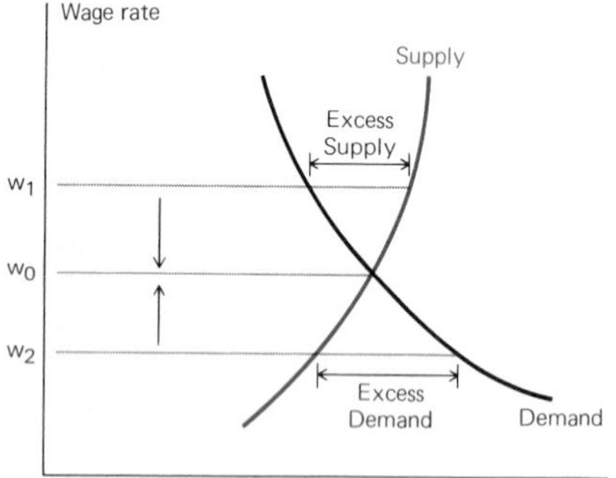

What about the following problem: When wage rates fall, incomes fall too. Will the output producible at full employment still be purchased at the reduced incomes? In the classical system, prices of goods as well as wages were assumed to be flexible. The prices of goods would always fall enough to ensure that all output would be taken at a wage level which would permit full employment.

There might, of course, be disruptions, such as wars, natural catastrophes, political changes, speculative crises, and other unusual events, to upset the smooth working of the classical system. These, it was believed, would only cause temporary deviations

[5] Notice that saving and investment are supposedly made equal in this theory by a market mechanism. They are not always and inevitably identical. Looking forward, or ex ante, they could be different. Looking backward, or ex post, the process is supposed to make saving and investment equal.

from the long-term full employment ceiling. With competition here, competition there, and competition everywhere, the classical economists concluded that there could be no lasting problem of unemployment and depression.

It was an attractive theory for several reasons. It seemed to be a natural extension to aggregate economics of the theory of behavior of competitive markets. It also provided the capstone to the doctrine that laissez faire capitalism was a fully self-regulating economic system. With full employment assured, there would never be any need for government intervention in the economy. The market economy would maintain prosperity by itself.

What is wrong with the classical theory? The first thing to be said about it has already been said: Its predictions were inaccurate. Even a casual acquaintance with the history of the period during which classical economics flourished reveals many recurring and often prolonged periods of unemployment and depression. Figure 9-1 provides a graphic description of recent ups and down. Figure 8-3 in the preceding chapter surveys the fluctuations in the United States economy since the turn of the century. The facts are against the classical theory. How did good logic like that go wrong? Or was the logic good? With minor amendments and additions, the classical logic was correct. That means that the basic assumptions must have been wrong; they were simply not close enough to reality to lead to good predictions.

The unreliability of classical price-wage flexibility

The classical theory assumed that aggressive competition would drive wages downward and deflate prices and restore full employment when there was a depression. Modern economies do not work that way. True, there is some shaving of wage rates and softening of prices when the economy slows down. But on the whole, both wages and prices tend to be "sticky" with respect to downward movements.

On the product side, in many industries, a good deal of market power is concentrated in the hands of a relatively few sellers. Often they choose to keep prices up even when there is a general slackening of economic activity and of demand for their product. They reason that it is easier to maintain their market control if they do not allow prices to fluctuate too much. They adjust their output instead to match reductions in demand at more or less constant prices.

On the labor side, unions are reluctant to allow wage cuts even though employment may be falling. The wage rigidity imposed by labor unions is reinforced by minimum wage laws which follow the upward trend of wages during periods of prosperity but do not lower the minimum during periods of economic softness.

The unreliability of the classical notion of wage-price flexibility has even deeper sources, however. A reduction in wages is a reduction in income, purchasing power, and effective demand for output. Prices of goods and services must also fall if *real* purchasing power in terms of goods and services is to be maintained. But if the prices of final goods and services fall as wages fall, then there is no increase in profits to stimulate an expansion in output and employment. Moreover, falling prices do not breed confidence, but just the reverse. When prices fall, businessmen are likely to postpone rather than increase investment and to reduce rather than expand output. This inclination will be reinforced if the interest rate is also sticky and does not adjust downward. Thus, while a low-price–low-wage full employment point might exist, the process of getting there would not be smooth and easy. It would involve bankruptcy and widespread dislocation. Critics of the classical theory who argue this way usually admit that wage and price flexibility might eventually work the system back to full employment, especially if adjustments were made on the financial side to stimulate spending. But "eventually" can be a long time, indeed. In the *short run,* wage and price flexibility do not guarantee full employment, and "In the long run," as John Maynard Keynes said in a slightly different context, "we are all dead."

The unreliability of the classical saving-investment connection

Let us remind ourselves, first of all, of the meaning of the terms saving and investment. That will help keep the logic straight. Saving is that part of current income which is not used for consumption. Investment is the expenditure on new capital goods and additions to inventories.

The motivations for saving and for investment are, for the most part, different; the decision-making processes are different and the individuals and groups who carry out the decisions are generally different. It is true that some saving is specifically allocated for investment projects. When individual business proprietors who are trying to build up their business plow back part of their income into equipment or inventory, they are saving in order to invest. Here the connection is short and direct. But it is not so for all businesses. Corporations save by not paying out all their net profits as dividends. They may or may not use that saving for investment in new capital goods. Instead they may pay off outstanding debts or buy some existing business.

Most individual income recipients and households who save have little thought of investment. They may lay away part of their current income for a vacation, for college expenses, for retirement, or for a new car. Or they may put their savings in a bank account, under the mattress, or in a piggy bank. They may buy stocks and bonds or insurance, which often has a substantial savings component. Or they may be paying back a loan on the installment plan or paying off a mortgage. These payments are, in large part, saving, since they are not used to buy new consumption goods.

Private investors, on the other hand, are in business to make money. It may be big business or small, but when they buy new capital goods they do so with the expectation of profits.

Federal, state, and local governments invest in such projects as new school buildings, hospitals, and highways. The motivation and decision-making processes for these investments are usually complex and sometimes obscure. It is certain, however, that they need have little to do with current saving by government or by private individuals or groups.

One question which sometimes bothers students is the following: How can investment be financed if the people doing it are not saving? In fact, there are many potential sources of *funds* with which to buy new investment goods other than current savings. The investors may have saved in past years and accumulated bank balances on which they can draw. Or they may be able to borrow from a bank or an insurance company or get cash by selling some other asset. Corporations can raise money by selling stocks, and both corporations and governments can sell bonds.

Now, does the fluctuation of interest rates act as a mechanism to make what people plan to invest equal to what other people plan to save, however different the processes and motivations lying behind the two types of activity? Is Figure 9-5 a reasonably good representation of reality? The facts tend to be against the theory. On the whole, savers do not appear to pay much attention to interest rates in making their savings decisions. Those who do are not likely to react uniformly. Some people may find that higher interest rates are an inducement to save more in order to receive more interest income. Others may find that higher interest rates only make it easier to reach their future income goals, and the higher rates may thus lead to reduced saving.

The responsiveness of investment to the interest rate is still a matter of debate among economists. Some types of investment hardly respond at all to changes in the interest rate. Other types may be slightly responsive. Investment that relies heavily on borrowed funds may be more responsive. Why these differences? Because interest charges are only one of the many expenses involved in a project, and not a major expense at that for most types of investment. So the leverage of the interest rate on investment varies from slight to substantial, depending on the kind of investment.

It is obvious now that the saving-investment connection put forward by classical theory is unreliable. Why was it not clear to the classicals? Not because of their logic. If the facts were as they assumed them to be, the theory would be all right. Unfortunately the evidence available, though not absolutely conclusive, does not confirm their assumptions. Saving is at most only slightly sensitive to the interest rate. Investment responds to interest rate changes only to a degree. The interest rate itself is now generally thought to be determined mainly by monetary factors at least in the short run, as will be explained in Chapter 15.[6]

The long-run germ of truth in classical economics

We cannot accept the classical notion of an automatic tendency toward full employment, but what determines the level of *potential GNP* plotted in Figure 9-1? The classical answer would be: Potential GNP is that producible with full employment of labor and other productive resources. The amount of labor available depends fundamentally on the size of the population, and the amount of productive capital available depends on the amount of saving and investment. Then drawing a breath, the classicals would add, the market economy operates so as to maintain full employment in the short run.

We do not have to agree with the last sentence to agree with the first part of the answer. The production of which an economy is potentially capable *is* increased by investment. The potential would be achieved if full employment could be maintained. That is the germ of truth in classical economics which we want to appreciate. Classical economics also bequeathed a good deal of useful analysis at the microeconomic level on which modern economics builds. It is at the macroeconomic level that its inadequacies are most severe.

In some ways it is rather a pity that the world does not work as classical economic theory predicted. If it did, life would be much simpler. Assured of a self-stabilizing economy, we could turn our attention to other problems. Unfortunately, the problems of macroeconomic stability and of unemployment are very much with us. Since the market economy is not self-stabilizing at full employment, public economic policy is required to maintain high levels of economic activity.

[6] Part of the popular confusion over saving and investment is a semantic one, though that was not the problem of the classical economists. Economists define saving as a leakage from the current flow of income. To the layman it may mean past accumulations of wealth in the hands of individuals, banks, or any potential lender. To us, investment is the purchase of new capital goods. To others, it is the amount of cash in banks or the amount of some financial transaction. It is a free country and anybody can make up and use his own definitions. But when we talk about the existence of a self-regulating mechanism in the economy, we must deal with saving as a *leakage* and investment as an *injection* of purchasing power. *If* we were to define investment as the amount people withhold from consumption and put into banks and financial instruments of all types – including piggy banks and IOUs – then saving and investment would be the same by definition. But that does not mean that there is an interest rate mechanism that always brings the nonconsumption leakage of purchasing power and the purchase of new investment goods into equality.

Summary

Macroeconomic records covering several decades indicate periods in which the actual GNP produced in an economy is substantially less than the potential GNP producible at full employment. The macroeconomic performance of the economy has a profound effect on all aspects of private and public life. In explaining the ups and downs of the economy, the New Economics emphasizes aggregate demand for real goods and services.

Classical economic theory denied the possibility of long-lasting depression. Say's Law of Conservation of Purchasing Power was at the heart of classical theory. This law argued that in the circular flow of income, there was never any *net* leakage of purchasing power for goods at full employment income. So full employment would be automatically maintained.

Classical economists recognized that the aggregate amount of output produced – and of income earned – depended on the aggregate demand for output. But they thought that the amounts of saving and investment would be adjusted by the rate of interest so that the saving leakage would always be exactly offset by the investment injection. Perfect competition and wage flexibility would ensure that this equalization of saving and investment took place at full employment.

The interest rate adjustment of saving and investment is not borne out by empirical studies. Experience shows that the interest rate has a small and uncertain influence on saving. Its effect on investment is often relatively minor. Limited wage and price flexibility impede the economy's adjustment toward full employment. Moreover, a reduction in wages is a reduction in income and leads to a reduction in purchasing power unless prices fall. But if prices do fall, the stimulus to expanded production and employment tends to disappear.

The important germ of truth in classical macroeconomics is that potential GNP is determined by the amount of labor and productive capital goods available. If full employment is maintained, saving and investment contribute to actual as well as potential GNP.

Questions for discussion and review

1. What determines potential GNP?

2. What does it mean to say that "supply creates its own demand"?

3. What is controversial about the "full employment equilibrium" conclusion of classical economics, the "full employment" part or the "equilibrium" part?

4. Why is saving in itself a reduction in purchasing power, and what, according to classical economic theory, is the mechanism by which it is always supposed to be exactly offset?

5. Suppose that for some reason, say, the demobilization of part of the army, a lot of new workers became available for work. How would classical economic theory explain the process by which they became employed?

6. Do you believe the classical price-wage flexibility mechanism? Explain your answer.

7. Do you believe the classical saving-investment mechanism? Explain.

8. Is there anything in classical macroeconomic theory that you do believe? Explain.

Concepts for review

Aggregate demand
Aggregate supply
Say's Law
Macroeconomic equilibrium and macroeconomic disequilibrium
Saving
Investment
Price-wage flexibility
Wage stickiness downward

10

Private aggregate demand: Consumption and investment spending

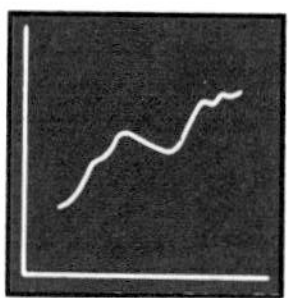

Classical economic theory proposed the conception of the economic system as a self-regulating mechanism which would tend to maintain full employment. Modern economists are critical of classical theory for the reasons set out in the preceding chapter. Yet it is difficult to escape the belief that classical theory was correct in singling out the saving and investment nexus as a strategic one for understanding the overall behavior of the economy. This chapter concentrates on the determinants of private saving and investment as an introduction to the exposition of the modern analysis of the determinants of national income to begin in the next chapter.

Since saving is simply what is left over out of income after current consumption expenditures, we will turn directly to an analysis of consumption. Actually the main lesson is a simple one: By far the most important determinant of consumption, and, therefore, of saving, is disposable income. In one way or another, this result comes out of every study made of consumer behavior.

Studies of family income and consumption

Over the years, a great deal of information has been collected on the expenditures of individual families with different levels of income. These data tell a story that is remarkably uniform from country to country and from time to time. Figure 10-1 shows the pattern of consumer expenditures and the relationship of expenditures to income in the United States.[1]

[1] These are called "Engel curves" after a nineteenth-century German statistican, Ernst Engel, not the collaborator of Marx, Friedrich Engels.

Figure 10-1

THE SHARES OF MAJOR CATEGORIES OF CONSUMER EXPENDITURE AND SAVING AT DIFFERENT LEVELS OF INCOME

The proportions of income spent on most categories of goods and services fall as income rises, and the proportion saved increases. But the absolute amounts spent on any category almost never fall as income rises. (Source: U.S. Department of Labor, Bureau of Labor Statistics.)

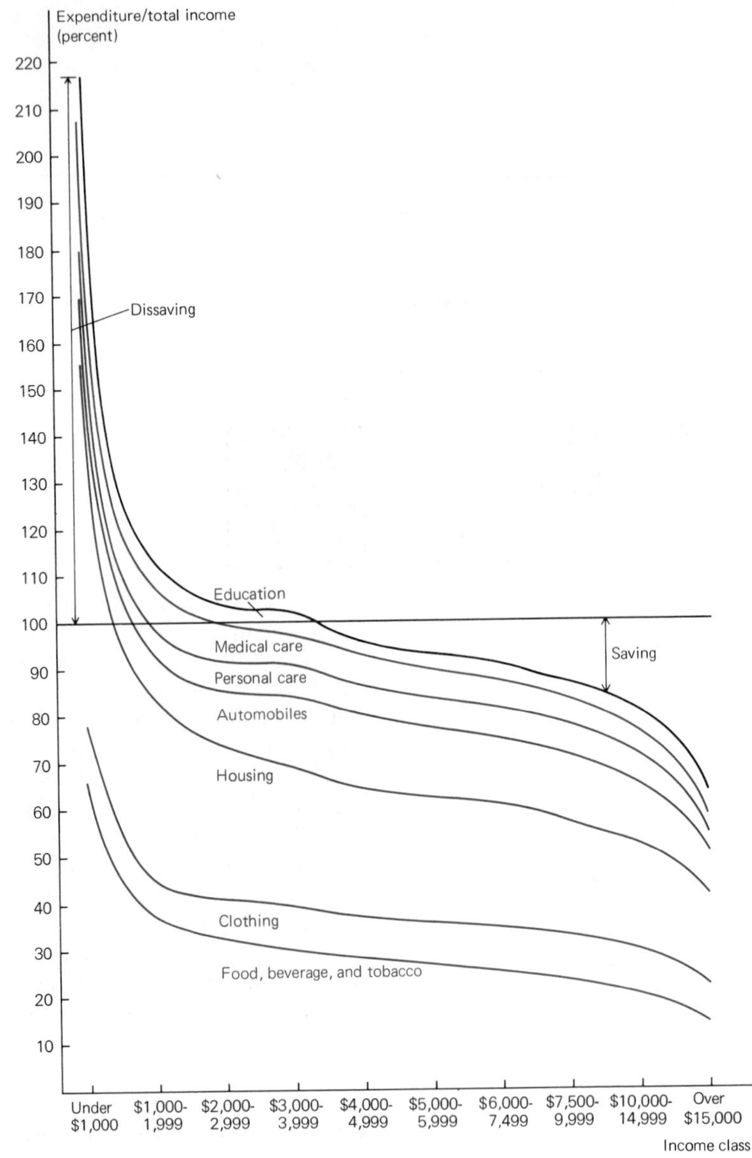

At low income levels, nearly all of a family's spending goes for food, shelter, clothing, and other necessities. By and large there is little saving. At the lowest income levels there is *dissaving*; consumption expenditures are greater than income. How? The difference may be financed out of past savings, by borrowing, or by gifts.

Saving is a "luxury" in the sense that there is more of it at high-income levels – both absolutely and as a percentage of income. That makes sense. Saving implies that income is not used for consumption. For lower-income people, there is little room for choice. Drowning men grasp at straws, and it should not be surprising that poor people find it necessary to use a larger proportion of their income for current consumption than people who are better off.

As incomes rise, expenditures on the so-called necessities of life fall as a proportion of disposable income. In addition, "necessities" are of a higher quality: more steaks and fewer hamburgers, for example, and, in general, a shift toward meat, vegetables, and dairy products and away from grains and other carbohydrate foods.

The basic consumption-saving-income relationship in family spending is clear and strong. Yet there is a good deal of variability in the relationship among individual families. There are spendthrift rich and thrifty poor. To some extent, the spending and saving done by a family are influenced by the way its income compares with that of the community or group with which it identifies. This tends to confirm the well-known "keeping up with the Joneses"

Figure 10-2

THE HISTORICAL MOVEMENTS OF REAL DISPOSABLE INCOME AND CONSUMPTION EXPENDITURES

The widening of the gap between disposable income and consumption in the World War II period indicates the high rate of saving then. That was associated with patriotic appeals to restrain consumption, goods shortages, and rationing. (Source: U.S. Department of Commerce, Office of Business Economics.)

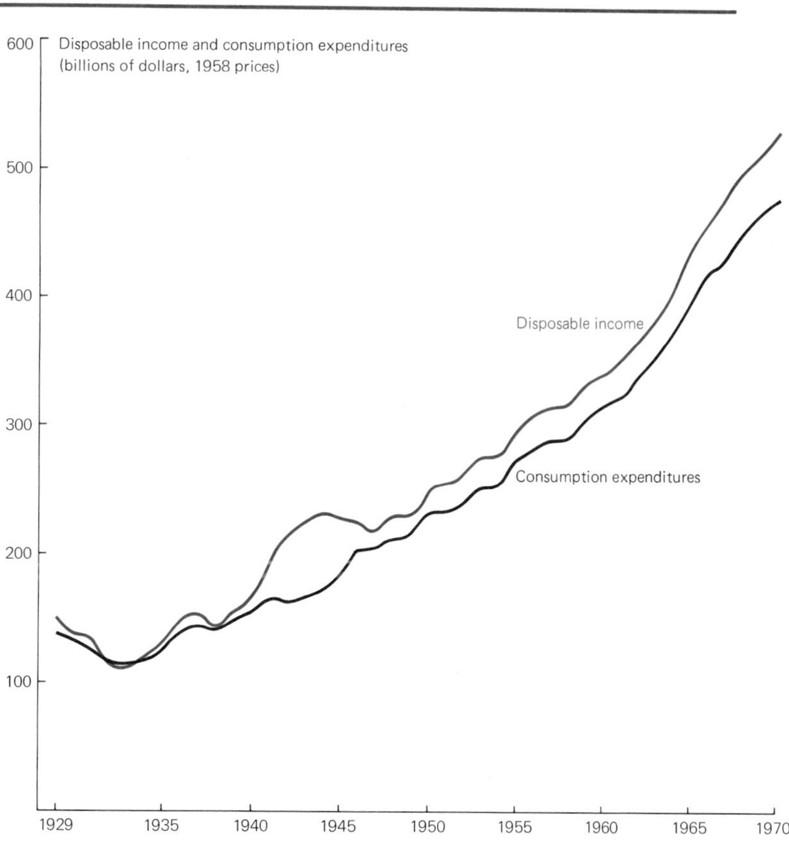

explanation of consumption behavior. That means not getting too far ahead as well as not too far behind. Who the Joneses are depends on where each family lives and the social group to which it regards itself as belonging.

Annual estimates of total income and consumption

The annual estimates of national income put out by the Department of Commerce throw a lot of light on consumption and saving behavior. Figure 10-2 plots the level of aggregate consumption and disposable income for each year since 1929. These magnitudes move along closely together. During the depression of the 1930s, consumption was greater than disposable income in 1933, which means there was *dissaving*. During World War II disposable income went up much faster than consumption, owing to goods rationing, shortages, and the success of patriotic appeals to restrain consumption and increase saving. To some extent, however, consumption was merely delayed, and rose more than normally in the immediate post-World War II years. After that, disposable income and consumption again began to march along together, though by no means exactly in step. Personal saving as a percentage of disposable income ranged as high as 7.5 percent in the early 1950s and fell as low as 4.9 percent in the early 1960s. In 1970 personal saving was about 7.3 percent of disposable income, but in 1969 it averaged about 6 percent.

In Figure 10-3, each point plots the national consumption of

Figure 10-3

AN AGGREGATE PROPENSITY TO CONSUME AND ACTUAL CONSUMPTION-DISPOSABLE INCOME OBSERVATIONS

The line C is fitted to the observed points statistically. The slope of the line C is 0.905, which indicates that, on the average, 90.5 percent of every additional dollar of disposable income is spent on consumption. (Source: Data from U.S. Department of Commerce, Office of Business Economics.)

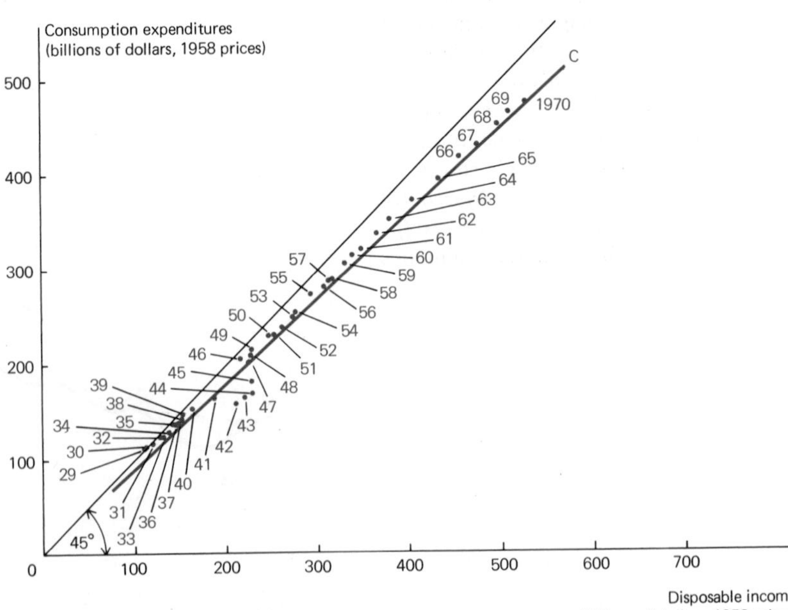

one year against the national disposable income of that year. The line drawn through the points indicates the approximate general tendency except during the World War II years when circumstances were particularly unusual. Another line goes out from the origin at a 45-degree angle to the consumption and income axes. If a point falls on this 45-degree line, it means that consumption is equal to income in that year. The distance by which any point falls *below* the 45-degree line is the amount by which consumption is less than disposable income, and that is the amount of personal saving that year.

The annual aggregate data confirm the impressions gained from the family budget studies. Consumption rises with income and so does saving. The *share* of consumption seems to fall and the *share* of saving seems to rise as income rises. A careful inspection of the separate points will show some apparent irregularities, to which we shall return below when we discuss extensions of the basic consumption and saving theory.

The aggregate consumption and saving schedules

So far we have discussed past relationships between consumption, saving, and income. These are pretty good indicators of what the future relationships will be. The relationship that *predicts* aggregate consumption from aggregate income data is called the *propensity to consume* or *consumption schedule*. The *propensity to save* or *saving schedule* predicts the total amount of saving from aggregate income data.

Figure 10-4 shows a somewhat idealized propensity to consume with an exaggerated amount of curvature. Figure 10-5 shows the corresponding saving schedule or propensity to save, and Table 10-1 presents the two schedules in numerical form. These schedules are so important that we can go no further in our macroeconomic analysis without understanding them fully.

The propensity to consume and the propensity to save are each a series of *if-then* statements: *If* disposable income is so much, *then* consumption expenditures and saving will be such and such. The propensity-to-save schedule is the mirror image of the propensity to consume, with the reflecting glass being the 45-degree line on the propensity-to-consume schedule. Thus, since the propensity-to-consume curve bends downward, the propensity-to-save schedule bends upward.

In Figure 10-4, the distance, XY, by which the propensity to consume is *above the horizontal axis* at $800 billion disposable income is the amount of consumption expenditures at that level of income. The distance, YZ, by which the propensity to consume lies *below the 45-degree line* when aggregate disposable income is $800 billion is $40 billion. That is the amount of saving at $800 billion

Figure 10-4

HYPOTHETICAL PROPENSITY TO CONSUME

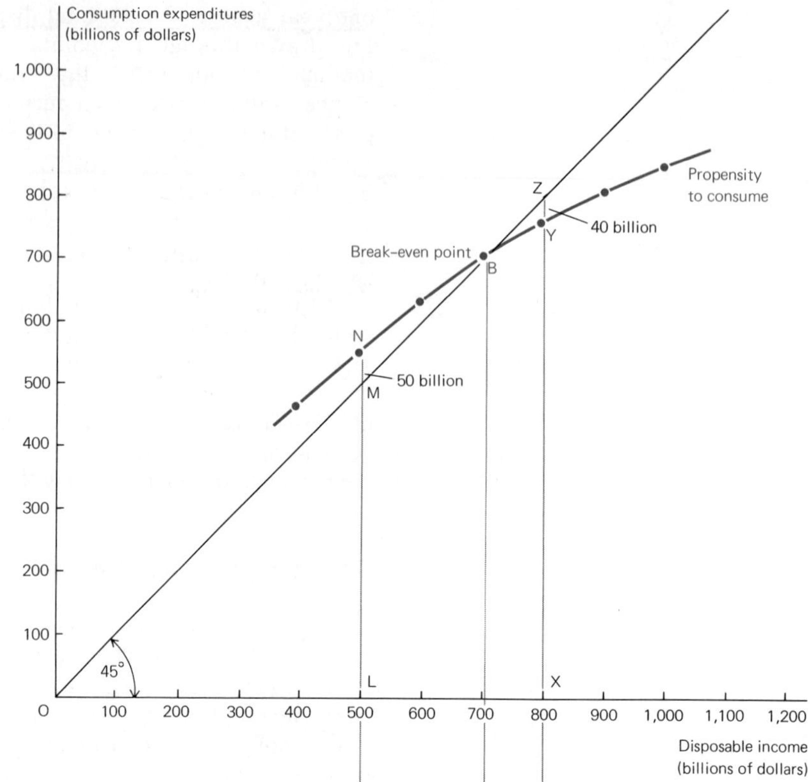

Figure 10-5

HYPOTHETICAL PROPENSITY TO SAVE

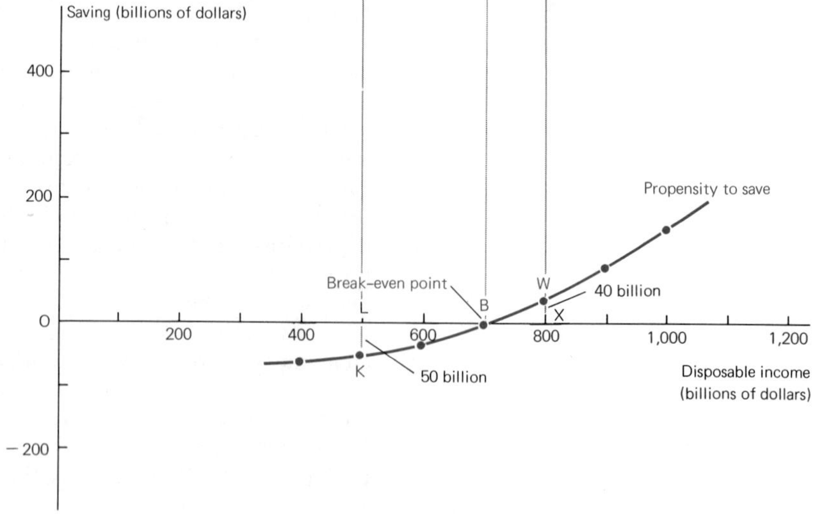

Table 10-1

THE PROPENSITY TO CONSUME AND THE PROPENSITY TO SAVE (HYPOTHETICAL DATA IN BILLIONS OF DOLLARS)

	DI		*C*	*S*
If	$1,100	then	$880	$220
If	1,000	then	850	150
If	900	then	810	90
If	800	then	760	40
If	700	then	700	0
If	600	then	630	−30
If	500	then	550	−50
If	400	then	460	−60

disposable income. *XW*, which is the distance by which the propensity to save is above the horizontal axis at $800 billion disposable income in Figure 10-5, is equal to *YZ* in Figure 10-4. At $500 billion disposable income, the *MN* distance in Figure 10-4 measures the amount of *dis*saving. That is equal to *LK* in Figure 10-5. The *break-even point B* in both figures is the level of disposable income at which consumption just equals income and there is no saving leakage. At the break-even point, in the aggregate all families and other spending units are spending just what they earn. There is no saving and no dissaving.

Consumption and saving concepts

The *average propensity to consume*, APC, is the average rate of consumption out of income. APC is just consumption expenditure divided by the corresponding disposable income, or C/DI. Likewise the average propensity to save, APS, or average saving rate, is total saving divided by the corresponding disposable income, or S/DI. There is a simple, necessary relationship between the APC and the APS. They must add up to one. Why? Since consumption and saving exhaust the disposable income, the sum of the shares of both in disposable income must be 100 percent.[2] Notice that the average propensity to consume is just the *slope* of a line from the origin *O* to the propensity-to-consume curve. The propensity to consume is redrawn in Figure 10-6 to help show this. At point Y, for example, the APC is the slope of the line OY. That is the length of the line XY divided by the length of the line OX. OX is the disposable income of $800 billion at which consumption, XY, is $760 billion. So the APC in this case is $760 billion/$800 billion or 0.95.

[2] Symbolically DI = *C* + *S*. If we divide through by DI, we get DI/DI = *C*/DI + *S*/DI or 1 = APC + APS.

Figure 10-6

HYPOTHETICAL PROPENSITY TO CONSUME AND THE APC

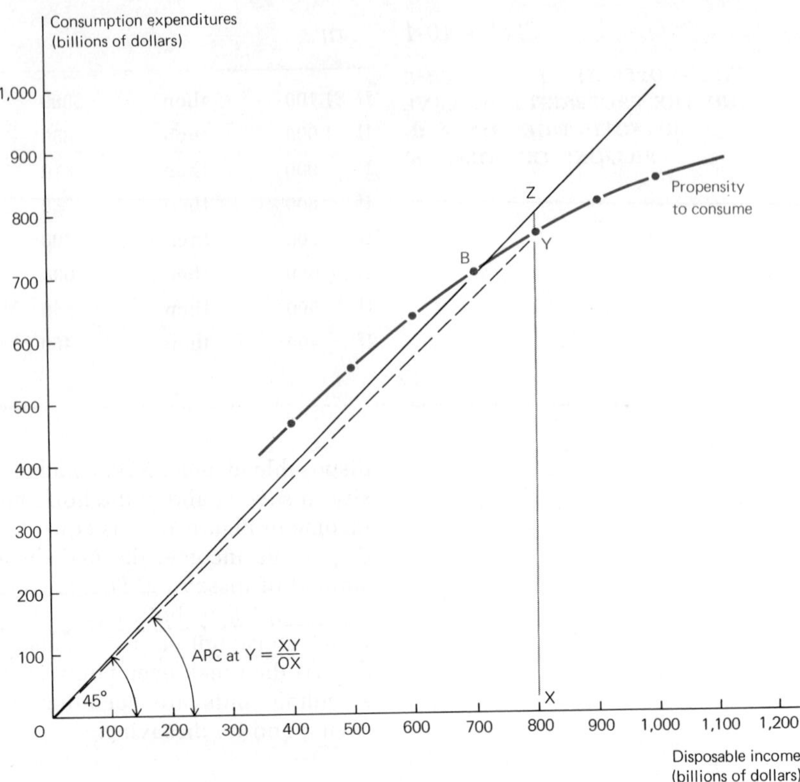

Figure 10-7

HYPOTHETICAL PROPENSITY TO SAVE AND THE APS

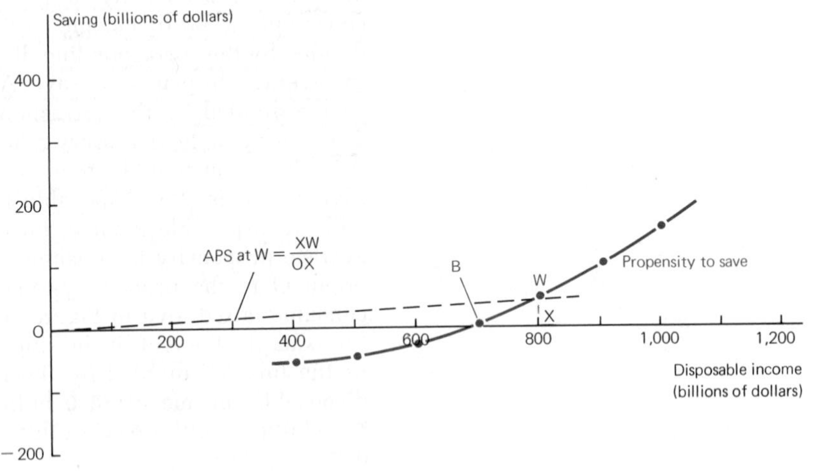

The propensity to save is redrawn in Figure 10-7. Here the average propensity to save, APS, is the slope of a line drawn from the origin to the propensity-to-save curve. At the level of disposable income of $800 billion (the distance *OX* in Fig. 10-7), saving is $40 billion (the distance *XW*, which is equal to *YZ*). So the APS is $40 billion/$800 billion or 0.05.

With the propensity-to-consume and propensity-to-save schedules like those presented in Table 10-1 and the figures plotted from that table, the average propensity to consume will fall as disposable income rises. Correspondingly, the average propensity to save will fall. This is shown in columns 3 and 6 of Table 10-2, reading from the bottom up.

We shall often be interested in the *change* that occurs in consumption expenditures when there is a *change* in disposable income. The ratio of these two changes is the marginal propensity to consume. Symbolically, Δ represents "change in." So, if ΔDI stands for the change in disposable income and ΔC is the change in consumption that it induces, then the marginal propensity to consume or MPC is ΔC/ΔDI. Similarly, the marginal propensity

Table 10-2

THE PROPENSITIES TO CONSUME AND SAVE (HYPOTHETICAL DATA, BILLIONS OF DOLLARS)

1 *DI*	2 *C*	3 *APC* = *C/DI*	4 *MPC* = *ΔC/ΔDI*	5 *S*	6 *APS* = *S/DI*	7 *MPS* = *ΔC/ΔDI*
$1,100	$880	0.80		$220	0.20	
			$\frac{30}{100} = 0.3$			$\frac{70}{100} = 0.7$
1,000	850	0.85		150	0.15	
			$\frac{40}{100} = 0.4$			$\frac{60}{100} = 0.6$
900	810	0.90		90	0.10	
			$\frac{50}{100} = 0.5$			$\frac{50}{100} = 0.5$
800	760	0.95		40	0.05	
			$\frac{60}{100} = 0.6$			$\frac{40}{100} = 0.4$
700	700	1.00		0	0.00	
			$\frac{70}{100} = 0.7$			$\frac{30}{100} = 0.3$
600	630	1.05		−30	−0.05	
			$\frac{80}{100} = 0.8$			$\frac{20}{100} = 0.2$
500	550	1.10			−0.10	
			$\frac{90}{100} = 0.9$			$\frac{10}{100} = 0.1$
400	460	1.15		−60	−0.15	

Figure 10-8

THE MARGINAL PROPENSITY TO CONSUME AS A SLOPE

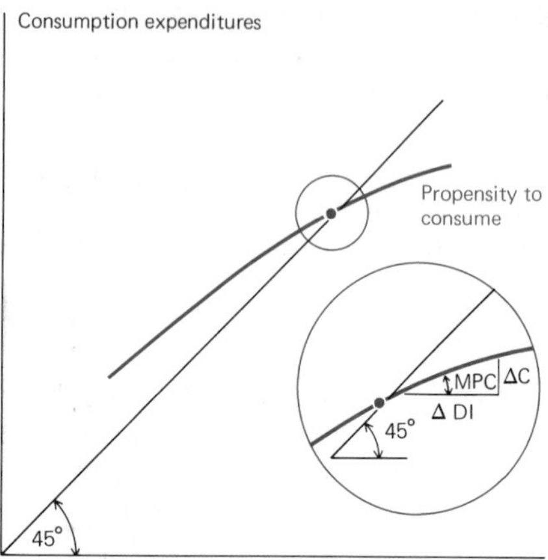

Figure 10-9

THE MARGINAL PROPENSITY TO SAVE AS A SLOPE

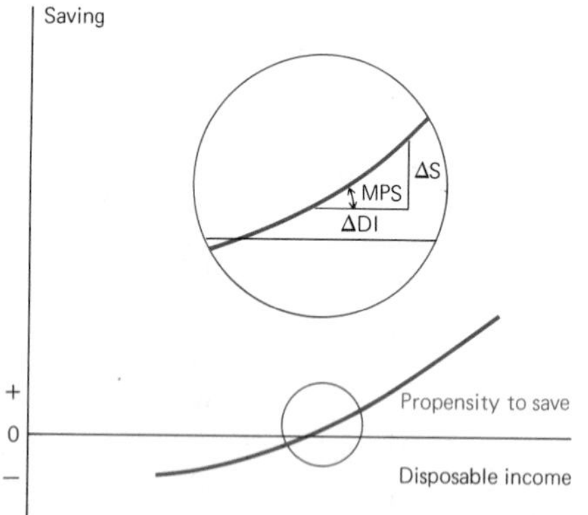

to save is $\Delta S/\Delta DI$. In Table 10-1 and Figures 10-6 and 10-7, for the \$100 billion change in disposable income from \$700 billion to \$800 billion, consumption changes by \$60 billion and saving changes by \$40 billion. So in this case the marginal propensity to consume, MPC, is \$60 billion/\$100 billion or 0.6, and the marginal propensity to save, MPS, is \$40 billion/\$100 billion or 0.4. Notice carefully that the *marginal* effects of a change in income on consumption and saving are different from the *average* rates of consumption and saving out of disposable income.

The marginal propensities to consume and save must add to unity for the same reason that the average propensities do. The change in consumption and change in saving resulting from any change in disposable income will just exhaust that change. Therefore, the sum of the shares of the consumption *change* and the saving *change* must again be 100 percent.[3]

The marginal propensity to consume can be interpreted geometrically as the slope of the consumption schedule for a short distance along it. That interpretation is shown in Figure 10-8. A small portion of the propensity-to-consume line is magnified to show more clearly ΔDI, the change in disposable income, and ΔC, the change in consumption that it induces. The ratio $\Delta C/\Delta DI$, which is the marginal propensity to consume, is just the slope of the propensity-to-consume line over a small distance. Similarly, in Figure 10-9, a portion of the propensity-to-save line is magnified, and MPS is shown as $\Delta S/\Delta DI$ – the slope of the saving schedule over a small distance. Marginal propensities to consume and save are calculated and presented in columns 4 and 7 of Table 10-2.

It is important to distinguish *movements along* a line from *shifts* in the schedules themselves. A shift in the consumption schedule would mean, for example, that we would have to write down a new table of numbers to describe consumption at each level of disposable income, rather than moving to a different row in a given table. Geometrically, a shift in the propensity to consume means that a new line has to be drawn. The two different kinds of changes, "movements along" and "shifts in" the schedules, are represented in Figures 10-10 and 10-11 on the next page.[4]

Extensions of consumption and saving analysis

The propensities to consume and to save have been studied intensively in the last twenty years. The analysis has become more

[3] In symbols, $\Delta DI = \Delta C + \Delta S$. Dividing both sides by ΔDI, we get $\Delta DI/\Delta DI = \Delta C/\Delta DI + \Delta S/\Delta DI$ or $1 = MPC + MPS$.

[4] If you want to set yourself some real puzzles, try to explain the year-to-year changes in consumption, or ΔC's, as compared with the year-to-year changes in disposable income, or ΔDI's, as implicit in Fig. 10-2. Professional economists have sometimes been baffled by variations in these ratios although there is considerable stability in them over long periods of time.

Figure 10-10

A MOVEMENT ALONG VERSUS A SHIFT IN THE PROPENSITY TO CONSUME

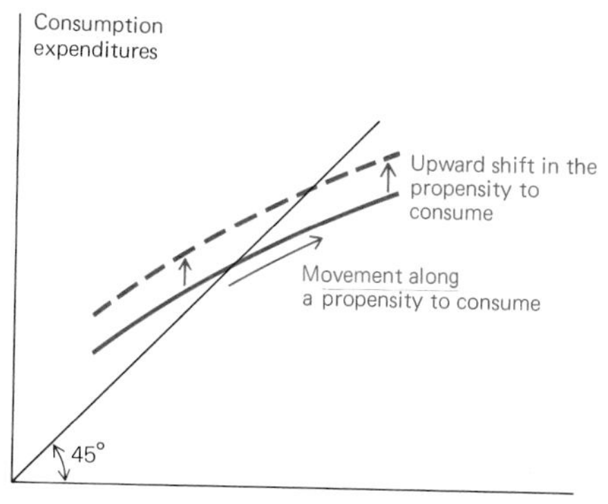

Figure 10-11

A MOVEMENT ALONG VERSUS A SHIFT IN THE PROPENSITY TO SAVE

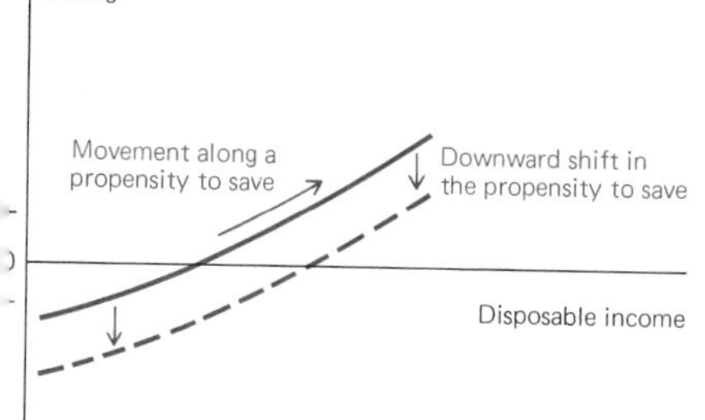

sophisticated and more successful in explaining the details of consumption. Here we shall merely indicate the directions in which the extensions and qualifications of the basic theory go.

First of all, other factors besides current income influence consumption and saving. The experiences of the period just after World War II illustrate some of these other factors. In the immediate postwar period consumption expenditures rose more rapidly than income in some years. This can be seen in Figures 10-1 and 10-2. It was as if the marginal propensity to consume were greater than unity in those years or as if a sharp upward shift in the propensity to consume had occurred. Many economists, like many bankers and businessmen, had predicted a post-World War II depression. They were wrong, in large part because they did not foresee this consumption splurge. Now most economists agree that two factors left out of the basic theory of consumption behavior were responsible for that splurge.

1. The amount of liquid assets, such as checking and savings accounts, stocks, and bonds, expanded greatly during the war as people accumulated these assets in place of consuming. This ownership made it easier for people to finance consumption after the war. Further, with more assets people have greater financial security, and as assets grow, people may become willing to reduce their current savings rate and consume more.
2. The stocks of durable goods owned by consumers – automobiles, washing machines, air conditioners, and the like – fell during World War II to abnormally low levels relative to what people desired. After the war, consumers wanted to make up the deficiency, and their unusually large liquid assets and increased willingness to spend made it possible. Effects of this kind are not confined to postwar years. Consumers appear to have some desired level of ownership of durable goods which grows over time. They will continually adjust their new purchases to stay around that level. Thus an unusually high rate of spending (or saving) in one year is likely to be followed by a somewhat lower than usual rate in the year immediately following.

Other nonincome determinants also affect overall consumption and saving patterns. For example, expectations of substantial price changes. There is some evidence that in late 1968 and early 1969 consumption rose more rapidly than was anticipated because consumers, expecting prices to go up, increased their rate of spending. Consumption rates also increase if consumers expect goods to become harder to get, perhaps because of a strike. If credit conditions change or even if they are expected to change, that, too, may affect consumption expenditures.

Some of the major extensions of consumption and saving theory have dealt with the influence of income itself. The basic hypothesis relates current consumption and current income, implying that, if income changes, consumption will change simultaneously. Yet, as a family's or an individual's income changes, there is generally a lag in adjusting to the new income. It takes people some time to change their spending habits. So this year's consumption expenditures depend not only on this year's income but on last year's income as well, and maybe even on the income of the last two or three years.

Another contribution to consumption theory has been the distinction of types of income. Income which is expected to persist and to be received regularly in the future is identified as *permanent income*. Income which is unexpected and regarded as not likely to continue to be received is called *transitory income*. The permanent-income consumption theory argues that spending and saving patterns are different for permanent and transitory income. People can and do make regular and predictable consumption plans for using their permanent income. But they cannot make such plans for transitory income, according to the theory. So reliable predictions of consumption based on transitory income cannot be made.

This approach can explain why the marginal and average propensities to consume which are observed over a short period can be quite different from long-term averages. In general the marginal propensity to consume out of transitory income is expected to be relatively low and the marginal propensity to save relatively high. Therefore, when income rises sharply, the saving rate out of total income increases. That is consistent, however, with more or less constant average consumption and saving rates over longer periods when the sharp changes average out. The permanent-income consumption theory is represented in Figure 10-12. The propensity to consume appropriate to permanent income is shown as a straight line that goes through the origin. Along it the average and marginal propensities to consume permanent income are constant and equal.

Figure 10-12

REPRESENTATION OF THE PERMANENT-INCOME CONSUMPTION THEORY

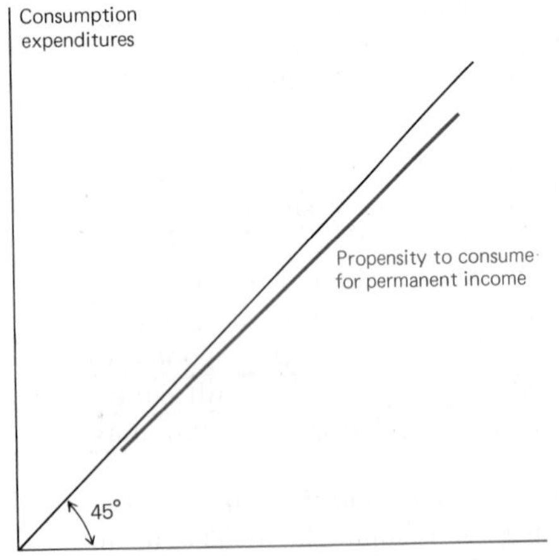

There is a good deal of controversy over the permanent-income theory. Some statistical tests seem to support it. Others do not. Nonetheless it is useful in reminding us of the importance of longer-term plans in short-run consumption decisions.

A related view of the consumption and savings decisions of families is that they follow certain regular life cycles. For a typical income earner, the ratio of consumption to income is higher at early and later ages than at in-between ages. Or, putting it another way, younger and older people are likely to spend a greater proportion of their income on consumption goods than are people in between. The aggregate average and marginal propensities to consume reflect the separate and somewhat different consumption-income ratios of income earners of different ages.

Both the permanent-income and life-cycle theories lead to the view that people follow different consumption and saving patterns for different types of income. It is argued, for example, that Vietnam War veterans do not treat their bonuses as if they would recur regularly; therefore, the consumption-income relationship for the bonus money is different from that for regular wage income.

Economists have studied consumption in great depth. It is a

good example of a field in which there have been important successes but in which substantial areas of ignorance remain. The fluctuations in the rate of consumption out of disposable income, as shown in Figures 10-1 and 10-2, are still hard to explain in spite of advances in consumption theory. The puzzles instill a proper humility in all professional economists working in this area. The evidence suggests that we should keep in mind the possibility that up and down shifts in the propensity to consume and propensity to save may depend on the forces we have discussed as well as on other influences that we now only dimly appreciate.

The patterns and determinants of investment behavior

Total investment consists of both that carried out by the private sector and that undertaken by government. When we turn to the determinants of private investment, we find it extremely difficult to arrive at a workable theory – much more difficult than in the consumption and saving area. Investment, we must remember, is expenditure on "fixed" capital goods and additions to stocks of goods held in inventories. Fixed capital goods include factory buildings and equipment as well as housing construction. A glance at the facts on private investment, as shown in Figure 10-13, verifies the common conclusion of bankers, businessmen, and economists: Private investment is highly volatile. Year-to-year changes of 10 percent to 15 percent have not been unusual in the past twenty years. It is the least stable of the major components of expenditure and output and it is also the hardest to predict. Why should that be so?

Investment results in the creation of new productive capacity or additions to inventory. It is undertaken in the expectation that over some future period it will yield a net return over and above the original cost. Because of their durability, fixed capital goods involve a commitment to a future that is always uncertain.

Figure 10-13

CHANGES IN INVESTMENT EXPENDITURES

(Source: U.S. Department of Commerce, Office of Business Economics.)

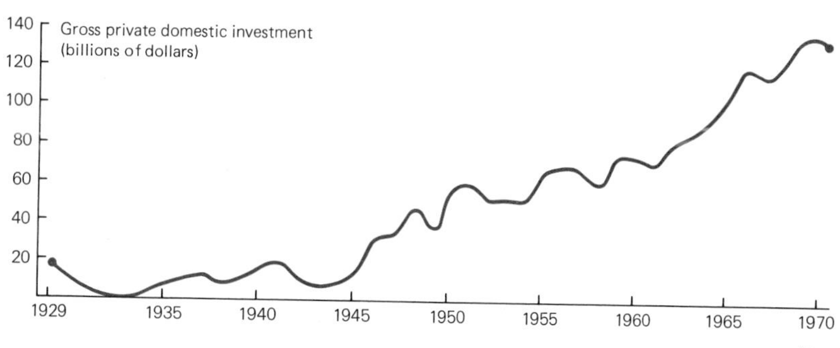

The objective of private business investment in plant and equipment and inventories is to make private profits, which are the difference between revenues and costs. Anything that affects either revenues or costs will influence business investment decisions. In fact, it is the *expectation* of profits which is important in determining those decisions. So anything that influences the general outlook and confidence of businessmen may affect private investment.

Changes in revenues may be the result of changes in demand that influence prices and sales. Behind this may be the slow growth of population, a change in income, or a change in tastes due to advertising campaigns or changes in fashion. Research and development activities that create new products and capture new markets are an important source of changes in business revenues.

Changes in costs have a variety of sources. The prices of the inputs used in production may change, and depending on the circumstances, both increases and decreases in input prices can stimulate new investment. If metal prices go down, for example, when new ore deposits are opened up, or if transportation costs fall, the reduction in costs is a stimulant to profitability and investment in the using industries. If metal prices go up when resources are depleted, that may stimulate investment in the producing industries; investors may hope to improve the rate of recovery from existing ores, or they may want to concentrate minerals or reclaim lower-grade or used inputs. Relative increases in wages stimulate the substitution of capital for labor where that is possible. Research and development activities develop new production processes and improve old ones, all of which may lower costs and stimulate new investment.

Federal, state, and local governments have a pervasive effect on private investment undertakings also. Their actions can directly affect business revenues and costs. The profits that motivate investment are those which accrue *after* taxes are deducted. So changes in business taxes can directly affect the investment motivating force. Governments are also important customers for everything from bombers to books.

Many businesses owe their livelihood to government purchases, and they expand as the public budget grows. The taxes that governments impose affect sales and influence prices and production. Government indirectly affects revenues and costs and private investment undertakings via its regulatory activity. Pollution controls, for example, force electric power plants to invest in smoke filters and regulators and thus stimulate investment by the companies that make these devices. Rent controls tend to reduce construction of new apartment buildings, because they lower expectations of profits. Urban redevelopment projects may raise expectations of high returns and thus stimulate investment.

Part of all the investment that goes on, such as that in roads, hospitals, and schools, is carried out directly by governments. Public investment is not motivated by profit. It is undertaken to

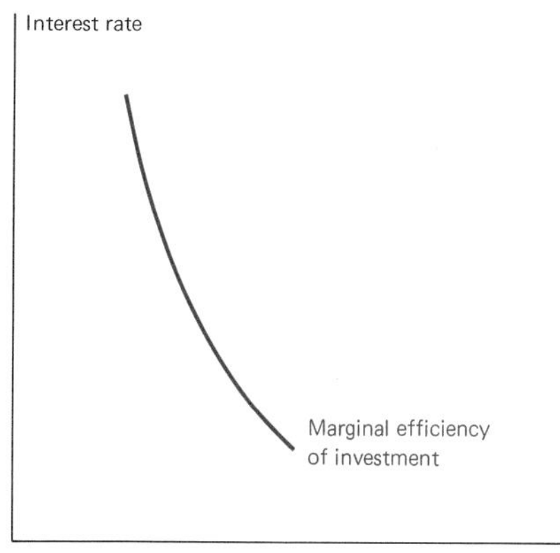

Figure 10-14

THE MARGINAL EFFICIENCY OF INVESTMENT SCHEDULE

provide public services. But the amounts and scheduling of public investment are as hard to predict as private investment. Government investment also stimulates private investment indirectly by providing facilities and services, such as highways and weather forecasts. In some localities the electric power systems are government-owned, and private investment is affected by the prices they fix.

The interest rate, which is at the center of the classical theory of investment, also plays a role in modern investment analysis, though not quite the leading part. The interest rate-investment relationship in modern economics goes under the rather cumbersome name of the *marginal efficiency of investment schedule.*[5] As shown in Figure 10-14, it posits that the rate of investment will increase as the interest rate falls. Why? Interest charges are an element of cost in new investment. Business has two choices: Either it pays out interest charges on the borrowed money it uses to buy new investment goods, or if it uses its own funds, it forgoes the interest it might have earned on those funds. That forgone interest is a cost, too, because it is a revenue that might have been earned, but is not.

Interest charges have a particularly important effect on investment in those sectors where borrowed funds are a large fraction of the total financing. This is true of new housing construction, where, typically, mortgage loans cover 75 percent or more of the total cost. Even in this area, however, fluctuations in the availability of funds may be a greater constraint on new investment than the interest rate. That availability is only imperfectly reflected by the level of the interest rate itself.

We return to some of the available investment theories and their implications in Chapters 11 and 16. But it is no secret that none of them are very reliable predictors.

We should spend an additional moment on one theory of private investment, however, because it is so widely held and so far off the mark. It also illustrates dramatically the dangers to clear thinking of multiple definitions of the same word. The theory is that the stock market determines investment expenditures. Actually the stock market does have some influence on investment, but it is not controlling. The error often results from a simple confusion of terminology. "Investment" in corporate stocks is *not* investment as defined here. We have been talking about purchases of real goods and services which create new productive capacity or new inventories and are a part of the national product. The stock exchange is a market where people buy and sell financial securities that reflect ownership of various kinds of assets. It is not even a place where *funds* for new investment are raised. Moreover, the stock market often behaves in a highly speculative manner, and

[5] This also appeared in Chap. 9 in the explanation of classical macroeconomic theory.

Figure 10-15
EXPECTED INVESTMENT EXPENDITURES AND ACTUAL OUTLAYS (BILLIONS OF DOLLARS)

(Source: U.S. Department of Commerce, Office of Business Economics.)

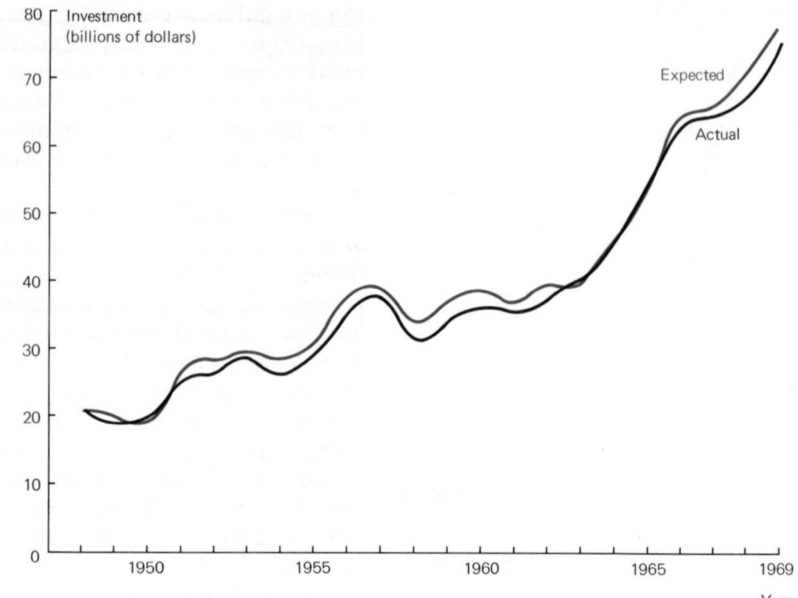

prices can sometimes run up and down more or less independently of the outlook for investment. Yet to the extent that the stock market affects or reflects business confidence, the price movements in it may be correlated with real investment. Sometimes they are not, and most businessmen know it.[6]

The best and currently the most widely used approaches to the short-term projection of private investment expenditures are the surveys of business intentions. The reports of the Department of Commerce and several private organizations that conduct regular surveys are followed closely by businessmen and economists. In these surveys businessmen are asked how much they expect to spend on investment goods during the next six months and next twelve months. To use some concepts developed previously, *investment intentions* are an ex ante, or forward-looking, concept. The investment that actually takes place in any year is an ex post, or backward-looking, concept. That is measured at the end of the year. Of course, businessmen are not obliged to carry out their intentions, though they would like to do so. Unexpected business changes always create differences between what is projected and what actually happens. Nonetheless, the surveys of investment intentions are reasonably good forecasts, as may be seen in Figure 10-15. They are the first place to turn for a projection of what inves-

[6] There is a deeper sense in which investment and stock prices may be related. Stock prices are a market valuation of assets. When that valuation is favorable relative to the cost of purchasing investment goods, that may stimulate investment.

tors intend to do during the next six months. We shall often refer to them.

A review of actual investment figures indicates that, while the surveys provide a good overall picture of what future investment will be, they tend to underestimate investment in periods when NNP is rising. Likewise they tend to overestimate future investment when NNP is declining. This suggests that there may, in some circumstances, be a relationship between the level of NNP and the level of investment. Alternatively, and more precisely, it suggests a relationship between investment and *changes* in the level of NNP. This corresponds to our previous argument that investment is a particularly dynamic phenomenon.

Summary

Modern macroeconomic theory originating with John Maynard Keynes rejects the classical economic view that the market economy has an inherent tendency to stabilize at full employment. The New Economics regards aggregate demand or spending as the factor determining national income and output. This focus leads to a modern concern, similar to that of classical economics, with saving and investment and their determinants.

Saving is the amount left from disposable income after consumption expenditures. Budget studies of individuals and families and annual aggregate data confirm that the most important determinant of consumption and saving is disposable income itself. The propensity to consume or consumption schedule relates consumption and disposable income. Typically, consumption rises with income, but not as fast. The propensity to save is the mirror image of the propensity to consume. The average propensity to consume, APC, is the ratio of consumption to income. The marginal propensity to consume, MPC, is the ratio of the *change* in consumption to the *change* in disposable income that caused it. Typically both ratios are less than 1. Over short periods the MPC is frequently less than the APC.

More sophisticated consumption theories take into account the influence, not only of income, but of other factors as well. They also distinguish between the effects of permanent income and of transitory income. This distinction helps explain why the APC and MPC tend to be more nearly constant and equal to each other over long periods than during short periods.

Private investment is a particularly volatile type of spending, because it depends on anticipations of profitability, which are affected by changes in expected costs and demand. Investment also depends on the interest rate. This relationship is called "the marginal efficiency of investment." In general the higher the rate of interest the lower the level of investment, and the lower the rate of interest the higher the rate of investment. The magnitude of the effect is not always large, however. The best projection of short-term private investment is probably a good survey of business investment intentions.

Questions for discussion and review

1. Why do people treat saving as if it were a luxury and allocate an increasingly large share of their income to it as their income rises?

2. Under what circumstances would you expect to observe families with negative savings? Would you ever expect a whole economy to dissave? Why?

3. Distinguish between a shift in the propensity to consume and a movement along the propensity-to-consume line. Describe the possible sources of each type of change.

4. What is the difference between permanent income and transitory income? Why might there be a different consumption-income relationship for each type?

5. Does it seem reasonable that private investment expenditures should be more difficult to predict than consumption expenditures? Why?

Concepts for review

Propensities to consume and save

Break-even point

Marginal and average propensities to consume

"Keeping up with the Joneses" effect on consumption

Permanent income and transitory income

Surveys of investment intentions

11

National income as determined by aggregate demand: The First Macro Model

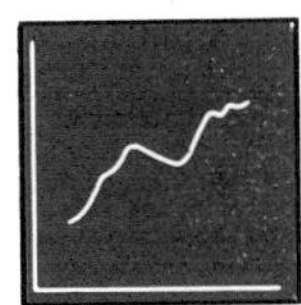

We are now ready to assemble the tools of macro analysis developed in the four preceding chapters and use them to get an idea of what determines national income, output, and employment. Prosperity and depression pose formidable theoretical as well as practical problems. We shall therefore again slice the overall issues into manageable parts by creating and analyzing simple models of reality. We shall examine the models from several points of view and find that each view adds to our understanding.

The First Macro Model

To strip the problem of national income determination to its essentials, we shall return to the First Macro Model. We assume that we are dealing with an economy that has no government and therefore no taxes or government expenditures. It has no foreign trade and therefore no exports or imports. There are no undistributed corporate profits and no business transfer payments, so production of final products equals income disbursements. We also assume that there is no depreciation. According to the national income accounting of Chapter 7, these assumptions imply that there is no difference between the gross and net national products, i.e., between GNP and NNP. Moreover, NNP is the same as national income, NI, since there are no indirect taxes. Finally, NI is the same as disposable income, DI, since there are no direct taxes, undistributed income, or transfer payments. In summary: GNP ≡ NNP ≡ NI ≡ DI.

We shall also assume that the system is below its full employment and full capacity levels of output and income. This helps assure that there are no upward pressures on prices, so there is one less thing to worry about. Finally, it will be assumed that, in general, prices are "sticky" with respect to downward movements.

In the First Macro Model there are only two uses of the national product: private consumption and private investment. That is, NNP $\equiv C + I$. Therefore, to explain the demand for GNP, we have to explain C and I. That was the focus of attention in the last chapter. Now we are going to put the pieces together. We shall at first use simple forms of the propensity-to-consume and propensity-to-save relationships, and we shall suppose that current consumption and saving depend only on current income, as in Figure 10-4 in the preceding chapter. For investment we will assume that we obtain information from a survey of business investment intentions. That indicates what businessmen intend to invest in fixed plant and equipment and in inventories. We shall assume that these intentions are *autonomous*, or *exogenous*; that is, they are not dependent on what is currently happening in the economy. They are determined by, say, technological change and population growth – influences outside the scope of the First Macro Model. Thus investment is not itself affected by the level of national income and output. These assumptions define the model exactly. Now how does it work?

The national product and national income as determined by aggregate demand

First, let us write down in the form of a table the propensity-to-consume and propensity-to-save relationships.

Table 11-1

PROPENSITY TO CONSUME AND PROPENSITY TO SAVE (BILLIONS OF DOLLARS)

Levels of NNP $\equiv NI \equiv DI$	C	S
$1,350	$1,090	$260
1,300	1,060	240
1,250	1,030	220
1,200	1,000	200
1,150	970	180
1,100	940	160
1,050	910	140
1,000	880	120

In Table 11-1 the marginal propensity to consume, which is the ratio of the increase in consumption to the increase in NNP that causes it, is always 30/50 or 0.6, and the marginal propensity to save is always 20/50 or 0.4. Since these rates are constants, the propensity to consume and the propensity to save are straight lines when plotted on a graph.

Next we will assume that intended investment spending is $200 billion. That is the amount businessmen want to invest, and we assume that their *intentions* do not change with the level of income.

Third, we ask: At what level of NNP will the plans of businessmen for the production of the total national product be consistent with the plans of consumers *and* businessmen for the purchase of the total product? To answer this, we prepare Table 11-2.

Column 1 is the aggregate supply of NNP. It shows the alternative amounts of NNP that businesses might produce. They would be willing to produce these amounts if their receipts, which in turn they pay out as income payments, were identical to their production. Column 2 indicates the level of consumption spending at each alternative level of NNP. So columns 1 and 2 together are the propensity to consume.

Column 3 is the autonomously determined level of private investment, which businessmen *desire* to maintain at $200 billion and which is assumed not to change with the level of NNP.

Column 4 is a critical one. It contains on each line the total *intended* spending on the national product, or the level of aggregate demand as determined by the propensity to consume and by autonomous investment decisions. It is an ex ante, or looking-forward, concept: the sum of what consumers and investors want to spend at each level of NNP.

Using Table 11-2 we can now answer the question: At what level of NNP are spending and output plans consistent? The only level of NNP at which this is true is $1,200 billion! Each line in column 5 shows the difference between the aggregate supply of NNP in column 1 and aggregate demand in column 4. Only when NNP is $1,200 billion does the difference between aggregate supply and aggregate demand disappear and become zero. This one level of NNP at which income and output plans are consistent is called the *equilibrium level*.

The next important question is: Is there any process or mechanism that moves the economy toward its macroeconomic equilibrium level, and if so, what is it?

One can reason the answer out in the following way: Suppose wages and salaries and other income were being paid out by businesses at a rate of, say, $1,300 billion. If that were the level of national income payments, spending on final products would be only $1,260 billion. Businesses could not and would not go on paying out more income than they received in spending on their

Table 11-2

NATIONAL PRODUCT AND NATIONAL INCOME AS DETERMINED BY AGGREGATE DEMAND (BILLIONS OF DOLLARS)

	1 *If NNP (≡ DI) were*	2 *Consumption spending would be*	3 *Investment spending is intended to be*	4 *Total spending would be*	5 *Difference between spending and income*	6 *Movement of income*	
A	$1,350	$1,090	$200	$1,290	− $60	Down	
B	1,300	1,060	200	1,260	− 40	Down	
C	1,250	1,030	200	1,230	− 20	Down	
D	**1,200**	**1,000**	**200**	**1,200**	**0**	**Equilibrium**	Aggregate supply = aggregate demand
E	1,150	970	200	1,170	+ 20	Up	
F	1,100	940	200	1,140	+ 40	Up	
G	1,050	910	200	1,110	+ 60	Up	
H	1,000	880	200	1,070	+ 80	Up	

output. They would cut back their rate of production and their use of productive resources and, therefore, the income payments for which they were liable. Income would then fall. The same would be true for *any* income above $1,200 billion. Any level of NNP higher than $1,200 would not be sustainable, and if, for any reason, the rate of production of NNP happened to be above $1,200 billion, it would fall back toward $1,200 billion.

Below $1,200 billion, at, say, a rate of payment of income of $1,100 billion, the rate of output would be greater than income (see column 5 of row *F* in Table 11-2). These expenditures on output would in turn become income to someone. Income paid out would rise and income received would rise. This is true of *any* income level below $1,200 billion, as shown in rows *F*, *G*, and H.

The analysis and the conclusions are perfectly general. The only level of income and output that will be maintained is the equilibrium level. That is the one at which aggregate income payments and total spending on output are consistent — where the level of aggregate demand is equal to the level of aggregate supply.

The graphic determination of national income and output

Anything that can be presented in a table like Table 11-2 can also be shown graphically, and sometimes people understand things better that way. In Figure 11-1 the aggregate supply line is the 45-degree line from the origin. It is equidistant from the axes, thus

Figure 11-1

GRAPHIC DETERMINATION OF NNP BY AGGREGATE DEMAND (BILLIONS OF DOLLARS)

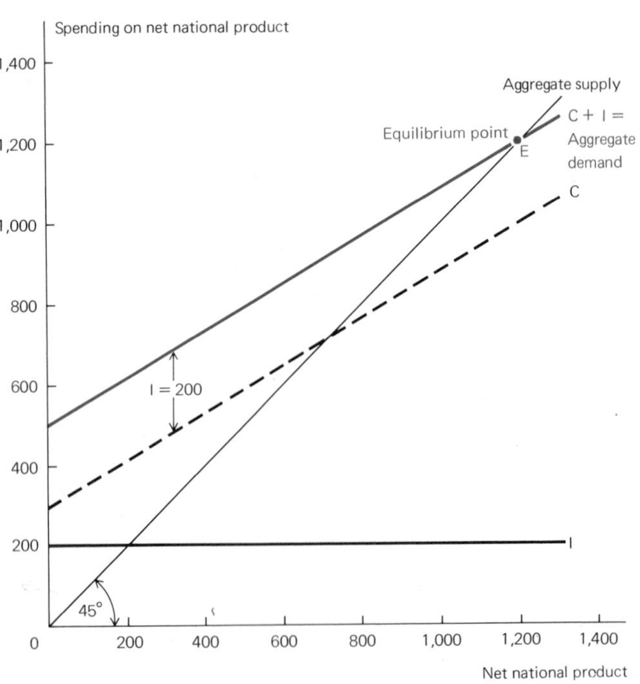

reflecting the fact that the total amount of final goods and services that will be offered for sale at each level of NNP is equal to that level of NNP.

The propensity to consume is plotted from Table 11-1 and comes out as the sloping straight line, C. Investment is also plotted. Since it is a constant amount, whatever the level of income, it is the straight horizontal line, *I*. Next we perform graphically the addition we did in each row of Table 11-2. At each level of NNP we add the amount of investment to the propensity to consume. This gives us the $C + I$ line. That line shows what the aggregate effective demand for output $(C + I)$ will be at each level of net national product.

Now what point in the graph simultaneously satisfies the two conditions (1) that the spending on the national product is equal to consumption plus investment spending, and (2) that the spending on the national product equals the national income, so that aggregate demand equals aggregate supply?

Only point *E* satisfies both requirements. First, everywhere on the $C + I$ line the net national product equals consumption plus investment. Second, everywhere on the 45-degree line the net national product equals the national income. At point E, where the $C + I$ line crosses the 45-degree line, both conditions are met. It is the equilibrium level of income and output.

At a *lower* level of income, spending on final goods would be *greater* than income, and income would rise. At a *higher* level of income, spending on final goods would be lower than income, and income would fall. The income and output would, therefore, tend to move to point E.

The determination of national income using equations

Anything that can be presented in a table like Table 11-2 or a graph like Figure 11-1 can be translated into equations. Those provide still another way of seeing what is involved, and for some purposes, are more convenient.

The propensity-to-consume relationship of Table 11-1 and Figure 11-1 relating consumption, C, and disposable income, DI, is

$$C = \$280 \text{ bilion} + (0.6 \times \text{DI}) \qquad (11\text{-}1)$$

This can be verified by multiplying some alternative levels of disposable income by the marginal propensity to consume, 0.6, and adding the product to \$280 billion. The result can be checked with Table 11-1.[1]

[1] This equation can be derived by first confirming that the marginal propensity to consume is, in fact, equal to 0.6. Note that, for every \$50 billion change in DI in column 1 of Table 11-1, consumption changes by \$30 billion. So the change in C divided by the change in DI which causes it is 30/50 or 0.6. Now multiply any level of DI by 0.6 and subtract the result from the corresponding level of C. The answer will always be \$280 billion, which is, therefore, the amount that has to be added to (0.6 × DI) to give the correct level of C.

Investment, I, according to our assumption will be carried out at the level of \$200 billion, so

$$I = \$200 \text{ billion} \tag{11-2}$$

The aggregate demand is defined as the sum of consumption and investment spending, so

$$\text{NNP} = C + I \tag{11-3}$$

Now, in place of consumption in Equation (11-3) we write the propensity-to-consume relationship, and in place of investment we put in the number from Equation (11-2). This gives us

$$\text{NNP} = [\$280 \text{ billion} + (0.6 \times \text{DI})] + \$200 \text{ billion}$$

$$\text{Or} \quad \text{NNP} = \$480 \text{ billion} + (0.6 \times \text{DI}) \tag{11-4}$$

The net national product in this simple economy is equal to national income and is also equal to disposable income:

$$\text{NNP} \equiv \text{NI} \equiv \text{DI} \tag{11-5}$$

So in place of DI in Equation (11-4), we use NNP and get

$$\text{NNP} = \$480 \text{ billion} + (0.6 \times \text{NNP}) \tag{11-6}$$

To find NNP, we first remember that if we subtract the same number from both sides of an equation, we maintain the equality. So we subtract (0.6 × NNP) from both sides of Equation (11-6) and get

$$\text{NNP} - (0.6 \times \text{NNP}) = \$480 \text{ billion}$$

$$\text{Or} \quad (0.4 \times \text{NNP}) = \$480 \text{ billion} \tag{11-7}$$

Remembering that if we multiply both sides of the equation by the same number, that will also maintain the equation, we multiply both sides of Equation (11-7) by 2.5 to eliminate the fraction on the left-hand side. That is

$$(0.4 \times \text{NNP}) \times 2.5 = \$480 \text{ billion} \times 2.5 \tag{11-8}$$

And

$$\text{NNP} = \$1{,}200 \text{ billion} \tag{11-9}$$

This is, not surprisingly, the same answer obtained before.

A cautionary note. We have worked out the aggregate demand approach to national income determination in three ways. It may well seem like a case of overkill, but the fundamental principle that the national income and product are determined by aggregate spending on final national product cannot be overstressed. We shall exploit this important insight again and again in our analysis.

A cautionary word about this approach, however: Nowhere in the analysis were we able to conclude that the equilibrium level of national income would necessarily be the full employment level. The full employment level depends on the productive capacity of the economy and the size of the labor force. Those two factors set upper limits to the national product, but below those limits it is aggregate demand that counts.

The national product and national income as determined by the equality of planned saving and investment

In Chapter 10, we examined the saving and investment approach to national income as used by the classical economists. One conclusion of that analysis was correct: National income is determined when the saving leakage and the investment injection are equal. If they are *not*, then income will move up or down. The crucial results of classical economic theory from which we had to dissent were that the equality of saving and investment was brought about by interest rate adjustments and that the equality would be achieved at full employment.

There is no doubt that changes in saving levels do occur, but modern macro theory makes saving depend on the level of disposable income via the propensity to save. To show this, we write down in the first two columns of Table 11-3 the same propensity to consume shown in Table 11-1. Then, subtracting the number in each row of column 2 from the number in the same row of column 1, we get saving in column 3. Columns 1 and 3 represent the propensity to save. Column 4 records intended investment expenditures, as indicated by the investment survey. Column 5 is the difference between saving and investment at each level of national income.

Whenever the planned saving leakage is greater than the investment injection, the rate of income payments cannot be main-

Table 11-3

NATIONAL PRODUCT AND NATIONAL INCOME AS DETERMINED BY THE EQUALITY OF SAVING AND INVESTMENT (BILLIONS OF DOLLARS)

	1	2	3	4	5	6
	If NNP (≡ DI) were	*Consumption would be*	*Saving would be*	*Investment would be*	*Difference between saving and investment would be*	*Movement of income*
A	$1,350	$1,090	$260	$200	+ $60	Down
B	1,300	1,060	240	200	+ 40	Down
C	1,250	1,030	220	200	+ 20	Down
D	**1,200**	**1,000**	**200**	**200**	**0**	**Equilibrium**
E	1,150	970	180	200	− 20	Up
F	1,100	940	160	200	− 40	Up
G	1,050	910	140	200	− 60	Up
H	1,000	880	120	200	− 80	Up

tained. In consequence, income *and* saving will fall. For example, even though at a rate of income payments of $1,350 billion per year, aggregate saving of $260 billion is planned or desired, it cannot be achieved. Investment at $200 billion is less than the rate of saving. As a result, goods produced for output would not be

Figure 11-2

GRAPHIC DETERMINATION OF NNP BY SAVING-INVESTMENT EQUALITY (BILLIONS OF DOLLARS)

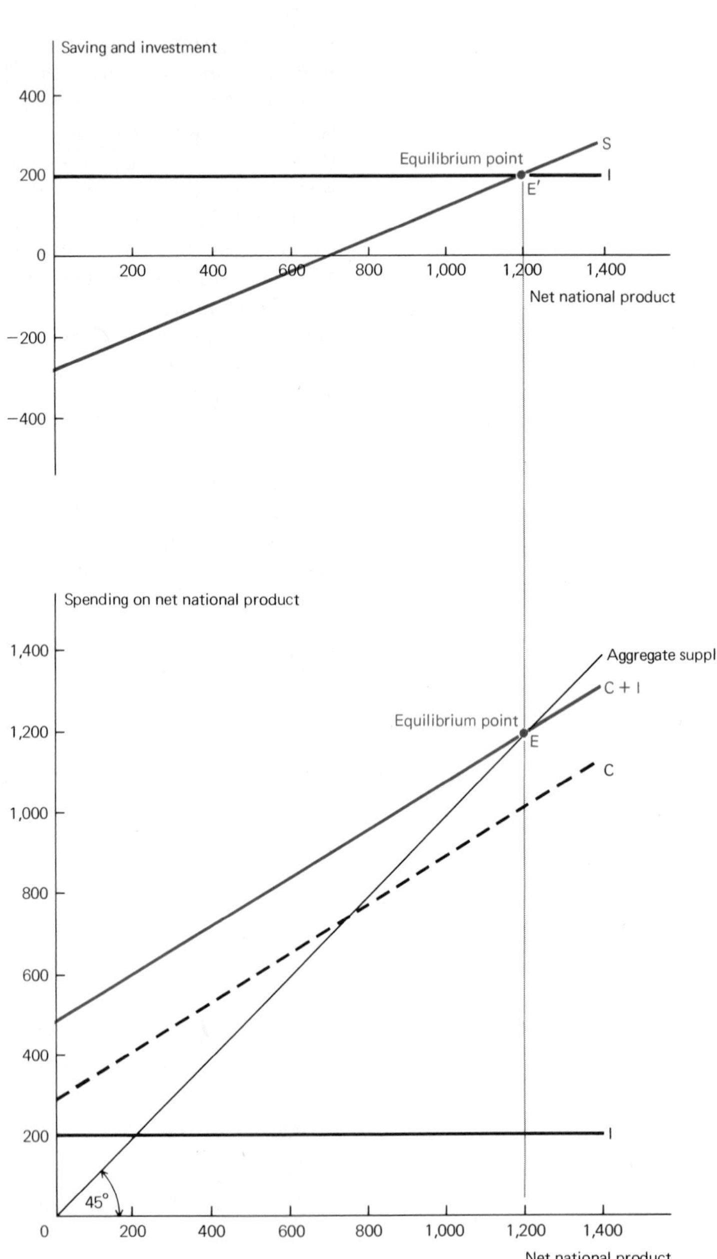

sold. They would tend to accumulate in inventories, and this in turn would force investment above the level which was intended and desired. In the face of this unexpected accumulation, businessmen would cut back on other investment to keep total investment at the planned levels. That means that the rate of production and income payments would be cut back. That in turn reduces saving.

Likewise income and output will not be in equilibrium whenever the planned saving leakage is less than the investment injection. Under these conditions income payments would rise, because the rate of production would be higher than expected income. At that higher income rate, saving would also be higher. The only maintainable level of income, the only level at which saving and investment plans are consistent, is, again, the $1,200 billion level.

Table 11-3 is translated graphically into Figure 11-2. To make the point that the saving-investment and aggregate supply-demand approaches are just two ways of looking at the same process, we reproduce Figure 11-1 as well.

On the saving-investment diagram, the propensity to save is the line S; the investment schedule is I. They intersect at point E′, which is the level of disposable and national income and net national product at which desired saving and planned investment are equal. That is the only level of NNP at which the planned saving is equal to the planned investment injection. If, for any reason, NNP were at a different level, it would move toward the equilibrium level.[2]

This analysis demonstrates that there is an economic mechanism that brings saving and investment into equality, but it is not the interest rate mechanism of classical economic theory. It is NNP, which adjusts to make planned saving equal to planned investment.

The saving-investment accounting identity and equilibrium equality

In Chapter 7 when we went through the national income and product accounts, we noted that one of the accounting results was that investment always came out to be identical to saving. This is true whether the accounting is done once a year, twice a year, or every month. It is a result of the manner in which the various components of national income are defined. Now we have worked through an analysis in which it is a condition of equilibrium that

[2] It is again possible to represent the arithmetic and graphic analysis in equations. The propensity to consume is $C = \$280 \text{ billion} + 0.6\ \text{DI}$.

Saving is DI − C, so the propensity to save is $S = \text{DI} - C = \text{DI} - (\$280 \text{ billion} + 0.6\ \text{DI})$ or $S = -\$280 \text{ billion} + 0.4\ \text{DI}$.

In this case $\text{DI} \equiv \text{NNP}$, so $S = -\$280 \text{ billion} + 0.4\ \text{NNP}$.

Investment is $I = \$200$ billion.

The equilibrium condition is $S = I$, or $-\$280 \text{ billion} + 0.4\ \text{NNP} = \$200 \text{ billion}$.

This is solved to give $\text{NNP} = \$1{,}200$ billion.

saving and investment be equal. How can the equality of saving and investment be a *condition* of equilibrium when in national income accounting they are defined always to be the same? It would not be surprising if this were a puzzling conjunction of ideas. So let us tackle the problem head on.

The precise statement of the national income accounting result is that, by definition, *measured* saving and *measured* investment must always and over every period be identical. This must be so, since every act of investment means that resources and output are not going to consumption. And saving is *defined* as just that part of income and product which is not consumed. These accounting definitions are ex post concepts, in which quantities are measured looking backward.

This does not mean that ex ante, looking forward, *desired* or *planned* saving and investment must always be equal. Nor do the *planned* levels have to be equal to the *actual* levels. Savers and investors, by and large, are different people with different motivations. It would be extraordinary if their *future* intentions should happen to coincide. What is true is that there is an economic mechanism which makes the plans coincide at an *equilibrium* level of income.

That mechanism is the movement of national income and product up or down to an equilibrium position in which the saving and investment planned at that equilibrium income level are equal. This equality is a condition of being at equilibrium. Away from equilibrium, measured saving and investment are identical, but planned saving and investment are not consistent. Only at the equilibrium level are measured saving and investment, which are identical, also equal to the levels of saving and investment which would be planned for and consistent with that level of NNP.

These are not easy ideas to grasp, as a large and tortuous professional economic literature can testify. We shall return to the issues again. When we have a few more tools at our disposal, we shall be able to analyze the issues in another and, perhaps, still more clarifying manner.

The significance of saving and investment equality. Just a final word at this point on the equality of saving and investment and the equilibrium of national income. The equality of S and I does not in itself necessarily mean that people are happy or unhappy or that business is good or bad. And, specifically, it does not mean that, necessarily, there is full employment of labor or full use of capacity. That was the claim of classical economics, but nothing in our analysis necessarily permits us to make that claim. The S-I equality is just a condition that must be met for NI to be in equilibrium. The national income equilibrium is a condition in which income receipts and production are consistent and have no inherent tendency to change. The equilibrium conditions do not mean any more than that — or any less.

The multiplier and the multiplied effects of a shift in investment in the First Macro Model

Nothing in life stands still, and changes in expenditure may come from a variety of sources. Our analysis would not be complete if we could not figure out the effects of such changes. So that is our next task. We shall continue with the First Macro Model in which there are only consumption and investment expenditures. Since investment is a particularly volatile type of spending we shall focus first on the effects of changes in it.

What happens to income if the desired level of investment rises, say, by $40 billion? Producers will probably not fully anticipate the increases in spending. They will find themselves running out of goods sooner than expected and their current rates of production will be too low to meet demand. In this case, or even if they anticipate the increases in spending, they will employ more labor and use more of other productive resources to increase output. That means more income. Remember, we assumed at the outset in the First Macro Model that there were excess capacity and unemployment, so that output could go up without prices having to change.

When income changes, the desired consumption changes. The marginal propensity to consume tells us what the change will be. In the earlier examples, the MPC is 0.6. Thus, when there is a $40 billion increase in investment spending, say, on new housing construction, there will be a 0.6 × $40 billion = $24 billion increase in consumption expenditures. This increase in consumption spending will be made by the people who receive the extra $40 billion spending as their earned income for producing the investment goods. But that is not the end of it. The $24 billion increase in consumption expenditures in turn means a $24 billion increase in income to the people working in the production of consumption goods. They, in turn, will spend part of their additional income, just 0.6 of it, or 0.6 × $24 billion = $14.4 billion. That becomes $14.4 billion in income to producers of consumption goods, and of that, 0.6 or $8.64 billion is spent on consumption, and so on. The additional "rounds" of income and consumption keep going. In a sense the ripples in the national income from the extra $40 billion of investment dropped into the economy go on forever. But like the ripples from a stone dropped into a quiet pool, they soon become too small to notice.

When does the process end and what is the final result? We can find the answer in a number of ways, and each approach adds some understanding. Let us start with a graphic analysis. In Figure 11-3 the initial equilibrium position E_1 is shown at the intersection of the propensity to save and the investment schedule of $200 billion. The new investment schedule of $200 billion + $40 billion =

Figure 11-3

THE EFFECT OF AN INCREASE IN INVESTMENT (BILLIONS OF DOLLARS)

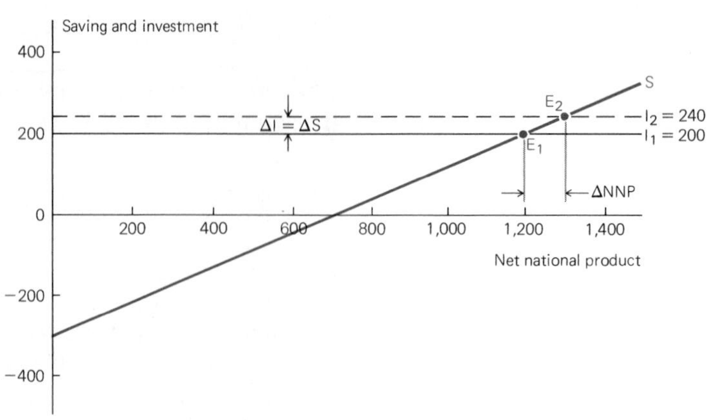

\$240 billion is shown. The intersection of the saving and the new investment schedule, E_2, is at \$1,300 billion. In the saving-investment diagram, the equilibrium point slides up the propensity-to-save schedule as investment shifts up. Using the symbol Δ again as a shorthand for "change in": ΔI of \$40 billion creates a \$100 billion change in NNP. The number M by which ΔI must be multiplied to calculate ΔNNP is called the *multiplier*. In this example, it is $\Delta\text{NNP}/\Delta I = M = \$100 \text{ billion}/\$40 \text{ billion} = 2.5$.

Looking closely at Figure 11-3, we can see that the distance by which the equilibrium level of NNP shifts to the right on the NNP axis depends on the slant or slope of the propensity to save. That slope is our old friend, the marginal propensity to save. The MPS is defined as the change in saving divided by the change in disposable income that brings it about. That is, MPS $= \Delta S/\Delta\text{DI}$. In the First Macro Model, DI $\equiv$ NNP, so MPS $\equiv \Delta S/\Delta\text{NNP}$. At the new equilibrium point, E_2, the total change in saving must be equal to the total change in investment, which is $\Delta I/\Delta\text{NNP}$. We recognize $\Delta I/\Delta\text{NNP}$ as the inverse of the multiplier, or $1/M$. If MPS $= \Delta I/\Delta\text{NNP} = 1/M$, then $M = 1/\text{MPS}$. This means that we can calculate the multiplier for this simple model if we know the marginal propensity to save.

We can put the multiplier relation in a slightly different form by remembering the connection between the marginal propensity to save and the marginal propensity to consume: They add up to one. That is:

$$\text{MPC} + \text{MPS} \equiv 1 \qquad \text{or} \qquad \text{MPS} \equiv 1 - \text{MPC}$$

If we put this relationship into the multiplier formula, 1/MPS becomes $\dfrac{1}{1 - \text{MPC}}$ and $M = \dfrac{1}{1 - \text{MPC}}$.

In the numerical example we have been using, MPS is 0.4. Then the multiplier $M = \frac{1}{1 - \text{MPC}} = \frac{1}{\text{MPS}} = \frac{1}{1 - 0.6} = \frac{1}{0.4} = 2.5.$

The final change in national income resulting from a $40 billion increase in investment spending is, therefore:

$$\Delta\text{NNP} = M \times \Delta I$$

or

$$\Delta\text{NNP} = (2.5)\ (\$40\text{ billion}) = \$100\text{ billion}$$

This is exactly what we obtained from Figure 11-3.

Let us reflect a bit: Is the multiplier relationship we have derived a plausible one? Does it make economic sense? The multiplier is 1/MPS or 1/(1 − MPC). The larger the denominator of the fraction, the smaller the multiplier will be. The smaller the denominator, the larger the fraction. A larger MPS or a smaller MPC, therefore, means a smaller multiplier. A smaller MPS or larger MPC means a larger multiplier. The following examples show this:

$$\text{If MPC} = 0.6 \text{ and MPS} = 0.4, \frac{1}{1 - \text{MPC}} = \frac{1}{\text{MPS}} = \frac{1}{0.4} = 2.5$$

$$\text{If MPC} = 0.5 \text{ and MPS} = 0.5, \frac{1}{1 - \text{MPC}} = \frac{1}{\text{MPS}} = \frac{1}{0.5} = 2$$

$$\text{If MPC} = 0.8 \text{ and MPS} = 0.2, \frac{1}{1 - \text{MPC}} = \frac{1}{\text{MPS}} = \frac{1}{0.2} = 5$$

A larger MPC means that a larger fraction of the original $40 billion increase in investment will be respent and a larger fraction of each succeeding round of income will be respent. In each round, there is less leakage into saving than there would be if the MPC were smaller and the MPS were larger. The resulting increase in

Figure 11-4

THE SIGNIFICANCE OF ALTERNATIVE MARGINAL SAVING RATES (BILLIONS OF DOLLARS)

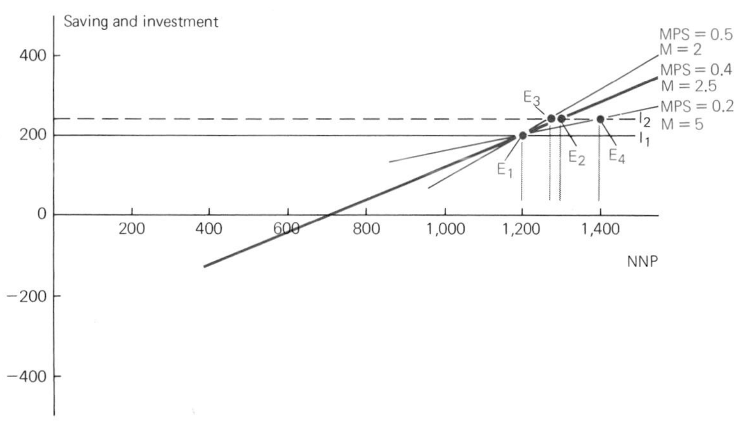

income in each round of spending is larger with the larger MPC, and the final, total effect will be larger. So the multiplier formula is indeed a plausible relationship.

Figure 11-4 shows graphically the effect of alternative marginal propensities to save on the multiplier and its induced effects on national income. The original equilibrium national income is at E_1. The equilibrium after a $40 billion increase in investment, with an MPS of 0.4, is at E_2. If the MPS from the original level of income were 0.5, the new equilibrium after the $40 billion increase in investment would be at E_3. The larger MPS would mean a larger saving leakage, a smaller multiplier, and a smaller increase in the marginal propensity to consume. A smaller MPS means a smaller saving leakage, a larger multiplier, and a larger increase in the national income. So in this case the new equilibrium is at E_4.

The multiplier process over time

We can obtain some additional insight into the adjustments that take place in the multiplier process if we go back to the original arithmetic of the multiplier and work it out with a slightly different and more realistic description of the propensity to consume.

When there is a change in output and income, it usually takes some time for this to result in a change in consumption. There is often a *time lag* between the earning of income and its payment. For example, wages and salaries may be paid only every other week or every month, so people may work longer hours and produce more and still have to wait some time for the extra income to show up in their paychecks. If a bonus is given for higher output, that may come only once a year. Rents and profits may be paid out quarterly.

There is also a time lag between a change in the amount of money received as income and the change in consumption spending that it induces. People get set in their ways, and when their income changes, they take some time to adjust to it.

The effect of time lags is such that, to a great extent, it is the income of a previous period rather than the current period which determines current consumption. To illustrate the effect of time lags, we will suppose that the propensity to consume takes the following form:

Current consumption C = $280 billion + (0.6 × DI or NNP of the previous year)

If there is no change in disposable income from year to year, we need not worry about the lag. But if there is a change, the effect of the lag becomes important.

With this new propensity to consume, we can work out in Table 11-4 the effects of a permanent $40 billion increase in investment. In this example, the change in investment is assumed to happen in 1971, supposedly after a period of equilibrium when there were no changes in national income.

Table 11-4

THE MULTIPLIER PROCESS OVER TIME (BILLIONS OF DOLLARS)

	Year	Investment	Consumption	Net national product	Change in net national product
	1969	200	1,000	1,200	0
Year of change in I	1970	200	1,000	1,200	0
	1971	240	1,000	1,240	40
	1972	240	1,024	1,264	24
	1973	240	1,038.4	1,278.4	14.4
	1974	240	1,047.04	1,287.04	8.64
	1975	240	1,252.224	1,292.224	5.184
	1976	240	1,255.3344	1,295.3344	3.1104
	:	:	:	:	:
New Equilibrium		240	1,060	1,300	0

We obtain the national income in each line of Table 11-4 by adding investment and consumption. We calculate consumption in each year by multiplying the preceding year's national income by 0.6 and adding $280 billion. How do we know what the new equilibrium will be after all the ripples have died down and there are no more changes in income? We can peek, which, as they say in playing bridge is worth a thousand finesses, and look back at Figure 11-3 and the calculations associated with it. Those tell us that the final increase in income from the change in investment will be $100 billion. We try out that new equilibrium in the last line of Table 11-4 and find that after the income of $1,300 billion is reached, there will be no further changes in income. Notice in the last column that, after the initial change in investment occurs, each subsequent change gets smaller and smaller just like those ripples in the pond. The size of the increases in income in successive rounds dwindles and finally disappears.[3]

How long does it take to complete all the rounds? Strictly speaking, forever. Yet because the successive changes get smaller and smaller, most of the effect is achieved quickly. For example, in Table 11-4, by 1973 almost 90 percent of the total change in national income induced by the first change in investment in 1970 is realized. With a shorter lag in consumption, we would get an even faster adjustment toward equilibrium.

Working out the multiplier process over time serves another

[3] We can also finesse the final result in the following way. The first *change* in income over the original level is 40. The second is 40 + (0.6 × 40). The third is 40 + (0.6 × 40) + (0.6 × 0.6 × 40). The fourth is 40 + (0.6 × 40) + (0.6 × 0.6 × 40) + (0.6 × 0.6 × 0.6 × 40), and so it goes. This is an infinite series with a finite sum which is given by the formula: 40 × [1/(1 − 0.6)]. That is just what we got out of the previous calculation using the multiplier.

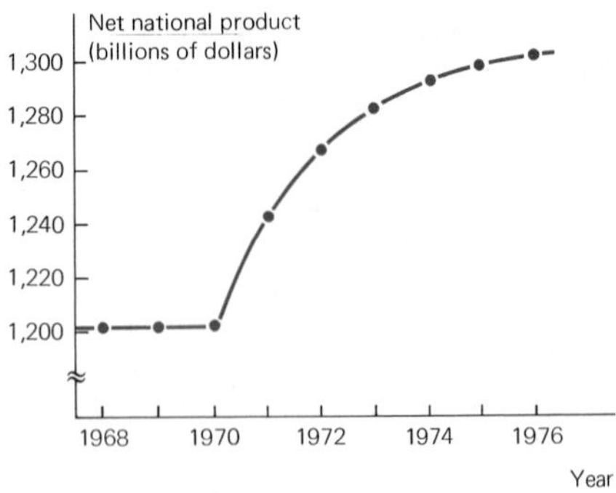

Figure 11-5

THE MULTIPLIER PROCESS OVER TIME

useful function: It introduces the idea of *dynamic* responses in the economy. Figure 11-5 shows the progression of the levels of national income after the initial change in investment. The change toward the final level of $1,300 billion is larger in the early than in the later years. In Figure 11-6 the year-to-year changes are shown; like the ripples in a pond, they die away toward nothing.

In actuality, changes are always occurring. Some types of investment are increasing; some are decreasing. Each change dropped into the pond causes a chain of ripples over time. But the multiplier can cut both ways. Increases in investment have multiplied effects in increasing income. Decreases in investment have multiplied effects in decreasing income in an exactly analogous manner. Sometimes the ripples cancel out. When there is a great flow of new investment, however, the multiplier-induced increases in income swamp all other effects.

We have analyzed the multiplier process for a change in investment. It works just as well for autonomous or exogenous changes in consumption and for other types of expenditures which have their source in other kinds of events not taken into account in our simple First Macro Model. We shall come to that extended analysis in the next chapter.

Shifts in the consumption and saving schedules and their paradoxes

Figure 11-6

YEAR-TO-YEAR CHANGES DUE TO THE MULTIPLIER PROCESS

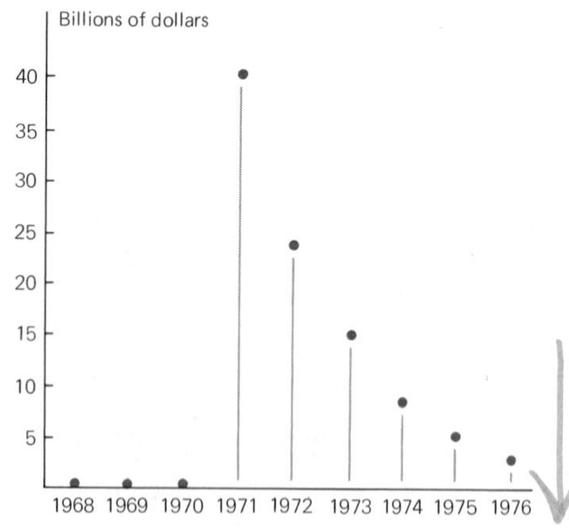

Occasionally there seems to be a shift in the overall propensities to consume and to save. In early 1969, when national income increased, consumption spending increased by more than was predicted by any reasonable estimate of the marginal propensity to consume. It was as if there had been an upward shift in the consumption-income relationship. It is useful to analyze the effects of such changes for their own sake and for the additional insight they provide into the national income determination process. We shall do this in the context of an assumed *decrease* in consumption spending, partly to practice working with declines in spending and partly to dramatize the effects.

We shall, therefore, assume that the propensity-to-consume relationship shifts downward, but in a straightforward manner that keeps the marginal propensity to consume constant. This is shown by the shift from C to C' in Figure 11-7(*a*). Instead of the former relationship, $C = \$280 \text{ billion} + 0.6 \text{ NI}$, we will now suppose that the propensity to consume is

$$C' = \$240 \text{ billion} + 0.6\,\text{DI} \quad \text{or} \quad C' = \$240 \text{ billion} + 0.6\,\text{NNP}$$

The decrease in consumption at each level of NNP is $40 billion. In the aggregate, people are trying to save that much more at each level of national income.

The *marginal* propensities to consume and save do not change,

Figure 11-7

EFFECTS OF SHIFTS IN PROPENSITIES TO CONSUME AND SAVE (BILLIONS OF DOLLARS)

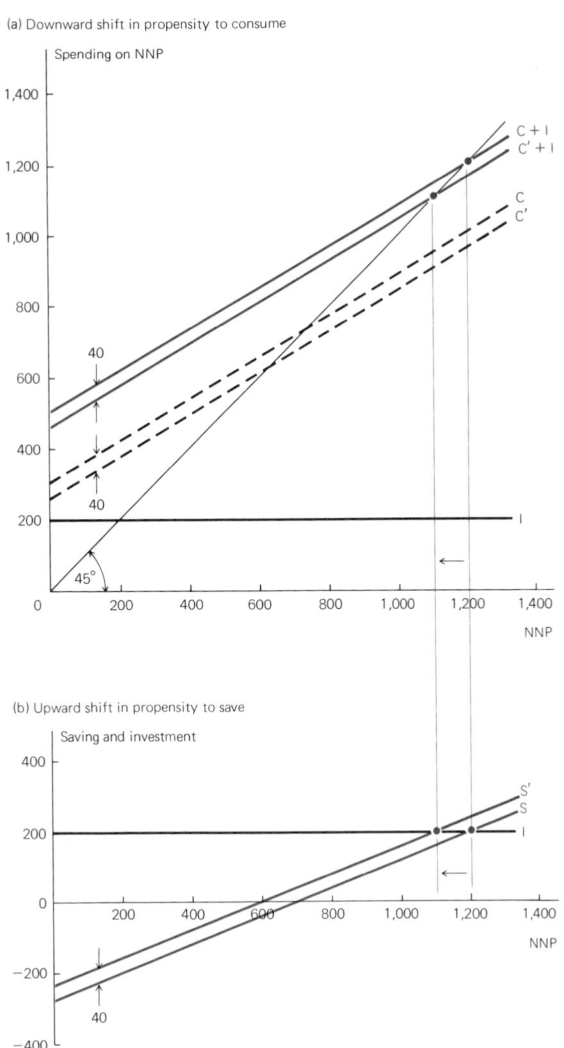

however. The multiplier is still $1/(1 - \text{MPC}) = 1/\text{MPS} = 1/0.4 = 2.5$. The total effect on NNP of the reduction in spending is, therefore, $2.5 \times (-\$40$ billion) or a $-$ \$100 billion *fall* in NNP, from \$1,200 billion to \$1,100 billion. At this new level of NNP, consumption will be \$900 billion, which is a fall not of \$40 billion but of \$100 billion.

On the other hand, saving, which is NI − C = \$1,100 − \$900, or \$200 billion, has not changed at all! This is our first apparent paradox. In the aggregate, people have tried to increase their saving and have succeeded only in reducing their consumption. What is the explanation?

When the propensity to consume shifted downward, income also fell, and that precipitated a further fall in consumption via the multiplier process. But the desired level of investment remained unchanged. As a result, in the new equilibrium, saving must be unchanged. This can be seen most clearly in Figure 11-7(*b*) which shows the shift upward in the propensity to save from *S* to *S′*. The paradox is resolved by observing that when consumption falls in the attempt to increase saving, income also falls by just enough to keep saving constant and equal to the constant level of investment.

Induced investment and more complicated multipliers and paradoxes

We have so far assumed that yearly investment plans, as revealed by our investment survey, are never altered once they are made. In Chapter 10, we noted that, actually, in periods of rising income, investment plans tend to be revised upward, and in periods of falling income, investment plans tend to be revised downward. That is, additional investment is *induced* or stimulated by higher incomes and discouraged by lower incomes. Let us include this point in our analysis and improve our description of the way the world works. We can do this by tilting the investment schedule upward. Now, if NNP should be above the equilibrium level of $1,200 billion, investment also would be higher. If the net national product should fall below $1,200 billion, investment also would be lower, as shown in Figure 11-8.

This new investment relationship is called the *propensity to invest*. Its slope measures the amount by which investment will increase when income increases. The slope is, therefore, called the marginal propensity to invest, MPI, by analogy to the consumption relationship. As shown in the inset in Figure 11-8, MPI $=$ $\Delta I/\Delta$NNP.

Figure 11-8

THE PROPENSITY TO INVEST (BILLIONS OF DOLLARS)

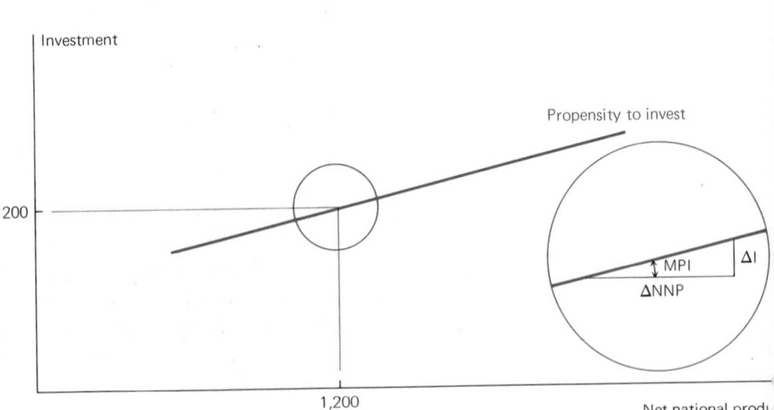

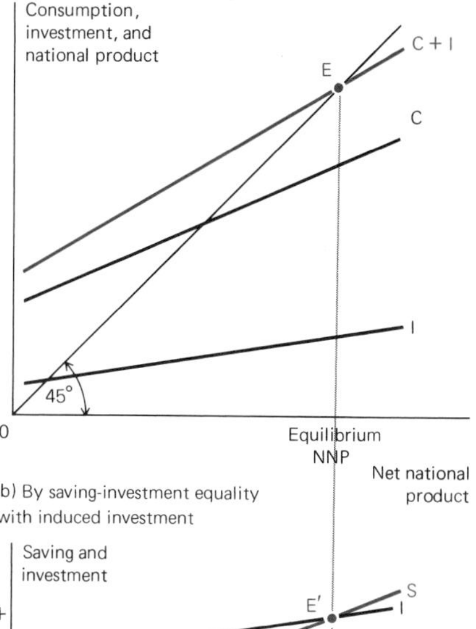

Figure 11-9

TWO WAYS OF DETERMINING NNP

Figure 11-10

THE PARADOX OF THRIFT

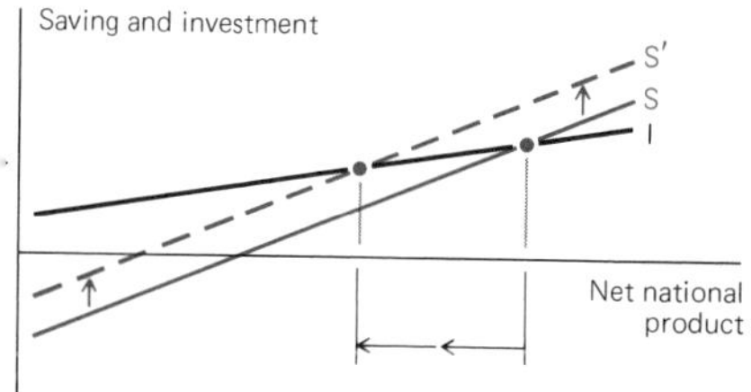

What difference does this new relationship make to our analysis? Figures 11-9 (a) and 11-9(b) show the *C-I* and *S-I* diagrams for this situation. The argument that income is determined in the *C-I* diagram at the intersection of the C + I line with the 45-degree line is the same as before. At that intersection and only there, aggregate supply is equal to aggregate demand, and producing and spending intentions are consistent. Likewise, in the S-*I* diagram the equilibrium level of NNP is at the intersection of the saving and investment lines. Above equilibrium NNP, the saving leakage would be greater than the investment injection. Below equilibrium levels, NNP would be raised, because the investment injection would be greater than the saving leakage.

The paradoxes related to the effects of a shift in the propensities to consume and save, with constant investment, are even more puzzling when there is induced investment. And since the investment schedule is somewhat more realistic, the explanation is even more important. Assume again that there is a decreased desire to consume at every level of disposable income and an increased desire to save. The propensity to consume shifts downward, and the propensity to save shifts upward. What is the result? As shown in Figure 11-10, there is now less consumption *and* less saving *and* less investment.

This result is the so-called "paradox of thrift." The paradox is that, in the attempt to save more, everyone ends up saving less. Why? Because the reduction in consumption spending reduces NNP, as before. But now, at lower NNP, there will be less investment, as indicated by the propensity to invest. With less investment there will be less income, and that, in turn, means less consumption *and* less saving, so income and output will fall further.

What accounts for these apparent paradoxes? They *seem* paradoxical because they deny that what is true for one individual is true for all individuals together. One individual can reduce his consumption spending and increase his saving without decreasing his income. But what is true for one is not necessarily true for all, though it is easy to fall into the trap of thinking it is so. That is the *fallacy of composition*. The effect on individual and aggregate income of one individual's actions can be ignored. The effect of an *overall* increase in consumption or saving by all individuals cannot be ignored, however, and is bound to have an effect on total spending and income. Once we are on the alert for the fallacy of composition, the apparent paradoxes disappear.

The multiplier when there is induced investment in the First Macro Model

The final effect of a shift in the spending schedules can be predicted by a multiplier when there is induced investment, just as it could be when there was a constant amount of investment. The multiplier is a different one, and as might be expected, it depends on the marginal propensity to invest, which reflects the response of investment to a change in income. To find the new multiplier, we first recall that the original multiplier formula without induced investment is

$$M = \frac{1}{1 - \text{MPC}} \quad \text{or} \quad M = \frac{1}{\text{MPS}}$$

In this relationship, only consumption spending responds to changes in income and output. The change in consumption is the marginal propensity to consume times the change in DI or NNP. It is MPC × ΔNNP. Now investment also responds to the change in national income. Induced investment, ΔI, is the marginal propensity to invest times ΔNNP, or MPI × ΔNNP. The total consumption and investment change associated with a change in net national product is

$$(\text{MPC} \times \Delta\text{NNP}) + (\text{MPI} \times \Delta\text{NNP})$$

Or $(\text{MPC} + \text{MPI})\,(\Delta\text{NNP})$

So in the multiplier formula, we must, in effect, replace the marginal propensity to consume, MPC, with MPC + MPI. The new multiplier relationship can now be written as

$$M = \frac{1}{1 - (\text{MPC} + \text{MPI})} = \frac{1}{1 - \text{MPC} - \text{MPI}}$$

or, using the relationship that 1 − MPC = MPS, we can also put it in the form:[4]

$$M = \frac{1}{\text{MPS} - \text{MPI}}$$

If, for example, the MPI were equal to 0.05 and the MPC were still 0.6, then M would be $\frac{1}{1 - 0.6 - 0.05} = \frac{1}{1 - 0.65} = \frac{1}{0.35}$ or about 3.15.

As before we should step back and ask if these relationships make economic sense and are plausible. They say that the larger the increase in investment at higher levels of NNP, the larger is MPI, the smaller will be the denominator, and the larger the multiplier. An antonomous increase in spending now results in larger succeeding rounds of induced spending because of both increases in consumption and increases in investment.

Induced investment, like an induced change in consumption, propagates ripples in economic activity and provides another explanation for the extended effects over time when there is a change in spending.

[4] This can be worked out as follows, noting first that $\Delta C + \Delta I + \Delta A$, where ΔA is any autonomous change in spending. Recalling $\Delta C = \text{MPC} \times \Delta\text{NNP}$ and $\Delta I = \text{MPI} \times \text{NNP}$, the first equation can be written as $\Delta\text{NNP} = (\text{MPC} \times \Delta\text{NNP}) + (\text{MPI} \times \Delta\text{NNP}) + \Delta A$.

Then: $\Delta\text{NNP}/\Delta\text{NNP} = 1 = \text{MPC} + \text{MPI} + \Delta A/\Delta\text{NNP}$.

So $\Delta A/\Delta\text{NNP} = 1 - \text{MPC} - \text{MPI}$

And $\Delta\text{NNP} = \Delta A \dfrac{1}{1 - \text{MPC} - \text{MPI}}$

An overview of the theory of national income as determined by effective demand

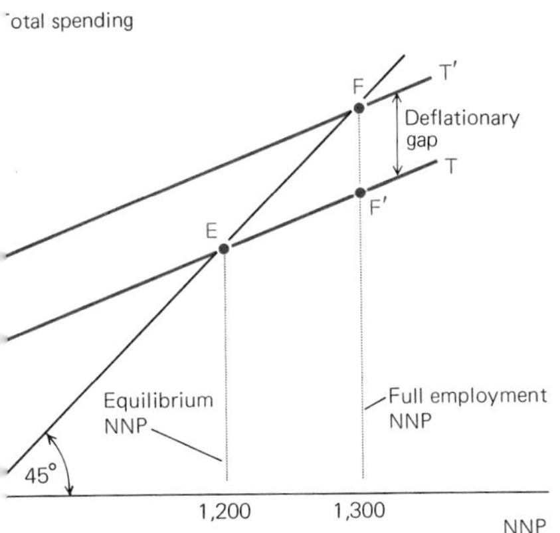

Figure 11-11

A DEFLATIONARY GAP (BILLIONS OF DOLLARS)

In the analysis presented here, aggregate output is determined by the effective demand for it.[5] This is different from the classical theory described in Chapter 6 in which aggregate output depends on the total productive resources available to the economy. Which theory should you believe?

The answer is: Both – but not as holding simultaneously. You have to determine which one is appropriate. And that depends on whether or not there is more or less full employment of labor and full use of capacity.

1. When there *is* full employment and full use of capacity, the availability of resources determines the output achieved.
2. When output is below full employment and full use of capacity, resources are not a binding constraint on the economy, and aggregate demand determines output.

In effect, the resources available to an economy set the ceiling to the output that can be produced. The level of aggregate demand determines where the economy operates, at or below the ceiling.

This can be appreciated with the help of Figure 11-11. We locate the full employment level of NNP at point *F* on the 45-degree line. We will suppose it to be $1,300 billion. The total spending line *T* cuts the 45-degree line at point *E*, which corresponds to a level of NNP of $1,200 billion. There is a *deflationary gap* in spending, because the economy is below full employment. That gap is the distance *FF′*, which is the amount by which the spending line would have to shift upward from *T* to *T′* if the economy were to operate at full employment. It is *less* than $100 billion because of the multiplier effects of any shift in spending.[6]

In Figure 11-12, a quite different situation is shown. The total spending line *T* cuts the 45-degree line at *E*, above the full employment NNP at *F*. In effect the economy is trying to buy more than it

Figure 11-12

AN INFLATIONARY GAP

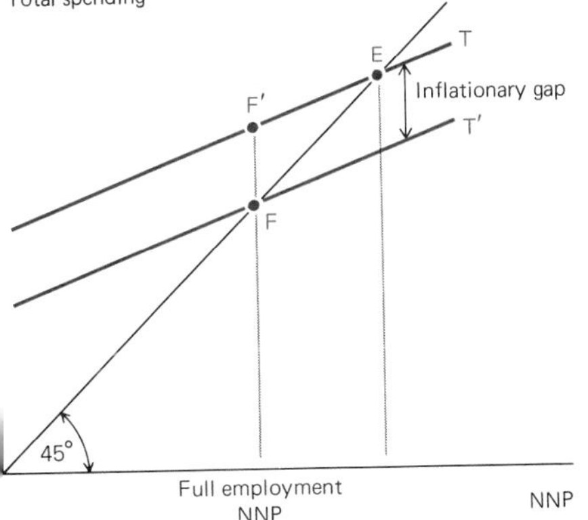

[5] A general algebraic formula for NNP can be worked out which encompasses all the special cases above. Suppose $C = A + \text{MPC (DI)}$, where A is a constant. Suppose also that $I = B + \text{MPI (NNP)}$, where B is another constant. Since $\text{DI} \equiv \text{NNP}$ in the First Macro Model and $\text{NNP} \equiv C + I$, then $\text{NNP} = A + \text{MPC (NNP)} + B + \text{MPI (NNP)}$. So $\text{NNP} (1 - \text{MPC} - \text{MPI}) = A + B$, and $\text{NNP} = A + B/(1 - \text{MPC} - \text{MPI})$. The special case of no induced investment is the result of setting $\text{MPI} = 0$. The denominator is just the multiplier when there is induced investment, but the entire formula predicts not just the change in NNP but total NNP, given the autonomous components of spending, A and B.

[6] The name "deflationary gap" does not mean that prices will not rise when there is unemployment. It just means that the real value of NNP is below that which is producible at full employment.

is capable of producing. The full employment ceiling sets the limit to how high NNP can be. The analysis shows that the economy will be at that limit. There is an inflationary gap now, since the excess aggregate demand, above the full employment levels of output, will create upward price pressures. The analysis does not tell us how far or how fast prices will move, however. We can also infer that, if the total spending line moved down by *F′F*, the inflationary gap would be removed.

The First Macro Model is a simplified economy with no government sector and no foreign trade. It can properly be interpreted as a model of the private business and consumer sectors of the economy with the effects of government and international economic activity somehow washed out. One of the most important morals of the analysis of this chapter is that there is no inherent tendency in this market economy for its aggregate output and income levels to be just at its full employment levels in any period. It may well generate either deflationary or inflationary gaps. Moreover, our review of the macroeconomic facts indicates that this potential inadequacy has often been a real deficiency. That does not mean that the whole system of a market economy is no good and beyond repair. It means that if we are to design offsetting public economic policies, we must recognize the deficiencies and understand their sources. We turn to the basic elements of public macroeconomic policies in the next chapter.

Summary

The determination of national output and income by the effective demand for the national product is analyzed in the context of the First Macro Model. This is a simple model with no government or foreign trade sectors and no depreciation. Business net revenues are equal to income payments. Under these assumptions, gross national product equals net national product, which is also equal to national income and disposable income. The simple economy is also assumed to be below its full employment and full capacity levels of output.

In the First Macro Model the net national product is the sum of expenditures on consumption and investment goods. Expenditures on consumption are determined by the propensity to consume. Investment is at first assumed to be determined autonomously, and the level of desired investment is assumed to be given by an investment survey. The condition of equilibrium for NNP is that aggregate supply and aggregate demand are equal, so aggregate production and spending intentions are consistent. This can be demonstrated numerically, graphically, and in an equation. The importance of the equilibrium NNP is that it is the level which will tend to be established in the economy.

Another way to look at the determination of the equilibrium NNP is that it satisfies the condition that the total amount of saving leaked out of the circular flow of national income is just equal to the total amount of investment spending injected into the economy. When these are not equal, there will be adjustments in the national income and product to make them equal.

The saving-investment equality as a condition of national income equilibrium is a condition in which planned or ex ante saving is equal to planned or ex ante investment. That is different from the ex post saving-investment identity of national income accounting in which realized or measured saving is identical to realized or measured investment.

Equilibrium is approached by means of adjustments in national income and product. This is different from the equilibrating process of classical economics, which relies on changes in relative prices. Further, classical economics argued that the process led to full employment. The equilibrium level of NNP as determined by aggregate demand need not be at full employment.

Multiplier analysis in the First Macro Model provides a means of predicting the effects on national income of a change in autonomous spending. The multiplier, M, is the number by which any change in autonomous investment, for example, must be multiplied to determine the resulting change in national income. If changes in national income induce changes only in consumption spending, then M is $1/(1 - \text{MPC})$ or $1/\text{MPS}$, where MPC is the marginal propensity to consume, and $\text{MPS} = 1 - \text{MPC}$ is the marginal propensity to save.

In actuality, the adjustment to a change in spending works itself out over time. This is because it takes time for consumption and saving to adjust to a change in income. Even so, most of the adjustment takes place in a relatively short time.

When investment as well as consumption depends on the level of NNP, the multiplied effects of any autonomous change in spending become larger. This is because changes in NNP now induce changes in both investment and consumption spending.

There are apparent paradoxes in the fact that attempts by everyone to reduce aggregate consumption and increase aggregate saving will not be successful. When investment depends on the level of NNP, the paradox of thrift is observed, and an upward shift in the propensity to save actually results in a decline in saving. The increase in aggregate saving means a reduction in aggregate consumption, a reduction in NNP, and further induced reductions in consumption and investment, which force income and, therefore, saving down rather than up. The apparent paradoxes are resolved, however, when it is noted that they arise from a comparison of aggregate behavior with the actions of an individual. Individually people can raise their saving without reducing income. All individuals acting in the same way cannot raise their saving without reducing aggregate consumption and, therefore, aggregate income.

Aggregate output in the theory presented is determined by effective demand. The maximum output producible with full employment and full use of capacity depends on the amount of labor, capital, and other resources available. If actual output is below this full employment output, there is a deflationary gap equal to the amount by which the spending function would have to shift upward to reach full employment. If there is an attempt to buy more output than can be produced, there is an inflationary gap. In that case prices will rise.

Questions for discussion and review

1. Reconstruct Table 11-1 under the assumption that, at each level of disposable income and NNP, consumption is $20 billion higher than indicated in column 2. Now insert this new propensity to consume in Table 11-2. What is the equilibrium level of NNP now? What is the multiplier for the new propensity to consume? Can you explain why? Suppose investment increased by $20 billion from the level in Table 11-2, with the new propensity to consume. Can you predict the new equilibrium NNP, using the aggregate supply-aggregate demand equilibrium condition? Can you get the same result using the saving-investment condition? Can you get the same result using a multiplier analyis?

2. Describe in detail the downward multiplier effects on national income and output of a reduction in, say, invesment spending.

3. Explain the difference between the national income accounting *identity* of saving and investment and the national income equilibrium *equality* of saving and investment.

4. What are time lags in consumption and income relations? How do they affect the economy's adjustment to changes in spending?

5. Explain the paradoxes that the attempt to increase saving either can lead to no change in saving if the level of investment does not change or can even lead to a reduction in saving if the level of investment is related to the level of income.

6. When there is a deflationary gap, it is sometimes wrongly identified as the difference between the actual level of NNP and the higher full employment level of NNP. Why is that wrong?

7. Would it be correct to say that one of the most important lessons of this chapter is that there can be less than full employment equilibrium in the economy? If you think that is not important, how would you have felt if we had turned up the opposite conclusion that the economy tended to maintain a full employment equilibrium? If the answers strike you as obvious, can you explain why?

8. Discuss the following quotation critically: *In both classical economics and modern economic analysis the equilibrum condition for*

national income and output is that aggregate supply and aggregate demand are equal. The theories differ in explaining how that equilibrium is achieved and the level of national income at which it will be achieved.

Concepts for review

Aggregate supply-aggregate demand equilibrium

Aggregate saving-investment equilibrium

The multiplier with and without induced investment

Time lags in consumption-income behavior

The paradox of thrift

Inflationary gap

Deflationary gap

12

The macro-economic effects of fiscal policy and foreign trade: The Second and Third Macro Models

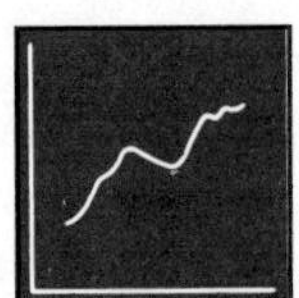

This chapter extends the analysis of the determination of income and output to make it more realistic and useful. The simple private economy that was examined in Chapter 11 had no government or international sector. This meant that we did not have to worry there about the effects of government spending or taxing or foreign trade, but we could not analyze those effects either. In this chapter the omitted sectors are brought into the analysis. A set of tools will be developed which will permit us to examine public macroeconomic policy in considerable depth and detail. The new macro models, like the first, are assumed to have less than full employment of labor and full use of capacity, so output is determined by effective demand. This makes plausible the assumption that prices do not change. Even with these remaining simplifications, we will still be able to analyze some of the sources of price inflation, though not all its processes and consequences.

The Second Macro Model

The Second Macro Model is similar to the first, except that there is a government sector. It includes all levels of government: federal, state, local, county, etc. The government sector buys goods and services for public use, and it collects taxes and borrows, if necessary, to pay for them. The Second Macro Model is still a closed economy, without foreign trade. To make the accounting easier, we continue to ignore depreciation.

By adding a government sector, we catch in this model the aggregate effects of government fiscal policy – which is its expenditure and tax policy. Analysis of the Second Macro Model will carry us a long way toward a realistic appreciation of the role of government in affecting aggregate demand.

The national income accounts of the Second Macro Model are shown schematically in Figure 12-1. The net national product is the sum of expenditures of the private sector on consumption, C, and net investment, I, and the expenditure of all levels of government on goods and services, G. Tax payments, T, to government are a leakage from the flow of income, but transfer payments, W, from government add to disposable income. Disposable income, in turn,

Figure 12-1

EXPENDITURE AND INCOME FLOWS IN THE SECOND MACRO MODEL

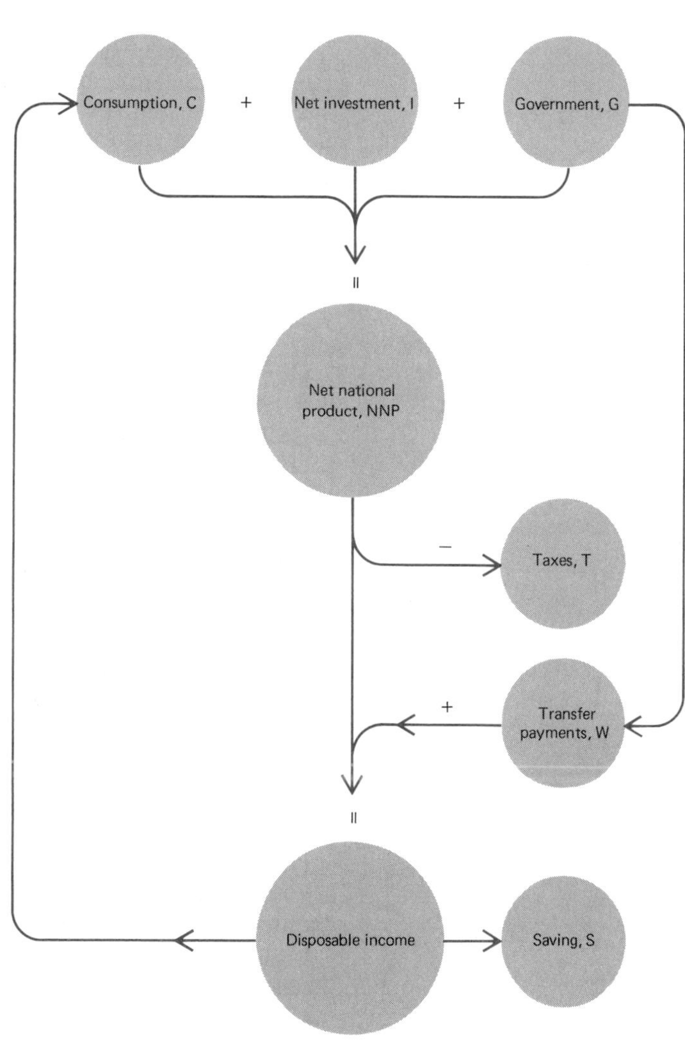

is divided between private consumption, C, and private saving, S.

Our income accounts are, therefore:

$$\begin{cases} NNP \equiv C + I + G \\ DI \equiv NNP - T + W \quad \text{or} \quad NNP \equiv DI + T - W \\ DI \equiv C + S \end{cases}$$

These are ex post concepts used to measure what has happened after it has happened. However, their careful examination will reveal in advance what the general effects of government spending and taxing must be. Government expenditures on goods and services are like consumption and investment spending in that they are a demand for output. To satisfy government demands, labor and other productive resources must be used to produce the goods and services wanted. An extra dollar of government spending is an addition to effective demand.

Taxes, on the other hand, are a leakage from the income stream, like private saving. They reduce the amount of disposable income available to individuals for purchasing goods and services. This is true of indirect taxes, such as manufacturers' excise taxes and sales taxes, and of direct taxes on income. A tax increase, therefore, tends to reduce effective demand. But a tax reduction increases purchasing power in the hands of private individuals. It thus stimulates consumption expenditures and aggregate effective demand.

Government transfer payments, W, for old-age security, welfare, etc., add directly to disposable income and can be used for any of the purposes for which individuals use their income. Another dollar of transfer payments, like a tax reduction, adds to effective demand by stimulating consumption.

The government sector as a whole will be in surplus if expenditures, which are $W + G$, are less than tax receipts, T; it will be in deficit if $W + G$ is greater than T. (Remember, G consists of purchases of goods and services, and W stands for transfer payments.) If there is a surplus, government is saving, just as the private sector is saving when its income is greater than its consumption expenditures. More commonly, all levels of government today seem to run deficits, which they finance by borrowing. If there is a deficit, government is *dis*saving. Although we may hear talk about governments "going bankrupt," there is no direct analogy between individual bankruptcy and government bankruptcy. As long as people are willing to accept government money, buy government notes and bonds, and/or sell to the government on credit, governments can spend more than they receive in taxes. We shall discuss the management of government debt in Chapter 18.

Before we get into the analysis of the Second Macro Model, it is useful to clarify the implications of the national income and government budget definitions. The definition of NNP on the "receipts" side makes it equal to disposable income plus taxes minus transfer payments, or

$$NNP \equiv DI + T - W$$

Disposable income is private consumption, C, plus personal saving. Personal saving will now be S_P, in order to distinguish it from government saving, S_G. In place of DI, we write $C + S_P$ and have

$$NNP \equiv C + S_P + T - W$$

That must be the same as NNP defined on the "expenditure" side as $C + I + G$, consumption plus investment plus government spending on goods and services. So

$$NNP \equiv C + S_P + T - W \equiv C + I + G$$

Since C appears on both sides of the identity, we can remove it without affecting the identity, and we can move G over to the left-hand side. This manipulation leaves us with

$$S_P + T - W - G \equiv I$$

$T - W - G$ is government saving, if it is positive, or dissaving if it has a minus sign (if expenditures are greater than taxes). So now

$$S_P + S_G \equiv I$$

This just says: *Total saving — the sum of private and government saving or dissaving — must be identical to investment.*

The sources and uses of saving for some recent years are summarized in Table 12-1.

Table 12-1

SOURCES AND USES OF SAVING (BILLIONS OF DOLLARS)

	1965	*1966*	*1967*	*1968*	*1969*	*1970**
Sources:						
Total saving	115.3	124.9	119.5	128.6	143.7	139.0
Gross private saving	113.1	123.8	133.4	135.9	135.0	148.6
Government surplus (+) or deficit (−)	+2.2	+1.1	−13.9	−7.3	+8.7	−9.6
Federal	1.2	−0.2	−12.4	−6.2	+9.3	−10.8
State and local	1.0	+1.3	−1.6	−1.1	−0.6	+1.2
Uses:						
Total gross investment	112.2	123.9	118.8	126.2	138.9	137.4
Gross private domestic investment	108.1	121.4	116.6	126.5	139.8	135.8
Net foreign investment	4.1	2.4	2.2	−0.3	−0.9	1.6
Statistical discrepancy†	−3.1	−1.0	−0.7	−2.4	−4.7	−2.5

*Provisional.
†The statistical discrepancy indicates an unexplained error in estimation. In the years shown, the negative statistical discrepancy indicates that the saving estimate is too high.
Note: Observe the surge in the federal deficit in 1967 and 1968 associated with the escalation of the Vietnam War.
Source: U.S. Department of Commerce, Office of Business Economics.

Income determination in the Second Macro Model

The general directions in which the economy is pushed by government spending and taxing, each taken separately, can be worked out from Figure 12-1. It is important to keep these general directions clearly in mind, just as it is useful to remember which way is North and which is South when traveling. But just as reading a map is more than knowing the points of the compass, appreciating the full effects of fiscal policy requires more than knowing the general tendencies suggested by Figure 12-1. Inspection of the figure will tell us, for example, that both additional government spending on goods and services and additional transfer payments will stimulate the economy. But are their quantitative effects the same? Are government dollars spent on goods more "powerful" in their effects on national income and product than transfer dollars? We can also deduce from Figure 12-1 that a tax reduction will stimulate the economy. But we would like to know more. Are tax reduction dollars more powerful in their effects on NNP than "spending dollars"?

Government spending with constant taxes

To work out the answers to these questions of fiscal policy, we shall take them up one at a time. First, we shall concentrate on the effects of government spending on goods and services by assuming that there are no transfer payments and that taxes are constant. This is the Mark I version of the Second Macro Model, an example of which is presented in Table 12-2. When we subtract taxes in column 2 (taxes are constant at $200 billion) from national product in each row of column 1, we get disposable income in column 3. (We might note here that column 2 can also be interpreted as $T - W$, taxes minus transfers. Taxes reduce disposable income and transfer payments increase it, and $T - W$ is the net effect.)

Table 12-2

THE DETERMINATION OF NATIONAL PRODUCT WITH CONSTANT GOVERNMENT SPENDING AND TAXES (BILLIONS OF DOLLARS)

	1 NNP	2 Taxes	3 Disposable income	4 Consumption	5 Intended Investment	6 Government spending	7 Total spending	8 Saving Government	9 Saving Private	10 Saving Total
A	$1,350	$200	$1,150	$970	$100	$220	$1,290	− $20	$180	$160
B	1,300	200	1,100	940	100	220	1,260	− 20	160	140
C	1,250	200	1,050	910	100	220	1,230	− 20	140	120
D	**1,200**	**200**	**1,000**	**880**	**100**	**220**	**1,200**	**− 20**	**120**	**100**
E	1,150	200	950	850	100	220	1,170	− 20	100	80
F	1,100	200	900	820	100	220	1,140	− 20	80	60
G	1,050	200	850	790	100	220	1,110	− 20	60	40
H	1,000	200	800	760	100	220	1,080	− 20	40	20

The propensity to consume is embodied in columns 3 and 4. It is the same one that we worked with in Chapter 11. The marginal propensity to consume out of disposable income is again 0.6. Intended investment is assumed to be a constant amount, at $100 billion, projected again from a recent survey of business intentions. Government spending on goods and services is set at $220 billion in column 6. Total spending is shown in column 7, each row of which is the sum of the entries in columns 4, 5, and 6. The government deficit in column 8 is $20 billion. Private saving in column 9 is disposable income minus consumption, and total saving in column 10 is the sum of government and private saving. Now using Table 12-2, we can work out the equilibrium toward which income and output will move.

The equilibrium level of NNP is $1,200 billion as shown in row *D* where the level of total spending (column 7) equals the net national product and where aggregate demand equals aggregate supply. We can also identify the equilibrium as the level of income at which total saving (column 10) equals total investment (column 5), remembering that total saving is now the sum of government saving and private saving. In this example government saving is a negative amount, since the government sector is always running a deficit.

The arithmetic of Table 12-2 is represented by Figure 12-2. The propensity to consume in this figure, line *C*, is plotted as consumption spending versus the NNP, so each point is taken from an entry in column 1 and the corresponding entry in column 4 of Table 12-2. Planned investment in column 5 is the line *I*, and government spending in column 6 is the line *G*. Both *I* and *G* are horizontal, reflecting the fact that they do not change with income in this example. Aggregate effective demand at each level of NNP is the sum of each type of spending. In Figure 12-2 this total is the vertical sum of lines *C*, *I*, and *G*, which is the $C + I + G$ line. It is obtained by adding *D*, *I*, and *G* at each possible level of NNP. The condition that NNP be equal to total spending is represented by the intersection of the aggregate demand line with the 45-degree aggregate supply line, which is equidistant from the spending and NNP axes. That is point D. A level of NNP higher than at *D* could not be sustained by the total spending at that higher level. A lower level of NNP would be pushed to *D* by the total spending.

The equilibrium condition can also again be thought of as one in which the planned investment injection is equal to the total saving leakage, or $I = S_P + S_G$. This condition is shown graphically in Figure 12-3, where *I* is the desired constant level of investment; S_P is private saving and S_G is government saving, which is here a deficit or dissaving of $20 billion. So the schedule that sums up private and government saving, $S_P + S_G$, is everywhere less than private saving by $20 billion. The equilibrium is at *D′*.

Finally, note that, as before, there is no reason why the equilibrium value of the NNP should have a special claim on our affections. In particular, the equilibrium NNP is not necessarily the

Figure 12-2

AGGREGATE SPENDING ON NNP WITH CONSTANT LEVELS OF TAXES AND GOVERNMENT SPENDING (BILLIONS OF DOLLARS)

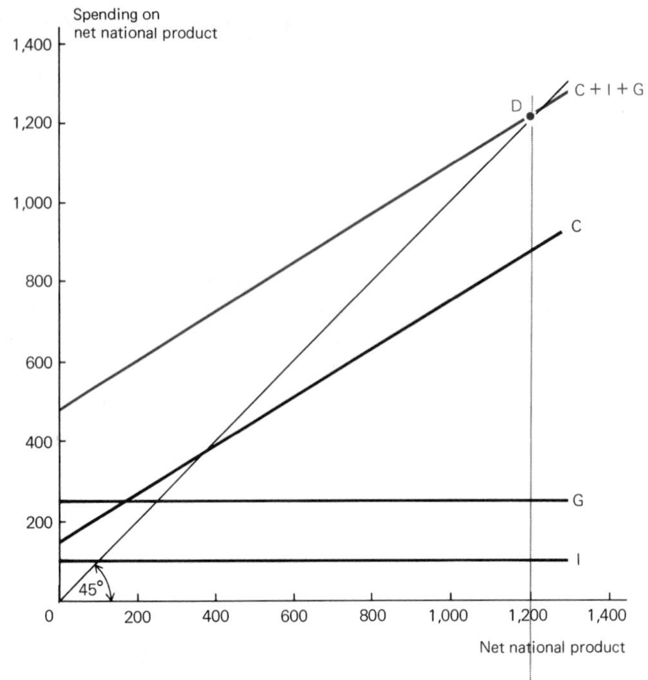

Figure 12-3

DETERMINATION OF NNP BY SAVING-INVESTMENT EQUALITY (BILLIONS OF DOLLARS)

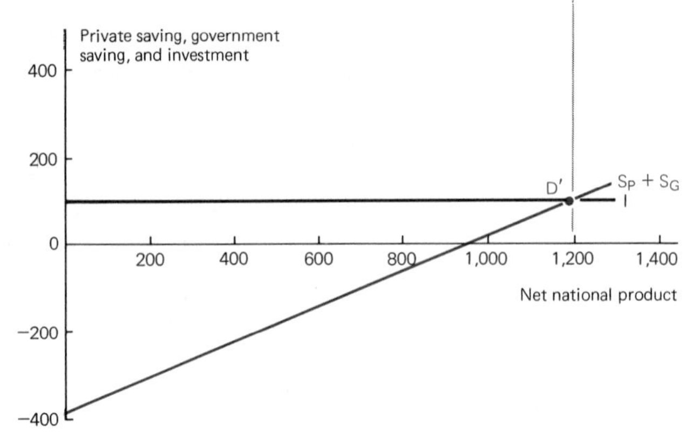

full employment and full capacity level of NNP. A government sector is not, in itself, a guarantee of prosperity and full employment — or of depression and unemployment.

What about the multiplier in this macro model? When taxes are constant and do not change with income, the multiplier analysis of the First Macro Model applies. The multiplier effects of a change in government or private spending can be worked out using the formula of the previous chapter, $M = 1/(1 - \text{MPC})$. The multiplier effects of tax changes are more complicated. That problem is taken up in the Appendix to this chapter.

Government spending and variable taxes

We go now to the Mark II version of the Second Macro Model. This version drops the assumption of a constant level of taxes. Instead, and more realistically, we recognize that to some degree taxes go up and down as income and output go up and down. The exact proportion of taxes in income at different levels of income depends on the specific rates of the various taxes. Figure 12-4 presents a rough description of the kind of relationship that prevails in the economy. The *marginal tax rate* (MTR) is the additional amount of taxes that must be paid when there is an additional dollar's income. It is the *slope* of the tax-NNP relationship in Figure 12-4 at a particular level of NNP. The specific relationship is embodied in a new arithmetical example in Table 12-3. Columns 1 and 2 of the table represent the tax-NNP relationship. A constant marginal tax rate is assumed.[1] For every $50 billion change in NNP, there is a $10 billion change in taxes. Therefore, the MTR is equal to $10 billion divided by $50 billion, or 20 percent. Disposable income in column 3 is just the difference between NNP and taxes.

Figure 12-4

A TAX-NNP RELATION WITH CONSTANT MARGINAL TAX RATE

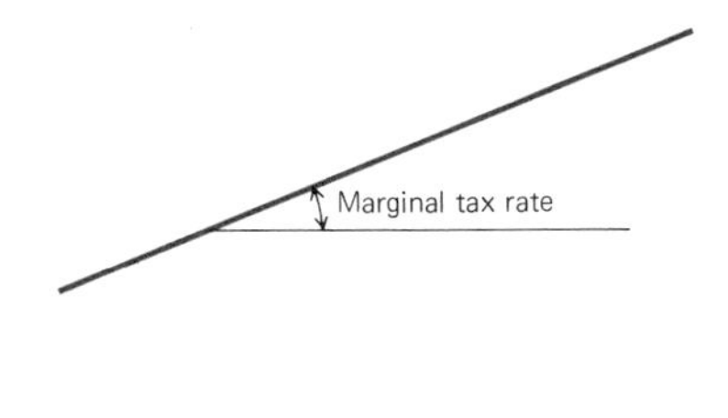

We can also interpret column 2 of Table 12-3 as the amount of taxes minus the amount of transfer payments at each level of NNP. Taxes go up with NNP, and transfer payments tend to fall, so the difference between them, $T - W$, tends to rise with NNP, as represented in columns 1 and 2.

The propensity to consume is embodied in columns 3 and 4 of Table 12-3. Again the marginal propensity to consume out of disposable income is assumed to be 0.6. Intended investment and gov-

[1] It should be emphasized that this is a simplification which makes it easier to understand the basic processes at work. Overall, the marginal tax rate tends to increase with income.

Table 12-3

DETERMINATION OF NNP WHEN TAXES RISE WITH INCOME (BILLIONS OF DOLLARS)

	1	2	3	4	5	6	7	8	9	10
								Saving		
	NNP	*Taxes*	*Disposable income*	*Consumption*	*Intended investment*	*Government spending*	*Total spending*	*Government*	*Private*	*Total*
A	$1,350	$230	$1,120	$952	$100	$220	$1,272	+ $10	$168	$178
B	1,300	220	1,080	928	100	220	1,248	0	152	152
C	1,250	210	1,040	904	100	220	1,224	− 10	136	126
D	**1,200**	**200**	**1,000**	**880**	**100**	**220**	**1,200**	**− 20**	**120**	**100**
E	1,150	190	960	856	100	220	1,176	− 30	104	74
F	1,100	180	920	832	100	220	1,152	− 40	88	48
G	1,050	170	880	808	100	220	1,128	− 50	72	22
H	1,000	160	840	784	100	220	1,104	− 60	56	− 4

Figure 12-5

DETERMINATION OF NET NATIONAL PRODUCT WHEN TAXES RISE WITH INCOME (BILLIONS OF DOLLARS)

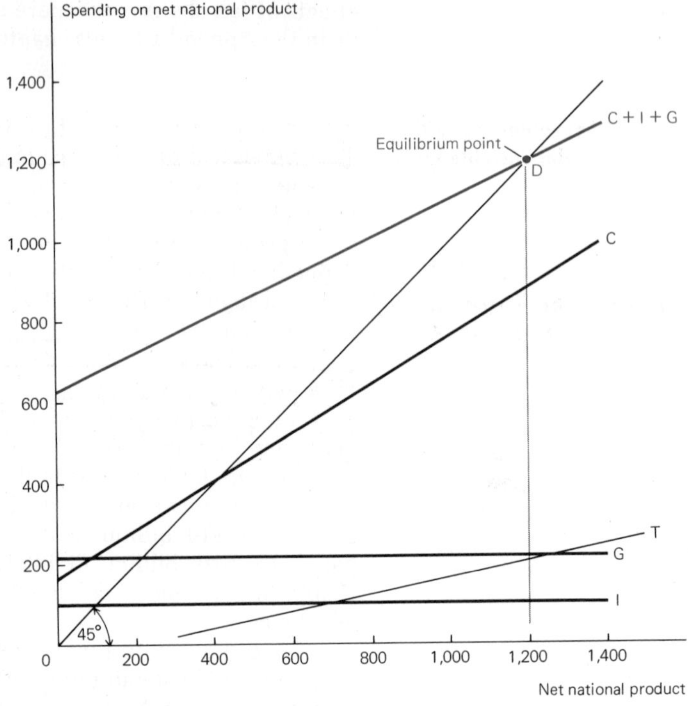

ernment spending are now assumed to be constant at $100 billion and $220 billion, respectively.

The equilibrium income level is again that level at which the total spending on the national product equals the total receipts by its producers. That happens to be at row *D*, as Table 12-3 shows.

We can also see in Table 12-3 that the size of the government deficit depends on the level of NNP. Government spending is always the same, but taxes increase as NNP goes up.[2]

Total saving (column 10) is the sum of the government deficit, or dissaving, in each row of column 8 and of the positive private saving in each row of column 9. At equilibrium, row *D*, total saving equals total investment.

The relationships in Table 12-3 are shown graphically in Figure 12-5. The propensity to consume is the *C* line; planned private investment is now assumed constant at $100 billion, and government spending is constant at $220 billion. The equilibrium income

[2] Taxes go up with spending but at a slightly faster *rate*, and transfers tend to fall with NNP. So with a given amount of government spending on goods and services, the size of the government deficit, or dissaving, would actually be less at a higher level of NNP than at a lower level.

is again at $1,200 billion, point D, at the intersection of the $C + I + G$ line with the 45-degree line, where aggregate spending on final goods equals the national product.

Fiscal drag and the full employment surplus

It was noted earlier that the existence of a government sector does not in itself ensure full employment. Government spending is an injection of purchasing power into the economy, but taxes are a leakage. Government expenditures are determined once a year in the budget-making processes, and they may or may not be adjusted later. Taxes are determined by the rate schedules. The schedules make taxes rise with income and, overall, more than proportionally. Transfer payments are determined by existing programs, and these tend to contract as NNP rises and the country becomes more prosperous. Conversely transfers increase as NNP falls. So the net leakage of taxes minus transfers increases with NNP.

Could the tax leakage be so high relative to government expenditures that it could retard overall expansion? *Once taxes are recognized as a leakage we must admit the possibility that they can be a "fiscal drag."* Moreover, experience has shown that this has actually happened.

How can one tell whether taxes are creating fiscal drag and tending to hold back employment and output or whether they are permitting too much fiscal stimulation and contributing to price pressures? Looking at *current* levels of taxes and expenditures and the *current* budget deficit or surplus is not enough. For example, in Table 12-3 there is a $20 billion deficit in the government budget at the $1,200 billion equilibrium level of income and output. That may suggest that taxes are low relative to expenditures and are not a retarding influence. Suppose, however, that the full employment level of NNP were actually $1,350 billion. Compare taxes at that level with taxes at $1,200 billion NNP. At $1,350 billion NNP, taxes would be $30 billion more. With unchanged government spending, there would be a budget surplus or net government saving of $10 billion at the full employment NNP of $1,350 billion. That government saving would have to be offset by additional spending in order to attain the full employment level. So in this example, taxes are indeed a fiscal drag, draining away larger and larger proportions of purchasing power as output rises.

Economists regularly make calculations such as those in Table 12-3 to determine whether, *at full employment,* there will be an overall surplus or deficit in the government budget. The result, naturally enough, is called the *full employment surplus or deficit.* Figure 12-6 presents the results of such calculations for the years 1956 to 1970. It indicates that fiscal drag has been an actuality in many years.

As might be expected, a higher marginal tax rate leads to a lower multiplier. It acts as a greater drag on the economy and

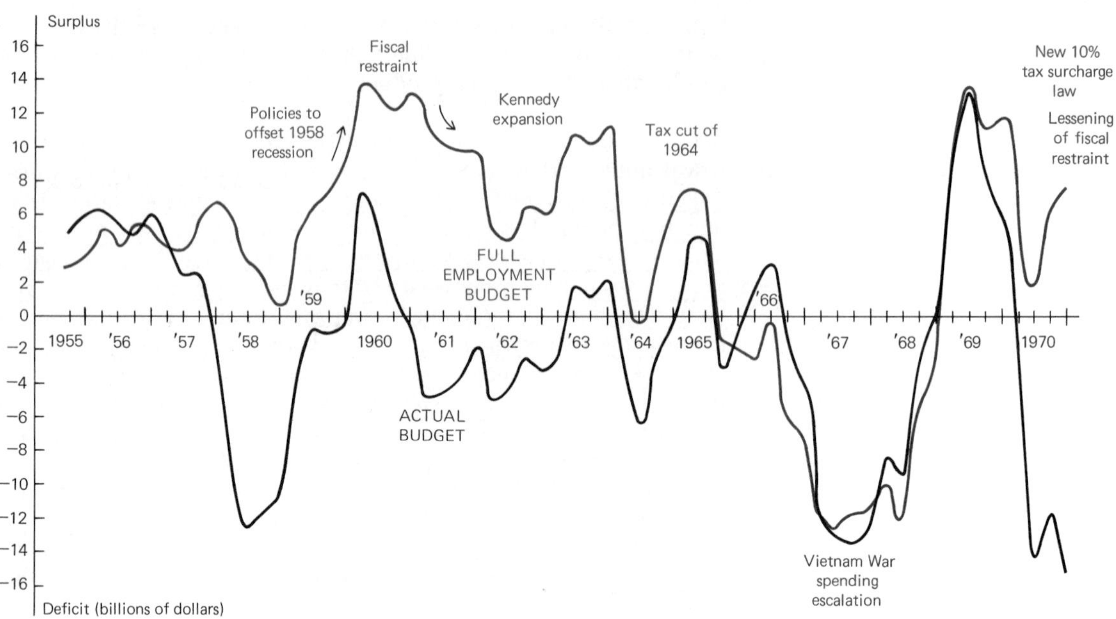

Figure 12-6

THE ACTUAL FEDERAL BUDGET SURPLUS OR DEFICIT AND THE FULL EMPLOYMENT BUDGET SURPLUS OR DEFICIT (BILLIONS OF DOLLARS)

The federal budget was in deficit through most of the period from 1955 to 1970. However, federal taxing and spending constituted a "fiscal drag" on the economy during most of this period, as indicated by the fact that the federal budget, if calculated as at full employment, would have been in surplus. The massive spending escalation in 1966, 1967, and 1968 drove the actual and full employment budgets deeply into deficit. That was followed by the fiscal restraint of 1969, which continued into 1970. President Nixon proposed in 1971 a federal budget which would show an actual deficit of $18.5 billion but would be in balance on a full employment basis. (Source: A. M. Okun and Nancy H. Teeters, "The Full Employment Surplus Revisited," Brookings Papers on Economic Activity, *No. 1, 1970, The Brookings Institution, Washington, D.C.; and Council of Economic Advisers,* Economic Report of the President, *February, 1971.)*

makes the system less responsive to private investment or government spending. If it generates a surplus in the government budget at full employment, that surplus or saving is a drain which must be offset by private spending in order to achieve full employment.

The effects of fiscal policy changes on expenditures and taxes

We can now turn to one of the most interesting and important questions in macroeconomics: What are the aggregate effects of *changes* in government expenditures and taxes? In the terminology of the preceding chapter, What are the multiplier effects of government spending and taxing? The answer will provide the basis for *designing* fiscal policy to achieve particular targets. If there is a deflationary gap and the economy is at less than reasonably full employment levels of NNP, the answer to the question will help us understand how to use fiscal policy to move the economy toward full employment NNP. On the other hand, if there is an inflationary gap and aggregate effective demand is above the real supply potential of the economy, we will be able to see how fiscal policy can be used to cool off the system and eliminate the gap.

Having mastered the essentials of macroeconomic analysis, we can now make the major points about fiscal policy with a few simple tables and graphs. First, we shall analyze the effects of a change in government spending with taxes constant. Then we shall work through the effects of a change in taxes with government spending constant. And finally we shall combine the two analyses.

Compare Table 12-4 with Table 12-2. The first five columns are the same, but column 6, government spending, is $20 billion higher in Table 12-4. With the higher level of government spending, total spending, or aggregate demand at each level of NNP in column 7, will be $20 billion higher in Table 12-4 than in Table 12-2. The new equilibrium level of NNP in Table 12-4 will be at $1,250 billion. As shown in row *D* of Table 12-4, at $1,250 billion NNP in column 1, aggregate spending in column 7 will also be $1,250 billion.

As we might expect, the increase in government spending has a multiplied effect on the level of NNP. *Additional government spending is an increase in demand for final goods and services, and production will expand to meet this additional demand as long as the economy is not at its full employment and full capacity ceilings.* But NNP expands by more than the increase in government expenditures. A close inspection of Table 12-4 will show that, at the new equilibrium level of NNP, not only is government spending higher than in Table 12-2, but private consumption spending is also higher. Why is that?

Table 12-4

DETERMINATION OF NNP WITH TAXES CONSTANT AND A HIGHER LEVEL OF GOVERNMENT SPENDING (BILLIONS OF DOLLARS)

	1	2	3	4	5	6	7	8	9	10
								Saving		
	NNP	*Taxes*	*Disposable income*	*Consumption*	*Intended investment*	*Government spending*	*Total spending*	*Government*	*Private*	*Total*
A	$1,350	$200	$1,150	$970	$100	$240	$1,310	− $40	$180	$140
B	1,300	200	1,100	940	100	240	1,280	− 40	160	120
C	**1,250**	**200**	**1,050**	**910**	**100**	**240**	**1,250**	**− 40**	**140**	**100**
D	1,200	200	1,000	880	100	240	1,220	− 40	120	80
E	1,150	200	950	850	100	240	1,190	− 40	100	60
F	1,100	200	900	820	100	240	1,160	− 40	80	40
G	1,050	200	850	790	100	240	1,130	− 40	60	20
H	1,000	200	800	760	100	240	1,100	− 40	40	0

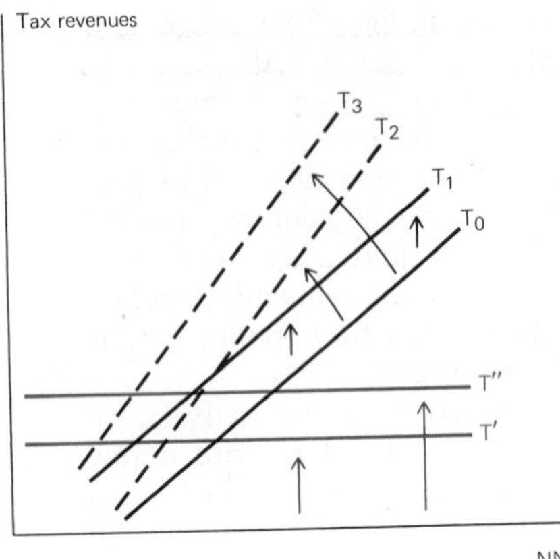

Figure 12-7

ALTERNATIVE CHANGES IN TAX SCHEDULES

The increase in government spending sets off an increase in output. That, in turn, means an increase in income to workers and owners of production facilities. They, in turn, spend part of their increased income on consumption goods and services. The increased demand for consumption goods means more output of these goods and more income earned in their production, and so on and on. The additional government spending initiates a whole set of new rounds of private consumption spending as well. That is why the increase in NNP is larger than the increase in government spending. There is a government spending multiplier at work which makes government spending dollars have a greater than one-for-one impact on NNP.[3]

A reduction in government spending, with everything else unchanged, leads to a reduction in NNP. A decline in government spending is, in itself, a decline in aggregate demand. In the simple example given here, the total effect of a one-dollar decline in government spending is equal but opposite to the effect of a one-dollar increase.

Now we can analyze tax changes. To find the effect of a tax change on NNP, we must first have the answer to another question, What kind of tax change are we talking about? There is no end to the ingenuity of man in taxing himself, and we could not hope to capture all the possible variations in a simple table or graph. Yet as a first approximation we can think of representing a change as one of the following:

1. A shift in the entire schedule, with the marginal tax rate remaining constant, shown as the movement from the original tax schedule T_0 to T_1 in Figure 12-7
2. A change in the marginal tax rate which swivels the tax relation from T_0 to T_2 in Figure 12-7
3. A change in both the general level and marginal rate of the tax schedule, as shown in the shift from T_0 to T_3 in Figure 12-7

It is possible to work out the effects of each of these types of changes. But since our purpose here is merely to appreciate the relative effects of a tax change, let us concentrate on a simple version. In the example of Table 12-4, taxes were constant at a level of $200 billion, corresponding to T' in Figure 12-7. We will assume now that there is an across-the-board tax *increase* of $20 billion, so that there is an upward shift in the tax schedule, as from T' to T''.

[3] The numbers in the example provide the basis for computing the multiplier for this simple case *with taxes constant.* A $20 billion increase in government spending led to a $50 billion increase in NNP. So the multiplier, the number by which we should have multiplied the change in government spending to predict the resulting change in NNP, is 50/20 = 2.5. This can also be calculated from the multiplier formula for the First Macro Model of Chap. 11. It should be emphasized, however, that this multiplier is appropriate only when taxes are constant. In actuality, taxes do vary with the level of NNP, as pointed out in the discussion of the Mark II version of the Second Macro Model. So this particular multiplier is not yet a realistic approximation.

Taxes are now at a constant level of $220 billion.

The general effect of a shift in the tax function can be inferred by looking at the propensity to consume with and without taxes. In Figure 12-8, C_0 represents what the propensity to consume would be before the tax change. Now suppose that there is a flat increase in taxes in the amount ΔT. At each level of the net national product, disposable income will be less by the amount of the tax change. And, therefore, *at each level of disposable income, consumption will fall by an amount equal to the marginal propensity to consume times the change in tax, MPC × ΔT*. The whole consumption function will drop from C_0 to C_1. Since consumption at each level of NNP is lower, owing to the tax, that in itself will tend to make NNP lower than it otherwise would be.

The effects of the specific change can be worked out numerically again, as in Table 12-5. As compared with Table 12-2, taxes are $20 billion higher at each level of NNP. Disposable income at each NNP level will be $20 billion lower. Since the marginal propensity to consume is 0.6, consumption at each level of NNP will be (0.6) × ($20 billion) or $12 billion lower. Intended investment and government spending are assumed to be unchanged and constant at their previous levels. A new row, *D'*, has been added to show the new level of equilibrium exactly. If NNP is $1,170 billion, aggregate spending will also be $1,170 billion, and saving will be equal to investment, so $1,170 billion is the new equilibrium after the tax change.

To summarize, the effect of a $20 billion *increase* in taxes is to *reduce* NNP by $30 billion. The change in NNP is greater than the tax change. The initial impact of the tax increase will be to reduce spending by 0.6, the marginal propensity to consume, times the tax change. But that reduction in spending on consumer goods means a corresponding reduction in income to producers of consumer goods. It will lead to a further reduction in consumer spending, a further reduction in income, a further reduction in consumer

Table 12-5

DETERMINATION OF NNP WITH A HIGHER LEVEL OF TAXES (BILLIONS OF DOLLARS)

	1 *NNP*	2 *Taxes*	3 *Disposable income*	4 *Consumption*	5 *Intended investment*	6 *Government spending*	7 *Total spending*	8 *Saving* *Government*	9 *Private*	10 *Total*
A	$1,350	$220	$1,130	$958	$100	$220	$1,278	$0	$172	$172
B	1,300	220	1,080	928	100	220	1,248	0	152	152
C	1,250	220	1,030	898	100	220	1,218	0	132	132
D	1,200	220	980	868	100	220	1,188	0	112	112
D'	**1,170**	**220**	**950**	**850**	**100**	**220**	**1,170**	**0**	**100**	**100**
E	1,150	220	930	838	100	220	1,158	0	92	92
F	1,100	220	880	808	100	220	1,128	0	72	72
G	1,050	220	830	778	100	220	1,098	0	52	52
H	1,000	220	780	748	100	220	1,068	0	32	32

spending, and so on and on in the customary multiplier manner. A tax increase, therefore, has a greater than one-for-one impact in reducing NNP.[4]

A tax reduction has an effect just opposite to a tax increase. A tax reduction increases disposable income and leads to an increase in income and output earned in the production of additional consumption goods and services, which means a still larger increase in consumption goods. In the simple example here, a one-dollar tax reduction leads to a change in NNP of the same magnitude as a one-dollar tax increase, but in the opposite direction.

The effects of a specific tax increase on NNP can be worked out graphically, as in Figure 12-8(*a*). C_0 is the propensity to consume that prevailed before the tax. I and G are the investment and government spending programs. $C_0 + I + G$ is the total spending line before the tax change, and D is the pre-tax-change equilibrium

[4] Again the numbers in the numerical example provide the basis for the calculation of a "tax multiplier" for across-the-board shifts in the tax schedule of the type shown. The change in taxes, ΔT, of \$20 billion led to a change in NNP, ΔNNP, of \$30 billion. So the tax multiplier is $M = -\Delta NNP/\Delta T = -30/20 = -1.5$. The minus sign indicates that a tax increase means an NNP decrease. It must be emphasized that this tax multiplier is appropriate only for the case in which the level of taxes does not itself vary with the level of NNP.

Figure 12-8

ANALYSIS OF THE EFFECTS OF AN INCREASE IN TAXES (BILLIONS OF DOLLARS)

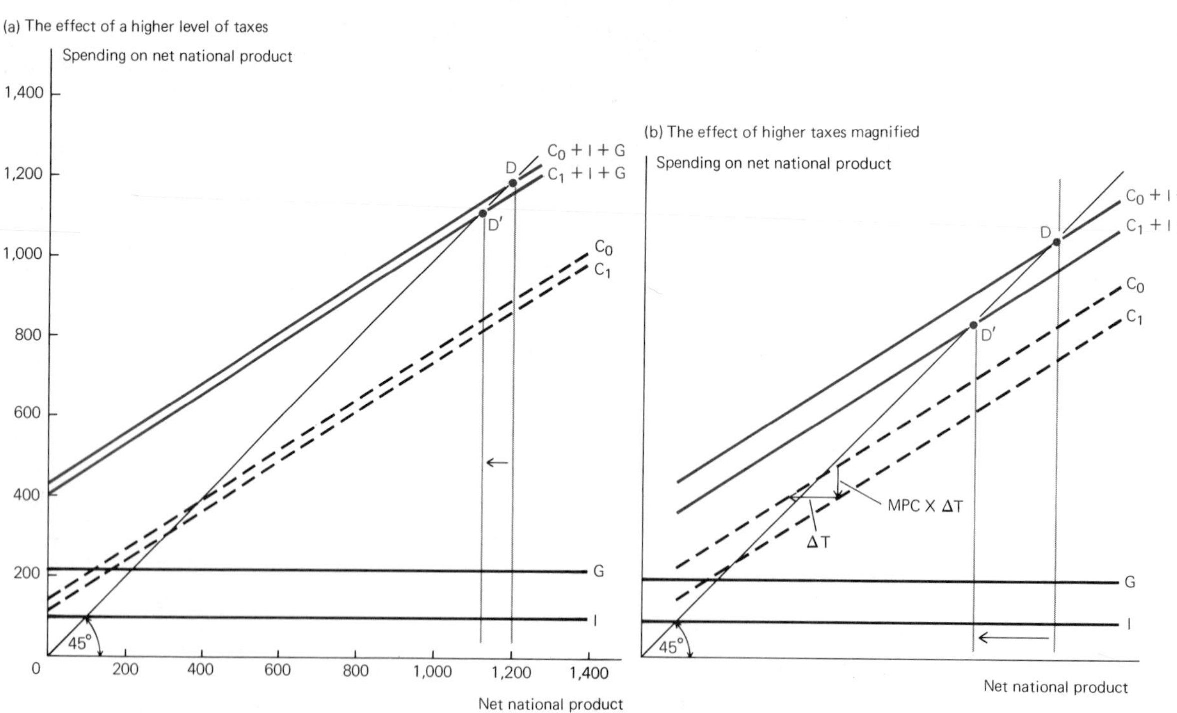

level of NNP. The effect of the tax change is shown in the shift in the propensity to consume from C_0 to C_1, and the new total spending line is $C_1 + I + G$. The after-tax-increase equilibrium level of NNP is at point D', which is less than before the tax increase. The effect of the tax increase is shown in a magnified way in Figure 12-8(b).

A tax increase shifts the equilibrium NNP downward, because it reduces the disposable income in the hands of consumers. The downward shift is the amount of the tax increase times the MPC. A tax decrease works just the other way. An increase in transfer payments operates like a tax decrease in that it increases disposable income. A decrease in transfer payments is like a tax increase. The above analysis can, therefore, be used to work out the general macroeconomic effects of changes in transfer payments.

Designing fiscal policy: Pure and mixed strategies

We have gone through a rather strenuous analysis of the income effects of government taxation and expenditures. The effort will pay off, because we can now tackle some of the great issues of public economic policy.

In Chapter 9 we worked out the argument that the spending decisions of individuals and private business will not automatically and always move an economy to full use of its capacity and full employment of its labor force. In Chapter 11 we analyzed the First Macro Model of a closed economy without government spending and taxing and again came to the conclusion that private spending decisions will not necessarily lead such an economy to full employment. There may be either a deflationary or an inflationary gap, as defined in Chapter 11.

When we add a government sector in the Second Macro Model, this conclusion remains unchanged: Just because there is government spending and taxing, that does not in itself mean that the economy will automatically avoid a depression. It is no guarantee that the economy will avoid inflation either. This is the conclusion of both distant and recent history, as well as of objective economic analysis. Yet when we add a government sector to our analysis, we see that its spending and taxing do affect the level of economic activity. This implies that fiscal policy can be used consciously to move NNP toward a desired level. But if it is not used wisely it can add fuel to inflationary fires or, alternatively, depress the economy.

Which is more powerful in its effects on NNP, a dollar of government spending on goods and services or a dollar of taxation? Of course, we should compare spending increases and tax reductions, on the one hand, or spending decreases and tax increases, on the other. The numerical examples of Tables 12-4 and 12-5 will lead us to the answer. A $20 billion increase in government spending in

Table 12-4, as compared with Table 12-2, led to a $50 billion increase in the equilibrium level of NNP. A $20 billion increase in taxation in Table 12-5 led to a $30 billion decrease in the equilibrium level of NNP, as compared with Table 12-2. So a $20 billion decrease in taxation would mean a $30 billion increase in equilibrium NNP. *It is clear that a spending change is more powerful than a tax change of the same magnitude.*

Why should a dollar of government spending on goods and services be more powerful than a dollar of tax change? The key to the answer lies in the fact that the first effect of, say, an increase in government spending on goods and services is to directly increase NNP. The next effects of government spending occur via the indirect stimulation of private spending. But the first effect of a tax reduction on NNP *is* the indirect effect of stimulating private spending. That does not mean that the tax effect is any less certain; it means that it is smaller than the spending effect, because it operates only through its effect on private spending. Part of any tax reduction is leaked off as an increase in saving.

Changes in government transfer payments, on the other hand, are similar in their effects to changes in government taxes. A change in transfer payments does not stimulate NNP directly. Its first effect is on disposable income, and the impact on NNP is the result of changes in private spending which result from the change in disposable income.

Look again at Tables 12-4 and 12-5 as compared with Table 12-2. In Table 12-4 government spending on goods and services was increased by $20 billion. In Table 12-5 taxes were increased by $20 billion. If both changes were made simultaneously, they would be offset in the government budget. What would happen to NNP? The spending increase would tend to make the equilibrium level of NNP rise by $50 billion; the tax increase would tend to make equilibrium NNP fall by $30 billion. The net effect would be a $20 billion *increase* in equilibrium NNP.

This result is known as the *balanced-budget theorem* because the effect *on the government budget* of the spending increase is exactly balanced out by the tax increase. The effects on NNP do not balance, however, because spending dollars are more "high-powered" than tax dollars.[5]

There is a popular tendency to think of fiscal policy in terms of the "pure" strategies of a change in government expenditures *or* a change in government taxes. The analysis above shows, however, that spending and tax changes *in combination* can be used to affect NNP. Does the combination have to be a balanced one? Not neces-

[5] The multiplier for a "balanced-budget" change in spending and taxes in this simple case is exactly unity. The $20 billion balanced change in spending and taxes leads to a $20 billion change in NNP. Or the multiplier can be computed by subtracting the tax multiplier of 1.5 computed in footnote 4 from the spending multiplier of 2.5 computed in footnote 3.

sarily, but even a balanced change will have an effect. Thus "mixed" fiscal strategies can be designed to find solutions for policy problems.

We should understand the potential of mixed tax and expenditure strategies not only for solving macroeconomic problems but also in dealing with microeconomic problems. Such strategies offer great flexibility in designing a policy to achieve macroeconomic goals. Why do we want that flexibility? Why are not two pure fiscal policy tools enough? Because we have other objectives for government spending and taxing besides the aggregate goals of full employment income and output without inflation: We want better schools, better housing, and job training, for example. *The ability to combine tax and expenditure policy tools gives us more freedom to achieve other, microeconomic goals.* The balanced-budget theorem says that it is possible to increase aggregate demand without unbalancing the government budget. Similar reasoning implies that it is possible to unbalance the budget, to increase government spending on urban problems, for example, without contributing to deflationary or inflationary pressures. Such a policy requires a careful design of both spending and taxing – in this case to have a budget surplus. Is such a careful design politically feasible? At times, the executive and legislative branches have acted in concert to design fiscal policies to achieve larger goals. So complete skepticism is not warranted, nor is general optimism. More understanding of the various options will increase the chances of intelligent policy.

These points will become more concrete if we consider particular kinds of macroeconomic problems for which fiscal policy can be used.

Fiscal policy for a deflationary gap

Suppose we anticipate a situation for next year like that represented in Figure 12-9 in a magnified form. The consumption, investment, and government spending schedules are labeled C, I, and G, respectively, and the total spending schedule is $C + I + G$. The equilibrium level of NNP is at E at $1,200 billion. The full employment level of NNP is assumed to be at point F and is equal to $1,250 billion. The difference between full employment NNP and actual NNP is $1,250 billion minus $1,200 billion, or $50 billion. There is a deflationary gap, FF', which is the amount by which the total spending schedule, $C + I + G$, has to shift up to intersect the 45-degree line at the full employment level of NNP.

We no longer believe that we have to throw up our hands and accept an undesirably high level of unemployment, however. We can use government fiscal policy to move the economy toward F by shifting the $C + I + G$ schedule. The amount, FF', by which the schedule must shift is not the same as the difference between full employment NNP of $1,250 billion and the equilibrium level of

Figure 12-9

EXAMPLE OF A DEFLATIONARY GAP (BILLIONS OF DOLLARS)

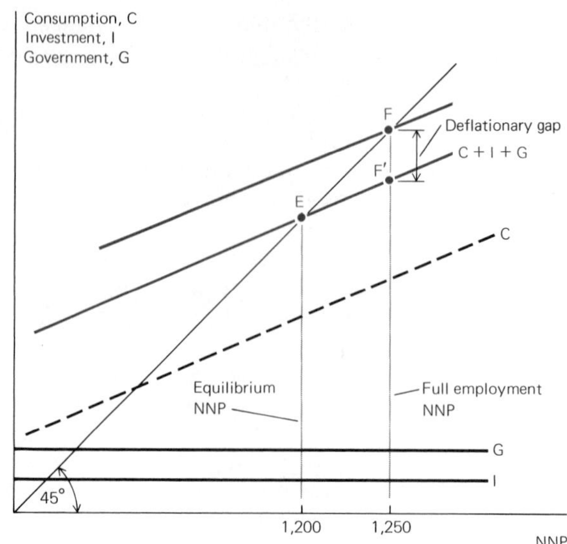

NNP of $1,200 billion. It is less. Why is it less? Because of the multiplier effects of any shift in the total spending schedule.

What fiscal policy will shift the total spending schedule so that it intersects the 45-degree line at *F*? The policy can be based on any of the following:

1. A change in government spending on goods and services
2. A change in government taxes or transfer payments
3. A "mixed" strategy of a change in spending *and* a change in taxes

There are only two *pure* strategies that will achieve full employment: a specific increase in government spending or a specific decrease in taxes. But there are any number of *mixed* strategies of spending and taxing. *Any* combination of expenditure and tax policies whose multiplied effects add up to $50 billion will move the economy to full employment.

Fiscal policy for an inflationary gap

Figure 12-10 shows a situation in which the total spending schedule cuts the 45-degree line at an NNP of $1,300 billion, which is a point above full employment NNP of $1,250 billion. Since the system cannot produce $1,300 billion of NNP, but only $1,250 billion, the demand for the greater amount will push up prices. Point E should not be regarded as an equilibrium position now, but only as representing the existence of inflationary pressures. There is an *inflationary gap* in the amount of *FF'*, and the total expenditure line must be shifted downward by this amount to eliminate those pres-

Figure 12-10

EXAMPLE OF AN INFLATIONARY GAP (BILLIONS OF DOLLARS)

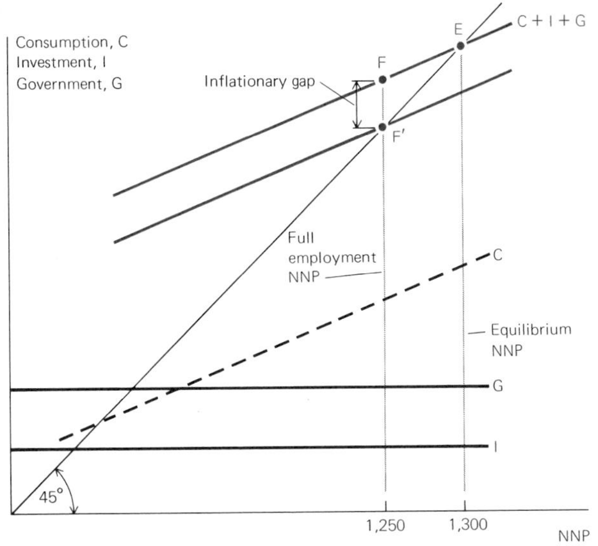

sures. A decrease in government spending will have that effect. A decrease of the required amount may be difficult, however, because of the various government programs requiring expenditures. Alternatively, an increase in taxes can be used to wipe out the deflationary gap, even if government spending remains unchanged. Finally, *expenditure and tax policy can be combined to achieve the desired macroeconomic goals*. Again, two pure and many mixed fiscal policy strategies can be used to moderate inflationary pressures.

The aggregate income effects of foreign trade

We shall now create a new model economy to take into account the effects of exports and imports on the national product. There is an intuitive appeal to the notion that people and businesses purchase goods and services from foreign countries because they can get better bargains than at home or can buy products not otherwise obtainable. In Chapter 32 we shall examine this idea and the factors that determine the composition of foreign trade. At this point, the intuitive rationale is adequate, as we shall concern ourselves only with overall effects.

The Third Macro Model is an open economy with both exports and imports as well as private consumption and investment and government expenditures. The aggregate national accounts identity is now net national product ≡ consumption + private investment + government expenditures + exports − imports, or NNP ≡ $C + I + G + E - M$.

With more justification than in the case of private domestic

Figure 12-11

ALTERNATIVE IMPORT FUNCTIONS AND AN EXPORT PROJECTION

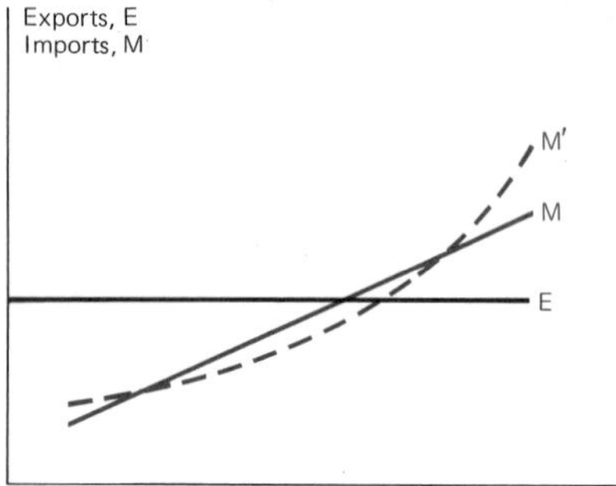

investment, we can regard the determinants of foreign spending on our exports as outside the economy or exogenous to the system. However this type of spending is determined, the demand for exports of goods and services is part of the demand for the national product. While exports are only about 6 percent of the United States gross national product, that is not a negligible figure. In some foreign-trade-oriented countries, such as the Netherlands, exports run as high as 46 percent or 47 percent of the national product.

Imports enter the national product accounts with a minus sign. Imports of goods and services represent the use of a part of the national income to buy goods and services from foreign producers. Like savings and taxes, imports are a leakage from the circular flow. What determines the total size of this leakage? As suggested previously, imports depend on relative prices in the various countries. Given those prices, the most important factor will be the level of economic activity in our own country, as measured by our national product or income. The relationship between imports and national income or product is the *propensity to import*. In general, the higher the level of income the larger will be the amount of goods and services imported, as shown by the solid line *M* in Figure 12-11. There may even be a tendency for imports to rise more rapidly than income, as indicated by the dashed line *M′*. For convenience, as with the other spending functions, we shall assume the linear or straight-line relationship, *M*. *Imports are a leakage and the propensity-to-import relationship indicates that the size of the leakage increases with NNP*. The slope of the propensity-to-import line is the marginal propensity to import; it shows the change in imports due to a change in NNP.

Exports, on the other hand, are an injection into the circular flow. Assumed to be exogenously determined, they do not vary with the level of NNP; so in Figure 12-11 they are the straight, horizontal line, E.

Now we must introduce these relationships into our income

Table 12-6

DETERMINATION OF NNP IN THE THIRD MACRO MODEL WITH A FOREIGN SECTOR (BILLIONS OF DOLLARS)

	1	2	3	4	5	6	7	8	9	10
	NNP	*Taxes*	*Disposable income*	*Consumption*	*Intended investment*	*Government spending*	*Exports*	*Imports*	*Total spending C + I + G + X − M*	*Total saving DI − C + T − G*
A	1,350	200	1,150	970	96	220	60	62	1,284	160
B	1,300	200	1,100	940	96	220	60	60	1,256	140
C	1,250	200	1,050	910	96	220	60	58	1,228	120
D	**1,200**	**200**	**1,000**	**880**	**96**	**220**	**60**	**56**	**1,200**	**100**
E	1,150	200	950	850	96	220	60	54	1,172	80
F	1,100	200	900	820	96	220	60	52	1,144	60
G	1,050	200	850	790	96	220	60	50	1,116	40
H	1,000	200	800	760	96	220	60	48	1,088	20

analysis. Since exports are an injection, we can expect them to stimulate the level of output and income. Since imports are a leakage, they tend to depress the level of output and income. To be more precise, we shall again work out some examples.

In Table 12-6, columns 3 and 4 embody the propensity-to-consume relationship with respect to NNP. Column 5 is private domestic investment, which is assumed to be constant. Column 7 presents exports, which are assumed to be exogenously determined and constant. Each row of column 8 shows the imports that will be purchased at the level of NNP shown in the corresponding row of column 3. Columns 1 and 8 embody the propensity to import.

The total spending at each level of NNP is shown in column 9. Each entry in the column is the sum along the row of consumption, private investment, government spending, and exports, with imports subtracted. The equilibrium position is at $1,200 billion, at *D*, where NNP is equal to total spending.

This is shown graphically in a magnified form in Figure 12-12. To find the total expenditure line, we add vertically the propensity to consume line, *C*, the investment schedule, *I*, government, *G*, and the export schedule, *E*, and subtract the propensity to import, *M*. The equilibrium level of NNP is again at the intersection of the total spending and 45-degree lines, which ensures the equality of desired spending and output.

We can also find the equilibrium level of NNP as that at which the total leakages and injections are equal. The leakages are saving and imports. The injections are domestic investment and exports. So the equilibrium condition is

Saving + imports = domestic investment + exports

Figure 12-12

DETERMINATION OF NNP IN THE THIRD MACRO MODEL WITH A FOREIGN TRADE SECTOR

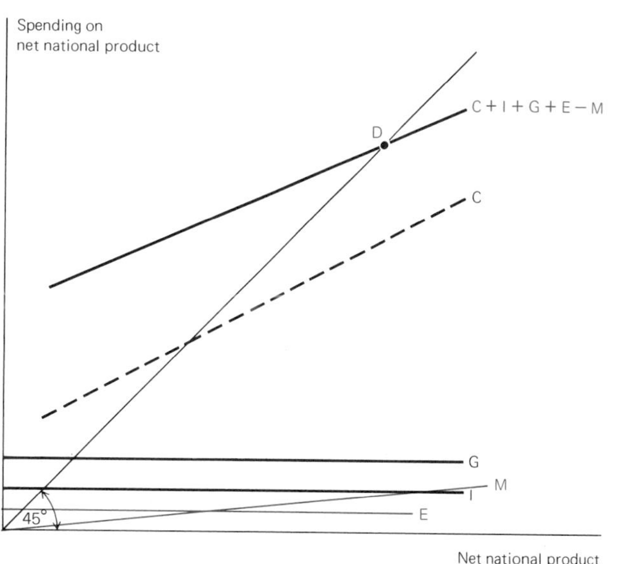

It will be convenient to rewrite this as

Saving = domestic investment + exports − imports

The quantity, exports minus imports, is called *net exports;* it represents sales abroad for which there are no corresponding purchases. This is also customarily called *net foreign investment*. The equilibrium condition is then:

Saving = domestic investment + net foreign investment

This equality can be seen in row *D* of column 10 in Table 12-6. Total saving of $100 billion when NNP is $1,200 billion equals desired private domestic investment of $96 billion plus net foreign investment of $4 billion ($50 billion − $46 billion).

Since exports are an injection of purchasing power demand for goods and services, any variation will tend to have an effect similar to the injection of government or private domestic investment spending. An increase in exports will stimulate the economy just as other types of spending increases do. This argument has been used to justify the "dumping" of goods abroad, i.e., selling abroad at lower than domestic prices, in order to stimulate the domestic economy. Similarly, since imports are a leakage, a reduction in the leakage will also stimulate the domestic economy. That reasoning has been used to justify tariff increases, such as those instituted in the summer of 1971, to maintain or increase the national product.

Export dumping and import restrictions are "beggar-thy-neighbor" policies, for whatever favorable effects they have in stimulating NNP in one country, they achieve them by depressing another economy. There is one overriding pragmatic objection to the policies: They will not work over a long period for a big country. Dumping abroad leads to retaliation. That will offset any temporary advantages that might be achieved. Likewise, when a big country raises its tariffs by a surcharge or by quotas, other countries will eventually retaliate by reducing their imports from the country that started it all. So the net effect of trying to manipulate trade as part of macroeconomic policy is likely to be that everyone ends up worse off because there is less trade all around.[6]

Qualifications to the theory

It is as important to learn the qualifications and extensions of the theory of income determination and fiscal policy as it is to learn the theory itself. Some of these qualifications and extensions will become clear in the next chapters. But a number of them can be appreciated now.

In working through the macroeconomic theory of income

[6] The 10 percent surcharge temporarily placed on imports in 1971 was advertised in part as a way of stimulating the economy. However, one of its major objectives was to force a change in the relative value of foreign currencies with respect to the dollar. This kind of policy issue is discussed in Chaps. 33 and 36.

determination, we ignored differential changes in particular sectors of the economy. But there may be fundamental differences in the way various sectors react to aggregate changes. For example, we made the point that the theory of income determination is relevant when aggregate output is determined by effective demand. Even when this is a reasonably good description in the aggregate, it need not be true for every sector. In some sectors, demand may exceed capacities. In these sectors output will be constrained by the specific capacities and and resources which are available.

In the analysis of the multiplier effects of government spending we did not go into any detail about what the composition of government expenditures was or should be. That does not mean that we are or need to be indifferent to the composition of those expenditures. It does not mean that we have to approve of digging holes in the ground and filling them up or approve of any other forms of waste in order to maintain employment.

There are challenging and useful things for all levels of government to do. *While expenditure policy may be designed for its macroeconomic effects, it can also be fitted into specific types of government programs.* Each type of program, however, is likely to have a somewhat different overall effect. Transfer payments to older people will almost entirely be respent on consumption. Most of the spending on a space program will *first* become income to well-educated and highly skilled workers with relatively high saving rates. Spending on highways or urban renewal programs will mean a higher proportion of income to construction workers and construction material producers.

Similarly, while the overall effects of tax policy are the major concern from a macroeconomic point of view, their specific impact on particular sectors and groups should not be ignored. Different taxes have different types of impact. This is clearest in the case of income taxes. They can be increased, if that is desired, with the burden being distributed among different income groups by careful adjustment of exemptions and tax rates. Or they can be reduced, with relief being either general or specific. The first effect of a tax reduction to corporations based on the amount they invest (investment tax credit) will be to increase corporate profits. The next effects will be to stimulate income and spending more widely. The desired macroeconomic effects can be achieved with a variety of different tax packages.

The analysis here has assumed that the economy is at less than full employment and that prices do not change. When demand presses against an output ceiling, prices begin to rise and that violates one of the assumptions we have made throughout. In that situation, the analysis is still relevant because it explains why output is at the ceiling. Yet it does not explain what happens at the ceiling other than that there will be upward price pressures. Likewise, it does not explain the sources of price inflation when there is substantial unemployment. In Chapter 17 we will develop an analysis to deal with situations in which price changes are important.

The theory we have learned, though unfinished, is powerful in explaining many of our aggregate phenomena. *The theory of income determination is a positive analysis*. It makes no value judgments about whether or not government budgets should be balanced, for example, or whether policies based on taxing are better or worse than those based on government spending. Such judgments require an appreciation of microeconomics – which we shall be concerned with in Part III—as well as macroeconomics. Also they depend on choices that each person must specify for himself.

Summary

In the Second Macro Model we extend the analysis to include government spending and taxing. Government expenditures are an injection into the circular flow of income, and taxes are a leakage. The former tend to stimulate output and income, the latter to reduce them. When tax receipts are less than government expenditures, the government deficit reflects government *dissaving*.

In this model the equilibrium level of net national product is again determined at the point where aggregate supply is equal to aggregate demand. Alternatively, equilibrium is at the output and income levels at which investment is equal to total saving, which is the sum of private and government saving.

In the Mark I version of the Second Macro Model, taxes do not vary with NNP. In the Mark II version, taxes do vary with NNP. The ratio of the change in taxes to the change in NNP that causes it is the marginal tax rate, MTR. When taxes increase as the national product grows, that creates a resistance to increases in the national product, because it means that the tax leakage also increases. This effect is called fiscal drag. It may exist even if there is a government budget deficit below full employment. To determine whether government expenditure programs and tax schedules are helping to keep the economy from reaching full employment, one must project the government budget at the full employment level of NNP. That projection reveals whether there is a full employment surplus or deficit. If there is a full employment surplus, fiscal drag is helping to keep the economy below full employment; if there is a full employment deficit, the budget is tending to stimulate the economy.

Comparison of the effects of government spending and taxes indicates that a dollar of spending has a greater effect on NNP than a dollar of taxation. The effect of taxes is felt indirectly through the changes in private spending that they induce. Government spending also has these indirect effects, but its first direct effect is to increase demand for goods and services.

The differential effects of spending and taxing on NNP make it possible to design mixed fiscal policy strategies to achieve macroeconomic targets. Mixed strategies are important because they allow greater flexibility in designing policy to achieve other objectives besides that of full employment without inflation. With mixed strategies, for example, expenditures can be maintained when the programs they are financing are urgently desired, even though the economy needs deflating. Such a policy requires that taxes be increased enough to more than offset expenditures. One particular mixed strategy involves the maintenance of a balanced budget while stimulating or deflating the economy.

In the Third Macro Model foreign trade is introduced into the analysis. Exports are exogenous, since they depend on foreign decisions to buy. Imports increase with the level of NNP via the propensity-to-import relationship. The marginal propensity to import is $\Delta M/\Delta NNP$. In the Third Macro Model, as in the first and second, equilibrium is at the point where spending on the national product is equal to the flow of output. Since exports are an injection of purchasing power into the circular flow of income and imports are a leakage, equilibrium can be described as the condition in which total injections, including exports, are equal to total leakages, including imports.

Increasing exports and decreasing imports will, by themselves, tend to stimulate output. But if these changes are induced artificially, just for this purpose, they tend to be self-defeating because they induce international retaliation. Their effect abroad is just the opposite of that at home.

There may be substantial differences in the reactions of particular producing sectors and population groups to changes in aggregate income and output. In particular, government fiscal policy has differential effects, depending on the specific types of expenditures made and taxes used. In a complete analysis, the microeconomic effects of macroeconomic policy must be appreciated.

Questions for discussion and review

1. Government spending on goods and services and government transfer payments both tend to stimulate the economy. Do they do so in the same way? Explain.

2. Does the amount of $T - W$ (taxes minus transfer payments) really increase with NNP? Why?

3. Discuss the following statement: *Because the net tax leakage of taxes minus transfer payments itself changes with the level of NNP, there is no way of telling whether any particular government tax and transfer policy tends to depress or stimulate the economy.*

4. The chapter argues that mixed fiscal policy strategies are important for dealing with deflationary or inflationary gaps. Why is that?

5. What is the balanced-budget theorem? Does it work both ways, for increases as well as decreases in NNP?

6. When the United States imports more goods and services than it sells abroad, does that have inflationary or deflationary effects on the economy? Why?

7. Can you explain why the saving-investment condition for income equilibrium is that private plus government saving must equal domestic plus net foreign investment?

8. Describe three fiscal policy strategies to eliminate an inflationary gap. Which do you prefer? Why?

Concepts for review

The marginal tax rate	Full employment surplus or deficit
Fiscal drag	Marginal propensity to import
Balanced-budget theorem	Net foreign investment
Mixed fiscal policy strategies	Microeconomic effects of fiscal policy

Appendix: More general multipliers

The numerical and graphic analysis of the macro models can be supplemented with an algebraic formulation that has some advantages in generality and precision. It is helpful to proceed by careful stages even in this more general approach, however.

The Mark I version of the Second Macro Model includes a constant level of investment, *I*, government spending *G*, and taxes, *T*. The propensity to consume can be written as

$$C = A + \text{MPC} \cdot (\text{DI}) \tag{12-1}$$

where disposable income, DI, is NNP − *T*. Therefore,

$$C = A + MPC \cdot (\text{NNP} - T) \tag{12-2}$$

The equilibrium condition of aggregate supply equaling aggregate demand is

$$\text{NNP} = C + I + G = A + \text{MPC} \cdot (\text{NNP} - T) + I + G \tag{12-3}$$

This can be rewritten as

$$\text{NNP} = \left(\frac{1}{1 - \text{MPC}}\right) \cdot [(-\text{MPC})(T) + A + I + G] \tag{12-4}$$

Equation (12-4) can be used to calculate the level of NNP for specified values of the propensity to consume, the constant level of taxes, planned investment, and government expenditures. In the example embodied in Table 12-2, there are the following values:

$A = \$280$ billion	$I = \$100$ billion
$\text{MPC} = 0.6$	$G = \$220$ billion
$T = \$200$ billion	

So $\text{NNP} = \dfrac{1}{1 - 0.6}[(-0.6)(\$200) + \$180 + \$100 + \$220]$ billion, or

$$\text{NNP} = (2.5)\,[-\$120 + \$180 + \$100 + \$220]\text{ billion}$$
$$= (2.5)\,(\$480\text{ billion})$$

Therefore, NNP = $1,200 billion.

The fraction 1/(1−MPC) is the multiplier for autonomous shifts in consumption, investment, or government spending in this simple example, since any one-dollar change in the level of taxes, investment, or government spending on the right-hand side of Equation (12-4) leads to a change $2\frac{1}{2}$ times larger in NNP.[7]

The multiplier for tax changes is different, however. A one-dollar change in taxes is multiplied by (− MPC) before it is multiplied again by 1/(1 − MPC). So the tax multiplier in the Mark I version of the Second Macro Model is − MPC/(1 − MPC). A little algebraic manipulation will show that this multiplier is equivalent to 1 − [1/(1 − MPC)]. The second term is the multiplier for spending changes. It becomes negative, and a one is added to get the tax multiplier. So in absolute value, the tax multiplier is one less than the spending multiplier.

In the Mark II version of the Second Macro Model, taxes change with the level of NNP, or

$$T = R + \text{MTR (NNP)} \tag{12-5}$$

where MTR is the marginal tax rate. This relationship replaces the constant level of taxes in the propensity-to-consume relationship, which becomes

$$C = A + \text{MPC [NNP} - R - \text{MTR (NNP)]} \tag{12-6}$$

The equilibrium condition becomes

$$\text{NNP} = C + I + G = A + \text{MPC [NNP} - R - \text{MTR (NNP)]} + I + G \tag{12-7}$$

This can be rewritten as

$$\text{NNP} = \frac{1}{1 - \text{MPC}\,(1 - \text{MTR})}\,[(-\,\text{MPC})\,(R) + I + G] \tag{12-8}$$

The first term is, again, the multiplier for private investment and government spending changes, and the multiplier for shifts in the tax function is − MPC/[1 − MPC (1 − MTR)].

Table 12-7 shows the calculation of the multiplier for alternative values of the marginal propensity to consume and the marginal tax rate.

[7] If a change in investment spending will be induced by a change in income, the multiplier for an exogenous change in government spending must be modified in the same way that the multiplier without tax leakage was modified when induced investment was introduced into the analysis. That leads to M being $\frac{1}{1 - \text{MPC}\,(1 - \text{MTR}) - \text{MPI}}$ where MPI is the marginal propensity to invest.

As might be expected, a higher marginal tax rate leads to a lower multiplier and makes the system less responsive to private investment or government expenditures.

Suppose imports, M, are related to NNP in the Third Macro Model by the relationship:

$$M = N + \text{MPM (NNP)} \tag{12-9}$$

where MPM is the marginal propensity to import and N is a constant number. Then, using the previous relationship for consumption, but neglecting taxes, and assuming that investment, government spending, and exports, E, are autonomously determined, we find that the NNP relationship is

$$\text{NNP} = C + I + G + E - M = A + \text{MPC (NNP)} + I + G + E - N - \text{MPM (NNP)} \tag{12-10}$$

This can be rewritten as

$$\text{NNP} = \frac{1}{1 - \text{MPC} + \text{MPM}} (I + G + E - N) \tag{12-11}$$

The multiplier for any autonomous shift in spending, including exports or imports, is the first term of Equation (12-11).

There is no end to the multipliers that can be worked out, and by now it is clear that they depend on what is to be multiplied, what is assumed to be constant, and what changes. The concept of the multipliers is important because it stresses that the first and immediate effects of a change in spending are not the final and full effects. The multiplier concept also helps us understand the processes of expansion and contraction in cycles of economic activity. Finally the multipliers help us to pinpoint the effects of particular fiscal policies and other aggregate spending changes.

Table 12-7

ALTERNATIVE VALUES OF THE MULTIPLIER IN THE THIRD MACRO MODEL: MARK II

Marginal propensity to consume out of disposable income	*Marginal tax rate on NNP*	*Multiplier for investment and government spending changes*
0.6	0.1	$\frac{1}{1-0.6(1-0.1)} = \frac{1}{1-0.6(0.9)} = \frac{1}{1-0.54} = \frac{1}{0.46} = 2.17$
0.6	0.2	$\frac{1}{1-0.6(1-0.2)} = \frac{1}{1-0.6(0.8)} = \frac{1}{1-0.48} = \frac{1}{0.52} = 1.92$
0.8	0.1	$\frac{1}{1-0.8(1-0.1)} = \frac{1}{1-0.8(0.9)} = \frac{1}{1-0.72} = \frac{1}{0.28} = 3.56$
0.8	0.2	$\frac{1}{1-0.8(1-0.2)} = \frac{1}{1-0.8(0.8)} = \frac{1}{1-0.64} = \frac{1}{0.36} = 2.78$

13

The functions of money and the demand for money

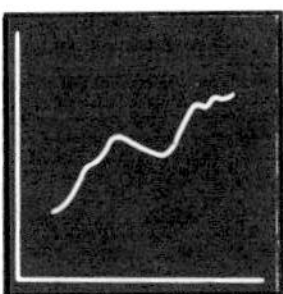

The objective of this chapter is to introduce money into the analysis of the determinants of the level of national income. It is none too soon either. Even if we do not believe everything we read in the newspapers, the billows of smoke there about the importance of money suggest that there really is a fire to be concerned about.

Monetary questions were explicitly put aside in the previous chapters by the assumptions which defined the macro models there. That is not because they are unimportant and easily ignored. On the contrary they are crucial to a realistic analysis of the determination of aggregate income and employment. The discussion of money was postponed partly because of its inherent complexity and partly because there is so much folklore and fantasy associated with money that it seemed wiser to work out other important relationships first. The analysis to follow will show that monetary influences are closely connected with the real spending decisions discussed in the previous macro models.

One of the ideas of classical economics that never really caught on to become public folklore was that money was only a "veil": It concealed but did not affect in an essential way the workings of the economic system. Instead, most people believe that "money matters," not only to them individually, but to the economy as a whole, without, of course, being too clear about why or how it "matters." Taxi drivers and financial columnists will say that too much or too little money is the source of all our problems without knowing what the "just right" amount would be. The mystique of gold has brought governments to disaster and humbled great nations.

Yet the relevance to our lives of many of the hoary traditions of money is remote, if not nonexistent, and we keep them alive only by repetition. Gold continues to fascinate us. We talk about hard money nostalgically, though we have always used paper. We may refer to a quarter as "two bits" and never stop to ask ourselves what one bit would be.[1] We regard banks as money warehouses and bankers as their stern but benign wardens who may out of graciousness take our deposits and, perhaps, give us a loan if we dare ask.

We are going to try to untangle these and other ideas about money and banking. The agenda in this chapter is the clarification of basic concepts and the examination of the demand for money. In Chapter 14 we shall turn to the supply of money and the structure of the banking system. But even to talk about monetary issues in terms of demand and supply is presumptuous and confusing until we master some fundamentals.

What is money? What does it do?

A good instinct, when faced with a complicated subject, is to start by defining the terms carefully. Following that lead, let us make clear what we mean by money. Our first impulse is to describe the coins and bills that we like to carry around in our pocketbooks and billfolds. A moment's reflection and a little history will show that this kind of description will not get us very far. The coins we have now look more or less the same as they have for many years, but the new ones have a lot less silver and more copper than the old ones. The paper bills nearly all carry the title, "Federal Reserve Note," whereas many of them formerly had "Silver Certificate" printed on them. The money substance at different times and in different societies has been animal, vegetable, and mineral. Cattle and horses have served as money. Beads, shells, cloth, tobacco, corn, and copper tablets – all have been used. If we rely on the physical characteristics of money, our definition is going to be a long and ever-changing list of natural and man-made objects.

Faced with that dead end, let us try another tack. Moving to a higher level of generality, we shall define money according to its *functions* – that is, *according to what it does*. Everything that performs these functions will be included in our definition of money. One implication of this idea is so widely accepted that it strengthens our confidence that the approach is a good one: Except for money misers, no one wants money in and of itself, but rather because of what it can buy, either immediately or in the future.

[1] It was one-eighth of a Spanish dollar, and circulated widely in the colonial period and for some time after.

The functions of money

Money is a social invention which facilitates the workings of the economy because it is useful in a number of ways. Economists long ago distinguished the separate functions of money and those distinctions are still valid.

Unit of account. Money serves as a *unit of account* or *standard of value*. In this function money is simply and only a *measure*, and all that is necessary for it to fulfill this function is the *idea* of a common measure.[2]

Money in dollars and cents is not indispensable as a unit of account or standard of value. It is merely a convenience. To show how we could dispense with it in this function, suppose that the prices of cigarettes, chewing gum, and pencils in money terms were:

Price of cigarettes = 30 cents per pack
Price of chewing gum = 10 cents per pack
Price of pencils = 5 cents each

Alternatively we could dispense with money for measurement purposes and value everything in pencils.

Price of cigarettes = 6 pencils per pack
Price of chewing gum = 2 pencils per pack

and, of course, the price of a pencil would be a pencil. Or we could use cigarettes or chewing gum rather than pencils as the *numeraire* or measuring unit. By the way, using pencils as the measuring unit would not require us to write with pencils or with ball-point pens.

There need not be any specific quantity of money circulating in the system for the unit-of-account function to be performed. This is often difficult to accept, largely because people have other uses of money in mind besides its unit-of-account function. We can cite as evidence the fact that in England some prices are quoted in terms of the guinea, a gold coin that has not circulated for more than 150 years. It is still used to price goods at 21 shillings. In the same way, in the United States, a bit has not circulated for 100 years, but casual pricing in terms of two bits and four bits, though less and less common, is still not unknown. The other functions of money, however, do make it necessary to have some amount of it on hand.

Medium of exchange. As a *medium of exchange*, money is a great improvement over barter, the exchange of goods directly for goods. To engage in barter or swapping, we must have what econo-

[2] This is how we used money in the analysis of the model economies and in supply and demand pricing. We used only the *idea* of money. Alternatively, we could have used some commodity as our measuring stick, as we occasionally did.

mists call a "double coincidence of wants." For example, an unusual combination of events is necessary for the advertisement "Young couple wants to swap motorcycle for twin baby carriage" to be successful. Not only must there be another couple who have had twins and now want a motorcycle, but both couples must agree that the one-for-one trade is acceptable. The transaction would be more "roundabout" but in the end much less time-consuming and more likely to result in the first couple getting the baby carriage if they sold their bike for money and used it to buy a baby carriage. Most transactions are carried out using money.

In simple and traditional economies, with only a limited exchange of goods or of labor, seeking out and preparing for successful barter arrangements might not impose too much of a burden on the economy. Barter activities might even provide the occasion for general socializing and partying on a regular annual or semiannual schedule. A modern, highly specialized economic system could not work that way, however, because of the overwhelming volume and complexity of transactions. People want not only final goods, such as bikes and baby carraiges, but intermediate products, such as hot-rolled steel and polyethylene film. Can there be any doubt that the production of steel would suffer if workers were paid off in steel (flat products or beams?) or if management had to barter steel for bread, meat, and potatoes to pay its workers?[3]

When we recognize the importance of money as a medium of exchange we are not reneging on the argument that the fundamental facts of economic life are the physical amounts of real goods and services produced and producible. In the same way, when we go to buy a car, the important facts about it are the performance of the motor and the safety and comfort of the body. We never ask about the oil in the engine, but we know the car will not run without oil and that too much or too little can be harmful. Money similarly "oils the wheels" of the economic system and helps it operate more smoothly, but it can also be the source of problems that would not exist at all in a primitive barter economy.

Store of purchasing power. Money serves as a *store of purchasing power.* It is one of a number of ways in which individuals can accumulate wealth, and it has some special advantages. It is the most "liquid" of assets, which means it is the most easily offered and accepted in transactions. It is, therefore, the best precaution against getting caught short if there are sudden and unforeseen expenses, from towing charges to tax payments. Being completely liquid, money is the best asset to have on hand in order to take advantage of unexpected bargains and opportunities. And the

[3] Something like this had to be done in West Germany just after World War II because of general distrust of the currency. A successful currency reform which provided a money people would accept in transactions increased productivity tremendously because it eliminated the need for barter.

"price" of money never changes. A dollar bill is always worth just a dollar bill, never more, never less.

Wealth may, of course, be stored in other forms: stocks, bonds, diamonds, real estate, oriental rugs, and so on. As compared with money, these other ways of accumulating wealth have a potential disadvantage. The prices of these assets can go down. If they do, the purchasing power the assets represent will then fall unless the prices of all the other things the wealth might have been used to buy also go down by the same amount or more. On the other hand, there is the possibility that the prices of stocks, bonds, diamonds, oriental rugs, and real estate may go up relative to other prices. That is one reason why some people prefer these assets over cash as a store of purchasing power. They are a *hedge* against inflation. They do have the disadvantage of being illiquid. That is, it takes time and effort to sell them – to convert them into cash which can be used to purchase other goods and services. And one can never be sure of their exact value until they are sold. Another advantage of stocks, bonds, and real estate, however, is that they can become income-earning assets. That is, they are forms of wealth that may provide an income return to their owners.

There are also advantages and disadvantages of holding wealth in the form of money. Cash is completely liquid, but it does not earn income. And the purchasing power of wealth held as money is not unchanging: One takes the risk that the prices of real goods and services may rise and thus decrease the real purchasing power of the money held. On the other hand if prices fall, which is rare, the real purchasing power of the money held rises.

Types of money

Now that we have described the functions of money we can come back to the question, What is money? The short answer is, *Anything that performs the functions of money.* The more complete, more sophisticated answer is longer and requires some working out.

What do we use as money? Coins, paper currency, certainly, and, less obviously but just as certainly, bank checking deposits. The last item may at first seem like an economist's trick. But it is no trick at all, or at least not one due to the economist. We shall examine each of these categories separately.

Coins and currency. About coins and paper currency there is no doubt. They are readily recognizable as performing all the functions of money. Coins and paper currency are "token monies," however, since the physical material of which they are made is not in itself worth the face value of the money. The metals in coins are not valuable enough to make it worthwhile to melt them down, separate them, and sell them in bulk. If they were that valuable, or became that valuable over time, the temptation to melt them would be well-nigh irresistible. In fact, when an upward trend in the price of silver began in the late 1950s, it became profitable to melt silver coins. The Treasury then decided to begin producing and placing in circulation coins made of nickel and copper. These metals account for the reddish tinge on the edge of our post-1966 dimes and quarters.[4]

Quantitatively, paper money is a much more important component of the money supply than coins, and each bill is worth far more than the paper it is printed on. United States paper money is now almost exclusively composed of Federal Reserve Notes. That is what is printed at the top on the darker green side. It also states there that the bills are legal tender, which means that they are legally qualified to be used in settlement of debts. On older notes, there is a meaningless statement that the bill "is redeemable in lawful money at the United States Treasury, or at any Federal Reserve Bank." That sort of thing only perpetuates confusion.

Remnants of older types of paper currency which are still in circulation are retired when they circulate back into the hands of the Treasury or a Federal Reserve Bank. These are the leftovers of former monetary practices. Two-dollar bills, which were printed until 1966 and still turn up occasionally, had their origin in the greenbacks issued by the federal government to help pay the costs of the Civil War when it was easier to run the printing presses than to tax. A National Bank Note, a relic of the days when national banks provided the paper currency, or a Federal Reserve Bank Note, issued by Reserve Banks until 1921, occasionally turns up. Even more rarely, we may come across a silver certificate. On its face there is a promise by the U.S. Treasury to deliver on demand one dollar's worth of silver. When the price of silver on the commodity markets of the world rose above the United States government price, it became profitable for people to collect silver certificates and turn them in to the Treasury for the metal itself. They could then resell the silver and make a profit. That process combed nearly all the silver certificates out of the system in 1967.

Gold coins and certificates, promising to pay gold to the bearer on demand, once circulated freely. They were called in by the Treasury and paid off at face value in paper currency in 1933 when the price of gold was raised from $20.67 an ounce to $35 an ounce for international transactions. Otherwise, holders of the gold certificates would have been able to obtain gold at $21 an ounce from the Treasury and hold it or sell it for $35 an ounce. They would have had windfall gains at the expense of other citizens, and the Treasury might have lost a substantial amount of gold to private hoards.[5] United States citizens are now forbidden by law to own

[4] Because of the increase in the price of silver, the "old" dimes and quarters with the higher silver content have virtually disappeared from circulation.

[5] The exchange of silver certificates for the metal was allowed because the profits were smaller, the holding of certificates more widespread, and the Treasury had relatively more of the metal.

gold except for jewelry, dental fillings, coin collecting, and manufacturing purposes.

Checking accounts. Why should checkable bank demand deposits be considered money? Because of our definition: Anything that performs the functions of money is money. *And anything you can do with coins and currency, you can do with checking accounts.*[6] They can serve as a standard of value, medium of exchange, and store of purchasing power. So they are part of our money supply.

Some people find it hard to regard checking accounts as money because they feel that the money supply (1) must have some kind of gold or silver "backing" to make it "sound" and (2) should be under government control. But, as has just been pointed out, neither our paper currency nor our coins are "backed" in the sense that the metal in the coins is worth their face value or that the paper currency is redeemable in metal. Like anything else, and whatever its form, money has value because of its scarcity. As to government control, this is not an essential requirement, although the government, especially the Federal Reserve System, can and does exercise a great deal of control over bank checking deposits.

Another problem that some people have with respect to checking account money is that it appears to involve some double counting. If a $10 bill is deposited in a checking account, are both the bill *and* the checking account part of the money supply? As long as the bank holds the bill, they are not. The depositor can have the bill or the checking account. He cannot have both. But we shall see in the next chapter how banks can affect the money supply.

It is important to appreciate that checking accounts really are money, because in total quantity they are much larger than the amount of coins and currency in circulation, as shown in Table 13-1. Individuals and families engage in many small transactions which use coins and paper currency, but they seldom use cash for substantial expenditures or keep cash on hand or in safes or storage vaults as a way of accumulating funds. Businesses keep a certain amount of cash on hand for minor transactions but it is called "petty" cash, and there is no "major" cash. Nearly all their expenditures are made by check, and their important accumulations of liquid funds are held in bank accounts.

In many ways, checking acounts are much more convenient than cash. They can be used to pay exact amounts without the necessity of making change. Checks can be mailed with little fear of loss, and canceled checks provide proof of payment.[7]

[6] You may object that you cannot cash your check in a strange town or in a store in which you are not a regular customer. That is true, but it is a relatively minor inconvenience, not much worse than the problem of trying to cash a $1,000 bill on Sunday. But note: It is the checking deposit which is money, not the check.

[7] Credit cards have in effect been a substitution of checking deposits for the use of cash in money purchases. Checking deposits are still the most common way of paying monthly bills.

Table 13-1

MONEY AND NEAR-MONEY IN THE UNITED STATES (BILLIONS OF DOLLARS)

	Dec., 1940	Dec., 1950	Dec., 1960	Dec., 1970
Types of money				
Coins	$ 0.6	$ 1.5	$ 2.4	$ 6.3
Paper currency	8.7	26.2	30.5	50.1
Subtotal	9.3	27.7	32.9	56.4
Demand deposits of banks (held by public)	30.4	92.3	114.8	171.1
Total cash and demand deposits	39.7	120.0	147.7	227.5
Near-monies				
Time and savings deposits				
Commercial	11.7	36.3	71.0	228.7
Other (includes mutual savings banks, postal savings, savings and loan agencies)	14.1	22.9	99.3	215.1
U.S. government bonds held by individuals and business	19.6	61.3	115.4	123.2
Subtotal	45.4	120.5	285.7	567.0
Total of cash, demand and savings deposits, and government bonds	85.1	240.5	433.4	794.5

Source: *Federal Reserve Bulletin.*

The top half of Table 13-1 shows the total amount of coins, currencies, and demand deposits on selected dates in recent years. The supply of coins continues to grow. While there are no more good 5-cent cigars or cups of coffee, there has been a growing need for coins to feed parking meters and vending machines. The supply of Federal Reserve notes has also grown, while the amount of other types of paper currency and silver certificates has declined. It is clear from Table 13-1 that the total amount of bank demand deposits is much larger than the total of coins and paper currency. We would certainly be missing something important if we left it out.

Near-monies. The idea of including items other than coins and paper currency in the money supply changes our whole notion of what constitutes money. Why stop at demand deposits? Why not include savings deposits in the money supply? Savings accounts serve many people as a way of storing purchasing power. It is true that they are not as liquid as cash or demand deposits, but in general they can very quickly be converted into cash or a demand deposit. While banks may require a thirty-day notice before they will make payment from time deposits and savings accounts, most banks will ordinarily pay out of these accounts on demand. Thus, savings accounts can be used almost like checking accounts. And if we include savings deposits in the definition of money, what about savings and loan shares, mutual savings bank deposits, or even government bonds? There is a saying on Wall Street that you can sell government bonds on Sunday. They are almost as liquid as savings accounts, and in that sense, there is no clear line between them. Nor is there a sharp distinction between savings accounts and government bonds and still other assets, such as private stocks and bonds or insurance policies on which one can obtain loans.

These assets fall into a category called *near-money. Near-money has to some extent, though not so completely, the qualities of cash and checking accounts.* The "moneyness" of assets depends on two characteristics: (1) the degree of liquidity, or the ease with which they may be converted into other assets, and (2) the degree to which their value may be fixed in dollar terms. Each type of money and near-money has some advantages and disadvantages, depending on the extent to which it possesses liquidity and fixity in dollar terms. These advantages and disadvantages of the various types of money and near-money are also associated with advantages and disadvantages of the assets as ways of holding wealth and earning income. Coins are heavy in any volume. Paper currency is light, but not safe to carry around or store. Demand deposits are safe and liquid but, compared with savings accounts, do not earn any interest. The interest on savings accounts helps compensate for their illiquidity, but that interest is not so great as the return on some bonds or other assets—which are still more illiquid and whose nominal value may vary over time.

There is no point in hiding the fact that economists disagree about what should be included in near-monies. Any distinction is necessarily somewhat arbitrary and a matter of judgment, which may change from time to time and from country to country as banking and business practices change.[8]

The lower half of Table 13-1 shows the total amount of savings accounts and some of the generally agreed-on near-monies. Note both the relative magnitudes and the changes over time. Time deposits and savings accounts of all types are now about $2^1/_2$ times as large as private demand deposits. That reflects the rapid growth of time deposits as compared with demand deposits during the last twenty years. In 1940, time deposits and demand deposits were about equal in size.

The amount of government bonds held publicly outside of banks was about equal to time and savings deposits in 1950. But the latter have grown much more rapidly and were about $3^1/_2$ times as large as public government bond ownership in 1970.

[8] In many countries, checks on personal demand deposits are not readily acceptable as a means of payment. In these countries personal checking accounts are closer to near-money than to money.

Semantic and logical confusions about money

Having described the functions of money and defined money as anything that performs those functions, we can clear up some misleading notions about money. The most frequent mistake is to confuse money as a *measure* with the things being measured and to confuse money as a *means* with money as an end in itself. The worst error is to confuse money and income. This confusion is repeated every time anyone other than a counterfeitor talks about "making money." When people say that, they really mean that they are "earning income."

Money is not income. It is used to *measure* income, which is the return for productive services, as explained in Chapter 7, and to *pay* income. Notice in Table 13-1 that the stock of money, narrowly defined, was only about $227.5 billion at the end of 1970. The gross national product in this year was about $977 billion. On the average, therefore, the money stock "turned over" about $3^1/_2$ times to pay for the gross national product produced in the country.

Money is not the only type of wealth, and it represents no specific physical type of wealth, precious metal or otherwise. It is an asset because it can be exchanged for other assets, including physical goods, but there is not and need not be any one-to-one correspondence between physical assets and money.

Money is not capital, at least not as the word "capital" is used here. We have stuck to the definition of capital as physical goods, such as buildings and equipment, which are capable of producing other physical goods and services. In the newspaper financial pages, capital may refer to stocks and bonds or other liquid assets and may or may not include money. But that is not what economists mean.

These distinctions must be kept clearly in mind. They are often the source of more confusion in economics than any other single set of semantic or analytic problems.

The demand for money

The descriptions of the functions of money permit the identification and the measurement of the different components of the stock of money in the economy. We will now use those descriptions to analyze the demand for money. This is part of our overall plan to integrate an analysis of the monetary system with the earlier analysis of the determination of the levels of income and output.

What determines the demand for money? The first reaction to this question is often a somewhat incredulous, Isn't it obvious? People want money to buy things. But that is not really a satisfactory answer. If it were, we would never find anyone keeping any type of money for more than the short time it takes to go to the appropriate store.

Since people do hold money, they cannot also want to spend it immediately. So, what does determine the demand for money? The correct answer is that people want to hold money to be able to spend it or give it away now or in the future. This answer is so sensible and yet so uninformative that we had better look back at the question and make sure we are interpreting it correctly.

Suppose we were to ask what determines the demand for a *gift of purchasing power*? The answer would be easy. Who would not want such a gift to spend now or later? But that is not what we are getting at in our question. We really want to know what part of their assets people will decide to hold in the form of money as compared with the amount they will hold in some other form.

The reasons for holding money lie in the functions it performs. It is not necessary for anyone to keep money on hand so that it can be used as a unit of account or standard of value. For this function, it is only necessary to have the idea of money. To perform its other functions, however, some amount of money must be kept available. As explained above, there are advantages and disadvantages in holding money as compared with other types of assets. The decision to hold money involves a balancing of these advantages and disadvantages.

The transactions demand for money (as a medium of exchange)

People hold money partly because they expect to spend it soon. *The money held for transactions purposes "bridges the gap" between the receipt of income and its current expenditure on goods and services.* It is more convenient to have some money readily available whenever we want to make a purchase than to have to sell or cash in a government bond. The average amount of money held by consumers to make purchases depends, first of all, on how much of a gap must be bridged. If a person were paid only once a year, he would, on the average, hold more money for transactions purposes than if he were paid once a week. The transactions demand also depends on the volume of transactions made by consumers. These transactions, in turn, are related to the overall level of economic activity in the economy as measured, say, by the NNP. Yet the transactions demand for money depends on other factors as well as the level of economic activity. Remember that money is a non-income-earning asset. If the rate of interest on savings accounts is high enough, some people will deposit their paychecks at the end of the month and will trot to the bank every day and withdraw just enough to get along that day. Other people will decide to make three trips to the bank every month rather than two trips. This will help them keep a larger average savings bank balance. But bank trips are a nuisance. The costs of making withdrawals, including lost time as well as any bank charges, will work against the influence of the interest rate. But as the rate rises,

people will try to maintain smaller money balances for daily transactions.

Businesses also hold money for transactions purposes. They keep some petty cash in the office, and like individuals, they keep substantial cash balances in their checking accounts. But businesses, like individuals, will try to keep smaller money balances for transactions as the return on savings deposits and other income-earning assets rises.

The demand for money for transactions purposes will be influenced, therefore, by the return that can be obtained from income-earning assets that can be purchased with money. In effect, the advantages of liquidity will be balanced by the *opportunity cost* of holding money. That opportunity cost is the net return that can be earned by holding an income-earning asset. When individuals and businesses put some of the funds they might otherwise hold for transactions purposes into income-earning assets, they are likely to want to be able to get their money out of those assets on short notice and with little risk. So the alternative return which is most relevant is the interest rate on savings deposits or on short-term government bonds, which are quite liquid and virtually riskless.

The sensitivity, or *elasticity*, of the transactions demand for money to the interest rate is likely to be high when the amounts of money held for transactions purposes are considered relatively large. Conversely, the sensitivity, or elasticity, of the transactions demand to the interest rate will be small when people think they are holding minimal money balances in relation to the level of transactions in which they are engaged.

The asset demand for money

As pointed out above, holding money is just one of many ways of holding wealth. The holding of money always has an opportunity cost, which is the return that can be earned on an income-earning asset that can be bought with money. Holding money also can be regarded as a speculation

1. That the prices of goods which are eventually to be bought will go up (or down) and, therefore, that the purchasing power of the money will go down (or up)
2. That the prices of the income-earning assets which can be bought with the money will go down (or up) and therefore become still more (less) advantageous than holding money

These ideas of money management are more clearly seen on a large than on a small scale. However, instead of asking, What would you do if you had a million dollars? we shall keep the issues impersonal by asking. How would we advise someone who has a million dollars on hand? Suppose it is a widow with several children or a business firm with a lot of stockholders. In either case one has to take account of future obligations as well as present needs.

We might act like "plungers," and instead of holding money we could wheel and deal in stocks or buy into a risky land speculation. The potential returns might be large but the risks of losing everything would be large too. The potential losses would leave our family destitute or the business bankrupt. Balancing the risks against the potential returns, we would probably decide not to chance everything on the turn of a few cards.

On the other hand, if we were to keep all the assets in the form of money, that would mean sacrificing some potential returns from income-earning assets. It would also mean taking the risk that goods prices will rise and that the purchasing power of the money will fall.

What we will probably do is to carry a *mixed portfolio of assets*. For the widow, we will buy some solid and safe income-earning assets with a virtually assured return, like government or American Telephone and Telegraph bonds. We may also buy some riskier but potentially higher-yielding stocks and even some apartment buildings to earn their rental incomes. We may even speculate just a little in real estate. For the business, we will purchase production equipment and inventories. Other purchases, like wildcat oil wells, are risky but have the potential of a high rate of return.

By deciding on a mixed portfolio, we have tried to balance risks and income-earning opportunities. With government and AT&T bonds, the risk of not earning income is virtually nil. And if they do not pay off, there will be bigger things to worry about than maintaining that portfolio. There *is* a risk that we may not be able to get back all the money we put into the purchases. For example, we may on occasion want to sell off a portion of our holdings in government bonds or our oil well stock in order to take advantage of some new and unusual opportunity or to meet college tuition expenses. We know that prices of government and private bonds and common stocks fluctuate, and the same is true for wildcat oil well sites. If we do not strike oil, the demand for those sites is not going to be impressive. In deciding what proportion of the portfolio we will put into any particular type of asset, we must balance our expectations of the income it will earn and its potential increase in value, on the one hand, against the risks of loss, on the other hand.

Shrewd managers will probably decide to hold some of their portfolio in the form of money. It is riskless with respect to its face value—unlike oil well stocks or government bonds—and it is liquid. Alas, its purchasing power will fall if prices go up. (But its purchasing power will rise if prices fall.) And money earns no income. Its liquidity, however, will permit us to take advantage of any unexpected bargains that turn up, and it will allow us to meet any unexpected contingencies.

This way of explaining the demand for money as an asset or store of purchasing power is called the *portfolio-balancing*

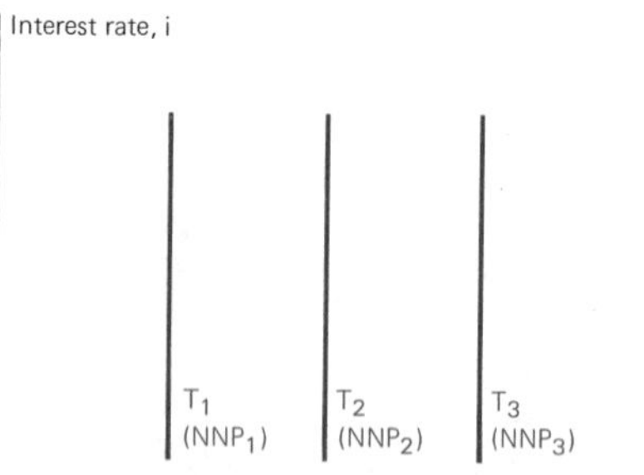

Figure 13-1

TRANSACTIONS DEMAND FOR MONEY WITHOUT INTEREST RATE EFFECTS

Figure 13-2

TRANSACTIONS DEMAND FOR MONEY WITH INTEREST RATE EFFECTS

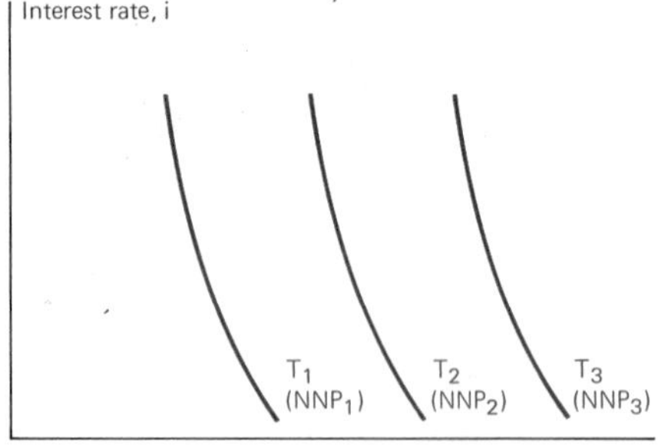

approach. Even if we abandon our game of managing a large portfolio, we can think of individuals or small businesses acting as if they were also "portfolio-balancing." One problem small investors formerly had was achieving *diversification* in order to reduce the risks associated with putting most of their eggs in one type of stock or bond. It is now possible to diversify easily by buying shares in mutual fund companies, which in turn invest in the stocks and bonds of a variety of companies.

The portfolio-balancing approach to the demand for money takes into account both the *precautionary* and *speculative* motives for holding money. The demand for precautionary balances arises because of the chance that, on some extremely rainy day, we might need to make greater expenditures than the transactions balances provide for. A hailstorm might break a lot of windows and we would then need money to pay for their immediate replacement. It is unlikely but not impossible, and prudence requires some allowance for the possibility.

The speculative demand for money has its source in two types of considerations. First, holding money is a way of hedging against a fall in the price of the assets we might otherwise buy with the money. If our funds are tied up in government bonds and their prices fall, we still get the annual interest payments, but the value of our portfolio declines. If we do not spend all our money on income-earning assets, but hold some cash, the power of that cash to purchase assets goes up when the price of the assets goes down. Second, by holding some part of our portfolio in cash we can take advantage of new business opportunities that we might otherwise have to pass by.

Holding cash has a cost even when it is held as part of a balanced portfolio of assets. That cost is the opportunity to earn income, as indicated by the interest rate yielded by income-earning assets. Typically, the higher the costs of maintaining liquidity, i.e., holding money, the smaller the proportion of assets that will be held that way. And the lower the costs, the larger the proportion of assets that will be held as money.

Demand schedules for money

The total demand for money balances is the summation of the demand of all individuals and businesses. It arises out of a variety of complex transactions and asset demand motives, and it changes as these influences change. Nonetheless it is useful to summarize the total demand for money in a schedule like the demand schedules for commodities in which we put quantity on one side of the diagram and price on the other side.

But what is the "price of money"? It is the amount per dollar one would have to pay to borrow from a bank or insurance company or some other source. Or, equivalently, it is the opportunity cost of holding money, the amount the owner of money forgoes by *not* lending it to a prospective borrower. It is summarized in the

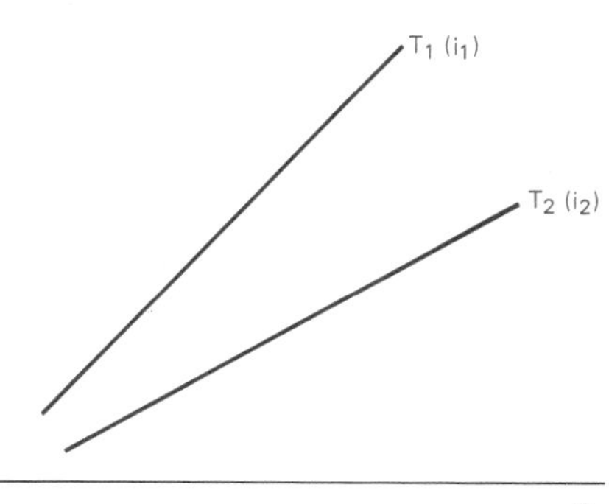

Figure 13-3

TRANSACTIONS DEMAND FOR MONEY WITH INTEREST RATE EFFECTS

Figure 13-4

SPECULATIVE DEMAND FOR MONEY

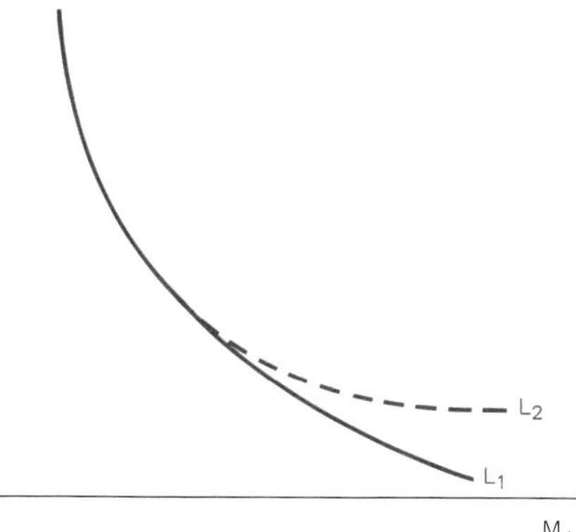

interest rate, which is the ratio of the cost of borrowing to a one-year loan.[9]

If the demand for money for transactions purposes, which we will call M_T, were dependent only on the level of transactions or aggregate income, then we would draw the demand curves like those in Figure 13-1. T_1, T_2, T_3 are demand curves for M_T associated with successively higher levels of NNP. The transactions demand would grow as the net national product increased from NNP_1 to NNP_2 to NNP_3, but the interest rate would have no effect at each level of NNP. Actually, there is some reason to believe that the interest rate in part determines whether people will hold more or less money for transactions purposes. To incorporate this effect, we draw the transactions demand curves for money as in Figure 13-2.

Alternatively, we can draw the transactions demand for money as a relationship between M_T and NNP. Then it would be like the curve T_1 in Figure 13-3 and would shift to T_2 if it were sensitive to changes, in this example an increase, in the interest rate.[10]

The asset demand for money, which we shall call M_A is also sensitive to changes in the interest rate. The rationale for this is that there is always a balancing of risks and returns in holding income-earning assets instead of money. If the returns on income-earning assets, as reflected by the rate of interest, go up, presumably the balance will shift somewhat away from money toward those assets. If the interest rate goes down, the relative attractiveness of holding money will increase. The asset demand for money will then look generally like the solid line L_1 in Figure 13-4.

The dashed part of the demand schedule, L_2, illustrates a hypothesis which some economists hold about the asset demand: that below some interest rate the asset demand for money no longer responds to the interest rate. The public will simply prefer money to any other kind of asset. That dashed portion of the curve has another one of those picturesque names that economists sometimes think up: the *liquidity trap*. We shall return to it in Chapter 16 and examine its possible significance.

The total demand schedule for money is developed by adding up, at each rate of interest, the transactions demand and the asset

[9] Actually there is not one interest rate but many, depending on the riskiness of the loan and its conditions (time to repayment, conditions of repayment, and so on). The range of the various interest rates is called the *structure* of the rate of interest. We shall avoid the complications of dealing with many interest rates by using just one, the "prime" rate on best-quality bank loans, as representative of all of them.

[10] The ratio of the total money stock to NNP is called the *income velocity of money*. If money were held only for transactions purposes, this ratio would measure the demand for money for transactions involving final products. The ratio plays an important role in some monetary theories and we shall return to it in Chap. 16.

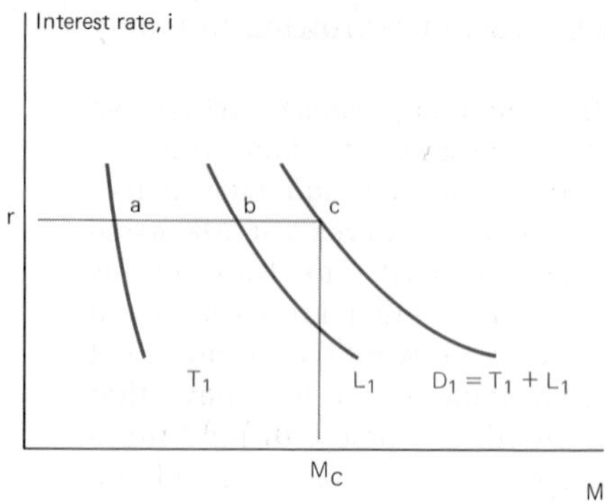

Figure 13-5

TOTAL DEMAND FOR MONEY

demand at that rate. This corresponds to summing horizontally the curves T_1 and L_1 in Figure 13-5. For example, the distance *rc* on the figure is equal to *ra* plus *rb*. This total money demand curve is given the name *liquidity preference*, because it literally describes the preference for liquidity or money. We should always be aware that the level of NNP is in the background of the transactions demand. If NNP should change, T_1 would shift and, therefore, D_1 would shift. That is why it is often more convenient to deal with T_1 and L_1 separately rather than combining them into the liquidity-preference curve.

We have dealt with only one side of the money markets, but we have gone far in removing the mystique associated with money. Though at the outset it may have appeared rather farfetched to talk about the demand for money it should now seem quite a reasonable approach. That ought also to help make the next step—analyzing money supply conditions—seem plausible.

Summary

In adding the influence of money to our macroeconomic analysis, we first identify the functions of money: (1) As a standard of value or unit of account, it serves to measure and compare the value of goods and services. (2) As a medium of exchange, it is much more efficient than bartering. (3) As a store of value or purchasing power, money is an asset which can be held as a means of buying goods in the future, as a precaution against unforeseen expenditures, or as a speculation on future prices. If prices of goods go down (up), the purchasing power of money rises (falls).

Money is defined as anything that performs these functions. Money includes coins and currency. Just as certainly, it also includes checking demand deposits, for they can do anything that coins and currency can do. Quantitatively, checking accounts are much more important than coins and currency in the money stock; they are about 3½ times as large. They are steadily becoming more important because of their convenience.

Other types of assets may be regarded as candidates for money. Near-monies are assets whose liquidity is almost as high as cash and checking accounts and whose face value is almost as fixed. Economists disagree about which assets should be brought into this category, but most accept savings deposits and some count government bonds as near-money.

The demand for money should be distinguished from the demand for income, as money and income are not the same thing at all. The demand for money is also not the desire for gifts of purchasing power. The demand for money represents a decision on how assets are to be held: in the completely liquid money form or in some other form.

The demand for money is distinguished according to its functions: (1) The transactions demand for money depends on the money volume of transactions to be carried out. It is affected by the frequency with which income payments are made and with which bills must be paid. It also depends on the rate of interest, because changes in that rate can induce people to get along with more or less ready money. (2) The asset demand for money derives from its function as a store of purchasing power. In this function money has the advantage of not losing face value, as other types of assets might, but there is the corresponding disadvantage of having no potential gain in face value — though its purchasing power might go up as prices go down. Holding money also means giving up the income that might be earned from other assets that can be purchased with money.

The price of holding money is the cost of borrowing it, or the opportunity cost incurred in holding it instead of some other asset. This is represented by the interest rate. Both the transactions demand and the speculative or asset demand are schedules that show an increase in quantity demanded as interest rate falls. Their sum is the total demand for money, or the liquidity preference.

Questions for discussion and review

1. Money has been described as the "root of all evil" and as a "useful social invention." Do these two phrases refer to the same thing?

2. Is money a useful social invention?

3. Would it be more efficient to have just one type of money than to have several kinds of monies and near-monies?

4. Do credit cards have any effect on the total demand for money?

5. If you lived, say, in Chile where prices go up from 15 percent to 30 percent a year, would your demand for money be any different from what it is in the United States, all other things equal?

6. Where would you draw the lines between money and near-money and between near-money and other types of assets? Why?

7. Explain carefully why the interest rate measures the opportunity cost of holding money and the price of money.

8. What reasons are there for believing that the demand for money depends on the level of NNP?

Concepts for review

Unit of account
Medium of exchange
Store of purchasing power
Token money
Near-money
Transactions demand for money
Asset demand for monies
Liquidity

14

Private banking and the supply of money

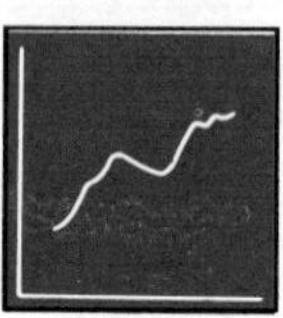

In Chapter 13, we described the functions of money and used these functions to identify the kinds of money. We turn now to an analysis of the determinants of the supply of each kind of money. When this is completed, we can combine the money supply and demand analyses with the income determination analysis to obtain a complete macroeconomic model.

We shall first investigate the determinants of the supply of coins and currency. To analyze the supply of deposit money, we shall have to make a detour to study the structure and functioning of the banking system. After that we can study the supply conditions for deposit money.

The supply of coins and currency

Coins At an early date in most countries the issuance of coins was assumed as an exclusive right by the prince, the king, the senate, or whatever the government happened to be. The minting of coins was not only one aspect of the trappings of power, but was also a handy way to finance government operations.

The government could issue a coin whose face value was less than the value of its metal content and use the actual or implied threat of government power to force its acceptance at face value. The coins could be used to pay off the army, buy supplies, reward friends, and so on. "Seignorage," the difference between the metal and labor costs of minting and the face value of the coins, was the right of the sovereign, or "seignor." It was an important source of revenue to governments when the major type of money was the coinage issued by them.

There is a long and checkered history of governments using their powers of coinage to divert purchasing power to themselves. They have "debased" coinage by adding "base" or nonprecious metals to their gold and silver content. They have reduced the weight of the coins, clipped off their edges to reclaim some of the metal for new coins, and plated copper and tin with silver and gold to fool the populace. In all this, the ingenuity of princes, kings, and parliaments has been matched, if not exceeded, by the ingenuity of their subjects. They also quickly learned to debase (as private enterprise, it is called counterfeiting), clip, and "sweat." Sweating is a little trick in which some of the metal is rubbed off the surface of coins. When coins contained the full face value of their metal, they would be hoarded and melted for the metal when its price rose above the face value of the coins. That caused inconvenient coin shortages, so governments began making token monies whose metal content was only a fraction of their face value.

Paper money

The historical origins of paper money are obscure, but paper money was probably an innovation of private enterprise. Quite likely, the first paper money was a kind of warehouse receipt. People owning coins and precious metals would prevail on the local goldsmiths, who had the best strongboxes and safes in town, to keep their treasure for them. The owners would naturally obtain receipts for whatever they placed in storage so that they could reclaim the precious metals when they wanted to do so.

Then the convenience of exchanging such a receipt for goods or using it to pay a debt must have been recognized. Such exchange avoided the necessity of going to the goldsmith, physically withdrawing the coins or metal to make a payment, which would often be returned to the goldsmith's vaults by the recipient.

In the dim recesses of monetary history, the warehouse receipts which became paper money started out as a currency—*fully backed* (by gold or silver) and *convertible* (into gold or silver). It could not have been long, however, before the goldsmiths discovered that most of the gold whose ownership was being transferred back and forth by the paper warehouse receipts never left the vaults. It was just stashed away. That undoubtedly created a temptation too strong to resist. Why not use the gold by lending it out for a small fee? Or, better yet, why limit the loans to the metal itself? The goldsmiths, who were always being asked for loans, began to make them by issuing warehouse receipts or notes *for which there was no gold or silver in their vaults.* Or to put it another way, the total amount of gold and silver backing was reduced to a fraction of the total amount of outstanding notes by the issuance of unsecured warehouse receipts. And that is how modern currency and banking were born!

But it was like trying to eat just one peanut. The goldsmiths-turned-bankers over and over again succumbed to the temptation to issue paper warehouse receipts in such volume as to create suspicion among the noteholders that there could not be corresponding amounts of gold and silver in the vaults. When the noteholders became alarmed and arrived to demand their specie, the goldsmiths could not pay all of them off. The embryonic bankers would be bankrupt and lucky to escape with their lives.

Nonetheless the idea was simply too good to be suppressed. Money changers who did business over benches, called "banques" in French and anglicized to "banks," got into the act. Then princes and parliaments who ran out of metal to coin and could not tax it out of their subjects learned from private enterprise. It was cheaper and easier to "debase" the currency by issuing paper money with only fractional backing than to alloy the silver and gold at the mint. Having learned this secret, governments generally used their power to establish a monopoly of paper currency also.

The metallic backing for paper currency issued by governments, though usually not more than a fraction of the outstanding currency, was considered for many years an essential condition for the "soundness" and "acceptability" of the currency. The paper currency was thought to have value because, if the owner wished, he could turn it in for the actual gold and silver. It was convenient to forget that not all owners could do this successfully. Yet people did forget it, and fractionally backed currency circulated with the mythology that it was the fractional backing which made it sound. When there were panics and all holders of paper currency tried simultaneously to turn it in for the precious metal backing, some, of course, were unsuccessful. They found that the purchasing power of their paper fell drastically.

Then some governments decided to stop paying out gold or silver on demand to paper currency holders. They would require by law that the currency be accepted in payment of debts. So it became pure *fiat money*, without metal (specie) backing. And lo, the world did not come to an end. To be sure, there have been occasions when governments ran the printing presses excessively and created a paper money inflation. But these rare events do not discredit the use of paper money. When a paper money inflation has occurred it has only been a symptom of deeper national social and political problems. In such extreme situations the essential question is why the nation's citizens could not or would not support the government by paying taxes to finance its operation.

The minting of coins and the printing of paper money were great economic issues in the last century and before, when these were the most important parts of the money supply. But that is no longer so. The supply of coins and currency is now managed by governments and/or central banks to provide enough to keep the vending machines humming and make small hand-to-hand transactions easy. Governments no longer have to print paper money to obtain purchasing power even when they cannot tax. They can obtain loans from the central banks which they control and write checks on the checking accounts created for them. When private citizens and businesses need money, they also rely mainly on checking accounts. Quantitatively, demand deposits are the most important kind of money. Since that is where the action is, we shall turn now to the factors determining their magnitude. Before we can proceed, however, we have to understand the structure of the banking system itself and how banks operate.

The structure of the banking system

Since demand deposits are accepted and paid out only by "commercial banks," we shall focus on them, as contrasted to "savings banks." Unless explicitly stated otherwise, when we use the term "bank," we shall mean commercial banks. As we shall see, these banks are able to create bank deposits just by doing what comes naturally, that is, by making loans.

Banks are private, profit-seeking corporations. State banks receive their corporate charters from the state governments; national banks receive their charters from the federal government. Of about fourteen thousand banks in the United States, approximately two-thirds are state banks and the rest are national. The national banks on the average are larger, however, and have around 60 percent of all deposits.

This multitude of individual unit banks is an unusual feature of the United States banking system. In most other countries, Great Britain and Canada, for example, there are only a few bank corporations, and these have branch banks around the country. California allows banks to establish branches anywhere within the state. Other states permit local branch banks near the head office, and still others permit no branch banking at all. Branch banking across state lines is not permitted.

It might appear that a banking system composed of a few banks with many branches would operate differently from a system composed mainly of separate unit banks. In essence, however, they work the same way, because the regulations they are subject to are similar and because the economics of banking requires both types of banks to operate as a *system*. Here is another example of interdependence which emerges not from legal requirements but from economic forces.

In addition to private banks, the banking "system" has a number of regulatory and service institutions and agencies at the state and federal levels. The most important of these is the Federal Reserve System, the Fed, to which all national banks must belong and to which many and usually the largest state banks elect to belong. Most banks are also members of the Federal Deposit Insurance Corporation (FDIC). These and other agencies regulate the credit policy of banks, supervise many bank operations, and provide other service functions.

The private banking business

Establishing either a state or national bank is a much more complicated procedure than obtaining an ordinary corporate charter. The incorporators are examined carefully by state or federal authorities to ensure their competence and financial responsibility. Usually an attempt is made to determine the needs of the community for additional banking facilities and the likelihood of success of the new business. Banks belonging to the Federal Reserve System and the FDIC must also meet the standards of these organizations with respect to incorporation and operation. Bank charters are more restrictive than ordinary corporate charters; they limit rather strictly the kinds of assets that banks can own and the kinds of activities they can pursue. A steel corporation, for example, can own farms or hotels and produce steel, bread, or cheese. A bank can do none of these things. It is limited to the banking business and those activities directly pertinent to it.[1]

Table 14-1

FIRST NATIONAL BANK OF DAYTON, OHIO STATEMENT DEC. 31, 1970 (THOUSANDS OF DOLLARS)

Assets	
Cash and reserves	$ 38,274
U.S. government securities	29,216
Other securities	26,864
Loans and discounts	114,921
Bank building, etc.	1,548
Other assets	18,752
Total assets	$229,575
Liabilities	
Allowances for losses on loans	$ 2,344
Deposits	
Demand	103,768
Savings and time	97,091
Other liabilities	10,909
Total liabilities	214,112
Net Worth	
Capital stock	$ 4,726
Surplus and undivided profit	10,737
Total net worth	15,463
Total net worth and liabilities	$229,575

Banks provide a number of services to their customers. They cash checks, rent safe-deposit boxes, accept time deposits, and pay interest on them. The fees charged for these services earn income for the banks, but only a small part of their total income. By far, banks earn the largest part of their income from loans and investments.

Though checking account funds are withdrawable on demand, banks seldom, on balance, lose any substantial amount of their deposits. In general, like the old goldsmith-bankers, modern bankers find that withdrawals are balanced by new deposits. Bankers do not expect the withdrawals made by their depositors to go to other of their own depositors. They do expect that their depositors will both withdraw and deposit, so on the average, their total deposits do not change much in any short period.

There may be gradual growth in a bank's total deposits, which bankers encourage, as it means they can loan out more funds to earn income. Or a bank may suffer from a gradual decline in deposits if it is located in a region of declining activity or does not compete aggressively for deposits. Bankers are alert to trends in withdrawals and deposits which indicate whether the average level of their accounts is tending up or down. They also keep some cash on hand against short-run swings in cash withdrawals by their customers. For example, banks always expect a substantial leakage of deposits into hand-to-hand circulating cash during the Christmas shopping period, and they prepare for it in advance.

Except for slow trends or temporary movements, banks can and do depend on the total amount of their customers' deposits

[1] In recent years this policy has been challenged by the incorporation of holding companies, which own a single bank corporation but also engage in other business activities.

being more or less stable. *Banks are not money warehouses. They earn profits by making loans. The greater their customers' total deposits, the more loans they can make. And the more loans they make, the more profits they earn.* That is why they watch carefully the balancing of withdrawals and deposits. Only in times of great financial crisis is there a common desire among depositors to withdraw their funds. And then they are doomed to find, like the goldsmiths' depositors, that those funds are not available in the banks.

It comes as something of a surprise to some people to learn these facts of banking life, for they still regard banks as money warehouses – as did the original goldsmiths' customers. Some people still think that, when they take their money to a bank, it is put in a safe-deposit box to be given back when they come for it or to be paid out when they write checks on it. Actually, the only part of the banking business which is warehousing is the safe-deposit box part, where customers store many kinds of valuables – wills, deeds, etc., and perhaps money. Bank employees never handle the contents of those boxes, and no one can write checks on their contents.

A bank balance sheet. We can obtain a good overall view of the banking business and how banks operate from a bank balance sheet. Table 14-1 presents a balance sheet for the First National Bank of Dayton, Ohio. Listed under Assets there are the cash and reserves which the bank holds against its deposits. Prudent management itself would dictate that a certain amount of reserves be kept, and there are legal minimum requirements as well. Notice that the reserves are only a fraction of the bank's deposits, which are listed under Liabilities. The bank has used most of the funds that depositors have left with it to make loans and buy securities from both of which it earns interest. The bank also has a small amount of assets in building and equipment and miscellaneous items. Under Liabilities are allowances for losses on loans. More importantly, there should be no doubt that deposits are liabilities; the bank owes them to its depositors. There are a few other miscellaneous liability items also. Net Worth is the residual item representing ownership in the bank. The bank's stockholders have put up only a small fraction of the funds which are earning income for the bank.

Table 14-2

CONSOLIDATED BALANCE SHEET FOR ALL FEDERAL RESERVE MEMBER BANKS, DEC. 30, 1970 (BILLION DOLLARS)

Assets	
Reserves	$ 29.2
Loans and discounts	255.3
U.S. government securities	45.1
Other securities	66.2
Other assets	66.7
Total assets	$462.5
Liabilities	
Demand deposits	$196.6
Time deposits	180.0
Other liabilities	52.1
Total liabilities	$428.7
Net Worth	
Total	$ 33.8
Total net worth and liabilities	$462.5

Source: Federal Reserve Bulletin.

Table 14-2 presents the consolidated balance sheet for all banks that are members of the Federal Reserve System. The cash and reserves under Assets must meet the minimum reserve requirements set by the Federal Reserve. The smaller the fraction of reserves held against deposits, the larger the proportion of assets the banks can put into income-earning loans and securities, also listed under Assets. Therefore, bankers are always tempted to stay close to the legal minimum reserve requirements. The Liabilities items are mainly the familiar deposits. Time deposits are almost as large as demand deposits. The total Net Worth is only about 9 percent of the income-earning assets.

Government regulation and support of the banking system

Private banking on its own is a "fair-weather" business. As long as everything goes well, life is sunny. Depositors use their checking accounts, borrowers obtain loans, and bankers make profits. If the least little cloud appears on the horizon to raise questions about a bank's stability, however, the climate can change drastically. As the balance sheet of Table 14-1 shows, not all depositors can obtain their funds simultaneously. If they try, the bank will simply have to close its doors and tell them to wait for their money while the bank liquidates its assets. Liquidation is a painful process for a single bank. On a large scale, it is certain to be unsuccessful, as it forces the businesses to which banks have made loans into liquidation of *their* assets in order to pay their bank loans. When businesses have to liquidate assets quickly, they take losses. Some fail. If banks cannot collect their loans, they cannot pay off depositors. Depositors at other banks begin to worry and may start new runs on other banks. On and on it can go and around and around. And it has.

There is a long, and sometimes sordid, history of bank failures. In 1933 the bank failure rate was higher than one in four. To be sure, personal mismanagement among bankers was probably no more widespread than among managers of other kinds of corporations. The waves of bank failures in the past were mainly the result of unregulated and uninsured banking and of frequent and often severe fluctuations in economic activity. It was primarily to prevent such recurring banking panics that the federal government moved into the bank regulatory field.

The Federal Reserve: A central banking system

The Federal Reserve System is the major regulatory agency in our system of money and banking. It is the product of the chaos and high failure rates of private banking during the nineteenth and early twentieth centuries. Prior to the establishment of the Federal Reserve System in 1913 there was only a limited amount of control of state-chartered banks by state banking agencies and of national banks by the standards set in their charters and regulations. There was no overall agency, however, that could act to break the vicious circle of liquidation and bankruptcy which set in with every depression. The panic of 1907 was the final straw. Public pressure resulted in a temporary currency reform bill in 1908 and the establishment of a National Monetary Commission. The Federal Reserve System evolved out of the report of that Commission and congressional and public debate in the election of 1912.

The most obvious structural feature of the Federal Reserve System is that there are twelve Federal Reserve Banks, one in each of the twelve Reserve districts into which the country is divided. This is somewhat misleading, because it gives the impression that there are twelve more or less independent central banks. *While each of the banks is a separate corporation, the System operates as a single central bank.* At the center of the Federal Reserve System in Washington is the seven-man Board of Governors, nominated by the President of the United States, subject to confirmation by the Senate. This Board is the focus of power in the Federal Reserve System. It sets policy, which is then carried out in each Reserve Bank under the direction of its own president.

The Board of Governors operates with the advice of the twelve Reserve Banks expressed through the Federal Advisory Council, which is composed of representatives of the Reserve Banks, and the Conference of Presidents of the Federal Reserve Banks. The powerful Open Market Committee, which is in charge of purchases and sales of securities by the System, is made up of the seven-man Board of Governors and five of the twelve presidents of the Reserve Banks. The Committee's decisions are binding on all the Reserve Banks and are a major force in controlling the supply of bank money. The structure of the Federal Reserve is shown in Figure 14-1, which indicates the relations among the various parts of the system.

What are the functions of the Federal Reserve System and how does it carry them out? First, it operates as a central bank. That means it is a banker's bank, where banks deposit funds and borrow funds, and through which interbank payments are made. The services it performs help tie the many individual banks together in a coherent system. Second, as a central bank the Fed-

Figure 14-1

THE FEDERAL RESERVE SYSTEM: ORGANIZATION

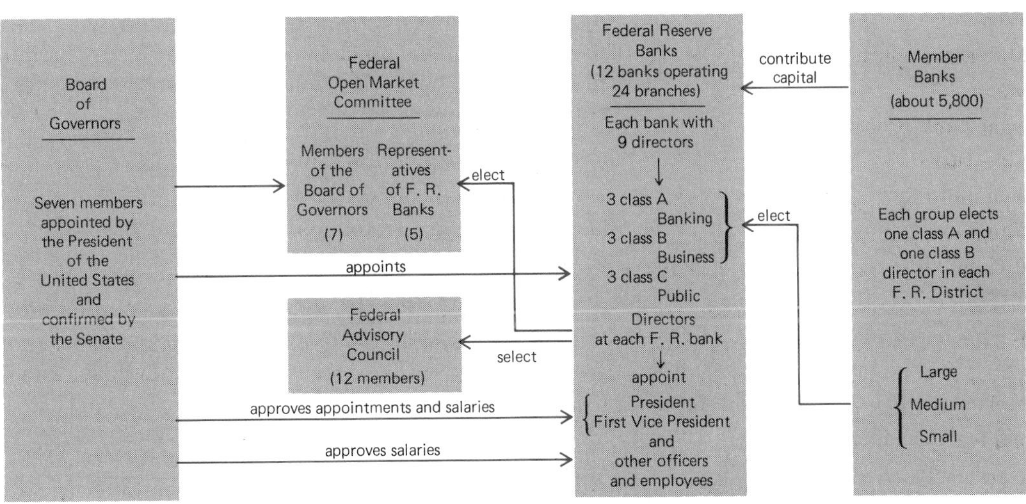

eral Reserve also operates as banker to the federal government. It holds most of the federal government's cash deposits, pays them out on government checks, and makes possible the easy transfer of government funds around the country. Federal Reserve notes are now our paper currency. In some countries, central banks make loans directly to the government. In the United States, the Federal Reserve does not do that. It does, however, profoundly influence the conditions under which the government can borrow from private individuals and institutions. Finally, as a central bank the Federal Reserve regulates the money supply; in doing so, it acts consciously to "lean against the wind" which at any particular time seems to be carrying the nation in the direction of excessively high or low rates of economic expansion. Sometimes it leans hard, at other times hardly at all. In general, rather than being a primary force for economic expansion or contraction, the Fed tries to modulate changes in the economy. In some circumstances, it acts with initiative and vigor to affect the overall economic climate, We shall see in the next chapter how it does this.

Table 14-3

CONSOLIDATED BALANCE SHEET OF THE TWELVE FEDERAL RESERVE BANKS, DEC. 30, 1970 (BILLIONS OF DOLLARS)

Assets	
Gold certificates and other cash	$11.1
U.S. government securities	62.1
Discounts, loans, and acceptances	0.4
Miscellaneous other assets (primarily uncollected items)	12.2
Total assets	$85.8
Liabilities	
Federal Reserve notes	$50.3
Deposits	
Member bank reserves	24.1
U.S. treasury	1.2
Foreign and other	1.3
Miscellaneous liabilities	7.5
Total liabilities	$84.4
Net Worth	
Capital	$ 0.7
Surplus	0.7
Total net worth	$ 1.4
Total net worth and liabilities	$85.8

Source: Federal Reserve Bulletin.

Table 14-3 presents the combined balance sheets of the twelve Federal Reserve Banks. Let us look first at the Liability items. The Federal Reserve notes, our paper money, are the major liability. These notes are essentially IOUs of the Federal Reserve System. They carry no interest and are payable with other, identical notes.

The other major liability of the Federal Reserve System is made up of the reserves that member banks keep on deposit. Most of these are the minimum required reserves that member banks must keep as a fraction of their customers' deposits. Some banks keep reserves in "excess" of the minimum. The reserve balances also provide means by which funds can be transferred among banks. To transfer funds, a bank need only direct the Fed to transfer a specific amount from its own account with the Fed to the account of another bank. In addition, the Fed's liabilities include the deposits it holds for the federal government and for foreign central banks and a few miscellaneous items.

The Fed's capital account reflects the legal ownership of the twelve Federal Reserve Banks by the member banks.

Among their assets, the Federal Reserve Banks own gold certificates, which are warehouse receipts corresponding to gold held by the Treasury. More important than its gold certificates in value, and more important from the standpoint of money management, are the government bonds that the Fed owns. In addition, the Fed has some loans outstanding to member banks whose notes it holds, listed under "Discounts, loans, and acceptances," and a variety of miscellaneous items.

The Federal Reserve System does not operate in order to make profits, but it does so. It earns income on its United States government bond holdings and its loans. On the other hand, it does not have to pay interest on its liabilities, which are mainly its notes and the deposits of its member banks, so its costs are relatively low. It now returns all of its profits to the U.S. Treasury.

The Federal Deposit Insurance Corporation

In addition to the Federal Reserve System, the Federal Deposit Insurance Corporation protects bank depositors and safeguards the banking system. The FDIC is a government-operated insurance system for banks to which all Federal Reserve members and most state bank nonmembers belong. FDIC-insured banks pay insurance premiums in return for the guarantee that their depositors will always be able to collect their deposits up to a maximum of $20,000. Thus, even if the unlikely should occur – if there should be a run on a bank and it had to close its doors and go into bankruptcy – depositors would always be able to collect their money, up to $20,000 in each account.

Bank safety

Though private banking on its own tended to be an unstable business, the system today is quite different, with the Federal Reserve and the FDIC standing behind it. *Banks are safe – that is, their depositors are safe – because the Federal Reserve can and will use its extensive powers to transfer funds and make loans to shore up any general weakness in the banking system. It also regulates the private banking system so that it does not become overextended.* The insurance provided by the FDIC eliminates the fear of most depositors that they will lose their money. These reinforcements of the private banking system were a response to the crises and panics that recurrently disrupted the economy up through the 1930s. The motive was not any special love that people and government have for bankers. Rather it arose from the desire to protect depositors from losses and from the critical role of banking operations in determining the money supply and affecting the overall level of economic activity.

The supply of bank money: A many-bank model of the creation (and destruction) of deposit money

We shall now go directly to our analysis of bank deposit money supply. To show where we are headed, we shall state the conclusion first: It is that in the ordinary course of their operations, by making loans, banks create bank deposit money. When they reduce total loans, they destroy bank money. The deposit money creation process is somewhat involved, and to understand it, we shall return to our old practice of making an initial simplification. We shall assume at the outset that all banks are members of the Federal Reserve System and face the same requirement that 20 percent of deposits must be kept as reserves. The banks always "loan up" as much as possible and keep their reserves at the 20 percent minimum requirement. We shall also assume that, after the initial deposit in our example, the amount of cash in hand-to-hand circulation does not change as the amount of deposit money changes. We shall ignore any problems related to the composition of the banks' portfolio of loans and investments and assume that banks simply make loans with their excess reserves.

With these assumptions, we start by focusing on the effect of a new deposit of $1,000 in cash in a particular bank, which we shall call the First Bank. Where does the cash come from? It is not important for our purposes. Perhaps it was discovered in an old sugar bowl or under a mattress. Anyway, there it is. We want to understand the effect of the new deposit on the First Bank's balance sheet, but to reduce the analysis to its essentials, we shall look only at the changes it produces. So only those changes will be recorded in the simplified balance sheets, which are sometimes called "T accounts." Remember that the Fed now allows a bank to count its cash on hand, sometimes called "vault cash," as part of its reserves. The initial effect of the deposit is shown in Table 14-4. Remember also that in the money supply, the only cash included is that which is outside of banks. So the new deposit does not change the total money supply, but it does change its composition. There is $1,000 less cash in circulation, but a new $1,000 demand deposit.

Now recall that the First Bank must keep 20 percent of the new deposit as required reserves against the deposit. So we will rearrange the balance sheet as shown in Table 14-5.

What will the First Bank do with those excess reserves? It will loan them out and earn interest on the loan. It makes the loan by creating a new deposit account for the borrower in the amount of $800, and it receives a note for $800 from him. Of course, with increased deposits of $800 the required reserves must go up by 20

Table 14-4

Assets		*Liabilities*	
Cash (reserves)	$1,000	Deposit	$1,000
Total	$1,000	Total	$1,000

Table 14-5

Assets		*Liabilities*	
Required reserves (cash)	$ 200	Deposits	$1,000
Excess reserves (cash)	800		
Total	$1,000	Total	$1,000

Table 14-6

FIRST BANK'S BALANCE SHEET NO. 3

Assets		*Liabilities*	
Required reserves (cash)	$ 360	Deposit (original)	$1,000
Excess reserves (cash)	640	Deposit (arising from the loan)	800
Loan	800		
Total	$1,800	Total	$1,800

Table 14-7

FIRST BANK'S BALANCE SHEET NO. 4

Assets		*Liabilities*	
Required reserves (cash)	$ 200	Deposit	$1,000
Loan	800		
Total	$1,000	Total	$1,000

percent of $800, or $160. Balance Sheet No. 3 shows the situation *immediately* after the loan.

Look quickly at the situation in Balance Sheet No. 3, because it will not stay that way long. Our borrower is not going to pay interest on an $800 loan and let it sit there. He is going to spend the money by writing an $800 check on his new account. It is most unlikely that whoever receives the $800 check will redeposit it with the First Bank. It will go to another bank, which we will call the Second Bank. Via the Federal Reserve System, the check will be delivered to the First Bank for payment. And in paying, the First Bank will lose $800 cash. At first glance, it may appear to be in trouble. To pay the $800 check it has to use $640 of its excess reserves and the $160 of required reserves. But at the same time, it cancels the $800 deposit as completely withdrawn and ends up all right, as shown in Balance Sheet No. 4 (Table 14-7), with its cash reserves just 20 percent of its deposits.[2]

[2] One thing the First Bank cannot do is to move all its cash into required reserves and make loans such that 20 percent of all deposits equals $1,000. That would mean loans of $4,000. Its balance sheet, as shown below *for the instant after the loans*, would be okay. But as the loans of $4,000 began to be withdrawn, as they surely would be, it would find that it simply did not have $4,000 to meet the required payments to other banks and individuals.

UNSUSTAINABLE BALANCE SHEET FOR THE FIRST BANK

Assets		*Liabilities*	
Required reserves (cash)	$1,000	Deposits (original)	$1,000
Loans	4,000	Deposits (arising out of loans)	4,000
Total	$5,000	Total	$5,000

Table 14-8

SECOND BANK'S BALANCE SHEET NO. 1

Assets		*Liabilities*	
Required reserves (cash)	$160	Deposits	$800
Excess reserves (cash)	640		
Total	$800	Total	$800

The change in the balance sheet of the Second Bank, where the payment by the borrower from the First Bank has been deposited, is shown in Table 14-8. The allocation of 20 percent of the new deposit to required reserves has been made.

Now let us add up the change in the money supply as a result of the new deposit and loan. All of the original $1,000 in cash is in the possession of the First Bank and the Second Bank; so it is not part of the money supply. There is still the original $1,000 deposit with the First Bank, which is part of the money supply. And now there is an $800 deposit with the Second Bank, which is also part of the money supply. So the money supply has increased

by $800! *The First Bank has created $800 more money—just by making a loan.*

The marvels do not stop there. Next the Second Bank will do just what the First Bank did—use its excess reserves to make a loan and earn interest. Likewise, the Second Bank can only loan out the amount of its excess reserves, as it must expect the loan recipient to use the loan by withdrawing the amount in cash or by writing a check to someone who will clear it through the Federal Reserve System. That check will be deposited, say, in the Third Bank. The final result of (1) the deposit in the Second Bank, (2) the new loan, and (3) its withdrawal from the Second Bank is shown in Table 14-9. The Third Bank's balance sheet is changed, as shown in Table 14-10.

Now if we total up the money supply, it includes the $1,000 on deposit in the First Bank, $800 on deposit in the Second Bank, and $640 on deposit in the Third Bank. That comes to $2,440. It is $640 more than after the First Bank had made its loan. *Another $640 has been added to the money supply by the Second Bank doing what comes naturally, i.e., using excess reserves to make loans.*

The Third Bank also does what comes naturally. It makes a loan of $512, which it expects to be withdrawn when the borrower uses it to make a payment to someone, who in turn will deposit the

Table 14-9

SECOND BANK'S BALANCE SHEET NO. 2

Assets		*Liabilities*	
Required reserves (cash)	$160	Deposits	$800
Loan	640		
Total	$800	Total	$800

Table 14-10

THIRD BANK'S BALANCE SHEET NO. 1

Assets		Liabilities	
Required reserves (cash)	$128	Deposits	$640
Excess reserves (cash)	512		
Total	$640	Total	$640

check in the Fourth Bank. The Third Bank's balance sheet ends up as shown in Table 14-11.

The Fourth Bank's balance sheet is shown in Table 14-12.

After the Third Bank's loan, the total change in the money supply is the $1,000 deposit in the First Bank plus the $800 deposit in the Second Bank plus the $640 deposit in the Third Bank plus the $512 deposit in the Fourth Bank, or a total $2,952.

We can now see where the whole process is going. Table 14-13 projects that in a consolidated balance sheet for all banks, showing the final position of the First Bank, the Second Bank, the Third Bank, the Fourth Bank, and successive banks.

There is a multiple expansion of bank credit in one bank after another. That successively reduces the excess reserves in each bank and shifts them into required reserves. The result is that *the banking system as a whole* makes

Total deposits = 5 × (all the new cash put into required reserves)

Or

Total deposits = 5 × $1,000 = $5,000

There is no doubt that a lot of new money has been created by

Table 14-11

THIRD BANK'S BALANCE SHEET NO. 2

Assets		Liabilities	
Required reserves (cash)	$128	Deposits	$640
Loan	512		
Total	$640	Total	$640

Table 14-12

FOURTH BANK'S BALANCE SHEET NO. 1

Assets		Liabilities	
Required reserves (cash)	$102.40	Deposits	$512.00
Excess reserves (cash)	409.60		
Total	$512.00	Total	$512.00

Table 14-13

CONSOLIDATED BALANCE SHEET FOR ALL BANKS: NO.1

	Assets		*Liabilities*
	Required reserves	*Loans*	*Deposits*
1. First Bank	+ $ 200.00	+ $ 800.00	+ $1,000.00
2. Second Bank	+ 160.00	+ 640.00	+ 800.00
3. Third Bank	+ 128.00	+ 512.00	+ 640.00
4. Fourth Bank	+ 102.40	+ 409.60	+ 512.00
5. Fifth Bank	+ 81.92	+ 327.68	+ 409.60
6. Sixth Bank	+ 65.54	+ 262.14	+ 327.68
7. Seventh Bank	+ 52.42	+ 209.72	+ 262.14
8. Eighth Bank	+ 41.95	+ 167.77	+ 209.72
9. Total of eight banks	+ $ 832.23	+ $3,328.91	+ $4,161.14
10. All other banks	+ 167.77	+ 671.09	+ 838.86
11. All banks	+ $1,000.00	+ $4,000.00	+ $5,000.00

all banks making loans based on their excess reserves – an extra $4,000, in fact. Where there was originally $1,000 in cash, there is now $5,000 in demand deposits. This implies the following formula:

$$\text{Potential change in total deposit money} = \frac{\text{initial change in bank deposits}}{\text{required reserves fraction}}$$

So the potential total of deposit money is $1,000/(1/5), or ($1,000)/(5) = $5,000.[3] The net *addition* to the money supply is the $5,000 of new deposit money minus the $1,000 of cash, all of which is now held completely inside the banking system as required reserves.

This model has demonstrated the following important points:

1. One bank, by itself, in the course of utilizing its excess reserves to increase its interest revenues by making loans, can create deposit money in an amount equal to (1 – required reserve fraction) times the amount of a new deposit made with it.
2. All banks, operating together, without any overall plan, but each utilizing its excess reserves to increase its interest revenue by making loans, can create deposit money in an amount equal to (1/required reserves) multiplied by the amount of an initial new deposit made with one of the banks.

Working exactly in reverse, the argument explains how bank deposit money can be destroyed. *If there were no excess reserves*

[3] This can also be worked out as the sum of the initial deposit plus the deposit money created by each successive bank as follows: $1,000 + $800 + $640 + $512 + . . . , which is equal to $1,000 + (4/5)($1,000) + (4/5)²($1,000) + ... This is an infinite series, whose finite sum is $1,000/[1/(1 – 4/5)] or $1,000 [1/(1/5)] or $1,000 × 5 = $5,000.

and a deposit were completely withdrawn from the banking system, deposit money would be destroyed in amounts as described above. Loss of cash from the banks' vaults means a loss of reserves of the banking system. The banks would have to reduce the amount of deposit money by canceling loans. That is the only way they could bring their deposits into the required ratio to their reserves.

Suppose, for example, that the man who found the $1,000 in a sugar bowl decides to withdraw his cash from the bank and go abroad. He spends it in France, and it never comes back as a deposit in a United States bank. Then, in an initial situation in which banks were fully loaned up and had no excess reserves, a permanent withdrawal of deposits would force a multiple contraction of credit and deposits in the banking system. We could work out in detail how that would happen. But the exposition of money creation can be used for monetary contraction also with the necessary change in words from "creation" to "destruction" and the change of the plus signs to minuses.

A monopoly bank model of deposit creation

We may supplement the explanation of the potential creation or destruction of bank deposits with another model. Suppose that the banking system consists of a single monopoly bank with many branches. Continue to assume that there is no change in the amount of cash in hand-to-hand circulation and that the monopoly bank always uses its excess reserves to make loans. Then an initial deposit at one branch will become the basis for a loan at that branch—or at any other, since all branches are part of the same bank. The withdrawal of a loan made at one branch will lead to a deposit at another branch, and there will be no loss of reserves. The monopoly bank could expand its loans and create deposit money in the same amount as the many-bank system, as indicated by the formula above. In fact the many-bank model can be used to demonstrate the process, with each bank now considered a different branch of the monopoly bank. Thus, the ownership of the banks does not alter the conclusion.

Reflections on deposit creation (and destruction)

The analysis of deposit creation and destruction by banks sometimes appears to be a sleight-of-hand trick that economists do with numbers, not really related to what happens in the world around us. This impression may be reinforced when a banker, asked if he creates money, denies it. He ought to know, shouldn't he?

The banker certainly does know what he is doing. He never starts out to create money. He is only trying to make profits from interest charges on loans. So he simply makes loans based on his excess reserves, and he expects to lose those excess reserves when the loan deposits are used. That is all we ever said was happening. Bankers make loans. We keep track of what happens and see the money supply change.

Is the deposit money that banks create real honest money? Well, it will do anything that money is supposed to do. Once a deposit is made, no one receiving a check drawn on that deposit knows whether its origins were cash found hidden in a sugar bowl or under a mattress or a loan. And no one cares.

Extensions and qualifications to the simple theory of deposit money creation

The simplifications and assumptions built into the models of deposit creation made the essentials of the process stand out clearly. The next task is to drop those assumptions and see what difference it makes. Dropping the assumptions will result in some extensions and qualifications of the theory. We will take up the extensions first, because the qualifications apply to them also.

Deposit money expansion based on Federal Reserve checks

We assumed that the initial change in the First Bank's reserves resulted from a deposit of currency. But suppose, instead, that the First Bank sells a $1,000 United States bond that it owns. It receives in payment a check drawn on a Reserve Bank. That would provide the First Bank with $1,000 of excess reserves, which could provide the basis for credit expansion. The whole process would work in the same way, in fact. The $1,000 of new reserves could support $5,000 of new deposits created by the banking system as a whole by making new loans. Table 14-13 can serve again to illustrate how the balance sheet of each bank and the entire banking system would look after the new reserves were fully utilized. This seems simple enough, but it is a significant extension. Excess reserves can be created by the Fed not only by issuing new paper money, which can be deposited in the banking system, but also by buying a government bond. Actually that is virtually the only kind of assets the Fed is allowed by law to own other than its own buildings and furniture, but – as we shall see in Chapter 15 – government bonds are important enough.

Turning the whole thing around again, suppose that a check is written by a private depositor to a Reserve Bank. That will force a contraction in deposit money, since it transfers a deposit completely out of the hands of private banks into the ownership of the Reserve Bank. Why would anyone write a check to the Reserve Bank? Well, if the Reserve Bank were selling government bonds, buyers would probably pay for them by check.

Bank portfolio management and deposit money creation

It was assumed in the analysis of deposit money creation that a loan was made to a private individual at each stage. The note for the loan can be regarded as an income-earning financial asset for the bank that collects interest on it. What if, instead of concentrating on loans, some banks purchased from businesses or individuals other types of income-earning financial assets, say, government bonds? In effect, individuals would exchange their bonds for bank accounts. It is the same as if the banks were making loans, and individuals exchanged promissory notes for bank accounts. More (deposit) money would move into individual ownership, and more income-earning assets would move into bank ownership. A bank's decisions to make loans or buy securities determines the composition of its "portfolio" of income-earning assets. Those decisions will depend on the current relative rates of return of the various kinds of loans and securities and on what the bank's managers expect to happen to these returns in the future.

Now let us turn to some important qualifications.

Drain of currency into circulation

We assumed in the models of deposit creation that there was no change in the amount of cash in hand-to-hand circulation as the amount of deposit money changed. In reality, while no strict proportion of currency to deposit money is maintained, there is a tendency for the amount of hand-to-hand currency to grow along with the amount of deposit money. *The effect of a cash drain from banks is very much like that of required reserves.* It reduces the amount of excess reserves that can be used as a basis for new loans and investments. Suppose there is a cash drain of, say, 5 percent. This means that, on the average, 1/20 of any new deposit is withdrawn and held as currency. As a good approximation, we can put the effect into our formula for the potential expansion of deposit money in the same way that the required reserves ratio goes in. The formula becomes:

$$\text{Potential total deposit money} = \frac{\$1{,}000}{1/5 + 1/20} = \frac{\$1{,}000}{0.25} = \$4{,}000$$

More generally, the approximate relation is:[4]

$$\text{Potential total deposit money} = \frac{\text{initial change in bank deposits}}{\text{required reserves fraction} + \text{cash drain fraction}}$$

We must be on guard, however, against thinking that the cash drain fraction is a constant. It does fluctuate, and in some years there has actually been a reduction in currency holdings as deposit money increased.

[4] The rationale of the formula is as follows. When banks fully utilize a new deposit of cash to expand their loans, their required reserves must be equal to RM, where R is the required reserve fraction and M is the total amount of their deposits. The total amount of reserves actually available will be the initial deposit, D, minus the amount lost into hand-to-hand circulation, FM, where F is the cash drain fraction. Since required reserves must equal available reserves when banks are fully loaned up, $RM = D - FM$. Rearranging makes $M = D/(R + F)$.

Holding of excess reserves by banks

To simplify the deposit money creation process, we assumed that banks never maintained any excess reserves but were always fully loaned up. It is a plausible assumption, because idle excess reserves do not make profits. Generally speaking, most banks keep excess reserves at a low level, because they can usually find relatively safe ways of putting those reserves to work. If nothing else, they can purchase short-term government notes or bonds. Even if the return is low, say, 3 percent a year or roughly 0.25 percent per month, it is better than nothing, and on a million dollars it is not a negligible amount. Banks even make loans to each other on a daily basis via a "federal funds" market. These funds are excess reserves held with the Federal Reserve Banks. This is another way the banking system as a whole gets as much mileage as possible out of its reserves.

But we should not think that every bank will always and automatically use up its excess reserves. Each bank tries to foresee what loan opportunities tomorrow and the days after may bring. The interest on government bonds is virtually a sure thing, as is the redemption of the bonds on their due date at face value. But the current market price is not a sure thing, and banks that may want to resell their bonds before the due date will worry about what might happen to the market price.

As part of their portfolio choice, banks may decide to keep some amount of excess reserves on hand as a fraction of their deposit liabilities. That would not break the cycle of deposit money creation, but it would reduce the stream in the same way that required reserves and cash drain do. Taking this into account, the approximation formula for potential expansion (or contraction) of deposit money now becomes:[5]

$$\text{Potential total deposit money} = \frac{\text{initial change in bank deposits}}{\begin{pmatrix}\text{required reserves}\\ \text{fraction}\end{pmatrix} + \begin{pmatrix}\text{cash drain}\\ \text{fraction}\end{pmatrix} + \begin{pmatrix}\text{excess reserves as}\\ \text{a fraction of deposits}\end{pmatrix}}$$

Again we should be on guard against thinking that excess reserves are in fact kept as a constant fraction of deposits. That fraction changes up and down, depending on the actual and expected level of interest rates on various types of financial assets, including business loans. Bankers are like other people and do not always agree. Not all bankers have the same expectations and not all face the same business conditions. Therefore, they behave differently with respect to use of their excess reserves. The point is that credit expansion is not an automatic process. It rests on the decisions of bankers. While their desire to increase their earnings

[5] Now the amount available for required reserves will be the cash deposit D, minus the cash drain FM, minus the excess reserves EM, where E is the ratio of excess reserves to total deposits. The formula derived in footnote 4 becomes $M = D/(R + F + E)$.

on loans and investments always pushes them in the direction of credit expansion, they may be held back both by prudence and uncertainty about the future.

Simultaneous versus sequential expansion or contraction of deposit money

For the sake of clarity, we have described deposit money creation as if it were a chain reaction working through the banking system from one bank to the next. In actuality, things happen simultaneously. All bankers pay close attention to what is happening to the level of their own deposits and to total deposits in the entire system. Substantial new deposits at any one time tend to be distributed across the banking system. Banks then tend to expand credit together, and as they do, their own deposit withdrawals are, on the average, balanced by new deposits. So the system as a whole can and often does expand or contract credit rather quickly. It does not have to wait for the effect of new deposits to work their way from one bank to the next.

Money is based on debt

To clinch the analysis of money supply, we shall raise the level of generality one more notch by considering the relationship between debt and money. When the government issues a bond with a fixed term and interest rate, it must repay the principal amount at the end of the term and the interest every year. Usually, when a bond comes due, the government pays for it by issuing a new bond. So the bonded debt is essentially permanent even when composed of short-term notes and bonds. In Great Britain, there are permanent bonds, which have no maturity date, but are perpetual interest-bearing government obligations. People are willing to buy and hold these bonds, which are called consols, because of the interest they pay.

What if consols earned no interest, but could be used to pay debts? They would be legal tender and people would be willing to hold some amount of them for that purpose. Then they would be called money. Thus, cash and currency can be regarded as permanent, non-interest-bearing debt of the government.

Now let us turn to deposit money. As we have seen, deposit money is created when banks make loans to businesses and individuals. Or, equivalently, it is created when banks buy notes and bonds. In either case, deposit money creation is the result of banks "buying" debts on which they earn interest revenue.[6]

[6] One major omission in our analysis concerns the creation and destruction of near-money. Yet we need not have too bad a conscience about it, as those processes are analogous to the creation and destruction of deposit money. The required-reserves ratios and other leakages will be different, of course, so the potential expansion of savings accounts or of savings and loan association shares is not the same as demand

So all the money in the system reflects one kind of debt or another. Does this come as a surprise? Does it make you uneasy? Do you feel we are floating on a rather unreliable and unruly "sea of credit"? You may feel all these things, because deep inside many of us there is a money mythology which says that "good" money is "hard" money or that money must have backing.

But very little money has ever been hard. The metallic backing of money held by governments never could satisfy all potential claimants. It was rarely, if ever, 100 percent. The real function of backing — when it was used — was to limit the amount of government (debt) money that could be placed in circulation. If law or custom required that 25 percent of the face amount of government notes be held in gold in the government vaults, that was a limit on currency issues. Was it the right limit? Are there other ways of controlling debt and the money supply? There are, and we shall take them up in the next chapter.

Banking institutions and the public interest

Some people think banks are the epitome of capitalist institutions. They would be surprised to find that banks also exist in noncapitalist countries, though they are not owned privately. The ubiquity of banks suggests that they have important functions in any kind of economy.

We have gone through the process by which banks can create money by making loans. We shall see in the next chapter how the process is controlled. Bankers do not think of themselves as creating money, however, but as making loans, using the reserves available to them to ration credit among businesses and individuals. This process is closely related to the banking functions of holding deposits and transferring payments in various personal and business transactions. These functions are fundamental in any economy. They require detailed expertise and complex institutional arrangements, just as other economic services do. That is why banks are found everywhere. In some countries they are quite specialized. They may be concerned only with making loans, perhaps just particular kinds of loans to industry or to agriculture. In other countries, as in the United States, they perform a variety of functions.

Although banks in the United States are private businesses, their influence on the economy is so great that there is a strong public interest in how they operate. That is the rationale behind

---

deposits. But the principle is the same. The differences in the potential expansion of the different types of money mean that the shifting of deposits among commercial banks and other types of financial intermediaries can itself affect the money supply. In recent years, there has been more intense competition for deposits among all types of banks, and that too has had an impact on the money supply.

the establishment of the Federal Reserve System and other bank regulatory agencies. These government agencies, in turn, wield great power through the control they have over private banks.

In the United States, there has been a conscious attempt to make the power of these agencies politically independent. The members of the Federal Reserve Board of Governors, once they are appointed by the President and approved by the Senate, cannot be removed by either and do not have to take orders from either. Does this, in fact, make the Board of Governors an independent, politically neutral group of financial and economic experts? More so than if they could be removed at will, but probably not completely. Undoubtedly the acceptability of their views to the President and the Senate is an important factor in whether their appointments are made and confirmed. Moreover, the powers of the President and the Senate are far-reaching, and by new laws, or even their threat, and through public opinion, both can influence the Fed.

But should the Federal Reserve be independent? Would it be better for the country as a whole if the Fed were responsive to public opinion or current political exigencies? Debate on these questions would take us further afield than we wish to go now. We shall return to them in the next chapter after taking up in detail the manner in which the Fed can control the money supply.

Summary

The coins in circulation are token money whose metallic content is only a negligible fraction of their face value. Coins as well as paper currency are fiat money, because they circulate and are accepted at face value only because of the fiat or decree of the government that this must be so. Coins and currency are no longer the most important part of the money stock. They now serve only for relatively minor, though frequent, transactions. Their supply is regulated by the government and the Federal Reserve System to provide enough to meet the requirements of the coin-operated vending machines and hand-to-hand circulation.

The most important type of money is deposit money created by banks when they make loans. The banking system in the United States is composed of many separately owned banks. These are corporations chartered either by the states or by the federal government; their activities are limited to banking, that is, receiving and paying out deposits. Deposits in commercial banks are mainly payable on demand by check. Savings deposits are longer-term deposits not payable by check, and savings banks are restricted to this type of deposit.

In general, withdrawals from banks by depositors are balanced by deposits, so that total depositors' claims do not fluctuate substantially over any short period. This balancing makes it possible for banks to keep only a fraction of their deposits on reserve to be paid on demand to depositors. They can use the remainder to make loans or buy bonds in order to earn income.

There have been no widespread bank failures for over thirty years, owing mainly to the regulation and support of the banks by the Federal Reserve System and the Federal Deposit Insurance Corporation. The FDIC insures depositors against losses up to $20,000 and, thus, reduces the danger that depositors will start a run on a bank to withdraw their deposits.

The Federal Reserve System is a central banking system with twelve regional banks; it is controlled by the seven-man Board of Governors in Washington, D.C. It acts as a banker's bank and holds deposits, makes loans, clears interbank claims, and sets overall banking standards for its members. In addition and, importantly, it regulates the supply of bank deposit money.

Bank deposit money is created when banks make loans by giving borrowers checking accounts. A single bank by itself can loan out only its excess reserves, those above the minimum reserve requirements. Loans withdrawn from one bank, as borrowers write checks, are deposited in another bank by the recipients of the checks. So the banking system as a whole does not lose deposits except for a minor trickle into hand-to-hand circulation. Therefore, the banking system as a whole can expand deposits by making loans. Each new $1 of deposits can support as much as $5 more in deposit money if the minimum reserve requirements are 1/5, or 20 percent. In general the maximum by which total deposit money can be expanded for *each* new dollar of deposits is initial deposit/required reserves fraction.

The potential expansion of bank deposit money can also be appreciated by thinking of the banking system *as if* it were a single monopoly bank. Then it becomes even clearer that the banking system as a whole does not lose deposits when it makes loans or buys bonds.

The major qualification to the story of bank deposit money creation is that banks may choose to keep some excess reserves above the legal minimum requirement. This desire for liquidity may reflect the bankers' uncertainty about the future. Since excess reserves generally mean that potential loans and investments and income will be forgone, banks tend to reduce reserves to the minimum required.

It is a surprise to some people to recognize that bank deposit money, the most important kind, is created by a fractional reserve banking system as banks make loans and investments. This type of money reflects the creation of some kind of debt. That is true of coins and currency, also, which can be regarded as non-interest-paying debt of the government.

The banking functions of making loans, holding deposits, and transferring payments are fundamental in any economy. The Federal Reserve and other regulatory agencies which control these functions have great power. Their economic responsibility and political independence are, therefore, important public issues.

Questions for discussion and review

1. How is a paper currency with a fractional backing of gold or silver equivalent to a debased coinage?

2. The lesson learned by the goldsmiths who issued fractionally backed warehouse receipts is the same as that which makes modern fractional reserve banking possible. What is the lesson? How true is it?

3. How do banks make profits for their stockholders?

4. Why do bank and business failures tend to be cumulative?

5. How do the Federal Reserve and the FDIC contribute to bank safety?

6. Using a series of bank balance sheets, trace out the effects on bank deposits of the permanent withdrawal of $1,000 in cash from the banking system. Assume reserve requirements of 20 percent, no excess reserves in the banking system, and no other changes in the holding of cash.

7. Why is it reasonable to assume that banks will keep their excess reserves at a low level? What difference will it make to the money supply if they do not?

8. Why is it reasonable to think of money as debt? At what stage in its evolution from gold and silver coins did it become debt?

9. Why don't banks disappear in socialist economies?

10. Do you think the Fed should be politically independent?

Concepts for review

Fiat money
Fractional reserve banking
Central bank
Deposit insurance
Required reserves
Excess reserves
Multiple expansion of bank deposits
Federal Reserve independence

15

Public policy and central bank control of the money supply

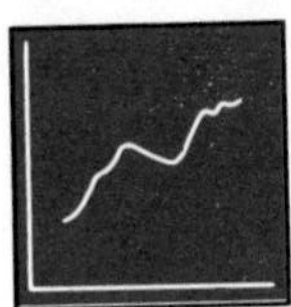

Chapter 14 demonstrated that the magnitude of bank deposits, the single most important kind of money, depends on the credits that banks are able and willing to extend. In this chapter we shall analyze the methods the Federal Reserve uses to control the money supply. We shall also investigate the limitations on the Fed's exercise of monetary control. We can then move on in the next chapter to integrate monetary analysis with national income analysis.

Federal Reserve control of the money supply

The Fed has a number of tools at its disposal with which it can regulate bank credit and the money supply. The most important operate directly on the total supply of money and are, accordingly, called "quantitative" controls. The others specify the conditions under which certain types of loans can be granted. These can control the uses to which bank loans can be put and are, therefore, called "qualitative," or "selective," controls, though they too have an effect on the total quantity of money.

Quantitative controls In order of their importance the quantitative controls are:

1. Open-market operations
2. Discount rate policy
3. Changes in minimum reserve requirements
4. Currency control

The order in which the controls can be most easily understood is probably the reverse, so we shall start with currency control.

Currency control. The most obvious of the Fed's tools is also the least important. The amount of currency in circulation is controlled by the Fed, because Federal Reserve notes are now the only kind of paper money being printed. All the other paper currency is moving out of circulation. In any case, currency in circulation is a much less important part of the money supply than is deposit money. Even so, though credit cards and checking accounts are used more and more, currency has not decreased as a proportion of the money supply. Other Federal Reserve quantitative controls operate on the deposit money creation process.

Changes in reserve requirements. Although changes in reserve requirements are relatively infrequent, they are a powerful tool and their effects are relatively straightforward. The ratio of reserves required against deposits for member banks is set by the Federal Reserve Board of Governors within limits established by Congress. The rates are different for Reserve "city" banks, located in the larger cities, and "country" banks, as shown in Table 15-1.[1]

When the Fed increases the reserve requirement ratio, that reduces the amount of deposits that any given amount of reserves can "back up." If there are excess reserves when the Fed increases the required reserves fraction, the result is a contraction in excess reserves and potential bank credit. When banks are fully loaned up and required reserves are equal to actual reserves, an increase in the required reserves ratio will force a contraction of credit and a reduction in deposit money. Individual banks going through this

[1] These are the rates for total deposits of more than $5 million. For banks with deposits of less than $5 million, the ratios are 17 percent and $12\frac{1}{2}$ percent for Reserve city banks and country banks, respectively. The difference in reserve requirements for city banks and country banks was due originally to the fact that city banks held deposits of country banks and paid interest on them. It was thought that the city banks were more vulnerable to panics and that potential runs on them would also endanger the country banks, and so they should have high required reserves. There are more effective protections now for city and country banks, but country-bank lobbyists are successful in keeping their requirements relatively low.

Table 15-1

PERCENTAGE RESERVE REQUIREMENTS FOR FEDERAL RESERVE MEMBER BANKS

	Net demand deposits						
	Reserve city banks		*Country banks*			*Other time deposits*	
	Under $5 million	*Over $5 million*	*Under $5 million*	*Over $5 million*	*Savings deposits*	*Under $5 million*	*Over $5 million*
Present	17	17.5	12.5	13	3	3	5
Legal maximum	10		7		3	3	3
Legal minimum	22		14		10	10	10

Source: Federal Reserve Bulletin.

process may think of it as a situation in which they must acquire additional reserves to credit to their account at their regional Reserve Bank. But for individual banks and for the banking system as a whole, it means that the volume of deposits must be reduced, because existing total reserves will "cover" a smaller volume of deposits.

To see how this works, recall the process of deposit money creation in Chapter 14. The amount of deposit money that can be created depends on the excess reserves available to the banking system and on the required reserves fraction. So a change in the reserve requirement fraction has an immediate impact on the private banking system's potential for deposit money creation.

Assume, for example, that member banks are fully loaned up, i.e., with no excess reserves, and with, say, an average reserve requirement of 20 percent of deposits. Table 15-2 is a simplified representation of that situation. In this illustration, the demand deposits are in the required 5 to 1 ratio to reserves.

Suppose that the Fed raised minimum reserve requirements to 25 percent. The existing required reserves of $20 could now stand behind or support only $80 in deposits, and the banks would have to adjust to a situation like that in Table 15-3. They could do it by calling in and not renewing loans and by selling some of their government bonds. Both borrowers and buyers of those bonds would pay by writing checks on their bank accounts, and this would reduce total bank deposits.

If banks are not fully loaned up – if they have excess reserves and these are reduced by an increase in reserve requirements – that in itself will not *force* a decrease in the deposit money. But member banks are likely to reduce their loans to maintain their desired portfolio proportions, including excess reserves. And they will become more sensitive to other monetary controls.

Table 15-2

BALANCE SHEET OF ALL MEMBER BANKS FULLY LOANED UP: REQUIRED RESERVES EQUAL TO 20 PERCENT OF DEPOSITS

Assets		*Liabilities*	
Required reserves	$ 20	Demand deposits	$100
Loans and investments	80		
Total	$100	Total	$100

Table 15-3

BALANCE SHEET OF ALL MEMBER BANKS FULLY LOANED UP: REQUIRED RESERVES EQUAL TO 25 PERCENT OF DEPOSITS

Assets		*Liabilities*	
Required reserves	$20	Demand deposits	$80
Loans and investments	60		
Total	$80	Total	$80

The effect of a *decrease* in reserve requirements depends in large part on the magnitude of existing excess reserves and, again, on bank portfolio management. If there is already a considerable volume of excess reserves, creating more may not induce much credit expansion and money creation. But it may push excess reserves above the level which banks desire and lead to more loans. If excess reserves are virtually nonexistent, creating more will almost certainly encourage credit expansion.

Changing reserve requirements is generally regarded as using a blunt instrument for an operation that requires a surgeon's scalpel. So the tool is used infrequently. Nonetheless it is used occasionally, mainly to create better conditions for the use of other scalpel-like tools.

Changes in the discount rate. When a bank makes a loan to a customer, it often discounts the loan. That is, it subtracts the first interest payment from the amount of the loan before it makes the money available to the customer. If the bank itself then takes the promissory note signed by the borrower to a Reserve Bank and borrows from it with the note as security, that is *rediscounting. The rediscount rate, or, for short, the discount rate, is the rate charged on the loan to the bank by the Reserve Bank.*

On what occasions do banks borrow from the Fed? When unusual conditions create a potential shortage of required reserves which a bank cannot meet by its own internal adjustments of its portfolio of assets. Then a bank may borrow from the Fed either by rediscounting a customer's promissory note or by giving the Fed its own promissory note, called an *advance.*

The discount rate is controlled by the Reserve Banks, though changes in it are usually instigated by the Reserve Board of Governors. By adjusting the discount rate up or down, the Reserve Banks can make borrowing by member banks more or less expensive for them. The Reserve Banks can in this way discourage or encourage the use of Reserve Bank credit to provide reserves for member banks.

A change in the discount rate is widely regarded in business and financial circles as having an "announcement effect." The change is interpreted as a clear signal of which way the Reserve Banks are going to lean – in the direction of tighter or easier credit. The announcement effect often has more influence than the change itself.

Open-market operations. *Open-market operations are far and away the Fed's most important means of controlling the money supply.* They function continually to maintain the monetary conditions the Fed desires. They are involved, however, and practically unknown to most people, so we shall work carefully through their operation.

Open-market operations are under the jurisdiction of the Open Market Committee of the Federal Reserve System. The Committee is composed of the seven members of the Board of Governors and

Table 15-4	Date	Owned by Federal Reserve Banks	Owned by all member banks
FEDERAL GOVERNMENT SECURITIES HELD BY FEDERAL RESERVE AND MEMBER BANKS (BILLIONS OF DOLLARS)	December 31, 1950	20.8	52.4
	December 31, 1955	24.8	50.9
	December 31, 1960	27.4	49.1
	December 31, 1965	40.8	44.9
	December 31, 1970	62.1	45.1

Source: Federal Reserve Bulletin.

five of the twelve presidents of the Reserve Banks. It usually meets every three or four weeks to decide whether to make credit and money a little tighter or a little easier or to maintain the existing situation. The "open market" in which the Fed operates is the market for transferable federal government short-term notes and longer-term bonds. The total amount of transferable government notes and bonds is large by any standards. About 64 percent of the roughly $370 billion federal debt is in bonds that can be privately bought and sold, unlike the Series E bonds, which are the most familiar type and which are nontransferable. The ownership of government securities by Federal Reserve Banks and member banks together was over $100 billion on December 31, 1970. The ownership of federal notes and bonds by the Federal Reserve Banks and member banks is shown for some specific dates in Table 15-4. Individuals, banks, insurance companies, businesses, and trusts purchase the transferable notes and bonds as long- and short-term investments. They may sell them to take advantage of higher returns on other uses of the funds, to realize possible capital gains on bond prices, to pay off debts, etc.

The market for these federal debt instruments is large, with a daily turnover of $2 billion to $4 billion. The "market" itself, however, is not a single physical location. It is a telephone network of bond dealers who buy and sell for their clients.

The face amount of a transferable note or bond is the amount for which the government will redeem it on its due date. But there is no law that says people must buy and sell the bonds at that face amount. On any day except the due date, the price at which a bond will sell on the open market may well be different from its face amount.

The Fed publishes the minutes of Open Market Committee meetings ninety days after the date of the meetings, so we know the Committee's decisions in detail only after some time lag. The decision of the Open Market Committee meeting on March 10, 1970, which moved toward an easier money policy was reported in the *Federal Reserve Bulletin* of June, 1970, as follows:

The information reviewed at this meeting suggests that real economic activity, which leveled off in the fourth quarter of 1969, is weakening further in early 1970. Prices and costs, however, are continuing to rise at a rapid pace. Market interest rates have declined considerably in recent weeks, partly as a result of changing investor attitudes regarding the outlook for economic activity and monetary policy. Both bank credit and the money supply declined on average in February, but both were tending upward in the latter part of the month. Outflows of time and savings funds at banks and nonbank thrift institutions, which had been sizable in January, apparently ceased in February, reflecting advances in rates offered on such funds following the recent increases in regulatory ceilings, together with declines in short-term market interest rates. The U.S. foreign trade surplus narrowed in January and the over-all balance of payments deficit has remained large in recent weeks. In light of the foregoing developments, it is the policy of the Federal Open Market Committee to foster financial conditions conducive to orderly reduction in the rate of inflation, while encouraging the resumption of sustainable economic growth and the attainment of reasonable equilibrium in the country's balance of payments.

> *To implement this policy, the Committee desires to see moderate growth in money and bank credit over the months ahead.* System open market operations until the next meeting of the Committee shall be conducted with a view to maintaining money market conditions consistent with that objective.

> Votes for this action: Messrs. Burns, Hayes, Brimmer, Daane, Heflin, Hickman, Maisel, Mitchell, Robertson, Sherrill, Swan, and Kimbrel. Votes against this action: None.

> Absent and not voting: Mr. Francis. (Mr. Kimbrel voted as his alternate.) (Italics added.)

To understand how open-market operations control the money supply, let us follow the effects of an Open Market Committee decision.

Suppose the Fed decides it must lean against the wind of inflation. It must find some way to reduce the growth of effective demand. The Open Market Committee does this by selling government bonds, which reduces the reserves of member banks. This in turn reduces the growth of effective demand for goods and services – in ways we have yet to spell out. First we must trace the relationship between the *sale* in the open market of government notes and bonds owned by the Federal Reserve and the consequent reduction in bank reserves.

Buyers of the notes and bonds sold by the Fed pay for them by writing checks to the Fed on their own bank accounts. The Fed charges these checks against the reserve balances of the member banks. The result is that member banks lose reserves and the means for sustaining the existing supply of deposit money.

A simple example will help. Suppose the Fed sells $100 million of its notes and bonds. Its balance sheet changes, as shown in Table 15-5.

Table 15-5

CHANGE IN FEDERAL RESERVE BALANCE SHEET (MILLIONS OF DOLLARS)

Assets		*Liabilities*	
United States government notes and bonds	–$100	Member bank reserves	–$100
Total	–$100	Total	–$100

Table 15-6

CHANGE IN MEMBER BANK BALANCE SHEETS (MILLIONS OF DOLLARS)

Assets		*Liabilities*	
Reserves with Federal Reserve Banks	–$100	Demand deposits	–$500
Loans and investments	– 400		
Total	–$500	Total	–$500

Banks feel the squeeze right away. Their reserves decline, and if they have no excess reserves, they must reduce their deposits in order to meet the minimum reserve requirements. The initial effect is a $100 million decline in reserve balances. The final impact will be as much as five times that if the ratio of required reserves to deposits is 1 to 5. Table 15-6 shows this final result.

The process also works in reverse. Suppose the Open Market Committee decides, as it did on March 10, 1970, that it must lean against a wind of *deflation* by expanding credit and the money supply. To do that, it must create excess bank reserves, which permit banks to expand credit and increase their loans and investments. So the Fed will *buy* government bonds. The individuals and businesses, including banks and insurance companies, who sell the bonds to the Reserve Banks will receive Federal Reserve checks, which they deposit in their banks. That results in an increase in the reserves that the banking system holds with the Fed. As far as the banks are concerned, the situation is just like that in Chapter 14 when the fellow deposited the cash he found in a sugar bowl. The increase in bank reserves creates a potential for monetary expansion which did not previously exist.

Figure 15-1

EFFECTS OF OPEN-MARKET BOND SALES

Using supply and demand analysis, we can see in Figure 15-1 what happens in the government bond market as the result of the Fed's open-market operations. There is a downward-sloping demand schedule for bonds, indicating that more will be bought and held at lower prices than at higher prices. At lower prices, the bonds are a more attractive investment, and just as safe, so they will be held in preference to other investments. The supply schedule has an upward slope, because owners who might be willing to part with their bonds will do so in increasing amounts only if the price they receive becomes more and more enticing.

If the Open Market Committee decided to start selling, the

supply schedule would shift to the right from S_1 to S_2. Bond prices would fall and the quantity exchanged would increase. *So tighter money and credit via open-market operations are associated with lower bond prices. And, in reverse, easier money and credit are associated with higher bond prices.*

Now let us tidy up one final aspect of open-market operations that has to do with their effect on interest rates. The interest rate on a government bond is printed right on it, so it cannot change. This means that the "owner of record" of the bond receives a fixed amount each year. If the face amount of the bond is $1,000, with a stipulated 5 percent interest payment, whoever owns it receives $50 per year. But, as we have seen, the purchase price of the bond can vary. Therefore, the effective rate of return *on the purchase price*, the "yield rate," or, simply, the yield, will change when the purchase price changes.

A $50 return on a $1,000 bond which will be due in a number of years is 5 percent only for the person who pays $1,000 for it. If the price should fall, say to $950, the effective yield to the person who buys it for $950 *rises* to about 5¼ percent ($50 return on $950). *Bond prices and yields move in opposite directions.* Lower bond prices, associated with monetary restriction due to open-market bond sales by the Fed, mean higher yield rates. And higher bond prices and open-market purchases mean lower effective yield rates.

The government bond market is a large and integral part of the entire market for funds and the bellwether for it. What rational man would take a lower return on a private bond than on a bond of the federal government? If a federal bond is not safe, nothing is. This means, first of all, that interest rates on government bonds are a standard for all other interest rates, and second, that anything that affects the prices and yields of government bonds will affect the prices and yields of all other bonds. Figure 15-2 shows the net

Figure 15-2

NET CHANGES IN FEDERAL RESERVE OWNERSHIP OF FEDERAL GOVERNMENT SECURITIES (MILLIONS OF DOLLARS)

The Federal Reserve has been a buyer of government bonds mainly. Its purchases create reserves for the banking system and provide for expansion of the money supply. That expansion, in turn, is related to the growth of the economy. (Source: Federal Reserve Bulletin.)

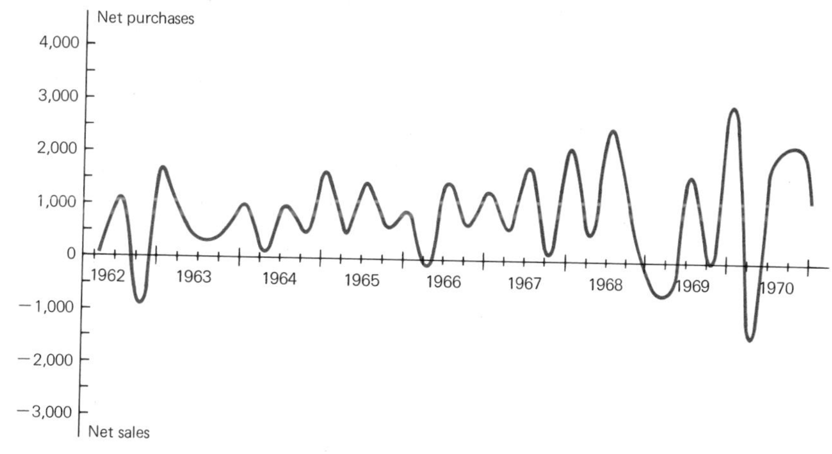

Figure 15-3

UNITED STATES GOVERNMENT BOND YIELDS AND FEDERAL RESERVE DISCOUNT RATES, 1950–1970

Compare 1966 with earlier years and you will see why it was called the year of the credit "crunch." But there was only a slight relaxation before an even greater degree of money tightness was engineered in 1969 and 1970. (Source: Federal Reserve Bulletin.)

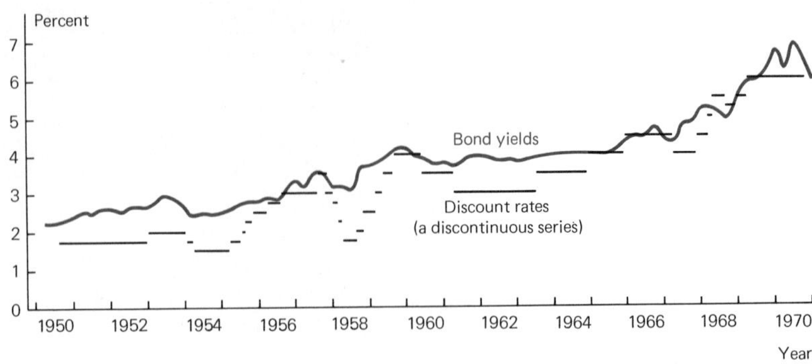

changes in the Fed's holdings of United States government securities since 1962. These changes are the results of its open-market operations. Figure 15-3 presents the history of United States government bond yields and Federal Reserve discount rates from 1950. The discount rates reflect policy announcements by the Fed. The United States government bond yields reflect the changing money market conditions created by the Fed's open-market operations and by private decisions to buy and sell government securities.

Open-market operations are the most convenient and flexible tool of monetary policy. They can be used vigorously or tentatively, delicately or forcefully. That does not mean they always have been or will be used correctly, however. The surgeon's scalpel still needs the surgeon's guiding hand. Critics claim that the Fed does not qualify as a surgeon. Supporters say that it is doing its best and that its policies usually turn out to be correct.

Qualitative controls

The Fed uses other instruments of regulation and control to strengthen or supplement its quantitative controls and to moderate their impact on particular sectors.

Margin requirements. The Federal Reserve can limit the percentage of the share price that can be borrowed for the purpose of buying common and preferred stock listed on the stock exchanges. The remainder, which must be put up by the purchaser, is called the *margin requirement*: It has varied between 50 percent and 90 percent in the last ten years. By raising margin requirements, the Fed discourages borrowing to buy stocks and thus controls the creation of money for speculative purposes. The regulation of excessive speculative movements in stock prices is, itself, one of the major motives for using this control.

Interest rate controls on time deposits. During the Depression of the 1930s, Congress passed a law prohibiting banks from paying interest on demand deposits. *The Federal Reserve, however, was* given the power under its Regulation Q to set the maximum interest rate member banks could pay on time deposits. Exercising this power, the Fed kept the rate at $2^1/_2$ percent until 1957. When interest rates on government bonds and in savings and loan associations began to rise, starting in the late 1950s, commercial banks found themselves at a disadvantage in the competition for funds. They lost deposits as investors switched to government bonds and to deposits in savings banks and savings and loan associations.

In the early and middle 1960s, the Fed moved to offset this competition and protect commercial banks from a drastic loss of time deposits. In several steps, it raised the maximum interest rate member banks were permitted to pay on such deposits. Member banks in turn quickly raised their own interest rates in order to seize the opportunity to pull in time deposits. That permitted a greater expansion of the money supply than would otherwise have been possible.

In 1961, the large New York banks made another innovation and introduced the "certificate of deposit." This is like a time deposit, but it can only be redeemed at a fixed date. Moreover, its ownership, indicated by a certificate, is transferable or "negotiable" – at a price, of course. Essentially it is a short-term bond or note. The certificate of deposit put the commercial banks one up in the competition for deposits, as these certificates carried interest rates up to $5^1/_2$ percent by 1965. That equaled or exceeded the return that many savings banks and savings and loan associations were able or willing to pay. As funds flowed out of the savings and loan associations and the specter of their bankruptcy appeared, the Fed applied the interest rate controls under Regulation Q to small-denomination certificates of deposit. That limited their attractiveness to small depositors and saved the day for savings banks and savings and loan associations.

Regulation Q applies only to commercial banks that are members of the Federal Reserve System, not to savings banks, savings and loan associations, and other nonmembers. The Fed and the FDIC and the Federal Home Loan Bank cooperate, however, in setting maximum rates for these savings institutions. In June, 1970, for example, the Fed relaxed the Regulation Q ceilings on interest rates on certificates of deposit of $100,000 or more to enable commercial banks to attract more funds to meet the demands for loans in that tight money situation. The report of the decision included the following statements:[2]

> The Board of Governors of the Federal Reserve System on June 23, 1970, suspended, effective Wednesday, June 24, ceilings on interest rates payable by member banks on certificates of deposit and other single-maturity time deposits in denominations of $100,000 or more with maturities of 30 through 89 days.
>
> . . .

[2] Federal Reserve Bulletin, July, 1970.

> In taking the action, the Board recognized that there could be unusual demands upon commercial banks for short-term credit accommodation as a consequence of current uncertainties in financial markets. . . .
>
> The Board's action was taken after consultation with the Federal Deposit Insurance Corporation and the Federal Home Loan Bank Board.

So the rate regulatory power can affect the distribution of deposits. Since different kinds of banks specialize in different kinds of loans, the rate regulatory power permits the Fed to influence the distribution of funds among major types of uses. Savings banks and savings and loan associations, in particular, specialize in housing loans. When Regulation Q limits the power of commercial banks to compete for deposits with savings banks and savings and loan associations, the Fed is not only protecting the liquidity of the latter institutions, it is also helping to sustain housing construction.

In the past the Fed had the power to control the terms of installment and mortgage loans. It stipulated the percentage of the total purchase price required as down payment on installment loans, and required repayment of those loans prior to the granting of additional credit. It also defined the down payment percentage and the length of the loan period for mortgage loans. These were powerful, if selective, instruments, which Congress allowed to lapse in favor of broader controls.

Moral suasion. The Board of Governors uses the tremendous prestige of the Federal Reserve System to influence banks and businesses to act in ways consistent with the Board's view of economic conditions. A Board member may, for example, use a speaking invitation to counter deflationary pressures. In addressing an industry convention or a chamber of commerce luncheon, he will say that banks and businesses should have "confidence in the future" and expand their investment activity. Or if the climate is inflationary, he may ask for "restraint and caution." These appeals may have some effect and, in any case, they are regarded as indications of the thinking of the Board of Governors and of its future actions.

Reserve System officials also exercise "open mouth" or "jawbone" control in earnest talks with member bankers who are "out of line" with Board policies. The Reserve System has power to make life a little easier or a little tougher for members. That does not mean that bankers are the pliable tools of the Board of Governors. They can make speeches, too, and appeal to their congressmen.

Not everyone agrees about the power of moral suasion. Some bankers and economists believe that only actions, not words, count. But in 1966, the Board asked bankers to voluntarily reduce their loans in foreign countries in order to control capital outflows, and that request did have an effect. It caused some resentment, too, as some bankers claim they were blackmailed with the threat of direct controls.

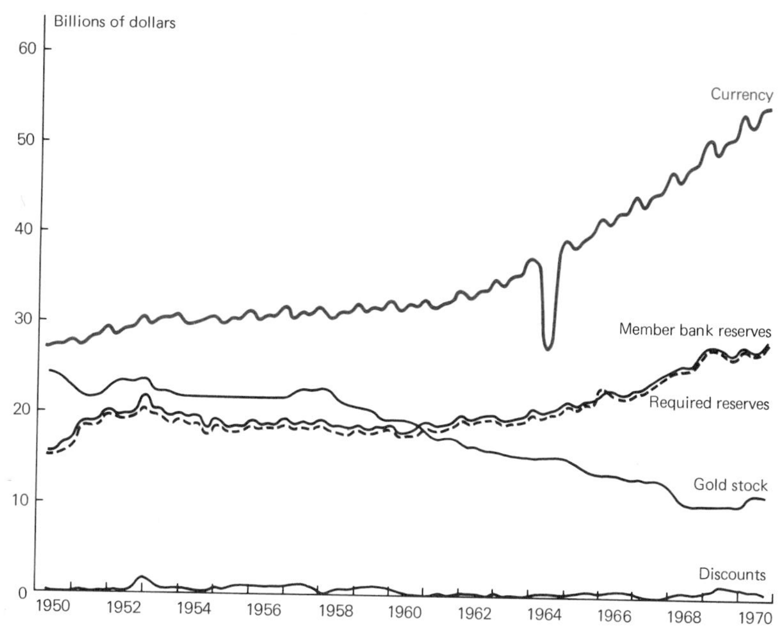

Figure 15-4

SOME IMPORTANT MONETARY VARIABLES

The decline in the gold stock reflects the demand for gold abroad and changes in the international economic position of the United States. The differences between member bank reserves and required reserves are excess reserves. On the infrequent occasions when the latter are larger than the former, the member banks have "borrowed reserves" from Reserve Banks. The discounts are one means by which the Federal Reserve provides credit to member banks. (*Source*: Federal Reserve Bulletin.)

Figure 15-4 traces some of the major monetary variables from 1950. These reflect developments such as the decline in the gold stock, over which the Fed has little control, and changes in member bank reserves and required reserves, on which the Fed has enormous influence.

Bringing together the monetary demand and supply analyses

The preceding analysis has demonstrated how the money supply can be regulated by the monetary authorities. We can now combine this supply analysis and the demand analysis of Chapter 14.

The demand for money was shown in Chapter 13 to be composed of two parts:

1. The demand for money for current *transactions purposes,* as determined mainly by the level of output in the economy but also, to some extent, sensitive to interest rates
2. The asset demand for money, as determined by the *precautionary and speculative motives* for holding it as compared with other types of assets, and also sensitive to the interest rate

In Figure 15-5 these two types of demand for money are represented in relation to the interest rate as M_T and M_A; their sum is the total demand for money, M_D, which is the *liquidity preference.*

Figure 15-5

DETERMINATION OF THE INTEREST RATE BY THE DEMAND FOR AND SUPPLY OF MONEY

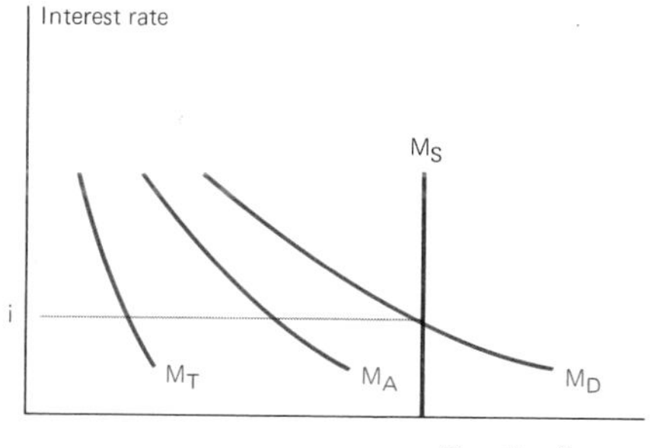

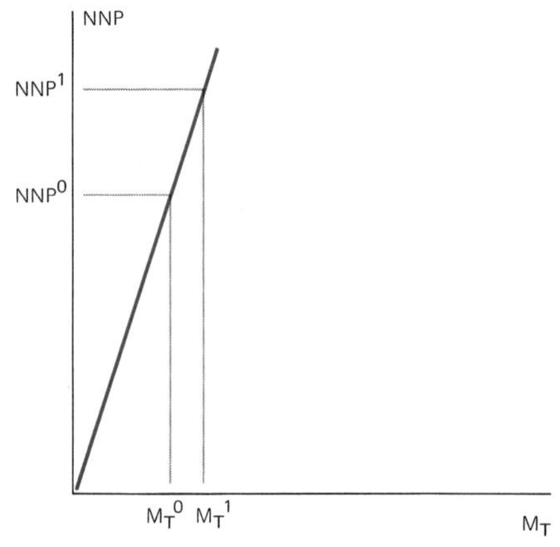

Figure 15-6

TRANSACTIONS DEMAND FOR MONEY

Let us assume that the supply of money is determined solely by the monetary authorities and is, therefore, insensitive to the interest rate. So the money supply is the vertical line, M_S. Its position on the horizontal axis is determined by the Federal Reserve.

Together the demand and supply of money determine the interest rate, which is the price of borrowing money. The interest rate is also the cost of holding money. It represents the income which could be earned by holding some interest-earning asset and which is forgone by holding the money itself.

With the money supply and demand curves, we can now work out the effects of changes in one or another of the components. For example, it was argued in Chapter 13 that the transactions demand for money, M_T, was determined mainly by the level of output in the economy. If the level of output should change, the transactions demand would change also. This can be seen clearly in an alternative depiction of the transactions demand for money, as shown in Figure 15-6. In this case NNP is on the vertical axis, and M_T, on the horizontal axis, increases as NNP increases.

If NNP shifted from the original level NNP^0 to NNP^1, more money would be demanded for transactions purposes at each level of the interest rate. Thus, the demand for money for transactions purposes would shift to the right, as shown in Figure 15-7. Therefore, the total demand for money, or the liquidity-preference schedule, would shift to the right, from $M_D{}^0$ to $M_D{}^1$. If the Fed held the money supply constant at M_S, the interest rate would increase from i_0 to i_1.[3] On the other hand, if the Fed engineered an

[3] Notice that, at that higher interest rate, the quantity of money demanded to satisfy the asset demand for money would be lower than originally. There would also be some economizing on money held for transactions purposes. Overall, however, there would be a shift of money from its use to satisfy assets demands and to its use to satisfy transactions demands.

Figure 15-7

THE EFFECTS OF AN INCREASE IN NNP ON THE DEMAND FOR MONEY AND THE INTEREST RATE

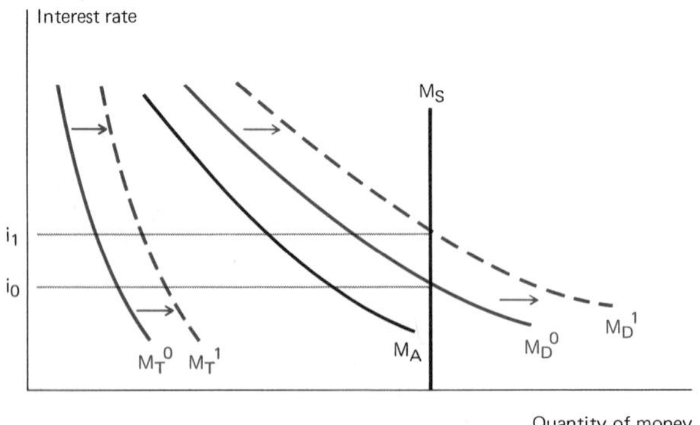

Figure 15-8

THE EFFECTS OF AN INCREASE IN THE SUPPLY OF MONEY ON THE INTEREST RATE

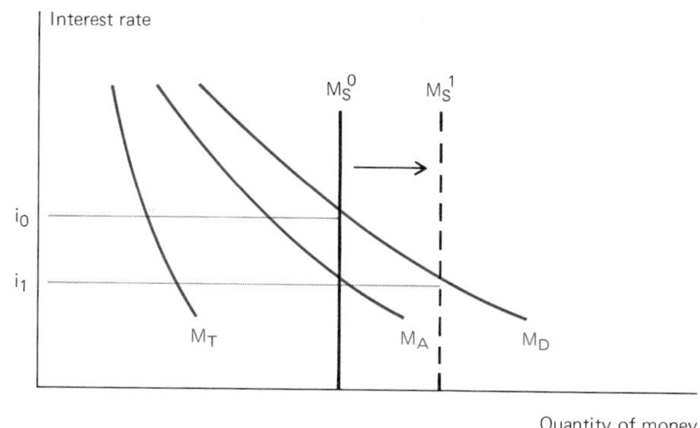

increase in the stock of money, from $M_S{}^0$ to $M_S{}^1$, and money demand were constant, that would decrease interest rates, as shown in Figure 15-8.

Open-market operations which increase the money supply also affect the price of bonds and their yield. Is that consistent with the change in the interest rate as shown in Figure 15-8? To increase the money supply, the Fed *buys* government bonds. That *raises* bond prices and *lowers* bond yields. That *is* consistent with the reduction in interest rates shown to be a result of the increase in the supply of money.

Constraints on monetary regulation: Real and otherwise

The analysis so far has given the impression that the Fed can do whatever it wants with the money supply. Before leaving the subject, we need to balance this view with an understanding of the limits or constraints on the Fed's powers. We shall start with the significance of gold in the money supply and then proceed to a discussion of other potential limitations.

The role of gold in the money supply

What about all that gold in Fort Knox and in the basement of the Federal Reserve Bank of New York? Doesn't it deserve some attention in a discussion of the money supply?

When the Federal Reserve was established, it had to meet certain gold reserve requirements: 35 percent of the total liabilities of Federal Reserve Banks and 40 percent of the Federal Reserve notes outstanding. In the 1930s, the United States acquired so much gold that the gold reserve requirements were for many years not effective as limits on the level of the money supply that the Fed wanted to maintain. Subsequently, the United States gold stocks declined substantially, as shown in Figure 15-4. Whenever it has appeared that those gold reserve requirements might become a constraint on Federal Reserve monetary policy, particularly since gold exports increased sharply in the late 1950s, Congress has passed a law reducing the requirements. Finally, in 1965, the requirement for gold as a backing for member-bank deposits held by the Fed was eliminated entirely. In 1968, the gold reserve requirement against Federal Reserve notes was dropped. Now there are no gold backing requirements and no gold constraints on the money supply.

Some people thought those old fractional gold requirements made the money safe and that without them the money supply could balloon to any amount whatsoever. Well, the reserve requirements were so fractional that they never offered much protection. Moreover, after the 1933 law got rid of gold coins, there has never been a hard gold money available to United States citizens. The lingering nostalgia for gold reserves may arise from the role they played as an upper limit to the height of the so-called "pyramid of credit" which could be built up in this country. Perhaps, the nostalgia reflects a mistrust of the "money managers" in the Federal Reserve Board of Governors. But the gold reserve limitations on the money supply were themselves quite arbitrary. *The view taken by Congress, and supported by nearly all banking and economic experts, is that careful management of the supply of money is much wiser than placing one's faith in the arbitrary limitations imposed by gold stocks.*

Gold is important as a means of settling international claims arising out of international trade and capital movements. A gold outflow occurs when a foreign central bank uses its accumulated dollar deposits to buy gold. The deposits are, therefore, canceled against the gold purchase. A loss of deposits by the banking system will, in itself, tend to contract the money supply. The Fed can offset or "neutralize" the transaction, if it wants to maintain the money supply, through open-market bond purchases. That will tend to raise bond prices and depress bond yield rates. It will, however, tend to encourage further movement of funds to foreign countries if higher interest rates are available abroad. So the Fed faces the choice: It can either neutralize the domestic effects of the gold outflow and tend to accentuate the out movement, or it can remain passive and accept a reduction in the money supply, which it may not want on domestic policy grounds.

On the other hand, a gold inflow increases bank deposits, and tends to increase the money supply. The Fed can "sterilize" the inflow by open-market bond sales. But that tends to lower bond prices and raise bond yields and stimulates further inflows. The Fed may be happy about the gold inflow but may not wish to raise the money supply. So, again, there can be a potential conflict between domestic monetary policy and the policy that would regulate gold movements.

We shall return to these issues in Chapter 34 after a discussion of balance-of-payments problems and international settlements, including gold movements.

Government debt management and economic policy

As pointed out earlier, the federal debt is a large amount, indeed, and about one-third of it is refinanced every year. We have also seen that when the Fed tightens the money supply, the yield rates on government bonds go up. That means that the interest rate on newly issued government bonds must also go up – which means increased interest costs in the federal government budget. During World War II and for some years after, there was a Federal Reserve-U.S. Treasury agreement under which the Fed maintained relatively low interest rates. This was a constraint on monetary policy which limited the Fed's freedom of action. The constraint was removed in 1951 in the famous Reserve-Treasury "accord," and since then the Fed has pursued a more vigorous and independent monetary policy. This has in recent years, in particular, resulted in interest rates on government debt almost twice as high as those which prevailed in the 1950s.

As an independent institution the Fed sometimes arrives at evaluations of economic conditions and policy prescriptions which are different from the views held in the executive and legislative branches of government. A presidential statement of "regret" for a certain Federal Reserve action has an effect on public opinion which the Fed cannot ignore. A statement by the head of a congressional committee deploring high interest rates or some other result of Reserve policy cannot be brushed off. It may portend a future legislative restraint on the Fed's freedom. There are risks – and potential benefits – in independence.

Monetary controls and money supply response

We have seen how the money supply can be manipulated by the Federal Reserve System. But we should not believe that the Fed is omnipotent. There are limits to what it can do. Monetary policy has been described as a string: You can pull on it but you cannot push. Translated, this means that the Fed can force a monetary contraction, if it tries hard enough, via open-market sales of its bonds and by increases in its discount rate and in minimum reserve requirements. But the Fed cannot *force* a monetary expansion. It can make an expansion possible and more attractive by creating excess reserves through open-market purchases, reductions in the reserve requirements, and lower discount rates. But the Fed cannot make people want to borrow and banks want to lend. We have to go further to see how those desires are determined. That requires combining our money supply and money demand analyses with our still earlier income analysis. That is on the agenda in Chapter 16.

Summary

The Federal Reserve System has a set of quantitative and qualitative tools with which to control the money supply and modulate excessive tendencies in the economy.

The quantitative controls of the Fed, in order of the frequency of their use, are (1) open-market operations in buying and selling government bonds, (2) discount rate changes on loans made by the Fed to member banks, (3) changes in the legal minimum reserve requirement ratio, and (4) currency control. The qualitative controls of the Fed are its ability to set interest rates on time deposits, to regulate borrowing for stock purchases, and to use moral suasion.

Control of the amount of currency in circulation is not an important tool of economic policy. The amount of currency available is regulated to meet the needs of the economy for an adequate supply of cash for hand-to-hand and hand-to-vending-machine transactions.

Changes in the minimum reserve requirement ratio act directly on the availability of reserves on which banks can make loans.

Discount rate changes up or down make it either more or less expensive for banks to borrow from the Fed and thus affect the use of Federal Reserve credit to provide reserves for member banks. There is also an announcement effect of changes in the discount rate, which indicates the direction of Federal Reserve policy.

Open-market operations are the most important instrument of Federal Reserve policy. They consist of Federal Reserve purchases and sales of government bonds, which, respectively, add to or subtract from the deposits of individuals, businesses, and banks. When the Fed buys bonds, that tends to push up bond prices and lower yields. That, in turn, affects the interest rate structure on all types of bonds and notes.

Qualitative controls change the terms and conditions of specific types of bank loans and, in this way, affect lending and borrowing.

The Federal Reserve, as a result of its powers and its overall view of the system, has great authority among bankers. So it can use moral suasion when it formally or informally announces to the financial community its opinion of the type of lending policy that should be pursued.

The interaction of the supply of money, as affected by the Fed, and the liquidity-preference demand for money determines the level of the interest rate. Since the demand for money reflects the level of economic activity, a change in NNP, by itself, will also affect the interest rate.

Though the Federal Reserve has powerful instruments of

monetary control, there are constraints on its use of them. Gold reserves are no longer required of the Federal Reserve against its deposits and notes. But international gold movements can affect the money supply. Contradictions can arise between the policies desired to control gold movements and the policies desired to control the domestic money supply.

Federal Reserve policies can also conflict with the Treasury's desire to maintain low interest rates on the federal debt. Federal Reserve independence means that it may not agree with the economic policies of the President or Congress. But the Fed is politically vulnerable, and that limits, though it does not destroy, its ability to act independently.

Questions for discussion and review

1. Why do changes in reserve requirements change the volume of deposits that the banking system can generate?

2. Should the Federal Reserve exercise more caution in increasing or decreasing reserve requirements?

3. What is Reserve Bank credit and how is it affected by the discount rate?

4. Do Federal Reserve purchases of government bonds tend to tighten or loosen credit? Why?

5. Why are open-market operations such a delicate tool in adjusting the money supply?

6. Why do Federal controls over interest rates on time deposits in member banks affect deposits with savings and loan associations?

7. How can the Fed control the interest rate? Are there any constraints on its control?

8. Discuss the following statement: *Gold has no role and no effect in our modern monetary system. We could save storage charges by getting rid of it all and not disturb the money supply at all.*

9. Why has monetary policy been described as a string that can be pulled, but not pushed?

Concepts for review

Reserve requirements
Open-market operations
Moral suasion
Discount rate
Qualitative controls
Margin requirements
Bond interest rates and yield rates
Regulation Q
Excess reserves
Gold inflow and outflow

16

Money, income, and prices: Alternative models

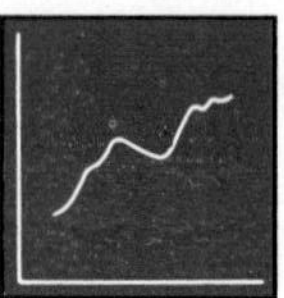

Does money matter? Those are the catchwords the professionals use to announce a debate on the macroeconomic effects of changes in the money supply. How do such changes affect the real production of goods and services? How do they affect employment? We are going to enter that debate now. We are at the culmination of our monetary analysis and are ready to analyze the relationships between the money supply and the overall performance of the economy. We shall start by tracing the effects of a decision by the Federal Reserve to change its monetary policy. In this analysis, we take the New Economics approach, sometimes also called "neo-Keynesian" or "post-Keynesian." Then we shall turn to an alternative explanation of the relationships between money and income — now known as the "monetarist" position. At the end of the chapter we shall reconcile the two approaches.

A schematic view of money in the New Economics

The argument can be followed more easily if we identify at the outset the major steps. Remember that the policy of the Federal Reserve is to moderate excessive tendencies in the economy. Suppose, for example, that the Fed thought effective demand was rising too rapidly.

1. It would reduce the reserves of the banking system.
2. This would lead to an even larger reduction in the demand deposits held by banks as they cut back on loans and invest-

ments in order to bring their deposits into line with their reserves.

3. A reduction in the money supply would mean less credit for borrowers and higher interest rates.

4. This situation would discourage both private spending and spending by state and local government agencies, reflecting their sensitivity to credit availability and interest rates. Effective demand, therefore, would be pushed in the direction the Fed wanted it to go. Output, income, and employment would follow.

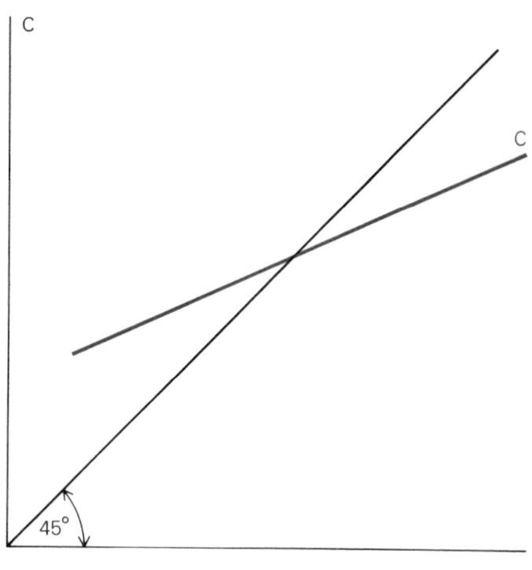

Figure 16-1

THE PROPENSITY TO CONSUME

On the other hand, if the Fed wanted to stimulate effective demand, all the steps would be reversed.

In preceding chapters, we went through steps 1, 2, and 3. Here we move to step 4 by putting all the pieces together. To avoid having to juggle too many balls at once, we go back to our simplest effective demand model, the First Macro Model, with no government and no foreign trade, and we add our monetary analysis to it.

In the First Macro Model, the net national product, NNP, is the sum of consumption, C, and investment spending, I. That is NNP $= C + I$. Consumption depends on disposable income, which is the same as NNP, since there are no taxes. The relationship between consumption and NNP is the propensity to consume, as shown in Figure 16-1.

To project investment expenditures, we shall use the marginal efficiency of investment relationship introduced in Chapter 9. This relationship is shown in Figure 16-2. The downward-sloping marginal efficiency of investment schedule, I, shows that the level of investment expenditure will be higher at lower rates of interest than at higher rates. This is due partly to the fact that lower interest rates mean lower costs of borrowing and, everything else the same, higher profits. Higher profits induce more investment. We also know from our monetary analysis that a greater availability of credit is associated with lower interest rates. That new credit can be used to finance the purchase of the new, durable physical plant, equipment, and inventories, all of which constitute investment.

Figure 16-2

THE MARGINAL EFFICIENCY OF INVESTMENT SCHEDULE

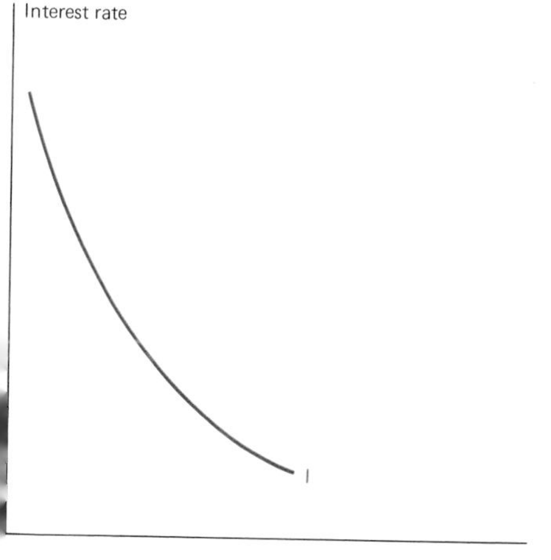

For convenience, we originally assumed that the interest rate was somehow given or determined and that the level of investment we observed was consistent with it. Now we do not take the interest rate as one of the "givens," but will determine it within our model system along with the other critical quantities.

The propensity to consume and marginal efficiency of investment schedules are effective demand relationships. They and the monetary demand and supply relationships provide all the pieces of the puzzle. We turn them around a few times, fit them together, and find the connections shown in Figure 16-3.

Figure 16-3 captures the essential interrelationships of a complete though simplified macro model. *The level of output depends on the total level of spending*—as in the models without monetary

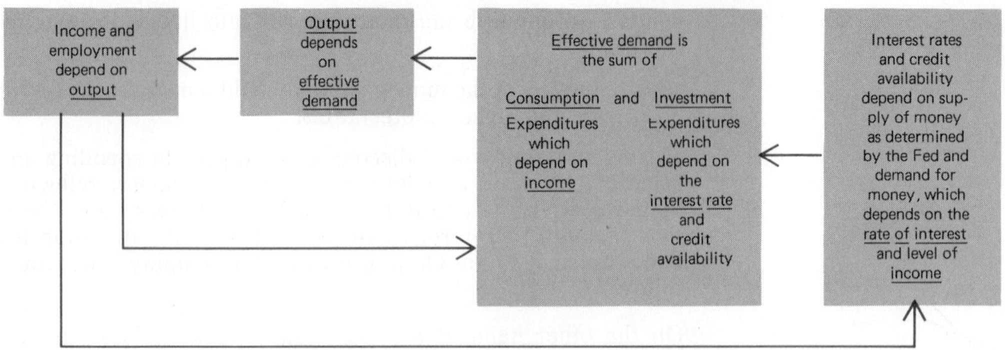

Figure 16-3

THE RELATIONS BETWEEN MONEY DEMAND AND SUPPLY AND REAL INCOME AND OUTPUT

effects. But now *the level of spending depends on the money supply via the effects of the interest rate on the level of investment. And the interest rate depends not only on the money supply but on the demand for money*, one component of which is the transactions demand, which in turn depends on the level of income.

The steps in Federal Reserve policy

With this more complete macroeconomic view, we can begin to appreciate in greater depth the way Federal Reserve monetary policy operates. Suppose the Fed wants to stimulate the level of economic activity. The processes through which its monetary policy operates are:

1. The Fed *increases* reserves by open-market purchases of government bonds and/or a reduction of reserve requirements. It may also lower the discount rate at which member banks can borrow, and it may announce publicly its desire to stimulate output and employment.
2. The increase in reserves makes possible a manyfold expansion of bank deposits. Banks, following the Fed's lead, adopt an easier policy toward loan requests. The interest rate on loans falls as the supply of money increases. Bank's loan officers, on their regular lunches and visits with customers, also let it be known that loans will be granted more readily.
3. The lower rate of interest and the easing of credit encourage a higher rate of investment in plant and equipment and inventories.
4. Owing to multiplier effects, the additional investment spending increases the level of NNP by an amount greater than the increase in investment itself.[1]

[1] The increase in national product results in an increase in the transactions demand for money, which tends to increase the interest rate. That tendency will have to be overcome by the Fed to make its expansionary policy more effective.

The qualification we must add to the story is that the increase in reserves engineered by the Fed in step 1 only *makes possible* the increase in bank loans and investments. The policy is permissive, not forcing. Usually banks and businesses hasten to take advantage of the new monetary freedom. But sometimes they do not do so fully. If business confidence is so shattered by a great depression that the Fed cannot force the interest rate down enough to stimulate investment, permissive policies will not stimulate the economy.

On the other hand, if the Fed wants to restrain spending and reduce the pressure on the economy, its powers are more positive. It can reduce the rate of growth of the money supply or even force an absolute reduction by open-market sales of government bonds and/or by increasing the minimum reserves requirement. It can make money more costly by raising the discount rate, and members of the Board of Governors can make speeches about the need for restraint. All this will force up interest rates and make credit less easily available. It will tend to reduce effective demand and, therefore, output and employment. The last effect – a reduction in employment level – is *not* desired, but the Fed is unable to maintain employment and at the same time reduce effective demand pressures. That, if it can be done at all, requires *combinations* of monetary, fiscal, and other policies which we will take up in Chapter 17.

This monetary and expenditure analysis is another example of interdependence in the economic system. Here, the interdependence is on the macroeconomic level: It reflects the varied interactions among the amount of each type of spending, the money supply, and the interest rate. All these are tied together in mutual relationships.

A diagrammatic analysis of the expenditure-money macro model and macro policy

The expenditure-money macro model is illustrated graphically in Figure 16-4. The diagrams show an interdependent equilibrium of money supply and of demand, investment and consumption spending, and NNP. Figure 16-4(*a*) presents the supply of and demand for money, which together determine the interest rate, *i*. *Given the marginal efficiency of investment schedule in Figure 16-4(b), the interest rate determines the level of investment, I. That level of investment and the propensity to consume in Figure 16-4(c) determine the equilibrium level of net national product, NNP.*[2]

It is worth stopping a moment to appreciate what has been achieved in Figure 16-4. This is an exceedingly simple system, and modern economics has gone far beyond it. Yet modern economics took a long time to get this far, and there is no need to be modest

[2] The transactions demand for money is part of the total demand for money and depends on the level of NNP. So for this system to be in equilibrium the demand for money *D* must be consistent with the level of NNP.

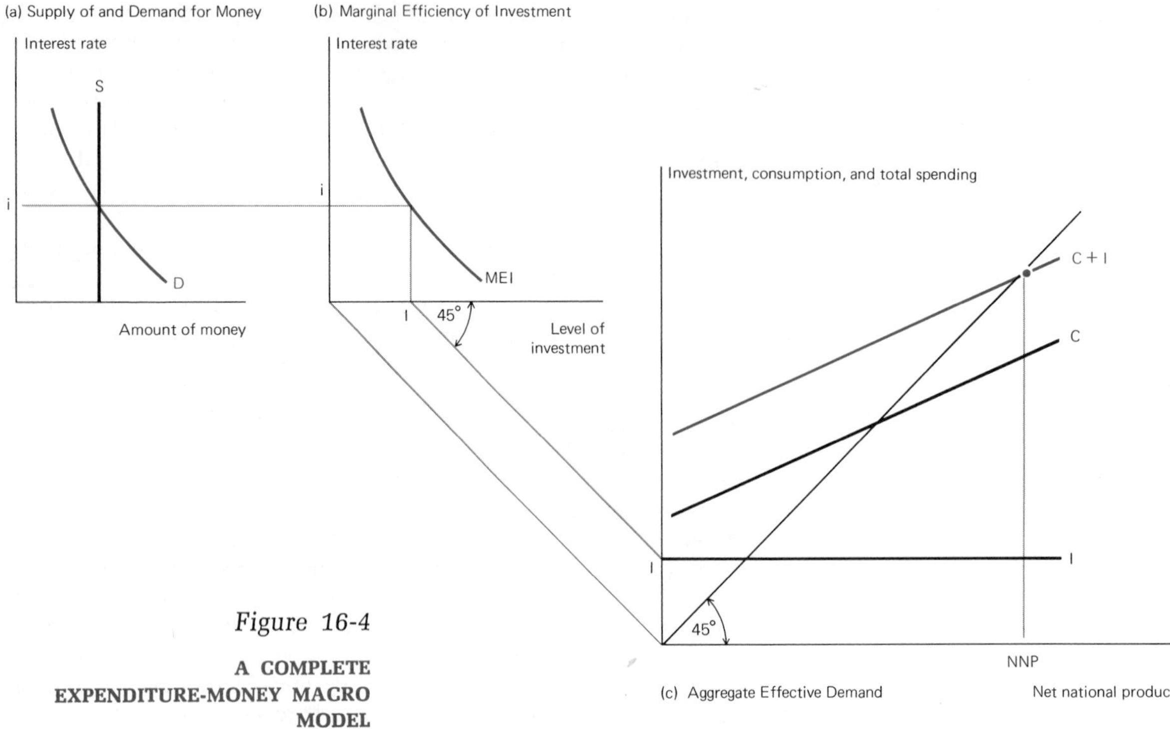

Figure 16-4

A COMPLETE EXPENDITURE-MONEY MACRO MODEL

about what has been accomplished. We have succeeded in integrating a monetary analysis with the earlier analysis of real effective demand in determining national income. The macroeconomic interdependence referred to above is shown graphically in this figure. We can now use this graphic analysis to explain in more detail the effects of alternative macroeconomic policies — fiscal policy, as determined by government taxing and spending, and monetary policy, as determined by the Federal Reserve.

Fiscal policy

In Figure 16-5 government spending, G, has been added to effective demand in part *(c)* of the diagram. With the initial level of spending, G, the system is in equilibrium at the NNP level of net national product. Suppose there was an increase in government spending, from G to G′, with no corresponding change in taxes. That would, as we have demonstrated, tend to lead to NNP′. But that, in turn, would tend to increase the transactions demand part of the total demand for money, as shown in Figure 16-5*(a)*. In turn, that would push up the interest rate and reduce private investment. At the new higher equilibrium NNP, there would be somewhat less

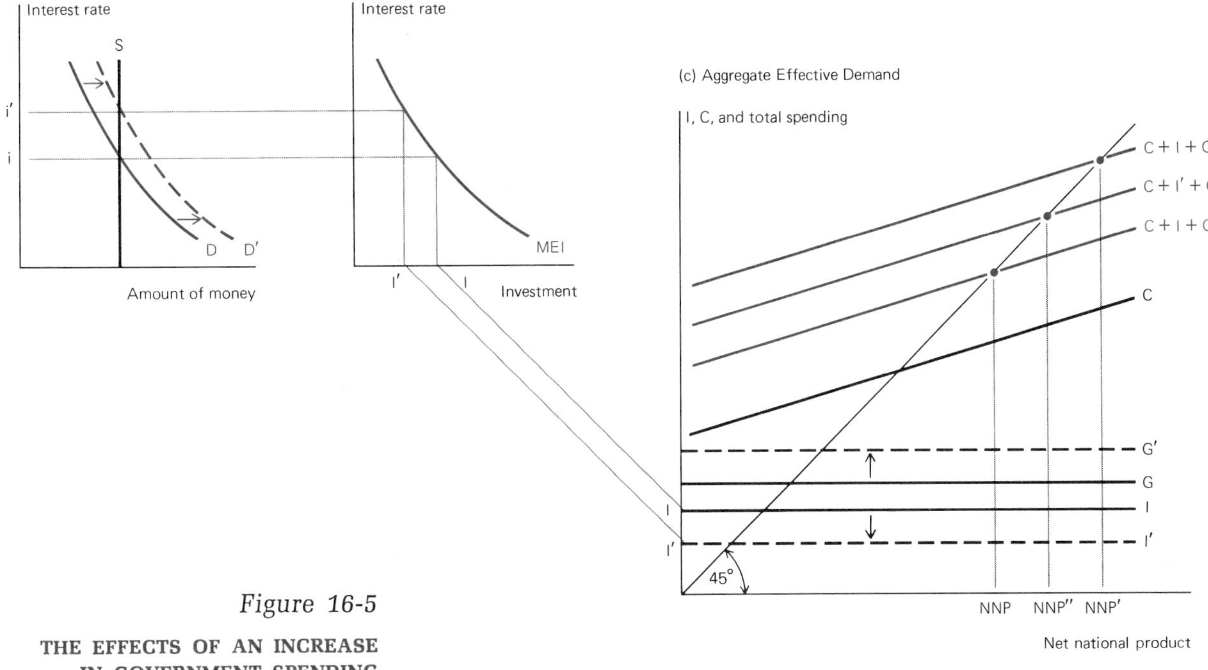

Figure 16-5

THE EFFECTS OF AN INCREASE IN GOVERNMENT SPENDING

private investment than originally and a new equilibrium at NNP″.

A word of caution should be injected, however. We pointed out in Chapter 10 that increases in investment tended to go with increases in national output. We could show this by shifting the marginal efficiency of investment schedule to the right in Figure 16-5(*b*). If such a shift occurred, the level of private investment would not fall as much as it would if interest rates were higher. In fact, investment might rise in spite of the higher interest rates and push NNP even higher. An effect like this seems to have taken place in 1969, for example, when investment rose sharply in spite of record high interest rates.

Monetary policy

Suppose that NNP were below the full employment level and the Fed decided to use monetary policy to stimulate the system. The money supply would, therefore, be increased. How would that affect NNP?

With more reserves available, interest rates would fall. Banks could expand their loans. Lower levels of interest would make investment more profitable. Investment would rise, and NNP would

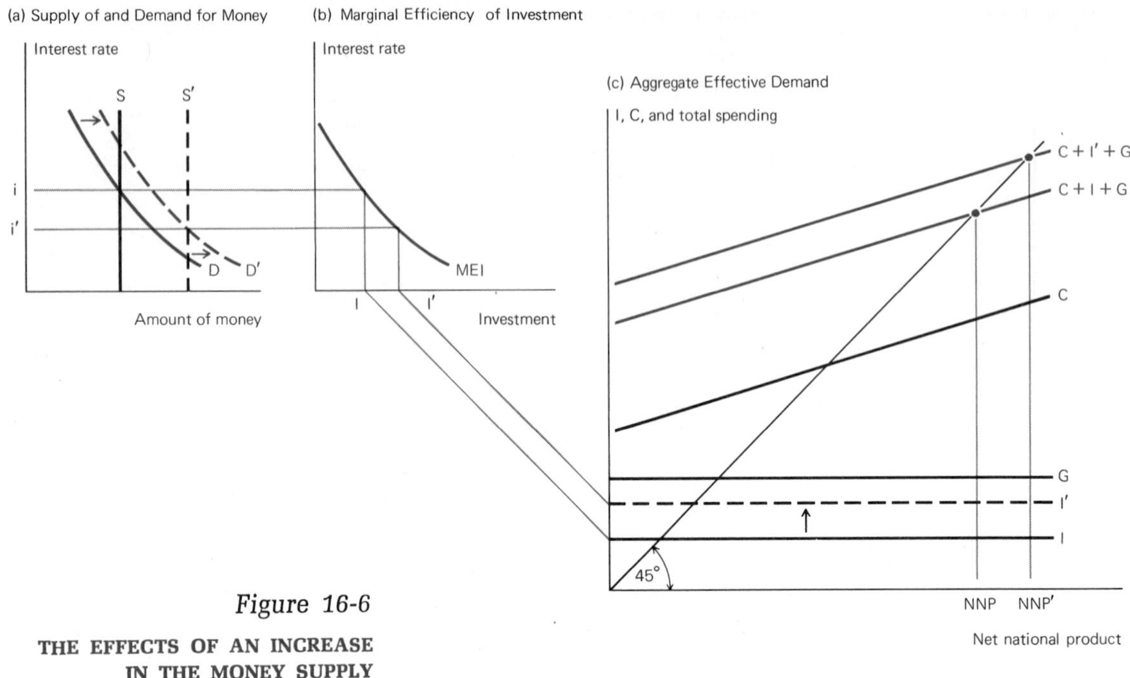

Figure 16-6

THE EFFECTS OF AN INCREASE IN THE MONEY SUPPLY

go up. The demand for money would also shift up slightly, tending to keep interest rates from falling as much as they otherwise would. That, in turn, would tend to keep investment and NNP from rising. But the Fed, if it kept increasing the money supply could overcome that effect. By engineering a shift from S to S', as shown in Figure 16-6(*a*), the Fed could reduce interest rates from i to i'. That would stimulate investment, which would rise from I to I', as shown in Figure 16-6(*b*). With a higher level of investment, aggregate demand would also be larger. There would be a new equilibrium level of net national product, NNP′, as shown in Figure 16-6(*c*), which would be larger than the original level of NNP.

Though both the monetary and fiscal policy examples describe expansionary policies, the analysis can just as well be used to demonstrate ways of reducing effective demand. You might, for example, reinforce your understanding of the analysis by tracing the effects of a decrease in government spending and a reduction of the money supply.

Does money ever not matter?

The integrated expenditure and money analysis indicates that, in general, money certainly does matter. There are circumstances, however, in which changes in the money supply have little or no effect on income and output. Our graphic analysis can illuminate these situations.

Suppose that the demand for money schedule looked like the one shown in Figure 16-7(*a*), with the money supply at *S*. An increase in the money supply from *S* to *S′* would not affect the interest rate. Therefore, there would be no tendency, as shown in Figure 16-7(*b*), to stimulate investment. This phenomenon is called the "liquidity trap." All the increased liquidity would simply be soaked up in idle cash balances. The Fed could buy bonds eight days a week and still not be able to force bond prices up and interest rates down. People would simply not care whether they held bonds or cash balances. The liquidity-trap phenomenon is thought to prevail, if at all, only at relatively low rates of interest.

Figure 16-8 illustrates another circumstance in which money does not matter. The demand for money in Figure 16-8(*a*) is downward-sloping throughout, so increases in the supply of money will bring about changes in the interest rate. Now, however, investment, in Figure 16-8(*b*), is simply not sensitive to changes in the interest rate. The completely vertical investment schedule shows that investment is inelastic with respect to the interest rate. Thus, no monetary policy operating through the interest rate will have an effect on investment spending and, therefore, on the national product.

Figure 16-7

IF THERE IS A LIQUIDITY TRAP, AN INCREASE IN THE MONEY SUPPLY HAS NO EFFECT ON THE INTEREST RATE

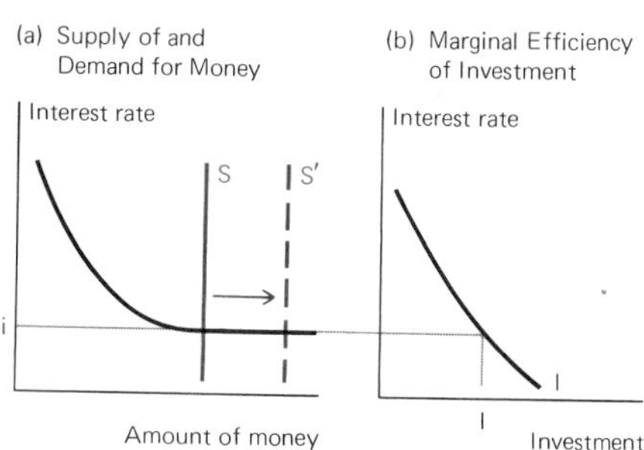

Figure 16-8

WHEN INVESTMENT IS NOT SENSITIVE TO THE INTEREST RATE, AN INCREASE IN THE MONEY SUPPLY HAS NO EFFECT

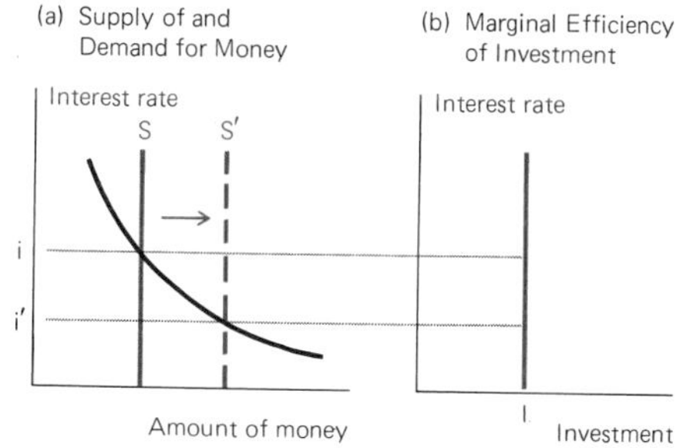

These are two "special cases" in which monetary policy would have no effect on the economy. *Monetary policy would be weak though not powerless if the liquidity trap did not turn so absolutely flat as in Figure 16-7(a). Also monetary policy would be weak though not completely powerless if the marginal efficiency of investment schedule were slightly responsive to interest, not so completely interest-inelastic as in Figure 16-8(b).*

Economists disagree about how real the liquidity-trap and interest-inelastic investment possibilities are. That disagreement underlies some of the argument over whether money matters.

An alternative macro model: The monetarist approach

An alternative view of the macroeconomic money-income relationship, the quantity theory, was widely held among classical economists. A related modern version, called "monetarism," has a small, though growing, and fiercely loyal following. The quantity theory, and monetarism, while not necessarily inconsistent with the money-income macro model, short-circuits the relationships and traces a direct connection between the supply of money and the level of output, when output is below full employment. When output is above full employment, the quantity theory and monetarism posit a direct connection between the supply of money and the price level.

The central role in the quantity theory is played by the velocity of circulation. This comes in two versions: the transactions velocity and the income velocity. Both are measures of the intensity of use of the stock of money.

The transactions velocity. The volume of transactions involved in the purchase and sale of a particular good is its price, p_1, times the quantity sold, t_1. The volume of transactions involved in all purchases and sales of all goods is the sum of all the p's times each of the corresponding t's or $p_1t_1 + p_2t_2 + p_3t_3 + \ldots$, for all goods or, in a shorthand way, PT. The number of times during the year that the money supply M must, on the average, be used for all purchases and sales is the transactions velocity, V_T. It is calculated by dividing PT by the money supply, M, or $V_T \equiv PT/M$. The three lines indicate that this is a definition of velocity, and so an identity. The terms, when rearranged in the form $MV_T \equiv PT$, become the "equation of exchange" – which is really an "identity of exchange."

The income velocity. If the NNP is divided by the money stock, the result is the income velocity, V_I, or $V_I \equiv \text{NNP}/M$. This can be regarded as the sum of the prices of final goods and services times the quantities of the final goods and services divided by the money stock. That is, it can be written as $V_I \equiv PQ/M$, where PQ stands for the sum of all price-quantity multiplications, with the prices and quantities referring to final goods and services.

The income velocity is the average rate at which the money stock turns over each year in purchases and sales of the national output.

Both of these velocity relations are definitions. As such they are "tautological": They are true by definition. If they are to be used to *explain* macroeconomic conditions and macroeconomic changes, we must add some information and postulate some empirical relationships. Let us concentrate on the income velocity, since we are most interested in influences on national income and product.

If we tried to explain what actually determines V_I, the average turnover rate of the money stock against NNP, we would have to investigate the monetary habits of the country. How frequently do people receive their paychecks? How much cash do they keep on hand and in their checking accounts? Do these behavioral characteristics change much over time? Are they influenced by other economic factors? For example, is the income velocity sensitive to the interest rate? Is it sensitive to the level of prices or expected changes in the price level? The answers to these questions raise considerable controversy among economists. Before going to the trouble of examining the evidence let us see why the income velocity might be significant.

The simple quantity theory predictions

Suppose that V_I were more or less a constant, that national output were at its full employment ceiling, and that we knew the money supply. Then with this empirical information we could turn the definition of income velocity into an equation, $V_I = PQ/M$, and usefully rewrite it as $P = V_I M/Q$. In this equation, under our assumptions each element on the right-hand side would be a number which we could specify. V_I would be constant; M would be some specific amount determined by the central bank. And Q would be at full employment levels. Therefore, we could calculate P, the price level. Morever, if M should change, since V_I and Q are assumed to be known and unchanging, prices, P, would change in the same direction and by the same proportion.

This idea has great intuitive appeal. Price inflation is commonly explained as "too much money chasing too few goods," which is not precisely the same, but can be translated into the quantity theory prediction about price changes.

Now suppose that real national output Q were *not* at full employment and full capacity levels. The quantity theorists would write $Q = MV_I/P$ and say that increases in M would lead to increases in Q, the real volume of final goods and services produced. With unemployed labor and unused capacity, Q could and would increase without causing price increases if M should increase.

Under some circumstances the simple quantity theory clearly catches the essence of the situation. Rapid and sweeping changes in the supply of money will carry everything along with them like a

Figure 16-9

INCOME VELOCITY OF MONEY

Income velocity is computed using GNP in current dollars for each quarter, seasonally adjusted. Monthly averages of the money stock, also seasonally adjusted, are divided into GNP. To assess the significance of changes in income velocity, suppose it were to be used to project GNP in the simple quantity theory of money. Then an unexpected change of 0.1 in the velocity of circulation would throw off the projection by about $20 billion.

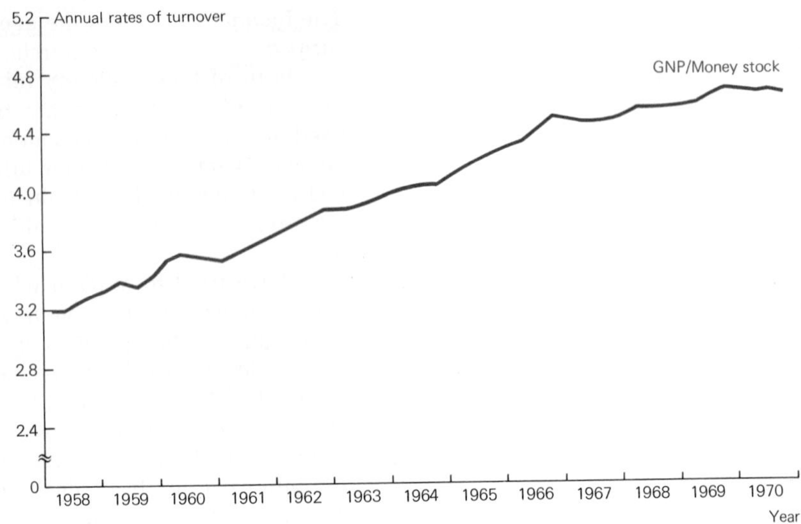

tidal wave. No plausible change in velocity of circulation or increase in output can offset a great monetary expansion, and prices are bound to rise.

The great hyperinflations of history – in which prices rose well over a thousandfold a year – occurred when there were vast and rapid expansions of the money stock. This happened, for example, in the South during the Civil War when Confederate notes were issued in great quantity. It occurred in Germany, in the 1920s, when inflation moved so fast that the government printing presses could not keep up with it. The government kept adding zeros to the digits on the old bills by overprinting. *When the money supply grows at an overwhelming pace, the quantity theory is a good predictor of price changes.*

Is the quantity theory useful when changes in the money supply are less overwhelming? Does it provide good predictions when annual changes in the money supply are within the range of 2 percent to 8 percent, as they have been recently in the United States? When *only* the money supply changes on the right-hand side of the equation $P = MV_I/Q$, and it grows very fast, then we have a predictor of price changes which seems to have worked reasonably well at various times recently. But it does not always predict so well. *The velocity of circulation has not been a constant and its changes have not always been predictable.* The chart in Figure 16-9 provides a picture of the changes in the velocity of circulation from 1958 to 1970. It rose by almost 50 percent during this period.

The quantity theory in terms of the complete expenditure-money model

Before we move on to a monetarist view that is more sophisticated than the simple quantity theory, it is useful to revert to our complete expenditure-money macro model and use it to answer the question: Under what circumstances is the economy highly sensitive to changes in the money supply?

Suppose (1) that the asset demand for money and the transactions demand for money are relatively insensitive to the interest rate, as shown in Figure 16-10(*a*). Then there will be only a small change in the holding of money if interest rates should change in response to a change in the supply of money. Suppose (2) that investment responds very sensitively to the interest rate. These conditions are represented in Figure 16-10(*b*).

Under the conditions shown in Figure 16-10, monetary policy would have powerful effects on the economy. Relatively small changes in the money supply from *S* to *S′* would bring about large changes in the levels of investment, from *I* to *I′*. That would, in turn, induce large changes in national product, from NNP to NNP′.

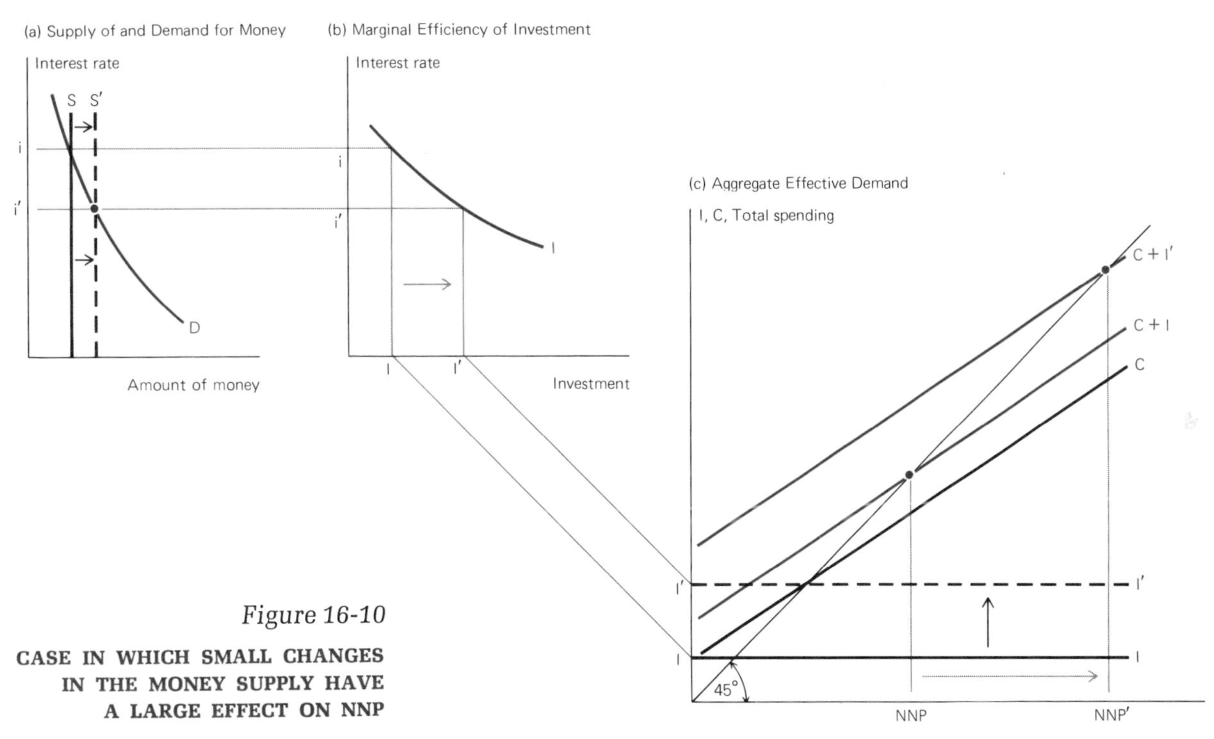

Figure 16-10

CASE IN WHICH SMALL CHANGES IN THE MONEY SUPPLY HAVE A LARGE EFFECT ON NNP

The new monetarism

According to the new monetarism, the essential macroeconomic relationship is a complicated but direct one between money, on the one hand, and income and prices, on the other. So the diagrammatic analysis presented in Figure 16-10 can be short-circuited. This point of view has been argued with power and persuasiveness in recent years by Prof. Milton Friedman of the University of Chicago. While still a minority view among bankers and economists, it has attracted many adherents and demands a hearing.

Part of the appeal of the new monetarist view has been its claim to superior predictive power. The predictive success of the monetarists in 1968, in particular, gave the theory a tremendous boost. In July of that year there was a major tax increase designed to stem the inflation which had its beginnings in the escalation of the Vietnam War in late 1965 and 1966. The analysis of the New Economics presented above would lead us to expect that a tax increase would reduce the pressures of effective demand. In turn, the reduction in disposable income ought to reduce consumption expenditures and have negative multiplier effects. That did not happen in 1968, although economists, businessmen, and bankers, including those in the Federal Reserve, expected it to.

Why? You can take your pick of explanations. The new economists point to the continued growth of government spending, a spurt in private investment spending, and a reduction in private saving which maintained consumption.

The new monetarists say: We told you so. The multiplier is not a reliable relation because the propensity to save is not stable. But most importantly, the Federal Reserve, wrongly expecting the tax increase to reduce effective demand pressures, allowed a substantial expansion in the money supply to take place. That itself was expansionary.

The ineffectiveness of fiscal policy and the seeming power of monetary policy in 1968 gave monetarism a new lease on life. It was, apparently, embraced by President Nixon's economic advisors at least in a mild form, and it received some support from Arthur Burns, who, on the President's appointment, became Chairman of the Board of Governors of the Federal Reserve in 1970.

Two aspects of the modern monetarist viewpoint can be distinguished: (1) a skeptical evaluation of the New Economics analysis, or neo-Keynesianism, and (2) a positive view of the role of money in the economy.

The skeptical attitude toward the New Economics dwells on the limitations of simple expenditure models, such as those presented in Chapters 10 and 11. And it is true that some economists seem to have stopped their economics course with those chapters.

The monetarists are skeptical about the stability of the propensity to save, and point to such evidence as the events of 1968. They are skeptical about the effect of the interest rate on the asset demand for money and about the predictability of the effects of fiscal policy.

The new monetarist view of the role of money argues that the demand for money is relatively stable. It finds a high correlation between changes in the supply of money and changes in national income. The monetarists argue that the velocity of circulation may not be an absolute constant, but that the income/money ratio does not fluctuate wildly and can be predicted.

The monetarists also claim that even when the new economists put money into their income analysis, they do not get the effects right. The preoccupation with the interest rate as an indication of monetary stringency can be particularly misleading. Why? *The interest rate is a partially controlled price – the price of using money.* It is difficult if not impossible to sort out (1) the real significance of the demand for investment goods, (2) the effect of general inflation, which influences this price just as well as other prices, and (3) the effects of efforts by the Federal Reserve to manipulate it. It is now recognized even outside monetarist circles that there is merit in this skeptical view of the role of the interest rate in the economy.

No amount of logic-chopping will reconcile the different viewpoints, though logic can help untangle the interconnections in the posited relationships on both sides. Finally, however, the issues depend on factual questions which have been answered differently by the new economists and the monetarists. Studies by the monetarists tend to support their views and demolish those of their critics. Studies by the new economists usually support their position and expose the weakness of monetarism.

On the one hand, we have the results of a monetarist study done at the Federal Reserve Bank of St. Louis:

> This [investigation] tested the propositions that the response of economic activity to fiscal actions is (I) larger, (II) more predictable, and (III) faster. The results of the test were not consistent with any of these propositions.
>
> The test results are consistent with an alternative set of propositions. The response of economic activity to monetary actions compared with that of fiscal action is (I′) large, (II′) more predictable, and (III′) faster.[3]

We also have contrasting results:

> . . . if one takes a general model containing both Keynesian and quantity theory parameters and uses some recent econometric estimates for these parameters, the results suggest

[3] Leonall C. Andersen and Jerry L. Jordan, "Monetary and Fiscal Actions: A Test of Their Relative Importance in Economic Stabilization," Federal Reserve Bank of St. Louis *Review*, November, 1968.

> that both autonomous expenditures and money are important. . . . Essentially our results support the intermediate (moderate Keynesian) position that it is incorrect to stress either autonomous expenditures or money to the exclusion of the other variable.[4]

What kind of science is it in which such conflicting claims can persist? Remember we cannot make controlled experiments in economics. We can observe the experimental evidence offered by history, but it is never complete; we never have all the facts we would like to have. And, too, the basic relationships may change in importance from time to time.

Rules versus authorities: An automatic pilot or a helmsman

The monetary debate is frustrating and often esoteric. But we cannot simply turn our backs on it and walk away. It involves a major issue of public economic policy.

Or does it? The approaches of both the new economists and the monetarists give weight to changes in the money supply. Can't we just agree on that and not worry about what lies beneath the agreement? No, because the two views lead to different policies.

The new monetarist, or, at least, Professor Friedman, thinks that the money supply is too hot a potato to handle. No one knows enough to "manage" it. *In particular, the monetarists believe that no policy directed at controlling the interest rate will be reliable, because, as pointed out above, the interest rate itself reflects a number of different forces.* What should be controlled is the stock of money, but even there, one should not yield to the temptation to "manage" it. The record of the Federal Reserve, according to Friedman, is replete with mistakes, caused not by bad intentions but by inadequate understanding. Therefore, the Federal Reserve authorities should not try to actively manage the money supply. Rather they should rely on a simple "rule" such as: Increase the money supply steadily at an annual rate of, say, 3 percent to 5 percent. That is the best one can do to generate stable full employment and steady growth at a corresponding rate.

The new economists, on the other hand, take a more active approach. It is not that they believe the Federal Reserve authorities have always steered just the right course in monetary policy. Some followers of the New Economics believe that the tight monetary conditions created by the Fed in late 1969 and 1970 were the result of carrying too far a policy which was, essentially, pointed in the right direction. Nonetheless, they argue, it is better to use all the skill and knowledge we have to set monetary and fiscal policy than

[4] Michael DePrano and Thomas Mayer, "Autonomous Expenditures and Money," *American Economic Review*, vol. 55, no. 4, September, 1965, p. 747.

to be constrained by an automatic rule. The automatic monetary-growth rule is not adequate. *Money matters in the complete expenditure-income analysis, but not in such a simple way that one can rely on a simple rule to always steer us out of trouble.*

The majority is not always right on economic issues. But in this case, the author must go along with the majority. Monetarists deserve credit for emphasizing monetary influences, which neo-Keynesians have too often ignored or undervalued. Our rejection of monetarism does not mean that money does not matter. It does, very much, but through the relationships of the complete money-expenditure macro model.

Summary

In the expenditure-money macro model of the New Economics, both spending and money affect national income. The monetary influences operate through the effects of the interest rate and credit availability on total spending. Monetary policy relies on these effects.

The quantitative controls operate in the following sequence: (1) The Fed uses its quantitative tools to change the reserves held by private banks. (2) This forces or induces a larger change in the ability or willingness of banks to make loans and, thus, changes the supply of bank deposit money. (3) The change in supply of bank money is reflected in a change in the interest rate. (4) The changes in the availability of credit and in the interest rate induce a change in investment spending, which leads to changes in output, income, and employment.

For a macroeconomic equilibrium to exist, all these interdependent relationships must be consistent with one another. This view of the interdependence of money supply and money demand and total spending makes it clear that, in general, money does matter. Except in the special circumstances when the interest rate is not sensitive to changes in the money supply (the liquidity trap) or when investment is not sensitive to the interest rate, monetary policy can be expected to have an effect on the economy.

This modern view of why money matters is different from the simple quantity theory. The velocity of circulation plays the key role in the quantity theory. The income velocity is defined as NNP divided by the money supply, and is a measure of the average annual "turnover" of the money stock. When the velocity of circulation is constant, there is a direct connection between the quantity of money and (1) the level of output when the economy is below full employment or (2) the level of prices when the economy is at full employment. When changes in the money stock are very large and rapid, the quantity theory rightly predicts resulting changes in the price level. In general, however, the velocity of circulation is not an absolute constant.

The new monetarism also gives money the primary role in determining the level of national income and denies the significance of spending changes, except as they are induced by monetary changes. According to this view, interest rates do not have much effect on the demand for money or the level of spending. The new monetarists claim that the evidence of history supports them. The new economists doubt it, and as yet there appears to be no decisive proof either way.

Though both the New Economics and the new monetarism give money a central role among the determinants of national income, their adherents come to different policy recommendations. The monetarists, led by Milton Friedman of Chicago University, want the Fed to follow the "rule" of maintaining a steady rate of growth in the money supply; they believe that will accommodate a similar steady growth in NNP. The new economists, while conceding past monetary policy mistakes, believe an activist monetary policy is less dangerous than completely forgoing short-term adjustments in the money supply.

The new economists are still in the majority, and the author believes that in this case the majority is correct – not because it is a majority, but because it proposes an eclectic theory not yet contradicated by the evidence.

Questions for discussion and review

1. Using a complete expenditure-money analysis, trace through the effects of a reduction in the money supply.

2. Using a complete expenditure-money model, trace the effects of a reduction in private spending.

3. Does fiscal policy have a monetary effect?

4. Does monetary policy have a fiscal effect?

5. What is the income velocity of circulation? About how large is it?

6. Under what conditions would you expect the velocity of circulation to be constant? Does it have to be an absolute constant to be useful?

7. Why did the economic impact of the tax increase of July, 1968, appear to be a confirmation of the new monetarism?

8. What is the positive aspect of the new monetarism?

9. What rule of monetary policy does Prof. Milton Friedman believe in? Why?

10. What kind of monetary policy do you believe in? Why? Is it closer to that of the monetarists or the new economists?

Concepts for review

- Money, expenditures, and net national product equilibrium
- Liquidity trap
- Interest-elastic and interest-inelastic investment
- Velocity of circulation
- The quantity theory
- Hyperinflation
- The new monetarism
- Monetary policy rules versus authorities

Appendix: Alternative approaches to a complete macro model

Alternative ways of presenting an integrated money-income macroeconomic model show in more detail some aspects of the interrelationships or are more convenient for some analytical purposes. We shall look at two approaches and illustrate their use.

The four-quadrant diagram

We can combine the components of the demand for money in a "four-quadrant diagram" which brings together the money supply and the major types of spending. To do this, we shall stand some of the diagrams on their side or upside down. They are just the same old diagrams, however, and the rotation should not confuse anyone. Figure 16-11 is an illustration. Before working out the interrelationships, let us make sure we see each separate relationship clearly.

Starting in the lower left-hand corner, Figure 16-11(*a*) is the transactions component of the demand for money taken from Chapter 13. It is turned so that the NNP axis points down instead of up, and the transactions demand for money increases with NNP to the left. It is presented as a relationship with NNP in its simpler form without any of the effects of interest on transactions demand. It is also simplified in that it is shown as a straight line without any changes in the ratio of money held for transactions purposes to the level of output or income.

Figure 16-11(*b*) is the asset demand for money, which was also derived in Chapter 13. It was argued there that this component of the total demand for cash balances is inversely related to the interest rate as shown. This relationship is drawn in its normal position.

Now for a critical and somewhat tricky feature of the way in which Figures 16-11(*a*) and 16-11(*b*) are drawn: They are positioned so that their *horizontal* axes point in opposite directions, and the

Figure 16-11

FOUR-QUADRANT DIAGRAM OF THE RELATION BETWEEN MONEY AND REAL EXPENDITURES

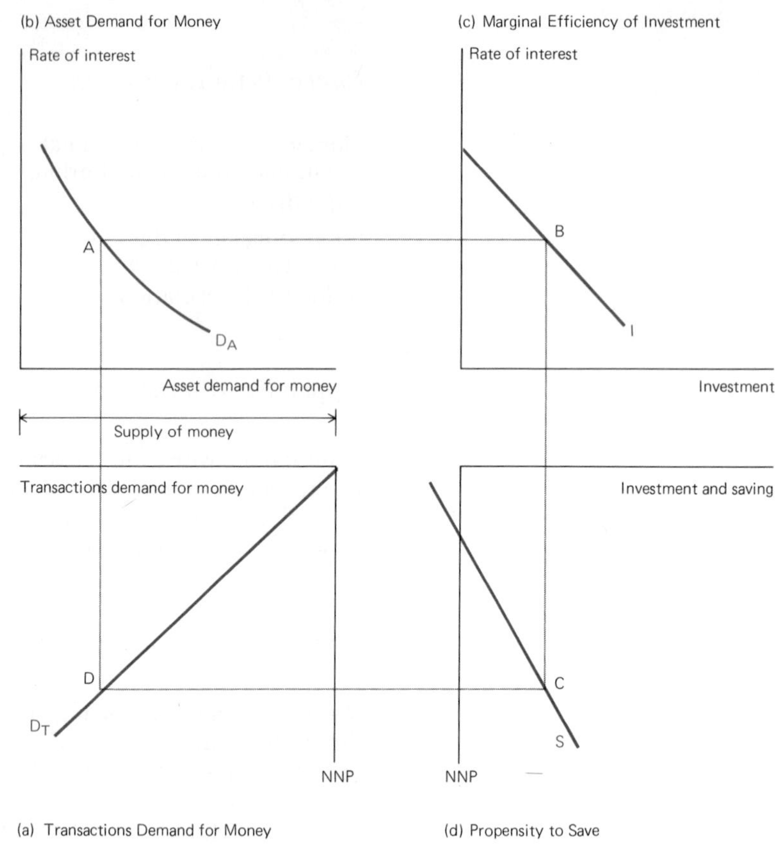

length of these axes is exactly equal to the total money supply as determined by the Federal Reserve System. This way of drawing the two components of the money demand means that the total money supply is absorbed either in the transactions demand or the speculative demand for money, and it ensures that *the total demand for money to satisfy both transactions and asset demands is equal to the total supply of money.*

Figure 16-11(*c*) is the marginal efficiency of investment schedule, which was first described in Chapter 10 and was in the background of the discussion about the effects of monetary policy on effective demand. It is also drawn in its customary position.

In Figure 16-11(*d*) the familiar propensity to save, or savings function, is turned on its side. The level of saving is now measured on the horizontal axis, and income on the vertical axis pointing down. We shall also measure the level of investment on the horizontal axis.

Looking at the four diagrams together, notice that the adjoining axes can be used to measure the same quantity. We can use them all together to ask: What levels of output, saving, rate of interest, investment, and transactions and speculative demands for money are consistent with the schedules as shown and the supply of money as indicated?

We can find the answer by trial and error by choosing some rate of interest and finding the level of investment it implies in Figure 16-11(c) and the level of NNP it generates in Figure 16-11(d), given the propensity to save. That level of NNP, in turn, generates a certain transactions demand for money, D_T in Figure 16-11(a). If that interest rate is not the same one with which we started, we go around again. We will find that the "equilibrium" values of all the quantities, the ones which are mutually consistent and which the system would tend to maintain in the absence of any changes in the fundamental data, are the values at points *A*, *B*, *C*, and *D*.

The four-quadrant diagram can be used to show the effects of an increase in the money supply. That increase, ΔM, appears in

Figure 16-12

ANALYSIS OF AN INCREASE IN THE MONEY SUPPLY

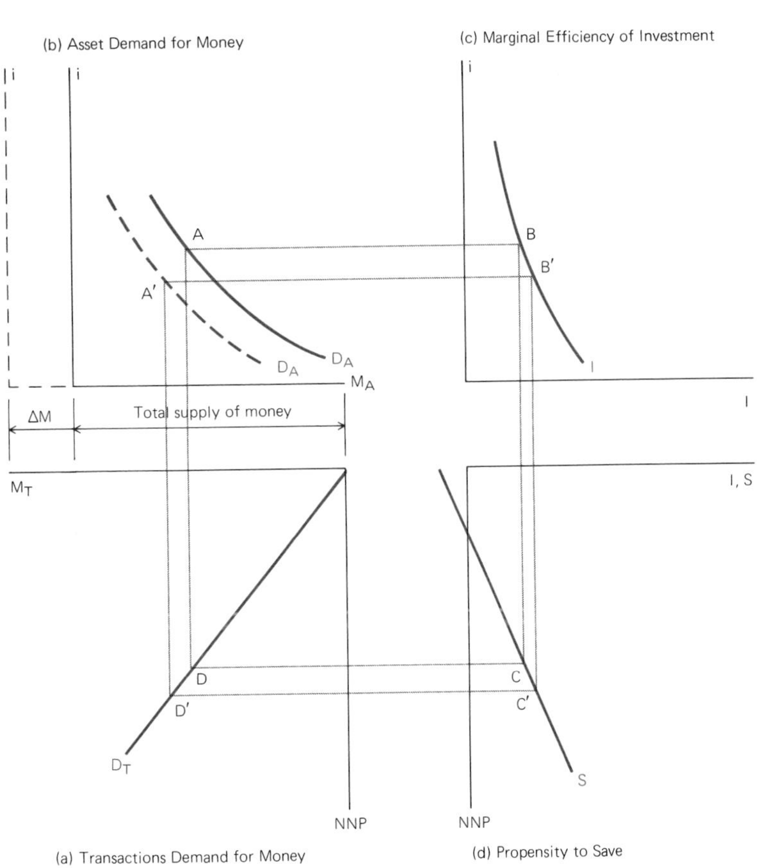

Figure 16-12(a) as a stretching of the horizontal axis. This means that the asset-demand-for-money curve shifts to the left relative to the transactions demand. The original set of equilibrium points – in which the levels of spending, NNP, the rate of interest, the money supply, and the money demand were consistent– was *ABCD*. The new set of equilibrium points after the increase in the money supply is *A′ B′ C′ D′*.

One must guard against the danger that the effect of an increase in the money supply may appear to be a shift in the liquidity-preference schedule, with the transactions demand being unchanged. Actually what is happening is that the increase in supply of money makes the transactions-demand and liquidity-preference schedules shift relative to each other in Figures 16-12(*a*) and 16-12(*b*). We will clinch our understanding and summarize the chain of effects by reviewing how they work when there is a *decrease* in the money supply:

1. With a decrease in the money supply, interest rates rise and credit becomes less available.
2. The higher interest rates and the change in credit availability tend to reduce investment.
3. When investment shifts down, the level of effective demand

Figure 16-13

DERIVATION OF THE LM CURVE

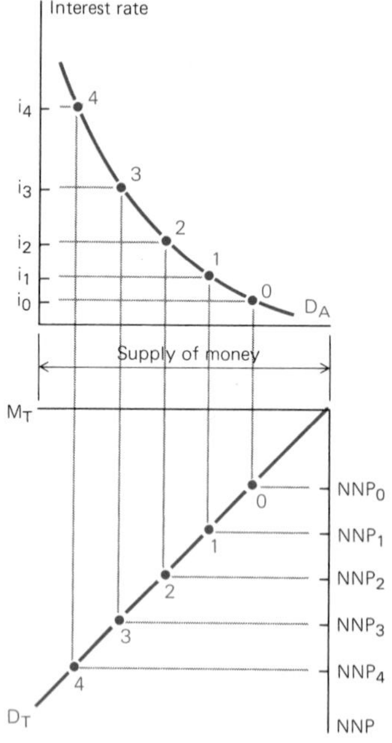

falls, and output will fall to a new, lower level at which saving and investment are equal.

The IS-LM curves

The four-quadrant diagram can be used to derive two synthetic relationships which, in turn, are often more convenient to use in analysis. Figure 16-13 brings together the asset and transactions demands for money.

If alternative rates of interest are stipulated, for example, i_0, i_1, and i_2, the amounts of money demanded for asset holding can be read from part (*a*). Given the money supply, the amounts of money left to satisfy transactions requirements can be found along the horizontal axis of part (*b*). With the transactions demand as indicated in (*b*), the corresponding levels of NNP that can be sustained can then be found. These are NNP_0, NNP_1, and NNP_2. Thus, in part (*c*), we can trace the so-called *LM* relationship between the rate of interest and the level of national product.

In Figure 16-14, the marginal efficiency of capital schedule in (*a*) and the savings-investment diagram in (*b*) are brought together.

Stipulation of alternative rates of interest i_0, i_1, and i_2 will

Figure 16-14

DERIVATION OF THE IS CURVE

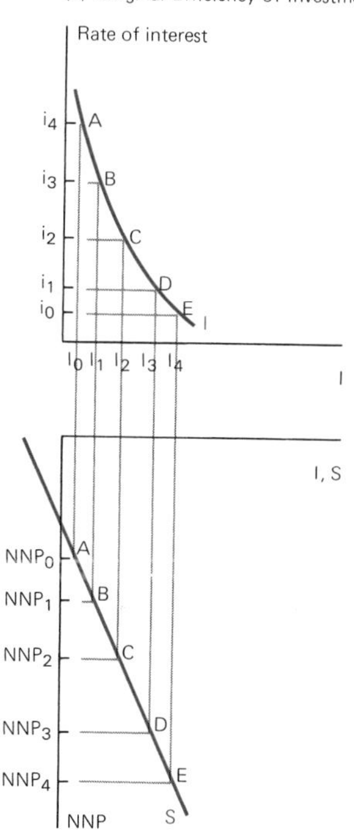

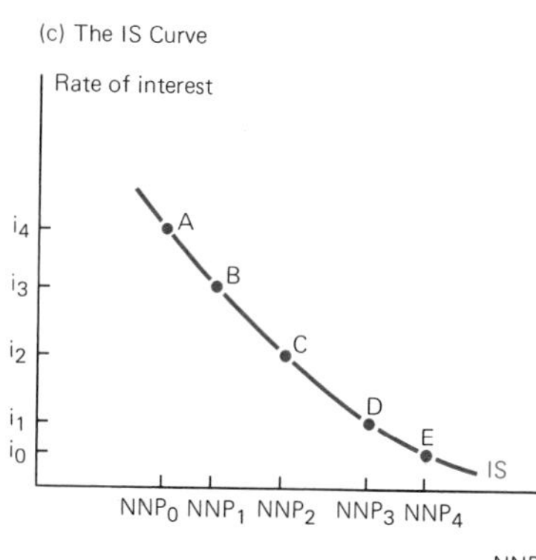

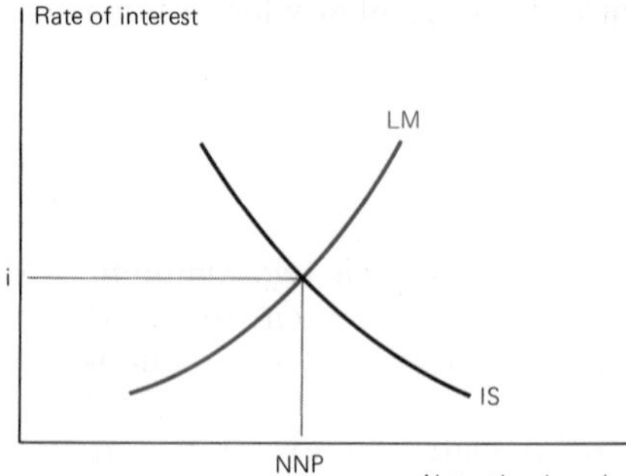

Figure 16-15

DETERMINATION OF THE INTEREST RATE AND NNP, USING IS-LM ANALYSIS

indicate the corresponding levels of investment in part (*a*) and the corresponding levels of NNP in part (*b*), given the propensity to save. In part (*c*) the alternative rates of interest and related levels of NNP are plotted. This is called the *IS* curve.

Figure 16-15 combines the *LM* and *IS* curves. Their intersection indicates the equilibrium rate of interest and NNP consistent with the money supply and money demand, the marginal efficiency of investment, and the propensity to save.

The *IS-LM* apparatus can be used to trace out the effects of various policies and changes in relationships. It would help in understanding these to verify that an increase in the money supply would shift the *LM* curve to the right. A technological change that generally improved investment prospects would shift the *IS* curve to the right.

Figure 16-16 represents the special cases of liquidity trap and interest-inelastic investment. Part (*a*) is the liquidity-trap case. An increase in the money supply which results in a shift from LM_1 to LM_2 does not increase NNP. Part (*b*) presents the interest-inelastic-investment case, and again an increase in the money supply has no effect on NNP.

Figure 16-16

APPLICATIONS OF THE IS-LM CURVES

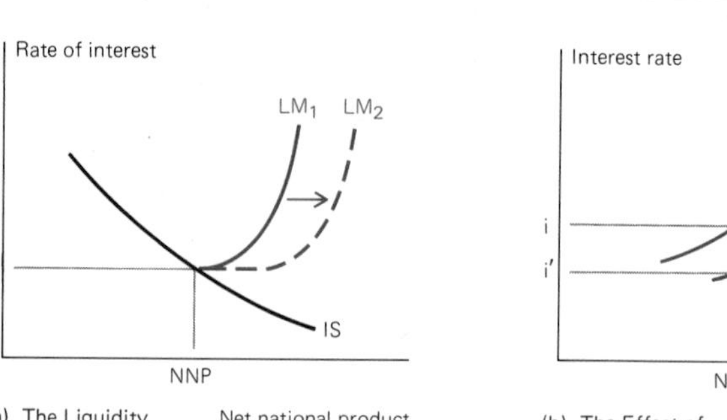

17

Economic fluctuations and price inflation

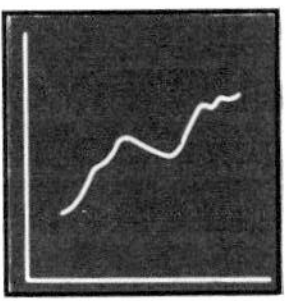

In the mid-1960s a period of rapid growth with stable prices produced a kind of economic euphoria. Many economists and politicians began to minimize the perils of economic fluctuations, inflation, or stagnation. More recent experience has demonstrated, however, that we cannot take for granted our freedom from boom and bust. The burdens of rapidly rising prices, of unemployment, and of slow recovery from a recession are now more freshly and painfully appreciated.

To better understand economic fluctuations, we shall in this chapter begin a more explicitly *dynamic* analysis. By comparison, the analysis of the preceding chapters was, for the most part, *static*. That is, it dealt with equilibrium conditions which were "timeless" in that they did not depend on a particular time sequence of events. "Static" is a bad word in some contexts, but the approach has served us well as a way of organizing and gaining insight into the relationships involved in the determination of aggregate income and output. Moreover, we did break out of the static mold on occasion. *An analysis is dynamic when it takes into account the particular time sequence in which events occur.* For example, at the very outset of macro theory, when we discussed the process by which the economy moves to an equilibrium of aggregate supply and demand, we distinguished between planned, or desired, investment and actual investment. Planned investment implies anticipation of some future event, and actual investment is that which did occur in some stated period. So events at different periods were examined. A dynamic analysis offers a better understanding of the causes of fluctuations in economic activity, of inflation, and of stagnation.

Theories of economic fluctuations

We know that the economy does not automatically tend to settle down at full employment. But why doesn't it at least settle down? Why is it always jiggling about, up or down? Faced with questions like these, we naturally look for a theory of economic fluctuations. As usual, we find a number of such theories, so we have to sort them out.

Theories of economic fluctuations fall into three categories: exogenous, endogenous, and mixed exogenous-endogenous. *The exogenous, or external, theories explain the fluctuations in terms of some influence outside the economic system itself which leads or forces economic activity up and down.* For example, an English economist, W. S. Jevons, argued almost a hundred years ago that there was a correspondence between the intensity of sunspots and the level of economic activity. He concluded (*post hoc, ergo propter hoc!*) that a causal relationship existed.

Another type of exogenous theory asserts a relationship between economic activity and weather patterns. It claims to find regular weather cycles and then traces a relationship between these and overall economic patterns via the effect of weather on output of the agricultural sector and the linkages of agriculture with the rest of the economy. That is a more plausible theory, since there can be little doubt that weather conditions affect farm output, and that has an effect on the rest of the system. It remains an unsatisfactory theory for several reasons: First, it is not clear that there are regular weather cycles. Second, the influence of the agricultural sector on the rest of the economy is too small in most modern economies to account for the fluctuations. Changes in agricultural output undoubtedly had important repercussions throughout the system in the early history of the United States. And they do today in agricultural countries. But for the United States, where the agricultural sector generates less than 4 percent of the national income, weather theories are not persuasive. Finally, recessions come in good crop years as well as in bad. There does not appear to be a one-to-one correspondence between farm output and general prosperity.

The endogenous business cycle theories find internal explanations for more or less regularly recurring fluctuations. A psychological theory, for example, argues that waves of economic optimism are inevitably followed by waves of pessimism. During the optimistic phase, investment and other types of expenditures increase and appear to justify more optimisim. But when optimism is unchecked, there are bound to be disappointments, and these eventually lead to unwarranted despair. That leads to cutbacks in economic activity. Pessimism grows and generates more pessimism. It becomes so excessive that any favorable sign is regarded as a basis for optimism, and a new cycle thus starts. A. C. Pigou, an English economist of the first half of this century, had a kind of psychological theory in which changes in expectations of profits provided the motive force. When business is profitable, good expectations keep businessmen investing. When storm clouds appear, some people run for shelter, and pretty soon everyone feels threatened. When the storm lets up, somebody with a good idea decides to try it. Success is contagious, and off we go again.

According to the endogenous theories, the economic system is inherently unstable. Its own internal structure contains relationships which tend to push it away from an equilibrium and generate cumulative movements that eventually reverse their direction.

A special, "explosive" endogenous theory of business fluctuations was advanced by Karl Marx. He believed that there were "internal contradictions" in capitalism. These would generate ever-wider fluctuations in economic activity.[1] Marx's prediction was that in the depths of a great depression, in despair, and with nothing to lose but their chains, the workers would rise up and overthrow the system. It has not worked out that way, of course, owing partly to a greater willingness to use government powers to control the cycle and partly also to a greater knowledge of how to use those powers. In addition, however, there has been no clear tendency toward ever-deeper and more drastic depressions.

Finally, some theories combine exogenous and endogenous elements. There are always exogenous influences impinging on the economy — changes in government spending due to a war or the end of a war, changes in other federal and state spending programs, or international crises that bring about domestic readjustments. It is also generally accepted that, in the intricate interactions of a modern economy, important endogenous propagating mechanisms tend to respond to outside forces by generating fluctuations in economic activity. The endogeneous elements are like the works of a clock: They go round and round and back and forth and up and down when the spring is wound. The exogenous forces wind the spring. Sometimes the clock slows drastically; at other times, everything speeds up far too much. There are internal limiting mechanisms, too, but nothing like an automatic regulator. We will now examine the important endogenous mechanisms that can propagate or dampen changes in economic activity.

The acceleration principle

The acceleration principle is one of the most basic of the propagating mechanisms. It helps to explain how changes in output in one sector generate changes in investment in that sector. These, in turn,

[1] In Marxian theory a war which creates inflation due to excessive aggregate demand is an endogenous event generated by the forces of capitalism. Most non-Marxians would argue that the political and ideological sources of wars are not related only to the levels of aggregate effective demand which determine whether NNP is high or low.

lead to changes in output by the industries producing investment goods.

It was pointed out in Chapter 10 that investment spending is a particularly volatile component of GNP. Typically the sectors producing investment goods show the greatest percentage changes during overall fluctuations. The so-called accelerator theory is a powerful explanation of this fact. It will be easier to understand if we start with a simplified arithmetical example.

Suppose there is a business firm whose production capacity is $1 million a year in output, for which it requires 100 machines. Each machine costs $20,000, and when used to capacity can produce $10,000 in output. (The firm could be a shoe producing firm requiring shoe machines, a paper products firm using papermaking machines, or a soft drinks company using bottling machines.) As long as its output remains unchanged, the firm will buy new machines only when old ones wear out. We will assume that the machines last twenty years and that the firm has been replacing 5 machines each year. Now, suppose demand for output rises, say, by 10 percent, to $1,100,000 in sales. The firm will need 10 new machines ($100,000/$10,000 output per machine). Its total annual purchases of investment goods (machines) will rise from 5 to 15 machines. So a 10 percent increase in output will lead to a tripling of investment! That is remarkable. But notice another remarkable fact. *Just to maintain* that rate of investment, *output must rise* again by $100,000, to a total of $1,200,000. To *increase* the rate of investment, output will have to increase by even more, or accelerate, say, to $1,400,000. Table 17-1 illustrates this point.

The table shows 1970 and 1971 as a base period with no change in output and an annual gross investment in new machines of $100,000. In 1972, sales rise by $100,000, and the firm buys 10 more machines to produce the additional output. That 10 percent increase in sales leads to a 20 percent *increase* in gross investment. Another increase in sales by the same amount in 1973 sus-

Table 17-1

AN EXAMPLE OF THE ACCELERATOR THEORY

	Year	*Sales*	*Machines required*	*Machines on hand*	*Additional machines needed*	*Replacement requirements*	*Total orders of machines*	*Money value of gross investment*
A	1970	$1,000,000	100	100	0	5	5	$100,000
B	1971	1,000,000	100	100	0	5	5	100,000
C	1972	1,100,000	110	100	10	5	15	300,000
D	1973	1,200,000	120	110	10	5	15	300,000
E	1974	1,400,000	140	120	20	5	25	500,000
F	1975	1,500,000	150	140	10	5	15	300,000

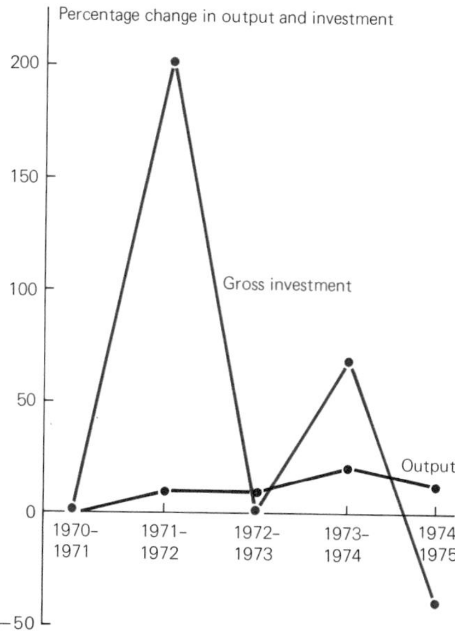

Figure 17-1

ACCELERATOR-INDUCED FLUCTUATIONS IN INVESTMENT

tains the *level* of gross investment but does not cause an increase over the 1972 level. If sales should jump by a larger amount in 1974, gross investment would rise again.

Notice, though, that the $200,000/$1,200,000, or 16.7 percent, increase in sales in 1974 over 1973 leads to only a $200,000/$300,000, or 67 percent, increase in gross investment. Comparing this with the effect on gross investment of the 10 percent increase in sales in 1972 shows the need for even more *acceleration* or increase in the rate of growth of output in order to *maintain* the rate of growth of output. In Figure 17-1 percentage changes in output and gross investment are plotted on the vertical axis. Notice in the last row of Table 17-1 what happens in 1975 when output increases but at a slower rate. Additional machines are still necessary and additional investment is required. But the level of investment in 1975 has fallen below that of 1974. Though output is still increasing, its rate of increase – or acceleration – has slowed. This simple example makes the following general points:

The *level* of output depends on the *level* of capital stock.

The *growth* of output determines the *new investment* in capital.

Changes in the growth of output determine the *changes in new investment.*

The argument has been made for a single firm, but it can be generalized to the economy as a whole. The economy, according to the acceleration principle, is like an Alice-in-Wonderland world where you must run as fast as you can just to stay where you are and even faster to get ahead.

The cumulating, accelerating, or "piling-on" phenomenon observed in fixed investment can also occur in investment in inventories of raw materials, semifinished products, and final products. When economic activity is booming along, businesses feel they should maintain a higher level of inventories to service the higher levels of production and sales. As a result, investment in inventories increases more than proportionately. Any slowdown in sales, however, raises the ratio of inventory to sales above what had been planned. To reduce inventories to "safe" levels, companies cut back sharply. They may cut out new orders altogether, or cancel existing orders, except for essential parts that are in especially short supply. Unlike fixed investment, which is often ordered on contract and whose production may take a year or more, inventory can be decreased or increased rather quickly.

Fluctuations in inventory investment are generally considered the major element in short economic cycles. They are unpleasant enough in themselves and their greater danger is that they may set off wider fluctuations.

We should note some important qualifications to the accelerator argument. First, it does not work the same way for decreases in output as it does for increases. Firms can reduce their investment levels to zero by halting new investment and not replacing machines. But they rarely, if ever, junk good equipment even if output declines very fast and far.

Second, when output increases, however fast, firms will not increase their investment if they have a great deal of unused capacity. Before buying new machines, they will want to utilize existing capacity. In the example above, the firm was assumed to start with full capacity.

Finally, there are other influences on investment besides changes in output levels, as argued in Chapter 9. Private investment depends on anticipated profitability, which is affected by costs as well as revenues. Anticipated costs and revenues depend on expectations of prices of inputs and outputs and on technology. The interest rate and availability of credit will also affect investment, as argued in the marginal efficiency of investment relation.

These qualifications make it difficult to test the empirical significance of the accelerator. In general, simple tests that do not allow for these qualifying factors attach little significance to the acceleration principle. But when the qualifications are taken into account, the tests often find the acceleration effects important.

Multiplier-accelerator interactions

The multiplier is another mechanism for propagating changes throughout an economy. *Whatever the original source of a change in income, that change will induce further changes in consumption expenditures via the multiplier*. That, in turn, leads to further changes in income and output. The final result is worked out over time in successive rounds of changes in income, changes in consumer expenditure, and further induced changes in income.

What happens when the economic waves propagated by the multiplier interact with the waves propagated by the accelerator? Many things *can* happen and we cannot trace them all in detail here. To appreciate the sources of potential instability, however, we should be aware of the possibilities.

One possibility is that multiplier-accelerator interactions will offset each other, depending on their timing and relative strengths. We know, for example, that saving is a leakage from the circular flow and, therefore, that a high marginal propensity to save or a low marginal propensity to consume means relatively low multiplier effects. This means that waves of spending and output induced by accelerator effects can be dampened by high saving rates.

On the other hand, the multiplier and accelerator waves may cumulate and lead to self-reinforcing movements. Suppose, for example, there is an increase in sales in a particular industrial sector. That results in a greatly magnified increase in investment if the acceleration effect is quite strong. That means a large increase in the output of the investment goods industries. The increases in output in turn mean increases in income and consumer expenditure. If the multiplier is large, it will magnify the effect and generate further large increases in income and output. There will be new accelerator-induced and magnified increases in investment. Round and round we go and where do we stop? Does anybody know?

Floors and ceilings on economic changes

The concepts of "ceilings" and "floors" which limit the up and down movements of the economy are important in many explanations of economic fluctuations. *The most common idea of a ceiling is that imposed by the limits of productive capacity and by limitations on the rate at which capacity can grow*. For example, when the economy is below full capacity and the capital stock is not fully utilized, output can expand relatively easily by putting idle capacity into operation. When the labor force is underemployed, output can be expanded by hiring more workers. But when the capital stock and labor force are both fully employed, the expansion of real GNP depends on the maximum rate at which capacity and labor force can be increased.

There are also *inherent limiting tendencies, or floors, which slow or prevent the decline of output*. One type of floor is set by the minimum consumption and investment expenditures of consumers, government, and businesses, all of which tend to maintain a minimum level of national income. Even when general business conditions are unfavorable, there is nearly always some sector which is expanding. The expansion may be due to a technical change that lowers costs or develops new products. It may simply be a response to consumer demands and government spending. These tend, in general, to sustain economic activity and set a floor under a decline.

Figure 17-2

FLOORS, CEILINGS, AND CYCLES

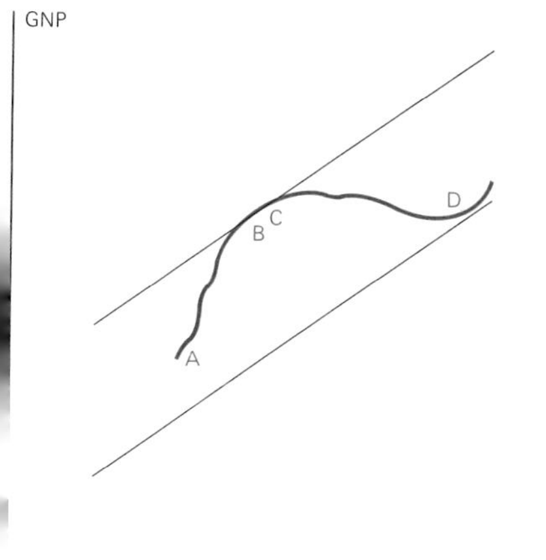

Many business cycle explanations combine theories of cumulative movements — which may originate in part in external factors — with the idea of floors and ceilings. Figure 17-2 represents such an eclectic theory. At point *A* the cumulative effect of the multiplier and accelerator is pushing the level of economic activity up at a rapid rate. This movement may be supported by expansion in the money supply and reinforced by spreading optimism.

When the expansion reaches point *B*, the system begins to run into the barriers of nearly full use of capacity and in some sectors nearly full employment of the labor force. As unemployment rates drop, productivity begins to fall. Costs begin to rise and profit expectations become less rosy. Nonetheless, the expansion of investment continues to increase the full capacity potential output. The ceiling slants upward to show that the economy's full employment and full capacity potential rises as time passes and as new and more productive facilities are installed. The rate of growth of the economy along its ceiling is less than before *and less than necessary to sustain the rate of growth of consumption and investment.* Business firms start announcing that times are good, but not good enough to increase next year's investment allocation by the same proportion as this year's. Profits grow, but managers who became accustomed to a 20 percent to 30 percent rate of return, from *A* to B, are disappointed over the prospect of a 10 percent return. As disappointments multiply and the rate of growth slows, the slower rate itself becomes unsustainable.[2] When the ceiling prevents the system from maintaining the rate achieved from *A* to *B*, the economy cannot stay where it is, just moving along the ceiling. At C a decline sets in, at first relative to the ceiling and then absolutely. The cumulative mechanisms take over and push the economy downward until it approaches the floor at *D*. At *D* the decline stops, and the economy begins to move along the slowly rising floor until the cumulative upward movement takes over again.

We do not have to swear allegiance to a fixed multiplier-accelerator mechanism to believe in cumulative movements. There are other sources of cumulative change in the economy, and the various business cycle theories are usually distinguished by their emphasis on a particular propagating mechanism. Joseph Schumpeter, the learned Austrian-born economist of Harvard University in the 1930s and 1940s, emphasized great new technical innovations as an initiating force in economic change. He regarded the extension and imitation of innovations as important propagating factors in economic fluctuations.

We pointed out in Chapter 15 that bank credit tends to expand when new reserves become available to the banking system and to contract when reserves are withdrawn. Moreover, *since economic expansion stimulates the demand for money, limits on the expansion of the money supply can be regarded as another kind of ceiling to overall expansion.* Milton Friedman of the University of Chicago has emphasized the susceptibility of the economy to monetary expansion and contraction. As noted in Chapter 16, Friedman argues that the economy is so sensitive to such changes that the Federal Reserve System should not try to make careful offsetting adjustments in the monetary supply. The best it can do is maintain a steady rate of growth of money. In Friedman's view, the Fed's penchant for activism has often contributed to economic instability.

The dangers of economic stagnation

Every age has its own set of worries. It seems a bit dated now to worry about stagnation. People with long memories or a historical turn of mind can review discussions of the slow recovery from the

[2] This is a manifestation of the accelerator effect. The economy has to run fast to keep investment constant. It must run even faster to make investment grow. The ceiling will prevent it from running fast enough to maintain existing investment; investment will fall, and that, in turn will induce negative multiplier effects.

Great Depression. At one time, the theory of secular stagnation advanced by Alvin Hansen, a leading innovator in the New Economics at Harvard until his retirement, enjoyed considerable popularity. It argued that new investment would never again rise to the inflated levels achieved during the prosperous 1920s because of the drying up of investment opportunities. Population growth, normally a source of new demand for goods and services, had slowed down. And new resources and technologies seemed to have limited future importance in the depression-induced pessimism. It strikes us as a bit odd now that anyone could put forward such a theory.

But a short period of slow growth will revive such ideas. During the late 1950s and early 1960s, the annual overall rate of growth of the economy was around 2 percent to 3 percent. Secular stagnation was brought out of the closet of economic ideas for another walk around. This time it had a more skeptical reception, but people were keeping their fingers crossed as the dull years went on and on. *Whenever recovery from a recession is slow, it is natural to begin looking for long-term causes, and secular stagnation will get a hearing.* Again in the slow recovery from the 1969–1970 recession, there was renewed speculation about secular tendencies toward stagnation.

Price inflation

Chapter 16 pointed out some important differences in the kinds of price inflation. There is "hyper" or "galloping" inflation when prices rise by 1,000 percent or 10,000 percent a year. Such inflation leads to a quick collapse of financial and credit institutions and necessitates major economic and social surgery. There are the inflations of 15 percent to 50 percent which, for lack of a better name but somewhat too broadly, we might call "Latin American." Brazil, Chile, and at times Colombia, have lived with inflations of this magnitude for many years. There are the relatively mild inflations of recent years in the United States and Europe, which are still rapid enough to force difficult adjustments on the systems. And finally there are "gentle" inflations of, say, 1 or 2 percent, which economic systems sustain without substantial adjustments.

Economists – as well as politicians and practically everyone else – debate the "livability" of these inflations, their overall consequences, and their effects on particular groups. People also hold divergent views on the proposition that inflation is like an epidemic disease, which must be stopped, else it will expand, grow more severe, and overwhelm everything.

The burdens of inflation

The general price increases of inflation place burdens on those who cannot prepare for them – and preparing for them is at best quite difficult. People with relatively fixed incomes suffer from loss in purchasing power when prices rise. That includes people on annually determined salaries which change slowly. It also includes older people living on pensions or annuity incomes which do not change at all when prices rise.

Creditors also suffer — people who have loaned out money, for example, by purchasing private or government bonds or putting money in a savings account (a loan to the bank). Why? Because a loan paid back with dollars with lower purchasing power for real goods and services represents a loss in wealth. Think, for example, about someone who bought a ten-year Series E federal bond in 1960 and held it to maturity. He would find in 1970 that the purchasing power of the principal he had loaned to the government had fallen by 29.8 percent. That is the amount by which the consumer price index, or cost-of-living index, rose from 1960 to 1970.

On the other hand, debtors and people whose incomes increase fairly quickly as prices change benefit from inflation. I pay back the mortgage loan on my house with dollars which have substantially less purchasing power than the dollars loaned to me ten years ago. People who own businesses that adjust their prices quickly can maintain — or even better — their position as their profits rise along with prices.

When prices go down (price deflation), the distribution of burdens and benefits is just the opposite. Does it all balance out? Not really. Look at Figure 17-3. From 1930 to 1970 there were a few periods of price decrease. These were slight, however, compared with the continuing upward trend in prices.

People play different roles in the economy and may be debtors and fixed-income recipients at the same time. So the burden of inflation on any specific individual may not be easy to determine.

Figure 17-3

CONSUMER PRICE INDEX, 1930–1970, FOR CITY WAGE EARNERS AND CLERICAL WORKERS (1967 = 100)

The downward price adjustment during the 1930s was large — nearly 25 percent from 1929 to 1933. Since then the downturns have been infrequent and small. The rapid increases in the mid-1940s resulted from World War II and the relaxation of price controls at its end. The increases in the late 1960s and in 1970 reflect the escalation of the Vietnam War without offsetting fiscal policy actions. (Source: U.S. Department of Labor, Bureau of Labor Statistics.)

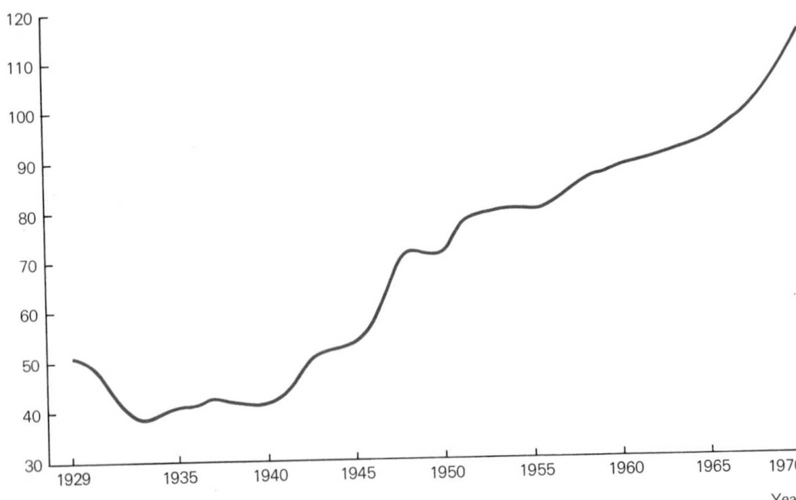

Nonetheless, in general, *recent inflation has shifted real income from older to younger people*. Older people tend, more frequently than younger people, to be creditors and to have relatively fixed incomes. So they get hit both ways.[3]

Theories of price inflation

It would be nice if another macro model could be presented which embodied a satisfactory theory of general price increases. However, the explanation of overall price changes is one of the most difficult problems of macroeconomics. There is no theory as satisfactory as the theories available for other economic phenomena. It is possible to give some reasons for rising prices, but they do not fully account for all the price inflation we observe, nor do they explain the rate or degree of price inflation.

Demand pull

Let us start by reviewing what we do know. *When the equilibrium level of aggregate real effective demand is greater than the output that can be produced with full employment and full use of capacity, prices will go up*. This is the inflationary gap phenomenon analyzed in Chapter 12. It is also known as "demand-pull" inflation. We may be tempted to draw the analogy between the inflationary gap and what happens in the market for a single commodity to make its price go up when the amount demanded is greater than the amount supplied. But in the case of a single commodity, we can expect price increases to reduce excess demand. That tends to check the price movement. The inflationary gap analysis does not tell us that, however. It just says that, when aggregate effective demand exceeds full capacity and full employment output, prices will rise. It does *not* say that the process will tend to be self-limiting, as it is for individual products in separate markets.

There is another difference between the aggregate effective demand analysis and the analysis of price changes in individual markets. In the latter, when the amount demanded is less than the amount supplied, the price falls. We never claimed, and the facts do not indicate, that the general level of prices will always fall when the aggregate demand for output is less than the amount that can be produced. Look again at Figure 17-3. There was a recession in 1949 and 1955, and prices went down slightly. But prices rose through the slowdowns in overall economic activity in the late 1950s and early 1960s when the economy was far below its full

[3] Notice that the argument made here is that the problems of inflation have their source in the inability of individuals to adjust to rising prices. If everyone could foresee inflationary pressures accurately and adjust their income payments and wealth so that they rode along with the price increases, then inflation would have relatively little deleterious effect. But such complete adjustment is not feasible, at least not in any short period.

employment potential. And they kept rising during and after the recession that started in the late 1960s and continued in the early 1970s. The fact that prices do not fall when aggregate demand is deficient reflects the downward "stickiness" of prices commented on in Chapter 9.

Another explanation for price inflation is an increase in the money supply. Chapter 16 argued that the relation is not an exact one, particularly for creeping or relatively slow increases in prices. In hyper, or galloping, inflation, when prices rise at extraordinary rates, they are being pushed along by drastic increases in the money supply. Such increases in the money supply were symptoms of deeper social maladjustment.

In both the demand-pull and the monetary explanations of inflation, causation emanates from the demand side. In both explanations, however, the story should be completed on the supply side. There are induced increases in the costs of production as capacity utilization and labor employment increase and as the prices of materials, capital equipment, and wages rise. These changes tend to induce further price increases as businesses struggle to maintain their margin of profits over costs. The increases in wages and other production costs mean higher incomes and lead to higher levels of demand. *As the inflationary process continues, it becomes increasingly difficult to determine the original cause, as demand pull and "cost push" feed on each other.*

Sellers inflation

Another group of theories of inflation locate the initiating factors on the supply or sellers' side. According to one "wage-push" theory, the impetus toward price increases emanates from the "excessive" wage increases demanded by labor and given by business. When is a wage increase excessive? According to this theory, prices rise whenever wage increases result in an increase in labor cost *per unit of output.* On the one hand, increases in output per worker do tend to reduce unit labor costs, on the average over the long run, by 3 percent a year. Suppose that wages rise by 5 percent a year, unit labor costs are then going to rise by 2 percent. Suppose now that business firms always raise prices enough to protect their profit margins and maintain other factor payments. Then prices will be pushed up by 2 percent per year. Again, the story has to be completed by telling what happens on the demand side. Increases in wages and other factor payments become increases in income and lead to increases in expenditure. These "validate" the price increase and make it just as difficult to isolate the origins of the inflationary process as before.

Several objections to the wage-push theory of inflation present themselves. One, falling back on supply and demand analysis in competitive markets, argues that wages will rise only when the quantity of labor demanded is greater than the quantity supplied at the existing wage. That means wage rates will not go up if there is unemployment. Yet there are periods of general unemployment in which wage rates do go up, and we must conclude that the assumption of competitive markets is not appropriate in this situation. It has in fact been argued that there is sometimes a kind of implicit collusion among employers and employees to raise wages and prices. Each side knows it cannot get a larger *share* of the value added generated *in the plant*. But both sides may believe that their mutual consent to wage and price increases can result in an increase in the price of their product relative to other prices. That would mean a larger total income for both employees and employers. If this belief is widespread and workers and management act on it, the attempts in each industry to get a larger share of GNP will tend to cancel out. No one firm will be able to increase its share as much as hoped, but the price level will be higher.

This last reasoning does not deny that price pressures can originate on the supply side, but says, in effect, Do not blame them on labor alone. *Management would not increase wages if it could not pass the increases on to consumers.* In fact, some people say that the real problem is lack of competition on the supply side. If businesses were more aggressive competitors, they would not give in so easily when faced with wage demands. When each firm can count on its rivals to fall into line on prices and wages, it is argued, no one firm really fights to keep costs down.

Another objection to wage-push reasoning – in fact to the whole supply-push argument – is that the price increase could not take place if the money supply did not increase to validate it. This objection can be understood at one level by assuming that the velocity of circulation of money is a constant. Then an increase in the value of output in money terms due to higher prices will require either a larger money supply or a smaller number of real transactions, i.e., a smaller real output. Or the validation argument can be made in terms of effective demand analysis: An increase in the value of output in money terms requires more money to satisfy the transactions demand for money. That forces up the interest rate and tends to reduce effective demand unless there is an increase in the money supply or an increase in money velocity reflecting an offsetting increase in effective demand from the private or government sector.

Offsetting changes often do seem to occur. The money supply increases. Or since rising prices mean higher profits to some businessmen, there is new investment. Consumer expenditures also rise. And off we go.

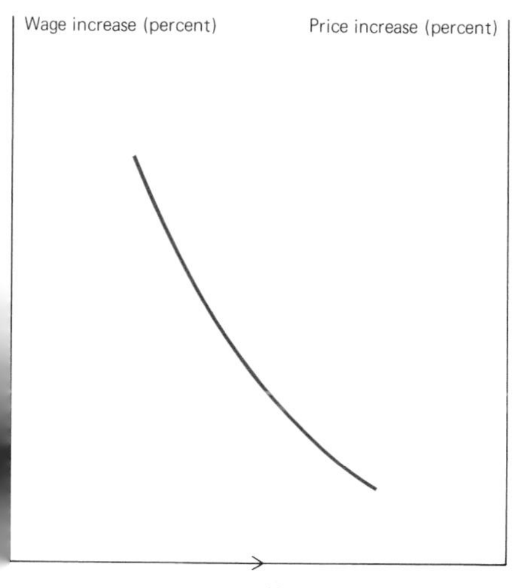

Figure 17-4

GENERALIZED PHILLIPS CURVE

The Phillips curve

A notable statistical analysis of these issues has found a significant relationship between the *level* of unemployment, or percentage of unemployment, and the rate of change in wages and prices. This relationship, called a Phillips curve after A. W. Phillips of the Australian National University, who first formulated it, is shown in Figure 17-4. The rate of unemployment is plotted on the horizontal

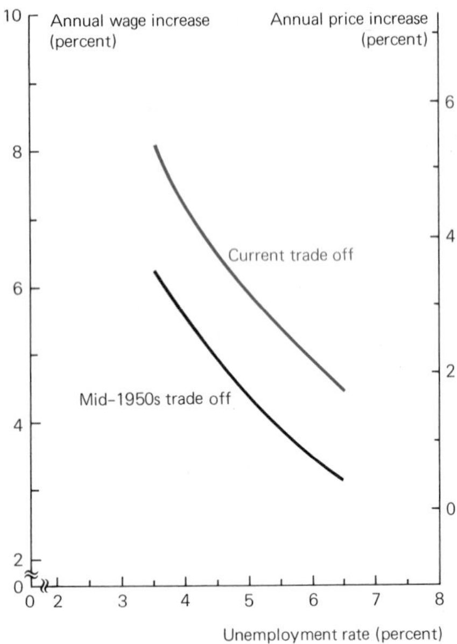

Figure 17-5

PHILLIPS CURVE ESTIMATED FOR THE EARLY 1970s, COMPARED WITH ONE FOR THE 1950s

An unemployment rate of $4^1/_2$ percent is now associated with price increases of almost 4 percent and wage increases of about $6^1/_4$ percent. In the 1950s, $4^1/_2$ percent unemployment meant price increases only slightly above 2 percent and wage increases of about 3 percent. (Source: George L. Perry, "Changing Labor Markets and Inflation," Brookings Papers on Economic Activity, *No. 3, 1970.*

axis, the rate of change in wages on the left-hand vertical axis, and the rate of change in prices on the right-hand vertical axis. The rationale of the relationship is that increasing wages generate increases in costs which are passed on as increases in prices. The increase in prices is less than the wage increase, however, because rising labor productivity offsets some of the impact of higher wages on costs. The line on the chart slanting from upper left to lower right shows that price and wage increases are lower with higher levels of unemployment. *The Phillips curve illustrates the characteristic trade off between unemployment and price stability.*

It should not be thought, however, that the Phillips curve is an immutable law of nature. It has shifted in the past and may well shift again in the future. For example, if the rate of increase of labor productivity should rise, then it would be possible for wages also to rise more rapidly without generating cost increases and price pressures. Further the shape and position of the Phillips curve depend in part on the success of government attempts to moderate the wage-price spiral—to which we shall return in Chapter 18.[4] Figure 17-5 illustrates the shift in the Phillips curve which one researcher has found to have occurred in the United States. An upward or rightward shift of the curve means a higher rate of inflation at a specified rate of unemployment—and, therefore, more difficulty in containing inflation.

There is in reality a difficult which-came-first-the-chicken-or-the-egg problem involved in identifying the sources of inflation on the supply side. We will not try to resolve the question but will simply follow the lead of Prof. A. P. Lerner of the University of California at Berkeley and avoid any judgment by calling the phenomenon "sellers inflation." It is important to remember, however, that sellers inflation must be validated on the demand side. *Price increases will not stand unless monetary and fiscal policies permit them to do so. Restrictive monetary and fiscal policies can reduce inflationary tendencies by reducing effective demand, but with the consequence of more unemployment.* Is there any way out?

In the next chapter we bring together what we have learned about the determinants of aggregate demand to gain a deeper appreciation of the issues of public economic policy to deal with the macroeconomic questions of unemployment and recession, on the one hand, and inflation on the other.

Summary

A dynamic analysis deals with the changes that contribute to economic fluctuations, stagnation, and inflation.

[4] It is useful in understanding the Phillips curve to note what it would be in extreme cases. If the labor market were like a competitive market and wage rates never rose when there was unemployment, the Phillips curve would be a vertical line at the full employment level. Any attempt to push above full employment would inevitably raise prices.

Theories of economic fluctuations are exogenous or endogenous, depending on whether they ascribe major significance to influences originating outside or inside the economy. Mixed exogenous-endogenous theories consider both types of influences. For example, weather theories of the business cycle are exogenous, while psychological theories are endogenous. Modern theories tend to be mixed; they give weight to exogenous forces, such as changes in government spending, and to endogenous mechanisms that propagate such changes so as to cause fluctuations.

The acceleration principle is one such mechanism. The accelerator theory argues that the level of new investment depends on the rate of change in output. So when output is constant, no new investment is necessary. But when output grows, new investment is generated, and its amount depends on the rate of growth of output. The theory must be qualified when there is excess capacity in order to take account of sources of investment. Nonetheless, it helps explain why fluctuations in inventory investment and in the output of those sectors of the economy which produce investment goods are generally greater than fluctuations in the gross national product.

The multiplier is another propagating mechanism which generates rounds of induced consumption expenditure and income and output from an original change in effective demand.

The multiplier and accelerator can interact in a variety of ways. There may be offsetting or reinforcing tendencies which can either dampen original changes or set off even more drastic movements in the economy. These movements are limited, however, by floors and ceilings, which are the capacity outputs and maximum rates of change of which the economy is capable.

An eclectic approach to the explanation of economic fluctuations recognizes the importance of external influences and combines the propagating mechanisms and the concepts of floors and ceilings. The various cycle theories differ mainly in the weight they give to alternative propagating mechanisms or external causes. The innovation theory of the business cycle gives great weight to the idea that the extension and imitation of major technical changes are the propagating factor which generates economic fluctuations.

The monetary theories place great emphasis on the effects of expansion and contraction of the money supply by the banking system when new reserves become available to it. This expansion and contraction can be a major propagating mechanism. The limits on the money supply may also constitute an effective ceiling to economic expansion.

Concern about secular stagnation, which received widespread attention in the 1930s, cropped up again in the slow 1950s and reappears whenever recovery from a recession does not go as fast as desired. Under such conditions, people look for long-run explanations in reduced investment opportunities.

The rapid growth of the 1960s dispelled most stagnationist

worries and replaced them with concern about inflation. The effect of inflation depends partly on its severity. Galloping inflations can virtually destroy existing economic structures. Short of that, inflation places a burden on an economy, owing to its differential impact on individuals. Creditors and people on fixed incomes suffer; people with variable incomes – especially profit recipients – and debtors benefit relatively.

The demand-pull theories of inflation say that price movements originate in the excess of effective demand over full capacity and full employment outputs. As inflations proceed, they lead to cost increases, and it becomes increasingly difficult to identify the first causes.

Sellers inflation theories find the sources of price increases in cost increases. Cost increases may result from wage increases. These, in turn, may be granted easily by employers who, because of some degree of product market power, can pass on the wage increases in the form of higher prices. Sellers inflation must also be validated on the demand side by increases in effective demand. It has been argued that monetary and fiscal policies often have not constrained these price-increasing influences.

The effect of lower unemployment in making it easier for workers to obtain wage increases with consequent upward price pressures is summarized in the Phillips curve, which relates unemployment and price increases. The existence of the relationship raises difficult issues of economic policy in achieving full employment without inflation.

Questions for discussion and review

1. Discuss the following statement: *The trouble with exogenous theories of economic fluctuations is that they make every cycle a special case, whereas economic fluctuations have many common features.*

2. Discuss the following statement: *The trouble with endogenous theories of economic fluctuation is that they give no weight to important forces which originate outside the workings of the private market economy and contribute to economic fluctuations.*

3. Describe how the accleration principle works and make up a simple numerical example to illustrate it.

4. Why does the accleration principle help explain how a slowdown in the rate of expansion of economic activity can turn into a real downturn?

5. Look back at the aggregate economic statistics of Chapter 7 and write out an explanation of the recession of 1969–1971, using whatever concepts of this chapter you think are appropriate.

6. Price inflation has a bad reputation. Do you think that is warranted, or is it simply another old-fashioned worry?

7. Why is the aggregate demand-pull explanation of inflation different from the explanation of price increases in particular markets?

8. What is the meaning of effective validation of sellers inflation?

Concepts for review

- Dynamic analysis
- Exogenous and endogenous theories
- Floors and ceilings to cumulative movements
- Propagating mechanisms
- Multiplier-accelerator interactions
- Demand-pull inflation
- Sellers inflation
- Phillips curve

18

Policies for full employment and price stability

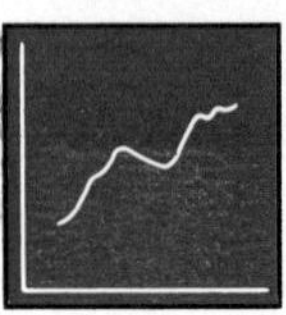

There are people who believe we are doomed to a future of perpetual boom and bust and, like Sisyphus, will always be pushing the heavy stone of the GNP up a hill only to have it roll back down again. There are other people who believe that the economic problems of scarcity and stability have been solved and we are about ready to enter a paradise of plenty if only we can fix up one or two nagging little problems, such as achieving world peace and universal brotherhood.

There are also people who believe that excessive attention is given to the macroeconomic problems of recession and inflation. They believe that the most pressing problems are at the microeconomic level—poverty, urban blight, depressed rural areas, economic racial inequities. The important point to remember in this respect is that while prosperity on a macroeconomic level will not itself solve all our problems it will ameliorate many of the most difficult ones. We have learned that we cannot rely on the private market economy to maintain high levels of employment and income. We have also learned that we cannot solve the aggregate problems of recession and inflation at the microeconomic level.

The design of policy to deal with these macroeconomic issues is one of the most critical areas of public economic decision making. This was recognized in the Employment Act of 1946 whose Declaration of Policy states:

> It is the continuing policy and responsibility of the Federal Government to use all practicable means consistent with its needs and obligations and other essential considerations of national policy . . . to coordinate and utilize all its plans, functions

and resources for the purpose of creating and maintaining . . . conditions under which there will be afforded useful employment for those able, willing, and seeking to work and to promote maximum employment, production and purchasing power.

A political realist recognizes that such ringing words may be interpreted in a variety of ways. Yet this kind of public commitment was never before expressed, and its statement imposed an obligation to which every administration since has given more than lip service.

The act also created the Council of Economic Advisers to the President and stated the responsibility of the President to submit an annual Economic Report to the Congress. With the passage of this act, macroeconomic policy moved out of the wings of the academic classroom and onto the main stage of government decision making and national action. Earlier chapters have provided enough expertise to let us appreciate the subtleties of the performance.

Public economic policies for full employment without inflation

It would be a mistake to believe that the United States has avoided severe depressions in the last twenty years through the efforts of a group of alert economists in high places who have been "fine tuning" the economy by adjusting this or that knob of fiscal or monetary policy. It is not even true that every adjustment has been of just the right amount. Yet there can be no doubt that the 1960s were different from the 1950s. Severe setbacks were avoided. Substantial growth was achieved. That was interrupted by the inflation of the late 1960s which had its origins in the escalation of expenditures on the Vietnam War without offsetting tax increases. But the New Economics cannot be blamed for that. The inflation was a stubborn one and the attempt to control it brought on the recession of 1969–1970. Even after recovery had started in 1971, inflation continued and drastic measures were taken to control it. Everything has not been for the best in this best of all possible worlds. There have been money crunches and liquidity crises, high unemployment, and slow growth. These have engendered continuing debate over the details of economic policy and whether it could have been wiser and more effective. To understand the debate, we must appreciate the strengths and limitations of the public policy tools available.

Economic policy instruments can usefully be distinguished as either automatic or discretionary, depending on whether they act without or with some new conscious decision on the part of a policy maker. We shall start with the automatic or "built-in" stabilizers. These have become much more important in the last thirty years than they were before and probably should be given much of the credit for the relative stability of the economy.

Automatic expenditure stabilizers

Automatic changes in transfer payments: Unemployment compensation, social security, and welfare payments. Unemployment compensation payments automatically increase whenever there is a slowdown in economic activity. They prevent disposable income and, therefore, consumption expenditures and effective demand from falling as rapidly as would otherwise happen when NNP falls. In periods of economic boom, they automatically tend to contract and, in this way, contribute to stabilization.

Social security (Old-age and Survivors Insurance) payments can and do vary automatically to make up some of the loss in income when unemployment increases. Not every person eligible for old-age or survivors benefits under the law actually elects to draw those benefits. When economic activity is high and jobs are relatively plentiful, many elderly people continue to work. If a slowdown causes them to lose their jobs, however, they can and do draw old-age or survivors benefits, which helps maintain their disposable income and consumption expenditures.

The same can be said about welfare payments. When unemployment increases, more people become eligible for these payments, and more eligible people apply for them, which again tends to maintain disposable income and expenditures. There is no conflict in these programs between their humanitarian and macroeconomic stabilization objectives.

Automatic changes in tax revenues. The federal tax system, with major reliance on personal and corporate income taxes, is a progressive one on the whole and tends to be stabilizing. That is, the proportion of income paid by individuals increases with their income. As overall economic activity and income levels rise, there is a general push into higher income brackets with higher tax rates. The result is that disposable income rises less rapidly than pretax income. That tends to make effective demand rise less rapidly than otherwise. It works the other way, as well. When there is a recession and incomes fall, people drop into lower tax brackets. Disposable income falls less rapidly than pretax income, so personal expenditures tend to be stabilized.

The state and local tax systems, which rely mainly on sales and property taxes, are much less stabilizing in their macroeconomic effects. The sales tax may go up and down somewhat less than disposable income, particularly if basic items such as food, clothing, and medicine are exempted. The property tax, however, is much more rigid. Assessments change infrequently, and tax levies do not fall by much, if at all, even when activity is slowing down.

Automatic changes in government subsidies. Industrial subsidy programs, the most important of which are in agriculture, operate to maintain income in the industries to which they are directed.

When prices fall, government expenditures help maintain farm production and absorb surpluses. This indirectly helps to sustain production and employment in other industries.

Changes in personal and corporate saving. Business saving rates vary with the level of national output so as to make changes in disposable income less than changes in national income. Many corporations, for example, have a policy of regular dividend payments to which they adhere even when their production falls. That helps stabilize the income of the stockholders.[1]

When individuals and families try to maintain their living standards in the face of falling income, their personal saving rates fall. When they are slow to adjust their consumption to rising income, saving rates rise. This type of behavior makes personal consumption expenditures vary less than disposable income and thus also tends to stabilize the overall levels of economic activity.

Advantages and disadvantages of automatic stabilizers

The great advantage of automatic stabilizers is that they *are* automatic and begin to operate without need for executive decisions or legislative action. They have one important limitation and one major disadvantage. First of all, they are not powerful enough to smooth out all the bumps. When the economy moves strongly in one direction or another, the automatic stabilizers slow down the movement but are not able to completely turn it around.

The major disadvantage is that there is no guarantee that the automatic stabilization will tend to occur at levels reasonably close to full employment. The First Macro Model of an economy without any government spending or taxing demonstrated that we could not count on the private sector to move the system to full employment. When government spending and taxing were added in the Second Macro Model, we reasoned that it was *possible* to use government fiscal policy to move the economy toward full employment. We did not conclude and should not have left with the impression that *any* set of taxes and expenditure programs necessarily *would* move the system to full employment.

One difficulty in working out the effects of a specific set of expenditure programs and tax rates is that their net impact on the economy is different at different levels of income. This point has not won acceptance easily. But the following phenomenon repeated several times has finally convinced most people: The President's budget specialists make their forecasts of government expenditures and tax receipts and project a government deficit. The economy grows more rapidly than expected; tax collections are also higher and the deficit smaller than expected. Or the economy grows less rapidly than forecast and the deficit is larger than projected.

[1] It is no criticism to say that the corporations are not being altruistic in doing this. A good, steady dividend will help make it possible for corporations to sell stock and finance themselves on more favorable terms in the future than would otherwise be the case.

A deficit projected at one level of national income can turn into a surplus at a higher level of income because of the revenue-generating capacity of our progressive federal tax structure. This aspect of automatic stabilization was called *fiscal drag* when first pointed out in Chapter 12. The tax system creates a resistance to changes in income up or down. Unless they are consciously offset, the net leakages of effective demand from the circular flow of income due to existing government fiscal programs become larger as income grows (or net injections become smaller) and thus hold back overall economic growth.

This is, by the way, a good example of new problems being created by the means chosen to resolve another set of problems. A progressive tax system was created on grounds of equity and, in the process, a tendency to automatic stabilization was created. But that also created a source of fiscal drag which can, if not compensated for, hold back the economy as a whole. This helps explain why automatic fiscal stabilization will, in general, not be fully satisfactory in maintaining full employment and why some amount of fine tuning is likely to be necessary.

Discretionary fiscal policies

A discretionary policy is one whose origin or implementation requires new decisions by individuals in positions of power and responsibility. In response to a presidential initiative, or on its own, Congress may pass a new tax law or expenditure program. The President has some optional powers to counteract recessions or inflations by his control of the timing of some expenditures. Three types of programs fall within the realm of discretionary countercyclical fiscal policy: changes in transfer expenditures; changes in expenditures for goods and services; and changes in the types and rates of taxes.

Changes in transfer expenditures. Present unemployment compensation laws limit the number of weeks during which an unemployed person can receive payments. When the incidence and average length of unemployment rise, this time limit is often surpassed. During the recession of 1958 the federal government made it possible for state governments to extend the period during which payments were made. This took a special legislative act by the Congress. It is an example of the discretion which has been and can be exercised in macroeconomic policy to achieve aggregate goals and microeconomic goals as well. The extension of unemployment compensation eligibility certainly reduces the burden of recession on low-income groups.

Congress has also made bonus payments to veterans during depressions or has accelerated refunds on their life insurance policies. It has increased farm price-and-income support payments. There is a good deal of inertia in such programs—once they are begun, they tend to become more or less permanent—but in principle they can be cut back during relatively prosperous periods.

Discretionary extension or retrenchment of unemployment insurance, depending on the amount of unemployment and slack in the economy, would add a desirable flexibility to such programs. Other kinds of welfare and transfer payments, however, are and ought to be independent of the overall level of economic activity. *The basic objectives of social insurance programs would be compromised if they were reduced or extended as part of countercyclical fiscal policy.*

Changes in expenditures for goods and services. Public works programs in which men are hired to work on construction projects were one of the earliest forms of discretionary policy. The government may act directly by organizing a project and hiring workers, or it may act indirectly by giving contracts to private firms. In theory, public works programs have great appeal, as they provide a means of using otherwise idle resources and manpower to create needed facilities. The practice has been less inspiring than the principle, however.

Efficient use of manpower and resources requires careful planning and able management. When planning is inadequate—and not many projects have been adequately worked out and blueprinted—and when emergency pressures prevent careful management, public works programs do not look so good. The Work Projects Administration (WPA) of the 1930s was charged with paying men for leaf-raking, ditchdigging and filling, and other make-work jobs. While these charges were much overstated, the WPA undoubtedly had many organizational problems.

Another major drawback to using public works programs to fight a recession is the delay entailed in getting them under way. After the initial decision to start a project, more than a year may pass before the actual employment of any substantial number of men. It takes time to make plans, issue contracts, and acquire land. It also takes some time before that to recognize a recession and additional time to make a decision to resort to public works. If the recession turns out to be a relatively short one, the impact of the public works programs might come after recovery is already well under way and the additional stimulation unnecessary.

Preparation and continual updating of a "shelf of blueprints" of important projects is authorized by law and will cut down the delays, but they cannot be eliminated entirely. So as a discretionary tool of countercyclical fiscal policy, public works programs are relatively inflexible. They are most useful during prolonged recessions. In any case, the basic justification for public works is public demand for the projects and their services. Schools, hospitals, slum clearance and public housing, highways and bridges are desired in themselves. Countercyclical policy requirements should not be the controlling factor in the supply of public services.

Many types of spending programs can be accelerated or

delayed to counteract the effects of deficient or excessive aggregate effective demand. In the early 1960s one justification advanced for the space program was that it would strengthen aggregate effective demand. The same argument, that spending generates employment, has been made for nearly every program put forward.

As an accusation against the United States economy, some groups have argued that our prosperity depends on government military expenditures, which in turn lead to military adventures. Without judging the conclusion, we can evaluate the first part of the statement. No doubt, government military expenditures generate income for the producers of military goods and have further multiplier effects. The real question is whether there are other ways in which income can be generated, and the answer is certainly Yes. Have the other ways been used? Many times; there was a high level of activity before the Vietnam War escalation. The Korean War came at the end of a recession, but the recovery had started before the war began. On the other hand, it was certainly the expenditures of World War II which brought recovery from the Great Depression.

Many, many worthwhile public projects could be undertaken at home and abroad. There are many unsatisfied public and private demands. *The United States economy need not depend on military spending to employ men and resources*.

Changes in taxes. Federal tax laws, according to the United States Constitution, must originate in the House of Representatives. The President can propose, however, and the entire Congress must agree. In principle, this can all be done relatively quickly, and tax changes can within a short time increase or reduce disposable income or corporate after-tax income and stimulate or restrain effective demand.

Tax changes can also be made selectively. Investment can be encouraged by giving tax credits to businesses that undertake new investment. Private consumption can be encouraged or restrained through income tax changes that affect disposable income.

In practice, public disagreement and congressional debate over tax policy can consume as much time as setting up public works projects. Disagreements about tax changes may stem from different diagnoses of the economic situation and what to do about it. Or the disagreements may have their origin in other political issues, so that tax policy becomes only one of several elements in a political settlement. In 1967 President Lyndon Johnson proposed a 10 percent surtax on income taxes to reduce inflationary pressures. At first, many members of Congress doubted that the situation called for deflation. Opposition to the Johnson administration's spending programs may have been equally important in blocking the tax increase. The bill was finally passed in May, 1968, after the President agreed to reduce government expenditures. By that time, the inflationary pressures had become well established. In the late summer of 1971, President Nixon proposed reductions in personal income taxes, an automobile excise tax, and investment tax credits in order to speed the slow recovery from the recession of 1969–1970.

The influential Committee on Economic Development, a private nonprofit group, has proposed that Congress give the President limited power to adjust personal income tax rates. This would represent the transference of Congressional discretion to the President and would almost certainly reduce the reaction time required for changes in tax policy.

Automatic versus discretionary monetary policy: Rules versus authorities

Chapter 16 describes the tools of monetary policy and how they can be used by the Federal Reserve to lean against the wind. Having reviewed the instruments of fiscal policy, we can now better appreciate the advantages and limitations of monetary policy. It *is* discretionary and can be implemented quickly by the Board of Governors of the Federal Reserve. By means of specific controls on particular kinds of credit, monetary policy can be used selectively to encourage or discourage particular kinds of spending. Overall monetary stringency or looseness affects mainly that type of investment spending which relies heavily on borrowed funds.

The critics of the use of monetary policy by the Federal Reserve Board of Governors do not doubt that it has an impact. They "only" doubt whether the Board of Governors or anyone else is wise enough or farseeing enough to use monetary policy consistently for the public benefit. They argue, for example, that in 1966, in trying to cool off the economy when expenditures on the Vietnam War were increasing sharply without corresponding increases in taxes, the Board of Governors forced an almost disastrous credit crunch.

But in 1967 and 1968, the Board of Governors allowed the money supply to expand at a 7.6 percent annual rate. The Board expected that fiscal policy would restrain the economy and therefore thought that monetary policy could be relaxed. The tax surtax bill passed in 1968 did not work as quickly as had been expected to reduce effective demand, and the expansion in credit facilitated by the Federal Reserve added fuel to the inflationary fires. Not until the very end of 1968 did the Board of Governors turn monetary policy around and begin to tighten credit in such a way as to restrict effective demand. The new year brought another period of extraordinary monetary stringency, and some people attribute this to the Fed's "overreaction." *Critics of the Fed cite the 1968–1969 decisions as evidence that no man, conservative, liberal, or what, can always be trusted to use monetary policy wisely.* It is like fighting a fire in a high wind. You not only need a fire hose, but you need to know how to use it.

The monetarist criticism of Federal Reserve discretionary

policy has been lead by Prof. Milton Friedman. He and other critics have proposed a rule to replace the discretionary actions of authorities. *The monetarist rule is: Increase the money supply automatically and steadily by 3 percent per year.* That will make possible a steady 3 percent rate of growth of output without price inflation.

The monetarists do not argue that the rule will necessarily bring the millennium, only that, with our limited knowledge, it is the best we can do. The rule represents a passive approach to monetary policy. Its critics – the new economists – feel that on some occasions an active policy can offset or shorten economic declines or take some of the steam out of an overheated economy. The monetarists argue that the dangers of misuse are so great that an active, discretionary policy should be avoided.

Behind the monetarist argument lurks the view that the economy has built-in tendencies to stabilize itself with reasonably full employment. Of course there are minor ups and downs and sometimes major ones. But the latter, according to the monetarists, have often been the result of enthusiastic but misguided monetary policy.

Many economists would agree with Professor Friedman's identification of the symptoms of the Fed's mistakes – even some of the Fed's economists themselves. Yet the remedy he prescribes is embroiled in controversy.

There is relatively little disagreement about the effect of monetary policy. But, the new economists ask, should we forgo using such a powerful tool when the situation cries out for remedial action? Yes, says Friedman, because we do not know how to act wisely. No, say his opponents. Though we are not superhuman and have no crystal balls, there are occasions when the correct monetary remedy is so clear that it would be a great mistake not to act. Forecasting is an imperfect art, to be sure, but it is not completely perverse. We can exercise foresight, and it would be foolish to let the opportunities to be constructive slip by.

While economists and bankers have never voted on the subject, it is doubtful that Professor Friedman's prescription would come close to obtaining a majority. That in itself does not mean he is wrong, but only that some caution is advised before the medicine is swallowed, as a lot of "doctors" are standing around shaking their heads.

Price and incomes policy

The dilemma of price stability versus unemployment illustrated by the Phillips curve was posed in Chapter 17. Attempts to deal directly with this problem have come to be known as *incomes policy.* The basic, underlying question relates to overall income distribution: Who is going to get how big a slice of the income pie? In effect, when workers demand wage increases, they are trying to hold on to their present share or get a larger share. When management raises output prices and attempts to hold wages and other costs down, it is trying to maintain or increase profits. Both management and unions in any firm and industry will want higher *relative* prices for their industry so that both higher wages and profits will be possible. Some degree of market power is necessary for their success. *Not everyone can have more, and the competition of all against all results in generally higher prices and in hardship for the groups whose incomes are fixed.*

In the 1960s, the Council of Economic Advisers formulated certain wage and price guideposts to help prevent inflationary wage-price spirals:

> The general guide for noninflationary wage behavior is that the rate of increase in wage rates (including fringe benefits) in each industry be equal to the trend rate of overall productivity increase. General acceptance of this guide would maintain stability of labor cost per unit of output for the economy as a whole—though not of course for individual industries.
>
> The general guide for noninflationary price behavior calls for price reduction if the industry's rate of productivity increase exceeds the overall rate—for this would mean declining unit labor costs; it calls for an appropriate increase in price if the opposite relationship prevails; and it calls for stable prices if the two rates of productivity increase are equal.[2]

The Council also recommended that the general guideposts be modified to permit larger wage and price increases in growing industries which needed to attract more labor and capital. Likewise, for declining industries, it recommended lower than average wage and price increases.

These recommendations did not have the force of law, but they did command widespread support when backed by President Kennedy in 1962. They justified the extraordinary efforts of Presidents Kennedy and Johnson to use the prestige of their office to prevent "excessive" wage and price increases. There is no way to measure the extent to which guidelines and executive pressure actually did hold down price increases during the next six years before the attempts were more or less abandoned after 1967. Yet *there is general agreement that in their early years the guideposts had a restraining effect.* The actual wage-price increases of the mid-1960s were less than one might have predicted. At that time no large business or union wanted to risk the public opprobrium of opposing a policy of restraint that the President declared to be in the public interest.

Voluntary restraints could not hold out against the growing demands for wage and price readjustment that, beginning in 1965, accompanied the price pressures generated by increased federal expenditures on the Vietnam War. "Jawboning" by the President

[2] *The Economic Report of the President,* January, 1962, p. 189.

and his close advisers stopped as it became apparent that it could not be successful. There was no desire to risk presidential prestige on the lost cause of price control.

As long as inflation is climbing at a substantial rate, there are pressures to use direct methods to stop it. On taking office, however, President Nixon declared that he would neither ask Congress to pass laws to control prices and wages nor try to use the prestige of his office, as previous presidents had, to restrain price and wage increases. This position was modified only slightly in early 1970 when a National Commission on Productivity was created to recommend measures to increase productivity and hold down prices. The Council of Economic Advisers was also charged with identifying inflationary price and wage increases in *Inflation Alerts.* These measures had no discernible effect.

In the summer of 1971, however, after a period of rapid price and wage increases, the President used his emergency powers to impose a ninety-day freeze on most wages and prices. This Phase I of the new attack on inflation was followed by Phase II in which price and wage controls were administered by special presidential commissions. New maximum guidelines of 2½ percent for prices and 5½ percent for wages were created to apply to the largest businesses and unions, with the pressures of competition counted on to force smaller firms and unions to conform.

The Phase I and Phase II controls represent a new departure in peacetime economic policy in the United States. They have attracted wide support as a necessary extension of price and incomes policy. They have also been bitterly attacked, especially by union leadership, as arbitrary and capricious extensions of government power. There have been predictions that Phase I and Phase II mean that the United States is backing into a system of widespread governmental controls over the economy. The best prediction, however, is that the country is still not finished with experimentation with the use of price and incomes policy to control inflation.

Constraints on stabilization policy

To recapitulate, no monetary or fiscal policy tool available used by itself will maintain both full employment *and* price stability. Further, there is intense disagreement about the use of direct controls. Besides these basic limitiations on policy formulation, there are also specific constraints on the use of fiscal and monetary policy. We shall now examine these.

The problems of forecasting levels of economic activity

It always takes some time for the effects of a stabilization policy to move through the economy. Unlike tuning a radio, the results are not immediately obvious in the quality of the reception. In making economic policy, we fiddle with the dials without knowing exactly what economic conditions are while we are making the adjustments. We do not even know for several months more what the effects will be. Whatever we may decide to do "today," we decide in expectation of what will happen "tomorrow." Actually some policy instruments have a more immediate effect than others, but there are always lags. *It is always necessary to forecast the future in order to decide what kind of policy effect will be desirable three months or six months or a year from now.*

Economists are no more clairvoyant than other people. When we talk about forecasting the future, we really mean "making guesses" about what is going to happen. Our inability to make absolutely accurate forecasts is a major limitation on policy making.

What is necessary to make good forecasts? Three things:

1. A theory that identifies the fundamental relationships in the economy and their interaction

2. Empirical estimates of the technical and behavioral relationships, such as the propensity to consume and the tax schedules

3. Estimates of exogenous conditions that impinge on these relationships, such as the government budget and changes in bank reserves

Forecasts can go wrong when any one of these elements is unsatisfactory. In particular, we should not assume that a bad forecast means a bad theory, since the error may be in item 2 or 3. Likewise a good forecast does not necessarily mean a good theory. Chance always plays a role in forecasts, and not one that can be predicted.

How close has the economics profession come to satisfying the three requirements for successful forecasting? Today's theory is a great improvement on that which existed, say, twenty-five years ago, but after the big breakthroughs that followed the "Keynesian revolution," progress has been slower. The theory is pretty good at providing explanations of the major trends in the economy, but it is far from perfect or complete, and occasionally the forecasts based on it have been badly off target. That has stimulated efforts to reformulate and refine the theory, and the theory-making process goes on and on. For example, many economists forecast a major recession at the end of World War II. The forecasts proved wrong. Their chief mistake was in the underestimate of consumption. As a result, there has been a great effort to refine the theory of consumer expenditures. A more recent example: In 1968, most forecasts predicted that the tax increase in the middle of the year would dampen aggregate spending enough to control inflation. Again the major mistake was in the estimate of consumption expenditures. There is a lesson in humility here for economists, but not a reason to give up. The stakes are too large to simply walk away from the game. We might be able to affect its outcome.

There is some evidence that part of the forecasting error is due to inadequate procedures for item 2: giving numerical content to the theory. This possibility has stimulated a great deal of work by econometricians, economists who use statistical techniques to measure economic relationships. Today, econometrics is an active research frontier, and large models requiring high-speed computers for their manipulation have been created and are being tested.

Element 3 in the development of forecasts, the specification of exogenous conditions — for example, government expenditures — may appear to be easy, but it is not. When government spending changes rapidly, as it did during 1965 and 1966 in the escalation of the Vietnam War, the forecasts can be left far behind.

Though sophisticated forecasting techniques are being developed, much still depends on the experience and judgment of the forecasters themselves. Forecasting is a continuous, not just a once or twice a year, process. Estimates must be revised as new information becomes available. There is a "market" in forecasts, also, as private and government economists, bankers, and businessmen meet in formal conferences and talk informally on the telephone to exchange views. Moreover, forecasters do a lot of figuring on the backs of envelopes, using some rough rules of thumb.

One of the useful rules is known as Okun's law — after Arthur Okun, now at the Brookings Institution and Chairman of President Johnson's Council of Economic Advisers in 1967 and 1968. This rule says that there is a "gearing" between unemployment and potential GNP: For every 1 percent *increase* in unemployment *above* the 4 percent rate, there is a 3.2 percent *decrease* in actual GNP *below* the potential full employment GNP.[3]

Economists also carry around with them some rough estimates of the multipliers for government expenditures or private investment and for tax changes. These are often taken to be around 3 and 2, respectively. But since only about two-thirds of the multiplier effects occur within a year, the corresponding short-term multipliers are closer to 2 and 1.5.

Practical forecasters watch carefully for the results of the surveys of business investment intentions described in Chapter 10. They follow the government budget discussions. They read the weekly descriptions of banking conditions and the speeches of members of the Federal Reserve Board of Governors to find out what the Fed is doing and what it may plan to do. With a modest amount of effort — and a good deal of fun — one can keep up to date on the state of the economy and on expected changes. There is less action than in most sports, but as you know, the stakes are higher.

[3] In the form of an equation Okun's law is: Full employment GNP = actual GNP $[1 + 0.032\ (U - 4)]$, where U is the unemployment rate.

In spite of all the serious effort that goes into forecasting, it still amounts to making a guess about the future, with many ways to be wrong. Forecasting errors will always present major barriers to the formulation of wise stabilization policies.

International balance-of-payments difficulties

For international trade purposes, it is desirable for a country to have stocks of gold. Gold is a means of making international payments, since all countries will accept it. *Although most international payments are made on a current basis from current earnings, gold reserves are "money in the bank."* They can be drawn on when current earnings are insufficient to cover current payments requirements.

As we pointed out in Chapter 12, the level of imports depends in part on the level of domestic income and on domestic prices. Thus, the demand for an international means of payment for imports – of which gold is one type – also depends on the levels of income and prices. *If the need to conserve gold seems to be quite urgent, then that in itself may become a reason to reduce effective demand and curb inflationary price pressures.*

From 1958 to 1970, the United States lost $13 billion in gold. Some people regarded this loss as dangerous: They thought that it represented a decline in backing for the money supply and that it was forcing the country close to the lower limit of the gold cover required by Congress. This latter aspect of the problem was eliminated in 1968 when Congress abolished the gold cover requirements, as explained in Chapter 15. In 1971, however, after an increase in the rate of outflow of gold, the United States stopped redeeming its dollars in gold, even those held by foreign central banks. This was part of a movement toward a change in the relative value of the dollar with respect to other currencies.

The international demand for means of payment, including gold, is also affected by the relative interest rates in different countries. A large oil corporation, for example, may shift some of its cash deposits from United States banks if the interest rate in Zurich is 1/2 percent higher. Even 1/2 percent on, say, $10 million is not to be sneezed at. When such a shift takes place, it may ultimately lead to a shift in gold holdings. The Fed must, therefore, take international interest rate differentials into account in determining its domestic monetary policy.

Government debt

Hardly any aspect of government operations is so fascinating as the public debt, partly because of its sheer size and partly because of the controversies that rage around it. Any discussion of the use of monetary and fiscal policy for stabilization sooner rather than later runs into the question, What about the government debt?

Figure 18-1

FEDERAL AND STATE AND LOCAL DEBT, 1929–1969 (BILLIONS OF DOLLARS)

By present standards the federal debt was small in the 1930s. It grew rapidly during World War II. After a postwar decline, its growth continued, with a few interruptions. State and local debt declined slightly during World War II. The postwar increase reflects expenditures postponed during the war and a growing demand for services. (Source: Economic Report of the President, *1971.)*

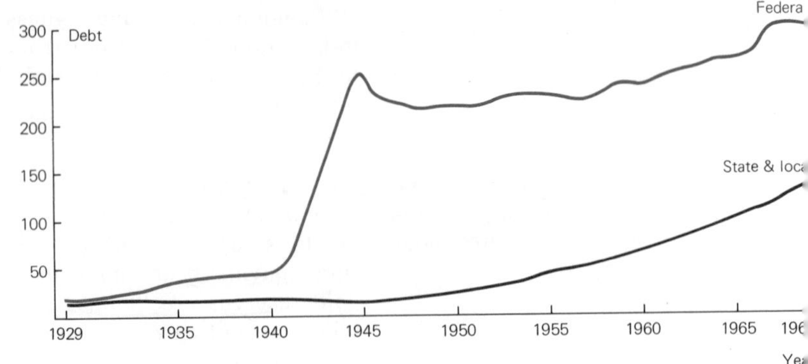

First the facts: Figure 18-1 presents a history of the public debt over the last forty years. The red line is the debt of the federal government. It is now close to $300 billion, which is a large sum by any standards. Notice that much of it, $196 billion, was accumulated from 1941 to 1945, during World War II. But the rate of increase from 1932 to 1941 was rapid; it more than doubled in those nine years. During the next five years, which covered the World War II period, the debt increased fivefold. After the war, there was a brief decline, and since then, the rate of growth has been relatively slow.

The debt of state and local governments, also shown in Figure 18-1, was $132 billion in 1969. It has been growing more rapidly than the federal debt since World War II, but is still only about 30 percent of the latter.

To keep everything in perspective, Figure 18-2 shows total private debt. Private debt is more than four times the federal debt and almost ten times that of state and local governments. Its growth rate, too, has been accelerating since the end of World War II. The comparison of public and private debt should not be accepted uncritically, however, as we shall see.

Invalid analogies and false burdens. Many people hotly disapprove of public debt. Since their hostility is often based on an implicit or explicit analogy with private debt, especially individual debt, it is useful to examine the analogy.

Individuals have limited lifetimes. Therefore, no creditor will lend to an individual for an unlimited period. Permanent and increasing debt for an individual means his eventual bankruptcy and inevitable losses by other individuals who are his creditors. A loan to an individual is based on his assets and on his ability to earn income. Suppose the individual does not use the loan to purchase or produce income-earning assets, and/or has no other means of repaying his debt. Then some part of the loan must be eventually defaulted, with resulting losses for his creditor. Perma-

Figure 18-2

PRIVATE DEBT, 1929–1969 (BILLIONS OF DOLLARS)

Private debt includes corporate and noncorporate debt, farm debt, and nonfarm mortgage credit and consumer credit. Corporate debt is about 55% of the total; mortgage credit, 24%; and consumer credit, 10%. Private debt has a faster growth rate than government debt. (Source: Economic Report of the President, *1971.)*

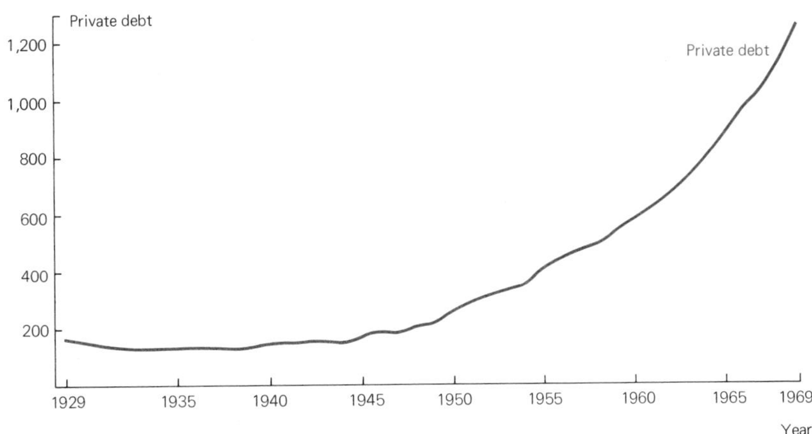

nent or unpaid individual debt inevitably means a permanent shifting of purchasing power from one person to another. Similarly, interest payments on individual debt imply such a shift.

How do these characteristics of private individual debt compare with public debt? Governments are immortal; that is, they do *not* have finite and limited lifetimes. The government debt, which is the collective debt *of* all members of the national community, is a debt *to* all members of the community who hold government bonds and notes. So long as the debt is an internal one, and not owed to foreigners, it is a debt of ourselves to ourselves. As we shall see, that does not mean the debt does not create problems, but they are different ones than commonly supposed. Moreover, governments, though they do not earn income or always buy tangible assets when the debt is created, do have the power to tax. *So long as the government enjoys the confidence and support of its citizens it can maintain its internal debt.* If it cannot, the inability to service the debt is a symptom of a deeper disaffection with the government.

A persistent critic might respond: Debt can be shifted—from one generation to another. But is this so? *As long as the debt is held internally, there is no way of transferring resources from the future to the present,* and we all agree it is resources that count. To be sure, we can make future generations less well off than they might otherwise be if we have such a high rate of consumption that the nation's capital stock is not replaced as it wears out. That—or the reverse, which is accumulation of capital stock via investment—can happen quite independently of changes, up or down, in the public debt.

As noted earlier, most of our federal debt was accumulated during World War II as we borrowed rather than taxed to pay for the war. Suppose we had taxed? Would there have been any more or fewer resources available now? Did deficit financing permit a higher level of consumption and investment for the war generation? If so, where did the extra resources come from? It is hard to support the simple argument that deficit financing leads to an intergenerational transfer of resources. There is, however, a related argument that has more substance.

True burdens. Though most of the arguments about the burden of the debt are without merit, some deserve serious consideration. *First,* an *external* debt is a burden, and the analogy to individual debt is appropriate. If the government bonds of country A are held in country B, then country A will have to transfer resources abroad to pay off the interest and principal. One generation can impose on a later generation or on itself in this way. Occasionally, after a revolution or coup, the new group in power will refuse to accept the inherited burden and will repudiate the foreign debt.

Second, even an internal debt requires some redistribution of income. A lot of people own a few government bonds, but only a comparatively few people own a lot of bonds, so ownership is relatively concentrated. Therefore, when taxes are collected on a general basis and used to make interest payments, some income redistribution inevitably takes place.

Third, a large public debt may well result in lowered incentives to work and to make somewhat risky investments. The taxes used to raise funds to make interest payments on the debt can distort individual incentives even when the individual receives back in interest what he pays in taxes. The distortion may be in the direction of less work and investment if each person acts as if his after-tax income is less of an inducement because it is lower. On the other hand, the distortion may be in the direction of more work if each person tries harder to reach a particular after-tax income objective.

Fourth, even though an internally held debt is "owed to ourselves," and not a *net* asset for the entire community, individual bondholders may consider their bonds a net asset and not balance against it the higher taxes they must bear in order to pay the interest charges. As a result, they may feel wealthier and may consume more and save less. This will restrict capital formation and retard growth if there is full employment and if investment is constrained by saving.

Fifth, the debt, its interest payments, and its management have at times been a constraint on monetary policy. From the end of World War II until 1951, the Treasury called on the Federal Reserve to support bond prices and keep interest rates at the low wartime levels in order to facilitate debt-refunding operations and reduce the debt interest charges in the federal budget. On March 4, 1951, the Treasury and the Board of Governors reached their famous Accord, which released the Federal Reserve from this obligation, provided for fluctuating short- and long-term interest rates, and freed the Fed to exercise an activist monetary policy.

In retrospect, the constraints on monetary policy imposed by the debt may not have been as necessary as the Treasury and the Fed believed prior to the Accord, but hindsight is nearly always better than foresight.

The real burdens of public debt are difficult to evaluate and weigh. It should not be thought, however, that the public debt involves only burdens.

Benefits. An externally held debt is not neccessarily bad. The governments of many countries, particularly in the less-developed areas, borrow abroad to obtain capital equipment and other foreign resources for investment. The state governments in the United States also borrowed externally on a large scale in the mid-nineteenth century. Here, the analogy to private business is valid: *Foreign borrowing by government is warranted when the loans have a productivity over and above the real cost of the interest payments and thus lead to economic growth that would not otherwise be possible.*

This argument illustrates the general point that evaluation of the net burdens or benefits of the debt requires an appreciation of the reasons behind its creation. Critics of the public debt sometimes claim that deficit financing of public expenditures is not an effective weapon against depression and unemployment. They point to the 1930s and say that deficit spending did not work then and that it was only the World War II expenditures which brought prosperity. Careful examination has shown this not to be wholly true. The deficits did generate income, just as modern multiplier theory would have predicted. They did not bring about a complete recovery because the deficits were relatively small.[4] The deficits of the 1960s also had the effects anticipated by our national income theory. This is true of both the tax reduction of 1964, which was "managed," and the Vietnam budget increases in 1965, which were "unmanaged."

We remarked above that a public debt, because it may make people feel wealthier, may stimulate consumption. That is a disadvantage for a full employment economy that is trying to mobilize savings for growth. It is an advantage in a slack period when effective demand needs to be sustained.

The debt serves other functions as well. Government bonds provide a virtually riskless way for widows and children to secure a future income with their inheritance. The bonds may encourage saving because of their low risk, and may thus make more resources available for investment. Finally, in the post-Accord period, the debt—held widely by banks, businesses, and individuals and with transferable instruments traded in an active market—has provided a powerful and flexible tool of monetary management. Whether one thinks that a powerful and flexible tool

[4] E. C. Brown, "Fiscal Policy in the Thirties: A Reappraisal," *American Economic Review*, vol. 46, pp. 857-879, December, 1956.

Table 18-1

FEDERAL DEBT AND NATIONAL INCOME (BILLIONS OF DOLLARS)

Year	Federal debt	Net interest charges on federal debt	National income	Federal debt*	Interest charges*
1930	$ 16.5	$ 0.38	$ 75.4	0.22	0.005
1940	44.8	0.72	81.1	0.55	0.008
1950	217.4	4.40	241.1	0.90	0.018
1960	239.8	7.00	414.5	0.58	0.017
1970	298.1	14.00	801.0†	0.37	0.017

*As percentage of national income.
†Preliminary.
Source: U.S. Department of Commerce, Office of Business Economics and Office of Management and Budget.

of money management is a benefit or a burden depends partly on whether one prefers authorities or rules, as argued in Chapter 16.

One way of assessing the significance of the debt and its interest charges is to compare it with the national income. Table 18-1 presents such a comparison for selected dates in the last forty years. As you can see, the federal debt and its interest charges have declined as a proportion of national income since 1950. This does not prove anything, of course. A confirmed debt-hater would point to the increase in the absolute magnitude and would say that any percentage is too high. But, at least, the numbers indicate that if the debt/income ratio, or the interest charges/income ratio, is worrisome, the worries should be decreasing.

Isn't there some fire blazing in all that smoke about the debt? If there is, it is probably this: *Those people who are worried about the debt are probably really worried about the level of government, particularly federal, expenditures.* They would be almost as unhappy — maybe more so — if taxes were high enough to balance the level of expenditures. So the essential issue is the one posed before for public economic policy: What obligations for providing services, maintaining welfare, and stabilizing the economy should the government assume? As we said, the answer depends on one's personal propensities.

An overview of stabilization problems and policy

A great deal has been learned about what determines aggregate levels of income and output and about the kinds of public policy that promote full employment and full use of capacity. These issues must be high on any economics agenda. *In fact, it might well be argued that the magnitude of public concern over other problems, such as pollution, economic racial discrimination, urban blight, pockets of poverty, is a function of our success in avoiding the devastating waste of recurring recessions.* The country cannot rest on its laurels, but we should appreciate its accomplishments in this regard.

It is well to reflect on this topic a moment, because there is some controversy about the significance of the accomplishments. It should never be claimed that macroeconomic prosperity is the be-all and end-all of economic policy. The evidence is clear that prosperity is not a universal economic panacea. More than that, prosperity itself creates some economic and social problems.

These facts, however, do not constitute an argument for unemployment and recession. Nor do they mean that we can stop trying to discover a public economic policy that can maintain high levels of employment and income. The personal and social costs of unemployment are not only large but fall most heavily on those already at the lower end of the economic scale. Recessions mean that people are living less well, not just in terms of having a year-older car or a year-older color TV. A recession means less nutritive diets; it means less medical care; it means that young people have to drop out of high school to scrounge for a job to help the family and that high school graduates have to give up a chance to go to college. These are facts of life, too, and warrant a constant concern with maintaining high employment and income. But these facts, in turn, do not justify ignoring the microeconomic and sectoral problems and the defects in the workings of the economy, which emerge most clearly in periods of prosperity.

The events of the recession of 1970 and 1971 are also a reminder that government economic actions can be the source of macroeconomic problems as well as a corrective. Opinions will differ as to whether the monetary and fiscal policies of 1970 and 1971 were the most effective which could have been designed to deal with the recession. But we would not have had the recession had there not been the prior inflation. That stemmed from the rapid increase in military expenditures in the late 1960s without accompanying tax increases. Moreover, the events of recent years suggest that we have not achieved the social consensus necessary for effective incomes policy. As in other fields, we have gained in scientific understanding; it is not clear that we have gained in wisdom in using that understanding.

Summary

Macroeconomic analysis helps us understand the use of public policy to achieve and maintain a high level of economic activity. Such an economic climate ameliorates many of the pressing problems of backward sectors, low income groups, and depressed cities and regions.

The economy has both automatic, or built-in, stabilizers and discretionary stabilizers. The former consist of relationships in the private and public sectors which tend to limit excessive movements in the economy. The latter require a conscious decision by a government authority.

Automatic stabilizers, like unemployment compensation, welfare and social security payments, and the progressive tax system, make disposable income more stable than earned income and, therefore, tend to stabilize consumer expenditures. Changes in personal and business saving have the same effect. When automatic stabilization via the tax system occurs below full employment levels of output and income, it then becomes fiscal drag.

Discretionary fiscal policies include changes in the overall level of taxes and transfers, which must be decided by Congress, and changes in government expenditures on goods and services, especially public works. They are powerful instruments, but entail an implementation lag.

In the debate over the use of monetary policy, the monetarist school of economic thought argues that the best thing the Federal Reserve can do is to follow a simple *rule* of holding the annual increase in money supply to a constant rate of about 3 percent. Reasoning via the quantity theory, this would be consistent with a constant 3 percent increase in the national income without price increases. Economists who believe in the power of monetary influences, but not in monetarist theory, argue that the monetary *authorities* should have more flexibility to use their discretion to offset the swings in the economy.

In the early 1960s, the President's Council of Economic Advisers formulated wage guideposts to restrain price increases by keeping wage increases consistent with the rate of labor productivity increases. These voluntary guidelines were influential in their early years, but lost power as they came to be increasingly violated. A price-wage freeze was imposed in 1971 in a direct attempt to control inflation.

Some of the limitations on the development of stabilization policies lie in the weakness of the policy tools and the conflicts of interest in their use. Another constraint is the difficulty of forecasting needed policy changes. Forecasting methods have become increasingly sophisticated and technical in their use of high-speed computers. But forecasting involves art as well as science, and forecasters still rely to some extent on approximative rules of thumb and a careful following of events.

The desire to maintain a sizable gold stock can also be a constraint on domestic fiscal and monetary policies. Gold is used in balancing international accounts, and without a substantial stock for this purpose, international trade and the acceptability of dollars abroad could be impeded.

The fact that fiscal policy may lead to deficits in the government budget and increases in the government debt is also thought by some to be an important constraint. For the most part, this view grows out of reasoning by means of invalid analogies that the debt is a burden on future generations or a danger to the stability of the country. As long as it is held domestically, the debt is more correctly seen as simply the result of a particular means of financing expenditure by selling bonds rather than taxing. There may be burdens in the form of the income redistribution effects of interest payments, since bond ownership is concentrated. There may also be some disincentive effects. By and large, however, concern about the public debt is a misconception of the essential issue. That issue is: What is the proper role of government in the economy?

Questions for discussion and review

1. Macroeconomic policy is usually thought of in terms of its effects on aggregate income and output. Describe the effects of aggregate expenditure policy designed to stimulate the economy as you observe them locally. Describe the effects of monetary policy to control inflation as they are observed locally.

2. How do automatic stabilizers work and what are their advantages and disadvantages?

3. If you had been the Chairman of the Council of Economic Advisers in 1969, what advice would you have given the President to deal with inflation?

4. If you were the Chairman of the Council of Economic Advisers now, what advice would you give the President?

5. In the 1930s there was a good deal of preoccupation with public works as a discretionary anti-inflation device. One hears relatively little about public works now. Why?

6. Do you agree with Professor Friedman that the Federal Reserve should stop trying to actively manage the money supply and settle for the 3 percent rule? Explain your answer.

7. Discuss the following statement: *No price and incomes policy has ever been successful for very long in a democratic environment, because the issues of income distribution pose essential conflicts of interest. Yet situations arise in which an incomes policy should be tried, even though we know it will not work permanently.*

8. What are the most important constraints on macroeconomic policy: ignorance. international economic relations, or conflicts of interest? Explain the content of each constraint and its significance.

Concepts for review

Automatic stabilizers
Discretionary fiscal policy
Rules versus authorities
Price and incomes policy
Wage and price guideposts
Economic forecasting
Okun's law
False burdens of the debt
True burdens of the debt

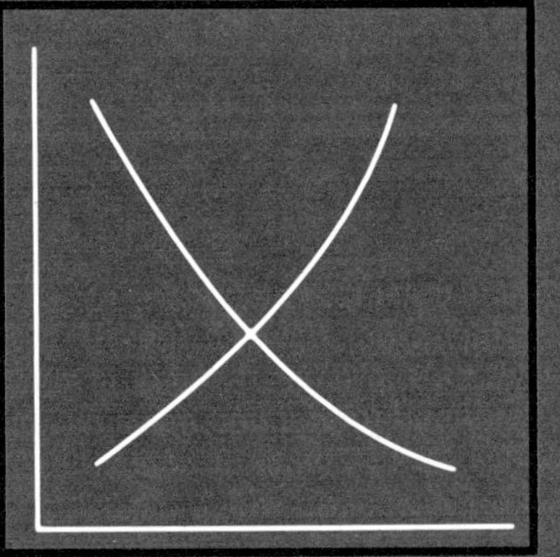

THREE

Microeconomic analysis of markets

In unplanned economies and, to some extent, in planned economies, prices are the signals which guide the decisions of business firms about what goods are to be produced and how much of them. Price formation and demand and production decisions are the subject matter of microeconomics. Part III takes up again the issues raised in Chapters 3 and 4 — the manner in which the many detailed Output, Input, and Distribution questions are resolved by market interactions.

Public economic policy enters at the microeconomic level when society decides that private market decisions have such undesirable consequences either for consumers or for producers that they should not be allowed to prevail. The rationale and the effect of government regulation of private firms and interference in markets are also examined in this part.

Chapters 19 and 20 work carefully through the economist's explanation of consumer demand. They also consider some of the important qualifications to consumer theory. Chapter 21 is a crucial link between consumer demand and the manner in which business firms perceive that demand. It argues that the perception depends on the structure of the market. Market "structure" refers to the quality of competition in an industry, the extent to which it approaches "perfection," and the character of the various imperfections.

Chapter 22 moves to the side of the business firm and examines the production cost conditions which affect the ways business firms react to the demands they perceive.

Then in Chapers 23 and 24 the demand and supply analysis is put together to explain the behavior of competitive markets. In Chapter 25 the analysis is extended to the case of monopoly and the cases between competition and monopoly which are labeled "imperfect" forms of competition.

Some of the issues of public policy toward the behavior of markets in which the assumptions of competition are reasonably appropriate are discussed in Chapter 24. Chapter 26 extends the discussion of public policy and business regulation to monopoly and imperfect competition.

19
The rationale of consumer choice

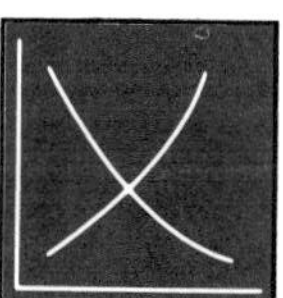

In an unplanned economy, the output of particular goods and services depends on the *demands* for those goods and services. Consumer demands, in turn, influence the demand for capital goods and other resources. If everyone eats frosty, flaky Energ-O, the breakfast cereal companies will demand a lot of frosting and flaking machines and frosting and flaking technicians. This chapter and the next are devoted to a deeper examination of consumer demand for particular goods. Chapter 4 introduced the concept of demand and described the major determinants of the relationship between the price of a commodity and the quantity that would be purchased at that price. Also that chapter first presented the Law of Demand. This law says that the quantity of a particular good purchased by a single consumer, and by all consumers together, will be greater at a lower price (and lower at a higher price), if all influences other than price remain unchanged. Some reasons were given for the plausibility of that law, including its agreement with commonly observed facts.

We have two objectives in pushing that analysis further. The first is to gain a better insight into the factors that determine the responsiveness of consumer purchases to price changes and other influences. If the analysis is to explain how markets operate to resolve the Output, Input, and Distribution questions, it must account for the sources and effects of changes on the demand side. Second, to understand the extent and significance of consumer sovereignty, we must understand how basic consumer choices are made.

The idea of consumer sovereignty, introduced in Chapter 3, is itself a complex one. It means, in general, that the economic activity of the private market sector is primarily directed toward satisfying consumer demands. In the theoretical world of perfect competition, consumer sovereignty leads logically to a close and precise relationship between production and consumer satisfaction. We shall develop that idea in Chapter 23.

Where the consumer is king, there is no tribal chieftain, feudal lord, or national planning commission who makes the Output decisions. Nor are there businesses with some degree of monopoly power which influence private consumer demand via large-scale advertising. In analyses of consumer demand, the power of advertising is a controversial subject. To fully understand the arguments, we must master the theory of consumer choice. Our discussion will be abstract, particularly at the outset, in order to be general. The analysis will deal with such standardized commodities as Food and Clothing. That will not be helpful to persons preparing advertising campaigns for Energ-O breakfast cereal, but it will help evaluate the effects of their efforts and even more important issues.

The consumer's budget-constraint or consumption-possibility line

Suppose that only two goods are produced in a simple economy: Food and Clothing. John Doe is a "typical" individual who lives with his family and works in that world and has an income of, say, $20 per week, which he spends on the two goods. The price of Food in the market is $2 per bushel and the price of Clothing is $4 per garment. With this information we can work out all the various combinations of Food and Clothing that Doe and family can *possibly* buy. (We note in passing that, since Doe's purchases are an insignificant part of the total market, his shifting of expenditures from one commodity to the other will have no effect on the prices of Food and Clothing.)

Table 19-1

THE CONSUMPTION-POSSIBILITY SCHEDULE IN A HYPOTHETICAL CASE

	Food purchases (bushels)	*Total food expenditures*	*Clothing purchases (garments)*	*Total clothing expenditures*	*Total expenditures*
A	10	$20	0	$ 0	$20
B	8	16	1	4	20
C	6	12	2	8	20
D	4	8	3	12	20
E	2	4	4	16	20
F	0	0	5	20	20

If Doe spent all his money on Food, he could buy 10 bushels each week; if he bought all Clothing, he could purchase 5 garments. Or he could buy any other combination that cost exactly $20. Table 19-1 lists a few of these consumption possibilities. They are also plotted in Figure 19-1 as points *A, B, C, D, E,* and *F*. The line drawn between these points is straight because, with prices constant, a shift of, say, $8 from one commodity to the other always means giving up the same amount of the one and gaining a constant amount of the other. To be precise, shifting $8 from Food to Clothings means giving up 4 bushels of Food and gaining 2 garments. Since the straight line from *A* to *F* represents all possible combinations of Food and Clothing purchases, it is called the *consumption-possibility* line or the *budget-constraint* line.[1]

The *slope* of the consumption-possibility or budget-constraint line can be calculated by dividing the vertical distance to the extreme point on the Food axis by the horizontal distance to the extreme point on the Clothing axis. It is 10/5, or 2, which is just the ratio of the Clothing price to the Food price, $4/$2. *The slope of the budget-constraint line represents the rate at which Doe can trade off Food against Clothing.* Since the trade-off rate is constant, because prices are constant for Doe, it can also be calculated between any two intermediate points, such as between *B* and *C*. In this case Doe would give up 2 bushels of Food to get 1 garment of Clothing ($2/1 = 2$).

The budget-constraint line does not tell us what Doe will do and how much Food and Clothing he will buy. Rather, it shows the limits of what he can do.[2]

Suppose Doe's income went up to $32 per week. He could then buy 16 bushels of Food, as at *A′* in Figure 19-1, or 8 garments, as at *F′*. Or he could buy any combination on the straight line *A′F′*. His consumption-possibility line would shift from *AF* to *A′F′*. His budget constraint would be somewhat less restrictive, but it would still be there.

The consumption-possibility line shows that a decision about purchasing Food is, inevitably, also a decision about purchasing Clothing. The need to make choices results from being constrained by a budget to be on a particular consumption-possibility line. This conclusion is immediately generalizable to a real world of many goods. As long as there is a budget constraint—which there always is—the decision *to purchase* one good is a decision *not to*

Figure 19-1

CONSUMPTION-POSSIBILITY OR BUDGET-CONSTRAINT LINE AND A SHIFT

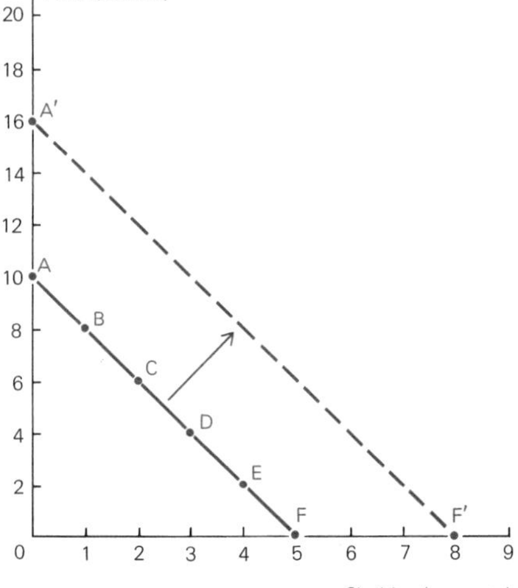

[1] If Doe did not spend all his income, a line could be computed which would represent all the consumption possibilities of the amount he budgeted to spend. For example, if Doe spent only $16, he could buy at most 8 bushels of Food or 4 garments or any combination of Food and Clothing whose total cost came to $16.

[2] The consumption-possibility line is analogous to the production-possibility curve of the First Model Economy of Chap. 3 in which the production trade off of one good against another good is fixed by the constant labor input ratios. In this case the line is straight because of the constant prices.

Table 19-2

CONSUMPTION POSSIBILITIES WITH A LOWER FOOD PRICE

	Food at $2/bushel	*Clothing at $2/garment*
A	10 bu.	0 garments
M	8	2
N	6	4
O	4	6
P	2	8
Q	0	10

Figure 19-2

CHANGES IN THE CONSUMPTION-POSSIBILITY LINES WITH PRICE AND INCOME CHANGES

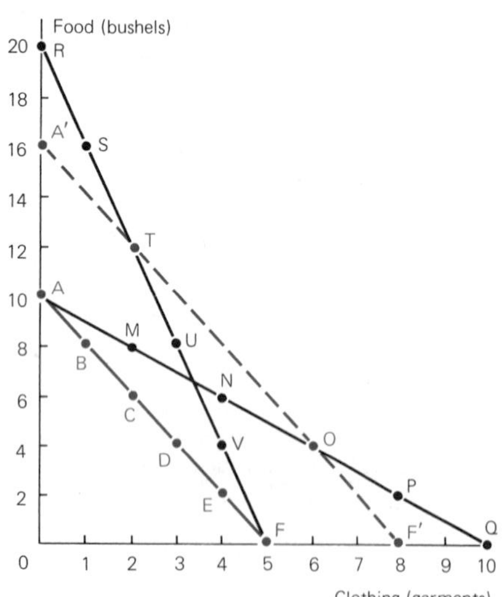

purchase some other. Though we do not always consciously balance out our alternatives so explicitly, choices are unavoidable. We do some "impulse buying," of course, but usually it represents a small part of our budget. Even so, we often reconsider the choice we made — sometimes with regrets — and decide not to repeat it. Any "mistake" limits our choices. It makes us forgo some other item which on reflection we might like more.

The budget-constraint concept can also be used to show the effects of price changes. Suppose that Doe's income is still $20 per week and that the price of Clothing falls from $4 to $2 per garment, but the price of Food remains unchanged at $2 per bushel. Table 19-2 shows a few of the new set of consumption possibilities, *A, M, N, O, P, Q*. These, as well as the original budget-constraint line *AF*, are plotted in Figure 19-2. The effect of the price reduction in Clothing is to create a new budget-constraint line, which is swiveled outward around point *A*. When *no* Clothing is purchased, at point *A*, the price of Clothing can change without affecting Food purchases, so point *A* is on both the old and new budget-constraint lines. When a lot of Clothing is purchased, as at points *O* or *P*, a change in its price makes a lot of difference *and makes it possible to have more of both Food and Clothing.*

Now suppose that, starting in the original situation, the price of *Food* dropped from $2 to $1, but the price of Clothing remained fixed at $4 per garment. Some of the new set of consumption possibilities are represented by *R, S, T, U, V*, and *F* in Table 19-3 and Figure 19-2. The budget-constraint line has swiveled out around point *F*. *The effect of the price change in one good is to make it possible to have more of both goods*, except right on the Clothing axis at *F*, when no Food is purchased.

These two examples lead also to the following conclusion: *A reduction in the price of one good (or both goods) is like an increase in income* in that it makes it possible to have more of both goods. To show this in another way, the budget-constraint line *A′F′*, which represented the consumption possibilities of Doe at the original prices but with a $32 income, is also drawn on Figure 19-2. The increase in income with no price changes also has the effect of increasing the Food and Clothing that Doe could purchase. Comparison of consumption-possibility lines *AQ* and *A′F′* shows that both permit the consumption of combination *O*, for example, composed of 4 bushels of Food and 6 garments of Clothing. Or the higher income and the old prices which generate *A′F′* and the lower income and prices of *RF* both permit consumption of the combination *T*, composed of 12 bushels of Food and 2 garments of Clothing. The comparisons also show, however, that *while price changes are generally like a change in income, they are not identical in their effects.*

Doe's *real income* is the purchasing power in goods and services of his income. It is represented by a set of consumption possibilities. We have shown in a formal way what every housewife

Table 19-3

CONSUMPTION POSSIBILITIES WITH A LOWER CLOTHING PRICE

	Food at $1/bushel	*Clothing at $4/garment*
R	20 bu.	0 garments
S	16	1
T	12	2
U	8	3
V	4	4
F	0	5

knows: that consumption possibilities depend both on money income and on prices. (It is legitimate to ask why we should go to so much trouble to figure out something so commonplace. The answer is that we are going to use the tools to probe more deeply into the issues of consumer demand and the significance of consumer choice.)

Consumer demand as consumer choice

While the consumption-possibility line describes all the choices open to a consumer, it does not show how he makes his choices. The theory of consumer choice deals with one of the most well-worked areas of economic analysis. It is open to a good many criticisms, many of which originate outside of economics. We must face up to these criticisms after we have looked at the theory itself. Actually there are at least two economic theories of consumer choice, and both come to the same practical conclusions about the relationship of prices and purchases. Of the two, the *marginal utility theory*, which we shall describe, is less fashionable among economists but it provides an intuitive grasp of the issues. It is also more restrictive and demanding in its assumptions and, therefore, more open to criticism. An alternative approach that avoids some of the criticism will be sketched out briefly in the chapter and developed in greater detail in the Appendix.

The utility plateau and diminishing marginal utility

Suppose that John Doe is questioned carefully about his desire for Food and that he is able to give these answers as he is asked about the alternatives of consuming 1, 2, 3, and more bushels:

> One bushel of Food a month keeps me and my family alive. Without it I would starve! Therefore I would have to say that it gives me a lot of satisfaction! On a *personal* utility scale, I would give it 100 points.
>
> Two bushels of Food pushes us above the barest subsistence and makes life a lot easier. Of course it isn't quite twice as important to me as the first bushel which kept us from starving. But if I could have two bushels of Food each month, my total personal utility would go up by 90 points to 190.
>
> Three bushels of Food permits us to begin to live it up a little. I can convert some of the wheat to cake flour and my wife can make a treat. The third bushel adds about 80 points, and my total personal utility from three bushels of Food would go up by 80, to about 270 points on my utility scale.
>
> Four bushels of Food begins to be a ball. I might even ferment a

little of that wheat. My total personal utility continues to rise, but at a declining rate, up 70 points to 340.

Five bushels of Food is a real party. I can invite in a few friends and we can enjoy life. My total utility continues to rise, but still the fifth bushel isn't worth what the fourth bushel was, so I'm up by 60 points to 400.

Doe clearly has two satisfaction or utility concepts in mind. The first is what happens to his *total utility* as his consumption of Food increases. The second is the *increment* in his total utility that results from increasing Food consumption by 1 bushel. That is called his *marginal* utility. We can make a table and draw charts to summarize his answers and extend them to 8 bushels of Food.

This is done in Table 19-4 and Figures 19-3 and 19-4. The table and the figures demonstrate *the principle of diminishing marginal utility*. This says that the marginal utility of Food consumption declines as Food consumption increases or, to put it more generally and at greater length:

> Total utility will rise as the consumption of a good increases. But the *increment* of extra utility from the consumption of an additional unit (marginal utility) will get smaller and smaller as consumption increases. So total utility will rise but at a decreasing rate.

Different people might give a different number of utility points to each additional bushel of Food. But the important question is this: Is the *principle* of diminishing marginal utility generally valid for *each* person? To the economists who first enunciated the principle over a hundred years ago, it seemed reasonable from their own introspection and observation. Modern economists criticize the principle because it assumes that Doe and other people can keep a

Table 19-4

HYPOTHETICAL SCHEDULES OF UTILITY FROM CONSUMPTION OF FOOD

Bushels of food	*John Doe's total utility of food*	*John Doe's marginal utility of food*
0	0	
		100
1	100	
		90
2	190	
		80
3	270	
		70
4	340	
		60
5	400	
		50
6	450	
		40
7	490	
		30
8	520	
		20
9	540	
		10
10	550	

Figure 19-3

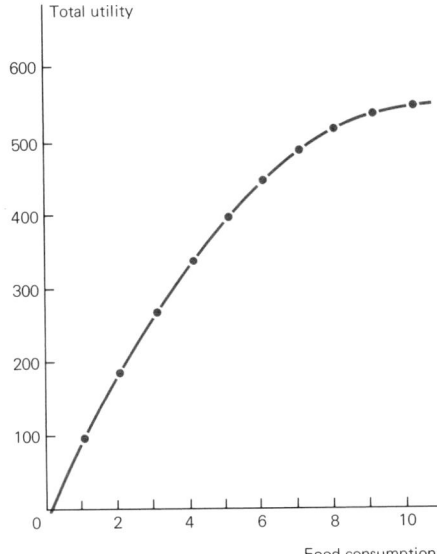

HYPOTHETICAL TOTAL UTILITY SCHEDULE FROM FOOD CONSUMPTION FOR AN INDIVIDUAL

Figure 19-4

MARGINAL UTILITY FROM FOOD CONSUMPTION FOR AN INDIVIDUAL

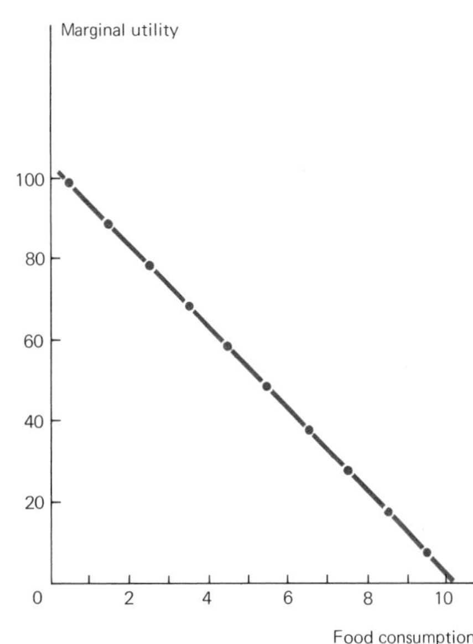

precise point score of their pleasure or satisfaction or utility. It provides a useful introduction to the theory of consumer choice, however. So, while retaining some skepticism, let us go along with Doe for a while and accept it if he says he knows how many utility points he gets from each of the alternative amounts of Food.

Doe also claims he knows how many utility points he gets from consuming different amounts of Clothing, and on questioning, he reveals the marginal utility schedules in Table 19-5 and Figures 19-5 and 19-6.

Table 19-5

HYPOTHETICAL SCHEDULES OF UTILITY FROM CONSUMPTION OF CLOTHING

Garments of clothing	*John Doe's total utility of clothing*	*John Doe's marginal utility of clothing*
0	0	
1	60	60
2	110	50
3	150	40
4	180	30
5	200	20

Figure 19-5

HYPOTHETICAL TOTAL UTILITY FROM CLOTHING CONSUMPTION FOR AN INDIVIDUAL

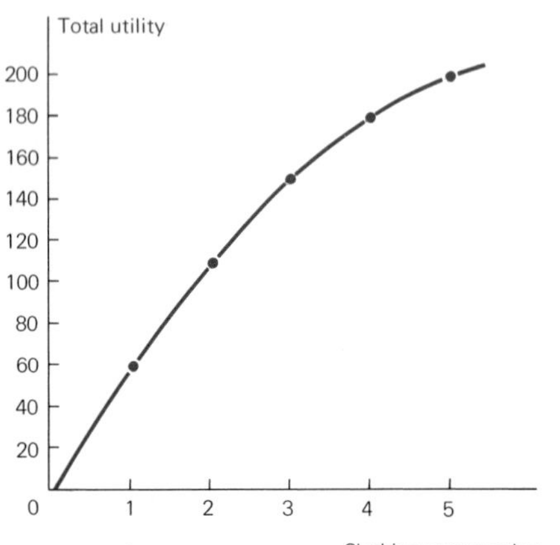

Figure 19-6

MARGINAL UTILITY FROM CLOTHING CONSUMPTION FOR AN INDIVIDUAL

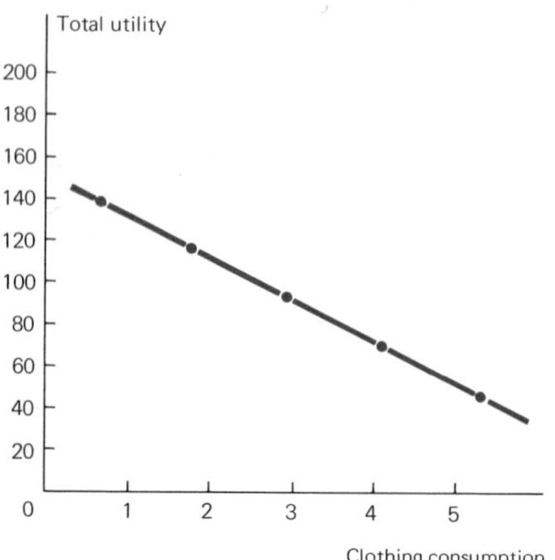

Making rational (optimal) choices

How is all this going to help Doe decide how to spend his income? That is, how is it going to help him choose among the possible combinations of Food and Clothing available to him, as indicated by his budget-constraint line? He could throw a dart at Figure 19-1 and choose the point on the consumption-possibility line closest to where the dart landed. But presumably, since he knows the total utility available from the various combinations, he will choose that combination which makes him most well off. That is what is meant by making rational or optimal choices.

What is the best choice Doe can make with the original set of prices? Suppose he computes the total utility associated with the alternative points on his original budget-constraint line *AF*. He refers to the utility schedules of Tables 19-4 and 19-5 and writes down for each consumption combination the utility points associated with it. That process generates Table 19-6. This table shows that, of all the combinations of Food and Clothing that Doe can afford to buy, row *B* delivers the maximum utility, and that is the one he will choose.

Computing total utility schedules is a cumbersome way of making choices even for an introspective calculator like Doe. He might use instead an equivalent procedure which involves compar-

Table 19-6

TOTAL UTILITY FROM CONSUMPTION POSSIBILITIES

	Food (bushels)	Food utility points	Clothing (garments)	Clothing utility points	Total utility points
A	10	550	0	0	550
B	**8**	**520**	**1**	**60**	**580**
C	6	450	2	110	560
D	4	340	3	150	490
E	2	190	4	180	370
F	0	0	5	200	200

ing the *marginal utility per dollar* of various expenditures. It yields the same result. He simply asks the sensible question each time he makes a purchase: How can I get the largest *extra* utility return for the dollars I spend? If there are only two goods, the question boils down to: Will the marginal utility of the next dollar I am going to spend be larger if I buy Food or if I buy Clothing?

Suppose that at the beginning of the week Doe buys 2 bushels of wheat. The first bushel will keep him and his family from starving. The second bushel yields 90 extra units of utility and, at $2 per bushel, gives 45 extra units of utility per dollar spent. The next day, however, Doe sees a shirt in a store window and decides to go in and buy it. That first garment provides 60 units of marginal utility, and at $4 per garment means that Doe is getting only 15 extra units of utility per dollar. That is a lot less marginal utility per dollar than he gets in buying Food. So he switches back to Food and buys 2 more bushels. On the fourth bushel, he gets 70/$2 or 35 units of extra utility per dollar. That is less marginal utility per dollar than on his first Food purchases, but more than on his Clothing purchase. So Doe stays with Food purchasing as long as the marginal utility per dollar in purchasing Food is greater than the marginal utility per dollar in purchasing Clothing. The marginal utility of Food will decline as his Food purchases increase. At some point it will be just equal to the marginal utility per dollar that he obtains from a purchase of Clothing. At that point – before the marginal utility of Food goes any lower – he ought to switch from Food to Clothing purchases.

All this is shown in Table 19-7. The marginal utility per dollar spent on each good, Food and Clothing, is the marginal utility divided by the price, or *MU/P*. That is computed in columns 4 and 8, respectively. At combination *B* (8 bushels of Food and 1 garment of Clothing), the marginal utilities per dollar of Food and Clothing purchases will be equal. That is the combination at which the total utility is maximized, as was worked out in Table 19-6. So Doe formulates the following rule to maximize the utility obtained from his purchases:

Buy Food if the:

$$\frac{\text{Marginal utility of Food}}{\text{Price of Food}} \text{ is greater than } \frac{\text{marginal utility of Clothing}}{\text{price of Clothing}}$$

Buy Clothing if the:

$$\frac{\text{Marginal utility of Clothing}}{\text{Price of Clothing}} \text{ is greater than } \frac{\text{marginal utility of Food}}{\text{price of Food}}$$

If John Doe has many goods among which to choose, this procedure is much more convenient than trying to compute the total utility of every possible combination of all the goods. Following this procedure, Doe just allocates each extra dollar of expenditure in such a way that he will get the largest possible extra or marginal return in utility per dollar. With many goods, therefore, the *equilibrium* position of maximum satisfaction is one in which:[3]

$$\frac{\text{Marginal utility of Food}}{\text{Price of Food}} = \frac{\text{marginal utility of Clothing}}{\text{price of Clothing}} = \frac{\text{marginal utility of each other good}}{\text{price of each other good}}$$

[3] Notice that since the condition for rational (optimal) choice is a comparative one, it does not depend on the utility units which Doe uses. If all utilities were multiplied or divided by arbitrary numbers like 10, the resulting choice would not change. That is because the *relative* marginal utility/price ratios would not change. And it is only the relative values of the ratios that matter, not the absolute values.

Table 19-7

TOTAL AND MARGINAL UTILITIES AND MARGINAL UTILITIES PER DOLLAR OF DOE'S CONSUMPTION POSSIBILITIES

	1 Food (bushels)	2 Food utility points	3 Food marginal utility	4 Food marginal utility per dollar (MU/P)	5 Clothing (garments)	6 Clothing utility points	7 Clothing marginal utility	8 Clothing marginal utility per dollar (MU/P)
A	10	550			0	0		
			10	5			60	**15**
	9	540						
			20	10				
B	**8**	**520**			**1**	**60**		
			30	**15**			50	12.5
	7	490						
			40	20				
C	6	450			2	110		
			50	25			40	10
	5	400						
			60	30				
D	4	340			3	150		
			70	35			30	7.5
	3	270						
			80	40				
E	2	190			4	180		
			90	45			20	5
	1	100						
			100	50				
F	0	0			5	200		

For each pair of goods this condition can also be written as

$$\frac{\text{Marginal utility of Food}}{\text{Marginal utility of Clothing}} = \frac{\text{price of Food}}{\text{price of Clothing}}$$

In this form the condition means that the consumer is in equilibrium when his personal trade-off ratio of the marginal utilities of two goods is equal to the market trade-off ratio, as indicated by the relative prices of the two goods.

Demonstrating the Law of Demand

The marginal utility analysis can now be used to show the rationale of the Law of Demand: an increase in the quantity of a good demanded as its price falls. Say that Doe's $20 weekly income and the $2 per bushel price of Food are constant but that the price of Clothing falls to $2. That will *not* alter the total or marginal utility associated with various amounts of Clothing consumption. But it will *increase* all the *marginal utility per dollar ratios* of Clothing consumption. This is shown in Table 19-8 where all the columns are the same as in Table 19-7, except column 8. The new price of Clothing leads to a new set of marginal utility per dollar ratios. The equilibrium choice of Food and Clothing will include more Clothing than before – row C rather than B. As the price of Clothing falls, the quantity demanded increases. *In effect, the fall in price leads Doe to substitute some Clothing for Food, because in that way he can increase his total utility.*

Tables 19-7 and 19-8 provide two points each on John Doe's

Table 19-8

TOTAL AND MARGINAL UTILITIES AND MARGINAL UTILITIES PER DOLLAR AFTER A REDUCTION IN THE CLOTHING PRICE

	1 *Food (bushels)*	2 *Food utility points*	3 *Food marginal utility*	4 *Food marginal utility per dollar*	5 *Clothing (garments)*	6 *Clothing utility points*	7 *Clothing marginal utility*	8 *Clothing marginal utility per dollar*
A	10	550			0	0		
			10	5				
	9	540						
			20	10			60	30
B	8	520			1	60		
			30	15				
	7	**490**						
			40	**20**			50	25
C	6	450			2	110		
			50	25				
	5	400						
			60	30			40	**20**
D	4	340			**3**	**150**		
			70	35				
	3	270						
			80	40			30	15
E	2	190			4	180		
			90	45				
	1	100						
			100	50			20	10
F	0	0			5	200		

Figure 19-7

TWO POINTS ON DOE'S DEMAND SCHEDULE FROM THE ANALYSIS IN TABLES 19-7 AND 19-8

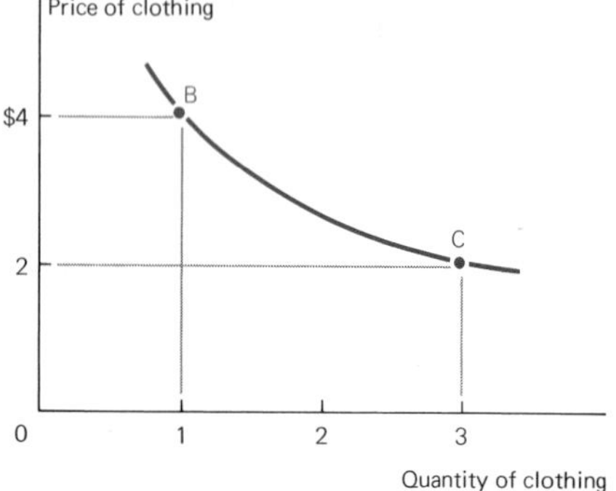

demand schedule for Clothing. These are shown as points B and C in Figure 19-7. Other changes in the Clothing price, with the Food price remaining constant, would generate still other points on Doe's Clothing demand schedule, as shown by the line extensions. These two points are enough, however, to demonstrate that the utility analysis leads to the Law of Demand: that the quantity purchased increases as prices fall.

What is true for John Doe will be true for everyone with utility schedules that show falling marginal utility with rising consumption. So, for each person, we can say that the Law of Demand holds: With everything else equal, when the price of a commodity falls, individuals will increase their purchases of it.

You may well think that this demonstration of a "law" that is perhaps intuitively plausible is not worth all the effort put into it. You may, like some economists, have doubts about the validity of utility analysis itself. The analysis makes one point that is not so obvious, however, and it deserves stressing. Explicitly or implicitly, consumer demand for any particular good involves choices among many goods. To express this in a way that emphasizes the more general result: There is interdependence in the demand decisions of individual consumers.

Substitutes, complements, income effects, and inferior goods

It is less obvious but also true that, in general, a change in John Doe's income will not necessarily affect his demand for the two goods in the same way. An increase in income makes Doe's budget constraint less restrictive and permits his consumption of both goods to rise. As consumption of Food and Clothing rises, the marginal utilities of both goods will fall. But they can be expected to fall at different rates just because the two goods are different. The marginal utility per dollar ratios will also change and will lead to changes in consumption proportions.

Likewise, the effects of price changes will be different for different goods. It was pointed out in the discussion of the consumption-possibility line that a change in prices is like, though not identical to, a change in income. A decrease in a price, for example, implies an increase in purchasing power. That is its *income effect*. In general, that will lead to an increase in the quantity demanded of the good whose price has decreased. It *may* lead to a decrease in the quantity demanded of other goods for which the original good is a *substitute*. And it *will* lead to an increase in the quantity demanded of other goods which are *complements* of the original good.

Is it ever true that a decrease in the price of a particular good will lead to a decrease in the amount demanded? Well, suppose that the good is an "inferior" one and its consumption would decline as consumers' income rose. In this case the income effect of a decrease in the good's price would not tend to increase the amount demanded but to reduce it. If that effect is strong enough, it can overcome the substitution effect of a price decrease. The quantity purchased will decline as the price declines. Potatoes are often assumed to represent such a case. The phenomenon is called the Giffen Paradox after a nineteenth-century English economist who claimed to observe its operation in the purchase of bread.

Abandoning marginal utility: The modern theory of consumer choice

Many people find the utility argument unpersuasive. It describes consumers in a special way. It assumes that consumers not only know when they are better off and when worse off, as their consumption changes, but that they know by exactly how much in some kind of utility points. This assumption is not necessary in an alternative approach to consumer choice which is described briefly here and developed in more detail in the Appendix.

Suppose that John Doe, still standing in as our typical consumer, knows *only* when he is better off or worse off as a result of a change in his consumption choices. That means he also knows when he is *indifferent* — a change one way or the other among consumption choices is not important to him. Without measuring satisfaction in utility points, Doe can recognize a situation where he can rearrange the composition of his consumption and be better off. He also knows when he is on the margin, that is, when he is indifferent to small changes. He may, for example, consider consuming 6 bushels of Food and 2 garments of Clothing. With that combination of goods he believes that a small trade off of, say, 1 bushel of Food for 1 garment of Clothing, or vice versa, would leave him equally well off. Then when he chooses 6 bushels of Food and 2 garments of Clothing, his personal marginal trading ratio for small changes in goods consumption is 1 to 1.

Now recall that the price ratio of Food and Clothing also represents the real ratio at which Clothing can be exchanged for Food. If, for example, the ratio of the price of Food to the price of Clothing is $4 per bushel to $2 per garment, that means that 1 bushel of Food trades for 2 garments of Clothing.

To bring all the facts together: By rearranging his purchases, Doe can trade 1 bushel of Food for 2 garments at going market prices. This would be trading at 1 to 2. He is willing, however, to trade at 1 to 1. Why then he certainly will trade, because he can do so at a rate even better than the rate at which he is indifferent. And he will not stop trading — which means he will not be in equilibrium — until he finds that combination of Food and Clothing at which his personal marginal trading ratio is equal to the market trading ratio. Notice that this condition is similar to that derived by utility theory when the ratio of marginal utilities is interpreted as a personal trading ratio. But the modern theory does not require the utility interpretation.

The paradox of value (prices) resolved

The theory of consumer choice can help resolve a paradox that preoccupied classical philosophers and economists. Why, they asked, do gold, silver, and diamonds, things which in themselves do not satisfy hunger or keep anyone warm and dry, have such a high value (i.e., price)? And why do bread and shelter and clothing, the very essentials of life, generally have a much lower price?

Adam Smith and others before and after him, including Karl Marx, recognized the paradox. They made a distinction between *use value* and *exchange value* and confined themselves to an attempt to explain exchange value, which we call price. The classical economists, of whom Marx can be regarded as the last, formulated a labor theory of value in which goods prices depended on the direct and indirect labor required for their production. The labor theory does not resolve the paradox of value, however. It is not true that the work of the gold miner is always much longer and harder than that of the farmer in the fields.

No one would deny that the *total* utility of food, clothing, and shelter, which permit people to survive, outweighs the *total* utility of a bit of glitter. But the theory of consumer choice does not claim and, in fact, would expressly deny, that it is the *total* utility of the commodity which determines willingness to purchase a loaf of bread or a diamond. In terms of utility theory, the willingness to purchase depends on the relative *marginal* utilities, or personal substitution ratios, of an extra loaf of bread versus an extra diamond. It is the marginal utility *per dollar* of *each* purchase which must be compared with other marginal utilities per dollar of outlay. The marginal utility per dollar of the "first" loaf of bread is greater than that for the "first" bit of diamond. But if any diamonds are purchased, the marginal utilities per dollar of bread and diamonds must be equal. Such comparisons lead to the largest total utility for a consumer from all of his purchases.

The modern theory of consumer choice also tells us that the consumer makes his decisions through an appreciation of the marginal effects of changing his decisions. Marginal comparisons are all that is necessary, and the theory does not involve the calculation and comparison of total utilities. The paradox of value is resolved by pointing out that the comparisons it makes are not the relevant ones for consumer choice.

Consumer's surplus

No consumer is ever asked whether the food he buys is the "first" unit, which will just keep him alive, or the "last" unit, with which he is going to have a party. He just buys his groceries and pays the same price for the last as for the first unit. In the process, he becomes the beneficiary of a free market process in which he gains a *consumer's surplus*. Recognition of the existence of this surplus provides additional insight into the paradox of value and the total satisfaction associated with alternative consumer choices.

To illustrate the concept of consumer's surplus, let us suppose that our typical consumer *must* buy all his goods at Simon LeGree's general store. Each John Doe comes in and, carefully comparing the marginal utilities per dollar, makes his purchases. LeGree, however, being a tough and unscrupulous monopolist sells in the following manner: After ringing up the cost of the purchases at the standard prices marked on the packages, he sets aside the bags of groceries and says, "O.K., now you must pay me what all these groceries are *really* worth to you. I know that if you don't get the first bag you starve today. The second bag has a few luxuries and has a slightly lower marginal utility. The third bag has a few party things and may be worth still less. Either you pay up for the total utility you get from these groceries or you get absolutely nothing." Poor John would have no choice and would pay up.

Imagine John's happiness when a supermarket opens up around the corner and he can get through the checkout counter paying just the standard prices. The difference between what LeGree was able to extort and what John would pay at the supermarket is a measure of the consumer's surplus John derives from being able to make all his purchases at the same price.[4]

The existence of consumer's surplus means that the price of a good does not measure the full benefit or utility that the consumer enjoys when he buys the product. This is an important idea. It helps explain the paradox of value. It also helps explain why it may be worthwhile to have goods and services made available by

[4] The concept of consumer's surplus is an important one, though it is not easy to measure. Some games analogous to the one above have been suggested as a possible approach to its measurement. If it were really true that utility could be measured with money and if the utility of income were constant, a measure of consumer's surplus could be obtained from the consumer's demand schedule. The demand schedule for, say, Food is represented by the line *BC*. Buying 4 units at $2, the consumer pays $8 total. But he would have been willing to pay much more than $2 for the first unit, somewhat more than $2 for the second, and slightly more than $2 for the third. The total utility he gets from all 4 units can be measured by the area under the demand curve *OABCE*. Subtracting his total expenditure, which is the area *OACE*, his consumer's surplus is measured by the area *ABC*.

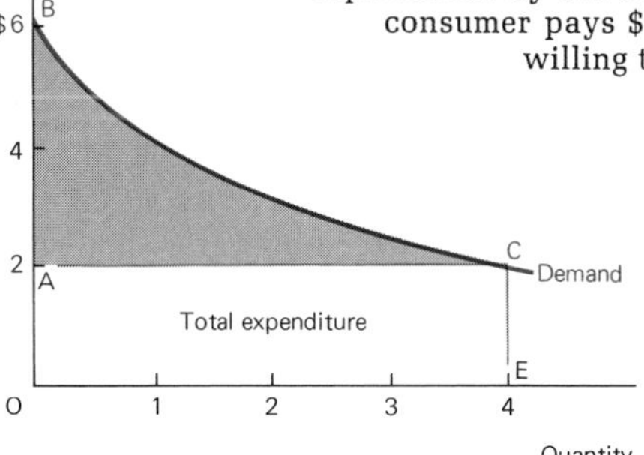

government even when no price can be charged — or when the price charged does not fully cover costs.

Suppose, for example, that a community was considering establishing a full-time, paid fire department to replace a volunteer company. It requires no special analysis to understand that, after a fire starts, the pricing process is not likely to be satisfactory to the "consumer" or even to the "producer." Moreover, the price at which consumers would be willing to subscribe to fire-fighting services on a regular basis might be too low to cover costs.

If there were a fire department and *no price were charged*, the total utility to each consumer of having the service available would be *entirely* consumer's surplus. Now imagine that we could somehow measure, compare, and add up the consumer's surplus that each person got from the existence of the fire department. If that total were greater than the cost of the department, its establishment would be justified. And some other way of paying for it (by taxes!) would be warranted.

Realism and relevance in the theory of consumer choice

It would not be surprising if the reaction to both the marginal utility theory and the modern theory of consumer choice were, "A plague on both your houses." It all seems quite abstract and unrelated to anything in the world. Yet both — and particularly the modern theory — can be interpreted quite realistically in the following way:

> The consumer is not a high-speed introspective computer, but he knows when he is better off and when he is worse off. He may not know what he likes — or dislikes — until he tries it. But in a trial-and-error way he tends to avoid the things he dislikes. He does not consciously try to make himself unhappy by buying goods he really does not want and not buying other goods he really does want. Nor does he always act in a random and inconsistent way and intentionally repeat mistakes.

These statements may seem much more plausible than the theory of consumer choice, but they are actually all that is necessary to provide the factual basis for that theory. The rest follows logically, as suggested above.

Yet some may still have more than a small doubt. How can we account for what appears to be inconsistent and irrational consumption behavior by so many people? Money is whooped off on fads and fashions and small pleasures and not enough is left for the "important things in life."

To a considerable extent such statements simply reflect differences in tastes. While we may say, *De gustibus non disputandum* — there is no arguing about tastes — in fact, we spend a good deal of time arguing about tastes and are often more than willing to praise or condemn. Human nature being what it is, and our neighbor's tastes being such an interesting subject, we should not expect the arguments to cease. Perhaps, however, we can come to distinguish differences in tastes from irrationality.

One particularly pervasive difference in individual tastes has to do with *time preference*. Some people worry more about what tomorrow may bring than others do. Given the alternative of a little more "consumption now" or a little more "consumption later," hardly anyone would accept the second choice unless the amount of consumption later were larger. But the size of the disparity matters more to some people than to others. A bird in the hand is worth two in the bush to some consumers of birds, but it may be worth three to others, or perhaps only one and a half.

Part of the seeming irrationality of consumption decisions stems from differences in knowledge. Sometimes the differences are objective; though the data one needs may in fact exist, they are not at hand when a decision has to be made. Some of the differences in knowledge are subjective, and the answers to our questions are hidden in the future. Do I know for sure how I will feel tomorrow if I consume pickles and ice cream today? In such circumstances we can expect people to behave differently – and to have different regrets. This is all part of the trial-and-error process envisioned in the theory of consumer choice.

Summary

The purpose of the theory of consumer choice is to explain consumer demands for particular goods and services, the relationships among them, and the sources of changes in those demands.

Each consumer's demand is constrained by the funds he has available for spending. When there are only two goods to be purchased, it is possible to show the budget constraint as a straight line, which is the consumption-possibility line. This does not show what the consumer will do, but represents the limits of what he can do in spending his income. It indicates the necessity of making choices and the range of the potential choices that can be made.

The utility theory of consumer choice assumes that the individual can measure precisely the amount of utility – or pleasure and enjoyment – that he obtains from consuming a particular good. If the consumer can do this, then consumer choice can be explained as picking the point on the consumption-possibility line which yields the highest utility. The consumer can find this point by comparing the extra or marginal utility per dollar which he gains from each alternative purchase. His rule for maximizing his total utility is to buy the good that provides the largest marginal utility per dollar. In equilibrium among his choices, the individual consumer will have equated the marginal utilities per dollar of the various goods and services he purchases.

When the consumer has an increase in income, his budget constraint relaxes somewhat and he can expand his consumption. The *degree* to which his purchases of various goods will increase will depend on the relative marginal utilities generated by the increased consumption of the goods.

A reduction in the price of one of the goods will increase the marginal utility per dollar of the good. That will ordinarily tend to increase the consumption of the good as it is substituted for other goods whose marginal utility per dollar has not changed. This substitution effect may be augmented or offset by the income effect, which is the increase in real purchasing power due to the price reduction. The offsetting occurs in the area of inferior goods whose purchases go down as real income rises. Except in the case of inferior goods the substitution and income effects both lead to the Law of Demand in which the quantity of a good purchased increases as its price falls.

The modern theory of consumer choice comes to the same conclusion as the utility theory, but does not assume that consumers can measure their satisfaction precisely. It only requires that consumers recognize when they are better off and when they are worse off. Suppose the consumer's personal or subjective trade-off ratio between two goods is not the same as the market or objective trade-off ratio between the goods, which is indicated by their relative price ratio. Then the consumer can make himself better off by adjusting the composition of his consumption, buying more of the relatively preferred good. He will be in equilibrium, according to this theory, when his personal trade-off ratio is equal to the market trade-off ratio.

The theory of consumer choice — both the utility theory and the modern theory — helps resolve the paradox of value. This is the paradox that essential goods like bread and water usually have low prices while nonessential luxuries have high prices. In both theories, it is the relative desirability of the *marginal* unit which is adjusted to price. Thus, in the utility theory, while the total utility of bread may be higher than that of diamonds, the marginal utility per dollar of bread is ordinarily much less than the marginal utility per dollar of diamonds. This also means that the total utility from a purchase is usually larger than the utility of the income spent on it. This difference is the consumer's surplus.

Questions for discussion and review

1. What is meant by consumer sovereignty? Is there full consumer sovereignty in the mixed economy of the United States?

2. Do you think consumers are actively aware of their consumption-possibility line? Would your answer change if we called the line the budget constraint?

3. Why is a reduction in the price of a single good that consumers buy like an increase in their income?

4. The theory of consumer demand is presented as a theory of consumer choice. Actually there appears to be a lot of buying on impulse and buying without consideration of alternatives. Do you think consumers make choices, conscious or subconscious, when they buy goods and services? Explain your answer.

5. Do you think that by introspection you could give point scores to the satisfaction you obtain from the consumption of various quantities of a particular good? If your answer is No, does that mean you think there is no substance whatever to the notion of declining marginal utility of additional consumption of any particular good?

6. Describe and distinguish between the income effects and the substitution effects of, say, an increase in apartment rents.

7. What is the paradox of value? Do you think the theory of consumer choice really resolves it? Explain.

8. Suppose you heard a man say, "I get a lot of consumer's surplus out of the educational system." How would you interpret that in plain English?

Concepts for review

Consumption-possibility or budget-constraint line

Theory of declining marginal utility

Equalization of marginal personal trade-off ratios and market-price ratios

Substitution effects of price changes

Income effects of price changes

Inferior goods

Consumer's surplus

Appendix: An introduction to the modern theory of consumer choice

The modern theory of consumer choice outlined here is a logical, sophisticated theory. It not only clarifies questions about consumer demand but is a quite general approach to many problems of choice.

You are in good company if you felt uneasy about the psychology implicit in the marginal utility approach to the theory of consumer demand. It is useful as a pedagogical device to assume that people can measure the satisfaction they receive from their consumption and assign utility points to it. But the theory goes further than most psychologists and economists are willing to go — and it is not really necessary. The modern theory of consumer choice avoids making the assumption of measurable utility. It only requires that individuals know when they are better off and when worse off, perhaps in anticipation, but at least from experience, from which they learn.

An indifference curve

Table 19-9

A SET OF FOOD-CLOTHING COMBINATIONS AMONG WHICH DOE IS INDIFFERENT

	Food (bushels)	*Clothing (garments)*
A	10	0
B	6	1
C	4	2
D	3	4
E	2	10

Let us go back to John Doe, who consumes only the two commodities, Food and Clothing. Suppose we ask him to express his preferences among alternative combinations of Food and Clothing. Or suppose we observe Doe as he actually makes his choices. He will clearly prefer some combinations of Food and Clothing to other combinations. There will be still other combinations among which he is *indifferent.*

We shall organize our observations as follows: From our record of his choices, we shall write down a set of Food-Clothing combinations among which he is indifferent and plot these on a Food-Clothing graph. These are shown in Table 19-9. The points are plotted in Figure 19-8, and something extra is added. A line is drawn connecting the points, and any combination of Food and Clothing on the line is assumed to be as much preferred as any other combination on the line. So John Doe regards himself as equally well off in terms of Food and Clothing with any combination along the line, and the line is called an *indifference curve.*

Are the results shown plausible observations of John as a typical consumer? Is it reasonable to expect that the indifference curve should look this way, sloping down from left to right and curving upward? The downward slope is plausible: If John is indifferent between combinations *A* and *D*, for example, then *D*, which has less Food than *A*, must have more Clothing.

Figure 19-8

A FOOD-CLOTHING INDIFFERENCE CURVE FOR DOE

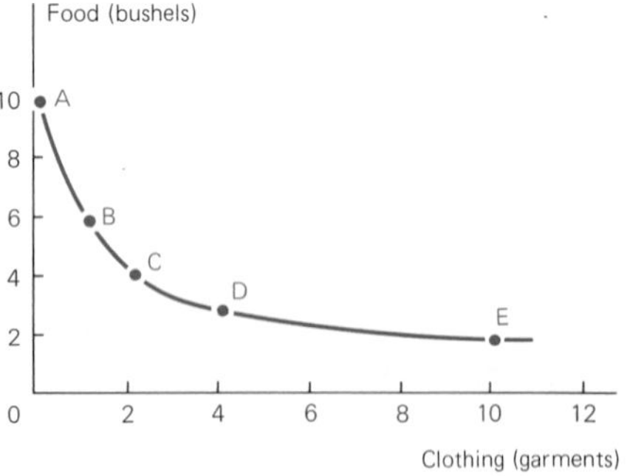

What about the curvature? The indifference curve starts out by falling very steeply. In effect, from *A* to *B* John is just willing to give up 4 bushels of Food to get the first garment of Clothing, and he will be indifferent between *A* and B. As between *B* and *C*, the second garment of Clothing is worth sacrificing only 2 units of Food. In effect, along the indifference curve there is a substitution or trade-off rate between Food and Clothing, as shown in Table 19-10. That rate is declining, which is simply the economic implication of the convex curvature of the indifference curve.

Some people are willing to accept this declining rate of substitution as axiomatic: The less there is of a good, the greater the rate at which other commodities must be substituted for it if the individual is to remain indifferent among alternative combinations. (In advanced texts it is shown that this condition must hold if we observe individuals continuing to make choices of both goods with which they are satisfied.) It is tempting but not necessary to

Table 19-10

SUBSTITUTION RATES BETWEEN ALTERNATIVE COMBINATIONS OF FOOD AND CLOTHING AMONG WHICH DOE IS INDIFFERENT

	Food (bushels)		*Clothing (garments)*	*Substitution ratio of food for clothing*
A to *B*	4	for	1	4
B to *C*	2	for	1	2
C to *D*	1	for	2	1/2
D to *E*	1	for	6	1/6

explain the declining substitution rate in terms of relative changes in the marginal utility of the two goods.

The calculated substitution ratios can also be interpreted as the slopes of straight lines drawn between each of the points *A*, *B*, *C*, *D*, and *E*. In each case they indicate the increase in garments of Clothing which just makes up for a specified decrease in bushels of Food and leaves Doe indifferent. The slope is Doe's personal or subjective trade-off ratio. If the changes in Food were made smaller and smaller, the trade-off ratio observed would approximate more and more closely the slope of the indifference curve itself. So the slope of the indifference curve at a point on the curve can be interpreted as the trade-off ratio for very small changes.

The indifference map

Figure 19-9

A FOOD-CLOTHING INDIFFERENCE MAP

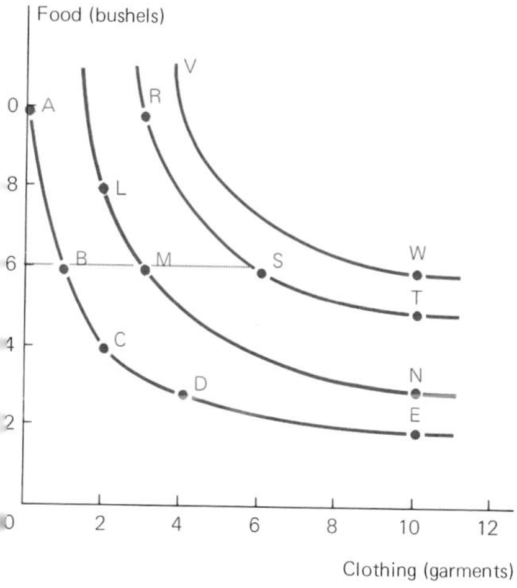

What if John were offered still another combination, say, 6 bushels of Food and 3 garments of Clothing? As shown at point *M* in Figure 19-9, that is the same amount of Food that Doe had at point *B*, but a lot more Clothing. He would probably prefer 6 and 3 at *M* to 6 and 1 at *B*. Since he is indifferent among *A*, *B*, *C*, *D*, and *E*, but prefers *M* to *B*, he will prefer *M* to any other point, e.g., *A*, *C*, *D*, *E*, which is on the same indifference curve that *B* is on.[5] By experimentation and observation we can find a set of combinations of Food and Clothing among which Doe is indifferent as compared with *M*, and we can draw an indifference curve through *M* connecting the points representing those combinations. That is the curve *LMN*. Since combination *M* is preferred to B, and all the points on *LMN* are indifferent with respect to *M*, then all points on *LMN* must be preferred to all points on line *ABCDE*.

Likewise, point *S* represents a combination of Food and Clothing preferred to *M*, because it provides still more Clothing and no less Food. And we can find a set of combinations of Food and Clothing among which, as compared with *S*, Doe is indifferent. There is still another curve going through point *S* which contains combinations among which Doe is indifferent. This is *RST*.

[5] This is the assumption of *transitivity of preferences.*

Actually the Food-Clothing space of Figure 19-9 is filled with indifference curves. The curves drawn can be regarded as only a few contours of John Doe's *indifference map.*[6]

Notice that, in working out the indifference map, we never claimed that the *LMN* indifference curve, for example, was better than the *ABCDE* indifference curve by any specific numerical amount. The only result we can strictly and honestly state from our experiments and observations is that *any* point on *LMN* is preferred to any point on *ABCDE*, and any point on *RST* is preferred to any point on *LMN* or *ABCDE*, and so on.

The consumption-possibility — budget-constraint line once again

Figure 19-10

A CONSUMPTION-POSSIBILITY LINE (FOOD AT $3/BUSHEL; CLOTHING AT $4/GARMENT; BUDGET OF $30)

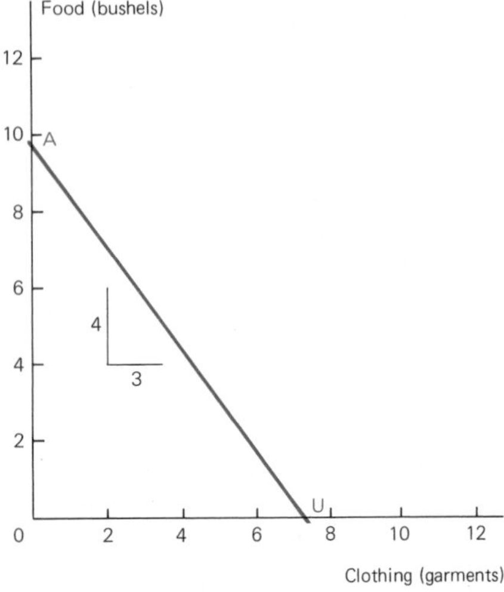

Earlier in this chapter, we worked out John Doe's consumption possibilities, as determined by (1) the prices of the commodities and (2) the budget that Doe had to spend on the commodities. For example, if the price of Food were $3 per bushel and the price of Clothing $4 per garment and Doe had $30 to spend on both, he could buy 10 bushels of Food or $7^1/_2$ garments of Clothing or any amount in between on the straight line *AU* in Figure 19-10. The *slope* of the consumption-possibility–budget-constraint line is 10/7.5 or 4/3, which is the ratio of the price of Clothing to the price of Food. As was pointed out earlier in the chapter, such a price ratio can also be interpreted as a trading ratio between Food and Clothing.

How Doe chooses the Food and Clothing he will consume

The next step is to combine the indifference map of Figure 19-9 and the consumption-possibility–budget-constraint line of Figure 19-10 and drawn them both in Figure 19-11. The indifference map organizes the information about Doe's preferences: his comparative likes and dislikes. The consumption-possibility line describes the constraint on his spending. Doe would like to get as far out in the Food-Clothing space as possible, but he cannot get "farther out" than the budget constraint will permit.

Now we ask: Which of all the Food and Clothing combinations that Doe *can* buy, as indicated by his consumption-possibility line, will he actually buy? And we answer: That combination which is farthest out on his indifference map!

Doe can purchase a combination like *C* or *D* in Figure 19-11, which is *inside* the consumption-possibility line, but he can also

[6] The transitivity condition guarantees that only one curve can go through each point, however.

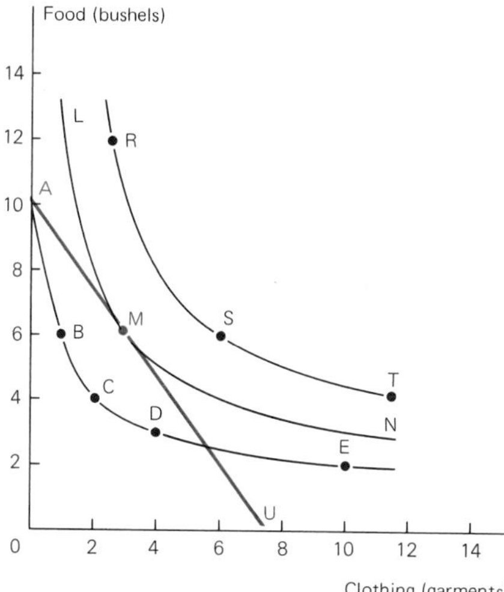

Figure 19-11

THE SOLUTION TO DOE'S CHOICE PROBLEM, USING HIS INDIFFERENCE MAP AND CONSUMPTION-POSSIBILITY LINE

purchase *M*, which is preferred to *C* or *D*. At point *M* he buys 6 bushels of Food and 3 garments of Clothing and spends his total budget of $30. He would prefer to have other combinations, say, *R* or *S* as compared with *M*, but he cannot buy them because he is constrained to be on or within his consumption-possibility–budget-contraint line. Given his indifference map and budget constraint, he cannot do better than point *M*. He can do worse, of course. But he will not if he is trying to enjoy his income as much as possible.

Another way of interpreting the consumption choice that Doe would make is given in the chapter: John will *not* settle down with any combination of Food and Clothing if he can trade (i.e., buy in the markets for Food and Clothing) at an objective market ratio which is different from his personal subjective substitution trade-off ratio (i.e., the slope of his indifference curve) and thus make himself better off. He *will* settle down when these two trade-off ratios are equal and he is as far out as possible on his indifference map. That means Doe's equilibrium will be at a point where the slopes of the consumption-possibility–budget-constraint line and indifference curve are equal. This is where they are just *tangent*, where they just touch but do not cross and therefore have equal slopes. In shorthand: In equilibrium, when Doe finds the best possible choice, his personal substitution ratio will equal the price ratio.

Again, this may all seem very abstract and far from reality. But it can all be reduced to a simple trial-and-error process in which John Doe tries to enjoy his income as much as possible. He may make mistakes, but he also learns from them and tries not to repeat them.

Income effects once again

We can use the tools to explain more rigorously the price and income effects mentioned earlier and also strengthen our understanding of the analysis.

Suppose Doe's income should go up by $10 to $40. His consumption-possibility–budget-constraint line would shift outward. He could buy $13^1/_3$ bushels of Food or 10 suits of Clothing or any combination in between on the line *VY* in Figure 19-12. The slope of the line would not change from the original consumption-possibility–budget-constraint line *AU* since the price ratios are assumed not to change. In effect, the budget constraint is relaxed somewhat and the income increase results in a *parallel shift* outward of the consumption-possibility line.

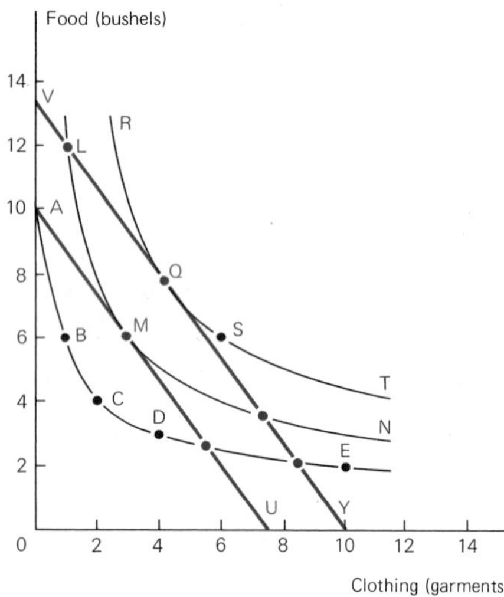

Figure 19-12

EFFECTS OF A CHANGE IN DOE'S BUDGET CONSTRAINT

As before, Doe would explore his way toward a new equilibrium position at Q at which his income is just exhausted and he is on the highest possible indifference curve. In the new equilibrium he will buy more of both Food and Clothing. Further increases in income would generate new, farther-out consumption-possibility lines and would lead to new equilibrium points for Doe.

Must it always work out that an increase in income results in some increase in consumption of both (all) goods? Not necessarily! If there is enough of the right kind of curvature in the indifference map, when the consumption-possibility line shifts outward as a result of an increase in income, consumption of a commodity may drop. This is shown in Figure 19-13. The consumption-possibility curve shifts out from CP_1 to CP_2 and moves from a tangency A_1 on indifference curve I_1 to the tangency A_2 on indifference curve I_2 At the new tangency, M_2 meat is consumed, which is greater than M_1 at the original tangency. But a smaller amount of potatoes P_2 is consumed than originally. Potatoes in this example are an *inferior good* whose consumption falls as income rises. Though such a phenomenon is not common, it is not unknown, and potatoes often fit the inferior good category.

Price effects

As explained earlier in the chapter, the effect of a change in the price of one of the commodities is to swing the consumption-possibility–budget-constraint line outward from the intersection on the axis of the commodity whose price has not changed. Suppose, for example, that the Clothing price does not change but the Food price drops and Doe's income stays constant. His consumption-possibility line will swing out from point *U*, as shown in Figure 19-14. There will be a new equilibrium position at *Q′* toward which he would grope from the initial equilibrium at *M*. At the new equilibrium he would consume more of both Food and Clothing. This clarifies the statement that a decrease in prices is to some extent like an increase in income and vice versa. The price change leads to an increase in consumption of both commodities in a manner analogous to the effect of an income increase. To see more clearly the significance of a change in prices, one might divide its effects into two parts whose total effect is the same as that of the price change: (1) a substitution effect and (2) an income effect.

Let us take the income effect first. Imagine a specific *income change* — with unchanged prices — which would permit Doe to make himself better off as compared with the original indifference contour on which he was located before the price change occurred.

Figure 19-13

EFFECTS OF AN INCREASE IN INCOME ON MEAT AND POTATO CHOICES, IF POTATOES ARE AN INFERIOR GOOD

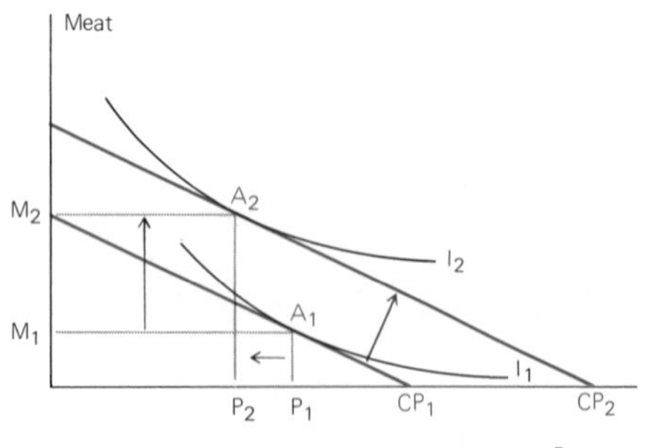

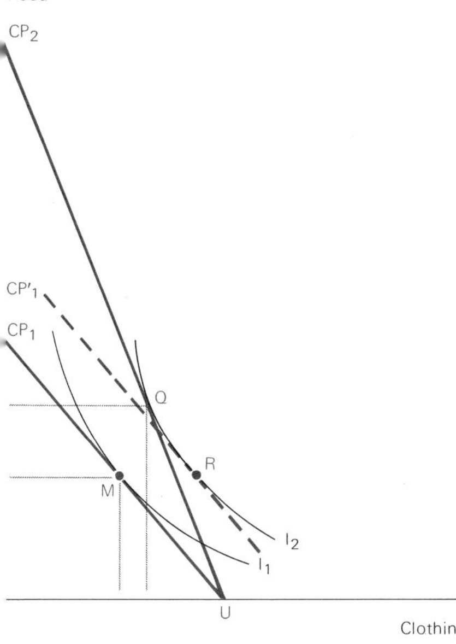

Figure 19-14

EFFECTS OF A REDUCTION IN THE PRICE OF FOOD

The income change is indicated by the shift of the consumption-possibility line from CP_1 to CP_2' in Figure 19-14. But this income change would leave Doe at R rather than Q', the point he reached after the price change. So now imagine a change in relative Food-Clothing prices that swivels the consumption-possibility line around the indifference contour to Q'. It always stays just touching or tangent to the indifference contour I_2 and ends up tangent at point Q'. This is the pure substitution effect due to price changes.

Notice that the income effect in this example leads to an increase in the consumption of both goods. The substitution effect tended to reduce the consumption of the good whose price increased and to increase the consumption of the good whose price stayed constant absolutely but went down relatively.

That statement should make us pause, however, for we found a case in which an increase in income led to a reduction in the consumption of inferior goods. Could a decrease in the price of a commodity, which is like an increase in real income, result in a *decrease* in consumption of the commodity? The answer is again Yes, for inferior goods. This is shown in Figure 19-15. The decrease in the potato price swings the consumption-possibility line out from C_1 to C_2. The equilibrium tangency moves from B_1 on indifference curve I_1, with M_1 meat consumed and P_1 potatoes, to B_2 on indifference curve I_2. In the new equilibrium, more meat M_2 is consumed than before, but a smaller quantity of potatoes P_2. The pure substitution effect for potatoes is outweighed by its inferior good income effects, and consumption drops.

A complete version of the Third Model Economy

In Chapter 3, some simple model economies were used to illustrate the essential economic problems, their interdependence, and the manner in which the problems are resolved. In those simple models, we assumed that the desired combinations of output were

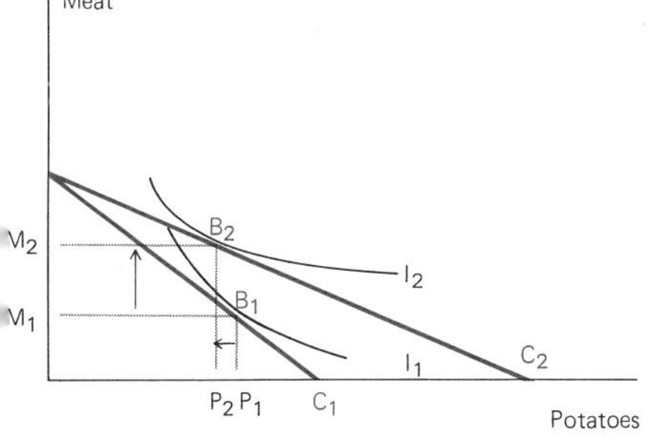

Figure 19-15

EFFECTS OF A REDUCTION IN THE PRICE OF POTATOES

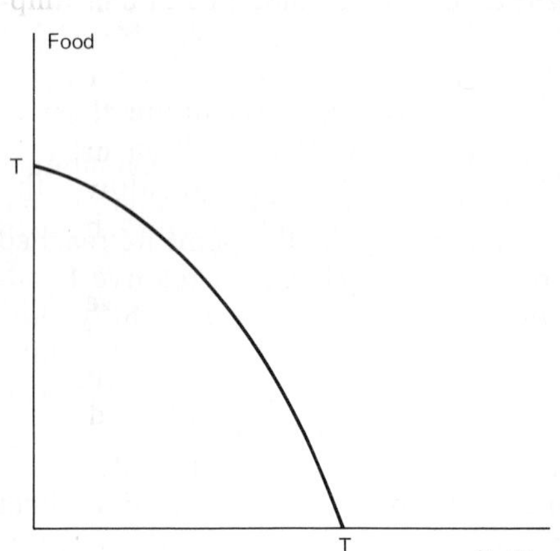

Figure 19-16

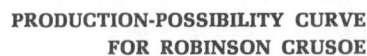

PRODUCTION-POSSIBILITY CURVE FOR ROBINSON CRUSOE

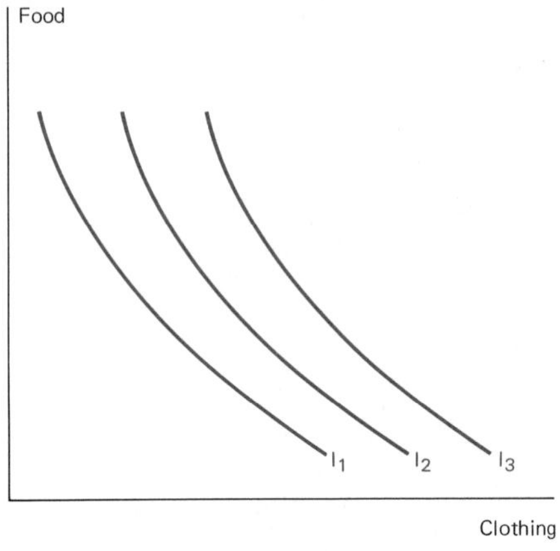

Figure 19-17

ROBINSON CRUSOE'S INDIFFERENCE MAP

chosen in some way, and we analyzed the reaction of the system to that choice. Since we now have a theory of choice, we can expand the analysis. But to keep the problem within modest limits, we will confine it at first to a single individual. So we shall assume a Robinson Crusoe version of a Third Model Economy.

Assume that Robinson Crusoe has two productive factors, Land and Labor, available for his use in producing Food and Clothing. His production-transformation curve is shown in Figure 19-16 as the line *TT*. He has also the indifference map for Food and Clothing represented in Figure 19-17. These are put together in Figure 19-18 and can be used to see how he decides what to produce and consume.

How does Crusoe decide? He chooses that output (and set of Labor and Land input allocations) which yields him the most satisfaction. This means that he tries to move as far out on his indifference map as possible. Perhaps he explores back and forth on *TT* to find that combination which he prefers most. His equilibrium posi-

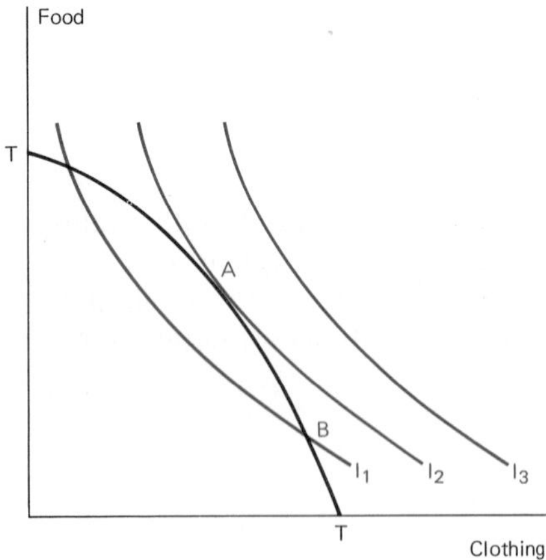

Figure 19-18

CRUSOE'S PRODUCTION-CONSUMPTION DECISION

tion will be at *A*, where the transformation curve just touches and is tangent to indifference curve I_2. That is the best he can do for himself.

At point *A* the trade-off ratio of the commodities in consumption will be just equal to the trade off in production. Why is that so? If in production Crusoe can trade off Food for Clothing, or vice versa, at a different rate than he is willing to substitute them in consumption — why then he should do so. At point *B* on his production-transformation curve, for example, if he withdraws the inputs necessary to produce 1 garment of Clothing, he may be able to produce 2 bushels of Food. At point *B* on his indifference curve I_1 the substitution ratio is, perhaps, 1 bushel of Food for 1 garment of Clothing. If 1 for 1 leaves him indifferent, 2 for 1 will make him better off. So he should move away from *B* and keep moving toward the equilibrium in which the trade-off ratios in production and consumption are equal.

20

Demand analysis: The theory and its qualifications

The theory of consumer choice provides the analytical basis for the generally valid observation that each consumer will tend to increase his purchases of a commodity when its price falls. Here we move on to the analysis of the total or market demand of all consumers for a particular product. This is a critical topic in understanding the operation of the private market sector of the economy, for it is demand expressed in markets to which the business sector responds. As we shall point out, the business sector tries to influence that demand through advertising. This chapter will also be a convenient place to discuss the demand for public goods and to contrast the manner of its expression with that for private goods.

The derivation of a market demand schedule

The market demand schedule for a specific good or service reflects the demand of all the consumers in the market. To determine the market or total demand schedule, we could go through the hypothetical experiment of changing prices and recording the purchases of each consumer. We could then add up the amounts purchased by all consumers at each price to obtain the market demand schedule. A simple example will help make the concept clear.

Suppose there are 20,000 potential purchasers of a particular commodity in a market. Of these, 10,000 have demand schedules like that of John Doe, and the other 10,000 have demand schedules like a certain Robert Roe.

John Doe's demand schedule is that of columns 1 and 2 in Table 20-1. The 10,000 consumers like John Doe have the demand schedule of columns 1 and 3 in Table 20-1. Column 3 is obtained by multiplying column 2 by 10,000. The demand of all consumers like John Doe is shown in Figure 20-1.

Robert Roe, who has a somewhat higher income, has the demand schedule of columns 1 and 2 in Table 20-2, and all consumers like him have the demand schedule of columns 1 and 3 of that table. Again column 3 is obtained by multiplying column 2 by 10,000. The demand schedule of all consumers like Robert Roe is shown in Figure 20-2.

The total demand schedule in this market is the sum of the

1 Price	2 Quantity purchased by John Doe	3 Quantity purchased by consumers like John Doe
$1.00	1	10,000
0.80	2	20,000
0.60	4	40,000
0.40	7	70,000
0.20	11	110,000

Table 20-1

1 Price	2 Quantity purchased by Robert Roe	3 Quantity purchased by consumers like Robert Roe
$1.00	4	40,000
0.80	6	60,000
0.60	9	90,000
0.40	13	130,000
0.20	18	180,000

Table 20-2

1 Price	2 Quantity purchased
$1.00	50,000
0.80	80,000
0.60	130,000
0.40	200,000
0.20	290,000

Table 20-3

DEMAND OF JOHN DOES

Figure 20-1

DEMAND OF ROBERT ROES

Figure 20-2

TOTAL DEMAND

Figure 20-3

demand schedules of the 20,000 potential consumers. It is obtained by adding up the amounts demanded at each price by everyone like John Doe and everyone like Robert Roe. That involves summing at each price the amounts in column 3 of Table 20-1 and column 3 of Table 20-2. That sum is shown in column 2 of Table 20-3. Graphically, the market demand schedule is the "horizontal sum" of all the separate demand schedules. This horizontal summing generates the market demand schedule in Figure 20-3 and is illustrated at a price of $0.40.

The market demand is a series of if-then statements for the entire marketplace. It indicates the entire amounts that would actually be purchased at alternative prices. Notice that to obtain – even conceptually in an experiment – the total demand schedule for each commodity, we do not need to compare the utilities or substitution ratios of individual consumers. It is only necessary to add up all the purchases at each price.

Market demand and income distribution

As pointed out in Chapter 19, the demand schedule of an individual consumer depends on (1) his tastes and preferences, (2) his income, and (3) the prices of other goods and services. In moving to the level of market demand, we must add (4) the number of consumers in the market and (5) the distribution of income among consumers. The need to include income distribution can be illustrated by extending the preceding example slightly.

Suppose that John Doe's income, and the income of every one of the 10,000 consumers with a demand schedule like his, is $8,000. So the total income of this group is $80 million. Assume also that Robert Roe's income is $12,000, and the income of every one of the 10,000 consumers who has the same demand schedule is also $12,000. Their total income is $120 million. The total income of both groups is $200 million.

Now suppose that the $200 million is distributed equally among the 20,000 consumers, with the result that each one has $10,000 and, furthermore, each one has the same demand schedule,

Table 20-4

DEMAND AFTER INCOME REDISTRIBUTION

1 *Price*	2 *Quantity purchased by either a Doe-type or a Roe-type consumer*	3 *Total demand of all consumers*
$1.00	3	60,000
0.80	4	80,000
0.60	6	120,000
0.40	9	180,000
0.20	13	260,000

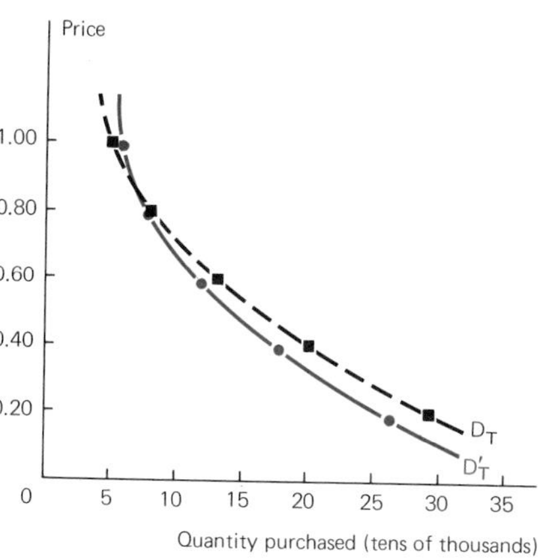

Figure 20-4

DEMAND AFTER INCOME REDISTRIBUTION

as shown in columns 1 and 2 of Table 20-4. The market demand schedule after the income redistribution is shown by columns 1 and 3 of Table 20-4. It is obtained by multiplying the quantity demanded at each price in column 2 of the table by the 20,000. The solid line in Figure 20-4 represents the market demand after income redistribution, and the dashed line, added for purposes of comparison, shows the market demand of Figure 20-3, before income redistribution.

The general conclusion to be drawn from this simple example is the following: *Market demand schedules reflect, for good or ill, the particular distribution of income that actually prevails.* It should not be presumed, however, that consumers are identical except for their incomes or that income equalization will generally have the effect shown.

Economists have used sophisticated statistical techniques to estimate market or total demand schedules for a wide variety of products. One of the classic examples was an estimate of the per capita demand for Food in the United States. This demand relation is represented by the equation:

$$\text{Quantity of Food purchased per capita} = 97.575 - 0.246\left(\frac{\text{price of Food}}{\text{average prices of all other consumer goods}}\right) + 0.298\,(\text{disposable income per capita})$$

Notice that although this is in per capita terms it can be transformed into a total demand schedule simply by multiplying Food purchases per capita by the population.

Note also that, as expected, the quantity of Food purchased will go down as the price of Food goes up. This is because of the minus sign in front of the 0.246 term which multiplies the price of Food. When other consumer goods prices go up, the ratio, price of Food/average price of other consumer goods, goes down. So the *minus term* becomes smaller. Therefore, the quantity of Food purchased becomes larger when other consumer goods prices go up, as would be expected.

Income also has just the effect on demand that we might have expected. If disposable income should rise, Food purchases would increase, owing to the plus sign in front of the income term.

The sensitivity of purchases to price changes: Demand elasticity

The theory of consumer choice provides the rationale for the general conclusion that the quantity demanded of any particular commodity will increase when the price is decreased. For each commodity, the *sensitivity* of its purchases to changes in prices will

Table 20-5

HYPOTHETICAL MARKET DEMAND FOR POUNDS OF BUTTER

Price	*Pounds purchased (per week)*
$1.25	0.75
1.00	1.0
0.75	1.25
0.50	1.75
0.25	2.50

Table 20-6

HYPOTHETICAL MARKET DEMAND FOR BUTTER IN QUARTER POUNDS

Price	*Quarter pounds purchased (per week)*
$1.25	3
1.00	4
0.75	5
0.50	7
0.25	10

Figure 20-5

HYPOTHETICAL MARKET DEMAND CURVE FOR POUNDS OF BUTTER

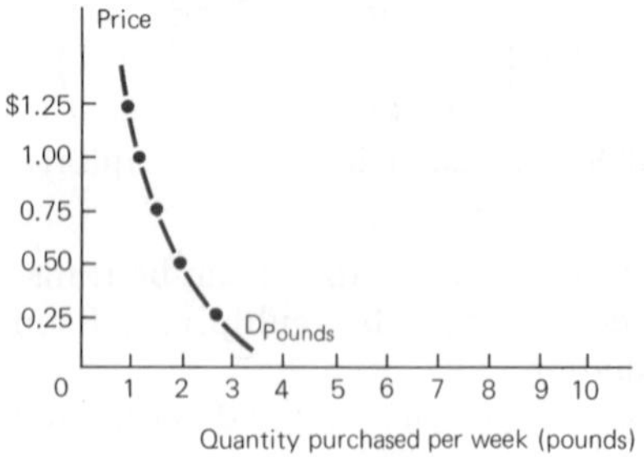

Figure 20-6

HYPOTHETICAL MARKET DEMAND CURVE FOR QUARTER POUNDS OF BUTTER

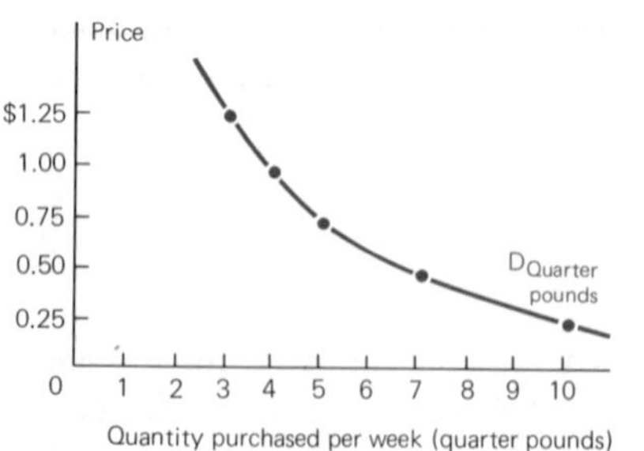

depend on all the factors that influence its demand. These may well result in different degrees of sensitivity at different price and income levels.

The concept of *demand price elasticity* was invented to provide a measure of the sensitivity of purchases to price changes. It is tempting to use the *slope* or slant of the demand schedule as drawn on a graph for this purpose. But that is unsatisfactory, because the slope of the demand schedule depends on the particular units used to measure the quantities. Suppose, for example, that a household's demand curve for butter measured in pounds and in quarter pounds were that in Tables 20-5 and 20-6 and in Figures 20-5 and 20-6. With quantity measured in quarter pounds or with a larger space for each pound on the horizontal axis, the demand schedule in Figure 20-6 is made to look flatter and much more sensitive to price changes than the demand schedule of Figure 20-5. Yet it is the same demand schedule. Thus, the slope is a misleading indicator of demand elasticity. This problem is avoided by defining demand elasticity as a measure of the sensitivity of the response of quantity demanded to price changes in terms of *relative changes* both in prices and quantities.

A numerical measure of the price elasticity of demand is computed in the following way:

$$\text{The price elasticity of demand, } e = \frac{\text{the percentage change in the quantity purchased}}{\text{the percentage change in price which caused it}}$$

Prices and quantities move in opposite directions, so this number, e, always has a minus sign if one is precise about it. Since elasticity is a little cumbersome to deal with when the minus sign tags along, we shall always refer to the *absolute value* of the elasticity, that is, the value without the minus sign. Even so, a problem arises in implementing this measure. The problem, which comes up in the calculation of relative changes, is, *Percentage change from what?* It is sometimes convenient to think of prices changing over time while everything else remains constant. Then there is a "first" and a "second" price and quantity. In the theory of consumer choice, however, the various prices and quantities are regarded as *alternatives,* with no specific "first" or "second." What does one do then? There are no perfect answers when we deal with real situations, but it is reasonable to split the difference when the differences are substantial. That is, when prices change from \$9 to \$11, the percentage change is *not* computed as (\$9 − \$11)/\$9 *or* (\$9 − \$11)/\$11, but as (\$9 − \$11)/\$10. The demand elasticity using this convention is, therefore, computed by the equation:

$$e = \frac{Q_2 - Q_1}{\frac{Q_2 + Q_1}{2}} \bigg/ \frac{P_2 - P_1}{\frac{P_2 + P_1}{2}}$$

When the quantity demanded is quite sensitive to price changes, then the percentage change in quantity will be greater than the percentage change in price which caused it, and the elasticity of demand will be greater than one. When quantity demanded is relatively insensitive to price changes, the percentage change in quantity will be less than the percentage change in price which caused it, and the elasticity of demand will be less than one. Right between them is the knife edge case of unitary elasticity in which price changes cause quantities to change in the same proportion as price. The range of elasticities can be represented as shown in Figure 20-7 for the absolute values of demand elasticity.

Figure 20-7

RANGE OF DEMAND ELASTICITY

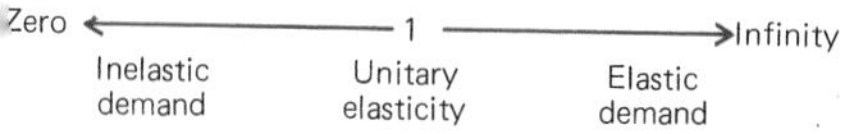

Elasticity is in general a characteristic *of a particular point on a demand schedule or of a movement along the schedule in a particular region.* There is no reason to suppose that, in general, demand schedules have the same demand elasticity at all points and in all regions. Only in special cases will that be so. This can be made most evident by computing the elasticity of demand at various points along a straight-line demand schedule. Table 20-7 is an example of such a schedule as shown in the plot of the points in

Table 20-7

PRICE AND QUANTITY DIFFERENCE BETWEEN POINTS ON A DEMAND SCHEDULE

	Price	*Quantity*	*Difference in Price*	*Difference in Quantity*
A	\$10	4		
			\$2	2
B	8	6		
			2	2
C	6	8		
			2	2
D	4	10		
			2	2
E	2	12		

Table 20-8

ELASTICITY CALCULATIONS BETWEEN POINTS ON A DEMAND SCHEDULE

Points	Percentage change in Price	Percentage change in Quantity	$e = \dfrac{\text{Percentage change in quantity}}{\text{Percentage change in price}}$
A–B	$\dfrac{\$10 - \$8}{\dfrac{\$10 + \$8}{2}} = \dfrac{2}{9}$	$\dfrac{4 - 6}{\dfrac{4 + 6}{2}} = \dfrac{-2}{5}$	$\left(\dfrac{-2}{5} \Big/ \dfrac{2}{9}\right) = -1.8$
B–C	$\dfrac{\$8 - \$6}{\dfrac{\$8 + \$6}{2}} = \dfrac{2}{7}$	$\dfrac{6 - 8}{\dfrac{6 + 8}{2}} = \dfrac{-2}{7}$	$\left(\dfrac{-2}{7} \Big/ \dfrac{2}{7}\right) = -1.000$
C–D	$\dfrac{\$6 - \$4}{\dfrac{\$6 + \$4}{2}} = \dfrac{2}{5}$	$\dfrac{8 - 10}{\dfrac{8 + 10}{2}} = \dfrac{-2}{9}$	$\left(\dfrac{-2}{9} \Big/ \dfrac{2}{5}\right) = -0.555$
D–E	$\dfrac{\$4 - \$2}{\dfrac{\$4 + \$2}{2}} = \dfrac{2}{3}$	$\dfrac{10 - 12}{\dfrac{10 + 12}{2}} = \dfrac{-2}{11}$	$\left(\dfrac{-2}{11} \Big/ \dfrac{2}{3}\right) = -0.272$

Figure 20-8. The elasticity of demand between the points is calculated as shown in Table 20-8.

There are only two cases in which simply by looking at a demand schedule one can tell what its elasticity is. Those are the extreme cases in which the elasticities of demand are zero and infinity, as shown in Figures 20-9 and 20-10. In Figure 20-9, the quantity purchased is fixed by influences other than price, and changes in price will have no effect on it. In Figure 20-10, an indefi-

Figure 20-8

ELASTICITIES AT DIFFERENT LOCATIONS ALONG A STRAIGHT-LINE DEMAND SCHEDULE

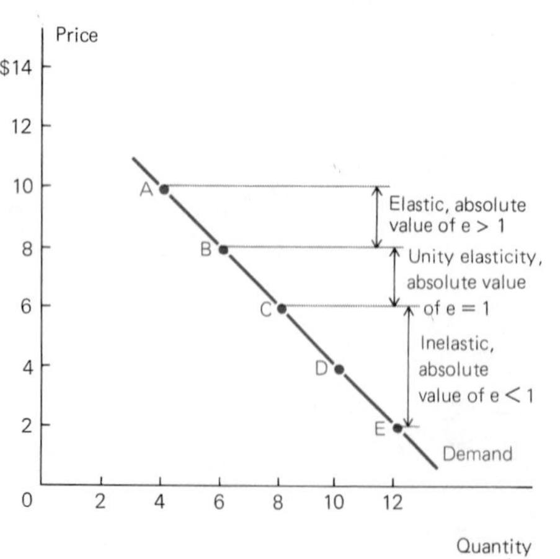

Figure 20-9

EXAMPLE OF COMPLETELY INELASTIC DEMAND ($e = 0$)

Figure 20-10

EXAMPLE OF COMPLETELY ELASTIC DEMAND (e = INFINITY)

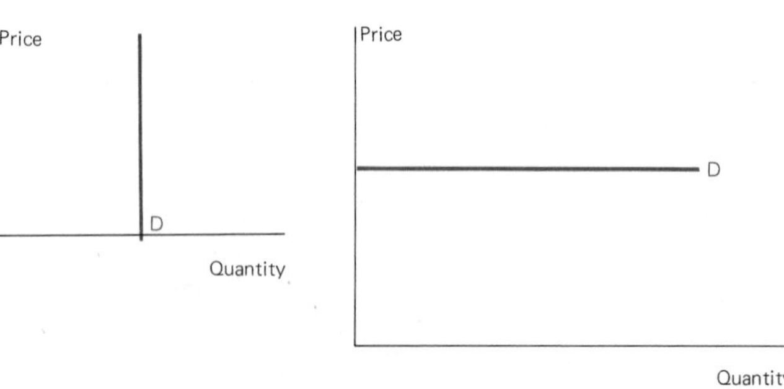

nitely large or small quantity would be purchased at the going price.

It is hard to find examples which correspond to these extreme cases except over some limited ranges. The demand for table salt is undoubtedly almost completely inelastic (elasticity of demand = 0) over most normal price ranges, but what commodity has an infinitely elastic demand?

Demand elasticity and total expenditures

Another way of thinking about demand elasticity is to associate it with changes in total expenditures. With an elastic demand, the quantity demanded is quite sensitive to price changes. Any change in prices, a reduction, for example, will be more than offset by the increase in purchases it induces. As a result, total expenditures will rise even though prices are lower. This is shown for a series of hypothetical cases in Figures 20-11, 20-12, and 20-13. In each, the total expenditure at price P_1 is P_1Q_1. That is the area of the rectangle P_1AQ_1O. When the price falls to P_2, total expenditure is P_2Q_2, which is the area of the rectangle P_2BQ_2O. In each figure, the initial total expenditure is the vertically shaded area. Total expenditure after the price change is the horizontally shaded area. When price goes down, revenue is gained in the amount $P_2(Q_2 - Q_1)$ and lost in the amount $Q_1(P_1 - P_2)$. If demand is elastic, as in Figure 20-11, the gains are greater than the losses, and the horizontally shaded area is greater than the vertically shaded area. The reverse is true for inelastic demand, in Figure 20-13. For unity elas-

Figure 20-11

TOTAL EXPENDITURE COMPARISONS WITH ELASTIC DEMAND

Figure 20-12

TOTAL EXPENDITURE COMPARISONS WHEN DEMAND ELASTICITY IS 1

Figure 20-13

TOTAL EXPENDITURE COMPARISONS WITH INELASTIC DEMAND

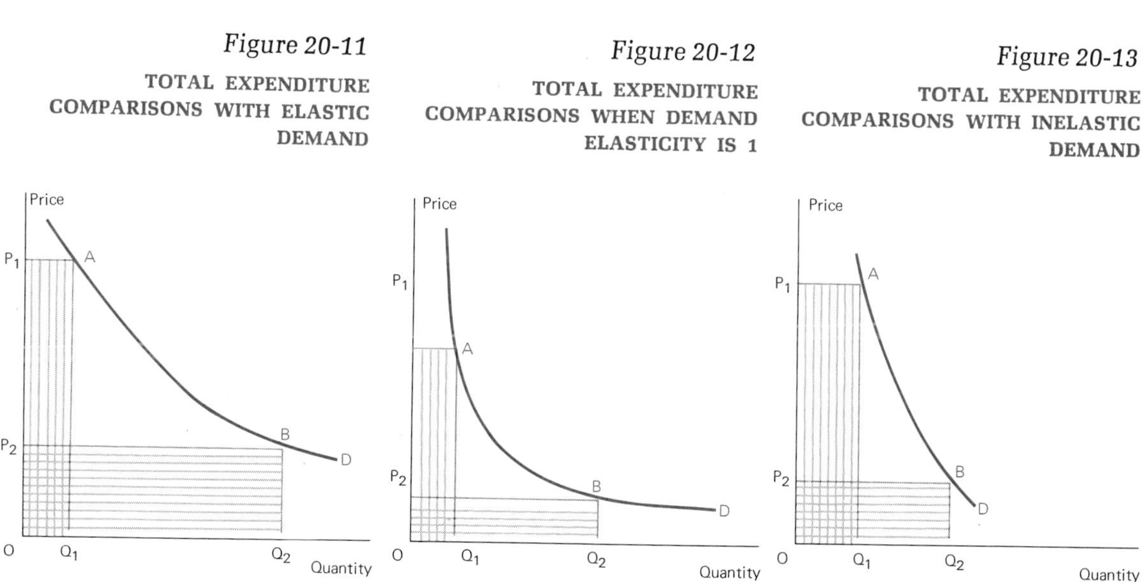

ticity of demand, in Figure 20-12, the two rectangles have the same size.

The income elasticity of demand

Figure 20-14

SHIFTS IN DEMAND DUE TO INCOME CHANGES

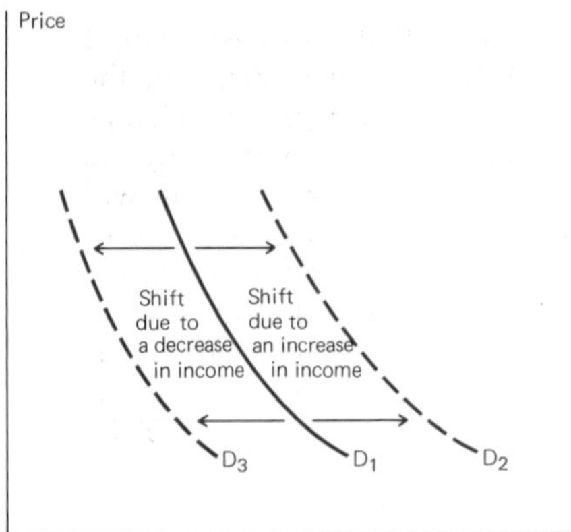

The demand curve of a commodity is drawn with everything *but* price kept unchanged. We know, however, that demand is also sensitive to income, and Figure 20-14 shows the normal relationship.

It is often interesting and important to measure the sensitivity of purchases of different commodities to changes in income. Automobile producers and sellers want to know whether people will continue to buy automobiles at the same rate as their incomes continue to rise. Public officials may want to project private expenditures on education and medical care as incomes increase. The *income elasticity of demand* is the appropriate sensitivity measure. It is defined analogously to the price elasticity:

$$\text{Income elasticity of demand} = \frac{\text{percentage change in quantity purchased}}{\text{percentage change in income which caused it}}$$

The "normal" case, as explained in Chapter 19, is for purchases to go up as income rises, though the extent to which this is so depends on the level of income. The quantity purchased of inferior goods will actually fall when income rises.

An exercise in demand elasticity with luxuries and necessities. It is tempting to think of necessities as commodities whose demand price is inelastic. The quantities needed may seem to be exactly so much and no more, and, therefore, quantities purchased will not respond very much to price changes. On the other hand, luxuries appear to be nonessential. It seems that they can and will be given up readily if their prices rise and, since they are much desired, quantities purchased may expand a great deal if prices fall.

This reasoning will not stand against a few observations. Cigarettes and beer, ordinarily classed as luxuries, have inelastic demands. Butter, which appears to be more of a necessity, has a more elastic demand. The truth is that price elasticity of demand is a characteristic of a narrow region of a demand schedule and will not necessarily reflect at all accurately a scaling of goods in terms of their necessity for survival. The same is true of income elasticity of demand: There is no necessary relationship between that number and survival requirements.

Cross elasticities of demand. What will happen to the sales of one commodity, say, Food, when the price of another, say, Clothing, changes? The cross elasticity of demand measures that type of sensitivity. It is likewise defined as:

$$\text{Cross elasticity of demand of Food to Clothing price} = \frac{\text{percentage change in quantity of Food purchased}}{\text{percentage change in price of Clothing}}$$

The cross elasticity of demand of one commodity for another can be used to measure quantitatively the degree to which one good is a substitute or complement for another. For example, suppose the price of one good, Food, goes up. That reduces the quantity of Food demanded. If it increases the quantity of Clothing demanded, then Food and Clothing are *substitutes*, and the cross elasticity of demand is positive. On the other hand, if the quantity of Clothing demanded went down when the price of Food went up, the goods would be *complements*, and the income elasticity of demand would be negative. Substitution relationships among goods are the most common, but some goods, like ham and eggs, go together and are complements.

Qualifications to the theory of demand

The theory of demand, particularly the modern version, starts from relatively simple and plausible assumptions about human behavior and draws the logical conclusions. The assumptions leave out some important phenomena which affect consumer demand behavior, however. These omitted influences require that we add certain qualifications to the theory.

Interactions among consumers: Bandwagon and snob effects

It is a common observation that some consumption is based on a desire to keep up with the Joneses. This is called a *bandwagon* effect in consumption, because when Jones buys something and Smith and Brown imitate him and then many more imitate them, there is a lot of jumping to get on the bandwagon.

It is difficult to estimate the quantitative importance of this effect in demand. It certainly upsets the logic of the *theory* of demand, however. That theory assumes that each person's or family's decisions are independent of others. Separate demands can, therefore, be identified and added up to compute total demand. Though this is a good approximation to reality for many types of goods, it can be quite untrue and misleading in other circumstances. Thorstein Veblen, the great iconoclastic American economist and sociologist, wrote at the end of the nineteenth century of the interacting motives for *conspicuous consumption* which lie behind some consumer choices. At the level of individual choice, that need not disturb the analysis, which does not inquire into how and why individual tastes are formed. At that level, it is only of incidental interest that the Joneses set the fashion for the rest of us.

The existence of the bandwagon effect, however, means that we cannot simply add up consumer demands based on individual decision making and obtain a total or market demand relationship. Why? Because when one person, say Jones, increases his consumption, others follow. In effect, individual demand decisions are interdependent.

How destructive is this point for the theory of demand? It is hard to estimate its quantitative significance, but even Veblen thought that conspicuous consumption was mainly in "wasteful" and "superfluous" goods. That leaves a wide range of products for which this qualification would have at most only a limited weight.

There are also certain goods that some consumers will buy *more* of, rather than less, when the price goes up. Why? Because that is a way of impressing other people. Such behavior produces *snob effects*, and these, too, tend to undermine the normal demand relationship described in the theory.

Interdependence in consumer choice: Public goods

Another source of interdependence among consumers in the choices they make is that some goods are not consumed by one individual or family *exclusively*. The theory of demand relates to *private goods* that are used up and enjoyed on an individual or family basis. Goods not consumed exclusively, but to some extent "used" collectively, are identified as *public goods*. For example, the streetlight that shines on me, and lights my way, also lights the way of my neighbor, and neither he nor I "uses it up." Neither person's consumption of it is exhaustive or exclusive.

The "joint use" characteristic of public goods means that *decisions about their purchase are not made independently by consumers*. Many people may want them but, because of the peculiar nature of the goods, will not buy them in markets in the same way they buy a loaf of bread or a bottle of wine.

If my neighbor purchases a pure public good, I can benefit just as much from his purchase as he does. Since I can, I may well encourage him to make the purchase and then sit back and enjoy it. Suppose, for example, my neighbors and I all wanted a fire-alarm box installed on our block. If one of my neighbors had the box installed on the curb in front of his house, I could use it also. So I might play a waiting game and hope that my neighbor, who is more of a worrier, will pay for it.

On the other hand, suppose I and all my neighbors answered honestly an interviewer who asked if we wanted the box installed and how much we would individually be willing to pay if that were the only way of obtaining it. The answers might be:

> Two of us would each be willing to pay $100 for a fire alarm.
> Four more would each be willing to pay $80 for a fire alarm.
> Eight more would each be willing to pay $60 for a fire alarm.
> Sixteen more would each be willing to pay $40 for a fire alarm.

The total demand for a fire-alarm box is not the conventional sum of the individual demands at each price. We can see this by asking how many boxes would (and should) be installed if the city charged \$60 to put one up. No one wants fourteen (2+4+8) red fire-alarm boxes standing along the street. We want only one, and we all want one a lot. The total amount we would all together be willing to pay for *one* box is:

$$(2 \times \$100) + (4 \times \$80) + (8 \times \$60) + (16 \times \$40) = \$1{,}640$$

That is far more than necessary to justify one box, and yet conventional market demand calculations would not show this.

The demand for public goods is not expressed primarily through markets, but through the political mechanism. A discussion of the effectiveness of that mechanism in reflecting the community's desires for public goods is beyond the scope of this book, except to point out that it is quite unlike the market demand mechanism. The political mechanism nearly always operates through elected representatives, and the demand for public goods is usually only one of the issues involved in their election. The expression of demand for public goods is often diluted and mixed with other political issues.

Advertising and consumer choice

Another criticism of the theory of consumer demand says that it is irrelevant in an age when consumer demands are created, molded, manipulated, and, occasionally, perverted by advertising. Under the tremendous pressures of modern advertising, it is claimed, nothing significant is left to free and rational choice. "The general effect of sales effort, defined in the broadest terms," J. K. Galbraith argues, "is to shift the locus of decision in the purchase of goods from the consumer where it is beyond control to the firm where it is subject to control."[1]

The objective of product advertising — in the jargon of economics — is to shift the product's demand curve out and twist it. The purpose is to be able to sell more than would otherwise be possible at the price charged or to permit the advertiser to increase his price without a loss in sales. Even if advertising can do this for a particular commodity — and apparently many advertising and other business men think it can — it does not follow that advertising will increase total consumer expenditures and reduce saving. We must beware of the logical fallacy of composition. What is true for one product, or even a great many products, may not be true for all. Unfortunately, we are as yet unable to measure the impact of product advertising on total spending.

The effects of advertising on consumer choices for particular products are difficult to sift out. There is a great deal of folklore, however. We are sometimes told — virtually in the same breath —

[1] *The New Industrial State,* Houghton Mifflin Company, Boston, 1967, chap. 18.

that, on the one hand, no one pays any attention to advertising anymore and, on the other hand, that it has made the consumer the pliable tool of business. While we cannot say which of these or other views is correct, we can organize the issues so as to identify them more clearly.

Figure 20-15

CHARACTERISTICS OF ADVERTISING

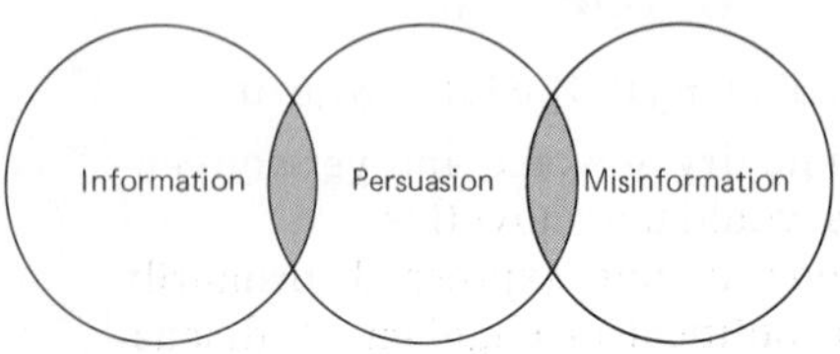

From the standpoint of the theory of consumer demand, it is *not* necessarily bad or good that advertising expands and twists the demand for a particular product. *An evaluation of advertising will surely depend on how and why it is done and on each person's appreciation of the mix of motives, costs, and results.* To make this point more clearly, let us organize product advertising into the not mutually exclusive categories of Information, Persuasion, and Misinformation, as shown in Figure 20-15.

Information about availability, prices, and qualities permits consumers to make more informed choices. It need not affect preference for beef or pork or for cotton or nylon clothing except insofar as it informs consumers about the true qualities of each. Much department store and grocery store advertising is primarily to inform consumers about availability and price. This, in itself, should not be enough to convince us that informational advertising is a "good thing." There is still a cost test. Product information has benefits which make it worth paying for, but it is not worth any price, however high. It can be provided with different degrees of efficiency. Perhaps all informational advertising could be carried in the classified columns. That would certainly reduce costs. Would it convey the same information?

At the other end of the spectrum, there are innumerable obvious and subtle ways that advertising can mislead. It promises qualities and prices which sometimes simply do not exist and which mislead consumer choices. Undesirable features that might turn consumers against the product are suppressed. Cigarette producers would not willingly publish the warning that is now printed on cigarette packages. It took a federal law to make them do it.

Advertisements also prey on our emotions, promising virility, sex appeal, power, and prestige – all of which are irrelevant to the product advertised. Yet we should not think that all such advertising is necessarily misleading. If driving a big fast car would make me feel successful, an ad which promises that does not deceive me. But I should not delude myself into thinking that feeling successful is the same as being successful.

Misinformative advertising distorts choices and makes people worse off. And to add insult to injury, they have to pay for it, too!

What about advertising that simply alters preferences? The cigarette, soap, and soft-drink jingles that we cannot get out of our heads may lead us to make purchases we otherwise would not make. Is that bad?

Yes, if due to misinformation.

No, if based on correct information.

Not so clear, if there is no information content at all.

If we really believe there is no point in arguing about tastes, we have to give up on this question. Yet much advertising does, in fact, argue about tastes, and most of us are willing to argue with it: whether movies are better than ever, or whether this year's model is the most beautiful car ever built, and so on. Much of the criticism of advertising is not really criticism of the act of advertising but of the tastes being promoted or of the techniques used. No doubt there are other important determinants of taste (long hair and beards were never advertised by any business), but the taste-setting power of advertising is a legitimate worry. Economists and other social scientists must simply work harder to provide more facts and analysis before we shall have an adequate basis for judging this form of advertising.

Where does all this leave the theory of consumer choice? The discussion might be summed up by saying that advertising men appear to regard the consumer more like a recalcitrant bucking bronco than a staid plow horse. They can occasionally get a saddle on him and stay on top a while, but it is a rough ride, and a lot of Madison Avenue cowboys fall off. That may reassure us a little about the independent-mindedness and rational thinking of the consumer, but it adds a worry about the costs involved and the effects on competition. Those will be dealt with later on in Chapter 26.

Market demand and consumer preferences

A discussion of the effectiveness of market demand in revealing consumer preferences provides the occasion for a final survey of the theory of demand.

The theory explains market demand as the sum of individual demands which express individual consumer preferences. How then shall we explain the common complaint that the system does not respond to consumer desires?

One explanation is that people have different tastes. That is understandable. But why should what one person consumes bother another person? There are *externalities* in consumption which arise from interdependence. A neighbor who loved neon lights so much that he outlined his house, doors, and windows with them would strain the patience of the most forbearing homeowner. It is not simply a matter of one man's taste. The neon lights shine not just on the one house but on the whole neighborhood, and the one man is to some extent imposing his tastes on a larger group.

Another explanation has its source in *social mores.* Some types of consumption which are not only personal but completely private are still subject to broad social approval or disapproval. It is argued, for example, that while some people are hungry and living in wretched housing, it is wrong to keep producing luxury goods. These are really complaints about the distribution of income, not about the system's lack of response to expressed demands.

Advertising, it is sometimes claimed, distorts consumer choices. The arguments were presented above. It should *not*, however, be thought that, before there was mass advertising, consumer choices rose from some deep and uncontaminated well of individual preferences. Social pressures expressed by the family and by religious, communal, and other social institutions have always had a powerful effect on consumer decisions. The issue with respect to advertising is not whether there should be social influences on individual consumption, but whether they should be of the sort now generated.

Finally, market demand will *not* reflect demands that are not expressed in markets. That is the case for *public goods*. If there is dissatisfaction with the balance between the amount and composition of private and public goods, the problem is not necessarily in the operation of the market. One must also ask whether or not the political system is adequately reflecting the demands for public goods.

Summary

The total or market demand for a good is the sum of the individual demands of all consumers for the particular good. Therefore, in addition to (1) tastes and preferences, (2) income of individual consumers, and (3) prices of other commodities, the determinants of market demand include (4) the number of consumers in the market, and (5) the distribution of income among consumers.

The elasticity of demand describes the responsiveness of quantities purchased to price changes. Demand elasticity is a characteristic of a particular point or small range of a demand schedule. It is measured by the ratio of the percentage change in purchases to the percentage change in prices. When quantity demanded is quite sensitive to price changes, the percentage change in quantity will be greater than the percentage change in price which caused the quantity change; in this case the absolute value of demand elasticity is greater than unity. When the percentage change in quantity demanded is less than the percentage change in price which caused it, demand elasticity is less than one in absolute value. In the just in-between situation, price changes and quantity changes will just balance, and demand elasticity will be unity.

When demand is elastic, a reduction in price, though it reduces the value of each unit sold, results in such a large increase in purchases that *total* expenditures rise. Or an increase in price reduces total expenditures. When demand is inelastic, the opposite is true. At the knife edge of unitary elasticity, price changes are just offset by changes in sales, so that expenditures remain constant.

The income elasticity of demand refers to the percentage

change in quantity demanded due to a particular percentage change in income. The cross elasticity of demand measures the degree of change in the quantity sold of one good due to a relative change in the price of another good.

The qualifications to the theory of demand arise in large part from interactions among consumers, whereas the theory assumes independent behavior. When there are bandwagon effects, consumers try to keep up with the Joneses. When there are snob effects, a higher price may induce greater sales, because paying it is a way of impressing others.

The theory of consumer choice does not apply to public goods, for which individual consumption is not exhaustive. In this case, the goods can be consumed jointly. Individual purchases then depend on the purchases of others, because their purchases can satisfy the first person's desires.

Advertising provides both useful and misleading information. Sometimes it provides no information at all, but is pure persuasion without information content. While advertising does not eliminate the role of consumer choice, it makes the theory irrelevant if it is true that consumers' tastes are simply manipulated by business. Though there are many contradictory statements about this, there is relatively little good evidence. Advertisers seem to regard consumers as buyers to be wooed and won rather than robots to be twisted and turned.

Questions for discussion and review

1. Do you think the market demand for most goods which consumers buy is at all sensitive to prices? Is it sensitive to income? Are your answers consistent? (Remember, a price change has income effects.)

2. Why does the distribution of income influence market demand? Can you give any examples of goods for which you believe the demand would change if there were a redistribution of income toward greater equality?

3. What does the following paraphrased statement tell you about the demand for hospital services? *East Coast physicians should learn from the practice of medicine on the West Coast that it is possible to discharge patients from hospitals more quickly than they are now doing. On the average, the stay of patients in hospitals is shorter on the West Coast than on the East. Of course, it is more important to patients of the West Coast to leave the hospital quickly, because the daily hospital charges are greater there. So total hospital bills are larger.*

4. The output of services such as medicine and education is growing more rapidly than income. What does that tell you about the income elasticity of demand for these products? Are there any products for which you think this is not the case?

5. Why is the presence of bandwagon and snob effects in principle so destructive to the theory of demand?

6. What are public goods, and why can't the theory of demand explain the demand for them?

7. Describe how demand price elasticity, income elasticity, and cross elasticity can be measured.

8. Discuss the following statement. *In spite of the criticisms of advertising and warnings about its effects, advertising still does not succeed in changing the Law of Demand. Even so, because advertising is such a powerful influence on demand, it changes the whole notion of consumer sovereignty.*

Concepts for review

Inelastic price elasticity of demand
Unity price elasticity of demand
Income elasticity of demand
Cross elasticity of demand
Bandwagon and snob effects
Interdependence in consumer choice
Nonexhaustive consumption

21

Business organization and motivation and the variety of market structures

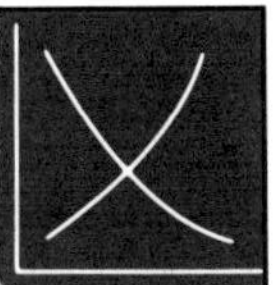

This chapter marks another of those critical points in our analysis of the private sector of the market economy. We have worked over the theory of demand in some detail, and it would appear natural to move on to a deeper analysis of the determinants of market supply. That is the plan, but our approach will have to be somewhat indirect. The supply responses of private businesses depend in part on how each firm perceives the market and on what it can do to affect the demands it faces. These in turn depend on the *structure* of the markets in which the firm operates.

The structure of markets refers to the *existence and comparative importance of monopolistic and competitive elements*. The subject of market structure is an interface between consumer demands and the supply responses of individual firms. A market structure itself has the effect of a sifting and sorting mechanism that channels the impact of total demand on each firm operating in the market. The market structure thus has a great deal to do with the profits a firm makes. From this observation we can infer that the individual firm may try to influence and change the structure of its market.

First, we shall discuss the organization and motivation of the business firm itself. Then the concept of markets and market structure. And finally, some of the most important types of market structures.

The organization and motivation of business firms

The business firm is the basic organizer of production in a mixed enterprise economy. To understand how production responds to consumer demands, we must understand the firm's motivation. The firm's motivation is, in turn, affected by how it is organized.

Organization

Business firms come in many sizes and forms of legal organization. There are small, informally organized proprietorships and partnerships turning out one or a few products or services, and there are large, intricately organized conglomerates producing many different types of goods. In the former, ownership and control are combined in the person or persons of the proprietors and partners. While some authority may be delegated to employees, typically the reins are held rather tightly in the hands of the owners.

In large corporations, the gap between ownership and control can be quite large. There may be thousands of stockholders, no one of whom has so substantial a share in the business that he can elect even one member of the board of directors in the annual stockholders' meeting. This is true for General Motors Corporation, for example. There are thousands of stockholders and no really big blocs. When ownership is widely distributed in this way, management may be more or less self-perpetuating. It may go on and on as long as its performance is not so bad that some group of "outsiders" – stockholders who disagree with the insiders' policy – can successfully organize a revolt.

In some large corporations, substantial blocks of stocks are owned by individuals or families or by private trusts on behalf of a few individuals. In these cases, there is no doubt who controls the board of directors, but the scale of the businesses requires extensive delegation of authority.

Between these extremes are many corporations in which ownership is not so concentrated. Substantial blocs may exist, yet they represent much less than 50 percent of the stock. In alliance with management, even a small bloc can control a corporation if the rest of the stock is widely scattered. When blocs compete with each other or with management for corporate control, they sometimes set off the spectacular financial battles reported in the newpapers.

Mergers and holding companies deserve a special word. Holding companies are organizational devices by which one corporation acquires a controlling interest in a number of other corporations and may, itself, be controlled by still another. They provide a means of pyramiding control; owners of a relatively small amount of stock can control several corporations. Figure 21-1 illustrates the principle. Firm M owns enough of the stock of the electronics firms

Figure 21-1

A CORPORATE CONGLOMERATE

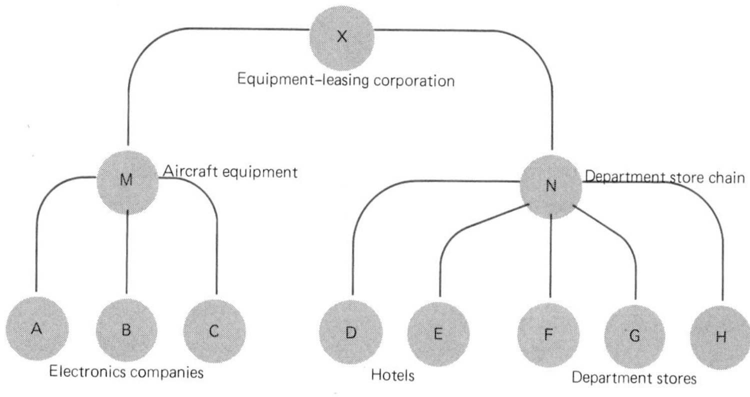

A, B, and C to control them. Firm N owns enough stock to control firms D, E, F, G, and H. Then firm X owns controlling interests in firms M and N. Thus, with just enough stock to control X, a stockholder or a bloc is able to control a large business empire.

In a merger: Firm M buys up enough stock of A, B, and C so that it can persuade the majority of stockholders to agree that A, B, and C should become an integral part of M. The stockholders of A, B, and C exchange their stock for stock in M. Likewise, N may persuade stockholders of firms D, E, F, G, and H to exchange their stock for stock in N. Finally, firm X merges with M and N.

In the merger process, the separate corporate identities of all firms except X may disappear, but some may remain as wholly owned subsidiaries of X. In the holding company, all the firms maintain their separate corporate identities and there continue to be other owners of stock of the operating firms besides the ownership of the holding company.

"Conglomerate" mergers took place on a large scale in the 1960s. The pace has slowed now, owing to attacks by the Justice Department and the effects of monetary restriction and recession in the late 1960s and early 1970s. As shown in Figure 21-1, conglomerate companies put together in a single firm a number of different kinds of unrelated products and services. These conglomerates are different from earlier "horizontal" and "vertical" combinations. The former joined firms producing more or less the same product. The latter joined firms whose products entered a single type of final product at various stages of production.

Motivations

The manner in which businesses react to consumer demands depends partly on the character of the markets in which they operate. But it depends partly also on *business objectives or motivations.* With the great variety in firm size and legal form, it would be natural to expect some variety in motivation.

There are surely great differences in the way businesses articulate their objectives. Yet the economist, in constructing his theories or models of market behavior, makes the same assumption about all firms. This is simply that businesses — all businesses — *try to maximize their profits.* That is not to say that they are always successful, but rather that they *try*. This is a powerful assumption: It is far-reaching in its implications and permits a detailed analysis of production and resource allocation. It is also a much discussed and much criticized assumption.

When economists assume profit maximization, that does not mean they believe that all firms actually behave the same way every minute of every working day. It is an abstraction of reality, an attempt to find and describe the most important and critical aspect of business behavior. Since it is an abstraction, we should not be surprised to find firms occasionally behaving as if they had some other primary objective. The proprietor of a neighborhood store or a small downtown business may only want a modest income and a quiet life, for example. On this rationale he may pass up profit-making opportunities. If his business and income are somehow protected from the attrition of competitors, he may be able to achieve his goal. If there is competition, however, he may wake up some day to find his business too quiet to yield that modest income any longer.

It does not seem unreasonable to say that most proprietorships and partnerships are trying to make themselves as well off as possible. That implies profit maximization, for their profits are their incomes. It would be quite a problem for microeconomic analysis if businesses regularly and systematically followed some other goal.

Since corporations produce roughly 57 percent of the national product, the more important question is, What goals guide this form of business enterprise? It has been argued, most recently in J. K. Galbraith's *New Industrial State*, that the separation of ownership and control in much of large modern enterprise means that the desires of the stockholder-owners for profits no longer guide the business. It is claimed that authority is so subdivided and delegated that the profit objectives of the stockholders get watered down. Decision makers at lower levels act to protect and advance the performance of their own divisions. That may or may not be consistent with profit maximization for the corporation as a whole. The head of a machine maintenance division may want to do the best job possible in maintaining the machines and keeping them in good working order. Unless someone above him has considered the relative cost of maintenance versus buying new machines and decided that maintenance is cheaper, good maintenance may be losing money for the business.

It has also been argued that even the top executives in modern corporations have other goals than profit maximization. They may have read a survey which shows that, on the average, the salaries of corporate executives are more closely related to the size of the firm than to its profitability. So, since salaries are larger in the larger firms, they may try to make their firm larger, even if it means sacrificing some profits. Or they may set certain growth objectives for the corporation in order to maintain or expand their share of the market. Or the top executives may conceive of themselves as business politicians, as mediators of the conflicting interests of bondholders, stockholders, white-collar personnel, unionized employees, and customers. They may just try to achieve survival.

There are chords of truth in all these refrains. Yet it is also true that these goals may be consistent with profit maximization and that profit maximization may be one of the best means of achieving them. Size and growth, for example, require investment. Profits and retained earnings from profits are one of the best sources of investment funds. Even if outside funds are used for growth, they are likely to be made available at lower real cost to the more profitable firms. The less profitable ones generally appear to be less desirable firms in which to put one's money. Moreover, relatively unprofitable firms are good targets for take-over attempts by "outsiders" who argue to stockholders that they can do better. Profit maximization does *not* mean sharp or shortsighted business practices. *It encompasses future as well as current profits and takes into account the future significance of current actions.*

The firm is constrained in its search for profits by the markets in which it operates as well as by its costs of production. We shall take up production costs in the next chapter. Our concern here is markets and market structure.

Markets

First, let us distinguish the popular definition of *market* from the economist's definition. People ordinarily think of a market as a *place* where goods are bought and sold. The economist extends this definition somewhat to say: *A market is composed of all the buyers and sellers of the same thing—a commodity, a service, a stock, or a bond.* A market is not necessarily a single place or even a collection of places so much as it is the means by which buyers and sellers confront each other. For United States government bonds, the market is essentially worldwide, and one can participate just by picking up the telephone and calling a bond broker. On the other hand, except for an occasional passing motorist, the local pharmacist seldom sells anything to anyone from outside the neighborhood.

What is critical is that the product sold in the "market" is the same for every prospective buyer. Appearances can deceive, however, and physically identical products are often bought and sold in different markets. A bag of cement in Boston is different from a bag of cement in Pittsburgh because of substantial differences in the costs of transporting the cement. So, strictly speaking, we often have to give the market a spatial dimension such that transport costs within it are negligible. The reason the United States bond market is worldwide is that the costs of making the purchase and of transporting the "commodity" are about the same everywhere.

For markets in which the spatial dimension is important, the boundaries are seldom clearly defined. Markets overlap and shade into each other as the transportation costs for buyers gradually increase. That is why arbitrary market boundaries tend to be erased by consumers as they try to find the best buys available. For example, a city sales tax will encourage consumers to go outside the city limits to make purchases on which the tax saving offsets the inconvenience of extra travel. If the city is big, with a large population concentrated close to its center – as in New York – that tendency will be less important.

We must also be aware that it is consumers who finally decide whether or not products are the same. The essential issue for market behavior is not the existence or nonexistence of "objective" differences in products, but "subjective" differences – as appreciated by the consumer. Two bottles of aspirin are different if consumers see different trademarks on the bottles and believe the contents are different, irrespective of the chemical analysis.

This does not mean that differences in consumer evaluations create a completely separate market for each product. The real or imagined differences may be relatively slight or quite significant. For example, people do act as if the various brands of aspirin were different. They also act as if the various brands of mouthwash were different. But the differences between aspirin and mouthwash are clearly greater than the differences within each category. So it makes sense to discuss the aspirin market as distinct from the mouthwash market.

Market structure

"Market structure" or "market organization" is a technical, generic concept of economists for which there is no equivalent layman's term. Briefly, it refers to all those organizational characteristics of markets which determine how the business firms buying or selling in the markets behave: whether and how they are competitive or monopolistic. For business firms, as for individuals, no *single* overriding characteristic determines how they behave. Height alone does not determine whether a boy will be a good basketball player, and score on an IQ test does not alone determine whether a person will make good grades. Likewise, the behavior of a business depends on the features of the markets in which it sells and also on its production costs. There is infinite variety among markets, just as there is among individuals. In general, however, the major features that distinguish one market from another can be discussed in terms of concentration of buyers and sellers, product differentiation, information availability and the quality of firm response, and barriers to entry.

Concentration of sellers and buyers. The number of potential transactors on each side of the market is one of the most significant market characteristics. It is a major determinant of the alternatives available to a transactor and, therefore, of the freedom each has from the influence of any other single buyer or seller. The existence of real alternatives depends on the relative size of the transactor, however, as well as on numbers. Suppose 3 firms have 95 percent of an industry's capacity and 997 firms have the other 5 percent. The alternative sellers for a big buyer are not 1,000 firms but only the few large firms. Any measure of concentration must take into account the *size distribution of firms as well as the total number.*

Product differentiation. There are not many products which buyers regard as absolutely identical. Some of the standard and staple foods might fit into this category. Products are differentiated by *real or imagined quality distinctions, by packaging, and by related services.* The significance of product differentiation is in its influence on buyers' preferences and on their willingness to pay a premium for the product and, if so, how much. In effect, the distinct identification of a product in consumers' minds gives the seller some control over his markets that he would not otherwise have.

Information availability and the quality of firm response. The degree to which the *actions of one transactor respond to the actions of others* is another important market characteristic. Interdependence of sellers and buyers depends largely on concentration and product differentiation. But it also depends on the amount of information available in the market. Moreover, every market has a history, and the different histories distinguish the markets even though the markets may have certain similar characteristics today, say, in number of firms and size distribution. A market reduced to five firms as a result of aggressive competition and elimination of other competitors is likely to be different from a market of five firms, four of which were allowed by government action to participate in a patent monopoly.

Barriers to entry. The conduct of individual firms depends not only on the actual or potential reactions of other firms already in the market but also on the *possible entry of new firms.* In some markets, entry may be relatively easy; in others, difficult. Ease of entry depends in part on whether production requires special, technical know-how that is relatively scarce. High fixed costs that must be met before new firms can begin producing discourage entry. Large-scale and aggressive advertising by existing firms can also create a barrier.

The varieties of market structure: Some market models

Each of the market characteristics described above can assume different patterns. Altogether they can be combined in a bewildering number of ways, and economists have not yet succeeded in bringing order out of this chaotic variety. That is why microeconomic analysis when applied to actual situations is still something of an art. Economists do not yet have a complete set of tools that anyone can apply to any market with assurance that he will come up with the correct understanding. We can, however, isolate a few "polar" or special cases and analyze them in detail. Then we can use them to round out our understanding of how other markets operate. The special cases are, in effect, "models" of different types of markets. They are not comprehensive in their description. For example, they lack any history, even a stereotyped or "model" history. As general models, they lose particularity. So in applying the market models to particular situations, we must exercise care. That is always necessary when interpreting reality with theories.

As a first approximation, it is useful to think of different kinds of market organizations *as different locations on a spectrum*. Along the spectrum, one type of market structure shades into another until it is clearly distinct from a type some distance away, but it is not so different from its neighbor. Only the extreme positions on the spectrum are uniquely identifiable. These represent perfect competition and pure monopoly.

Monopoly

Pure monopoly is the easiest model to identify, though its causes, methods, and effects are not so obvious. In a monopoly, there is *only one seller of a commodity for which there are no close substitutes*. The last part of the definition is important. The person who patents a square doughnut and obtains an exclusive right to its production has a monopoly in square doughnuts, to be sure. What is it worth? If square doughnuts attract some buyers because of the novelty, because they dunk better, or because they do not roll off the plate, the exclusive patent *is* worth something. But if square doughnuts are considered more or less identical to round doughnuts, the exclusive right hardly deserves to be called a monopoly.

There are potential substitutes for almost every kind of commodity: beef and pork are substitutes; so are beer and wine. Movies and television are. So are radio and television. If the ballgame is not shown on local TV, some people will listen to it on the radio. But some products are closer substitutes than others. How "distant" must the substitutes be for the single seller to be a monopolist? This is not an easy question to answer. Essentially, the definition of monopoly hinges on *whether the seller has the power to affect the price of the product by controlling the amount he sells* and whether, in this sense, the seller is a *price maker*.

When there is only one firm in an industry, the firm *is* the industry, and the demand schedule faced by the monopolist is the aggregate demand schedule for the industry's output. If we keep in mind that every monopoly has its own demand schedule, which is a constraint on its operations, we can avoid an elementary confusion about monopoly. That is the notion that the monopolist can charge whatever price he wants to charge *and* sell whatever amount he wants to sell. He cannot do both! The quantity of a commodity purchased by consumers depends on many factors, as explained in Chapter 20, including the tastes and income of consumers – and the price of the commodity. The aggregate demand schedule tells us how much all consumers will buy at each price. It also tells us that price and sales are tied together. The monopolist is a price maker and can set the price by deciding how much he chooses to sell. Or he can determine his sales by setting his price. But he cannot set his price and his sales independently of each other. We shall study in Chapter 25 just how the monopolist actually does set his price.

Pure monopoly is sometimes created by law. For example, exclusive franchises given to public utility companies create monopolies. These "natural monopolies" are justified by the technological and cost advantages that a single firm can achieve. These monopolies created by law are also regulated by law. Government bodies determine the prices they charge and their conditions of service.

The patent laws also confer exclusive rights for production and sale. These are a reward for new inventions. But the courts do not permit firms to buy up patents in order to establish monopolies.

Economic warfare of one firm on others, which results in the defeat and disappearance of all but the victor, has been used to create monopoly. Such warfare has a vivid and dramatic place in capitalist folklore. It seems to have been relatively rare in national markets, however, owing partly to the counterattacks of the antitrust laws. We shall understand the conditions of pure monopoly better by contrasting it with other types of market structure. The contrast will be sharpest if we move at once to the other extreme on the spectrum, perfect competition.

Perfect competition

The essence of perfect competition, as an economist would define it, is that *no seller of the commodity has any influence on the price of the good.* Each one is a *price taker.* As compared with the monopolist who can influence the price by changing his output, the perfectly competitive firm can do nothing to manipulate price, by changing its output or by any other means. The conditions of perfect competition are so stringent that they are almost never fully met. But if they were met, what would they be?

There would have to be a great many sellers, each acting independently and not colluding with any other. How many is "a great many"? No specific number, but so many that the production of each seller would be a drop in the ocean of the competitive industry. That means that, like a drop in the ocean, a perfectly competitive firm could increase or decrease its size, even enter or leave the industry, and no one would notice the difference.

If there are ten fairly similar firms producing an identical commodity in an industry, the entry or withdrawal of one firm will result in a 10 percent average change in the sales of each of the others. That kind of change is certainly large enough for a firm to feel. If there are 1,000 firms of about the same size producing the same good, when one firm enters the industry or withdraws, the change in the sales of the other firms will average only 0.1 percent, which is barely noticeable. If there are 10,000 similar firms, a change in production by one firm would probably have no noticeable effect on the others, and, thus, would exactly fit the model.

Also like a drop in the ocean, *the output of any single perfectly competitive firm is indistinguishable from the output of any other firm in the industry*. Or, to use the jargon, the product is standardized, homogeneous, and undifferentiated among firms. The buyer is completely indifferent about where he makes his purchase. That is ensured by the model's requirement that all the services associated with a purchase, such as delivery conditions and credit terms, are absolutely the same for every seller. Since a pleasant smile and a friendly word may be enough to turn a consumer's head, we must insist that all transactions be completely impersonal.

It is conceivable that, even in an industry of many firms of roughly similar size producing a standard product, there could be temporary collusion. The markets could become fragmented and unorganized. Such conditions would forestall efficient interaction of supply and demand forces and might result in prices and quantity which are not the same for all sellers. To avoid this, the model requires that all the participants, both buyers and sellers, have access to the same market information and know the prices being quoted. A competitive market is, therefore, well organized in the sense of quick and full transmission of information and accomplishment of transactions. An auction market or an open bidding market, such as a commodity exchange, is a realistic approximation.

Can you think of any industries that even approximate these strict conditions? The examples most frequently given are of agricultural commodities such as wheat, corn, and cotton. Though some farms are large by absolute standards, they are still small in comparison with the total size of the crops marketed. When a grain elevator operator or cotton warehouser sets the price for the commodity, it is based on a judgment about a market in which his purchases and sales are just a drop in a bucket. The farmer, big or small, can sell to the warehouse operator or not, but he cannot force the price up by withholding his crop or force it down by selling.[1] Other industries, such as the production of standard textile goods and some wood products, also come fairly close to the competitive norm.

[1] The farmer can decide to *speculate* that prices will go up and withhold his crop on that basis. In itself, however, that will not make prices go up. But if many farmers withhold their output, prices will go up. Competitive price setting prevails in agricultural commodity markets only when government price-support programs do not create barriers to its operation.

The competitive firm's demand schedule. One of the least obvious features of the perfectly competitive model is the nature of the demand schedule faced by the individual firm. The concept of the industry's demand is familiar to us. It is the demand of all consumers for the particular product, and, as we have come to expect, total purchases are larger at low prices than at high prices. But no one of the relatively small firms in the competitive model faces that total demand, as evidenced by the following test: Any firm can expand its output manyfold and still have no effect on the price charged in the industry. As far as the individual, price-taking producer in a perfectly competitive industry is concerned, his demand schedule *shows no variation of price with his sales! It is a straight horizontal line at the going price,* whatever that price happens to be.

Figures 21-2 and 21-3 help to demonstrate this. Suppose the price of wheat is $1.75 per bushel as shown in Figure 21-2. In that price range about 1.5 billion bushels are sold every year in the United States. There are about 2 million farms producing wheat. No single farm is big enough to make the slightest dent on the market. Thus, each perfectly competitive producer is a *price taker* rather than a *price maker.* The individual, perfectly competitive farm-firm can sell a little or a lot and the price will not change, as is shown in Figure 21-3. No one will buy at a price higher than that prevailing in the market. Everything the farm-firm wants to sell at the going price will be sold, so there is no reason to sell at a lower price. A quick reference to Chapter 20 will help in recalling that a demand schedule like that in Figure 21-3 has an infinitely large elasticity. Sometimes it is called a "perfectly" elastic demand. If the firm increases its price at all, for example, it will lose all its sales.

Figure 21-2

HYPOTHETICAL MARKET DEMAND AND SUPPLY SCHEDULES FOR WHEAT

Figure 21-3

DEMAND FACED BY INDIVIDUAL PRODUCER

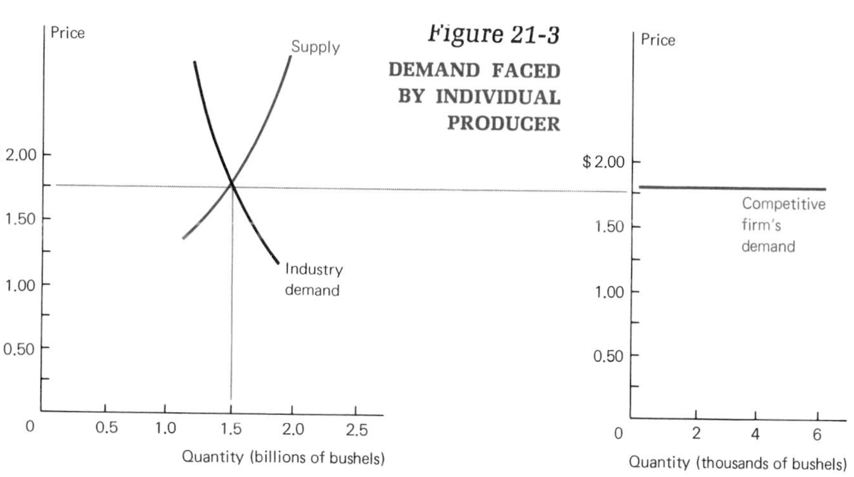

A final warning: While no *single* firm can affect the going price in a perfectly competitive industry, the actions of *all* firms will. The reason for this will become clear in the next chapter.

Imperfect competition

Between the extreme models of pure monopoly and perfect competition lie the diverse types of market organizations that we find in reality. There are industries with a few giant firms and a lot of small ones producing similar products (steel). There are those with only a few big firms (autos). There are those with many firms producing a wide variety of products, some of which are quite different and many quite similar (pharmaceutical drugs). There are industries with a moderate number of firms producing a few virtually identical products (lumber). Nearly every industry has its own somewhat unique pattern, and no simple classification scheme can capture and organize the tremendous variety.

All these in-between market forms are labeled *imperfect competition*. They are "blemished" types of competition. An alternative name for them which is sometimes used is "monopolistic competition." That suggests that they contain monopolistic elements in a competitive structure. We shall use *imperfect competition,* and reserve *monopolistic competition* for a special case to be described below. It should be clear that the terms are used descriptively, not pejoratively. The social and economic consequences of the alternative market forms will be examined in later chapters.

The essential and distinguishing feature of imperfectly competitive industries is *the power the individual firm has to "make" prices by adjusting its sales — without, however, having the complete power of a monopolist.* In our shorthand terminology: The demand curve faced by a firm in an imperfectly competitive industry is not horizontal at the going price; it has some slope, but is not the demand curve of the industry.

It is understandable that a firm would want to have some control over its price, rather than having to accept the industry price, as a perfectly competitive firm must. Perfect competition is a rigorous world of cold, hard calculation. Life would certainly be cozier for the firm if it could somehow get some power to set its own price, and it is natural that it should try to get to that position. There are many different ways to achieve this control, and it is possible in a variety of market structures. The two most common types are: (1) oligopoly — an industry of relatively few firms and (2) monopolistic competition — an industry of relatively numerous firms, each one of which sells a product that consumers regard as somewhat different. We will describe these in some detail.

Oligopoly

Oligopoly comes in two forms: *differentiated* and *undifferentiated*, depending on whether or not the products sold are generally regarded as noticeably different. In an oligopoly, there are only a few firms, all relatively large. The industry may have evolved in this way due to the relative efficiency of large-scale production. Or cost advantages in advertising may lead to this pattern, or patent barriers may limit the entry of new firms. When there are economies of large-scale production, entry of new firms on a small scale is difficult even if the established firms do not engage in economic warfare against newcomers.

The aluminum industry, in which there are only four producers of aluminum from the ore, is a reasonably good example of an undifferentiated oligopoly, because there is relatively little difference among the firms' aluminum products. Until 1945 there was only one aluminum producer, Alcoa, the Aluminum Company of America, which had an absolute monopoly, based primarily on the original patents for the production of aluminum. Since 1945 three new primary producers have entered the field, partly by purchase of government production facilities built during World War II. And there are six new producers at the next stage of the production process. As a result, none of the ten aluminum metal producing firms has complete monopoly power, but none is simply a price taker either. The firms are closely interdependent in their business decisions whether they like it or not and whether they consciously exploit the fact or not. Unlike in a perfectly competitive industry, *the actions of one firm in an oligopoly in changing its output or its price have an immediate effect on the output and prices of the others.* Each firm knows this and expects a reaction to its own actions.

The automobile and cigarette industries are examples of differentiated oligopolies since the few firms in each sell products that people think are different. It does not matter whether a laboratory test would show them to be different or not. If advertising or any other influence makes a substantial number of people think the products are different, that is enough, for our present purposes, to make it so. Advertising thus gives the firm some control over its price and sales that it would not otherwise have. It is understandable that oligopolies would want to insulate or isolate their markets. Interdependence does not necessarily make for a comfortable and easy life. The intensive interdependence in oligopoly even makes it difficult to generalize about the demand curve for the individual firm, as we shall see in Chapter 25.

Monopolistic competition

In a monopolistically competitive industry, *the firms are relatively numerous and they sell products which are roughly similar, but not regarded as identical.* The industry is easy to enter; the firms are usually small or, if large, they are diversified and have a relatively small share of each market in which they operate.

Product differentiation, like beauty, exists in the eye of the beholder. It may be justified by some modest technical and quantifiable difference among the products. It may only be the result of a distinct brand image. The brand image may be created by different packaging, intensive advertisement, or word-of-mouth consumer evaluation. It may result from some service associated with the product, a guarantee, or a more convenient location of the seller.

Product differentiation gives the seller a certain amount of monopoly power with respect to his product. It may not be a power he can exploit intensively, however. On the fringes of the loyal band of customers are some who will transfer their loyalty to another product if the price differential makes a difference to them. More and more customers will slip away as the price differential increases.

The demand curve of the monopolistically competitive firm will, therefore, have some slope to it. Unlike under perfect competition, an increase in price will not cause the firm to lose all its sales. Nor will it be able to sell unlimited amounts at the going price. To some extent the monopolistically competitive firm is a price maker rather than a price taker, but it is always under the pressure of the "quality" changes and price manipulations of its actual and potential competitors.

Other market structures

The great variety of market structures cannot be captured in the few models described so far, although these include the most important types. Other types may have local, regional or even national importance. For example, in some industries, a few large firms and a substantial number of small firms produce an only slightly differentiated product. In these industries the sales of the large firms are so great relative to the industry as a whole that each behaves somewhat like an oligopolist, taking into account the reactions of other large firms to its price and quality competition initiatives. At the same time, the many small firms are sniping at the markets of the large firms and, occasionally, in mass, forcing a price and policy change in the industry. The steel industry approximates this pattern.

In other industries, such as book publishing, there are many firms, but a pattern of competition has evolved in which price changes play only a minor role. "Quality" changes and aggressive advertising are the major means of enlarging a firm's market share. In the computer industry, IBM is overwhelmingly the largest firm, but there are many small firms which snipe at it, especially in the production of auxiliary equipment.

This variety is reflected in Table 21-1, which reports on one important aspect of market structure: the concentration of output in firms. The table is confined to a relatively few examples of manufacturing industries and omits the agricultural, financial, and other service sectors entirely. Notice the great range in the number of firms in the industries surveyed, from 8 cigarette producers to 10,000 sawmills. And notice also the range in the concentration of output in the 4 largest firms. The locomotive and flat-glass industries lead among those tabulated, but a number of other industries are not far behind. Some industries with fewer firms are not as

Table 21-1

CONCENTRATION RATIOS: PERCENTAGE OF VALUE OF SHIPMENTS BY LARGEST MANUFACTURERS IN 1967

		Percentage of value of shipments accounted for by			
Industry	*Number of companies*	*Four largest companies*	*Eight largest companies*	*Twenty largest companies*	*Fifty largest companies*
Food and tobacco					
Cheese	891	44	51	61	72
Chocolate	27	77	89	99	100
Cigarettes	8	81	100		
Meat packing	2,529	26	38	50	62
Textiles, shoes, and clothing					
Cotton weaving mills	218	30	48	68	88
Men's and boy's suits	904	17	27	43	59
Shoes	676	27	34	46	51
Women's and misses' dresses	5,008	7	9	14	23
Women's hosiery	302	32	44	64	82
Wood and paper products					
Wood furniture	2,934	12	18	29	44
Paper mills	203	26	43	65	86
Saw mills	10,016	11	15	22	31
Chemicals and petroleum					
Fertilizers	85	35	55	84	98
Petroleum refining	276	33	57	84	96
Plastic materials	508	27	43	64	86
Pharmaceuticals	791	24	40	73	90
Synthetic rubber	33	61	82	100	
Glass and clay products					
Cement	66	29	49	82	99
Flat glass	39	94	98	99	100
Vitreous plumbing fixtures	34	62	84	99	100
Steel and nonferrous metals					
Blast furnaces and steel mills	200	48	66	83	96
Copper	15	77	98	100	
Metal cans	96	73	84	94	99
Pipe and fittings	356	17	27	48	68
Machinery and equipment					
Ball bearings	88	54	73	90	99
Electronic computer equipment	134	66	83	92	98
Farm machinery	1,526	44	56	68	77
Machine tools	865	21	33	54	77
Transportation equipment					
Aircraft	91	69	89	99	100
Locomotives	26	97	99	100	
Truck trailers	147	48	64	82	85
Tires	119	70	88	97	100
Household goods					
Dolls	331	19	31	51	72
Household appliances	71	44	65	92	99
Radio and TV sets	303	49	69	85	95
Watches	45	68	81	97	100

Source: U.S. Department of Commerce, Bureau of the Census.

concentrated in this respect. But notice also that the 4 largest women's and misses' dress producers get only 7 percent of the market. There is also a great range in the shares of the 8 largest firms and the shares of the 20 and 50 largest. This variety must always be kept in mind and respected in any generalizations about market structure.

All the ingenuity of man is reflected in the variety of market structures and market practices. We shall analyze them in more detail after mastering one more aspect of firm demand schedules.

The revenue schedules of price makers and price takers

The type of market structure in which a firm operates has a special implication for the demand schedule the firm faces. *The firm's attempt to obtain some "protection" against competition is an attempt to obtain some control over its prices.* As far as the firm is concerned, the payoff for the ability to control price lies in the relationship between its price and its sales and revenues. So let us explore that relationship for the various types of firms, starting with the pure monopolist, who is a price maker.

The monopolist The revenues of a monopolist at alternative prices can be calculated from his demand schedule, which is the aggregate demand of the industry.

Table 21-2 presents an illustration of a monopolist's (industry) demand schedule in columns 1 and 2.

The total revenue that would be earned at each price is the price times the quantity sold, as shown in column 3. If the demand schedule is elastic, total expenditures by consumers — which for

Table 21-2

A HYPOTHETICAL MARKET DEMAND SCHEDULE FACED BY A MONOPOLIST

1 *Price*	2 *Quantity*	3 *Total revenue*	4 *Marginal revenue*	5 *Average revenue*
$2.50	1	$2.50		$2.50
			$2.00	
2.25	2	4.50		2.25
			1.50	
2.00	3	6.00		2.00
			1.00	
1.75	4	7.00		1.75
			0.50	
1.50	5	7.50		1.50
			0	
1.25	6	7.50		1.25
			− 0.50	
1.00	7	7.00		1.00
			− 1.00	
0.75	8	6.00		0.75

the monopolist are equal to total revenues—will increase if prices are reduced. Looking carefully at the revenue schedule, we can see that over the price range $2.50 to $1.25, the demand is elastic: As prices drop, the total revenue goes up until the price of $1.25 is reached. As prices fall below $1.25, revenue falls, indicating demand inelasticity in that lower price range. This is shown in Figure 21-4.

Figure 21-4

HYPOTHETICAL TOTAL REVENUE SCHEDULE OF A MONOPOLIST

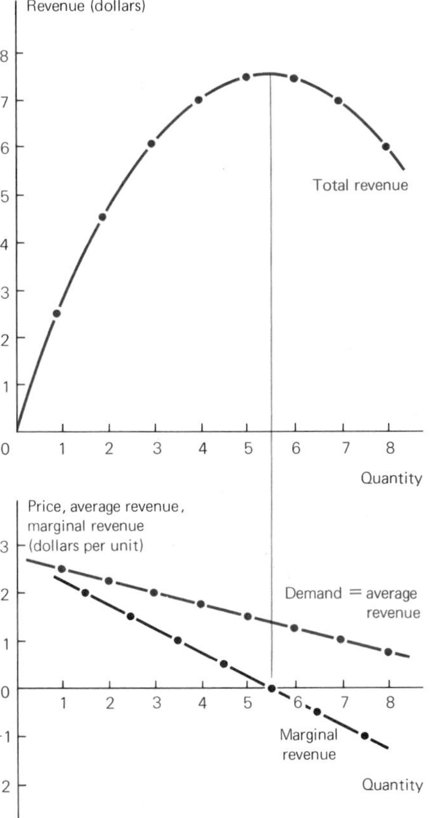

Figure 21-5

AVERAGE AND MARGINAL REVENUE SCHEDULES

Now we can calculate what an extra sale is worth to the monopolist. That is the marginal revenue. *Marginal revenue is the change in total revenue when sales change by 1 unit.* That extra revenue due to an extra sale is shown in column 4 of Table 21-2. As prices drop from $2.50 to $2.25 and sales increase from 1 to 2, revenue increases by only $2. So that is the marginal revenue between those prices and quantities. As sales increase from 2 to 3, the marginal revenue is only $1.50 and so on. The marginal revenue schedule is plotted in Figure 21-5 along with the average revenue. The latter can be calculated by dividing total revenue by quantity sold; it will be just the price, and so the average revenue schedule is the same as the demand schedule.

Notice that the marginal revenue is a positive number as long as demand is elastic, because when demand is elastic, and price falls, revenue rises and marginal revenue is positive. When demand is inelastic, as price falls and sales rise, revenue decreases, which means that the marginal revenue is negative.

Figures 21-4 and 21-5 are drawn so that the quantity axes are lined up. This helps make the point that total revenue increases as long as marginal revenue is positive and total revenue decreases when marginal revenue is negative.

If we look again at Figure 21-5, we notice that the marginal revenue schedule is *always* below the average revenue or demand schedule. That is, marginal revenue is always less than the price! That is a little paradoxical and is worth thinking about. To sell a bit more, the monopolist must lower his price—not just on the extra unit, but on every unit! So the extra revenue from each extra sale is always less than the price charged!

This is an important result. Consider what it implies in terms of the theory of demand. According to the utility theory of Chapter 19, it means that the marginal utility of an extra unit purchased by a consumer (= price) is always more than the marginal revenue of an extra unit sold by a monopolist. Or, in more ordinary language: *The value of an additional unit of a commodity to a consumer, which is worth to him the price he pays, is greater than the contribution of an additional unit of output to the revenue of a monopolist.* This means there is an essential difference in the interests of a monopolist and the interests of consumers!

How did it happen? The monopolist did not seem to do anything bad, and yet it is so. The explanation is right there—in the sloping demand schedule; the result will be the same for a monopolist, an oligopolist, or any firm in an imperfectly competitive industry who is a *price maker*. This will become more apparent if we move now to the other end of the spectrum and take up the case of the perfectly competitive firm, which is, necessarily, a price taker.

The perfectly competitive firm

The demand schedule of the perfectly competitive firm is a straight horizontal line at the price level prevailing in the industry's market. The firm "takes" the price and can sell as much or as little as it wants at that price.

Table 21-3

HYPOTHETICAL DEMAND SCHEDULE FOR A COMPETITIVE FIRM

1 *Price*	2 *Quantity*	3 *Revenue*	4 *Marginal revenue*
$2	1	$2	
			$2
2	2	4	
			2
2	3	6	
			2
2	4	8	
			2
2	5	10	

Suppose, for example, that a firm in a competitive industry faced a price of $2. Table 21-3 presents a few examples of its possible sales and revenues at that price. Total revenue is calculated in column 3. The marginal revenue, the addition to total revenue from an additional unit sold, is calculated in column 4. That marginal revenue is always equal to the price *because* the price is constant as sales change!

The firm's demand and marginal revenue schedule is shown in Figure 21-6. The total revenue line in Figure 21-7 is straight because the firm's selling price is not affected by its sales. The price line is the demand schedule, and in the perfectly competitive case, it is the marginal revenue schedule. In the perfectly competitive model, therefore, and using utility theory again, we see that the marginal utility of a good (= price) is always equal to the marginal revenue it earns for the firm.

To describe the point in the longer way, the contribution of an additional unit of output to the revenues of a perfectly competitive firm (price = average revenue = marginal revenue) is equal to the value of the additional unit of the commodity to the consumer (= price). This means that the disjunction of interest of consumer and producer, which was present in the monopoly, is not present in competitive industries. And this is not because competitors have more noble characters and the public interest at heart. It is because the structure of the industry and the horizontal demand schedule faced by competitive firms make it so.

The imperfectly competitive firm

Imperfectly competitive industries comprise such a broad range of market situations that, without investigating each industry separately, we cannot describe a firm's demand schedule. Even with such an investigation, a precise description is not always possible, as it is in monopoly and perfect competition. Yet a general qualitative appraisal can be based on the foregoing analysis.

Imperfectly competitive firms in general have downward-sloping demand schedules over some range, reflecting their limited power to determine market prices. They are to some degree like monopolists. Therefore, their revenue schedules will in a qualitative way be like those of monopolists. Because their prices will fall as the quantity they sell increases, the marginal revenue of an

Figure 21-6

HYPOTHETICAL DEMAND SCHEDULE FOR A COMPETITIVE FIRM

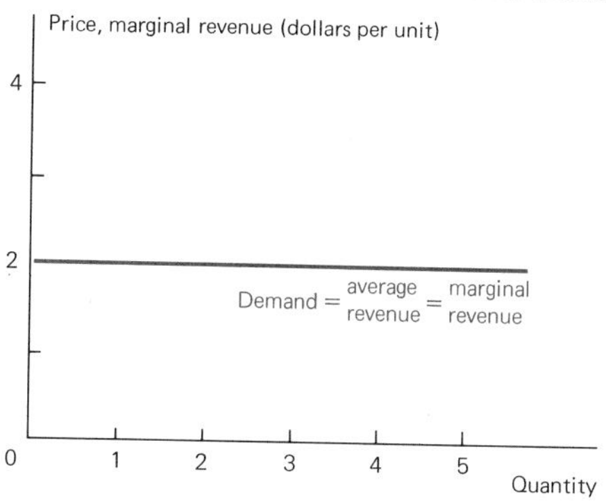

additional unit sold to such a firm will be lower than price or average revenue. As for pure monopolists, the value to the firm of an additional unit sold will be different from its worth to a consumer.

As we shall see in Chapter 23, the "invisible hand" will lead business firms to operate in such a way as to improve the general welfare when a unit of output is worth the same to a producer as to a consumer. When that is not the case, the operation of the private market sector is no longer so reliably in the interest of the public as a whole, as Adam Smith argued. As a consequence, there will be a greater role for public economics.

We have seen the significant differences among the various types of market structures and the implications of these market structures for the revenue possibilities faced by the firm. But the production and, therefore, the supply decisions of the firm depend on costs as well as revenues. So before we can analyze those decisions and their relation to price determination, we must work through the analysis of costs. That is the task of the next chapter.

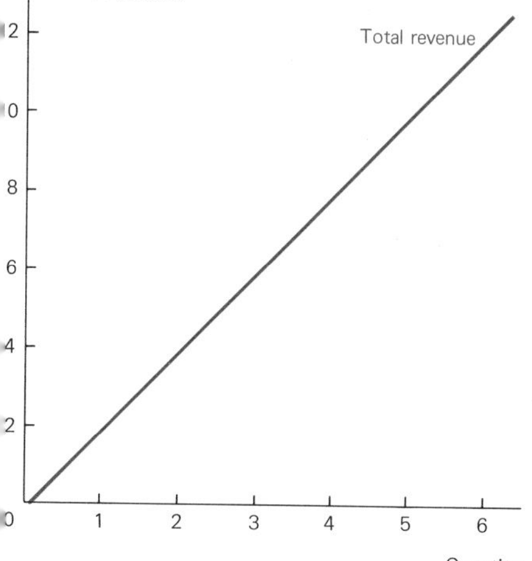

Figure 21-7

HYPOTHETICAL TOTAL REVENUE SCHEDULE FOR A COMPETITIVE FIRM

Summary

Business firms—the basic units for the organization of production in a mixed economy—take on many forms. Proprietorships and partnerships are the most numerous, but corporations are more important in terms of their assets, employment, and share of output. Business firms differ in the degree to which the owners are also the actual controllers of the business. In proprietorships and partnerships, though there may be some delegation of authority, ownership and control are usually identical. In corporations with widely dispersed ownership, control may be exercised by a substantially self-perpetuating management. In other corporations in which some stock holdings are concentrated, top management may be closely supervised by—or actually consist of—the important stockholders.

Mergers and holding companies are ways of pyramiding corporate ownership so that relatively small ownership of stock in a parent company can exercise control over a number of other firms. In mergers, the other firms are owned outright by the parent company, whereas in holding companies, the parent company may own only a partial though controlling share.

The behavior of businesses depends on their motives, the character of the markets in which they operate, and their cost constraints. The third topic is discussed in Chapter 22.

Economists usually assume that businesses are motivated by the desire to maximize their profits, taking into account the future as well as the present. In proprietorships and partnerships this may seem plausible, because the firms' profits are the income of the owners. Even in these firms, however, there may be conflicting motives. In the modern corporation, the separation of ownership and control creates the possibility of a conflict of motives. Management may simply want to survive and grow, whereas the owners are interested in profits and dividends. Such differences are sometimes important, but they become less significant when it is realized that making profits may be the best means of achieving growth.

The market in which a firm operates describes not so much a place as the set of circumstances in which buyers and sellers carry out their transactions. The critical feature for defining a particular market is that the product is the same for all buyers and sellers. Markets may differ because of location and transport costs or because of differences in the commodities, as perceived by the buyers and sellers.

The structure of markets is the result of the character and degree of competition, and that in turn depends on: (1) the number of buyers and sellers and the degree to which they are of relatively similar or dissimilar size; (2) the degree to which the product is standardized or differentiated; (3) information availability and the quality of firm response; (4) the barriers to the entry of new firms. These features are combined in a great variety of ways in actual markets. Economists work with models of markets which attempt to capture the essential features. Economic analysis is most successful, however, with the most unrealistic cases, pure monopoly and perfect competition.

The alternative market structures can be described as a spec-

Table 21-4

CHARACTERISTICS OF MARKET STRUCTURE

	Type of market structure	*Concentration*	*Product differentiation*	*Interdependence of decisions*	*Barriers to entry*	*Control over price*	*Occurrence*
	Pure monopoly	One seller	One product with no close substitutes	None	Complete	Considerable control over output decisions	Rare, mainly controlled utilities
Imperfect competition	Oligopoly						
Imperfect competition	Differentiated	Few sellers	Considerable	Considerable	Some	Some	A number of consumer goods
Imperfect competition	Undifferentiated	Few sellers	Little or None	Considerable	Some	Some	A number of producer and consumer goods
Imperfect competition	Monopolistic competition	Many sellers	Substantial	Slight	Slight	Some	Many consumer goods
	Perfect competition	Many sellers	None	None	None	None	Rare, a few in agricultural sector

trum of a number of dimensions, as is indicated in Table 21-4. The pure monopolist at one end of the spectrum is a rare case in which there is a single seller for whose product there are no close substitutes. The demand faced by the monopolist is the industry demand, the total of the demand of all consumers of this product. The monopolist is a price maker and can control his price by the amount of goods he offers for sale. But he cannot sell all he wants at any price he sets, for he is constrained by the price-quantity relationship of the market demand schedule.

The firm in a perfectly competitive industry is too small to affect the industry's price. It is a price taker which must accept the industry price, but it can sell as much or as little as it wants at that price. The perfectly competitive firm, therefore, faces an infinitely elastic demand, a straight horizontal line at the going market price.

Oligopoly is one of the in-between cases. There are only a few firms, so few that each must take all the others' actions and reactions into account in making its own decisions. Oligopoly comes in two forms: undifferentiated, in which a fairly standard product is sold, and differentiated, in which the product of each firm is regarded by consumers as somewhat different. In a closely interdependent way, oligopolists share among themselves the power to make prices.

Under monopolistic competition, there are many sellers, but each has succeeded in differentiating its product slightly. This gives each seller some control to make its price, but it is limited by the fact that substitutes, though not perfect, are available.

There are many different kinds of market structures between the extremes of pure monopoly and perfect competition. Oligopoly and monopolistic competition represent only a few points in this most important area of imperfect competition.

The relationship between a firm's revenues and sales depends on the structure of the market in which the firm sells. Its total revenue is just its price times the quantity it sells at that price.

The important marginal revenue concept is defined as the change in revenue (plus or minus) due to a 1-unit change in sales.

The total revenue schedule of the monopolist can be derived from the industry demand schedule it faces. Its marginal revenue schedule will always be lower than its demand schedule, because to increase its sales by 1 unit, it must lower its price on all units.

The price of the perfectly competitive firm does not change with output, so its total revenue schedule is a straight line and its marginal revenue from an additional sale is always constant and equal to the price.

The theory of demand indicates that an additional unit of a commodity is worth to a consumer the price he pays for it. That is also what it adds to a competitive firm's revenues. But it is more than what it adds to the revenues of a firm with some degree of monopoly power, because price is greater than marginal revenue in this latter case. The differences among market structures have a significant effect on pricing and allocation.

Questions for discussion and review

1. Comment on the following statement: *Businessmen are not in business for their health. They are out to make money any way they can — without getting caught breaking the law. But they can't maximize their profits because they aren't smart enough to do that.*

2. Comment on the following statement: *Businessmen must take into account the social consequences of their actions. If they try to squeeze the last drop of profit out of their operations and "let the consumer be hanged" they won't last long in this modern world.*

3. What is meant by market structure? How do market structures differ?

4. Can you give some examples from your personal and local experience of the various types of market structures?

5. What effect does product differentiation have on the interdependence of producers? Is your answer for oligopolies the same as for firms in a monopolistically competitive industry?

6. Why is a perfectly competitive firm's demand schedule perfectly elastic?

7. Why is the marginal revenue schedule of a monopolist below its average revenue schedule?

8. Discuss the following argument. *Monopolists are no more grasping than any other type of businessmen. They have only been successful in doing what other businessmen would like to do. The fact that the value to consumers of their output is different from the value of the output to the monopolist himself is simply an unfortunate consequence of the slope of the industry demand schedule.*

Concepts for review

Price makers and takers
Profit maximization
Market structure
Product differentiation
Imperfect competition
Monopolistic competition
Perfect competition
Oligopoly
Marginal revenue

22

Resource use and cost factors behind supply decisions

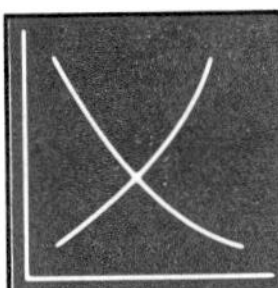

The concept of supply – of alternative amounts that firms will offer for sale at corresponding alternative prices – was introduced in Chapter 4.[1] Analysis of a particular price and market requires more than merely saying that they are governed by a Law of Supply and Demand. Most of what is important about prices and markets depends on the detailed specification of prevailing demand and supply conditions. To understand the basic determinants of supply, we are now going to embark on a long and complicated chain of reasoning. Like Theseus entering the labyrinth to find the Minotaur, we will put out a thread to help us find our way out of the maze. The line of thought is as follows:

1. The goal is to understand how prices are determined and the significance of that determination for the allocation of resources and goods.
2. In a mixed economy prices are determined essentially by the interaction of supply and demand forces.
3. The two preceding chapters dealt with demand, as determined by consumers and as seen by firms. We turn now to supply.
4. The goods and services businesses offer for sale depend on the profits they can make.
5. Profits are the difference between revenues and costs.
6. Revenues depend on demand and market structure.

[1] A review of that chapter will keep the detailed analysis in which we are about to engage in perspective.

7. Costs of production depend on the amounts of the inputs used in production and their prices. The dependency is both direct and indirect.

a. It is direct and obvious, since the total cost of purchasing a productive input is its price times the quantity purchased.

b. There is indirect, but important dependence, since the production technique chosen may depend to some extent on the prices of the inputs.

Inputs and production

The explanation of costs of production starts with the conditions of production and the use of productive resources or inputs. Business firms trying to maximize their profits will try to be *technically efficient* in order to be *economically efficient*. Technical efficiency in the production of a *particular level of output* means that no other combination of inputs can produce the output level without using more of at least one of the productive inputs. Achieving technical efficiency is no mean task. It occupies most members of the engineering profession. For some types of goods and services, there may be only one technically efficient combination of inputs for producing a particular level of output. In most areas of production, however, there are a number of technically efficient combinations: One combination, compared with another, may require more of one input but will use less of one or more other inputs. For example, technically, electric power can be produced in a number of ways which require different combinations of natural resources and capital and labor inputs. Water power can be used as the energy source where it is available or coal or oil can be used as a source of thermal energy, or nuclear reactions. Whatever method is chosen, engineers try to be technically efficient and not use more of any input than is required for a particular level of output.

Economic efficiency requires the choice of a least-cost combination of inputs for a particular output level from among the technically efficient alternatives. The supply decision by producers – of the amount they will offer at any price – depends on the economic efficiency with which the output can be produced. The decision to build a hydro, thermal, or nuclear electric power generating station depends on the economic costs of the alternative technically efficient methods. The analysis of supply must, therefore, probe into the relationship between production conditions and cost.

The qualitative and quantitative relationships between inputs and outputs vary greatly from product to product. One generally valid qualitative production characteristic is that described by the Law of Diminishing Returns (Chap. 3). This law states that, as one variable input is added to one or more fixed inputs, output will increase, but the increments in output associated with each additional unit of the variable input will become smaller and smaller. That also implies that the average output per unit of the variable input will decline.

The Law of Diminishing Returns has important implications for the behavior of an individual firm's costs. Consider a firm producing a single type of output. It uses a fixed input, land, and a variable input, labor.

Table 22-1 provides a numerical illustration of diminishing returns at the firm level. Just enough man-hours of labor are added at each step to increase the firm's output by 1 unit. Notice in column 4 that the amount of labor necessary to do this first decreases and then, reflecting the Law of Diminishing Returns, increases. Correspondingly, the average physical product of labor (APP_L) in column 6, which is output divided by the labor input, first increases and then decreases in obedience to the Law of Diminishing Returns. The average physical product of land always increases, as that input is constant and more and more labor is used on it.

The marginal physical product of labor (MPP_L) is the *change in output* due to a *change in the labor input by just 1 unit*. That is calculated in column 5. Since the variable labor input is not added

Table 22-1

VARIATION OF OUTPUT WITH CHANGING LABOR INPUTS AND LAND CONSTANT AT 1 ACRE

1 Output	2 Land input (acres)	3 Labor input (man-hours)	4 Additional units of labor	5 Additional output for each additional unit of labor (MPP_L)	6 Output per unit of labor (APP_L)	7 Output per unit of land (APP of land)
0	16	0				
			6	$\frac{1}{6} = 0.167$		
1	16	6			$\frac{1}{6} = 0.167$	$\frac{1}{16} = 0.063$
			4	$\frac{1}{4} = 0.250$		
2	16	10			$\frac{2}{10} = 0.206$	$\frac{2}{16} = 0.125$
			3	$\frac{1}{3} = 0.333$		
3	16	13			$\frac{3}{13} = 0.231$	$\frac{3}{16} = 0.188$
			4	$\frac{1}{4} = 0.250$		
4	16	17			$\frac{4}{17} = 0.236$	$\frac{4}{16} = 0.250$
			7	$\frac{1}{7} = 0.143$		
5	16	24			$\frac{5}{24} = 0.208$	$\frac{5}{16} = 0.313$
			12	$\frac{1}{12} = 0.083$		
6	16	36			$\frac{6}{36} = 0.167$	$\frac{6}{16} = 0.375$
			19	$\frac{1}{19} = 0.052$		
7	16	55			$\frac{7}{55} = 0.127$	$\frac{7}{16} = 0.438$
			28	$\frac{1}{28} = 0.036$		
8	16	83			$\frac{8}{83} = 0.096$	$\frac{8}{16} = 0.500$

one man-hour at a time, but rather in just those amounts needed to increase *output* by 1 unit at a time, it is necessary to approximate the increase in output due to a *1-unit* change in man-hour inputs. To do this, we divide the 1-unit change in output by the total change in labor input that caused it. For example, the increase from the fifth to the sixth unit of output required twelve *additional* man-hours of labor. So the marginal physical product of labor in this range as shown in column 5 is averaged out to be 1 unit of output/12 units of labor or 0.083 additional units of output per additional man-hour.

The average and marginal physical products of labor calculated in Table 22-1 are plotted in Figure 22-1 on page 456. The initial increase and then steady decline in both the average and marginal products of labor as labor inputs increase are shown. As long as the *MPP* of labor is above the *APP* of labor, then labor's *APP* curve rises. When labor's *MPP* is less than its *APP,* then the *APP* of labor is pulled down.

Table 22-1 and Figure 22-1 provide an example of the variation of output as one input is increased and the other is kept constant. The numbers of the example do not represent any particular production process. They are, however, in a general way and in the diminishing returns phase, especially, representative of many types of production processes.

Costs and production

The costs of production can be calculated from the production data once the prices of the factors are specified. Assuming that these prices are constant,[2] total costs for each level of production can be computed in the following way:

$$\text{Total costs} = (\text{amount of fixed input}) \times (\text{price of fixed input}) + (\text{amount of variable input}) \times (\text{price of variable input})$$

The costs of the fixed input are, naturally enough, called fixed costs, *FC,* and the costs of variable inputs are variable costs, *VC.* So

$$\text{Total costs} = \text{fixed costs} + \text{variable costs} = FC + VC$$

It is also useful to put these costs on an average basis per unit of output. If we divide total costs at any particular level of output, *Q,* by that output, we have the average total cost (*ATC*) of that level of output. In the same way we can compute average fixed cost (*AFC*) and average variable cost (*AVC*) for a particular level of output. Their sum is the average total cost of that output level:

[2] This assumption will be examined in Chap. 27. It is equivalent to assuming that the firm hires the inputs in a competitive market so that it has no effect on the input prices.

$$\frac{TC}{Q} = \frac{FC}{Q} + \frac{VC}{Q} \quad \text{or} \quad ATC = AFC + AVC$$

One other definition will be useful: *The extra cost of an additional unit of output is called the marginal cost, or MC.* That is calculated as the change in total cost due to an extra unit of output. Since only the variable cost changes as output changes (fixed cost is really *fixed!*), marginal cost is equally well calculated as the change in variable cost for a 1-unit change in output.

These definitions will become clearer if we go back to the production example and actually calculate costs. Suppose that it costs $9 to rent each acre of land and $4 for each man-hour of labor. The costs at each level of output can be computed by multiplying the required fixed and variable inputs by their prices. This is done in Table 22-2. The total costs of each level of output are computed by adding the costs of the fixed and variable inputs. This is shown graphically in Figure 22-2 on page 456.

Table 22-2

VARIATION OF COSTS WITH OUTPUT

1 Output	2 Fixed costs (land inputs × land price = FC)	3 Variable cost (labor inputs × wage = VC)	4 Total costs (TC = FC + VC)	5 Marginal costs (MC)	6 Average fixed costs (AFC = FC/Q)	7 Average variable costs (AVC = VC/Q)	8 Average total costs (ATC = TC/Q)
0	(16 × $9 =) $144	(0 × $4 =) $ 0	$144				
				$ 24			
1	(16 × $9 =) $144	(6 × $4 =) $ 24	$168		$144/1 = $144	$24/1 = $24	$168/1 = $168
				$ 16			
2	(16 × $9 =) $144	(10 × $4 =) $ 40	$184		$144/2 = $72	$40/2 = $20	$184/2 = $92
				$ 12			
3	(16 × $9 =) $144	(13 × $4 =) $ 52	$196		$144/3 = $48	$52/3 = $17.33	$196/3 = $65.33
				$ 16			
4	(16 × $9 =) $144	(17 × $4 =) $ 68	$212		$144/4 = $36	$68/4 = $17	$212/4 = $53
				$ 28			
5	(16 × $9 =) $144	(24 × $4 =) $ 96	$240		$144/5 = $28.80	$96/5 = $19.20	$240/5 = $48
				$ 48			
6	(16 × $9 =) $144	(36 × $4 =) $144	$288		$144/6 = $24	$144/6 = $24	$288/6 = $48
				$ 76			
7	(16 × $9 =) $144	(55 × $4 =) $220	$364		$144/7 = $20.57	$220/7 = $31.43	$364/7 = $52
				$112			
8	(16 × $9 =) $144	(83 × $4 =) $332	$476		$144/8 = $18	$332/8 = $41.50	$476/8 = $59.50

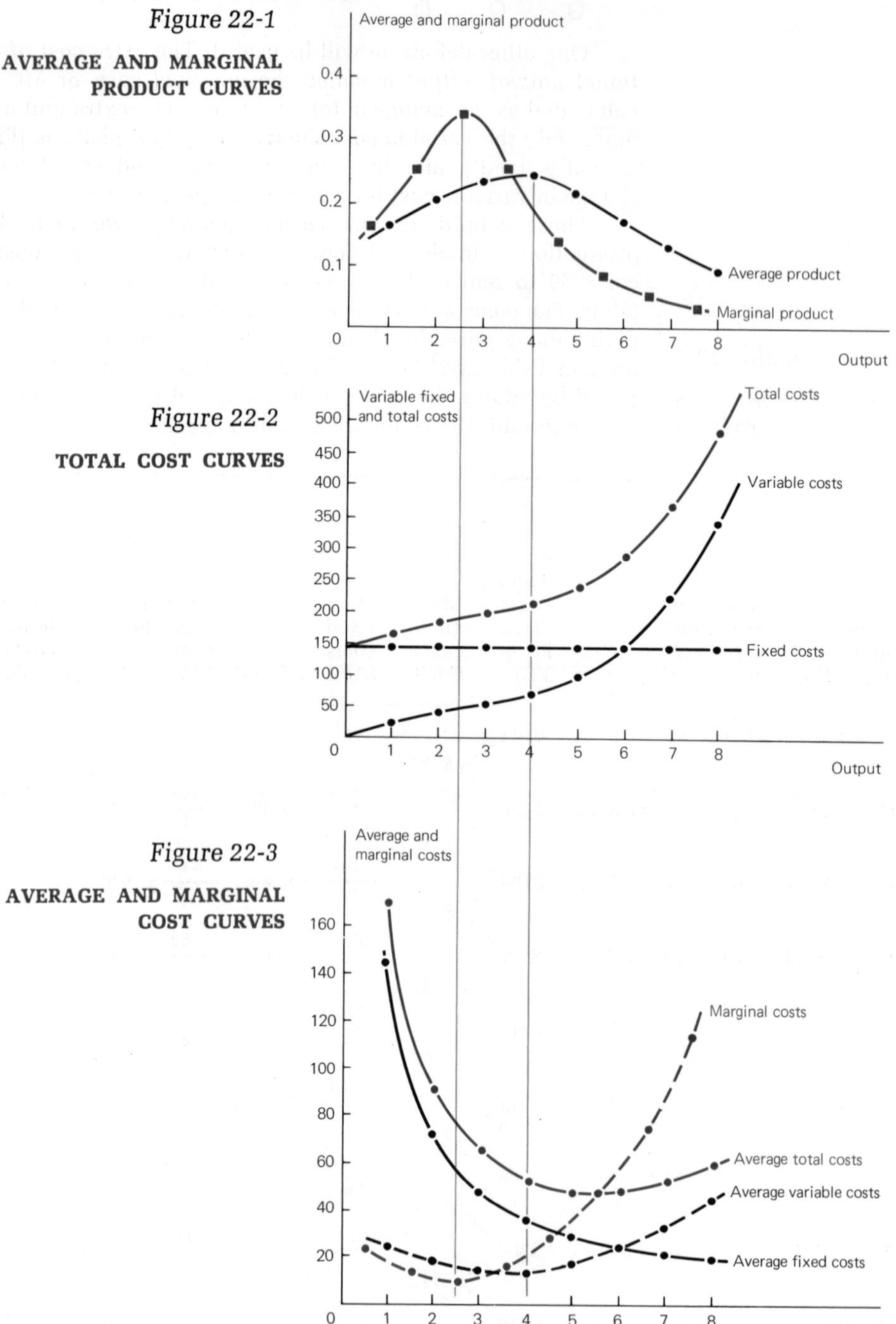

Figure 22-1

AVERAGE AND MARGINAL PRODUCT CURVES

Figure 22-2

TOTAL COST CURVES

Figure 22-3

AVERAGE AND MARGINAL COST CURVES

Total cost always increases with output, but the movements of average total cost reflect the cross currents which occur over some output ranges in average fixed cost and average variable cost. *AFC* declines steadily as fixed costs are spread over a larger and larger output, but *AVC* falls and then rises as the average physical product of labor rises and then falls. As shown in Figure 22-3, there is a range of output, from 3 units of product to 6 units, over which *AVC* rises. But since *AFC* is falling sufficiently rapidly, the net effect is for *ATC* to fall. For still higher levels of output, though *AFC* continues to fall, *AVC* rises so rapidly as to pull up *ATC*.

Note that behind these cost patterns are the more fundamental patterns of variation of outputs and inputs. Figures 22-1, 22-2, and 22-3 are arranged one above the other so that we can easily compare what is happening to inputs and costs at each level of output. Observe the following relationships:

> As the average output of the fixed input *rises*, the fixed cost per unit of output, *AFC, falls.*
>
> When the average output of the variable input is *rising*, the variable cost per unit of output, *AVC falls.*
>
> When the average output of the variable input is *falling, AVC rises.*
>
> When the marginal product of the variable input is *rising*, the extra cost of a unit of output, *MC*, *falls*, and *AVC* falls as long as *MC* is less than *AVC*.
>
> When the marginal product of the variable input is *falling*, *MC* is *rising*, but *AVC* rises only when *MC* is greater than *AVC*.
>
> As the average product of labor first *rises* and then *falls*, the variable cost of expanding output first *falls* and then *rises*. The output at which the average product of labor is at its highest level is, therefore, the output at which the average variable cost reaches its lowest level.

The significant marginal cost and marginal product concepts

Most of the cost and output concepts introduced here are fairly straightforward totals and conventional averages. The unconventional ideas, which will be extremely important in the analysis to follow, are the concepts of *marginal* changes in output and cost. To review them:

> Marginal physical product (*MPP*) is the change in *total output* due to a *1-unit* change in one *input*, with other inputs unchanged.
>
> Marginal cost (*MC*) is the change in *total cost* due to a *1-unit* change in *output*.

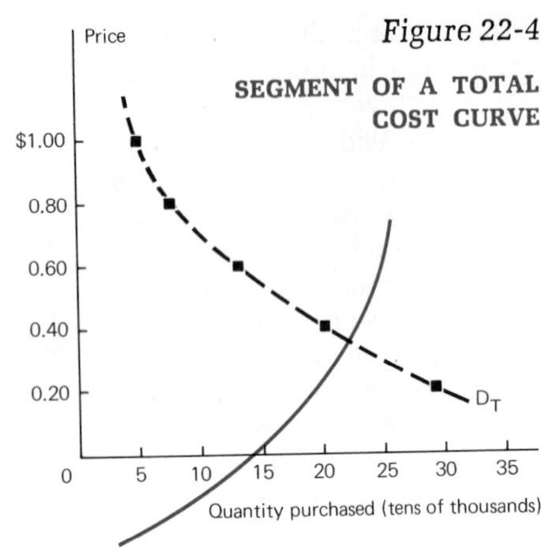

Figure 22-4

SEGMENT OF A TOTAL COST CURVE

These marginal concepts provide the basis for a realistic analysis of decision making. No business manager anywhere is so all-wise and knowledgeable that he can always exactly forecast the results of changes in production scheduling. What he can do is try a change and observe the results. Unplanned economies – and planned ones as well – are trial-and-error systems; how well they work depends in part on whether there are incentives for managers to recognize and learn from errors. *The concepts that measure the effects of trial changes in inputs and outputs are the marginal concepts.*

In Figure 22-4, part of the total cost curve drawn in Figure 22-2 is cut out and enlarged to obtain a magnified picture of the total cost curve.The marginal cost of a change in output from *a* to *b* is the increase in the total cost, *bc*, divided by *ab*, or *bc*/*ab*. This estimates the change in total cost for a 1 unit change in output. As Figure 22-4 indicates, the marginal cost is a measure of the slope of the total cost curve over a particular short range of output. (As the range of output is reduced, marginal cost will approach the slope of the line *ss*, which is tangent to the total cost segment at point *a*.)

The short run, the long run, and input choice

In our explanation of the cost structure of a simple firm, we assumed that it had and was committed to a specific land input but could vary its labor input. Yet no firm is committed, forever, to any input. Given enough time, it can buy or rent more of the fixed input, if it decides that is reasonable. Or it can decide not to renew its lease on land it rents. Over some period, it can wear down, use up, sell, or junk whatever fixed inputs it owns. Fixed inputs are fixed only in the *short run*. In fact, we distinguish the short and the long run in just this way:

> The *short run* is the period during which the amount of some input which is available for use by the firm cannot be changed.
>
> The *long run* is the period long enough to change both (all) inputs.

With all but one input fixed in the short run, the only way to change output is to change the variable input. In the long run, however, all inputs are variable, and more than one set of inputs may be capable of producing the same output. Since there may be more than one set of inputs capable of producing a certain output, there may also be more than one level of costs of production associated with that output! In the long run, profit-maximizing firms will choose that input combination for each level of output which has the lowest total costs. This principle provides a guideline for the next section.

Choosing a least-cost input combination in the long run

An example will clarify the rationale of long-run input and cost adjustments. Table 22-1 showed that it was possible to produce 6 units of output with 16 acres of land and 36 man-hours of labor. Suppose that output can be produced with two other input combinations: (1) 24 acres of land and 24 man-hours of labor, and (2) 36 acres of land and 16 man-hours of labor. These alternative combinations are shown in Table 22-3 and Figure 22-5 as *A*, *B*, and *C*. Assume that other input combinations which lie along the line through *A*, *B*, and *C*, are also capable of producing 6 units of output. *That line is called an equal-product curve, or a production isoquant, because everywhere along it the input combinations will produce 6 units of output.*

Figure 22-5

EQUAL-PRODUCT LINE FOR PRODUCING 6 UNITS OF OUTPUT

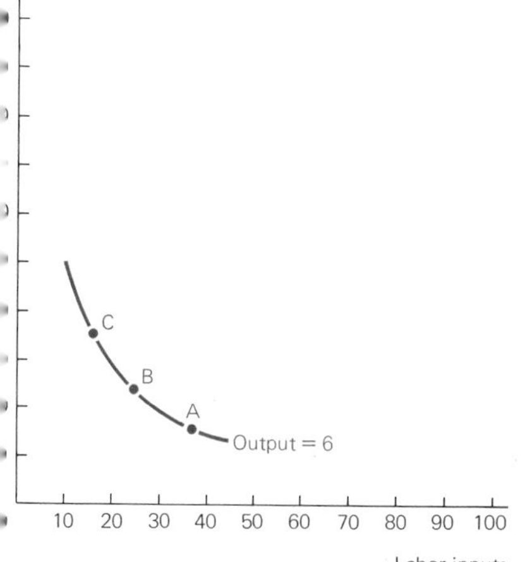

For each of the three different input combinations *A*, *B*, and *C*, we can figure out the total costs, as shown in Table 22-3, with land at $9 per acre and labor at $4 per man-hour.

Combination *A* is the cheapest of the three alternatives, *A*, *B*, and *C*. But of *all* the potential combinations on the equal-product line through *A*, *B*, *C*, which is the cheapest? And for other outputs, how does a firm go about finding the lowest-cost input combination? These questions may seem rather technical, but they are important. Their resolution by firms determines the resolution of the Input question in the economy as a whole. What determines the amounts of resources and the technology that will be used to produce any particular output?

The answer again starts with the working assumption that firms try to maximize their profits. They try to *minimize the costs* of whatever output they decide to produce so that the spread between revenues and costs will be as wide as possible. So the Input question can be rephrased as follows: How will firms choose the input combination and technology to minimize the costs of whatever they decide to produce?

We can proceed in two ways. We can assume that firms know everything there is to know about the technology they use and the inputs necessary to achieve a certain output. Alternatively, we can

Table 22-3

ALTERNATIVE INPUT COMBINATIONS AND THEIR COSTS

	Land	*Labor*	*Land costs*	*Labor costs*	*Total costs*	*Output*
A	16	36	(16 × $9 =) $144	(36 × $4 =) $144	$288	6
B	24	24	(24 × $9 =) $216	(24 × $4 =) $96	$312	6
C	36	16	(36 × $9 =) $324	(16 × $4 =) $64	$388	6

assume that in a trial-and-error way firms will try to minimize the costs of their output, using whatever knowledge they can develop. This approach is usually the more realistic. Though engineers and executives are getting better all the time, they will usually be the first to assert that production is not a cut-and-dried matter of following the recipe in some engineering cookbook. Rather it is often a matter of constant rearrangement and adjustment to keep costs down. So let us first take the more realistic road. Then we can show how the results are consistent with those which would be achieved with perfect knowledge.

Cost minimization by marginal adjustments

The simplest rearrangement in production is to fit in an additional unit of one input, say, labor, in the most efficient way possible. The resulting increment in output is the marginal physical product of labor, MPP_L. The *cost* of that increment in output is the price of the additional unit of Labor, p_L. Therefore, the additional *output per dollar of expenditure* on the unit of labor is the marginal productivity of labor divided by its price, or MPP_L/p_L. For example, one extra man-hour of labor, with everything else unchanged, might add, say, 1/10 of a unit of output. With labor's wages at $4 per man-hour, the extra output per dollar of expenditure on labor, or MPP_L/p_L, would be $1/10 \div \$4$, or 1/40, or 0.025 units per dollar.

Similarly the increment in output per dollar spent on land would be MPP_T/p_T. If an acre of land rented for $9 and an extra acre added 3/10 of a unit of output to production, then MPP_T/p_T would be $3/10 \div \$9 = 1/30$ or 0.033 units per dollar.

Now suppose you were in charge of production – trying to produce 6 units of output at the lowest possible cost – and you had these facts before you. What would you do? Use more land in production in place of labor! *Each dollar spent on land would add more to output than a dollar spent on labor, so it would make sense to substitute land for labor in production.*

To minimize costs of a particular output, a firm will be guided by the following trial-and-error rules:

> If the MPP_T/p_T is greater than MPP_L/p_L, substitute land for labor.
>
> If MMP_L/p_L is greater than MMP_T/p_T, substitute labor for land.
>
> If $MPP_L/p_L = MPP_T/p_T$, no further adjustment will lower cost and the production process will be in equilibrium.

Finally, if there were many inputs, the condition for cost minimization could be generalized to say: *The marginal physical product per dollar spent on each input must be the same.*

Cost minimization by comparison of total costs

Let us now compare cost minimization by marginal adjustments with a procedure which assumes full knowledge. A new concept will be helpful: the *equal-cost*, or iso-cost, line or schedule. This line

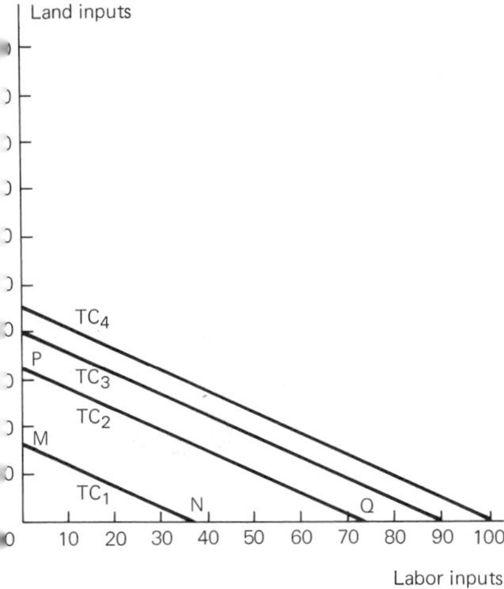

Figure 22-6

EQUAL-COST LINES: INPUT COMBINATIONS THAT COST THE SAME

shows all the combinations of inputs that have the same total cost. The equal-cost line is like the consumer's budget constraint introduced in Chapter 19. When there are just two inputs, say, land and labor, each iso-cost line can be computed by asking how much of both can be purchased for a specific total expenditure. For example, with land at $9 per acre and labor at $4 per man-hour, for a total cost of $144, a firm could purchase 16 acres of land at point *M* in Figure 22-6 *or* 36 man-hours of labor at point *N*. Or it could purchase any combination on line TC_1 between *M* and *N*. For a total cost of $288, it could purchase either 32 acres of land at *P* or 72 man-hours of labor at *Q*, or any combination in between *P* and *Q* on line TC_2. There is a different equal-cost line for each level of total expenditure. Four equal-cost lines are drawn as examples in Figure 22-6. All the input combinations along line TC_1 cost $144. Along TC_2, all the input combinations cost $288. Along TC_3, all input combinations cost $360. Along TC_4, all input combinations cost $400, and so on.

Figure 22-7

USING THE EQUAL-PRODUCT AND EQUAL-COST LINES TO FIND A MINIMUM-COST INPUT COMBINATION

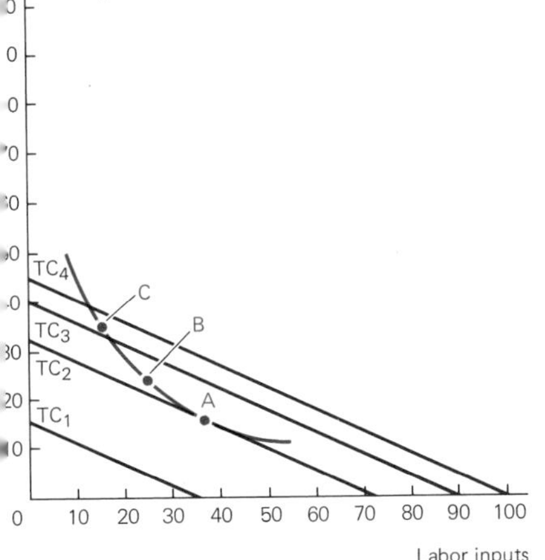

We again ask: What input combination will be the least-cost way of producing 6 units of output? To answer, we combine Figures 22-5 and 22-6 in Figure 22-7. Everywhere along the equal-product line *ABC*, the input combinations will produce 6 units. The various equal-cost lines crossing line *ABC* indicate the costs of each input combination. If, figuratively speaking, we move along line *ABC* seeking the lowest equal-cost line, we come again to point *A*. At that point any move up or down, to the right or left, to another input combination which will also produce 6 units will lead to higher total costs. At *A*, the equal-product line just touches but does not cross – it is *tangent* to – the equal-cost line TC_2 on which total costs are $288. This means that *minimium cost is where the slope of the equal-cost line is equal to the slope of the equal-product line*. For if the two lines did not have the same slope, they would cross.

Therefore, with the technical possibilities indicated by the equal-product line and the prices of $9 per acre for land and $4 per hour for labor, in the long run, the combination of inputs that would be used to produce 6 units of output would be just that at *A*.

Consistency of the two approaches to cost minimization

The two approaches to cost minimization are consistent. The key to appreciating this is to notice again that at the minimum-cost point for any output, the equal-cost and equal-product lines for that output are just tangent to each other, which means they have the same slope.

The slope of the equal-cost line is equal to the ratio of the prices of the inputs p_L/p_T. This can be figured out as follows: The maximum amount of land which can be rented for, say, \$144, is \$144 divided by the price of land, \$144/\$9 per acre, or 16 acres. The maximum amount of labor which can be hired for \$144 is \$144/\$4 per hour, or 36 man-hours. The slope of the equal-cost line is 16/36, or 4/9. That is the ratio of the labor price to the land price.

Next we must work out the slope of the equal-product curves. For each equal-product curve, that slope is essentially a trade off or *substitution ratio* between the land and labor used in producing that particular output. Let us call it *S.R.* The change in output for a small change in the use of *land* is its marginal physical product, MPP_T, and the change in output for a small change in labor inputs is MPP_L. Output is constant along an equal-product curve, so the *change* in output for a small change in land use must be balanced by the change in output due to a change in labor use. That means that MPP_T must be equal to the substitution ratio times MPP_L, or $MPP_T = S.R. \times MPP_L$, or $MPP_L/MPP_T = S.R.$

The *condition for cost minimization*, that the equal-cost and equal-product curves be tangent — or have the same slope — can now be written as $p_L/p_T = MPP_L/MPP_T$, or $MPP_L/p_L = MPP_T/P_T$. This is just the condition derived from the reasoning about the marginal adjustments of inputs.[3]

Input substitution due to input price change

Having come this far in production and cost theory, let us detour a bit and analyze the effects of a change in input prices. This is one of the most common changes a business firm experiences. The theoretical apparatus developed above can be used to explore the effects of such a change.

Suppose labor's wages *increased* from \$4 an hour to \$6 and the rent of land *dropped* from \$9 to \$6. Table 22-4 shows the new costs of the alternative input combinations *A*, *B*, and *C*.

As a result of the change in the prices of labor and land, which changed their *relative* prices from 4/9 to 6/6, the least-cost input combination has changed from *A* to *B*. This result is also shown in Figure 22-8. As a result of the price changes, the slope of the equal-cost lines changes, and there is a new tangency at *B*.

[3] The arithemetic of the procedure can be worked out as follows. For an output of 6 units, the equation of the equal-product line is: $6 = \frac{1}{4} \cdot \sqrt{\text{labor inputs} \times \text{land inputs}}$. It takes a little math or a good eye with a ruler to figure out that the *slope* of the equal-product line at points *A*, *B*, and *C* are, respectively, 16/36, 24/24, and 36/16. In this quite special case, the slope of the equal-product line at each point is just the land/labor ratio at that point. The slope of an equal-cost line is always the ratio of the prices of the inputs, just as it was for a consumer's budget-constraint line, as shown in Chap. 19. So when the prices of the inputs are \$4 per man-hour and \$9 per acre, the equal-cost line has a slope of 4/9. At a tangency of an equal-product line and an equal-cost line, their slopes must be equal. That can only be at point *A*, whose slope of 16/36, or 4/9, matches the 4/9 slope of the equal-cost lines.

Table 22-4

ALTERNATIVE INPUT COMBINATIONS AND THEIR COSTS WITH DIFFERENT INPUT PRICES

	Land	*Labor*	*Land costs*	*Labor costs*	*Total costs*	*Output*
A	16	36	(16 × \$6 =) \$ 96	(36 × \$6 =) \$216	\$312	6
B	24	24	(24 × \$6 =) \$144	(24 × \$6 =) \$144	\$288	6
C	36	16	(36 × \$6 =) \$216	(16 × \$6 =) \$ 96	\$312	6

Figure 22-8

EFFECT OF A CHANGE IN INPUT PRICES ON THE CHOICE OF THE LOWEST-COMBINATION COST INPUT

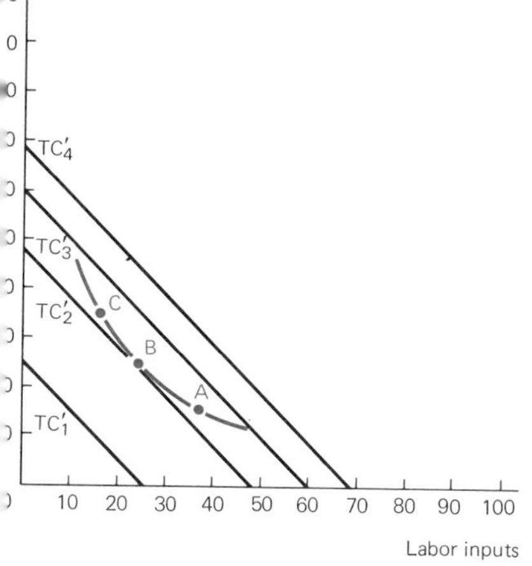

Notice that much less labor is used per unit of land at *B* than at *A*. At *A* the labor/land ratio is 36/16, or 2.25 to 1, while at *B* the ratio is 24/24, or 1 to 1. This warrants the observation: *A change in input prices will lead to the substitution of the input which has become* relatively *less expensive for the input which has become* relatively *more expensive, when such substitution is possible.*

This is an important point. It was introduced in Chapter 3 when we discussed the role of prices in resolving the Input question. Here the mechanism is made more explicit, and we shall return to it again in Chapter 27. It is another example of interdependence in the economy—in this case between output costs, input prices, and the choice of production techniques.

Choosing the long-run least-cost input combination for various output levels

The procedure for finding the long-run least-cost combination for a single output level can now be generalized. Figure 22-9 shows a whole family of equal-product curves, each for a different level of output as labeled: $X_1 = 6$, $X_2 = 8$, $X_3 = 10$, and so on. *The family of equal-product curves sums up all that is known about the technically efficient production of the particular good.* It represents the *production function* for the product. In Figure 22-10, a number of equal-cost lines are added. These reflect the prices of the inputs and the combinations of them that could be purchased for the specified alternative levels of costs.

The least-cost input combination for each possible output level is at the tangency of an equal-product line with an equal-cost line. That tangency for successive output levels occurs at points *B, D, E,* and *F* in Figure 22-10. In the long run, therefore, as the firm expands its output and can choose the best of all possible input combinations, it will use inputs in the amounts indicated at just those points. The minimum cost for which it can produce each output is just that cost on the equal-cost line through each of the points *B, D, E,* and *F*. The line through the minimum-cost points is called the *expansion path* of the firm. Along the expansion path, the scale of both inputs will change to make possible a larger-scale output at the lowest possible cost.

Figure 22-9

MAP OF EQUAL-PRODUCT CURVES

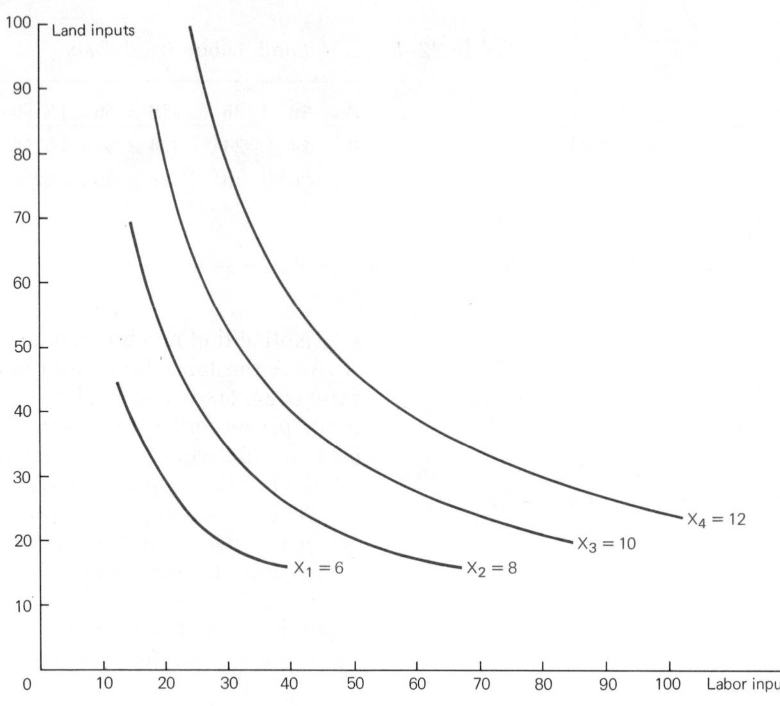

Figure 22-10

CHOOSING THE LONG-RUN MINIMUM-COST INPUT COMBINATIONS FOR ALTERNATIVE OUTPUT LEVELS

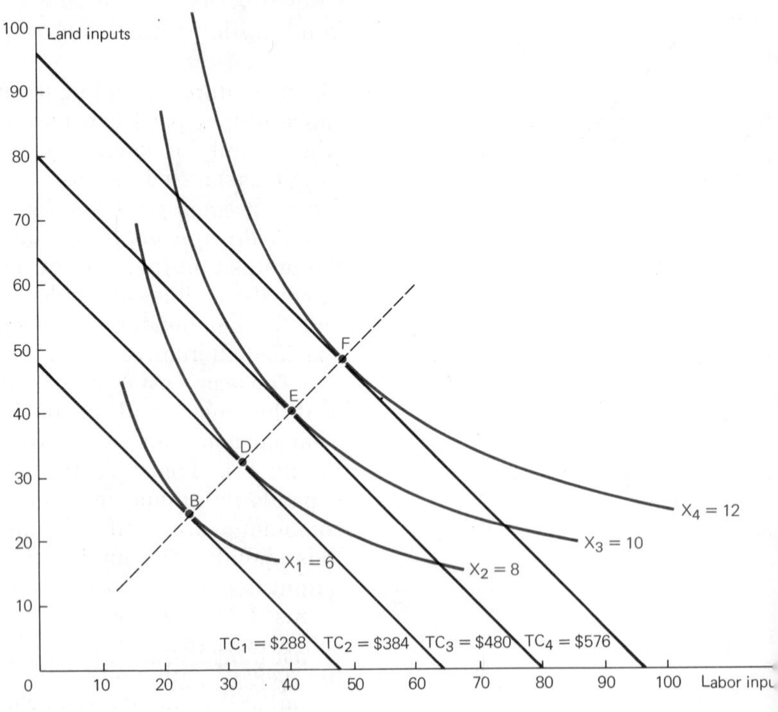

Figure 22-11

HYPOTHETICAL LONG-RUN TOTAL COST LINE

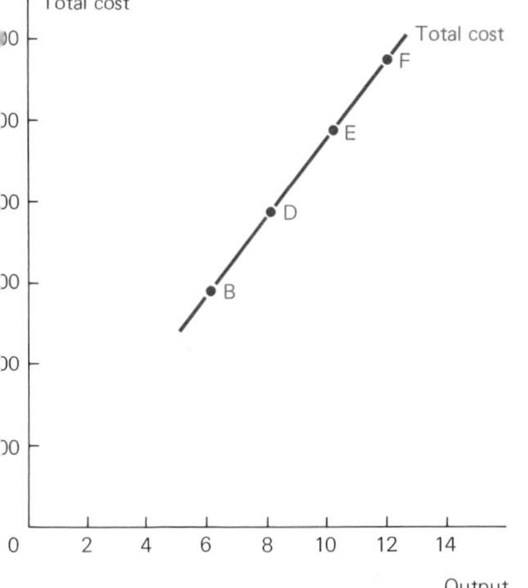

If the minimum total cost associated with each output is plotted, as on Figure 22-11, we have a picture of the long-run cost curve of the firm. This cost curve reflects all the possible adjustments that could be made to lower the costs of producing each output. The straight-line shape of the relation should not be generalized. While it is not unknown for total costs to behave this way, there is nothing necessary about it.

Long-run and short-run output expansion paths and cost schedules

The equal-product curves and equal-cost curves can be used to contrast the adjustments made by a firm in the short run and in the long run. Suppose, for example, that a firm faces the input prices embodied in the equal-cost line TC_1, as shown in Figure 22-12 on the next page. The firm makes a long-run adjustment to use inputs at point *B*, where TC_1 is just tangent to an equal-product curve. In the short run, adding only the variable input labor, *with land, the fixed input, constant*, the firm will have to move along line *BMNQ*.

When the firm has time to adjust its fixed as well as its variable input to produce, say, output X_2 at minimum cost, it will be at *D*. After making that long-run adjustment, if it then wants to increase output in the short run, it will have to move along line *DRST*, with a constant level of land input.

For each of the short-run expansion paths, *BMNQ, DRST, EUV,* and so on, there is a short-run total cost schedule. These are shown in Figure 22-13. They interweave in a rather complex way and have a special relation to the long-run cost schedule. They can be sorted out by tracing each one from the origin. Notice that for the range of outputs up to output X_1, TC_1 has the lowest total costs of production. For the output range from X_1 to X_2, note that TC_2 has the lowest total costs of production. Above X_2 for some range, TC_3 has the lowest total costs. *Each short-run total cost curve contributes one point to the long-run cost curve derived from the firm's long-run expansion path.* That long-run total cost curve, remember, is derived in the following manner: Given enough time and with specified factor prices, the firm can adjust its land and labor inputs to achieve the lowest possible cost of producing each output, as shown by line *BDE*. This long-run total cost curve embodies the assumption that long-run average costs rise, at least after some point.

It is helpful to think of line *BDE* as a "planning" cost curve. The firm is able to achieve any point on it by long-run adjustments. The firm is also always on a particular short-run cost curve, however, only one point of which need coincide with the long-run cost curve. *The long-run cost curve is called an envelope curve, because it just touches each of the short-run cost curves at the lowest cost for each output.*

Figure 22-12

LONG-RUN AND SHORT-RUN EXPANSION PATHS

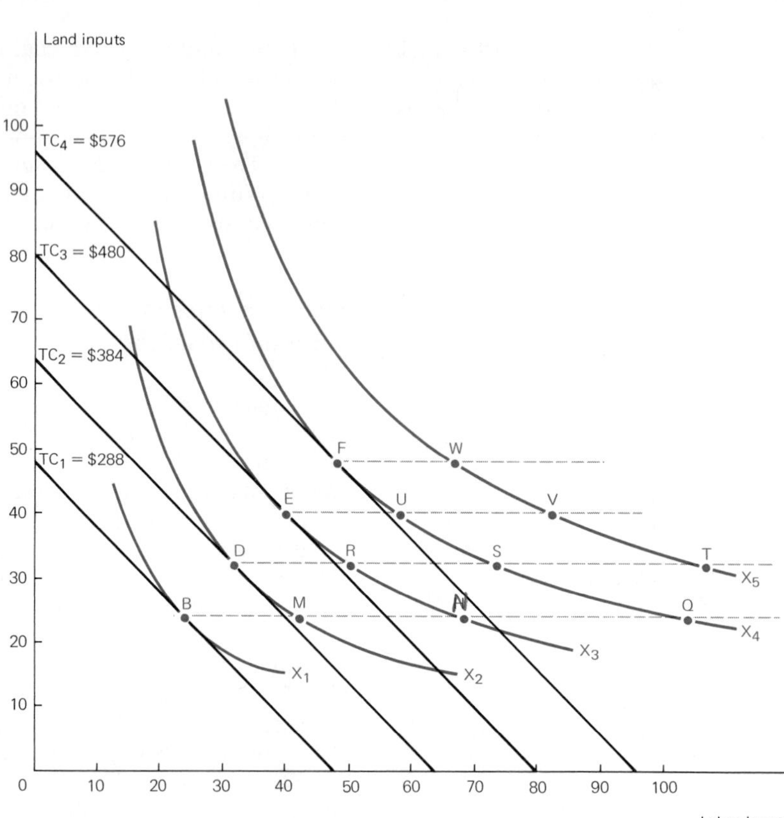

Long-run average and marginal cost curves

The same set of relationships between long- and short-run costs can be presented in terms of average and marginal costs. This is done in Figure 22-14.

For each amount of the fixed input, there is a short-run average total cost curve, which is calculated in the same way as the average total cost curve of Table 22-2, plotted in Figure 22-3. Some of these are ATC_A, ATC_B, and ATC_M, indicating the amount of the fixed input of land used in each case. There are also corresponding short-run marginal cost curves plotted as MC_A, MC_B, and MC_M. In addition, there are short-run average fixed cost and short-run average variable cost curves, which are not plotted.

Total costs

Short-run total costs

Long-run total costs

N R E M D B

Output

Figure 22-13

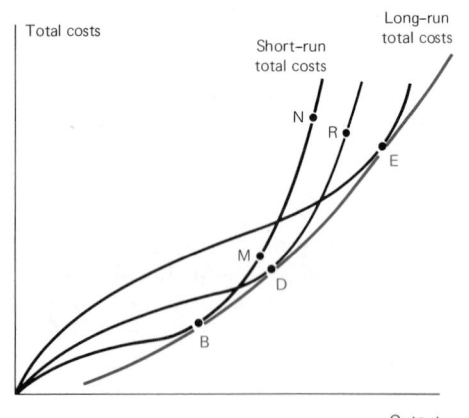

RELATION BETWEEN SHORT-RUN AND LONG-RUN COST CURVES

Figure 22-14

HYPOTHETICAL LONG-RUN AVERAGE COST CURVE WITH THE SHORT-RUN COST CURVES THAT GENERATE IT

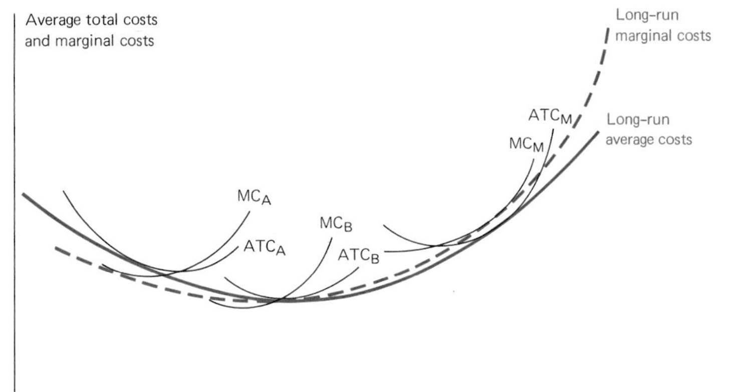

The *long-run* average total cost curve, *LRAC*, is again an *envelope curve. Each short-run average total cost curve which gives the lowest unit cost for each possible output level contributes a point* on the *LRAC*. No short-run *ATC* can cross below the long-run *ATC*. So the short-run *ATC* curves will be just touching the long-run *ATC* from above. Notice that the long-run average cost curve, like the short-run curves, is "U-shaped" in this case. The long-run average costs fall over some range of output and then rise. This is a common assumption whose empirical basis will be discussed in the next section.

Why isn't there a long-run average fixed cost curve, and why isn't there a long-run average variable cost curve? Because *in the long run all costs are variable*! Therefore, in the long run, the average total cost curve is also an average variable cost curve.

We *could* compute and plot the land costs per unit of output and the labor costs per unit of output which correspond to each point on the long-run average total cost curve. But we *could not* legitimately call them long-run fixed cost and long-run variable cost relations.

There is, however, a long-run marginal cost, *LRMC*. Analogously to the short-run marginal cost, it can be defined as the extra cost of an additional unit of output, but with a difference. On the long-run marginal cost curve, both inputs are capable of being varied to minimize that additional cost. The points on the long-run marginal cost curve could, in principle, be located on Figure 22-14 in the following manner: Go back to the long-run total cost curves in Figure 22-11 or 22-13. To obtain those curves we would have to figure out the additional cost of an additional unit of output when both labor *and* land can be varied. That was done explicitly for Figure 22-11, and the result was generalized in Figure 22-12. The additional cost of a unit of output when all inputs can be varied to minimize the cost of output is the *long-run marginal cost of that increment in output.*

Costs when there are many inputs

The cost analysis has been carried out in the context of a simple model of a firm with one short-run variable factor and one short-run fixed factor. The fixed factor, however, can be varied in some specific longer-term period. What happens to the analysis if it is transposed into a real world of many different kinds of inputs that can be adjusted with varying speeds and whose adjustment imposes different costs on the firm?

An ordinary small manufacturing business, for example, will own or rent its business and parking space. It will own or rent some production and packaging machinery. It may own or rent some materials-handling equipment, some trucks, and cars for salesmen. It will have some inventories of materials and products. It may employ some men by the hour, it may have to give a month's notice to some workers, and it may employ some officials on annual or even longer-term contracts. Each of these different types of inputs will be fixed to a different degree in the sense that the time required for adjustment of each will be different. There may be a one-year lease on the building and a six-month lease on the machines. The firm may get new equipment delivered in three months, but new inventory in only a week. Some more labor can be hired tomorrow, but it might take a couple of months to find another good quality-control man.

On further thought, however, one can see that those adjustment times are not really fixed. They can be speeded up if the firm is willing to pay the necessary costs. If it wants badly enough to move to a better site without waiting for the lease on its present building to expire, it will pay the costs for breaking the lease as prescribed in the penalty clause of the contract. It may be willing to buy more costly equipment than it really needs if that is the only kind immediately available. It may be willing to accept raw materials with a higher proportion of rejects if those materials can be obtained more quickly. Or the firm may not be willing to pay these extra costs for quick adjustment of its inputs and may decide to keep its costs down by adapting more slowly.

These considerations make the concepts of short-run and long-run and fixed and variable costs less definite than they are in the simple two-factor model. There are *many different short runs,* and the variabilty of factors is usually *not* determined once and for all by technical or legal contractual constraints, but by *cost considerations.*

Nonetheless, the concepts of short and long run and of fixed and variable costs are useful; in one form or another they are used by all businessmen in planning and managing their businesses. Managers talk about *overhead* costs and mean what we have called fixed costs, though they know as well as we do that such costs are not absolutely fixed. They are only *relatively* inflexible — at least over the range of output they are discussing. And businessmen also distinguish variable costs, or *running* costs. These are costs which vary with output. They are not completely unique for each level of output, but depend to some extent on the adjustment expenses the firms are willing to bear.

Long-run cost patterns

Three alternative patterns of *long-run cost* behavior can be distinguished:

> *Constant-cost* firms whose long-run average costs are virtually constant as their output increases
>
> *Increasing-cost* firms whose long-run average costs increase as their output increases
>
> *Decreasing-cost* firms whose long-run average costs decrease as their output increases

These alternatives are presented in Figure 22-15.

Figure 22-15

ALTERNATIVE LONG-RUN AVERAGE COST PATTERNS

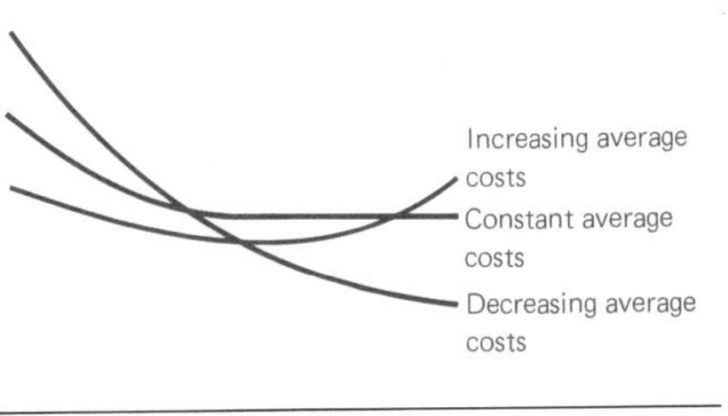

A plausible case for long-run constant costs can be made in the following way: Suppose a firm, by good engineering and cost studies, worked out the least-cost method of producing its product, taking into account all possible adjustments of its inputs. Then, if it wanted to double or triple its output, it could do so without increasing its average costs in the long run just by duplicating or triplicating the original facilities. (As long as the market is large enough to absorb such an expansion of output, all an acute observer would see is production at constant average costs.)

One argument made against this idea of maintaining constant costs by replicating inputs is that there is, finally, one necessary ingredient which simply cannot be replicated. That is the brain of the man who must manage and coordinate all the replicated fixed and variable inputs. The top manager, therefore, can be regarded as a "fixed input" that finally forces diminishing returns to all other inputs and rising average costs in production. On the other hand, management efficiency has been increased by modern organizational and communications techniques, so this factor may not actually be limitational. This is not the kind of argument that can be settled in principle. The essential question is, What do the facts show? While the "facts" are almost never unequivocal in such studies, the limitations imposed by management bottlenecks now seem relatively unimportant in many industries.

In some types of production, however, long-run average costs of production do increase with output. At first blush, long-run increasing costs may seem to be a plausible result of the Law of Diminishing Returns. This law says that as more and more units of one variable input are added to one or more fixed inputs, average output per unit of the variable input will fall. But in the long run, the firm is free to vary *all* the inputs, both fixed and variable, within whatever limits are set by the technology and fundamental resource availabilities of the economy. Yet not all inputs may be capable of indefinite expansion. Or the availability of some inputs may be increased only at substantially higher prices. In such circumstances, the long-run average total cost curve will tilt upward as output increases.

Strictly speaking, a firm with decreasing costs should have an average total cost curve which falls over all conceivable ranges of output. All we can say is that in some industries average costs fall over all observed ranges of output. Industries of this type are popularly known as having *economies of large-scale production*. Typically, in these industries, expensive but highly specialized methods and machinery are used which are so tremendously productive when operated at full capacity that the costs per unit of output are lower than unit costs at lower output levels with less expensive (and less productive) equipment. Sometimes the least-cost scale of output can be achieved when a single firm covers a single market, thus avoiding expensive duplication of effort and facilities by two or more firms. Two electric power companies in the same region, each with its own transmission lines going to next-door neighbors, will have higher "delivery costs" than one company. This is a case of natural monopoly. It helps explain the exclusive franchise given to electric and other utilities to achieve lower costs for the consumer.

Empirical evidence on cost curves

The *break-even chart* that business firms often use to project their revenues and costs in the short run is illustrated in Figure 22-16. Over the relevant range of output, revenues are often assumed to rise with production and sales in a straight-line fashion: $R = pQ$, where R is revenue, p is the price of the product, and Q stands for quantity produced and sold. Likewise over the relevant output range, total costs are assumed to move along a straight line. But if the total cost line is projected backward to the zero level of output, there will still be some costs to be borne. Those are the fixed costs. And when the firm's capacity is fully utilized, costs are assumed to rise abruptly. So up to capacity, the total cost line follows the equation: $TC = FC + vQ$, where TC stands for total costs; FC stands for fixed costs, v is the *increase* in cost for a unit increase in production, and Q is the quantity produced. The point A is the *break-even point* of operations for the business firm. *Above A, the firm begins to make profits, and below A, it takes losses.*

Let us draw out the implications for the behavior of unit production costs of the conventional cost line of the break-even chart. That will tell us how businessmen often see their own cost situation. With the total cost line $TC = FC + vQ$, then average total cost

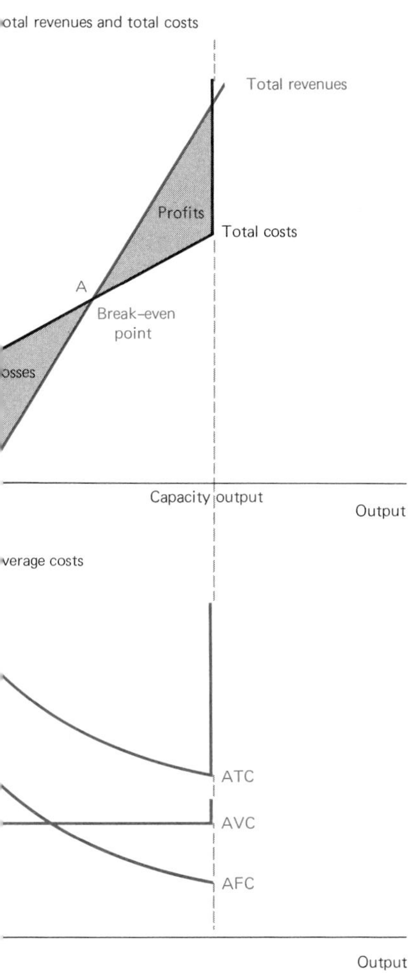

Figure 22-16

TYPICAL BREAK-EVEN CHART

Figure 22-17

AVERAGE COSTS IMPLIED BY BREAK-EVEN CHART

or unit cost is $ATC = TC/Q = FC/Q + v$. Notice that as output increases, up to capacity, average fixed costs, FC/Q, will fall steadily, but average variable costs, $vQ/Q = v$, will be constant at the level v. So *ATC*, which is the sum of average fixed costs and average variable costs, will fall until capacity is reached, and then will rise abruptly. This is shown in Figure 22-17. The pattern of cost variation implied by the conventional break-even cost curve has frequently been found in many careful studies of production costs: slowly falling average fixed costs and more or less constant variable costs as output increases. The two together lead to slowly falling average total costs up to full capacity. Many studies, however, show that unit costs begin to rise somewhat even before an absolute capacity limitation is reached.

Studies of the variation of costs with output in the long run, when the size of plant and other fixed factors can be adjusted, also often show a *relatively constant unit cost*. In some industries, there is a slight tilt downward. This seems to be especially typical of railroads, electricity generation, and natural gas transmission. These are industries whose production technology has inherent increasing-returns-to-scale characteristics. These give rise to lower and lower long-run unit costs as the scale of plant is adjusted.

Steel production also seems to have important economies of scale and, therefore, lower unit costs with size up to several million tons of output annually. After that, though unit costs do not rise, they do not seem to fall substantially. Similar patterns prevail in the chemical industry and in cement production. On the other hand, there is evidence that unit costs in quite large meat-packing plants may actually be larger than in smaller plants, and the same may be true in bakery products.

Cost investigation is difficult, largely because good data are hard to obtain. Nonetheless, it is an important area of research.

Long-run cost patterns and market structure

An industry's market structure is often intimately related to its production cost patterns. It is no accident that the industries cited as examples of long-run decreasing costs are industries with relatively few firms and, sometimes, even complete monopoly. In long-run decreasing-cost industries, competition, in the sense of the

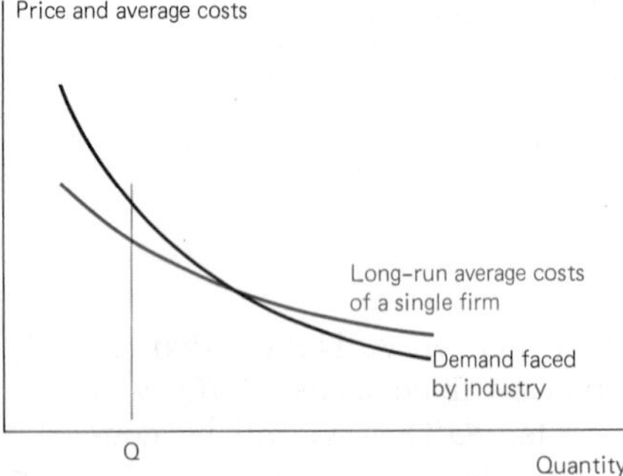

Figure 22-18

DEMAND AND COSTS OF A DECREASING-COST INDUSTRY

existence of a large number of firms which provide alternatives for the buyer, cannot survive. When firms *can* reduce costs by increasing their size and *try* to do so, the less efficient firms and those which are growing more slowly are going to be squeezed out. The process may or may not go all the way to complete monopoly. It depends on (1) whether the long-run cost curves fall continually or turn up at some point and (2) whether a *modus vivendi* is found among the final few giant firms or whether they struggle to the death of all but one of them.

Figure 22-18 combines on one diagram the total demand for the product of a decreasing-cost industry and the continually falling long-run average cost curve of a firm in that industry. The firm which produces the largest output will have the lowest costs. No other firm can compete with it by producing at lower costs.

On the other hand, if several firms grow to, say, point Q, they may decide to live and let live rather than face the life and death struggle involved in growing larger. Then the industry will end up as an *oligopoly*. Oligopoly can also develop even if the long-run cost curves do not fall continually, but the minimum-cost point at M is a large fraction of the quantity demanded, Q, at the going price. This is shown in Figure 22-19.

Figure 22-19

AN INDUSTRY IN WHICH MINIMUM-COST OUTPUT IS A LARGE FRACTION OF THE QUANTITY DEMANDED AT THE GOING PRICE

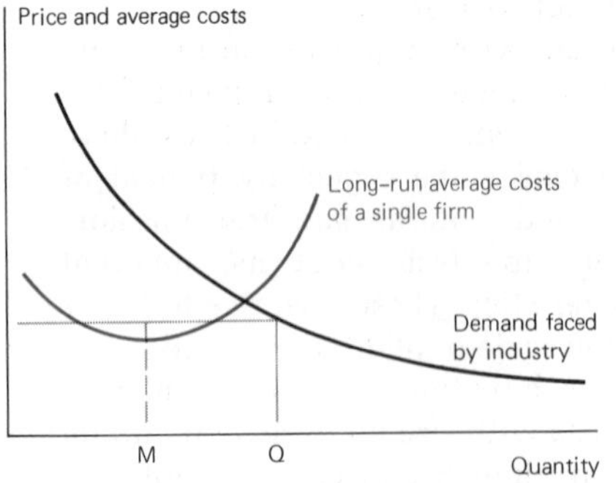

If there are constant long-run average costs or sharply increasing costs, however, competition may be maintained. There may be large firms in industries whose firms have long-run constant costs. But they have no cost advantage over smaller firms which can enter the industry easily and compete on equal terms. This possibility is shown in Figure 22-20.

When long-run unit costs increase with size of output, there are definite disadvantages to large-scale production. Then it is more likely that competition and many relatively small firms will survive as alternative sources of supply.

While long-run cost conditions are important influences in determining market structure, they are certainly not the only relevant and determining factors. For example, long-run costs of production in the automobile industry seem to decline up to an annual output of about 800,000 to 1 million cars and to be more or less constant after that. In an automobile market such as the United States where 8 million or so cars are sold each year, there is room for maybe eight to ten efficient-sized firms.[4] In smaller and poorer nations, the automobile market may not be large enough for one

Figure 22-20

AN INDUSTRY IN WHICH FIRMS OF VARYING SIZES HAVE THE SAME MINIMUM COSTS

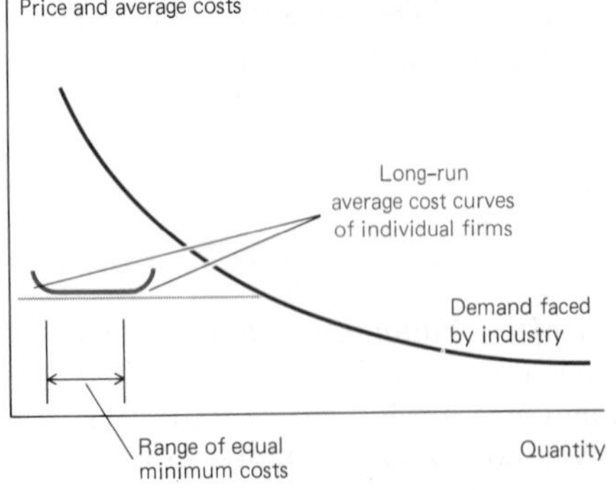

[4] See, for example, George Maxcy and Aubrey Silberston, *The Motor Industry*, Allen & Unwin, Ltd. London, 1959.

firm to achieve minimum efficient scale. But there are not eight to ten efficient-sized auto producers in the United States today. There are only four. Likewise there is no evidence which suggests that long-run decreasing costs account for the existence of only 8 firms in the cigarette industry. These facts require an explanation which goes beyond cost structure. It will have to be put off to Chapter 25.

A final note on catching all the costs: Private and social

If every factor that contributed to a firm's production were rented for just the period it was used, then all of its costs would be explicit and borne only by the firm. The firm's accountants could put down a specific dollar figure for every productive input for each period. In practice, a variety of circumstances prevent cost calculations from being so explicit and straightforward.

Implicit costs. Resources owned by the firm and used in production do not have to be paid an annual rent. Still no one would think of them as *free*. Legal ownership is not the criterion of whether the use of a factor involves a cost. The criterion is whether an explicit payment would be required to hire the factor if it were not owned. If it would be, then there is an *implicit* cost, which is equivalent to the explicit cash payment that would otherwise have to be made. Accountants and businessmen must be alert to implicit costs. Such costs do not involve a cash payment in the short run, but in the long run, they well might if the resources are depleted or wear out.

Implicit costs are most commonly overlooked in small-scale proprietorships. The man who owns and works in his own small business should count as a cost of doing business the interest he would have to pay if he borrowed the funds he has tied up in his concern and the rent he would have to pay if he did not own his place of business. He should also count as a cost the wages he would have to pay if he had to hire someone as good as himself to work the long hours he puts in. Those are real even if not explicit costs of doing business. One way of estimating them is to ask: What income could be earned by the funds tied up in the business if they were put into some good stocks or bonds? And what wages could the owner-operator earn if he took a job which required his special abilities? The implicit costs could then be estimated as *opportunity costs* – i.e., the costs of the forgone alternative opportunities to earn income with the resources available.

Profits. One particularly important opportunity cost is the *"normal" minimum profit level which will attract people to invest their funds in an industry*. There is no law requiring a corporation to make profits or pay out dividends. If it does not, however, the firm will not attract future investors. It will even be hard to keep its current owners. They will want to recover their invested funds, if possible, and place them where they will earn an income. Normal profits are, therefore, often considered part of the "costs" of a business. They are also an opportunity cost of the owners' resources tied up in the firm.

Social contributions and external diseconomies. As pointed out in Chapter 4, there are some *social contributions to the production process for which there are no exactly corresponding implicit or explicit individual costs.* Local, state, and national government organizations provide a variety of services to private individuals and to business for which there are usually no precisely corresponding payments. For example, a business firm may fire a night watchman when the local police department decides to send a police car around the plant every hour during the night. The night watchman's salary was an explicit cost. Virtually the same service is provided by the police cruiser without any explicit cost to the firm. To be sure, the firm pays taxes, but there is usually no one-to-one correspondence between taxes paid and services provided.

There are also *individual and social costs due to private production for which businesses may make no payments whatsoever,* exactly corresponding or not. These are *external diseconomies*, discussed first in Chapter 1. They are borne widely by the community, but not by the private producers when they are able to shift the costs away from the firm. When manufacturers dispose of the waste products of their production processes by dumping them into lakes and rivers or burning them, they save the costs of providing other disposal methods. In effect, such firms are shifting some of their costs to the public at large. Where there is not much industry and population is sparse, use of the atmosphere and rivers for smoke and waste disposal may create no diseconomies or costs. The growth and concentration of industry and urban population change that and create a problem and costs where none existed before.

Opportunity costs once again

The opportunity cost idea is a central and important one in economics. It came up in the First and Third Model Economies in which only two goods were produced. In those models, it was clear that, when resources were fully employed, if the economies wanted to produce more Clothing, they would have to shift the resources from producing Food. The cost of the increased Clothing production could legitimately be said to be the Food that had to be sacrificed when the resources were shifted. Analogously, in an economy of many goods, when there are full employment and efficient use of resources, the costs of expanding the production of one good are the opportunities lost to produce other goods. As we shall see, only under the special conditions of perfect competition and full accounting of all resources used by firms can we be sure that the costs of using resources for one type of production will reflect the opportunities lost for using the resouces in other types of production.

Summary

The amounts of output which firms are willing to produce and offer at any price depend on their costs of production. These costs, in turn, depend on the characteristics of the particular production process and the prices of the inputs.

In the short run, a firm is committed to certain costs which are fixed and will not vary with output. In the long run, all inputs and costs are variable.

In the short run, the total costs of various outputs can be calculated once the variation in output with the variable inputs is known. For each output: total cost (*TC*) = *fixed cost* (*FC*) + *variable cost* (*VC*). Fixed cost = fixed inputs × their price, and the variable cost = variable inputs × their price. Marginal cost (*MC*) is the additional cost or the change in total cost due to a 1-unit increase in output. *MC* can also be interpreted as the slope of the total cost curve. *MC* is important because it is the cost concept which businessmen watch to observe the effects of a change in output.

Total cost always increases with output even in the short run, but the average total cost, *TC*/output, may fall over some range before it starts rising. Average variable cost, *VC*/output, in the short run will eventually increase, owing to the Law of Diminishing Returns. For the same reason, the marginal cost of additional output will at some point begin to rise with output.

In the long run, all inputs can be adjusted and, therefore, all costs are variable. The existence of alternative input combinations for a particular output level is another way of saying that inputs can be substituted for each other in production. When this is possible, firms will substitute inputs that have higher marginal physical products per dollar of cost (*MPP*/input price) for inputs with a lower *MPP*/input price. The choice of a least-cost input combination for a particular output can also be explained by the concept of the equal-product, or iso-product, curve and that of the equal-cost, or iso-cost, line. The equal-product curve shows the alternative input combinations that will produce the same output. So everywhere along it, output is constant. The equal-cost line shows all combinations of inputs for which the total expenditure is the same. The choice of the least-cost input combination for a particular output can be described as if it were a movement along an equal-product curve, crossing lower and lower equal-cost lines. The movement will stop when it is no longer possible to move to an input combination that will have lower costs for that particular output level.

The long-run total cost curve of a firm is generated by finding the least-cost input combination for each output level. In the short run, however, the firm may use a different input combination until it has time to adjust its fixed inputs to their most desirable level.

If in the long run, when all inputs can be varied, the unit cost or long-run average cost (*LRAC*) of a firm tends to rise, this is known as an increasing-cost firm. If its *LRAC* stays more or less unchanged as output expands, this is a constant-cost firm, and that is the result of constant returns to expansion of the scale of all inputs. There may also be decreasing-cost firms, where the economies of large-scale operation, or increasing returns to scale, more than offset the cost of using additional inputs.

Empirical studies commonly find that unit costs are more or less constant over wide ranges of output when there is time to adjust input combinations. There are cases of increasing costs as well, and also cases in which there are decreasing costs over all the observed output ranges of firms in existence.

The behavior of costs with output is an important determinant of industrial market structure. When there are constant costs, it is relatively easy for new firms to compete with established firms, as size and previous experience give no particular advantage. Increasing-cost conditions tend also to be favorable to competition, as there are actually disadvantages to large size. Industries whose firms have decreasing costs over a range of outputs that is large relative to the market understandably have difficulty in maintaining competition. In this case, firm growth can create a cost advantage.

In accounting its own costs, a firm should include those costs which do not involve explicit payments but nonetheless have an opportunity cost. If the resources were not owned or otherwise available, they would have to be purchased or rented, with payment of an explicit charge. One type of opportunity cost is the normal profits investors expect to make if they are to continue to provide funds for a business. Costs of production, such as pollution, which a firm avoids bearing itself, are external diseconomies to other firms or to the community as a whole.

Questions for discussion and review

1. Describe in your own words the difference between technical and economic efficiency. Can technically efficient production ever be economically inefficient? Can economically efficient production ever be technically inefficient?

2. Interpret in the language of the chapter the following statement made by a businessman in discussing his production cost problems: *The only way I can bring down my average overhead costs is to expand output. But in my business the direct labor and material costs per unit of output go up quite rapidly. Therefore, I have a particularly difficult job balancing these costs.*

3. Translate this statement of another businessman: *I can't hope to minimize my costs of production. The whole process is much too complicated. Anyway it wouldn't be worth the time of my engineers to figure out all the possible input combinations for a particular output that economists talk about in the production function concept. All I can do is try one or another technique and see what happens. And besides I get along pretty well that way.*

4. Describe in your own language the rationale of the cost-minimizing condition – that the substitution ratio of inputs in producing a constant level of output must be equal to the ratio of the prices of the inputs.

5. Explain the following statement: *Every point on a long-run cost curve is also a point on a short-run cost curve. But not every point on a short-run cost curve is also a point on a long-run cost curve.*

6. If the short run is defined as the period during which some costs cannot be changed, there must be many different short runs. Still there is only one long run in which all costs can be varied. Do you agree or disagree? Why?

7. Why is competition more difficult to maintain in decreasing-cost industries than in increasing-cost industries?

8. "All costs are opportunity costs." Do you believe it? Explain.

Concepts for review

Fixed, variable, marginal, and total costs
Average fixed, average variable, and average total costs
Substitution ratio of inputs in production
Equal-product and equal-cost curves
Short run and long run
Increasing-, decreasing-, and constant-cost industries
Implicit, explicit, and opportunity costs
Private and social costs

23 Supply decisions and pricing in competitive markets

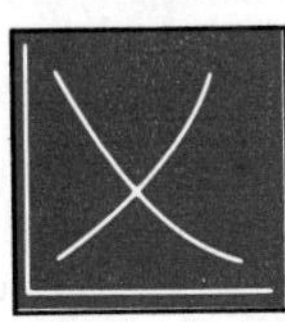

Most of what is interesting and important in supply and demand analysis goes on behind the face of the diagram on which the supply and demand curves appear. In Chapters 23 and 24 we put everything together to work out supply-demand interactions in price determination in the perfectly competitive model, and in Chapter 25 we move on to monopoly and the various types of imperfect competition.

The procedure will be to work out the firm and industry supply schedules in different adjustment periods. Then we shall use the industry supply and demand schedules to obtain some general insights that can be tested in particular cases.

Supply schedules and the adjustment period

The amount offered for sale in a perfectly competitive industry depends on the actions of the multitude of firms producing identical products. Yet each firm acts independently and, as a price taker, regards the price of its product as one which the firm itself cannot affect. That does not mean the firm thinks the price will never change. Quite the contrary, the industry may well have a history of price changes with which the firm is familiar. *For a price-taking firm, price changes are exogenous; that is, they originate outside the firm.* The price-taking firm has no control over them; it can only react to them.

The supply curve for a perfectly competitive industry depends, therefore, on the reactions of all the firms in the industry to the going price and to changes in the going price. For each firm, the supply schedule is a series of if-then statements: *If* the price is ——, *then* the quantity produced and sold by the firm will be ——. The supply schedule for the *industry* is, therefore, also a set of if-then statements which sum up the quantities offered by all firms at each price.

The supply reactions of a firm depend importantly on the time it has in which to react. The important measure of time here is not years or months or days — but the period required by the firm to adjust its inputs and outputs. Three such periods can be distinguished: (1) the *momentary* supply period — which is too short to permit any change in inputs or outputs; (2) the *short-run* supply period — in which the firm can change its output only by adjusting the variable inputs in its production processes; and (3) the *long-run* supply period — in which the firm can vary output by adjusting all inputs in the production process.

We shall take up supply and price determination in each of these three periods.

The momentary supply schedules of competitive firms and the industry

"Momentary period" is an unwieldy but conventional term. It is a *period which is so short that the firm has no time to adjust its production if there should be a change in the price it faces.* All the firm has to sell is the stock of goods it has on hand. The portion the firm will sell at the market price depends on its own *reservation price.* That is a kind of floor price or minimum price for the firm. If the current market price is below the reservation price, the firm will just hold over for sale in the future the inventories currently on hand. But if the going price is above the reservation price, the firm will start to sell from its currently available stock of goods.

The reservation price of each firm depends on (1) its expectations of future prices, (2) its need for current revenue from sales, and (3) the storability of the good. If the firm thinks that prices are going to be higher in the future, it will tend to hold back its sales now. If the firm needs cash rather desperately now, it will be more willing to sell its stocks. If the product is perishable and cannot be stored, then the stocks will be worthless in the future. At prices above the reservation price, the amount of its stocks that each firm offers for sale will depend on these same factors. Typically, the higher the price, the greater the amount each firm will offer to sell.

Figure 23-1 illustrates this point. It shows three different kinds of firms with three different reservation price levels and three different schedules of amounts which they would be willing to offer above their reservation prices. The lines that start from the reser-

Figure 23-1

HYPOTHETICAL MOMENTARY SUPPLY SCHEDULES OF THREE TYPES OF FIRMS

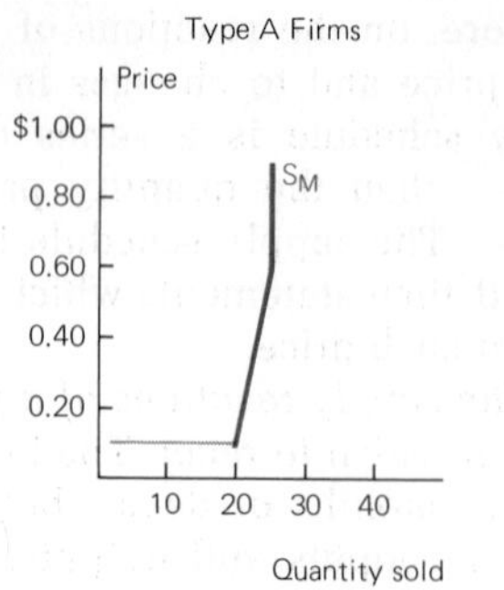

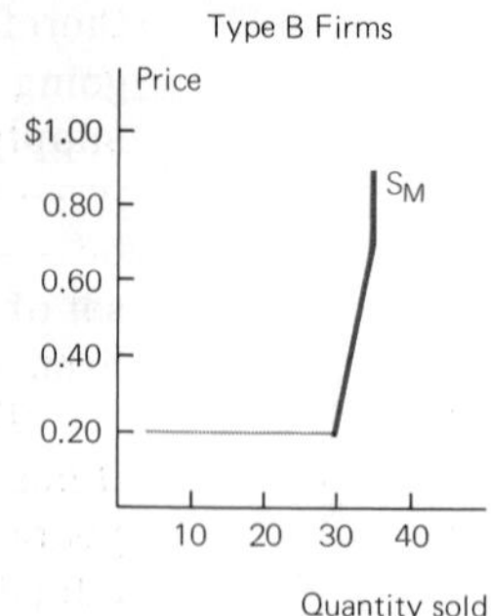

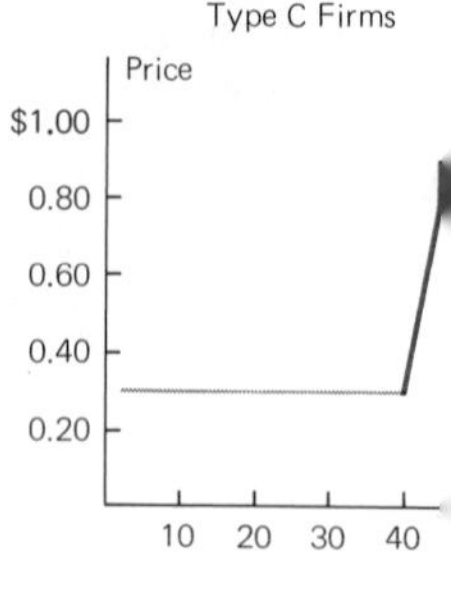

vation price of each type of firm are the momentary supply (S_M) schedules for each firm of that type. For example, the Type A firm would not offer anything for sale below $0.10. It would slowly increase its offers up to a price of $0.70, when it would reach its maximum quantity supplied, which is 25. The reservation prices of Type B and Type C firms are $0.20 and $0.30, respectively; they have a maximum quantity supplied of 35 and 45, respectively.

In Table 23-1, we work out the industry supply schedule, assuming that there are 1,000 firms of each type. To obtain the industry supply schedule, we multiply the amount offered by each type of firm at each price by 1,000, and then add up the separate amounts offered at each price. This corresponds to a horizontal addition of the supply schedules of the 3,000 firms represented by the three supply schedules in Figure 23-1. The industry supply schedule, which is taken from columns 1 and 5 of Table 23-1, is shown in Figure 23-2.

Table 23-1

HYPOTHETICAL MOMENTARY SUPPLY SCHEDULES OF ALL FIRMS OF EACH TYPE

1 Price	2 *1,000 Type A firms*	3 *1,000 Type B firms*	4 *1,000 Type C firms*	5 *All firms*
$0.10	20,000	0	0	20,000
0.20	21,000	30,000	0	51,000
0.30	22,000	31,000	40,000	93,000
0.40	23,000	32,000	41,000	96,000
0.50	24,000	33,000	42,000	99,000
0.60	25,000	34,000	43,000	102,000
0.70	25,000	35,000	44,000	104,000
0.80	25,000	35,000	45,000	105,000
0.90	25,000	35,000	45,000	105,000

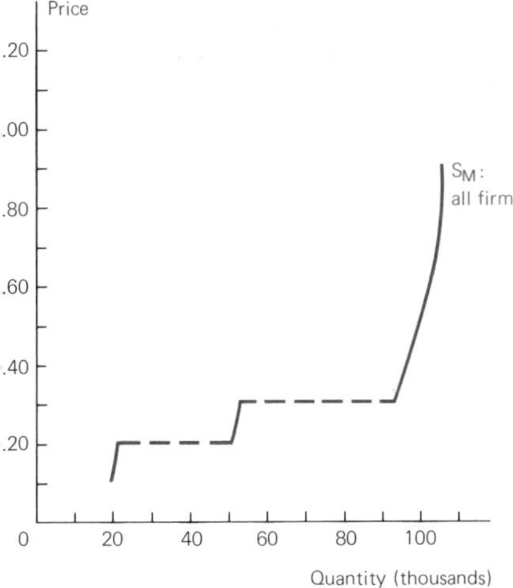

Figure 23-2

MOMENTARY SUPPLY SCHEDULE OF ALL FIRMS

Figure 23-3

COMPETITIVE PRICE DETERMINATION IN THE MOMENTARY PERIOD

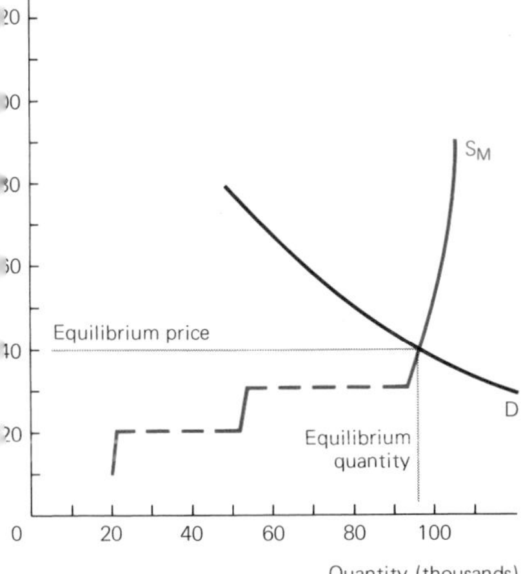

Competitive price determination in the momentary period

The industry demand schedule together with the industry's momentary supply schedule provides enough information to determine the price. Such a demand schedule is shown in Figure 23-3 along with the industry supply schedule. The equilibrium price of $0.40 can now be read off at the supply-demand intersection, as explained in Chapter 4. At a higher price, the firms would offer more than buyers would purchase, and competition would force the price down toward the equilibrium. So a price above $0.40 could not prevail. At any price below $0.40, a greater quantity would be demanded than supplied, and competition among buyers would push the price up. So the market price would always move toward the equilibrium price of $0.40, and sales of all firms would tend toward 96,000.

Notice that, at the equilibrium price, all types of firms – A, B, and C – would be selling from their stocks. But at a price of $0.20, only Type A and Type B firms would be selling.

The distinction between movements along each of the schedules and a shift of the schedules themselves must be kept in mind. For example, if the demand *curve* shifted upward to intersect the momentary supply curve at a price of $0.50 and a quantity of 99,000, there would be a change in quantity supplied, but not in the supply schedule itself. The firms of each type would change the amounts they offered. Type A firms would sell 24,000 units; B firms would sell 33,000 units, and C firms would sell 42,000 units.

It is useful to review the procedure by which we analyzed price determination in this simple case of the momentary period, because the same procedure is used in much more complicated cases.

1. A series of if-then questions were asked and answered about how much each firm would offer for sale at each price. That provided the firm supply schedules.

2. The firm supply schedules were added to obtain the industry supply schedule by asking, If the price is ——, then how much will *all* firms offer?

3. The industry supply schedule was compared with the industry demand schedule. The origins of the demand schedule were explained in Chapters 19 and 20. The industry demand schedule is the result of an analogous process of adding up the answers of individuals to a set of if-then questions: *If* the price is so much, *then* how much will each *person* purchase and what will *total* purchases be?

4. The intersection of the supply and demand schedules indicated the market-clearing price and quantities. *At the market-clearing price,* the if-then questions for both industry supply

and demand give the same quantity answer for the same price question. At no other price will the quantity answer to both the demand and supply questions be the same.

The short-run supply schedule of the competitive firm

In the short run, the competitive firm can change its output by changing the amount of its variable factor inputs. As its output changes, its costs as well as its revenue change. As a result, the firm's sales decision is much more complicated in the short run than in the momentary period. In the latter, the maximum amount available for sale is fixed, and the firm need only decide on its reservation price and how much it will offer from its stocks at prices above the reservation price.

What determines how much a firm will produce and offer for sale at various prices in the short run — when both its costs *and* its revenues will change for each level of output? The key to the question is that, though the firm is a price taker, it can and will always try to do as well for itself as possible. It will try to maximize its profits, as explained in Chapter 21. Therefore the firm supply question is, *What volume of production will maximize the profits of a firm in a perfectly competitive industry in the short run at a spe-*

Figure 23-4

DETERMINATION OF THE SHORT-RUN MAXIMUM-PROFIT OUTPUT LEVEL FOR A COMPETITIVE FIRM

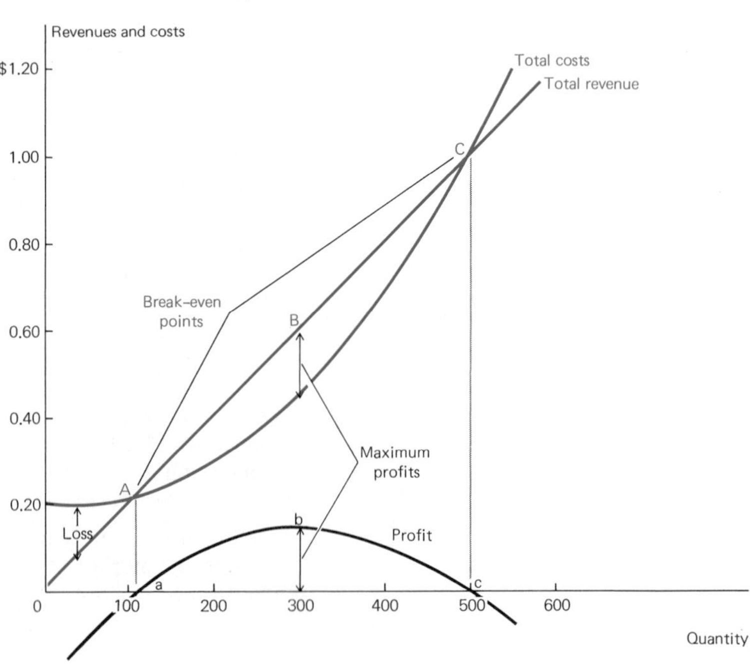

Figure 23-5

DETERMINATION OF THE PROFIT-MAXIMIZING OUTPUT BY MARGINAL ANALYSIS

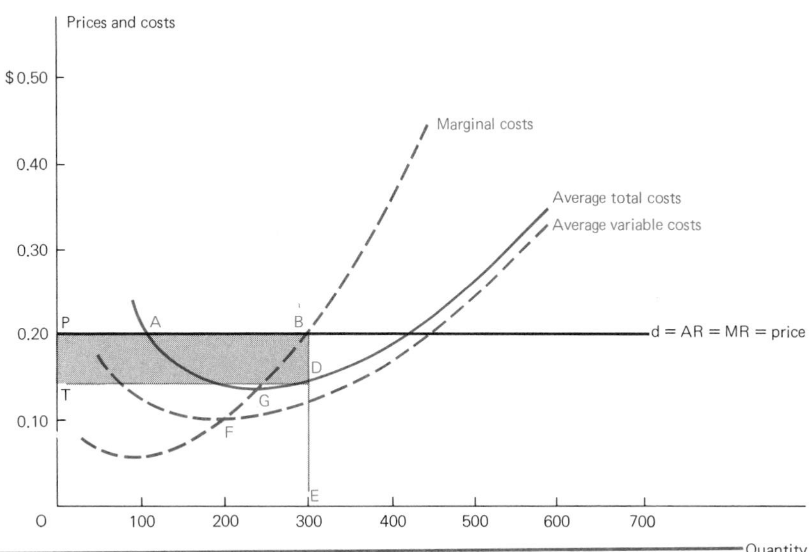

cific price? The question can be answered with the help of Figures 23-4 and 23-5.

Figure 23-4 shows the total revenue and total cost curves for a typical perfectly competitive firm. The total revenue curve reflects a particular price for the product. This price is constant for the price-taking firm no matter how much it offers, as explained in Chapter 21. The price is set at $0.20. So the total revenue line is straight, and goes up by $0.20 for each additional unit sold.

The short-run cost curves derived in Chapter 22 reflect input prices, technology, and the amount of the fixed inputs used with the variable inputs. In the short run, there will be some fixed costs even if there is no output. Above zero output, costs rise, first slowly and then more rapidly.

Profits are the difference between revenue and costs. In Figure 23-4, the profit made by the firm at each level of output is the distance by which the revenue curve lies above the cost curve. That clearly varies with output. Points *A* and C are break-even levels of output. Costs and revenues are equal and there are no profits. Between *A* and *C*, revenues are greater than costs, and there are profits. At outputs below *A* and above C, there are losses. At point *B*, profits are at a maximum. The profits curve is also shown in Figure 23-4 as the line *abc*, with *b* at the top of the profit mountain.

So the answer to the question, If the price is $0.20, then how much will the firm offer? can be read off Figure 23-4. It is 300 units, because *that is the quantity that will bring in the maximum profits!*

The same answer can be obtained from Figure 23-5. The figure may look formidable, but it is actually more convenient and in some ways more realistic than Figure 23-4. The use of Figure 23-4 and the numbers behind it might seem to imply that the firm knows in advance what its costs will be at each level of output. In practice, although the firm makes some projections, it ordinarily learns what its costs will be by actually producing. So a realistic explanation of how firms decide what to produce and offer for sale at each price should reflect that learning process. Figure 23-5 can be interpreted in this spirit.

First of all, we have the firm's demand schedule, line *D*. As explained in Chapter 21, that demand schedule is straight and horizontal at the going market price, because the competitive firm is a price taker and is too small to affect price. The demand line for the competitive firm is also its average revenue schedule and marginal revenue schedule. We have plotted on Figure 23-5 the firm's average total cost, average variable cost, and marginal cost schedules, as derived in the preceding chapter. The average total cost at each output is the total cost of that output divided by the output level. The average variable cost is the variable cost divided by the output. And the marginal cost is the *increment* in total cost (or variable cost) due to an additional unit of output. (If there is any doubt about these schedules, a little review of Chap. 22 is in order.)

Now we can ask and answer the following question: Is there a decision-making procedure for maximizing profits which does not require that a firm have full knowledge of its costs at all levels of production before it starts to produce anything, a rule that a firm can follow in a step-by-step manner?

There is such a procedure, a reasonable approach when one stops to think about it. *The firm should just figure out whether it is making profits or losses at its current output level, and also what happens to its revenues and costs when it changes its output.* It can increase output by 1 unit and look at the extra revenue (marginal revenue) and extra costs (marginal costs) associated with the change. Keep in mind that the marginal or extra revenue from selling an additional unit for a price-taking firm is just equal to the price. So if the price or marginal revenue is greater than marginal costs, the firm has made some additional profit on that unit and it should expand output further. It should then go on, step by step, in the same way. If it comes to a point where expansion of output raises marginal costs above marginal revenue or price, that step reduces profits. The firm should then retract that step and decrease production.

The profit-maximizing rules for the firm can be summarized as follows:

> If the firm is making profits *at a price which is greater than MC*, it should *expand output* to make more profits.
>
> If the firm is making profits *at a price which is less than MC*, it should *contract output* to make more profits.
>
> If the firm is making profits and *price equals MC, it should not change output*. Profits are being maximized.

On Figure 23-5, point *B* is the profit-maximizing output at the price of $0.20 with the cost curves shown. At a lower level of output, say, at 100 units, price (= *MR*) is greater than *MC*, and profits can be increased by expanding. At a higher output, say, 400 units, *MC* is greater than the price (= *MR*) and some profits are being lost. At point *B*, with output equal to 300 units, price (= MR) = *MC*.

Point *B* is the profit-maximizing equilibrium condition. The total revenue at point *B* is the price *BE* times the quantity *OE*, or the area of the rectangle *OPBE*. The total cost is the average total cost *DE* times the quantity *OE*, or the area of the rectangle *OTDE*. Total profit is the difference between the total revenue rectangle and the total cost rectangle, which is the shaded area *PBDT*.

Minimizing losses and shutting down in the short run

When a firm can make any profits at all, it can maximize its profits by adjusting its output to the point at which price (= *MR*) = *MC*. Unfortunately for the business firm, situations may develop in which the price is so low that it can make no profit at all. What will it do then?

If the price falls below the lowest average variable cost at which the firm is capable of producing in the short run, it ought to shut down. If it does, its loss will be equal to its fixed costs in the short run. That loss will be smaller, however, than if it produced and took a loss on its fixed costs plus something on its variable costs. In Figure 23-5, the minimum average variable cost is at point *F*. That indicates the firm's "shutdown" price. *If the price falls below minimum average variable cost, the best thing the firm can do for itself is shut down.* At any price above *F*, the firm can adjust its output to more than cover its average variable cost and to partially cover its fixed costs. At any price above *F*, the firm should operate – even if it is temporarily losing, owing to its inability to fully cover fixed costs. Its losses will be less than if it shut down completely.

If the price is less than the minimum *average total cost*, but greater than the minimum average variable cost, the firm will have to take a loss. In this range, between *F* and *G* in Figure 23-5, the rule which led to profit maximization will also ensure loss minimization. If price is greater than marginal cost, the firm can make more profits or further reduce losses by expanding output. If price is less than marginal cost, the firm should contract output. If price is just equal to marginal cost, the firm will be doing as well as possible for itself.

Tracing the firm's short-run supply schedule

Once we know how the firm will react to a given price to maximize its profits or minimize its losses, we can work out how it will react to many alternative prices. This will permit us to fill in the blanks in the "if price is ——, then output will be ——" statements which constitute the firm's supply schedule. We just ask:

Figure 23-6

DERIVATION OF THE SUPPLY CURVE OF A COMPETITIVE FIRM

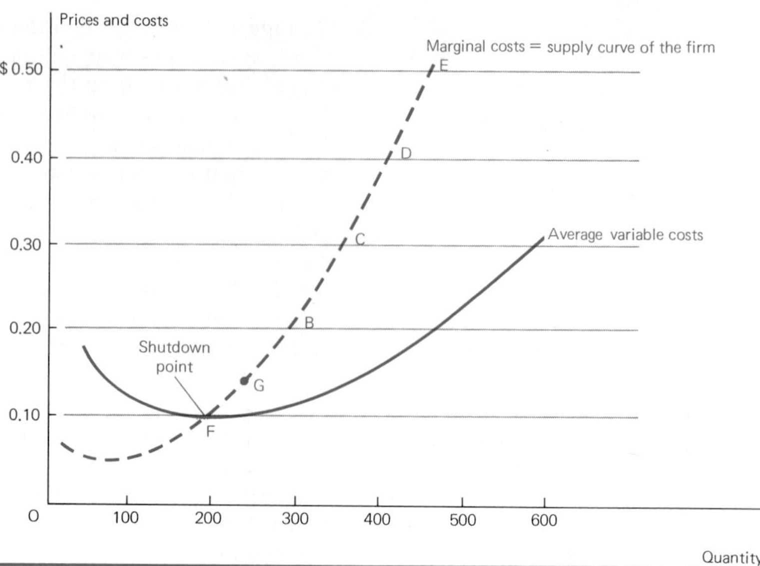

If the price is $0.05, then how much will the firm offer?
If the price is $0.10, then how much will the firm offer?
If the price is $0.20, then how much will the firm offer?
If the price is $0.40, then how much will the firm offer?

And we answer each question by applying the profit-maximizing rule. For each price, that will lead us to the intersection of the price line and the marginal cost curve, as long as the price is greater than the average variable cost. In Figure 23-6, the intersections of the successive price lines and the marginal cost curve are the points *F, G, B, C, D*, etc.

The short-run supply curve of the perfectly competitive firm is just its marginal cost curve above the shutdown point. It tells us how much the competitive firm will offer at each price!

The industry's short-run supply schedule

Going from the firm's supply schedule to the industry's supply schedule requires one more step. Conceptually we can imagine the following process. We ask of each firm in the industry: If the price is so-and-so, how much will you offer? Then by adding the quantities for each firm, we have the total quantity that will be supplied at that price. We keep changing the price question and tabulating the answers of all firms to each question. This tabulation generates the industry supply schedule.

In effect, the short-run supply curve in the perfectly competitive industry is the *horizontal sum of the short-run supply curves of all firms in the industry*. The concept of adding up firm supply schedules to obtain an industry supply schedule is illustrated in Table 23-2 and Figure 23-7. The marginal cost curves of three types of firms are presented. For easy calculation, these are assumed to be straight lines. The marginal cost curve of each firm above its *AVC* is its supply curve. As shown in Figure 23-7 the shutdown price is different for Type X, Type Y, and Type Z firms. That is not at all unreasonable. All the firms will pay more or less the same prices for their inputs, but they may have been established at different times and be using different technologies. Thus, there will be differences in the level and composition of their costs.

In Table 23-2(*d*) the offers of each type of firm at each price are added up. That is the industry supply schedule in Figure 23-7(*d*).

When the industry demand schedule is added, as in Figure 23-8, we have the basis for short-run price determination. The equilibrium price of $0.50 and the equilibrium quantity offered of 50,000

Figure 23-7 **SHORT-RUN MARGINAL COST AND SUPPLY CURVES**

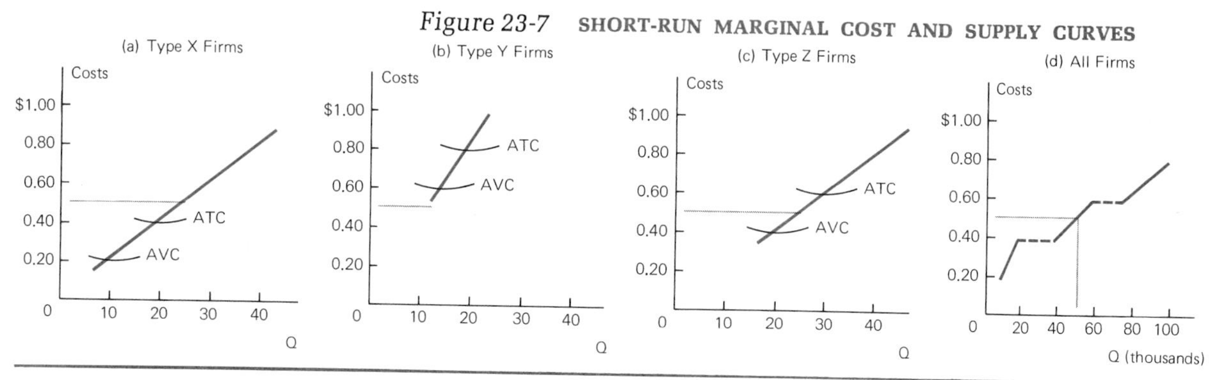

Table 23-2 **SHORT-RUN MARGINAL COST AND SUPPLY SCHEDULES**

(*a*) Type X firms			(*b*) Type Y firms			(*c*) Type Z firms			(*d*) All firms	
	Supply			*Supply*			*Supply*			
Price	*One firm*	*1,000 firms*	*Price*	*One firm*	*1,000 firms*	*Price*	*One firm*	*1,000 firms*	*Price*	*Supply*
$0.20	10	10,000	$0.20	0	0	$0.20	0	0	$0.20	10,000
0.30	15	15,000	0.30	0	0	0.30	0	0	0.30	15,000
0.40	20	20,000	0.40	0	0	0.40	20	20,000	0.40	40,000
0.50	25	25,000	0.50	0	0	0.50	25	25,000	0.50	50,000
0.60	30	30,000	0.60	15	15,000	0.60	30	30,000	0.60	75,000
0.70	35	35,000	0.70	17.5	17,500	0.70	35	35,000	0.70	87,500
0.80	40	40,000	0.80	20	20,000	0.80	40	40,000	0.80	100,000

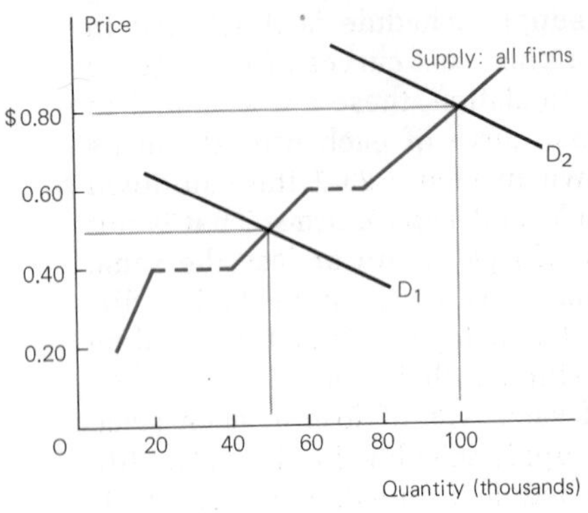

Figure 23-8

COMPETITIVE PRICE DETERMINATION IN THE SHORT RUN

units are the result of competition among firms and require short-run adjustments of variable inputs on the supply side.[1]

The short-run supply curve, it should be emphasized, is composed of *the offers of all firms in the industry at each alternative price when each firm is in short-run profit-maximizing (or loss-minimizing) equilibrium.* But equilibrium is more sought after than achieved. Events are constantly creating new conditions which require adjustments in inputs and outputs. The firms in a reasonably competitive industry do not lead a quiet life. They are always trying to adjust their outputs and their costs to make a little more profit. They are always reacting to price changes too. Suppose, for example, that demand should shift upward from D_1 to D_2, as in Figure 23-8. There would be a new equilibrium price at $0.80 and a new equilibrium quantity bought and sold of 100,000. But how is it achieved? No firm or consumer knows the industry supply and demand schedules and just where that new intersection is. No one knew where the first price-quantity intersection had to be either before it was achieved. *Firms must do the adjusting, and buyers must also, and in the process of trial-and-error changes they move toward a market-clearing price.*

Though competitive firms are price takers, and not price makers, they nonetheless will change prices when they find themselves accumulating unsold production or running out of inventory at the going price. They may overadjust and then have to adjust again. Understanding the process of adjustment is essential to understanding how the system operates. The equilibrium conditions indicate the direction in which adjustment takes place and its "final" result. In a perfectly competitive industry, the equilibrium position is not "chosen" by the individual firms, however. They are driven inexorably toward it by the market processes set in train by consumers shopping around and producers trying to maximize their profits.

The long-run supply schedules of the competitive firm and industry

The constant-cost industry

In moving from the short run to the long run, we must take account of another type of adjustment process: *change in short-run fixed factors.* These include capital in plant and equipment owned by existing firms. In addition, long-run changes may include the *entry of new firms or the withdrawal of established firms* – all depending on profitabilities.

Figure 23-7 illustrates the point. In the short-run situation which was first depicted, the equilibrium price was $0.50, with equilibrium sales of 50,000 units. The short-run cost and price data

[1] Is the amount supplied at $0.60, 60,000 or 75,000? It is either. If the demand schedule intersected the supply schedule at a quantity of 60,000, what would the equilibrium price be?

in the figure indicate the long-run tendencies that will operate in the industry. At the short-run equilibrium price of $0.50, Type X firms with their new technology make above-normal profits: The price is above their average costs at that output, and we include in costs some "normal" profit rate. Type Y firms will not operate at all, since the $0.50 price is below their shutdown point. Type Z firms are taking losses, since they are not covering their average total costs. They are doing better, however, then if they shut down entirely.

Certainly, in the long run, Type Z firms are not going to continue to take losses. They will either leave the industry or adopt a technology like that of Type X firms, or they will try to do even better. Type Y firms, who will not produce at a price of $0.50 will also look enviously at X's technology and try to adopt it or do better. Type X firms will not sit on their profits but will look around for other ways to cut costs. And since there are no barriers to entry, enterprising businessmen outside the industry will see Type X firms making above-normal profits and will say to themselves, I can do as well as that. And they will try to establish new firms in the industry.

The profit-maximizing (loss-minimizing) rules for the firm's adjustment process are the same in the long run as in the short run – with an important difference in interpretation of the long-run shutdown price. In the short run, the firm continues to operate if the price is less than average total cost but above *average variable*

Figure 23-9

SHORT- AND LONG-RUN TYPE X FIRM COST CURVES

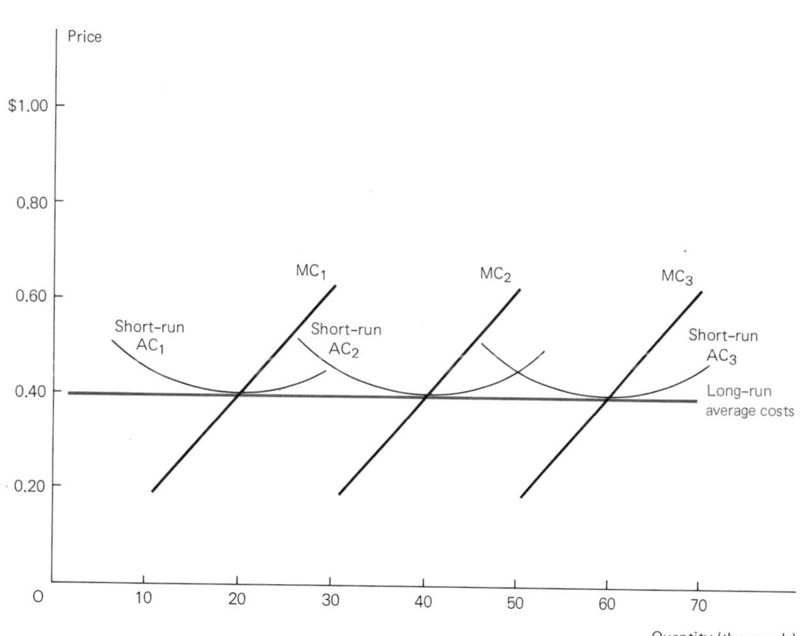

cost. In its long-run adjustment, no firm will operate unless the price is above the lowest *average total cost* that can be achieved after all possible adjustments of all inputs.

Where will it all end? What will it be like, this final equilibrium toward which all these long-run adjustments are moving? Ultimately, the answer depends on the long-run cost curves of the firms in the industry. Suppose that the technology of Type X firms is the most efficient that can possibly be found. Assume also that this is an industry characterized by constant costs in the long run *as long as the prices of the resource inputs do not change.* It will be recalled from Chapter 22 that this means that the *long-run* average total costs of the firm remain constant as output is expanded or contracted. The long-run cost curve of Type X firms then looks like that shown in Figure 23-9, along with successive short-run cost curves. In the long run, old firms can adjust to that technology and those costs, and new firms can enter and achieve the same results. Such adjustments and new entries will continue as long as firms can make at least normal profits. As a result, *the long-run constant-cost industry supply curve is a horizontal line!* In this case, it is at $0.40. All firms producing at higher average costs than $0.40 per unit are going to be squeezed out.

Figure 23-10

SHORT- AND LONG-RUN INDUSTRY SUPPLY CURVES

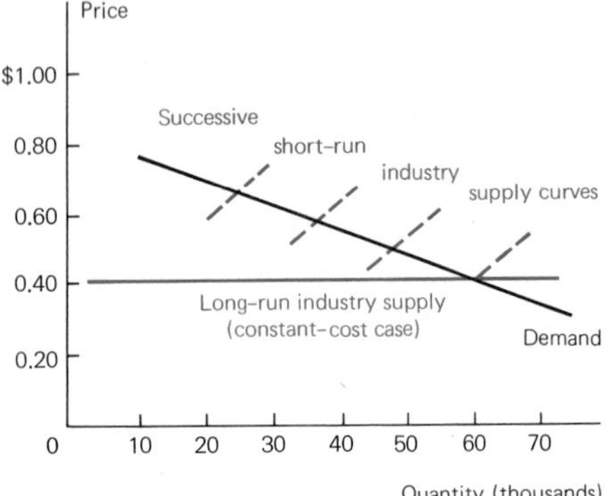

As more and more firms achieve Type X costs and supply schedules, the amounts offered by such firms will increase and prices will fall toward $0.40. In effect, the short-run industry supply curves will keep shifting to the right, as shown in Figure 23-10, as the total supply is made up of more and more Type X firms. Finally, only Type X firms will be left in the industry. Their long-run supply curves, which are horizontal at $0.40, will make up the industry supply schedule.

The same long-run horizontal industry supply schedule could be achieved under somewhat different circumstances. Suppose each firm could at best achieve the long-run average cost curve shown in Figure 23-11. Whenever industry price was above the minimum average total cost on this schedule at output *M*, there

Figure 23-11

HYPOTHETICAL SHORT- AND LONG-RUN COST CURVES FOR A COMPETITIVE FIRM

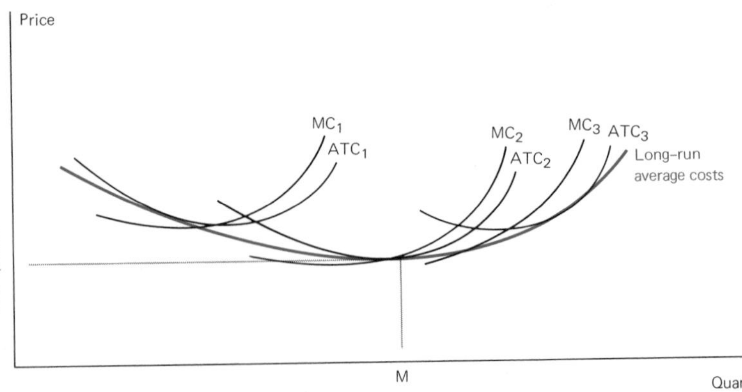

would be above-normal profits. New firms would enter and old firms would adjust. Suppose, however, that input prices did not change in this process. Then the long-run supply schedule for the industry would still be like the one shown in Figure 23-10. It would be a straight horizontal line at the minimum average total cost which could be achieved by any firm – even though each firm's long-run average total cost increased with output above the *M* level of output. This horizontal supply curve would result from the entry or withdrawal of firms, each striving to produce at the lowest possible unit costs.

In the long-run equilibrium position of a competitive industry, there are no above-normal profits and no losses. If there were profits, new firms would be attracted. Output would expand and prices would fall and wipe out the excessive profits. If there were losses in a long-run equilibrium, firms taking those losses would leave the industry or adjust their sales and costs.

The importance of the long-run equilibrium position is not that it is actually achieved, but that *it is the target toward which adjustment takes place.* In reality, changes in technology, changes in factor prices, and changes in demand occur frequently. They change the long-run equilibrium conditions. So the long-run equilibrium is a moving target. But knowing its characteristics helps us to understand the adjustments that business firms continually try to make in a competitive environment.

The horizontal long-run industry supply curve of Figure 23-10 requires that the prices of the resource inputs remain constant as long-run adjustments occur. If that does not happen it's a different ball game.

The increasing-cost industry

If the prices of inputs rise as new firms enter an industry and output expands, the costs of each firm in the industry will rise. Let us assume that only variable costs increase and that minimum-cost output does not change. This is represented for a single firm in Figure 23-12. When this happens, the long-run industry supply curve will rise with quantity, as shown in Figure 23-13. This is in spite of the fact that each firm in the long run will be producing at its minimum-cost point. It would happen even if each firm separately had long-run constant costs.

It would not be surprising for the prices of resources used in a competitive industry to rise as the industry expanded and increased its use of inputs. While each firm in the industry is too small to affect prices, the industry as a whole may be quite large. If the industry requires a particular input of only limited availability, the price of that input will rise as demand for it rises. No one wheat farm in Kansas would have much effect on land prices if it expanded. If all wheat farms were to try to increase their output and bring more land under cultivation, they would force up the price of the good land. That, in turn, would force up the costs of all farms. In addition, a substantial expansion of wheat production

Figure 23-12

EFFECTS OF INCREASING PRICES OF PRODUCTION INPUTS WITH ENTRY OF ADDITIONAL FIRMS

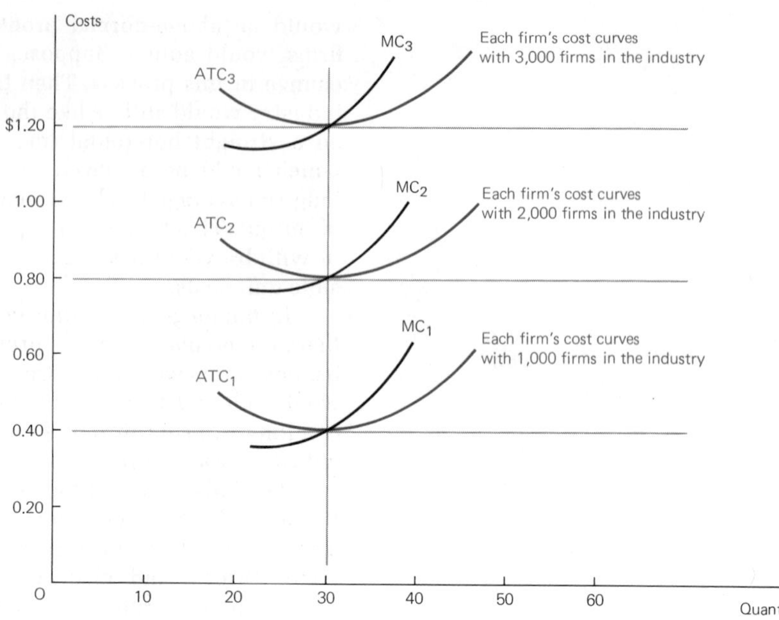

would not only divert good land, but also higher-priced land, from, say, corn production. It would also draw into production marginal lands whose yields were lower and costs of production higher. The effect of each of these — the higher land prices of the better lands and the lower yields on the marginal lands — would be to tilt the long-run industry supply schedule upward after some output level were reached.

The decreasing-cost industry

It might seem natural after dealing with horizontal and rising supply schedules to close the ring and discuss the case in which the industry supply schedule slopes downward — and the price decreases as the quantity offered increases. But is this consistent with competition? *Can there be a long-run downward-sloping supply curve for a competitive industry?* Only under special circumstances.

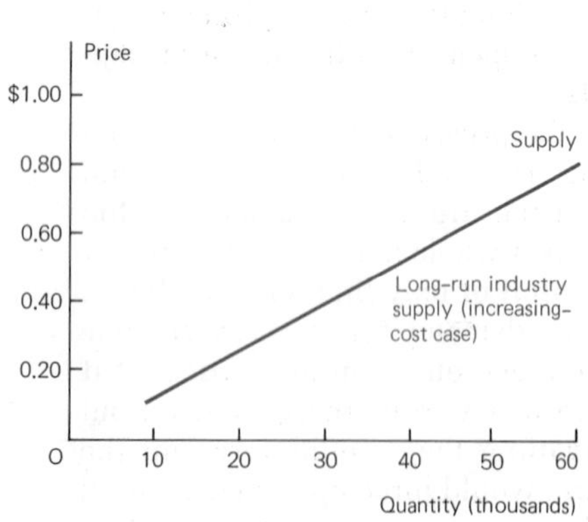

Figure 23-13

LONG-RUN INDUSTRY SUPPLY (INCREASING-COST CASE)

It is certainly possible for costs to decrease as the scale of output increases, if the technology permits greater and greater economies of large-scale production. This case was discussed in Chapter 22 as the decreasing-cost firm. The marginal cost curve of the firm would *always* slope downward and lie below the average total cost curve. The additional cost of an additional unit of output would always be less than the cost of the previous unit.

Under these circumstances, however, competition could not survive. If there were a number of firms in the industry at an early stage of its growth, all would try to increase their output to lower costs. In the process, the firms which adjusted more slowly would be driven out by the larger, more vigorously expanding and lower-cost producers. The last few firms would continue this deadly competition until only one survived, or they would come to some agreement to split the market among themselves. *In either case, decreasing costs destroy competition.*

On the other hand, suppose the industry were in the fortunate position of being able to procure some of its most important inputs at lower and lower prices as its output expanded. This could be the result of increasing returns to scale in an industry supplying the resources. Then the cost curves of each firm in the industry would shift downward with increasing output, and the supply curve of the industry would also slope downward with output. Under these conditions, however, competition would be maintained because no single firm could gain an advantage.

Technological change and downward shifts in supply

Downward or rightward shifts in supply schedules due to technological improvements are possible. We often observe such changes. This is illustrated in Figure 23-14 in the shift from S_1 to S_2. A new process or machine which lowers all or some costs will lower the supply schedule (or shift to the right). As a result, price will fall over time. As explained above, however, it would be a mistake to observe prices falling over time and conclude that the supply schedule was downward-sloping. Here again it is important to distinguish *shifts* in a schedule from *movements along* it.

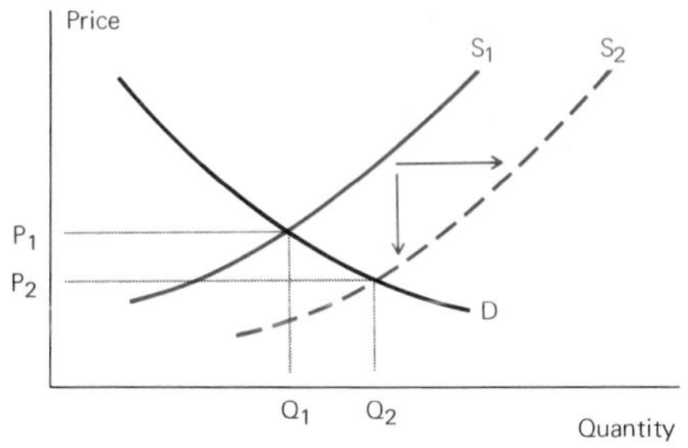

Figure 23-14

EFFECT ON COMPETITIVE SUPPLY OF COST REDUCTIONS FROM TECHNICAL IMPROVEMENTS

Supply elasticity and the adjustment period

Supply elasticity, which is a measure of the responsiveness of amounts offered for sale to changes in prices, is analogous to demand elasticity. It is simply the *percentage change in quantity offered divided by the percentage change in price which induced the change in offerings.* This elasticity, like demand elasticity, can vary from zero to infinity. Inelastic supply means a supply elasticity of less than unity. The amounts that firms offer are relatively insensitive to price changes, so percentage changes in quantities offered are less than percentage changes in prices. When supply elasticity equals unity, offerings and prices change in the same proportions. When supply is elastic, the percentage change in offerings is greater than the percentage change in prices.[2]

In general, one expects that the responsiveness of firms to price changes will be greater the longer the period in which firms have to adjust to price changes. Therefore, in the momentary period, supply is likely to be relatively inelastic. In the short run, it will be somewhat more elastic, and in the long run, it will tend to be even more elastic still.

The usefulness of supply and demand analysis in understanding markets

Professional economists use the supply and demand concepts and market analysis to explain the price levels and market sales in particular markets. But for the nonprofessional, the utility of the concepts and analysis is not in such particular applications. *The supply-demand analysis provides a general understanding of the economic forces operating in markets.* This can be illustrated by analyzing a market that exists in spite of its illegality: the market for marijuana. Application of supply and demand concepts to this market also illustrates the *value neutrality* of these analytical tools. Their use does not imply approval or condemnation of the market being analyzed.

There is relatively little precise and detailed knowledge about the marijuana market because it is illegal. But general qualitative information organized in supply and demand concepts will permit some insights. First of all, the market in urban areas may not be too far from being a competitive market. The nature of the product and the conditions under which it can be produced and "imported" encourage competition among suppliers. It is light, takes up little volume, and can be easily transported. Apparently it can be cultivated intensively or extensively, on large or small plots, with little specialized technology. These factors contribute to the existence of a number of alternative sources of supply.

The effect of the illegality of the market, however, is to increase the costs of the supply. The penalties for breaking state and federal laws regarding marijuana are heavy in order to dis-

[2] The measure of supply elasticity which reconciles the problem of deciding the base from which to measure the quantity and price changes is

$$e = \frac{Q_2 - Q_1}{\frac{Q_2 + Q_1}{2}} \div \frac{P_2 - P_1}{\frac{P_2 + P_1}{2}}$$

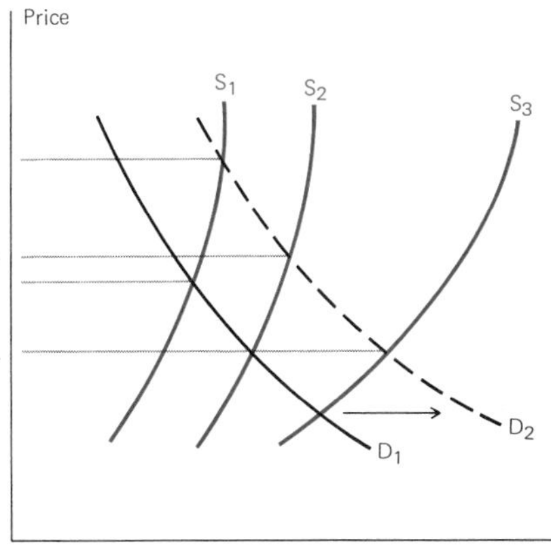

Figure 23-15

ANALYSIS OF THE EFFECTS OF DEMAND AND SUPPLY CHANGES ON MARIJUANA PRICES

courage its production and sale. The returns to suppliers must, therefore, cover the risks of fines and imprisonment. The continuation of supply suggests the profitability of the undertaking.

An apparent increase in demand over time has been accompanied by an increase in supply. This has been facilitated by easy "entry" into the import "business." It has occurred in spite of the high "costs" of arrest and conviction. This is just another example of a market working out as we would by now expect it to work, even though it is an illegal market. The process is represented in Figure 23-15. The increase in demand is shown by the shift from D_1 to D_2, with a consequent increase in price from p_1 to p_2. When prices go up, the profitability increases. This stimulates an increase in the quantity supplied from available sources. In addition, it leads to an enlargement of the scale of operations of existing "firms" and brings new "firms" into the industry. The consequent shift in the supply curve from S_1 to S_2 is shown also in Figure 23-15. That in turn leads to a new equilibrium price at p_3. Effective police action against suppliers may shift the supply schedule back to S_1, with a consequent increase in price.

How would legalization affect the price and sale of marijuana? Would it lead to increased usage? Legalization would mean a substantial shift in the supply schedule, say, to S_3 in Figure 23-15, because the "costs" of the present penalties on supply would be eliminated. If the demand curve for marijuana showed the conventional downward slope, more would be purchased at a lower price. Would the total expenditures on marijuana then be greater? That would depend on the elasticity of demand. If demand were elastic, expenditures would increase; if inelastic, total expenditures would fall; and if the elasticity of demand were unity, expenditures would be constant.

Can the Law of Supply and Demand be repealed?

We are told in the financial columns that "the Law of Supply and Demand cannot be repealed." Is it true? The marijuana example showed that government regulation, if it cannot repeal the operation of supply and demand, can certainly tamper with the system. But just what is the Law of Supply and Demand anyway?

It is certainly not a physical law like the Law of Conservation of Energy, for the process of supply and demand interaction need not take place at all. It is not a moral law either. It was never claimed that the price resulting from supply and demand interaction in a competitive market was Right or Just or even that it would Make Everyone Happy.

On the supply side, the analysis assumes that firms are profit maximizers and that there is perfect competition. The first assumption means that firms try to use resources as effectively as possible in searching for their short- and long-run equilibrium positions. The assumption of competition means that firms are price takers and cannot affect the market prices to which they react. It is also assumed that technology is constant and that the prices of productive resources, if they change at all, change only because of expansion and contraction of industry operations. With these assumptions it is possible to work out the relationships between the costs of the firm and the amount it would offer at alternative prices.

On the demand side, we assume that individuals work out their satisfaction-maximizing composition of consumption at each price. As long as they keep searching around, the demand schedule itself will keep shifting. In addition, we must be aware that the amounts demanded at each price reflect the distribution of income.

These reminders and qualifications are a warning against thinking of supply and demand schedules as forever fixed and immutable. *Each supply-demand picture we draw is like a single picture in an animated cartoon in which the characters shift their positions slightly from picture to picture.* Usually in the foregoing analysis only the first and last pictures in the sequence have been drawn.

Nor is the process invulnerable to "outside" interference. Government has actively interfered with the operation of supply and demand in competitive markets. Private business that grows too large for competition or succeeds by product differentiation in achieving some degree of monopoly power can also interfere, as we shall see in more detail in the next chapter.

What is true is that *every interference has a consequence*! This is an important grain of truth in the notion of the immutability of the Law of Supply and Demand. Governments can pass laws which set prices or constrain market sales. But without coercing *individual* buyers and sellers, governments cannot force purchases and offers to be anything other than what the free demand and supply would be at the price government sets. If the price is anywhere except at the free-market equilibrium, the price set by the government will not clear the market and there will be shortfalls or surpluses. What if a government program set both prices and quantities to be purchased and sold? At any other price than the equilibrium price, enforcement of an arbitrary price and quantity of sales would require coercion of the free decisions of buyers and sellers. So the Law of Supply and Demand *can* be repealed, *but not without further consequences for production and consumption.*

The notion of the immutability of a Law of Supply and Demand is best interpreted as recognition of *general interdependence* in the economic system. An interference with supply and demand in one market will have effects on other markets for resources and products. Rather than say that the Law of Supply and Demand cannot be repealed, it is better to say that, where there is general interdependence, the effects of one market cannot be isolated, nor can the effects of interfering with that market.

Competition and efficiency

It is also true that price-quantity determination by competitive supply and demand *encourages economic efficiency and ensures a responsiveness to expressed consumer demands.*

What do we mean by efficiency? Not the use of the most labor-saving or capital-saving or resource-saving or fuel-saving or timber-saving methods of production. But the use of techniques which employ each input in just the "right" proportion so as to place the economy on its overall transformation surface, as described in Chapter 3.

This leads us to an important concept: When prices are determined competitively, they are equal to the *marginal costs* of production, including in costs all the relevant implicit costs as well as the explicit ones. We label this condition the price-equals-marginal-cost equilibrium. To some people there is an intuitive appeal in the idea that the value (price) of a product should be just equal to the extra cost involved in its production. It is much like the commonsense notion that a good should be worth what it costs to make it. That notion can be misleading, but it has a rough nugget of truth which, if refined, will yield a golden rule. The commonsense statement can be interpreted as combining two conditions. The first is the long-run equilibrium condition of a competitive industry. In long-run competitive equilibrium, the price of the product is just equal to its average cost of production, including normal profits. If that long-run equilibrium condition is not met, the industry will use more or less resources in the course of changing output and moving toward the equilibrium.

The second condition is that an *extra* unit of output of a good should be worth just the *extra* cost of making it.

The significance of this condition can be illustrated by asking, What would happen if it were *not* met? Production of an extra unit of output that is worth *less* than the extra cost of production is an inefficient use of resources. The value of the output to the consumer is less than the productive value of the resources that go into it. On the other hand, if an extra unit of output is worth more to consumers than its extra cost of production, then more of that output should be produced. In an equilibrium of maximum efficiency, the marginal-cost–price equality prevails.

The long-run equilibrium toward which a competitive industry tends to move is one which satisfies the two conditions: (1) production at the lowest possible average cost for the output, and (2) price equals marginal cost. As is shown for a typical firm in Figure 23-10, in long-run equilibrium:

Minimum long-run average total cost = marginal cost
= marginal revenue = price

The efficiency of marginal cost pricing has a general validity independent of any particular setting. In the Soviet Union, Eastern Europe, and the less developed countries of the world, some economic planners are rediscovering and consciously using this test of efficiency. It is also used by some corporate planners to achieve maximum internal efficiency *within* their corporations.

In a perfectly competitive industry, however, the condition would tend to prevail as an intrinsic feature of the industry's operations. That, as we shall see, is a unique characteristic of perfect competition.

Efficiency and equity

Competition, like some customs, is honored more in the breach than the observance. The breach is sometimes due to private business that tries to escape the rigorous life of competition by gaining some control over prices. But not all the breaches of competition are private ones. For example, there are government interferences in agriculture, where competition is otherwise closely approximated. There are also government price controls, which limit competition in retailing. And there is increasing interest in rent controls, such as those which prevail in New York City. What is the rationale of such controls in more or less competitive sectors?

Interference with competition, as a matter of public and private business policy, can be explained in several ways. As has been pointed out, the environment of competition is an impersonal, cold, and difficult one in which only the fittest survive. It is natural that producers in such circumstances would like to erect a little noncompetitive shelter for their businesses. If they can persuade enough consumers or legislators that it is all in the public interest, they may be able to get laws passed maintaining prices and restraining competition. Higher prices permit higher-cost producers to survive and lower-cost producers to make more money. In effect, such a public interference with competition represents nothing more or less than a successful attempt on the part of businessmen to get a larger share of the income pie.

It is also true that there is more to life than being efficient. The argument that the life values in rural areas deserve preservation is one reason advanced for the laws which restrain or offset the effects of competition in agriculture. On the basis of the argument that small retail shops require and deserve protection, resale price-maintenance laws have been passed in some states to restrict retail price cutting by large chains, for example. Tenants have succeeded in a few places in obtaining rent control laws. The intent of all these is to modify the distribution of income toward a more "equitable" or "fair" pattern than would be achieved under competition. There are unfortunate consequences for efficiency, to be sure. But if people want it that way, who is to say they are wrong? There is nothing holy about competition, not even efficiency.

We can say, however, that it is not possible to have one's cake and eat it too — to interfere with competition and also have its efficiency characteristics. Yet it is human to want to have one's cake and eat it too. Are there any means by which the distribution of income created by competition can be modified and the efficiency of competition be preserved? In principle the answer is, Yes — by shrewd tax and income transfer schemes. But whether such schemes are feasible in practice is another of those political issues which we raise and put aside at this point.

Summary

In a competitive industry, the amount supplied at each price is the sum of all the offers of each firm at that price. The amount each firm offers depends on its costs and the time it has to adjust to the quoted price.

In the momentary period the only amounts available for sale by the firm are those it has on hand. The amount it sells from this stock depends on: (1) its reservation price, the minimum price at which it will sell anything, and (2) its expectations of future prices.

In the short run, the firm can adjust output by changing its variable inputs. The amount each firm will offer at each price depends on the output that will maximize its profits or minimize its losses at that price. If the price will not fully cover the average variable cost of any output, the firm will minimize its losses by shutting down. At market prices above the shutdown price, the firm will maximize its profits or minimize its losses by adjusting its inputs to produce the output at which price equals marginal cost. So the firm's short-run supply schedule is its marginal cost schedule above average variable cost. The short-run *industry* supply schedule is the horizontal sum of the supply schedules of all firms — which is found by adding up the amounts offered at each price.

The long-run industry supply schedule will depend on the amounts offered by firms when they have ample time to adjust all their inputs. In the long run, firms cannot and will not take losses. The price must cover their average total costs. There will be a long-run horizontal supply schedule at the minimum average total cost if firms can expand in the long run without raising their average total costs. This will happen if they have a constant-cost technology and if the prices of the resources they use do not rise. A long-run horizontal supply schedule will exist even though the technology leads to increasing costs for larger-scale production for old firms, *if* new firms can enter at the optimum scale — again with constant input prices. If input prices rise as the industry's scale of output increases, the long-run supply schedule will slope upward. If one or more input prices fall enough as the industry's output expands, the long-run industry supply curve can even decline as output increases.

On the other hand, if there are continuing economies of scale to *single* firms, they will tend to grow large and eliminate slower-growing and higher-cost competitors. That is the end of competition. Technological change that lowers all costs can result in the downward – or rightward – shifting of the supply schedule without destroying competition.

Supply elasticity reflects the responsiveness of offerings to price changes. It is measured as the ratio of the percentage change in offerings to the percentage change in prices.

Analysis of the effects of various types of changes in supply and demand must take into account the period of adjustment. An increase in demand, for example, will increase price in the momentary period. In the short run, price will tend to fall somewhat, with an increase in output as the short-run supply schedule shifts. With a shift toward the long-run industry supply schedule, output may expand more and price may fall even further.

Shifts in supply also occur in response to input price changes and changes in technology. When demand is growing at the same time that supply is growing, it is difficult to predict the final effect on prices.

The Law of Supply and Demand is simply a statement that there will tend to be a market-clearing price in a competitive market. It is not immutable, but can be interfered with in many ways by taxes and price-control programs. Since there is general interdependence, each interference has a consequence.

An important characteristic of competitive markets is that their price-equals-marginal-cost equilibrium condition is also an efficiency condition. When this condition prevails all around, the economy is using its productive resources in the most efficient way possible. If it does not prevail, efficiency can be increased by moving inputs into industries where prices are greater than marginal costs and out of industries where prices are less than marginal costs.

While efficient use of resources is important, the competitive life in which efficiency is achieved is a tough one. Businesses often try to soften it by winning some degree of monopoly power. Society may try to ameliorate it by various laws. These latter interferences are often justified in the name of greater equity in income distribution, the preservation of the particular way of life of a special group, such as farmers, or the protection of a particular interest group, such as tenants. Appraisal of public interferences with competitive markets requires the balancing of such goals against the costs in lost efficiency.

Questions for discussion and review

1. Comment on the following statement, explaining why you agree or disagree: *For products that are made to order, such as hand-*

tailored suits, the concept of the momentary supply period is irrelevant, since in the very nature of such things there are no stocks on hand. The only relevant supply period is the long run.

2. Explain in your own words the rationale of the $MR = MC$ condition as a profit-maximizing equilibrium position for the individual firm.

3. Why should a firm continue to produce in the short run if the market price is less than the minimum average *total* cost it can achieve but greater than the minimum average *variable* cost it can reach? And why, under the same conditions, should it shut down in the long run?

4. What is meant by the description of the industry supply schedule as the horizontal sum of the supply schedules of the individual firms in the industry?

5. Tell why you agree or disagree with the following statement: *The long-run supply schedule of a perfectly competitive industry is always horizontal at the lowest possible average total cost for any firm. That is because, with complete freedom of entry, it is always possible for a new firm to enter the industry at the optimum scale of output.*

6. If decreasing long-run costs to a particular firm will finally destroy competition, why doesn't technological change, which also results in lower costs, destroy competition?

7. Is there any meaning to the statement that "the Law of Supply and Demand cannot be repealed"?

8. If competition can guarantee efficiency in the use of resources, why can't it guarantee equity?

Concepts for review

Momentary, short-run, and long-run market periods
Reservation price
Marginal revenue = marginal cost
Shutdown price
Constant-cost industry
Supply elasticity
Competitive efficiency
Long-run equilibrium of the firm and the industry

24

Extensions and applications of supply and demand analysis

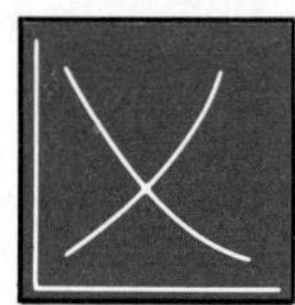

The supply and demand concepts and market analysis should rightly be seen as a model of buyer and seller interaction in markets. Such a model or theory is applicable only where the market conditions are described reasonably well by the competitive assumptions of the model. Where that is true, supply and demand analysis is one of the most powerful and useful sets of tools economists have developed. In this chapter, we will extend the analysis and apply it to particular sectors and problems.

Analyzing agricultural prices and support programs

Agriculture is the sector that most closely approximates the assumptions of perfect competition. Some people think of farm life as stable and more or less unchanging except for the weather. Actually modern agriculture is a dynamic sector. *It faces shifting demands and generates continuous changes in supply under the impact of changes in growing conditions, technology, and the price of inputs: fertilizers, insecticides, machinery, etc.* Changes in agricultural productivity have been rapid. Reflecting these changes, agricultural prices have fluctuated more than prices of industrial commodities. Moreover, in spite of growing population and rising income, farm prices have fallen relative to other prices. These changes are represented in Figure 24-1, which presents measures of the prices received by farmers for the sale of their products and prices paid by farmers for the productive inputs they buy. From 1929 to 1969 the former went up by 86 percent while the latter went up by 133 percent. From 1950 to 1970 farm prices rose by

Figure 24-1

PRICES RECEIVED AND PAID BY FARMERS AND THE PARITY RATIO

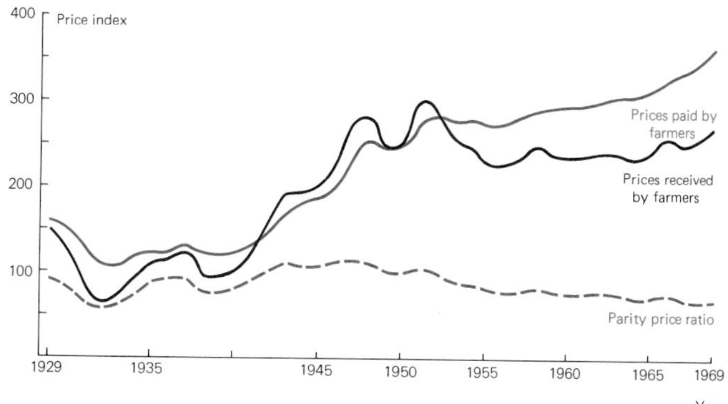

The base year for both price indices is the period 1910–1914 when the indices were equal to 100. The parity ratio is obtained by dividing the index of prices received by farmers by the index of the prices they pay. Since the high point of farm prices at the end of World War II, the prices farmers receive have declined relative to those they pay, though both have gone up. Consequently, the parity index has fallen since 1952. (Source: Dept. of Agriculture.)

---

only 7½ percent while the prices farmers pay rose by 46 percent. During the last several years of the 1960s, however, the prices that farmers receive rose as fast as the prices they pay.

An analysis of the long-term changes in farm prices is presented in Figure 24-2. Demand has shifted from D_1 to D_2 as the result of population and income growth. Supply has shifted from S_1 to S_2, owing largely to technical change and increased use of fertilizer and equipment. Prices have fallen from p_1 to p_2. The shift in supply has been substantial; the shift in demand less so, which requires some explanation.

Figure 24-2

AN ANALYSIS OF THE SOURCES OF CHANGES IN FARM PRICES

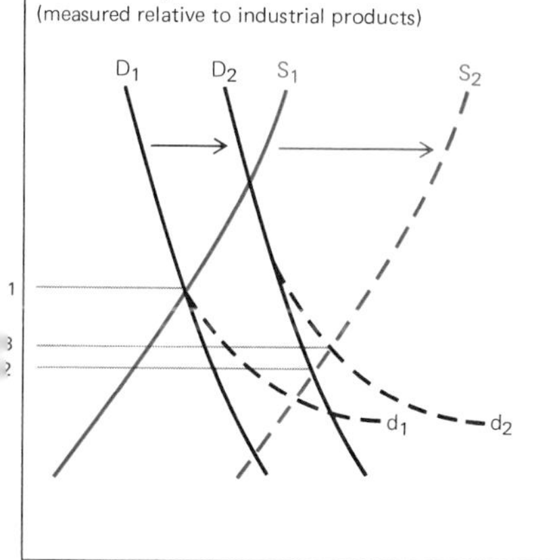

On the whole, the demand for agricultural products—particularly the staple crops—tends to be inelastic with respect to *income* changes. That is, for a given percentage change in income, the percentage change in quantity demanded will be smaller. In addition, the demand for agricultural products tends to be inelastic with respect to *price* changes. The price inelasticity of demand is partly responsible for the magnitude of the price decline as supply curves shift to reflect productivity increases. If the demand were more price-inelastic, as in D_1d_1 and D_2d_2 in Figure 24-2, prices would have fallen only to p_3 as the supply curve shifted from S_1 to S_2.

Falling prices and incomes in agriculture during the Great Depression of the 1930s provided the main impetus for the present government programs designed to aid the sector. The original programs have been continued through many transformations. Using the supply-demand analysis developed in the previous chapters, we can work out the major consequences of the government programs.

Price-support programs

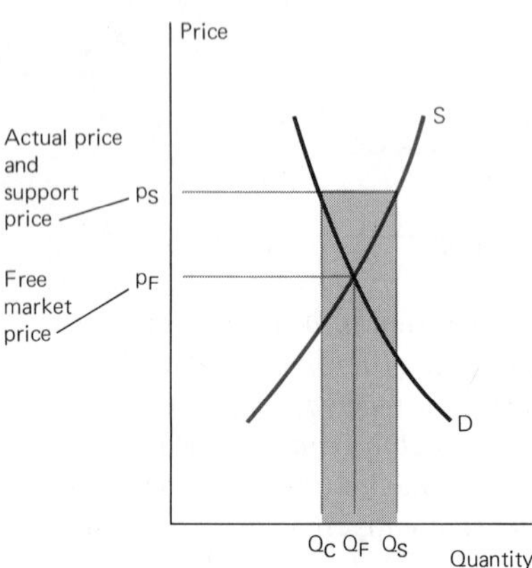

Figure 24-3

SUPPORT OF AN AGRICULTURAL COMMODITY PRICE ABOVE THE FREE MARKET PRICE BY GOVERNMENT PURCHASES

Figure 24-4

SUPPORT OF AN AGRICULTURAL COMMODITY PRICE ABOVE THE FREE MARKET PRICE BY CROP-RESTRICTION PROGRAMS

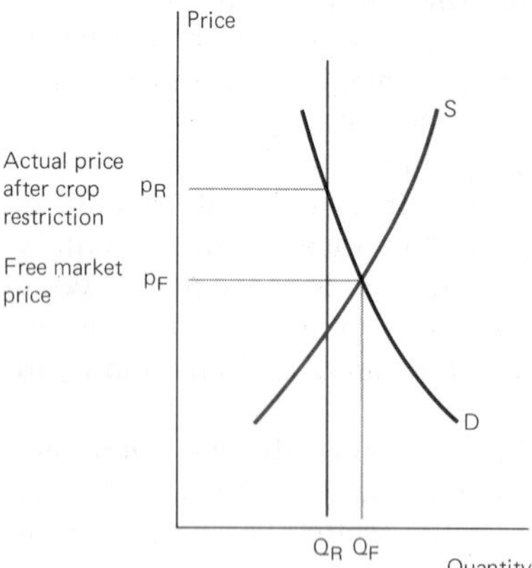

Agricultural income-support policies constitute a set of programs for government interference in markets. We can understand the reasons for this better after first understanding the methods. In its price-support programs, the government fixes a minimum price level for the supported commodity by standing ready to buy enough of that commodity to maintain that price level. The government uses a variety of legal devices to carry out its programs. Sometimes it gives loans at a specified price against the security of the stored crop. The farmer-borrower can then default on the loan and let the government keep the wheat, corn, cotton, etc., if the market price is less than the loan price. Or he can pay off the loan and sell the commodity on the open market if the market price is greater than the loan price. So the procedure is equivalent to a sale at the specified loan price, which is the support price.

The support price itself is computed by first determining a *parity price*. That is the price necessary to maintain a constant relationship between the prices the farmer receives for his products and the prices he pays for the goods he purchases. The relationship enshrined in the law is that which prevailed from 1909 to 1914. Why these years? They were chosen because they were thought to represent a golden period of American agriculture. The movements in the parity price ratio are also shown in Figure 24-1 as the dashed red line. The actual support price is set by Congress at, say, 90 percent of the parity price.

Figure 24-3 illustrates how the program works for a particular commodity. Points p_F and Q_F would be the free market price and free market purchases and sales without government intervention. The total expenditures by individual consumers at p_F would be equal to $p_F Q_F$. The support price is p_S. At this price, consumers buy only Q_C, with total expenditures of $p_S Q_C$. With price-inelastic demands, the total consumer expenditures at p_S will be greater than at the lower free market price p_F.[1] To maintain the price at p_S, however, the government must buy everything offered at that price that is not taken by private purchasers. That amount is the difference between Q_C and Q_S. At price p_S the government is spending an amount equal to $p_S \times (Q_S - Q_C)$, which is the area of the shaded rectangle in Figure 24-3. The amount $(Q_S - Q_C)$ accumulates in government warehouses. Under the price-support program, total receipts by farmers from sales to private purchasers *and* government is the amount $p_S Q_S$, which is certainly greater than $p_F Q_F$, the amount that would be spent by consumers if there were no support program.

In some years in the past, the agricultural price-support program in the United States resulted in the accumulation of enormous inventories of surplus commodities and, occasionally, but rarely, in shocking waste. Drought, sales and gifts to poor countries, and free

[1] Remember that, if demand is price-inelastic, total expenditures increase as price goes up.

food programs to our own poor have reduced the surpluses drastically. Even so, *a support program does not solve the long-run farm problem. It only preserves the problem by not letting conditions become worse.* The farmers stay on the farms, the inefficient ones are not prodded by the market to become more efficient, and surpluses accumulate unless given away. Moreover, the farmers who benefit most are the largest ones with the most to sell. And these are usually the ones who need the aid least. This experience with price supports has led to the development of other programs.

Crop-restriction programs

By persuasion, by law, and with payments for not putting land into production, the government has limited farm output. One of the methods has been the "acreage-allotment" program in which cultivated acreage is reduced as a condition of price-supporting actions by the federal government. In this program the government estimates the crop acreage which is consistent with the support price, and that acreage is divided among individual farmers. Under the "soil bank" program, the federal government makes a payment to farmers to retire some part of their land from production. These programs have been used to move free market prices to levels which are closer to the parity price. The process is shown in Figure 24-4. Points p_F and Q_F are again the prices and purchases which would exist in a free market. Q_R is the restricted production which results in a higher price, p_R. Since demand is inelastic, the total receipts by farmers under the crop-restriction program, p_RQ_R, are greater than if there were a free market, which would lead to total receipts of p_FQ_F.

A crop-restriction program reduces the surplus accumulation problem and has the desirable result of promoting soil conservation practices. But it also generates a variety of abuses and inefficiencies. Farmers tend to put their least-good lands into the conservation programs and then farm their better lands even more intensively than before. They seed the plants closer together and use more fertilizer and insecticides; hence output is not reduced by nearly as much as the acreage reduction would seem to indicate.

Figure 24-5

SUPPORT OF FARM INCOMES BY A SUBSIDY PAYMENT AT A PRICE ABOVE THE MARKET PRICE

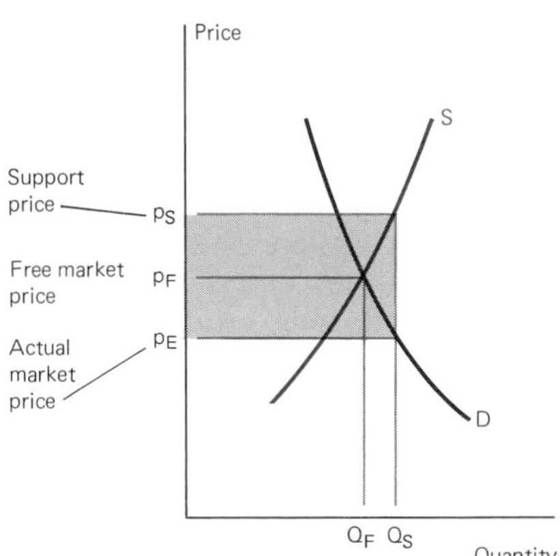

Government subsidy payments

In the late 1950s the government tried briefly a subsidy plan for wool which took a different tack. Under the subsidy plan the government *paid directly to farmers an amount which made up the difference between farm income at a free market price and farm income at the subsidy price.* The operation and the effects of such a plan are shown in Figure 24-5. The government guarantees the subsidy price to farmers, so they supply Q_S, as indicated by their supply curve. The actual price is then determined by the market without intervention. The price at which Q_S will be purchased by consumers is indicated by the demand curve to be at p_E. The government then pays directly to farmers the difference between the amount they receive at the market price p_E and the amount they would have received if the price were p_S. The total amount paid out is equal to the shaded rectangle $p_SQ_S - p_EQ_S$. Again, farm receipts are higher than they would have been in a free market. In this case, the difference is between p_FQ_F and p_SQ_S.

Evaluating agricultural assistance programs

What is the rationale behind all these schemes to help agriculture? Why does this sector get so much attention? The answers are a tangle of objective economic arguments, self-serving rationalizations, hardheaded back-scratching politics, and widespread and nostalgic sympathy for the difficulties and the virtues of rural life. This is not the place to try to untangle those knotted threads. It is a good place, however, to recognize both the potential and the limitations of economic analysis. Our analysis *can* help us understand the economic consequences of alternative policies. It *cannot* weigh economic, political, sociological, and cultural factors in a balance and say that the economic costs and benefits of one or another policy outweigh the noneconomic benefits and costs.

Briefly, then, a summary: No doubt, each of the alternative farm programs can raise farm income, but each program has different consequences for consumer satisfaction and for efficiency. First, under all the programs, the consumer ends up with a different expenditure and consumption than would be generated by free markets. The price-support and crop-restriction programs are *regressive, because food and other agriculture-based products are a larger proportion of the expenditures of low-income groups than of higher-income groups.* Moreover the larger, richer farmers receive most of the government payments. This is shown in Table 24-1, which tabulates the distribution of government payments among

Table 24-1

DISTRIBUTION OF PRICE SUPPORT AND ACREAGE DIVERSION PAYMENTS TO FARMERS IN 1969

1	2	3	4	5
			Government payments to maintain prices and incomes	
Size of Farms (acres)	*Percentage of total farms*	*Percentage of total acreage*	*Total ($1,000)*	*Percent of total*
Up to 50	72.02	23.98	924,551	28.06
50–100	17.44	27.47	805,737	24.45
100–200	6.46	19.44	614,497	18.65
200–500	3.53	20.60	646,827	19.63
500–1,000	0.45	5.80	193,903	5.91
Over 1,000	0.10	2.71	108,716	3.30
Total	100.00	100.00	3,294,231	100.00

Source: U.S. Department of Agriculture.

farmers. Notice that the payments per acre are made reasonably equal among both large and small farms, as shown by the fact that the percentages in columns 3 and 5 march along together fairly well. But farm acreage is concentrated in large farms, so payments are also concentrated in large farms. Farms above 200 acres – about 4 percent of the total number – receive about 29 percent of the payments and contain about 29 percent of total acreage.

These are important conclusions. They are true in spite of the fact that none of the programs impose any direct control on consumers. Furthermore crop-restriction policies tend to promote inefficiency of resource use in production. To be sure, the soil conservation and other agricultural productivity programs that are part of the total package tend to offset that effect. But there is no point in denying the inefficiency that results from an arbitrary limitation on one of the inputs. In terms of our earlier analysis, the economy is pushed inside its production-possibility surface. The factors of production cannot be combined freely, depending on their true relative availability, because the use of land is constrained.

The price-support programs, either of government purchase or government subsidy, require government expenditures.[2] The relative costs of the two plans can be determined from a little exercise with demand elasticities. If the final price to the farmer is the same in both purchase and subsidy programs, the relative *government* costs can be compared by determining in which case the *private* consumer pays more. In the government purchase program, the consumer pays p_S, as shown in Figure 24-3, which is the final price to the farmer. In the subsidy program, represented in Figure 24-5, the consumer pays p_F, a lower price.

If demand is inelastic, consumer expenditures at p_S – the area $p_S Q_S$ in Figure 24-3 – are greater than at p_F in Figure 24-5, where total expenditures are represented by the area $p_F Q_S$. The government's total payments to farmers are, therefore, less under a support program than under a subsidy program. On the other hand, if demand is elastic, consumer expenditures at p_S, in Figure 24-3 equal to the area $p_S Q_S$, are less than expenditures $p_R Q_S$ at price p_F in Figure 24-5. In this case, government payments to farmers are greater under a support program than under a subsidy program. In addition to the direct costs, the government must pay the costs of storage under the price-support scheme.

Are there any specific benefits from government price-support programs other than increased farm income? There are, of course, the accumulated surpluses, which can be used to offset shortages in drought years and to help feed the poor in our own country and in less developed areas. And there are the conservation and other farm improvement programs.

[2] If government must pay farmers to take their land out of production, expenditures are also involved in crop-restriction plans. These are usually set at a fraction of what the farmer might earn if the land were used.

One important economic issue is whether these benefits could be achieved with fewer distortions of production and consumption. There is one alternative program that has not been tried. Why not have the government just give farmers — by transfer payments — whatever income is necessary to make up the difference between what they earn from producing and selling in a free market and what the country as a whole thinks they should have? The payments would come out of general government revenues, as payments for the income-support program would. Some distortion would be involved there, as the result of taxes, but that would be the only source. Consumers would not have to pay high support prices and producers would not be given incentives to be inefficient.

The answers to why the transfer payment alternative has not been used are probably more political than economic. One argument made against it is that it gives "something for nothing." Another argument, not made by farmers but no doubt important, is that a direct payment scheme would probably not give as much income to large farmers as they now receive — and they are presently the major recipients of government support payments.

The present price-support and crop-restriction programs obstruct long-run adjustments which might eventually reduce or eliminate the need for large-scale programs. What are those adjustments? Abandonment of farming on relatively unproductive land and movement of even more of the population and labor force out of agriculture. That is a bitter pill for some people to swallow, though it is the same pill other industries have swallowed. The country has, in effect, decided not to force it on agriculture.

Rent controls

Another sector in which there is general dissatisfaction with the operation of free markets is urban housing. Public recourse to rent control laws and housing subsidies of various kinds reflects this dissatisfaction. The many interconnections between urban housing and other urban problems make it, like agriculture, too complex an issue to resolve in a short economic analysis. Nonetheless, as in the case of agriculture, a little supply and demand can carry us a long way.

First of all, is it appropriate to use supply and demand analysis? Is the perfectly competitive model a reasonably good approximation of the apartment rental sector, say, in a moderate-sized city? You may be impressed by the apparent imperfections in that market. There are many quality differences among apartments; certainly they are not a completely standardized and uniform commodity. Location is one of the most important differentiating factors. There are strong preferences for certain locations. Sometimes they are so strong that a particular corner or neighborhood commands a premium. Landlords also differ. Some know the "market" pretty well and get as much as they can. Others seem less knowledgeable or less determined. Some are good managers; others are not. Some will try for high rents quite out of line with the general market. They will have high vacancy rates, but occasionally get the rentals they ask, because tenants also vary in their knowledge of the market and in their determination to do as well for themselves as possible.

Nonetheless, it is not too far off the mark to think of apartment housing as a perfectly competitive sector. Though some people may have strong loyalties to a certain housing development or strong preferences for colonial architecture, there is a lot of moving around by people whose preferences can be changed by a rent differential. For most renters there are a number of more or less equally satisfactory alternative locations. Of course, the ordinary distinctions according to the number and size of rooms and the floor of the building on which an apartment is located must be taken into account. The differentials for each of these features are often fairly standard. Moreover, in the apartment rental business, one hears frequent references to "the market" — as if there were some "standard" set of prices (rents) that could be attached to a "standard" apartment. So we shall assume that this is true and apply supply and demand analysis to this sector.

Unlike public policy in agriculture, which holds prices *up*, rent controls for urban housing aim at holding prices *down*. One of the most common devices is a rent ceiling, a maximum price that can be charged, usually set at the level prevailing in some earlier year.

Figure 24-6

ANALYSIS OF THE SHORT-RUN EFFECTS OF RENT CONTROL

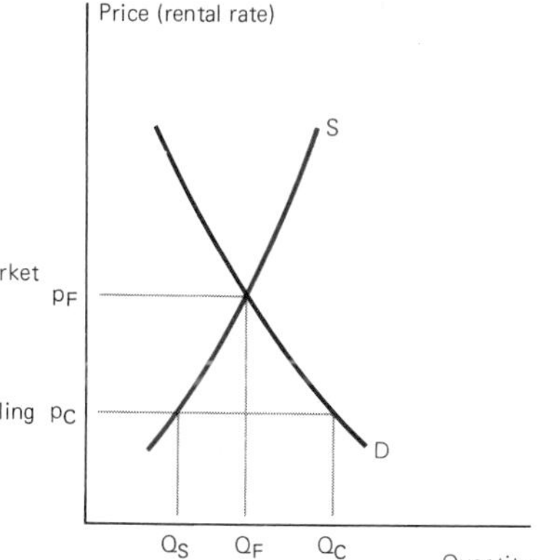

Figure 24-6 illustrates the short-run supply and demand for the standard apartment. The supply schedule reflects the fact that the stock of housing cannot be changed substantially in the short run. Point p_F is the rental that would be set in an uncontrolled market, and p_C is the rent ceiling below the free market price. At the rent ceiling, the demand for standard apartments is Q_C; the supply is only Q_S, and there are some potential tenants willing to pay the controlled rent but unable to find an apartment. At the free market rental rate, the amounts offered and demanded coincide at Q_F. If the supply schedule is only slightly elastic, as shown in Figure 24-6, the number of apartments available at the controlled rental will be only slightly lower than the number available at the free market rental. Total expenditure will be different, however. At the free market price, it would be $p_F Q_F$. If the demand is inelastic, as commonly presumed, at the rent ceiling price, total expenditure will be lower, at $p_C Q_S$. *The major short-run effect of rent control is to change the relative real incomes of landlord and tenant in favor of tenants.* (By contrast, the effect of agricultural price-support programs is to change the income distribution in favor of landowners.) In addition, since somewhat fewer apartments are available, there are potential tenants who are doubling up with friends or family who would get an apartment if there were no rent controls.

Figure 24-6 can also show why some tenants as well as landlords are tempted to cheat on rent control. There are always potential tenants willing to pay more than the ceiling rent, and it would be surprising if the landlords did not also want a higher rent. It will not be long before one of the people on the waiting list for the next free apartment slips a little tip to the building manager to move him higher on the list. If that sort of thing becomes common, then rent control is bypassed.

The story does not stop with the short run. In Figure 24-7, the short run is contrasted with the long-run. The long-run supply schedule is more elastic than the short-run schedule. The short-run free market price p_F is above the long-run equilibrium price p_S. If a free market set the price at p_F, that would induce additional construction in the long run and would tend to bring the price down to the long-run supply price p_S. More apartments Q_S would be available at a rental of p_S, but still not as many as would be demanded at the rent ceiling price p_C.

Notice that if the ceiling level is below the long-run supply price as shown, no additional apartments will be built. The rent ceiling simply freezes the existing supply. When rents are uncontrolled, long-run adjustments will ameliorate housing "shortages." But if rents are controlled at prices below the long-run supply price, those adjustments will not take place. Moreover, if rents are completely fixed and costs of construction rise from one year to the next, new construction will look less and less appealing to potential landlords. As demand continues to rise, owing to population and income growth, the housing shortage will itself grow steadily larger, and the "need" for rent control, that is, the gap between the control price and a free market price, will grow.

If rent control creates problems of nonprice rationing, stimulates evasion and cheating, and blocks long-run adjustments toward increases in supply, why does it have any supporters?

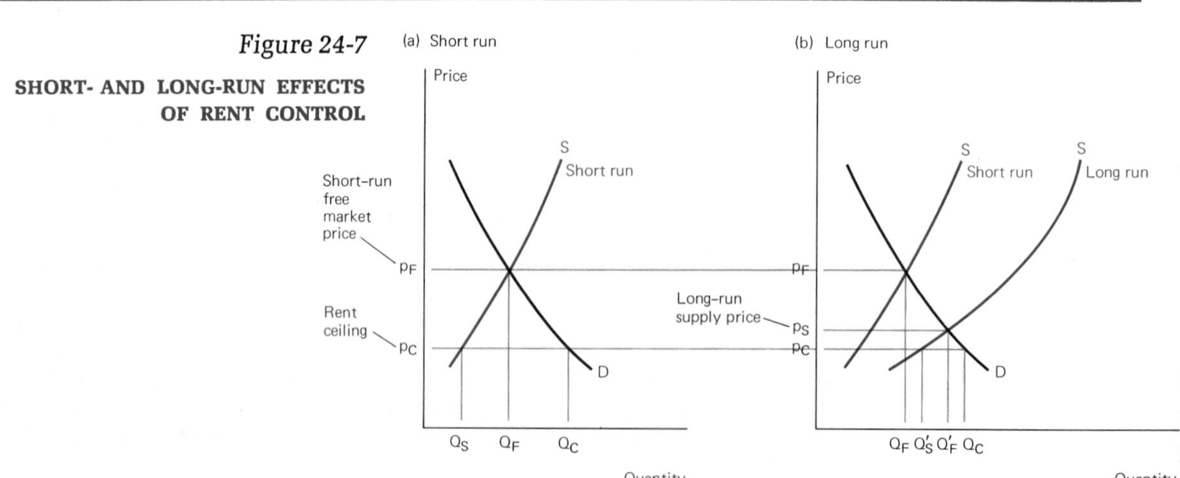

Figure 24-7

SHORT- AND LONG-RUN EFFECTS OF RENT CONTROL

Ignorance is one reason. The consequences are simply not clearly foreseen. But there is also room for honest differences of informed opinion. Even if the consequences are clear, a rent control proponent can claim that the inefficiency and cheating in this sector are smaller evils than rationing by prices. He might believe that uncontrolled rent changes would create great hardship for persons with low incomes. He would give greater weight to these hardships than to inefficiencies due to market interference and to the hardships suffered by landlords – and by people who cannot obtain apartments.

As for long-run adjustments, a rent control proponent may hope for new public housing projects or greater private housing subsidies. There are costs in both rent controls and free market adjustments. The latter differ from rent controls as a policy choice, however, because the market contains a mechanism which helps resolve short-run shortages. Rent controls *may* prevent some short-run hardships to some tenants – at the expense of hardships for others. But, in themselves, they do *not* contain any means of resolving the problems of relative housing scarcity. Rent controls, in fact, exacerbate the long-run housing scarcity problem.

Suppose that, after a landlord remodels, he can adjust his rents. Also suppose, as is often true, that the rent per square foot is higher in small apartments than in large ones. Then landlords will tend to remodel and subdivide large apartments and increase each building's population. If office rentals are not controlled but apartment rentals are, owners will tend to change the use of the land, by remodeling or by new construction, from apartments to offices. If suburban rents are not controlled, new residential construction will tend to be concentrated in suburban areas.

Rent control will not bring new apartment construction into a city. That could be achieved, however, by providing construction subsidies, either directly or through special construction loans with subsidized interest rates. Alternatively, or additionally, public housing projects could be used to add to the total supply of apartments.

We see again that government can interfere with supply and demand and set rents, but the consequences, especially in the long run, may be the opposite of what is desired.

Dynamic adjustments of supply to demand

In the supply and demand analysis developed so far, the final results of a supply-demand intersection or price control have been identified. But the processes by which price and quantity move toward equilibrium have not been explained or even described in detail. Actually such an explanation or description is one of the more difficult parts of economics. It is much easier to do static economics, where time has no essential role and only final results

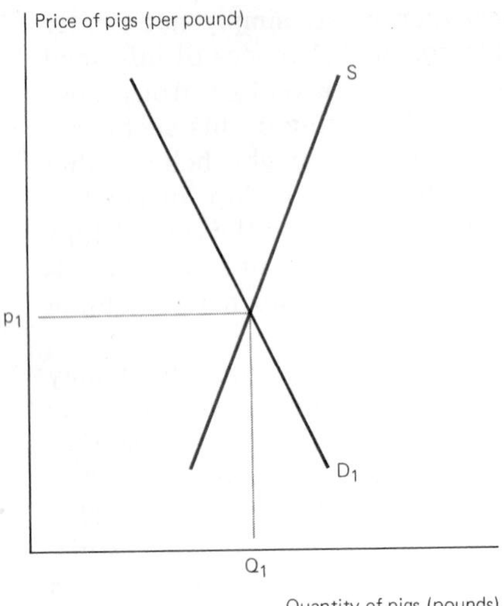

Figure 24-8

EQUILIBRIUM OF PRICE AND QUANTITY

Figure 24-9

DYNAMIC ADJUSTMENT TO A NEW EQUILIBRIUM

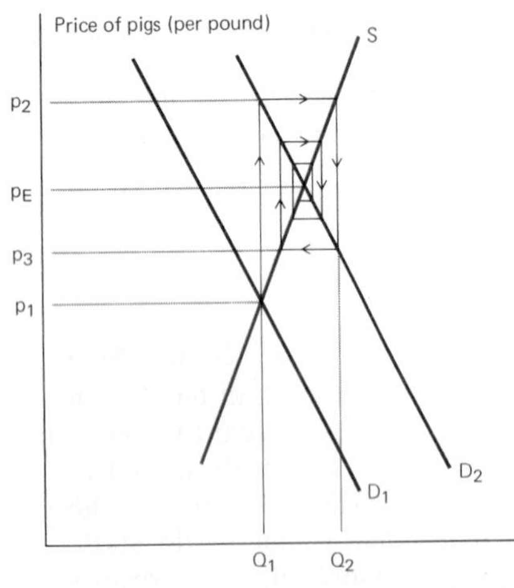

are identified, than to do dynamic economics, where time is of the essence. We can, however, extend the static supply-demand analysis to describe a rather interesting type of dynamic adjustment.[3]

In some kinds of production there is a long time *lag* between the decision to produce and the actual output. During that interval, prices may change. The price that led to the production decision and the price that prevails when the output is marketed may be quite different. A classic example of such production is the raising of hogs for pork. It takes seven to ten months to fatten a pig for marketing, depending on the weight desired. So the farmer's decision to buy little pigs and fatten them may well be based on a price that is substantially different from that which prevails at the time the fat pigs are carried to market.

To understand the implications of the situation, let us examine Figure 24-8. In this figure, D_1 is the conventional demand curve. The supply curve is reinterpreted, however. The quantity of pigs supplied in one period will depend on the price in the preceding period. The period is set by the length of time required for growing and fattening.

If the price and quantity sold in this market happened to be at the equilibrium position, p_1 and Q_1, then they would stay there. The price p_1 in each period would call forth the quantity supplied Q_1 in the next period. And the quantity Q_1 would sell at the price p_1.

Suppose, however, that there were an increase in the price of beef. Since pork is a substitute for beef, the demand for pork and pigs would shift, say, from D_1 to D_2, as shown in Figure 24-9. The quantity supplied in the period in which the shift occurred would continue to be Q_1, because that would depend on the price p_1 in the period before. With the new demand curve D_2, the quantity Q_1 would command the price p_2. The price p_2 would, in the next period, elicit the production of Q_2. When Q_2 is offered on the market, it would sell for the price p_3. That, in turn, would lead to a reduction in the quantity supplied, which would lead to a higher price. The sequence of high price and high production, low price and low production, etc., goes on and on.

Where does it stop? In this case, right at the new equilibrium price, p_E. *The tendency to move toward equilibrium is called dynamic stability.* Since the pattern looks like a spider's cobweb, it is called the *cobweb cycle.*

Does the story always have a happy ending at the supply-demand intersection? Not always. It did here because the supply curve has a steeper slope than the demand curve. If the demand curves were steeper than the supply curves, we would obtain the divergent price-quantity movements shown in Figure 24-10 if ever there was a displacement from the equilibrium p_E and Q_E.

[3] The 1970 award of the Nobel Prize in economics to Prof. Paul A. Samuelson of M.I.T. was based in part on his pathbreaking contributions to this difficult area of dynamic analysis.

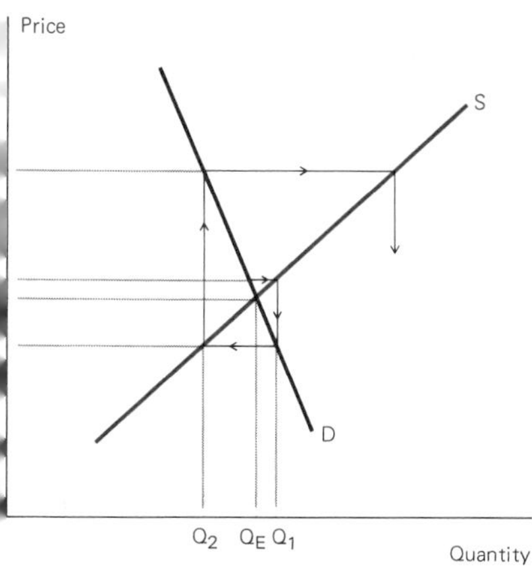

Figure 24-10

UNSTABLE DYNAMIC PRICE-QUANTITY ADJUSTMENTS

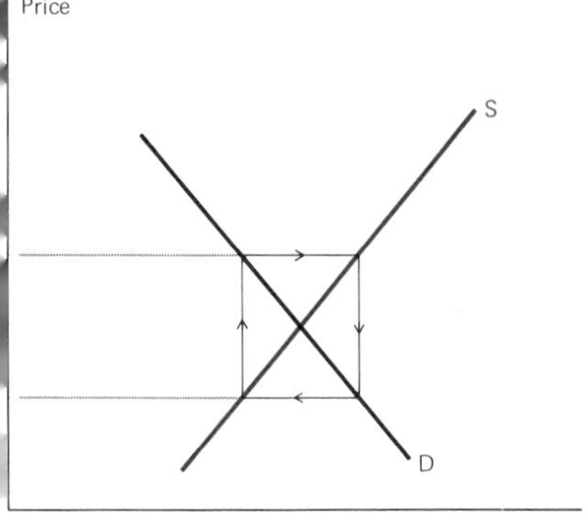

Figure 24-11

NONCONVERGENT PRICE-QUANTITY ADJUSTMENTS

This is a case in which an equilibrium price and quantity exists, but an unstable equilibrium.

An example of equal demand and supply schedule slopes is shown in Figure 24-11. Here the price and quantity changes never grow larger but never become smaller. There may be other types of price-quantity interactions as well. Everything depends on the slopes of the two curves.

Is price stability, therefore, in the lap of the gods? Is it true that, if we are lucky, we will get a movement toward the supply-demand intersection? But if we have a little bit of bad luck with the slopes, off we go?

Not quite. In the cases above, it was only on the supply side that there was any reaction over time. Suppose that a big pig crop led to a low pig price in the present, but on the demand side there were people willing to bet that prices would be higher in the future. Such *speculators* would put slaughtered hogs in cold storage until the next cycle of low production resulted in higher prices. Action by speculators to increase demand in periods of large supply and to increase supply in periods of low production *tends to stabilize prices and dampen their ups and downs.*

Speculation is not always stabilizing, however. Under certain conditions it can accentuate price movements. When it is stabilizing it can perform an important economic function.

Summary

The economic problems of the agricultural sector have their source in continuing growth in farm productivity but an inelastic demand. As a result, total expenditures on farm products do not rise as prices fall. Adjustment of production by movement of labor out of agriculture and voluntary reduction in acreage tilled has been slow.

Government programs to help the agricultural sector concentrate primarily on price maintenance. First a parity price is established that is intended to permit the farmer to maintain his income relative to that of other sectors. Then, under its price-support programs, the government steps into the particular market and supports the price at the desired fraction of parity. Alternatively or additionally, via acreage restriction and soil bank programs, the government reduces production and, in this way, maintains prices. Finally, the government could pay the difference between what the farmer would earn if prices were determined in free markets, without government controls, and what he would earn if he produced at the parity price.

While the various government programs maintain farm incomes, they do so at the expense of accumulated surpluses and/or inefficiency in the use of resources. They also have the effect of raising food prices, a burden which falls most heavily on lower-income consumers.

Rent controls grow out of dissatisfaction with the operation of the housing market. They set maximum prices which can be charged. While protecting existing tenants from price increases, they make it more difficult for potential new tenants to find housing and represent a transfer of income from landlords. In addition, rent controls obstruct the long-run adjustments which would relieve housing shortages by providing new housing. Therefore, while rent controls prevent some hardships, they create others. Complementary measures are required if longer-run solutions to housing shortages are to be worked out.

Static supply and demand analysis looks only at the equilibrium price and quantity conditions and not at the detailed adjustment processes by which the equilibrium conditions are reached. The possible patterns of dynamic adjustment are exemplified by the cobweb cycle process. In this process the quantity supplied in one period depends on the price in a previous period. On the other hand, the quantity demanded in any period depends on the price in that period. Under these conditions, if price and quantity are not at their equilibrium positions, there will be cycles of price and quantity changes. These cycles may move toward or away from the equilibrium position, depending on the relative shapes of the supply and demand curves.

Questions for discussion and review

1. Do you believe there should be special government programs to maintain the income of farmers? Should other sectors have such programs? Explain your answer.

2. Why do price-support programs tend to lead to the accumulation of agricultural surpluses?

3. Is it reasonable for farmers who participate in acreage reduction and soil bank programs to attempt to increase the productivity of the land which they do use?

4. Why do crop-restriction and acreage-reduction programs lead to inefficiencies in the use of resources? Does that mean that price-support programs do not generate inefficiencies in the use of resources?

5. If you were a congressman from an urban district, what kind of farm program would you support?

6. Why do both landlords and tenants cheat on rent control laws? How do they do it?

7. What is the strongest case you can make for rent control laws in crowded urban areas?

8. Is there any reason to expect that the price cycling effect observed in pig prices might also occur in housing rentals? Explain your answer.

Concepts for review

Parity prices
Acreage restriction
Price supports
Crop subsidy payments
Rent ceilings
Cobweb cycle
Lags in response to price changes

25

The economic consequences of monopoly and imperfect competition

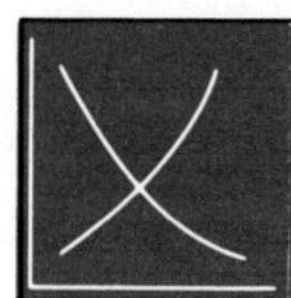

A brief review of the objectives and strategy of our analysis will indicate our progress so far and the road ahead. First we established that prices are the signals to which businessmen respond in buying and hiring productive resources to produce goods and services in order to make profits. Therefore, we had to understand how prices are determined. Next we established that prices depend on the supply and demand influences in the markets faced by each firm. These influences, in turn, depend on the cost structure of each firm and on the *structure* of the markets in which the goods and services are bought and sold. The structure of markets refers to a complex of characteristics: the number and size distribution of buyers and sellers, the degree of standardization of the goods exchanged, information availability and the quality of firm response, and barriers to the entry of new firms. Market structures range from perfect competition to pure monopoly, with a multitude of in-between types.

The model of perfect competition that was analyzed in Chapters 23 and 24 is at an extreme position in the spectrum of market structures. In this chapter we will move to the opposite extreme — pure monopoly. We will then work back and forth between perfect competition and pure monopoly in that vast intermediate area of imperfect competition.

Table 25-1

DEMAND FOR THE PRODUCT OF A MONOPOLIZED INDUSTRY

1 *Price*	2 *Quantity*	3 *Total revenue*	4 *Marginal revenue*
$260	0	$ 0	
			$240
240	1	240	
			200
220	2	440	
			160
200	3	600	
			120
180	4	720	
			80
160	5	800	
			40
140	6	840	
			0
120	7	840	
			− 40
100	8	800	
			− 80
80	9	720	

Monopoly

Price and output determination: The short run

One of the conclusions of Chapter 21 was that a monopolist's sales are constrained by the demand curve the firm faces. *A pure monopolist can set his price at whatever level he wants. But he cannot sell whatever he wants to at any price he sets. Alternatively, the monopolist can set his sales, and take the price he can get, as determined by the demand schedule.* The problem now is to understand how a monopolist actually sets his price — or his sales.

Presumably a monopoly, like a competitive firm, will try to do as well for itself as possible, making as much profit as it can. It will be a profit-maximizing producer. Recall, however, that profit maximization is not the same as maximizing the amount of goods sold or the revenue from goods sold. It is maximizing the *difference between total revenues and total costs.*

To understand how a monopolist *would* set prices, we ask how he *should* set prices to maximize profits. We shall approach the question in two ways. First, we assume that the monopolist has complete knowledge of his revenues and costs for each level of sales and output and we work answers out under that assumption. Then, more realistically, we analyze the price and output determination process as a method of trial-and-error exploration of revenues and costs at alternative levels of output and sales. As we shall see, the two approaches lead to the same result.

The full knowledge approach. For a monopolist to know his revenues at each price, he would have to be fully informed about his demand schedule. Suppose he is so informed and that Table 25-1 reproduces his demand, revenue, and marginal revenue schedules.[1]

Figure 25-1

TOTAL REVENUE CURVE OF A MONOPOLIST

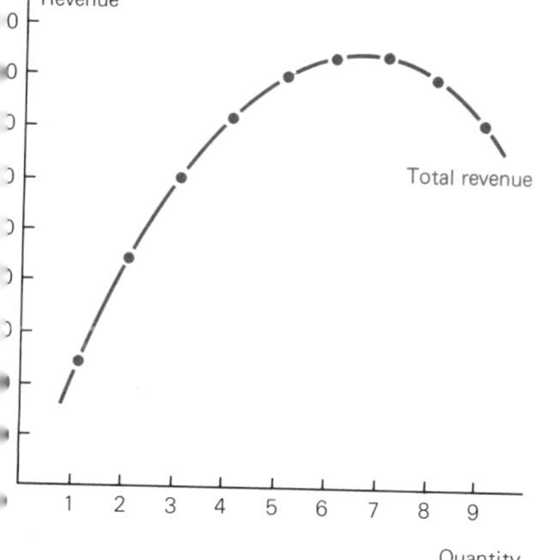

The *total revenue* earned, as listed in column 3, is the product of the price and the quantity sold at that price. The *marginal revenue* is the change (plus or minus) in total revenue due to the production of an additional unit of output.

The total revenue schedule is plotted in Figure 25-1. Its curvature is strikingly different from the total revenue schedule of a perfectly competitive firm, which is a straight line. The perfect competitor is too small to affect prices, and he can expand his sales, with a constant price on each sale. The monopolist faces the *industry* demand schedule, and the Law of Demand illustrated in Table 25-1 says that, everything else remaining equal, prices fall as sales expand. His revenue from each additional unit, i.e., his marginal revenue, will also fall with increasing output. In the range

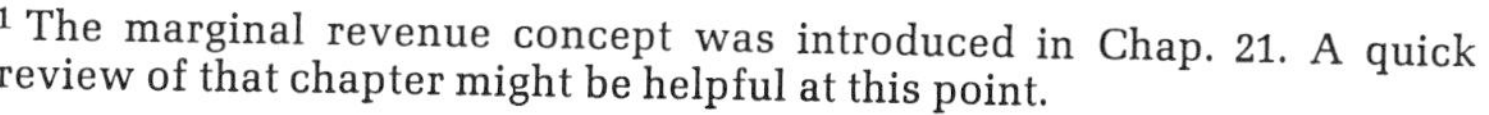
[1] The marginal revenue concept was introduced in Chap. 21. A quick review of that chapter might be helpful at this point.

Table 25-2

COSTS OF PRODUCTION IN THE MONOPOLIZED INDUSTRY

1 *Quantity*	2 *Fixed costs*	3 *Variable*	4 *Total costs*	5 *Marginal costs*
0	$400	$ 0	$ 400	
				$ 40
1	400	40	440	
				30
2	400	70	470	
				35
3	400	105	505	
				45
4	400	150	550	
				60
5	400	210	610	
				80
6	400	290	690	
				105
7	400	395	795	
				135
8	400	530	930	
				170
9	400	700	1,100	

of prices in which demand is elastic, an extra unit of output will add more to revenue than is subtracted by the fall in price. So total revenue will rise as sales increase. That is between outputs 6 and 7 on the revenue schedule. When the monopolist's demand curve becomes inelastic, after that point, total revenue falls even though sales increase. At that point, marginal revenue becomes negative.

We assume that, in addition to revenue information, the monopolist knows his costs for each level of output. Cost data are provided in Table 25-2. The fixed costs, variable costs, and total costs are tabulated separately. Marginal cost, which, again, is the extra cost of an additional unit of output, is listed in column 5. The fixed, variable, and total costs are plotted in Figure 25-2.

Figure 25-2

TOTAL, VARIABLE, AND FIXED COST CURVES OF A MONOPOLIST

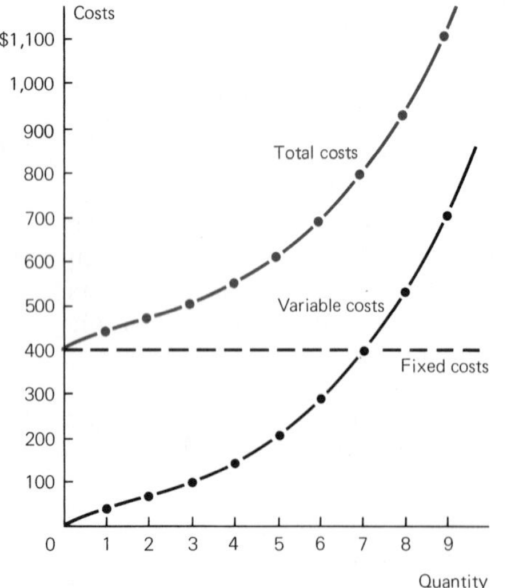

Now the revenue and cost information can be put together to calculate the profits expected at each level of output. That is done in Table 25-3 and Figure 25-3. In column 4 of the table, profits are calculated by subtracting costs from revenues. That amount is equivalent to the vertical distance between the total revenue and total cost curves in Figure 25-3 on page 520. The figure includes a plot of profits at each output level. Assuming, as we have, that the monopolist has full knowledge of his demand and cost data, all he has to do is to pick out and produce the output which yields him the largest profit. This is the production level of 5 units, which generates profits of $190 at point E on the profit curve.

This way of looking at monopolistic behavior, assuming complete knowledge and considering only total costs and total revenues, is perfectly legitimate under our assumptions. Yet it is not realistic. It assumes that the monopolist has information that ordinarily is not available, at least not in detail. The approach does yield an important insight, however: *There is no concept of a supply curve for a monopolistic industry analogous to the supply curve of a competitive industry*. For the pure competitor, recall, the supply schedule is a series of if-then statements: If the price is such-and-such, the amount supplied will be so-and-so. But it is not relevant to ask if-then questions about the price and output of a monopolist. The monopolist can exercise his discretion to *choose* whatever price and output combination is needed to maximize his profits.

The trial-and-error approach. Now we will develop a more realistic, trial-and-error procedure. It will lead the monopolist to the *same* price-quantity decisions he reached with complete knowledge of his cost and revenue schedules. The approach of systematically changing output and observing what happens to profits can get the monopolist to his maximum profit position.

A 1-unit increment in output leads to a change in revenue; that is called marginal revenue, *MR*. It also leads to a change in costs, which is labeled marginal costs, *MC*. As a result, there is a change in profits, which might as well be called marginal profits. Now all the monopolist has to do is to follow the commonsense rules:

> If an increase in output leads to an increment in revenue that is greater than the increment in cost, there will be an increment in profits, and the monopolist should keep going. Translated into economic shorthand, if *MR* is greater than *MC*, there will be an increase in profits from expanding output.
>
> If *MR* is less than *MC*, profits can be increased by reducing output.
>
> If *MR* just equals *MC*, profits will be at a maximum.

There is one further condition: The price charged must cover at least the average variable cost of the output produced. Otherwise the firm will be better off shutting down completely. If this

Table 25-3

COMPARISON OF REVENUES AND COSTS AT ALTERNATIVE OUTPUT LEVELS TO FIND THE MAXIMUM PROFIT OUTPUT

1 *Quantity*	2 *Revenues*	3 *Total costs*	4 *Profits (+) or losses (—)*
0	$ 0	$400	— $400
1	240	440	— 200
2	440	470	— 30
3	600	505	+ 95
4	720	550	+ 170
5	**800**	**610**	+ **190**
6	840	690	+ 150
7	840	795	+ 45
8	800	930	— 130
9	720	1,100	— 380

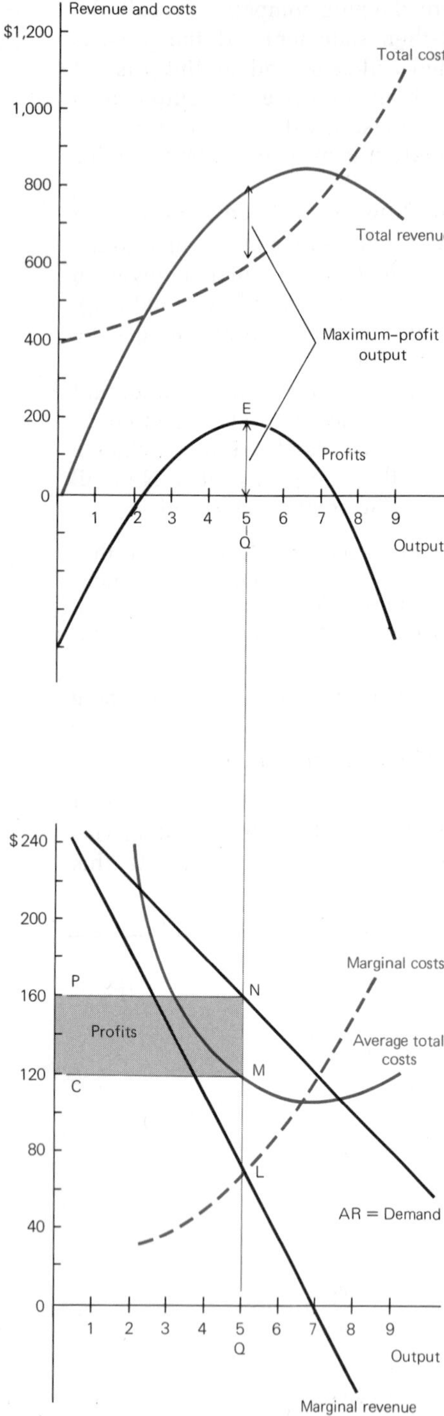

Figure 25-3

COMPARISON OF TOTAL REVENUE AND COST CURVES TO MAXIMIZE PROFITS

condition is met, however, the commonsense marginal rules will maximize profits or minimize losses.

The marginal rules are shown in operation in Table 25-4 and Figure 25-4. As long as *MR* is greater than *MC*, profits can be increased by expanding output. If output should be expanded to a level at which *MR* is less than *MC*, profits can be increased by reducing output. The changes in Table 25-4 are too large to permit us to find the fractional level of output around the fifth unit at which *MR* is just *precisely* equal to *MC*. But the logic of the rules tells us that, at that output level, profits will be at a maximum. Close inspection of Figure 25-4, on which the output levels are smoothed, indicates that the *MR* and *MC* curves intersect and have the same value at output level *L*.

The cost per unit at the maximum profit output level can be read off the *ATC* curve. It is at *M*. The revenue per unit is found by moving up to the *AR* line at *N*. That is the price at which the output will be sold. The profit per unit is the distance between the *AR* and *ATC* curves, which is *MN*. The total profit on all units is the profit per unit, *MN*, times the output Q, which is the same as the distance *PN*. That is equivalent to the area of the rectangle *pNMC*.

As in the analysis of competitive firms, we find that the commonsense marginal rules lead to the same result that would be achieved if there were full knowledge of costs and revenues. The output at which *MR* = *MC* in Figure 25-4 corresponds with the output level at which the profit mountain peaks in Figure 25-3.

These marginal rules for profit maximization are quite analogous to those worked out for the perfectly competitive firm in Chapter 23, but with one—big—difference. The marginal revenue for the perfectly competitive firm was the price of the product, since that did not change with output. That is not true for the monopolist, and it explains the important difference in the economic significance of the behavior of the two types of firms. This conclusion, however, does not imply that businessmen in competitive and monopolistic firms behave differently as managers of their firms. They are all profit maximizers, but they face different market conditions.

Figure 25-4

COMPARISON OF MARGINAL REVENUE AND MARGINAL COST CURVES TO MAXIMIZE PROFITS

Table 25-4

COMPARISON OF MARGINAL REVENUES AND MARGINAL COSTS TO MAXIMIZE PROFITS

1 Quantity	2 Marginal revenue	3 Marginal cost	4 Marginal profits (+) or losses (−)
0			
	$240	$ 40	+ $200
1			
	200	30	+ 170
2			
	160	35	+ 65
3			
	120	45	+ 75
4			
	80	**60**	+ **20**
5			
	40	**80**	− **40**
6			
	0	105	− 105
7			
	− 40	135	− 85
8			
	− 80	170	− 250
9			

Price and output determination by a pure monopolist: The long run

In the short run, the monopolist can adjust only his variable inputs to maximize his profits. He is committed to and cannot vary his fixed inputs. In the long run, however, he may be able to find a better plant size and a lower cost curve on which to operate. The monopolist's long-run maximum profit position is at *the output level at which long-run marginal cost is equal to marginal revenue.* This is shown in Figure 25-5. If the monopolist found himself with the short-run average and marginal cost curves ATC_1 and MC_1, he would produce Q_1, the output at which MC_1 intersects and is equal

Figure 25-5

LONG-RUN ADJUSTMENT BY A MONOPOLIST TO MAXIMIZE PROFITS

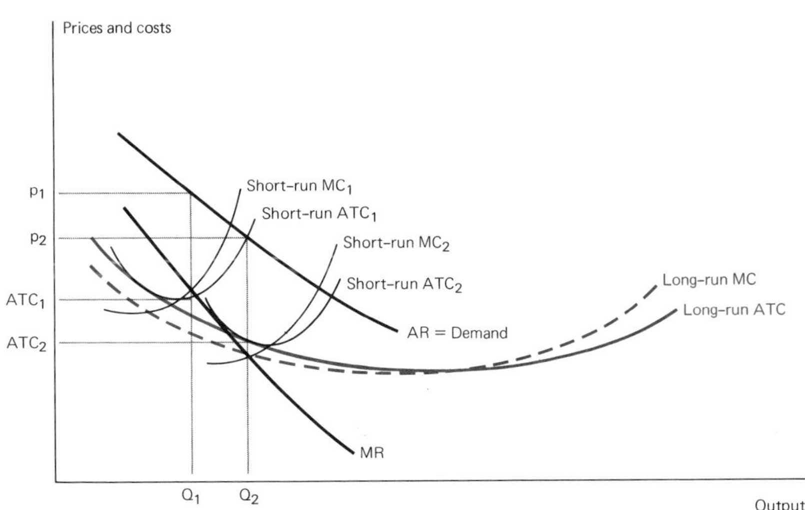

Figure 25-6

CASE IN WHICH A MONOPOLIST CANNOT MAKE PROFITS

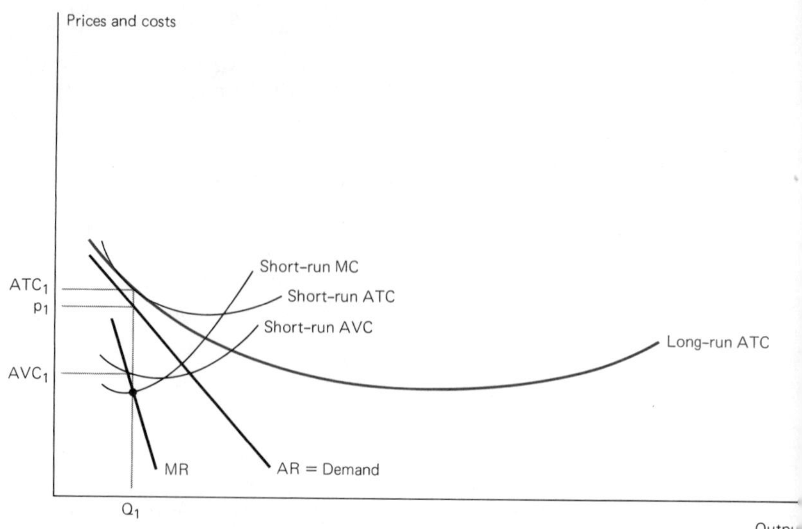

to his marginal revenue. The unit costs of producing that output are ATC_1. For that output he would charge price p_1 The profits *per unit*, therefore, are $p_1 - ATC_1$, and the total profits are $(p_1 - ATC_1) \times Q_1$.

The *long-run* marginal cost curve intersects the *MR* curve at Q_2, which is a larger output than Q_1. Making the marginal revenue–long-run marginal cost comparisons, the monopolist would decide that he could improve his profit position by expanding his plant. Therefore, in the long run, the monopolist would acquire more fixed factors in order to be able to produce Q_2 with the scale of plant which leads to the marginal costs at Q_2. His average total costs would then be at ATC_2 and he would charge price p_2. His profit per unit would be $p_2 - ATC_2$, and his total profit would be $(p_2 - ATC_2) \times Q_2$.

One should not think, however, that the existence of a monopoly in itself guarantees profits either in the long run or in the short run. That is how it happened to come out in the examples shown so far, but we can certainly find real situations in which it does not happen. A monopolist whose demand has fallen, owing to the development of other goods and services, *may* have to take short-run losses while reducing the scale of his output. If his product is completely obsolete and demand has fallen drastically, he can even be forced out of business. That is what happened to the interurban street railways in the 1920s and 1930s after the use of buses and automobiles became widespread.

Figure 25-6 presents graphically an example of a monopolist who will face long-run losses if he continues to produce. Demand has fallen so drastically that the demand schedule lies below the long-run average total cost curve at every output level. Yet, in the short run, if the monopolist found himself with the short-run average total costs shown, he would be doing as well as possible by producing Q_1 and charging p_1. He would have some fixed costs to bear in the short run even if he shut down his plant. If he produced Q_1 and charged p_1 he would minimize his losses, because p_1 is greater than AVC_1, variable costs per unit. His revenue would cover some part of his fixed costs, but not all of total unit costs ATC_1. On the other hand, in this situation he will not reinvest or add to his plant. The future holds no hope of covering total costs of production. The monopolist will thus let his equipment wear out, and finally shut up shop.

Resume and evaluation of monopolistic behavior

Let us consolidate our analysis of pure monopoly before we push on. In a sense the most important conclusions are negative ones.

The consequences of price being greater than marginal cost. A monopolist maximizing his profits will move toward an output at which *marginal cost equals marginal revenue.* But this is *not* the output at which the price or value of the good to a consumer is equal to the marginal cost of its production. Figure 25-7 helps demonstrate the implications of the difference in monopolistic and competitive behavior. The pure monopolist will tend to produce Q_1 where $MR = MC$. But the output at which the value of an incremental unit of output to the consumer is equal to its incremental cost is Q_2, where $MC = AR$.

In effect, the monopolist is making goods scarcer than they would be if the industry were competitive. He is restricting output

Figure 25-7

MONOPOLISTIC OUTPUT DIFFERS FROM COMPETITIVE OUTPUT

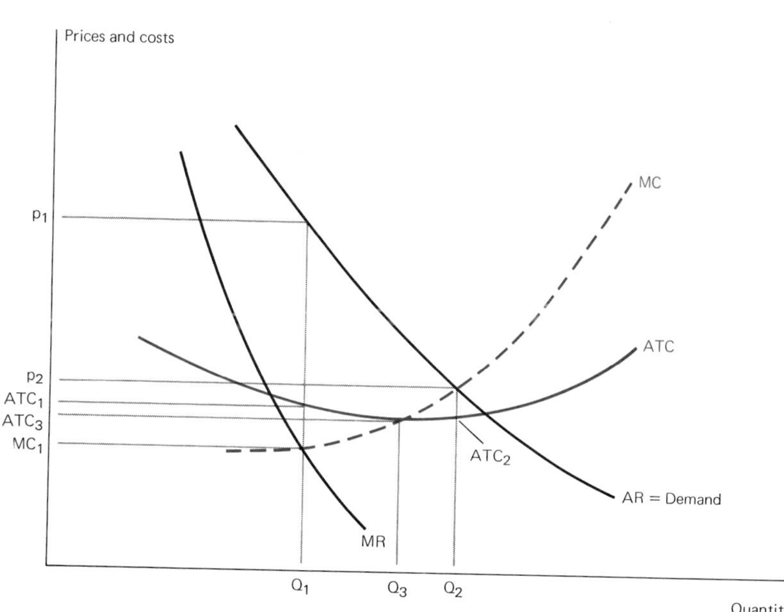

to Q_1 rather than expanding to Q_2. It is a *contrived* scarcity, because output could grow to Q_2 and consumers would then be better off. This contrived scarcity means that less resources are being used in producing the product than would be used if output were expanded to Q_2.

As stated in Chapter 21, the very fact that the monopolist faces a downward-sloping industry demand schedule creates a difference between what a sale is worth to him, his marginal revenue, and what it is worth to a consumer, the price or average revenue. For the firm in a perfectly competitive industry, however, the price, which is the value of an extra unit of output to the consumer, is equal to the marginal, or incremental, cost of the extra unit. That marginal-revenue-equals-price relationship for the perfectly competitive firm is a consequence of the horizontal demand curve which it faces.

This means that monopolized markets have no automatic market mechanisms which lead them to promote the general interest of consumers. Competitive markets do have such mechanisms.

The tendency not to produce at the cost-minimizing output. In a monopolized market, there is *no tendency* for the firm to move in the long run toward an output at which unit costs of production, *ATC*, are minimized. That is Q_3 in Figure 25-7. The monopolist's long-run profit-maximizing output is where long-run $MC = MR$, at Q_1, and in general that will not be equal to the output, Q_3, *at* which long-run average total cost is as low as possible. Again, this means that, in the long run, the wrong combination of resources will be used in production — "wrong" in the sense that it is not the resource combination that minimizes costs in the long run.

This does not imply that monopolists will use old-fashioned and high-cost technology or that they will waste manpower and material resources. Far from it. They may be as "modern" as can be, automated and computerized from head to toe, with the most efficient management practices in using their labor and other factors. But it will all be directed toward reducing the cost of the "wrong" output — an output which is not at the minimum long-run average total cost point.

Monopoly, income inequality, and efficiency

The cliché adjective used to describe a monopolist is "grasping." It conjures up a picture of an aggrandizing, powerful firm seizing every opportunity to exploit consumers for its own profit, making the rich richer and the poor poorer. No doubt, fortunes have been created by monopolistic practices. The Rockefeller fortune, for example, was based on the aggressive monopolizing of the early oil industry by the original John D. Rockefeller in the 1890s. The monopoly that the Aluminum Company of America enjoyed for many years was based on exclusive patents and was the origin of the Mellon fortune. Many examples can be given, and their effects on income distribution cannot be ignored. They raise questions of equity which we have touched on before.

Moreover, the effects of monopoly profits can be quite far-reaching. As was first pointed out in the discussion of interdependence in Chapter 3: The resolution of the Output questions, related to level and composition of production, is closely related to the resolution of the Distribution questions. In turn, the Input questions, related to the use of productive resources, are related to Output and, therefore, again to Distribution issues.

On the other hand, in analyzing the effect of monopoly on the efficient use of resources, we did not come to our negative conclusions by asking who owned the monopoly. We did not ask whether it was a family firm or a corporation in which widows and orphans had invested. We simply found that a monopoly creates inefficiencies in *resource allocation*. The inefficiencies exist so long as a monopolistic firm acts in a profit-maximizing manner. It would make no difference in this respect if the ownership of stock shares were distributed equally among the entire population. Moreover, we never claimed that monopolists were more single-minded profit maximizers than competitive firms. We simply assumed that both monopolists and competitors try to make themselves better off. That is what the widows and orphans, if they owned stock in a monopoly, would want their management to do. *The inefficiencies and evils of monopoly cannot be avoided just by distributing its ownership widely. They are built into its market structure, and their elimination requires either the elimination of the monopoly position or some kind of direct control or intervention.*

The limits to monopoly power

Are there any constraints on monopolistic practices? Are there forces which can move monopolies toward competitive uses of resources? Firms with monopoly power sometimes ask us to believe that they have only the consumers' interests at heart; in an altruistic way, they set prices that just cover their costs and yield a little profit. That is a story for the gullible. Certainly their stockholders do not believe it. If they did, they would turn the management out for another group which would make more profits. Yet the extent and freedom of monopoly power is constrained in several ways.

First of all, the demand curve of the monopolist may not have much slope to it because there are a variety of substitutes that consumers can switch to as the price goes up. Our square doughnut producer has a patent monopoly which does him a little good, but not much. Aluminum, on the other hand, has sufficient advantages over other metals in so many uses that its demand schedule has a significant slope, and its monopoly had real power.

Second, even monopolies have to worry about *potential* competition. They are rarely completely invulnerable. Competitors can break patent monopolies by exploiting more or less equivalent foreign patents or by finding an equally effective, but not identical, way of producing the good. Attacking a monopoly can be an expensive undertaking, however, and competitors will not attempt it unless the potential profits warrant. To avoid having to fight off new entrants, existing monopolies may expand their output, charge a lower price, and be content with lower current profits. That strategy, they figure, will pay off in the long run. As we shall see, this kind of situation, where the actions of one firm are affected by the actual or potential behavior of another, will come up again in the section on oligopoly.

Finally, monopolies must be sensitive to the political climate and the possibility of government regulation. Whether their concern will force them to moderate prices and expand output depends on political influences, which we cannot explore here. But it also depends on the product itself. A monopoly in gold-plated plumbing does not have to worry much. But monopolistic actions in milk pricing generate a good deal of public attention and outcry.

Is there anything good to be said for monopoly? As pointed out earlier, one of the sources of monopoly is the cost advantage that may result from larger and larger scale production. Under such conditions it is not possible to maintain competition in a free market, though the industry can be forced into a competitive mold by a limitation on the size of the firm. Such a limitation would also force higher costs and, perhaps, higher prices. Figure 25-8 illustrates this possibility. It shows the long-run average total cost and marginal cost curves. The monopolist would move toward output Q_M – where MR equals long-run MC. The price would be p_M, which maximizes profits. If the size of the firm were limited by government decree to guarantee competition, the competitive firm's cost curve would be much higher, as shown. If enough competitive firms entered the industry to just cover minimum long-run costs of firms of the size shown, they would generate the total supply curve

Figure 25-8

OUTPUT AND PRICES OF MONOPOLISTIC AND COMPETITIVE FIRMS WHEN MONOPOLIST HAS COST ADVANTAGE

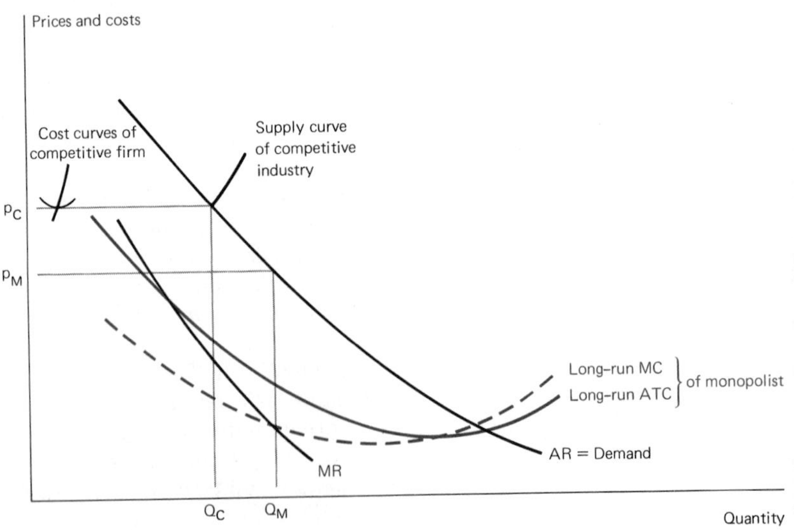

depicted. The price would be p_C, which is greater than p_M, and the quantity supplied would be Q_C.

This is the argument for natural monopolies in the electric power and telephone industries. There can be little doubt that, if competition were forced on these industries, the cost of services would go up substantially.

What other social advantages are claimed for monopoly? For one thing, it is claimed that monopoly firms are more willing and able to undertake technological research and innovation from which there are widespread benefits. The evidence for this assertion is far from conclusive. In fact, most of the evidence suggests that large, but not dominant, firms contribute more to research and innovation than do monopolists or the very largest firms.

A final word on monopoly and its ubiquity

Pure monopoly is rare, so rare that one can find it about as often as one can find perfect competition. Why then spend so much time on monopoly? Because it is common for businesses to have *some degree* of monopoly power. Our analysis of pure monopoly tells us what businesses would like to do and, in fact, try to do with the monopoly power they have. When their monopoly is not complete, they are constrained in their exercise of monopoly power by the actions of other firms. We now turn to other types of market structures in which there are different sources of monopoly power and different constraints on its exercise.

Monopolistic competition

The rather self-contradictory name of monopolistic competition is given to industries that have *some major features of both monopoly and competition.* In such industries, entry is easy, so there are a large number of firms, each with a relatively small share of the market. That is the competition part. The monopoly part arises from the fact that each firm sells a somewhat differentiated product, so its demand schedule has some downward slope.

Products are differentiated by the unique qualities associated with them or by the special services that accompany their sale—their durability, their fashion appeal, the credit terms on which they are sold, etc. Actual differences may be real, large or small, or completely nil, with the illusion of difference created by advertising. The important thing is that consumers act as if the products were somewhat different.

Monopolistic competition is a reasonably good model for industries producing many types of consumer products—some small appliances, for example, some types of clothing, canned foods, cosmetics, paper products. Among such industries there may be great variation in the degree to which monopoly and competition are mixed. As a result, our analysis will have to be rather general.

Even so, we can work out the major characteristics of such industries.

With a large group of sellers of close but not perfect substitutes, no *one* firm can directly affect the price and sales of any other firm. As in perfect competition, there are no direct interactions among the decisions of individual firms. Many firms acting separately, compelled by the same market forces, determine industry output and price levels.

Short-run pricing

To predict how a firm in a monopolistically competitive industry will determine its output and price, we again ask how the firm *should* behave in trying to maximize profits.

The answer is by now familiar. If the firm can cover its variable costs at any output, it can work toward the profit-maximizing output by following the marginal rules:

If MR is greater than MC, expand output.

If MR is less than MC, contract output.

If $MR = MC$, profits are at a maximum.

Each firm is like a little monopoly and will behave as if it were, as shown in Figure 25-9. It will move toward output Q_1 at which $MR = MC$, and charge price p_1. With unit costs of ATC_1, it will make profits on each unit of $(p_1 - ATC_1)$ and total profits of $(p_1 - ATC_1) \times Q_1$.

Figure 25-9

SHORT-RUN PROFIT-MAXIMIZING EQUILIBRIUM OF A MONOPOLISTICALLY COMPETITIVE FIRM

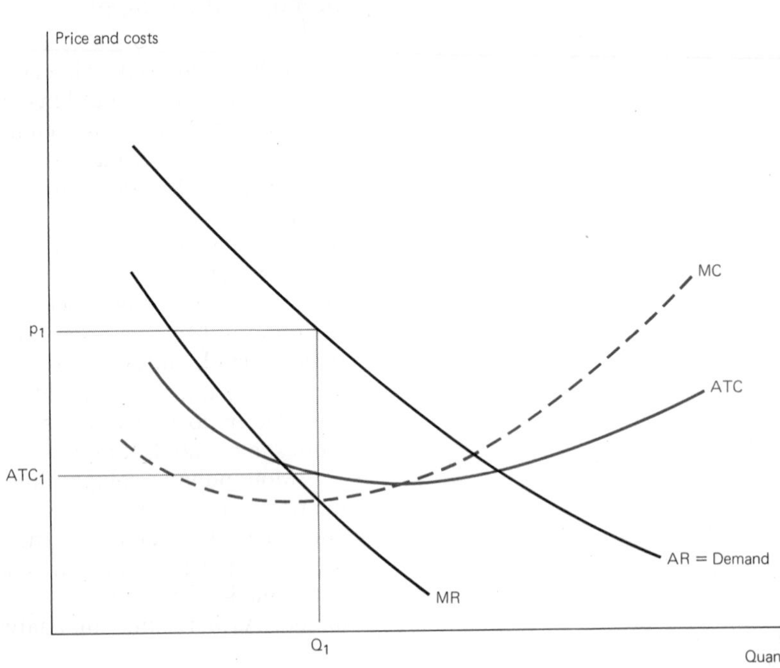

Long-run adjustments Unlike in pure monopoly, there is *free entry* into monopolistically competitive industries. The sight of profits will attract imitators and competitors, each of whom will try to slice off a share of the market by some differentiation of its own product. As that happens and the market is divided among more and more firms, the demand curve of each firm will be shifted downward (or to the left). *The end of the adjustment process will come when there are no more profits to attract more firms.* In that final long-run equilibrium, the price charged will be equal to the unit costs of production: The demand curve will be just touching the average total cost curve. For that to be the best that the firm can possibly do, *MR* must also be equal to *MC* at that equilibrium output. Before long-run equilibrium is achieved the typical firm facing the demand schedule D_1 in Figure 25-10, with the cost curves shown, would maximize profits by producing Q_1 (where $MR_1 = MC$) and selling at price p_1. As new firms entered the industry, the original demand schedule would shift toward D_2. With demand curve D_2, the firm would produce Q_2 (where $MR_2 = MC$) and sell at price p_2, which would just be equal to the average total cost of that output. That is the final equilibrium toward which each firm in the industry would move, even though it might never be reached because of the constant shifting of demand and cost conditions.

The equilibrium output in a monopolistically competitive industry is not characterized by monopoly profits, but is characterized by monopolistic waste and inefficiency in the use of resources.

Figure 25-10 also shows the long-run equilibrium output Q_3 at

Figure 25-10

ADJUSTMENT TOWARD LONG-RUN EQUILIBRIUM BY A FIRM IN A MONOPOLISTICALLY COMPETITIVE INDUSTRY

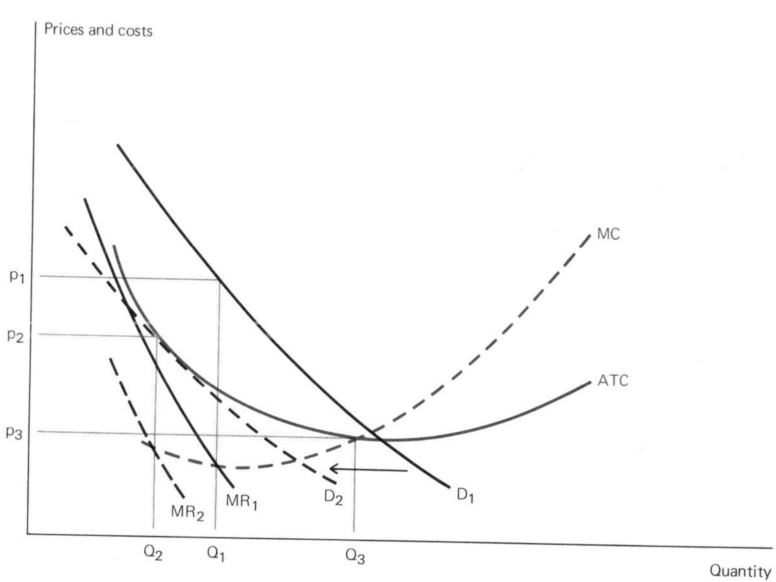

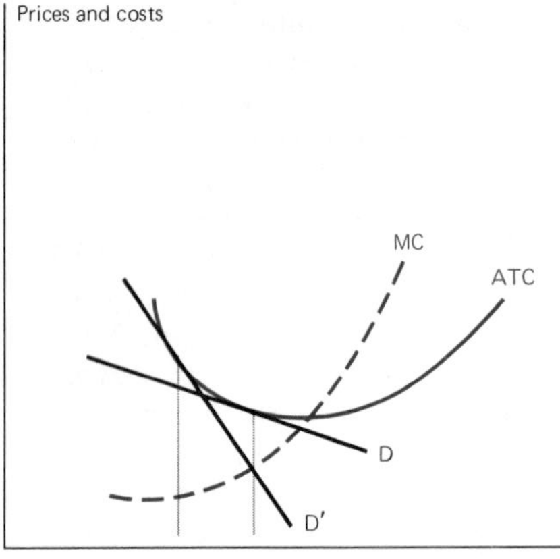

Figure 25-11

EFFECT OF DIFFERENT DEMAND SCHEDULES IN THE LONG-RUN EQUILIBRIUM OUTPUT OF A FIRM IN MONOPOLISTIC COMPETITION

which price = MC = ATC, which would tend to be achieved by a perfectly competitive industry. The long-run equilibrium output of a monopolistically competitive industry at Q_2 is less than that. This means there is the same kind of inefficiency in monopolistically competitive industry as in pure monopoly. Each firm in monopolistic competition has the capacity to produce at a lower cost, but it does not do so, because it would not be maximizing profits. Instead of a long-run equilibrium tangency for the firm at the lowest point of the average total cost curve, the tangency is on the side of the firm's average total cost curve. If it were not for product differentiation and the downward slope of the demand schedule, the output of each firm could be expanded. There would then be fewer firms, less excess capacity, and more efficient use of resources in the industry.

An important implication of this analysis is that freedom of entry is not enough to guarantee competitive efficiency in the use of resources when there is monopolistic competition. It will only eliminate "monopoly profits" as total demand is divided among more and more firms. The quantitative importance of the inefficiency in the use of resources depends on the slope of the firm's demand schedule and the shape of cost curves. An average total cost curve with a great deal of curvature in a limited output range is drawn in Figure 25-11, along with two examples of demand schedules with different slopes. The demand schedule with the steepest slope moves the no-profit tangency output farthest from the least-cost point. The output shift is also larger when the cost schedules are shallow rather than deep U shapes, as shown in Figure 25-12, though the price shift is smaller.

Figure 25-12

EFFECT OF MORE GRADUALLY CHANGING AVERAGE TOTAL COSTS ON THE LONG-RUN EQUILIBRIUM ADJUSTMENT, WITH ALTERNATIVE DEMAND SCHEDULES

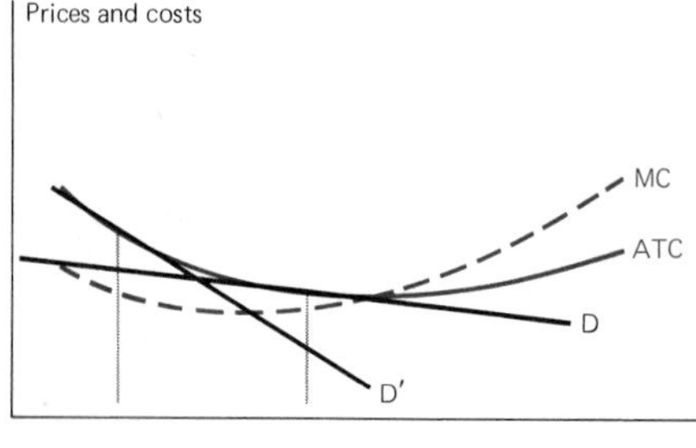

At this point someone who thinks that variety is the spice of life might argue that he is willing to give up some of the meat and potatoes of economic efficiency for the spice of product differentiation. *De gustibus non est disputandum*; there is no arguing about tastes.

Oligopoly

The oligopoly category of market structure covers a multitude of market conditions. The essential feature of oligopoly is that *the number of firms in the industry and participating in the market are so few that the actions of any one will directly affect the profits of others.* Each firm will take this mutual interdependence into account when it makes its price and output decisions. The tightness of the interdependence depends on: (1) the number of firms in the industry and (2) the extent to which products are differentiated. If firms are few and their products are regarded as more or less the same by users, the interdependence will be close. If firms are more numerous and their products are considered somewhat differentiated, the direct interdependence will be looser.

The degree of interdependence is also affected by the manner in which the firms have accommodated themselves to living together. As in some extended families in which there are warm and close relations among the members, so also in some oligopolies with fairly numerous firms, effective methods of accommodation have been worked out. On the other hand, there are small families, and, analogously, small oligopolies, in which the members continue to live together but in continuous warfare.

A parable of direct interdependence

A fictitious but not unrealistic example will help to illustrate the possibilities. Suppose there are only four tire firms producing and selling in a particular market area. One of them, firm A, has just replaced its old tire-making equipment with some new machines which will lower its costs at its current production rate and give it even lower unit costs if it can increase production. So firm A decides to have a sale. It will cut the price of its tires by 25 percent.

A's sale amounts to a price reduction, which will increase the total purchases of tires. In addition, the sale will directly affect other firms in the industry. It will induce some of the formerly loyal customers of firms B, C, and D to switch to A. Actual and projected industry sales are shown in Table 25-5 on the next page.

Table 25-5(*a*) represents the before-sale situation. The industry sells 8,000 tires a week at $40 per tire, and the total receipts of all firms are $320,000 per week. The firms are of different sizes, however, and have different proportions of the market.

Table 25-5(*b*) represents firm A's calculations or best guesses of what will happen if it announces its sale – *and all the other firms maintain their prices*. Firm A's sales will go up substantially, from 2,000 a week to 3,600 a week – by 80 percent – as it pulls customers away from B, C, and D *and* induces more sales in the industry. Total weekly tire sales of the industry rise to 8,400. Firm A's revenues rise by 35 percent, from $80,000 to $108,000, and the revenues of the other firms fall. Total industry sales receipts fall by $20,000, however, indicating that the industry demand is inelastic. A comparison of the increase in A's sales and revenues with what happens to the industry as a whole indicates that most of A's improvement comes at the expense of the other firms.

The other firms would really be hit hard in the situation described in Table 25-5(*b*). Firm B, formerly number one in the industry, would lose 25 percent of its sales and revenues. Firms C

Table 25-5 ACTUAL AND PROJECTED LEVELS OF SALES IN THE TIRE INDUSTRY

Firm	Price	Quantity sold per week	Revenue
(a) Before the sale			
A	$40	2,000	$ 80,000
B	40	2,400	96,000
C	40	1,900	76,000
D	40	1,700	68,000
Total		8,000	$320,000
(b) If only Firm A has a sale			
A	$30	3,600	$108,000
B	40	1,800	72,000
C	40	1,600	64,000
D	40	1,400	56,000
Total		8,400	$300,000
(c) If all firms react to the sale			
A	$30	2,800	$ 84,000
B	30	2,800	84,000
C	30	2,800	84,000
D	50	1,600	80,000
Total		10,000	$332,000

and D, who are the smaller ones, would also lose, though not by so large a proportion as B. No doubt, the officers of these firms would be angrier than a nest of wet hornets. The next time B's president met A's president on the golf course, he would either cut him dead, or curse him out, or smile politely and step on his ball. C's president might try to reason with him back at the clubhouse bar, pointing out what he is doing to total industry receipts. D's president might call up and threaten to sue on antitrust grounds and ask for triple damages.

Of course, A is sitting there with the new machinery that gives it lower costs than the others, so A's president might just smile and say, "That's business, boys. We aren't in it for our health." But B has a lot of liquid assets and is prepared to teach A a lesson by meeting A's lower price. Firm B may have to take losses for a while, but it has the cash to carry it over. Firm C has been toying with the idea of installing a revolutionary new foreign process which will give it even lower costs than A anyway. It may go out and get a bank loan to put in the new machinery. Firm D's back is to the wall. So it calls in a product and marketing consultant, hires a hotshot advertising firm, and announces a new line of "four-ply nylon, dacron, fiberglass, and rayon tires — guaranteed as long as you own your car,"* which it sells at a higher price. (*Allowance made for actual use if replacement becomes necessary.)

Before firm A ever announces its sale, therefore, it will try to think through the reactions of the other firms. It might embody its best guesses in a table such as Table 25-5 (*c*). If B and C retaliate by lowering their prices, A's sales will rise when its own prices are lowered, but not by nearly as much as they would in the absence of retaliation. The revenues of A, C, and D rise, and those of B fall.

In spite of these reactions, firm A might decide to go ahead, depending on how much its costs have been reduced by its new equipment. If the retaliation resulted in such a small net gain in sales that it could not make more profits at the lower price, firm A might give up the whole idea — and wonder whether it had been smart to buy the new machinery. Since firm A's foresight is no better than that of the rest of us, however, its advance calculations might well be faulty and it might be unpleasantly — or pleasantly — surprised when it cuts prices.

If the actions and reactions did work out as shown in Table 25-5(*c*), firm B's strategy might pay off, though it might cost a substantial amount in current losses. Firm C might have even lower current operating costs but a bank loan to pay off. Firm D would have larger revenues, but we do not know the costs of its advertising campaign and consultants and the extra costs of those new fiber cords in the tire.

We could continue to make up alternative scenarios for this industry and other such industries, and it is rather fun to do so. Why are there so many possibilities? *The human element and the playing out of market strategies and responses to them have a large role in markets where there is direct, mutual interdependence among a few firms.* Yet, however much effort we put into the construction of alternative scenarios, we could never capture all the possibilities. Too many things can happen, and they depend in part on the unique history of each industry as well as on new events, which may also be unique. It would be like trying to map out everything that could happen in a long poker game. There are many, many different card combinations. In addition, the personality of each player will manifest itself in different ways as the game goes on. Each player bluffs and retreats and establishes a pattern of play which may change intentionally or unintentionally as he wins or loses. We simply cannot catalog all the possibilities. Moreover, we cannot predict which of the many alternative scenarios will apply in a particular case.[2]

[2] Oligopoly is just one of many situations in which the development of rational strategies requires A to take into account B's reaction to A's actions and reactions and maybe C's, D's, etc. The furthest development of the theory of such strategy formation is John von Neumann and Oscar Morgenstern, *The Theory of Games and Economic Behavior,* Princeton University Press, Princeton, N.J., 1953. An amusing introduction to this field is provided by J. D. Williams, *The Compleat Strategist,* McGraw-Hill Book Co., New York, 1954.

Price and output determination

Economists have no general theory of oligopoly. All we can do is set out some guidelines and analyze some special cases. The situation is not hopeless, however. The guidelines have a good deal of predictive power and the analysis covers some of the most important cases. We know, of course, what each firm wants to do. It wants to make as much profit as possible. But there are no general rules for how it should behave to do this, and, therefore, we can make no general prediction of how it will behave.

Table 25-5 can be used to illustrate one general point: In making their decisions, oligopolistic firms will take into account *the effects they will have both on the combined profits of all firms in the industry and on the profits of each firm*. We know also, from the simple example in Table 25-5, that oligopolists are pulled in two directions. One way for each firm to increase its own profits is to make the profits received by the industry as a whole as large as possible. This goal will be achieved if the industry as a whole behaves as if it were a single monopoly. That will create the largest total profit pie to be divided among the individual firms. So there is a tendency for each firm to cooperate in overall monopolistic behavior. The sticky point in such cooperation is always the sharing out of the pie. Firms do not readily agree on how that is to be done, and their joint efforts to maximize total industry profits may well break down on the issue of who is to get how much.

The other way for an oligopolistic firm to increase its profits is to attempt to get larger profits for itself out of a smaller total industry pie. That is what firm A started out to do in the example in Table 25-5. In trying to make more profits for itself, its actions tended to reduce the total revenues and profits earned in the industry. This angered its rivals and provoked reactions whch partially offset firm A's actions.

Allocation and efficiency in oligopoly

It is hard to predict just where on their cost and revenue curves oligopolists will produce. We can be reasonably sure that oligopolists will *compare marginal revenues and marginal costs and try to maximize their profits, taking their rivals' reactions into account.* There are now two reasons why an oligopolist's demand schedule slopes downward and why an oligopolist can affect the industry price by changing his output and sales. First, the oligopolist is such a large part of the total market that his output and sales decisions have repercussions throughout the industry. Second, the oligopolist's rivals may retaliate and cut their prices also.

As a result, we should expect that an oligopolist trying to maximize profits by equating marginal revenue to marginal cost will arrive at a different output from that at which price equals marginal cost, as in a competitive industry. In effect, the oligopolist has some degree of monopoly power. He must share it, and the general indeterminacy of the sharing arrangement makes it impossible to predict the price and output position at which he will end up. We can be sure, however, that there is nothing in the market that necessarily pushes the oligopolist to the efficient point that would be achieved by perfect competition.

Because of the interdependence among oligopolists and the uncertainty created by rivalry, no firm has a safe and sure guide to maximum profits. On the one hand, each firm is attracted by the possibilities of joint action, and on the other, each is tempted to strike out on its own. Our analysis of monopolistic behavior helps us understand the appeal of individual action. Let us now think about the ways and means of joint decision making.

Methods of collusion

Overt collusion or explicit agreement. Firms may simply get together and talk over what they are going to do and how they will do it, what prices they will charge and how they will share out the market. They may not always reach an agreement, but, within the circle, each player announces his intentions as clearly or as vaguely as he sees fit. Thus the firms reduce the risk of accidental and mutually undesired economic warfare.

Overt collusion takes many forms. Judge Elbert H. Gary, president of the United States Steel Corporation around the turn of the century, held his famous dinners in Pittsburgh until 1911. These gathered together the presidents of the leading steel companies to discuss steel pricing and market policy issues. In the nineteenth century, some industries drew up formal collusion agreements; these were, however, unenforceable in the courts. In 1961, forty-five executives of twenty-nine companies in the electrical equipment industry were convicted of price fixing. They also held meetings to plan their maneuvers. One of these was a system for determining which company would make the low bid on a particular contract—according to the phases of the moon. The ordinary telephone is, of course, an instant "hot line" for executives trying to avoid economic warfare.

The federal antitrust laws are hard on explicit collusion among firms to set prices and control markets. Since overt agreements leave so much evidence behind them, they generally are avoided by colluding firms in favor of *tacit arrangements*.

Tacit collusion or implicit agreements. Oligopolistic firms do not have to be told about their mutual interdependence. Nor do they need to make explicit agreements in order to work out mutually acceptable modes of behavior. They employ a variety of unspoken, unwritten, and indirect means of communicating. Long after the Gary dinners were held, for example, it was accepted practice in the steel industry for U.S. Steel Corporation to act as the "price leader." It set prices and the rest of the industry followed. The company's position in the industry has been eroded in recent years. Other firms now frequently play the role of price leader, with the rest of the industry sometimes following and sometimes not.

Isn't that like competition when the "leader" may or may not be followed? The answer is, No, because the leader and the potential followers are all looking carefully at interfirm reactions.

In the courts, implicit collusion agreements have been called a *conscious parallelism of action*. A speech by the president of one company about the difficulty of holding prices against rising costs may be the tip-off to other firms in the oligopoly that the company is willing to go along on a price increase. Or an increase in the price of a relatively unimportant service or product may be a signal that the company thinks the overall price structure should change. If the other firms follow, the next step will be a change in a still more important price. If other firms do not go along, the erstwhile leader can retract the price increase without much embarrassment and without much harm to profits.

The incentives for firms in oligopolistic industries to act as a monopoly, to work out some *modus vivendi* for avoiding economic wars of all against all, are powerful. But business is business, and when one firm thinks it can win an advantage and get a larger share of the pie, it may try. Which path an oligopolistic firm will follow depends on a number of factors. We cannot be quantitatively precise about the influence of each factor, but we can describe the qualitative effects.

The number of firms in each oligopolistic industry, the size distribution of firms, and the similarity of their products will affect the degree of interdependence and its recognition. Five firms are more likely to feel intense interdependence than twenty firms. An industry of two large producers and twenty small firms is more likely to play follow-the-leader than an industry of twenty-two medium-sized firms. When the various firms' products are recognized as more or less identical (as, e.g., in the copper, aluminum, and steel industries), interdependence will be recognized as close. *The greater the interdependence and the greater its recognition, the more likely it is that the oligopoly will behave as if the industry were a monopoly and maximize joint profits.*

Relative stability of technology, costs, and demand is more likely to be conducive to consensus than is instability and uncertainty. But overt efforts at collusion tend to increase with falling demand or reduction in the rate of growth of demand, when economic life becomes more difficult for the oligopolist.

Barriers to entry make it easier for oligopolistic firms to preserve monopoly profits. If established firms have to fight new firms for profits, however, the economic warfare is likely to spread. Some entry barriers, such as patents, have already been discussed. Economies of large-scale production are a barrier, because a new firm must be large from its outset if it is to match the costs of already-existing firms. Established brand names and aggressive advertising are also barriers to entry. Recognition that barriers of this kind help to preserve monopoly profits will explain some otherwise puzzling behavior. For example, each of the tobacco companies in the United States has several brands of cigarettes which it advertises aggressively. Some of each company's advertising is counterproductive, because it offsets not only the advertising of rival companies but also some of its own advertising of different brands. All of its advertising works to prevent new firms from gaining a foothold, however, and serves as a barrier to entry.

A history of successful concerted action, even when forbidden and punished in an antitrust action, can make a conscious or unconscious parallelism of action more effective in the future. Explicit agreements, though long abandoned, may still mold expectations and influence behavior.

A special case: The kinked oligopoly demand schedule

It is tempting but not quite accurate to describe our analysis of oligopoly as an anything-can-happen type of analysis. It would be more accurate to call it a many-things-can-happen anlysis. Though general predictions about price and output in an oligopolistic industry are impossible, a detailed examination, using the tools of analysis of the firm, will usually permit one to evaluate just what is going on in terms of efficient use of resources.

Oligopolistic prices often tend to be relatively inflexible; they do not change very much in spite of changes in production costs. The hypothesis of the *kinked oligopoly demand* schedule has been advanced to explain this behavior. The essential notion is that the demand schedule faced by a single firm is more elastic for upward price movements than for downward movements. This is shown in Figure 25-13. The D_1D demand schedule would apply if the firm were to increase its price and no other firm followed suit.

Figure 25-13

HYPOTHESIS OF THE KINKED OLIGOPOLY DEMAND CURVE

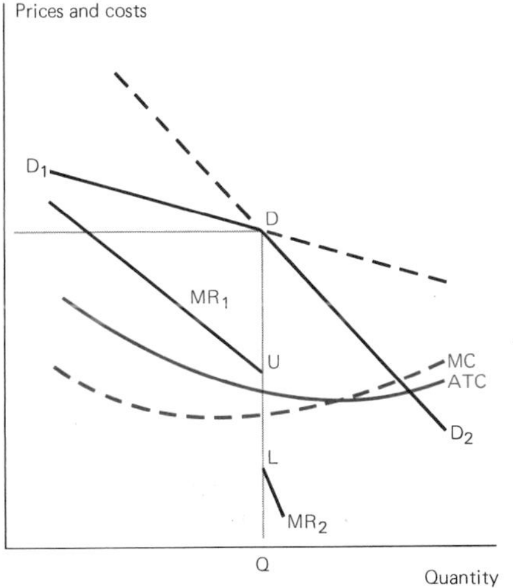

On the other hand, if the firm decreases its price and other firms match that decrease, its demand will be relatively inelastic, as shown by DD_2. The firm's sales will increase, but by so little relative to the price decrease that revenues will decline. Other firms will believe they have to follow a price decrease to avoid losing sales, so the original price cutter's sales do not rise by much. If these asymmetric conditions prevail for price increases and decreases, the firm's demand schedule will be D_1DD_2. With that kink in the demand schedule, the marginal revenue schedule associated with the demand curve also follows an unusual path. The marginal revenue associated with the D_1D portion of the demand schedule is MR_1-U; it slopes gradually downward as price and sales change smoothly along the assumed demand schedule D_1D. The marginal revenue schedule associated with the DD_2 portion of the oligopolist's demand is L-MR_2; it also slopes gradually, but it does not start at the level where MR_1-U leaves off! That is because the additional revenue from an additional sale is much lower at the right of the kink than at the left of the kink. The effective marginal revenue schedule for the firm is MR_1-U and L-MR_2, with the discontinuity UL at the quantity Q.

If the firm follows the profit-maximizing rule of producing where marginal revenue equals marginal cost, it will produce Q as long as marginal cost falls *anywhere* in the interval *UL*. So costs can shift up or down, with marginal cost shifting up to *U* or down to *L*, and output will not change. And, as long as output is at Q, the price charged by a profit-maximizing firm will stay at *p*. So this kind of kinked demand schedule helps explain why prices may change only infrequently in an oligopoly. It does *not* explain why the price is at *p* to begin with, however. For that explanation, we would have to undertake a detailed analysis of the industry. Nor should this special case be interpreted as a general prediction that all oligopoly prices will be sticky in the face of cost changes. Even in this case, if the marginal cost curve intersected the marginal revenue just at *U*, any further increase in costs *would* lead to price increases. In other oligopolistic situations, there could well be a substantial industry consensus on any price changes up or down provoked by cost changes.

Evaluation of alternative market structures

When students are first exposed to the economic analysis of alternative market structures, they tend to remember the polar cases of perfect competition and monopoly and forget the in-between types. Economists themselves may contribute to this tendency by spending so much time on the polar cases.

The polar cases of competition and monopoly *are* important. For some industries, the models we have presented are reasonably good approximations. The analysis is fairly straightforward and provides useful insights.

Far more important, however, and far more numerous are the in-between cases. Even so, we have no general theory that applies to all the types of imperfect competition. While we can treat the special cases of monopoly and monopolistic competition rigorously, we cannot enumerate the market patterns or provide a general analysis for all types of oligopoly. That does not mean that anything can happen and that we are helpless in understanding what does happen. It only means that when we try to explain the market structure and performance of an industry, we have to study that *particular* industry. We cannot give a standard diagnosis and write a standard prescription that will cure every industry's problems. Economics, like medicine, is both art and science. From the welter of events, the economist-artist tries to pick out the critical pieces of evidence; and with these, the economist-scientist carefully formulates and tests hypotheses.

If we recognize the limitations as well as the potentials of our tools of analysis of the firm, we will be better able to apply the theory. A disturbing question, however, must now be faced head on: How should we evaluate a private enterprise system in which imperfect markets are a more characteristic feature than are perfect markets? There are no easy answers, but the question is too important to be put aside.

In perfectly competitive industries, market forces push the firms to meet consumer demands with utmost efficiency. There is a built-in tendency for the price to the consumer of the goods he buys to become equal to their marginal cost in production. But these tendencies cannot be claimed for most industries. It is not that monopolists, oligopolists, etc., do not want to make profits as much as perfect competitors do. Rather, our analyses show that business firms with some degree of monopoly power will in their attempt to maximize profits *not* be led, "as if by an invisible hand," to promote the public interest. We can cite the following economic charges against monopoly power:

1. Output will be restricted to levels at which the value to the consumer of the goods he buys will be higher than the marginal cost of their production.
2. Monopolies and oligopolies can operate to preserve inefficient firms whose costs are higher than need be for the output produced.
3. The profits associated with monopoly power are one source of inequality in the distribution of income.
4. The factual evidence suggests that the protection afforded by some degree of monopolistic power may be a disincentive to technological progressiveness.

The following points can be made against these charges:

1. The relatively small number of firms in some industries may be the result of economies of scale and may lead to lower costs than could prevail in perfect competition.
2. Some advertising provides useful information, and product differentiation provides a variety of choice to consumers, but both tend to create monopoly power over prices.
3. Some degree of monopoly power, as in patent grants, may be a strong incentive to technological innovation.
4. The existence of only a few firms in an industry does not free the firms from the indirect competition of firms in other industries and other countries which try to develop substitutes that will attract purchasers who resent monopoly prices.

Though firms in imperfect markets may fall short when judged against the ideal performance of perfectly competitive firms, that does not mean that such markets do not "work" or that the industries are chaotic. Resources are allocated to production. Prices are set, and goods are sold. There may be a number of alternative sellers of not too dissimilar products, substantial responsiveness to consumer demands, technological progressiveness, and technical efficiency. *The imperfect competition may be "workable" though not optimal.*

How can we determine when competition, though restricted, is workably effective? Can monopolistic or oligopolistic power ever serve the public interest?

These are difficult questions to which there are no uniform and easy answers. The pros and cons listed above have different weights in each industry. And there is no point in disguising the fact that information is often so limited and the analysis often so difficult that professional economists of good will can have vigorous differences of opinion. In such circumstances, what, then, is the student or the citizen to do? Many decisions – perhaps most – have to be based on imperfect knowledge and understanding, and we can only do our best. One guideline can be kept in mind: The burden of proof is on those who defend monopoly or oligopoly power, for our analysis has shown that *such power has built-in threats to consumer interests without any sure guarantees of offsetting benefits.*

Summary

The prediction of a monopolistic firm's price and output behavior follows from the explanation of how such a firm should behave in order to maximize its profits. It would move toward the output at which its marginal revenue was equal to its marginal cost. Once at the output where $MR = MC$, the firm could make no change without reducing its profits. At that output point, however, the *price* of the product is different from the marginal cost. There is, moreover, no tendency for monopolistic firms to move toward the long-run least-cost production point. These are the fundamental disadvantages of monopoly, and they emerge whenever there is any degree of monopoly power. On the other hand, in industries with strongly increasing returns to large-scale production, the costs of a monopolist might be lower than those which could be achieved if competition were forced on the industry. The monopolist may also face competition from other products and services outside his industry. By making the demand schedule he faces more elastic, this competition restrains his power to raise prices.

Monopolistic competition is the name given to industries in which there is free entry, but in which each firm has some degree of monopoly power, owing to its ability to differentiate its product and reserve some share of the market for itself. The short-run result is qualitatively the same as for monopoly, since each firm will move toward its $MR = MC$ output. At this point, price will be greater than MC, as in pure monopoly. Quantitatively, all operations may be on a smaller scale, owing to free entry. The long-run result will certainly tend to be different from monopoly, since, with free entry, new firms will try to enter the industry as long as profits are being made. The entry of new firms will tend to eliminate profits, but will result in the creation of capacity which is not used at the rate that would minimize costs of production. The long-run equilibrium of the monopolistically competitive firm is on the side of its average total cost curve, not at its bottom.

Oligopoly is the name for the market structure in which there are so few firms in the industry that the decisions of one directly affect the profits of the others. It is impossible to predict in general the precise price and output tendencies of the oligopolistic industry. Output and price adjustments are more like the events in a poker game than the results of inexorable market mechanisms. All the firms acting together can maximize the industry's profits if they collaborate and act like monopolists. Each firm trying to get a larger piece of the profit pie is tempted to act somewhat independently, however, so the result may not be the same as would be achieved by joint action. There can, in fact, be competition in price, quality, and technology, but in general, the results are not those which would be achieved by perfect competition. The kinked oligopoly schedule, where demand is more elastic for an upward change in price and less inelastic for a downward change, is a special case of oligopoly which contributes to price rigidity.

Though the high standards of perfect competition may not be met, many industries may nonetheless be reasonably effective and efficient. This "workable" competition is achieved when the consumer can choose among alternative sellers, when prices are not fixed by explicit or implicit agreement, and when sellers respond to consumer demands.

Questions for discussion and review

1. Explain in your own words why the $MR = MC$ condition provides a good prediction of the output at which monopolistic firms will choose to operate.

2. Why isn't there a supply curve in a monopolized industry?

3. Is it true that a monopolist can and will charge whatever price he wants to charge and always make profits and get away with it? Explain your answer.

4. Discuss the following quotation: *However technically progressive they may be, monopolistic firms are always inefficient.*

5. If monopolistically competitive firms have a "little bit" of monopoly power, why aren't they always sure to make at least a little profit?

6. Discuss the following quotation: *The operation of firms in a*

monopolistically competitive industry is satisfactory neither to their owners, who are always fighting to remain profitable, nor to consumers, who always complain about their inefficiency.

7. If the operation of an oligopolistic industry has elements of a poker game, does that mean it is impossible to predict any of the characteristic features of the operation of the industry? Explain.

8. After surveying the economic disadvantages and possible benefits of monopoly power, give your own personal evaluation.

Concepts for review

Monopoly and monopolistic competition
Oligopoly
Product differentiation
Monopolistic inefficiency
Natural monopoly
Direct interdependence
Overt collusion and implicit agreements
Kinked demand schedule

26

Market structure and the requisites of public economic policy

In a mixed economy the fundamental economic questions are, for the most part, resolved by private decisions mediated through markets. Unless the markets are self-regulating to the satisfaction of the community as a whole, public economic policy is required to influence and regulate private decision making. This chapter takes up the questions of the design of such public economic policy: What type of market structure and performance should be maintained? The Appendix to the chapter takes up the subject of the regulation of public utility rates.

It is easy to be for virtue (competition) and against sin (monopoly) when these are abstract market qualities. But, to repeat, the virtues and sins found in the theoretical models are not exactly matched in the market structures of the complex world of business practices. Moreover, after one has decided what to be for and against, we must still find ways to put our ideals into practice. Before taking up the design of public economic policy, we must examine some special problems of market performance.

Market structure and sick industries

One set of economic symptoms often associated with an industry marked by ease of entry and a number of relatively small firms is the so-called *sick industry* syndrome. In such an industry, profits or the returns to one or more of the resource inputs have fallen below the normal or going rate. This phenomenon is not an exclusive disease of competition. It is also seen in monopolistically competitive industries. The sick industry syndrome is not simply a characteristic of a particular kind of market structure. Rather, it reflects a peculiar lack of responsiveness to economic incentives. This kind of negative behavior may be found in a variety of markets. We realize, therefore, that a sociology, as well as an economics, of industry performance must sometimes be called upon to explain conditions.

The fishing industry of New England, for example, is largely an industry of small-scale owner-operators of fishing boats producing a standard fish commodity. In these respects, it is not too far from the competitive norm. Yet it has continued to use an outmoded side trawling technology long after the stern trawling methods of European vessels have been proved superior. It uses wasteful and inefficient pitchforking methods for unloading. It has been unable to attract young workers, and more than two-thirds of the labor force in the Boston fishing fleet are over fifty years of age.

This may be a declining industry in which price is less than average total cost but greater than average variable costs. New investment is not warranted, but the existing capital might as well be used until it is worn out. Likewise the old labor force may stay with it for lack of other skills. On the other hand, evidence shows that new techniques could make the industry profitable. Why aren't they used? Perhaps because the industry operates in an imperfect capital market that will not finance this kind of small-scale enterprise. Or perhaps the explanation lies in the sociological factors that determine the attitudes of the shipowners and the labor force.

Small-scale garment manufacturing presents a somewhat different case of industry sickness. There are many relatively small and unprofitable firms, yet new firms enter all the time and, in general, remain small and unprofitable or even collapse. This is an industry where the product is differentiated. It corresponds more to monopolistic than to perfect competition. The new producers hope to strike it rich with different and better styling, rather than through efficient organization and lower-cost production. As a result, free entry does not lead to efficiency, but to overcrowding and waste, as each firm has some overcapacity. Prices tend to move toward unit costs – not at the point of lowest unit costs – but on the upward-sloping side of the unit cost curve, as shown in Figure 25-10 in the preceding chapter.

Another example is the railroad industry. This is an industry of large-sized firms. On the whole, but with exceptions, it has been a rather depressed sector, especially the eastern railroads. Recently it began to show signs of recovery, but was hit hard by the general slowdown of 1969 and 1970. Railroad technology has been relatively static for many years and railroad management unaggressive in seeking out business. In the face of vigorous competition from airlines and the trucking industry, the railroads lost revenue traffic on a large scale. Reorganization for more efficient use of facilities, new techniques for operating and coordinating trains, and the development of "piggy back" hauling of truck trailers for long-distance shipments have begun to revive the rail freight portion. Passenger traffic is still in the doldrums, though again new technologies and reorganizations hold some promise.

Advertising and nonprice competition

The economic analysis of firms and industries emphasizes the importance of price competition. But "nonprice" competition, is such a widespread and important feature of modern economic life that it deserves a closer look. Broadly defined, nonprice competition is effected through advertising and "product policy."

Nonprice competition has no role in perfectly competitive industries. All the products are homogeneous. Perfect competitors would like to be able to differentiate their products and achieve some control over price. But they cannot. Only informative advertising has a role in perfect competition.

Advertising designed to achieve some degree of control over at least a part of the total market by creating product differentiation is an important form of nonprice competition. Firms with monopoly power use advertising to try to shift their demand schedules and make it more difficult for new firms to enter and obtain a share of the market. Firms with a degree of monopoly power may develop a variety of somewhat differentiated products; in this way, they cover a wider portion of the market, deter the entry of potential competitors, and put pressure on existing competitors.

In oligopolistic industries, firms may try to avoid direct price competition for fear of setting off price wars which end in mutual disaster. Nonprice competition is a more diffuse kind of attack, and, therefore, more likely to evoke a diffuse response from rival firms.

In monopolistically competitive industries, nonprice competition is the only way a firm can stave off the inexorable pressures that new entries place on its demand curve. By advertising and product differentiation, the monopolistic competitor tries to shift his demand schedule or change its slope.

We can now see why firms are willing to incur the costs of nonprice competition rather than use the funds to expand or streamline productive activities.

Price competition is relatively straightforward. The competitive issue is a single number: the price. Nonprice competition stresses qualities, some of which cannot be compared or measured. That is part of what makes nonprice competition attractive to businesses. For consumers, however, it makes life more difficult, because, in general, they lack the means and the expertise to resolve conflicting product claims.

Nonprice competition is not all bad. As was pointed out in Chapter 21, some advertising does perform a service. Every once in a while there is an amusing TV commercial, and, besides, what pays for television programs anyway? A wide variety of products means that consumers have a wide range to choose from. Technological research to develop or modify new products has brought many useful improvements. These achievements cannot be ignored.

But do we really need all the consumer choice offered by thousands of different kinds of breakfast cereals, soaps, and soups? This is not an idle question, for product differentiation has a cost. Three outstanding economists estimated that, from 1949 to 1960, annual model changeovers in American automobiles added a total *extra* cost of about $5 billion per year, or about $700 on the average car purchase price. Were new styling and extra horsepower and other features of the changeovers worth the cost to the consumers? Well, we paid for them. But we did not have much choice about it either.

Questions about the value to consumers of nonprice competition are difficult. We have no *general* answers, only general *pros* and *cons*. That does not mean there are *never* any answers. Close study of a particular case will lead to conclusions for that case.

The uses and abuses of monopoly power

A firm can exercise some degree of monopoly power even when, strictly speaking, it is not the only source of a particular product. When there is monopoly power, prices are relatively high. High in relation to what? Not necessarily in relation to what they would be if there were competition. Competitive firms might not be able to develop the technology or reach the scale of operations necessary to produce at the low absolute costs achieved by a large firm with some monopoly power. But even so, the prices of the firm with monopoly power will be *relatively* high – relative to the opportunity cost of the resources used in production. That opportunity cost is the marginal cost of the firm's output. (If any doubt on this point remains, a review of Chaps. 22 and 25 would be in order.) If a firm can eliminate and block competition, it can raise its price above what it would be if there were rival sellers. These effects of monopoly are not necessarily redeemed by technical change and economies of scale.

One common and widespread characteristic of monopoly power is *price discrimination*. Price discrimination exists when different prices are charged to different buyers and the price differences are not due to actual cost differences in supplying the buyers. Our analysis indicates that such differentials could not exist in a competitive industry.

Some examples will illustrate the ubiquity and significance of this market tactic:

At movies and concerts, it is common to find lower admission prices charged for children than for adults. Yet there is little reason to believe that the costs of admitting children are lower. In fact the reverse is often true.

Doctors and dentists may have a sliding scale of fees, charging wealthy patients more than poorer ones for the same treatment.

Alcoa at one time sold aluminum cable for electrical power transmission *at a lower price* than it sold the aluminum ingot from which the cable was made.

Discounts given for purchases in large quantity may be due to lower costs in production or delivery of larger orders, but they may also reflect price discrimination against small buyers.

What is the rationale and significance of price discrimination? In effect, the price-discriminating firm divides its total market into categories, each one of which has a different demand elasticity. To do this successfully, the firm must (1) exercise monopoly power in controlling the supply to the different segments of the market, and (2) be able, via monopoly power or other constraints, to prevent transactions among the market segments. If trade among the various segments flowed freely, prices would tend to be equalized. By separating the markets, the price discriminator is able to take advantage of the particular demand characteristics of each of the market segments. Without going into detail, we can suggest why price discrimination might pull in more profits. Suppose there are just two market segments: one with a quite inelastic demand and the other with a relatively elastic demand. If the price to the inelastic demand segment is pushed up, sales will not fall proportionately, and there will thus be an increase in revenues. If the price to the relatively elastic demand segment is reduced a little, revenues there will fall only slightly, or they may increase, owing to a larger volume of sales. The shrewd price discriminator can find a combination — a price increase in the first sector and a price decrease in the second — which will permit him to make higher profits than if he sold at the same price to both sectors.

Discrimination is a bad word, but is its odious reputation always deserved when practiced with prices?

When the doctor discriminates and raises his prices to his wealthy patients, they lose some consumer's surplus, i.e., some satisfaction over and above what they pay for. On the other hand, the poorer patients pay less for the same services and have more consumer's surplus. Is the net effect better or worse than it would be if the doctor did not discriminate? And if you trust doctors to discriminate, do you trust all sellers?

Retired persons living in a housing development for the elderly cannot walk far for their groceries. A supermarket chain that takes advantage of that source of demand inelasticity and raises its prices in its neighborhood store will be subtracting from total welfare.

Pharmacies sell medicines at different prices. If a product is asked for by its trade name, it costs less than when ordered by its scientific name on a prescription. What do you think of that price discrimination?

Price discrimination may be used to create monopoly power by eliminating rivals or reducing their access to part of the market. A trucking firm may give rebates to customers who agree to use its services exclusively for intercity haulage. Or a chemical firm may sell pigments at lower prices to a paint company which buys other supplies from it. The customer paying the higher price is buying the commodity at more than its opportunity cost (marginal cost) of production. The customer paying the lower price may even be able to buy at less than marginal cost of production. Both practices represent an inefficient use of resources.

Technological progressiveness, firm size, and industrial concentration

Technological progressiveness is one of the special advantages often claimed for large firms – and, by implication, for industries with a high degree of concentration. Actually our understanding of many aspects of research and development (R and D) is quite limited. The best we can do is look hard at the facts. First, R and D activities are not spread evenly across all sectors of the economy. As shown in Table 26-1, they are concentrated in a relatively few industries, with the aircraft and missiles and electronics and electrical equipment industries leading the list. The overwhelming part of the R and D in these industries is done on government defense contracts. Relatively little is being done in industries producing food products and general metal fabrication, which are neither highly concentrated nor dominated by large firms. On the other hand, there is relatively little R and D in the petroleum and steel industries, which are highly concentrated.

The proportion of the labor force devoted to R and D is often smaller in giant firms than in somewhat smaller firms. Whether or not the largest firms innovate more effectively is not known precisely but the available evidence does not favor the largest firms. Their patents cost more in terms of dollar expenditure on R and D. In addition the largest firms use fewer of their patents. In some industries, such as petroleum and coal, the largest firms have often accounted for a larger share of major innovations than their share of the market. But the reverse is true in other industries, such as steel and chemicals.

A good deal of the technological progressiveness of large firms is based on inventions which originate outside the firms and which the firms buy or lease. Many important innovations are the work of individual inventors and small firms. A widely accepted bit of folklore states that very large firms are the special vehicles and

Table 26-1

FEDERAL AND COMPANY FUNDS FOR RESEARCH AND DEVELOPMENT, BY INDUSTRY (MILLIONS OF DOLLARS)

Industry	1958			1968		
	Federal	*Private*	*Total*	*Federal*	*Private*	*Total*
Aircraft and missiles	2,276	333	2,609	4,503	1,148	5,651
Electrical equipment and communication	1,337	632	1,969	2,272	1,766	4,038
Chemicals and allied products	126	666	792	200	1,440	1,640
Machinery	343	438	781	421	1,198	1,619
Motor vehicle and other transportation equipment	296	560	856	414	1,116	1,530
Petroleum refining and extraction	12	234	246	75	463	538
Professional and scientific instruments	137	157	294	214	376	590
Food and kindred products	6	77	83	1	172	173
Fabricated metal products	57	105	162	11	162	173
All other industries	374	781	1,155	450	1,033	1,483
Total, all industries	4,964	3,983	8,947	8,561	8,874	17,435

Source: National Science Foundation.

agents of technological change in the economy. They have been both praised and condemned for this, depending on whether technological change is regarded as generally desirable. The folklore is misleading, however. One cannot make a case for or against the largest firms on the basis of the argument that they are technologically the most progressive.

Managerial Capitalism and The New Industrial State

One branch of the economic mainstream rearranges and gives different emphasis to the elements of the analysis of market structure and behavior which has been presented above — and adds a few new ideas. This is the creed now associated with the names of John Kenneth Galbraith of Harvard as its high priest, Robin Marris of

Cambridge, England, as its chief minister, and Adolf Berle and Gardiner C. Means as its ancient patriarchs.[1] Only Galbraith has made the best-seller list, and he is, therefore, the most convenient source and target.

According to Galbraith, the economy is divided into two quite different sectors. One is the province of "small and traditional proprietors" governed by market competition. The other, the Industrial System, is "the heartland of the modern economy" and "the world of the few hundred technically dynamic, massively capitalized and highly organized corporations." To understand the operation of the heartland, one must abandon the "accepted sequence" of economic analysis, which starts with the assumption of free consumer choice to which producers respond. Instead, one must recognize a "Revised Sequence," which starts with the motivations of the Technostructure. This is the business bureaucracy composed of technical and managerial specialists who participate in the group decision making that characterizes modern corporations. In the Revised Sequence,

> The mature corporation has readily at hand the means for controlling the prices at which it sells as well as those at which it buys. Similarly, it has means for managing what the consumer buys at the prices which it controls. This control and management is required by planning. The planning proceeds from use of technology and capital, the commitment of time that these require and the diminished effectiveness of the market for specialized technical products and skills (page 222).

All this is consistent with the dominant motivations of the members of the Technostructure in their role as managers. Their motivations, according to Galbraith, are, first, to help the corporation survive, and, second, to help it grow.

In colorful and persuasive language, with appropriate quotations from economists who have seen glimpses of the promised land, Galbraith has provided a richly detailed view of the system within which he claims we live. Should we believe it?

Though Galbraith has tried to differentiate his own product, it is in many ways not so dissimilar from aspects of the "accepted sequence." It is easy to ridicule the polar cases of perfect competition and monopoly, though the fundamental insights they provide cannot be denied. The patterns of differentiated oligopoly, though described in different words in Chapter 25, are closer to the Galbraithian vision. It is, however, not really important for serious scholars and students of the economy to decide whether or not

[1] When Berle and Means wrote *The Modern Corporation and Private Property*, Commerce Clearing House, Inc., New York, 1932, it was taken seriously as an important, realistic qualification to much of economic analysis. Marris, in *Managerial Capitalism*, The Free Press of Glencoe, New York, 1964, and Galbraith, in *The New Industrial State*, Houghton Mifflin Company, Boston, 1967, have attempted to make the qualification into a system.

Galbraith is the original prophet. The critical issue is whether his vision is correct. Let us examine some of the key elements of the Revised Sequence.

On the existence and power of the Technostructure. The staff and managerial groups of business have certainly expanded greatly. The management groups in many corporations have only an insignificant share of ownership, as Galbraith and others point out. On the other hand, numerous managerial groups have been turned out by stockholders who found their performance inept. When corporate weakness creates a substantial chance of takeover, other management groups are usually waiting on the sidelines to do the job.

On the motivation of business managers. Short-run maximization of profits that does not take future possibilities into account is never rational. Yet corporations that do not survive the short run have no future. Is there a difference between profit maximization over a long horizon and growth maximization? Possibly, but not necessarily. No doubt growth in sales can be traded off against increased profits by creating unprofitable ventures in which to increase sales. But unprofitable ventures, or even ventures which are profitable but not so much as others, reduce the potential rate of growth: They eat up the internal funds for financing new ventures. Low profitability also reduces the ease of securing bank loans and increases their cost. These qualifications do not demonstrate that Galbraith is, on balance, incorrect. It will require a good deal more research to determine that. Rather the logic of the qualifications is that, even if he is correct, the difference between profit maximization and growth maximization may be minor. But more research will be required to evaluate that, too.

On the pervasiveness of planning and control by modern corporations. Although Galbraith asserts that modern corporations achieve their goal of autonomy from market forces, he is widely challenged by other careful investigators. Many economists will agree that perfect competition does not rule the firm in many markets. But they will not go to the other extreme and argue that market forces generally have little or no influence on the modern corporation. One can cite the management-labor conflicts, which indicate neither perfect competition nor complete control of the labor market by the corporation. One can also cite the competition of resource inputs, such as fuel and coal, which indicate lack of market control.

On the output side, it would be pointless to deny the magnitude and social impact of advertising. But it is far from clear that advertising creates the degree of control that Galbraith claims. For some more or less standard products, such as steel, copper, aluminum, and industrial fuels, advertising is simply irrelevant. Of course, other market-controlling arrangements have existed in some of those markets, but while they restrain intraindustry competition, they do not limit competition across industries.

The issue is not whether modern businesses "plan," as Galbraith argues they do. The exercise of foresight is a human condition. The real question is whether modern businesses "control." Although Galbraith has won many followers to his party, the opposition remains vigorous and vocal.

The debate on the Galbraithian propositions continues to be a heated one, and the issues, fundamental as they are, are not yet resolved. Nor will they be without much more careful investigation. Yet there can be no doubt of the significance of those issues. This can be seen from the nature of some of Galbraith's predictions: a tendency toward convergence of the United States and Soviet societies; the merging of the private (industrial) and government (bureaucratic) technostructures; an increasing degree of management of economic wants, education, and social morality by the industrial system. Against these predictions of the evolution of the industrial system, Galbraith raises the possibility that the intellectual and scientific community will subordinate economic goals to aesthetic goals and the industrial system to larger social purposes. These are social questions on the grandest scale.

Public policy for the maintenance of competition

Public hostility to monopoly has an old tradition in the common law. Yet it was not until 1890 after a period of exposés of price-fixing and market-sharing agreements and a wave of mergers and "trust" formations that this hostility was embodied in federal legislation in the Sherman Antitrust Act.[2] This law is still the fundamental statement of policy on the maintenance of competition. It applies to interstate commerce, but has its counterpart in state laws on intrastate commerce. Its words are brief but ringing:

> Every contract, combination in the form of trust or otherwise, or conspiracy in restraint of trade or commerce . . . is hereby declared to be illegal.
>
> . . .
>
> Every person who shall monopolize or attempt to monopolize or combine or conspire . . . to monopolize . . . shall be deemed guilty . . . .[3]

The law's significance has rung less clear.

[2] Trusts were formed when corporate stock was turned over to a group of trustees in exchange for trust certificates. The trustees could then run the companies in such a way as to exercise whatever market control the joint operation created. By the end of the century, this device was largely replaced by the corporate "holding company" which exercised control of other corporations by outright ownership of their shares.

[3] But only of a misdemeanor. Yet the law made monopolization illegal and, therefore, permitted the government to act to eliminate it and provide for triple damages by injured parties.

The Sherman Act itself did not define what constituted "restraint of trade" or monopolies, and for some years the federal courts took a narrow view of what the law prohibited. Application of the Sherman Act has, in fact, proceeded in cycles of activity and passivity depending on: (1) the inclination of the President and his Attorney General to be vigorous or permissive in fighting monopoly power, (2) the funds provided by Congress for the Antitrust Division of the Justice Department, and (3) the attitude of the Supreme Court toward the meaning of the law.

After the turn of the century, there were a number of successful antitrust prosecutions. The main targets were such large and obvious combines as the American Tobacco Company and the Standard Oil Company. At the height of their power, these two firms controlled 93 percent and 85 percent of their respective markets. In the course of finding these firms guilty, however, the Supreme Court enunciated the famous "rule of reason." The Court stated that it was not the possession of monopoly power that was illegal, but rather its acquisition by predatory and coercive attacks on rivals. Thus government suits against the American Can Company (90 percent of tin cans) and International Harvester (65 percent of farm machinery) were disallowed. The Court held that their actions did not represent overt and "unreasonable" restraints of trade. In the famous U.S. Steel case, the Supreme Court held that "the law does not make mere size an offense or the existence of unexerted power an offense." Owing to the rule of reason doctrine and the indulgent attitude toward business after World War I, antimonopoly actions under the Sherman Act were relatively limited during the 1920s and early 1930s.

The legal basis for government action to maintain competition was strengthened in 1914 with the passage of the Clayton Antitrust Act and the Federal Trade Commission Act. The former prohibited specific business practices which tend to lessen competition – price discrimination, exclusive-dealing contracts, acquisition of the corporate stock of competitors. The latter act established the Federal Trade Commission (FTC), gave it broad investigatory powers, and declared "unfair methods of competition . . . unlawful." The Commission itself was to decide what was unfair. In 1938, the Wheeler-Lea Act specifically outlawed "deceptive" business practices so that the FTC could move against misrepresentation in advertising.

Not until the late 1930s were these acts vigorously enforced. A new cycle of antimonopoly activity began in 1938 when Franklin D. Roosevelt appointed Thurman Arnold to head the Antitrust Division. The most significant suits of this period were not fully resolved until after World War II. Since then, each President has supported a large and vigorous Antitrust Division.

In their interpretation of the antitrust laws, the courts have increasingly focused on the existence of monopoly power and given less and less weight to how it was achieved. This is the direction that economic analysis indicates is important.

In the Alcoa case, started before World War II and decided in 1945, the company was declared in violation of the Sherman Act. No aggressive monopolizing practices were demonstrated, but monopoly power was simply inferred from its preeminent market position. The U.S. Shoe Machinery Company has been forced to divest itself of important divisions and to sell machines it once only leased to users. Du Pont was forced to divest itself of a 23 percent interest in General Motors which it had held since 1922.

The Clayton Act has been used against competition-lessening practices even when the firms involved had only a small share of the market. The Celler-Kefauver Act of 1950 strengthened the Clayton Act. It extended the government's power to deal with mergers created by outright purchase of assets if the effect of such mergers would be "substantially to lessen competition or tend to create a monopoly." Using this weapon, the government is able to prevent horizontal merger – of companies in the same stage of production – even when they monopolize only a small part of the market. For example, Bethlehem Steel was not permitted to acquire Youngstown Sheet and Tube. Vertical mergers – of companies at successive stages of production and sale – have also been blocked. Brown Shoe manufacturing, for example, was forced to divest itself of Kinney, a retail shoe store chain. The rationale here was the preservation of independent retailers and producers against the market strength of vertically integrated firms.

"Conglomerate" mergers – of firms in quite different industries – are the most spectacular recent manifestation of the combination movement. These mergers led to the rapid formation of new giants during the 1960s. But in 1967 the Supreme Court checked the movement when it forced Procter & Gamble to divest itself of Clorox. The Court argued that, by its very size, Procter & Gamble, which makes soap and detergents, reduced competition when it entered the household bleach industry in which Clorox already had a major share. Yet, on the whole, public policy has dealt gingerly with conglomerate mergers, largely because their effects on market performance are often far from clear.

The government has also moved against trade practices that interfere with competition but do not change the number of firms. During the 1960s it successfully challenged price-setting conspiracies among electric equipment manufacturers, asphalt producers, rubber hose and plastic pipe makers, and others.

Government policies to restrain competition

Not all public policy has been directed toward preserving competition. The Robinson-Patman Act of 1936 was drafted by the Wholesale Grocers' Association with the object of protecting small retailers. It forbade quantity discounts that lessened competition *and* harmed competitors. The two are not necessarily the same: Effective competition may require that some firms be harmed. The law also tried to prevent other forms of price concessions. Its effect has been uneven. While eliminating some monopolistic pricing practices, it has probably also reduced the scope of price competition.

Many states have laws against "unfair practices." Such laws prohibit a retailer from selling goods below cost — as "loss leaders" which attract customers into the store. And most states have passed resale price-maintenance laws, which permit manufacturers and retailers to agree on minimum prices. The Miller-Tydings Act of 1937 exempted such agreements from the federal antitrust laws. The intent of this act also was to preserve retail distributors and maintain competition. The competition of such small distributors, however, is often what we have called monopolistic competition. The small retailer differentiates his services by means of his location, credit terms, and store-to-home delivery. Frequently the costs of these services make it impossible for him to match the economies of large self-service stores.

Fair trade and resale price maintenance are now, for the most part, dead letters. Manufacturers can enforce such agreements only on a limited range of items that have achieved unique market positions. Retailers have found that the laws are no protection against aggressive competition.

There are, however, other important exemptions from the antitrust laws:

1. Labor unions are exempt except when they form restrictive agreements with nonlabor groups.
2. Agricultural cooperatives and marketing organizations are, by and large, exempt.
3. Export associations which engage in price fixing in trade abroad are exempt.

The dilemmas of policy to maintain competition: Market structure versus performance

One line of thought argues that government policy to maintain competition has not been and cannot be effective. Looking at the whole sweep of antitrust legislation, we find that its enforcement has been spasmodic and in some cases perhaps inequitable. Yet if we focus on the last twenty-five years, a more encouraging picture emerges. Antitrust action has been more vigorous and the courts' interpretations have been broader.

It is difficult to establish a cause and effect relationship between the government's stance at different times and the pattern of growth of monopoly power. But the evidence seems to show that, on balance, concentration in the United States economy as a

Table 26-2

AVERAGE CONCENTRATION RATIOS (SHARE OF TOTAL SALES OF FOUR LARGEST FIRMS)

Industry	1 *1901*	2 *1947*	3 *1947*	4 *1954*	5 *1958*	6 *1967*
Food and kindred products	39.1	18.8	34.9	33.8	32.6	34.2
Tobacco manufactures	49.9	77.7	76.2	73.4	74.1	76.8
Textile mill products	20.3	9.0	24.3	26.5	29.2	33.8
Apparel and related products	–	2.2	12.6	13.0	13.4	19.0
Lumber and wood products	0.5	2.0	11.2	10.8	12.8	15.9
Furniture and fixtures	–	8.1	21.9	20.3	19.0	18.6
Pulp, paper, and products	71.0	1.6	21.2	24.8	25.9	31.2
Printing and publishing	1.0	0.0	19.7	17.7	17.6	18.8
Chemicals and related products	24.3	33.7	51.0	48.6	45.7	41.5
Petroleum and coal products	46.8	13.6	39.5	36.6	31.6	32.8
Rubber products	100.0	59.9	58.6	54.1	51.3	22.0
Leather and leather products	26.3	0.0	26.2	26.4	25.0	25.6
Stone, clay, and glass products	13.3	43.9	43.4	46.4	40.3	39.9
Primary metal products	45.7	21.0	43.8	49.5	46.8	42.4
Fabricated metal products	–	8.4	25.3	26.1	25.5	25.5
Machinery, except electrical	41.4	18.5	38.0	33.2	35.5	34.1
Electrical machinery	–	53.2	54.1	48.2	46.9	46.6
Transportation equipment	57.3	84.2	54.4	58.7	61.3	63.8
Instruments and related products	–	45.0	45.3	47.4	47.8	48.9
Miscellaneous manufactures	2.7	21.2	34.9	16.1	22.6	27.5
Total, all industries	32.9	24.0	35.3	36.9	37.0	37.7

Note: In calculating the ratios for a large industry made up of subindustries producing a variety of products, one must strike an average. The average should reflect the relative size of the subindustries, so each subindustry's concentration ratio is "weighted" by its contribution to national income. That was done for columns 3, 4, 5, and 6. Because of incomplete data for 1901, column 1 is calculated with weights which are the share of the total valued added in the industry produced by firms with concentration ratios above 50 percent. Column 2 was calculated the same way to have a comparable figure for a later date. There are slight differences from year to year in the makeup of each industry.

Source: Morris A. Adelman, "Monopoly and Concentration: Comparisons in Time and Space," *Essays in Honour of Marco Fanno,* CEDAM, Padua, 1966.

whole has not been increasing by very much, if at all, during this century. Table 26-2 presents the average concentration ratios by major industry for four years since 1901. Columns 1 and 2, which are prepared on a comparable basis, suggest that overall concentration actually fell substantially from 1901 to 1947. Columns 3, 4, 5, and 6 are calculated on a basis different from columns 1 and 2. They show that there may have been a slow and slight increase in overall concentration from 1947 to 1967. It is clear that in a number of industries concentration has declined. Look at what has been happening in the rubber industry, for example. There have been cross currents over time in other industries, such as lumber and nonelectrical machinery. In industries which were originally dominated by small-scale handicraft producers, such as apparel and furniture, and in textiles and lumber, there has been a steady trend toward greater concentration. This is also true in the transportation equipment industry, with big firms producing trucks and autos, aircraft, and railroad equipment.

The fundamental question is, What policy should the government follow in the future with respect to antitrust? Some economists focus on the features of market structure: the number of firms, their relative importance in the market, and the existence of collusive agreements. These economists believe that if enforcement of the antitrust laws centered on preserving competitive industrial structures, that would go as far as is possible in maintaining efficient performance.

Other economists put performance itself at the center of the stage and say the courts should worry less about how firms achieve it. The consumer, they believe, may benefit more from the competition of a half dozen large supermarkets than from 200 small grocery stores. These economists deplore, for example, the success of the government suit against A & P in 1954. That suit forced the company to divest itself of a buying subsidiary, in spite of evidence that efficient buying practices of the subsidiary were a source of A & P's efficiency and relatively low prices. Those economists concerned with performance emphasize the potential advantages of such large-scale operation and the possibility of effective though not perfect competition among a relatively few firms.

Can the courts enforce standards of performance? Performance is, necessarily, more vague than a measure of the share of the market. In the history of antitrust, narrow criteria of the mere existence of monopolizing actions as grounds for conviction have given way to a broader look at the prevalence of monopoly power whatever its source. There is probably room for criteria of both structure and performance. Rather than automatically applying formulas, the courts, lawyers, and economists will have to delve deeply into each case to determine what is in the public interest.

It can be noted that supporters of the New Industrial State would argue that the antitrust laws are an anachronism. Firms not only control prices now, but they *should* do so, because that is one means of effective planning—which, it is argued, also brings the benefits of modern production.

An examination of the regulatory commissions

In certain types of industries, state and federal commissions exercise regulatory powers over prices and conditions of sale. The industries so regulated are characterized by natural monopoly or contain only a few firms or have special features that justify a direct public interest. The state commissions, for the most part, regulate only public utilities: electricity, gas, telephone, and, occasionally, railroads. There are four such federal regulatory commissions: The Interstate Commerce Commission (ICC), which was the first to be established, regulates railroad rates and service, interstate trucking firms, interstate petroleum pipelines, and some kinds of shipping. The Federal Power Commission (FPC) regulates the business of the interstate transmission of natural gas through pipelines and the interstate transmission of electrical energy. The Federal Communications Commission (FCC) controls the allocation of broadcasting channels and has some power over the radio and television industry's use of its broadcast time. It also regulates interstate telephone and telegraph rates and service. The Civil Aeronautics Board (CAB) controls the fares and allocates routes and services of domestic airlines.[4]

The objective of commission regulation of natural monopolies is supposedly to secure a satisfactory level of service without permitting monopoly profits. Direct regulation is also intended to ensure efficiency and prevent discrimination among customers. The rationale for regulation by the federal commissions is to avoid "chaotic competition," to maintain high standards of safety, and to ensure the use of natural "resources," such as broadcast channels and airspace, in the public interest.

Consumer dissatisfaction with both state and federal regulatory commissions has become quite vocal. Dissatisfaction at the state level has several sources. Evidence in some cases and over some periods shows that the profit rates of local utilities have been relatively high. A comparison of regulated and nonregulated utilities indicates that the former have not, on the average, had either lower costs or lower prices. With some justification, critics of the state commissions charge that they have become partisans of the industries they regulate rather than impartial supervisors. In fairness to the state commissions, it should be pointed out that they

[4] There are other federal regulatory agencies which exercise some control over segments of private industry. These include the Securities and Exchange Commission, the Federal Maritime Board, and the Department of Agriculture.

have often had to work under grave handicaps. In general, they have been underfinanced by the state legislatures. Their rate setting has, until relatively recently, been conducted under detailed judicial review, and they have often faced the frustrating problem of attempting the local regulation of operations that are essentially interstate. But more fundamentally, the problem is that the state commissions can regulate prices but not costs. The guarantee of a fixed return on investment means that the utility's incentive to operate efficiently and minimize costs is reduced if not eliminated.

Compared with the state commissions, the federal regulatory commissions have a wider scope and handle even more complex problems, largely because they are not confined to natural monopolies. Often two or more railroads and many trucking firms serving the same area come under ICC regulation. Several airlines may be assigned to essentially the same route by the CAB. A number of radio and television stations broadcast in most areas, all under the regulation of the FCC.

Consider the following classic "weak and strong road" problem. Two railroads carry freight between the same two cities. Railroad A, with an aggressive management and modern techniques, has lowered its costs. Railroad B, using older equipment and less efficient methods, has higher costs. The ICC is supposed to set a rate which yields a "fair return on fair value." A single rate for both railroads that permits A a fair return might well be too low to permit B to stay in business. A single rate for both that permits B to earn a fair return on its investment will lead to relatively high profits for A. It would also completely eliminate any incentive for shippers to use the railroad with lower costs, and that means there would be a waste of resources. If there were two rates – a lower rate for A than for B – the former would capture all of the freight business.

What is the answer to the problem? There is none – not within the present structure and mode of operation of the regulatory commissions. Can one imagine ways of forcing the inefficient railroad to become efficient? That would call for direct interference by government, perhaps to replace one management with another. It might also call call for government loans to the weak railroad. These things are not impossible, but they would require an approach that is not at the present time embodied in the commission structure.

Consider another type of regulatory problem, which might be called the "unsatisfied minority" problem. Suppose there are two television stations in a broadcast area. From a viewer survey, the stations learn that 80 percent of their audience rate "adult westerns" highest on their preference list while 20 percent prefer "cultural programs." The two competing stations can each hope to capture 40 percent of the market if they show adult westerns. Neither station has any incentive to show cultural programs, and the minority which prefers them gets less of the "product" than its relative proportion in the audience would warrant.

What is the answer to this problem? Again, there is none within the present mode of operation of the FCC.

Let us be clear about the reasons these problems and many similar ones have not been resolved. It is not that the commissioners and their staffs are lethargic, venal, or stupid. They are, on the whole, vigorous, honest, and well qualified. The problems have their source in the inappropriateness of the standards that are applied and in the regulatory methods that are used. The commissions are agents, not the source of new concepts for regulation. New concepts, including the possibility of abandoning some types of regulation, need to be provided for the commissions; without them, problems such as those described cannot be resolved satisfactorily. This area of public economic policy abounds with unsettled issues. There are no markets to resolve them, and the government-political machinery has not been working well.

Summary

Market structures that are not self-regulating to the satisfaction of the larger community must be regulated by public economic policy.

Sick industries are usually characterized by a number of relatively small firms operating at prices which do not cover costs. In effect, the returns to one or more of the factors of production are below the going rate. For reasons that may be better explained by sociology than economics, the resources do not move away from the industry, and the firms in the industry do not adopt technical improvements that might raise profits.

Nonprice competition refers to methods by which firms try to increase their market share without cutting prices, for example, by advertising, product differentiation, and services. These methods are attractive to firms as means of gaining consumer loyalties and some degree of monopoly power to affect price. Monopolists use the methods to establish barriers to the entry of new firms. Nonprice competition appeals to oligopolists as a more diffuse and less risky type of competition than direct assault by price changes. Product competition, however, has the virtue of appealing to and satisfying consumer demands for variety in consumption and is a stimulus to product innovation.

Price discrimination is the charging of different prices to different consumers even though the different sales involve no cost differences. Such discrimination is evidence of monopoly power, as it could not exist under competitive conditions. Price discrimination usually leads to economic inefficiency, because the same good with the same production costs is sold at two or more different prices. But it may result in higher output and some gains, as well as losses, in consumer satisfaction.

Some evidence suggests that market structure has an effect on the technical progressiveness of an industry. Yet it is not the largest firms that have been most effective in innovation, but rather those which are slightly smaller. Even small firms and individual inventors have contributed some significant inventions. Moreover, in many sectors, little research and development is done by any firm, whether large, medium, or small.

A view of firm behavior, market structure, and economic performance which deemphasizes the importance of profit maximization as the goal of business management has recently been put forward again. This interpretation is now most prominently associated wih the name of John Kenneth Galbraith. The theory starts with the identification of the Technostructure – the bureaucracy of technocrats required to handle the complex engineering and managerial problems of modern economic life. The objectives of the Technostructure that operates the major companies are, first of all, survival and, second, achievement of the maximum possible growth rate. To achieve these goals, a firm effectively plans and controls not only its production operations, but the prices of the inputs it buys. It also uses modern advertising techniques to control the prices, quantities, and qualities of the products it sells. In effect the role of the market is superseded by planning.

While Galbraith and his compatriots have provided new insights, or at least a new emphasis, as a counterweight to conventional analyses, much of their argument is already contained in the theory of differentiated oligopoly. The goals of profit maximization and growth maximization often lead to the same policies. On the ability of firms to control their purchases and sales by planning and advertising, Galbraith's claims have encountered strong opposition.

The public hostility toward monopoly and the desire to maintain competition are expressed in the antitrust laws. From their inception in 1890 (the Sherman Antitrust Act) until just before World War II, the enforcement of the laws was sporadic and uneven. Fluctuations in presidential interest and the nature of some Supreme Court opinions led to ups and downs in enforcement activity. In the last twenty-five years, however, there has been more vigorous enforcement by the Justice Department and a broader interpretation of the intent of the laws by the courts. There is little evidence that business concentration has increased in the United States, but it is difficult to determine whether this is attributable to the antitrust laws. The most difficult policy issue in antitrust is the extent to which the enforcement of the laws should rely on criteria of market structure or of market performance. The former set of criteria depends on the number of firms in the industry, their relative importance, and evidence of collusion. The advocates of performance criteria place efficiency and prices at the center. They say that it is not market structures, but the effective results in the market that count most. Both types of criteria probably are needed.

State and federal regulatory commissions are becoming more obviously unsatisfactory because of their narrowly defined goals and ineffective methods of dealing with the problems they face. The state commissions set public utility rates to prevent monopoly profits; they are also supposed to ensure the efficient operation of the utilities, but are not empowered to enforce standards of efficient performance. The federal regulatory commissions cover railroads, oil and gas pipelines, some interstate shipping and trucking, interstate electrical transmission, radio and television broadcasting, telephone and telegraph rates, and civil aviation. In these industries there is often some degree of competition. The federal commissions have not been entirely successful in encouraging or controlling it, however, to ensure low-cost operation and satisfactory response to consumer demands. Again the problem has been mainly a narrow frame of reference and limited means.

Questions for discussion and review

1. Small-scale retailing is sometimes characterized as a sick industry. Do you see any signs of that sickness in the stores you know or have known? If so, what distinguishes these stores from others that are not "sick"?

2. Galbraith argues that firms can use advertising to control their markets. Do you agree? Think of the products you and your family buy and consider the degree to which your level and composition of consumption are affected by advertising. Does this lead you to a different opinion?

3. Do you think that price discrimination in favor of children at the motion pictures is justified? Do you think such discrimination on buses and airplanes is justified? Do you think it leads to inefficient use of resources?

4. What is the Technostructure, according to Galbraith, and what is responsible for its existence?

5. List carefully the points in the Galbraithian argument which you think differ from the "accepted sequence," including in the latter the theory of differentiated oligopoly.

6. Why was the rule of reason a barrier to the effective enforcement of the Sherman Antitrust Act for so many years?

7. What is the argument between those who believe that the most important criterion for antimonopoly action on the part of government should be market structure and those who believe that it should be market performance?

8. What are the differences and the similarities in the problems faced by state and federal regulatory commissions?

Concepts for review

Sick industry	The rule of reason
Price discrimination	Vertical, horizontal, and conglomerate mergers
Nonprice competition	Resale price maintenance
The Revised Sequence	The weak and strong road problem

Appendix: The regulation of public utilities

The potential advantage of monopoly in achieving economies of large-scale production has had one important result. The government has granted private and public corporations exclusive production franchises in a number of industries. These include electric power production and distribution, bus and rail transportation, telephone communication, radio broadcasting, and others. While the creation of a monopoly may have certain advantages, it also has certain dangers. Public utility commissions have been established to oversee the business practices of companies operating under exclusive franchise and to control their prices. There is a vast literature on public utility regulation. We cannot even summarize that literature here, but we can mention a few essential principles.

It is clear that if we let a monopoly – public franchised or private – do what comes naturally, it will try to maximize profits. It will do this by "restricting" output to a level less than that at which the price or rate is equal to marginal cost. In Figure 26-1, the monopoly price and output would tend to be P_M and Q_M, determined where $MR = MC$, and profits per unit would be $P_M - ATC_M$.

If you were on the public utility commission, what rates or rate-setting procedure would you recommend?

You may decide not to allow monopoly profits but only a 7 percent return on investment. Assume that the 7 percent is already built into the average cost curve as the normal profit, which is also the opportunity cost of attracting firms into the business. Price is equal to unit cost of production (including now opportunity cost profits) at Q_R, where the demand curve intersects the ATC curve. You might have some satisfaction from not allowing monopoly profits to be made if the price were set at P_R, and it appears to be a fair solution to the problem of rate setting. But you are nagged by the thought that you learned in your college economics course that overall efficiency requires that price equal marginal costs. The price of a good or service should be equal to the additional or incremental cost of production. At Q_R, the price of the

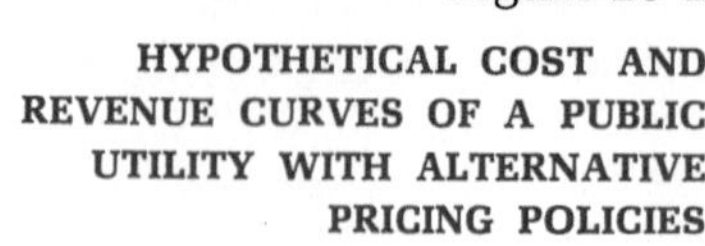

Figure 26-1

HYPOTHETICAL COST AND REVENUE CURVES OF A PUBLIC UTILITY WITH ALTERNATIVE PRICING POLICIES

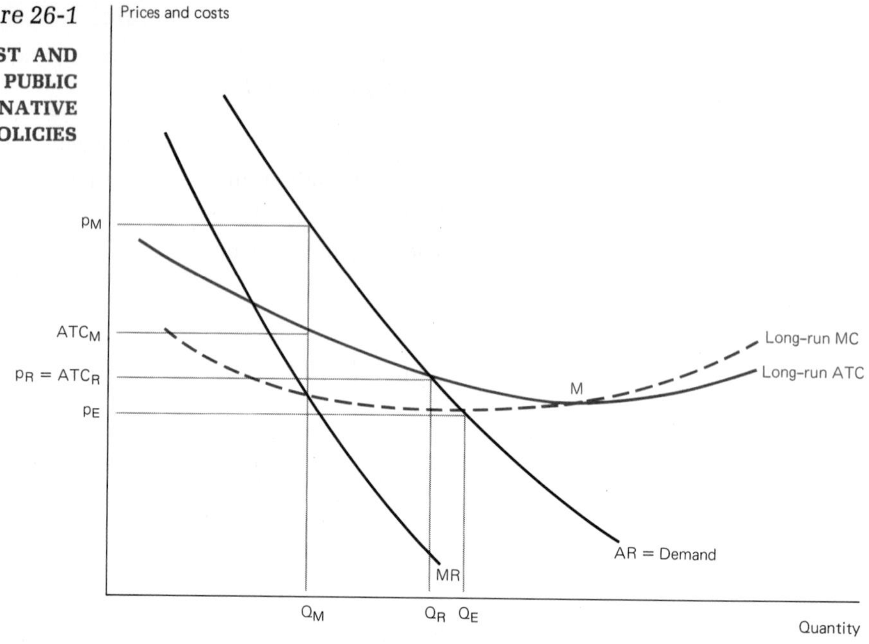

good, P_R, is equal to ATC_R, the *average* cost of production of the output, not MC_R, the *additional* or incremental cost of producing that output.

The output at which price is equal to marginal cost is Q_C. Q_R is closer to Q_C than Q_M is, so the proposed rate would move the firm in the right direction.

But why not go all the way? Why not rule that the utility can charge no more than the rate P_E? At that price Q_E will be demanded, with marginal cost of production also equal to P_E. That would satisfy the efficiency condition which seems so important. But if you set that rate, you will have all the utility executives after your scalp. They will argue, absolutely correctly, that if they charged only P_E they could not cover their costs of producing Q_E. Looking back at Figure 26-1, you can see that P_E is less than the full average costs of producing Q_E.

What is to be done? The full costs of producing Q_E must be borne somehow if that output is to be produced. The utility obviously cannot and will not subsidize that level of output by taking losses. The answer must be: If the public wants that level of output – at which the price of the output is just equal to its marginal costs – the public is going to have to pay for it. Therefore, as a public utility commission member, you must go before the state legislature and ask for a budget to *subsidize* the private utilities!

What an extraordinary conclusion. It is going to take some

explaining, so better have it clear in your own mind. First, why did we get this result by following the efficiency rules? The answer lies in the relative positions of the demand and cost curves. In the case shown, the demand curve intersects the marginal cost curve to the left of — and, therefore, *under* — the long-run average cost curves. If the intersection of demand and marginal cost were at or to the right of point C, the results would be quite different, as will be shown shortly. The subsidy is intended to just make up the losses incurred by the utility in producing Q_E and selling it at P_E. That is all. It will not contribute to monopoly profits. To be sure it is justified, you may want to examine the costs of operation of the utility more closely.

You should also be prepared for the following arguments, which have merit:

1. The subsidy will have to be raised by taxes, and taxes may also be the source of distortions in the production process and departures from perfect efficiency.
2. There are other claims on the public budget, and legislators may feel that other projects are more important than eliminating this inefficiency.

Figure 26-2 presents the alternative case, when the demand and long-run marginal cost schedules intersect to the right of the minimum long-run average cost point. Here, the monopolistic price would be at P_M and the corresponding output at Q_M. The regulated price which just covers unit costs, including normal profits, is

Figure 26-2

EFFICIENT PRICING IN A PUBLIC UTILITY WHEN AN EXCESS PROFITS TAX WOULD BE JUSTIFIED

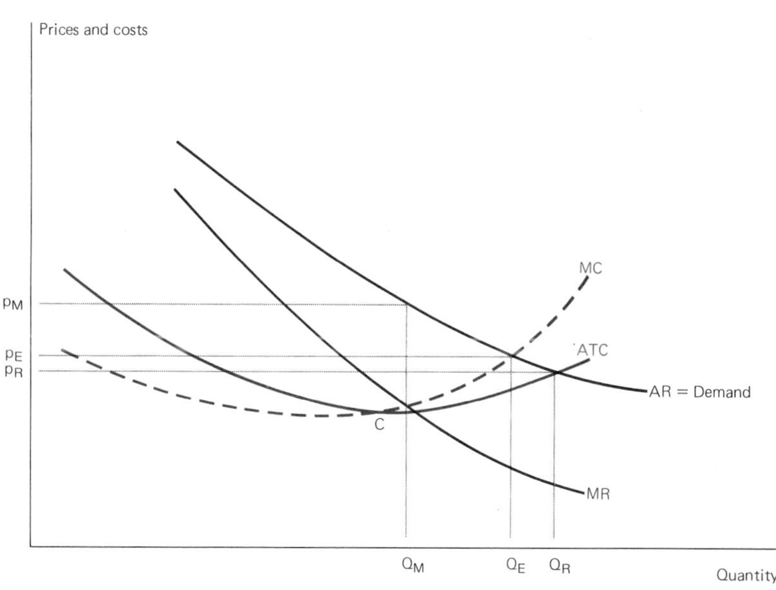

P_R, with output Q_R. At this latter price and output, however, the price is below the marginal costs of production. Again the efficiency condition would be violated. The condition is met at the lower output Q_E, with price P_E. At this price and quantity, however, the utility would be making above-normal profits. To be consistent in our pursuit of efficiency, if we proposed the rate P_E, we would also have to ask for an "excess" profits tax to take away the above-normal profits the utility would earn at that price and with output Q_E.

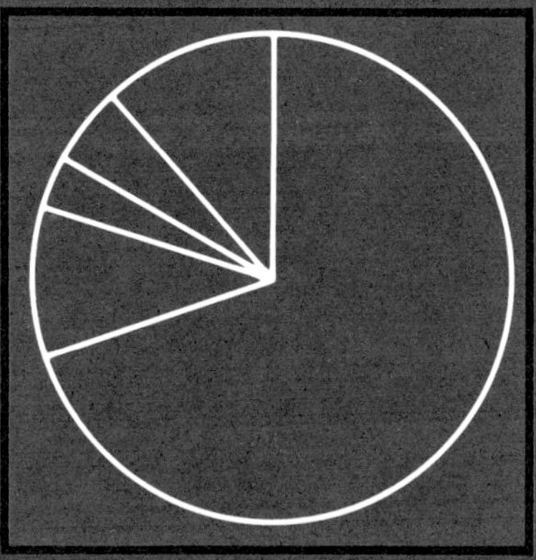

FOUR

The functional distribution of income

Who will get the hamburger? Who will get the steak?
Who will get the real fur? Who will get the fake?

This jingle sums up the Distribution question: How are the goods and services produced to be apportioned? The question is as old as time, and it is what a lot of the shouting is about today. In this area it is important to distinguish positive and normative analysis, because the questions strike close to what is near and dear to the hearts of most of us. Normative analysis asks: How should society distribute goods and services? However, we must first answer as well as possible the positive question: How is the Distribution question actually resolved?

The task of Part IV is to explain distribution of earned income. That is called the functional distribution of income and depends on the rates at which resources are paid for the services they perform. The personal distribution of earned income depends also on the distribution among individuals of earning abilities and the ownership of income-generating assets.

The determination of the rates of pay is, therefore, at the heart of the functional income distribution questions. Once again the tools of supply and demand analysis will be brought to bear. They will be extended and given content in their application to resource markets.

Chapters 27 and 28 develop the basic supply and demand approach to the pricing of productive services. Chapter 29 takes up the special conditions of wage determination and the role of labor unions in labor markets. Chapter 30 analyzes the difficult subjects of capital and the determination of the interest rate, and Chapter 31 discusses profits.

27

The functional distribution of income and factor pricing

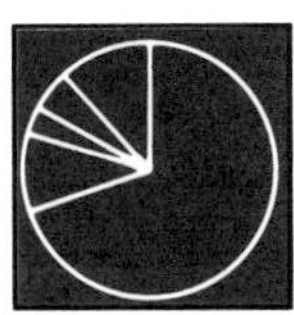

In the interdependent structure of the economy, the resolution of the Distribution questions depends on the manner of resolution of the Output and Input questions. And there is "feedback," or influence in the opposite direction as well.

The functional distribution of income questions are not abstract problems, however. They are closely related to issues in which we all have a close personal interest. As current or future wage and salary recipients, we are interested in the share of wages in the total national income. As potential house owners or apartment dwellers, we are interested in the share of rents. Figure 27-1

Figure 27-1

DISTRIBUTION OF INCOME AMONG WAGES, RENTS, INTEREST, CORPORATE PROFITS, AND INCOME OF UNINCORPORATED ENTERPRISES

(*Source:* U.S. Department of Commerce, Survey of Current Business.)

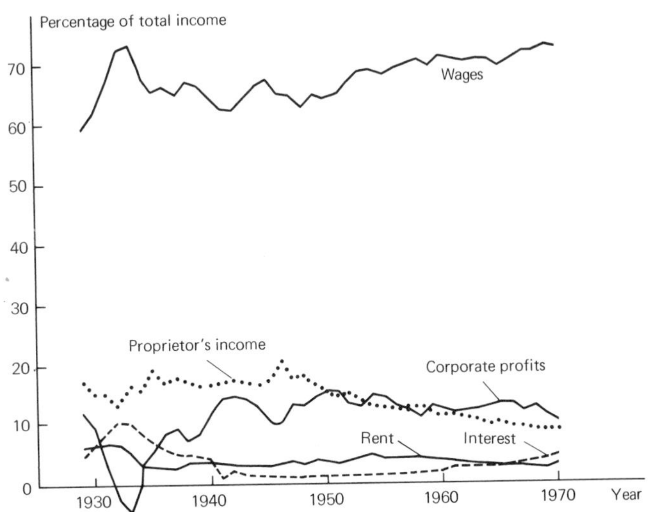

provides some facts on the functional distribution of income in the United States and its changes. Notice that the categories, wages, rents, and interest, correspond to the tripartite classification of Labor, Land, and Capital. Corporate profits are readily identifiable as what is left over to corporations after all other income payments have been made as costs. The income of unincorporated enterprises cannot in general be divided among the various productive resources.

The functional income distribution facts of Figure 27-1 are, in turn, closely associated with some of our most pressing social problems. Table 27-1 shows the so-called "poverty levels" and the number of families that fall below these levels. The poverty levels represent the minimum amounts necessary to provide the basic essentials of a decent life. They contain little if anything to raise the quality of life above the bare minimum. They are inevitably arbitrary, and, in truth, vary among families, depending on particular circumstances, such as health and wealth. Nonetheless the pov-

Table 27-1

POVERTY LEVELS AND POOR HOUSEHOLDS, MARCH, 1970

Average poverty levels

Number of family members	Average, all families	Nonfarm: Average	Nonfarm: Male head	Nonfarm: Female head	Farm: Average	Farm: Male head	Farm: Female head
1 member	$1,914	$1,921	$2,008	$1,868	$1,634	$1,674	$1,584
Under 65 years old	1,969	1,975	2,060	1,905	1,698	1,750	1,619
65 years old & over	1,824	1,832	1,850	1,825	1,563	1,573	1,552
2 members	2,464	2,486	2,497	2,420	2,092	2,099	1,991
Head under 65	2,546	2,564	2,578	2,476	2,187	2,193	2,055
Head 65 & over	2,285	2,310	2,312	2,299	1,964	1,965	1,952
3 members	3,026	3,049	3,064	2,943	2,585	2,593	2,482
4 members	3,881	3,905	3,907	3,886	3,334	3,334	3,317

Number of persons below poverty levels (thousands)

Age of family head	All races: Total	All races: Number	All races: Percent of total	White: Total	White: Number	White: Percent of total	Black & other nonwhite races: Total	Black & other nonwhite races: Number	Black & other nonwhite races: Percent of total
Under 35	14,132	1,477	10.4	12,437	1,001	8.1	1,696	475	28.0
35–44	10,884	870	8.0	9,752	591	6.1	1,132	279	24.6
45–54	10,829	703	6.5	9,803	483	4.9	1,026	219	21.4
55–64	8,314	658	7.9	7,516	465	6.2	798	193	24.2
65 & over	7,078	1,243	17.6	6,515	1,014	15.6	563	228	40.6
Total	51,237	4,950	9.7	46,022	3,555	7.7	5,215	1,395	26.7

Source: U.S. Department of Commerce, Bureau of the Census; *Current Population Reports*, Series P-60. Updated from 1969 by use of consumers price index. Numbers may not add to totals because of rounding.

erty levels provide an indication of the scope of the poverty problem.

The proportion of the population under the poverty levels has been declining in recent years but is still substantial. Table 27-1 suggests some of the sources of the poverty problem. The high rates of poverty among blacks are the effect of racial discrimination. The high rates of poverty among older people indicate the inadequacy of the present social provisions for that group.

Analysis of the functional distribution of income will not explain all aspects of the poverty problem. It will not, for example, cover those aspects of the personal distribution of income which depend on the distribution of income-earning abilities and assets, transfer payments, and labor market conditions such as discrimination. Functional income analysis is an essential part of any explanation or solution of the poverty problem, however.

Factor pricing and factor incomes

The first step in the analysis of the functional distribution of income is to *think of the income paid for the use of a productive resource, or "factor of production," as the product of a price multiplied by a quantity*. The income of a worker is his hourly wage times the number of hours he works. The rental income paid on a piece of land is the rental rate per square foot times the number of square feet. The interest income paid on a savings account is the interest rate times the number of dollars in the account. Once the essential role of *factor pricing* in the determination of the functional distribution of income is appreciated, all the artillery of supply and demand analysis can be brought to bear on the problem. To use the supply and demand analysis, we must assume that factor markets are reasonably competitive. We will do that in this chapter and modify the assumption in the next chapter.

Figure 27-2

HYPOTHETICAL SUPPLY AND DEMAND CURVES FOR A PRODUCTIVE INPUT DETERMINING ITS PRICE, USAGE, AND INCOME

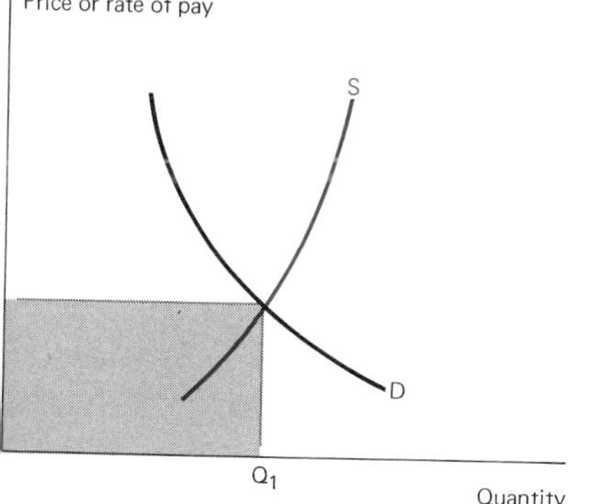

Without being specific about the type of factor, suppose that the demand curve *D* in Figure 27-2 represents the rates or prices that would be paid for the use or hire of various amounts of the factor in a perfectly competitive market. The supply curve *S* shows the amounts of the factor that would be offered for use at various prices. Assume also, as is usual in such supply and demand analysis, that the prices of other productive resources and products do not change as the prices in this particular factor market shift around.

With all these assumptions, the equilibrium price toward which the market will move is at the intersection of the supply and demand curve, at p_1, and the corresponding amount of the factor used at Q_1. The *total income* paid to and earned by the factor is the product $p_1 \times Q_1$, which is the area of the shaded rectangle. A shift in the demand or supply curves will change the price received by the factor for its services. It may also change the total income that the factor receives, depending on the elasticities of the demand and supply schedules and on any offsetting shifts.

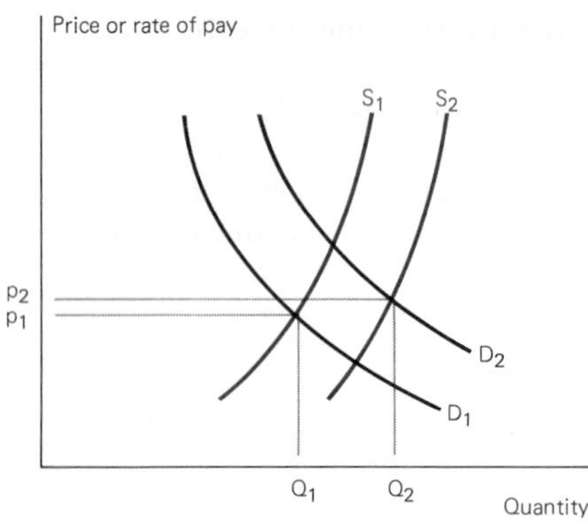

Figure 27-3

EFFECTS OF SHIFTS IN DEMAND AND SUPPLY FOR A PARTICULAR PRODUCTIVE FACTOR

Suppose, for example, that Figure 27-2 is a rough representation of the market for computer programmers. The demand for programmers is growing with the increasing use of computers in private and public institutions. On the other hand, the increasing versatility and flexibility of computers is reducing the amount of programming that has to be done and the skill required in programming. These conditions affect the demand side of the computer programmer "market." Suppose that over some period there is a net increase in the demand for programmers so that the demand curve shifts from D_1 to D_2 in Figure 27-3. On the supply side, a lot of things are happening too. There are more training schools for computer programmers; some high schools and colleges are giving programming courses. People are drawn into the field from other occupations. These changes may be represented by an increase in supply, shown as a shift in the supply curve from S_1 to S_2. In the case shown, the average salary level rises. This has occurred in recent years, though it is not necessarily a prediction of what will happen in the future. To make a prediction, we would have to make some projections about future relative shifts in the demand and supply schedules, and we would have to know more about their elasticities.

As in other uses of supply and demand analysis, analyzing the returns to productive factors requires that one go behind the supply and demand curves to see what determines their position, their shape, and the changes in them. That will be the procedure here in analyzing the functional distribution of income. First, we shall look at competitive factor markets, and then other types of markets. Initially, the analysis will be general and will not go into the special characteristics of particular types of factors. Subsequent chapters will become more specific.

The demand for productive resources by a competitive firm

To be blunt about it, resources are demanded not for themselves but for what they can produce. The rolling farmland may be beautiful; the mathematician may be a wizard; the steam turbine may be a marvel of ingenuity. But those qualities, in themselves, will not earn a dime. It is what the qualities contribute to the value of output that makes land, mathematicians, or steam turbines worth renting, hiring, or leasing. *Resources are needed for production, and the demand for resources is derived from the demand for the goods they produce.*

The basic producing units are firms. The *total* demand for any particular kind of productive resource is just the sum of the demand of all firms for that resource. The demand of each firm for the productive resources it uses will depend on: (1) the effectiveness of the resource in producing the firm's output and (2) the demand for the firm's product. Therefore, to get to the bottom of factor demand, we must move to the level of the individual firm and answer in detail the following question: What determines a firm's demand for a particular factor of production?

The dependence of the demand for resources on the demand for the goods they can produce is itself a fundamental insight. Note, however, that "goods" is plural. Iowa farmland can be used to produce wheat or corn or soybeans or a number of other crops, and somehow all these possibilities affect the demand for the land.

A second point to remember is that *there is almost never a simple and commonsense way of distinguishing the unique contribution of one particular resource from that of another.* We can make this even more explicit by going through a kind of reasoning that seems to be on the right track but does *not* get to the bottom of the issue. Suppose you were an observer in a labor-management bargaining session and you heard the following argument from the union side:

> Well, we really should have an extra $5 million divided among the 1,000 workers in the plant, because that is how much output went up last year, and it only went up because the working force has become more skilled and productive. And certainly without us nothing could have been produced.

On the management side they may respond by saying:

> Output went up because we installed some new equipment. Without the machines to work with and the factory and the engineering personnel and the sales and advertising staff, the effort of the labor force would not be worth anything. Therefore, you really don't deserve to get anything extra at all.

How should this dispute be resolved (recall the discussion of Chap. 4)? The following reasoning is true:

> In fact, each needs the other.
> On the one hand, labor cannot produce without machines and material, and on the other hand, the machines and material supplied by management cannot produce without labor.

The moral of this story is by now familiar: There is extensive interdependence in economics. In this example, there is interdependence in production. For any particular factor, the quantity demanded depends on its contribution to the value of output. *But the contribution of any one factor to the value of output depends on the other factors of production with which it is combined.* It is this interdependence in production which is the source of most of the difficulty in the analysis of the functional distribution of income. This point can be appreciated more deeply by referring again to the First Model Economy of Chapter 3. In that simplified economy, the sole factor of production was labor. And the distribution problem was trivial: Labor received all the output produced. When there are two or four or many productive resources, then it is not so obvious just how the contribution of one particular factor

Table 27-2

DERIVATION OF THE DEMAND CURVE OF A COMPETITIVE FIRM FOR LABOR

1 No. of workers	2 Output	3 Marginal physical product	4 Price of output	5 Revenue	6 Marginal revenue product
0	0		$1	$ 0	
		20			$20
1	20		1	20	
		14			14
2	34		1	34	
		10			10
3	44		1	44	
		8			8
4	52		1	52	
		6			6
5	58		1	58	
		5			5
6	63		1	63	
		4			4
7	67		1	67	
		3			3
8	70		1	70	

to the value of output can be identified and derived. To determine that, we need to go back to fundamentals.

Suppose a firm in a competitive industry was considering using more of a particular productive input, say, labor. The firm would ask itself, What is it worth to the firm to hire an extra worker? What will the worker contribute to revenues? To find an answer, the firm must first identify what a worker contributes to physical output and then figure out the value of that contribution to the firm's dollar revenues.

Figure 27-4

MARGINAL PHYSICAL PRODUCT OF LABOR WITH OTHER RESOURCES OF THE FIRM FIXED

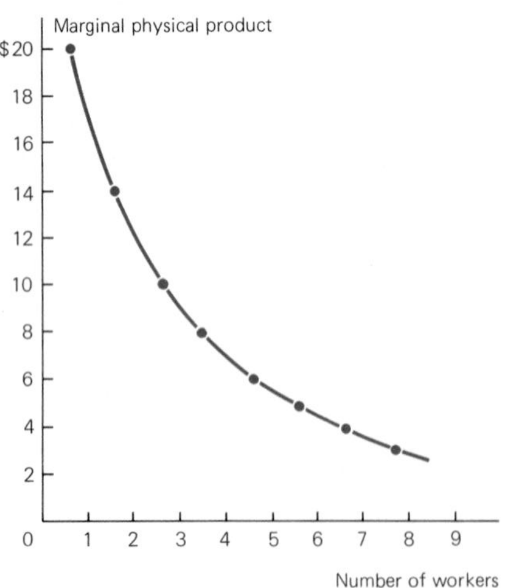

If the firm keeps all the other resources at a constant level and adds one more worker, output will go up by the *marginal physical product* of the worker. That is what the term means. (A reference to Chap. 22 might be helpful.)

The Law of Diminishing Returns, however, tells us that as more and more workers are added, with all other factors held constant, the marginal physical product of each additional worker becomes smaller and smaller. This is shown in a simple example in Table 27-2. As the number of workers used goes up (column 1), output goes up (column 2). The marginal physical product of each additional worker falls, as shown in column 3 and in Figure 27-4.

Since the firm is operating in a competitive industry, its output cannot affect the industry's price, which is assumed to be $1. *The market value of each additional worker's output is called the marginal revenue product.* Strictly speaking, it is the *marginal product of the additional worker times the marginal revenue that the firm obtains from selling that additional output.* This firm is selling in a competitive industry, so the marginal revenue from a sale is constant and equal to the price. In this case, therefore, the marginal revenue product from hiring an additional worker, using him in the production process, and selling the increased output is the marginal physical product times the price of the product. That is shown in

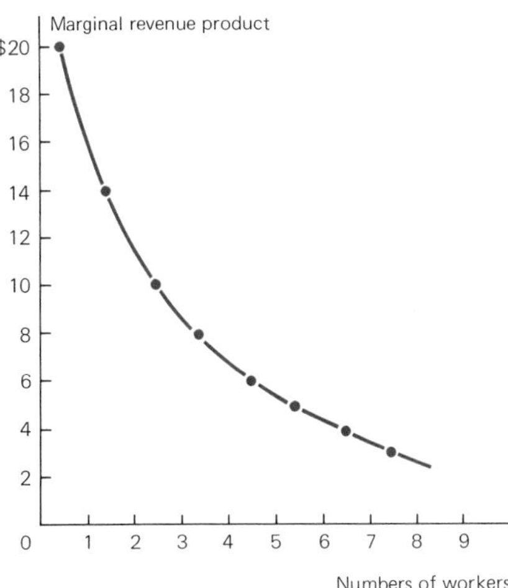

Figure 27-5

MARGINAL REVENUE PRODUCT OF LABOR FOR A COMPETITIVE FIRM WHOSE OUTPUT SELLS FOR $1

column 5 of Table 27-2. It is also depicted in Figure 27-5. There is only one difference between Figures 27-4 and 27-5. On the vertical axis of Figure 27-5, the marginal physical product of the labor shown in Figure 27-4 is multiplied by the product price of $1.

To understand this firm's demand for labor, ask yourself what maximum wages the firm would be willing to pay to a worker. The answer is, No more than the amount the worker can contribute to the earnings of the firm, i.e., the marginal revenue product. But in a competitive labor market, labor would tend to receive that maximum. In the competitive pricing process, firms would bid against one another for the labor and force the wage up to the marginal revenue product. Therefore, *the marginal revenue product curve of labor in the firm is just the demand of the firm for labor.* Why? Because it indicates what an additional worker is worth in the only terms important to the firm: What does the worker add to the firm's revenue?

Notice that, since the output price is constant, the downward slope of the marginal revenue product curve is due solely to the decline in the marginal physical product of labor. And that decline is due to the Law of Diminishing Returns.

What is true for labor is true for any other productive resource: *The firm's demand for a resource depends on what it contributes to the firm's revenues.*

The competitive market demand for a productive resource

We have now worked through the argument that the firm's demand for labor or any other resource depends on what it adds to the marginal revenue product of the firm. The essential fact of that first step in our analysis is that the demand for any resource by any firm depends on what the resource can add to the firm's revenues.

The next step is to look at the demand for the resource by all firms in the market area. Conceptually that is straightforward. *The total demand for a particular productive resource in a market area is the sum of the demands by all firms for the resource.* One can imagine sending a questionnaire around to ask each firm in the market how much of a particular resource it would want to rent or hire at each of many rates. By adding up the amounts reported at each rate, we would get the total amount demanded at that rate.[1] The total amounts demanded at alternative rates would be the market demand for the resource.

Can we obtain any insights into the general relationship between total product demand and the factor demand derived from

[1] It is important to keep this total demand concept restricted to a particular factor market area which is small in comparison with the total amount of the factor used in all markets. As will be explained in Chap. 29, since factor incomes vary with factor prices, "all other things" would not remain equal if an aggregate schedule were attempted.

it? There are a couple of useful propositions which are true for noncompetitive as well as competitive markets.

First, *the more inelastic the product demand, the more inelastic the demand will be for the factors that produce it.* Suppose that for some reason there was an increase in the rates of factor payment such that it would raise costs and, all other things equal, reduce product supply. In turn, product prices would rise and the quantity of the good demanded would fall. But the fall in sales would depend on the elasticity of product demand. Sales would fall less if product demand was relatively inelastic. They would fall more if product demand was relatively elastic. So when factor payment rates rise, the demand for the factors to produce the output will fall less when product demand is relatively inelastic than when it is relatively elastic.

Second, *the smaller the proportion of a particular factor's cost in total costs, the more inelastic will be the demand for that factor.* If the payments to a particular input are only a tiny part of total costs of production, those payments can change substantially without affecting total costs very much. A change in the rates paid to such a factor will, therefore, have only a relatively small effect on the product's supply, on the price of the final product, and on the quantity of the product demanded – and, therefore, on the derived demand for the input.

Actually estimating and computing the total demand schedule for a factor would not be an easy task. But for our present purposes of getting the central concept straight, we need not worry about the practical difficulties.

The supply of productive resources

What determines the amount of resources that will be offered for use in a particular market at alternative prices, wage rates, rental rates, or lease rates? Stating the supply question carefully helps to dispose of one appealingly simple and true but inadequate answer – that the supply of productive resources at any moment is fixed. The rationale of the answer is that there is just so much arable land in the world, so much oil, coal, iron ore, etc., in the ground. Even though we do not know the exact population of the world, it is just *some* number. And there is just so much capital equipment of all types in buildings, dams, machines, highways, etc. All this is true, but it is not enlightening. The response is not an answer to the question posed. Let us look at the question again and italicize the word *offered*. Not all the world's land or oil or labor or equipment is going to respond to prices in a particular market. Though the world's resource endowment is in some sense a fixed amount, in any given period of time it may yield more or less productive services. Thus, it is necessary to probe deeper into the supply problem than this easy answer goes.

In analyzing the supply of productive resources, we can no longer be content to stick to the completely general level at which we discussed demand. Productive resources are demanded by business firms not for themselves but for their contribution to revenues. The supply of productive resources, however, rests on a more diverse set of motivations. *Each of the factors has a somewhat different rationale in its supply*. Each, therefore, really requires a separate treatment. That will be the object of Chapters 29 and 30. Here we shall give each type of factor supply a once-over-lightly treatment.

Labor

"Labor" is a code word for many different kinds of skill and effort. Some skills can be developed only with many years of training. Some can be acquired relatively quickly. The amount of any particular type of labor that will be offered in a particular market in return for a specific wage or salary depends on two things: the total pool of that type of labor and the willingness of the labor to work at that wage. In general, the higher the wage, the greater the "participation rate." That rate is the ratio of active members of the labor force to the total population. If there is to be an increase in the amount of effort put in or the number of hours worked by the people employed, it is in general necessary for the wage to rise.

Figure 27-6

ALTERNATIVE COMPETITIVE SUPPLY CURVES FOR LABOR

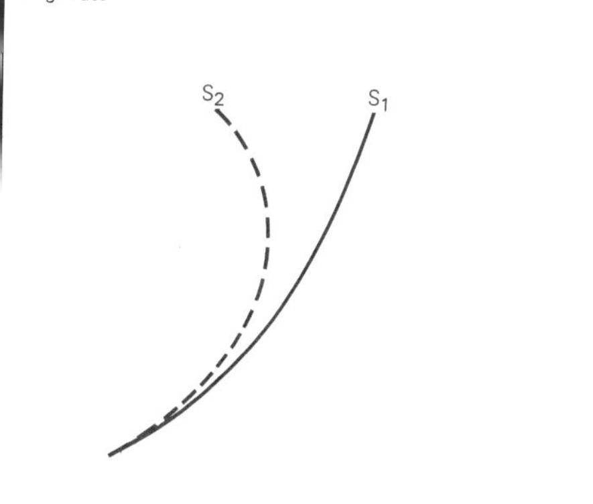

The supply of labor in competitive markets is just the sum of the amounts offered by each person at each wage rate. Unions or professional associations have an important influence on supply conditions, however. A professional association with the support of the law and with the rationale of raising the standards of the profession can restrict supply by requiring professional tests and licenses. A union can do the same thing and, in addition, often bargain for a large part of the total work force of a particular employer or group of employers. In these circumstances, the supply of labor is not simply the sum of the independent decisions of each of the potential workers.

If we were dealing with competitive labor markets, the most plausible supply schedule would be one in which the amounts of labor offered increased with the wage rate, as shown by the curve S_1 in Figure 27-6. As we shall see in Chapter 28, in some circumstances the amounts of labor offered at higher wage rates will increase up to a point, and after that will decrease. This happens if workers choose more leisure over earning more income. Then the supply curve of labor will "bend backward," as shown by the curve S_2.

Land and natural resources

At one time land and natural resources were described by economists as "the original and indestructible powers of the soil." The total supply was considered fixed and unresponsive to the price or rent offered. So the supply "curve" of land was visualized as a

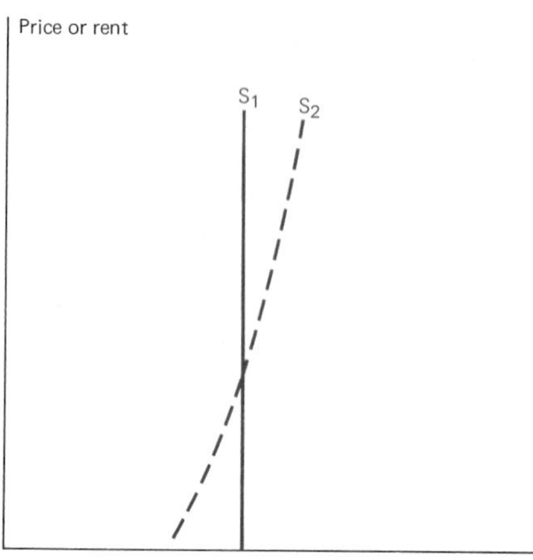

Figure 27-7

ALTERNATIVE COMPETITIVE SUPPLY CURVES FOR NATURAL RESOURCES

straight vertical line at the maximum quantity available. By now we know that *very few of the productive qualities of natural resources are "indestructible." The productivity or quantity available of most resources declines with their use.* This is most obvious with things like oil and coal. It is just as true for farmland; fertility will decline unless it is continually restored. But soil productivity can also be increased by grading, irrigating, and fertilizing. The significance of this observation is that the "original" powers of the soil may not be so original either, but are subject to improvement by the use of other resources. Similarly, oil, gas, coal, and other mineral deposits cannot be exploited until they are found. Exploration involves prospecting and test drilling. In turn, the amount of "improvement" and exploration undertaken depends on the payments offered for the use of natural resources. If the price offered is high enough, it may well pay to extract more ore from a particular deposit or to use farmland more intensively.

"Land" has one quality that, it is sometimes argued, "fixes" its supply: its location. There is only one northeast corner of Fifth Avenue and Forty-second Street in Manhattan, and that uniqueness contributes to its value. Location is usually more important for urban land, although it is often significant even for farmland and ore deposits. Location, for example, is likely to affect access to other resources and transport costs for other inputs and outputs.

The supply curve that represents the idea that the supply of land and other natural resources is fixed is S_1 in Figure 27-7. The curve S_2 represents the view that the offerings of productive features associated with land and natural resources will respond to prices.

Capital resources

The theory of capital is one of the most complicated parts of economics. At this point, the objective is only to get the main ideas clear. First of all, capital means man-made factors of production: machines, buildings, and other facilities which are themselves produced and used for further production.

At any particular moment, a certain "endowment" or "stock" of such man-made productive resources is available for use. So one might think of this endowment just as one thinks of the endowment of land and other natural resources. The stock itself is more or less fixed in the short run. But, just as for natural resources, the capital stock available may not be used at all or it may be used more or less intensively.

Capital stock can also be replaced and increased by investment – by the production of additional machines and buildings and other facilities. That part of total or gross investment which offsets depreciation is called "replacement"; the rest is net investment, which results in new additions to productive capacity.

Over a period long enough to carry through new investment, the supply of capital will depend on the amount of investment

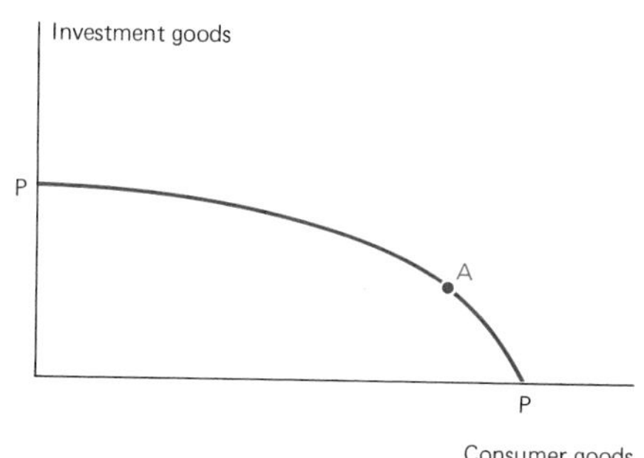

Figure 27-8
ECONOMYWIDE PRODUCTION-POSSIBILITY CURVE

undertaken. Many of the influences affecting investment in the economy as a whole were discussed in Chapters 10 and 16. We can also make use of the production-possibility curve analysis of Chapter 3. If we think of the total production of the country as composed of either consumer or capital goods, then the production-possibility curve, *PP* in Figure 27-8, shows all the possible output combinations. If the economy were producing at full employment and full capacity, if its original output point was at *A*, and if the amount of investment goods supplied were increased, then the amount of consumer goods produced would have to decrease. Or to say this another way: *If there is full employment, the rate of saving will have to increase in order to free resources for the production of investment goods. In these circumstances, the supply of new investment goods depends on the rate of saving.* One way to induce more saving is to make it more rewarding, and one way of making it more rewarding is to increase the price paid for the use of capital goods. So, again, there is reason to believe that the supply of real capital will increase with the increase in returns paid to it.

Factor mobility and factor supply

The operation of competitive factor markets is facilitated when factors are *mobile* among alternative uses. Factor mobility means that *the "owners" of productive resources are willing to shift them from one use to another to take advantage of earnings differentials.* If wages are high in the computer programmer field, workers will tend to move into that field and out of lower-paying fields that use more or less the same set of skills. If land earns less in cotton production than in rice, its owners will tend to shift it to the higher-paying use.

Factor mobility tends to reduce the price *differentials* of factors in their various uses. Notice that the factors do not necessarily move around physically. The programmers have to change jobs, but they may or may not move from one city to another. The land surely stays in one place; only its use changes. Factors differ in their mobility. To some extent the differences reflect the technological characteristics of the factors and of the production processes in which the factors are used.

Specialization is one source of factor immobility. Labor, on the whole, is a multipurpose resource, but it may take some time to train workers for a new job. There are impressive examples of the mobility of land among alternative uses. In the Middle Western states, farmers shift acreage from wheat to corn to soybeans as they compare the returns in these alternative uses. But there are unique land qualities as well. On cannot grow bananas in New Hampshire or snow ski in Florida.

Whether capital is mobile or not depends on its own technical characteristics as well as those of the goods produced. New investment goods come in many forms and embody widely differing technologies. But once the capital is committed, its range of uses is limited. Though the trend seems to be toward specialized types of capital, some capital goods have a variety of uses. Modern high-speed digital computers are increasingly specialized to the particular functions for which they are most often used. But computer-controlled metal machining tools may be more versatile than some hand-controlled metal-cutting equipment.

Noneconomic influences also contribute to factor immobility. For example, the story is told about the Berkeley physicist who was offered a professorship at M.I.T. but would not move because there was no good Chinese restaurant close to the M.I.T. campus. Presumably the "good Chinese restaurant" was a metaphor. He didn't move even when such a restaurant was established within a couple of blocks of the campus. Man does not live by bread alone, or egg rolls. Climate, political attitudes, the location of one's friends – all such nonmonetary influences affect labor mobility and, therefore, the amounts of labor offered at various wages in a particular market. In addition, job conditions other than wages affect labor mobility: the reputation of the firm, the fact that a cousin works with you – or does not. These are not neatly embodied in the wage offered.

In the economy as a whole, such nonmonetary influences often balance out. Just as some people do not want to leave Berkeley, others have an intense preference for Cambridge, Massachusetts. On the other hand, they do not *exactly* balance, and, in many occupations, we find important regional differences in salaries.

As a result of the technological and nonpecuniary barriers to factor mobility, we should expect to find differences in the prices that are paid for more or less the same factor service in otherwise perfectly competitive markets. To some extent the differences may be temporary; they may represent a stage in the movement of the factor market toward a new equilibrium. *Where wage differentials persist, economists have described the situation as one in which there are noncompeting groups in the labor market.* These are groups between which there is, at best, limited factor mobility so that the wages of the groups are not equalized.

Economic rent and transfer earnings

An example of the way demand and supply interact to determine the rates of pay of productive resources will help consolidate our understanding of the basic analysis. How would you resolve the following argument between a basketball fan and the owner of a professional basketball team?

> Fan: I would like to see more games but the prices of your tickets are too high. Why don't you reduce the price?

Owner: I would like to, but I can't. I have to charge high prices to cover the high salaries I have to pay the players.

Fan: Why pay them so much? After all, how much can a 7-foot athlete earn outside of professional basketball? They would settle for less than the $100,000 per year they are now getting.

Owner: If I don't pay the $100,000, some other team owner will. There is a lot of money being made in basketball because there are so many people like you who want to see the games and are willing to pay our ticket prices

Fan: First you said the high prices were due to high costs, and now you are saying the high prices are due to a high demand. Which is it? Make up your mind.

The problem of economic analysis contained in this dialogue is not an unusual one when there are interdependent relations. With a few definitions, the issues can be posed in a more general form. The price of a factor service can be thought of as composed of "transfer earnings" and "economic rent." *Transfer earnings are the minimum necessary to keep a factor from shifting to an alternative use or job. Economic rent is the amount earned by a factor over and above its transfer earnings.* (Notice that economic rent can be paid to any kind of productive factor. "Rent" is the payment made for the use of property — real estate, buildings, or equipment.)

Now the issues in the conversation can be stated as follows: Are goods prices determined by factor prices, or are factor prices determined by the prices of goods and services? What determines the amount of transfer earnings and economic rent in any factor payment?

These important questions are often posed about food prices. They were first raised in modern form in England in the early nineteenth century about the price of wheat. Was it so high because the rents on farmland were high? Or, asked David Ricardo, an English stockbroker who became the leading economist of his time, was the price of land high because the price of wheat was high? If so, the way to meet the problem would be to somehow increase the supply of wheat, since the demand could not be reduced. And in England at the time, increasing the supply of wheat meant reducing or removing the tariff on grain.

Figure 27-9

EFFECT OF INCREASING DEMAND ON THE RENT OF A RESOURCE IN FIXED SUPPLY

To begin the analysis, suppose that we are dealing with a factor whose supply is completely fixed and unresponsive to price changes, as was often assumed for English wheat land. This is represented in Figure 27-9 as the vertical line S at the land quantity level, Q_1. The demand for land is its marginal revenue product, as indicated by the line D_1. The equilibrium price or rental of land services is at p_1, the intersection of D_1 and S. An increase in demand, from D_1 to D_2, will raise the rental to p_2, but will not change the amount of land available for use. A reduction in demand to D_3 will reduce the price but still have no effect on quantity offered. *We can conclude that the price of the factor (land)*

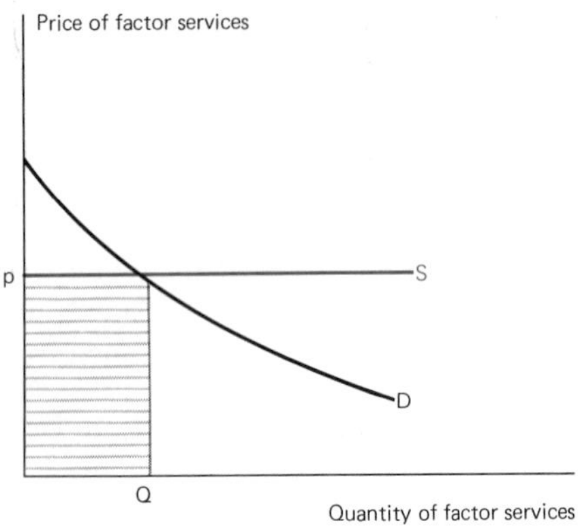

Figure 27-10

DETERMINATION OF THE QUANTITY USED OF A PRODUCTIVE SERVICE WITH PERFECTLY ELASTIC SUPPLY

Figure 27-11

DETERMINATION OF THE PRICE OF A PRODUCTIVE SERVICE WHOSE QUANTITY SUPPLIED RESPONDS SOMEWHAT TO PRICE

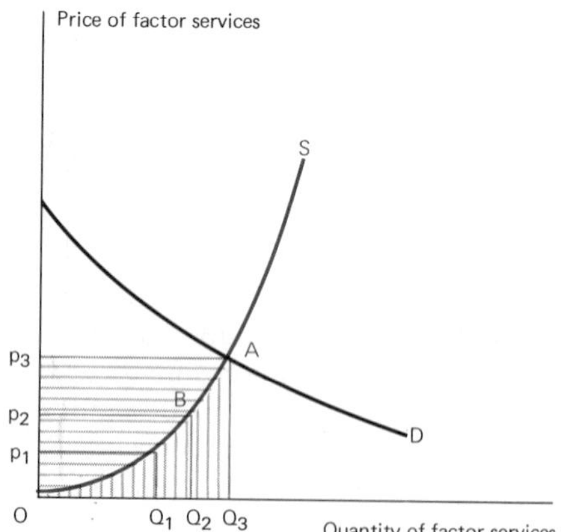

services in this case is a pure economic rent. The total economic rent at factor price p_1, is the vertically shaded area. Remember that the demand for land is *derived* from the demand for wheat, so changes in the demand for wheat will be the source of changes in the demand for land.

Thus we can almost completely agree with Ricardo that the price of land was high because the price of wheat was high, rather than the reverse. The qualification "almost" is necessary, because it still takes both a supply and a demand schedule to determine prices. If Figure 27-9 were representative of England in the nineteenth century, the only way to get more wheat and bring down its price was, as Ricardo said, to import it.

Suppose we move to the opposite extreme and think of a case in which the price of factor services is entirely transfer earnings. That is represented by Figure 27-10. *S*, the supply curve of the factor is "perfectly" elastic with respect to the factor price. The demand curve *D*, therefore, determines the quantity, *Q*, made available. Shifts in demand will change the amount available, but not the price. If the price is somehow forced below *p*, no factor services will be available. Therefore, the factor price, *p*, is entirely transfer earnings rate, because if it is not paid the factor will either not be used at all or will be transferred to some other use. Total transfer earnings for services in the amount Q are shown by the horizontally shaded area.

Finally, Figure 27-11 illustrates the more common situation in which the supply of services of a factor is somewhat responsive to factor prices. The factor price at which Q_1 of factor services is made available is p_1, which is what those services can earn in alternative uses. So p_1 is the transfer earnings rate for Q_1 services, p_2 is the transfer earnings rate for Q_2 services, and so on. The total receipts of Q_3 are $p_3 \times Q_3$, or the rectangle p_3AQ_3O. But suppose a separate bargain could be made for Q_3 inputs, and the higher payment rate did not also have to go to Q_2 and Q_1 inputs. The total extra payments for Q_3, as compared with Q_2 inputs, would be AQ_3Q_2B. Since Q_2 is willing to work at p_2, anything above that rate is economic rent. Therefore, the total transfer earnings of all factors hired up to Q_3 are shown by the vertically shaded area $OBAQ_3$. The difference between the rectangle p_3Q_3 and total transfer earnings is the horizontally shaded area. And that is the economic rent involved in the earnings of Q_3 of the factor.[2]

But of what use is this demonstration – to paraphrase the question asked by Gladstone on visiting Faraday in his laboratories and seeing an experiment with electricity. We can appreciate Faraday's answer, "Well I suppose you may one day put a tax on it." That is what Henry George proposed to do with land rents, and we can now analyze the proposal.

[2] "Quasi rent" is sometimes used to indicate an economic rent due to a temporary fixity in supply. It will tend to disappear as supply increases with time.

Taxing rents

The single-tax movement of Henry George — an American printer-publisher turned economist — gained many adherents in the last decades of the nineteenth century and still has organized groups in some cities. Its central economic proposal was that government should be financed by a single tax on land. George's justification for such a tax was that landlords benefited from general economic progress. That progress steadily increased the returns to land, which according to George represented an "unearned increment" to landlords. This is shown in Figure 27-12 as the result of increases in demand from D_1 to D_2 to D_3, with land in completely fixed supply.

Now suppose a tax was imposed, taking away the amount indicated by the horizontally shaded area. Notice the following important result, based on the previous analysis: A tax on economic rent would not affect resource allocation. The amount of the land offered and used would be the same after the tax as before. This was part of the appeal of the single-tax proposal. *A tax on economic rent would only take away "unearned increments" and would not distort the use of resources in fixed supply.*

It sounds like a good idea. What, if anything, is wrong with it? First, it is necessary to identify the *economic rent* portion of rentals paid. That is, at best, difficult, though not necessarily impossible. If there are buildings or other improvements to land, rentals will not be entirely economic rent, for the amount of the improvements supplied does depend on price, at least in the long run. Yet in some countries, for example, Australia, sites are valued independently of the buildings on them, as the basis for a site tax that would be imposed on pure economic rent.

Figure 27-12

INCREASES IN RENTS DUE TO INCREASES IN DEMAND

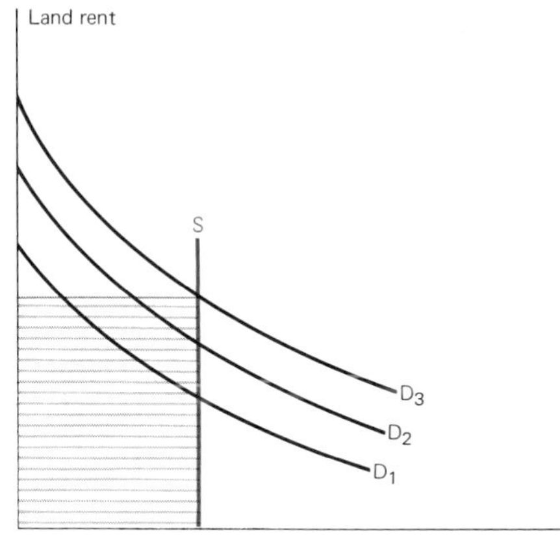

Second, a tax on economic rent on land may not take the unearned increment from the owner who benefited from it. The land may have been bought and sold many times, with each seller benefiting from the last increase in demand. The owner who is taxed can well say, "Why me? I just got in line. Go and get the ones who sold me the land at prices which capture most, if not all, of the benefits." But there is no way of going after previous owners with the single land tax.

Finally, the landowner may also say, "Why me? I'm not the only one receiving economic rents (which you should not confuse with ordinary land rents). Every factor except those whose supply schedule is horizontal — as in Figure 27-10 — is getting some economic rent. It's not equitable just to tax me." There is something in this argument also.

The high point of the single-tax movement is long past. Its very simplicity was appealing. Unfortunately, as we keep learning, life is hardly ever simple.

Rents, opportunity costs, and price signals

The demand for a resource reflects its real marginal contribution to output. Therefore, the price paid for its services in competitive markets is the opportunity cost of using those services. *If a unit of the resource were transferred from one line of production to another, the value of output in the first line would go down by the marginal contribution of the resource unit.* That is what is meant by the *opportunity cost of using a resource.*

But how does this fundamental observation square with the analysis of economic rents? That analysis showed that the rent of a resource in fixed supply could be taxed without disturbing its use. Would not such a tax distort the opportunity cost calculation? The answer is, No, because the factor *is* in fixed supply. Its use in one line or another depends only on the *relative* rate of earnings in one or another line of production, not on the absolute amount it receives.

From the standpoint of the individual firm, the rent paid to any resource whether or not its supply is fixed is undoubtedly a real cost. From the standpoint of the economy as a whole, rent paid to a resource in fixed supply is not an opportunity cost. What is the source of this apparent paradox? The fallacy of composition again. A resource in fixed supply can be used in a number of alternative ways in various firms. But for the economy as a whole, it is there to be used in its total amount at whatever price is paid.

But let us take one more step. For a resource in fixed supply – or for one whose supply varies with price – the price paid for its services is a rationing device necessary for its efficient use. If there were no such opportunity-cost price, there would be no way of determining where the productivity of the resource was highest. *The fact that the price of a productive service as determined in competitive markets is equal to the value of its marginal product means that the price serves as an effective signal controlling its use.* In this case, the price serves to guide the resource to where it will make the greatest contribution to the value of output.

Summary

The distribution of income determines the distribution of output among individuals. Income distribution in the United States is such that 12.2 percent of the population lived below the poverty level in 1969. The evidence suggests, however, that the distribution of income is not becoming more unequal and that there has been a decrease in the number and proportion of families below the poverty level.

The personal distribution of income depends: (1) on the earnings of productive resources and (2) the distribution of the ownership of the resources. The functional distribution of income is concerned only with the first of these aspects. It, in turn, depends on the price of the factor services and the quantity of services hired, rented, or leased. This means that, with the assumption that the prices and quantities are determined in competitive markets, the tools of supply and demand analysis can be used to explain the functional distribution of income.

The total demand for any particular productive resource is the sum of the demands of the individual firms that use the resource. The demand of an individual firm for a particular factor of production is derived from the demand for the firm's output and depends on the factor's contribution to the firm's revenues. The productivity of any resource depends, however, on the other resources with which it is combined in production.

The maximum price a firm would be willing to pay for an additional unit of a particular input in competitive factor markets would be equal to the contribution of the resource to the firm's revenues. That is the marginal revenue product of that additional unit. It can be calculated as the change in revenues due to the sale of the additional output produced when the additional unit of input is used with the other factors available to the firm.

The demand curve of a firm for an input is, therefore, the relationship between the marginal revenue product of the input and the quantity of the input used. The total demand schedule for the productive resource is the sum of the demands of all firms in a particular market.

The supply schedule of a particular kind of productive resource is unique to that resource. The amount of labor offered at various rates in competitive markets depends on the rate of participation of the population in the labor force and the willingness of the labor force to give up leisure to earn income. In general, participation rates are positively related to wage rates. Hours of work tend to go up with wage rates, but in some circumstances the amount of labor supplied will fall as wage rates rise, and the supply curve of labor will bend backward.

One possible but unenlightening view of the supply of land and other natural resources is that the supply of each type is fixed at the maximum conceivable amounts that might exist. If this amount is not sensitive to prices, the supply schedule will be a straight vertical line. It is more useful, however, to think of the amounts of such natural resources that are made available by their owners as depending on the price offered for them. Higher prices are necessary to cover the costs of bringing more land into cultivation and of finding coal, oil, and other mineral reserves and bringing those resources to markets. Thus, the supply schedule for productive resources of this type also generally shows larger amounts offered at higher prices than at lower.

The supply of capital – that is, man-made plant and equipment used for production – depends on the stock that has been accumulated, but it is reduced by depreciation and can be increased by new investment. The amount made available at various prices depends – as is true for other productive resources – on the period allowed for adjustment. In a short period, not much can be done to change the services of the capital available except to change utilization rates. Over longer periods, new plant and equipment can be produced, and the supply of such goods will increase with their price. Fundamentally, in a full employment economy, an increase in the output of investment goods requires a diversion of resources from the production of consumer goods. That means an increase in saving.

The prices of resources are determined by the interaction of demand and supply in competitive factor markets. Each factor will tend to receive its marginal revenue product when factor markets are competitive.

Economic rent is the return to factors over and above their transfer earnings, which is the amount they can earn in alternative employment. When a factor has a completely fixed supply, all its earnings are economic rent. More generally, when the amounts offered increase with price, only part of the factor earnings are pure economic rent. The attractiveness of the Henry George proposal for a single tax on economic rents was that such a tax would not affect the use of resources. But economic rents are not the same as rents, which may include some returns to buildings and other improvements. A tax on rents on land also ignores the economic rent elements in other factor earnings and is, therefore, subject to criticism on grounds of equity.

The price for the service of a productive resource as determined in competitive factor markets is equal to the value of its marginal product. It is, therefore, equal to the opportunity cost of its alternative uses. Thus, resource prices signal the most effective allocation of resources to meet market demands.

Questions for discussion and review

1. Describe in your own words the difference between the functional and personal distributions of income and how they are related.

2. Why is a purely economic analysis of the personal distribution of income certain to be incomplete?

3. Explain in your own words why the demand for the services of a productive resource depends on its marginal revenue product.

4. Why does the marginal revenue product of a factor used by a firm decline as the factor use increases?

5. Why does an industry facing an inelastic demand for its product tend to have an inelastic demand for the resources it uses?

6. Why would a supply curve of labor ever "bend backward"?

7. What determines the supply of capital?

8. Does the price of corn-producing land determine the price of corn, or does the price of corn determine the price of corn-producing land? Or would you explain both prices differently? If so, how?

9. What are the pro and con arguments for the Henry George single-tax proposal?

10. How do factor prices set by competitive markets for the services of productive resources help to allocate those resources efficiently?

Concepts for review

Marginal productivity
Marginal revenue product
Factor mobility
Transfer earnings and transfer payments
Economic rent
Inelastic supply curve of a productive resource
Functional distribution of income
Backward-bending supply curve of labor

28

The marginal productivity theory of factor pricing

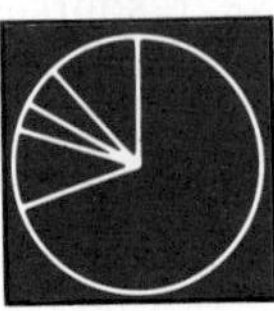

The objective of this chapter is to analyze in more detail the manner in which supply and demand forces interact to determine the prices of productive services and the functional distribution of income. In addition, the analysis of Chapter 27 will be extended to noncompetitive factor markets.

It is easy enough to say that in competitive markets the price of a factor is determined by the interaction of supply and demand and that the price will tend toward the equilibrium, where the supply and demand curves intersect. By now supply and demand analysis is familiar, and it can be used to understand what causes changes in factor prices. The statement also puts market forces where they belong – at the center of the analysis. By relating demand to marginal revenue product, as was done in Chapter 27, the analysis helps establish the relationship between factor pricing, on the one hand, and the prices of goods and the choice of production methods, on the other.

What has not yet been done – and still must be done carefully – is to relate factor price determination by supply and demand interaction to the Distribution question: the division of the output produced and the income earned among the factors of production. That is the next task.

The determination of factor prices in competitive markets

Assume that we are back in the Second Model Economy in which only one good is produced; thus, we can measure income and output unambiguously in terms of the single good. We will again call it

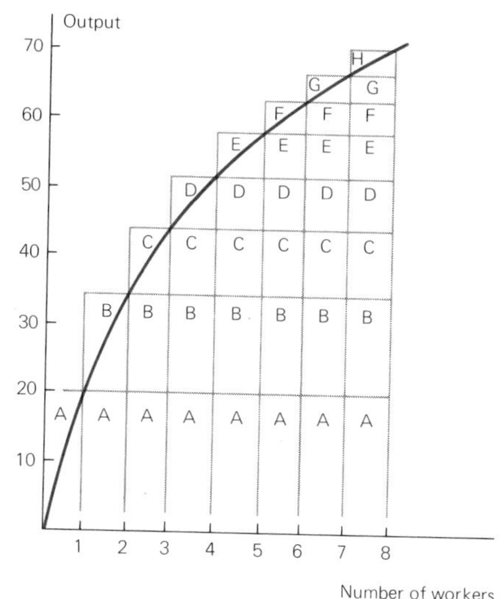

Figure 28-1

RELATIONSHIP BETWEEN MARGINAL PRODUCTS AND TOTAL PRODUCTS

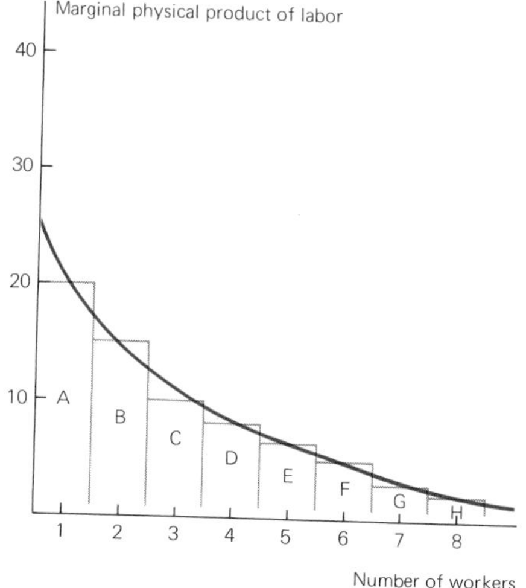

Figure 28-2

DECLINING MARGINAL PHYSICAL PRODUCT OF LABOR

food. Assume again that two factors of production, land and labor, are used to produce food. To make life even simpler, assume also that the total amounts of land and labor available for production are fixed and that firms buy and sell in competitive markets.

Though the *total* amounts of land and labor are fixed, we can imagine experiments in which different amounts of the two factors are combined in production. If the amount of land were constant and only the use of labor were varied, the total product curve of labor and the related marginal physical product curve of labor could be traced out. These two curves are shown in Figures 28-1 and 28-2. Notice that the marginal products of each additional unit of labor in the total product picture of Figure 28-1 are labeled *A, B, C, D, E,* etc. So the total product when 5 workers, or units of labor, are used is the height of the output column at 5 units of labor; this is $A + B + C + D + E$. In the marginal product picture, each block identifies the marginal product of that unit of labor. Now notice the following interesting and important fact when there are 5 units of labor: The area under the marginal product curve in Figure 28-2, as estimated by the area of blocks *A, B, C, D, E,* is just the total output of 5 units of labor, as shown on the total product curve in Figure 28-1. This particular result is true in general: *The area under a marginal physical product curve up to a particular level of input is equal to the total output produced using that input.*

Next, remember the conclusion reached in Chapter 27: The marginal revenue product curve of a factor is its *demand* curve. Since there is only one product in this model, everything can be measured in terms of that product. Therefore, the marginal revenue product curve is just the same as the marginal physical product curve.

The final step in analyzing the determination of wages is to provide the supply curve of labor. Assume that the labor supply of this model economy is fixed at, say, 5 units. It is shown as the straight vertical line in Figure 28-3 on the next page. With this supply curve of labor and the demand curve for labor as shown, labor's wage will tend to be fixed at the level of *W* in Figure 28-3, the marginal productivity of the fifth unit of labor.

Why, you may ask, does the fourth unit of labor accept the wage paid to the fifth unit, when the marginal productivity of the fourth unit is higher than that of the fifth? Well, all labor is alike and the only difference between the fourth and fifth units is the order in which they were hired. If the fourth unit protested too much, he could be told that he was the fifth unit, and the fifth unit would become the fourth. The point is that, if all labor is alike, and there are competitive markets, no laborer, the fifth or the fourth or whatever, can receive a wage different from that paid to any other.

With the wage rate determined at *W*, the total wage bill or income received by labor, in terms of food, can be calculated as the wage rate times the amount of labor employed. In Figure 28-3, that is the area of the shaded rectangle, *VWXO*. Thus, the amount of income that goes to labor has been determined!

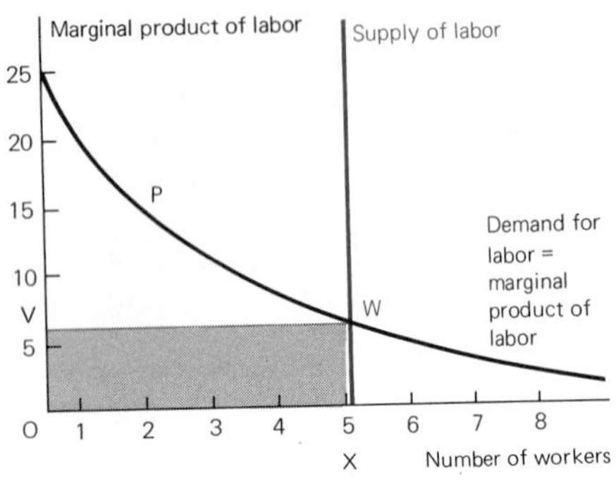

Figure 28-3

WAGE AND RENT DETERMINATION WITH FIXED LABOR SUPPLY

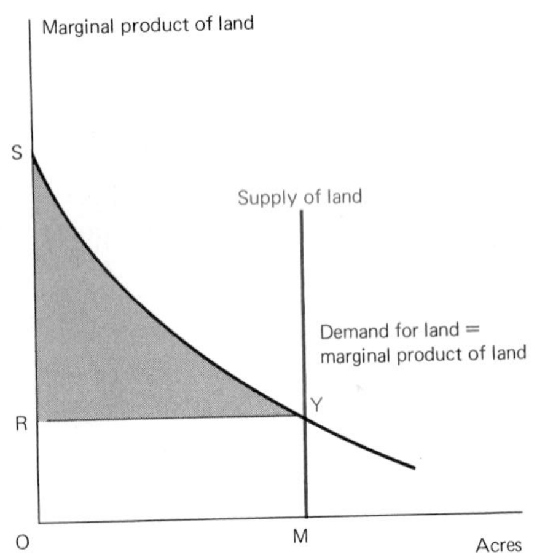

Figure 28-4

RENT AND WAGE DETERMINATION WITH FIXED LAND SUPPLY

There is an important and not so obvious implication of the above analysis: *In the process of determining the wage rate and the share of income going to labor, we have also determined the share of income received by landowners and the rental rate on land.* How does this come about? The total output produced with all the resources available is the area under the marginal product curve, as stated earlier. It is the area *PWXO* in Figure 28-3. When *VWXO* is distributed to labor, the part left for land is just *PWV*, the triangular area. So *PWV* is the share of income that goes to land. Divide that share by the total land available, and the result is the rental rate paid on each piece of land.

Now for a still less obvious extension of the argument. Suppose that instead of working out the marginal physical product curve of labor and combining it with the supply curve of labor, we had been dealing with land, as shown in Figure 28-4. The equilibrium land rental rate would be determined at the intersection of the supply and demand curves at Y, and the total amount received by landowners would be the area of the rectangle *RYMO*. The marginal productivity of the last available unit of the land would be *OR* (= *MY*). Since the total output of all the land and labor is the area under the marginal physical product curve up to Y, the amount left to labor after the total rental was paid would be *SYR*. That would have to be equal to the amount *VWXO* in Figure 28-3. We must be able to switch the roles of land and labor in the diagrammatic analysis. The conclusion that *labor must in equilibrium receive a wage equal to its marginal product must be consistent with the conclusion that land must also receive a rent equal to its marginal product! This is the marginal productivity theory of factor pricing and functional income distribution.*[1]

[1] There is one more question which may have occurred to you: If labor receives its marginal product and land receives its marginal product, and, in a world with still other factors, each type receives its marginal revenue product, how can we be sure that the total payments to all factors are just equal to the total value of output produced? In short form the question is: When the factor payment rates are equal to their marginal products, do the factor incomes just exhaust the total product, with neither more nor less being claimed? One quite acceptable way of answering the question is as follows. If each factor receives its marginal product and something is left over, that represents some extra profit which goes to whoever owns the enterprises. Supernormal profits stimulate new entrants and increase supply, which tends to reduce profits and make total income just equal to factor payments. On the other hand, if payment of the marginal revenue product to each factor would more than exhaust the product, then obviously not every factor could receive its marginal revenue product. Someone would have to take some losses and no firm will do that, not in the long run in any case. But in competitive markets, every factor would insist on that payment. So products in which there would be overexhaustion could not be produced without a subsidy of some kind. When there are constant returns to scale, marginal revenue product factor pricing will always just exhaust the product. When there are decreasing returns to scale, marginal revenue product factor pricing will leave something over for profits, except in the long-

The analysis of the simple Second Model Economy with just one good and two factors is generalizable to a complex economy of many goods and many factors as long as there are competitive markets all around. Income can still be measured in terms of one good, but it is more convenient to use money. The general result is still that the services of each productive factor will tend to be priced at the level of its marginal revenue product, which is the value of its marginal contribution to the revenues of the firm that employs it.

One final point: *The equilibrium tendency will be for the marginal revenue products of each factor to be the same whatever the good being produced and whichever the firm using the factor.* Why? Because if the factor has a higher marginal revenue product and, therefore, receives a higher rate of pay from one firm than from another, it will tend to move toward the high-paying firm, increasing its availability and use there and tending to bring down the rate of pay. This shift will also reduce the availability and use of the factor in low-paying firms and thus tend to push up the payment rate.[2]

Reflections on the marginal productivity theory

In their enthusiasm for the neat analytical results of the marginal productivity theory of factor prices, some economists, often on the Right, claim certain normative qualities for those results. They identify the marginal product of a factor as its "actual" and "specific" output and thus regard its payment as "natural" and "morally justifiable." On the other hand, some economists, mainly from the Left, criticize the theory, saying that it justifies the exploitation of labor and condemns people to poverty – people who, through no fault of their own, are not personally productive and do not own resources. Explicit analysis of these views will help clarify the theory.

First, the theory is a "positive" one; that is, it tries to explain how factor prices are actually determined and how income is actually distributed functionally among productive resources. It is not a complete explanation of income distribution, because it says nothing about the distribution of ownership of the factors

---

run equilibrium of competitive industries. In that equilibrium condition, the entry of new firms drives prices down so far that profits are wiped out. If there are increasing returns to scale, paying each factor its marginal product would more than exhaust the total product of a competitive firm and such firms simply could not survive. But, as we pointed out in Chap. 22, increasing returns to scale tends to destroy competition because it creates continuing incentives for the growth of firms.

[2] It may be useful to review Chap. 22 at this point. The condition derived there for the most economical combined use of factors is that the marginal physical products per dollar of cost of each factor must in equilibrium all tend to be the same.

of production. It is not a normative theory, because, in itself, it does not contain any judgments about what the functional or personal income distribution *ought* to be. Like other positive theories, it starts by making some descriptive assumptions. It assumes, for example, perfect competition in factor markets. Then it draws out the implications of that assumption. Thus, the theory does not predict competition, but assumes it. On the other hand, the theory does not assume the equalization of prices of the same factor in all uses; it predicts the equalization.

According to this theory, landlords are not paid rents because they are morally deserving, and capital is not paid interest because capitalists have political power with which to force its payment. Factors receive factor payments because the factors are *scarce* in relation to the demand for them. And that demand is derived from the demand for their outputs. *The factor payment rates indicate the relative scarcity of the productive resources and lead firms which are trying to do as well for themselves as possible to use the factors as efficiently as possible in production.*

As far as this theory is concerned, all productive resources could be owned by the state, or just the land, or both the capital and the land. The theory merely says that, whatever their ultimate ownership, if the resources are hired and used as in competitive markets, the payments for their use will tend to be as the theory predicts.

The marginal product of any factor depends on the other cooperating factors being used. So it cannot really be claimed that the marginal product of a factor is its *own* "actual" or "specific" output. As to whether any factor is "morally" entitled to its marginal product – that is a matter of individual opinion. It is true that when the functional distribution of income is determined by marginal products, then the factors will be used with maximum efficiency in the production of the output demanded. That, however, says nothing about what the ownership of resources and, therefore, the personal distribution of income ought to be.

Does the theory justify the exploitation of labor? That depends on what is meant by "exploitation." If exploitation means that labor as a factor of production will not receive all the output it helps to produce, that is a prediction from the theory, to be sure. If other factors are scarce, they will "receive" a share of the income generated. What happens to the income after it is "allocated" to scarce factors, whether it is redistributed or concentrated or taxed away, is not a concern of the marginal productivity theory of distribution.

Is the theory "inhuman" in that it does not take into account the special character of labor? It is – as a result of the assumption of perfect factor markets in which only labor's productivity, not its humanity, counts.

The most important economic question to ask about the marginal productivity theory is: Does it provide good descriptions and predictions of reality? The answer is, Sometimes yes and sometimes no. As with all theories, we must appreciate its limitations as well as its strengths. The theory *does* get at the basic market forces. It does *not* provide good predictions when there are important market imperfections. These may include monopoly power in the selling of services or monopsony power in the buying of services. Factor markets with these characteristics are discussed below.

There is one other qualification to the conclusions of the marginal productivity theory of distribution. The marginal productivity theory conclusions do *not* hold up when some of the costs of providing factor services are left out of the price at which the services are offered. Suppose, for example, a factory disposes of its waste products by dumping them into a river. Otherwise it would have to haul them away. The stream is a productive resource which provides some services to the factory. As long as no payments – and no penalties – are imposed for those services, why shouldn't the profit-maximizing factory use the stream for waste disposal? That is, in brief, the explanation for a lot of water and air pollution. The costs for the factory's use of the river are borne by the *community*. If taxes were imposed for such waste disposal, that would provide a means by which the costs of the services of the river could be charged to the factory.

But will taxes on waste disposal in public waterways eliminate pollution? Just make the price, i.e., the tax, high enough and that will do it.

Demand for resources by a monopolist

The analysis can be extended to the firm which has some degree of monopoly power in the sale of its product but which hires resources in competitive markets. In this case, when the firm's output and sales change, the price of its product changes. As more and more workers are used along with fixed amounts of other inputs, output rises as before and the marginal physical product of labor falls as before, as shown in Table 28-1. Now, however, the price at which the firm sells falls as output rises, since the firm is large enough to affect the market price.

The marginal revenue product, which is the addition to the firm's *revenues* due to an additional worker, can be calculated in two ways, as before: (1) as the change in total revenue due to the addition of another worker or (2) as the marginal physical product times the marginal revenue from the sale of an additional unit. The marginal revenue product curve is the demand of the firm for labor, just as it was for the perfectly competitive firm, because the marginal revenue product is what the addition of a worker is worth to the firm. The demand curve for labor of the monopolist falls for two reasons: (1) the Law of Diminishing Returns, which causes the marginal physical product of the firm to decline, and (2) the decline in the price of the product as output increases, because the firm's sales are sufficiently large relative to the industry to have a noticeable effect on the market price as its sales expand.

Table 28-1 illustrates the two ways of calculating marginal revenue product in a monopolistic firm. The physical production relations are shown in columns 1, 2, and 3. The falling demand schedule is represented by columns 1 and 4. The revenue the firm would earn from using the labor in production and selling the output at the price indicated by its demand schedule is computed by multiplying the entry in each row of column 2 by the entry in the same row of column 4. The result is tabulated in column 5. Since the change in revenue from row to row of column 5 is the result of using 1 additional unit of labor, that change is the marginal revenue product. It is tabulated in column 7. The marginal revenue is the increase in total revenue due to a 1-unit increase in output. It is calculated by dividing the marginal revenue product by the corresponding change in output. The result is shown in column 6. Multiplying the marginal revenue in column 6 by the marginal physical product in column 3 is another way of obtaining the marginal revenue product tabulated in column 7.

Again, what is true for labor is true for other productive inputs: The monopolistic firm's demand for them depends on what they contribute to the firm's revenues.

The monopolistic firm's demand for labor, which is its marginal revenue product, is shown in Figure 28-5 along with a labor supply schedule. The two together determine the wage paid to labor and how much labor will be hired. A similar analysis would determine the price of other productive services and the quantity used by the monopolist. Unlike the competitive equilibrium case, there may also be some profits.

The marginal revenue product of the labor input becomes less and less than the value of the marginal product of the labor as output increases. That value can be calculated by multiplying the

Table 28-1

DERIVATION OF THE DEMAND CURVE OF A MONOPOLIST FOR LABOR

1 *Labor*	2 *Output*	3 *Marginal physical product*	4 *Price*	5 *Revenue*	6 *Marginal revenue*	7 *Marginal revenue product*	8 *Marginal value product*
0	0		—	—			
		20			$1.00	$20.00	$20.00
1	20		$1.00	$20.00			
		14			0.66	9.24	12.04
2	34		0.86	29.24			
		10			0.42	4.20	7.60
3	44		0.76	33.44			
		8			0.24	1.92	5.44
4	52		0.68	35.36			
		6			0.05	0.60	3.72
5	58		0.62	35.96			
		5			—0.01	—0.05	2.85
6	63		0.57	35.91			
		4			—0.10	—0.40	2.12
7	67		0.53	35.51			
		3			—0.17	—0.51	1.50
8	70		0.50	35.00			

Figure 28-5

DEMAND FOR LABOR INPUTS BY A FIRM MONOPOLIZING A PRODUCT MARKET

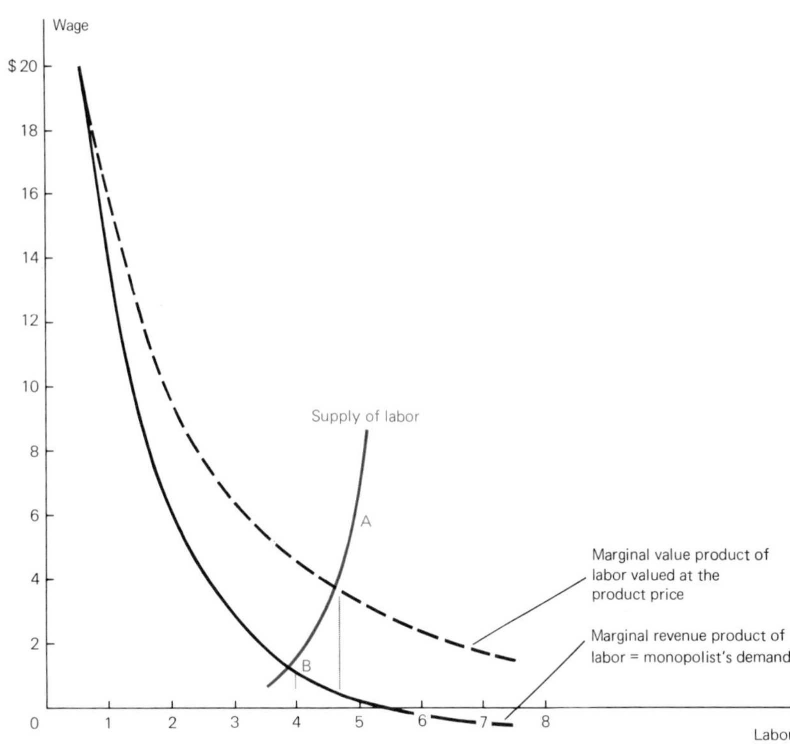

price of the product at each level of output by the marginal physical product of labor. The results of such a calculation are shown in column 8 of Table 28-1 and are plotted in Figure 28-5. *If the industry were organized competitively instead of being monopolized, the wages of labor would be higher and the amount of labor used would be larger.* The equilibrium would be at point *B* instead of point *A*. The difference reflects in another way the tendency of a monopolist to restrict output and the use of inputs.

Prices in noncompetitive resource markets

The theory of factor pricing and the functional distribution of income has been worked out in the context of perfectly competitive *factor* markets. The tools that have been developed can now be extended to other market models. Each of the factor market models is a simplification of reality. Each is also an extreme case, whereas in reality most factor markets are in between. Nonetheless, the models will add to our insights about factor pricing.

Perfect competition: Many buyers and sellers. It is worth repeating that each participant in a perfectly competitive market is

Table 28-2

FACTOR SUPPLY AND FACTOR COST TO A MONOPSONIST

1 Factor price	2 Factor quantity	3 Total cost	4 Marginal cost
$2	100	$ 200	
			$700/200 = $ 3.50
3	300	900	
			$700/100 = 7.00
4	400	1,600	
			$650/50 = 13.00
5	450	2,250	
			$750/50 = 15.00
6	500	3,000	
			$675/25 = 27.00
7	525	3,675	

a price taker, not a price maker. This means that the sellers and buyers of the services of a factor are so numerous that no one buyer or seller has a perceptible influence on the price. For some labor markets, this is not a bad approximation. Clerks and stenographers fit this category pretty well. They are numerous, and so are their employers. In general, their unions are not strong. Wage differentials for the same type of labor are for the most part explained by the nonmonetary factors discussed in Chapter 27. Many kinds of capital goods, farmlands, and industrial sites also fit this model reasonably well.

Monopsony: One buyer and many sellers. Labor markets which approximate monopsony include the mill or the mining town, where there is just one big employer for miles around. The category is usually cited as the "classic" model of labor exploitation. But it can also be used as an approximation to markets for other kinds of factors for which there is only one major buyer, or just a few buyers, but many sellers.

In a monopsony, the buyer of the factor is aware that if he increases his use of the factor he "pushes the price against himself"; that is, the price climbs up the supply curve. Why? Because to obtain a little more of the factor he has to pay a higher price for all units. Table 28-2 shows this. The first two columns constitute a conventional supply schedule showing that increasing amounts of the factor are offered at higher prices. In column 3, the total cost that the monopsonist would have to incur for each quantity of the factor is calculated as the product of the price in column 1 and the quantity in column 2. Column 4 is just the *marginal cost* of hiring an additional unit of the factor. It is calculated as the change in total cost divided by the change in the amount of the factor hired. Note that the marginal cost of hiring additional factors goes up as the number used increases.

Figure 28-6

ANALYSIS OF RESOURCE PAYMENT AND USE BY A MONOPSONIST

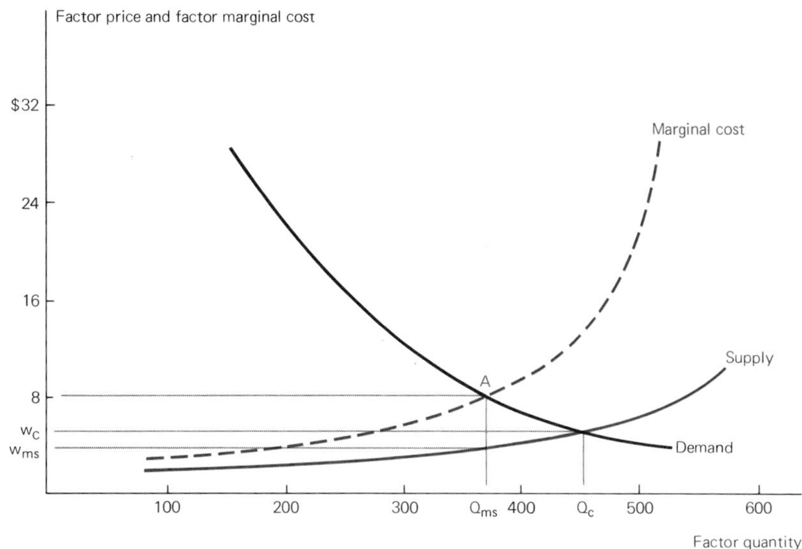

How will the price and the amount of the factor used be determined? The monopsonist, following the familiar commonsense rules for profit maximization, will hire factors so long as the amount they add to his revenue (marginal revenue product) is greater than the marginal cost of hiring and using them. The equilibrium tendency would be for the amount of the factor used to be at the intersection of the marginal cost curve and the demand curve, which is the firm's marginal revenue product curve. That is at point *A* in Figure 28-6, which contains the supply and marginal cost curves of the factor from Table 28-2 and a demand curve for the factor. The amount of the factor used in this equilibrium is Q_{ms}, and price charged is w_{ms}. By comparison, the prices and quantities that would prevail if the factor market were competitive, with the same supply and demand, would be w_c and Q_c, which are, respectively, larger than w_{ms} and Q_{ms}. This is the basis for the argument that employers in single-factory towns can exploit their labor force. The conclusion is *not* that they will necessarily pay starvation wages, but that *they will pay less than the wage that would prevail in competitive markets.* Actually there are limits to which wages — or factor prices in general — can be driven down by monopsony power. If a monopsonist tried to drive the wage too low, he might find that workers would leave town to look for jobs in the big city and that they might be willing to commute long distances to work at higher-paying jobs. Low wages might make workers more susceptible to union organization. With respect to other kinds of factors, a monopsonistically low price might also result in resources being transferred into other uses.

Monopoly: Many buyers and one seller. Another extreme case is the one in which there are many users of a factor but only one

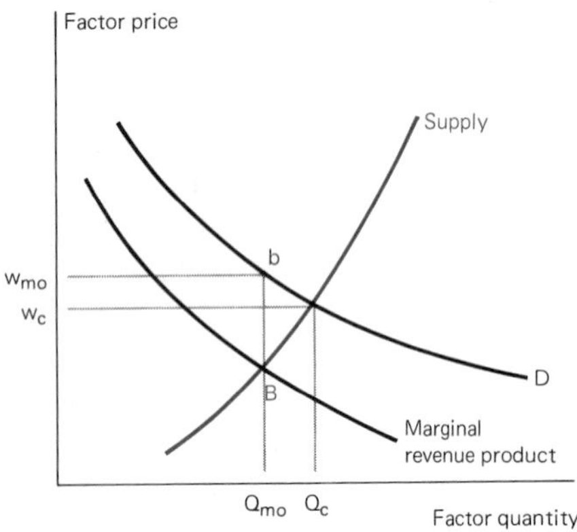

Figure 28-7

ANALYSIS OF RESOURCE PAYMENT AND USE BY A MONOPOLIST

seller, who has complete control over the supply. This might be approximated by an extremely strong union that was able to keep all nonunion labor out of the market. It could also describe markets for certain types of capital or scarce resources which were effectively controlled by patent monopoly or property ownership.

The determination of factor prices and factor use in a monopoly market is illustrated by Figure 28-7. The demand curve D is the sum of the demand of all the many buyers of the resource, none of whom has any effect on the market price of the good being produced. The resource monopolist knows, however, that, as the use of his resource expands and output grows, the price of the good will fall. Thus, the marginal revenue product of the resource will fall with increases in its use. At Q_{mo} the supply price of the resource will be equal to the marginal revenue product of the resource. But the monopolist seller will be able to extract from producers the factor price w_{mo}. That is the value to a producer of an additional unit of the resource, because each single producer can assume that his output has no effect on the product price. Each producer will, therefore, evaluate the marginal physical product of the resource at the product price. That price is higher than the marginal revenue of additional sales when output as a whole expands. The factor price w_{mo} is higher than the competitive factor return, w_c. And Q_{mo}, the amount of the resource employed, is lower than Q_c, the amount that would be employed if the resource market were competitive.

Bilateral monopoly: One buyer and one seller. Bilateral monopoly is another extreme case, but again a useful approximation to some situations. Where there is industrywide bargaining by a single labor union with a single group representative of all employers, it is a roughly accurate representation. There are also certain kinds of highly specialized capital equipment produced by only one or two suppliers and used by just a few potential buyers. What does the theory predict would happen under such circumstances?

Figure 28-8

BILATERAL MONOPOLY IN A RESOURCE MARKET

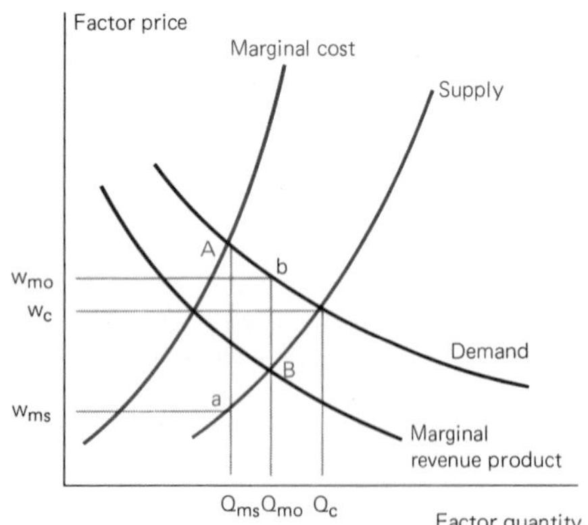

We know what price the monopsonist single buyer would like to prevail. That is at point A in Figure 28-8 and is w_{ms}. The rationale corresponds to the argument made for Figure 28-6. On the other hand, the monopolist single seller would like to be at point B in Figure 28-8 and charge w_{mo}. That corresponds to the argument made about Figure 28-7. Would the twain ever meet? Actually, they would be better off by striking some bargain than by continuing to argue. We know the limits to the bargain each would be willing to strike. But we do not know where within these limits the price will settle down. There is an essential indeterminacy to our economic analysis in these conditions. That does not mean that the market will never settle down, but rather that this analysis will not predict where it will settle.

An appraisal of the theory of functional income distribution

It is not too early to review the relevance of the economic theories of income distribution. First of all, from among the alternative theories of factor pricing and income determination, it is essential to use the theory whose assumptions most nearly fit the facts. For some factors, the assumption of a perfectly competitive factor market is a reasonably good approximation. But for many others, the imperfections in the market are of great significance.

Second, as in other analyses, the conclusions of the theory depend on the assumptions made. In particular, the equalization of the returns to identical productive services and the equality of those returns to the value of each factor's contribution to revenues are implications which are valid only in competitive factor markets. In markets with imperfections, those equalities need not obtain.

Third, the theory is an objective one and attempts to explain and predict the returns to productive resources. Its conclusions on the personal distribution of income are limited because it does not attempt to explain the *ownership* of productive resources. The theory is not normative. It offers no judgments on whether the functional or personal distribution of income is fair and equitable.

Finally, a question: Does economic theory do reasonably well in actually predicting factor returns? As in other types of microeconomic analysis, the theory here is quite abstract and requires a good deal of art in its applications. It gains content in particular applications and provides considerable insight, as we shall see.

Summary

The demand by a firm hiring a resource in a competitive market depends on what an additional unit of the resource can add to the firm's revenues. That is the marginal revenue product of the additional unit of input. If the firm also sells in competitive markets, the marginal revenue product of an additional unit of input will be equal to the value of the marginal physical product at the market price. But if the firm sells in monopolistically controlled markets the value at market prices of the marginal physical product of the services of the resource will be greater than the marginal revenue product which it generates to the firm.

The total demand for the resource is the demand of all the firms using it and, conceptually, is the result of adding up the amount which each firm would purchase at alternative prices. That total demand with the total supply of the resource will determine the resource price.

While the price and use of one resource are being determined, the price and use of other resources are also settled in a mutually interdependent process. The total income paid to each factor will be the total amount of the factor offered and demanded times the factor sales price or rental rate. On the supply side, resources will shift around to get the highest possible return, and in the process, the quantity supplied will increase where rates are high and decrease where rates are low. On the demand side, producers trying to minimize costs will also tend to shift the use of resources from high-cost to low-cost inputs to find the lowest cost of producing any output. This will tend to equalize the marginal revenue product of a resource in all types of production.

The marginal productivity theory of factor pricing and functional income distribution is a positive theory. The theory does not imply that the resulting functional distribution has normative content, except that it leads to a maximum of efficiency in satisfying the demands for goods. Those demands, however, reflect the existing distribution of ownership of resources.

Factor markets can depart from competitive conditions in a variety of ways. In a monopsony, where there is a single buyer of a productive factor, the factor price tends to be lower than in a competitive market, and the quantity used tends to be less. In a monopolistic market with a single seller of a factor, the factor price is higher and the quantity sold is less than in a competitive market. If there is bilateral monopoly—a single buyer and a single seller—economic analysis can tell only the range within which the final factor price will fall, but not exactly where within that range.

Questions for discussion and review

1. Why is the equalization of the marginal revenue products of the same resource in all of its uses a condition for the efficient use of resources?

2. Explain in your own words the marginal productivity theory of income distribution.

3. Do you believe the marginal productivity theory of income distribution is an inhuman justification for the exploitation of labor? If you answer Yes, do you think that the theory is also an inhuman justification for the exploitation of land and capital resources? If you answered No, what do you think is particularly "human" about it?

4. All other things equal, will the demand of a monopolist for productive resources be greater or less than the demand of a competitive industry at the same product price level?

5. What are the effects of monopsonistic practices in resource markets?

6. What are the effects of monopolistic practices in resource markets?

7. What is the source of the indeterminacy of factor prices when there is bilateral monopoly in the factor market?

8. Do you think that colleges and universities take advantage of their position as large employers and pay student labor less than the competitive wage?

Concepts for review

Derived demand for productive services
Bilateral monopoly in factor markets
Monopsony in factor markets
Efficient resource allocation
Marginal revenue product
Marginal product valued at market prices

29

Wages, labor unions, and labor demand

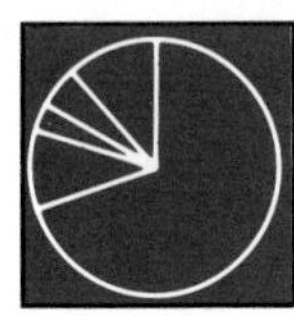

A reasonable self-interest leads most people to have a special concern for the share of income going to labor. As demonstrated in the last chapter, the forces that influence the pricing of factors of production and the distribution of income among factors can be analyzed in general terms. But for deeper understanding, the structure and the operation of the markets for each factor must be examined individually. This chapter focuses on the returns to labor.

The share of the national income received by labor varies somewhat from year to year. After staying close to two-thirds of total income for many years, it has risen above 70 percent in recent years. At the same time the national income has been growing, so the absolute amounts earned by all labor as well as the earnings per worker have been rising.

Though income from productive labor makes up, by far, the largest share of most individuals' income, labor incomes vary widely. Table 29-1 shows median incomes for a number of occupations. Columns 1 and 2 list the income for all members of each occupation in 1968. It is no surprise that incomes in the professions and in management are higher than in other occupations. But did you realize that blue-collar craftsmen and foremen average more than white-collar clerical and sales personnel?

Labor incomes within each occupation also vary. A lot of that variation is associated with color and sex. Columns 3, 4, 5, and 6 in Table 29-1 list the median incomes within each occupation by sex and race. They show that black males are less well paid than whites and that females are less well paid than males. White females and black workers of both sexes tend to receive less pay

Table 29-1

MEDIAN EARNINGS OF WHITE AND BLACK YEAR-ROUND WORKERS IN METROPOLITAN AREAS CURRENTLY EMPLOYED IN SELECTED OCCUPATION GROUPS, 1968

Occupation group	1 Total Male	2 Total Female	3 White Male	4 White Female	5 Black Male	6 Black Female
Professional & managerial workers	$10,492	$6,425	$10,572	$6,404	$7,046	$6,607
Clerical & sales workers	7,633	4,522	7,763	4,545	6,346	4,354
Craftsmen & foremen	8,441		8,598		6,407	
Operatives	7,111	3,988	7,339	4,093	5,956	3,457
Nonfarm laborers	5,607		5,826		5,251	
Service workers except private household	5,965	3,139	6,340	3,118	4,760	3,172
Private household workers		1,174		740		1,487

Source: U.S. Department of Commerce, Bureau of the Census.

for the same work. But they tend also to be less qualified because of prior discrimination in education and training. The results of the discrimination practiced against females and nonwhites, however, are even greater than the table indicates. Not only are they less well paid within each occupation, but their access to the better-paying occupations and to the better-paying jobs within each occupation is restricted.

A general explanation of wage levels and the share of income received by labor must be flexible enough to account for the occupational differences shown in Table 29-1. That is one of the beauties of the supply and demand framework. It provides a means of organizing all the relevant data, yet it provides scope for great variability in the way different forces interact and influence the final outcome.

Analysis of the supply side of labor markets must take into account such overall matters as the size of the population, its growth rate, and the proportion of people actively seeking work. It must also consider the influence of education and training and the distribution of particular aptitudes in the labor force.

The demand side of the analysis must consider the growth of the economy and of particular sectors with different labor demand characteristics. Capital accumulation increases labor productivity but may substitute for labor. Technical changes and new products also have an effect.

A realistic appraisal of wage determination must recognize the importance of "imperfections" in labor markets. Often there is no significant competition on the hiring side; there may not be many alternative employers and/or there may be explicit or implicit collusion among them. Unions restrict competition on the supply side, as does individual labor immobility. Discrimination against nonwhites, against females, against older workers and people with the "wrong" accents — all these imperfections must be kept in mind.

The character of wage differences

Before undertaking a detailed examination of labor supply, let us note the distinction between *equalizing* and *nonequalizing* differences in wage and salary rates. This will add a new dimension to our understanding of how supply and demand conditions interact.

Equalizing differences. Some jobs are performed in pleasant surroundings; some must be carried out in ugly, noisy, dirty, very hot, or very cold places. Some jobs are nerve-racking; some are easy-going. Some jobs are dangerous; in others the only risk is falling out of a chair. Some jobs require years of specialized training; others can be learned in a few days or weeks.

With such job differences, one would naturally expect differences in income. *Higher incomes that compensate for relative unpleasantness, danger, longer training periods, and so on represent equalizing differences.* They tend to offset the nonmonetary differences among jobs. The relatively higher incomes of craftsmen and kindred workers as compared with clerical workers are, in part, the result of equalizing differences in earnings. White-collar work typically requires less physical effort, enjoys more pleasant inside working conditions, and entails little danger as compared with blue-collar working conditions. Moreover some crafts require long years of training and apprenticeship.

Nonequalizing differences. If all the differences in wage incomes were equalizing, foundrymen who work in hot, dirty, and sometimes dangerous conditions would receive higher wages than most other workers. Garbage collectors would also be highly compensated to make up for the unsavoriness of their tasks. It is common knowledge, however, that, with some important exceptions, *many of the higher-paying jobs are also those with better working conditions. Higher incomes in such cases reflect nonequalizing differences in pay.* How can one account for them?

Widespread imperfections in labor markets are one cause. They account for wage differences based on sex and race discrimination. But in addition, not all people have the same labor qualities. Their different qualities are scarce to different degrees and, therefore, command different wage rates. Sometimes the distinctive qualities are obvious, as in the case of 7-foot basketball players. (If the rules were changed and the basket were lowered, what do you think would happen to the income of 7-footers?) More often the particular, scarce qualities are not so readily apparent, and a long period of training and testing is necessary to determine the extent to which they exist. The last violinist in the last row of a large symphony orchestra may have had as much training and practice as the first violinist, but the latter receives the higher income because the system pays off on performance. The differentials in performance and in income are partly the result of certain qualitative differences in individuals.

The *qualitative differences among people,* in effect, create somewhat distinct categories of labor. A number of years ago economists gave the name "noncompeting groups" to these categories. The name is picturesque, and it has stuck. It is misleading, however, because the existence of such qualitatively different types of labor is consistent even with a perfectly competitive labor market as long as there is competition among the members of each group. It is also misleading because it suggests that the groups do not compete at all with one another. They may compete where, in fact, members of one group can substitute for those of another. Few talents are absolutely unique, and fewer still have no reasonably good substitutes. While being 7 feet tall provides unique advantages to a basketball player, shorter players can, to some extent, substitute speed, jumping ability, and shooting accuracy for height.

Determinants of the supply of labor

The availability of labor for use in production depends on (1) the size of the population, (2) the proportion of the population in the labor force, and (3) the number of hours that members of the labor force are willing to work. At a less global and more particular level, it is necessary to add (4) the education and training systems – including on-the-job training – which create both generalized and special skills.

Population growth Population growth rates in the United States have ranged from 1 percent to 1.9 percent per year in the last thirty years. Though the variations have been extensively studied by demographers, their sources are still not well understood. For example, there is some evidence that population growth varies with economic conditions. During depressions, marriages and children tend to be postponed. When economic conditions improve, the rate of family formation and the birthrate tend to go up. Yet during the relatively stagnant 1950s, the rate of population growth averaged about 1.7 percent, while during the more buoyant 1960s, it fell to about 1.4 percent. In societies where population growth is constrained by a scarcity of the bare necessities of life, an increase in income and an improvement in sanitary conditions and health care will result in a higher rate of population growth. But in these cases, continued income growth generally results in a decline in the rate of population growth. In any case, *the effect of population growth on the availability of labor is not felt in the short run, but is of basic significance over long periods.*

Immigration

Another potential source of population change is immigration. The rate of migration tends to respond to economic incentives both within a country and among countries. There are net population movements from relatively low to relatively high average income areas in the United States and from relatively poor to relatively wealthy countries. Immigration to the United States has been tightly restricted in the last fifty years, so that it has averaged around 300,000 persons per year, or less than two-tenths of 1 percent of the population. By comparison, at the beginning of the century, immigration was about 800,000 persons per year or around 1 percent of the population at that time. Even this number understates the immigrant addition to the labor supply during the turn-of-the-century years, because an unusually large percentage of immigrants were males in their prime working age.

No doubt, one of the chief arguments used to justify the clampdown on immigration to this country was based on economics. *Limiting immigration is one way to restrict the supply of labor.* Our analysis tells us that, all other things equal, restricting the labor supply will tend to raise the level of wages.[1]

Labor-force participation

The labor-force participation rate, or the proportion of the population in the labor force, tends to vary directly with the wage rate. As wages increase, an increasing number of women, young persons, and older persons will stay in or move into the labor force and a decreasing number will move out. This is a well-known and consistently recurring phenomenon. *A decline in wages and the number of jobs available will correspondingly result in a decline in the number of persons looking for work*; older persons and women will find it less attractive to keep looking for work and to accept lower wages, and younger people will stay in school longer. This kind of change in labor-force participation is, by the way, one of major problems in estimating unemployment. The official unemployment rate – people out of a job *and* looking for one – includes

[1] The effect of population growth and immigration on labor incomes and on labor's share of the national income depends on the elasticity of demand for labor and the ease with which it can be substituted for other resources. Suppose, for example, that a country was in a phase of overall increasing returns to the scale of production. That might be true of a relatively sparsely populated area. Then a larger labor force achieved via population growth and immigration could lead to larger average returns to all factors, including labor, even if labor's *share* declined.

the effects of an adjustment which takes into account the fact that the number of people actually looking for work changes with economic conditions.

Hours of work

The number of hours an individual is willing to work depends in large part on the wage rate offered. Individuals may react to wage increases *either by increasing or by reducing the amount of labor they will supply*. And changes in either direction can be rationalized.

If wages go up, a *substitution effect* will tend to induce people to give up some of their leisure in order to increase their incomes. That permits a higher level of consumption of goods and services.

The opposite tendency is for people to work shorter hours as wages rise. At the higher hourly rates, they can work less and continue to earn the same or even more income. With more income, they may want to "buy more leisure." This is called the *income effect*.

The substitution effect tends to increase the amount of labor supplied as wage rates rise. The income effect tends to reduce the amount supplied as wages rise. What will the net effect be? We have no generally valid answer, but it is likely to depend on the period of adjustment. There is a good deal of evidence that higher wages will induce longer hours of work in the short run. On the other hand, the evidence of the twentieth century leaves little doubt that, on the average, hours of work have fallen as wages and incomes have risen. Even in the short run, if wages rise far enough, the supply curve may bend backward as the income effect outweighs the substitution effect.[2]

[2] This is shown in Fig. 27-5 on p. 575. The indifference curve technique of the Appendix to Chap. 16 can be used to illustrate this point. In the accompanying figure, the indifference curves indicate the relative preferences of the individual between income, on the horizontal axis, and leisure, on the vertical axis. Leisure is the difference between 24, the number of hours in the day, and h, the number of hours worked. A budget-constraint line such as AB indicates the various combinations of leisure or income that the individual can have. The distance OB is the maximum income which could be earned at the wage rate w_1. If the wage rate should rise to w_2, the maximum income earned would be OC. If the new tangency of the budget-constraint line with an indifference curve were at Y, the individual would settle for less leisure than at X, his initial position. In effect he would be offering more hours of work. On the other hand, if the indifference map was such that the new tangency was at Z, the individual would be working fewer hours.

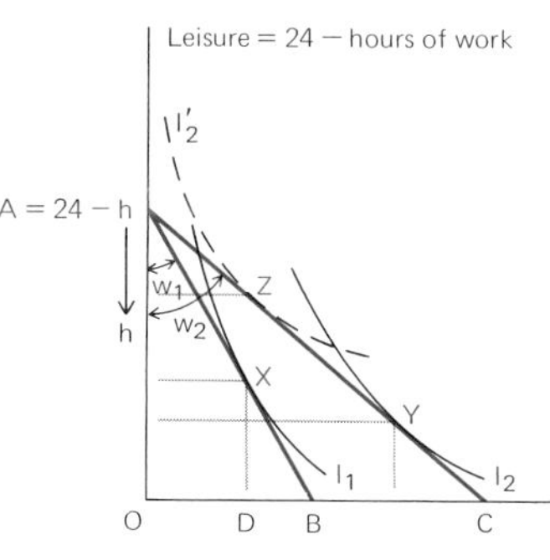

Education and training Attendance in school is required by law up to a minimum school-leaving age. That still does not guarantee a high school education for everyone in the United States. Education above the minimum school-leaving age involves costs to the individual and his family—the opportunity costs of the income that is not earned when he is in school. Above the high school level, tuition costs and travel to and from college can also be significant. Since education has a cost, one might expect the demand for education—and the supply of educated persons—to be responsive to economic incentives. Those incentives are the income differentials that can be earned with additional education. There is, in fact, evidence that persons demanding education do respond to economic incentives. *It is difficult, however, to separate the effects of income incentives on the demand for education from other social pressures and individual aptitudes.*

Unionism and the supply of labor

The vigor with which labor unions are both praised and condemned emphasizes the special role they have in affecting the labor supply.

Early unionism. Labor unionism in the United States is still influenced by its early history. In the first decades of the nineteenth century, unionism had a tenuous hold on life. It appealed to small groups of workers only and lost membership drastically in the recurrent economic depressions. Moreover, unionism had an equivocal legal position. For many years and in many courts, strikes for higher wages or better working conditions were considered criminal conspiracies.

The first labor unions were locally organized "craft unions" composed of members of particular trades, such as printers, shoemakers, hatters, tailors, weavers, and carpenters. The first permanent national unions were formed in the 1850s and were made up of local unions in the same craft. An attempt to found an overall labor organization in 1866 resulted in the National Labor Union, but this lasted only six years. The severe depression of the early 1870s not only cut sharply into union membership, but actually destroyed many organizations that could not hold their membership together in the face of widespread unemployment. In the late 1870s a new national organization, the Knights of Labor, had a number of initial successes, particularly in strikes for recognition and against wage cuts in the railroad industry. These much-publicized successes brought in many new members in the mid-1880s. The Knights of Labor cast its net widely and admitted almost anyone, excepting only such "enemies" as bankers, doctors, lawyers, and saloonkeepers. The organization was highly centralized, with a program which emphasized the development of cooperative producing organizations. These were to be achieved primarily by political action and social education. The Knights were first associated in the public mind with the movement for an eight-hour day. However, when the national leadership failed to support the widespread strikes that took place in 1886 to achieve that goal, the organization lost much of its popularity. By the early 1890s, the Knights of Labor had virtually disappeared.

Business unionism. While the Knights of Labor was emerging from obscurity and returning to it, another national labor organization was growing quietly. The American Federation of Labor became the dominant force in United States unionism for the next half century. *The principles upon which the AFL was based are regarded by most union leaders as the major source of its success in bringing unionism out of the wilderness and giving it a lasting place in the economy.* The character of modern American unionism cannot be understood without appreciating this fact.

The first and long-time president of the AFL was Samuel Gompers. He and his associates attributed the weakness of American unionism to a diffusion of interests and energies into general "uplift" programs and political action. Their prescription for a healthy trade union movement was "business unionism": (1) organization along craft or trades lines, with each national trades union having exclusive jurisdiction in its field and complete autonomy in internal affairs; (2) no permanent political commitments, but a tactic of "supporting friends and punishing enemies"; (3) bread and butter unionism, which means a primary concern with the improvement of wages, hours, and working conditions of union members via direct negotiations with employers.

With these principles and with effective organization, the AFL weathered the depressions that virtually wiped out other unions. "Industrial unions" organized at the beginning of the century to include all the members of an industry, regardless of craft skills, were defeated in major strikes in the iron, steel, and railway industries. The fate of the "Wobblies" (the IWW – International Workers of the World) also seemed to confirm the success of the business unionism prescription of the AFL. The IWW was a radical labor organization with some initial success in strikes against the textile industries of the East and the mining and lumber camps of the West. Its radicalism provoked reaction, often bloody, and it did not survive the political witch-hunting of the post-World War I period.

Life was not smooth for business unionism, however, in the first decades of the century. The Sherman Antitrust Act was used against labor unions until, in 1914, a new law gave them more protection. Employers often insisted on a yellow-dog contract, in which workers agreed not to join unions. Nonetheless, union membership expanded until the early 1920s when it leveled off.

The development of modern unionism. The Great Depression of the 1930s was at first a severe blow for labor unions, but it brought in its train an enlarged public concern for the welfare of workers. That in turn led to a major change in unionism. New federal laws in the 1930s, especially the Wagner (National Labor Relations) Act of 1935, greatly strengthened the bargaining position of labor unions. The use of the injunction against unions in labor disputes was restricted; yellow-dog contracts were made unenforceable in federal courts; discrimination against labor union members was outlawed, and, most importantly, the *right* of employees to bargain collectively with their employers was established.

With this encouragement, labor union membership grew rapidly in the middle 1930s, spreading to major industries and increasingly taking place along industrial rather than craft lines. A new organization, the Committee for Industrial Organization, was formed within the AFL to promote this development. But the AFL, insisting on craft organization, regarded the new committee as "dual unionism" and expelled its members. The expelled unions then became the nucleus of the Congress of Industrial Organizations (CIO), which conducted vigorous organizing campaigns in steel, automobile, rubber, and other major industries, using unconventional tactics such as the sit-in strike. Though the sit-in was declared illegal, it was an important device in winning public attention and support. Yet not all CIO campaigns were successful, and many were not peaceful, as both employers and unions resorted to violence. But the overall result was clear; unionism was spread far beyond the boundaries within which it had operated earlier. The AFL, reacting to the new organization, itself began to organize more vigorously and expand its membership, though again not always with success.

The World War II period was one of consolidation and growth. Union leadership pledged the unions not to strike during the war and received the continuing support of the federal government — in organization and in gaining recognition as the collective bargaining representatives of their members.

The new unions of the thirties and forties evoked widespread concern over radicalism, but, for the most part, the leaders were men brought up in the business unionism of the AFL. No doubt, on occasion Communist labor organizers were used. They were often hard-working and effective, sometimes so effective that they won control of a union. In 1948 the CIO expelled several of its member unions which it accused of Communist domination. In general, however, the union movement in the United States has continued to regard business unionism rather than political ideology as its cornerstone of success.

In 1948 the Taft-Hartley Act was passed with the rationale of making the government more neutral in labor-management disputes. The act made it possible for management to bring unfair

Table 29-2

TOTAL EMPLOYMENT AND UNION EMPLOYMENT AS A PERCENTAGE OF TOTAL EMPLOYMENT, 1968

Unions	*Total employment (1,000)*	*All unions*		*Union employees as a percentage of total employment*
		Number	*Members (1,000)*	
Manufacturing	19,740	103	9,218	46.7
1. Food, beverage, and tobacco	1,866	34	919	49.3
2. Clothing, textiles, leather products	2,759	32	1,192	43.2
3. Furniture, lumber, wood products, paper	1,774	48	915	51.6
4. Printing, publishing	1,063	19	375	35.3
5. Petroleum, chemical, rubber	1,777	54	724	40.7
6. Stone, clay, glass	638	20	295	46.2
7. Metals, machinery and equipment, except transportation equipment	7,062	85	3,022	42.8
8. Transportation equipment	2,026	21	1,333	65.8
9. Other manufacturing	777	60	443	57.0
Nonmanufacturing	40,953	101	8,125	19.8
1. Mining, quarrying	625	12	321	51.4
2. Contract construction	3,259	28	2,323	71.3
3. Transportation	2,701	47	2,429	89.9
4. Telephone, telegraph	991	8	437	44.1
5. Electric, gas utilities	657	17	305	46.4
6. Trade	14,111	18	1,217	8.6
7. Finance, insurance	3,357	7	61	1.8
8. Service industries	10,504	27	981	9.3
9. Agriculture, fishing	4,749	6	40	0.8
Government	12,202	59	1,453	11.9
1. Federal	2,737	56	897	32.8
2. State, local	9,465	18	556	5.9
Total	72,895	189	20,210	27.7

Source: U.S. Department of Labor, Bureau of Labor Statistics.

labor practice charges against labor unions. It increased the power of the nonunion worker by banning the closed shop, which restricts hiring to labor union members. State governments were given the power to ban the union shop, which requires membership of all employees after they are hired. The act also included provisions for "cooling off periods" and for court injunctions against strikes in labor disputes involving a "national emergency."

Union leaders labeled the Taft-Hartley Act a "slave labor" law and predicted grave consequences for unionism. In general, however, it does not appear to have reduced labor union strength, though it probably slowed the expansion of unionism into industries and regions where it was not already well established.

Labor unionism in the late 1940s and in the 1950s and 1960s also became more active politically. Though labor unions are forbidden to make direct contributions to any political party or candidate, they have created new political "wings" to express their opinions. Still, the major political technique is the one laid down by Gompers: Support labor's friends and punish its enemies.

In 1955 the AFL and CIO reunited and formed a single federation. This did not eliminate craft and industrial unionism conflicts, however. While the AFL-CIO is a spokesman for the labor movement and initiates some organizing campaigns, most of the economic and political power is still in the individual crafts and industrial unions which make up the national federation. Table 29-2 shows total employment by major industry and union membership as a percentage of the total. The high unionization rates of transportation and contract construction are due to the organizing effectiveness of the railroad unions and the Teamsters Union. But there are many industries, mainly in the nonmanufacturing and government sectors, with less than half of their workers in unions.

The tactics of labor union power

Labor union organization seeks to replace person-to-person negotiations between employers and employees with collective bargaining, in which the union acts on behalf of all or most employees. Yet it is *not* correct to regard a union as a monopolist "selling" labor. A union's ability to affect the wage bargain gives it some degree of monopoly control. But, in general, it does not have the power to "sell" various amounts of labor at different wage rates. How do unions exercise power? To what extent can they affect the labor market?

Strikes. The *organized strike* is by far a union's most important source of power. It is a potent weapon to the extent that it succeeds in denying employers the labor necessary to carry on production. Until about twenty-five years ago, many employers tried to break strikes by bringing in nonunion labor, strikebreakers or "scabs." That often led to violence and bloodshed when nonstriking workers crossed picket lines or when the police tried to enforce a court injunction prohibiting picketing. Public condemnation of strikebreaking is now so general that it is seldom tried unless a large proportion of the labor force opposes the strike.

Strikes become wars of attrition, and victory depends on who can hold out longer — the employer who is taking losses while not operating or the workers who must go without their regular pay. To shore up their bargaining position, unions often accumulate strike funds from which they pay their striking members a weekly or monthly strike benefit. Some unions will even make loans to help another striking union through a difficult period.

Where strikes are forbidden by law, as in certain public service and government employment, labor unions lose much of their effectiveness. Rather than forgo this weapon entirely, the union officers may choose to accept the consequences of an illegal strike — fines and imprisonment.

During a strike of any magnitude, someone always comes up with a statement about what each day on strike costs the average worker. For example, at $4.50 per hour, the worker would lose $36 a day in wages. A strike that lasts four weeks or twenty working days would cost the striker $720. A 5 percent wage increase would add only $450 to the annual prestrike earnings of about $9,000 — much less than the amount lost in wages during the strike. Is it worth it? Well, that depends in part on what the union and its members are trying to prove and what they are after.

Even if the income arithmetic works out as shown for one year, the gains go on and on for a number of years. In addition, a long, successful strike may make the next set of negotiations easier for the union, as it has demonstrated its will and ability to stop work. Other issues besides wages may be at stake in the negotiations, and the strike may help achieve them. Finally, however, labor-management negotiations and strike preparations may release deep personal emotions. These, rather than any rational balancing of gains and losses, may come to dominate the proceedings.

By the way, what would the type of cost calculation made above show for the company? Remember that many fixed costs go right on piling up even when a plant is shut down. Output and, eventually, sales and profits will fall. On the other hand, the firm may also lose more in a strike than the annual cost of the wage settlement. It may have to agree to provide certain "fringe" benefits to its employees, such as additional health insurance and paid vacations. The higher labor costs will go on and on, and unless prices and/or productivity rates change, the company's future profits will be lower than if there had been no strike and wage increase. The firm will take present and future gains and losses into account in its wage bargaining. It will also fight for changes in labor practices which will raise labor productivity.

An organized strike is one authorized by a vote of the union or its strike committee. A *wildcat strike* is "unauthorized" and sometimes "illegal" in the sense that it is a violation of the labor-management contract. A "slowdown" is a reduction in the pace of work, sometimes justified by "following the rule book," rather than cutting the usual corners to speed up the work flow. Increased absenteeism when workers call in sick, higher rates of rejection of parts for failure to meet quality standards – all are ways of disrupting the flow of output. They can be carried on so subtly that, while management knows what the result is, no individual worker can be singled out for violating accepted work practices.

While organized strikes are the union's "ultimate weapon" in collective bargaining, workers can demonstrate their strength in many ways. Since these subtle means of work disruption are often explicitly forbidden in labor contracts, union officers cannot condone them. But they can argue that such disruptions are the result of legitimate grievances that must be resolved in a new contract.

Wildcat strikes may result from worker dissatisfaction with employer policies, but sometimes they reflect rank and file dissatisfaction with union leadership. When union leaders lose touch with their members, they may not be able to induce them to abide by a labor contract. The wildcat strike is then a means by which union dissidents put pressure on the leadership. Unannounced work stoppages, ostensibly a protest against management, may in reality have the objective of embarrassing the official union leadership. Management is caught in the middle of internal political maneuvering within the union.

Picketing. Union members can publicize a strike by carrying signs in front of the struck plant. They urge nonunion workers to stay out and employees of other firms making deliveries or providing services not to cross picket lines. Obstructive picketing can usually be stopped if the employer seeks a court injunction. But when the workers are sharply divided, there may be violence between those who want to work and those who want to strike.

Boycotts and union labels. In *consumer boycotts*, unions urge consumers not to buy products sold by firms whose workers are on strike or which hire nonunion labor. On the other hand, *union labels* identify products made with union labor and are intended to encourage consumption. Boycotts can be an effective union weapon, especially in local situations where union members constitute a large proportion of the total market. They can also be successful in national campaigns if public sympathy is aroused. Though union labels are used in many industries, they seem to have little influence on consumer expenditures.

In *secondary boycotts*, unions involved in labor disputes urge the employees of other firms not to handle or buy the products of their firm. They may appeal to union solidarity and brotherhood and promise future help in labor-management confrontations.

Public pressure. Unions attempt to mobilize public pressure and government intervention in their behalf, just as management does. Public opinion has often been a powerful force, and its explicit or implicit sanction of court actions and of the use of the police in labor disputes in the nineteenth and early twentieth centuries was a major deterrent to the growth of union power. In the late 1930s and early 1940s, government support was a major source of union strength. Popular support has wavered, and one can only say that public opinion is changeable, and both labor and management must contend for it.

In any large-scale labor dispute, local or state or national government officials are under some pressure to intervene. Their powers are quite varied. They may only be able to mobilize public opinion in favor of one or another type of settlement. In certain industries they have the legal power to ask for court injunctions to end a strike or force arbitration. Specialists in labor-management relations disagree about the effect of government intervention. Some regard it as a necessary part of an incomes and price policy aimed at avoiding inflation while passing on to labor a share of the gains in productivity. Others argue that government intervention dilutes and distorts the economic forces that should determine the outcome of labor-management negotiations.

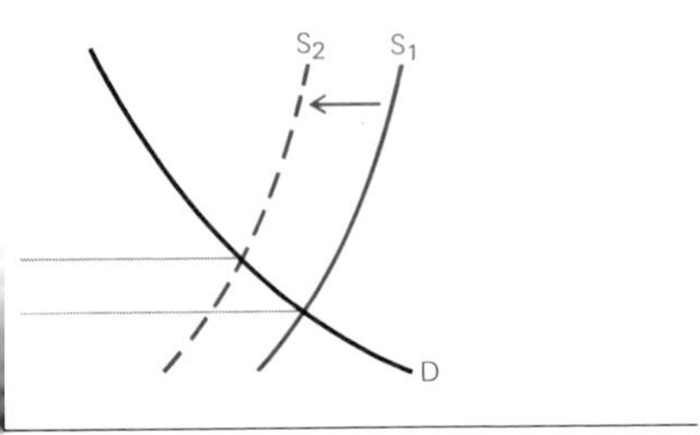

Figure 29-1

TO RAISE WAGES RESTRICTION OF LABOR SUPPLY

The economics of union tactics

Even though unions are seldom if ever complete monopolists, they are able to change the nature of competition in labor markets. Three approaches to achieving higher wage rates can be distinguished: *restricting the labor supply, raising wages directly, and increasing or maintaining the demand for labor.* Our analysis of each of these approaches will assume that, except for union activities, the labor markets are competitive.

Restricting the labor supply. If the union can effectively shift the supply curve of labor so that less is available at each wage level, then wage levels will tend to rise. This is shown by the shift from S_1 to S_2 in Figure 29-1, with an increase in wages from w_1 to w_2. How can that shift be accomplished? On the national level, barriers to immigration will have that effect. At the local level, unions may try to impose high initiation fees, which will limit entry or enforce unduly long apprenticeship programs. These practices will also act to reduce the supply of labor. Charges that some craft unions have followed such practices appear to be justified.

Raising wage rates directly. Suppose that through collective bargaining unions win a standard wage increase for all workers. That forces employers to hire fewer workers than they would hire in a competitive labor market. This is shown in Figure 29-2. If the labor market were competitive, wage w_c would be paid and L_c amount of labor would be hired. If unions succeeded in raising the wage to w_u, only L_u amount of labor would be used. This direct increase in wages has been the most common approach of industrial unions, which contain relatively few highly skilled workers and have no tradition of apprenticeship.

Figure 29-2

EFFECT OF WAGE INCREASES ON EMPLOYMENT

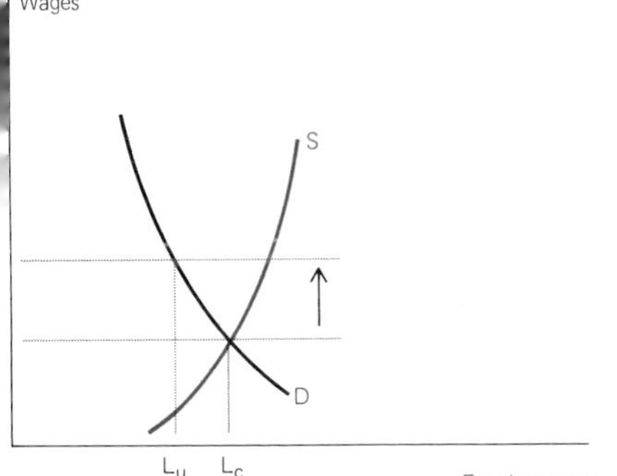

Increasing or maintaining the demand for labor. By identifying the goods produced with union labor and trying to shift consumer demand toward those goods, unions are, in effect, trying to increase the demand for union labor and, thus, maintain or increase wages. This approach is shown in Figure 29-3. The upward shift in demand from D_1 to D_2, with the given labor supply curve, results in a higher wage and increases employment. The appearance of the presidents of textile unions and steelworkers' unions before congressional committees to ask for an increase in tariffs to keep out or reduce imports is an attempt to maintain or increase the demand for union-produced goods.

Wages versus employment

Only the third approach to wage policy leads to an increase in employment along with the increase in wages. *Either shifting the labor supply schedule downward or increasing the standard wage rate would reduce employment in otherwise competitive labor markets.* Of course, if for other reasons the demand curve for labor should be shifting upward, that would tend to offset the employment-reducing effect. Then the employment-reducing effect would be "virtual" rather than actual, for if the wages were not increased, employment would rise.

It is easy for union membership to overlook the employment-reducing effect of wage increases. If anyone is actually laid off, it will probably be the younger workers and the newer men in the union rather than older workers with more skill and seniority. The employment-reducing effect of wage increases is also likely to be gradual. Firms may not fire workers immediately; they may just not replace workers who quit or retire. They may decide to adopt laborsaving machinery, which will take some time for delivery and installation. During that time, the normal turnover and quit rate will result in labor force reductions.

Figure 29-3

EFFECT OF INCREASES IN DEMAND FOR UNION-MADE PRODUCTS

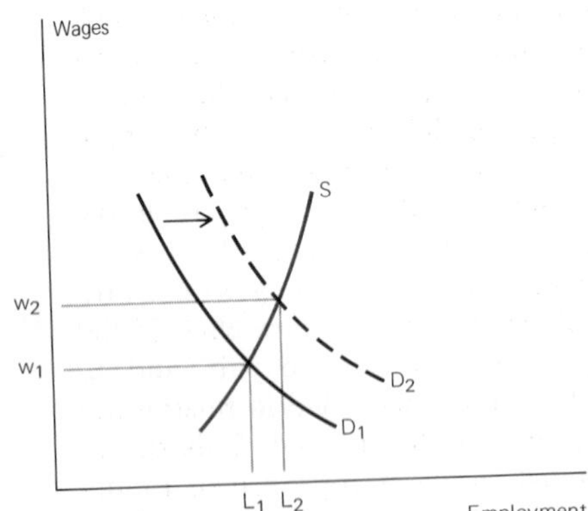

The employment effects of increases in wages depend on the elasticity of demand for labor in particular lines. For any given level of output, the demand for labor will be more inelastic (1) the smaller the proportion of the particular wage costs in total costs of production and (2) the less likely it is that other labor, machines, or material can be substituted for the labor whose wage has gone up.

Some union policies are intended primarily to preserve jobs and maintain employment, at least for certain groups. The most obvious of these policies is "featherbedding." Here, the union uses its collective bargaining power to force employers to use more labor than they otherwise would want to. Featherbedding is often associated with the preservation of jobs after a technological change eliminates the need for some of the workers. For example, when coal-fired locomotives were replaced by diesel-electric trains, the need for firemen to stoke the coal-fired locomotives disappeared. Sometimes unions completely block technological change in order to preserve employment. Thus, most painters' unions will not let their members substitute rollers or pads for brushes to spread paint, even though labor productivity is lower with brushes.

The issues are seldom clear-cut. Locomotive firemen are not needed to tend the nonexistent boilers of diesel-electrics, but workers with that title had other functions as well, such as serving as a general assistant and lookout for the engineer. Was it a coincidence that yard accidents went up when firemen were taken off diesel-electrics? Was it no coincidence but a real effect, which could be offset by better safety practices on the part of the engineers? Is the quality of brush painting superior to that of roller painting?

There are instances of unions cooperating closely with employers when technical innovations change the requirements for labor skills. The International Typographical Union, for example, has retraining schools for its members, so that they can learn to use new techniques of printing and reproduction.

Union and management bargaining

Labor-management relations in unionized firms are guided rather strictly by the terms of a contract, which is renegotiated on specified dates. Let us assume that it is now contract time. To put the various claims and disputes in perspective, we shall sit in on a collective-bargaining session.

> *Tough but shrewd union leader:* We have looked at the situation as it has developed since our current contract was signed and found that things have gotten out of line. Our present demands are for an additional 25 cents per hour in wages and increased employer contributions to worker health insurance and pension funds. We know we must take into account both the company's circumstances and our workers' welfare, and after careful study we believe our demands are just and reasonable. The things we are asking for are based on the following considerations:
>
> 1. *Worker productivity.* Output per worker has gone up this year at a rate about equal to the wage increase requested. Thus, the wage increase would not contribute to inflation.
>
> 2. *Ability to pay.* Company profits have risen by 15 percent, while wage rates have not changed since the last contract negotiations, twelve months ago. The company has increased its dividend payout, however, and its retained earnings.
>
> 3. *Keeping pace with price increases.* As prices have gone up, the previous gains in the workers' standard of living have been lost. To maintain their living conditions, they must have a wage increase.
>
> 4. *Meeting national, local, and industry standards.* Other firms in the industry have granted wage increases similar to those being demanded. Nationwide, as well as locally, similar settlements have been made in other industries.

5. *Higher wages are necessary for prosperity.* Higher wages help maintain effective demand by increasing consumer purchasing power. Therefore, they contribute to the nation's and the company's prosperity.

The union demands will be met by a counter offer by management, represented by the head of the personnel division or the vice president in charge of labor relations. He will have his rationale, which may simply deny the union's arguments or may develop new arguments.

Steely but shrewd management negotiator: We have followed developments carefully over the last year. Keeping in mind the interests of our stockholders as well as the legitimate concerns of our employees, we are willing to offer an additional 15 cents per hour in wages and one day of extra paid vacation each year. This offer is based on the following considerations:

1. *Staying competitive.* If the firm is to stay competitive and grow and continue to provide employment, costs must be kept down. Productivity has not gone up as much as represented, and if the requested increase were granted we would have to raise prices.

2. *Investing to increase productivity.* Increases in productivity are due to management investment in new equipment. Reduced profits due to higher labor costs will reduce the company's savings and ability to borrow to continue such investment.

3. *The firm's benefits offset higher wages elsewhere.* The firm carries on special training programs of benefit to its employees. Its convenient location on the turnpike makes it easier for employees to come to work, and the regional average wage level is lower than the national average anyway.

4. *Wage increases force price increases.* Labor's request for excessive wage increases is only self-defeating. If granted, the wage increases will only have to be passed on in price increases, which contribute to higher living costs and erode the worker's standard of living.

5. *Tending one's own garden.* Labor's arguments about maintaining national prosperity are beside the point. This firm cannot be expected to stick its neck out and raise wages to sustain the whole economy. We have to consider just those issues about which we can do something positive in relation to company profits.

Which side wins? The arguments on both sides are plausible. Can we judge them like a debating contest on content, organization, and presentation? Or does all this talk count for nothing? Are the real issues the unspoken questions on both sides: How badly do you want to avoid a strike? How long a strike can you tolerate?

There is no general answer. *It is impossibile to predict the outcome of bilateral bargaining. But the issue does not hang simply on the spoken or unspoken threats of strikes by unions or shutdowns by management.* Most of the arguments presented above have at least a grain of truth in them, as each side might privately admit. And that truth will affect the potential success of a strike and the eventual settlement.

Labor will make an estimate of the company's inventory position and try to predict the effect a strike might have on the company under current economic conditions. Management will speculate on how strong the union leadership is and whether a hard battle will weaken it or possibly lead to its being replaced by an even more hard-nosed bunch.

Each side will call in its economists and lawyers and will issue public statements praising its own reasonableness and questioning that of the other side. Management may offer to compromise by giving more fringe benefits in place of the extra paid holiday or in return for more freedom in setting incentive rates on piecework. Labor might indicate its willingness, not to give up, but to postpone, say, 5 cents of its hourly wage request. What will the outcome be? We really cannot predict.

Do unions raise wages?

After all this, can it be said that unions have been successful in raising real wages? Let us be sure about the question. We know that unions have won many wage increases. But remember that even in completely competitive labor markets a reduction in the labor supply curve or an increase in the labor demand curve would result in wage increases. Have the wage increases won by unions been greater than would have been achieved in any case? And do they more than make up for price increases, so that real wages have gone up?

Unionists answer affirmatively. They point to the battles unions have had in winning wage increases. If they would have been granted anyway, what was all the fighting about? Moreover, statistics show that heavily unionized industries have higher average wages than industries with little union membership. The statistics, say union advocates, even underestimate the success of union activism, because the wage increases earned by labor unions have "spillover" effects in nonunion industries, raising their wages too.

On the other hand, skeptics point out that the unionized industries often paid relatively high wages even before they were unionized. Such industries tend to employ skilled workers who have higher productivity and who could expect to receive higher wages. Table 29-3 shows that, among manufacturing firms, nonunion establishments have raised wages faster in some years than union establishments. Moreover, in some nonunion occupations in the service sector, wages have gone up more rapidly in recent years than average union wages. Demand has been shifting toward the service sector, and the relative wage trends reflect that shift and the fundamental forces in labor markets.

It is difficult to answer the question unequivocally. *There is*

Table 29-3	Year	*All establishments*	*Union establishments*	*Nonunion establishments*
PRECENTAGE WAGE INCREASES IN MANUFACTURING	1955	3.7	3.6	4.0
	1966	4.2	4.1	4.4
	1967	5.3	5.5	5.0
	1968	6.0	6.5	5.0
	1969	6.2	6.9	6.0

Source: U.S. Congress, Joint Economic Committee: *The Federal Budget, Inflation, and Full Employment*, 91st Cong., 1st Sess. Data from U.S. Department of Labor, Bureau of Labor Statistics.

evidence that wages increase relatively fast just after an industry is unionized and that unions in declining industries keep wages from falling. But results seem to vary from one industry to another.

Special features of labor demand

We could simply repeat at this point that the demand for labor, like the demand for any other productive input, is a derived demand. It depends on the factor's marginal additions to a firm's revenue (marginal revenue product). Each kind of factor has unique qualities associated with it, of course, and those were discussed in Chapter 27. Some issues in labor demand, however, require further consideration.

What do businessmen know about their labor demand schedule?

Wage theory is sometimes criticized on the ground that employers do not really know their labor demand schedules in detail. But it would be a mistake to interpret the theorizing about demand and supply conditions for labor as requiring such knowledge. One need only suppose that, as in other markets, businesses know when they are better off and when they are worse off (i.e., making more or less profits) and that they try to be better off. It is not even true, or need not be true, that businessmen think about this in terms of their entire labor force. What is necessary and generally true is that employers consider the various processes and services that have to be carried out and try to achieve the combination of labor – and other inputs – which will do that best.

Monopsony power in labor markets and offsetting union power

The monopsony power of employers is not necessarily the result of active attempts to control labor markets. The natural immobility of labor contributes to it. Workers do not move from one job to another with the same ease that consumers change the kind of soap

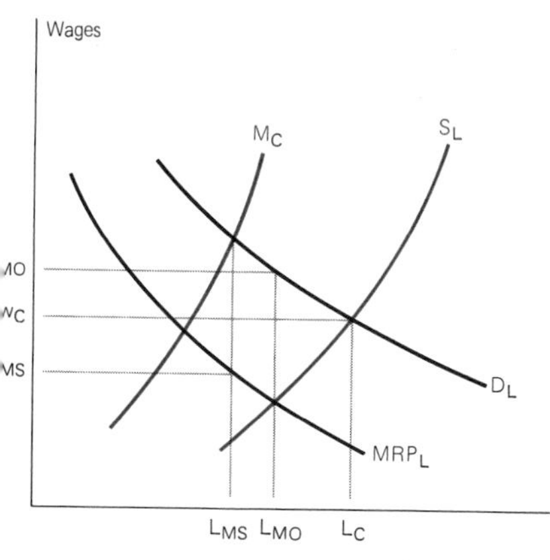

Figure 29-4

BILATERAL BARGAINING OVER WAGES

they use. Changing jobs entails important psychological and monetary costs. It means losing the comfort of familiar surroundings. It may require learning new skills. Going to a new locality means moving costs. All these tend to reduce labor mobility and give employers special bargaining power.

Employers may, of course, explicitly or implicitly follow commonly agreed-upon wage practices. "Present a united front to labor union organization and wage demands. Don't let them pick us off one at a time." These exhortations to reduce employer competition are just as understandable as the impulse to unionization.

A "united front" of employers or other sources of monopsony power deprive labor of the protection of competitive markets. Under such circumstances, *union bargaining may conceivably lead to a closer approximation of a competitive wage and level of employment than if there were no union to face employer monopsony power.* This is illustrated in Figure 29-4, which is the diagram of bilateral monopoly and monopsony presented in Figure 28-8 of the preceding chapter. With the labor demand curve D_L and the supply curve S_L, the competitive wage would be w_C, with L_C the equilibrium quantity. L_{MS} would be purchased at the intersection of the monopsonist's marginal cost of labor and demand schedules, with a wage w_{MS}. If the labor union could act as a single seller to many buyers of labor, it would "sell" L_{MO} man-hours, at the intersection of the supply and marginal revenue product curves of labor, and charge w_{MO}. If the labor union monopoly faced the employer monopsony, the resulting wage would be between w_{MO} and w_{MS}, and the corresponding employment level would be between L_{MO} and L_{MS}. The precise outcome is indeterminate but it could be closer to the competitive outcome than if there were no union and if monopsony power alone prevailed.

Technology and the demand for labor

One of the fragments of economic folklore states that there is only a limited amount of work to be done in the world and that it should be jealously protected against new techniques and "outsiders." This is called the *lump-of-labor fallacy* by economists. Why is it a fallacy? Because, given the technology, the demand for labor is derived from the demand for final goods and services. When the demand for goods and services grows, as effective macroeconomic policy can help ensure, the demand for labor will grow.

But what if engineers and businessmen are always busy trying to develop laborsaving devices to replace labor? Won't that reduce the demand for labor? First, it is not clear that technological change is always "biased" toward laborsaving changes. Some changes, such as the introduction of blown oxygen into steelmaking furnaces, seem to be as "capital saving" as they are "labor saving," if not more so. Though the evidence is not strong one way or another, there is some indication that, overall, technological change has tended to be "neutral" in its effects.

Yet the demand for particular labor skills is reduced by particular technological changes. One can hardly argue about this with the expert welder who is displaced by an automatic welding machine or the garment cutter displaced by automation. But the fallacy of composition would lead us badly astray if we concluded from such single examples that technological change *must* be accompanied by a reduction in the demand for *all* labor.

When technical change displaces workers, it also increases the productivity of the remaining employed labor. Effective macroeconomic policy to maintain aggregate demand and microeconomic policy to help keep labor — and other resources — mobile to meet that demand can offset the labor-displacement effects of technical change. That may also mean retraining workers and a certain amount of shifting about. It is likely to be painful to those workers who must shift, and that is a cost to them which must be balanced against the general benefits of higher productivity.

Another fallacy of composition: A general demand curve for labor

We have developed the concept of the demand of a single firm and of a group of firms for labor in a restricted labor market. It might now seem the most natural thing in the world to think of adding up all such demand schedules and, thus, move to the concept of a total demand for all labor based on wage rates. But at this point the fallacy of composition would rear its ugly head again. Remember that those separate demand schedules are derived on the assumption of "all other things equal." What other things? Well, specifically and importantly, the demand for the final product and the prices of other inputs.

Suppose we tried to construct a total demand curve for labor in relation to the wage rate. Would those other things remain constant if the wage rate changed? No! Wages are both incomes and costs. When *all* wage rates change, incomes will change — and costs — and, therefore, prices of goods and services. We would be trying to construct our aggregate demand curve on shifting sands and we could not do it.

A little example will indicate how important it is to get our thinking straight on this apparently abstract question. Suppose there is a recession with widespread unemployment. Someone suggests lowering wages. Thinking in terms of some aggregate demand schedule for labor, he argues that the quantity of labor demanded will be higher at lower wages than at higher wages. But lower wages mean lower incomes. Prices will have to fall to maintain sales. That means the derived demand for labor will fall. Is there any end to the process? The end is not necessarily that of full employment. Whether or not that outcome is achieved will depend on the macroeconomic questions discussed in Part II.

What if someone were to suggest raising wages so as to increase purchasing power to maintain demand and employment? Isn't that just as plausible? But higher wages again mean both higher money incomes and higher costs and possibly, therefore, higher prices. Labor may end up with no change in real income and, perhaps, with no more employment, but, perhaps, no less. Again it all depends on what happens to effective demand.

Drawing an aggregate demand curve in which the total quantity of labor demanded depends on wage rates *cannot* be justified. Too many other things can change for such a relationship to be warranted.

Labor discrimination

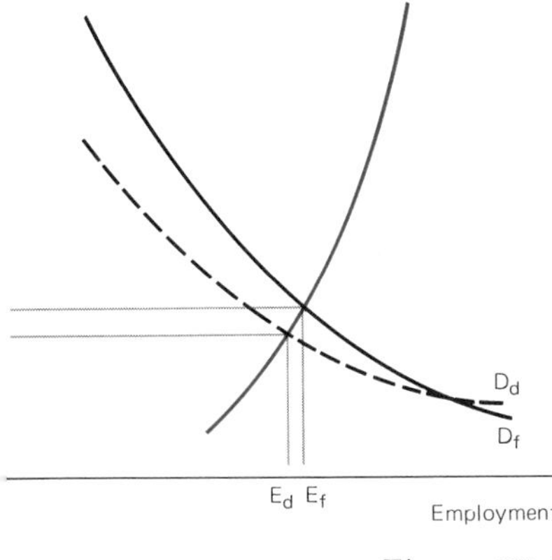

Figure 29-5

AN ANALYSIS OF THE EFFECTS OF DISCRIMINATION

Discrimination in the sense of excluding individuals from jobs on the basis of color, sex, or religion is widespread. Is it solely a sociological and political phenomenon, or does it have economic effects — and, perhaps economic origins? Does it make everyone worse off or only the persons discriminated against? Economic analysis can help answer these questions.

In Figure 29-5 the amount of labor offered by a particular group discriminated against — such as blacks or females — in a particular local market is indicated by the curve S_d. The line D_f indicates what the demand for that labor would be if there were no discrimination. The equilibrium wage would be at w_f and employment at E_f. What is the effect of discrimination? Better-paying jobs are rarer. Promotions are more difficult to get. On the other hand, relatively low-paying jobs may become more abundant as the groups not discriminated against move out of competition for such jobs. So the demand curve for the groups discriminated against may both shift and twist, as shown by D_d. *The equilibrium wage when there is discrimination* is at w_d, which is lower than at w_f, where it would be *if there were no discrimination*, and the employment at E_d of the groups discriminated against is lower than at E_f.

When certain groups are discriminated against, the demand for other labor groups increases. That is shown in Figure 29-6 by the shift in the demand for labor from the "other groups" from D_o to D_n. Their wages and employment increase from w_f to w_o and from E_f to E_o, respectively. They benefit from discrimination.

What is the economic balance? Discrimination is a market imperfection. It lowers the productivity of the system and reduces the output and income producible with a certain amount of labor. Getting rid of it could make those discriminated against better off *and* increase the output and income of the system as a whole. But no

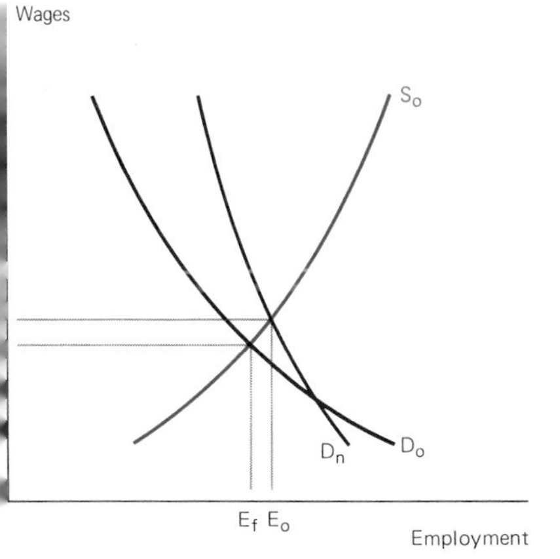

Figure 29-6

SOME GROUPS BENEFIT FROM DISCRIMINATION

means of making transfer payments now exists which would ensure that, in the process, no one was made worse off while those previously discriminated against were made better off. General economic growth would help. But that promise may not reassure those threatened by increased competition for jobs. It would probably be wrong to claim that the individual economic advantage gained from discrimination completely explains why some people want to preserve it. There are, unfortunately, other social and political influences. The economic effects are, however, a reinforcing element which should be recognized.

Minimum wage laws

The rationale of minimum wage laws is that *they prevent the exploitation of labor—particularly at the bottom of the wage scale.* On the other hand, one increasingly hears criticisms of such laws. Critics argue that the laws make low-paid labor groups worse off than they otherwise would be.

The best case for minimum wage laws is illustrated by Figure 29-7. Here, we have monopsony in the labor market and competition in the product markets. The supply of labor is S, and its marginal cost to the monopsonist is MC. The demand for labor is also the firm's marginal revenue product curve. The monopsonist would tend to hire labor at point A, where the marginal cost of an additional worker equaled his marginal revenue product, that is, L_M amount of labor. He would pay the wage rate w_M. This should be compared with the wage rate w_C and the employment rate L_C which would prevail if the market were competitive.

Figure 29-7

EFFECTS OF MINIMUM WAGE LAWS ON A MONOPSONIST

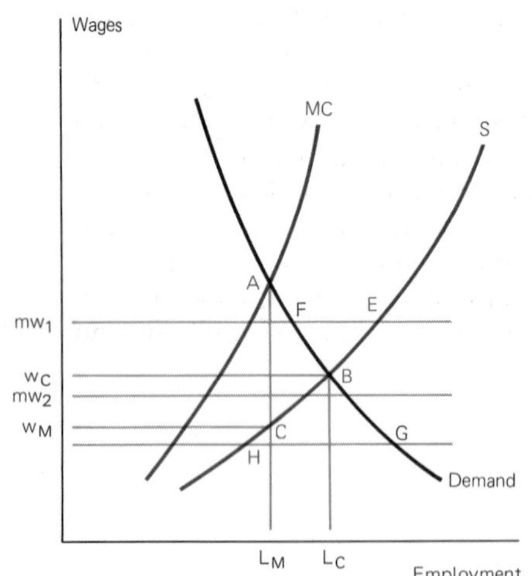

If a minimum wage were established in this market, say, at a rate between points A and B, wages and employment would be higher than otherwise. At the minimum wage mw_1, labor would be demanded at point F, though the amount offered would be at E. If the minimum wage were mw_2, labor would be demanded at point G, but only the amount H would be supplied. Either mw_1 or mw_2 would lead the labor market closer to the competitive equilibrium point at B than it would be if monopsony power prevailed.

But what if the labor market were more or less competitive, as represented by Figure 29-8, with the labor demand schedule D and supply schedule S and the equilibrium wage and employment tendency at w_C and L_C? A minimum wage at mw_1, below the competitive wage, would have no effect. But if it were set to raise the wage level, at mw_2, employers would hire at point B, with only L_2 labor being used. The effect of the minimum wage here would be to *reduce* employment.

Critics of the minimum wage laws argue that *the least-favored labor groups sell their labor in labor markets which are approximately competitive. The effect of the laws on these groups is to reduce employment opportunities,* as shown by Figure 29-8. It is

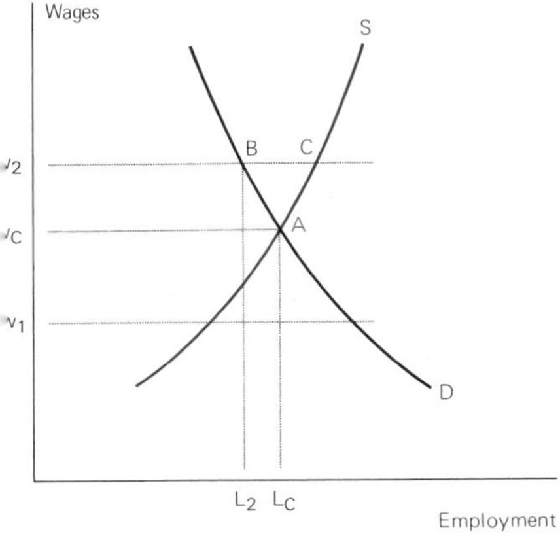

Figure 29-8

EFFECTS OF MINIMUM WAGE LAWS IN COMPETITIVE MARKETS

true that employment opportunities may be increased in imperfect labor markets. It is suggested, however, that either the increased opportunities do not balance the losses or that discrimination and skill requirements restrict access to the jobs anyway. So the rationale of a minimum wage is a clouded one. The danger—for which there is some supporting evidence—is that minimum wage laws reduce employment opportunities.

Summary

Though the share of labor in total national income has varied from about 60 percent to 70 percent, there are wide differences in the incomes of particular occupations and in the median wages paid in various industries. These median wages and the variations can be analyzed via a supply and demand organization of the various influences if the significant "imperfections" in the labor markets are taken into account. These include the monopsony power of some employers, monopsony power of some unions, labor immobility, and discrimination against particular groups.

Labor supply depends fundamentally on population size, labor-force participation rate, and individual decisions about hours of work. Supply changes due to population growth and immigration respond slowly and erratically to economic forces. Labor-force participation and hours of work respond more positively to wage rates, though under certain conditions people may prefer to increase their leisure time and reduce their working time as their incomes rise. That has been the historic trend.

Income differences result from individual supply reactions and particular job conditions. Differences in wage rates due to dissimilar working conditions are called equalizing differences. Differences in wage rates that reflect greater or lesser skills or other worker qualifications are nonequalizing. In this case the differences are the basis for distinguishing noncompeting groups in the labor force. Such groups need not be a source of labor market imperfection if there is competition within each group.

Labor unionism in the United States went through unsuccessful phases of political activism and attempts to create broad-based union organizations in the nineteenth century. The AFL, which emerged at the turn of the century as the first permanent overall labor organization, was founded on pragmatic principles of business unionism: (1) concentration on bread and butter issues of wages and working conditions; (2) organization along craft lines;

(3) forgoing permanent political commitments and remaining free to reward labor's friends or punish its enemies by giving or withholding local political support. The success of business unionism principles also shaped the policies of the CIO after it was formed in the 1930s to encourage the organization of unions along industrial lines. Today the AFL-CIO, combined in one single federation, serves as a spokesman for the labor movement in the United States.

The ultimate union method of exercising bargaining power is the withholding of labor through the organized strike. Picketing makes strikes more effective. Wildcat strikes, slowdowns, and boycotts are also tools of labor power.

Government intervention usually changes the outcome of labor-management negotiation, though the effects are not uniformly favorable to either side. They depend on the sympathies of political leaders, public attitudes, and economic conditions. In general, government intervention dilutes the economic forces that, in the absence of intervention, would determine labor-management decisions. But some intervention may be necessary as part of an overall policy of controlling prices.

Unions do not sell labor, but they can achieve higher wages by reducing the supply of labor available, by raising wage rates directly, and by increasing the demand for labor. The first two approaches lead to lower employment than would otherwise prevail. Unions sometimes also try to maintain employment by featherbedding rules and restrictions on the introduction of laborsaving technology. On the other hand, unions and management may cooperate in the introduction of technological innovations.

Unions and management pose many arguments to justify their proposals. But a union's power to control management's access to labor and the employer's power to control access to jobs are the ultimate weapons. Evidence on the effect unions have had in raising wages is not unequivocal. Wages in unionized industries seem to go up rapidly just after unionization, but wages in many nonunion industries have risen just as rapidly.

A long as businessmen keep trying to increase profits, they need not know their labor demand schedules in order to find the best combination of labor and other factors. They can be expected to take advantage of whatever monopsony power they can exercise because of labor immobility and employer collusion.

Technical change may displace labor, but it also increases productivity. So, if effective macroeconomic policy maintains labor demand, total output and income can be increased.

It is erroneous to think in terms of a total demand schedule for labor based on wages. The everything-else-equal assumption, which is necessary for such a demand schedule to be valid, would not be warranted in this case, because wage changes lead to income changes, which in turn change the demand for labor.

The economic effects of discrimination in labor markets can be analyzed as a reduction in the demand for the labor of the groups being discriminated against. Other labor groups may correspondingly benefit from discrimination which reduces competition in the labor markets.

Minimum wage laws may offset any monopsony power in labor markets and move wages and employment closer to the competitive norm. But minimum wage laws in competitive markets will have a distorting effect and may, in fact, particularly injure those groups which are relatively low on the wage scale by restricting their employment opportunities.

Questions for discussion and review

1. Think of the jobs you and people you know have held. To what extent are the differences in the incomes earned in these jobs the result of equalizing or nonequalizing differences in pay?

2. Analyze the following quotation: *The way to become wealthy is to become a member of a noncompeting group.*

3. How would you account for the success of business unionism in the United States in the past eighty or ninety years? Do you think that will continue to be the formula for union success?

4. Discuss critically the following two position statements: (*a*) *Government must step in to protect the public when private collective bargaining would result in strikes which would damage the economy.* (*b*) *Government should stay out of private collective bargaining and let market forces operate to settle disputes, because that is the only guarantee of efficiency and of meaningful labor peace.*

5. To what extent do you think national price and wage trends are of significance in local labor disputes, and if you were a labor or management negotiator, would you introduce them into your arguments?

6. To what extent are the costs and benefits of technological change borne by labor?

7. Some young people argue that one of the most important kinds of discrimination is that which is practiced by one generation against the next. Do you agree or disagree? Why?

8. On balance, do you think minimum wage laws are a desirable economic policy?

Concepts for review

Equalizing and nonequalizing differences in wages

Noncompeting groups

Bread and butter unionism

Craft and industrial unions

Wildcat strikes

Primary and secondary boycotts

Featherbedding

Lump-of-labor fallacy

30

The pricing and the use of capital and interest incomes

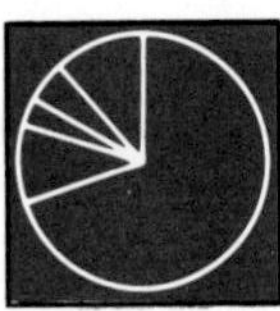

A parable of the economist's view of productive resources could be written in the following way:

> In the beginning there was only land and all good things flowed from the endowment of natural resources. Then there was only labor which was the means and the measure of all output. And finally there is only capital, for all inputs themselves require processing, are durable, and their pricing requires comparisons of values at different times.

It *has* become increasingly popular among economists to apply capital concepts to all productive resources. Most resources are durable. And like capital equipment, they require some processing before they can be used effectively. This is clearly true of land and other natural resources. They are not productive until a certain amount of work has been done on them. Farmland must be improved, mines must be opened up, and the power of rivers must be harnessed.

It is even possible to think of "human capital" as created by "investing" in education. Education, like investment in physical capital, requires time and uses resources. The skills and expertise it creates, like capital equipment, last a long time. This view of education, as a capital creation process, has come to be one of the dominant approaches to the economics of education.

Capital formation, capital pricing, and interest present some of the most difficult conceptual problems in all of economics. That is partly due to the intrinsic complexity of the issues: Input and output decisions at different times are involved in an essential way. Nothing is static. Everything is dynamic. Part of the difficulty, however, stems from semantic confusions and the emotional and ideological overtones of the words "capital" and "interest." Those are hard to put aside.

On the other hand, the very ubiquity of the capital concept suggests that it is a useful one. And the persistent ideological preoccupation with capital and interest suggests that the issues are important.

Our approach can be outlined briefly. First, some concepts and definitions. Then a "real" theory of interest will be presented in terms of the net productivity of capital and saving decisions. Next, a theory of interest rate determination in money markets, called a "loanable funds" theory of interest. Then the interdependence of these two approaches, the real and monetary theories of interest, will be explained, and the theories reconciled. With this background it will be possible to clear up some common misapprehensions regarding interest and capital.

Capital and interest

The word *capital* will be used in this chapter as it has been in the rest of the book, but occasionally it will be given a broader interpretation. So far, capital has referred to durable physical goods produced in the economic system to be used for the production of other goods and services. In its broader interpretation, capital can mean *any* durable increase in productive capacity, whether embodied in newly produced goods or in land or other natural resources or in labor. For the most part, we will use the narrower meaning, knowing, however, that we can extend it when we need to.

If we were to add up the nation's "stock of capital goods," we would add the values of all the plant and equipment, bridges, highways, hospitals, schools, etc. All these are durable produced "goods" which can be used with labor and other inputs to produce a flow of services. Suppose, for a moment, we focus on corporations. Should we add to the value of plant and equipment owned by the corporation the stocks and bonds shown on its balance sheet? No, that would clearly be double counting. Capital goods yield a flow of productive services over their lifetime. There are also financial assets like private and government bonds and corporation stocks which yield income to their owners. That makes it tempting to call these financial assets "capital," and in popular usage that is often done. The temptation should be resisted as it can be a source of confusion.

Payments made for the productive services supplied by capital goods are sometimes called *rentals*. This distinguishes these returns from the "rents" paid to productive factors in absolutely fixed supply. More commonly these rentals are measured as a percentage, or as a ratio of their annual amounts to the value of the capital goods. That percentage is the interest rate!

But the returns on strictly financial assets that yield income to their owners are also called interest payments, and their rate or yield is measured as a percentage of the price of the financial assets. *So interest refers to the percentage return of income to asset value for two different kinds of things, capital goods and income-earning financial assets.*

Interest has also been described as a payment for the use of money or loanable funds. Is that another, different use of the word? No. Because the loan of money can be regarded as a purchase of a financial asset. When a bank makes a loan, for example, that can be considered a purchase of an IOU or a note from the borrower, which is just a kind of financial asset. The interest on the loan paid by the borrower is the price paid for the use of the money. In the same way, the purchase of a government bond is like loaning money to the government, and the interest paid on the loan is just the price for the use of the loanable funds.

The structure of interest rates

The analysis of interest rates will be carried out as if only one rate prevailed at any one time. This is a convenient simplifying assumption, though not strictly true. Turn your newspaper to the financial pages some day and look at the range of rates quoted there. A number of rates are quoted even on government bonds. Those rates differ with the "maturity" of the bond, and they depend on various other special features. The rates on utility bonds differ from the rates on industrial corporation bonds, and they also differ among themselves. Banks charge the "prime rate" to their soundest customers, a different rate to other businesses, still another on car loans, and maybe a different one on home improvement loans. Still other rates are charged by personal finance companies, department stores, and so on. What accounts for this diversity of interest rates?

First of all, actual interest rates may include a payment or a charge for something besides the costs of borrowing funds with certain repayment at the end of the year. A bond may be "convertible" into common stock, and if that privilege is valued, the bond will be priced higher than otherwise and the interest yield will be lower than otherwise. Or a bond may or may not be "callable" and repayable at the issuer's option at the end of a certain period; that condition will be reflected in the price and interest rate.

Second, and, perhaps more important, different degrees of risk are associated with various bonds and with investment in physical assets. Government bonds may or may not be riskless, depending on your point of view. What is certain, however, is that if those obligations are not met, no other obligation can be counted on. But is a new three-month government note less risky than a new three-year government bond? In a sense, yes. Remember, you can count on getting your money back when the note or bond comes *due*. But you cannot count on getting your money back if you decide to sell the bond before its due date. How much you will be able to get before the due date will depend on the market price. Yet, even if general conditions in the money market change, that will not affect the price of the three-month bond very much, because you need wait at most only three months to collect its face value. Since over the next three months the market price of a three-month bond will vary less than that of a three-year bond, you may have to pay something for that advantage. So you will get a lower interest return on the three-month bond.

Is a five-year AT&T bond more risky than a United States government bond? Well, suppose someone invents a cheap substitute for telephones, say, a wrist radio that can be dialed to call any other wrist radio. What then would happen to AT&T?

The "structure" of interest rates refers to the various interest rates that exist on different types of income-earning assets. Though the discussion in most of this chapter will be conducted in terms of a single interest rate, it is important to interpret that as merely representative of the whole structure of interest rates.

The valuation of income-earning assets

Before taking up interest rate determination, let us investigate the valuation of assets which earn income over time. We will assume that we live in a world of well-organized financial markets, so the interest rate itself is already known to us. We will further suppose that there is just a single type of capital good or income-earning asset. The annual income which accrues to this asset is also known and fixed at a certain amount. What is left unknown about this income-earning asset? Do we know what it would sell for? Do we know what a rational person trying to do as well as possible for himself would pay for it?

To make the problem even more concrete, suppose that the income-earning asset is a financial asset. Say that it is a note which guarantees that at the end of one year it will be paid off at its face value of $100. In addition, at that time, the owner of the note will collect $5 from the payer. What is this note worth today, one year before the payment date?

To answer the question, first ask yourself what amount put into a savings account or some other equivalent asset—at the current rate of interest—would pay back $105 at the end of the year. Or, *what price placed on the asset would make its value equal to the opportunity cost of using those funds in an equivalent way?* If the going rate of interest were just 5 percent, then $100 placed in a savings account would give you $105 at the end of the year. But if the going rate of interest were greater than 5 percent, say, 7 percent, then $100 in a savings account would bring you $107 at the end of the year, or $2 more than $105. At a going rate of 7 percent, some amount less than $100 placed in a savings account would be worth \$105 at the end of the year. How much exactly? We can figure it out. Suppose V is the amount we want to determine. Then

$$V + (0.07)V = \$105 \qquad \text{or} \qquad 1.07V = \$105$$

So

$$V = \$105/1.07 \qquad \text{or} \qquad V = \$98.13$$

This amount is the *price which would be placed on the financial asset if the rate of interest were 7 percent.* It is the *opportunity cost of buying the asset rather than using the money in an equivalent way.* Even though the note pays off only \$5 plus principal at the end of the year, it will, if it is purchased for \$98.13 at the beginning of the year, yield 7 percent to the owner. Buying the note for \$98.13, therefore, is equivalent to putting the money into a savings account and getting 7 percent.

Is the difference between \$98.13 and \$100 enough to worry about? It is \$1.87 difference on \$100. What if it was a matter not of \$100 but \$1 million? The difference would be \$18,700. Not an amount to sneeze at.

The amount V which was calculated is called the *capitalized value* or *present discounted value* (PDV) of the financial asset. In general, in good asset markets, *the price of any income-earning asset will tend to equal its present discounted value*! Why? Because the PDV measures the opportunity cost of purchasing the asset instead of using the funds to earn the going rate of interest in some other way.

Calculation of the PDV of an asset that yields a *stream* of payments in the future takes two steps. First, divide the amount that will be returned in *each* year by $(1 + i)^n$, where n is the number of years to the date at which the amount will be paid. Second, add up the discounted payments of all years. That sum is the PDV of all the future income payments. For example, if an asset were to yield \$Y only once, n years from now, its present discounted value would be $\$Y/(1 + i)^n$.

Looking carefully at this formula for present discounted value, we can see that the PDV of any income-earning asset will go up if the annual payments it generates should for some reason increase or if the market interest rate should decrease. The PDV would go down if the annual payments should decrease or if the interest rate were to increase. This all makes sense. The higher all annual payments, the greater the present discounted value. But the higher the interest rate, the smaller the amount anyone would be willing to pay for an asset with a fixed return, because the greater the opportunity cost of tying up one's funds.

The concept of the capitalized or present discounted value of an asset is extremely important. It is often necessary to compare *two or more streams of income payments which have different magnitudes at different times and are maintained over different periods of time. The calculation of the present discounted value of each provides a sure means of establishing comparability.*

To calculate the PDV, one must know both the interest rate and the stream of income payments. But what determines the interest rate? That is the next, and fundamental, question.

Real capital assets and their net productivity

The attractiveness of real capital goods is not in their aesthetic qualities, if any, but in their productivity. Capital-using methods are sometimes said to be more "roundabout" than direct methods of production. For example, wheat is not grown by farmers scratching the ground with their fingernails to put in seed, and then pulling out the weeds by hand and collecting the stalks one by one. Rather, an extremely indirect approach is taken. Steel is made with ore and coal and lime taken from the ground in different locations and transported to iron and steel mills. Then the steel is taken to equipment and tractor factories to make farm machines, which are sold to farmers. With these farm machines and other modern inputs, also produced with industrial capital equipment, the land is plowed, seeded, fertilized, tilled, and harvested. Though the process is roundabout, it is immensely more productive than direct hand methods, even after all the costs of the indirect, more capital-intensive approach are taken into account.

Each farm machine added to the land, labor, and other capital resources available adds something to output. That is its annual marginal product. The Law of Diminishing Returns assures us that the marginal product of capital falls as more and more is used in conjunction with fixed amounts of other productive resources. But farm machines and other capital assets vary in many ways. Some wear out relatively quickly. So their annual marginal products will terminate after a short time, though they may be high initially. Other machines have quite long lifetimes and perhaps lower annual marginal products. Farm buildings may last fifty or a hundred years or more. How can capital assets with such different characteristics be compared? But, first of all, why is it important to compare them? Farmers and other businessmen want to increase their incomes and would like to use more capital to do it. They know they cannot buy more of every type of capital good, however. They must make choices, and that implies comparisons.

As with financial assets, *calculating the present discounted values of future net income streams generated by real capital goods will provide a foolproof method of comparing capital assets, new or old, which have different costs, returns, and life-spans.* The PDV computation can, therefore, be used to indicate which machines are most worth buying and which projects are most worth undertaking. A simple example will show how it can be used.

Suppose you are offered a chance to invest $100 in a project that will last just one year. You know, with complete certainty, that at the end of the year it will pay back $106. That sounds pretty good. But suppose that the going rate of interest is 7 percent. The PDV of the revenues of the project is $106/1.07 = $99.07. That is less than the initial $100 you put up, so you lose on the project. In what sense? Not absolutely, since you end up with more than you started, but relatively. At the going rate of interest of 7 percent, you should make $7 on every $100. On the other hand, suppose the project paid $110 in a year. The present discounted value of that return is $110/1.07 = $102.80. That is $2.80 more than the $100 you had to invest and you would end up ahead of the game. The moral of this simple tale is: *Any such project with a present discounted value greater than the initial costs of the investment is worth undertaking!*

Suppose now the calculation is turned around and the question is asked: At what rate of interest would you become just indifferent about borrowing and investing in the project? Or the same thing, What rate of interest would reduce the PDV to the initial cost of the project? We can answer the question by finding the rate of interest that makes the PDV equal $100. This interest rate is called the *internal rate of return* to distinguish it from the rate of interest at which one can borrow in the market. Looking at the question this way, we let the internal rate be the unknown quantity in the equation

$$\$100 = \frac{\$110}{1 + \text{internal rate of return}}$$

With just a little manipulation we can solve this:

$$1 + \text{internal rate of return} = \frac{\$110}{\$100} = 1.10 = 1 + 0.10$$

Therefore, the internal rate of return is 10 percent. This leads to the rule: *If the internal rate of return of an investment project is greater than the market rate of interest, it will pay to undertake the project.* If the internal rate of return is less than the market rate, the project should not be undertaken.[1]

The rule follows from the way the internal rate of return was calculated – to make the present discounted value equal to the initial cost. If the internal rate were less than the market rate, the actual present discounted value would be less than the initial cost, and one would lose on the undertaking, at least in an opportunity sense.

Remember now an important conclusion from Chapter 28: If the capital market is competitive, the returns that the real capital assets generate will tend to equal their marginal productivities.

[1] It is shown in advanced courses that in some circumstances when costs and returns fluctuate, the internal rate of return rule can give equivocal results. And a ranking of a number of projects by their internal rates can be less reliable than a ranking by their present discounted values. But the rule will do for the simple projects considered here and as a first, pretty good approximation.

Why? Because the marginal productivity theory of distribution tells us that capital goods, like labor and other productive resources, will be employed up to the point at which each receives its marginal contribution to output.

The internal rate of return is, therefore, a measure of the productivity of investment projects over and beyond all costs — or the net productivity of the investment! In any year or month, there will be projects whose net productivity is relatively high and projects whose net productivity is somewhat lower and projects whose net productivity is quite low. This is a general implication of the Law of Diminishing Returns. The productivity of capital at any time depends on the existing technology and the other resources available to be used with the capital goods. If more and more capital goods were used, with these other conditions fixed, the productivity of the capital would fall.

Figure 30-1

A DEMAND SCHEDULE FOR CAPITAL

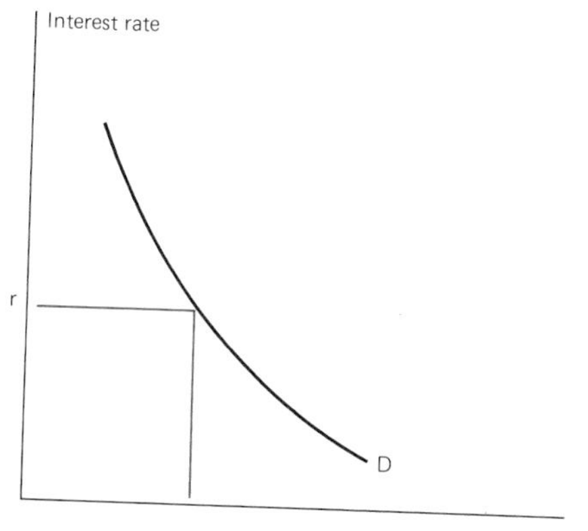

The demand for capital goods

The ranking of capital projects by their internal rates of return can be used to develop the concept of *a demand curve for capital.* Suppose that information were available which would permit the calculation of the internal rate for all the kinds of capital-using projects which exist and which could be created through investment. Then ask how much capital would actually be desired at an interest rate of, say, 10 percent. The answer would be found by adding up all those projects whose internal rate exceeded 10 percent. Now repeat the process and ask how much capital would be desired at an interest rate of, say, 8 percent. And find the answer in the same way. Keep on doing this, and at each rate of interest tabulate the amount of capital stock that would be desired. Lo and behold, you have a demand schedule for real capital, such as that shown in Figure 30-1.

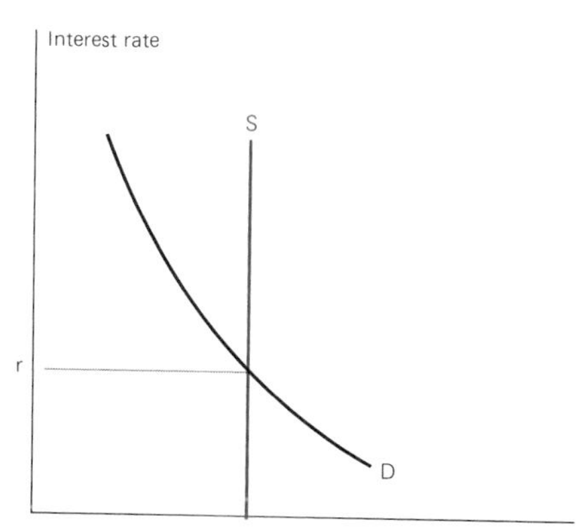

Figure 30-2

DETERMINATION OF INTEREST RATE BY THE REAL CAPITAL SUPPLY AND DEMAND

Demand and supply interaction and interest rate determination

After wandering around a while in the wilderness of present discounted values and internal rates of return, we are beginning to recognize the terrain. There, standing in Figure 30-1, is a familiar-looking demand schedule that reflects the resource's net marginal productivity. All we need now for price analysis is a supply schedule.

We know that it takes time to produce new capital. At any moment, there is some fixed stock, *S*, on hand, as shown in Figure 30-2. *The demand and supply schedules together determine the rate of interest r.* But the diagram is not going to stand still. It is going to flick to another picture within a short time. Why? For reasons on both the demand and supply sides.

This shifting *must* be going on because in almost every year we have net new investment, which means growth in the capital stock. That, in turn, implies that the desired amount of capital is greater than the existing amount of capital at the going rates of interest. The shift in the capital stock is shown in Figure 30-3. In the case shown in Figure 30-3, the demand and supply shifts balance so that the market rate of interest does not change. But this is a special case which need not prevail.

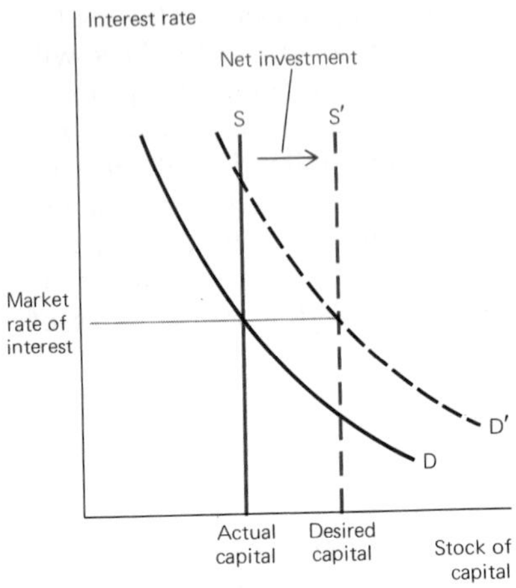

Figure 30-3

CHANGES IN INTEREST RATE DUE TO SHIFTS IN DEMAND AND SUPPLY

It is essential to understand the true implication of net investment. It means that businesses want more real capital plant and equipment than is now available. This may be the consequence of (1) growth in demand for the goods that the capital produces, or (2) reduction in other costs, which increases profitability, or (3) technological change that reduces the costs of producing old products or develops new products.

On the supply side, the stock of capital which grows via new investment wears out via depreciation. The stock of existing capital can also be made more productive and longer-lived through technical change.

This concept of the determination of the interest rate in a market that is continually subject to growth and change is not easy to comprehend. *Supply-demand analysis helps us understand that the interest rate we observe is likely never to be in equilibrium. Any observed rate is likely to be a way station in the movement toward an equilibrium, which, itself, is continually moving.*

Investment, saving, and the interest rate

The identification of new investment in the interest rate picture raises explicitly the issues that are involved in determining the level of new investment. Since we have discussed this topic already in several places, we need only tie some loose ends together. We pointed out in Chapter 3 that, in any economy, one of the important trade offs is between the use of resources for producing new investment goods or for producing consumer goods. The alternatives are indicated schematically by the production-possibility curve *QP* in Figure 30-4.

Figure 30-4

CONSUMPTION-INVESTMENT PRODUCTION-POSSIBILITY CURVE

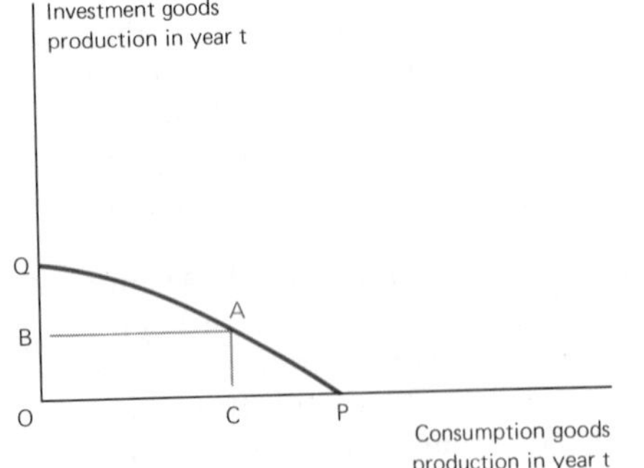

But the basic reason for producing investment goods in any year is *to have more consumption goods in the future.* So the production-possibility curve between consumption goods and investment goods in any year can be appreciated more fundamentally as a trade-off line between consumption *now* and *more* consumption in the *future*. In Figure 30-5, this is shown by the production-possibility line *PP'* as a trade off between two periods. Notice that along the 45-degree line in this figure the amount of consumption "now," in period *t*, and the amount of consumption in the "future," in period $t + 1$, would be equal. The effect of investment in period *t* is to lift the economy's *future* consumption *above* the 45-degree line.

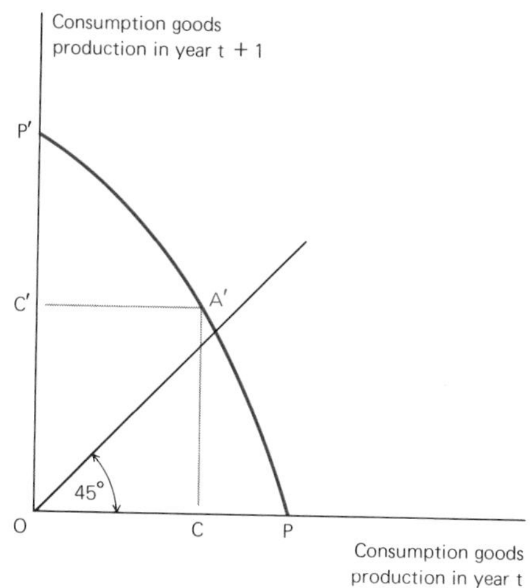

Figure 30-5

CONSUMPTION NOW VS. CONSUMPTION LATER PRODUCTION-POSSIBILITY CURVE

The choice of a particular combination of consumption and investment goods in a particular year is represented by point *A* in Figure 30-4. The investment goods produced in the amount *AC* (=*OB*) at point *A* in period *t* make it possible to raise the output of consumer goods in period $t + 1$. In Figure 30-5, the total consumption output available in period $t + 1$ would be *A′C* (=*OC′*). *The net productivity of the investment is the increase in consumption available in period t + 1 over what it would have been without the new investment. And that would determine the interest rate that could be paid on the new investment projects which increased the future availability of consumption goods.*

Producing investment goods requires saving — or forgoing present consumption. If the combination at *A* in Figure 30-4 is chosen, the investment goods production *AC* (=*OB*) means that saving in the same amount must be taking place. The productivity of new investment can also be interpreted as the reward for saving. That is why interest is sometimes called a reward for "waiting" or "forgoing consumption." In this interpretation, it is the bribe that has to be paid to offset people's "impatience to consume now." We should be careful about making too much of this point, however. While it is true that there must be saving if there is to be investment, we pointed out in Chapter 10 that evidence on the responsiveness of saving to the interest rate is equivocal.

The market for loanable funds and the interest rate

The interest rate analysis we have been going through is not only complex, it is rather abstruse. It might even generate a certain amount of uneasiness. After all, what about the effect of the money supply on the interest rate? Much of Chapters 15 and 16 was devoted to a discussion of the powers of the Federal Reserve to control the interest rate and what the effects might be. Yet monetary processes have not come up at all in this chapter. How do those processes and monetary analysis square with the "real" interest theory of the preceding section?

The monetary interest rate theory of Chapters 15 and 16 is often described as the "loanable funds" theory of interest. Interest, in that analysis, is the price paid for the use of money and is the result of the interaction of the demand for and supply of money. The other side of that coin is the determination of the interest rate in the interaction of the demand for and supply of credit or loanable funds.

The Federal Reserve in controlling the money supply effectively controls the amount of credit that banks — the major source of short-term loans — can extend. The Fed's monetary controls also influence the availability of long-term credit — directly through Federal Reserve purchases and sales of long-term government bonds and indirectly through the interaction of the short- and long-term credit markets. The demand for loanable funds stems from a variety of sources: households, business firms, and all levels of government.

Households. Families and individuals demand credit to buy consumer goods. Consumer credit is a means by which the timing of the purchase of consumer goods can be made different from the timing of the receipt of income. Young couples can purchase and enjoy houses, cars, and baby clothes even though their current incomes are typically inadequate to pay the entire costs of such goods. They pay something extra for the privilege of buying with credit, and that "something extra" is the interest rate on the funds they borrow.

Business firms. Fundamentally, the demand for credit by businesses is connected with the real net productivity of capital, as described in the preceding pages. *When the market rate of interest is below the real net productivity of capital, businesses can make profits on the difference by using borrowed funds to acquire real capital.*

We must keep the "big picture" of a firm's business in mind, however. Businesses borrow to pay taxes, to pay insurance premiums, to sponsor advertising campaigns. They also borrow to carry inventories and meet payrolls, because payments on the contracts they hold and their sales receipts do not exactly match in time the expenditures they must make.

Some of the business demands for credit are rather remote from the real net productivity of capital. In fact, sometimes no real physical capital is involved. Then, business credit, like consumer credit, is a means of adjusting the flows of receipts and expenditures over time.

Governments. All governments borrow. They use credit to finance the building of physical facilities, such as schools, highways, hospitals, or a new city hall. But, often, they borrow to meet general expenditures that are not covered by current tax receipts. When governments borrow to build physical facilities, they sometimes prepare a careful accounting of the expected social payoff of the facilities. This kind of cost-benefit analysis was described in Chapter 5. Often, however, they do not make such a computation. Somehow people decide that the old city hall is a disgrace to the community – and anyway inadequate – and a new one must be built. In decisions of this sort, the connection between government demand for loanable funds and the net physical productivity of publicly owned capital facilities is quite tenuous.

In many instances, government borrowing is a means of achieving a timing of expenditures which is different from the timing of tax receipts. If the debt incurred is never paid off, but is "rolled over" by new borrowing, the borrowing is simply another way of financing government expenditures.

The interaction of real and monetary influences in the interest rate

This brief description of the supply of and demand for loanable funds and the determination of the interest rate in money markets is closely connected to the macroeconomic monetary analysis of Chapter 16. It has a realistic ring to it. Yet it seems quite remote from the real interest rate theory discussed above. Are the monetary and real theories mutually consistent, or do we have to take sides and choose one approach or the other?

The influences and interactions on which each approach focuses are interdependent in some obvious ways but also in some subtle and difficult ways. First, the obvious interactions: (1) The demand for loanable funds is, in part, based on the net productivity of physical capital. This is the case for some business borrowing and that part of government borrowing which is based on careful comparisons of social costs and benefits. (2) The supply of loanable funds is, in part, dependent on the willingness of individuals to save – to forgo the use of current income for current consumption.

The subtle interactions between real and monetary factors in interest rate theory are not so easy to catch. As one example, suppose that major technical changes in the next decade raise the real net productivity of capital. The demand for loanable funds based on real capital productivity would rise, and businesses would try to divert resources to new investment. That would tend to raise the interest rate, as it would represent an increase in demand.

As another example of the interaction of real and monetary influences, suppose there were strong deflationary forces in the economy. The Fed could lean against them by increasing the money supply and available credit and, thus, lowering the interest rate. That would make it easier for businesses to borrow funds and use them to demand new capital goods with which to carry out investment projects. That, in turn, would affect the real productivity and the real rates of return of the additional capital created.

On the other hand, if the Fed thinks that the greater danger is inflation, it will tend to tighten the credit markets and raise the money rate of interest. Its actions will again interact with the demands of businesses for credit based on the real net productivity of capital and their desires to make the time pattern of their expenditures different from the time pattern of their receipt of funds.

If the real demands for new capital based on the real net productivity of investment are not consistent with the interest rate determined in monetary markets, something will have to give. Imagine, for example, that you – and others – could borrow funds at 4 percent and buy real assets that earned 6 percent. That is such a good deal that the demand for funds would drive the monetary interest rate up from 4 percent. And the additions to real capital stock would drive its real rate of return down from 6 percent. So the monetary and real rates would tend to be equalized. That is, *there cannot be an indefinitely continuing disparity between the real and monetary interest rates in well-organized capital and funds markets unless the government consciously interferes to maintain the disparity.* The government can do so, just as it can interfere in the markets for corn and wheat. Apart from this possibility, however, the real and monetary interest mechanisms have built-in tendencies toward equalization. That does not mean that equalization will occur rapidly or will ever be achieved. There are continuous changes in demand and supply in both markets. But both monetary and real interest determination will be appreciated better if their interconnections are recognized.

Interest: Exploitation or allocation

If we think of interest as a payment for the use of real capital, then, like other kinds of prices, it measures the opportunity costs of using resources in a particular way. It is simply a device for rationing and allocating goods among competing uses. But interest payments have a bad reputation in certain quarters, or at least not so good a reputation as "honest wages." In some states, interest income is taxed at a higher rate than wage income, perhaps because its receipt is thought to be relatively concentrated among upper-income groups. That is true, but poor widows and children as well as Wall Street bankers clip bond coupons.

Marx thought that "capital is dead labour, that, vampire-like, only lives by sucking living labour, and lives the more, the more labour it sucks."[2] On the basis of such beliefs, no interest charges were made for the use of capital in the Soviet Union after the October Revolution of 1917.

To understand the problems that created, put yourself in the position of a planner in the Soviet Electric Power Ministry in the 1920s. A proposal is made to build a big dam and use the stored water to run electric generators. Everyone knows that *after the dam is built* the generators will run on the annual flow of water and it will really cost very little to produce electric power: just the wages of a few operating personnel and some annual maintenance. But everyone also knows that it is going to cost a lot to build the dam; that is, it is going to require a lot of real resources to construct the real capital. By comparison, if a couple of coal-burning power stations are built with equivalent generating capacities, the initial real resource costs will be lower. There will, of course, be much higher annual costs as compared with the hydro station, as coal will have to be continually purchased as fuel inputs. Suppose,

[2] K. Marx, *Capital*, vol. 1, part III, Chap. X.

to make life a little easier, the hydro and coal-fired stations had the same lifetimes. Now, how would you decide whether to build the hydroelectric plant or the two coal-fired power stations?

Both projects produce the same amount of power, so the decision really depends on cost comparisons. After reading the first part of this chapter, you might be tempted to calculate the present discounted values of the revenues and costs of the two projects at the going rate of interest and pick the one with the highest PDV. The net contribution to the total present discounted value of, say, the tenth year's revenues and costs would be:

$$\frac{\text{Revenues of 10th year} - \text{costs of 10th year}}{(1+r)^{10}} = \frac{\text{revenues of 10th year}}{(1+r)^{10}} - \frac{\text{costs of 10th year}}{(1+r)^{10}}$$

Revenues would be the same whatever the type of generating plant built; only costs would differ. So focus on them. The lower the rate of interest, the smaller the denominator and, therefore, the larger the weight of discounted future costs in present discounted value. Since the coal-fired stations would have higher costs in the tenth year than the hydro plant, as coal would have to be purchased for fuel, a lower rate of interest would tend to support the decision for a hydro station. Conversely the higher the rate of interest the larger the denominator, and the smaller the weight of discounted future costs in the present discounted value calculation. That would tend to encourage the construction of the coal-fired installation.

In general, a higher rate of interest would tend to discourage projects that require a relatively large amount of capital to get started. A high rate of interest, remember, reflects the high real net productivity of capital. So it is reasonable to be reluctant to put a lot of capital resources into a dam when you can build coal-burning stations instead which use less capital, even though their operating costs are substantially larger.

It is clear that the interest rate is an essential part of the capital allocation decision. But you are in the early years of the Soviet Union, and there is no rate of interest. What then will you do? If you do not have to take into account the opportunity costs of capital, as measured by the interest rate, you may just add up and compare costs without discounting them. That can lead to major errors. Published self-criticisms in the Soviet Union suggest that there were such mistakes. By now, however, the Soviet Union has found ways to get around the Marxian view that the interest rate is a source of labor exploitation. Essentially, projects are ranked according to calculations like the present discounted value estimation.

Turning to another illustration of the importance of the interest rate in capital allocation decisions, suppose you are in the United States Corps of Engineers and making decisions about building public dams for irrigation. The alternative would be the private drilling of deep wells from which water would be pumped. The issue is again one of high capital costs and low operating costs of dams versus the lower capital and higher operating costs, in this case, of wells. You know that you should take interest charges into account. So you calculate the present discounted values of the alternatives, using the rate of interest on government bonds as a measure of capital costs on the dam project. On the privately drilled well projects, however, you use the prime bank rate on private loans to farmers which will be assumed to reflect the true opportunity cost of capital. But is that the right thing to do? Is it appropriate to use two different rates of interest in the comparison? Not at all. *The real resource allocation decision can be made properly only if one correct opportunity cost of using capital (interest rate) is used to value the alternatives.*[3]

These are good examples of the significance of the capital price in making Input decisions, i.e., decisions about the choice of technology. Not only must the price exist, but the right price must be used. The examples also make another important point: *The functional distribution of part of income to interest is necessary for efficient resource allocation purposes. Unless interest costs are calculated explicitly, it is impossible to make correct decisions about projects which require durable capital inputs.* On the other hand, there need not be a corresponding personal distribution of interest payments as income. In the Soviet Union, the thermal stations are not owned by private utilities and no interest is received by private investors in such plants. Likewise, dams built by the Corps of Engineers will not generate interest payments to individuals, but privately owned tube wells will. In both cases, correct decisions must take interest "costs" into account.

Consumption loans, interest, and usury

Moral condemnation of the taking of interest on loans has an ancient history. Aristotle preceded Marx. The Old Testament and the New and the Koran all inveigh against it. Is our general acceptance of the practice of charging interest just one more bit of evidence of our fall from grace? It takes a Biblical scholar and a theologian to understand fully the historical and doctrinal issues involved in the religious injunctions. It is clear, however, that the most vigorous condemnation is made of the taking of interest on consumption loans where the lender has some monopoly power over the borrower. In such circumstances interest rates of 60 percent, 100

[3] In advanced analyses, there are discussions of conditions under which it is appropriate to use a different interest rate for public and private projects. The answer depends largely on whether the returns are the same, as in this example, or are different.

percent, 200 percent, or more have been and still are charged. That is called *usury.* When such interest charges are made, the lender's object is often not to encourage quick payment, but to establish a kind of "debt slavery" or "debt peonage." It still goes on in some parts of the world – and in the United States in those dark corners where loan sharks operate.

As pointed out earlier, *consumption borrowing allows individuals and families to achieve a time distribution of consumption which is different from the time distribution of their income.* Presumably they are the happier for it. Of course, people can make unwise decisions about consumer credit as well as about other things. But, in itself, there is nothing wrong with consumer credit.

Lending money to consumers is a highly competitive business. Stores sell on credit. Banks make loans for consumption purposes. Personal loan companies are anxious to lend money; that is how they make their profits. All these alternatives can be confusing and even deceptive unless one keeps firmly in mind the importance of finding out the true simple annual interest rate on credit or on a loan. For example, suppose you buy a $120 suit at a department store and agree to pay for it in equal monthly installments over the next ten months plus a "$1 per month carrying charge on each $120 of credit." Well, $1 per $120 sounds like less than 1 percent. That is pretty good. But $1 per month is $12 per year. That appears to be $12/$120, or 10 percent. But wait. After the first month's payment, though you are going to owe only $110, you still have to pay the $1 carrying charge. By the last month you will owe only $10 – and will still be paying the $1 carrying charge. The average size of the outstanding loan over the entire year is $60, not $120, and the $12 paid on it means an effective rate of interest close to 20 percent!

The so-called "Truth-in-Lending" Law (Title I of the Consumer Credit Protection Act of 1968) now requires that every credit contract state plainly the true simple annual interest implicit in credit arrangements. It often comes to 15 percent or 20 percent a year. Consumers are the despair of their protagonists when they pay such rates; most could borrow much more cheaply at banks.

Human capital

Capital theory is useful in explaining decisions about the accumulation and use of durable resources. The power of this approach can be illustrated in the economics of education. *Getting an education can be compared to making an investment in physical assets. It takes some time to complete the "project," and the result is a "durable" increase in earning power.*

The costs of creating that human capital are most obvious at the college level, perhaps. There are tuition charges, books, travel to and from home, and so on. But the most important private cost of education is *the opportunity cost of the earnings forgone by*

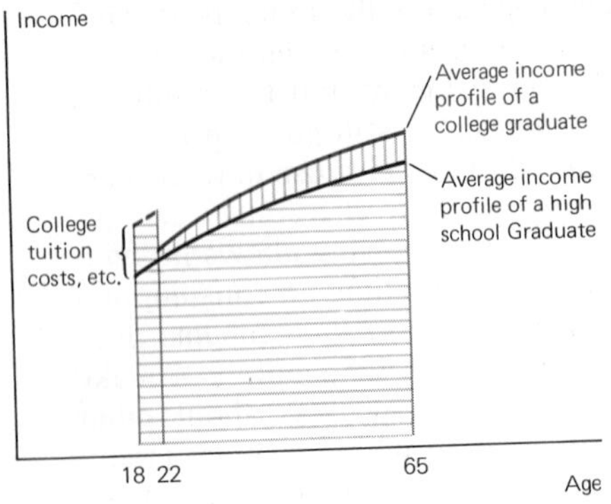

Figure 30-6

RELATIVE POSITION OF INCOME-AGE PROFILES ASSOCIATED WITH HIGH SCHOOL AND COLLEGE EDUCATION

being a student instead of a job holder. The costs can be quite substantial. For example, if an eighteen-year-old high school graduate employed full-time received the average factory wage rate, he would have earned about $7,700 per year in 1971. Some high school graduates earn more, some less. The point is that all who go to college sacrifice some income to do it. Since college students can earn some income while in college and during the summer months, we should deduct that income to obtain a better measure of the opportunity costs in forgone earnings. Then we must add the direct and explicit costs of tuition, etc., to obtain the total costs of a college education.

What are the returns for investment in a college education? The solid red line at the top of Figure 30-6 represents the average income a college graduate may expect over his working career. The horizontally shaded area includes the average lifetime income of a high school graduate plus the direct costs of a four-year college education. It covers, therefore, the opportunity costs that the college student incurs between the ages of eighteen and twenty-two. The vertically shaded area is the difference between an average high school graduate's income and an average college graduate's income. That difference can be considered a rough measure of the returns to a college education.

It is natural to try to compute the rate of return on "investment" in education. This has been done by a number of economists – with a variety of further adjustments to the data – and a variety of results. The average private rate of return on college education for white males has consistently been estimated around 10 to 12 percent. There is a great deal of variability in the results, and some people obviously do much better than others.

The precise numbers are suspect, however. It has probably already occurred to you to wonder whether the differences in income of high school and college graduates should be attributed wholly to education. Perhaps many of the people who go to college have greater innate intellectual abilities or, on the average, are in better physical health than the ones who do not. Or, perhaps, they go to college in part because they have better high school records to which both innate ability and socioeconomic background have contributed. These influences would tend to create income differences independently of the "investment in education."

While the precise quantitative results are still somewhat in doubt, the qualitative insights one gets from this approach are nonetheless useful and important. For example, why don't more people at middle age or after go back to school for refresher courses? Two reasons emerge from the human capital approach: (1) The *opportunity cost* of forgone income at age 40 is quite high. (2) At age 40 the number of years over which one will benefit from the additional education is relatively low. But again, we should not try to claim too much for the economic analysis. Other influences discourage middle-aged and older people from returning to school.

The social status of the student – particularly the older student – is not a high one. That in itself is a discouragement.

Thinking of education as an investment helps to explain the high incomes of persons in professions with relatively long training periods, such as lawyers and doctors. The opportunity costs of the income forgone while they were in training make their investment quite large. Unless their incomes after graduation were also relatively large, that investment would not pay off. Again, however, one should not claim too much for the approach. Economists have not untangled from the returns to such professionals the part that is due to education, the part due to innate abilities, and, perhaps, some part due to "monopolistic" limitations on entry into the professions.

The quality of capital markets

It is tempting to think of the market for capital funds as a reasonably close approximation to perfect competition. After all, "funds" are homogeneous: A dollar is a dollar, and dollars are relatively easy to transfer around the country. For certain classes of borrowers and lenders, the funds market is probably reasonably competitive. A moderately large business can tap a variety of sources of funds: banks, insurance companies, and stock and bond markets. An individual who has a good income and some wealth and wants to get a personal loan can also get a good reception at a number of lending agencies. But small businesses and individuals of only modest means often find their alternatives quite limited. The local businessman in a small town is not likely to find many, if any, alternatives to the local bank. By comparison, the local bank will have many potential borrowers for its funds.

Imperfections in capital markets can have far-reaching effects. To the extent that small businesses have few alternative sources of funds and face monopolistic "pricing" (interest rate) practices, their investment and growth are discouraged. To the extent that agriculture and service industries have fewer specialized lending agencies to which they can turn, they also suffer. The significance of these imperfections must be kept in mind. We must avoid the mistakes that arise when the theory of perfectly competitive markets is inappropriately applied.

Summary

Capital goods are durable productive resources which are themselves produced with other resources. Natural resources and trained and educated labor are similar to physical capital in that they require inputs to become more productive and their increased productivity is durable.

Interest payments are the return to real capital; the name is also used for the payments made by income-earning financial assets. The ratio of the annual amount of interest payments to the value of the real or financial asset is the interest *rate*. There are differences in the contract provisions which provide for interest payments, including differences in the period over which they are to be paid. There are also differences in the certainty of their yield. All these differences account for a broad range or structure of interest rates. In developing a theory of the interest rate, however, economists, for convenience, assume that there is only a single rate.

The present discounted value of an income-earning asset is estimated as equal to the opportunity cost of owning the asset instead of using the funds in some other way to earn the going rate of interest, as, for example, in a savings account. Calculation of the present discounted values, therefore, provides a way of comparing income-earning assets that have different lifetimes and patterns of returns.

If, at the going rate of interest, the present discounted value of the stream of future returns from some real capital assets is greater than their costs, there will be a net demand for the assets. This means that present discounted value calculations at various interest rates can be used to determine the demand schedule for real capital assets.

Alternatively, a rate can be calculated for each real revenue-yielding project which would make its present discounted revenues just equal to its present discounted costs. This rate is called the internal rate of return, and is a measure of the real net productivity of the capital. It pays to acquire real assets when the market rate of interest is less than the internal rate of return on the real assets.

The supply of real assets depends on the capital stock available and on new investment. Thus, the supply schedule of real capital is continually shifting: growing by new investment and being worn out by depreciation. The demand is changing, too, as the real net productivity of assets changes, owing to changes in demand for final products, technological innovations, and changes in the amount and quality of other resources used with the capital. Supply and demand interaction determines the present discounted value of real assets and their net productivity, which will be equal to their internal rate of return and also the market rate of interest.

Saving has an effect on interest rates, because, in a full employment economy, the production of new investment goods depends on the amount of resources freed by abstaining from using them to produce consumption goods.

The loanable funds theory of interest concentrates on interest rate determination in money markets, as analyzed in Chapter 16. The demand for loanable funds is derived partly from business demand for real financial assets. It derives in part from consumer, business, and government demands for funds, because their patterns of desired expenditures do not match the timing of their receipts. The supply of loanable funds is ultimately controlled by the Federal Reserve through its influence over the money supply.

The real and monetary influences in interest rate determination are intimately interwoven. The net productivity of real assets is an important factor in the demand for loanable funds. The real savings of individuals may affect the supply. Changes in the supply of money will affect ability to purchase real assets. Any Federal Reserve macroeconomic policy of tightening or loosening monetary constraint will, therefore, have an effect on the valuation of and the returns from real assets.

The interest rate has an important role in the efficient use of capital resources. Unless the relative scarcity and productivity of such resources – measured by the interest rate – are taken into account, such resources will not be used effectively.

The taking of interest on consumption loans is often condemned, and monopolistic moneylenders have a long history of exacting usurious rates whenever they can. But consumer credit increases the freedom of the consumer to spread his consumption over time in a pattern which is different from, and presumably preferable to, the time pattern of his income receipts.

The insightfulness of the capital theory approach can be illustrated by its application to education. Education can be regarded as a capital creation process which requires resources and creates a durable increase in productivity. Education decisions are, therefore, in part like investment decisions and depend on the level of returns and the period over which they will accrue, as compared with the costs. The most important costs of education are the forgone opportunities of earning income while going to school.

Questions for discussion and review

1. What is the rationale of the view that all productive resources, including labor and so-called "natural" resources, are really capital?

2. What accounts for the different interest rates that exist at any one time in financial markets?

3. Describe in words the meaning of the present discounted value of an income-earning asset and its internal rate of return. How are these concepts actually calculated?

4. Describe in your own words the real theory of the determination of the interest rate.

5. Analyze the following statement: *The only valid theory of the interest rate is the monetary theory, because the Federal Reserve System can control the interest rate on borrowed funds and the federal government can regulate the rest of the economy, including real investment, to make the monetary interest rate prevail throughout the system.*

6. Resource prices are supposed to be guides to the efficient use of resources. How does the interest rate operate to guide the efficient use of capital resources?

7. Consumer credit has a bad reputation in some circles, because it appears to be an easy way for people to go permanently into debt. What do you think about this attitude and about consumer credit generally?

8. Do you think of your education as an investment? If so, when did you start thinking of it that way? If not, why not? If so, did you investigate the costs and returns as carefully as you would the purchase of, say, corporate stocks?

Concepts for review

Net productivity of capital
Present discounted value
Internal rate of return
Usury
Human capital
Return to investment in education
Capital market imperfections
Structure of interest rates

31

The sources and significance of profits

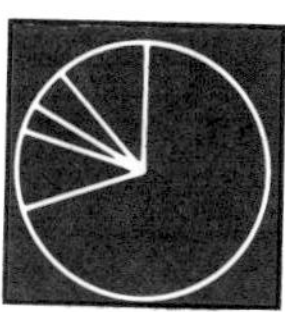

Profits are certainly a kind of income, so they ought to be considered in the chapters on income distribution. But are they a return to a particular productive resource, as wages are the return to labor, and rents the return to land, and interest the return to capital? Doesn't that exhaust the list of all the productive inputs? If it does, are profits a surplus, extracted somehow from the earnings of real resources? Do they always reflect the existence of monopoly power? This chapter will take up such questions and analyze the role of profits.

Defining and measuring profits

One of the things we have had to learn is to be careful about using common words in precise ways. Profits are the difference between revenues and costs. That sounds straightforward. But does everyone agree on what revenues are and – more of a problem – on what to include in costs?

If you turn to the financial pages of your newspaper, you may read in an article that X corporation's profits this year are $600,000 above or below last year's level of $2.5 million. Are those reported figures profits? If you read on, the article is likely to say something about profits being the return on assets. It is also likely to refer to the "profitability" of a new plant or process. Such comments should warn you that those reported "profits" are, in some part, a return to capital, and that part ought to be called "interest."

Or suppose you talked to your local druggist and dry cleaner about the "profitability" of their little unincorporated businesses. They are likely to tell you how much they "clear" after meeting "out-of-pocket" expenses, such as rent, hired help, materials costs, and the interest on the bank loan they got to redecorate their store. Then the druggist might tell you that he could do better by working as a pharmacist or chemical technologist for some other business. That should lead you to suspect that what he is calling profits may to some extent really represent returns on his labor and on the funds he has tied up in the business.

The general point is that *there are a lot of implicit returns to land, labor, and capital in all the reported profit figures*. This is a major source of difficulty in interpreting profit data. The corporate profits figure is the most unequivocal number, and even it will typically include some interest return to corporate assets. Only if *all* the corporation's assets have been leased or purchased with borrowed funds on which interest charges are explicit can we be reasonably sure that the interest elements have been taken out of reported profits. That is seldom the case, of course. Likewise, to arrive at the true profits figure of an unincorporated enterprise, we should charge off all the costs of self-owned inputs and the proprietor's labor.

The difficulty in separating profits from other returns was recognized earlier when we included "normal" profits in the "costs" of business enterprises. *Normal profits were defined to include the minimum returns that would keep owners from withdrawing their funds or real capital from the business.*

Suppose, however, we could do what is practically impossible and deduct all returns to particular resource inputs from revenues. We would then have a figure for profits (or losses). Let us imagine we can do that and try next to understand the sources of profits.

Profits as the return to monopoly

"Monopoly profits" is one of the clichés of the language and, like many clichés, has at least a grain of truth in it. It doesn't take a complete and absolute monopoly to make monopoly profits. It only takes some degree of monopoly, enough to be able to control price by adjusting the level of sales. Yet even that will not *guarantee* monopoly profits. If there is relatively free and easy entry, as in the situation called "monopolistic competition" in Chapter 25, that can wipe out monopoly profits. Or low demand may make monopoly unprofitable. But if entry is restricted, the possibility of making profits increases because of the monopolistic power to control price.

How does the monopolist do it? (A review of Chap. 25 might help here.) He restricts output below the level at which a competitive industry would operate. In effect, *the monopolist creates a scarcity which would not exist if the industry were competitive. He creates that relative scarcity of output by limiting the resources employed in the production of the output.* We know from the discussion of rents that they are the result of "natural" scarcities; pure economic rent is the return to a factor with absolutely fixed supply. Analogously, monopoly profits can be considered the result of a "contrived" scarcity of resources used in the production of output. The owners of the resources, however, can appropriate only the returns due to their *natural* scarcity. The returns due to contrived monopolistic scarcities are profits.

To help understand this, consider the virtual monopoly of diamond production exercised by the De Beers Consolidated Mines, Ltd., which controls the diamond-bearing lands in South Africa. Some of the "profits" of that monopoly should be called rents on the naturally scarce diamond-bearing lands. The monopoly restrictions on output from those lands, however, create an additional return, which is monopolistic profits.

The paradox of monopoly profits is that they generally do not confer any special benefits on the owners of the company with monopoly power. The reasoning behind this important point can best be explained by a specific example. Our local television stations operate under broadcasting licenses granted by the Federal Communications Commission. These licenses allocate TV channels to a restricted number of corporations and, thus, allocate some amount of monopoly power to those corporations. The owners of a corporation that receives a license have to buy equipment and bear substantial costs, but generally they reap even more substantial returns. Their returns reflect both the net productivity of the purchased equipment and the monopoly power granted in the license to broadcast. But, if the owners of the TV station sell their corporation to another firm or sell additional stock in it, they do not need to offer a higher rate of return on the company's shares than do the owners of some other more or less equivalently safe (or risky) enterprise. Thus, they set the selling price of each share sufficiently high that the rate of return on each share will be more or less equivalent to the rate of return on other similarly risky shares in the market. So, if you reproached a new shareholder with getting monopoly profits, he could rightly answer, "I'm getting only about 7 percent on my money tied up in television broadcasting stocks. That is what I get from investing in the stocks of other more competitive companies. You are shaking your finger at the wrong person."

And in an important sense he is right. The television corporation still has monopoly power, and part of the dividends each shareholder receives is, therefore, monopoly profits. But those profits have been "capitalized." *Capitalization of profits means that the ownership of the firm with monopoly power has been so subdivided and priced that now the stockholders receive only a "normal" return on their shares.*

In this sleight of hand, who got away with the big money? The original owners! Instead of raking in their monopoly profits each year, they decided to turn some of those expected returns into wealth by selling off a lot of claims to those returns (corporate shares). They could and did, however, set a price on the shares such that the returns per share would be about the going rate on comparable corporate securities.

It is misleading to think of monopolists as a bunch of sinister men smoking fat cigars. The present owners of monopolistic enterprises include widows and children, trust funds, and insurance companies, who usually bought in late, long after the original owners "absconded" with the profits by capitalizing them.

Profits as the return to enterprise and risk taking

Not all profits are monopoly profits. We have pointed out that *profits have an important role as an incentive to businessmen to start new enterprises, innovate with improved techniques, and make plans to meet future demands.* All this is compatible with perfect competition and essential for the progressive and efficient operation of a mixed economy.

The business world is full of uncertainties about future prices, quantities demanded, resource costs, and new techniques. There are opportunities to be seized in meeting emerging demands, in taking advantage of new resources, and in testing technical innovations. And there are risks of being wrong, of losing time and wealth – even of going bankrupt. Profits can be considered the economic reward for innovation, enterprise, and risk taking.

The enterprising people who face these uncertainties head on are called *entrepreneurs.* How would you know an entrepreneur if you saw one? It is not easy, because they come in many sizes, shapes, and functions. But essentially, the entrepreneur is a *risk taker.* Where there is uncertainty, he is the one who is taking an exposed position with real chances of losses. He can insure his business enterprises against fire and theft. He can try to balance his risky business with less risky investment, but there is an irreducible uncertainty which he is willing to face. He is, in sum, willing to bet on his own estimate of the future.

The innovator may back a new invention worked out in someone's basement or garage and may spend his evenings and weekends getting a new company started. He may finally quit his regular job to try to make the thing go. He is also an entrepreneur. The real estate developer who starts a new construction project is betting with his time and money that urban expansion will make a new subdivision a desirable place to live. He, too, is an entrepreneur. So is the merchant who makes plans to meet the demand for new fashions or for staple products whose prices may change because of a drought, a freeze, or a flood. So is the corporate executive who decides that his firm will back a new product, adopt an unproved technique, or open a new chain of stores. "Oh," you may say, "the corporate executive is different because he isn't risking anything of his own. He is risking the corporation's assets." But he is taking the chance of losing his job, since unsuccessful corporate risk takers are often fired. He is also taking a chance on the bonuses he may get in addition to his salary.

A caution is in order, however. The line between entrepreneurial and more conventional management decisions is not always easy to draw. Some decisions, in both big and small enterprises, hardly require the risk taker to go very far out on a limb. That does not mean they do not require a lot of skill and expertise. The laboratory chemist who does the tests that control the quality of a firm's inputs and outputs will need his Ph.D. Moreover, his decisions to accept or reject large batches of inputs and outputs must be based on small samples. He may make a very costly decision incorrectly when, strictly by chance, his sample happens to contain an unrepresentative percentage of good or bad items. He can "insure" himself in the sense that, in the long run or on the average, his decisions will turn out to be correct in a certain minimum proportion of trials. Management — and the risk takers in the management — must decide what they want that proportion to be. Will it hurt the firm's reputation if the quality control man rejects 0.5 percent of the sample? Will the firm lose sales? What if the proportion is 5 percent? That is an entrepreneurial decision.

Entrepreneurial profits and losses can and will be made even in a perfectly competitive system — except in the final condition of long-run equilibrium. In that situation, free entry of competitors and flexible prices of resources and products will have eliminated all returns over and above — or below — competitive wages, rents, and interest payments. Long-run competitive equilibrium will never be achieved in this world, however. Something is always happening. Population is growing; demands are changing. New resources are being found; old ones are being depleted. New techniques are being evolved, and old ones displaced.

The profits earned by entrepreneurs in a competitive industry are "temporary" in the sense that imitation and the free play of supply and demand forces will always tend to eliminate them. They are "permanent," however, in the sense that something new is always happening to generate profit-and-loss situations from which entrepreneurs can benefit — or suffer. Profits are the carrot and losses are the stick which drive entrepreneurial decisions. Competition as a form of economic organization does not rely on the individual good will of men or their ability to see what contributes most to the greater good of mankind. It relies on responses to material incentives. The wage, rent, and interest payments to resources are part of the incentive system for the efficient use of those resources. Profits and losses are also part of

Table 31-1

ANNUAL RATES OF PROFITS AFTER TAXES ON STOCKHOLDERS' EQUITY, BY INDUSTRY (PERCENT)

Industry	*1969*	*1968*	*1967*	*1966*	*1965*
All manufacturing corporations	11.3	12.8	12.5	13.4	13.7
Durable goods:	11.1	13.3	12.5	14.1	14.6
Transportation equipment	11.8	17.2	14.0	16.9	20.3
Motor vehicles & equipment	13.4	18.5	14.0	17.8	21.4
Aircraft & parts	9.5	14.9	14.7	14.4	17.2
Electrical machinery, equipment, & supplies	10.7	13.9	14.1	14.6	16.0
Other machinery	11.4	12.1	12.0	14.0	14.3
Other fabricated metal products	10.7	12.3	12.1	12.8	12.5
Primary metal products	10.3	9.2	9.2	12.0	9.5
Stone, clay, & glass products	7.9	9.1	9.5	8.4	10.8
Furniture & fixtures	12.6	14.6	13.3	14.1	16.0
Lumber & wood products except furniture	8.0	15.1	9.6	6.2	10.1
Instruments & related products	16.8	18.4	20.3	23.2	21.5
Miscellaneous manufacturing & ordnance	13.0	15.0	13.9	19.6	14.1
Nondurable goods:	11.4	12.2	12.5	12.7	12.8
Food & kindred products	11.2	11.4	11.8	11.1	11.2
Tobacco manufactures	15.1	14.8	15.0	14.0	13.6
Textile mill products	7.8	9.3	9.5	9.5	12.0
Apparel & other finished products	10.1	15.3	15.1	13.6	15.0
Paper & allied products	9.9	10.6	9.3	11.0	10.7
Printing & publishing	14.1	13.8	12.2	15.3	14.7
Chemicals & allied products	12.0	13.3	13.3	13.9	15.1
Petroleum refining & related industries	11.6	12.1	13.0	13.1	12.4
Rubber & miscellaneous plastic products	10.4	12.9	13.7	12.5	13.7
Leather & leather products	11.0	14.4	14.6	13.1	13.8

Source: Federal Trade Commission, Securities Exchange Commission. Fourth quarter converted to an annual rate.

the incentive system to reward entrepreneurship when it is successful and discourage it otherwise.

Extensive interdependence in the economy has been emphasized again and again. It leads to an intimate intermingling of different types of *functional* incomes in the personal distribution of income. Life would be simpler if we could identify profits and say that so much was due to monopoly and so much was reward for enterprise, innovation, and risk taking. But we cannot, and we must face up to the consequences.

Table 31-1 shows the reported rates of profit on stockholders' equity for a number of industries in the fourth quarter of each year. Remember that even for corporations this return includes some rent and interest elements as well as profits. In almost all industries, 1965 was the best of the years covered. Several industries had a 20 percent return in that year. The trend in profit rates from 1965 to 1969 was generally downward, with exceptions in some industries.

Public attitudes toward profits

No one loves a profit maximizer, and not many businessmen would admit publicly to being one. On the other hand, no corporate management could well go before its annual stockholders' meeting and admit that it was not trying to earn as much as possible for its stockholders over the long run as well as the short run. What accounts for these inconsistencies? Well, "profits" is a bad word in much conventional usage. It evokes images of long-armed monopolists, of slick wheeler-dealers engaging in sharp, speculative practices, of "capitalists" living off the "surplus value" created by labor.

Yet, as has been pointed out, one cannot equate measured profits with monopoly profits. That does not mean that the latter do not exist, but just that they are usually "capitalized" and transformed into wealth which may be quite separate from the monopoly. Moreover, it is clear that profits have an important function even in a competitive economy. It may be tactful for businessmen and politicians not to make too much of the importance of profits under prevailing public attitudes. But as long as we have a mixed economy, it is dangerous to overlook the role that profits have in its operation.

At this point, we might ask whether profits are the one type of income payment that can be dispensed with in a socialist system, either decentralized or centrally controlled. Some people believe, for example, that workers are morally entitled to all the output they help produce. Yet even these people must recognize that capital and natural resources are scarce and need to be allocated carefully if they are to be used efficiently. Charging competitive prices for their use is one way of achieving such efficiency, and it is a method with which there is increasing experimentation in the Soviet Union and Eastern Europe.

Enterprise and innovation are also important in the Communist economies. Can one rely on the revolutionary socialist spirit to pervade the consciousness of managers and workers and lead them to make the right innovations? The answer to such a question goes far beyond mere economics. We can only report that *"incentive payments" to managers appear to be more and more widely used in socialist and Communist systems.*

Public policies toward profits: Taxation

Public attitudes toward different types of income are expressed in the tax system. Corporate income taxes and progressive personal income taxes are commonly justified, in part, because they are thought to fall largely on profits. This rationale requires careful consideration. We have just shown that it is extremely difficult to identify what is or what is not profits. But suppose we could identify profits correctly. What are the effects of profits taxation on the efficiency and progressiveness of the economy?

Corporate profits taxation

Corporate profits usually include elements of implicit interest. It is hard to say how much these amount to, because monopoly or innovative profit income is "capitalized," as explained above. Corporate income taxation is, therefore, to some extent taxation of implicit interest. The explicit interest paid on corporate bonds is not taxed as corporate income because it is considered a cost of operation.

The effects of not taxing the explicit interest on bonds and of taxing the implicit interest on corporate stocks can be seen in the methods adopted for corporate financing. When corporations need to raise funds, they tend to issue bonds or borrow from banks and insurance companies rather than issue stocks. They do not follow this tendency all the way, because some forces are working in the opposite direction as well, but the tendency is certainly created by the corporate income tax.

Corporate income taxation may also affect management's enterprise and innovation. Why? Because no matter how successful it may be, the corporation reaps only part of the benefits. On the other hand, losses on a risky venture can be offset against profits earned in a successful venture. This is an incentive for corporations to grow large enough by purchase or merger to be able to offset losses in one line against profits in another. In fact, it has been a powerful force behind the creation of mergers and conglomerate corporations. *On the other hand, corporations may be able to shift all or part of the burden of the corporate income tax to customers and thus reduce the disincentive effects of the tax.*

Does corporate income taxation discourage monopoly? Probably only slightly, if at all. As noted above, monopoly profits are easily capitalized and converted into wealth and other kinds of income. Thus, only a fraction of the profits need be subject to taxation.

Personal income taxation

The personal income tax takes a progressively larger fraction in taxes as income rises. It makes only minor distinctions among the various types or sources of income. Thus the personal profit income earned on a risky innovation will be taxed just the same as income earned from clipping bond coupons in an easy chair. *This tax policy tends to discourage new enterprise and risky undertakings.* The personal income tax law permits only a limited averaging of losses in one year against gains in another year. In addition, the individual typically has a much more limited range of activities than a corporation. He cannot as readily merge or consolidate his losses in one venture with gains in another – unless he is in the upper-income brackets and has a lot of irons in the fire. *So it is particularly the people in lower-income tax brackets who face the disincentive effects of the income tax laws on enterprise and risk taking.*

There is a somewhat offsetting effect in the favored treatment of capital gains. These are increases in wealth resulting from increases in asset prices. Until the tax reform law of 1969, long-term capital gains (on assets held more than six months) were taxed at a maximum rate of 25 percent. That provided a big loophole through which individuals in upper-income brackets could report profits capitalized as increases in wealth, without paying more than a 25 percent tax rate on them. The tax reforms of 1969 reduced the size of that loophole by raising the minimum tax rate on capital gains to the tax rate on normal income or to 50 percent, whichever is lower.

Profits, taxation, and incentives

Every so often one can read in the newspaper, usually on the financial pages, an article or a speech warning that high corporate and personal taxes seriously reduce individual and business incentives. It is argued that these taxes work against the undertaking of new enterprise, the production of new products, and the use of new and risky techniques. That is a serious charge if it is true, as such activities are important determinants of the vigor and growth of the economy.

But is the charge true? This is another of those terribly difficult questions about which little can be said except "Be skeptical about any strong assertions on the issue." There is, no doubt, a great deal of innovation and enterprise in the United States. It is not obvious that any other country has a higher proportion of such activity. All that is true. But would there be even more if the tax laws were more favorable? That cannot be answered conclusively.

Try the next question then: Should there be a larger proportion of innovation and new enterprise in the economy? Once we recognize that the effect of tax laws can be good or bad for innovation, we must face the issue: What is "good" and what is "bad" in this respect?

Some people think the pace of economic and technical change is already too fast. They believe it is changing the context of life so rapidly that our social and political institutions cannot successfully cope with it and that "excessive change" is a source of social chaos. They think that if we cannot stop the world and get off we should at least slow it down.

On the other hand, a contrasting line of argument goes as follows: (1) The existing behavior norms and social and political institutions have many inadequacies. So why not use economic and technical pressure to change them rapidly? (2) Rapid change creates opportunities for relatively disadvantaged individuals and groups to advance themselves. A stagnant economy is one in which economic and social mobility is limited; the "haves" can hold on to what they have, and the "have nots" are denied access to channels of improvement.

These are some of the great issues of the times. No text can resolve them. But we can say that their eventual resolution is very likely to be related to something as mundane as the structure of taxation.

Summary

Profits have several sources. They can originate in the contrived scarcities due to monopolistic power. They will, however, also be present in perfectly competitive systems, except in that always-sought-and-never-achieved position of long-run equilibrium. In competitive as well as in monopolistic industries, profits can originate in the willingness of individuals to take entrepreneurial roles and bear the risks of losses as well as the chances of gains in situations of danger and uncertainty.

In practice, it is difficult to identify profits and even more difficult to identify their sources. Reported profits figures for corporations include some elements of interest return. "Profits" in unincorporated businesses usually include some implicit returns to labor and, perhaps, implicit interest and rents on assets.

It is seldom easy to identify the profits of monopoly, as these will be "capitalized" before they come to public notice. Since monopolists do not have to offer corporate stock buyers more than the going rate of return on their funds, monopolistic profits above that level need not be shared. Rather, the original owners of a firm in a monopolistic situation will sell as much corporate stock as necessary to bring the return to each stockholder down to the going level. They may even sell out their claims entirely and turn all the monopoly power they have created into additional wealth.

While profits do not have a good reputation, they play an important role in a mixed economy. The vigor of any economy depends in large part on the speed and discrimination with which new technologies are adopted and changes in demands are met. If the economy, socialist or capitalist, relies on economic motivations, then payments, which may be called profits or simply incentive payments, must be made for entrepreneurship.

Taxation of profits will affect the proportion of funds that a corporation raises by bonds, the interest on which is considered a cost, rather than by stocks. Taxation of the income of corporations and individuals may also have disincentive effects on risk taking and entrepreneurship. Corporations more than individuals are able to avoid income taxes on successful ventures by offsetting profits against losses or by averaging profit income over a number of years. The incentive and disincentive effects of tax policy provide a means for affecting the rate at which the economy changes.

Questions for discussion and review

1. Why are reported profits, either by corporations or by unincorporated business, almost never "pure" profits?

2. How do you explain the fact that, even when a monopoly can be identified, the owners of shares in the company usually do not seem to be getting an unusually high rate of return?

3. Explain in your own words how a monopolist manages to make monopolistic profits and then to "capitalize" them.

4. If entrepreneurs and innovators are to get profits from their successful enterprises, must they become monopolists?

5. Do you think that incentive payments in a socialist system can play the same role that profits play in a capitalist system?

6. Businessmen often complain that the corporate profits tax reduces their incentive to undertake new enterprise. What is the rationale of that complaint? Do you believe it?

7. Should taxes on profits be reduced to encourage a higher rate of economic and technical change?

8. A number of years ago, a member of the President's Cabinet said that "what is good for General Motors is good for the country." In view of the role of profits in a mixed economy, do you believe that the Cabinet officer was correct if what he said referred to General Motors' profits?

Concepts for review

Normal profits
Monopoly profits
Capitalized profits
Entrepreneurship
Contrived scarcities
Disincentive effects of taxation

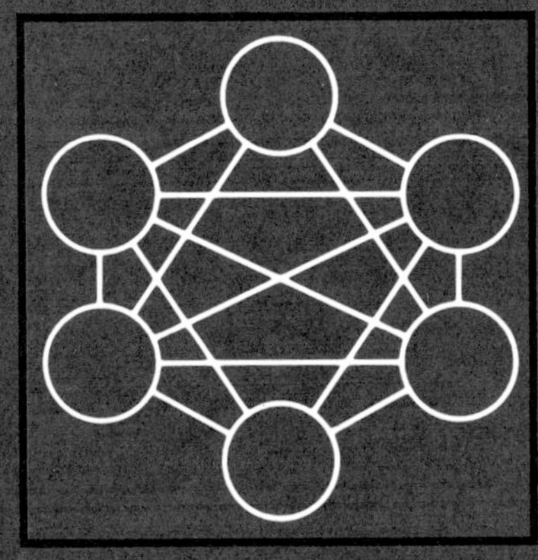

FIVE

International economics

Behind the drama of international high finance, gold movements, and trade in exotic products lie many intriguing economic issues. These require special care in their unraveling in part because they are the focus of a great deal of ideological argument and the special pleading of political and economic pressure groups.

Arguments from the Left claim that capitalist countries use international trade to exploit the rest of the world. Some capitalist and labor groups argue that international trade is a competition between cheap foreign labor and high-paid United States labor. We cannot win, they say, so we would be better off without it. Still others maintain that international trade permits a country to increase the real returns to the use of its productive resources and thus makes the country better off. One of the objectives of our analysis of international trade is to identify its benign and/or insidious influences and see what truth there is in the arguments.

Chapter 32 will develop some general background information and an accounting method for following international transactions. Chapter 33 will examine the determination of the rates at which foreign currencies exchange. In Chapter 34 the international Output, Input, and Distribution questions with respect to international trade will be analyzed. Finally, in Chapters 35 and 36 a number of problems of public economic policy toward international trade and finance will be taken up.

These chapters on international trade are, in a sense, an application of the micro- and macroeconomic theory which has been worked out in the context of the domestic economy. The study of international economic relations, therefore, provides an opportunity to review as well as extend and refine the concepts developed in earlier chapters.

32

The balance of payments and its equilibrium

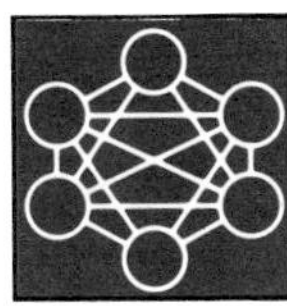

While trade in goods is the most obvious aspect of international economic relations, there are other important features of such relations. The buying and selling of "invisibles," which are nothing but services, is far from inconsequential. Tourism is the biggest industry in a number of countries. There are foreign investments in productive facilities. There is talk of "funds" moving internationally.

The objective of this chapter is to explain the content of all these international economic relations and the mechanisms through which they operate. Once we have mastered these details we can begin to analyze with more sophistication the balance-of-payments problems which often seem to dominate the international economy. The Appendix to the chapter provides a summary of alternative ways of assessing the viability of a country's balance of payments.

International trade in goods and services

The flows of international trade are responsible for the exchange of thousands and thousands of goods and services among nations. The United States imports asbestos, bananas, coffee, perfume, spices, tea, wine. It exports airplanes, bacon, coal, computers, corn, machinery, and wheat. We bank in London and Zurich. We pay restaurant bills in Paris, tourist guides in Rome, and oil tanker rentals in Tokyo. And we collect similar payments from foreigners.

Figure 32-1 presents a summary picture of trade in goods and services among the major trading areas. It is an intricate web of

Figure 32-1

INTERNATIONAL TRADE FLOWS, 1969 (BILLIONS OF DOLLARS)

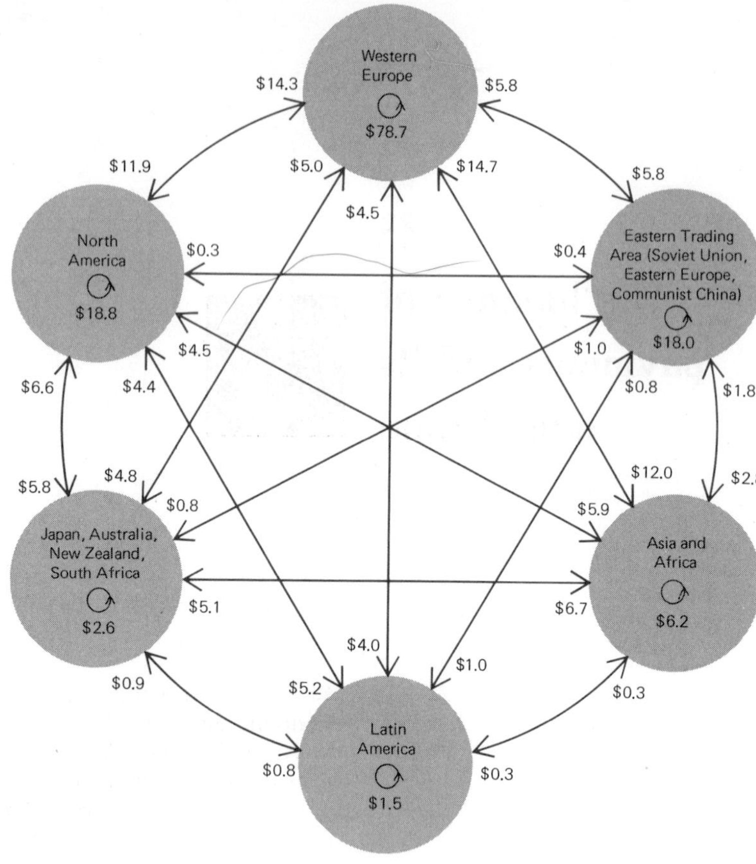

(*Source: United Nations,* Yearbook of International Statistics, *1970.*)

transactions but a little study will verify the following facts, some of which may come as a bit of a surprise:

1. The United States typically exports more to Western Europe – and to the rest of the world – than it imports.
2. Trade among the relatively advanced countries of the world is greater than trade between the advanced countries and the less developed areas of Latin America, Asia, and Africa.
3. Trade among the less developed countries is less important than trade between the less developed and the advanced countries.

Figure 32-1 embodies other interesting tidbits, and a more detailed flow chart and history would reveal still more information that is not generally appreciated. For example:

1. Trade among advanced countries is growing faster than trade between advanced and less developed countries.

2. Many of the poorer countries of the world import more than they export.

3. Trade in manufactured goods and finished products is larger and is growing faster than trade in food products and industrial raw materials.

International capital movements

In addition to trade in goods and services, there are large-scale private and governmental movements of capital among nations. These may be direct investments, loans, gifts, or grants. United States oil companies invest in oil wells and pumping equipment in North Africa and the Arabian peninsula. Arab sheikhs with their oil royalties buy stocks on the New York Stock Exchange. United States companies have joint ventures and subsidiaries abroad, like Goodrich Tire Company's factory in India and English Ford in Britain. European emigrants in North and South America send remittances back to their families in Europe, and Algerian and Turkish workers in Europe send remittances to their homes. The United States government makes loans and grants of several billion dollars annually to less developed countries. The Canadian government has a similar but smaller foreign aid program, and so on. The origin and destination of capital flows are more difficult to trace than trade flows, but a good deal is known. For example:

1. The United States is the world's giant in terms of loans and grants supplied to foreign countries and also in terms of funds received from other nations.

2. The movement of capital among the more developed countries is much greater than capital movements from these countries to less developed countries.

3. Most of the United States private capital investment in less developed areas goes to the oil-producing countries of the Mid East and to Latin America, and relatively little goes to Africa and Asia.

The mechanics of international transactions

Since most of us do not import or export goods or invest capital abroad, we are unfamiliar with the mechanics of international trade. We know how to buy a dozen eggs, a refrigerator, or a hundred shares of General Motors stock, but how do you go about buying 10 tons of Turkish chrome ore or a hundred British government bonds? Actually these are straightforward operations at the "how-to-do-it" level, and we can begin to clear up some of the mysteries of foreign trade and capital movements if we follow some of the transactions.

Suppose you are a buyer in one of the local department stores planning your merchandise for next Christmas. You will be looking at catalogs of domestic producers and writing out orders. You may also look at the catalogs of, say, British bicycle manufacturers. The prices of the bicycles are quoted in pounds (£), so you look in the financial pages of the morning paper or call your bank to find out how much you would have to pay in dollars for a British pound. Then you make a simple calculation: A bicycle with specified equipment costs £10. Each pound will cost you, say, about $2.40. So the wholesale price of the bicycle in Britain is $24. Then there will be the freight, insurance, and delivery charges as well. But English bikes have always been popular and you think they will sell well at Christmas. So you decide to order directly. You write out an order to the manufacturer for fifty specified bicycles. Then you realize that he will want payment in pounds, since all his prices are quoted that way. You call your banker back and ask him what to do. He says, "Have the British firm send the bill of lading,[1] which it will have stamped by the freight company when it ships the bikes, to our correspondent bank in London. We will arrange for our correspondent bank to make the payment on presentation of the bill of lading. Then your account will be charged here." Well, that is not so bad. And then your banker recommends an insurance firm in London to insure the shipment, a steamship line, a customshouse broker to clear the shipment through United States customs, and a local delivery company. Finally he suggests a reliable British freight-forwarding company that will handle all those details, and you breathe easier. So you specify in your letter to the manufacturer that he use the freight-forwarding company. It seems a little complicated the first time. The second time around it is a snap. To get those cottons, ceramics, transistor radios, and wickerwork pieces from Hong Kong, however, you decide to buy directly from a New York importing firm, which has its own catalog with dollar prices.

International trade is more complicated than domestic trade, and specialized import and export firms exist to handle the foreign exchange and foreign language problems, the domestic and foreign duties, quotas, and other trade regulations, and international shipping details. They do essentially what the department store buyer learned to do but with more frequency and on a larger scale so that it becomes just another, though different routine.

What about capital transactions? Suppose you come across the catalog of a Japanese firm selling a line of low-priced radios, television sets, and appliances that you think will really catch on in the United States. Having a little savings, you decide to try to get a piece of the action and invest in the firm. How can that foreign investment be accomplished? Again relatively simply. You look up a stockbroker in the Yellow Pages whose advertisement says

[1] The bill of lading is nothing more than a description of the goods delivered, where they come from, where they are going, and who is doing the delivering – all on a standard form.

"foreign branches." You explain to the "customer's man" what you want to do. He looks up the Japanese firm and finds that it is listed on the Tokyo stock exchange. The stock prices are quoted in yen, so he finds the dollar price of yen in the financial pages or from his bank. He then figures the stock price in dollars and tells you that your savings will buy, say, 100 shares. If you decide to go ahead, you place an order for the 100 shares with your new broker and send him a check to cover the cost and the commission charges on the transaction. The broker then arranges with his correspondent or branch brokerage firm in Tokyo to buy the stock in your name. The brokerage firm maintains a Tokyo bank account from which payment can be made, and if the account needs replenishing, that will be arranged with a United States bank or a Japanese bank in Tokyo.

These explanations should not really satisfy you that you understand all the "how," much less the "why," of foreign trade. For example, where did those foreign bank balances that you used indirectly as purchaser or investor come from? And how and where was the exchange rate between pounds and yen and the dollar determined? And, more fundamentally, why were the prices of English bicycles in London lower than English-style bicycles made in the United States? Why were the prices of Japanese transistor radios lower than United States radios? What do foreigners buy in the United States and why? There are a lot of questions like these to answer. Before we go into them, however, we must develop a way of accounting for international transactions. That will give us an overall picture of international economic relations and a way of measuring their absolute and relative importance.

The balance of payments

A country's balance of payments is simply a record of all economic transactions between its own residents and the residents of all foreign countries during a specified period, usually a year.[2] Being a record of all transactions, it provides a comprehensive guide to why people want to make transactions.

While it is often convenient to talk about trade and capital movements among nations, we must remember that trade and capital movements are, for the most part, conducted by and for individuals and businesses — not by governments. Government-

[2] Notice that the distinction between "United States" and "foreign" in the balance of payments is not a matter of citizenship but of permanent residence. So by this definition, United States citizens residing permanently abroad are foreigners, and foreign citizens residing in the United States are not foreigners. To avoid confusion, we shall usually refer to United States residents, on the one hand, and foreign residents, or foreigners, on the other hand, meaning by the latter, persons residing in foreign countries.

Table 32-1

THE STRUCTURE OF A BALANCE OF PAYMENTS

	Credit (+)	*Debit (−)*
1. Current account		
Private		
Merchandise trade	Exports	Imports
Invisibles		
Services: transportation, shipping	Sales	Purchases
Insurance	Sales	Purchases
Tourist expenditures	Foreign residents in the United States	United States residents abroad
Investment income: interest and dividends	Earned by United States residents investing abroad	Earned by foreign residents investing in the United States
Private remittances (gifts and grants)	Sent by foreign residents to the United States	Sent abroad by United States residents
Government		
Merchandise transactions	Exports of military goods by the United States government to foreign governments	Expenditures on military goods abroad by the United States government
Grants and income payments	Receipts	Payments
2. Capital account		
Long term		
Private	Inflow	Outflow
Government	Inflow	Outflow
Short term		
Private	Inflow	Outflow
Government	Inflow	Outflow
3. Gold movements	Outflow	Inflow
4. Errors and omissions	(Either)	

directed trade and capital movements are not inconsequential, but even so, they are usually a small part of the total. The balance of payments is a summary of individual, private business, and government transactions.

Like other types of accounting balance sheets, the balance of payments is defined so that it will always balance. *Transactions that create claims by residents on the foreign exchange of foreigners are called credits. Transactions that create claims by foreigners on domestic funds are called debits.* Credits and debits must balance, because what is not paid for is owed for. "Owings" — *net* debits or credits — are also included in the balance of payments. The principles are the same for every country, but for convenience we shall refer to the United States balance of payments.

A balance of payments has three parts: the Current Account, the Capital Account, and the Monetary Gold Account. These are explained below. The major components of each account are enumerated in Table 32-1, and the proper accounting of each type of transaction as a debit or credit is shown. An "errors and omissions" line is added, for it is impossible to catch every transaction and measure it precisely. Be warned, however, that it is not this line that makes the balance of payments actually balance. The balancing is guaranteed by the way the accounting is done.

The current account

Starting with merchandise trade in the current account will help to clarify how we decide what is a debit and what a credit.

An export is a credit: It creates a claim on foreigners who purchase United States goods. Foreigners can pay by drawing down the bank accounts of U.S. dollars which they may own. Alternatively, *exports are a source of foreign currencies,* if United States exporters will accept them in payment. Those foreign currencies will, in turn, be deposited to the accounts of United States businesses and banks abroad.

An import is a debit: It creates a claim by foreign residents on the United States residents who purchase foreign goods. *Imports can be a source of dollar accounts held by foreigners,* if they accept payment in dollars. Or if United States residents have bank accounts in the currency of the country from which they are importing, these can be used for payments.

Any other type of transaction can be judged by the same criteria used to decide that exports are credits and imports are debits. In the time period considered, does the transaction create a source of foreign currency (or a reduction in dollar balances held by foreigners) — a credit — or does it create a source of dollars for foreigners (or a reduction in foreign currency balances held by United States residents) — a debit?

When United States businesses use *foreign shipping and commercial services* and United States *tourists* sip coffee in the cafes of Rome and Paris, they create debits in the U.S. balance of payments. When United States residents earn *income on their investments abroad,* that is a credit, since it is a source of foreign currency. When foreign residents living abroad collect *dividends* on stock purchased on the New York Stock Exchange, that is a debit in the U.S. balance of payments, since it provides them with a claim against U.S. dollars. When an American sends a money order as a gift to a grandmother in Italy, that is a debit because dollars are made available to a foreign resident. The recipient can use the dollars to buy Italian lira.

The capital account

The current account is reasonably straightforward, though not obvious. The capital account is even less obvious and requires more explanation.

Capital outflows are debits: Like imports, they can increase the supply of United States currency available to foreigners.

Capital inflows are credits: Like exports, they can be a source of foreign currency to United States residents.

Suppose, for example, you are a corporate officer in an American bicycle manufacturing firm. After hearing about all the orders that an English manufacturer is receiving, you persuade your company to buy into it. To do that, your company will need pounds with which to purchase the stock shares from their English owners. So you go to your local bank, which will arrange with its correspondent in Great Britain or with a British bank to sell you pounds for dollars. Your payment in dollars increases the supply of dollars available to foreigners. If your company has an account in a British bank – in pounds – it may, of course, make the payment in pounds. This would reduce the holdings of pounds by United States residents. In this respect, this *foreign investment* is like an import – a debit in the U.S. balance of payments. Your firm hopes to make a profit on its investment and receive dividends. That is in the future, however. If dividends are paid, they will be a current account credit in the U.S. balance of payments. But we cannot count them until they are in hand.

The purchase of the Japanese firm's stock on the Tokyo stock exchange was also a debit. On the other hand, if an oil sheikh makes a *purchase of United States securities*, that is a capital inflow. It is a credit in the U.S. balance of payments because it increases the supply of foreign currency available to United States residents or reduces the amount of dollars held by foreigners. The sheikh exchanges his dollars for the securities.

The only difference between long- and short-term capital movements is in the period for which the loan or investment is expected to be made. The arbitrary dividing line is a year. So when the balance of payments is drawn up, the loans outstanding are considered short-term if, when made, they were expected to be liquidated within a year. Otherwise, they are considered long-term. If a United States company were to give a foreign buyer six months to make payment on an order of spare parts, and that account was outstanding at the end of the year when the balance of payments was drawn up, it would enter as a short-term capital outflow. The purchase by the United States bicycle company of a share of the English bicycle manufacturer is a long-term capital outflow. In many cases, the distinction is essentially arbitrary.

Gold movements Gold is a means of international payment as long as it is acceptable as a way of buying foreign currencies. In this case, gold reserves are like money in the bank. They are like a checking, not a savings, account, however, because they do not earn interest. Therefore, while every country wants gold reserves, there are limits to the amounts a country would want to hold – just as an individual does not keep all his assets in cash. Venezuela, for example, instead of holding gold, could keep reserves in the form of dollars in time deposits in United States banks. Every $100 million kept in this way would earn, say, $4 million or $5 million interest annually – whatever the going rate of interest is – not an insignificant amount. On the other hand, $100 million of gold reserves earns nothing. But like cash it is liquid and it provides a more secure way of preserving the international purchasing power of reserves.

Gold exports can be thought of as commodity exports, and like commodity exports, they are a credit.[3] To obtain gold, a country must buy it with dollars or with its own currency. If it uses its own currency, that clearly increases the supply of foreign currency available to United States residents. If it uses dollars, that decreases the foreign holdings of U.S. dollars.

Before 1969 the United States exchanged gold dollars with both foreign private and central banks. After 1969 such exchanges were restricted to foreign central banks, and even these were suspended in the foreign exchange crisis of 1971. When gold trading was more extensive, the connection between gold movements and foreign currency availabilities was more direct. Now central banks can and do exchange gold, but they can regulate its effect on the supply of foreign currencies.

The balancing of the balance of payments

Why does the balance of payments balance? The essence is:

> Imports come in and exports go.
> What a country doesn't pay, a country must owe.[4]

[3] Though there have been about $14 billion of gold "exports" by the United States in the last fifteen years, only a small amount has left our shores. Generally an export of gold means only that some gold bars are moved from a room labeled United States in the basement of the New York Federal Reserve to another room in the basement with another country's name on it.

[4] With apologies to John Heywood, *Be Merry Friends.*

> Let the world slide, let the world go;
> A fig for a care and a fig for woe!
> If I can't pay, why I can owe,
> And death makes equal the high and low.

There are three ways of "paying" for imports: (1) by exporting goods and earning foreign exchange, (2) by exporting gold and buying foreign exchange, or (3) by borrowing foreign exchange or using up past accumulations of it. Importers who do not buy or earn foreign currencies to pay off their bills must still *owe* those bills, and that means there is a capital *inflow*, either long-term or short-term. Exporters who are not paid off must be extending credit, i.e., undertaking a capital *outflow*. Or purchasers of exports may borrow from banks in order to make payment, and in that case the banks are financing a capital outflow. The banks, in turn, may have the foreign funds on deposit, that is, on loan, from private firms or individuals. One way or another, *those bills which are not paid are owed, and the balance of payments, which records the owings as well as the payments, must always balance.* The errors and omissions line does not affect this fundamental logic. That line only means that we have not fully succeeded in measuring all transactions.

The U.S. balance of payments and its role in world trade

The balance-of-payments picture of the United States for 1960 and 1970 is presented in Table 32-2. Though foreign trade is a small fraction of GNP – about 4 percent or 5 percent, depending on what measure is used – United States international trade and capital movements are a large fraction of the world total. So when the U.S. balance of payments is not quite up to par, a number of other countries will reach for the headache tablets.

It may be surprising to find that the United States surplus of exports of goods and services over imports is usually substantial.[5] The private surplus on trade in goods and services, investment income, and gifts and remittances is largely offset, however, by the government current account deficit. The latter is mainly due to military expenditures and grants abroad for military purposes.

There is a large deficit on long-term capital movements in the capital account. That means that the United States was investing abroad on a long-term basis much more than it was receiving in investments by foreigners. The total current account and long-term capital account together generate an even larger deficit.

Short-term capital inflows and gold exports balance the net deficit from the current account and long-term capital account. The United States special role in world trade shows up in its capital accounts in particular. *The U.S. dollar is a "reserve currency," and much of the rest of the world uses the United States – or rather its banks and financial markets – as a banker.* The "reserve currency" role of the dollar means that other countries find it convenient to maintain deposits in U.S. dollars – analogous to the way private

[5] The net exports of goods have been declining.

Table 32-2

U.S. BALANCE OF PAYMENTS, 1960, 1970 (MILLIONS OF DOLLARS)

	1960		1970	
	Credits	Debits	Credits	Debits
Current				
Private:				
Merchandise	19,650	14,744	42,041	39,856
Invisibles				
Transportation	1,782	1,915	3,665	4,032
Travel expenditures	919	1,750	2,318	3,916
Income on investments	3,402	731	10,244	4,054
Private remittances		382		925
Miscellaneous services	898	482	1,944	813
Current private balance	26,651	20,004	60,212	53,596
United States governmental:				
Export of military goods and services (+)	335		1,479	
Military aid (—) to allies		335		1,479
Other military transactions	1,765	2,752	615	3,358
Other grants and payments		3,643		2,724
Miscellaneous governmental transactions	501	645	1,271	1,782
Current government balance	2,601	7,375	3,365	9,343
Net balance on current account	**+1,873**		**+ 638**	
Capital account				
Long-term loans (—) or borrowings (+)				
Private	148	1,867	1,852	5,350
Government	663	1,213	2,442	3,909
Net long-term foreign investments		**—2,269**		**—4,965**
Net balance on current accounts and long-term investment ("basic deficit")		**— 396**		**—4,327**
Short-term loans (—) or borrowings (+)				
Private	1,630	1,440	2,153	1,118
Purchase of equities	482	863	2,782	1,457
Government	126	528		103
Net short-term foreign investments		**— 593**	**+2,257**	
Net changes in gold and foreign currency holdings				
Gold	1,703		787	
Foreign currency reserves	442		1,690	
Net change in gold and reserves	**+2,145**		**+2,477**	
Allocation of special drawing rights (SDR)			+ 867	
Errors and omissions		—1,156		—1,274
Offset to "basic deficit"	**+ 396**		**+4,327**	
Total	34,446	34,446	76,150	76,150

Source: U.S. Deparment of Commerce, *Survey of Current Business.*

individuals find it convenient to maintain checking and savings deposits in banks. Dollars are generally accepted in international payments, and United States banks have effective systems for transferring funds. In addition, via time deposits or purchases of securities, foreigners can earn income on funds they may be accumulating. The large size of the United States financial markets is itself an important attraction in this respect. Foreign funds can usually move in or out without substantially affecting financial conditions in the United States itself. Thus, many short-term capital inflows and outflows are, in their origins, independent of United States trade and long-term capital movements. As will be pointed out below, this situation makes it difficult to evaluate the health of the U.S. balance of payments.

There were substantial gold outflows in 1960 and a smaller outflow in 1970. These outflows were characteristic of the period starting in 1958 during which the United States lost almost $14 billion in gold. Foreign currencies held by the Federal Reserve System serve the same function as gold reserves, and therefore, changes in these holdings are recorded in the same account as gold.

The errors and omissions entry which was a small negative amount in 1960 became a larger negative item in most of the 1960s, as it was in 1970. The usual and probably correct explanation for the persistence of a negative errors and omissions is that not all short-term capital outflows are being measured. Some of the outward movements are illegal, but even some legal ones are hard to capture. For example, a United States tourist living in Switzerland for a while may establish a bank account there. That is perfectly legal. But a United States resident regularly depositing money in Swiss accounts without paying United States taxes on such movements is acting illegally.

Deficits, surpluses, and equilibrium in the balance of payments

The newspapers carry a good deal of talk about the balance-of-payments deficit. And, as is usual with any economic concept discussed in the newspapers, controversy prevails. The controversy is not simply a matter of ignorance. Rather it represents essential differences on two questions: What do the facts mean? And what international economic position is desirable?

If the balance of payments always balances, what meaning can there be in the concepts of balance-of-payments equilibrium, deficit, and surplus? The key to the identification of equilibrium is the notion of "maintainability" or "sustainability." A balance can be achieved in many ways. If an unbiased expert could examine a country's balance of payments and say, Yes, that is an indefinitely maintainable condition, then that balance of payments is in equilibrium. But anticipating disagreement on who is an unbiased expert, shouldn't we establish some rules by which anyone could decide what is maintainable? As might be expected, there is disagreement about rules as well as about who is an expert. Our discussion of balance-of-payments equilibrium can be applied to any country. It will concentrate on the United States, not only because of a parochial interest, but because of the special difficulties of interpretation the United States accounts raise.

The mercantilist doctrine of the seventeenth and eighteenth centuries, of which we still hear an occasional echo, held that the only good or "favorable" balance of payments was one in which exports of goods were greater than imports of goods. In the simpler days of the mercantilists, that meant a surplus on current account that would be balanced by a gold inflow, inasmuch as services and capital movements were negligible. Since having more gold was, *ipso facto,* A Good Thing, a trade surplus was desirable.

This mercantilist doctrine was vigorously attacked by Adam Smith, David Hume, and others who argued that:

1. A trade surplus does not necessarily lead to a gold inflow.
2. Even if there is a gold inflow, economic forces are automatically set in motion to stop and then reverse the flow.
3. Accumulation of gold is in any case a sterile achievement except for misers. It is goods and services which provide satisfaction. A preoccupation with gold movements ignores the fundamental point that international trade can provide goods at a lower real cost than that for which they can be produced domestically and, therefore, more goods than otherwise from the same amount of resources.[6]

One particularly narrow version of the old mercantilist doctrine is that, if the merchandise trade between any two countries does not balance, the surplus country is profiting at the expense of the trade deficit country. This complaint is sometimes made in the United States with respect to our trade with Japan, and it is made in Latin America and Canada about their trade with the United States. The argument evaporates, however, when we recognize that since international trade is multilateral, or many-sided, the condition of one country's balance of payments cannot be judged just by looking at its commercial relations with one other country. Each country's balance of payments must be evaluated with respect to *all* countries. Moreover, a *trade balance,* surplus or deficit, is not by itself the only determinant of the condition of a country's balance of payments.

The mercantilist position was that the balance of payments was not in a desirable state unless

$$\text{Exports of goods and services} - \text{imports of goods and services} = \text{gold inflow}$$

This overlooks completely the role of capital movements.

[6] The determinants of the advantages in trade are analyzed in Chap. 34.

A more modern view of balance-of-payments equilibrium that takes account of the role of capital movements is called the *basic balance*. The condition for a *basic balance* adds long-term capital movements to the left side and short-term capital movements to the right side and requires that the sum on each side be equal to zero. The basic balance states:

$$\begin{array}{l} \text{Exports} \\ \text{of goods} \\ \text{and} \\ \text{services} \end{array} - \begin{array}{l} \text{imports} \\ \text{of goods} \\ \text{and} \\ \text{services} \end{array} - \begin{array}{l} \text{net} \\ \text{long-term} \\ \text{capital} \\ \text{outflow} \end{array} = 0 = \begin{array}{l} \text{net} \\ \text{short-term} \\ \text{capital} \\ \text{outflow} \end{array} + \begin{array}{l} \text{gold} \\ \text{inflow}^{7} \end{array}$$

Two types of equilibrium cases can be distinguished. First, if exports of goods and services are greater than imports of goods and services, that can balance a net long-term capital outflow. Second, if exports of goods and services are less than imports, that can be balanced by a net long-term capital *inflow*. Suppose exports are greater than imports and the difference is *not* made up by a net long-term capital outflow. Then the left-hand side of the basic balance definition will be positive and, therefore, the right-hand side also. There is a *basic surplus*. On the other hand, if exports are less than imports and the difference is not made up by a net long-term capital inflow, there is a *basic deficit*. In the latter situation, for example, the difference will have to be made up by a short-term capital inflow or a gold outflow.

Short-term capital movements are often regarded as particularly volatile and, therefore, not a reliably maintainable way of financing a left-hand side deficit. Or if the balance is achieved by means of gold outflows, that is also regarded as not sustainable, since there is always a limit to gold reserves.

Evaluating the condition of the balance of payments of most of the countries of the world is not difficult, and the various definitions do not lead to major differences in opinion. But the United States is not just one among many trading nations. Not only is it the largest in terms of its trade, but it also serves as the major banker to the world. Flows of funds and transactions are not always motivated primarily by the trade and transactions of the United States itself, but by trade and transactions among foreign nations. Nonetheless, some of these transactions have an effect on the accounting in the U.S. balance of payments. And they affect the ability of the United States to finance its own transactions. Differing judgments about the role of the United States as an international financial center are a major source of differences in evaluating the condition of the U.S. balance of payments. Suppose that short-term capital inflows are like private deposits in commer-

[7] If the long- or short-term capital movements are on balance *inflows*, the algebraic sign in front of them would change. The same would be the case if there were a gold outflow. The long-term capital movements include remittances and government foreign aid.

cial banks and on the average are maintained indefinitely. Then a balance achieved by means of short-term capital inflows will be regarded as sustainable. But if short-term capital movements are regarded as volatile and unreliable, a balance of payments that relies on them to finance a trade deficit or long-term capital outflows will not be considered in equilibrium.

As always, when the facts are in doubt, the diagnosis is in doubt. In this case the facts include not just the explanation of the various individual transactions, but also a projection of whether they are likely to continue. In Chapter 36, when we turn to a deeper analysis of the recent U.S. balance-of-payments difficulties, we shall find that they are related to some of the most basic features of our economy.

Summary

International economic transactions represent trade in goods and services and capital movements among countries. These transactions are carried out like domestic purchases, with one important difference: At some point domestic currency must be exchanged for foreign currency in order to make payment.

A country's balance of payments is a record of all transactions between its residents and the residents of all foreign countries in a particular time period. The current account includes private trade in goods and services as well as government exports and grants. The capital account includes private and government loans, both short-term – i.e., expected to be liquidated in a year or less – and long-term. There is a separate account for gold movements.

Transactions that create claims on foreign currency, or are a source of supply of foreign currency, enter the balance of payments as credits. Transactions that create claims on domestic currency, or are a source of supply of domestic currency to foreigners, enter as debits. Thus, exports, capital imports, and gold outflows are credits. Imports, capital exports, and gold inflows are debits. The balance of payments must always balance, because every transaction is either paid for or owed for, and both payments and debts (capital movements) are recorded.

Since the balance of payments must always balance, there is no simple calculation which indicates whether or not it is in equilibrium. The important issue is whether the flows which are recorded are maintainable. A trade surplus of exports over imports, which generates a gold inflow, is not in itself a sign of health. It means that goods and services are being exported on balance simply to acquire stocks of gold bullion. While some amount of gold is desirable as reserves, its indefinite accumulation is not necessary for this purpose.

The basic balance concept of balance-of-payments equilibrium requires that total exports minus total imports plus long-term capital outflows be equal to zero. Likewise the sum of short-term capital outflows and gold inflows should be zero. If there are short-term capital inflows and gold outflows which finance a net trade deficit and capital outflow, there is a basic deficit in the balance of payments.

The differences in the various definitions of balance-of-payments equilibrium stem from differing views of the United States role in the world economy. The United States is not simply another trading nation, since it is the major banker for world trade. That, in turn, means that many transactions appear in its balance of payments which reflect trade and capital flows among other nations. Nonetheless, these transactions affect the manner in which the United States transactions are balanced. The problem of maintainability, therefore, becomes one of judging the persistence of the world banking role of the United States and how it is accomplished.

Questions for discussion and review

1. What are the various types of international transactions? Give examples.

2. Describe how the following transactions for goods and services are treated in the balance of payments: (*a*) Insurance purchased from a London firm, (*b*) bananas imported by a United States-owned company from its plantation in Central America, (*c*) payments by Mexicans for refining Mexican zinc in Missouri and then exporting it from the United States.

3. Describe how the following transactions for private capital are treated in the balance of payments: (*a*) Purchase of farmland in Australia by a United States citizen planning to migrate, (*b*) purchase of stock in Canadian firms by United States citizens, (*c*) payments by the Peruvian government for expropriated United States firms in Peru, (*d*) United States government loans to India for development purposes, (*e*) United States government loans to Taiwan to finance the purchase of military goods.

4. Discuss the following statement: *The balance of payments balances because the government is always watching it, and if it is not going to come out right at the end of the year, the government steps in to make it balance.*

5. Do you believe that a trade surplus means that the balance of payments of a country is in good shape? Do you think that this is true for the United States?

6. What is the rationale of the definition of the "basic balance" for balance-of-payments equilibrium?

7. Does balance-of-payments equilibrium require that gold reserves remain unchanged?

8. How does the role of the United States as the center for financing international trade complicate the definition of equilibrium in our balance of payments?

Concepts for review

Balance of payments
Debits and credits in the balance of payments
Gold reserves
Trade surplus
Basic deficit
Capital outflows and inflows
Government capital outflows
Maintainability in the balance of payments

Appendix: Alternative definitions of balance-of-payments equilibrium

Differing views of the role of the United States in international trade and of the facts of international finance lead to different definitions of balance-of-payments equilibrium. Two alternative definitions have received a good deal of attention: the *liquidity balance* and the *official reserve transactions balance.*

The *liquidity balance* distinguishes between domestic and foreign short-term capital flows. For the United States, the balanced condition would be:

$$\begin{array}{c}\text{Exports of}\\ \text{goods and}\\ \text{services}\end{array} - \begin{array}{c}\text{imports of}\\ \text{goods and}\\ \text{services}\end{array} - \begin{array}{c}\text{net long-}\\ \text{term capital}\\ \text{outflow}\end{array} - \begin{array}{c}\text{short-term}\\ \text{United States}\\ \text{capital outflow}\end{array}$$

$$= 0 = \begin{array}{c}\text{short-term}\\ \text{foreign capital}\\ \text{outflow}\end{array} + \begin{array}{c}\text{gold}\\ \text{inflow}^{8}\end{array}$$

The logic of the distinction between United States and foreign short-term capital movements is that, in times of monetary crisis, the former will not change as readily as the latter. Thus short-term foreign capital movements and changes in gold reserves should be equal to zero by this criterion. If there is a "deficit," the sum on the left-hand side, and, therefore, on the right-hand side, is negative. The implication of a deficit is that transactions that are relatively stable are being maintained by transactions that cannot be relied on to persist indefinitely. On the other hand, if the totals on each side are positive, there is, by this definition, a balance-of-payments surplus.

[8] Again the algebraic signs would change if the net movements of capital and gold changed direction.

The official reserve transactions balance is:

Exports of goods and services	−	imports of goods and services	−	net long-term capital outflow	−	net short-term *private* capital outflow

= 0 =	net short-term foreign official capital outflow	+	gold inflow[9]

This definition is based on the reasoning that, when there are private short-term capital movements, some company or individual has decided to make a loan or hold foreign currency. But official capital movements, among central banks, are required when private transactions are no longer enough to maintain the balance. Suppose, for example, that the left-hand side of the official reserve transactions balance added up to a minus, or deficit. That would mean that private transactions of all types were not balancing, and central bank loans would be required to rescue the situation. Because of the unwillingness of foreign central banks to continue rescue operations indefinitely, the left-hand side should balance to zero if the balance of payments is to be in equilibrium by this criterion.

[9] Any *official* short-term capital movements would be included in the short-term private movements. The algebraic signs would change if the net movements changed direction.

33

Foreign exchange rates and their determination

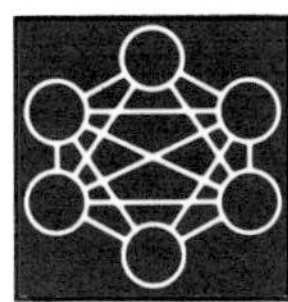

The balance-of-payments statement discussed in Chapter 32 is not only an accounting device. It is a panoramic view of the size and diversity of international economic transactions. Behind every transaction is an explicit or implicit exchange of currencies. The ratio at which one currency exchanges for another is just the price of the one in terms of the other. Supply and demand tools can be used to show how this price is determined. As in other applications of supply and demand, the heart of the analysis lies in the explanation of what determines the shape and position of the supply and demand schedules.

Foreign exchange availability and pricing

The balance-of-payments statement suggests the close interdependence of many international economic transactions. The various transactions add to the quantity of foreign exchange supplied or demanded and, thus, affect the foreign exchange that is available for other transactions and the price of foreign exchange as well. The balance of payments helps resolve many of the questions left unanswered in the last chapter: Where does the foreign exchange come from — the pounds, the yen, etc., that banks and brokers use to pay for the purchases of goods and securities? What determines the prices of those currencies in dollars or rupees or francs? And is there a connection between price and availability?

The foreign exchange used by United States residents in any single transaction can arise from any of the types of credit transactions which create claims on foreign exchange. The British pounds held by a United States correspondent bank in London might have had their source in exports from the United States to Great Britain or even an export to, say, Hong Kong, a British colony, for which payment was arranged in London. The British and Hong Kong importers go to United States bank branches and ask to buy U.S. dollars to be used, in turn, to buy United States goods. They pay for the dollars with pounds. This payment – like other credit-generating transactions – provides foreign exchange, which United States residents can use in their transactions abroad. A Zurich businessman who wants to deposit funds in a New York bank to get the high interest rate there or wants to buy United States bonds for the same reason may buy dollars at a Swiss bank. The Swiss francs with which he pays then become available through the bank for use, say, by United States importers who want to buy them to pay for Swiss cheese. Or a United States firm might buy the francs in order, in turn, to buy shares in a Swiss watch factory.

Similarly, *transactions which are debits create claims on United States exchange by foreigners and provide the dollars needed by buyers of United States goods and by persons wishing to send funds to the United States.* There is nothing in international trade like Newton's Third Law, which says that for every action there must be an equal and opposite reaction. Nothing says that the credits and debits created by sustainable transactions must automatically be equal. There are, however, economic processes which act to adjust such credit and debit transactions *toward* equality. Since we know that the influence of prices is ubiquitous, it will come as no surprise to realize that changes in the prices of foreign currencies can be one of the basic adjustment mechanisms. Other important adjustment processes are due to changes in income.

Foreign exchange markets and arbitrage

Before we develop the supply and demand apparatus to be used in analyzing the determination of foreign exchange rates, a more precise picture of the markets in which foreign currencies are traded will be helpful. We also want to understand the mechanics of foreign exchange pricing.

Foreign exchange markets are not located at any one place. Dealers in foreign exchange are spread around the world, though they concentrate in such major financial centers as New York, London, Hamburg, Paris, Zurich. Yet all these markets constitute one large market which is close to being perfectly competitive.

1. Each private buyer and seller is too small for his transactions to have a noticeable effect on prices though the transactions of all together do affect prices.

2. The separate markets are closely connected by telephone and teletype and have good arrangements for the international transfer of funds, so that prices in all markets must be more or less the same.

3. A dollar is a dollar, a pound is a pound, and all the other currencies are each the same. Each of the currencies traded is a homogeneous item.[1]

Foreign exchange prices are foreign exchange *rates* because they imply the ratio in which one currency trades for another. Suppose, for example, we had the following dollar quotations on the pound, the deutsche mark, and the French franc, as might be excerpted from the *Wall Street Journal*:

Great Britain (pound)	$2.41
France (franc)	0.18
West Germany (deutsche mark)	0.28

These prices also mean that you could get 1/2.41 or 0.415 of a pound, 1/0.18 or 5.55 francs, and 1/0.28 or 3.57 deutsche marks for a dollar. Though it is increasingly common in financial circles to quote foreign exchange rates in terms of the dollar, they could just as well be quoted in terms of the pound, the franc, the deutsche mark, or the Honduran lempera. It is the trading *ratios* which matter, and those do not depend on the particular currency that is used for pricing the other currencies.

How can we be so sure that foreign exchange prices will be the same in all markets in which they are freely traded? In the foreign exchange markets, there are people called *arbitragers* who will pounce on any price difference and try to make a profit on it by means of simultaneous purchases and sales. Suppose that you called up your broker before breakfast, as John Maynard Keynes was said to do, and got the following price quotations in London and Hamburg:

London		*Hamburg*	
Pound	$2.38	Pound	$2.40
Deutsche mark	0.28	Deutsche mark	0.26

The differences in prices mean that the currencies are trading at slightly different ratios in London and Hamburg. The broker tells you that the differences were larger when the markets opened. Remember that, like Keynes, you are dealing with your broker in

[1] The exception to this statement is that promising to pay a dollar or a pound a month or a year from now *is* different from paying a dollar or a pound now. "Forward" exchange to be paid in the future carries a different price from "spot" currency which is deliverable immediately.

London, and your account is in pounds. A little rapid calculation, dividing $2.38 by $0.28 and $2.40 by 0.26 tells you that you can get 8.50 deutsche marks for each pound in London and 9.23 deutsche marks for each pound in Hamburg. So quick, you order your broker to buy £1,000 of deutsche marks in Hamburg and sell the deutsche marks in London. That means you buy DM9,230 in Hamburg and sell them for (9,230/8.50 =) £1,086 in London. You make £86. It is not a lot of money, but it is pretty good for a phone call before breakfast and, best of all, it is virtually riskless. You would do it again if there were time, but by now the prices have moved to equalize the trading ratios in the different markets. Your action and that of other arbitragers have increased the demand for deutsche marks in Hamburg and their supply in London and moved the trading ratios to equality in the two markets. Too bad you slept late.

Determination of foreign exchange rates

Arbitrage only equalizes the foreign exchange rates prevailing in the various markets and ensures their consistency. It is the buying and selling, as if seen under a microscope, around the intersection of the supply and demand curves. The buying and selling keep the price and quantity at the intersection, but, in itself, arbitrage does not determine the level of the intersection.[2] To understand that, we must push our analysis deeper. Most foreign exchange markets are hidden under a mass of official regulations which make them difficult to understand. Rather than tackle these complex markets and regulations directly, we shall start with some simple models. First we shall develop the model of foreign exchange markets without government or central bank control. In this model, we have "freely fluctuating" or "flexible" exchange rates. Then, in the "classical" gold standard model, we have an example of fixed rates. Finally, with the insights gained from the simple models, we can study exchange rate determination in the system which has prevailed for most of the recent past.

Freely fluctuating exchange rates

Suppose that the pound-dollar price or trading rate were determined in a free market without government intervention to fix the rates. The price of pounds in dollars would be determined in this model by the *supply of pounds for dollars* and the *demand for pounds in dollars*. All we have to do now is understand the sources of this supply and demand. The answers come out of the analysis of the sources of credits and debits in the balance of payments.

[2] Arbitrage is not confined to foreign exchange markets. It can and does occur whenever the same commodity is traded in many markets and can be transported among them.

The *demand* for pounds with payments in dollars depends on all those kinds of transactions which create *debits* in the U.S. balance of payments. For example, the demand for English bicycles in the United States depends on the dollar-pound exchange rate. The influence is reciprocal. The dollar-pound exchange rate depends on the demand for English bicycles in the United States. Why? Because if you want to buy English bicycles, you must buy pounds. The demand for pounds also depends on the demand for other British goods and services, the demand for British stocks and bonds, the demand for pounds to buy into British companies and to hold deposits in British banks, and so on.

The *supply* of pounds for dollars depends on all those kinds of transactions vis-à-vis holders of pounds which create *credits* in the U.S. balance of payments. The *British demand* for our goods, for United States stocks and bonds, for dollars to invest in the United States or to hold in bank deposits in New York – all influence the *supply* of pounds for dollars.

If we added up all the amounts of pounds which would be demanded at each possible pound-dollar foreign exchange rate, we would derive the demand curve for pounds in dollars. Adding up all the amounts of pounds which would be supplied at each pound-dollar exchange rate would give us the supply curve for pounds in dollars. What reasons are there to believe that these curves would have the conventional shapes shown in Figure 33-1?

A demand schedule is a series of if-then statements. What would happen on the demand side, *if* the price of pounds in dollars should *rise*? It would mean, for example, that the price of the pound would go up in dollar terms. It would reduce the quantity of English bicycles demanded and, therefore, the quantity of pounds demanded with which to buy English bicycles. An increase in the price of pounds in dollars would also increase the price of British stocks and bonds in dollar terms and make them less attractive. Investments in Great Britain would be less profitable. All this would reduce the quantity of pounds demanded with dollars as the price of pounds increased. A reduction in the price of pounds would have the opposite effects.

Figure 33-1

FREELY FLUCTUATING EXCHANGE RATES DETERMINED BY SUPPLY AND DEMAND

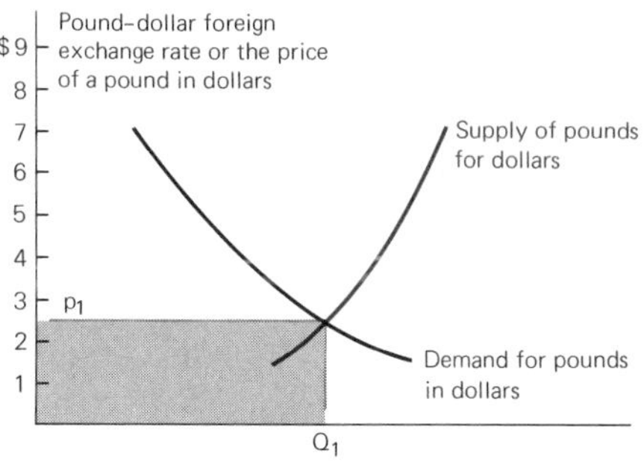

A supply schedule is likewise a series of if-then statements. So what would happen to the quantity of pounds offered for dollars if the dollar price of a pound were to go up? It is a little less obvious, but true, that the price of United States goods to an Englishman would go down. Each of his pounds would buy more dollars. Instead of a pound being worth, say, $2.40, it might be worth, say, $2.60. At $2.40 per British pound, a $3,000 American car would cost £1,250. At $2.60 for each pound, the $3,000 car would cost only £1,154. As the price of pounds in dollars went up, the pound price of American cars, coal, jet airplanes, etc., would fall. British importers would tend to buy more, offering more and more pounds for dollars as the dollar price of pounds rose, as shown in Figure 33-1.

With the conventional slopes for the demand and supply

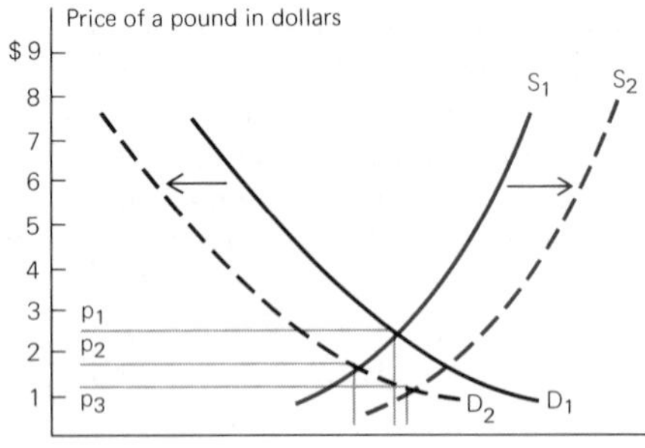

Figure 33-2

EFFECTS OF RELATIVELY RAPID INFLATION IN GREAT BRITAIN ON FREELY FLUCTUATING EXCHANGE RATES

Figure 33-3

EFFECTS OF INCREASED UNITED STATES INVESTMENT IN GREAT BRITAIN ON FREELY FLUCTUATING EXCHANGE RATES

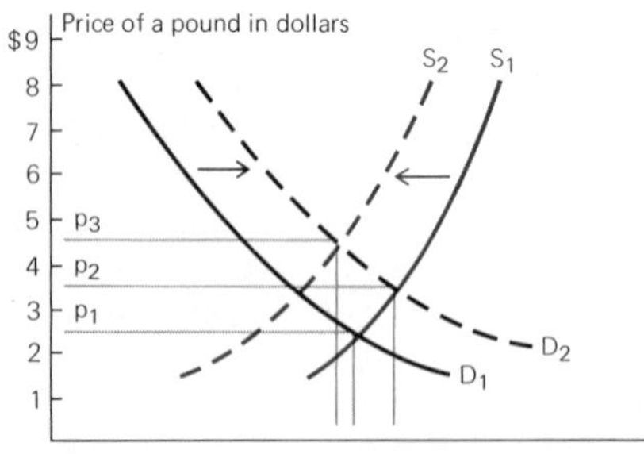

schedules in markets in which the foreign exchange rate was free to change, the rate would tend to move toward the equilibrium price and quantity, p_1 and Q_1, at which the total dollar amount spent on pounds would be the shaded area in Figure 33-1.

The supply and demand analysis of freely fluctuating exchange rates can be used to explain several important features of foreign trade and exchange rates. If the price of a country's currency falls in terms of other currencies, that is a *depreciation* in its price and an *appreciation* in the prices of the other currencies. Suppose, for example, that, as a result of inflation in Great Britain, prices there rise relative to prices in the United States. English bicycles become relatively more expensive in pounds. At *each* exchange rate, the quantity of English bicycles demanded would fall, and, therefore, the demand for pounds would fall. The demand curve for pounds would shift from D_1 to D_2, as shown in Figure 33-2. If the supply schedule of pounds for dollars S_1 did not change, the price of the pound would fall from p_1 to p_2 as shown.

But would the supply schedule S_1 remain constant? Now we come to a new wrinkle in supply and demand analysis: *A change in prices within a country which affects one side of the market for foreign exchange is likely to affect the other side of the market also!* British buyers also will purchase fewer English bicycles when the price goes up. Like Americans, they will to some extent shift their purchases to "English-style" bicycles made in the United States. That will increase the *supply* of pounds offered for dollars. This means that the supply curve will shift from S_1 to S_2. The price of pounds will drop further below p_1. The final exchange rate and the quantity of pounds and dollars exchanged will depend on how far the shifts in the demand and supply curves go and the elasticities of the schedules.

The effects of other events which change the demand for one or both of the currencies can also be traced with the help of the foreign exchange supply and demand apparatus. For example, an increase in the desire by Americans to invest in Great Britain would mean a rightward shift in the dollar demand for pounds. This is shown in Figure 33-3 in the shift from D_1 to D_2. That would tend to raise the dollar price of pounds from p_1 to p_2. Would there be any corresponding shift in the supply schedule of pounds for dollars? There might or might not be. Suppose the same factors that motivated the original change in the direction of United States investment also caused British investors to reduce their investment in the United States. Like the Americans, they would want to increase their investment in Great Britain. Then the supply schedule of pounds for dollars would shift to the left, from S_1 to S_2, and the price of the pound would rise further to p_3. In general, there is no reason why in the process the quantities of currency bought and sold should be unchanged. The first and the final quantities are likely to be different, as shown in Figures 33-2 and 33-3.

One final summary point about a flexible exchange rate: In such a system, any change in the domestic economy of the nations participating has an immediate impact on the foreign exchange markets through its effects on the demand for imports, supply of exports, and capital and gold movements. Domestic and foreign trade are not isolated. Does that make for more stable or less stable foreign trade? We will answer this question after analyzing other types of foreign exchange markets and the rationale for trade.

Foreign exchange rates under a gold standard

The United States abandoned a close approximation to the gold standard in 1933. Nonetheless an analysis of foreign exchange under the gold standard will further our understanding of other fixed exchange rate standards.

Under a real, old-fashioned, classical gold standard, all the participating countries agree to buy and sell gold in unlimited amounts at a fixed price in their own currency. That means that *anyone* can take, say, a dollar to the U.S. Treasury or a Federal Reserve Bank and get a gold coin with a specified gold content. Likewise anyone in Great Britain can exchange his pound note at the Bank of England for a gold coin with a specific gold content. As long as this is so, the price of each currency is fixed in terms of every other currency, except for some relatively minor qualifications that have to do with the costs of shipping gold.

Assume, for a moment, that there are no shipping costs and that countries adhere to a classical gold standard, with their currencies defined in gold as follows:

1 ounce of gold can be bought and sold in London for £12.

1 ounce of gold can be bought and sold in New York for $36.

1 ounce of gold can be bought and sold in Paris for fr.180.

1 ounce of gold can be bought and sold in Hamburg for DM144.

The relative gold content or price of each currency implies the following *fixed* exchange rates:

£1 = $3 = fr.15 = DM12

These are the rates at which the currencies must trade for each other. Why? Because there are now two ways of obtaining a foreign currency:

1. A direct purchase of currency for currency
2. An indirect purchase by first buying gold and then using the gold to buy the foreign currency

Arbitrage would ensure that no one would pay more or could pay less in a direct purchase of currency for currency than in an indirect purchase of currency — for gold — for currency!

When the transport, insurance, and forgone interest of

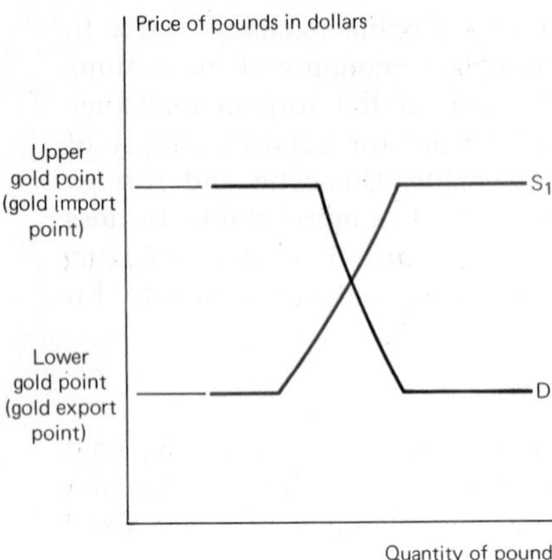

Figure 33-4

GOLD STANDARD FOREIGN EXCHANGE RATE DETERMINATION IN LONDON BETWEEN GOLD POINTS

shipping gold are taken into account, some slight variations in foreign exchange rates do become possible under a gold standard. Suppose, for example, that the price of a pound in London rose above $3. Then a smart trader would try to buy gold with his dollars and use the gold to buy pounds. But the only place he could buy gold with dollars would be in New York, and it would cost, say, 3 cents to ship gold from New York to London. Therefore, the price of a pound in London could rise as high as $3.03 but no higher before it became profitable to ship gold from New York to London. For analogous reasons, the pound price could fall below $3.00 but not below $2.97. Thus, the pound price could fluctuate between $3.03 and $2.97, which are called the upper and lower *gold points* determined by supply and demand schedules, as shown in Figure 33-4. Between the gold points, the price is set by the intersection of the demand and supply schedules, and this need not be at $3.00. In effect, there is a freely fluctuating exchange rate mechanism between the gold points.

Suppose now that there is a shift in the supply for pounds, perhaps because inflation in Great Britain makes United States goods relatively inexpensive as compared with British goods. This is shown in Figure 33-5 as a shift of the supply schedule to S_2 and a shift in the demand schedule to D_2. As a result of this shift, the demand and supply schedules coincide from *A* to *B*, and the price of pounds will move to the lower gold (export) point. Remember that these schedules have their flat portions because the possible shipment of gold constrains the price within the gold points.

The gold flow adjustment mechanism

The attractive aspect of the gold standard for foreign trade lies in its fixed exchange rates. Thus one major source of uncertainty about effective prices is eliminated, and buyers can be more confident in planning future purchases. The fixed rates, however, raise one puzzle.

When supply or demand conditions change in a market of flexible exchange rates — or in any market with flexible prices — the exchange rate or price will change as part of the process of adjustment to the new conditions. If a gold standard creates stable prices, what kind of adjustment process can there be if basic supply or demand conditions change?

To clarify the issue, assume that the same change occurs in a classical gold standard situation as was assumed in the flexible exchange rate model: the internal prices in Great Britain rise relative to those in the United States. In the flexible exchange rate model, a general price increase in Great Britain led to a fall in the price of the pound. That, in turn, led to further changes which maintained an equality between the quantity of pounds supplied for dollars and the quantity of dollars supplied for pounds.

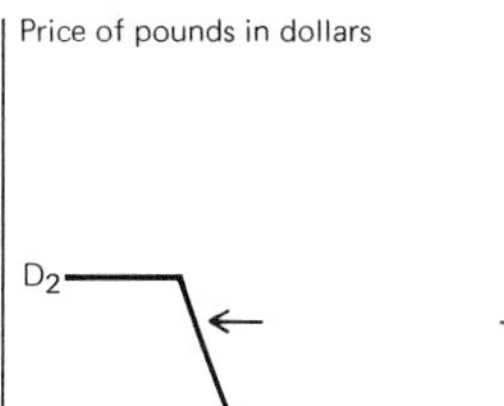

Figure 33-5

FOREIGN EXCHANGE RATES IN GREAT BRITAIN DETERMINED AT LOWER GOLD POINT UNDER GOLD STANDARD

In the classical gold standard, however, price inflation in a country will not lead to a substantial change in its foreign exchange rate. As British goods become relatively more expensive, the quantity demanded at home and abroad will certainly fall. The quantity of foreign goods demanded by British buyers will rise. The dollar demand for pounds will decrease, and the pound supply for dollars will increase. Eventually, the supply of dollars available at the gold standard exchange rate will not be enough to meet the demand for dollars at that rate. In order to buy more dollars with which to purchase the relatively cheaper American goods, British buyers will ship gold from Great Britain to the United States. All this is represented by Figure 33-5. The shipment of gold will go on and on, to buy more and more dollars to buy more and more American goods, until finally Great Britain will run out of gold – unless, that is, some adjustment process exists to stop and finally reverse the gold outflow.

The *gold flow mechanism* or *price-specie flow* was first elaborated by David Hume to explain how adjustment takes place under a classical gold standard.[3] It is easy to explain, using the simple quantity theory of money which guarantees that prices will be directly proportional to the stock of money. Assume, for the purpose of getting the main argument straight, that gold coins are the only kind of money used. Under these conditions, the adjustment process is as follows:

1. An increase in imports relative to exports (without compensating changes in the capital accounts) will finally lead to a loss of gold from the deficit country. That means a reduction in its money supply.

2. The reduction in its money supply leads to a fall in prices in the deficit country. That follows from the quantity theory.

3. As bicyles and other goods become cheaper and cheaper in the deficit country as its gold flows out, it will become a more attractive place in which to buy, both for foreigners and its own residents. Its imports will decline, and its exports will rise.

4. In the surplus country, the inflow of gold is in effect an increase in its money supply. The result, again according to the simple quantity theory, is an increase in its prices.

5. As the surplus country's prices increase, it becomes a less attractive place in which to buy goods. Its exports will fall and imports will rise.

6. As the deficit country's exports rise and imports fall and as the surplus country's exports fall and imports rise, the gold flow from the deficit country to the surplus country will fall and finally be reversed.

And that is the house that David Hume built.

Notice the important contrast between this type of adjustment

[3] Hume was a nineteenth-century English philosopher-economist.

mechanism and that of flexible exchange rates. *Under a flexible exchange rate system, the exchange rate fluctuated to bring about adjustment. Domestic prices which prevail in the economy could be relatively untouched by such fluctuations. Under the gold standard, the exchange rate stays constant, and domestic prices and the domestic economy go through the wringer to bring about adjustments in international transactions.*

Suppose, however, that the two countries use paper money and checking accounts instead of, or in addition to, metal coins, but that gold reserves must be kept as a minimum fraction of the coins and currency outstanding. This system is called a "gold exchange standard." The price-specie flow mechanism would operate as in the simple gold coin system, with modest changes. If the deficit country had gold reserves in excess of the minimum required backing, a gold outflow would not necessarily at its outset have any effect on the money supply. After the gold reserves fell to the minimum required backing, the mechanism would begin to work. On the other hand, the monetary authorities could decide to "play the gold standard game" and reduce the money supply as the gold stock fell, even before it reached the minimum reserve levels.

Under the gold exchange standard, however, the monetary authorities could act to slow down the drain of gold and the consequent reduction in coins and currency. What could they do? They could provide for additional paper and demand deposit money. Chapters 15 and 16 explain how that could be done. But what would the consequences of such offsetting action be? The equilibrating adjustment process would not take place. Gold would continue to flow in one direction — from the deficit country — until finally it had no more gold and could no longer exchange gold for its currency on demand. It would be forced "off the gold standard." That would certainly annoy those of its citizens who thought they had a right to buy gold from their government. In addition, the deficit country would have to restrict its imports to whatever limited amount of foreign exchange it earned. If *all* the goods it produced were available elsewhere at lower prices, and its foreign exchange cupboard really became bare, the deficit country would simply have to give up importing! Its monetary authorities would never let the situation get that bad. If a nation unknowingly or mistakenly approached such a condition, the monetary authorities would act swiftly and forcefully to limit imports and conserve foreign exchange.

Rather than let the situation deteriorate into a breakdown of foreign trade, the monetary authorities might decide to *devalue*. Devaluation means *reducing* the amount of gold that can be purchased with a unit of currency, reducing it from, say, 1/20 to 1/25 of an ounce. That is equivalent to raising the price of gold in terms of the currency. If other countries do not also devalue, that means a *depreciation* of the first country's currency in terms of other currencies. Depreciation also reduces a currency's *relative* prices. Devaluation and depreciation, however, are not sure panaceas for balance-of-payments difficulties.[4]

As an alternative to devaluation – which in this case would mean that the country continued to observe the gold standard rules but with a different gold content for its currency – the country in trouble could "go off" the gold standard. That includes several possibilities. It might mean a switch to a freely fluctuating exchange rate mechanism. Or it could mean a controlled foreign exchange rate, with the domestic economy managed to prevent a breakdown in trade. Or the government could force all holdings of foreign exchange to be sold to it at a specified price in domestic currency. It would then ration the available foreign exchange among potential domestic importers. The two latter patterns are the most common. Before discussing them, however, we must describe another adjustment process.

Income adjustments and sophisticated monetary adjustments

Frank W. Taussig, the great international trade specialist of the Harvard economics department of forty years ago, remarked with some mystification after intense study that international adjustments were affected more quickly than he would have expected. He did not have the benefit of modern monetary and income theory to help explain the rapidity of the adjustment processes.

Suppose there is an increase in imports into the United States which displaces the purchases of domestically produced goods. That implies a decrease in aggregate effective demand. In Chapter 12 it was pointed out that imports are a leakage in the circular flow of income. An increase in that leakage has *multiplied downward* effects on national income, as indicated by the foreign trade multiplier. The reduction in effective demand for domestically produced goods means an overall reduction in income and employment. That leads to a further reduction in demand for imports. If domestic business firms try to maintain revenues by diverting into foreign trade some of the goods originally intended for domestic markets, there may also be an increase in exports. So we come full circle: *An increase in imports creates a chain of effects on domestic and foreign incomes, and these tend to reduce imports and expand exports.*

Similarly, an increase in exports leads to an increase in imports, because it means an increase in income and an induced increase in effective demand for nearly all goods, including imports. The induced increase in effective demand can also lead to a diversion to domestic markets of goods originally intended for

[4] Whether or not they will correct a balance-of-payments deficit depends on the elasticities of demand and supply as well as other adjustment processes. We shall take this issue up again in Chap. 36.

export and, therefore, a reduction in exports. *So an increase in exports will also set off a chain of effects which will tend to increase imports and reduce exports.*

Induced income effects are powerful forces; they tend to offset any changes occurring in the balance of payments. Though, in general, they may not completely eliminate any disequilibrium in the balance of payments, they can be expected to reduce the magnitude of the disequilibrium.

One does not have to accept the simple version of the quantity theory to believe that an imbalance in foreign transactions can also have important monetary effects. These induce changes which will reduce the imbalance. Suppose that gold is used in the settlement of international debts, as under the gold standard or the gold exchange standard. When money in the form of currency or deposits is used to buy gold from the central bank, that money is, in effect, removed from the money supply. If that removal is not offset, the decrease in the money supply will have a depressing effect on the economy. The mechanism was explained in Chapter 16. Interest rates would tend to increase, and investment and other types of aggregate demand would tend to decrease. That, in turn, would tend to reduce imports; if price reductions occurred, that would stimulate exports and tend to correct the foreign imbalance.

Both the income and monetary adjustments of foreign trade conditions can be somewhat offset by domestic monetary and fiscal policies, or they can be accentuated. Offsetting may, however, require changes which are not desirable from the standpoint of domestic policy. It was pointed out in Chapter 18 that a nation's international economic policy could in this sense be a constraint on domestic policy. Suppose, for example, that domestic economic conditions called for expansionist monetary and fiscal policies at the same time that there was a serious deficit in the balance of payments. Domestic expansion would tend to stimulate imports and capital exports and aggravate the payments deficit. What can be done in such circumstances? Economic policies to deal directly with international trade and capital movements are likely to be required. These will be taken up in Chapter 36.

Modern foreign exchange rate determination and adjustment mechanisms

Most of the nations of the world now belong to the International Monetary Fund, which was established in 1944 in the so-called Bretton Woods agreements. Notable exceptions are the Soviet Union, Communist China, and a number of Eastern European nations. *In joining the IMF, a country commits itself to a stipulated par value of its currency either in terms of gold or the U.S. dollar.* That commitment leads to a fixed rate of exchange of each currency against the currencies of all the other IMF countries, just

Figure 33-6

ANALYSIS OF OVERVALUED RUPEE EXCHANGE RATE

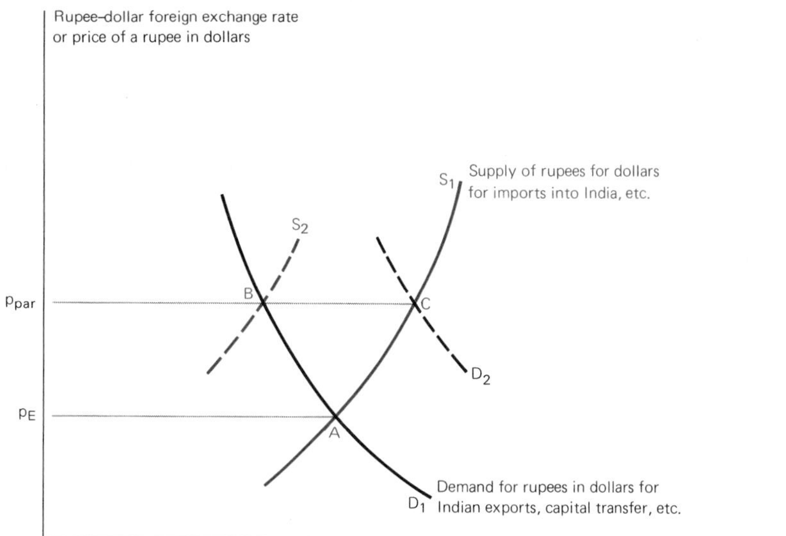

as if each country committed itself to a gold content for its currency. Each country also agrees to maintain that rate in all officially sanctioned transactions. Changes in the rate are permitted in order to adjust to a "fundamental disequilibrium" in the balance of payments.

But foreign exchange rates do *not* become stable just because nations sign an agreement. The underlying supply and demand forces in each country's balance of payments may or may not sustain the country's announced par value. If they do not, the country will find itself losing reserves of gold and foreign currencies which it had accumulated. The country will also find it necessary to rely on short-term capital inflows to balance its imports.

In Figure 33-6, for example, the rate of exchange consistent with equilibrium in the Indian balance of payments is represented by the dollar price for the rupee, p_E. In 1971 that equilibrium rate was commonly estimated to be lower than the pegged par value exchange rate, p_{PAR}. That was slightly over 13 cents per rupee. At the par value, the quantity of rupees demanded abroad was less than the quantity that would be supplied. This is an "overvalued" exchange rate, because the par value of the currency is *higher* than the equilibrium rate. For some years before the dollar crisis in 1971, the dollar was also widely considered overvalued. An "undervalued" exchange rate is one in which the par value is *less* than the rate that would be established by independently motivated transactions.

Overvalued and undervalued rates arise from quite different

sources and present quite different problems. An overvalued rate can be maintained as long as there are short-term capital inflows or gold reserves to pay out, as in the case of the overvalued dollar. Or it can be maintained by rationing foreign exchange, as in the case of the Indian rupee. For example, as shown in Figure 33-6, a short-term capital *inflow* that increased the amount of rupees demanded for dollars in the amount *BC* would maintain the par value. This has the effect of shifting the demand curve in Figure 33-6 to D_1.

What about undervalued exchange rates? Isn't that a comfortable condition? When its exchange rate is undervalued, a country does not run out of foreign exchange. It is likely to accumulate holdings of gold or foreign exchange and become more attractive to foreign investors. That might make some people feel better. But the country is also probably not earning as much from its exports as it would with a higher exchange rate, and its imports are more expensive.

Under the IMF agreements, a change in par value of more than 10 percent requires prior approval of the IMF Board of Directors. But this provision has been breached often and widely. Many IMF countries have revised the value of their currency more than once. The changes have both disadvantages and advantages for the country changing its currency par. When is a depreciation or an appreciation of a country's currency warranted? This question is a controversial one. Depreciation lowers the effective price – in terms of foreign currency – of a country's exports. Whether or not that leads to larger or smaller foreign exchange earnings depends on the elasticity of demand for the country's exports and the reaction of supply. If a country has debts abroad, and many do, depreciation also increases the size of those debts, as valued in domestic currency.

Although technically in violation of IMF rules, a number of countries, including the United States, have allowed their currencies to "float" freely for a period of time, with their values set by the play of international supply and demand forces. Canada, the Netherlands, and West Germany did this before the United States tried it.

Many countries decide to live with overvalued exchange rates. They use tariffs to discourage imports and subsidies to encourage exports, and they tax or completely outlaw capital exports. They may commandeer all private foreign exchange holdings or earnings at the stipulated par price and distribute this foreign exchange by their own rationing criteria. If the direct controls do not work, then something has to give, because gold reserves and short-term capital will not last indefinitely. The exchange rate will be adjusted; the country will devalue.

Still other international exchange rate policy problems remain to be discussed: foreign exchange speculation, the dollar problem, and the "two-tier" prices for gold. The explanations above have to be expanded, but that will be easier after we have analyzed the fundamental rationale of international trade and the patterns of trade.

Summary

The price of a country's currency in terms of another currency is called its foreign exchange rate. The foreign exchange rates of all currencies which are exchanged freely are brought into consistency in foreign exchange markets by arbitrage. This is the simultaneous buying and selling of currencies so that the price of, say, dollars in British pounds and the price of dollars in French francs will be consistent with the price of pounds in francs.

The levels at which all these prices become consistent depend fundamentally on the demand and supply forces operating in the foreign exchange markets. The balance of payments is a guide to all the sources of demand for a country's currency by foreigners and to its sources of supply to foreigners. The manner in which the foreign exchange rate is determined, however, depends on the particular exchange rate determining system to which a country adheres.

When there are freely fluctuating exchange rates, the price of each currency is determined in an open market by supply and demand forces without any constraints. Under these conditions the conventional supply and demand tools can be used to analyze exchange rate determination.

Under a classical gold standard, each country agrees to buy and sell gold in unlimited amounts at a fixed price. That also determines the official rate of exchange among currencies. The actual price at which currencies exchange cannot vary from this official rate by more than the costs of transporting gold from one country to another. Otherwise gold would be moved in or out to take advantage of any larger discrepancy. That movement would keep the currency price within the range set by transportation costs; the upper and lower limits of that range are called the gold points.

Under a system of flexible exchange rates, the foreign exchange price can fluctuate up or down when there are changes in demand for or supply of foreign exchange, resulting, for example, from domestic inflation or deflation. Since foreign exchange prices cannot change enough to guarantee balance-of-payments equilibrium under a gold standard, some other adjustment process is necessary. Classical economists relied on the price-specie flow or gold flow mechanism. In this explanation gold exports generated by an excess demand for goods imports mean a reduction in money supply. This, in turn, via the quantity theory of money, leads to a reduction in domestic prices and an increase in prices in the countries receiving gold. These changes stimulate exports, reduce imports, and eventually establish equilibrium.

The income-adjustment trade equilibrating mechanism does not rely on the quantity theory. Increases in imports induce reductions in domestic income, which tend in turn to reduce imports. Increases in exports stimulate income and therefore additional imports.

Countries belonging to the International Monetary Fund are supposed to peg their currencies in terms of gold. That determines their exchange rate with other currencies. If, at these official rates, the demand for *foreign* currency exceeds supply, the par value is too high and the currency is overvalued. Countries with overvalued currencies use their own gold and foreign exchange reserves, or they borrow foreign exchange reserves or gold. When those possibilities are exhausted, as is true for many countries, their supply of foreign exchange – from export earnings, loans, and grants – is rationed among importers by some official organization. Countries with undervalued currencies tend to accumulate holdings of foreign currencies and/or gold.

When prices of currencies change relative to one another, those currencies whose prices go up relative to others appreciate; those whose prices go down relatively depreciate. When currencies change their price in terms of gold, that is devaluation or revaluation.

Questions for discussion and review

1. An importer can buy or borrow foreign exchange from his bank. List half a dozen possible sources of that foreign exchange.

2. Make up an example to describe how arbitrage works.

3. It was pointed out in the discussion of freely fluctuating exchange rates that a change in the demand schedule for the foreign currency of a country was likely to be accompanied by a change in the supply schedule of the currency for foreign exchange. Why is this so? Are the two shifts likely to be offsetting or not?

4. What keeps the foreign exchange rate fixed under the gold standard? Or is it fixed?

5. Describe the price-specie flow adjustment mechanism under the gold standard. Do you think it would be a comfortable process to live through? Explain.

6. Describe the income-adjustment process for imbalance in international trade. Is that a comfortable process?

7. How can monetary authorities facilitate or offset the adjustment processes of either price or income changes to eliminate foreign exchange imbalances?

8. Most countries now have fixed foreign exchange rates without being on a gold standard. Does that mean there are no adjustment processes or that there are no more foreign exchange imbalances or what?

Concepts for review

- Flexible exchange rates
- Gold standard
- Price-specie flow mechanism
- Appreciation and depreciation
- Devaluation
- Arbitrage
- Gold points
- Overvalued and undervalued exchange rates

34

The theory of international trade and comparative advantage

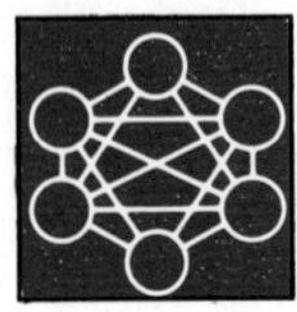

The fundamental questions of international economics are again those of Output, Input, and Distribution. What quantity and composition of the *output* of each country will move into international trade? What quantity and composition of *inputs* will be devoted to producing for trade, and how is this related to the Output question? What gains will there be from trade, and what will be their *distribution* among the trading nations and within each country?

Let us be clear that these three questions are, in fact, the fundamental ones. All the concern over balance-of-payments deficits and surpluses, foreign exchange rates, gold movements, and monetary standards assumes that there *is* trade in goods and services and that, on the whole, it is a good idea. If international trade were not desired, the financial headaches could easily be avoided. We must, therefore, buttress our analysis of the financial issues of trade with an understanding of its basic rationale. That rationale needs to be understood if there is to be a serious discussion of the political issues of international economic relations, of economic imperialism, and of the relative benefits from trade for the rich and poor countries.

The analysis which will be presented is the *theory of comparative advantage*. The words, themselves, are suggestive. The idea that the composition of trade depends on the relative or comparative efficiency with which goods are produced in different countries is a powerful insight. More specifically, *the theory of comparative advantage states that the goods which a country can and should export are those which it can produce at the lowest relative cost.*

The argument that a country can gain from specializing in the production of the goods in which its relative efficiency is greatest and by trading those for other goods is an extension to international trade of a commonplace observation for individuals. A colleague down the hall is a good mathematician, but it would be a mistake for him to earn his income teaching calculus, because he is a great economist. An Italian tenor who can make a fine spaghetti sauce is wiser to do that only as a hobby and to earn his income on the opera stage. The greatest comparative or relative advantage of these men, the field in which they can earn the most income, is in their professions. They are induced to specialize by their *comparative* advantage, and so are regions and countries.

The theory of comparative advantage in international trade will first be worked out in the context of some simple models constructed so as to eliminate influences extraneous to the central argument. The theory will then be extended to more complicated systems.[1] The Appendix presents a synthetic view of the rationale of trade.

A two-country–two-good model of trade

We shall assume that there are only two countries. Each produces only two goods, bread and wine. Let us follow up the suggestion above that foreign exchange rates and international finance are not the most fundamental aspects of international trade and put these aside. So we shall assume at the outset that the two countries trade goods for goods. Thus, we do not have to worry about foreign currencies and exchange rates. To be provocative, let us call the countries the United States and France.

Each country has only land and labor resources and each produces only bread and wine. The land, however, is not completely settled and farmed in either country, so it is not scarce. Further, we shall assume that, within each country, all the land is absolutely uniform. Labor is scarce.[2] Land, of course, cannot be shipped back and forth across the "national" boundaries, and labor, we shall assume, does not migrate. We shall also assume that the conditions of production and sale in both countries are those of pure competition.

The conditions for producing both goods are assumed to be better in the United States than in France: The land is better suited; the rainfall is better timed, and so on. Thus, a producer in the United States can always get more wheat and more grapes per man-hour of work than a producer in France. The United States, therefore, has an *absolute advantage* in the production of both

[1] The models will be like those of Chap. 3, which might be reviewed as background for this chapter.

[2] In the terminology of Chap. 28, the marginal product of land is zero and the marginal product of labor is positive.

Table 34-1

HYPOTHETICAL LABOR PRODUCTIVITIES AND LABOR SUPPLIES IN A TWO-COUNTRY–TWO-GOOD MODEL OF TRADE

	United States	*France*
Output per man-year		
Bread	900 loaves	500 loaves
Wine	600 bottles	500 bottles
Number of producers	1 million	1 million
Maximum output		
Bread	900 million loaves	500 million loaves
Wine	600 million bottles	500 million bottles
Slope of production-possibility line	$\frac{900}{600}=\frac{9}{6}=1.5$	$\frac{500}{500}=\frac{5}{5}=1$

bread and wine, because its labor productivity in the production of each commodity is higher. Finally, we shall assume that the quality of bread and wine produced in each country is the same.

A numerical example will help to illustrate these assumptions. Table 34-1 provides some hypothetical data on labor productivities for the United States and France which embody the assumption that the United States has an absolute advantage in both goods. Since labor is the only scarce factor, and land is absolutely uniform and free, the labor productivities in Table 34-1 are constants. To simplify the arithmetic, assume that there are a million producers in each country.

Figure 34-1

UNITED STATES PRODUCTION-POSSIBILITY LINE

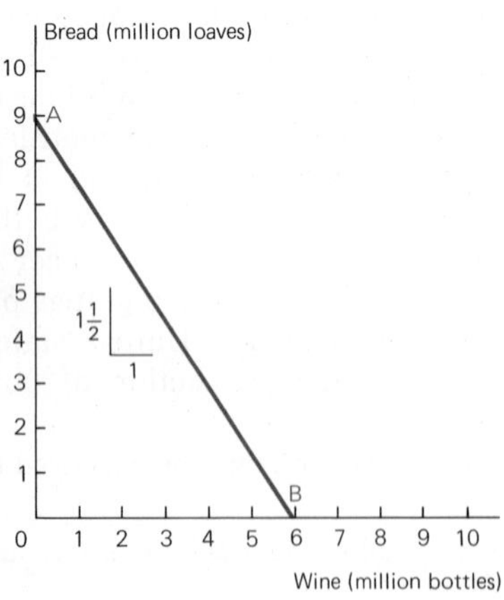

The production-possibility schedules showing all the alternative outputs of bread and wine can now be worked out. Suppose that all land and labor in the United States were devoted to bread production. A maximum of 900 million loaves could be produced, as indicated at point *A* in Figure 34-1. If total production were devoted to wine, the maximum output would be 600 million bottles, as at point *B*. With labor productivities and land yields absolutely constant, the trade off in production of bread and wine is also absolutely constant, and all the possible combinations of bread and wine that can be produced in the United States are on the straight line between *A* and *B*. A man-year taken out of bread production in the United States will always reduce bread production by 900 loaves and increase wine production by 600 bottles. So the production-possibility frontier between bread and wine is a straight line between *A* and *B*. The trade-off rate in production is the ratio 900 loaves of bread to 600 bottles of wine, or $1^1/_2$ loaves of bread to 1 bottle of wine. This trading ratio is the *slope* of the production-possibility line *AB* in Figure 34-1. Equivalently, 1 loaf of bread is worth $^2/_3$ bottle of wine.

The domestic trading ratio is a price ratio in which one of the goods is used as the standard. In equilibrium, the "price" of a good

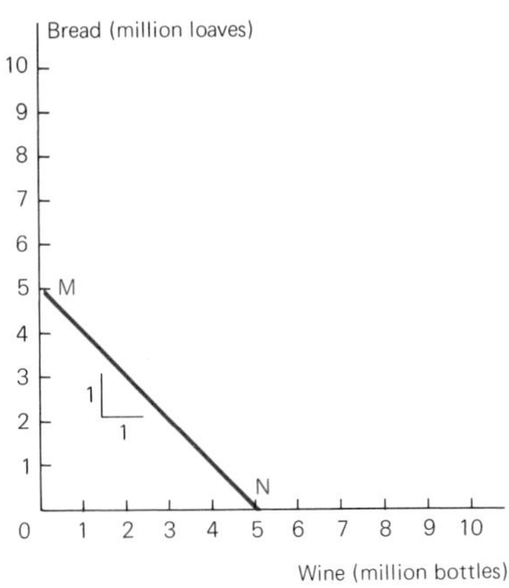

Figure 34-2
FRENCH PRODUCTION-POSSIBILITY LINE

via production must be equal to its price in exchange. If that is not so, production will shift from one good to another, changing the relative supply and bringing the trading ratios into equality.

We can derive the production-possibility frontier for France in a similar manner. If all labor in France were devoted to bread production, a maximum of 500 million loaves could be produced, as indicated at point *M* in Figure 34-2. If all labor were concentrated in wine production, 500 million bottles could be produced, as at point *N*. Again, all the possible *combinations* of bread and wine producible in France are represented by the straight line between *M* and *N*, reflecting the constant trade off in production. A man-year taken out of bread production would reduce output by 500 loaves, and when put into wine production would increase output by 500 bottles. The bread/wine trading rate in France, therefore, is 500 loaves of bread to 500 bottles of wine or 1 loaf of bread to 1 bottle of wine. Again this trade-off ratio is just the slope of the production-possibility line *MN*.

Now let us imagine that, as the result of some old antagonism, the United States and France have developed without any trade between them. In each country, both bread and wine are desired, so farmers produce enough of both in each country to satisfy internal demands. One day, however, a French merchant, without the traditional national animosities, notices the different trading ratios between bread and wine in the two countries. He remembers what his father taught him: *When prices for the same goods differ, you can buy cheap and sell dear and make a profit.* How would he do it?

If he ships French bread to the United States, then for every, say, 100 loaves he can get ($^2/_3$) (100) = 67 bottles of wine. But he can do better than that in France where 100 loaves will get him 100 bottles of wine.[3]

The merchant has made no commitments, so he thinks next about selling French wine in the United States. For every 100 bottles of French wine which he sells in the United States, he can get ($1^1/_2$) (100) = 150 loaves of bread. In France, for 100 bottles of wine he can get only 100 loaves of bread. That's it! He sees how he can make a profit and starts exporting wine to the United States and importing bread.

Since this trade makes a profit for the merchant, it will attract other French and United States traders. Farmers in France will find that the demand for wine is growing; they will also face the growing competition of the imported bread. They will react by switching their land and labor from bread production to wine production. In the United States, just the reverse will happen. United States wine producers will find French wines being imported and sold at prices they cannot meet, while the demand for United States bread grows. So United States producers will switch their production from wine to bread. A flourishing "international" trade would de-

[3] Transportation costs are neglected at the outset.

Table 34-2

HYPOTHETICAL U.S. AND FRENCH LABOR INPUT REQUIREMENTS IN PRODUCTION OF BREAD AND WINE

Good	U.S. labor requirements	French labor requirements
1 loaf of bread	$\frac{1}{900} = 0.00111$ man-years	$\frac{1}{500} = 0.0020$ man-years
1 bottle of wine	$\frac{1}{600} = 0.00167$ man-years	$\frac{1}{500} = 0.0020$ man-years

velop, with the United States tending to specialize in bread production and France in wine production even though *United States farmers are more productive in producing both bread and wine.*

Absolute and comparative advantage

United States producers have an *absolute advantage* in producing both goods, as shown by their higher labor productivity. But the *comparative advantage* of the United States — as compared with France — is in bread production, because that is where the United States productivity is, *relatively* speaking, greater.

We can figure out for ourselves the good in which France has its *comparative* advantage and the product in which the United States has its *comparative* advantage by comparing the *input requirements per unit of output.*[4] This is done in Table 34-2 above.

The ratio of United States labor requirements to French labor requirements for a loaf of bread is:

$$\frac{0.00111}{0.0020} \quad \text{or} \quad \frac{1/900}{1/500} = \frac{500}{900} = 0.555$$

The ratio of United States labor requirements to French labor requirements per bottle of wine output is:

$$\frac{0.00167}{0.0020} \quad \text{or} \quad \frac{1/600}{1/500} = \frac{500}{600} = 0.833$$

Therefore, the United States labor requirements are, relatively speaking, lower in bread production than in wine production as compared with French labor requirements. *The relative labor requirements determine comparative advantage.*

For France, the relative advantage is in wine production. But notice that the smart merchant who started the business did not have to calculate the comparative advantages of the two countries. All he had to do was to look at the trading ratios and figure out whether and how he could make a profit by trading.

Figure 34-3 demonstrates this point. The French production-

Figure 34-3

FRENCH PRODUCTION AND TRADE

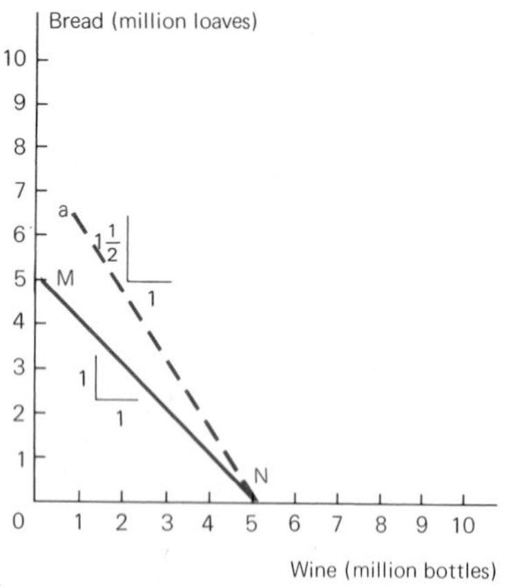

[4] Remember that, although land is necessary for production, we have assumed that it is not scarce in either country and, therefore, we do not have to worry about how much is necessary for production.

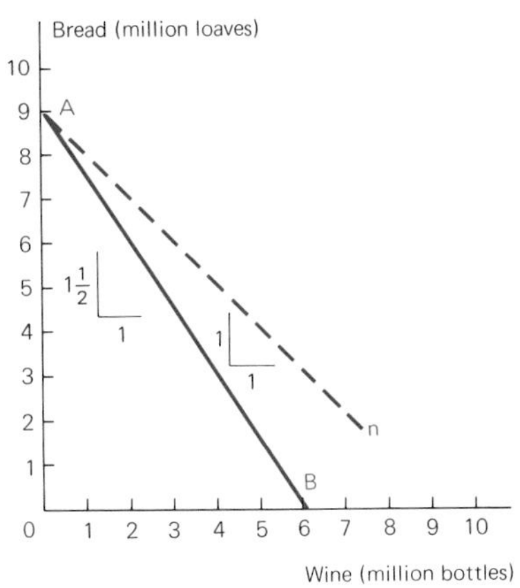

Figure 34-4

UNITED STATES PRODUCTION AND TRADE

possibility line is MN. *If* France specialized in wine production, it would produce at *N*. Then, *if* it could trade at the United States bread/wine trading ratio, it would in effect move out along line *Na*, which has the slope of $9/6 = 1\frac{1}{2}$, to obtain just the combination of bread and wine desired. The possibility of trading along line *Na* at the United States ratio would mean that Frenchmen could have more of both bread and wine than would otherwise be feasible. By specializing in the good in which they have a comparative advantage and exchanging that good at a price ratio different from their own production trade-off ratio, Frenchmen can make themselves better off.

If the United States specialized in bread production, it would produce at *A* in Figure 34-4. Then, *if* it could trade at the French bread/wine trading ratio, it would move along line *An*, which has the slope of 1/1, to obtain the bread/wine combination desired in the United States.

Between the French local trading ratio of 1 loaf of bread to 1 bottle of wine and the United States local trading ratio of $1\frac{1}{2}$ loaves of bread to 1 bottle of wine, there is a lot of scope. Suppose, for example, the trading ratio ended up at $1\frac{1}{5}$ loaves of bread to 1 bottle of wine. Then Frenchmen, specializing their production at *N* in Figure 34-5, could trade along the line *Nt*, with slope equal to $(1\ 1/5)/1 = 1.2$. In the United States, with bread specialization at *A* in Figure 34-5, there could be trade along the line *At*, with slope equal to 1.2. *Trade makes it possible for both countries to get outside their production-possibility curves and to be better off as a result!* That is the powerful conclusion of the theory of comparative advantage.

This conclusion is illustrated in Table 34-3, which presents a

Table 34-3

BEFORE-TRADE AND AFTER-TRADE PRODUCTION AND CONSUMPTION IN THE UNITED STATES AND FRANCE

	Bread			*Wine*		
Country	*Production (million loaves)*	*Labor requirements*	*Consumption (million loaves)*	*Production (million bottles)*	*Labor requirements*	*Consumption (million bottles)*
Before trade						
United States	570	$\frac{570}{900}$ million = 633,000	570	220	$\frac{220}{600}$ million = 367,000	220
France	280	$\frac{280}{500}$ million = 560,000	280	220	$\frac{220}{500}$ million = 440,000	220
Total	850	1,193,000	850	440	807,000	440
After trade						
United States	900	$\frac{900}{900}$ million = 1,000,000	600	—	—	250
France	—	—	300	500	$\frac{500}{500}$ million = 1,000,000	250
Total	900	1,000,000	900	500	1,000,000	500

Figure 34-5

FRENCH PRODUCTION AND TRADE

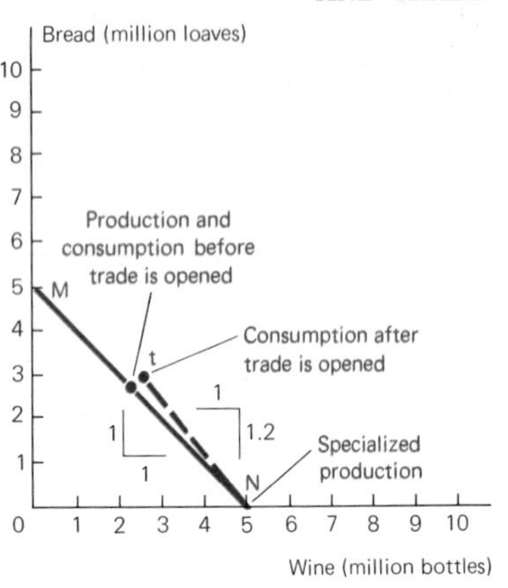

hypothetical "before-trade" and "after-trade" set of output and consumption levels. Before trade, the United States produces and consumes 570 million loaves of bread and 220 million bottles of wine, using all of its 1 million workers in both types of production. In France, before trade, 280 million loaves of bread and 220 million bottles of wine are produced and consumed with its million-man labor force. Notice the somewhat greater preference of Frenchmen for wine as compared with Americans; this is revealed by the larger wine/bread consumption ratio in France.

After trade is opened up, each country specializes and trades at a trading ratio determined by demand and supply conditions. In the new condition, shown in Figures 34-5 and 34-6, after trade is opened up, in this example, *both* countries consume more of *both* goods. The United States produces 900 million bushels of wheat, consumes 600 million at home, and trades 300 million bushels for 250 million bottles of wine from France. France specializes in wine output, produces 500 million bottles, consumes 250 million, and trades 250 million for the 300 million bushels of wheat from the United States.

Terms of trade

There is one loose end to tidy up, but an important one. What will determine the actual terms on which bread and wine are exchanged between the United States and France? The extra demand from the United States for French wine will tend to raise its price in terms of bread in France. The extra demand from France for United States bread will tend to raise its price in terms of wine. What will the final prices be?

The *limits* to which the prices can move are clear. Frenchmen will pay no more for 1 loaf of bread than 1 bottle of wine, which is their domestic trading ratio in isolation. In the United States, the limit to the bread price per loaf is 1.5 bottles of wine, the United States trading ratio in isolation. Local production and trade set the limits on the terms of trade in international commerce. *The final trading ratios must be at or within the domestic trading limits and will depend on the relative strengths of demand for bread and wine in the United States and France.*

Figure 34-6

UNITED STATES PRODUCTION AND TRADE

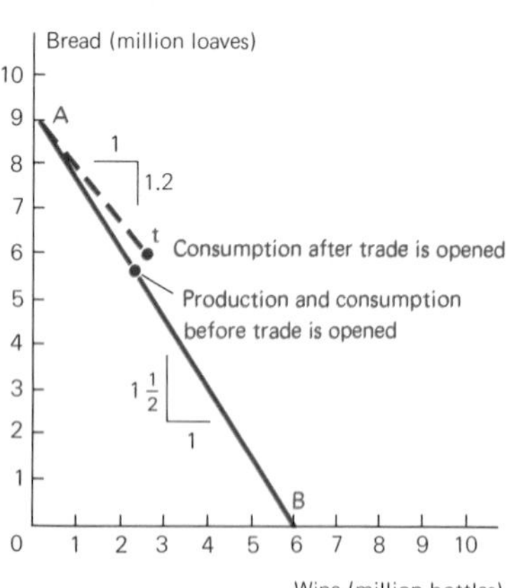

The relative strengths of demand, in turn, depend on (1) bread-wine preferences in both areas and (2) the relative size of the two areas. An extreme example will help in understanding this point also. Suppose France were a tiny region by comparison with the United States. Then, even if Frenchmen used all their wine to buy bread, their demand would be too small to have any effect on relative prices in the United States. They would specialize in producing wine at point *N* on their production-possibility frontier (Fig. 34-2) and would trade at the United States prices until they had just the amount of bread they wanted.

In these unequal circumstances, all the *gains from trade* would go to the small country, France, because it could exchange at

United States prices. The amount of wine that the United States would get from France would be too small to make a difference to the United States, and international trade would bring no benefits to it.

In less extreme circumstances the final trading ratio, or terms of trade, will be somewhere between the United States and French production ratios. The gains from trade will also be distributed between the United States and France, and both will be better off than if there were no possibility of trade!

This simple two-country–two-good example has served us well, as it has served others before. It is essentially the theory presented in 1817 by David Ricardo, the English stockbroker-economist. It is time to go beyond it now and make the theory more realistic by taking into account other sources of trade and the gains from trade.

An expanded view of the bases for trade

The guide to further analysis will be the observation that individual traders react to differences in prices at home and abroad. They do not have to understand *why* prices are different to be successful traders. The economist wants to, however, in order to better understand all the sources of trade and the potential gains from it. In the original example, the bread/wine trading ratios were different in the United States and France before trade because of persistent differences in the labor productivities of the two goods in the two countries.[5] Let us now turn to a more comprehensive view.

Geographic differences

Diverse geographic conditions, broadly construed, are a major source of differences in conditions of production and supply. These, in turn, create differences in the price of the same good in different countries. (In the Ricardian United States-France bread-wine example, the differences in climate and land quality were the source of the original price differences in the two areas.) Climate, land quality, and resources explain why Central America exports bananas, Brazil ships coffee, and India and Ceylon export tea. Great pools of oil underlie parts of the Arabian peninsula and Venezuela, and rich deposits of copper ore abound in the Congo and Chile – and these are the sources of the major exports of these countries. A less obvious but good example of the influence of the local natural endowment is the refining of aluminum ores in Norway. Such refining requires a lot of electricity, which Norway produces cheaply in generating plants using its abundant supplies of water power.

Trade based on specific kinds of natural endowments accounts

[5] In terms of our production terminology, we would say it was because of differences in production functions.

for a substantial share of all international trade. United States imports in this category come to about 17 percent of the nation's imports. For the world as a whole, trade in primary products based on specific kinds of natural endowments accounts for about one-third of the total. In some countries, this kind of trade literally dominates national economic life. Without oil, the Arabian peninsula would be mainly desert and a few oases. Without fish harvested from its nearby Humboldt Current, Peru would lose 20 percent of its total exports and 4 percent of its national product.

Differences in relative capital-labor availabilities

What if the basic technologies and geographic conditions were the same in all countries but the relative amounts of the productive inputs available were different? Could these conditions give rise to international trade? Yes! In fact they are one of the most frequently cited sources of trade. *Aside from natural endowments, one of the most striking differences among countries is the relative amounts of labor and capital which are available.* On automobile assembly lines in Italy, fewer automatic tools are used than in the United States, and more human effort is applied to hand tools. Even the most casual visitor to Hong Kong and India can hardly fail to be struck by the intensive manner in which labor is used in many activities — from cutting grass to producing electric fans.

The differences in the relative amounts of capital and labor among countries are an important source of trade. The hand-wired transistor radios from Japan and the handwoven wicker furniture from Taiwan, which are in effect traded for such products as jet aircraft from the United States, reflect these different factor intensities.

It is important, however, to avoid the simplistic view that all labor is alike and that all capital is the same kind of plant and equipment. Relatively uneducated and unskilled workers can wire radios and weave wicker, but they cannot design and build high-speed digital computers. Some of the comparative advantages which countries possess are based on specific types of labor skills. These skills may be created by college education, as in the case of the electrical engineers in the United States who build computers, or by tradition and special trade schools, as in French wine making.

Economies of scale

National production advantages in some commodities do not appear to be determined by geographic differences or relative capital-labor availabilities. In many cases, *the explanation for international trade on the production side seems to lie in the economies of large-scale production that have been achieved in a particular country.* Sometimes these economies of scale and the resulting trade are based primarily on selling to a large domestic market. The worldwide sales of the aircraft industry of the United States are an example. When the market is divided among two or three firms, however, a firm may have to obtain a large share of the world market, as well as the domestic, to achieve maximum economies of scale.

The hope of achieving the benefits of larger-scale operations is one of the main motivations in the formation of "free-trade" or "common market" areas. The European Common Market brought together in a relatively unrestricted trade area the economies of Belgium, France, Italy, Luxembourg, the Netherlands, and West Germany and created a market which approaches in size that of the United States. The rationale of achieving economies of large-scale production via a common market is even more compelling for many of the Latin American countries. The individual economies of these nations, with the exception of Argentina and Brazil, are much smaller than those of most European countries.

Differences in tastes or demands

The reasons why tea and coffee are grown in India and Brazil rather than in Great Britain and the United States are on the production side. The reasons why Great Britain is a much larger importer of tea than of coffee, and vice versa for the United States, are on the demand side. *The differences in consumption habits among nations are a major determinant of the directions of trade.* Consumption habits are influenced by income levels and prices, as discussed in Chapter 19, The Rationale of Consumer Choice. They depend in a fundamental way also on tastes and preferences, and these are the major explanation of the predominance of tea imports into Great Britain and coffee into the United States.

In international trade, the idiosyncracies of consumer demands are by far the best explanation for the direction of movement of many goods and services: rock records from Great Britain, cheese and wine from France, clothes from Italy, beer from Germany, and so on. Trade makes available a wider variety of differentiated products than exists in any single country alone. Consumers take advantage of this, and different kinds of cars, cloth, food, bicycles, etc., are shipped back and forth.

Imperfect competition and trade

So far very little has been said about the relationship between trade and the *structure* of domestic and foreign markets. Yet that is clearly important, for we know that monopoly and other types of restrictive market practices can profoundly affect both absolute and relative prices.

Suppose, for example, that before there was any trade, the wine producers in France had organized a wine cartel and priced wine monopolistically. That would force *up* the wine price in France. (It would force *down* the price of bread in terms of wine.)

It would make the possibility of trading wine for bread in the United States even more attractive to France.

What if there were a bread cartel in France which forced up the bread price in terms of wine. Would France then import wine and export bread, which is just the reverse of what would happen if domestic markets were competitive? Certainly. *Market imperfections that are bad enough can create a basis for trading in directions opposite to fundamental comparative advantage.* We should be clear, though, that the fault in such circumstances does not lie with international trade, but with domestic market imperfections. In this example, there would still be gains from international trade because it would reduce the power of the domestic monopoly.

We can generalize these conclusions: *Market imperfections can distort domestic prices, and international trade can provide an alternative source of supply.* This is another source of gains from trade. Understandably, it can be particularly important for small and/or poor countries whose markets are too small to support vigorously competitive firms.

Finally, what are the effects of monopoly power in international trade itself? Monopoly power tends to restrict sales and output and to result in higher prices. The total benefits from international trade will thus be lower when it is to some extent monopolized. This does not mean that all the trading partners will be worse off. It may mean that countries and companies exercising some monopoly power will benefit more than if the trade were competitive. We shall return to this point below when we talk about tariffs, quotas, and export taxes.

An expanded view of trade

In the original two-country–two-good model, international trade was based on fixed differences in the productivity of a single scarce productive resource, labor. The discussion above indicates more realistically that there are a number of different bases for trade. We shall not trace the effects of all of these in detail in theoretical models. But we can describe the conditions of trade more fully.

Many countries engage in multilateral trade in many commodities. Figure 32-1 (p. 664) presents a picture of international trade. Referring to it again, we see that in only a few cases is trade roughly balanced between any two areas. *Moreover, bilateral balancing is not even desirable.* The example of one of the famous international trade triangles in United States economic history will help make this point. In the seventeenth, eighteenth, and early nineteenth centuries, New England traders took timber, wheat, and salt cod to the Caribbean sugar-producing islands and sold them for sugar. The sugar, in turn, was carried to Great Britain and Europe and sold for a variety of textiles and other manufactured items which were brought back to America. Everyone benefited from this exchange, though to different degrees. There was certainly more trade and more benefit than there would have been if exchanges had been restricted to back and forth, bilateral shipments between New England and the Caribbean, on the one hand, and Europe and America, on the other.

Every country produces many goods, using many kinds of productive resources that are available at different relative prices in different relative amounts. Though exports may be highly specialized, no country devotes its resources entirely to the production of just one or a few products. Typically, because of transport charges and conditions of production and use, some goods and services do not enter international trade at all. These include such things as most personal services, domestic transport, electric power, and fresh bakery products. On the other hand, some goods may be produced solely for export, or some may be available only from foreign countries. The Congo uses almost none of the copper it produces, and Peru consumes very little fish meal. But these two countries import all the locomotives they use. In some countries, many goods are both produced domestically and imported as well as exported. The patterns of production and trade are different for each country.

For any particular good of a specific type and quality, we can tell whether it will be imported or exported by comparing its world market price with its domestic price.

Figure 34-7 presents a supply and demand analysis for a typical product. Shoes serve as a good example. The demand schedule, in Figure 34-7(*a*) is the United States demand for shoes – and it will be assumed that we can think in terms of some standard quality and fashion. The domestic supply schedule S_d is based on the United States industry. The price that would prevail in the absence of imports, with only the domestic supply to satisfy the domestic demand, is p_d, determined at the supply-demand intersection at *A*.

Figure 34-7

RELATION BETWEEN THE WORLD PRICE AND DOMESTIC PRICE OF A GOOD WITH AND WITHOUT TRADE

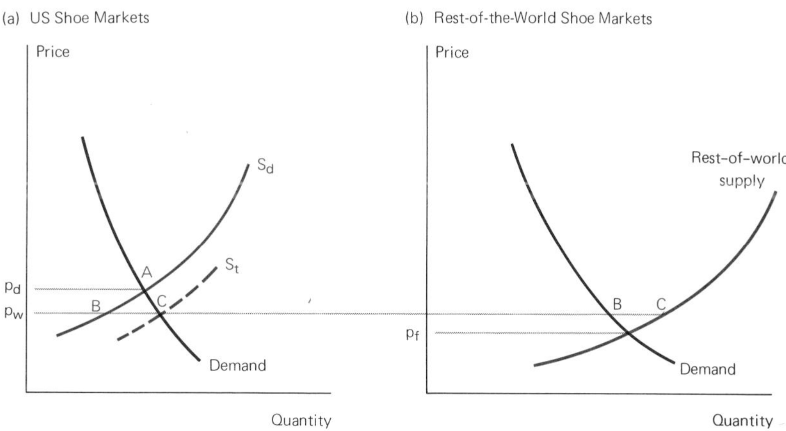

The price at which shoes can be imported, however, is p_w, the world price. *In effect, a foreign source of supply is added to the domestic supply by trade and this becomes the total supply for the United States market.* This is indicated by the curve S_t. The total supply and the demand schedules intersect at the world price, p_w. At that price only the amount at *B* is supplied domestically and the amount *BC* is imported. In equilibrium, the world price p_w will prevail in the domestic market and the rest of the world, as shown in Figure 34-7(*b*), with the amount *BC* being supplied from the rest of the world. (Transport costs and import tariffs are assumed to be zero.)

Notice that when there are imports we cannot directly observe p_d, the price that would prevail if there were only a domestic supply. But if imports are increasing, as they have been in the shoe industry, we can infer that p_d is high relative to p_w, the world price, owing to shifts in demand or supply or both.

Trade as a substitute for factor movements

Those shoe imports look rather threatening for the shoe industry, which is not an insignificant part of the United States economy. In some cities and regions it is quite an important source of income and employment. When imports are hurting a domestic industry, can we still believe in comparative advantage and the gains from trade?

The principle of comparative advantage says: A country should specialize in those goods in which its comparative efficiency is greatest. If it does, its citizens will be able to buy their goods at lower prices and their real income will be larger than if trade were inhibited.

Let us review the argument once again. Even if a country had an absolute advantage in the production of *all* goods, there would still be differences in its own *relative* efficiency in producing the various goods and differences in its *relative* prices for the goods. Because of these differences, trade becomes mutually beneficial to all parties. International trade, in fact, is like a technological improvement in the production of the goods that are imported. Our original two-country–two-good example will suffice to demonstrate this point. Let us look again at Figures 34-3 and 34-4. France, with its comparative advantage, specialized in wine and got more bread by trade than by producing it itself—just as if there had been technical progress in France in bread production. The United States specialized in bread production and received more wine in trade than if wine were produced domestically—as if there were technical progress in wine production in the United States. In the shoe example, imported shoes are less expensive than domestically produced shoes. For consumers, the ability to import is like a domestic technological improvement that reduces shoe costs.

This is another example in which economic theory may appear to be pulling a rabbit out of a hat. So we had better make absolutely clear how the rabbit got in there.

Since the assumptions always put the rabbit in the hat and logic always pulls it out, we must go back and look at the assumptions. The United States and France are assumed to be two separate countries which can trade with each other. Factors of production, however, cannot move back and forth. That is obviously true of the land and climate, but not so obviously true of labor. Still, intercountry immobility of labor is not a bad descriptive assumption, even though some small amount does migrate. Further, only limited amounts of capital are exported from areas in which capital is abundant. The assumption of limited factor mobility is the key to understanding the gains from trade.

We can turn the key by dropping that particular assumption for a moment. Assume that labor can move back and forth freely between the United States and France without political or cultural obstacles. Will it move? Yes, indeed! If a man working in France can produce more wine or bread in the United States, he will move to the United States, because he can make himself better off that way.

Suppose we also drop the assumption that land is not scarce. As labor moves to the United States, the land will be used more intensively in the United States and less intensively in France. The marginal and average productivities of labor in the United States will fall, owing to the Law of Diminishing Returns. These productivities will rise in France as the remaining producers have more land to work with per man. Moreover, labor will keep moving until the value of each man's marginal productivity in bread and wine is the same in the United States and in France! Though output falls in France as each worker moves, output increases by a larger amount in the United States as long as there is a productivity differential. The result of the labor movement is that the combined two-country output of bread and wine will be higher than before labor started emigrating from France.[6]

Now suppose the film is run backward so to speak. Assume that we start all over again with the differential in labor productivity *and* the reimposed assumption of labor immobility. These create the basis for trade. *That trade in goods tends to substitute for the movement of factors. The gains from trade are the counterpart of the gains in total output which would result if there were labor mobility.*

International factor immobilities are like an "imperfection" whose removal will increase output. Though all factors cannot become internationally mobile, many goods can be transported and traded. The gains from that trade are gains which the factor mobil-

[6] Equalization of the marginal productivity of labor in alternative uses is the condition for output maximization developed in Chap. 15.

ity would create if factors *could* move. Put succinctly, international trade tends to be a substitute for those factor movements which would lead to the production of the largest value of output.

Trade and foreign exchange rates

Our analysis of the bases of trade and the gains from trade has been conducted as if all that mattered were the real trading ratios of goods imports and exports. Yet importers and exporters do not trade goods for goods. They buy and sell at money prices which not only reflect the domestic price of each good but the foreign exchange rate. In the preceding chapter, we saw how foreign exchange rates were determined, and we related that analysis to the demand for goods. The links between these analyses can now be established.

In the two-country–two-good example, the trading ratio between bread and wine in each country in isolation is equal to the trade-off ratio in production. That is equal to the *slope* of each country's production-possibility line. That line, in turn, is equal to the ratio of the labor requirements per unit of output of each product. Table 34-4 shows the labor outputs per man-year of bread and of wine in each country and computes the trading ratios in isolation.

Table 34-4

LABOR OUTPUT AND GOODS TRADING RATIOS IN THE UNITED STATES AND FRANCE

	United States	*France*
Output per man-year		
Bread (loaves)	900	500
Wine (bottles)	600	500
Trading ratio in isolation: Bread for wine	$\frac{900}{600} = 1.5$	$\frac{500}{500} = 1$

Suppose that the currency used in France is francs and that used in the United States is dollars. The absolute money prices of the two goods in the two countries can be set as shown in Table 34-5. These prices must be in the correct ratio in each country, as indicated by the relative labor input proportions. If the foreign exchange rate or price of a franc were $0.25, the prices *in dollars* of bread and wine in each "country" before trade would be as shown in Table 34-6.

Table 34-5

DOMESTIC MONEY PRICES FOR BREAD AND WINE IN THE UNITED STATES AND FRANCE

Good	*U.S.*	*France*
Bread	$0.40	fr. 2
Wine	0.60	2

With the domestic prices of Table 34-5 and the foreign exchange rate of fr. 1 = $0.25, the United States is the place to buy bread and France is the place to buy wine, and each country will tend to specialize in the commodity in which it has a comparative advantage. Unless one country is very small relative to the other, the final prices of bread and wine will end up some place between the prices shown in Table 34-6.

Table 34-6

DOLLAR PRICES OF BREAD AND WINE AT 1 FRANC = $0.25 EXCHANGE RATE

Good	*U.S.*	*France*
Bread	$0.40	$0.50
Wine	0.60	0.50

What will happen to trade if the United States has a price inflation *and* the foreign exchange rate is pegged by a gold standard or international agreement? Suppose the dollar prices in Table 34-6 become those of Table 34-7, as the result of a general 50 percent price increase in the United States. The exchange rate does not change. Clearly, United States producers will be out of business. Frenchmen will now find it cheaper to buy at home. Not even Americans will want to buy their bread or wine in the United States. At the pegged rates, it will be cheaper to buy in France.

Table 34-7

DOLLAR PRICES OF BREAD AND WINE AFTER UNITED STATES INFLATION WITH FIXED EXCHANGE RATE

Good	*U.S.*	*France*
Bread	$0.60	$0.50
Wine	0.90	0.50

Table 34-8

DOLLAR PRICES OF BREAD AND WINE AFTER UNITED STATES INFLATION AND DEPRECIATION OF THE DOLLAR RELATIVE TO THE FRANC

Good	*U.S.*	*France*
Bread	$0.60	$0.75
Wine	0.90	0.75

Americans will use all the francs they have to buy bread and wine in France. Unless something happens – a price-specie flow adjustment or an agreed change in the pegged rates – the United States will eventually lose all the francs its residents own, and the United States will no longer be able to import. That will be the end of trade. The comparative advantage conditions have not changed, but the pegged rates block trade.

If there were a flexible exchange rate system, this would not happen. The foreign exchange price would also reflect the real demands for bread and wine. An increase in domestic prices in the United States would be just offset by a decline in the foreign exchange rate price of the dollar in francs. Exporters and importers might find the fluctuation of the exchange rate disconcerting, however. In the example of Table 34-7, instead of a franc being worth $0.25, the price would rise, say, to $0.375, and at that new foreign exchange rate, trade prices in U.S. dollars would be as shown in Table 34-8.

The simple example makes the point that comparative advantage does not in itself prevent the imports of any country from being priced out of the market by domestic price increases. When prices in nearly all countries are going up, the country whose prices are increasing most rapidly will be in the most difficult position. An "overvalued" foreign exchange rate – one whose price is too high in terms of other currencies – can reduce the scope of a country's trade whatever its basic comparative advantage.

An appraisal of the theory of international trade and the distribution of its benefits

One way of appraising the theory of international trade and the supposed benefits of trade is to consider the criticisms leveled against the theory.

Critics point out that the theory of comparative advantage is a *static theory* and *does not take into account the potential development of productive capacity.* For example, just because a country does not now have the capacity to produce high-speed computers does not mean it cannot produce them in the future and possibly at lower cost than they can be produced in the United States or Western Europe. The criticism is just; the simple theory is static. Conditions may change over time and what is true now may be different in the future. The expanded list of the bases for trade presented above does, however, include economies of scale and differences in capital-labor availabilities, two "technical" determinants of relative production costs which can change over time. *Potential changes in production capabilities may well make the long-run comparative advantage of a country different from its short-run advantage.*

Therefore, it can make sense for a country to begin to specialize in some type of production which is not immediately justified on grounds of static comparative advantage.

A quite different criticism of the theory of international trade is that it "condemns" the less developed countries of the world to a future of continued specialization in primary agricultural and mineral products and simple manufactures. The theory, it is said, also consigns less developed countries to continued economic "dependence" on advanced countries for most manufactures. These criticisms contain a mixture of truth and falsity. First the falsity: As indicated above, the theory of international trade does *not* assume that production and demand conditions will remain constant over time. If they do change, and if comparative advantage changes, then the patterns of trade should also change. Moreover, a number of the less developed countries have successfully reduced their dependence on more advanced countries for manufactures. Some are even competing successfully with the products of the more advanced countries in all markets, both foreign and domestic.

The grain of truth in the criticisms is that *specialization in primary products is to the advantage of many of the less developed countries now and probably will continue to be for some time.* It is mere wishful thinking to say that most of the oil-exporting countries of the Near East will become diversified, industrialized nations in the near future. The Central American countries that devote their resources to bananas and coffee are more productive in doing that than in attempting to compete in manufactures with the larger nations to the south or the giant to the north. So it is likely to be in their self-interest to continue to specialize. True, it is risky to specialize in a few commodities whose prices are subject to great fluctuations. So an important question of equity arises: Should these specialized countries alone bear the burden of fluctuations in world market prices? One proposal under active consideration is the possibility of creating common markets or free-trade areas which can help small countries reduce their dependence on one or two products.

Finally, while the theory of international trade indicates how a country's resources can be used most productively, *it says nothing about the personal distribution of the benefits of trade.* The oil sheikhdoms are much richer from producing and exporting oil than they would be from any other conceivable use of their resources. And the Central American countries' resources are most productively used in growing bananas and coffee. Neither statement implies that there is or is not equity in the distribution of the benefits of the use of those productive resources. Likewise, neither statement says that the resources and the producing companies should or should not be foreign-owned. The theory of international trade is a positive theory. In the interests of clear thinking on all sides, it should be distinguished from normative judgments which are embodied in emotionally charged words like "imperialism."

Summary

The fundamental issues of international trade are the Output, Input, and Distribution questions of foreign commerce: What goods will be produced by each country and with what resources? What goods will be traded? And what will be the distribution of benefits?

The theory of comparative advantage is used to answer these questions. The theory states that it is not absolute efficiency, or advantage, which determines the goods each country tends to specialize in and export. The composition of goods traded depends on comparative advantage or relative efficiency. If each country specializes in the production of goods in which it has the greatest relative efficiency or comparative advantage and trades them for other goods, then the total output of all countries together will increase.

The opportunity for a country to specialize and exchange goods at a trading ratio different from its own can be of great benefit to it. The international trading ratios must lie at or between the domestic trading ratios. The actual trading ratios that prevail and the distribution of the benefits of trade depend on the relative strengths of demand in the various countries for the goods imported and exported as well as on the conditions of supply.

National differences in domestic goods exchange ratios originate in a number of ways. (1) Differences in land, climate, and natural resources account for a great deal of the world's trade. (2) Differences in the relative capital-labor availabilities also influence comparative advantage. (3) Countries that have achieved economies of large-scale production have an advantage in international trade. (4) National preferences for certain goods affect trade patterns. (5) Monopoly and the various forms of imperfect competition can distort international trade just as they distort domestic trade.

The patterns of international trade are complex and many-sided. Comparative efficiency and the other bases for trade account for differences in relative prices. But merchants and manufacturers engaging in trade need observe only the domestic selling prices, the transport costs, and the foreign exchange rate to determine whether goods can and should be exported or imported.

The possibility of gains from trade arises from the fact that trade is a substitute for international movement of resources. If resources were fully mobile, they would tend to move wherever their productivity was highest. In the process, output would increase as the intercountry differentials in the marginal productivities of factors were reduced. When resources cannot or will not move, the differences in the factor productivities are the basis of trade and of the gains from trade.

The potential for mutually beneficial trade can be reduced or eliminated by foreign exchange rates that do not reflect the real trading ratios among countries. The theory of comparative advantage, therefore, does not contradict, nor is it contradicted by, the analysis of factors determining foreign exchange rates.

Questions for discussion and review

1. What is the difference between absolute advantage and comparative advantage?

2. Comment on the following statement: *The theory of comparative advantage explains what goods countries would like to trade but does not explain the terms on which goods will be traded.*

3. Is it true that small countries always gain more from trade than big countries? Explain your reply.

4. Explain why differences in the relative availabilities of capital and labor can create the basis for trade.

5. Analyze the following statement: *If all productive resources could move easily from country to country, there would be no reason for international trade. Trade arises because some productive resources are immobile.*

6. Is it possible for foreign exchange rates to be at values which eliminate the international trade of a country? Explain.

7. Do businessmen who buy and sell in international trade know the production-possibility curves and domestic trading ratios for goods in each country? How does this knowledge or lack of it affect international trade?

8. If international trade displaces some domestic production, how can it make a country better off?

Concepts for review

Absolute advantage
Comparative advantage
Terms of trade
Multilateral and bilateral trade
Gains from trade
Factor immobility
Relative factor availabilities
The bases for trade

Appendix: A synthetic view of the rationale of trade

It is possible to use the production-possibility curves and indifference curves of Chapters 3 and 19 to obtain a synthetic view of international trade theory just as we did for a closed economy in the Appendix to Chapter 19.[7]

[7] The graphic analysis to be used was first developed by Prof. W. Leontief of Harvard University.

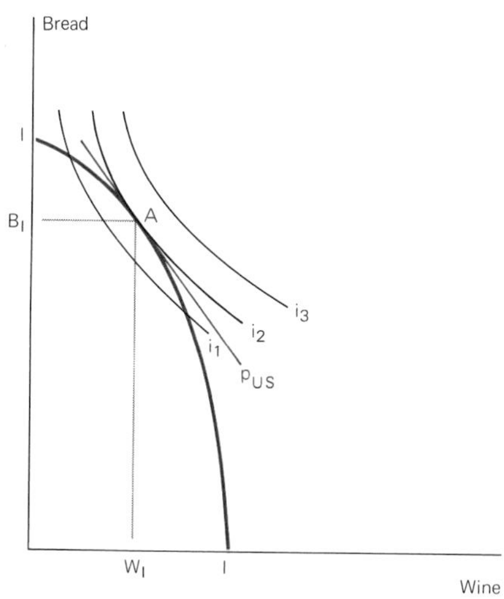

Figure 34-8

UNITED STATES PRODUCTION AND CONSUMPTION DECISIONS IN ISOLATION

Figure 34-9

FRENCH PRODUCTION AND CONSUMPTION DECISIONS IN ISOLATION

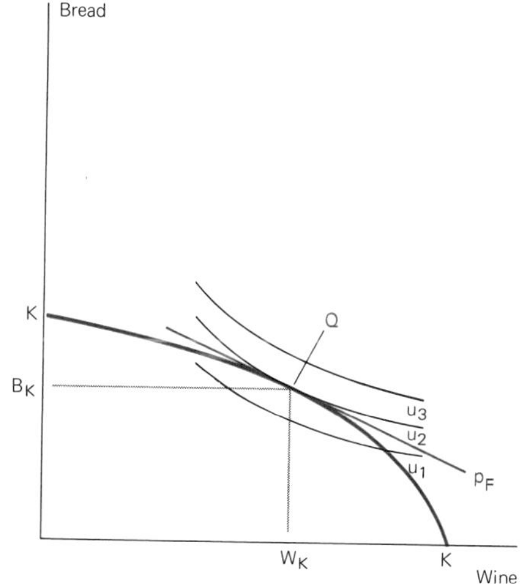

We shall stick to the assumption that only two goods, bread and wine, are produced and that they may be traded by only two countries, the United States and France. Now, however, we take into account the fact that a number of scarce resources are used in producing each commodity. That means that the bread-wine production-possibility frontiers for the two countries will be curved lines, analogous to those originally drawn in Chapter 3. These are the lines *II* and *KK* in Figures 34-8 and 34-9.

We shall also assume that we can draw two sets of indifference curves which represent the preferences of *all* Americans and *all* Frenchmen, respectively. These are represented by the set of lines i_1, i_2, i_3, etc., for the United States and u_1, u_2, u_3, etc., for France.

In isolation each country would tend to produce and consume that feasible combination of bread and wine which it most preferred. Without trade, Americans would end up at point *A* in Figure 34-8, and Frenchmen at point *Q* in Figure 34-9. At these points, each country is on its transformation curve and tangent to an indifference curve. At these tangency points the marginal rate of transformation in production is equal to the marginal rate of substitution in consumption. The relative prices of the two goods are equal to these transformation rates. In the United States, the relative prices are indicated by the slope of the line p_{US}, which is the slope of the transformation curve and indifference curve at the tangency. In France, the corresponding price line is p_F.

The conditions which will be met when trade between the two countries is in equilibrium are shown on the next page in Figure 34-10, where it is also assumed that there are no transport costs. Relative prices of bread and wine must be the same in both countries, and again these relative prices must be equal to the marginal rates of transformation in production and the marginal rates of substitution in consumption in both countries. In Figure 34-10, that price line is p_T. At that price, the United States produces at point *B*, as compared with its original production in isolation at *A*. In shifting from production at *A* to production at *B*, the United States specializes somewhat more in bread and produces less wine, but it still produces both goods. At price p_T, France shifts from its isolation production point *Q* to its trade production point *R*, producing less bread and more wine, but still some of both.

The United States trades along the price line p_T, moving to the highest indifference line it can possibly reach, i.e., to i_3 at point *C*. Likewise, France trades along p_T to reach its highest indifference curve at *S* on u_3.

The United States and France must also meet the condition that the amount of bread that the United States is willing to sell for wine at relative price p_T is just the amount of bread that France is willing to take for its wine. So *BD*, the amount of bread the United States trades for wine must be equal to *ST*, the amount of bread that France is willing to take. Likewise *DC*, the wine the United

Figure 34-10

UNITED STATES AND FRANCE PRODUCING AND TRADING

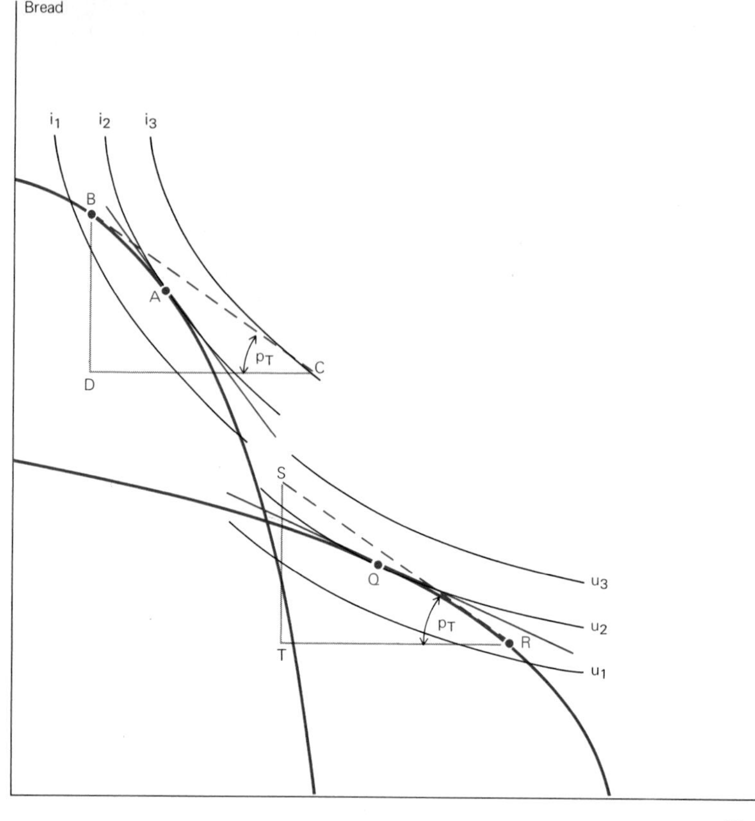

States receives, is equal to *RT*, the wine France trades. *B* and *R* are the final equilibrium production points, and *C* and *S* are the final equilibrium consumption points.

This analysis combines the effects of diminishing returns and differences in factor intensities and the effects of differences in tastes in determining patterns of trade. A little experimentation with alternative assumptions will help to clarify the sources of trade. If the United States and France had the same production-transformation curves, but differences in tastes — as described by their indifference curves — that could generate trade. So could identical tastes and differences in transformation curves.

35 Public policy on tariffs and trade

The issues of public economic policy toward trade stand in the forefront of international economic analysis. National governments have regularly assumed the prerogative of taxing and otherwise regulating international trade. In this chapter, we shall analyze the use of tariffs and quotas to regulate trade and the potential advantages of relaxing trade restrictions in free-trade areas.

Intellectuals, hopefully including economists, speak eloquently of the power of ideas. Powerful ideas, they say, can move men, and through them, their governments. If that is so, the theory of comparative advantage and the gains from trade would appear to be a weakling among economic arguments. Although this theory has remained at the center of international economic analysis for more than 150 years, nearly every country has a plethora of trade restrictions. There are not many activities in which the gap between "conventional wisdom" and prevailing practice is so great and so persistent. To explain this gap, we shall begin by evaluating the arguments put forward by the advocates of tariffs and other trade restrictions.

Tariffs and quotas and their effects

Tariffs are taxes or duties imposed on imports either *ad valorem*, i.e., as a percentage of value, or *specific*, as a flat amount on each item. *Export duties* are taxes on exports. *Quotas* are quantitative limits on imports, often imposed according to the country of their origin. Their effect is much like that of tariffs, so we shall concen-

Figure 35-1

FISH PRICES AND THE EFFECTS OF A TARIFF ON FISH IMPORTS

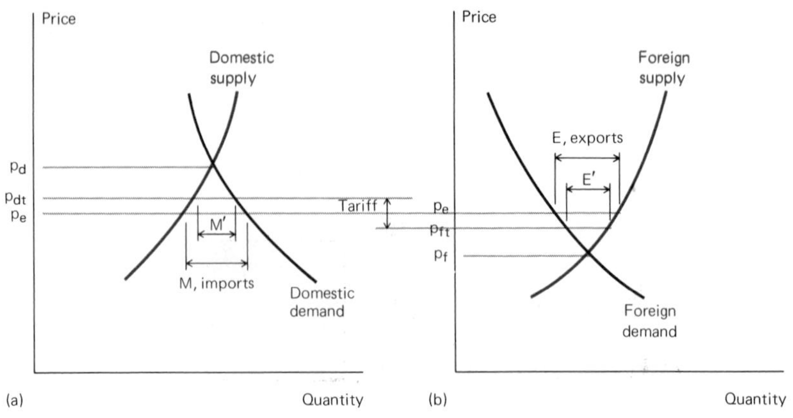

trate on the latter. *Export subsidies* are sometimes used as a means of encouraging the sale of specific products to foreign buyers.

A general analysis of the effects of tariffs can be made with the aid of a supply and demand diagram. Figure 35-1 gives an idea of United States domestic and foreign supply of and demand for fish caught in the North Atlantic. Note that, for similar amounts, the cost of the foreign supply is lower. By and large the foreign fishing industry uses larger boats, has more efficient techniques, and pays lower wages. If the United States demand were satisfied solely by the domestic industry, the landed price of fish would be at p_d, as shown in Figure 35-1(*a*). Without trade with the United States, the foreign price would be lower, at p_f in Figure 35-1(*b*). If fish could be landed without tariffs, the landed price in the United States would be at p_e. At that price the export supply, *E*, of the foreign fishing nations would exactly match the United States import demand, *M*. The length of the line *M*, which measures United States imports, is equal to the distance *E*, which measures foreign exports.

If a specific tariff were to be placed on fish imports, then import prices at p_{dt} in the United States would be higher than foreign prices p_{ft} by the amount of the tariff. At the new set of prices, the amount of imports, *M′*, would again equal foreign exports, *E′*. Notice that the price rise in the United States as a result of the tariff would, in this example, be less than the amount of the tariff, as would the price decrease abroad. The relative impact of the tariff on domestic and foreign prices and on the amount of imports would depend on the elasticity of the domestic and foreign supply and demand curves and could be verified by a little experimentation with alternative curves.[1]

[1] The analysis here is analogous to that in Chap. 6 of the incidence of a sales tax.

The arguments for trade restrictions

Arguments for trade restrictions are of two types: (1) noneconomic arguments, which admit either explicitly or implicitly that trade restrictions entail some economic losses to the community as a whole, but claim that the noneconomic gains are more important; (2) economic arguments, which are either wholly wrong or are correct only to some degree in special cases.

Noneconomic arguments

Periodically the argument is made that the United States must place a tariff on Swiss watch movements. This is necessary, it is claimed, to preserve the United States watch industry, which is of strategic military importance. Without the tariff and without the industry, we would not be able to build the timing and other precision devices that we would need in the event of a war. The same kind of argument is made for fuel oil import quotas: Unless fuel oil imports are limited, cheaper foreign oil imports will drive many United States producers out of business and discourage exploration for new oil reserves in the United States. As a result, if there should be a war, the United States would not have the known oil reserves needed for national defense. It should be noted that, although the arguments have been couched in terms of United States tariffs and quotas, similar arguments are made in nearly every other country in which there is any industry of potential military significance.

Adam Smith, a noted free trader himself, said, "Defense is of much more importance than opulence," and to arguments for tariffs based on defense requirements there can be no response based simply on economics. The issue is the military and political significance of the industry being protected. On the other hand, the economist can ask whether there are not better and less costly ways of achieving the same ends – if they are of overriding importance. A tax, or a tariff, on the price of a good changes the value of the good for all potential users. It, therefore, distorts the use of the good for everyone.

If the nation decides, on political and military grounds, that a particular industry should be maintained, a subsidy payment is usually a more efficient and less distorting device than a tariff. The government would simply pay the domestic producers a subsidy making up the difference between the market price when there were imports and the price necessary to keep the industry going. Goods would be available to users at final prices which reflected their true opportunity costs, as affected by foreign supply. The burden of supporting the industry with subsidy payments would be borne by general tax revenues rather than by the users of the product.

The fact is that the general public is usually not willing to bear such tax costs. Subsidies appear to be politically more difficult to get through a legislature than tariffs. This is one source of the suspicion that the national defense argument has often been a rationalization for the protection of particular industrial interests whose military significance is, at best, slight.

Noneconomic arguments have also been made for tariffs to protect industries desired on grounds of national prestige. In some of the less developed countries, for example, a steel industry is a symbol of modernization, and a steel tariff is justified as a means of creating and maintaining the symbol. It can be expensive!

Economic arguments

It is no trick to make up an argument for tariffs which demonstrates that they will make some industry or group better off. The real question is, Are they in the economic interests of the general public? Though there is essentially only one argument for free trade – comparative advantage and the gains from trade – there are any number of protariff arguments. Some contain a kernel of truth, but only for special cases and conditions. They are offered, however, as arguments having general validity. The next step is to survey those arguments in order to separate the kernels from the chaff of protectionist folklore.

Protecting established industries. *A tax on imports whose prices are lower than those of products in a domestic industry will almost certainly make the protected industry better off,* at least in the short run. Because the domestic output will sell at higher prices than could otherwise be charged, the labor and the owners of other productive resources employed by the industry can receive higher incomes. Indeed, some industries simply could not survive without the tariff. All this is achieved by making consumers worse off, because they must pay the higher prices. In effect, because of protection, resources are used in less productive ways than they otherwise might be used, and costs are higher as a result. In the long run, even those resources which are used in the protected industry might be better off without protection if they could move to other industries where their productivity would be higher.

Protection is sometimes justified in terms of a "scientific tariff" which just equalizes the domestic and foreign costs of production. That, of course, is the end of trade and any gains from trade, for an equalization of prices eliminates the basis of trade. Tariff laws often provide for the determination of "peril points." These are tariff rates below which the very existence of a domestic industry would be threatened. These too restrict trade and the gains from trade, because they prevent the domestic economy from adjusting to its sectors of comparative advantage.

"Scientific" protariff arguments recognize the protective effect of tariffs but avoid the implications. To the extent that tariffs are successful in protecting domestic industries and restricting imports, they are likely to induce retaliation abroad. Foreign countries will be tempted to put up their own tariffs partly as a bargaining ploy. If it doesn't work to roll back tariffs, everyone will be worse off.

These arguments against protectionist tariffs do not imply that it is easy for an industry to adjust to foreign competition. Such adjustments entail hardships just as the adjustments to aggressive domestic competition do. These are real problems and we shall return to them below.

Protecting domestic labor. The counterpart of the argument that tariffs protect domestic industry is that they protect domestic labor. The particular form this argument takes in the United States is that high-wage United States labor cannot compete with cheap foreign labor. Interestingly the reverse argument is often made in foreign countries: Their slow hand labor cannot compete with efficient, highly paid, capital-using United States labor. Both arguments ignore the point of the theory of comparative advantage, that benefits will be greatest for everyone when each country specializes in producing those goods in which it has a *comparative* cost advantage. And no country can have a *comparative* advantage in everything! Both arguments also ignore the fact that *comparative advantage depends on all costs, not just labor costs.* If only labor costs per hour mattered, the United States could sell nothing abroad, and India with perhaps the lowest *hourly* labor costs in the world would dominate all international trade. Once the point is made in this way, the weakness of the protariff argument becomes apparent.

The kernel of truth in the argument lies in the fear that imports can affect the total returns to domestic labor. As we know, international trade tends to be a substitute for international factor movements. *If the United States imports goods made in foreign countries with cheap labor, that is a substitute for the migration of that labor.* If the foreign labor could migrate to the United States, that would certainly tend to reduce wages in the United States or keep them from rising so rapidly — and trade tends to have the same effect. Of course, cheaper goods would be available, but, even so, total real wages in the United States might be lower than they otherwise would be. Whatever is lost in total wages is more than made up in the returns to other productive resources. The kernel in the argument is not that trade will lower the national income, but that it may tend to redistribute it. For example, in 1965 the movement of Mexican field workers into the Southwest and West was curtailed by a law based mainly on the rationale that such migration lowered the wages of United States field workers. One effect of curtailing the international movement of labor has been an increase in the amount of fruit and vegetables imported from Mexico. This tends to have the same effect on the wages of United States field workers as the former migration of labor. The example makes clear, however, that without the free import of Mexican produce, the protection of United States labor is at the expense of the general consumer of fruits and vegetables. The next step against the consumer, which has already been taken, is the restrictive regulation of imports of Mexican produce.

"Keeping money in the country" and macroeconomic stabilization. One argument states that, by discouraging imports, tariffs keep money in the country and increase domestic prosperity and employment. This goes back to the mercantilists, for whom money was gold. The argument is based primarily on an elementary confusion: that trade is an exchange of money for goods. Mainly, however, trade is an exchange of domestic goods and services for foreign goods and services.

A New Economics version of the argument has validity in some quite special and unlikely circumstances. It goes like this: Tariffs will increase domestic employment (1) if a country is at less than full employment, (2) if the demand for imports is shifted to domestic products, and (3) if there is no retaliation by foreign countries. Then domestic employment and output will rise when tariffs are imposed. The redirected demand will be an increase in domestic spending which will spread through the economy via the miltiplier effects.

When domestic output and employment rise as the result of a tariff, employment and output in foreign countries will correspondingly fall. That is why it is a *beggar-thy-neighbor* policy and is virtually certain to evoke retaliation. Even though retaliation only further reduces the benefits of trade, it is a potential bargaining point and the temptation to retaliate is virtually irresistible. In the Great Depression of the 1930s many countries desperately trying to save their own necks imposed tariffs, which did evoke retaliation and reduce trade all around.

Improving the balance of payments. When a country is having balance-of-payments problems, one of the most natural policies to think of is the imposition of tariffs to reduce imports. As we have seen, many special interests are always standing on the sidelines, ready to hop on the tariff bandwagon if it should get rolling. *No doubt, the first effect of a tariff is to reduce imports of the taxed goods. There are other somewhat offsetting effects, however.* Domestic income will tend to rise, as explained above. That will tend to increase imports and to reduce the amounts of domestic products available for export. In addition, a tariff imposes a sacrifice on domestic consumers — loss of access to cheaper foreign production.

Again, the policy invites retaliation. If it improves one country's balance-of-payments position, it causes a deterioration in the balance of payments of other countries. It is not likely to be successful unless other countries agree to it.

Raising revenue. *Tariffs, it is rightly argued, can be used to raise revenue, and many countries impose them for this purpose.* In fact, until the end of the nineteenth century, tariffs provided more than half of the United States federal tax revenues. In many less developed countries, tariffs are still an important tax. They can be collected rather easily, and this is not a negligible consideration.

Admitting that tariffs *can* be used to raise revenue does not imply that they *should* be used. Tariffs are a sales or excise tax — a selective one on imported goods. Applied indiscriminately, they can be regressive and distorting. Applied in a discriminating manner, however, on luxury imports of high-income buyers, they can become a progressive tax.

Are tariffs a way of "making the foreigner pay"? The description of tariffs as taxes indicates that a problem of tax incidence is involved. *In general, the incidence of tariffs will lie on both the foreign exporter and the domestic buyer.* The distribution of the burden will depend on the same practical issues of demand and supply elasticity which determine the incidence of domestic excise taxes. Figure 35-1 shows that the tariff both raises the price of imports and lowers the price received by exporters.

Export taxes are the analogue of tariffs on the selling side. They are also used by governments to raise revenue. In some instances, they are, in effect, a tax on the operations of foreign companies exploiting domestic resources. Export taxes are distorting, too, for the world as a whole and for the use of the resources domestically. Can they make the exporting country better off? The answer depends on the nature of the exporting industry. If it is competitive, export taxes must come out of the earnings of the industry. That will discourage investment and employment in the industry. *If an industry has a complete or partial monopoly vis-à-vis the rest of the world, export taxes can be used to appropriate part of those monopoly profits.* Most of the less developed oil-producing nations of the world impose a tax on their oil exports. Though some part will be passed on to world consumers of their oil products, some part comes out of the monopoly profits of the international oil companies.

Improving the terms of trade: An optimum tariff rate. The argument set forth in the preceding paragraphs suggests the question: Is it possible that the incidence of tariffs could fall so heavily on foreign suppliers that the terms on which imports are obtained are improved? The answer is, Yes, and the analysis of tax incidence suggests the conditions under which it might be so. First, the supply of the imported good must be relatively insensitive to price, that is, relatively inelastic. The imposition of a tariff, which raises the price, will then reduce the quantity offered by a relatively small amount. Second, the demand for the particular import must be relatively elastic, which means that consumers will be willing to reduce its consumption and substitute other goods in the face of price increases.[2]

[2] The construction of some extreme cases may help in understanding the general point. If supply is perfectly (infinitely) elastic and demand completely inelastic (zero elasticity), the full burden of a sales tax falls on the consumer.

Such a tariff changes the "terms of trade" or relative price of the taxed good in just the right amount to obtain the maximum gain. *Since the gains from tariff revenue and improvement in terms of trade might offset the disbenefits due to reduced availability, it is possible in principle to design an "optimum tariff."* This theoretical possibility seems to be of limited importance for two reasons. First, tariffs — whatever their rationale — invite retaliation, and the losses from retaliation can offset the gains from the terms-of-trade effect. Second, the political process which generates tariffs does not in general appear to be conducive to the fine adjustments necessary for "optimum" tariff making.

Protecting infant industries. Some industries — if they could get firmly established — would have a comparative advantage and could survive. It is for these industries that the *infant-industry argument* is proposed. The argument is a particularly popular one for less developed countries. Essentially it goes as follows: A young industry has many problems to overcome even if it is basically sound: training new workers and managers, obtaining adequate financing, establishing a sales organization and penetrating markets, and so on.

Once the industry is established, it might produce and sell at lower prices than those charged for imports and might thereby increase consumption. *A tariff may thus be justified to help get an industry to efficient production levels by protecting the industry in its tender infancy.* In this case the burden of higher current prices would be offset by lower future prices.

Unfortunately, tender infant industries usually grow up to be frail adult industries that can never face foreign competition. Examples are so numerous that any list is inadequate: automobile plants and paper mills whose scale of production is too low to be efficient, steel mills working with high-cost coal and low-grade iron ores, and so on. Nonetheless, the infant-industry argument is, in principle, a valid and important one.

A variation of the infant-industry argument which is not always recognized as such is the "tariff-factory" argument, also popular in less developed countries. It says that the way to encourage capital imports and industrialization is to set the tariff so high that it will be more profitable to produce at home than to import. That is possible, of course, but the real question is: What effect would such a tariff have on the real consumption and income of the country? Would the people as a whole be better off if cheaper goods were imported than if relatively expensive goods were produced at home?

A generalization of the infant-industry argument might be called the infant-economy argument. In the poorer countries, there are many domestic barriers to modernization which must be overcome. It has been argued that tariffs which create new incentives to industrialization and help upset old stagnant patterns of life will have long-run benefits that more than offset short-run losses. It is a difficult argument to evaluate because the claimed effects are so diffuse. As modern experience with development accumulates, however, more and more policy makers are impressed with the inefficiency of protected industries and the difficulty of removing protection once given.

Promoting diversification. In many of the less developed countries, production, especially for export, is concentrated in a few primary products, such as wheat, meat, coffee, sugar, copper, and oil. A small decrease in the international price of one of the commodities can endanger the entire economy of a highly specialized producer. The fall in price of a major export can prevent the country from earning enough to pay for the import of many of its requirements. Diversification stimulated and protected by tariffs can reduce the risks of specialization. *A tariff policy designed to promote diversification entails a cost – which is the loss of some potential gains from trade. But that cost is like an insurance premium* against violent fluctuations in export earnings, and the benefits, it has been argued, are worth the costs.

Another aspect of the diversification argument is the claim that, in the long run, the prices of the typical primary exports of the less developed countries tend to decline relative to the prices of the typical manufactured goods they import. It is argued that the demand for the primary product exports simply does not grow as fast as the demand for manufactures. Moreover, such new manufactures as nylon and other synthetic fibers are substitutes for natural fiber exports, such as silk, cotton, and wool. And the development of such substitutes tends to depress the demand for natural primary products.

Evidence on the diversification argument is equivocal and difficult to evaluate. It had a great vogue in the 1950s but seems less fashionable now, though it is far from dead. Again, however, tariffs are generally not the best means of accomplishing the desired diversification.

Adjustment to tariff changes

What do you say when someone argues that without tariff protection an industry simply cannot survive? If it folds up, workers will lose their jobs. State and local tax collections from the industry will disappear. The efforts of generations of owners and managers will perhaps be lost. Some industries face such a prospect. The United States shoe and textile industries are in an advanced stage of decline, partly as the result of foreign competition. Can you just say, "Too bad. Better luck next time. Remember that everyone else will be better off, even though you are worse off"? Those are harsh words, and the issue is not hypothetical.

Whatever the errors of logic or the power of special interests which lead to the imposition of a tariff, eliminating the tariff or even reducing it is going to cause somebody pain. Since tariffs protect, removal of a tariff harms the protected industry. There should be no blinking at this fact. It explains much of the hue and cry against tariff reduction. It also exposes the false promise sometimes made that no one will be hurt by tariff reduction. Resources become committed to certain regions, and workers acquire special skills. Transferring resources and moving to other jobs will impose hardship.

No one should want to impose hardship on another, but preserving a domestic industry which is inefficient by world standards also imposes hardships — on consumers as a whole. The real question is: In what circumstances are the hardships least and how can the pain of any necessary adjustments be reduced? The theory of comparative advantage tells us how to minimize total hardship by getting as much as possible of the gains from trade.

The Trade Expansion Act of 1962, often called the Kennedy Trade Act, contains provisions for facilitating the adjustments to lower tariff levels. Special employment benefits, retraining programs, loans to business, and tax relief are provided. These are necessary to reduce the burden of tariff adjustments on particular groups and, by reducing this burden, to reduce the opposition to lower tariffs.

Tariff policy in the United States

Recent tariff history, except for the 10 percent surtax of 1971, marks a retreat from the high levels of protection of the 1930s. Many countries, in desperate attempts to reduce the impact of the Great Depression, imposed tariffs, and many others retaliated. The consequence was a worldwide reduction of trade. The United States began to reduce those high tariffs in the late 1930s by negotiating reciprocal trade agreements for tariff reduction.

The General Agreement on Tariffs and Trade (GATT) of 1947 is a vehicle for multilateral tariff reduction among the more than two dozen countries which participate in it. Since 1947, a number of important "rounds" of tariff reduction have been negotiated. United States tariffs are now relatively low as compared with many other nations.

The Kennedy Trade Act of 1962 pointed toward further tariff reductions. But Congress can always reverse the trend, and the late 1960s and early 1970s have already seen major debates on tariffs sparked by new proposals for protection. Table 35-1 shows some of the recent tariff rates on a range of goods, not including the 10 percent surtax. Some of the industries protected are hardly infants and some of the effects on prices must be substantial.

Table 35-1

UNITED STATES TARIFFS ON SELECTED COMMODITIES, 1970

Commodity	*Rate of tariff*
Cameras	20% ad valorem
Radios and televisions	35% ad valorem
Automobiles	10% ad valorem
Large electric generators	35% ad valorem
Steel bars for reinforcing concrete	20% ad valorem
Crude petroleum*	0.5¢ per gallon
Motor and gas fuel*	2.5¢ per gallon
Natural rubber	Free
Synthetic rubber	20% ad valorem
Cocoa beans	Free
Sweetened chocolate	4¢ per pound
Coarse cotton textiles	35% ad valorem
Medicinal drugs in dosage form	7¢ per pound + 45% ad valorem
Cheeses	35% ad valorem
Tomatoes†	3¢ per pound

*Also subject to import quotas.

†Tariff charged if import enters during the period from March 1 to July 14, inclusive, or the period from September 1 to November 14, inclusive in any year.

Source: U.S. Tariff Commission.

Quotas

Quotas are regulations limiting the quantity of imports of particular commodities. They have come to be more and more common in the last thirty years. This is in part because special interest groups have found tariff protection increasingly difficult to secure. Less political attention is paid to quota regulation. *Nonetheless, the effect of quotas is to protect domestic industry from foreign competition and to raise prices to higher levels than they otherwise would be.*

Quotas raise new problems, however. For example, if only limited amounts of sugar or oil imports are permitted, which countries will be allowed to send how much? The awarding of shares of the allowed trade among nations has become an important instrument of international economic and political policy. The limits on imports become domestic political issues as well and can involve intense bargaining, since the President of the United States and the chief executives of foreign governments often have some discretion in the quota-setting limits. The United States has obtained voluntary agreements from certain countries to abide by quota limits even in the absence of formal, legal restrictions on imports. In recent years the United States and Japan have bargained intensively over the level of voluntary quotas on Japanese textile exports to the United States. One of the United States counters in the bargaining was the threat of a new tariff law, and such a law was almost passed in 1970. In the United States the oil industry argues that quotas are necessary to maintain economic conditions in which the industry can survive and grow and provide reserves for the national defense. There can be little doubt, however, that the concentration of the industry in the Southwest has strengthened its political influence on quota decisions.

Free-trade areas

The European Common Market (European Economic Community) was formed in 1957 by Belgium, France, Italy, Luxembourg, the Netherlands, and West Germany. The aim was to achieve the benefits of freer trade among its members by reciprocal tariff reduction and quota elimination. At about the same time, seven other European nations, Austria, Denmark, Norway, Portugal, Sweden, Switzerland, and the United Kingdom, formed the "Outer Seven" (European Free Trade Area), but with less extensive plans for tariff and quota elimination. There is also active consideration of the creation of free-trade areas in Latin America or in some part of it, in Central America, and, possibly, in Africa and Southeast Asia.

Virtually since the inception of the European Common Market there have been negotiations toward broadening it to include the United Kingdom and other countries of the Outer Seven. These negotiations have often broken down. Usually the sticky issues have been the conditions under which the United Kingdom would come in and, specifically, how much of its special trading arrangements with the Commonwealth it would sacrifice. In early 1971, however, the negotiations were successful, and the last obstacle was the unfavorable attitude of a large segment of British public opinion.

The rationale of a free-trade area is *to secure for its members the economic advantages of a large trade area without sacrificing national political identity.* The internal tariff cut within a free-trade area is a move toward freeing trade and, therefore, has a "trade creation" effect. Nations outside the free-trade area worry that an internal tariff cut discriminates against outside trade. That effect is called "trade diversion" and is a form of trade distortion. So there is a mix of good and bad economic effects. In any case, there is widespread political support for the idea of free-trade areas.

The creation of a free-trade area does not mean the end of special interest pleading. In 1965 the European Common Market almost broke up over the issue of protecting the relatively inefficient agriculture of France, in particular. The Common Market survived, but at the cost of conceding that protection—and higher costs for agricultural products.

Summary

Tariffs are taxes on imports. In general they raise the price of imports in the receiving nation and lower their price in the exporting nation. The arguments for tariffs fall into noneconomic and economic categories.

The most popular noneconomic argument is that certain industries which are essential to national defense must be preserved. Sometimes it is argued that an industry should be protected because of its contribution to national prestige. Since noneconomic arguments set a political rationale against an economic one, they cannot be settled on economic grounds alone. Economic analysis can point out the costs of tariff protection, however.

While the economic arguments for tariffs do not make a universally valid case for protection, they often contain a kernel of truth in that tariffs benefit special groups or have general benefits in special circumstances.

Tariffs protect established industries from foreign competition and preserve investment and jobs in the protected industries. The cost of the protection is the higher prices which consumers as a whole must pay. So-called scientific tariffs, which just equalize foreign and domestic prices, destroy the benefits of trade.

Tariffs are sometimes justified on the ground that high-wage domestic labor cannot compete with cheaper foreign labor. This argument ignores other costs of production and differences in labor productivity. It is true, however, that imports may reduce labor's relative income share.

Tariffs which restrict imports may stimulate the internal economy if demand is shifted to domestically produced goods and if there is no international retaliation. Retaliation is almost certain, however. Under such circumstances, tariffs are not only an ineffective tool against unemployment, but one which makes everyone worse off. Similarly, tariffs used to reduce imports in order to improve a balance-of-payments deficit invite retaliation.

Tariffs can be used to raise revenue. The incidence of the tax seldom falls entirely on the foreigner. In general, the burden will be distributed between the consumer and the seller, just as with other excise taxes. But a tariff can be used to improve the terms of trade on which a country imports if supply of the import is relatively inelastic and demand for the import is relatively elastic. Then, the tariff will change quantity traded by relatively little but will change the selling price net of tariff by a relatively large amount.

When a country has a long-run comparative advantage in a particular industry which needs time to achieve international levels of efficiency, a tariff can be justified to protect the infant industry. Tariffs can also be justified as ways of promoting the diversification of a country in order to reduce the risks of specializing in primary commodities whose prices are subject to great fluctuations. It has been argued that tariffs to promote diversification are also justified because in the long run the prices of primary products deteriorate relative to those of manufactured products.

Though free trade may be in the general public interest, adjustment to tariff reduction is nonetheless a real burden to the labor and the owners of resources in the affected industries. Recent tariff policy in the United States has retreated from the high tariff levels of the 1930s and has provided help to industries caught in the adjustment squeeze. United States tariffs are now relatively low as compared with those of many of the other major trading nations. The General Agreement on Tariffs and Trade provides for international cooperation in tariff reduction and has been successful in promoting several rounds of tariff reduction in the last twenty years.

Quotas are limitations on the quantities of imports. They are similar to tariffs in their protection of domestic industry since they limit foreign competition. They have attracted less political attention than tariffs and have been used more and more widely as instruments of trade restriction.

Trade liberalization has been achieved within Europe by the formation of the Common Market, and the creation of free-trade areas is being discussed in other regions. Though free-trade areas stimulate trade within the area, they may divert trade from the rest of the world.

Questions for discussion and review

1. If the argument for international trade is valid, what accounts for the persistence of tariff and quota restrictions?

2. Why would a scientific tariff destroy the advantages of free trade?

3. Since United States labor receives higher wages than foreign labor, how do you account for our export not only of electronic equipment, which requires special skills, but also of corn, wheat, and coal, all of which are produced in low-wage countries?

4. Discuss the following statement: *Tariffs intended to stimulate the domestic economy or improve a nation's balance of payments can work only if other nations are forbearing — and that cannot be counted on.*

5. How can tariffs be used to improve the terms of trade of a nation?

6. Why do economists concede some validity to the infant-industry and diversification arguments for tariffs?

7. How can you explain the growing use of quotas to restrict trade during a period of general tariff reduction?

8. What are free-trade areas and why do countries outside such areas often feel threatened by them?

Concepts for review

Ad valorem and specific tariffs
Scientific tariffs
Tariff retaliation
Optimum tariff
Infant industry
Diversification effects
Quotas
Free-trade areas

36

Balance of payments and exchange rate policy and international finance

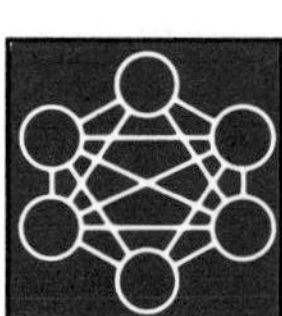

The world is always being plagued by international economic crises. If the current crisis is not in Asia or Africa or Latin America, it is in Europe or the Near East or some other quarter of the world. Recent difficulties in the U.S. balance of payments have shown that this country is not immune itself. Such crises are in part problems of private international markets adjusting to new patterns of demand and conditions of supply. The crises in part reflect changing domestic economic conditions and strains induced by government foreign policies. Whatever their origins, international economic crises become issues of public economic policy. That is because foreign exchange rates and international financial transactions are regulated by government policy and often by intergovernment agreement.

The survey of current international economic problems in this chapter will include an analysis of balance-of-payments difficulties, foreign exchange adjustment mechanisms, and the rationale of international finance. Many of the analytical tools developed earlier will be brought to bear on these issues.

Alternative sources of balance-of-payments disequilibrium

There are more ways than one to be sick – or to have a balance-of-payments disequilibrium. *The chronic deficits in the balance of payments of many of the less developed countries stem from their attempts to accelerate their economic growth rates.* To do that, they need foreign resources of equipment and material. Their traditional exports, however, are usually not growing fast enough to supply the foreign exchange needed to finance ambitious growth plans. The demands for such exports are often price-inelastic, so price cutting will not generate additional revenue. The less developed countries often try to earn foreign exchange by producing new goods (export promotion). But setting up the new production facilities requires even more foreign exchange, at least in the short run, and it is, moreover, difficult to penetrate existing markets. When the less developed countries try to reduce their foreign exchange requirements by producing more of what they need themselves (import substitution), that too requires foreign equipment and material. It also takes time. Further, it often calls for a larger scale of operations to match the lower cost of foreign-produced goods than is warranted by the domestic market. Price inflation is often a concomitant of the growth pressure, and this tends to make the products of the less developed countries less attractive in international markets.

Yet it is a mistake to think that the pattern of trade problems is the same in all the less developed countries. India, for example, fits most of the above description, but has been relatively free from inflation except that caused by drought. Chile has not grown very rapidly, but has had a high rate of inflation.

The balance-of-payments problems from which some of the European countries have suffered at various times, while superficially similar to those of less developed countries, usually have different sources. In some cases, the deficit has been due to relatively rapid increases in domestic prices. That may reflect overall pressures of effective demand. But as pointed out in Chapter 18, domestic price inflation may have other origins than simply excessive real demand: It may be caused by an excessive rate of growth of the money supply. Or the competition of labor and the owners of other resources for a larger share of the national income may generate general price increases. Whatever its sources, domestic inflation tends to reduce exports and increase imports and create balance-of-payments difficulties. In some industries the comparative advantage in the production of particular products has shifted relatively rapidly from one country to another. Unless domestic resources are shifted to new areas of comparative advantage, the country will find itself without new sources of foreign exchange earnings.

The symptoms and cures for balance-of-payments disequilibrium

When a balance-of-payments problem shows up, a country will typically first use its foreign currency reserves to meet its deficit. The currencies most widely accepted include the West German deutsche mark, the Swiss franc, and the U.S. dollar. It will also draw on its gold reserves. But if the disequilibrium continues, the country will worry about exhausting its foreign currency and gold reserves. It will want to avoid that, since it would have to put all trade on a cash basis and thus have no cushion against unforeseen difficulties. Before exhausting its reserves, therefore, the deficit country will often do one of two things: (1) reduce its currency's price relative to other currencies, in the hope of eliminating the disequilibrium problem, or (2) resort to the rationing of the foreign exchange available to it. These are always controversial measures and their rationale needs to be examined.

Depreciation to restore balance-of-payments equilibrium. *A persistent deficit in a country's balance of payments means that its currency is overvalued.* As a result, its own exports are too expensive and foreign goods are cheap. Depreciation which lowers the price of the domestic currency and raises the price of foreign currencies also raises the price of foreign goods and discourages imports. At the same time, the prices of domestic goods in terms of foreign currencies are reduced, and exports are stimulated. These changes, *if* they go far enough, will tend to resolve the balance-of-payments problem. The "if" is a big one and the occasion of vigorous debate. Since it is easier to discuss the issues in terms of an actual set of events, we shall use the French devaluation of 1968 as an example. The discussion will provide some new insights into the general argument.

Actually the French balance of payments appeared to be in relatively good condition prior to the student riots and general strike of 1968. But when the labor unions obtained the wage increases they were after, there was a general feeling that widespread price increases would follow. French managers would hardly be content to take the wage increases out of profits. *The anticipation of price increases on French goods was quickly transformed into an expectation of lower exports, higher imports, balance-of-payments difficulties, and eventual devaluation of the franc. That, in turn, set off immediate speculation against the franc.* Foreign holders of French francs sold them for gold or other hard currencies. Frenchmen, themselves, sold francs, speculating that they would be able to buy them back later at a lower price and make a profit. The French central bank attempted to maintain the value of the franc by selling gold and hard currencies from its own reserves, hoping in that way to stem the tide of speculation. But the plan did not work. The speculator ran little risk in betting that the price of the franc would fall, since the chance that it would rise was almost nil. Eventually, the franc was devalued, but before that happened, France had lost a substantial portion of its gold and foreign currency reserves. *One moral of the story is that devaluation or depreciation, if either is to be done at all, is done most successfully when not fully anticipated.*

While the speculation against the franc and the loss of reserves were painful for France, there was a general belief that devaluation would be successful in the sense that it would resolve the balance-of-payments problem. Likewise the devaluation of the dollar in 1971 was intended to reduce United States imports and stimulate its exports.

Exchange controls to manage balance-of-payments deficits. India has lived for many years with a balance-of-payments problem and an overvalued rupee. It has been widely believed there that devaluation would not succeed in earning more foreign exchange. This was because India's important traditional exports of tea, jute, and cotton have inelastic demands, so a price decrease would not earn more foreign exchange. *Instead of devaluation, India has relied mainly on comprehensive exchange controls. Though a devaluation did occur in 1966, the government has retained these controls.*

The Indian government requires everyone owning and earning foreign exchange to sell it to the Indian central bank at the official exchange rate. Then the government sells the foreign exchange at the official rate to importers who have agreed to use the foreign exchange for government-approved purchases abroad. This policy permits India to live with an overvalued exchange rate and keep its balance of payments under control. Is it bad for a country to live with an overvalued foreign exchange rate? It does have some undesirable effects, as pointed out in Chapter 34. The foreign exchange rate is a price, and an overvalued rate is a price which does not reflect the real relative scarcity of foreign exchange. On the other hand, adjusting the foreign exchange rate to eliminate a deficit may have a real cost to the economy. In the Indian case, the official view has been that the costs of adjustment are greater than the benefits which would accrue from recurring devaluations.

The problems of balance-of-payments surpluses. The discussion thus far would suggest an apparent asymmetry: Balance-of-payments deficits are "bad" and balance-of-payments surpluses are — well, nothing has been said about them. Chronic surpluses result in the accumulation of gold and foreign currency. There *is* an asymmetry in that the accumulation process can go on and on without the surplus country being forced to change its currency value or control its use of foreign exchange. But a chronic surplus makes little economic sense. It occurs when a currency is undervalued. That means that the country's exports are relatively inexpensive and, therefore, particularly attractive abroad, while imports are relatively expensive and, therefore, unattractive. In effect, the surplus country gets less imports of goods in return for its exports than could otherwise be obtained. That condition is a cost to the domestic economy, even though it is a disguised one.

The West German deutsche mark was widely regarded as an undervalued currency when the decision was made to raise its price by 9.3 percent in 1969. That decision was provoked partly by the rapid accumulation of gold and foreign currency reserves in West Germany. It was also part of a policy to reduce domestic inflationary pressures. By reducing the price of foreign currencies, the West German government lowered the price of imported goods.

The deutsche mark was also regarded as overvalued in the spring of 1971 when the decision was made to let the mark "float" freely. As a result, the mark did appreciate by about 5 percent relative to the dollar. The Japanese yen also came to be regarded as an overvalued currency in 1970 and 1971 as Japan's accumulation of dollars and gold reserves proceeded at a high rate.

The U.S. balance-of-payments problems

The U.S. balance-of-payments problems are complicated by the nation's role as world banker. The dollar has been used as a reserve currency by foreign countries as if their dollar reserves were "money in the bank." This means that the resolution of the U.S. balance-of-payments problems, unlike those of India, for example, involves a great many other trading nations of the world. The U.S. dollar problem is closely bound up with the great issues of international liquidity. This section will focus narrowly on balance-of-payments difficulties which have their origins in the United States economy itself.

Starting in 1933, the United States began to accumulate stocks of gold. Other countries sent gold here for safekeeping as World War II became more obviously imminent. Foreign buyers also used gold to pay for United States exports when this country was the major source of many scarce military and civilian goods during and after World War II. Until 1958, the problem of the dollar appeared to be one of "shortage," and the nation accumulated gold in exchange for dollars. Since 1958 a change has taken place. Dollar "shortage" has turned into dollar "glut," and the gold has drained away, as shown in Figure 15-4 on page 313.

The U.S. balance of payments has balanced since 1958, with a shrinking current account surplus and gold outflow and a large short-term capital inflow, all of which offsets a long-term capital outflow. In the 1960s the gold outflow in some years was slightly more than $1 billion per year, but had fallen slightly by the end of the decade. The "deficit" in the balance of payments can be computed in various ways, as explained in Chapter 32, and appears to be a somewhat different problem, depending on how it is computed. What accounts for it and what can be done about it? To answer the question we shall go through the U.S. balance of payments and discuss the status of each account and how it can be "improved."

Current account problems and policy. In part, the shrinking of the current account surplus has been due to (1) decreasing attractiveness of United States exports and (2) increasing attractiveness of foreign imports. These changes are to some extent the result of relative inflation of United States prices, but only in particular sectors. Up until 1966, average prices in the United States rose *less* than in most of the other important trading nations. After the escalation of the Vietnam War, price inflation accelerated in the United States, and the U.S. balance of payments suffered from it. The cure for this particular problem lies in the achievement of domestic price stability. As argued above, domestic price stability would bring other benefits as well. Alternatively, one could hope for price increases abroad. But simply hoping is not a rational economic policy. Yet it is important not to fall into the trap of thinking that balance-of-payments equilibrium at all times is so important that it justifies any measure to achieve it. Domestic policy changes to achieve balance-of-payments equilibrium may well have some undesirable side effects. Those must be balanced against the benefits.

In particular sectors, United States prices had become relatively high as compared with foreign prices even before the post-1966 inflation. This fact suggests another explanation for the shrinking of the United States current account surplus: a change in comparative advantage due to a more rapid increase in the productivity of resources abroad than in the United States. Japan provides the example par excellence of such a change. The old stereotype of Japanese products was that they were cheap copies of foreign goods made with low-wage labor. Japanese goods are no longer copies, however, but well-designed originals. And Japanese factories are low-cost not just because of relatively low-wage labor but because they get more out of their capital. Japanese steel mills, for example, often exceed United States mills in productivity. *United States productivity has not increased fast enough in many lines to offset the good design and production engineering as well as the lower-cost labor of many foreign countries.* That does not mean that the United States has lost its comparative advantage in all lines; that is impossible. Nor does it mean that lost comparative advantage cannot be recovered. But it does mean that adjustments are required to achieve a sustainable balance of payments.

What can domestic policy do? Sponsor research. Give tax credits for investment in new technologies. These are the devices used in other countries. Again, however, the costs must be balanced against the benefits. The supersonic transport (SST) airplane, for example, is a major technical change for which the argument has been made that its sales abroad would earn foreign exchange for the United States and help the balance-of-payments problem. But most economists looking at the SST project have concluded that the domestic costs of achieving that technical change more than outweigh the value of the foreign exchange which it would earn.

One reason United States exports have not grown faster is that there is foreign discrimination against United States goods. During the dollar shortage period, many foreign countries discouraged imports from the United States by tariffs and quotas and other regulations. Such policies were intended to reduce their demand for U.S. dollars. The discriminatory regulations still exist in some places and for particular commodities, though they are being gradually eroded. Undoubtedly, their removal would help the U.S. balance of payments.

Other ways of improving the current account would sacrifice some of the benefits of international trade. Increasing our tariffs and quotas, for example, will reduce imports. This was one motivation for the 10 percent surcharge on dutiable imports announced by President Nixon in the late summer of 1971. Threats of retaliation helped to induce its removal later in the year. Restricting foreign travel would reduce expenditures abroad. Such measures are less desirable than a policy that would improve export capabilities and increase competition between domestic products and imports.

Long-term capital movements. Turn now to the long-term capital account. *The private outflow reflects the eagerness of United States business to take advantage of foreign profit opportunities.* The European "miracle" growth rates of the 1950s and 1960s meant high profit rates in Europe, and United States companies wanted to take advantage of them. The stirrings in the less developed countries also opened up new profit opportunities which stimulated new investment by United States companies. Part of the movement of capital abroad has been associated, both as cause and effect, with the growth in foreign productivity remarked above. United States capital has often been accompanied by United States know-how, which has increased foreign productivity. United States capital has also been attracted by the possibility that increased foreign productivity would provide a means of producing for the United States market at lower costs than could be achieved in the United States.

The long-term capital outflow on government account includes the substantial contributions that the United States has made to help the economic development of the poor countries of the world. These contributions have been made both through international agencies and through direct grants and loans. In addition, there have been large-scale grants and loans for military equipment. In recent years, long-term government grants and loans have been almost entirely "tied" to the purchase of United States goods and services, so a dollar of such capital outflow virtually means a dollar of exports.

Should these long-term capital movements be curbed? Again the answer depends on the relative benefits and costs of such a policy. If it were not for the balance-of-payments deficit which inspires the question, the private outflows would be generally regarded as mutually beneficial to both the United States and the recipient countries. The profits earned would help the U.S. balance of payments when repatriated. The United States capital abroad provides resources and technology useful there. Long-term government development loans and grants similarly provide needed resources for faster economic growth abroad.

The long-term outflows can be curbed if necessary. Congress has already imposed an 11½ percent tax on the purchase of foreign stocks and bonds by a United States resident from a nonresident. A program of voluntary restriction on capital investment abroad by banks and corporations was instituted in 1965 and made compulsory in 1968. *Though they may help the balance of payments, these interferences with free movement of factors are counterproductive of real goods and services in a literal sense.* That is why they are usually not regarded as desirable long-term policies.

Short-term capital and gold movements. A review of U.S. balance-of-payments problems should conclude with an analysis of the role of short-term capital movements and gold outflows. This analysis transcends the U.S. balance of payments itself, however, and involves the entire international financial system. That system will be the subject of the next section, so we shall only point out here the connections between United States short-term capital movements and the larger issues.

As noted in Chapter 32, the role of short-term capital movements in the U.S. balance of payments is unique. In other countries short-term capital inflows are credits which are expected to be liquidated within a year. They are not, therefore, a reliably sustainable way of financing a current plus long-term capital account deficit. The United States, however, plays the role of world banker. Other countries often *want* to send short-term funds to the United States to take advantage of United States capital markets while maintaining a high degree of liquidity. *A "cure" for the U.S. balance of payments which permanently eliminated the net short-term inflow to zero might not be regarded favorably by all those foreign countries that want to use United States banking facilities and financial markets.*

The need for improved balance-of-payments adjustment mechanisms

Each country's balance-of-payments accounts are constantly adjusting to domestic and foreign changes. Some of these changes are short-term, such as "cyclical" unemployment at home or abroad, bumper crops or a drought, or an international political crisis that cuts off or diverts normal sources of fuel. Some of the changes are longer-term, such as inflation in some countries or changes in comparative advantage. *In a world of constant change, adjustment mechanisms are of paramount importance.* Alternative adjustment systems are, therefore, one of the dominant themes of international economic debate.

Alternative automatic adjustment systems. The *price-specie flow adjustment mechanism* of the gold standard required domestic prices to move up or down to change imports and exports and to establish balance-of-payments equilibrium. No country now adheres to a gold standard. Many prices tend to be relatively inflexible, especially downward, and the response to price changes cannot in any case be relied upon to achieve the requisite quantity changes. Furthermore, few central bank authorities are brave enough to provoke a domestic deflation to achieve balance-of-payments equilibrium.

The *income-adjustment mechanism* operates through changes in domestic incomes rather than prices. It requires income, output, and employment to fall when imports are excessive. And, to be effective, it too requires at least the tacit consent of the central bank authorities and of the fiscal authorities as well. Again, few officials are willing to sacrifice domestic prosperity for international equilibrium. Rather, over and over again, they have maintained the expansionist domestic policies, which often brought on the balance-of-payments deficits, and resorted to a variety of exchange controls to maintain international economic viability.

Freely fluctuating exchange rates would permit domestic prices to remain relatively stable and bring about balance-of-payments adjustment through changes in the foreign exchange rate. The dangers of a destabilizing speculation and the fear of the unsettling consequences of continual and one-sided changes in the foreign exchange rate have discouraged reliance on this mechanism. However, the deutsche mark was allowed to float freely in both the exchange crises of 1971, with the announced intention by the West German government of fixing the price after some period. In this case the West German dollar and gold reserves were so large and the West German trade conditions so strong that in the short run at least it was quite unlikely that speculation could force the deutsche mark price down radically. Other countries, such as France and Austria, appreciated their currencies relative to the dollar by a fixed amount rather than run the risks of a freely floating exchange rate. The U.S. dollar was also allowed to float freely later in 1971 when the United States government suspended payment for dollars in gold.

International policies for balance-of-payments adjustment. If every automatic adjustment mechanism is rejected, how can balance-of-payments equilibrium be achieved? One of the instrumentalities intended to help is the International Monetary Fund established after World War II. At that time policy makers and economists generally thought that most of the balance-of-payments adjustments needed to maintain equilibrium would be relatively minor, much like short-term swings in the need for credit on the part of business. The International Monetary Fund was established with contributions from its members to provide that short-term credit. The IMF was also supposed to supervise and consult with countries having exchange rate difficulties so that orderly and *managed* changes in exchange rates could be made if changes became necessary.

The Fund was relatively passive through most of the 1950s. Its inactivity was due to the initial strains in the international exchange system. The necessary adjustments were far larger than had been envisaged. The resources of the Fund were simply too limited to cope with them. In the early 1960s, however, the IMF had a more active role in international adjustments. Yet IMF rules have often been ignored when a country decides to change its currency's relative value. This was the case in 1971 when the United States stopped redeeming its currency in gold for foreign central banks.

Though foreign exchange crises recur, their nature has changed. There has been the reversal of the U.S. balance-of-payments position mentioned above. As dollar shortage changed to dollar glut and United States gold stocks flowed into other hands, the reserve positions of many other countries improved. There has been intermittent adjustment of foreign exchange rates, downward for deficit countries and upward for surplus countries. In retrospect, at least, and often in prospect, the adjustments were frequently delayed too long, so their palliative effects were less than they might have been. The foreign exchange crisis of 1971 was the occasion for a general realignment of exchange rates and reexamination of the adjustment mechanisms.

It is widely believed that the international economy ought to be able to do better than adjust by "fits and starts." But there is also disagreement about what the adjustment mechanism ought to be. Economists divide into two principal camps on this subject: Some advocate freely fluctuating exchange rates and others wish to stick with fixed exchange rates or, at most, a "crawling peg."

The advocates of freely fluctuating exchange rates make the important point that, with the demand and supply conditions of international trade constantly changing, it is not reasonable to insist on a completely fixed price of foreign exchange. Adjustments will always be necessary, they argue, and it is better for them to occur continuously rather than intermittently. Freely fluctuating exchanges, it is argued, would provide the continuous adjustments desired. As to the worries about wild speculative fluctuations in exchange rates, good futures markets in foreign exchange would help prevent that, just as futures markets generally lead to relatively smooth adjustments in commodity markets. Traders and capital exporters could also use a foreign exchange futures market to "hedge" their transactions against loss due to foreign exchange rate fluctuations.[1]

[1] In futures markets for foreign exchange, contracts for future delivery of particular currencies would be bought and sold. For example, a contract for the delivery of, say, £100 in three months would be purchased by an importer who had to make a £100 payment on a shipment of English bicycles at that time. Suppose the price of the pound were to go up in three months, so that the bicycles were more expensive than had been anticipated. The extra cost would be offset by the profit that the purchaser could make on selling the futures contract he had bought as a hedge. If the price of the pound were to drop, the bicycles would be less expensive, but there would be a corresponding loss on the futures contract. Long-term capital transactions would be more difficult to hedge, as futures contracts rarely extend beyond one year. But fixed exchange rates cannot be relied on to remain unchanged either in the face of balance-of-payments disequilibrium.

Arguments against freely fluctuating exchange rates claim that exchange rate stability encourages trade and capital movements. When exchange rate adjustments are necessary, it is better to have them occur in a once-and-for-all fashion (at least for a year or so) than to have the uncertainty of continuously fluctuating flexible rates.

The compromise position between freely fluctuating exchange rates and fully fixed rates — the "sliding" or crawling peg with widened gold points — is gaining adherents. This plan actually has two parts. It would (1) widen the range within which exchange rates are allowed to fluctuate and (2) allow the parity exchange rate itself to move by some stipulated maximum amount during the year. The first part of the proposal has the object of achieving some of the flexibility and market-clearing advantages of the freely fluctuating exchange rate scheme while setting limits on how far the rate changes are allowed to go. It was proposed officially by the United States in 1971 as part of the attempt to resolve the U.S. balance-of-payments problems. The second part of the scheme provides for continuous though slow adjustment in the parity rate. It would, therefore, say its advocates, eliminate the big, discontinuous changes that have characterized most devaluations.

The range of exchange rate fluctuation that is set by the gold points — the costs of shipping gold among countries — is about 2 cents or 3 cents above and below the parity rate. For the U.S. dollar, this would permit only a 2 percent or 3 percent fluctuation in rates under the fixed exchange rate rules. Under the sliding-peg scheme, a range of fluctuation of up to 10 percent above and below the fixed rate has been proposed. That itself would permit a substantial "depreciation" or "appreciation" of the rate in any year. The parity rate itself would "crawl" at approximately 1 percent or $1^1/_2$ percent a year.

The sliding-peg scheme has gained widespread support as a means of moving away from the rigidities and crisislike discontinuous changes of the present fixed exchange rate system. If it were ever instituted, there would be some immediate changes as some rates moved up or down toward their ceilings or floors. One of the problems of making any change in the exchange rate system is simply the transitional one: getting over the uncertainty created by the change itself.

There is another, quite different attitude toward the sliding-peg proposal and other reform proposals, however. Some economists say that other currencies can very well change their par rates up or down or go on a sliding-peg basis, but not the dollar — not without disturbing all of world trade. So the real question is, What would happen to the dollar's value?

That question concerns the liquidity of the entire international financial system, and no clever scheme of limited changes in exchange rates can deal with it. To understand this argument, we must take up the matter of international finance.

International monetary reform and gold

The fundamental facts of economic life are real productive resources, the manner in which they are used to produce goods and services, and the way that production is distributed. But a complex modern economy is far from a barter system, and money plays an essential role in making production and distribution more efficient. Or if monetary policy is unwise, it can make the real economy work badly indeed.

Analogously, international trade is fundamentally an exchange of the goods and services of one country against the goods and services of other countries. The international economy is likewise far from a barter system, however, and the international financial system can make foreign trade and capital movements go more smoothly — or can constrain them if the system works badly. In recent years, signs of increasing strain in the system of international money and finance have led to a number of proposals for reform.

The analogy between international money and banking, on the one hand, and domestic money and banking, on the other, is not fully valid, particularly since there are no regulations for international banking and money creation. Nor is there a central bank or deposit insurance agency to protect the system. Nonetheless the analogy provides some useful hints for our analysis.

The demand for international money is related to *the volume of international trade,* just as the demand for a domestic money is related to *the level of the domestic output.* International trade as a whole is growing relatively rapidly — at about 7 percent or 8 percent per year. That, in turn, means a growing demand for international money.

Stretching the gold supply by general devaluation. What can satisfy the growing demand for international money? Gold can, at least partially. Its worldwide acceptability makes it an international money. Like coins and bills in domestic circulation, it is the most liquid international asset. The supply of gold that can be used for international money, however, depends on the amount that has been scratched out of the ground in the past and is not locked up in private hoards, but is available for the settlement of international claims. Gold production has been increasing at about 2 percent per year, which represents a smaller increase in the available gold stock than in the past. And not all of the additional supply becomes available as international money, because some of it is drained into private hoardings and diverted to industrial use.

Though the gold stock cannot be increased rapidly, it can be stretched in a monetary sense by raising its price. If all countries *devalued* their currencies by the same percentage in terms of gold, no country's currency would depreciate or appreciate in terms of other currencies. And the same amount of gold stocks would represent much more international money. This seems to be an easy way out of any international liquidity shortage. But there is a catch. The benefits of mass devaluation would *not* be spread equally even though all currencies remained at the same relative price. The major gold-producing countries in particular would be much better off as a result of the general devaluation. It would give their gold production greater purchasing power in terms of the real goods and services of other countries. Most of the world appears to believe that there is no reason to confer such a windfall gain on these gold-producing countries. They are, of course, South Africa (an IMF member) and the Soviet Union (not a member).

The dollar as an international money. *"Hard" currencies constitute another major type of international money. These are foreign currencies that other countries are willing to hold as part of their international money reserves.* These countries maintain demand or time bank deposits in the hard currencies or buy short-term securities payable in the currencies. The former are quite liquid; the latter are slightly less liquid but give somewhat higher interest returns.

The U.S. dollar has clearly been the most important of the international reserve currencies in terms of volume of foreign holdings. But the British pound in the "sterling bloc" countries, the French franc in the "franc bloc," and the West German deutsche mark and the Swiss franc in many countries also serve as hard, reserve currencies.

The dollar has been the most important reserve currency for several reasons. One is that the sheer volume of United States international transactions makes it the most readily available reserve currency. In addition, United States banks have excellent facilities for transferring funds around the world, so maintaining accounts in these banks makes payments and receipts relatively easy. Finally, the United States capital markets are by far the largest in the world, and that makes it easier for foreigners as well as United States residents to buy short-term securities and earn interest on short-term accounts.

With this background, we can now make the connection between the U.S. balance-of-payments problems and international liquidity. The United States has contributed toward satisfying the increasing world demand for international money in two ways. First, the gold drain from the United States can be interpreted as a desirable redistribution of the total stock of gold among the trading nations. Second, the U.S. balance-of-payments deficit has made increasing amounts of dollars available for holding by foreign countries. This holding of dollars abroad or their deposit by foreigners in United States banks or their use by foreigners to buy short-term securities constitutes the short-term capital inflow which is so important in balancing the United States accounts. *The U.S. balance-of-payments "problem," therefore, has been the means by which the increasing demand for international money has been satisfied.*

Changes in the international monetary system. The international gold and dollar monetary system was not planned; it just grew. It has been vulnerable to crises for two reasons. First, the connection between gold and the dollar has made the system susceptible to speculative attacks. And second, the countries holding dollars as a reserve currency have on occasion come to think that perhaps there has been too much of a good thing. On occasion they have come to doubt that the U.S. dollar would maintain its price in terms of gold. They have withdrawn their deposits in such large amounts that they have endangered the use of the dollar as an international currency and tended to create the situation they feared. The vulnerability of the system has led to major changes in recent years. These changes have strengthened it substantially, but new problems have arisen even before the old ones have been fully resolved.

The discontinuous adjustments of foreign exchange rates made by many countries have often been forced by the attack of foreign speculators, as described above in the case of the French franc. The adjustments usually occurred after prolonged adherence to an overvalued exchange rate drained away gold and foreign exchange reserves. In 1968 it seemed that the hour had struck for the dollar. United States gold reserves had been steadily draining away since 1958, and it appeared to many that devaluation was imminent. In anticipation of a change in the price of the dollar, foreign speculators sold foreign holdings of dollars for gold. Those sales tended to push the price of gold up. To maintain the official price of gold, the Federal Reserve sold gold to foreign central banks, some of which in turn sold it to the private speculators. The resulting gold drain seemed only to confirm and hasten the need for an eventual devaluation, and the speculation grew more intense.

Finally, in March, 1968, the ten leading trading nations, with the exception of France, suspended gold payments by their central banks to private purchasers and created a "two-tier" gold system. The suspension of payments to private individuals and businesses plugged the leakage of gold out of United States and foreign central bank ownership. Henceforth, within the group, which was eventually broadened to include France and other members of the IMF, no gold was to be sold to or bought from the free private markets.[2]

On the official tier, gold is used in international settlements among the central banks of IMF member nations, with all the exchanges being made at official parity rates. On the unofficial or free market tier, the price of gold is set by supply and demand like the

[2] France at first stayed outside the central bank agreement, but joined when the French gold reserves were depleted in the run on the franc and after the student and labor riots later in 1968. South Africa, as the major gold-producing nation within the IMF, was given special rights to deal in gold, but can sell only limited amounts to the central banks of members of the IMF.

price of any other commodity. Just after the formation of the two-tier system, when there was doubt how effective it would be, the price of gold rose as high as $44.41 per ounce in the Zurich market, as compared with the official price of $35.20 per ounce. Speculators bid for available supplies in anticipation of United States devaluation. After the formation of the two-tier system, the price of gold fell gradually until it came down to virtually the official United States price of $35.20.

Some experts feel that these events show that the United States called the bluff of those who claimed that the dollar was overvalued. It is true that central banks around the world had a strong interest in maintaining the price of the dollar. Their large holdings of dollars meant that any change in the dollar price would result in substantial losses. However, again in the summer of 1971 there was extensive speculation against the dollar, and this time the hour had struck. Payments of gold to central banks against dollars were halted by the United States government, and the value of the dollar was allowed to float for almost four months. Then, in December 1971, it was depreciated against the other major currencies and devalued against gold.

The dollar reserves that foreigners own are called "Eurodollars," though large amounts are also held by Japan. Their total volume is quite large and their movement among countries has been almost completely unregulated until recently. While they are a useful means of facilitating international transactions, they are also a vehicle for speculative money movements. And they are regarded as a threat to the domestic monetary policy of the countries among which these dollar deposits are moved. For example, in the early 1971 speculation against the dollar, individuals and businesses abroad which held Eurodollars sold them for deutsche marks, francs, etc., in great volume. That tended to force down the price of the dollar in terms of these other currencies. To maintain the IMF rules, the central banks of the European countries had to buy dollars with their own currencies. That, in turn, meant a large increase in their money supply — an increase which was not desired in terms of the domestic economic conditions in these European countries.

European monetary authorities now fear that through Eurodollar movements they may have lost control of their own money supply. To regain control, some countries have already imposed new reserve regulations on Eurodollar deposits.

But does the United States deserve the right to supply dollars in unlimited amounts to the rest of the world and use the short-term capital inflows to finance its long-term capital outflows? Shouldn't the rest of the world have some of the benefits that the banker acquires when he creates money — in this case international money? Many foreign central bankers think so. In effect, as a result of the two-tier system, the gold supply has become more limited as a means of international payments. And foreigners generally do not want to rely so heavily in the future as in the past on U.S. dollars as an international money. These conditions led to an international agreement in 1969 to create "paper gold" – called Special Drawing Rights (SDRs).

SDRs are created annually by a vote of IMF members. They are a new international money, because IMF members agree to accept them in exchange for goods and services and in payment of international obligations. They are as "good as gold" in international transactions, except that no resources were expended to dig them out of the ground and no country has a preeminent position in supplying them. This new asset is distributed among IMF members in proportion to the quota of each member in the IMF. The quota of each member country was established on its admission. It determines the amount of help the country can obtain from the IMF in terms of foreign currencies, by loan or purchase, and also the amount of gold and its own currency it has to contribute.

The SDRs are a notable achievement in international finance because they represent a concerted effort to break away from the folklore of gold and create an international money which can grow to meet the expanding needs of world trade.

There is, for example, a widening debate over the possibility of creating an international central bank. The IMF already carries on some of the functions of such a bank, and the creation of SDRs gives it even more central bank-like power. The major issue in such a debate is whether sovereign nations are willing to surrender any degree of control over their domestic economies to such an institution.

What then will become of the dollar as a reserve currency? The advantages of holding dollars are still important. But there can be disadvantages. *The dominance of the dollar as a reserve currency has increased foreign susceptibility to changes in the domestic economic policy of the United States.* When the Federal Reserve tightens credit and raises interest rates, e.g., dollars held abroad are attracted back to the United States in search of the higher interest return. That creates monetary problems for foreign countries. Finally there are widespread suspicions abroad that the use of the dollar as a reserve currency has permitted the United States government, and private companies as well, to maintain long-term capital outflows in spite of a shrinking current surplus – outflows that may be beyond what is justified and desirable from a foreign point of view.

The distribution of the international financial reserves held by countries in 1960 and early 1970 is shown in Table 36-1. The United States held almost 20 percent of total world reserves in March, 1970, but that was down absolutely and relatively from its 30 percent share in 1960. The decrease in United States reserves supplied part of the increase in reserves of other countries from 1960 to 1970. In addition, a large part of the foreign exchange reserves held abroad are dollars. The less developed countries held only 20 percent of total reserves in March, 1970, but that was a big increase

Table 36-1

COUNTRIES' OFFICIAL RESERVES, ADJUSTED, 1960, FIRST QUARTER, 1970 (IN MILLIONS OF U.S. DOLLARS)

			Composition of reserves at end of March, 1970			
Country	*1960*	*March, 1970*	*Gold*	*SDRs*	*Reserve position in IMF*	*Foreign exchange*
Total developed areas	52,149	61,807	35,714	2,566	6,557	16,978
United States	19,359	15,400	11,903	920	2,577	
United Kingdom	5,094	2,710	1,469	305		936
France	2,272	4,126	3,544	166		417
Germany	7,032	7,366	4,079	222	302	2,763
Italy	3,251	5,080	2,978	120	885	1,097
Belgium and Netherlands	3,369	5,200	3,250	176	666	1,108
Switzerland	2,324	3,587	2,659			928
Other industrial Europe*	1,838	3,287	1,054	126	369	1,741
Canada	1,991	3,598	879	133	515	2,070
Japan	1,949	4,058	469	133	684	2,773
Other European countries†	2,358	4,475	2,158	113	134	2,074
Australia, New Zealand, and South Africa	1,312	2,920	1,272	152	425	1,071
Total less developed areas	9,730	16,750	3,450	699	621	11,985
Western Hemisphere	2,955	5,150	1,115	306	356	3,380
Africa‡	2,170	3,370	420	156	111	2,675
Middle East§	1,415	3,080	1,015	31	68	1,965
Other Asia	3,090	4,985	735	206	86	3,960
Grand total	61,879	78,557	39,164	3,265	7,178	28,963

*Austria, Denmark, Luxembourg, Norway, and Sweden.

†Finland, Greece, Iceland, Ireland, Malta, Portugal, Spain, Turkey, and Yugoslavia.

‡Excluding South Africa and the United Arab Republic.

§Cyprus, Iran, Iraq, Israel, Jordan, Kuwait, Lebanon, Saudi Arabia, Syria, and the United Arab Republic.

Note: Excludes U.S.S.R., socialist countries of Eastern Europe, mainland China, etc.; also excludes United States holdings of foreign exchange but includes U.K. dollar portfolio. Totals may not add because of rounding and because some area totals include unpublished data.

Source: International Monetary Fund.

over 1960 both in absolute amounts and as a percentage. Half of total reserves are still gold, but the foreign exchange component is quite large and increasing more rapidly.

The pros and cons of long-term foreign investment

Long-term foreign investment occurs in several forms. First of all, there is the distinction between government grants and loans and private investment. The former is represented by the loans for economic development which the governments of the advanced countries make to the poorer nations. Private investment includes the purchase of foreign securities and the setting up of foreign producing subsidiaries. It covers the activities of both small investors and large corporations. A useful distinction is that between "portfolio" investment and "direct" investment. The former is simply the purchase of securities. The latter means operating control and responsibility and often involves sending physical equipment and managers and technicians.

The potential advantages of foreign investment have already been pointed out. *For the receiving country, foreign capital is an addition to the country's resources.* It permits more imports than would otherwise be possible. It can assist in the country's development by permitting a more rapid exploitation of its natural resources. It is often accompanied by skilled managers and engineers who provide technical know-how. In return, the country must allow some of the profits from the investment to be repatriated, but even so, the country can be better off if the increases in output associated with the investment exceed the profits taken out.

What then is the source of the bad reputation of foreign investment? It is called "economic imperialism" and "foreign intervention and control." It is accused of draining away the natural resources of poor countries and exploiting their peoples. It is Dr. Jekyll or Mr. Hyde, depending on whom one talks to.

The fears of foreign investment are understandable. For example, when the United States government sets up an economic assistance agency in one of the less developed countries, ten or twenty specialists may be brought in when loan negotiations are started. It will be only one of perhaps a hundred such field operations for the United States, but in a small country it can represent a major addition to expertise and resources — under the control of a foreign government. The mission representatives may try hard to be unassuming and cooperative, but they are still foreign. The same thing may be said about the foreign employees of corporations that come in to set up a plant. A big multinational corporation has a budget which approaches in size that of the governments of many nations. It may come in with unspecified but hinted-at recommendations from the still larger and more powerful government of its home country. For a small nation, dealing with such a business can be almost like carrying out a diplomatic negotiation. And too often and in too obvious ways, the foreigners appreciate their economic power. But beyond these real human problems, what are the economic reasons for resenting foreign investment?

A foreign corporation is frequently not just one among a group of many small producers, both foreign and domestic. It often exercises a good deal of monopoly and monopsony power. That is always resented. And it is particularly resented when it is foreign. The locally hired workers may feel that the bargaining power of a giant foreign corporation prevents them from receiving higher wages. Local businesses may believe — often correctly — that the foreign corporation receives special tax and operating privileges. The foreign corporation may have gained exclusive operating or exploration rights in private bargaining sessions with local government officials who do not protect the interests of their country as a whole. There are, no doubt, many cases in which a foreign corporation has been able to use its economic power to gain favored political and economic treatment from a local government or a national government and helped maintain that government in order to gain favors. Sometimes a foreign corporation is able to mobilize the tacit or overt support of its home government to sustain it. Such practices are the substance of economic imperialism, and the history of foreign investment is replete with examples. Foreign investment, therefore, carries a heavy burden of often justified prejudice.

On the other hand, *alert and aggressive domestic business firms, governments, and unions have often been able to gain special advantages from a foreign corporation.* Workers may organize and strike. Depending on the significance of the producing facility in world markets and in generating profits for the foreign corporation, the labor union may succeed in gaining wages substantially above those paid in the rest of the economy. Local businesses may secure laws which require local participation, even majority ownership, in the operation and, thereby, gain access not only to the profits of the operation but to technical and managerial expertise. And local governments may succeed in bargaining effectively for substantial tax or royalty payments, which can make a major contribution, not just to financing the government, but also to supplying the investment resources required for national economic development.

Foreign investment in the past has not always meant political reaction and economic exploitation, and it need not mean that in the future. Recognizing the inequities that have existed and the resentments that have been created, most international corporations now try to operate in a more enlightened fashion. *The problem for the countries in which they operate is to obtain the benefits of foreign investment without suffering either political intervention or economic exploitation from monopolistic practices.* That is often as much a matter of domestic politics as of foreign politics or trade.

Summary

Balance-of-payments deficits may arise from attempts to accelerate the rate of economic growth, with consequent inflation. They can also be the result of the monetary and fiscal policies followed by governments in financing their budgets, or they may result from the competition of social groups for a larger share of the national income. Deficits can also arise when there are changes in comparative advantage to which adjustment has not been made.

Persisting balance-of-payments deficits imply overvaluation of the currency. Depreciation of the currency may be forced by speculation against it when the private purchase and sale of the currency is not fully controlled. Depreciation can remedy the deficit if the demand for exports is sufficiently elastic and if the supply of exports is sufficiently responsive. Rather than depreciating their overvalued currencies, some countries have resorted to extensive exchange control and have rationed the foreign exchange that becomes available from exports and capital inflows.

The U.S. balance-of-payments problem is to some extent also a result of domestic price inflation and changes in comparative advantage. In addition, the U.S. balance of payments has had a large long-term capital outflow, which includes both private investment abroad and government loans and grants for military supplies and for development purposes. The U.S. balance of payments also reflects, however, the widening use of the dollar as a reserve currency. This use shows up in the U.S. balance of payments in part as a short-term capital inflow.

Foreign exchange rate adjustments in the post-World War II period to help achieve balance-of-payments equilibrium have been discontinuous, often made in crisis circumstances and often too long delayed. The large-scale reversal of the U.S. balance of payments from dollar shortage to dollar glut has made large amounts of gold and dollar reserves available to foreign countries. This condition and the discontinuous exchange rate adjustments of other countries have contributed to a reduction in balance-of-payments disequilibrium around the world. Nonetheless, there is active interest in the development of an improved balance-of-payments and foreign exchange rate adjustment mechanism.

A shift to a fully flexible exchange rate system has been advocated as a means of achieving the advantages of continuous relatively small-scale adjustments. Opponents believe it would create uncertainties which would reduce foreign trade and long-term capital movements. A compromise plan calls for a crawling or sliding peg, with widened gold points. Under this system, the range within which exchange rates would be allowed to fluctuate would be increased in order to achieve some of the advantages of market clearing by price fluctuations. The parity exchange rate would also be allowed to move slowly up or down at some specified maximum rate each year to correct over- or undervaluation.

Continuing growth in international trade creates a growing demand for international money. Gold production grows relatively slowly. While an across-the-board increase in the price of gold would make the available stock go further as an international money, such a worldwide devaluation is opposed because it would bring large windfall gains to the major gold-producing nations, South Africa and the Soviet Union. While the U.S. dollar has served as a reserve currency, it is felt in some countries that the United States has exploited its position to avoid taking steps to correct its balance-of-payments disequilibrium and to continue a long-term capital outflow.

The U.S. balance-of-payments deficits have provided large amounts of dollars to foreigners who hold them abroad and use them in international transactions. Transactions in these Eurodollars have been unregulated until recently and have been the means of large-scale speculative movements. These, in turn, have forced domestic monetary changes on some countries which have not desired them. This is another source of the impetus for reform of the international monetary system.

The movement for reform in the international monetary system has led to the creation of Special Drawing Rights, SDRs, which are an international money administered by the International Monetary Fund and allocated to members in proportion to their quota in the Fund. Debate on further reform, including the possible creation of an international central bank, is continuing.

Long-term foreign investment can contribute needed resources to the development of a country. It has often also been accompanied, however, by monopolistic practices and exploitation of their economic power by foreign corporations in order to gain special advantages. This is the substance of charges of economic imperialism against foreign business. Increasingly vigorous and alert local unions and governments and businesses have forced concessions from some international corporations.

Questions for discussion and review

1. Explain in detail how domestic inflation or a loss of comparative advantage in a major industry can lead to a balance-of-payments deficit.

2. What are the disadvantages of a persisting balance-of-payments surplus?

3. How can rationing its foreign exchange enable a country to live permanently with a balance-of-payments deficit? What kinds of decisions must the rationing agency make?

4. Destabilizing speculation can force a depreciation of foreign exchange rates if reserves are not adequate to dampen speculative

purchases of foreign currencies or gold. How does this work? Can speculation ever force an appreciation of a currency?

5. What are the sources of the U.S. balance-of-payments problems? Or do you think that there is a U.S. balance-of-payments problem?

6. How has the U.S. balance-of-payments problem made life easier for the balance of payments of many of the other important trading nations?

7. Explain how the trading nations of the world can create an international money, as they did in the SDRs. Is it as good as gold? Is it as good as the dollar?

8. What is meant by international economic imperialism? Do you think it warrants the elimination of international investment?

Concepts for review

Overvaluation and undervaluation

Reserve currency

Two-tier gold system

Sliding-peg system

Special Drawing Rights

International money

Direct and indirect investment

Economic imperialism

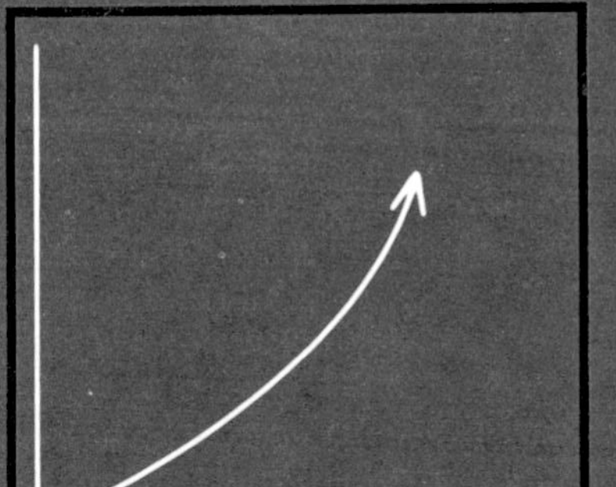

SIX

Growth and development

The economics of growth focuses on the sources of increases in total and per capita output and income. It may seem to be an abstract discussion of the overall effects of capital accumulation, technological change, and population growth. Yet economic growth is also about improvements in the standard of living and increases in employment opportunities. These are not abstract subjects at all but touch the lives of everyone.

There is an extraordinary amount of speculation and theorizing about the sources of economic growth. Writers on the subject base their conclusions on everything from folklore to sophisticated intellectual theories. Is economic growth the result of the stimulating climates of the temperate zones? Does it result from the spread of the Protestant ethic? Is it capitalism and/or democracy or simple frugality which makes all the difference?

Certainly not all of these interesting though difficult questions can be answered in two chapters. But we can and will clear away some of the underbrush and get the fundamental economic relations straight. This will permit a clearer view of the effects of noneconomic factors in growth.

When the economics of growth is put into the context of the poor countries of the world, it becomes the economics of development. It then encompasses all the interrelated kinds of economic changes which occur as a country is transformed from a traditional to a modern society. The relations which are important in a less developed economy are often different from those which are important in an advanced one. For example, Malthusian population growth no longer threatens the ability of advanced economies to provide the essentials of life for their peoples. (Population growth may have deleterious effects on the quality of life even in the advanced economies, however.) In some of the less developed countries, rapid population growth is still a real threat to the possibility of economic advancement. Therefore, the analysis of economic development must go into the relations which can create a vicious circle of poverty and population growth.

The subject of development also naturally focuses on economic policy: What can and should be done to alleviate the terrible conditions of poverty in which so many of the people of the world still live? What can foreign economic assistance contribute? These are also grand questions, but not so grand that we cannot make a beginning in understanding them in the chapters that follow.

37 Growthmanship

The fashions of economics follow the worries of the world. In the 1950s, when economic growth in the United States was relatively slow, discussions of public economic policy to accelerate growth commanded a lot of attention. Then in the mid-1960s, when the economy was booming along at real growth rates of 5 percent or more per year, it became common to downgrade the significance of the performance, to stress other problems, and to regard growth as an issue only for the less developed countries. Then in the late 1960s, as inflation climbed and the rate of real growth slowed, it again became fashionable to worry about the need for economic growth to help resolve some of our own problems and about policies to promote that growth.

While no panacea, economic growth can be an important social solvent. This feature of economic growth and its costs as well as its benefits will be discussed first. After that, a detailed analysis of growth will be undertaken. The most fundamental sources and mechanisms of growth are common to both advanced and less developed countries. The analysis of this chapter will, therefore, be of help in the next chapter, which deals with the less developed areas.

The benefits of economic growth

Why grow? Why concentrate on "more" rather than "better"? Why not emphasize greater equity at our present scale rather than more affluence? The United States as a whole is already much more affluent than any other country. These are reasonable questions, and they have been answered in a number of ways.

Advantages of growth *Most of the "pro growth" arguments deny that there is a trade off between equity, on the one hand, and growth, on the other.* They claim that growth actually makes equity easier to achieve. Essentially they take the following line: First there are important demands for additional output. Second, equity is more readily achieved by producing and distributing additional output than by redistributing a constant amount of output. These are plausible arguments, but are hard to prove or disprove. More specific pro arguments for growth fall under three headlines: national security, international policy, and domestic economic and social reform. The rationale of each will be reviewed briefly. Each has different degrees of persuasiveness for different people.

National security. *Why is slow growth a national security issue? Because military security requires the allocation of resources to military goods production.* The amounts involved in various weapons systems are large. The price tag on an antiballistic missile system, for example, has been estimated at $12 billion (which is more than 1 percent of the 1971 GNP). Some opponents of the system think the actual cost would be even higher if the system were ever built. Reference to antiballistic missile systems is enough to remind one of the heated debates over the technical methods that should be used to maintain national security and over the balance of "conventional" and "nuclear" forces that is desirable. Disagreement is understandable when the issues are so complex and the conflicting claims for resources are so powerful. The arguments cannot be evaluated here, but the disagreement should be recorded.

International policy. *The growth performance of the United States, or any other country, affects its international posture.* First, trade – to take advantage of international specialization – requires adjustments to changes in comparative advantage. These adjustments have costs which are more easily met, it is argued, in a growing than in a stagnant economy. Second, it is easier for the United States to find resources to aid poor countries if such economic aid does not require the domestic economy to make absolute sacrifices. Finally, an expanding United States economy is likely to be a better market for the products of the less developed countries than is a stagnant economy.

The view of the United States economy abroad is likely to be strongly affected by its growth performance. While that is not the only, or even the most important criterion of economic performance, it is one of the most obvious criteria and one to which many people abroad respond. It does make a difference in the international relations of the United States whether the country is regarded as healthy and progressive or as stagnant.

Domestic economic and social reform. There are many, but conflicting, arguments about the directions economic and social reform should take. Some changes can be made without a substantial increase in the use of resources, but many others require additional resources. Pollution abatement, for example, is not simply a matter of getting some bad guys to behave themselves. *Nearly everyone contributes to pollution, and limiting pollution requires nearly everyone to bear some additional costs. Those costs are easier to bear when the economy is expanding and individual incomes are growing than when they are stagnant.* Discrimination against nonwhites and women is deplorable, but it is less likely to be overcome when those who benefit from such discrimination are required to give up something than when they are not. It would be easier to eliminate discrimination if those whom discrimination hurts could be given opportunities to raise their income without hurting anyone else's income.

Population in the United States is growing at a rate slightly above 1 percent per year. Just to maintain per capita income, the GNP must expand at that rate. While redistributing income can help eliminate poverty, providing more opportunities for productive work must play at least as important a role. And opportunities for productive work are greater when the economy is expanding.

This kind of reasoning leads economists to think of economic growth as a catalyst or social solvent which makes change and reform easier. As noted above, "more" is not inconsistent with "better," and a little growth has a big impact in an economy the size of the United States. With GNP running above $1,000 billion a year, an increase of just 1 percent is more than $10 billion. The difference between a $2^1/_2$ percent rate of growth, such as characterized the late 1950s, and a 5 percent rate of growth, which was achieved in the mid-1960s, would now amount to more than $25 billion per year in additional output. It may help in appreciating what $25 billion means to know that the GNP of the whole country of India with 500 million people is only about $40 billion.

The costs of growth

What about the "con" arguments? As pointed out in Chapter 8, some of the costs of producing GNP are not included in the national income accounts – particularly the external *diseconomies* of economic activity. These fall on the community as a whole, rather than on individual producers, and are not subtracted from the gross value of production: air, water, and noise pollution, especially.

Another argument against taking the GNP figures at face value says that much of consumption does not represent an increase in the "fundamental" satisfactions received and enjoyed by consumers. Advertising and social competition may persuade consumers that they are better off with more goods, but some people claim that everyone would be just as happy with fewer goods and services. With less emphasis on material production there could be, it is said, more emphasis on self-realization and more happiness. This claim, in turn, plays down the significance of economic growth.

In fact, relatively few people seem to be willing to sacrifice *their* car or TV set. The pro argument should be remembered at this point — that growth makes it easier to establish programs to alleviate poverty and improve welfare as well as provide more color TV sets.

Finally, and importantly, growth implies some current sacrifice in a full employment economy. As will be explained in more detail below, there must be investment in additional capital stock and in the development of new technologies — both of which often require resources. There must also be additional education and training. All these mean that some present consumption must be forgone in order to have more consumption in the future.

In addition to requiring consumption sacrifices, efficient growth requires continuing adjustment of resources and people to new demands and new technologies. The economic costs of such adjustment can be taken into account. The personal and social costs are not so easily identified.

We might make some progress in evaluating the growth pros and cons if we used more comprehensive income accounting which made allowance for diseconomies. Fundamentally, however, there is no way of objectively resolving the arguments, because the issues are essentially normative. Individuals differ in their preferences, and countries differ in the importance they place on growth. Interestingly enough, in the less developed countries this kind of debate is generally regarded as a luxury they cannot afford. Though there are many differences in these countries with respect to ideology and methods, there is virtually unanimous agreement on what their objective should be: economic growth.

The sources of growth

Economic growth like organic growth is a complex process. Fortunately, much of the analysis of this book can be used to support an understanding of economic growth. Our procedure, again, is to formulate and exploit a series of growth models. It is useful, however, to review the fundamentals. Thinking in simplified terms, as if all goods were either consumption goods or investment goods, we can draw a production-possibility curve for an economy for a particular year, like the line *MN* in Figure 37-1. The position and shape of that production-possibility line depends on the resources available to the economy. It also depends on the productivity of those resources which, in turn, depends on the goods produced and the technology and efficiency with which the resources are used.

Suppose the economy produces the mix of consumption goods and net investment indicated by the point X on line *MN*. That

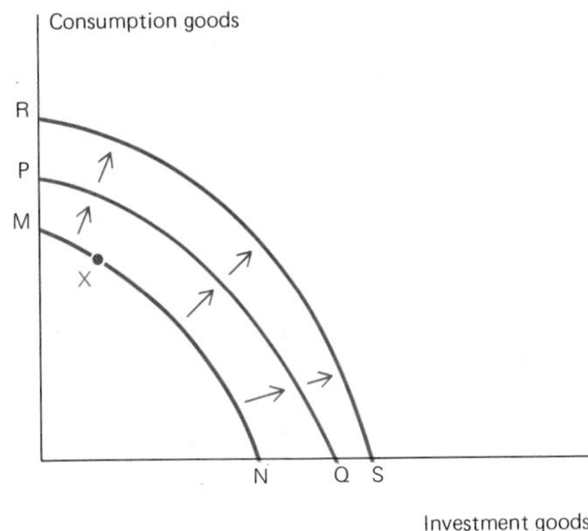

Figure 37-1

EFFECTS OF GROWTH AND TECHNICAL CHANGE IN SHIFTING THE OVERALL PRODUCTION-POSSIBILITY CURVE

means that next year more capital goods will be available as the result of the investment. The labor available will also increase as the result of population growth. These increases in the productive resources available will shift the production-possibility curve of the economy outward to, say, line *PQ* in the next year. If there should be technological innovations or other changes that increase the productivity or efficiency of the resources, the production-possibility curve would shift still further outward to, say, the line *RS*.

This brief review provides us with a list of the sources of economic growth:

1. An increase in the availabilities of productive resources
2. A change in the productivity of the available resources which can result from

a. An improvement in technology

b. A change in the efficiency with which resources are used

c. A change in the composition of output

The next step is to see just how these factors influence growth.

Growth in fixed proportions: The First Growth Model

The First Growth Model to be described was developed by Sir Roy Harrod of Oxford University, England, and Prof. Evsey Domar of M.I.T., Cambridge, Massachusetts. It has greatly influenced economic thought about growth and has directly affected actual planning in some countries. Though it is quite simple, it produces some powerful insights. As we shall see, however, it has its limitations.

Full capacity growth. The First Growth Model, like the Second Model Economy presented in Chapter 3, has just one good, which is produced with two inputs, capital and labor. The good can be used either for consumption or to form new capital, i.e., for investment. The growth of the labor force depends on the rate of growth of population, which in this model is not affected by consumption or other economic forces. The rate of growth of the capital stock depends on the rate of new capital formation via investment.

The first production relationship in the model is that between total *potential* output, X, and the capital stock, K. It is a straight-line relationship:

$$X = \frac{1}{v} K \qquad (37\text{-}1)$$

where v is a constant number called the "capital coefficient." Rearrangement of Equation (37-1) will show that v is just the ratio, assumed not to change, of K to X. Therefore, v is the amount of capital required per unit of total output. And $1/v$ is the productivity of capital, the output per unit of capital input. If there should be an increase in the capital stock ΔK, which is just investment I, that would lead to a change in the level of potential output, ΔX. The precise relationship would be

$$\Delta X = \frac{1}{v} \Delta K \tag{37-2}$$

Now notice another interesting relationship. *Under the conditions assumed, the rate of growth of potential output, which is $\Delta X/X$ is the same as the rate of growth of the capital stock, which is $\Delta K/K$.* This comes from dividing the left-hand side of Equation (37-2) by the left-hand side of Equation (37-1) and the right-hand side of Equation (37-2) by the right-hand side of Equation (37-1). That operation is

$$\frac{\Delta X}{X} = \frac{1/v\ (\Delta K)}{1/v\ (K)} = \frac{\Delta K}{K} \tag{37-3}$$

Now we turn to the determinants of *total demand* for output. The macroeconomic analysis of the First Macro Model, which can be adopted here, indicated that aggregate income, Y, is determined by aggregate effective demand and is the sum of consumption spending, C, and investment spending, I. So

$$Y = C + I \tag{37-4}$$

If consumption is assumed to be a constant proportion, c, of total income, then

$$C = cY \tag{37-5}$$

Using Equation (37-5) in Equation (37-4),

$$Y = cY + I \quad \text{or} \quad Y(1 - c) = I \quad \text{or} \quad Y = \frac{1}{1 - c} I \tag{37-6}$$

Since consumption is a constant proportion of income, saving, S, is also a constant proportion $(1-c)$ of income, and the number $(1-c)$ will be indicated by s. So total effective demand, Y, can also be written as $(1/s) \times I$. Since $I = \Delta K$, this is also $(1/s) \times \Delta K$. This is just a variation of the multiplier formula derived for the First Macro Model in Chapter 11.

Suppose now that there was full use of capacity so that actual income and output as determined by effective demand were equal to potential output. Then $Y = (1/s) \times I$ or $Y = (1/s) \times \Delta K$ would be equal to $X = (1/v) \times K$. A little rearranging of the terms leads to the growth relationship consistent with full use of capacity:

$$\frac{\Delta K}{K} = \frac{s}{v} \tag{37-7}$$

As shown above, the rate of growth of the capital stock in this

Table 37-1

GROWTH RATES CONSISTENT WITH SPECIFIED SAVING AND CAPITAL COEFFICIENTS

s \ v	2	3	4	5
.10	5.0%	3.3%	2.5%	2.0%
.15	7.5%	5.0%	3.8%	3.0%
.20	10.0%	6.7%	5.0%	4.0%
.25	12.5%	8.3%	6.3%	5.0%

model is also equal to the rate of growth of output. Therefore, the growth rate G_W of output which "warrants" or justifies the investment that is undertaken because it generates an equally fast rate of growth of effective demand is

$$G_W = \frac{\Delta X}{X} = \frac{s}{v} \tag{37-8}$$

The special character of this growth rate is emphasized by the name Harrod gave to it, the "warranted rate of growth." *If the system starts with full use of the capital stock and grows at the G_W rate, it will continue to maintain that full use of capacity.* Notice that the analysis does *not* lead to the claim that the warranted rate of growth will necessarily prevail in the economy. Rather, G_W is a particular growth rate which satisfies a special, but important, condition.

Though the warranted rate of growth as derived above must be interpreted carefully, it can be used to illustrate some important relationships. This rate of growth is positively related to the rate of saving: *the higher the saving rate, the faster the rate of growth.* Saving provides the resources for investment, and investment provides the increases in capacity which permit increases in output. If this seems to contradict the lessons of Chapter 11, remember that the problems analyzed in that chapter were those of unemployment and less than full use of capacity. When there is less than full employment, the warranted rate of growth analysis is not appropriate.

The warranted rate of growth is also inversely related to capital requirements per unit of output, or directly related to the productivity of capital 1/v. *The lower the capital requirements per unit of output — or the higher the productivity of capital — the larger the increments of output which can be produced with an extra unit of capital.* Table 37-1 shows the results of some calculations with s and v to compute the warranted rate of growth. Notice the "trade off" illustrated there between capital productivity and saving rate; a 5 percent warranted rate can be achieved with a 10 percent saving rate and a capital-output coefficient of 2. A 15 percent saving rate and a capital output ratio of 3 will also produce a 5 percent warranted growth rate, and so on.

Full employment growth. What about the relationship of labor to output and to output growth? To start, suppose that the labor force, *F*, has a constant relation to the population, *P*. Thus,

$$F = r \times P \tag{37-9}$$

where r is a fraction called the "participation rate" of the population in the labor force. Suppose also that population is growing at some constant rate, g, which is not affected by the level or rate of growth of the economy as a whole. In symbols,

$$\frac{\Delta P}{P} = g \tag{37-10}$$

Since the labor force, F, is a constant fraction, r, of the population, the labor force must also grow at the rate g. This can be seen by writing $\Delta F = r \times \Delta P$ or $\Delta P = (1/r) \times \Delta F$. Using these relationships and Equation (37-9), Equation (37-10) then becomes

$$\frac{1}{r} \times \frac{\Delta F}{(1/r)F} = \frac{\Delta F}{F} = g \qquad (37\text{-}11)$$

Turning to the productivity of labor, suppose there is a constant relationship between output, X, and labor employed, L, which is

$$X = b \times L \qquad (37\text{-}12)$$

where b is the productivity of labor or output per unit of labor employed. Notice that the distinction is made at this point between the labor employed, L, and the labor force available, F. If there is to be an increase in output, ΔX, there must be an increase in the amount of labor employed, $b \times \Delta L$. *The rate of growth of output must, therefore, be equal to the rate of growth of employed labor.* That is

$$\frac{\Delta X}{X} = \frac{b \times \Delta L}{bL} = \frac{\Delta L}{L} \qquad (37\text{-}13)$$

Finally, we can ask and answer the following question: If the economy somehow manages to be at full employment of the labor force so that $F = L$, what rate of growth of output will maintain that full employment? Under these conditions $\Delta L/L$ will be equal to $\Delta F/F$, which is equal to the rate of population growth g. So $\Delta L/L$ must also be equal to the rate of population growth g. But with a constant productivity of labor, the rate of growth of the employed labor $\Delta L/L$ will also be equal to the rate of growth of output $\Delta X/X$. So the rate of growth of output G_N which would maintain full employment of labor is

$$G_N = \frac{\Delta X}{X} = g \qquad (37\text{-}14)$$

This growth rate must again be interpreted carefully. *G_N is the rate of growth that must exist if there is to be full employment, with labor productivity constant.* Its special character is again emphasized by the name Harrod gave to it: the "natural rate of growth." Why "natural"? Because this growth rate provides enough employment to keep the labor force that is created by the "natural" rate of population growth fully employed. Notice an interesting and perhaps unexpected fact about the natural rate of growth: It does not depend on the productivity of labor. Why? Because that productivity is assumed to be constant. The rate of population growth is a powerful factor in any economy, because it provides additional members of the labor force who can generate additional output. In this case, with the participation rate and productivity of labor constant, population growth and economic growth are completely linked together.

Are full employment and full capacity growth compatible? Two growth rates have now been derived; they fulfill special and different conditions. The warranted rate of growth, G_W, guarantees full use of capital capacity; the natural rate of growth, G_N, guarantees full employment of the labor force. *And there is no reason for G_W and G_N to be equal in the model specified here.* G_W is equal to s/v; s, the saving rate, and v, the capital coefficient, are specified as constants. G_N, the natural rate of growth, is equal to the rate of growth of the population and labor force, g, as long as there is a constant labor-force participation rate, r, and productivity of labor, b.

Just suppose there is an output level, X*, at which there is both full use of capital capacity and full employment of labor. Then the amount of capital capacity used at such a full capacity-full employment level of output can be worked out from the relationships:

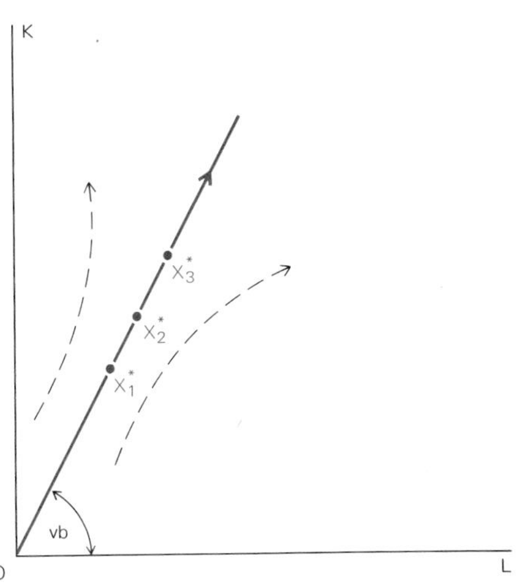

Figure 37-2

HARROD-DOMAR FULL EMPLOYMENT-FULL CAPACITY GROWTH PATH

$$X^* = \frac{1}{v} K^* \tag{37-15}$$

and

$$X^* = bL^* \tag{37-16}$$

where K^* and L^* are full capacity and full employment amounts of capital and labor, respectively. If both these relationships are to be satisfied then, under Equations (37-15) and (37-16), the relationship between K^* and L^* can be seen to be

$$X^* = \frac{1}{v} K^* = X^* = bL^* \qquad \text{or} \qquad K^* = vbL^* \tag{37-17}$$

This aspect of the First Growth Model is illustrated by Figure 37-2. The two inputs, capital, K, and labor, L, are plotted on the axes of the graph.

The relationship in Equation (37-17), in turn, means that the slope of a line from the origin in Figure 37-2 to a full capacity-full employment point, say, X_1^* is

$$K/L = vb \tag{37-18}$$

And that slope is a fixed number, since v and b are fixed numbers. This is just another way of saying that the First Growth Model represents a "knife-edge" case. *Capital and labor must stay in a fixed relationship to each other if full capacity utilization and full employment are to be maintained in the First Growth Model.* And that, in turn, means that the warranted and natural rates of growth must be equal. That is, s/v must come out to be the same as g. As long as the warranted and natural rates of growth are equal, and capital and labor maintain the fixed relationship $K = vbL$, then the economy represented by this model can move out along the growth path $0 - X_1^* - X_2^* - X_3^*$, etc., to higher and higher levels of output while maintaining full capacity and full employment. But that is the only path which would guarantee these conditions. If the economy should ever slip off the full employment-full capacity path, it would move away from it, further and further away, as indicated by the dashed arrows. Since slight movements in s, r, and b are always likely to occur, this model economy cannot be expected to maintain both full employment and full capacity growth.

While the First Growth Model permits some fundamental insights into the conditions for growth, its instability finally makes it a theory which is not really satisfying.

Flexible growth: The Second Growth Model

The Second Growth Model overcomes the instability of the First Growth Model and generates some additional insights. Professor Robert Solow of M.I.T. is its modern progenitor. The Second Growth Model is like the first, except for the conditions of production which prevail in it. In the First Growth Model, output was related to capital capacity by a fixed number and was related to labor by another fixed number. That meant that capital and labor would not be substituted for each other in production. That is really not a good description of many production processes, and that inaccuracy in depicting reality is, fundamentally, the source of the instability in the First Growth Model.

Figure 37-3

SUBSTITUTION POSSIBILITIES IN THE PRODUCTION OF ALTERNATIVE LEVELS OF OUTPUT

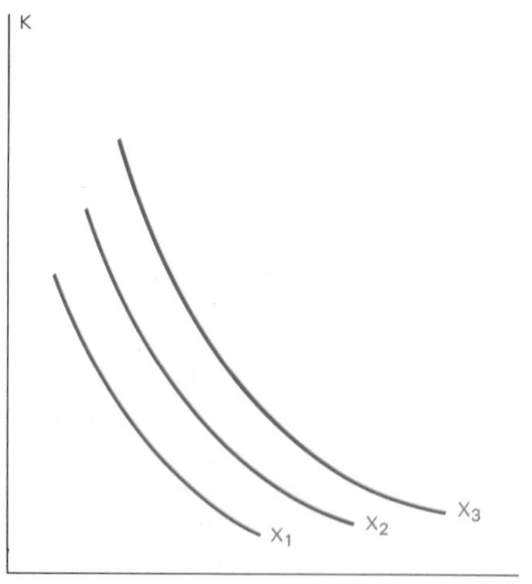

In the Second Growth Model, on the other hand, capital and labor can be substituted for each other in production, as shown in Figure 37-3. Each line in the figure represents the various combinations of capital and labor that can be used to produce a particular level of output. (Note that this is just a representation for an entire "model" economy of a "production function" of the type postulated in Chapter 22 for a particular firm.) So there are a set of combinations of capital and labor inputs which will produce output level X_1, and a different set of input combinations which will produce output level X_2, and so on. The existence of a set of alternative inputs for any particular level of output means that there are trade offs or "substitution possibilities" in production. The trade off is not constant, as indicated by the fact that the slope of each substitution-possibility line changes along its length.

What are the rules of growth in the Second Growth Model? A complicated analysis can be avoided by relying on some reasonable, though intuitive relations. *Output grows in the Second Growth Model by growth in capital and by growth of labor. Moreover, labor and capital can grow at different rates and still maintain full use of capacity and full employment.* That is illustrated by the fact that there are any number of growth rays, shown by the dashed lines on Figure 37-4, which move across the various substi-

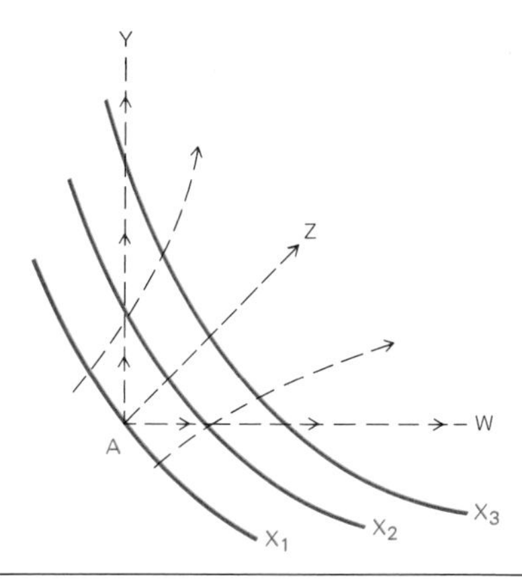

Figure 37-4

FULL EMPLOYMENT-FULL CAPACITY GROWTH PATHS IN THE FLEXIBLE GROWTH MODEL

tution-possibility lines. There can be full employment of both inputs at each point on each dashed line. It only requires using the resources in production in the proportions in which they are available, and production substitution possibilities exist to make that feasible.

Suppose, however, that, for some reason, capital capacity did not grow, but that the labor force did as the result of population growth. Then the model economy would move along line *AW* in Figure 37-4. The rate of growth of output, which is $\Delta X/X$, would in this situation plausibly be some fraction of the rate of growth of the available labor $\Delta L/L$. Why a fraction? *With capital held to a constant level and only labor growing, there would be diminishing returns to labor. So the rate of growth of output would be smaller than the rate of growth of labor.* That is, in this case,

$$\frac{\Delta X}{X} = S_L \frac{\Delta L}{L} \tag{37-19}$$

where S_L is a fraction.

On the other hand, suppose that for some reason the labor force did not grow, but that capital capacity did, through new investment. The economy would, in this extreme case, move along a growth ray *AY*. *The rate of growth of output would be a fraction of the rate of growth of capital.* In this case, there would be diminishing returns to the new investment, so the percentage increase in output would be less than the percentage increase in the capital stock. Or

$$\frac{\Delta X}{X} = S_K \frac{\Delta K}{K} \tag{37-20}$$

where S_K is a fraction.

Now suppose that both capital and labor grow: capital by the percentage $\Delta K/K$ and labor by the percentage $\Delta L/L$. *Then output would also grow by an amount which is the sum of the growth due to increase in the labor force and the growth due to increase in the capital stock.*

That is shown by

$$\frac{\Delta X}{X} = S_L \frac{\Delta L}{L} + S_K \frac{\Delta K}{K} \tag{37-21}$$

This is the fundamental growth relationship for the Second Growth Model. Here growth occurs as a result of increases in either capital or labor inputs, or both, *and* it is possible to maintain full use of both productive resources. This last point can be put another way to contrast it with a conclusion from the First Growth Model: When substitution of factors in production can take place, as in the Second Growth Model — *and in reality* — it is possible to have overall growth in output without inevitably creating unemployment in one or more of the resources used in production.

The relationship shown by Equation (37-21) for the growth in output when there is growth in both capital and labor is called a "weighted average" of the growth rates of the two factors. It differs from a simple average in that the two components do not have equal weights in affecting the result. The fractions S_L and S_K are called the "weights" of the separate components.

One of the important and interesting questions about the growth relationship is: What determines the relative weights of the labor and capital growth percentages in the overall growth percentage? A detailed analysis would take us into deep water. But a hint that will move our thinking toward the right answer in some special cases comes from noticing that the shares of total income received by capital and labor resources, whoever owns them, are not equal. Most rough estimates for the United States suggest that about 60 percent of total income is paid to labor and about 40 percent is paid to capital, including land rent. *If the shares of the two factors are not equal, it is reasonable to expect that their contributions to overall growth will also not be equal.* And it is plausible that the contribution of each factor to growth in total output depends on the share of total output each factor receives.[1]

Table 37-2 presents the results of some simple calculations based on Equation (37-21) in which S_L is set at 60 percent and S_K is set at 40 percent in columns 1 and 3 and the values of the weights are reversed in columns 2 and 4. A labor-force growth rate of 1 percent is stipulated for columns 1 and 2 and a labor-force growth rate of 2 percent is stipulated for columns 3 and 4. Alternative growth rates for capital of 2 percent, 3 percent, and 4 percent are stipulated in successive rows. With these conditions, the rates of growth of total output implied by the growth Equation (37-21) are calculated and entered in the table.

[1] This can be demonstrated rigorously for some special types of production relationships, but requires an analysis beyond the scope of this book. Essentially, the production relationships must be of the constant-returns-to-scale type, as described in Chap. 22.

Table 37-2

OVERALL GROWTH RATES CONSISTENT WITH SPECIFIED CAPITAL AND LABOR GROWTH RATES AND WEIGHTS

Labor growth rate, G_L / Capital growth rate, G_K	1	2	3	4
	1 percent		2 percent	
	$S_L = 0.6$, $S_K = 0.4$	$S_L = 0.4$, $S_K = 0.6$	$S_L = 0.6$, $S_K = 0.4$	$S_L = 0.4$, $S_K = 0.6$
2%	1.4	1.6	2.0	2.0
3%	1.8	2.2	2.4	2.6
4%	2.2	2.8	2.8	3.2

Table 37-2 illustrates the point that the rate of growth of output depends on the labor and capital growth rates *and* the relative weights given to these separate growth rates. It indicates the trade offs in capital and labor growth for the achievement of any specified overall growth.

The table also suggests another problem, however. The actual historical growth rates of the labor force in the United States have been around 1 percent per year, sometimes a little more, sometimes a little less. The actual growth rates of the capital stock have usually been around 3 percent per year. With these numbers, we should, according to Table 37-2, expect an overall growth rate of 1.8 percent. By comparison, the United States economy has historically grown at an overall rate close to 3 percent. There is a difference, or "residual," which the Second Growth Model does not explain. In this case, labor growth and capital accumulation would account for 1.8/3, or only 60 percent, of the actual growth observed!

Economists who have studied this situation carefully have come up with a variety of answers to the question: *What part of total growth can be accounted for by simple increase in the amount of productive resources? The answers range from 20 percent to 90 percent or more.* That range of answers in itself suggests that we should keep looking for sources of growth.

The ultimate growth model?

A reference to the list of growth sources on page 763 will emphasize the point that the First and Second Growth Models really embody only the first of those listed sources: increases in the amount of resources available. Unfortunately, it is easier to enumerate the other influences than to explain how they arise and include them in a neat and simple theory. Still, a good description is no mean accomplishment and will provide at least an intuitive appreciation of other growth factors.

Technological change and growth

Technological change as a source of growth is one of the most obvious omissions from the First and Second Growth Models. *A change that increases the productivity of existing resources and makes newly produced equipment more productive than old equipment will make growth easier.* In a sense it is "factor-augmenting" in that having technical change is equivalent to having more resources. It is like multiplying the available factors by some number such as 1.2 or 1.5 or 2, or whatever the degree of change is.

The First Growth Model can be used to illustrate the significance of technical change. The equation for the warranted rate of growth is $G_W = s/v$, where s is the saving rate and v is the capital/output ratio. Technical change which increases the productivity of capital reduces v because it reduces the amount of capital required per unit of output. A reduction in v, with s unchanged, means an increase in G_W, the rate of growth that can be achieved with, and warrants, full use of capital.

Education

Although the simple growth models treat labor as if it were all the same and as if its productive qualities were independent of any social influence, no one really believes that is so. There is a lot to technical education at all levels whose purpose and effect is to increase the productivity of labor. Moreover, an argument often given to justify general education is that it is the broadest kind of vocational education which exists. The claim is that general education prepares people to do better work in a wide variety of jobs. In this sense, *more and better education is like technical change which increases the productivity of the available resources.*

Another way of looking at the effect of education on economic growth is suggested by some analysis in Chapter 30. In that chapter, education was treated as a process of "human capital formation." This suggests that when computing the growth in all kinds of capital, we should add the growth of "human capital." Considered in this way, the effect of education is like the effect of net investment in physical capital goods in that it increases the amount of a particular kind of capital available to the economy.

Increases in the efficiency with which factors are used

More effective organization of resources and better management, though they might be credited to better technology and better education, deserve a separate headline. For example, computers which digest a tremendous flow of data and use it for improved scheduling of production are a product of new technology. And the people who use computers are the product of a new kind of education. On the other hand, *the use of new methods requires different attitudes toward the organization and management of production enterprises than existed fifty or even twenty years ago.* New production management techniques may also require or create new organizational methods.

It is not really so important whether changes in efficiency can be identified separately from changes in technology and the skill created by education. The important thing is to recognize that the changes are a source of growth.

Changes in the composition of output

Growth due to changes in the composition of output is one of the most difficult growth processes to comprehend in an intuitive way. Some of the analysis already presented can be interpreted under this headline, however. For example, in the First Growth Model the warranted rate of growth is directly related to the rate of saving. And the rate of saving in that model determines the rate of invest-

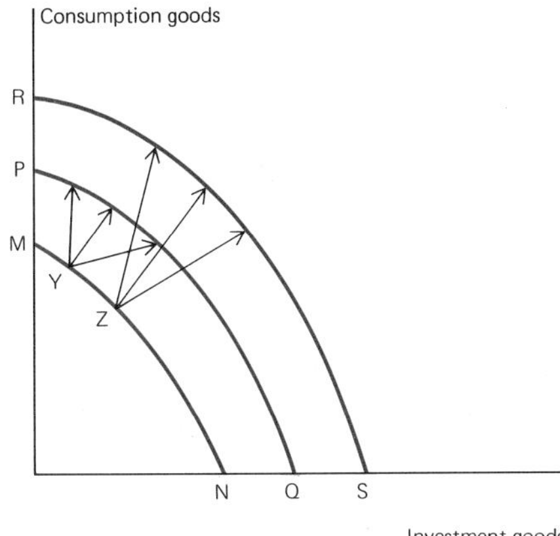

Figure 37-5

EFFECTS OF ALTERNATIVE CHOICES OF OUTPUT COMPOSITION ON GROWTH

ment which is possible. Or, to make the point another way, *the composition of output — its division between consumption and investment goods — directly affects the rate of growth.*

The production-possibility curve can be used again to illustrate the idea. In Figure 37-5 the production-possibility curve *MN* represents the alternative combinations of consumption goods and investment that can be produced by an economy in a particular year. The points Y and Z represent specific alternative combinations, with Y having a smaller proportion of investment goods in the output mix than Z. Thus, the rate of growth of capital stock would be higher with the Z combination than with the Y combination. As a result, the choice of the Z combination in one period would make it possible for the economy to be on the *RS* production-possibility curve in the next period, while choice of the Y combination would only make the attainment of the *PQ* curve possible.

But besides the aggregate investment-consumption goods choice, there are other "composition effects" which affect growth. For example, during the period in which the Soviet Union's rate of growth of output was most rapid, its total investment goods output had a large component of heavy industry construction and a relatively small component of investment in new housing. The high proportion of investment in heavy industry — steel and machinery building — in turn made possible the relatively high rates of growth in other industries producing capital goods. Investment in housing would "only" have made more consumption possible.

This last observation recalls the point made at the outset of the chapter: *While economic growth is important for a variety of reasons, economic performance should not be judged by growth alone.* Most people would want to judge an economy by its contribution to individual welfare, in some sense. However difficult it is to define that welfare precisely, it is clear that it includes among other things housing in the "present" as well as housing in the "future." The relative preference for consumption "now" and consumption "later" is one of the most important growth-determining decisions.

Foreign trade and growth

While foreign trade is less important for the United States than for other countries, it would be unduly parochial to leave it off the list of growth influences. It could be sneaked in under the "composition of output" headline, but it is just as well to make it explicit since it is so important for many countries. The opportunity to trade and to reap the benefits of comparative advantage is of great importance for countries like the United Kingdom, more than 20 percent of whose GNP is earned in foreign trade.

International trade can be thought of as an efficient kind of production. Instead of "trading" resource inputs for outputs, as in domestic production, international trade exchanges goods for goods. *That is a way of making domestic resources more productive.*

Economic policy for growth

As the list of growth influences indicates, all aspects of an economy affect its growth performance. Just how the various influences are interrelated and are exerted is difficult to work out in detail, however. What makes the Japanese economy, which has been growing at rates above 10 percent per year, so buoyant? Japan's growth is partly due to high saving and investment rates and a high rate of population growth. In addition, the Japanese economy has been absorbing and producing a high rate of technological change in production methods. Education is at a high level; management is efficient, and the economy takes extensive advantage of foreign trade possibilities. Having said all this, we must still admit that Japan's remarkable performance remains inadequately understood.

What public economic policies will contribute to United States growth? Investment in new capital and the development of new technologies will help. So will improved education and more efficient management. All this is straight-forward, and some of it is always going on. Occasionally new policies are tried. In 1962, for example, a federal law permitted corporations to deduct as much as 7 percent of the amount they invested from their income taxes. This did encourage more investment and undoubtedly contributed to the growth performance of the 1960s. A similar law was proposed in 1971.

What is the proper mix of growth policies? This is another point at which economists must admit that they do not know all the answers. It is not simply a defensive reaction, however, to point out that the issues are difficult. How can the development of new technologies be encouraged most efficiently? Not many scientists and engineers will claim that they know the answer. How can education be improved? We all have ideas, but we have to admit a lot of ignorance about education as well. Exhortations to improve management are common, but beyond exhortation what can be done?

Even more basic than finding the right set of growth-stimulating policies is the question, How much growth is desirable? But that, in turn, requires knowing and evaluating the costs and effects of growth policies so that we can balance growth benefits against costs. Those were the difficult issues with which the chapter started. Essentially, they involve personal preferences as well as careful accounting.

The sources of growth in the United States and Northwest Europe from 1955 to 1962 are shown in Table 37-3, as summarized from a heroic investigation by Edward F. Denison of The Brookings Institution. The overall growth rates during the period were 2.67 percent in the United States and 4.11 percent in Europe. In the United States, more than half of the growth, 1.70 percent, was due

Table 37-3

SOURCES OF GROWTH IN TOTAL NATIONAL INCOME IN THE UNITED STATES AND NORTHWEST EUROPE, 1955–1962 (CONTRIBUTIONS TO GROWTH RATE IN PERCENTAGE POINTS)

Sources of growth	*United States*	*Northwest Europe*
National income growth rate	**2.67**	**4.11**
Growth due to increase in amount of resources	**1.70**	**1.62**
Changes in labor	0.97	0.62
Increases in employment	0.73	0.57
Reduction in hours of work	−0.20	−0.26
Changes in age-sex composition	−0.08	0.08
Increases in education	0.52	0.23
Changes in capital	0.73	1.00
Increases in residential housing	0.25	0.08
Increases in international assets	0.06	0.03
Increases in nonresidential structures and equipment	0.35	0.70
Increases in inventories	0.07	0.19
Growth due to increases in productivity of resources	**0.97**	**2.49**
Advances of knowledge	0.76	0.76
Reduction of lags in application of technology, reduction in age of capital, and improved balancing of capital stock		0.23
Improved allocation of resources	0.25	0.62
Economies of large-scale production	0.30	0.88
Effects of irregularities in growth of total effective demand and in agricultural output and effects of deflation procedures	−0.34	

Source: Edward F. Denison, *Why Growth Rates Differ,* The Brookings Institution, Washington, D.C., 1967.

to increases in the amount of productive resources available. In Northwest Europe only 1.62 percent growth, or only 40 percent of the total growth, was due to increases in resources. Notice that increases in the labor force were more important in the United States than in Northwest Europe, where the effects of capital accumulation were somewhat larger. Where minus signs appear, the effect of the change was to reduce growth.

In the United States slightly more than a third of the growth performance was due to increases in the productivity of resources, and most of that was due to advances of knowledge. In Northwest Europe that source of growth was equally important in absolute growth terms, but less important relative to other sources. The achievement of economies of large-scale production was more important in Europe during this period, because they had already gone quite far in the United States. The effect of recessions in slowing growth in the United States was substantial.

One must be cautious about the exact numbers in the table and even more cautious about drawing policy conclusions from them. As Denison points out, the better European growth performance was due partly to the fact that the European economies were at a relatively earlier stage of exploiting growth possibilities than the United States. Nonetheless the results are quite suggestive.

Summary

There are advantages and disadvantages to economic growth. It is likely to make social reforms easier because it can provide the necessary resources from *increments* in output rather than requiring a redistribution of existing income. It has also been argued that economic growth is necessary to maintain national security, because of increasing military costs, and that growth facilitates United States international policy by making it easier to carry out assistance programs abroad and by creating a better image of the economy. On the other hand, costs as well as benefits are associated with economic growth. Some of the costs are the diseconomies of production which are external to the market and not subtracted in the conventional national income and output totals. In addition, there is an argument that people really do not want more goods and services but are only persuaded that they do by high-pressure advertising. According to this argument, with less preoccupation with material things, people would give more time to the pursuit of self-realization.

Growth does require direct sacrifices in a full employment economy so that there can be investment. It also requires continuing adjustments if it is to be efficient. Adjustments have personal and social costs as well as the more readily accounted economic costs. The evaluation of the pros and cons of growth cannot be completely objective because it inevitably requires value judgments.

Growth models are used to gain insight into growth processes. In the First Growth Model, both capital and labor are required to produce output which can, in turn, be used for either consumption or investment purposes. Growth in the capital stock via investment and growth in the labor force from population growth will generate growth in output. If the saving rate is s and the capital/output ratio is v, then the warranted rate of growth, G_W, will be s/v. This is the rate which will always generate enough effective demand to fully utilize the capital stock. On the other hand, the natural rate of growth, G_N, is that which fully utilizes the available labor. The rate of growth of labor in this model depends on the rate of growth of the population, since a constant fraction of the population is assumed to be in the labor force. The rate of growth of population is to be a constant, g. The productivity of labor is assumed to be another constant, b. Because productivity is assumed constant, the rate of growth of output which maintains full employment of the available labor, G_N, is just g.

The dependence of output growth on the rate of saving, the productivity of capital, and the rate of growth of the labor force is demonstrated by the First Growth Model. But, there is nothing in the model to make the warranted and natural rates of growth equal or to ensure growth at either rate. Should there be changes in s or v, the warranted rate would change. And if the warranted and natural rates should somehow happen to be the same, a change in s, v, or g would make them diverge. The instability of growth in the First Growth Model results from the lack of substitutability between capital and labor in production. As a result, should one factor grow faster than the other, unemployment of the faster-growing one is inevitable.

In the Second Growth Model, growth in output is again the result of growth in both labor and capital, but now it is possible to maintain full employment of both inputs because of substitution possibilities which exist in production. The rate of growth of output in this case is the weighted sum of the rate of growth of the two inputs. That is, $\Delta X/X = S_L \times \Delta L/L + S_K \times \Delta K/K$, where S_L and S_K are the weights. In the production conditions assumed here, these weights are the shares of income of labor and capital in total output.

The Second Growth Model does not have the instability of the First Growth Model and is, therefore, more satisfactory. If the numbers that approximately describe the United States economy are substituted into the growth equation, however, it can be seen that growth in inputs accounts for only a fraction of the total growth in the economy.

Technological change is another source of growth because it increases the output that can be produced from additional resources and, in some cases, from the resources already available. Education increases the efficiency of labor and contributes to growth. Alternatively, education can be considered an additional type of investment whose effects should be added in the growth equation of the Second Growth Model. Organizational and managerial changes that increase the efficiency with which resources are used are also a source of growth. While many of these are due to technological changes and greater knowledge, they deserve separate identification. Changes in the composition of output can also contribute to growth. Changes in the proportions of output going to investment and to consumption can be interpreted as changes in the composition of output. But changes in the investment-consumption proportion are important since they determine how much additional investment can be undertaken in a later period. International trade is also a way of making resources earn more than they otherwise would and, therefore, contribute more to economic growth.

The formulation of growth policies requires the balancing of the benefits of growth against the costs of the various growth-encouraging policies. The decisions are difficult, not only because of differences in growth preferences but because our knowledge is relatively limited.

Questions for discussion and review

1. Discuss the following statement: *Growth is a good thing. It oils the wheels of the economy and the society and makes everything work better. Politics, social adjustments – all the problems in these areas – are tougher when the economy is stagnant.*

2. Reproduce for yourself the reasoning that leads to the result that the warranted rate of growth in the First Growth Model is s/v and the natural rate of growth is g.

3. Explain what is meant by the "instability" of growth in the First Growth Model and what its source is.

4. In the Second Growth Model, it is possible to grow with full use of capital and full employment of labor. Is that a surprising result or an artificial result? What is its explanation?

5. Why isn't the increase in the amount of resources available an adequate explanation of economic growth?

6. Discuss the following statement: *Technical change and education are alike in their effects on economic growth in that they both increase the efficiency of the resources used.*

7. What are the costs of economic growth?

8. What policies could you suggest to increase the rate of economic growth in the United States?

Concepts for review

The benefits and costs of growth
The warranted rate of growth
The natural rate of growth
The capital coefficient
A weighted average of input growth rates
The composition of output
Full employment and full capacity growth
Unstable growth

38 The economics of development

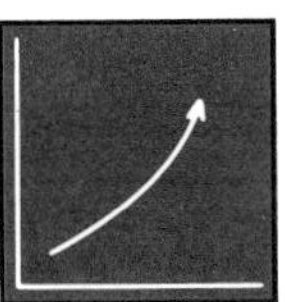

Ye have the poor always with you, according to the New Testament. Most of us do not fully realize just how much the poor *are* with us. Table 38-1 on the next page provides an impression of the pervasiveness of poverty. In 1965 almost 70 percent of the people of the world lived in countries in which the average GNP per head was approximately $170. In the early 1970s that average would still not reach $200 per capita. By contrast, the GNP per capita in the United States in 1970, measured in 1965 prices, was $3,930. The comparisons are rough and, as pointed out in Chapter 8, averages can be quite misleading. In all of India, which is close to the bottom of the income scale, the per capita GNP in 1965 was only about $95. Even in a less developed country with the average GNP per capita of $170, most of the people would be living well below that level owing to inequality in the distribution of income. In the same way, most people in the United States live below the $3,930 GNP per head level. However, the estimates may somewhat overstate the differences between rich and poor countries. The internal prices of the goods usually purchased by individuals or families are often lower in the less developed countries than in the more advanced countries.

But suppose that the differences are not 40 to 1, as between the United States and India, but only 20 to 1 or 10 to 1. Most people in the United States do not believe they are so wonderfully well off that—if their incomes were merely cut in half—they would not feel it. Yet, if that should happen, they would, on the

Table 38-1

COMPARATIVE WORLD INCOMES IN 1965 (U.S. DOLLARS)

World GNP per capita	*$ 750*
Less developed market economies	
GNP per capita	$ 170
Share of total world population	69.5%
Share of total world GNP	15.8%
Africa (excluding South Africa)	
GNP per capita	$ 124
Share of total world population	13.9%
Share of total world GNP	2.3%
Caribbean and Latin America	
GNP per capita	$ 390
Share of total world population	10.9%
Share of total world GNP	5.7%
Asia (excluding Japan)	
GNP per capita	$ 120
Share of total world population	41.6%
Share of total world GNP	6.6%
Middle East (excluding Israel)	
GNP per capita	$ 297
Share of total world population	2.9%
Share of total world GNP	1.2%
Developed market economies*	
GNP per capita	$2,070
Share of total world population	30.5%
Share of total world GNP	84.2%
North America	
GNP per capita	$3,476
Share of total world population	9.7%
Share of total world GNP	45.2%
Europe†	
GNP per capita	$1,590
Share of total world population	14.6%
Share of total world GNP	31.1%
Oceania‡	
GNP per capita	$1,660
Share of total world population	0.8%
Share of total world GNP	1.8%
Israel	
GNP per capita	$1,400
Share of total world population	0.1%
Share of total world GNP	0.2%
Japan	
GNP per capita	$ 901
Share of total world population	4.5%
Share of total world GNP	5.3%
South Africa	
GNP per capita	$ 544
Share of total world population	0.9%
Share of total world GNP	0.7%

*Europe (except Communist countries), North America, Oceania (Australia and New Zealand), Israel, Japan, South Africa.

†Excludes Communist countries.

‡Australia, New Zealand, Fiji Islands.

Source: U.N. Statistical Yearbook.

average, still be many times better off than most of the people of the world.

The differences in average incomes between the rich and the poor countries are so great that some effort is required to appreciate their significance. What does profound and widespread poverty mean?

A high death rate: In many countries one out of fifteen children do not survive their first ten years.

A short life expectancy: In India, for example, the life expectancy is less than 42 years for males and less than 41 years for females.

Frequent hunger: The calorie consumption per capita in much of the world is less than 2000 per day as compared with more than 3000 in Western Europe and the United States.

And many deprivations: Clothing is usually inadequate to keep out cold and rain much less to provide color and variety. Housing is bad. Medical care is poor. Education is limited. Opportunities for self-development, as we understand the term, are restricted or nonexistent.

Poverty in rich countries is an anomaly. *Poverty for most of the people of the world is the normal, commonplace, and seemingly eternal condition of life.* It is sometimes romanticized, and eulogies have been written of the life of the "poor but happy peasant," close to the earth and nurtured in the bosom of an extended family and close community. The important social values of traditional society should never be overlooked, and their preservation is a matter of real concern. Yet changes in economic aspirations must also be recognized. The "revolution of rising expectations" is by now a cliché. Like many clichés it contains a good deal of truth: People of the poor countries want "more and better" and their desires are increasingly a world force.

In addition, more and more people in the richer countries agree with Lady Barbara Ward Jackson that "if morals have any meaning at all, they must entail that the hungry are fed, the naked are clothed, the homeless sheltered and all the sons of men are given some little share in the world's great patrimony of knowledge and opportunity, of health and hope."[1]

This chapter can be only an introduction to development economics. The first step will be a closer look at the characteristics of the less developed countries. This will clear up some of the more simplistic explanations of their lack of development and lead to a deeper study of the real reasons. Then, a discussion of development policy, drawing on the growth analysis of Chapter 37, and a look at the economics of foreign aid will conclude the chapter and the book.

[1] Quoted in Benjamin Higgins, *Economic Development,* 2d ed., W. W. Norton & Company, New York, 1969.

Terminology and the social setting of poverty

The current United Nations euphemism for the poor countries of the world is "developing." That is polite, hopeful and, unfortunately, inaccurate for many of them. Before they were "developing," they were "less developed"; before that they were "underdeveloped"; and before that, "backward." There has been more progress in the gentility of the nomenclature than in the conditions of many of the countries. We shall use the term "less developed countries" or the current shorthand, ldc's.

Why isn't "poor" good enough? The question is reminiscent of a conversation reported to have taken place between F. Scott Fitzgerald and Ernest Hemingway. To a comment by Fitzgerald that "the rich are different from us," Hemingway replied, "Yes, they have more money." It is a rather enigmatic exchange, but with respect to the poor countries of the world, the award for insight would go to Fitzgerald. *The differences in income and wealth between the more and less developed countries are just one aspect of wider social dissimilarities.* That is not to imply that all advanced countries are cast in the same mold. But Japanese, Western European, and United States businessmen can meet and make effective plans together. A village leader in India or a peasant in Latin America may also respond to economic incentives, but they do so in different ways—ways which reflect their different views of individual and social responsibilities. The anthropological and sociological literature of the less developed countries provides insight into the variety of social structures and motivations of their peoples. These social structures and motivations, which are in part an accommodation to and a protection from poverty, can also be barriers to economic improvement.

Using the word "poor" to describe the less developed countries might suggest that only economic changes are necessary for their economic growth. "Development," on the other hand, connotes wider changes. Thus, although this chapter will continue to concentrate on economics, use of the word "development" will be a reminder that the issues of growth are examined in a context in which growth has been a rare and unusual occurrence.

Economic conditions in less developed countries

A common stereotype of less developed countries is that they are crowded with illiterate and unsophisticated people, scratching out a bare subsistence from farming, generally with only limited mineral and fuel resources, but sometimes profiting from oil or copper deposits. This stereotype does catch some of the most important features of many of the less developed countries. (1) Their populations do tend to be concentrated in agriculture. (2) Employment and output in the manufacturing sectors are relatively limited. (3) There are often concentrations of labor and capital in certain extractive industries. (4) The capital available per worker is relatively low and the technologies used are crude, except where modern plants have been installed. (5) Expenditures of the people tend to be concentrated on the essentials of food, clothing, and shelter. (6) Saving rates are low and most saving is done by a small upper-income group. (7) Both domestic and international trade tend to be at relatively low levels, though some countries specialize heavily in a few primary products. (8) Credit and marketing facilities are quite limited. (9) There are high fertility rates and high mortality rates. (10) There are often high rates of unemployment both open and "disguised" in the sense that many people are not working full time. (11) Nutrition tends to be inadequate. (12) Hygiene and public health conditions tend to be rudimentary. (13) Illiteracy rates are high. (14) Women generally are limited to a quite inferior role in the society. (15) Decision making tends to be guided by traditional methods.

The next lesson to learn quickly is that these features do not apply to all the ldc's. Conditions in the less developed countries range from the teeming poverty of Calcutta to the sparsely populated barren uplands of the Andes. Both images, though extraordinarily different, are correct.

The concentration of the population in agriculture is one of the most typical conditions of the less developed countries. The characteristics of their agriculture sectors vary enormously, however.

In some ldc's, where the agriculture is rich and the land not crowded, the people eat well. In Turkey, over 3000 calories per capita are consumed daily. In Ecuador, with a sparse population and less productive farming, the comparable figure is about 2000.

There is also great variety in mineral and fuel deposits. Some of the less developed countries are well endowed with such resources. These include such oil-rich countries as Venezuela, Iran, Libya, and the countries of the Arabian peninsula; the copper-rich countries of Africa and Latin America; and tin-rich Malaysia. On the other hand, some ldc's have quite limited mineral and fuel deposits. Haiti and Ecuador apparently fall into this category. India has iron, coal, and bauxite, but little copper and oil have been found. Not every Middle Eastern and North African country floats on a pool of oil; Syria, Jordan, Tunisia, and Morocco apparently have no deposits. It is always a bit risky to describe an area as poor in mineral and fuel resources, however. One aspect of the limited development of many countries is that for various reasons there has been no systematic search for such resources.

The differences among the less developed countries go further. India has a large and vigorous manufacturing sector. Afghanistan has relatively little in the way of manufacturing capacity.

Literacy rates vary widely. In Burma, 42 percent of the population is illiterate; in Algeria, 80 percent; and in Haiti, 89 percent. In some less developed countries, the people are still struggling to establish their national identity. In others, they are the proud descendants of an ancient civilization which had a sophisticated political structure when Western Europeans were still forest nomads.

Population densities vary enormously. In Zambia, there are about 5 people per square kilometer; in Kenya, about 13. The comparable number for India is 160, and for the Barbados, 586.

It is not possible to say whether a country is or is not overcrowded, from an economic point of view, without knowing something about its resources. The natural resource endowment is especially important. That includes the quality of the land, the rainfall, and other conditions affecting agriculture, as well as mineral and fuel deposits. Some of the densely populated countries have fertile lands from which two or even three crops a year are harvested. This is so in Indonesia and Ceylon. In other less densely but still heavily populated areas, such as India, the land is rich, but the rainfall, generally, is less reliable. And, of course, there are relatively sparsely populated countries whose land supports only a limited amount of agriculture because it is mountainous or infertile or has limited water or short growing seasons.

Dualities in less developed countries

Part of the variety within and among the less developed countries can be described in terms of "dualities": The existence of two major contrasting sets of institutions, modes of organization, or behavior. While such contrasts are to be found in every economy, they are more pronounced in the ldc's. Recognizing these dualities will aid our understanding not only of the less developed countries, but incidentally, the advanced economies as well.

One of the most widely noted dualities is the *modern-traditional sector duality.* In the traditional sectors, decision making is prescribed by long-established customs and patterns. Rational calculation and planning to maximize goal achievement is not paramount and may even be discouraged. That is not to say that traditional sectors are not responsive to external incentives, but that they do not respond in the reasoned manner of the modern sector. The modern sector may also preserve some traditional conventions, but they are much less significant interferences with the achievement of its goals.

The modern sector of the ldc's is often identified with the central and provincial governments, and the traditional sector with village government. The duality may be between the profit-seeking, newly emerging manufacturing sectors, on the one hand, and the old handicraft industries and small traders, on the other. Duality may also be associated with large- as compared with small-scale industry, though there are examples in Hong Kong and the Indian Punjab of small-scale industry that is just as nontraditional, rational, and gain-oriented as large-scale industry.

Another duality often of great importance in the ldc's is the *rural-urban distinction.* Even in developed countries the differences between rural and urban life are a well-known part of the folklore. But modern communications have made rural areas part of the mainstream of life in developed countries. In some of the less developed countries, however, to drive outside the city limits is to move back 200 or 300 years in the amenities of life and patterns of behavior. Again, it should be emphasized that this is by no means always so. In many ldc's as, for example, in Malaysia, a large part of agriculture is thoroughly commercialized and has been for many years. In such places, rural life is closely tied to urban life by marketing and credit arrangements for the supply of farm and plantation output and for the sale of manufactured goods from the cities.

Technological dualism is often associated with the dualities already mentioned, but is conceptually and in some cases practically distinct. *Technological dualism is observed when the technologies used in different sectors create quite different factor productivities.* Technological dualism may be associated with the difference between the modern and traditional sectors. Electric power and irrigation water, for example, may be provided from modern dams and equipment operated by a few skilled technicians with a high contribution to the value of output. The water may be used, however, with otherwise traditional agricultural methods in which labor's contribution to the value of output is small. Technological dualism may also be associated with a wage dualism and an employment dualism, but these may exist separately. In the urban industrial and government sectors in less developed countries, wages are often substantially above the returns received by labor in the rural, handicraft, and private commercial sectors. This may be the result of technological dualism or of modern unions exercising the monopoly power their organization gives them. Differences of this kind are also observed in developed countries, but are usually not so profound.

Unemployment dualism is the "permanent" unemployment or underemployment which characterizes some ldc's. There often seems to be a kind of structural unemployment which is not absorbed even by an increase in effective demand. It may result from a fundamental imbalance in the resources available to be used with labor and/or an inability to substitute abundant labor for other resources. Or it may result from other limits on labor absorption. Economists disagree over how widespread such unemployment is — or whether it exists at all. But many observers consider it an essential aspect of labor conditions in some of the less developed countries.

The rules for growth and the lack of development

While there is great variety among the less developed countries, they share one common attribute: They are poor. Many of them now share two other attributes: Ancient patterns are changing and per capita incomes are rising. What explains the past stagnation and what explains the more recent growth? It is rather a puzzle. Chapter 37 describes the sources of growth and, by implication, how to grow. And it does not give away any secrets. Just follow the rules: *Be efficient. Accumulate capital. Educate and train the labor force. Introduce more productive technologies. Find the right output composition.* Is there more to it than that? And if there is, why didn't it turn up in the chapter on growth? Let us, first of all, clear away some of the underbrush of the folklore which attempts to explain lack of development.

Climate One argument that is still around explains lack of development in terms of climate, particularly tropical climate. It is argued that hot humid weather saps incentives, is debilitating, and even corrupting. The argument will not wash. Some of the great early civilizations were in tropical areas, and in recent years Israel and Lebanon have prospered in climates once thought inhospitable to modern development. West Bengal, an area of monsoons and extreme heat, was one of the first industrial areas in India.

To deny the overriding importance of climate is not to argue that climate has no importance. It is one of the "natural" conditions affecting development. But man is an adaptable animal and has shown that he can flourish even close to the extremes of climate.

Custom and culture Another bit of chauvinist folklore that was formerly popular and can be heard occasionally even now is that economic development is a white, Northern European monopoly. It is a narrow reading of history. True, Max Weber and R. H. Tawney and others explain the head start of Western Europe's modern economic development in terms of the emergence there of the Protestant ethic. Their argument is involved and controversial and can again be met most easily with counterexamples. Modern economic transformation took place in the Catholic areas of the Rhineland and northern Italy as early as in Protestant England, Germany, and the Low Countries. The Armenians, Lebanese, and Jews in favorable conditions were ethnic centers of modern economic practices. The Japanese, with no trace of the Old or New Testament in their cultural background, managed to transform their society and enter into a modern phase of development almost as early as parts of Protestant Scandinavia and earlier than Catholic Spain.

In any case, we need not settle the argument about the nineteenth century. There are many contemporary examples of economic development under a wide range of cultural conditions. Indian and Taiwanese merchants and industrialists, Nigerian and Colombian businessmen, and Iranian economic government specialists — all have proved themselves capable of promoting economic development effectively.

To deny that Western society has a monopoly of the potential for economic development is not to argue that custom and culture are irrelevant to development prospects. In some countries, the systems of belief and the social structure have been and probably still are barriers to economic development. The positive conclusion implied by the discussion here is that economic development has been achieved within a wide variety of custom and culture systems. The peoples of the world will not become Europeans or Americans in order to develop, and it is not necessary.

Capitalist exploitation

Still another explanation sometimes given for the lack of development in many countries is that it is the result of the conscious and unconscious policies of capitalist exploitation by the more advanced countries. According to the argument, favored by if not originating with Marxists, this exploitation is an inevitable concomitant of the expansion of the private, profit-seeking businesses of Western Europe and the United States. The capitalist spirit, it is argued, led to political imperialism as a means of extending economic imperialism.

This argument is even more difficult to evaluate than the preceding ones. *There can be little doubt that Western capitalist enterprise has often exercised its monopoly power to its own advantage and to the disadvantage of the peoples of the less developed areas.* There also can be little doubt that Western — and sometimes Eastern — political and military pressures have been used to gain economic advantages. Foreign economic power has also corrupted local governments, who on many occasions showed themselves more than willing to be corrupted.

On the other hand, counterexamples can again be given of countries which developed in spite of foreign capitalist pressures (Japan, Argentina) or which did not develop even though foreign capitalism was excluded or was unimportant. Western capitalists were simply uninterested in the Arabian peninsula until the emergence of markets for oil and its discovery there. So Western capitalism can hardly be blamed for the earlier lack of development of that area. Western capitalist intrusions have also brought important benefits to the less developed countries. The foreign-built railroads in China and India may not have been located optimally for the internal development of those countries and their cost was probably too high. But most likely, they would not have been built until much later if foreign companies had not constructed them. Education and training, as well as exploitation and, occasionally, savagery, have accompanied colonialism. And though the benefits from international trade have not been distributed equally, there have been important local benefits.

The capitalist exploitation argument – like the climate and culture arguments – is too simple. Again that does not mean it is irrelevant. Sometimes it does catch the essential features of the history of a less developed country. Yet it does not encompass the full variety of political, economic, and social conditions that have retarded development.

Vicious circles and growth traps

Turning from grand historical theories to more narrowly economic analysis, we come to the idea that there are "vicious circles" of poverty. *These vicious circles tend to make poverty self-reinforcing.* Failure breeds a lack of confidence, which breeds more failure. Ignorance breeds a lack of appreciation of the potential benefits of education, which breeds more ignorance.

One of the most important vicious circles of poverty alleged to exist in less developed countries is of the following type: Because of their poverty, people in the ldc's are not able to save a substantial part of their income by abstaining from consumption. That, in turn, means that the proportion of resources that can be diverted from consumption to investment is relatively low. Capital accumulates at a slow rate. Therefore, output can only grow slowly, and poverty persists.

This is a suggestive line of thought, but not quite conclusive. Even a little bit of saving each year will add to the capital stock and make the economy more productive. And as it becomes more productive, slightly more can be saved and slightly more added to the capital stock to make the economy somewhat more productive and to increase income and saving slightly again. It is like putting a dollar in a savings account and plowing back part of the interest every year. The savings account will grow slowly, but after a long enough period it will be quite substantial. The rate of growth which the economy as a whole can achieve will depend on the rate of saving and the productivity of new investment. (The Harrod-Domar First Growth Model of Chap. 37 can be used to make a rough guess about the growth rate if the marginal capital/output ratio and saving rate are known.) But, no doubt, there will be overall growth and not a vicious circle – unless something important has not been taken into account.

Figure 38-1

RELATIONSHIP BETWEEN POPULATION GROWTH AND PER CAPITA INCOME

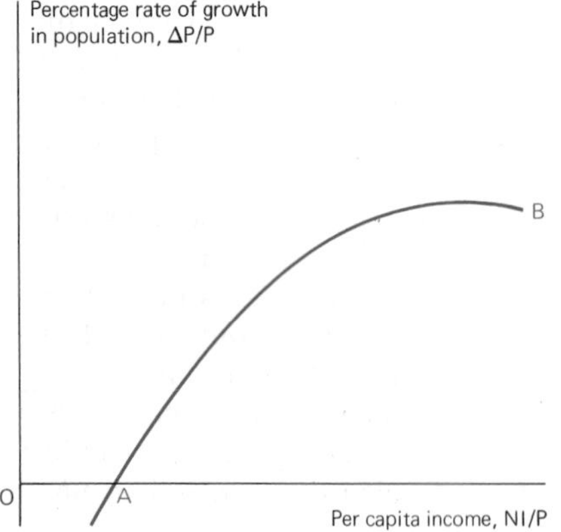

The important element omitted from the simple vicious-circle-of-poverty argument is the effect of higher incomes on population growth. It is frequently observed in the ldc's that one of the first effects of increase in per capita income is an increase in the rate of population growth. Improvements in individual nutrition and public and private health care combine to increase the rate of infant survival and to prolong life. Though higher incomes may have some slight effect in reducing the birthrate, the positive

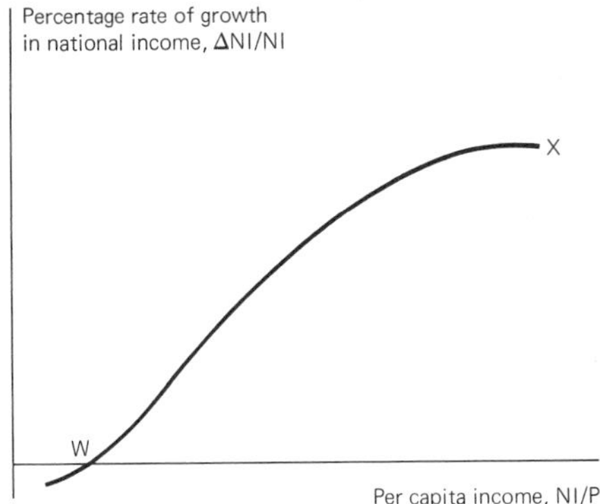

Figure 38-2

RELATIONSHIP BETWEEN PER CAPITA INCOME AND INCOME GROWTH DUE TO SAVING AND INVESTMENT

Figure 38-3

EXAMPLES OF THE LOW-LEVEL EQUILIBRIUM TRAP AND ESCAPE FROM IT

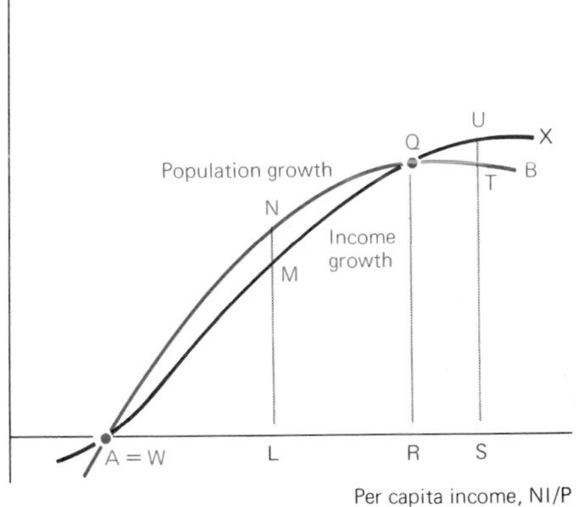

effects of higher incomes will swamp the original birthrate-reduction effect at first and the rate of population growth will rise. Typically, however, if per capita income continues to increase, the positive effects on the birthrate and on prolongation of life will tend to become less and less strong. That change does not lead to a decline in population, but to a decline in the rate of population growth.

Suppose P stands for population and ΔP for population change. The relationship between the rate of population growth, $\Delta P/P$, and the level of per capita income, NI/P, is, therefore, approximately like that shown in Figure 38-1 by line AB. As the line is drawn at point A, there is a zero rate of population increase and, therefore, no change in the population. Point A is a minimum subsistence level of per capita income. Below that, the rate of growth is negative and population will decline; above point A, the population will grow at increasing rates until it reaches a maximum growth rate, after which the rate of growth of population will decline.

When the relationship between population growth and per capita income is joined to the reasoning about saving, investment, and per capita income, a true vicious-circle or "trap" analysis emerges. But, first, we must be more explicit about the relationship of saving, investment, and income growth, on the one hand, and per capita income, on the other.

The rate of personal saving, according to the argument, depends on the level of per capita income. So the higher the level of per capita income, the higher will be the rate of saving and investment and the subsequent rate of growth in income. This relationship between income growth and per capita income is represented by the line WX in Figure 38-2. The percentage growth rate of income, ΔNI/NI, on the vertical axis is plotted against the level of per capita income, NI/P, on the horizontal axis. In the background of the WX relationship are the constraints of natural resources and technology as well as saving rates. As the relationship is drawn, point W divides stagnation and decline in total income from growth and improvement. To the right of point W in Figure 38-2, there will be growth in total income. The relationship is drawn to bend over to the right in order to suggest the effects of diminishing returns, which reduce the productivity of saving and investment with the existing resources and technology of the country. With technological improvements in production, the relationship of income, growth, and per capita income could shift or pivot upward.

Figure 38-3 combines Figures 38-1 and 38-2. At each level of per capita income, Figure 38-3 indicates what the rate of growth of income, ΔNI/NI, and the rate of growth of population, $\Delta P/P$, will be. Remember that *if the rate of growth of income is greater than the rate of growth of population, then per capita income will increase. But if the rate of growth of income is less than the rate of growth of population, then per capita income will decrease.* If the

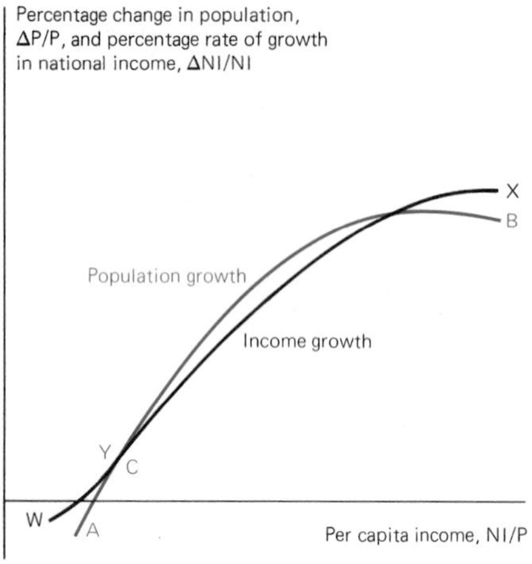

Percentage change in population, $\Delta P/P$, and percentage rate of growth in national income, $\Delta NI/NI$

X

B

Population growth

Income growth

Y

C

W

A

Per capita income, NI/P

Figure 38-4

A LOW-LEVEL EQUILIBRIUM TRAP WITH OVERALL GROWTH AND PER CAPITA STAGNATION

two rates are the same, the per capita income will not change, and, in this sense, the economy will be stagnant. At the per capita income level *A*, which is assumed here to be the same as the per capita income level *W*, both the rate of population growth and the rate of total income growth will be equal to zero, or $\Delta P/P = \Delta NI/NI = 0$. That means that the change in per capita income will also be equal to zero.

But look at per capita income at a level like L in Figure 38-3. The rate of population growth, $\Delta P/P$, is equal to *LN*, while the rate of income growth, $\Delta NI/NI$, equal to only *LM*, is less than that. Therefore, since the rate of income growth at L is less than the rate of population growth, per capita income must fall! *The disturbing conclusion of a rigorous argument along the vicious-circle-of-poverty lines is that ecnomic growth can set in motion forces which will inhibit and even reverse that growth.* In the language of the professional economics literature there is a *low-level equilibrium trap.*[2] An increase in per capita income from $A = W$ to L will be self-defeating, because population growth will push per capita income back toward the $A = W$ level.

But notice that it is a low-level trap. If per capita income can only be raised enough, the vicious circle can be broken. At a level of per capita income to the right of point *R*, for example, at *S*, the rate of growth of income, *SU*, will be higher than the rate of growth of population, *ST*, and, as a result, per capita income will rise. So the problem is to somehow raise per capita income enough to escape from the low-level trap. Economic policies to do that will be taken up in the next section.

Before moving on, however, we should note one more point about the vicious circles which restrain development. First of all, stagnation of per capita income need not be characterized by a zero rate of growth in both income and population. Figure 38-4 illustrates the possibility that the low-level equilibrium trap with no growth in *per capita* income can occur with positive growth in both population and *total income*. In Figure 38-4 the population growth curve rises above the national income growth curve at point Y = C, where both national income and population are growing at the same rate. But that means that per capita income remains stagnant.

How to develop: The issues of policy

The rules of growth listed above are just the beginning of a policy for development. To each of them, the response should be, How? Detailed answers to that question form the essence of development

[2] The analysis, though referred to in a number of places, was made most explicit and the terminology was introduced by Prof. Richard Nelson of Yale University.

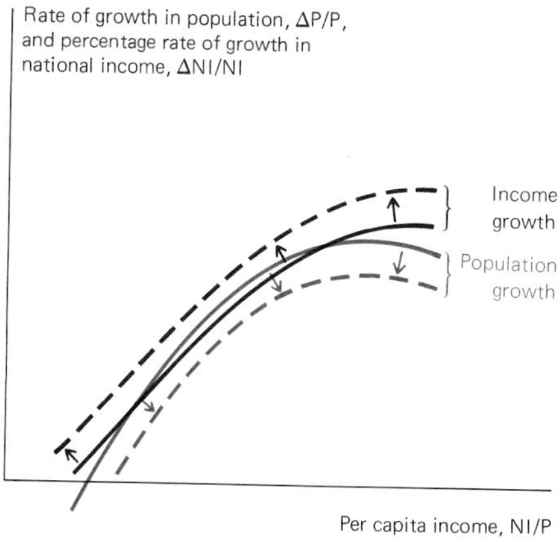

Rate of growth in population, $\Delta P/P$, and percentage rate of growth in national income, $\Delta NI/NI$

Income growth

Population growth

Per capita income, NI/P

Figure 38-5

EFFECT OF POLICIES TO RAISE INCOME GROWTH AND LOWER POPULATION GROWTH

policy. This is another of those situations that we were warned about in the very first chapter of the book. *The great problems of development are composed of a mass of prickly and difficult "little" problems with which development policy must deal.*

It is not easy to be efficient. It is not enough for the political leaders of an ldc to say, "We should be efficient," and for the people to respond, "We would like to be efficient." Achieving efficiency requires many specific and often painful changes in the economy and in the larger society. Accumulation of capital requires sacrificing consumption in an economy when there is full use of capacity and full employment. That sacrifice can be painful, and the capacity creation calls for special skills and organization, which cannot be had for the asking or wanting.

The general objective is illustrated in Figure 38-5, using the diagrams first drawn to illustrate the low-level equilibrium trap. If the line for income growth and per capita income can be shifted or rotated upward and the line for population growth and per capita income shifted or rotated downward, the trap is destroyed. This section will examine policies that can be followed to carry out in detail the rules for growth.

How to be efficient

Efficiency requires rational organization of production and distribution, and that, in turn, often requires a break with traditional products and traditional methods. There may well be agricultural societies in which "peasant wisdom" has evolved an optimal adjustment to growing conditions and needs. Yet new seeds, fertilizer, and new technology will demand a reorganization of production. A goverment can encourage change and can provide education and training but, short of coercing its citizens, cannot force changes on them.

Economic efficiency means more than avoiding obvious waste, though that is itself important. *Efficiency requires combining resources in the most effective ways and using the capacity created fully. If that goal is to be achieved, the price signals to which enterprises respond must reflect the true relative scarcities in the economy.* Yet a number of sources of distortion of prices are likely to be particularly important in less developed countries. Importers and firms producing manufactured goods are likely to have some degree of monopoly power, because there are relatively few of them and the total size of the markets is small. Since markets are not well organized, information about prices and quantities is not so generally available. Transport costs are high, and this will also tend to break the country into small market areas. The money markets are embryonic and subject to monopolistic influences.

Government economic policies in the ldc's are themselves often the source of price distortions. If the government maintains an overvalued foreign exchange rate, as it might for reasons touched on in Chapter 36, that will underprice the goods produced abroad and overprice the goods produced at home. That, in turn, will tend to encourage imports and discourage exports. The government, through the central bank, may maintain a relatively low interest rate to stimulate investment. But that will tend to stimulate substitution of capital for labor, when in reality, labor may be relatively abundant and capital relatively scarce.

Attempts have been made in the ldc's to estimate prices which reflect the true relative scarcities of foreign currencies, goods, and resources. These are called "shadow prices." They do not actually prevail in any market, but are the "shadows" or images of the prices that would prevail if there were efficient allocation of resources and products. Shadow prices which indicate true relative scarcities provide better guides to policy than actual prices. But they are difficult to enforce and require shrewd government tax and subsidy policies to make them effective.

How to accumulate capital

Poverty, so the saying goes, begets poverty. How can it beget savings? In less developed countries, most of the people are poor, but some are not. Those in the highest-income groups can and sometimes do save a substantial proportion of their incomes. The problem is to channel these savings into the uses that will contribute most to overall economic growth. As just pointed out, it is not always possible to rely on markets to do that. Tradition and custom may associate social status with the life of the country gentleman or the town barrister, and thus discourage the relatively well off from directing their savings into innovative domestic investment.

On the other hand, it is impressive that, even at quite low levels of income, some small amount of saving can be generated out of whatever *increases* in income may occur. As economic jargon puts it: *The marginal rate of saving out of additions to income may be positive and substantially larger than the average rate of saving.*

Nonetheless, a greater burden for saving is likely to fall on the government in the ldc's than in the more advanced countries. Government saving may be voluntary in a political sense if the people freely choose to have a government that will tax and use other measures to generate saving. Yet *saving is forced in an economic sense if it requires taxing.*

One should avoid the pitfall of thinking that a government must run surpluses in its budget, with tax revenues greater than expenditures, if it wishes to force saving on the nation. It may raise taxes in order to raise revenues and then spend those revenues to finance public or private investment. There is saving in this case, because consumption is reduced; the saving is channeled directly into investment expenditure. But the government budget may never be in surplus.

Inflation is another way of forcing saving that is often used in less developed countries. Governments which find it politically inconvenient — or maybe impossible — to raise taxes can nevertheless often finance investment expenditures by loans from the central bank. Such deficit spending will increase the money supply. Moreover, when imposed on an economy already straining at the boundaries of its productive potential and unwilling to release resources for investment by forgoing consumption, it will create an inflationary gap. In such circumstances, both monetary and expenditure forces will generate inflationary pressures which are the concomitant of the technique used to force saving.

Education, training, and technological innovation

At least the ldc's ought to be able to educate their populations and provide the technical training necessary for development, one might think. Well, education requires resources too — resources which must be diverted from other productive uses. Teachers in engineering schools could be working as engineers in manufacturing establishments. Teachers in schools of humanities and business could use their trained intelligence in the government and in business enterprise. Schools require bricks and mortar which could be used in bridges and dams. *When resources are terribly scarce, a careful accounting of the costs and benefits must be made, even of education.*

In a number of less developed countries, there is no shortage of educated labor, though often the education is not of the kind most required for development purposes. India graduates tens of thousands of English literature and economics majors every year, but there are shortages of technically trained workers. Again, the powerful effects of culture and tradition divert the flow of resources from the uses that would contribute most to development.

Planning the educational and training programs that will provide the kinds of labor necessary to sustain development and equalize opportunities for advancement is another difficult policy-making task. Educational systems in the more advanced countries provide little help in this task, for they too have usually grown in a helter-skelter fashion and reflect all the quirks and idiosyncrasies of each country's culture and society.

But at least, one might think, it should be possible to find the technology most suited for the development of production in each country. Again, it is not easy. The menu of technologies from which the ldc's can choose is, for the most part, a menu produced in the advanced countries. They have different kinds of resources, or they have resources available in different proportions. Maybe it is the best menu that could be created for the less developed countries. But we do not know for sure.

Unfortunately, the ldc's often do not have a free choice from the technological menu. The choice may be dictated by whatever advanced country is providing funds or expertise. For example, there has been a debate in India over accepting an outmoded steelmaking technology for the steel mill that the Soviet Union is underwriting at Bokaro in West Bengal. But India must accept that technology or not have the steel mill. It is, by the way, the same type of technology which a United States company intended to provide when it made a preliminary study.[3]

Though the ldc's face major difficulties in making good technological choices, there is also a major advantage for them. They did not themselves have to develop the rich and varied technical menu from which they choose. The costs of research, development, and technical evolution have been borne abroad. Even though in many cases the ldc's pay royalties on patents and employ foreign know-how, they are the beneficiaries of foreign technical progress.

Finding the right composition of output

The distribution of output between consumption and investment goods is related to the rate of saving, as pointed out in Chapter 37. But the exact balancing of the relationship raises another difficult set of issues for the ldc's where markets and information are particularly imperfect.

One of the tough decisions regarding output composition is the amount and timing of the proportion of investment to be made in "infrastructure." This consists of the public capital goods that provide services for a wide range of industry and consumption. Infrastructure includes roads, water and sewer systems, port facilities, public lighting, etc. Typically the investments are relatively large and often "lumpy"; that is, they have to be carried out in big, indivisible projects. The facilities cannot be built a little at a time as a little more of the services they provide are needed. Since infrastructure investment is important for other economic activity, it must be carefully timed and implemented in advance, but not too far in advance, because it absorbs so much capital resources.

Another major decision with respect to the composition of output is the relative emphasis to be placed on encouraging agricultural expansion as compared with industrialization. One of the clichés of development is that it must be accompanied by rapid industrialization. A special version of this cliché is that there must be heavy industry, such as steel and heavy machinery plants and heavy chemical refineries. *While it is true that there must be some industrialization in the course of development, its optimal amount, composition, and timing can vary greatly among countries.*

The optimal amount and composition of industrialization will in part depend, again, on the rate of saving. All other things equal, the higher the rate of saving and, therefore, in a sense, the greater the willingness to postpone consumption, then the larger the

[3] Instead of providing for the new technique of continuous casting of the slabs fed into the rolling mills, both the Soviet and the United States designs call for the older, more expensive process of casting ingots and then rolling them into slabs.

proportion of industrial investment which should go into capital-producing sectors, such as steel and heavy machinery. Creation of capital in these sectors does not directly create the capital to produce consumption goods, but rather the capacity to create the capital which can produce consumption goods.

In making decisions about the composition of output, the ldc's must take into account the relative costs of producing a good at home or buying it abroad. Cost criteria may well lead to an emphasis on agriculture, as occurred in Argentina and Denmark, rather than a wholesale rush into industry.

A less developed country must also decide what proportion of its investment will go into import-substituting industries – industries whose output can take the place of imported goods. Alternatively, export-promoting sectors can be pushed. The latter are sectors whose products can be sold abroad to earn the foreign exchange necessary to pay for imports. The decisions again depend on the relative costs and returns associated with the various sectors.

The rationale of foreign aid

Foreign aid represents the policies made in advanced countries to help the less developed. It consists of loans and grants made available on special concessionary terms which are more favorable than would be provided by private business. Table 38-2 presents at the bottom of the first column the total amount of foreign aid that was provided by the advanced countries to the less developed from 1950 through 1968.

The \$73.2 billion is a substantial amount by any standard. It has been a crucial component of the investment carried out in the less developed countries. As Table 38-2 shows, government-sponsored foreign aid has been more than 60 percent of total foreign-financial resources available to ldc's from 1956 to 1969. What is the rationale of aid?

Actually a number of alternative rationalizations have been advanced for foreign aid. It has been argued in the United States that foreign aid is a way of encouraging allegiance to our foreign policy – or, crudely, a way of buying votes in the United Nations. On occasion, it probably has been used in such ways by the United States and by other aid-giving nations. While such things would not happen in the best of all possible worlds, economic pressures of this sort may be less reprehensible than some other kinds of foreign policy pressure and tactics.

Evidence suggests that foreign aid does not itself produce reliable allies. Rather, when used as a pressure tool in this way, it encourages bargaining and a playing off of one nation against another. It also generates resentments and antagonisms.

The Left argues that foreign aid is an instrument of imperial-

Table 38-2

NET FLOWS OF FINANCIAL RESOURCES BY CATEGORY TO LESS DEVELOPED COUNTRIES: 1950–1968 (IN BILLIONS OF U.S. DOLLARS)

Year	Total official aid flows	Private investment		Total aid and private investment
		Direct	Portfolio investment & export credits	
1950–1955	1.9			
1956	3.3	2.4	0.6	6.3
1957	3.9	2.7	1.0	7.6
1958	4.4	2.0	1.0	7.4
1959	4.3	1.8	1.0	7.1
1960	4.9	2.0	1.2	8.1
1961	6.0	2.0	1.1	9.1
1962	5.9	1.5	1.0	8.4
1963	6.1	1.7	0.8	8.6
1964	5.9	1.9	1.3	9.1
1965	6.2	2.7	1.5	10.4
1966	6.5	2.4	1.5	10.4
1967	7.0	2.1	2.1	11.2
1968	6.9	2.8	3.1	12.8
Total flows	73.2	28.0	17.2	116.6

Source: OECD, Development Assistance Committee, *Statistical Tables for the 1969 Annual Review, Efforts and Policies of the Members of the Development Assistance Committee; The Flow to Financial Resources of Less-developed Countries, 1961–65;* OECD Secretariat.

ism. If so, it is an expensive one, as Table 38-2 indicates, and one with dubious returns. For the United States, a careful investigation will show that there is no one-to-one relationship between foreign aid flows and foreign trade and investment flows. By comparison, that relationship is much more closely approximated by French aid.

Another argument for foreign aid that has had a good deal of weight in the past is that helping the less developed countries can reduce economic tensions in the world which contribute to totalitarian governments and political unrest. It is a hopeful argument, but an inconclusive one. Examples can be given pro and con.

Humanitarian motives, such as those expressed in the quotation from Barbara Ward Jackson at the beginning of the chapter, have probably played an important but unmeasurable role in the foreign aid programs of many countries. It is on humanitarian grounds that the proposal has been made that each of the advanced countries contribute at least 1 percent of its GNP to the less developed countries for their development.[4] That, it should be noted,

[4] For example, Lestor B. Pearson et al., *Partners in Development: Report of the Commission on International Development,* Frederick A. Praeger, Inc., New York, 1969.

would not correspond to progressive taxation. The foreign aid donations of the advanced countries show a wide variation in the absolute magnitudes contributed and a wide variation also in the ratio of each country's foreign aid donation to its gross national product.[5] The United States aid program, which is large in absolute terms, is relatively small as a share of GNP, and that share has been declining in recent years.

Prospects for development

In the Victorian view of the world, poverty and backwardness were the fated future of the less developed countries. After World War II, political independence and the change in expectations in many of the ldc's put many of them on the road to development. By the mid-1960s the determination for development and the initial optimism seemed to be waning, and there was a spate of rather pessimistic evaluations. These need to be put into perspective. Table 38-3 on page 798 summarizes the growth rates in both the industrialized and the less developed countries. Comparatively, the ldc growth rate in this period is quite a respectable performance; it is remarkably better than most ldc's achieved in any previous period. The evidence of Table 38-3 indicates that development is by no means a hopeless undertaking.

Summary

Improving economic conditions in the less developed countries usually requires social as well as economic changes. There is, however, great variety in the economic conditions of the ldc's, in their relative population densities, and in their natural resource endowments. The ldc's are also characterized to varying degrees by dualities. There are often profound differences between the traditional and modern sectors of government and of economic organization. The urban-rural differences are often great. Great differences exist also in the techniques used, in the ability of industry to provide employment, and in the wage rates paid among the sectors.

Lack of development has been explained in terms of unfavorable climate, inadequate resources, lack of the Protestant ethic, and unfavorable cultural conditions. While such arguments are often difficult to refute, because they are couched in vague or conditional terms, impressive counterexamples can be given to all of them. Another kind of explanation offered for lack of development is that it is the result of capitalist exploitation by the businesses and governments of advanced countries. It is true that the

[5] The amounts reported in Table 38-2 are a little misleading, because the manner in which each country gives foreign aid affects the amount of concession it contains. There is no international truth-in-lending law that makes each country reveal this amount.

Table 38-3

GROWTH RATES OF DOMESTIC PRODUCT, POPULATION, AND GROSS DOMESTIC PRODUCT PER CAPITA, 1950–1967 (PERCENT PER YEAR)

Area	*1950–1960*	*1961–1965*	*1966–1969*
Less developed countries*			
GDP	4.6	5.1	5.7
Population	2.2	2.6	2.6
GDP per capita	2.3	2.5	3.1
Africa			
GDP	4.0	4.3	4.3
Population	2.3	2.4	2.5
GDP per capita	1.7	1.9	1.8
South Asia			
GDP	3.6	3.5	5.2
Population	1.9	2.5	2.5
GDP per capita	1.7	0.9	2.4
East Asia			
GDP	4.7	5.5	7.4
Population	2.5	2.8	2.8
GDP per capita	2.1	2.7	4.5
Southern Europe			
GDP	5.2	7.3	6.1
Population	1.4	1.4	1.5
GDP per capita	3.7	5.8	4.5
Latin America			
GDP	5.0	5.0	5.4
Population	2.8	3.0	3.0
GDP per capita	2.1	1.9	2.3
Middle East			
GDP	6.0	7.4	7.7
Population	3.0	2.9	2.8
GDP per capita	2.9	4.4	4.8
Industrialized countries			
GDP	4.0	5.1	4.8
Population	1.2	1.3	1.0
GDP per capita	2.8	3.8	3.8

* Eighty ldc's covering approximately 97 percent of GDP of all ldc's.

Note: Gross domestic product is the gross national product plus the earnings of foreigners sent abroad.

Source: International Bank for Reconstruction and Development.

monopoly power and superior economic bargaining strength, as well as the political and military strength, of the Western countries were often used to gain special advantages for them at the expense of the ldc's. It is also true that trade and investment by capitalist businesses and Western governments often brought economic and educational advantages to the ldc's which would not otherwise have been available. Moreover, there are examples of ldc's which developed with intensive participation from the capitalist countries and of ldc's which developed without such contacts. These indicate that the capitalist exploitation argument is too simple to account for the variety of conditions actually observed.

An economic theory for the lack of development must identify those forces which tend to act against economic expansion. The low-level equilibrium trap theory argues that increases in per capita income lead to increases in saving and investment and economic growth. But such increases also generate growth in population. Whether or not development is successful, according to this theory, depends on whether the rate of growth of per capita income can be achieved which is greater than the rate of growth of population. If not, the economy is caught in a vicious circle or trap.

The rules of growth derived from Chapter 37 must be given detailed and somewhat different content in forming development policy in each of the less developed countries. Efficiency requires not only rational organization of production, but also prices which reflect the true relative scarcities in the economy. The markets in less developed countries are often not well enough organized to generate such prices, or there are government-generated distortions. So such prices must be estimated as a guide to policy. Estimated prices are called shadow prices because they do not actually prevail in markets.

To plan for the accumulation of capital, governments of the less developed countries must often play an important role in generating saving. They can do this via the tax system or by permitting the central bank to lend funds to support private or public investment programs. In neither case is the government likely to maintain a surplus in its budget, and in the latter case it will clearly have a deficit. That may be an important contributing factor to the inflationary pressures which characterize many less developed countries.

Education, training, and technological innovation are also necessary to improve the productive techniques used in less developed countries. Education and training require diversion of resources and must be planned carefully to meet the manpower requirements for development. The choice of technology must usually be made from the menu developed in the advanced countries, and that may not contain alternatives that would be most appropriate for less developed countries. Moreover, the choice is often constrained by the fact that it is tied to loans or grants made by advanced countries.

The optimal output composition for the less developed countries must reflect the rate of saving as well as the real costs and returns that can be earned in various sectors by investment for domestic use and for export. While development most certainly includes some degree of industrialization, it need not mean a concentration on heavy industry. Depending on relative cost and comparative advantage, countries have developed successfully with reliance on agriculture and participation in international trade.

Foreign aid helps make up some of the scarcities in development. It has contributed importantly to the economic development of some countries. The history of the less developed countries since World War II indicates that they have in many cases substantially improved their conditions.

Questions for discussion and review

1. Do you believe that the less developed countries are just the same as the advanced countries of the world except that they are poor?

2. Comment on the following statement: *The less developed countries have a dense, illiterate population, limited natural resources, and nothing to trade abroad. No wonder they are poor.*

3. What is meant by the phrase "dualities of the less developed countries"?

4. Describe and explain in your own words the theory of the low-level equilibrium trap.

5. How important do you think capitalist exploitation is as an explanation of the conditions of the less developed countries? How does your answer account for the Japanese success story?

6. What is forced saving? How can inflation be used by the government of an ldc to force saving?

7. Comment on the following statement: *For a country to develop and modernize itself, it must industrialize and acquire the same industries on which the advanced countries have built their economic progress.*

8. What are shadow prices and why may they not be the same as actual prices?

Concepts for review

Modern-traditional, technological, and wage dualisms
Growth trap
Shadow prices
Forced saving
Infrastructure investment
Import promotion and export substitution
Industrialization
Rules for growth

Index